THE NEW INTERNATIONAL COMMENTARY
ON THE
OLD TESTAMENT

General Editors

R. K. HARRISON
(1968–1993)

ROBERT L. HUBBARD, JR.
(1994–)

The Book of
GENESIS

Chapters 18–50

VICTOR P. HAMILTON

WILLIAM B. EERDMANS PUBLISHING COMPANY
GRAND RAPIDS, MICHIGAN

255 Jefferson Ave. S.E., Grand Rapids, Michigan 49503

Printed in the United States of America

00 99 98 97 96 95 7 6 5 4 3 2 1

Library of Congress Cataloging-in-Publication Data

Hamilton, Victor P.
The book of Genesis: chapters 18-50 / Victor P. Hamilton.
cm. — (The New international commentary on the Old Testament)
Includes bibliographical references and indexes.
ISBN 0-8028-2309-2 (cloth)
1. Bible. O.T. Genesis XVIII-L — Commentaries.
I. Title. II. Series.
BS1235.3.H34 1994
222′.11077 — dc20 94-24076
CIP

To

Heather
Paul
Dawn
David

CONTENTS

AUTHOR'S PREFACE

One of the archetypal homileticians and clergypersons of this century, the late Dr. Paul Rees, himself a productive and eloquent writer, was once asked: "Do you like to write?" His answer was: "Yes, I like to write, but I like better to have written."

I can identify with that dictum. When I accepted this assignment a number of years ago, I knew it would be an extended one, and would take a good while to produce. But now I have written. I started. I progressed. I finished.

But the completion of this manuscript would have been impossible without the assistance of many individuals. Accordingly, I must express my gratitude to our former general editor, Dr. R. K. Harrison. Now that he is "absent from the body, but present with the Lord," may he look approvingly from above on this commentary. All of us who are contributors to this NICOT series, as well as to other publishing projects, know how his heart beat with concern for involvement on the cutting edge of biblical scholarship. He was inimical to few things as he was to shabbiness and slovenliness.

Additionally, I would extend a large thank you to the library staff of Asbury Theological Seminary here in Wilmore, Kentucky, that made available materials and resources not available in our own undergraduate college library. On numerous occasions they helpfully directed me to or through the labyrinth of bibliographic sources.

As with the first volume of this commentary, Mr. Gary Lee has been my editor. He has been thorough, professional, sagacious enough to save me from egregious errors, and stimulating enough to interact creatively and probingly with my manuscript. I thank him for thoroughly excavating the commentary I submitted to him, and for his suggestions and recommendations.

Finally, I must one more time thank my dear wife Shirley for her constant support and encouragement. While she goads me still to write something "we ordinary people can understand," she has been at my side constantly. She is responsible for typing the bulk of vol. 1 and all of the larger vol. 2, all on our old-fashioned Apple IIe computer, which I understand has now been dubbed "the Model T of the industry."

As this commentary is consulted by scholar and nonscholar, may our Lord be pleased to bless it as a vehicle that brings a deeper understanding of his word, and beyond that, a deeper understanding of him.

VICTOR P. HAMILTON

PRINCIPAL ABBREVIATIONS

AASOR	*Annual of the American Schools of Oriental Research*
AB	Anchor Bible
ABD	D. N. Freedman, et al., eds., *Anchor Bible Dictionary.* 6 vols. New York: Doubleday, 1992
AJSL	*American Journal of Semitic Languages and Literatures*
Akk.	Akkadian
AnBib	Analecta Biblica
ANEP	J. B. Pritchard, ed., *The Ancient Near East in Pictures.* 2nd ed. Princeton: Princeton University, 1969
ANET	J. B. Pritchard, ed., *Ancient Near Eastern Texts Relating to the Old Testament.* 3rd ed. Princeton: Princeton University, 1969
AnOr	Analecta Orientalia
ANQ	*Andover Newton Quarterly*
AOAT	Alter Orient und Altes Testament
AOS	American Oriental Series
Arab.	Arabic
Aram.	Aramaic
ARM	Archives royales de Mari
ASTI	*Annual of the Swedish Theological Institute*
ATR	*Anglican Theological Review*
AusBR	*Australian Biblical Review*
AUSS	*Andrews University Seminary Studies*
AV	Authorized (King James) Version
BA	*Biblical Archaeologist*
BAR	*Biblical Archaeology Review*
BASOR	*Bulletin of the American Schools of Oriental Research*
BDB	F. Brown, S. R. Driver, C. Briggs, *Hebrew and English Lexicon of the Old Testament.* Repr. Oxford: Clarendon, 1959
BeO	*Bibbia e Oriente*

BETS	*Bulletin of the Evangelical Theological Society*
BHK	R. Kittel, ed., *Biblia Hebraica.* 3rd ed. Stuttgart: Württembergische Bibelanstalt, 1937
BHS	K. Elliger and W. Rudolph, eds., *Biblia Hebraica Stuttgartensia.* Stuttgart: Deutsche Bibelstiftung, 1967-77
Bib	*Biblica*
BibOr	Biblica et Orientalia
BiTod	*Bible Today*
BJRL	*Bulletin of the John Rylands University Library of Manchester*
BKAT	Biblischer Kommentar: Altes Testament
BN	*Biblische Notizen*
BR	*Biblical Research*
BRev	*Bible Review*
BSac	*Bibliotheca Sacra*
BSOAS	*Bulletin of the School of Oriental and African Studies*
BT	*The Bible Translator*
BTB	*Biblical Theology Bulletin*
BWANT	Beiträge zur Wissenschaft vom Alten und Neuen Testament
BZ	*Biblische Zeitschrift*
BZAW	Beihefte zur *Zeitschrift für die alttestamentliche Wissenschaft*
CAD	I. J. Gelb, et al., eds., *The Assyrian Dictionary of the Oriental Institute of the University of Chicago.* Chicago: Oriental Institute, 1956-
CBQ	*Catholic Biblical Quarterly*
CBQMS	Catholic Biblical Quarterly Monograph Series
CHAL	W. Holladay, *A Concise Hebrew and Aramaic Lexicon of the Old Testament.* Grand Rapids: Eerdmans, 1971
CNFI	*Christian News From Israel*
ConBOT	Coniectanea biblica, Old Testament
CT	*Christianity Today*
CTA	A. Herdner, *Corpus des tablettes en cunéiformes alphabétiques.* 2 vols. Paris: Imprimerie Nationale, 1963
CTJ	*Calvin Theological Journal*
CTM	*Concordia Theological Monthly*
CTQ	*Concordia Theological Quarterly*
CurTM	*Currents in Theology and Mission*
DD	*Dor le Dor*
Egyp.	Egyptian
EncJud	C. Roth and G. Wigoder, eds., *Encyclopaedia Judaica.* 16 vols. Jerusalem: Keter, 1971-1972
ETL	*Ephemerides Theologicae Lovanienses*
EvQ	*Evangelical Quarterly*

ExpTim	*Expository Times*
fem.	feminine
Fest.	Festschrift
FOTL	Forms of the Old Testament Literature
GKC	*Gesenius' Hebrew Grammar.* Ed. E. Kautzsch. Tr. A. E. Cowley. 2nd ed. Oxford: Clarendon, 1910
GTJ	*Grace Theological Journal*
HALAT	W. Baumgartner, et al. *Hebräisches und aramäisches Lexikon zum Alten Testament.* 4 vols. Leiden: Brill, 1967-90
HAR	*Hebrew Annual Review*
HBT	*Horizons in Biblical Theology*
HeyJ	*Heythrop Journal*
HKAT	Handkommentar zum Alten Testament
HS	*Hebrew Studies*
HSM	Harvard Semitic Monographs
HSS	Harvard Semitic Studies
HTR	*Harvard Theological Review*
HUCA	*Hebrew Union College Annual*
IBS	*Irish Biblical Studies*
ICC	International Critical Commentary
IDB(S)	G. A. Buttrick, et al., eds., *The Interpreter's Dictionary of the Bible.* 4 vols. Nashville: Abingdon, 1962. *Supplementary Volume.* Ed. K. Crim, et al. 1976
IEJ	*Israel Exploration Journal*
IJT	*Indian Journal of Theology*
Int	*Interpretation*
IRT	Issues in Religion and Theology
ISBE	G. W. Bromiley, et al., eds., *International Standard Bible Encyclopedia,* 4 vols. Rev. ed. Grand Rapids: Eerdmans, 1979-88
ITQ	*Irish Theological Quarterly*
JAAR	*Journal of the American Academy of Religion*
JANES	*Journal of the Ancient Near Eastern Society of Columbia University*
JAOS	*Journal of the American Oriental Society*
JASA	*Journal of the American Scientific Affiliation*
JB	Jerusalem Bible
JBL	*Journal of Biblical Literature*
JBLMS	Journal of Biblical Literature Monograph Series
JBR	*Journal of Bible and Religion*
JCS	*Journal of Cuneiform Studies*
JEA	*Journal of Egyptian Archaeology*
JES	*Journal of Ecumenical Studies*

JETS	*Journal of the Evangelical Theological Society*
JJS	*Journal of Jewish Studies*
JNES	*Journal of Near Eastern Studies*
JNWSL	*Journal of Northwest Semitic Languages*
JPOS	*Journal of the Palestine Oriental Society*
JPT	*Journal of Psychology and Theology*
JQR	*Jewish Quarterly Review*
JRT	*Journal of Religious Thought*
JSNT	*Journal for the Study of the New Testament*
JSOT	*Journal for the Study of the Old Testament*
JSOTSup	Journal for the Study of the Old Testament — Supplement Series
JSS	*Journal of Semitic Studies*
JTS	*Journal of Theological Studies*
KB	L. Koehler and W. Baumgartner, *Lexicon in veteris testamenti libros.* Leiden: Brill, 1958
KD	*Kerygma und Dogma*
KTU	M. Dietrich, et al., *Die keilalphabetischen Texte aus Ugarit.* Vol. 1. AOAT 24. Neukirchen-Vluyn: Neukirchener, 1976
Lat.	Latin
Leš	*Lešonénu*
LTQ	*Lexington Theological Quarterly*
LXX	Septuagint
masc.	masculine
mg.	margin
ms(s).	manuscript(s)
MT	Masoretic Text
NAB	The New American Bible
NCBC	New Century Bible Commentary
NEB	New English Bible
NICNT	New International Commentary on the New Testament
NICOT	New International Commentary on the Old Testament
NIGTC	New International Greek Testament Commentary
NIV	New International Version
NJB	New Jerusalem Bible
NJPS	New Jewish Publication Society Version
NKJV	New King James Version
NovT	*Novum Testamentum*
NT	New Testament
NTS	*New Testament Studies*
OBT	Overtures to Biblical Theology
Or	*Orientalia*

OT	Old Testament
OTL	Old Testament Library
OTS	*Oudtestamentische Studiëen*
PEQ	*Palestine Exploration Quarterly*
Pesh.	Peshitta
PIBA	*Proceedings of the Irish Biblical Association*
pl.	plural
PRU	C. F. A. Schaeffer, et al., eds., *Palais royal d'Ugarit.* Paris: Imprimerie Nationale, 1955-
PTR	*Princeton Theological Review*
PTMS	Pittsburgh Theological Monograph Series
RA	*Revue d'assyriologie et d'archéologie orientale*
RB	*Revue biblique*
REB	Revised English Bible
RefR	*Reformed Review*
REJ	*Revue des études juives*
RestQ	*Restoration Quarterly*
RevExp	*Review and Expositor*
RevQ	*Revue de Qumran*
RSP	L. Fisher, et al., eds., *Ras Shamra Parallels.* 3 vols. AnOr 49-51. Rome: Pontifical Institute, 1972-81
RSV	Revised Standard Version
SAOC	Studies in Ancient Oriental Civilization
SBLASP	Society of Biblical Literature Abstracts and Seminar Papers
SBLDS	Society of Biblical Literature Dissertation Series
SBLMS	Society of Biblical Literature Monograph Series
SBT	Studies in Biblical Theology
ScEs	*Science et Esprit*
SEÅ	*Svensk Exegetisk Årsbok*
sing.	singular
SJT	*Scottish Journal of Theology*
SNTSMS	Society for New Testament Studies Monograph Series
SOTSMS	Society for Old Testament Studies Monograph Series
SP	Samaritan Pentateuch
SR	*Studies in Religion/Sciences Religieuses*
ST	*Studia Theologica*
StBTh	*Studia Biblica et Theologica*
Sum.	Sumerian
Symm.	Symmachus (ancient Greek version)
Targ.	Targum
T.B.	Babylonian Talmud
TD	*Theology Digest*

TDNT	G. Kittel and G. Friedrich, eds., *Theological Dictionary of the New Testament.* 10 vols. Tr. G. W. Bromiley. Grand Rapids: Eerdmans, 1964-76
TDOT	G. Botterweck and H. Ringgren, eds., *Theological Dictionary of the Old Testament.* Vols. 1-. Tr. D. Green, et al. Grand Rapids: Eerdmans, 1974-
TGUOS	*Transactions of the Glasgow University Oriental Society*
THAT	E. Jenni and C. Westermann, eds., *Theologisches Handwörterbuch zum Alten Testament.* 2 vols. Munich: Kaiser, 1971-76
TJ	*Trinity Journal*
TJT	*Toronto Journal of Theology*
TNTC	Tyndale New Testament Commentaries
TOTC	Tyndale Old Testament Commentaries
TS	*Theological Studies*
TUSR	*Trinity University Studies in Religion*
TWAT	G. Botterweck and H. Ringgren, eds., *Theologisches Wörterbuch zum Alten Testament.* Vols. 1-. Stuttgart: Kohlhammer, 1970-
TWOT	R. L. Harris, et al., eds., *Theological Wordbook of the Old Testament.* 2 vols. Chicago: Moody, 1980
TynBul	*Tyndale Bulletin*
TZ	*Theologisches Zeitschrift*
UF	*Ugarit-Forschungen*
Ugar.	Ugaritic
USQR	*Union Seminary Quarterly Review*
UT	Cyrus H. Gordon, *Ugaritic Textbook.* AnOr 38. Rome: Pontifical Biblical Institute, 1965
Vulg.	Vulgate
VT	*Vetus Testamentum*
VTSup	Vetus Testamentum, Supplements
WC	Westminster Commentaries
WMANT	Wissenschaftliche Monographien zum Alten und Neuen Testament
WTJ	*Westminster Theological Journal*
ZA	*Zeitschrift für Assyriologie*
ZAW	*Zeitschrift für die alttestamentliche Wissenschaft*
ZDMG	*Zeitschrift der deutschen morgenländischen Gesellschaft*
ZDPV	*Zeitschrift des deutschen Palästina-Vereins*
ZPEB	M. Tenney, et al., eds., *Zondervan Pictorial Encyclopedia of the Bible.* 5 vols. Grand Rapids: Zondervan, 1975
ZTK	*Zeitschrift für Theologie und Kirche*

TEXT AND COMMENTARY

G. YAHWEH'S VISIT TO SODOM (18:1-33)

1. ABRAHAM THE HOST (18:1-15)

1 *Yahweh appeared to him by the terebinths of Mamre; he was sitting at the opening of the tent as the day grew hotter.*

2 *He looked up and spotted three men standing beside*[1] *him. Upon seeing them he rushed from the opening of the tent to meet them, and bowed to the ground.*

3 *He said: "My lord,*[2] *if I have found favor in your eyes, please do not pass by your servant.*

4 *Let a bit of water be fetched so that you may bathe your feet and rest yourselves under the tree.*[3]

5 *I will get a morsel of bread so that you can be refreshed.*[4] *After that you may go on — now that you have come by your servant." They answered: "Very well, do as you have spoken."*

6 *Abraham went quickly back to the tent to Sarah. "Hurry," he said, "three seahs*[5] *of fine flour, knead and make cakes."*

1. Cf. Gen. 28:13 for the combination *nāṣaḇ ʿal* to express again the appearance of a divine being to a mortal; also Amos 7:7; 9:1. For *nāṣaḇ bᵉ* involving theophany, see Num. 22:23, 31; Ps. 82:1; 119:89; for the related verb *yāṣaḇ* (only Hithpael) in similar contexts see Exod. 34:5; Num. 22:22; 1 Sam. 3:10. See also *nāṣaḇ* (Niphal) in Exod. 33:21; 34:2; Deut. 29:9 (Eng. 10); and *yāṣab* (Hithpael) in Exod. 14:13; 19:17; Deut. 31:14; Josh. 24:1; Ps. 2:2.

2. The MT here has *ʾᵃḏōnāy*, "Lord," implying thereby that from the beginning Abraham recognizes God as God. My translation "my lord" reads the text as *ʾᵃḏōnî*. It is unlikely that Abraham, had he known his visitor to be God himself, would have offered him water for his feet and food for his stomach. Such an early recognition by Abraham of God would also run against the idea of the gradual revelation of God's identity to Abraham in this narrative (vv. 10, 13, 17-22). See the lengthy note by Speiser, *Genesis,* p. 129. He harmonizes the sing. of v. 3 and the pls. of vv. 4-5 by suggesting that Abraham through some means identified one of the three as leader, and spoke to him in v. 3. Out of courtesy he included the other two in vv. 4ff. It is also possible to read the consonants as *ʾᵃdōnay,* "sirs," as if Abraham is addressing all three men, but to do so one would have to change "your eyes," "do not pass," and "your servant" in the rest of the verse from sgs. (as in the MT) to pls. (as is done by SP).

3. *ʿēṣ* occurs approximately 320 times in the OT, the vast majority of which the LXX translates by *zýlon.* On the few occasions that *ʿēṣ* is translated by *dendron* (as here, v. 8; 23:17; Num. 13:21; and about 12 more times), what is meant is a big tree. See B. Paradise, "Food for Thought: The Septuagint Translation of Genesis 1:11-12," in *A Word in Season: Essays in Honour of William McKane,* ed. J. D. Martin and P. R. Davies, JSOTSup 42 (Sheffield: JSOT, 1986), p. 194.

4. The verb *sāʿaḏ* means "to sustain (with food)" in Judg. 19:5, 8; 2 Sam. 24:15 ("time of sustenance, dinnertime"); 1 K. 13:7; Ps. 104:15.

5. The seah is a measure for flour and cereals (1 Sam. 25:18; 1 K. 18:32; 2 K.

7 *And Abraham ran to the flock, and took a tender and choice calf, gave it to the young man, and he quickly prepared it.*

8 *He then took curds and milk, and the calf which he had prepared, and placed these before them. He was standing by them*[6] *under the tree while they ate.*

9 *"Where is your wife Sarah?" they asked. "In the tent," he replied.*

10 *One (of them) said: "At this time next year*[7] *I will surely return to you, and by then*[8] *Sarah your wife shall have a son." Sarah had been eavesdropping at the opening of the tent which was just behind him.*

11 *Abraham and Sarah were elderly, advanced in days;*[9] *Sarah had reached menopause.*[10]

12 *Sarah laughed inwardly,*[11] *saying: "Now that I am worn out,*[12] *shall I*

7:1, 16, 18); its exact size is uncertain. Suggestions range from about one-tenth of a bushel to one-third of a bushel (*IDB,* 4:834-35), or from about 7 to 12 dry quarts (*ISBE,* 4:1050-51).

6. Or, "he himself waited/was waiting on them."

7. The exact force of *kāʿēṯ ḥayyâ* here and in v. 14 (and in 2 K. 4:16, 17) — "about the living time"(?) "at the time of life"(?) — is open to question, although all agree that it refers to some time in the near future. Is it a reference to the period of pregnancy, i.e., 9 months (see Skinner, *Genesis,* p. 301; see also A. B. Ehrlich, *Randglossen zur hebräischen Bibel* [Leipzig: Hinrichs, 1908], 1:72, who gives "the time required for the embryo to be born"). Support for the translation "at this time next year" is found in the Akkadian expression *ana balaṭ,* lit., "to life," used in the sense "next year." See R. Yaron, "KAʿETH ḤAYYAH AND KOH LEḤAY," *VT* 12 (1962) 500-501; O. Loretz, "*kʿt ḥyh* — 'wie jetzt ums Jahr' Gen 18,10," *Bib* 43 (1962) 75-78. If *ḥayyâ* is an adjective, the absence of the article is strange. Accordingly, Yaron reads *ḥayyâ* as a noun, not an attribute of *ʿēṯ,* "at this time, next year." G. R. Driver ("A Lost Colloquialism in the Old Testament," *JTS* 8 [1957] 272 n. 2) notes that the omission of the article before *ḥayyâ,* whether adjective or participle, is correct, since it is not merely a descriptive epithet but has predictive force. He cites Gen. 37:2; Ps. 94:3; Jer. 16:16; Ezek. 34:13; Hag. 1:3. Cf. GKC, § 118u; BDB, p. 312a; O. Margalith, "More Samson Legends," *VT* 36 (1986) 397 n. 2; idem, "Some Aspects of Terms Denoting Time in the Bible" (Hebrew), *Beth Mikra* 89-90 (1982) 198-200. The translation "at this time next year" is supported by the parallel phrase in 17:21 *baššānâ hāʾaḥereṯ,* which clearly means "by this time next year."

8. On the use of *wᵉhinnēh* with temporal force, see D. J. McCarthy, "The Uses of *wᵉhinnēh* in Biblical Hebrew," *Bib* 61 (1980) 337.

9. For the phrase "goes/going in days" see Gen. 24:1; Josh. 13:1; 23:1; 1 K. 1:1. Days are seen as something through which one moves. Cf. S. J. DeVries, *Yesterday, Today and Tomorrow* (Grand Rapids: Eerdmans, 1975), p. 44 n. 60. The use of the participle indicates that the process of aging is not yet fully completed, suggesting that Sarah may be able yet to bear a child. But the next phrase in the verse ("had reached menopause") precludes that possibility.

10. Lit., "there ceased to be for Sarah the way of [as?] women." The problematical *ka-* in *ʾōraḥ kannāšîm* is best explained as an illustration of construct *k* in Biblical Hebrew. See F. Andersen, "A Short Note on Construct *k* in Hebrew," *Bib* 50 (1969) 69.

11. For Heb. *tiṣḥaq śārâ bᵉqirbāh* cf. *UT,* 75:I:12-13: *ʾil yẓḥq bm lb wygmś bm kbd,* "El laughed in his heart and exulted in his inward parts." See H. L. Ginsberg, "Baʿlu

experience pleasure,[13] *even though*[14] *my husband is old?"*

13 *Yahweh said to Abraham: "Why did Sarah laugh, saying: 'Will I indeed*[15] *really give birth even though I am old?'*

14 *Is anything too demanding for Yahweh? At the appointed time I will return to you, at this time next year, and for Sarah there will be a son."*

15 *Because she was afraid, Sarah lied, saying, "I did not laugh." But he said, "No,*[16] *you laughed."*

For a last time Abraham is given advance notice of Isaac's forthcoming birth. This happens while Yahweh and his entourage journey to Sodom to inspect the situation there. Abraham appears in two distinctly different roles within this chapter. In the first half he is the polite, deferential host who treats his visitors with the greatest respect. In the second half of the chapter he appears as the outspoken intercessor who pleads before Yahweh on behalf of Sodom. There is also a blatant contrast between how Abraham hosted his visitors (ch. 18) and how the Sodomites hosted the same delegation (ch. 19).

1 At the completion of an earlier revelation Yahweh had vanished from Abraham's sight (17:22). Now he reappears, this time in the heat of the day, as Abraham rests by his tent, located in a cluster of trees at Mamre.[17]

---

and his Brethren," *JPOS* 16 (1936) 140 n. 3. See also M. Niehoff, "Do Biblical Characters Talk to Themselves? Narrative Modes of Representing Inner Speech in Early Biblical Fiction," *JBL* 111 (1992) 583-85.

12. The verb for "worn out," *bālâ,* occurs again in Deut. 8:4 and 29:4 (Eng. 5) to refer to the clothing and shoes that did not wear out as the Israelites traversed the wilderness. The word is used only one more time (in adjectival form) in reference to a woman. Ezek. 23:43 mentions a woman who is grown old or jaded with adultery.

13. The word for "pleasure" *(ʿeḏnâ)* has strong connotations of sensual and sexual pleasure. See BDB, p. 726b. It is also to be associated with the primeval garden, Eden *(ʿēḏen),* "the garden of delight."

14. Lit., "and." Here and in v. 13 *waw* introduces a circumstantial clause of concession, which is best translated "even though, although." See GKC, § 141e.

15. H. L. Ginsberg (*The Legend of King Keret* [New Haven: American Schools of Oriental Research, 1946], pp. 42, 44) cites Gen. 18:13, 23, 24 and Amos 2:11b as instances of *'ap* indicating a question in the OT. In each of these cases, however, *'ap* is prepared by a *he*-interrogative, showing that *'ap* itself does not indicate a question. See BDB, p. 65a.

16. The expression *lō' kî,* to express denial, is found here and in 19:2; 42:12; 1 Sam. 8:19; 1 K. 3:22. Y. Hoffmann seems to go too far when he says that never in Biblical Hebrew is absolute denial expressed only by the use of *lō'* as an independent clause, but that with *lō'* is required an additional word ("Did Amos regard himself as a *nāḇī'*?" *VT* 27 [1977] 209-10). Here we have an adversative element introducing the positive statement after the negative one: "No [your denial in v. 15a is untrue], but you did laugh." See Z. Zevit, "Expressing denial in Biblical Hebrew and in Mishnaic Hebrew, and in Amos," *VT* 29 (1979) 505-8, and p. 508 n. 6.

17. For other references to "terebinths/oaks" of Mamre cf. 13:18; 14:13. Both of

The visit of Yahweh to Abraham in the hottest part of the day (cf. 1 Sam. 11:11; 2 Sam. 4:5) contrasts with his "visit" to Adam in another garden in the cool of the day (Gen. 3:8).

2 To his surprise Abraham sees[18] *three men* in front of him. Yet, for reasons unclear to us, he addresses only one of them in the following verse. Indeed, one of the interesting features of this section is the shift back and forth from singular to plural. Thus: v. 2, three men; v. 3, all singular; v. 4, second person plural; v. 5, again the second person plural; v. 9, plural; vv. 10-15, singular; v. 16, plural; vv. 17-21, singular; v. 22 begins with the plural but ends with the singular; vv. 22b-33, singular.[19]

A similar shift from plural to singular, or from angels to God, occurs in ch. 19. At Sodom Lot is met by two angels whom he addresses (v. 2) as "my lords" *(ʾ^{a}ḏōnay).*[20] A few verses later (v. 17) we read: "when they [the angels, Lot's *ʾ^{a}ḏōnay*] had brought them outside [Lot and his family], one of them said. . . ."[21] Then follows v. 18: "He [Lot] replied to them [the angels], 'Oh, no, my lord' " (sing., *ʾ^{a}ḏōnāy*)!

The same fluidity between God and angels is found in 21:17 (the angel is distinct from God) and 18 (the angel is identified with God). Judg. 6:7-24 provides the lengthiest illustration of this dynamic transfusion between angel

---

these verses designate this spot as Abraham's dwelling place. In 14:13 Abraham receives at Mamre a human visitor with chilling news (Lot has been captured). In 18:1ff. he receives divine visitors with happy news (Sarah will shortly have a child). 13:18 is the only text that refers to Mamre as a place of worship. 23:17 locates Mamre near the cave of Machpelah where the patriarchs and their wives were buried. The OT does not refer to Mamre outside Genesis. After citing postbiblical references to Mamre, R. de Vaux suggests that the silence in the rest of the OT about this site is due to the embarassment of orthodox Yahwism over a syncretistic cult that flourished there (*Ancient Israel,* 2:292-93). Note that Jerome's rendering of Heb. *ʾēlôn* ("terebinth, oak") by *convallis* (in 12:6; 13:18; 14:13; 18:1) and *vallis* (Deut. 11:30; Judg. 4:11), "plain, valley," is anticipated by Targ. *mysr.*

18. Lit., "he lifted up his eyes and saw. . . ." On the idiom "to lift up one's eyes" see S. C. Reif, "A root to look up? A study of the Hebrew *nśʾ ʿyn,*" *Congress Volume: Salamanca, 1983,* ed. J. A Emerton, VTSup 36 (Leiden: Brill, 1985), pp. 230-44. Reif notes (p. 243) that "there is some conscious intellectual decision associated with the element of sight in the phrase *nśʾ ʿyn.* This may take the form of an understanding that arises out of the sight." He then refers to Gen. 18:2, 4 as illustrations of this point.

19.

Singular	Plural
v. 1	v. 2
v. 3	vv. 4-9
vv. 10-15	v. 16
vv. 17-21	v. 22a
vv. 22b-33	

20. In contradistinction from Abraham's "my Lord" in 18:3 *(ʾ^{a}ḏōnāy).*

21. LXX, Vulg., and Pesh. read "they said." But MT has the sing. form, and I suggest for the sing. the translation "one (of them) said," as in 18:10.

and deity. The angel who greets Gideon is distinct from Yahweh (6:12). Gideon addresses him as "sir" (*'ᵃḏōnî,* 6:13). But from v. 14 on the angel and the deity are the same. In fact, in 6:15 Gideon addresses him as "my Lord" (*'ᵃḏōnāy,* the form used only of God). In 6:20 "the Lord" becomes "the angel of the Lord" again (see esp. v. 22). In vv. 23ff. the angel is once more the Lord. Finally, we note that the divine visitor to the mother of Samson is variously identified throughout Judg. 13 as "the man of God" and "the angel of Yahweh." Manoah fears for his life, for he says: "we will certainly die, for we have seen God" (Judg. 13:22).[22]

Scholars have accounted for the shift between plurals and singulars in Gen. 18 in several ways. One suggestion is that two variants of the story have been intertwined. One emphasized the visit by three individuals to Abraham. The second emphasized a visit by one messenger to Abraham.[23] E. A. Speiser offers a second suggestion (see the reference in n. 2); he harmonizes the singulars and plurals by having Abraham at times address the group and at other times address only the leader. Noting that 19:1, 15 refer to two of the three visitors to Abraham as *mal'āḵîm* ("messengers, angels"), A. R. Johnson has advanced the idea that Gen. 18 provides another illustration of the oscillation between the one and the many in the Israelites' conception of God.[24] *'ᵉlōhîm* is both one and more than one, and on this concept the NT doctrine of trinitarianism is built.

The progression of events in Gen. 18 is written in typical Hebrew narrative style. The writer first describes what has happened from the author's perspective (v. 1). Then he proceeds to narrate how the discovery was made by the one involved directly in the story (vv. 2ff.). The same progression is found in ch. 19. One may also compare the glow on Moses' face after his meeting with God (Exod. 34:29). Only eventually did Moses himself learn of this glow. The author and reader know why the scrub bush near Horeb is aglow (Exod. 3:2). But Moses does not immediately realize the significance of the burning bush. Similarly, the author and reader know why Job is suffering (Job 1), but Job does not.

The simple description of the visitors as *three men* is intriguing. No attempt is made to delineate the form or the appearance of them. Nor is any comment offered on the significance of three visitors, as opposed to one or two, or more than three. The next chapter, ch. 19, suggests that the trio is really Yahweh and two of his messengers.[25] But that information is not forthcoming

22. See M. Takahashi, "An Oriental's Approach to the Problems of Angelology," *ZAW* 78 (1966) 346-48.

23. Westermann, *Genesis,* 2:278.

24. A. R. Johnson, *The One and the Many in the Israelite Conception of God* (Cardiff: University of Wales, 1961), pp. 30-31.

25. Westermann (*Genesis,* 2:275-76) notices that earlier commentators cited the

in ch. 18. That Gen. 18 does not identify the visiting party beyond calling them "men" may in fact be intentional. "Obscurity is story's way of telling us the truth about this God with whom we daily have to do, by reminding us of God's hiddenness, of the concreteness of God's revelation, and of the impossible possibilities that are open to all who believe."[26] All that is told is the words they uttered. That they are described as *standing* (for deity "standing" [*niṣṣāḇ*] cf. Gen. 28:13; 1 Sam. 3:10; Amos 7:7; 9:1) implies, but does not prove, erect human form. In the OT God may assume human form and allows himself to be seen in such form by human beings; indeed, when God does appear in a form at all, the human form is the characteristic one for him to assume.[27]

This is the one theophany in the Abraham cycle in which Yahweh appears to Abraham with others at his side. Older Christian interpreters seized upon the number *three* in v. 2 and identified them with the Trinity. Obviously, such a statement reads a considerable amount into the text, and forces on the text an interpretation the text itself will not yield.

3-5 The emphasis here is on Abraham's solicitude as host. His actions include giving water to his guests so that they may wash their feet,[28] and offering them rest and food. Once they are *refreshed* (v. 5), they may continue on their journey. Such hospitality in the ancient Near Eastern world would not be strange. Indeed, its absence would be strange and disturbing. The host is responsible for his guest's needs and safety as long as the guest remains under his roof. This custom explains Lot's actions in the following chapter when it is his turn to host a visitor.[29] On an earlier occasion Abraham, when he himself was the visitor, received anything but a hospitable reception from the Egyptians (12:10-20).

---

passage from Ovid (*Fasti* 5.494ff.) in which a childless Hyrieus is visited by three gods (Zeus, Poseidon, and Hermes) who dine with him, but Westermann offers reasons why he does not believe it to be either the source of Gen. 18 or even a legitimate parallel.

26. W. M. Alston, Jr., "Genesis 18:1-11," *Int* 42 (1988) 400.

27. See J. Barr, "Theophany and anthropomorphism in the Old Testament," in *Congress Volume: Oxford, 1959,* VTSup 7 (Leiden: Brill, 1960), p. 32; S. Terrien, *The Elusive Presence: Toward a New Biblical Theology* (New York: Harper & Row, 1978), pp. 79-81.

28. For other illustrations of offering water to a guest and inviting him to wash his feet cf. Gen. 19:2; 24:32; 43:24; Judg. 19:21; 1 Sam. 25:41; 2 Sam. 11:8. In each case, except for 1 Sam. 25:41, the host merely provides the water — the guest washes his own feet. For possible connections with Jesus' washing the disciples' feet, see A. J. Hultgren, "The Johannine Foot-washing (13:1-11) as Symbol of Eschatological Hospitality," *NTS* 28 (1982) 539-46.

29. At the heart of Ps. 23, at least the second half, is this law of hospitality in operation. In Ps. 23 God acts as Abraham does in Gen. 18. God is the host; we sit at the table he has prepared while a helpless enemy looks on. Thus Ps. 23 pictures God as shepherd and host. Both metaphors suggest the idea of providing for the physical needs of another and providing for the protection of those for whom the host is responsible (sheep/those who sit at his table).

The masquerade is perpetuated by the visitors. They accept Abraham's offer: *Very well, do as you have spoken.* They eat! Like Joseph, who conceals his identity from his brothers, Yahweh and his angels conceal their identity from Abraham. He does not know that he is "entertaining angels unawares" (Heb. 13:2).

It is not necessary to push this story as far as do some commentators, who understand 18:1-15 as a story diluted by the Yahwist from the idea of God eating food to the idea of a meal given to angels unawares.[30] Rather, the eating is a concession by God to Abraham's ignorance of the one who stands in front of him incognito. In OT thought God inhales the pleasing odor of sacrifice, but he does not consume the sacrifice. Surely it is not without significance that only when Yahweh is in the guise of a wayfarer does he partake of food (18:8; 19:3).[31]

The presentation of food sacrifices to the gods is standard in the ancient Mediterranean world, Israel excepted.[32] The Ugaritic texts in particular provide instances in which a childless couple or father present food to their god in the hopes of alleviating childlessness. In the Keret Epic, Keret has lost his wife before she can provide him with an heir. He implores El to help him get her back, that through her he may have children to carry on the line. Part of El's instructions to Keret are:

"Take a lam[b in thy hands]
A kid in b[oth]
Loaves of [thy] b[read] of —
Take the entr[ails] of a bird of sacrifice
P[our] wine [from a c]up of silver
Honey from a cup of [g]old
Rise to the top of the [to]wer
Ride the shoulders of the wal[l]
Lift thy hands heavenward
Sacrifice to Thor, thy Father, El
Bring Baal down with thy sacrifices
Dagon's Son with thy victuals!"[33]

30. See W. Eichrodt, *Theology of the Old Testament,* tr. J. A. Baker, OTL, 2 vols. (Philadelphia: Westminster, 1961-1967), 1:144.

31. See Y. Kaufmann, *The Religion of Israel,* tr. and ed. M. Greenberg (New York: Schocken, repr. 1972), p. 70n.

32. See W. Herrmann, "Götterspeise und Göttertrank in Ugarit und Israel," *ZAW* 72 (1960) 205-16; P. A. H. de Boer, "An Aspect of Sacrifice. I. Divine Bread," in *Studies in the Religion of Ancient Israel,* VTSup 23 (Leiden: Brill, 1972), pp. 27-36.

33. Translation by C. H. Gordon, *Ugarit and Minoan Crete* (New York: Norton, 1966), p. 103.

Later in the narrative El blesses Keret with "a cup in his hand, a goblet in the right," that is, the benediction with a cup of wine (provided by Keret).

In another Ugaritic text, the Epic of Aqhat, Aqhat's father Danel and his mother Danatay serve a feast to express appreciation for the bow that the god Kothar-wa-Ḫasis has just presented to their son Aqhat:

Thereupon Danel, Man of Rp',
Straightway the Hero, Man of Hrnmy,
Picks himself up
Yea he sits
In the enclosure of the gate
Under the dignitaries which is in the threshing floor
He judges the case of the widow
Adjudicates the cause of the fatherless.
On lifting his eyes
He perceives
By the thousand acres
Myriad nectares
He spies the going of Kothar
He spies the course of Ḫasis.
Lo he brings a bow
Behold he fetches an arc.
Thereupon Danel, Man of Rp',
Straightway the Hero, Man of Hrnmy . . .
Shouts aloud to his wife: "Hear, Lady Danatay!
Prepare a lamb from the flock
For the soul of Kothar and Ḫasis
For the appetite of the Skilled of Handicraft!
Feed, give drink to, the gods
Serve and honor them." Lady Danatay hearkens
She prepares a lamb from the flock . . .
Thereupon Lady Danatay
Feeds, gives drink to, the gods
  She serves and honors them . . .
Kothar departs to his tents
  The Skilled departs to his tabernacles.[34]

34. Ibid., pp. 124-26. P. Xella ("L'épisode de Dnil et Kothar [*KTU* 1.17 (= *CTA* 17) v 1-31] et Gen. xviii 1-16," *VT* 28 [1978] 483-88) notes eight parallels between 2 Aqhat V:2ff. and Gen. 18:1-16: (1) both Abraham and Danel are seated; (2) the appearance of one or more divine beings; (3) an offer of hospitality, which is accepted; (4) an order by the man to his wife to prepare a meal; (5) the prompt execution of the order; (6) the divine beings eat and rest; (7) hospitality is rewarded (with an ark, with a son); (8) the divine beings depart. Y. Abishur ("The Story of the Angels' Visit to Abraham [Gen. 18:1-16] and

Now, it is difficult to compare the offering of food by mortals (Keret, Danel, and Danatay) to gods (El, Kothar-wa-Ḫasis) with Abraham's actions in Gen. 18. First, Abraham is not aware of the true identity of this visiting triumvirate, as are the human beings in the Ugaritic epics. Second, while Sarah is still childless, and while that motif will shortly emerge in the narrative, there is no indication that those circumstances dictate Abraham's actions. He acts as a gentleman and as a gracious host. He is not engaging in any ritual action, nor has he any hidden motive.

6-8 Sarah will provide the *cakes* for the meal, using *three seahs of fine flour.* 1 Sam. 25:18 tells us Abigail made sufficient provisions for David and his band of outlaws with five seahs of parched grain. The trench Elijah dug around the base of the altar at Mt. Carmel, which was then filled with twelve jars of water, was large enough to hold two seahs of seed (1 K. 18:32). These two references suggest that Sarah's three seahs is a large amount, which will yield much more bread than the three visitors, Sarah, and Abraham can possibly eat.

Abraham's extravagance continues. He provides *curds and milk* (side dishes to bring out the taste of the meat and to diminish their thirst), together with the meat of *a tender and choice calf.* In other entertainment scenes the host is content to provide "kids of goats" (Gen. 27:9; Judg. 6:19; 13:15).[35] That Abraham provides a *calf* shows either his relative prosperity and social standing, or his desire to give his best to his guests, or both. Abraham apparently does not share the meal with the threesome: *He was standing by them under the tree while they ate.* He is both waiter and host.

9 Sarah also does not join around the table. Abraham is standing aside, but Sarah is not seen at all. She is still inside the tent. Perhaps it was not proper for females to eat with males. Later, Rachel would be in a tent and would protest to her father that she was not able to rise so that he could search the entire tent because "the manner of women" (lit.; *dereḵ nāšîm*) was upon her (31:35). Sarah too is in a tent, but for her "the manner of women" (lit.; *'ōraḥ kannāšîm*) has ceased (18:11).

Readers may be surprised that the visitors know Abraham is married, and further, they know his wife's name, for nothing in the narrative has indicated that Abraham has introduced her to them, or even spoken of her to them. Abraham, however, shows no surprise. Perhaps the narrator makes a

its Parallel in Ugaritic Literature [2 Aqhat v:4-31]," *Beth Mikra* 32 [1986/87] 168-77 [Hebrew]) notes five parallels between the two stories, all of which were observed in Xella's earlier article except for the use of the idiom "lift one's eyes and see" in both accounts. Such parallels support the view that Gen. 18:1-16 is a cohesive unit, rather than the result of a fusion of sources.

35. Cf. also Gen. 38:17, 20; 1 Sam. 10:3; 16:20 for other references to small cattle, esp. goats, as a prime source of meat.

deliberate contrast between the three men who know who Sarah is and Abraham who does not know who they are.

One may compare the visitors' question, *Where is your wife Sarah?* with the deity's earlier question, "Where is Abel your brother?" (4:9). Abraham's response is a bit more respectful than was Cain's.

10 All previous promises of a son to Abraham were, to say the least, nebulous and unqualified (e.g., 15:4; 17:16). Now the announcement is more specific. *At this time next year* Sarah is to have a child. Possibility now gives way to specificity.

It is not clear all that is meant by the phrase *I will surely return to you.* What does the return of the divine presence to Abraham have to do with Sarah's conception of Isaac? Gen. 21:1 picks up on this promise: "Yahweh visited Sarah as he had said, and Yahweh did to Sarah as he had promised." A number of OT texts use *šûḇ* with God as subject, and the idea is to return for the sake of showing favor.[36]

11 Abraham's earlier protestations regarding fathering a child had focused on his problem (15:4), or on the advanced age of both prospective parents (17:17). Also, such protestations occurred in Abraham's direct discourse. But here it is the narrator who speaks. He knows Abraham and Sarah are advanced in years and Sarah has *reached menopause.* This phrase reinforces the advanced stage of Sarah. She was not just old or older, but at a point where her menses had ceased. This verse and the following two place special emphasis on the ages of Abraham and Sarah by the three-time use of the root *zqn.* The narrator calls both of them "elderly" (*zᵉqēnîm,* v. 11), a point made by Sarah about Abraham (*zāqēn,* v. 12) and about herself (*zāqantî,* v. 13). The narrator simply states the biological facts. The narrator, while he does not succumb to an outburst of laughter as Abraham did, and as Sarah shortly will, through such asides, injects his own sense of humor and the incredulous into the story. As Sternberg has said, "In his interpolated aside on the age of the prospective parents, he [v. 12, the narrator] goes out of his way to give color to Sarah's laughter at the visitor's forecast: the more natural her doubt, the stronger our sense of God's supernatural prescience."[37]

12 Sarah's display of shock is not as skeptical as that of her husband. At least she does not fall on her face, laughing. Her response is more of a bemused reflection after she overheard the visitor announce her forthcoming

36. Here and again in v. 14; 2 Chr. 30:6; Zech. 1:3; Mal. 3:7 (all followed by the preposition *'el*); Ps. 6:5 (Eng. 4); 80:15 (Eng. 14); Isa. 63:17; Jer. 12:15; Joel 2:14; Jon. 3:9 (all without the preposition *'el*).

37. M. Sternberg, *The Poetics of Biblical Narrative* (Bloomington: Indiana University, 1985), p. 91.

pregnancy to Abraham. Given the hard realities of the situation, she cannot imagine the possibility of such pleasure.[38]

13 Sarah has overheard the anonymous visitor talking to her husband. Now the tables are turned — the visitor overhears Sarah talking to herself. Here the speaker is identified: *Yahweh.* That explains how he knew Sarah's name, and how he hears her quite distinctly here, even though she *laughed inwardly* and was probably muttering to herself.

For such a response Yahweh takes Sarah to task, through her husband: *Why did Sarah laugh?* She is not spoken to directly. Furthermore, Yahweh knows quite well what Sarah had meant by "pleasure," as is evident from his interpretative quotation of her: *Will I really give birth, even though I am old?* That is what Sarah had in mind, but that is not exactly how she said it. She had drawn attention to both her own age and her husband's advanced years (v. 12). Yahweh has Sarah drawing attention to her own advanced age. He discreetly avoids any reference to Abraham the centenarian, for conceivably a man might father a child even at such an age.

It may seem odd that Yahweh rebukes Sarah for her reservations but does not challenge Abraham for his doubts. We had mentioned earlier that 18:10b and 17:19 would, together, suggest that Abraham kept the announcement of Isaac's conception from Sarah. She hears about it (18:10b) quite by accident. Perhaps the rebuke aimed at Sarah indicates that Abraham had shared the news about Isaac with Sarah, but that she still persisted in unbelief. She was not convinced by her husband.[39] Or perhaps, following Speiser, one should translate *ṣāḥaq* in 17:17 as "smile," rather than as a laughter of disbelief (see commentary on 17:17).

14 Here Yahweh himself promises to return to Sarah. Sarah's laughter and display of incredulity provoked this question from Yahweh: *Is anything too demanding* [difficult, impossible] *for Yahweh?*[40] It is a question that neither

38. My translation "Shall I experience pleasure" renders, somewhat unusually, a *qāṭal* form *(hāyᵉṯâ)* by a future. One translation renders the passage, "after my wearing out, have I had sexual pleasure. . . ?" (R. B. Coote and D. R. Ord, *The Bible's First History* [Philadelphia: Fortress, 1989], pp. 118, 125). GKC, § 106n, cites *hāyᵉṯâ* in Gen. 18:12 as an instance of the perfect "to express facts which are undoubtedly imminent, and, therefore, in the imagination of the speaker, already accomplished."

39. See Kidner, *Genesis,* p. 132.

40. W. Brueggemann traces the trajectory of the theme of the possibility/impossibility of God throughout Scripture, beginning with Gen. 18:14, in " 'Impossibility' and Epistemology in the Faith Tradition of Abraham and Sarah (Gen. 18,1-15)," *ZAW* 94 (1982) 615-34. See also his *Genesis,* pp. 159-62. For all the nuances contained within the Hebrew root *pl'* (here translated "demanding"), see R. Albertz, *THAT,* 2:413-20. BDB, p. 810b, cites Gen. 18:14 as an illustration of the meaning "be beyond one's power, difficult to do" for *pālā'*. On many occasions the verb means not "to be difficult" but "to be wonderful." Thus, one might render 18:14a "is a matter too wonderful for Yahweh?" But almost all

Abraham nor Sarah tries — or has a chance — to answer. The guest's first question pointed to Sarah. His second question points to himself. In the latter half of this chapter Yahweh is moved out of the role of interrogator and into the role of respondent when Abraham asks him a rhetorical question: "Shall not he who judges all the earth give right judgment?" (v. 25).

Yahweh's question to Abraham is designed to shift the patriarchal couple's obsession beyond their own hopeless situation and their own limited resources to the limitless resources of their God. Note that Sarah's unbelief does not abort, or sidetrack, or slow down the promise of God. She will still conceive, whether she thinks she can or cannot. To reinforce this certainty, not only does the text repeat in v. 14 the *kāʿēṯ ḥayyâ (at this time next year)* of v. 10 but it adds *lammôʿēḏ, at the appointed time.*

15 *Because she was afraid.* Fear moves people to do things that are irrational and uncharacteristic of them. Adam hid because he was afraid of God. Abraham deceived because he was afraid of what the Egyptians might do to him. Now Sarah is afraid because she has challenged the authenticity of a divine promise and because she has irked the divine visitor. Thus she lies: *I did not laugh.* A second sin is committed (lying) in an attempt to cover up a first sin (unbelief).

Sarah speaks aloud only once in vv. 1-15 — "I did not laugh," (v. 15), and softly once (v. 12). Only once is she addressed: "No, you laughed." The conversation stops quickly. Abraham makes no contribution to the dialogue between Yahweh and Sarah. By ending on such a note, Yahweh intends for Sarah not to dismiss quickly remembrance of her laughter over the announcement of her forthcoming conception. In effect, Yahweh is providing Sarah with a "recondite hint of the name of the child."[41]

2. ABRAHAM THE INTERCESSOR (18:16-33)

16 *The men got up to leave and looked toward Sodom. Abraham accompanied them to send them on their way.*

17 *Yahweh mused: "Shall I conceal from Abraham what I am on the verge of doing,*

18 *for Abraham is to be an enormous*[1] *nation, and all the nations of the earth will be blessed in him?*

19 *For I have covenanted with him so that he may instruct his sons and*

instances of *pālāʾ* meaning "be wonderful" are confined to Niphal participles and uses of the verb in the Hiphil stem.

41. Westermann, *Genesis,* 2:282.

1. I take *gāḏôl wᵉʿāṣûm,* lit., "great and vast," as a hendiadys.

family-to-be to observe the way of Yahweh by practicing righteousness and justice, to the end that Yahweh may bring to fruition that which he spoke concerning him."

20 *Yahweh said: "The clamor of Sodom and Gomorrah is so*[2] *loud and their sin so very grave,*

21 *I must go down and observe whether what they have done is at all*[3] *like the cry*[4] *that has come to me. I intend to find out,*[5] *one way or another."*[6]

22 *The men departed from there and went on to Sodom, but Abraham still stood before Yahweh.*

23 *Abraham came forward and remonstrated: "Will you indeed sweep away the innocent*[7] *with the guilty?*

2. Following GKC, § 148d, I take the two *kî*s in this verse as corroborative ("so . . . so") or emphatic; this explanation seems preferable to that in BDB, p. 473b, which suggests that the *kî*s are causal. See M. J. Dahood, "Northwest Semitic Notes on Genesis," *Bib* 55 (1974) 79; J. Gray, *The Legacy of Canaan,* VTSup 5 (Leiden: Brill, 1957), p. 203. Note also the presence of the formulaic *rb . . . kbd* ("loud . . . grave"), which appears three more times in the OT (Jer. 30:19; Nah. 3:3; 3:15b-16, all poetry). See J. S. Kselman, "*rb//kbd:* A new Hebrew-Akkadian formulaic pair," *VT* 29 (1979) 111-12. Given that all other examples of *rb . . . kbd* in the OT are in Hebrew poetry, that the verse is an ABC/AC bicolon with a syllabic meter of 11:10, and that the emphatic *kî* is present in both parts of the bicolon, often a feature of Hebrew poetry, Kselman argues for the possibility that this verse is a bicolon of poetry. For a contrary position on the two *kî*s in this verse (and thus arguing for "because"), see B. L. Bandstra, "Word Order and Emphasis in Biblical Hebrew Narrative: Syntactic Observations on Genesis 22 from a Discourse Perspective," in *Linguistics and Biblical Hebrew,* ed. W. R. Bodine (Winona Lake, IN: Eisenbrauns, 1992), p. 121.

3. MT *kālâ* is difficult. As a substantive it means "destruction, annihilation." That meaning may be retained here: "whether (the) destruction they have done is like the cry that has reached me." Or it may be taken as an adverb, "thoroughly, completely," with the emendation of *kālâ* to *kulâ.* See *HALAT,* 2:455a.

4. MT *hakkeṣaʿaqāṯāh,* lit., "like her outcry," is problematic, for the fem. pronominal suffix has no antecedent unless it be Sodom and Gomorrah, which are treated as fem. in the previous verse. Several ancient mss., including LXX and Targ. Onqelos, read final *m* for *h,* hence "their outcry." D. Irvin (*Mytharion,* AOAT 32 [Neukirchen-Vluyn: Neukirchener, 1978], p. 21) understands the *k-* after the interrogative as the "K *veritatis*" — "the especially loud cry which has come to me."

5. A proposal has been made to relate *ʾēḏaʿâ* to a verb other than *yāḏaʿ,* "to know." D. W. Thomas ("Julius Furst and the Hebrew Root *ydʿ,*" *JTS* 42 [1941] 65) relates it to an Arabic verb meaning "to punish, humiliate," and revocalizes it as a Hiphil: *ʾōḏîʿâ.* (Cf. the translation of Targ. Onqelos: *ʾytprʿ,* "I will call to account, take revenge.") But there is no strong reason to reject the meaning "to know," in the sense of "to find out, discover." Cf. J. A. Emerton, "A Consideration of Some Alleged Meanings of *ydʿ* in Hebrew," *JSS* 15 (1970) 171.

6. The phrase *weʾim-lōʾ ʾēḏāʿâ* provides an illustration of the *ʾîm-lōʾ* of asseveration, combined with the cohortative (GKC, §§ 108e, 149a, e).

7. Lit., "(the) righteous" *(ṣaddîq).* "Innocence and guilt are always defined in relation to each other. In this narrative the behavior of the Sodomites has been defined as

24 *Perhaps there are fifty innocent in the city; would you still sweep away the place, rather than spare it because there are fifty innocent in it?*

25 *It would be a desecration*[8] *for you to do such a thing, to slay the innocent with the guilty, so that the innocent fare as do the guilty. It would be a desecration for you! Shall not he who judges all the earth give right judgment?"*

26 *Yahweh said: "If I find in Sodom fifty innocent in the city I will spare the entire place on their account."*

27 *Abraham answered: "I venture to speak to the Lord, I who am but dust and ashes.*

28 *Perhaps the fifty innocent lack five. Would you destroy because of those five the entire city?" He responded: "I would not destroy it if I find there forty-five."*

29 *Again he spoke to him: "Perhaps if forty were found there?" He replied: "I will not do anything on account of the forty."*

30 *He said: "Let not the Lord be angry if I speak. Perhaps if thirty were found there?" He replied: "I will not do anything if I find thirty there."*

31 *He persisted: "I venture again to speak with the Lord. Perhaps if twenty were found there?" He replied: "I would not destroy it on account of the twenty."*

32 *He said: "Let not the Lord be angry if I speak one more time. Perhaps ten will be found there?" He replied: "I would not destroy it on account of the ten."*

33 *Yahweh departed, as soon as he finished talking with Abraham. Abraham returned to his own place.*

A number of emphases unite vv. 1-15 with vv. 16-33. The "men" arrive in v. 1 and prepare to depart in v. 16. The action starts in Mamre (v. 1) and ends in Mamre (v. 33). The quiet, gracious, scurrying host (vv. 1-15) becomes the bold and brash inquisitor of God (vv. 16-33). A rhetorical question in each section — "Is anything too demanding for Yahweh?"; "Shall not he who judges all the earth give right judgment?" — sounds the major motif of each unit. Abraham does not feel constrained to be arbitrator between Yahweh and Sarah, but he does place himself between Yahweh and Sodom, concerned as he is that God not unjustly,

---

wicked. Hence, the innocent are not intrinsically just or righteous, only in contrast to the Sodomites" (Coote and Ord, *Bible's First History,* p. 129 n. 9).

8. Translations of *ḥālilâ lāḵ* as "far be it from you" are too weak, and miss the force of the verb *ḥālal. ḥālilâ* is normally used with the 1st person. Two passages use it with the 3rd person (Gen. 44:7-9; Job 34:10), and two with the 2nd person (here and 1 Sam. 20:9). See J. Milgrom, *Cult and Conscience* (Leiden: Brill, 1976), p. 87 n. 306.

not precipitously, destroy the righteous along with the wicked. In both units it is some kind of noise that provokes Yahweh — Sarah's laugh and Sodom's groans.

16 Their respite finished, the men now prepare to move on to Sodom. They could look *toward Sodom* only from some spot in the hill country of Judah. Although it cannot be ascertained with certainty, tradition identifies this vantage point as the elevated village of Beni Naʿim, three miles east of Hebron. The Dead Sea, eighteen miles to the south, could be discerned on a clear day through gaps in the hills. Always the perfect host, Abraham escorts his guests on a portion of their journey. In a literal sense Abraham, like Enoch, "walked with God."

17 It is possible to read the end of v. 16, skip vv. 17-19, and continue smoothly with v. 20. For this reason some commentators have suggested that vv. 17-19 are a later addition to this narrative.[9] Apart from the lack of textual support for such an excision, the deletion of these three verses would omit a major theme — God's daring to adopt Abraham as his confidant — which throws into bold relief a second theme — Abraham's daring to be Sodom's intercessor before Yahweh.

In this narrative, both God and Abraham express mutual concerns. Can God trust Abraham? Can Abraham trust God? The answer to both questions is yes.

Yahweh's question, directed to himself, prepares the reader for Abraham's intercession, which is forthcoming. The question *Shall I conceal from Abraham what I am on the verge of doing?* resurfaces in later biblical literature, in the form of an affirmation. Through Amos (3:7) Yahweh says: "Surely Yahweh God does nothing, without revealing his secret to his servants the prophets." To Abraham, and to his prophetic successors after him, inside knowledge of divine operations is revealed.

But what is God about to reveal to Abraham? God's question is not: "Shall I conceal from Abraham what I am about to do to Sodom?" As is stands, the question could just as well be about Abraham's future. In fact, the next two verses (18 and 19) are precisely about Abraham's future and the future of his descendants.

18 This is not the first time that God has spoken about his promises to Abraham. But this is the first time — and the only time — when the divine promises to a patriarch are couched in a soliloquy. The significance of this form is that it reinforces that the earlier divine disclosure to Abraham is authentic, unadulterated, and truthful. The soliloquy underscores the word of God as infallible, for will God, when speaking to himself, attempt to deceive himself? What God says is what he is thinking.[10]

9. Accordingly, R. A. F. Mackenzie ("The Divine Soliloquies in Genesis," *CBQ* 17 [1955] 277-86, and esp. p. 159 n. 7) omits vv. 17-19 from his discussion. But he is opposed by R. Lapointe, "The Divine Monologue as a Channel of Revelation," *CBQ* 32 (1970) 177.

10. See Lapointe, *CBQ* 32 (1970) 179-80. W. Brueggemann labels God's address

Verse 18b supplies the motive for God's decision not to withhold information from Abraham: *all the nations of the earth will be blessed in him.* This is, of course, a repetition of the promise of 12:3. Abraham is concerned with the judge of all the earth, but God is concerned with the nations of the earth. For the first time since ch. 12 (except for ch. 14) Abraham finds himself involved with the affairs and destiny of a people who, geographically, are among the nations of the earth. And for the first time one of the nations of the earth, the Sodomites, is "blessed" because of Abraham. To *be blessed* in this context means to have one who intercedes before God regarding one's destiny, to have one who "makes intercession for the transgressor" (Isa. 53:12).[11]

19 The previous verse discussed Abraham's future in terms of effects: an enormous nation and the means of blessing to the world. Now this verse supplies the cause for those effects. Why will Abraham's influence be so enormous and worldwide? The simple explanation is that God has *covenanted with* (*yāḏaʿ,* lit., "known") Abraham.

One obvious thrust in Yahweh having "known" Abraham is that Abraham is intimate with God and vice versa. But the choice of this verb may have further implications. For one thing, there is a growing consensus among OT scholars that *yāḏaʿ* is, in places, a technical term in treaty or covenant terminology that refers to mutual legal recognition on the part of the suzerain and the vassal. Of particular interest here are those passages where the subject of the verb is Yahweh himself. For Yahweh to "know" someone may mean not "take notice of, be aware of, look after," but "recognize as a legitimate servant, grant recognition."[12]

The choice of the verb "know" may be deliberate in the light of the context. Yahweh knows Abraham; yet he goes to Sodom in order to know (v. 21b) what is going on there. Certainty and uncertainty are placed alongside each other. Or again, perhaps the narrator wants to draw a contrast between Yahweh who knew Abraham and the Sodomites who wanted to "know" Lot's

---

to himself about Abraham and Abraham's destiny "an extravagant credentialing of Abraham, perhaps the most extravagant of all scripture" ("A Shape for Old Testament Theology, II: Embrace of Pain," *CBQ* 47 [1985] 411).

11. H. W. Wolff traces the various ways in which the theme of the blessing on the nations through Abraham affects the biblical narratives in Genesis–Exodus ("The Kerygma of the Yahwist" [tr. W. A. Benware], in W. Brueggemann and Wolff, *The Vitality of Old Testament Traditions,* 2nd ed. [Atlanta: John Knox, 1982], pp. 41-66, esp. pp. 55-56).

12. See H. B. Huffmon, "The Treaty Background of Hebrew *Yādaʿ*," *BASOR* 181 (1966) 31-37, esp. pp. 34-35; Eichrodt, *Theology of the Old Testament,* 2:290-94. In addition to Gen. 18:19, relevant texts include Exod. 33:12, 17; Deut. 9:24; 34:10; 2 Sam. 7:20 (= 1 Chr. 17:18); Jer. 1:5; 12:3; Hos. 13:5; Amos 3:2. See also J. Bergman and G. J. Botterweck, *TDOT,* 5:448-81, esp. p. 468.

guests (19:5). Here benign knowledge and diabolical knowledge are juxtaposed.

With Abraham's position as a covenant vassal of Yahweh comes certain responsibilities. He is to *instruct his family . . . to observe the way of Yahweh by practicing righteousness and justice.* Sandwiched between Abraham's role as host and intercessor is that of instructor. The reference to *righteousness and justice* has a double thrust. One, it provides a second ironical twist in the narrative. We have already compared Yahweh's knowledge of Abraham with his need for a closer look at Sodom. Now here we have God's charge to Abraham to teach his descendants about *justice (mišpāṭ).* But Abraham's concern is whether Yahweh himself will practice *mišpāṭ* (v. 25)!

A second thrust provided by the phrase *righteousness and justice* is that it places Abraham, proleptically, in the role of a prophet. For the message of Abraham to his children is the same as the message of the prophets to their contemporaries. They too were concerned for the practice of these two virtues.[13] Thus, before Abraham the prophetic intercessor emerges in this narrative, we encounter Abraham the prophetic exhorter. Implicit in this charge is the fidelity of Abraham and his offspring in meeting their covenant responsibilities. To that end, Gen. 18:19 is much like 17:1, 9-14 before it, and 22:15-18; 26:2-5 after it. In a context that overwhelmingly emphasizes the unilateral nature of the covenant with the patriarchs, the voice of conditionality and mutality is occasionally heard.

20-21 God's earlier hearing of Sarah's laugh is balanced by his hearing Sodom's *clamor* or "cry" *(zeʿāqâ).* It is not only the loud cry of Sodom that comes to Yahweh's attention but also its grave sin.[14] The first term, by itself, would not necessarily point to moral wrong, but the addition of "their sin" removes any doubt. In the very next verse (v. 21) Yahweh mentions only the cry, and not the sin, as the reason for his descent. It appears that sin is the cause, and the clamor of Sodom and Gomorrah is the result produced by this cause.

After making known to Abraham his diagnosis of the cities' ills, Yahweh declares to Abraham his intention to go down[15] and inspect the cities.

13. The phrase *ṣeḏāqâ ûmišpāṭ* appears less frequently (Ps. 33:5; Prov. 21:3) than *mišpāṭ ûṣeḏāqâ* (2 Sam. 8:15; 1 K. 10:9; Isa. 32:16; 33:5; 56:1; 59:9, 14; Jer. 9:23; 22:3, 15; 23:5; 33:15; Ezek. 18:5, 19, 21, 27; 33:14, 16, 19; 45:9; Amos 5:7, 24). The two words occur in a nonprophetic source in Neh. 2:20; 1 Chr. 18:14; 2 Chr. 9:8; Ps. 99:4.

14. Another reference to sin/iniquity that uses the root *kbd* is Ps. 38:5 (Eng. 4), "my iniquities . . . like a heavy burden they are too heavy for me *(ʿawōnōṯay . . . kemaśśāʾ kāḇēḏ yiḵbeḏû mimmennî).*

15. For the idea of Yahweh "going down *(yāraḏ)* cf. Gen. 11:5, 7; Exod. 3:8; Num. 11:17; 2 Sam. 22:10 (= Ps. 18:10 [Eng. 9]; Isa. 63:19 (Eng. 64:1); 64:2 (Eng. 3); Mic. 1:3. For his descent/manifestation in a theophany cf. Exod. 19:11, 18; Neh. 9:13; Isa. 31:4.

Thus Yahweh intends to set out on a mission of verification. Will what God sees confirm what he has already heard? Again, we have in this section a bold anthropomorphism — Yahweh will reconnoiter Sodom as investigator — that balances the anthropomorphism of vv. 1-15, viz., Yahweh stops off for rest and food at Abraham's home as guest. The modern reader may think it strange that Yahweh knows what he is about to do with Sodom (v. 17), he knows about its sin (v. 20), yet he announces his intention to make a judicial inquiry into the state of affairs in the city (v. 21). Is Yahweh fully informed about Sodom's turpitude or is he not? Had vv. 20-21 been a further soliloquy by Yahweh, then we would have no recourse but to suggest that vv. 20-21 are intrusive in the narrative.[16] Yet this is not a soliloquy but a speech made to Abraham. Later in the narrative Abraham will raise the issue of whether God is always and consistently just. Almost in anticipation of that interrogation, seemingly almost on the defensive, Yahweh informs Abraham not only of Sodom's state but of his intention to buttress that observation with a fact-finding mission. Thus, already Yahweh dilutes some of Abraham's concerns by letting the patriarch in on the thoroughness of his analysis of the situation at the two cities.

The Hebrew word for *clamor* in v. 20 *(zeʿāqâ)* differs only slightly from the word for *cry* in v. 21 *(ṣeʿāqâ),* that is, the initial letters (both interdentals). The first one is used twenty times in the OT, and the second one twenty-one times. The two words are interchangeable, as Gen. 18:18, 20, and other passages make clear.[17]

Both narrative and legal sections of the OT provide evidence that the basic nuance in this word is the cry of the oppressed because of harsh treatment.[18] For legal evidence we may turn to Exod. 22:22-23, the cry of the widow or the orphan who have been oppressed; Deut. 14:25, the cry of the

16. This is the view of L. Schmidt, *"De Deo": Studien zur Literarkritik und Theologie des Buches Jona, des Gesprächs zwischen Abraham und Jahwe in Gen 18:22ff. und von Hi 1,* BZAW 143 (Berlin: de Gruyter, 1976), pp. 131-64.

17. Thus, 1 Sam. 4:13-14, "all the city cried out [*zāʿaq*]. When Eli heard the outcry [*ṣeʿāqâ*]. . . ."; Jer. 25:34, 36, "wail, you shepherds, and cry [*zāʿaq*]. Hark, the cry [*ṣeʿāqâ*] of the shepherds"; Isa. 65:14, 19, "You shall cry out [*ṣāʿaq*] for pain of heart . . . no more shall be heard the cry of distress [*zeʿāqâ*]." Texts closest to Gen. 18:18, 20 with the interplay of the two substantives include Jer. 48:3-5, "a cry [*ṣeʿāqâ*] from Horonaim . . . a cry [*zeʿāqâ*] is heard as far as Zoar . . . the cry [*ṣeʿāqâ*] of destruction they have heard"; and Neh. 5:1, 6 "now there arose a great outcry [*ṣeʿāqâ*] . . . when I heard their outcry [*zeʿāqâ*]." See also G. Hasel, *"zāʿaq," TDOT,* 4:112-22. According to him *zeʿaqâ* and *ṣeʿāqâ* represent "the loud and agonized 'crying' of someone in acute distress, calling for help and seeking deliverance" (p. 115).

18. For a broad discussion of OT terminology for oppression, see Thomas D. Hanks, *God So Loved the Third World: The Bible, the Reformation, and Liberation Theologies,* tr. James C. Dekker (New York: Orbis, 1983), esp. pp. 3-40.

oppressed hired servant.[19] The root occurs in narratives such as the Cain-Abel story, with the voice of the blood of murdered Abel crying to God (Gen. 4:10), and in the story describing the oppression of the Israelites in Egypt (Exod. 2:23; 3:7, 9); it is also the cry that results from the divine judgment on Egypt (Exod. 11:6; 12:30). Similar to these references is the use of the root in Jeremiah to refer to the scream of terror that is heard when an individual or city is attacked and ravaged (Jer. 18:22; 20:16; 25:36; 48:3-5, 34; 49:21; 50:46; 51:54). In summary, the *clamor* or *cry* in Scripture is the cry of those who receive, illegitimately or legitimately, brutal punishment.

In the Sodom story the cry God hears cannot be one for which he is responsible. Then the cry must be either the cry rising from the city itself or else the cry about the city by nonresidents. The issue may be determined by how one understands the pronominal suffixes on *ṣaʿ^aqāṯāh,* "its/her cry" in v. 21 and *ṣaʿ^aqāṯām* "their cry" in 19:13. Thus one may understand "its/her cry" of 18:21 as either objective (i.e., the cry about the city, made by nonresidents) or subjective (i.e., the cry the city is making). The same goes for 19:13. The noun in "the clamor of Sodom and Gomorrah" (18:20) has no pronominal suffix; it is difficult to interpret this phrase as meaning anything other than the clamor that the city and its occupants are making. Because the verbs *ṣāʿaq/zāʿaq* are intransitive, it is impossible to read the pronominal suffixes as objective. Accordingly the cry of Sodom and Gomorrah mentioned in 18:20, 21 and 19:13 must be the cry that the city and its inhabitants are making.[20]

Sarna describes the sin of Sodom as "heinous moral and social corruption, an arrogant disregard of elementary human rights, a cynical insensitivity to the sufferings of others."[21] This is precisely the adumbration of Sodom and Gomorrah's sins given by Ezek. 16:49 — "pride, surfeit of food, prosperous ease, but did not aid the poor and the needy." This is not the total explanation of their sins, as Gen. 19 will make manifest, but it is a major part. Social immorality plays as large a role in the Sodom story as does sexual immorality.

Scholars have not missed the opportunity to compare the cry motif in Gen. 18–19 with the emphasis on noise *(rigmu)* in certain cuneiform stories. It is well known that the opening section of both the *Enuma elish* and the Atrahasis Epic cite the noise and commotion of the lesser gods and humanity, respectively, that prevented the chief god from getting his proper sleep.[22] Action was then

19. Cf. Job 34:28, which refers to the cry of the oppressed that attracts God's attention to the oppressor. As a result, divine wrath consumes the tyrant. Isa. 5:7 clearly delineates "outcry" as the negation of righteousness and justice.

20. Irvin, *Mytharion,* pp. 20-21.

21. Sarna, *Understanding Genesis,* p. 145.

22. In *Enuma elish,* Apsu and Tiamat engender two gods Lahmu and Lahamu, who in turn engender Avisher and Kishar. They gave birth to Anu (the god of heaven), and Anu became the father of Nudimmud (= Enki/Ea, the god of running waters, rivers, and

taken to solve the problem. It is, however, fanciful speculation to suggest that the Sodom-Gomorrah story in Genesis developed from these Babylonian stories.

---

marshes). These several generations of gods come together to dance, but in the process make too much noise for Apsu to tolerate. The story says:

By dancing they had the heart
of heaven's foundation worried.
Apsū could not subdue their clamor,
And Ti'mat kept silent before them.
Though their doings were noisome to her,
and their ways not good, she indulged them.

Later Apsu says to Tiamat:

Their ways have become noisome to me!
I am allowed no rest by day;
by night no sleep.
Let me abolish, yea, let me smash to bits
their ways
that peace may reign (again) and we may sleep.

(Translation of T. Jacobsen, *The Teasures of Darkness* [New Haven: Yale University, 1976], pp. 170-71. See also *ANET,* p. 61.)

Similarly the Atrahasis Epic draws attention to the increasing noise that humans were making, thus depriving the god Enlil of his sleep and inciting him to send a plague on the world.

Twelve hundred years [had not yet passed]
[When the land extended] and the peoples multiplied.
The [land] was bellowing [like a bull],
The god got disturbed with [their uproar].
[Enlil heard] their noise
[And addressed] the great gods,
"The noise of mankind [has become too intense for me],
[With their uproar] I am deprived of sleep
[. . . .] let there be plague."

(Translation of W. G. Lambert and A. R. Millard, *Atra-ḫāsis: The Babylonian Story of the Flood* [Oxford: Clarendon, 1969], p. 67. See also *ANET,* p. 106.)

Jacobsen has translated a cuneiform text from Nippur that dates back to Old Babylonian times (ca. 1600 B.C.). He calls it the "Eridu Genesis." A bilingual fragment of that text (Sumerian with Akkadian translation) from Ashurbanipal's library in Nineveh, and dated to ca. 600 B.C., begins with a list of kings and reigns, with a mention of the noise humans made. The din was so great it kept Enlil awake day and night until he finally decided to rid himself of these tormentors by sending a flood: "Enlil took a dislike to mankind, the clamor of their shouting . . . kept him sleepless." See T. Jacobsen, "The Eridu Genesis," *JBL* 100 (1981) 520. It is interesting to compare these references to divine sleeplessness with Elijah's mocking the prophets of Baal with the idea that Baal is sleeping (1 K. 18:27), versus the claim of the Psalter that Yahweh never needs sleep (Ps. 121:4), though some of the pious had their doubts at times (Ps. 44:24 [Eng. 23]).

Indeed, both the Genesis text and the Babylonian stories do emphasize the noise and the consequent destruction. But Genesis contrasts with the Babylonian stories in two ways: on the one hand, Genesis does not refer to the deity's problem with insomnia; on the other hand, the nonbiblical accounts do not have any moral overtones connected with the noise. To be sure, one would not be able to discern any moral understanding of the use of "cry" per se in v. 20. But its juxtaposition with "sin," in v. 20, and Abraham's later plea that Yahweh not destroy the innocent *(ṣaddîq)* with the wicked *(rāšāʿ)* would indicate that Yahweh's concerns reach beyond the volume of noise rising from the cities.

22 The "men" now continue their journey to Sodom, but *Abraham stood yet before Yahweh.* Earlier he had walked with him (v. 16); but now he stands before him. Earlier Abraham stood "by" Yahweh (v. 8, *ʿal*). Now he stands "before" *(lip̱nê)* him.

The expression *stand before (ʿāmaḏ lip̱nê)* is common in the OT. To stand before God may mean to worship him (Jer. 7:10), to enter his presence (Deut. 19:17; 29:14), or to serve him (1 K. 17:1; 18:15; 2 K. 3:14; 5:16). A special use of this phrase is to designate the intercessory ministry of the prophet. Thus, Yahweh says to Jeremiah, "Even if Moses and Samuel were to stand before me, my heart would not go out to this people" (Jer. 15:1). Later in the same chapter, after one of the prophet's outbursts, Yahweh says to Jeremiah, "If you return I will restore you that you may stand before me" (v. 19). In the light of Abraham's importunity before God that follows (Gen. 19:23-33), it should be apparent that when Abraham stands before God he is a precursor of the mediating prophet.

There is, however, some evidence that the text originally read: "Yahweh stood before Abraham." The Masoretic tradition has preserved a list of eighteen of the most ancient scribal corrections of the text, with the note "Ezra corrected eighteen words (of the Bible)," "eighteen words are euphemisms due to the scribes," or "eighteen words have been emended by the scribes."[23] Such changes are known as *tiqqûnê sōp̱ᵉrîm,* "emendations of the scribes." The purpose of these changes was to avoid what was considered irreverent, idolatrous, or blasphemous expressions.[24] Such changes were done, for example, by avoiding the juxtaposition of "curse" with God (1 Sam. 3:13), by changing the pronoun (Num. 11:15; Jer. 2:11; Ezek. 8:17), or by changing the word order (Gen. 18:22).

23. The texts are Gen. 18:22; Num. 11:15; 12:12; 1 Sam. 3:13; 2 Sam. 16:12; 20:1; 1 K. 12:16; 2 Chr. 10:16; Jer. 2:11; Ezek. 8:17; Hos. 4:7; Hab. 1:12; Zech. 2:12 (Eng. 8); Mal. 1:12; Ps. 106:20; Job 7:20; 32:3; Lam. 3:20.

24. See C. McCarthy, "Emendations of the Scribes," *IDBS,* pp. 263-64; G. E. Weil, "Qere-Kethibh (QK)," *IDBS,* pp. 717-18; J. D. Barthélemy, "Les tiqquné sopherim et la critique textuelle de l'Ancien Testament," in *Congress Volume: Bonn, 1962,* VTSup 9 (Leiden: Brill, 1963), pp. 285-304. See also Gen. Rabbah 49:7, "The men went on from there to Sodom while Abraham remained standing before the LORD. R. Simon said: 'This is a correction, for the *Shekinah* was actually waiting for Abraham.'"

Did the scribes think it too daring to have Yahweh standing before Abraham, that is, in the role of a servant? To avoid that possibility did they invert the word order and place Abraham before Yahweh? Note that the ancient versions (LXX, Targ., Vulg., Peshitta) give no hint of the supposed "original" reading. Also, in some of the earliest midrashim the verse is not marked as a *tiqqun.*[25] If someone felt that the idea of Yahweh standing before a mortal in Gen. 18:22 needed emendation, why was Exod. 17:6 not similarly treated: "I will stand before you there on the rock"? Finally, Gen. 19:27 supports the traditional rendering. It may be that discourse grammar (sentence structure, paragraph structure, and chiasmus) is an argument for the emendation of Masoretic tradition. But even here the evidence is inconclusive.[26]

23-33 In the first half of this chapter Yahweh raised the questions ("Where is Sarah"; "Why did Sarah laugh?") and Abraham supplied the answers. Now Abraham raises the questions (twice "Would you . . ?"; four times "Perhaps . . ?"), and Yahweh supplies the answers. Sarah's denial ("I did not laugh") is matched by Yahweh's denials here ("I would not destroy it").

Abraham begins by asking whether Yahweh would spare the city because of fifty innocent or righteous in Sodom, i.e., the faithful members of the community. When he consents, Abraham presses Yahweh to mitigate punishment if forty-five innocent were there. (The verb I have translated as "I venture" in v. 27 is *hô'altî,* the Hiphil of *yā'al,* "to begin." At times it refers to a new move, one associated with initiative and boldness [Josh. 7:7; Judg. 17:11; 1 Sam. 12:22].) With this Yahweh agrees also. Three times Abraham lowers the number by five (50 to 45 to 40). As his boldness grows he lowers it three more times, but now by tens (40 to 30 to 20 to 10)! No reason is given why Abraham stops at ten. Why not continue down to five, or even one?[27] It appears that Abraham's

25. See W. E. Barnes, "Ancient Corrections in the Text of the Old Testament *(Tikkun Sopherim),*" *JTS* 1 (1900) 387-414, esp. pp. 397, 404-5.

26. See F. I. Andersen, *The Sentence in Biblical Hebrew,* Janua Linguarum, Series Practica 231 (The Hague/Paris: Mouton, 1974), pp. 84-85; he has a lengthy note in support of the reading of the *tiqqun:* "This episode [viz., vv. 19-21] ends by stating what the travellers do in a chiastic sentence in which Yahweh is matched more appositely with the other two than Abraham is. Then Yahweh's tarrying with Abraham . . . is matched by Abraham's initiative in approaching with his intercessions" (p. 85).

27. J. Blenkinsopp ("Abraham and the Righteous of Sodom," *JQR* 33 [1982] 123) summarizes suggestions of earlier commentators. He notes the suggestion of L. Schmidt (*De Deo,* pp. 151-56) that 50 and 10 have a special significance as military and judicial subunits. Schmidt's proposal is that 50 stands for an extended family and 10 for the smallest unit constituting a group in the city. Perhaps for Abraham 10 was a sufficient figure to make his point, and to go beyond this number was unnecessary. Brueggemann (*CBQ* 47 [1985] 410) says that "In its outcome the narrative is thoroughly Jewish because the bottom line is the minimum often, a minyan." J. L. Crenshaw (*A Whirlpool of Torment: Israelite Traditions of God as an Oppressive Presence,* OBT [Philadelphia: Fortress, 1984], p. 20

concern is twofold. His first concern, as expressed in v. 23, is whether Yahweh would indiscriminately kill the innocent along with the guilty. Thus, in v. 23 the emphasis is on the preservation of the *ṣaddîq*. But in vv. 24ff. Abraham expands his concern to include the preservation of the city/the place *(hāʿîr/lammāqôm)* because of the presence of a remnant of *ṣaddîq*.

Nowhere does Abraham challenge God's evaluation of Sodom's moral turpitude. That judgment is not up for debate. Nor does he at any point turn to Sodom to urge repentance. Rather, he turns to God to ask for divine mercy. In so doing he becomes the pattern for other intercessors: Samuel (1 Sam. 7:5-9; 12:19-25), Elijah (1 K. 17:17-23), Elisha (2 K. 4:33; 6:15-20), Job (Job 42:7-9), Amos (Amos 7:1-6), and especially Moses (Exod. 32:11-13, 31-34; 33:12-15; 34:9; Num. 12:11-13; 14:13-19; Deut. 9:16-29).

The only reason Abraham can appeal to Yahweh's mercy is because of what Abraham knows about Yahweh's character. Yahweh can be merciful because he is righteous and just. Abraham's confidence in Yahweh's character is expressed in his stunning question: *Shall not he who judges all the earth give right judgment?* (v. 25b).[28] This question may be interpreted as a challenge hurled by Abraham toward God,[29] or it may be understood as a testimony by Abraham about his belief in his God's integrity and predictability.

Abraham's concern is: Which affects God more regarding Sodom's future — the many who are wicked or the few who are innocent? The transparent answer that is given is that it is the few who are innocent. Not only are the ten righteous more important, but they become a holy remnant[30] and the means of the entire community's preservation. Just as the nations of the earth find blessing in Abraham and his seed, so the guilty of Sodom and Gomorrah find mercy in the lives of their fellow citizens who are innocent.

Later prophetic tradition both affirmed and challenged the indubitable effects that the lives of one group have on another. For affirmation we may consider God's word to Jeremiah (5:1): "Run to and fro the streets of Jerusalem, look and take note! Search her squares to see if you can find a man,

---

n. 38) suggests that in halting at 10, Abraham "stopped short of pushing the deity to the limit."

28. See J. Crenshaw, "Introduction: The Shift from Theodicy to Anthropodicy," in *Theodicy in the Old Testament,* IRT 4, ed. Crenshaw (Philadelphia: Fortress, 1983), p. 7; idem, "Theodicy," *IDBS,* p. 895; R. P. Carroll, "Theodicy and the Community: The Subtext of Jeremiah v 1-6," *OTS* 23 (1984) 27-28.

29. See J. Crenshaw, "Popular Questioning of the Justice of God in Ancient Israel," *ZAW* 82 (1970) 385; C. S. Rodd, "Shall not the judge of all the earth do what is just? (Gen. 18:25)," *ExpTim* 83 (1971/72) 137-39; S. E. Balentine, "Prayers for Justice in the Old Testament: Theodicy and Theology," *CBQ* 51 (1989) 597-616.

30. See G. Hasel, *The Remnant* (Berrien Springs, MI: Andrews University, 1974), pp. 147-52.

one who does justice and seeks truth, that I may forgive her." The presence of one righteous person would suffice to spare Jerusalem.[31] But the same Jeremiah (31:29-30) — as well as his junior contemporary Ezekiel (14:12-23; 18:2-4) — suggests that each generation stands on its own with regard to the consequences of guilt. Ezek. 14:12ff. is especially strong in denying the fact that a righteous person had influence with God to the point of nullifying a divine decree. "Thus, with one sharp stroke, the theological presupposition of Genesis 18, in which YHWH himself acknowledges the theoretical possibility that a minimum number (ten) of righteous men could save a sin-filled city by virtue of their merits, is thoroughly rejected."[32]

THE NEW TESTAMENT APPROPRIATION

a. Gen. 18:12 and 1 Pet. 3:6

In 1 Pet. 3:1-6 the author addresses himself to the issue of wives and their relationship with their husbands. On the part of the wife, he encourages submissiveness, exemplary behavior, and inner adornment. V. 1b would suggest that the purpose behind these exhortations is a missionary one: "though they [the husbands] do not obey the word, they may be won without a word by the behavior of their wives." Such evangelization is accomplished not through oral persuasion but through exemplary conduct.

This is how "holy women" (v. 5) ought to behave. To provide an antecedent for such behavior Peter appeals to Gen. 18:12: "as Sarah obeyed Abraham, calling him lord."[1] The pertinent words of Sarah in Gen. 18:12 are "my husband/lord is old" *('ᵃḏōnî zāqēn),* which the LXX rendered as *ho de kýrios mou presbýteros.* It is the LXX's use of *kýrios* that Peter picked up and focused on. Peter's reference to Sarah's obedience to Abraham is not mentioned per se in Genesis. But because Peter puts the word "obeyed" in the aorist tense, he had a specific incident in mind, and Gen. 18:1-15 is that incident.

Peter goes on to suggest that those wives who conduct themselves like

31. For a wisdom text that makes this same claim see Job 22:28-30, esp. v. 30. M. Pope (*Job,* AB, 3rd ed. [Garden City, NY: Doubleday, 1973], p. 168) provides references in rabbinical literature to the idea of saving the wicked out of consideration for the righteous.

32. M. Fishbane, "Sin and Judgment in the Prophecies of Ezekiel," in *Interpreting the Prophets,* ed. J. L. Mays and P. J. Achtemeier (Philadelphia: Fortress, 1987), p. 175. I have corrected an obvious typographical error: Fishbane referred to "Genesis 19" rather than Gen. 18.

1. D. L. Balch draws attention to Jewish texts that reversed the order of obedience (*Let Wives Be Submissive: The Domestic Code in I Peter,* SBLMS 26 [Chico, CA: Scholars, 1981], p. 114 n. 80). Abraham "obeys" Sarah in taking Hagar as a wife (Jub. 17:6; Philo *Cherubim* 9; *Preliminary Studies* 68; *Allegorical Interpretations* 3.244-45).

Sarah become her children (v. 6b). As Abraham is the father of the faithful (Rom. 4:11), so also Sarah is the mother of the holy, virtuous wife.

b. Gen. 18:11-14 and Heb. 11:11

Hebrews 11:11 makes the first mention in this chapter of the faith of a woman. Sarah, she who is famous for her skeptical laughter, is presented as a faith model. It was by faith that she received strength to conceive. The use of Sarah as an illustration contrasts strongly with Paul, who nowhere, in all his allusions to the faith of the patriarchs, mentions the faith of Sarah.

The text has, however, textual and interpretative problems. One problem is immediately observable in that some versions have Abraham as the subject of the sentence (e.g., NIV), and others have Sarah as the subject (e.g., RSV). The main problem concerns the presence of "even Sarah" (in the nominative case) and "she received power to conceive." This second phrase *(dýnamin eis katabolēn spérmatos élaben),* literally, "(s)he received power for the deposition of seed," refers to the act of a male.

To get out of the impasse of female subject and male activity, two changes in the text have been suggested. The more radical is simply to excise "even Sarah." In this way the problem is neatly removed, and Abraham becomes the subject of both sentences. Another solution is to read "even Sarah" as dative rather than nominative: "by faith he [Abraham] also, together with Sarah, received power to beget a child when he was past age, since he counted him faithful who had promised."[2]

One can make a plausible case for retaining Sarah as the subject throughout the entire verse. The phrase "even Sarah" may give one an insight into the author's perspective on Gen. 18. R. V. G. Tasker suggests: "It is surely just the paradoxical character of the illustration which is a sign of its genuineness. . . . Even Sarah'a acceptance of a promise which at first she seemed to hear with indifference is to the mind of the *auctor ad Hebraeos* a venture into the unseen world which faith makes real."[3]

Another factor weighing in favor of the Sarah interpretation is the phrase *kai para kairón hēlikías,* literally, "even beyond the season of life."[4]

2. See F. F. Bruce, *The Epistle to the Hebrews,* NICNT (Grand Rapids: Eerdmans, 1964), pp. 301-2.

3. R. V. G. Tasker, *NTS* 1 (1954-55) 182-83 (quoted by Bruce, *Hebrews,* p. 300; and by T. Hewitt, *The Epistle to the Hebrews,* TNTC [Grand Rapids: Eerdmans, 1960], p. 175).

4. See J. Moffatt, *A Critical and Exegetical Commentary on the Epistle to the Hebrews,* ICC (Edinburgh: T. & T. Clark, 1924), p. 171. G. W. Buchanan (*To the Hebrews,* AB [Garden City, NY: Doubleday, 1972], p. 190) says of *hēlikías* that "it refers to the age of maturity, the prime of life. It generally distinguishes adulthood from childhood. In early

Although the phrase could refer to Abraham, the reference to a woman who has passed her years of childbearing is more bold and dramatic. A woman loses her ability to conceive before a man loses his ability to inseminate. This, then, is what made Sarah's faith so authentic — not her advanced age per se but that she had gone beyond the period of fertility. It may be that the writer of Hebrews observes a bit more faith on Sarah's part, as she reflects on the possibility of becoming pregnant, than does the narrator in Gen. 18.

H. THE ANNIHILATION OF SODOM AND GOMORRAH (19:1-38)

1. LOT AS HOST AND GUARDIAN (19:1-11)

1 *Two messengers reached Sodom in the evening. Lot, sitting by the gate of Sodom, saw them and arose to greet them; bowing down with his face*[1] *to the ground,*

2 *he said: "My lords, please come aside to your servant's house and spend the night, and bathe your feet. You can rise early and be on your way." They said "No, we will spend the night in the square."*[2]

3 *He was so insistent, however, that they turned aside to his place and entered his house. He prepared for them a meal.*[3] *He baked unleavened cakes, and they dined.*

4 *But even before they retired,*[4] *the townspeople, the men of Sodom,*

---

years it would mark the beginning of menstruation for a woman, but it also refers to the entire period from the beginning of menstruation to the beginning of menopause, namely, the period of fertility."

1. Here *'appayim,* "face," follows *yištaḥû,* but it is lacking in 18:2, where the same verb is used with Abraham when he bows before his visitors. The inclusion of *'appayim* in 19:1 may indicate that Lot's greeting of the two messengers was more pronounced than the greeting extended by Abraham to the three men in 18:2.

2. *rāḥôḇ,* lit., "broad place," refers to the town square (see NAB, NIV) and not to the street (see AV, RSV, NEB). Cf. Judg. 19:15, 17, 20; Jer. 9:21; Amos 5:16; etc.

3. *mišteh* often means "feast, banquet." What Lot prepared was decidedly less modest. Speiser (*Genesis,* p. 139) remarks, "The description is meant to contrast with the semolina biscuits of xviii:6; hurriedly baked flat flaps of bread are the daily fare of the region." This might suggest that the author is contrasting the lavish dinner that Abraham (a tent dweller) served his guests with the nonexceptional dinner that Lot (a city dweller) served his guests. The offer of hospitality is greater in a village context than in an urban one.

4. The verb for "retire," *šāḵaḇ,* means "lay down"; some OT texts use it in decidedly sexual situations. For example, Potiphar's wife asked Joseph to "lie" with her (39:7). Its use at the beginning of v. 4 may be deliberate in setting the stage for what follows.

young and old[5] from every quarter, had circled the house.
5 *They called to Lot and said to him: "Where are the men who came to you tonight? Bring them out to us so that we may know them."*
6 *Lot went out to them at the entrance, but the door he closed behind him.*
7 *He said: "Please, my brothers, do not act wickedly.*
8 *Look, I have two daughters who have never known a man. Let me bring them out to you, and you may do to them as you wish. But to these[6] men do not do anything, forasmuch[7] as they have come under the shelter of my roof."[8]*
9 *They retorted: "Stand back![9] This one,"[10] they said, "came as a transient, and now he would play judge![11] We will deal worse with you than with them." With that, they jostled the man Lot, and surged forward to break down the door.*
10 *But the men extended their hands and pulled Lot inside with them, and the door they slammed shut.*
11 *The men who were at the house's entrance, small and great,[12] they*

5. Another clear case of merism. The expression does not mean that Lot's house was surrounded by elderly men and children. Rather, it indicates that all, or most, adult males took part in the incident. See A. M. Honeyman, "*Merismus* in Biblical Hebrew," *JBL* 71 (1952) 12.

6. *hā'ēl* is an abbreviation for *ha'ēlleh,* used also in 19:25; 26:3, 4; Lev. 18:27; Deut. 4:42; 7:22; 19:11. Cf. 1 Chr. 20:8 and Num. 24:23, which demonstrate the use of *'ēl* for *'ēlleh.*

7. The use of *'al kēn* meaning "forasmuch, because" is rare. See Num. 14:43; 2 Sam. 7:22. Normally the expression connotes purpose, i.e., "therefore."

8. *qorâ* is a rare word appearing here and in 2 K. 6:2, 5; 2 Chr. 3:7; Cant. 1:17. It means "log" or "beam." BDB, p. 900a, suggests "my roof-tree" for Gen. 19:8, and "rafters" for 2 Chr. 3:7. "Beam" is the meaning in 2 K. 6:2, 5.

9. *hāleʼâ* may have either a positional meaning, as here, or a temporal meaning, "from then on," with the former meaning more likely the original one. See G. Brin, "The Formulae 'From . . . and Onward/Upward' (*m . . . whl'h/wm'lh*)," *JBL* 99 (1980) 161. *nāgaš* normally means "to come forward, nearer," and that is its meaning in the latter part of the verse (which I have translated "they surged forward"). The adverb that follows *nāgaš* in the first part of the verse permits the translation "stand back!"

10. What is the function of the *h* on *hā'eḥāḏ*? My translation takes the *h* as the definite article, used to draw attention to Lot's solitary position (as in German *der Eine da*). It could also be the interrogative *h* if one takes *hā'eḥāḏ* as evidence that before *aleph* there was a tendency to vocalize the interrogative *h* with full vowels. See R. Gordis, *Koheleth: The Man and His World,* 3rd ed. (New York: Schocken, 1968), p. 238; and J. Milgrom, *Leviticus 1–16,* AB (New York: Doubleday, 1991), p. 627 ("the interrogative *heh* is vocalized as a definite article only when the question is rhetorical and the answer is certain").

11. The use of the infinitive absolute after a finite verb is rare. For examples see GKC, § 113r, and Ezek. 17:10 *(tîḇaš yāḇōš).*

12. For other instances of *miqqāṭōn weʻaḏ-gāḏôl* cf. 1 Sam. 5:9; 30:19; 2 K. 23:2; 2 Chr. 15:13; 34:30; Esth. 1:5, 20; Jer. 6:13; 31:34; 42:8; Jon. 3:5; cf. in the NT John 8:9.

struck with a blinding flash[13] *so that they became exhausted*[14] *trying to find the door.*

We would argue most strongly against the position that views Gen. 18 and 19 as two originally independent narratives that were only subsequently sutured.[15] First, the two chapters share a great deal of similar vocabulary. For example, Van Seters presents no less than seventeen illustrations of similarities.[16] Second, the shift from action in the heat of the day (18:1) under a tree (18:8) to action in the evening (19:1) inside a house (19:3) fits the parameters of the story quite nicely. That is, the tent-dwelling (i.e., outside a city) Abraham of ch. 18 contrasts with the house-dwelling (i.e., inside a city) Lot of ch. 19; furthermore, the ability of these two messengers to make the trip from Mamre, just north of Hebron (18:1) to Sodom (19:1, a journey of some forty miles that would normally take at least two days) in just several hours (from the midafternoon of 18:1 to the evening of 19:1) reinforces the supernatural nature of these messengers. Third, the emphasis on the two angels/messengers in ch. 19 is consonant with the presence of the three emissaries in ch. 18. For, according to the narrative, Yahweh has sent his two companions on ahead of him (18:22a), while Yahweh himself stayed behind to converse with and hear out Abraham (18:22b). Fourth, in ch. 18 it is Yahweh who lingers — to talk with Abraham. In ch. 19 it is Lot who lingers, unable to leave Sodom. Finally, we note that potential destruction (ch. 18) becomes actualized destruction (ch. 19).[17]

Again, this expression is a merism; the reference is not to "small and great" but to everyone, regardless of rank or of age.

13. *sanwērîm* is used only here and in 2 K. 6:18. Speiser (*Genesis,* p. 139) explains it as a loanword based on Akk. *šunwurum,* an adjective form with superlative or elative force: "having extraordinary brightness." The more common Hebrew word for "blindness" is *'iwwārôn.* W. von Soden ("Hebräische Problemwörter," *UF* 18 [1986] 341-44) relates *sanwērîm* in Gen. 19:11 and 2 K. 6:18 to Akk. *sinnurbû* ("defect of eye") and translates the Hebrew word "temporary blindness."

14. Some (e.g., Speiser, *Genesis,* p. 140) emend MT *wayyil'û* (Qal) to *wayyillā'û* (Niphal), "they were unable to find" or "they wearied themselves in vain trying to find." But this changes seems unnecessary. Exod. 7:18 illustrates that the Niphal of this root may carry the same meaning and syntax as the Qal. See M. J. Dahood, "Scriptio defectiva in Judges 1,19," *Bib* 60 (1979) 570. Pope's translation of the Qal of *lā'â* in Job 4:2 also illustrates the meaning "be weary" or "become exhausted" "Should one dare a word, could you bear it?" (*Job,* AB, 3rd ed. [Garden City, NY: Doubleday, 1973], pp. 34-35), i.e., "would you be weary?"

15. As argued by R. Kilian, "Zur Überlieferungsgeschichte Lot," *BZ* 14 (1970) 23-27; M. Noth, *A History of Pentateuchal Traditions,* tr. B. W. Anderson (Englewood Cliffs, NJ: Prentice-Hall, 1972), pp. 151-54.

16. J. Van Seters, *Abraham in History and Tradition* (New Haven: Yale University, 1975), pp. 215-16. I would add to this list the dual emphasis on "know" in 18:19 and 19:5, 8.

17. Ibid., p. 216: "The notion that these stories could gradually come together and develop such similar vocabulary and thematic dovetailing through a complex process of

1 The two *messengers* (a term used only here in the narrative) moved quickly! They were at Sodom by evening. The *evening* of 19:1 must be the same day as the midafternoon of 18:1. The location of *Sodom* is uncertain. Local tradition favors a site at the southern end of the Dead Sea, either on the west side (cf. the Arabic name Jebel Usdum, lit., "mount of Sodom") or the east side (perhaps near Bab edh-Dhraʿ). Sodom's connection with Zoar (Gen. 13:10; 14:2, 8) supports a site in the south, for Zoar is in the Jordan Valley (Deut. 34:3) near Moab (Isa. 15:5; Jer. 48:34). A few scholars have searched for Sodom and Gomorrah at the northern end of the Dead Sea. No indubitable archeological evidence has yet emerged to substantiate either a northern or a southern location.

If Sodom is at the northern tip of the Dead Sea, the messengers still had to travel eighteen miles from Mamre/Hebron to reach it (see our comments above at 18:16). If Sodom is at the southern tip of the Dead Sea that journey would be extended to forty miles. In either case, to walk eighteen miles or forty miles between midafternoon and evening is no small feat (angels excepted!). Perhaps the alacrity with which the messengers moved not only reinforces their supernatural nature but also provides a stunning contrast with Lot, who moves slowly and hesitantly. Thus the context permits the translation of *mal'āḵîm* as "angels," that is, supernatural messengers.[18] Although some do render *mal'āḵîm* as "angels" in 19:1 (KJV, NKJV, RSV JB, NJPS, Speiser), others opt for "messengers" (von Rad, Westermann) on the basis that this rendering is more appropriate to the Hebrew. Indeed, since the word frequently applies to human messengers (see, e.g., Gen. 32:4 [Eng. 3]) as well as supernatural messengers, "messenger" adequately represents all uses of the word. Furthermore, the Hebrew noun *mal'āḵ* derives from the verb *lā'aḵ,* which does not occur in the Hebrew Bible but does occur in Ugaritic ("to send"), and this derivation argues for *mal'āḵ* as meaning "one sent."

Thus the Hebrew Bible does not distinguish between human and supernatural *mal'āḵîm;* one word covers both groups. The LXX also uses one word, *ángelos,* to render *mal'āḵ* in reference to both human and supernatural messengers. It is the Vulg. that first used a special word, *angelus,* when the text referred to a messenger of God, an "angel" (19:1, *duo angeli*), and *nuntio* when the text referred to a human messenger. But the bifurcation by the Vulg. of *mal'āḵ* into *angelus/nuntio* is purely arbitrary. That the *mal'āḵîm* of 19:1 are elsewhere in chs. 18 and 19 called "men" (*'ᵃnāšîm,* 18:2, 16, 22; 19:5,

oral tradition is complete fantasy. All of these features are indications of deliberate literary composition."

18. For studies on *mal'āḵ,* see A. Boling, *TWOT,* 1:464-65; R. Ficker, *THAT,* 1:900-908.

8) suggests that the writer of this story conceived of the messengers that appeared to Lot as human beings, not as winged, supernatural beings.[19]

Their arrival in Sodom finds Lot sitting by the gate of Sodom. The *gate* is a common place for meeting in the East, either for conversation, for business, or for the administration of justice.[20] It is normally a place where the town leaders (Deut. 21:19; Josh. 20:4) and kings (1 K. 22:10) assemble to adjudicate the business at hand. Yet Lot is among them, even though he is a "transient" (v. 9, *gûr*).

Two of Lot's actions are commendable. First, he alone (assuming he is not the only one sitting by the gateway of Sodom, for what would he be doing there by himself?) acknowledged the newcomers. Second, his acknowledgment was anything but cold and formal. He essentially did obeisance, *bowing down with his face to the ground!* Such action by Lot toward the newcomers who approach him would be strange. It is the newcomer who is expected to genuflect, as does Abraham the outsider when he approaches the sons of Heth (Gen. 23:7, 12). Here Lot actually outdoes his uncle in his show of welcome to the newcomers. Lot's actions may be dictated by more than courtesy. Perhaps the strangers appeared to Lot to be important men.

2 Lot is extremely courteous but equally ignorant. While Lot shares his uncle's penchant for courtesy, he does not share his uncle's concern for Sodom's future. He appears to be quite comfortable as a town resident, and the outcry that God has heard Lot has not heard. Abraham knows full well why his two visitors are continuing on to Sodom. Lot does not share that knowledge. He assumes that they are travelers who wish only to spend the night in town. Accordingly, he offers them a night's lodging. Little does Lot know that his overnight guests will play a part in destroying Sodom until they inform him of that fact in v. 13.

3 Because of Lot's persistence,[21] the visitors abandoned their original intention to stay outside, and instead accepted his offer of overnight lodging in

19. J. Akao, "Yahweh and *Mal'ak* in the Early Traditions of Israel: A Study of the Underlying Traditions of Yahweh/Angel Theophany in Exodus 3," *IBS* 12 (1990) 72-85; Irvin's excursus on "The Theological Meaning of Angels in the Genesis Narratives," in *Mytharion,* pp. 90-104.

20. For "gate" as a gathering place cf. Gen. 23:10, 18; Deut. 21:19; 22:15; 25:7; Ruth 4:1ff., 11; 1 K. 22:10; Job 5:4; Ps. 127:5; Prov. 31:23; Amos 5:10, 12, 15. It is possible that Lot sits at the city gates as a solitary figure, but given the nature of the gates as a place of community activities and given the fact that all these references to "gates" mention the presence of some kind of a group that has convened at the gates, it is most likely that Lot is there mingling with a larger group.

21. The root used to describe Lot's persuasiveness with the angels *(pṣr)* is used again a few verses later (v. 9), but this time to describe how the townspeople "jostled" Lot. Lot pressured the angels, and the Sodomites pressured Lot.

his home. Here is another parallel between uncle and nephew. Abraham persuades Yahweh to change his mind about the indiscriminant annihilation of Sodom. Lot persuades two supernatural beings to change their mind about where they will spend the night. But Lot was apparently not equally persuasive regarding the Sodomites. His presence there failed to have a redeeming influence.

Gracious host that he is, Lot insists that his guests eat with him as well as sleep in his home. The light meal he serves them consists of *unleavened cakes,* that is, a kind of biscuit which could be baked rapidly. Unlike Abraham, who assigned kitchen duties to his wife (18:6), Lot assumes these responsibilities himself. In such behavior he is like Gideon (Judg. 6:19), who offers to his divine visitor a meal consisting of a kid and unleavened cakes.[22]

4-5 Here for the first time the nature of Sodom's sin is clearly revealed. An earlier statement (13:13) was content to evaluate the Sodomites as "evil" and "sinners." The story that is about to unfold will substantiate that statement with specific details.

Before the guests can retire, the house of Lot is surrounded[23] by the townsmen, who want to *know* Lot's guests. This situation is somewhat ironical. The Sodomites want to "know" two men whom Lot himself does not really "know." We know that he does not know their identity or the reason for their mission to Sodom.

Much debate has focused on these two verses and the meaning of *know.* In the OT the Hebrew root *yd'* and its derivatives occur 1,058 times. Fifteen of the 948 instances of the verb refer to sexual knowledge.[24] These fifteen passages include instances where the man is the subject, where the woman is the subject, and where man is both subject and object.[25] While it is well known

22. The possible textual and interpretative problems in Judg. 6:19, and how this verse is clarified by Gen. 18:6 and 19:3, are discussed by D. R. Ap-Thomas, "The Ephah of Meal in Judges VI.19," *JTS* 41 (1940) 175-77.

23. Speiser (*Genesis,* p. 139) notes that a number of Hebrew verbs *(sāḇaḇ, qāhal, kāḇēḏ)* when used in the Niphal and followed by the preposition *'al* convey hostile intentions. To capture that nuance, he translates *nāsabbû 'al habbayiṯ* in the later part of v. 4 as "they closed in on the house." See Josh. 7:9 for the same construction, and Judg. 19:22 for an approximate construction (accusative instead of preposition): *nāsabbû 'eṯ habbayiṯ.*

24. These statistics are taken from G. J. Botterweck, *"yāḏa',"* *TDOT,* 5:453.

25. A man is the subject in Gen. 4:1, 17, 25; 24:16; 38:26; Judg. 19:25; 1 Sam. 1:19; 1 K. 1:4; a woman is the subject in Gen. 19:8; Num. 31:17, 18, 35; Judg. 11:39; a man is both subject and object in Gen. 19:5; Judg. 19:22. Heterosexual intercourse is in view in all but the last two references, which refer to homosexual intercourse. Interestingly, in Gen. 19:5 but not in Judg. 19:22 or anywhere else, the LXX renders *yāḏa'* with *syngin̄ōskō* ("to meet, converse with") instead of the usual *ginṓskō.* The LXX has here chosen a word capable of innocuous interpretation in the context. See J. A. Lee, "Equivocal and Stereotyped Renderings in the LXX," *RB* 87 (1980) 109-10.

that Heb. *yāḏaʿ* can connote sexual knowledge, what is not as well known is that Hebrew shares this feature with other Semitic languages.[26]

What is its meaning in Gen. 19:5? Some maintain that *know* in this verse should not be included with the fifteen passages mentioned above. Rather, a case is made that *yāḏaʿ* carries here its normal meaning of "become acquainted with."[27] This viewpoint argues that the sin of the Sodomites is a violation of the rules of hospitality. Because he is only a sojourner, Lot has exceeded his privileges. Since he has no authority to monopolize the time of these visitors, the men of Sodom request the opportunity to meet and get to know these two outsiders.

This interpretation can only be evaluated as wild and fanciful. For when Lot responds by offering his daughters "who have never known a man" (v. 8), it becomes clear that the issue is intercourse and not friendship.[28] Lot would never have made such an unusual suggestion if the request was only for a handshake and moments of chitchat.

Among those who agree that the issue is sexual, the question arises whether the issue is homosexual relations per se or homosexual rape. The answer depends on how one chooses to translate *yāḏaʿ*. For instance, compare Speiser's "bring them out to us that we may get familiar with them" with JB's "hand them over to us so that we may abuse them."

We see at least four problems with the view that the prohibition here is only on homosexual rape. First, nowhere in the OT does the verb *yāḏaʿ* have the nuance of "abuse" or "violate." Second, the OT uses unmistakable language to relate rape incidents. Thus the Shechemites "seized" and "lay with" and "humbled" Dinah (Gen. 34:2). Amnon "forced" and "lay with" his half-sister Tamar (2 Sam. 13:14). Similarly, the biblical laws about rape also use these terms: "seize," "lie with" (Deut. 22:25-27). Third, this interpretation forces one meaning on "know" in v. 5 (i.e., "abuse") but a different meaning on "know" three verses later (i.e., "have intercourse with"), for it is unlikely that Lot is saying: "I have two daughters who have never been abused." Fourth, such an

26. Law 130 in the Code of Hammurapi reads: "If a seignior [a free man, perhaps a noble] bound the (betrothed) wife of a(nother) seignior, who had had no intercourse with [lit., "had not known"] a male . . ." (*ANET,* p. 171). For other references to this idiom in cuneiform literature see W. von Soden, *"edû," Akkadisches Handwörterbuch,* 3 vols. (Wiesbaden: Harrassowitz, 1965-81), 1:188; and *CAD,* 7:28. But neither von Soden nor *CAD* lists many references for this use of *edû/idû.*

27. See D. S. Bailey, *Homosexuality and the Western Christian Tradition* (London; Longmans, 1955), pp. 4ff. This is also the position of J. J. McNeill, *The Church and the Homosexual* (Kansas City, KS; Sheed, Andrews and McMeel, 1976), pp. 42-50.

28. See Kidner, *Genesis,* pp. 136-37; P. M. Ukleja, "Homosexuality and the Old Testament," *BSac* 140 (1983) 260-62; D. L. Bartlett, "A Biblical Perspective on Homosexuality," *Foundations* 20 (1977) 134.

interpretation forces these incredible words in Lot's mouth: "Do not rape my visitors. Here are my daughters, both virgins — rape them!" Clearly, then, the incident frowns on homosexual relations for whatever reason.[29] Note that in the often-cited parallel to Gen. 19, viz., Judg. 19, the host offers both his own virgin daughter and his guest's concubine to Gibeah's city dwellers with the statement "and sexually mistreat them" (*w^{e}ʿannû ʾôṯām,* v. 24). By contrast, Lot avoids using any verb that has clear-cut indications of sexual aggression. Still, the reader of this narrative cannot avoid puzzlement over Lot's willingness to make his daughters available to the people of Sodom for their sexual pleasure, even if he acts out of a desire for hospitality for his guests. In any case, his action is unsuccessful, unheroic, and it "may even make the audience of the story relieved not to be among the daughters of Lot."[30]

6-8 Lot now becomes a mediator. The two messengers are behind him, and many men are in front of him. But as a mediator Lot's approach is to strike a compromise. Rather than attempt to raise the moral conscience of the Sodomites, he offers to assuage their lust by handing over his two virgin daughters. He is willing to make his daughters vulnerable for the sake of his guests, but he is not willing to offer himself. The motif of the female who is exposed for the sake of some male(s) appeared earlier in ch. 12. There Abraham placed Sarah at the mercy of Pharaoh in the hopes of saving his own skin. Just as Sarah was not solicited either for approval or disapproval for her part in her husband's proposed ruse, so the daughters of Lot are not consulted by their father about their willingness to be substitutes for the messengers in Lot's house.

Lot's approach to the situation bears in two ways on the larger context of chs. 18–19. First, the proposal of Lot that the daughters be surrogates for the guests points to a theme common to both of these chapters. One group (the wicked Sodomites, the two visitors) will be spared because of the presence of another group (the innocent Sodomites, Lot's daughters). Second, Lot's proposal regarding his daughters is later turned around via the daughter's proposal in relation to their father (vv. 30-38). If he is so willing to turn them over as pawns to a sexually aroused mob, then they, when their chance comes,

29. R. Gordis observes that "it is difficult to see how the clear indication in both Genesis and Judges that homosexuality is worse than rape can be ignored" ("Homosexuality and the Homosexual," in *Homosexuality and Ethics,* ed. E. Batchelor, Jr. [New York: Pilgrim, 1980], p. 250 n. 10). Or, I might add, that homosexual rape is as vicious as heterosexual rape.

30. G. Coats, "Lot: A Foil in the Abraham Saga," in *Understanding the Word: Essays in Honour of Bernhard W. Anderson,* ed. James T. Butler, et al., JSOTSup 37 (Sheffield: JSOT, 1985), p. 122. Note also this comment: "The proposition is, to put it mildly, disgusting. . . . Two young women, captive to their father's will, dragged from what they may have supposed was the security of their home, in exchange for two grown men who arrive uninvited, of their own accord, at night in a strange city" (D. N. Fewell and D. M. Gunn, *Gender, Power, and Promise* [Nashville: Abingdon, 1993], p. 58).

will not hesitate to get their father drunk and have intercourse with him. One licentious act deserves another, with villain and victim exchanging roles.

It may well be that Lot is not following the path of least resistance or stooping to the level of the townsmen. Oriental ethics decreed that a host is responsible for the safety of his guests. If anything happens to his guests while they are under his roof, the host is culpable. This is a concept the Hebrews shared with their neighbors. In the opening lines of the Epic of Aqhat from Ugarit, Baal intercedes on behalf of Aqhat that Aqhat may have a son. Baal lists the qualities and responsibilities of a model son with respect to his father. The son (1) sets up the stela of his ancestral gods in the shrine; (2) lays his people to rest on earth; (3) sends out his incense from the dust; (4) is the soldier of his post (i.e., protects his father's tomb); (5) heaps the tablets of his office;[31] and (6) drives out those who would abuse his houseguest.[32] Lot's conundrum in this situation is to decide which of his two options is the lesser (or greater) evil: exposing his guests to the crowd, and thus withdrawing his hospitality and the protection of his roof, or exposing his two daughters to deflowering, and thus quenching the thirst of the mob for sexual gratification through females rather than through males.

One should not use this custom, however, to exonerate Lot. His actions are as inexcusable as those of Abraham in Egypt (ch. 12) and those that follow in Gerar (ch. 20). Abraham's uncertainty about how he will be received by the Egyptians equals Lot's uncertainty as he faces the rapacious mob that surrounds his house. Both are confronted by potentially hazardous situations. To ameliorate an explosive situation both uncle and nephew degrade themselves by proposing something unconscionable.

9 The townsmen disqualify Lot's setting himself up as a judge because he is a newcomer, a *gēr.* The same Hebrew form (preposition plus infinitive construct, *lāgûr*) was used in 12:10 to describe Abram's short-lived trip to Egypt to escape the famine in Canaan. A sojourner is one who lives, either permanently or briefly, among people to whom he or she is not related by blood. In cases where Abram or his descendants are the *gērîm,* then the stay is always a temporary one. As such, they depended for their well-being on the gracious hospitality of their host, were denied privileges extended to the native born, and normally did not have a voice in community affairs. Gen. 19:9 is one of the few places in the OT that refers to someone as a *gēr* in a

31. This phrase is particularly difficult to translate with confidence. J. C. L. Gibson (*Canaanite Myths and Legends* [Edinburgh: T. & T. Clark, 1977], p. 104) renders *ṭbq lḥt niṣh* as "one to shut the jaws of his detractors."

32. 2 Aqhat I:30 (*CTA* 17.I.30): *grš d ʿšy lnh.* I am following the translation of M. J. Dahood, "The Root *ʿzb* II in Job," *JBL* 78 (1959) 304 n. 5, rather than that of C. H. Gordon, *Ugarit and Minoan Crete* (New York: Norton, 1966), p. 122: "expels him who eats the supper of his spending the night." Gibson (*Canaanite Myths,* p. 104 n. 8) links this last line with Gen. 19:1-11.

patronizing and denigrating fashion. What right does Lot have to judge that having sexual relations with his daughters would be preferable to having sexual relations with his visitors? Incidentally, this theme is reversed in the parallel story in Judg. 19. There the Levite, whose concubine was abused, sets himself up as judge and summons the other tribes to avenge the crime (19:29-30; 20:4-7). Nobody faults him for doing that, although he too is a sojourner.

Lot's pompous attitude in overstepping his bounds aggravates the Sodomites. Their words *We will deal worse with you than with them* suggest that they are prepared to have coitus with Lot. They will take Lot himself as a substitute sex partner rather than his daughters.

10 The townsmen put forth their hands against Lot (v. 9). But now *the men* extend their hands, pull Lot back inside the house, and slam the door. The concept of a divine door shutter is familiar from Gen. 7:16b, "and Yahweh shut him in" (again the verb *sāgar*). In the end he who attempts to save his guests is saved by his guests. Has it dawned on Lot yet who his visitors really are?

11 The visitors perform a work of salvation (they save Lot from the mob) and a work of judgment (they smite the mob with blindness). But as the subsequent story shows, this is only a preliminary judgment.

The only other OT occurrence of *sanwērîm, blinding light* (2 K. 6:18), indicates that the blindness was not physical, that is, the total deprivation of physical sight. Elisha called on Yahweh to strike with "blindness" the Aramean troops who were about to invade Israel. V. 19 is ironic and comedic. It relates that Elisha led the Arameans to Samaria. They are ignorant of the fact that the person leading them is Elisha, the very man they seek.[33] The problem is not that they are blind, but that their vision is faulty — it does not correspond to reality.[34]

The same phenomenon takes place in Gen. 19:11. It is unlikely that a mob suddenly smitten with blindness but only a few feet from the door would be unable to find the door, unless the shock of sudden blindness caused

33. See R. LaBarbera, "The Man of War and the Man of God: Social Satire in 2 Kings 6:8–7:20," *CBQ* 46 (1984) 642-43. LaBarbera quotes A. Jirku, "Materialen zur Volksreligion Israels," in *Von Jerusalem nach Ugarit: Gesammelte Schriften* (Graz: Akademische Drück- u. Verlagsanstalt, 1966), p. 234: this passage "does not deal with an organic blindness but with a temporary removal of the normal sight function and perception of the eyes."

34. A number of commentators on Kings understand *sanwērîm* as literal "blindness" rather than "blinding light." See, e.g., J. A. Montgomery, *A Critical and Exegetical Commentary on the Books of Kings,* ICC (Edinburgh: T. & T. Clark, 1951), p. 383; J. Gray, *I & II Kings,* OTL, rev. ed. (Philadelphia: Westminster, 1970), p. 517. Yet even Montgomery suggests that the word is a Safil intensive of the verb "to dazzle" *(wārîr).* For those favoring the idea of "blinding light" see C. F. Burney, *Notes on the Hebrew Text of the Books of Kings* (Oxford: Clarendon, 1903), p. 286; A. F. Kirkpatrick, *The Second Book of the Kings* (Cambridge: Cambridge University, 1911), p. 28 ("it means here blindness of mind, as the sequel shews, not of eyes"); and *HALAT,* p. 718.

inestimable confusion. The blindness of the Sodomites does not deter them from trying to break into Lot's house. Rather, it makes it impossible for them to find the door. The mob wants to "know" the men who have come to Lot's home, but now they do not even know where the door of that home is.

In many ways Gen. 19:1-11 parallels Judg. 19–20, the story of the Levite and his concubine. The visitors who come to stay with Lot parallel the Levite who stays with an old man in Gibeah. Both of the hosts are cordial and polite to their guests. Both have their home surrounded by a mob who demands that the host surrender his guest(s) so that the mob may "know" them. After futile attempts to dissuade the crowd, the host turns over a female occupant in his house. The difference between the two accounts is their conclusion. In Gen. 19 the guests are supernatural and are able to prevent any kind of a scenario. In Judg. 19 the Levitical guest can only surrender his concubine, who is shamelessly ravished throughout the night.

The literary relationship between these stories is not clear. Earlier criticism suggested that Judg. 19 is a late, and worthless, imitation of Gen. 19.[35] A more recent suggestion is that Judg. 19 is the earlier of the two stories.[36] Between these two extremes is a moderating position which suggests that the similarity is due "to the use of a standard episode from a traditional stock of commonly used material in oral narration of prose."[37] The canonical witness is that the sin of non-Israelites (Gen. 19) was practiced later on by Israelites, particularly Benjaminites (Judg. 19). The sins of the nations became the sin of the chosen nation. Violations of social and sexual improprieties cannot go unchecked, regardless of whether the villains are Sodomites or Benjamites.[38]

35. See J. Wellhausen, *Prolegomena to the History of Ancient Israel,* tr. A. Menzies and J. Black (repr. Cleveland/New York: World, 1965), pp. 235-37.

36. See S. Niditch, "The 'Sodomite' Theme in Judges 19–20: Family, Community, and Social Disintegration," *CBQ* 44 (1982) 375-78. She appeals to style, plot, integrality, and theology to establish her case. Her last criterion — theology — is the least convincing. I do not discover a simplistic, moralistic theology in Gen. 19 as opposed to more sophisticated theological emphases in Judg. 19–20. See also S. Lasine, "Guest and Host in Judges 19: Lot's Hospitality in an Inverted World," *JSOT* 29 (1984) 38-41; M. Brettler, "The Book of Judges: Literature as Politics," *JBL* 108 (1989) 411-12; and P. Trible, *Texts of Terror,* OBT (Philadelphia: Fortress, 1984), pp. 74-75; these three scholars present convincing evidence for establishing the dependence of Judg. 19 on Gen. 19. P. M. Arnold ("Hosea and the Sin of Gibeah," *CBQ* 51 [1989] 451) avoids establishing Judg. 19's dependence on Gen. 19 or vice versa by suggesting that both sex crime stories represent a variant of an early stock story popular throughout Israel.

37. See R. C. Culley, *Studies in the Structure of Hebrew Narrative* (Philadelphia: Fortress; Missoula, MT: Scholars, 1976), p. 59.

38. Sarna (*Understanding Genesis,* pp. 145-46) comments, "As with the Flood, the Sodom and Gomorrah narrative is predicated upon the existence of a moral law of universal application for the infraction of which God holds all men answerable."

2. LOT AND HIS SONS-IN-LAW (19:12-14)

12 *The men then said to Lot: "Who else belongs to you here? Son-in-law,*[1] *your sons and your daughters, anyone you have in the city — take them away from here!*

13 *We are on the verge of destroying this place; the outcry against them*[2] *is so great before Yahweh that he has sent us to destroy it."*

14 *So Lot went out and spoke to his sons-in-law who were to marry his daughters*[3] *and urged them: "Up, abandon this place, for Yahweh is on the verge of destroying the city." To his sons-in-law he seemed as if he were clowning.*[4]

12 The supernatural visitors (SP reads "angels" instead of MT "men" here) do not know all the members of Lot's family. If they have omniscience they do not exercise it. They know nothing of Lot's family, just as Lot knows nothing of them.

The reference to a *son-in-law (ḥāṯān)* at this stage is strange. The only previous mention of children in Lot's household was his two virgin daughters, neither of whom had known a man (v. 8). Also, the mention of relatives by marriage before the mention of immediate relatives is unusual. For this reason many commentators delete *ḥāṯān* at this point as a gloss, a deletion supported by some ancient manuscript evidence.[5] (See further below on v. 14.) Note the

1. MT is sing., *ḥāṯān.* Yet the pl. is used (twice) two verses later *(ḥᵃṯānāyw).* LXX kept the number consistent by reading the Hebrew sing. as a pl. *(gambroí).* Speiser (*Genesis,* p. 140) and Westermann (*Genesis,* 2:296) suggest that the presence of *ḥāṯān* in v. 12 is an error, an inadvertent intruder from v. 14 and therefore ought to be deleted. But it may be that the narrator wishes to show the messengers' sense of urgency about the situation, even to the point that they are not consistent with the use of number (son-in-law, sing.; sons/daughters, pl.) and pronominal suffix (son-in-law, no pronominal suffix; sons/daughters, pronominal suffixes used).

2. Lit., "their outcry" *(ṣaʿᵃqāṯām),* i.e., the inhabitants of Sodom. Speiser (*Genesis,* p. 140) translates, "the outcry to Yahweh against those in it." On MT "the outcry against them" and on the pronominal suffix in *ṣaʿᵃqāṯām* he remarks that it refers not to "the place" *(hammāqôm hazzeh),* "which is the actual antecedent, but —by extension— to the inhabitants."

3. Lit., "takers of his daughters." See commentary on v. 14. For participles with future meaning, see GKC, § 116d.

4. For *mᵉṣaḥēq* in the sense of "clowning," see J. Sasson, "The Worship of the Golden Calf," in *Orient and Occident,* Fest. Cyrus H. Gordon, ed. H. Hoffner, Jr. (Neukirchen-Vluyn: Neukirchener, 1973), p. 155. The Piel participle occurs in Genesis again in 21:9 (to describe Ishmael's behavior); 26:8; 39:14, 17. There seems to be a wordplay between the sound that comes from Sodom to God, expressed by *ṣāʿaq,* and the sound that comes from Lot to his sons-in-law, expressed by *ṣāḥaq.*

5. *BHK* suggests reading *bāneyḵā* and deleting *ḥāṯān,* with 37 mss. and SP, "Your sons and your daughters . . . — take them away from here!"

absence of any inclusion of Lot's wife in this survey of potential members of the family. Her identity is subsumed under that of her husband. Or possibly these messengers know that Lot's wife will not leave Sodom behind (v. 26).

13 For the first time the visitors reveal their identity and mission to Lot. What they have heard is now confirmed by what they have seen. Yahweh would not destroy Sodom until he had heard Abraham out (ch. 18), and the rationale for destroying Sodom is not given until Yahweh's emissaries have disclosed their intentions to Lot.

The messengers' use of the word *outcry* links the narrative with the earlier narrative (18:20-21). There has been no specific allusion to "cry" in 19:1-11, but perhaps the mob surrounding Lot's house, a disorderly, shouting group, represents another form of noise that Yahweh hears.[6]

14 Lot now speaks, not to his daughters or putative sons, but to his *sons-in-law,* urging them to leave the city promptly. Heb. *ḥāṯān* refers to the men who were either betrothed or married to Lot's daughters.[7] They are his sons-in-law either in prospect or in fact. They cannot be his sons-in-law in fact unless (a) we are prepared to accept a flat inconsistency between v. 14 and v. 8; or (b) the sons-in-law had not yet consummated their marriages with Lot's daughters (much as Joseph with Mary); or (c) the sons-in-law are husbands of other daughters of Lot. As stated (see n. 3), I am inclined to attribute to the participle a futuristic meaning: "who were to marry his daughters," because the daughters are still living in their father's house (though it is not unheard-of for a son-in-law to live with his father-in-law; recall Jacob and Laban). Thus I find (b) more appealing than (a) or (c).

who were to marry. The Hebrew form used here is a participle *(lōqᵉḥê),* and as such is without a specific tense reference. Even the ancient versions differed on how to render the participle, with the Vulg. opting for a future tense, and the LXX opting for a past tense.[8]

It may not be accidental that the sons-in-law's response to Lot's imperative is described by the use of the verb *ṣāḥaq.* The same verb described Sarah's response in the preceding chapter (18:12, 13, 15) to something she heard. Both hear incredible announcements. She is to become pregnant; Sodom is to be destroyed. What Sarah and Lot's sons-in-law hear is, in their judgment, ridiculous.

Lot's sons-in-law (to be) clearly do not take him seriously. What is

6. Cf. a similar mob scene in which the crowd cried out: "Give us Barabbas; away with this man" (Luke 23:18).

7. See T. C. Mitchell, "The meaning of the noun *ḥtn* in the Old Testament," *VT* 19 (1969) 93-112, esp. p. 96.

8. Vulg. *qui accepturi erant* (cf. Luther's *nehmen sollten*); LXX *toús eilēphótas.*

- Don't copy - (DC)

not clear is a reason why they do not. Do they suffer from a false sense of security, like the Jerusalemites in Jeremiah's day: "Nothing can happen to us as long as we have the temple"? Or has Lot's performance, described in vv. 1-11, deprived him of any sense of respect and believability? Should an individual who offers to surrender his daughters to a group bent on assault be taken seriously by the (future) husbands of these women? Should a father-in-law who is himself saved only because he is pulled inside his own house now be viewed as a bearer of vital information? Lot wants them to leave the house now, but he is safe only because he is inside. What about that mob outside? Or maybe the sons-in-law think that Lot is overreacting to his own rough treatment and calling down a divine judgment on Sodom for being so treated.

If the use of the verb by Sarah in the preceding chapter (i.e., to express her incredulity upon overhearing that she herself is to become a mother) is the same as here, then the reason for the sons-in-law's inclination to ignore Lot, not to take their father-in-law seriously, is rooted simply in the ridiculousness, the implausibility, of the message, rather than in the messenger.[9]

3. LOT'S DEPARTURE FROM SODOM (19:15-22)

15 *As dawn was breaking the messengers urged*[1] *Lot, saying: "Up, take away your wife and the two daughters who are here lest you be swept away in the punishment*[2] *of the city."*

16 *Lot dawdled.*[3] *The men grabbed his hand and the hands of his wife and his two daughters — Yahweh being merciful*[4] *to him — and led him to safety outside the city.*

9. Almost all translations and commentators understand *kimṣaḥēq* to convey something stronger than simply "like one laughing." Thus, cf. "jesting" (RSV); "joking" (Westermann, Speiser); "like a fool/a fop" (Coats). Coote and Ord (*Bible's First History,* pp. 119, 131) alone read "thought he was laughing," but understand "laughing" to mean that Lot made a pass at them.

1. In 19:3 and 9 the root *pṣr* was used to describe urging, or putting pressure on somebody to do something. Here the root for "urge" is *'ûṣ*. Cf. Jer. 17:16; Exod. 5:13. This verb conveys the idea of doing something hastily in Prov. 19:2; 21:5; 28:20; 29:20.

2. Another instance of *ʿāwōn* indicating not only the trespass but the punishment that comes because of that trespass (see Gen. 4:13).

3. A verb used only 8 other times in the OT: Gen. 43:10; Exod. 12:39; Judg. 3:26; 19:8; 2 Sam. 15:28; Ps. 119:60; Isa. 29:9; Hab. 2:3. As if to accentuate Lot's hesitation, the verb is followed by a *paseq,* a vertical line between words that is the Masoretic sign for a pause. No doubt exegetical homily played the major role in its placement here.

4. Behind the root *ḥml* is the idea of "to spare." The form here is a fem. infinitive construct.

17 *When they had brought them outside, one of them said:*[5] *"Flee for your life! Do not look behind you or stop anywhere on the plain. To the hills flee, lest you be swept away."*

18 *But Lot replied to them, "Oh, no, my lord!*[6]

19 *Indeed, your servant has found favor in your sight and you have shown me great protection in saving my life. But I cannot flee to the hills to prevent the disaster from overtaking me and dying.*

20 *Look, this town ahead is near enough to flee to, and it is only a tiny place. Let me flee there — it is a tiny place, isn't it? — and my life will be spared."*

21 *He answered: "I will show deference to you*[7] *in this matter. I will not overthrow the town about which you speak.*

22 *Hurry, flee there, for I am unable to do anything until you arrive there." That is why one calls the town Zoar.*[8]

15 Throughout the Abraham cycle certain events have been introduced with a time frame. Yahweh instituted his covenant with Abraham "as the sun was setting" (15:12, 17). The three visitors came to Abraham in "the heat of the day" (18:1). Two of them went on to Sodom "in the evening" (19:1). Lot is urged to exit Sodom "when dawn breaks" (19:15). The destruction starts at "sunrise" (19:23). And three subsequent events in Abraham's life are introduced with "early the next morning" (19:27; 21:14; 22:3).

No reason is given why Lot and his family are to be spared. As in the case of Noah, a household head is delivered from certain death along with his wife and children. But, unlike Noah, Lot is not singled out as righteous. We will have to wait and let the narrative tell us later (v. 29) why Lot was spared. The text here does not mention any sons of Lot, though v. 12 alluded to them. Since the sons-in-law have sealed their own destiny (v. 14), they are omitted from the angel's announcement.

16 Apparently the messengers' command to Lot had no more impact on him than his similar command had on his sons-in-law. They joked and he

5. The sing. form of the verb (as in MT) may be maintained if it is understood that one of the two angels becomes the spokesman, as in 18:10.

6. MT reads "Oh, no, Lord" (*'ᵃḏōnāy*). The translation "my lord" is arrived at with a minor change in vocalization (reading *'ᵃḏōnî;* cf. *BHS*), as in 18:3 (see commentary there). The translation "my lords" (*'ᵃḏōnay*) is also possible if one understands the vocalization as due to a pausal position.

7. Lit., "I have lifted up your face." For the various nuances conveyed by this expression, see M. I. Gruber, "The Many Faces of Hebrew *nś' pnym* 'lift up the face,' " *ZAW* 95 (83) 252-60, esp. p. 255. For this idiom in the sense of "grant the request of" see Deut. 28:50; 2 K. 3:14; Job 42:8, 9; Lam. 4:16.

8. Zoar (*ṣōʿar*) is here connected with *miṣʿār,* "a trifle."

balked. Note Lot's inconsistency. He urges his sons-in-law to flee, but finds it hard to flee himself. He is better at giving directives than receiving them. We do not know why he hesitated. One would think that in the light of the atrocities almost committed outside his house he would be more than happy to leave. Is he afraid that if he leaves the security of his house he will be sure game for the mob? Westermann notes that "Lot's dallying is not so much an indication of his character as a description of the city dwellers' way of life; they feel more secure in the city."[9]

For a second time, then, his visitors grab him. First they grabbed him and pulled him inside his house (v. 10). Now they grab him and pull him *outside the city.* Against his better judgment Lot is led to his only possible point of salvation. In biblical thought to be led *outside the city* sometimes carries the idea of abandonment and loneliness, the place where the sinner or sin bearer goes (Lev. 16:21; John 19:17; Heb. 13:12). But here it is the place of deliverance from judgment.

17 For a second time (cf. v. 15 earlier) the possibility is raised about Lot being *swept away* (see also Num. 16:26). Twice in the preceding chapter (18:23-24) Abraham had used this verb when speaking to Yahweh about Sodom's future.

The reference here (and in v. 25) to *the plain (hakkikkar)* designates the same place referred to in 13:10 as "the plain of the Jordan" (*kikkar hayyardēn;* cf. RSV, which renders *kikkar* as "valley" of the Jordan in both 13:10 and 19:17). Deut. 34:3 demonstrates that this plain extended from Jericho to Zoar. This reference in Deuteronomy suggests that the catastrophe about to beset Sodom will spread well beyond Sodom. To that end, an exit for Lot only as far as Sodom's suburbs will do him no good. As with Noah, his only salvation will be on top of a mountain (in Moabite territory).

The verb the messenger uses for *flee* or "escape" is the Niphal of *mālaṭ*. It is used five times in this section (vv. 17 [twice], 19, 20, 22). Perhaps it was selected because of the closeness in sound between "flee" *(mālaṭ)* and "Lot" *(lôṭ).*

18 Lot's rebuff *Oh, no, my lord,* is a strange way for a human being to address a supernatural being, or any messenger who informs one that one's life is in imminent danger. But it is no more surprising than Peter's word to Jesus: "No, you shall never wash my feet" (John 13:8), and "Surely not, Lord!" (Acts 10:14).

19-20 Lot recognizes that he is alive only because these angels have protected him.[10] But still he persists in bickering. Believing that he has not

9. Westermann, *Genesis,* 2:303.

10. *ḥesed* is normally translated "kindness, mercy," but I note that in the AV alone it is translated 48 different ways! For its use here see C. F. Whitely, "The Semantic Range of *Ḥesed,*" *Bib* 62 (1981) 523-24. See also K. D. Sakenfeld, *The Meaning of Ḥesed in the*

enough time to make it to the mountains, he requests that he be allowed to take refuge in some nearby hamlet. The irony in this whole situation is that catastrophe is about to strike Sodom, and Lot is arguing about the escape route![11] Furthermore, he had at first hesitated even to leave Sodom. Now he speculates whether he has adequate time to flee far enough.

21 To Lot's request the angel acquiesces. He withdraws his earlier ultimatum that Lot flee as far as the hills, and modifies his plan to overthrow every settled territory of the plain. In so speaking Lot resembles the Abraham of ch. 18. In response to Abraham's plea, Yahweh agreed not to destroy the entire population of Sodom if a righteous nucleus was living there. Here, Lot too persuades a divine representative to scale down his intentions because of extenuating circumstances.

22 This last verse supplies an etymology for *Zoar.* As pointed out above, there is a play on the acoustical similarity between "Zoar" *(ṣōʿar),* v. 22, and "tiny place" *(miṣʿār),* v. 20. Lot's "I cannot" (*lōʾ ʾûḵal,* v. 19) is now matched by the angel's "I am unable" *(lōʾ ʾûḵal).* Lot feels he cannot flee to the hills, and the angel cannot unload punishment on Sodom until Lot is satisfactorily out of the way.

Many commentators have regarded vv. 17-22 (23) as originally an independent etymology of Zoar that was only later attached to the Lot-Sodom story.[12] Three supporting lines of evidence have been brought forth to substantiate the intrusive nature of these six (or seven) verses. One argument is that they break the continuity between v. 16 and v. 24. A second argument revolves around whether Lot is speaking with one (v. 18b, vv. 19-22) or more (v. 17a, v. 18a) individuals. A third argument is that the etymological motif is subordinated to the main theme of 19:1-28.[13]

One can hardly say that the leap from v. 16 to v. 24 would be a smooth one. For the intervening verses supply fundamental information to the narra-

---

Hebrew Bible: A New Inquiry, HSM 17 (Missoula, MT: Scholars, 1978), pp. 97-99. Sakenfeld suggests that the second *miṣʿār hîwʾ* may not be a further reference to Zoar, but to Lot's suggestion that saving him from destruction would be a small act in comparison to the earlier and greater act of rescuing him from Sodom. The Masoretic punctuation does not support this interpretation. For an excellent treatment of *ḥeseḏ,* see F. I. Andersen, "Yahweh, the Kind and Sensitive God," in *God Who Is Rich in Mercy,* Fest. D. B. Knox, ed. P. T. O'Brien and D. G. Peterson (Grand Rapids: Baker, 1987), pp. 41-88 (esp. pp. 52-53 on Gen. 19:19).

11. See E. M. Good, *Irony in the Old Testament* (Philadelphia: Westminster, 1965), p. 94.

12. See, e.g., von Rad, *Genesis,* p. 220: "It is probable that the section vv. 17-22 did not yet belong to an earlier version of the narrative. It has a certain independence because of its aetiological tradition."

13. See B. O. Long, *The Problem of Etiological Narrative in the Old Testament,* BZAW 108 (Berlin: Töpelmann, 1968), pp. 20-21.

tive (e.g., the removal of Lot from Sodom and his reception of divine protection from the divine judgment). In fact, the transition between vv. 16 and 17 is much smoother than between vv. 16 and 24. In addition, there are clear vocabulary links between vv. 17-22 (23) and the rest of the chapter. For example, Yahweh was merciful to Lot, a fact that both the narrator (v. 16) and Lot himself (v. 19) mentioned.[14]

Interestingly, the wordplay of v. 20 that explains the significance of "Zoar" is separated from the actual etymological statement (v. 22b) by intervening material (vv. 21-22a). Where etymological statements are most patently redactional, such lacunae between the explanation of the name and the etymological formula ("That is why one calls . . .") are rare.

4. DOOMSDAY AT SODOM (19:23-29)

23 *The sun*[1] *rose upon the earth just as Lot reached Zoar.*

24 *Then Yahweh deluged Sodom and Gomorrah with sulphurous fire from Yahweh in heaven.*

25 *He overthrew those*[2] *cities and the entire plain, together with all the inhabitants of the cities and the vegetation on the ground.*

26 *His wife, (who followed) behind him,*[3] *looked back,*[4] *and she turned into a pillar of salt.*

27 *Early the next morning Abraham hastened to the spot where he had stood before*[5] *Yahweh.*

14. See Van Seters, *Abraham in History and Tradition,* pp. 217-18.

1. Here *šemeš* is treated as a masc. noun, and is followed by the 3rd masc. sing. form of the verb, *yāṣā'*. In 15:17 it was treated as a fem. noun *(haššemeš bā'āh).* Both genders for "sun" are reflected in Ps. 104: masc. in v. 19, but fem. in v. 22. Although *špš* is always fem. in Ugaritic (at least in the texts published thus far), that language (along with Hebrew) provides other instances of the same noun in both masc. and fem. gender. Accordingly the suggestion to emend *yāṣā'* to *yāṣᵉ'āh* is unnecessary. See the earlier discussion between G. R. Driver, "Theological and Philological Problems in the Old Testament," *JTS* 41 (1946) 165-66; and A. Guillaume, "A Reply to Professor Driver," *JTS* 49 (1948) 56.

2. The same form of the demonstrative *(hā'ēl)* appeared in v. 8.

3. To what does *mē'aḥᵃrāyw* refer? Does it refer to the wife's position behind the husband as they head for Zoar, "behind him"? It cannot refer to the wife herself, i.e., "she looked behind her," for the form would have to be *mē'aḥᵃreyhā*. I inserted "who followed" in parentheses only for sense. I take the MT as it stands, indicating that in the exodus from Sodom Lot's wife was behind Lot.

4. The verb *nābaṭ* (in the Hiphil) means simply "to look, gaze." When followed by the preposition *'aḥar,* it clearly means "to look behind" (here; Gen. 19:17; 1 Sam. 24:9 [Eng. 8]).

5. The correspondence between *'āmaḏ lipnê* in 18:22 and *'āmaḏ 'eṯ* here establishes for *'eṯ* the meaning "before." Cf. 1 Sam. 2:18; Ps. 16:11.

28 *As he looked down toward Sodom and Gomorrah and the whole area of the plain, he spotted smoke*[6] *over the land rising like the smoke of a furnace.*[7]

29 *So it was that, when God destroyed the cities of the plain, he was mindful of Abraham by sending away Lot from the upheaval*[8] *in which he overthrew the cities where Lot had been dwelling.*

23 The destruction of Sodom is not completed at sunrise but begins at sunrise. Of its duration we cannot be sure. This point has been missed by commentators (e.g., Gunkel and Skinner) who in their own haste to explain Lot's haste have suggested that the judgment must be carried out in the night when the demons come out of hiding (Gen. 32:24-26; Exod. 4:24; 12:22, 29-31; 2 K. 19:35).[9] Indeed, many of the judgment scenes in the Bible are nocturnal events. (Does this explain the darkness that came upon the land at Jesus' crucifixion, Luke 23:44?) But this one happens in emerging daylight. That the event took place in daytime explains why Abraham could see the rising smoke from many miles away (v. 28). Flames would be seen from a long distance at night, but smoke would not.

24 The actual description of the catastrophe is limited to two verses, 24 and 25. To be more precise, v. 24 relates the event and v. 25 relates the consequences. The repetition of the tetragrammaton at the end of the verse should not be dismissed as a doublet or a gloss. The twofold use of the tetragrammaton reinforces the fact that the disaster that struck Sodom and its environs was not a freak of nature. Rather, it was sent deliberately by Yahweh himself. The verse adds further that the disaster was sent from Yahweh *in heaven.* Throughout chs. 18–19 Yahweh has been pictured as moving to and fro on the earth. He rests under a tree near Mamre and has a meal. He engages in conversation with Abraham. His angelic entourage are overnight guests of

6. The word for "smoke" is *qᵉṭōr,* one that is used but a few times to indicate either thick, black smoke as in Ps. 119:83, "I have become like a wineskin in the smoke" (RSV; i.e., after hanging in a house a wineskin shrivels and blackens), or some other kind of substance that is a screen, as in Ps. 148:8, either "frost" (RSV) or "mist" (JB). It is close to the word *qᵉṭōreṯ,* which is the smoke/odor rising from a burning sacrifice.

7. The same simile occurs in Exod. 19:18, where the smoke on Sinai rose "like the smoke of a kiln" (RSV). The expression in Gen. 19:28 is *kᵉqîṭōr hakkiḇšān,* and in Exod. 19:18 it is *kᵉʿešen hakkiḇšān.*

8. This is the only place in the OT where the noun *hᵃpēḵâ* occurs. The more common noun derived from *hpk,* "overturn," is *mahpēḵâ* (Deut. 29:22; Isa. 1:7; 13:19; Jer. 49:18; 50:40; Amos 4:11).

9. It is not necessary to infer from this point that Gen. 19:23ff. originally portrayed the destruction of Sodom by Shemesh the sun-god, as is done by O. Keel, "Wer zerstörte Sodom?" *TZ* 35 (1979) 10-17. Note the double use of the tetragrammaton in the following verse, which accentuates the source of the sulphurous fire.

Lot. Now suddenly Yahweh, from his heavenly position, unleashes a catastrophe on Sodom.

Then Yahweh deluged. This is the third time in Genesis that Yahweh is the subject of the verb *māṭar* (in the Hiphil), "to send rain" (see 2:5 and 7:4). The first rain (2:5) is a life-bringing rain. The second (7:4) is a life-denying rain. The third is also a life-denying deluge.

What Yahweh rains on Sodom is *goprîṯ wā'ēš.*[10] While "brimstone and fire" (AV, RSV, JB; cf. NEB) has gained notoriety, we follow the majority of modern commentators who see here a hendiadys — hence *sulphurous fire* (NAB), or "burning sulphur" (NIV). The disaster has often been explained as an earthquake, a phenomenon to which the Jordan Valley with its series of rift valleys would be particularly prone. Lightning would ignite the compressed gases and the petroleum/asphalt that escaped through the fissures in the ground.[11] But those who embrace this interpretation must ignore the phrase "from Yahweh in heaven/the heavens." The clear impression created by the addition of this phrase, if in any way it contributes meaningfully to the narrative, is that Yahweh hurled blocks of burning sulphur on the cities. For the concept of a rain of heavenly fire that consumes the wicked see Ezek. 10:2.

25 The possibility that an earthquake is involved might be suggested by the use of the verb *hāp̱āḵ,* "overthrow," and the noun *h^a^pēḵâ,* "upheaval" (v. 29). To overthrow means "to turn upside down."[12] This happens in an earthquake, but not in a volcanic eruption, unless the eruption was under the sea floor. Perhaps we need not limit "overthrow" to actions precipitated only by an earthquake. As Westermann has noted, "as it [viz., the verb *hāp̱ak̲*] is a fixed image for a divine judgment it is no more to be attached to a definite event than is our word 'catastrophe'."[13]

The casualties include all the residents of this area and the vegetation. No reference is made to the loss of livestock. Ch. 13 had informed us that Lot had taken his herds to this location. Is the livestock included among *all the inhabitants of the cities (kol-yōš^e^ḇê he'ārîm)*? The inclusion of vegetation

10. The same combination appears in Ps. 11:6 and Ezek. 38:22, but in reverse order.

11. See the extended notes here by S. R. Driver, *Genesis,* pp. 202-3; Skinner, *Genesis,* pp. 310-12; Vawter, *On Genesis,* pp. 239-41; Sarna, *Understanding Genesis,* p. 142; von Rad, *Genesis,* pp. 220-21.

12. In postbiblical incantation texts written on the inside of inverted bowls, *hpk* was a favorite verb of the magicians. As the bowls are turned upside down so may the powers of the demons be turned upside down or overturned. See J. A. Montgomery, *Aramaic Incantation Texts from Nippur* (Philadelphia: University of Pennsylvania Museum, 1913).

13. Westermann, *Genesis,* 2:307.

as one of the victims of this inferno is another graphic detail that underscores the totality of the destruction that fell on Sodom.

26 Sodom is overturned and Lot's wife is metamorphosed. Her action in "looking back" was in direct defiance of the order given in v. 17. We are not told why she looked back. The text nowhere suggests that her affection for the city had a stranglehold on her, and that she now entertains a wistful thought toward Sodom. Perhaps she looked back simply because of the noise and the bright horizon of the city behind her. But if that is the case, why does she lose her life? The action seems to be more than simple curiosity. She lost her life for only one reason: because she overtly ignored the directive of v. 17 (which, admittedly, was directed just to Lot). In spite of the messenger's *'al tabbîṭ* ("do not look behind"), Lot's wife did *tabbēṭ* ("she looked behind"). As von Rad states, "before divine judgment there is only the possibility of being smitten or of escaping, but no third alternative."[14]

The Hebrew word *n^eṣîḇ* is translated "pillar" only here in the OT. Its usual translation is "prefect/governor" or possibly "garrison/outpost" (1 Sam. 10:5; 13:3; 2 Sam. 8:6, 14 [twice]).[15] The noun is formed from the verb *nāṣaḇ,* "to set, station, erect," and indicates something or someone that has been placed in position, formed. One cannot judge from the verb *watt^ehî* whether Lot's wife became a pillar of salt instantaneously or subsequently. The narrator certainly depicts her as a person who, in pausing to look back, was stopped, trapped, and overcome by a sulphur cloud, either suddenly or gradually. The existence of salty marl at the southwest end of the Dead Sea that forms odd-shaped hillocks in the salt cliffs of the area more than likely provided the inspiration for the tradition found in Wis. 10:7, "and where, monument to an unbelieving soul, there stands a pillar of salt," and in Josephus (*Ant.* 1.11.4), "Lot's wife . . . changed into a pillar of salt; for I have seen it and it remains at this day."[16]

14. Von Rad, *Genesis,* p. 222. Cf. Fewell and Gunn, *Gender, Power, and Promise,* pp. 64-65, 67 for a more sympathetic interpretation of Lot's wife and her looking back.

15. For the juxtaposition of *n^eṣîḇ* and *melaḥ,* "pillar of salt," cf. the account of David's victory over the Edomites in the Valley of Salt (*gê' melaḥ,* 2 Sam. 8:13) after which he stationed projects (*n^eṣiḇîm,* 2 Sam. 8:14) in Edom.

16. See D. J. Wiseman, "Lot," *ISBE,* 3:172. R. T. Boyd (*Tells, Tombs, and Treasure* [Grand Rapids: Baker, 1969], pp. 85-87) compares the fate of Lot's wife to what happened when Pompeii was destroyed in A.D. 79. First, a volcanic gas settled over the city, asphyxiating many of the citizens while they slept. The city was then covered with heavy deposits of volcanic ash up to a depth of about twenty feet in which human and animal life was entombed. In the process of archeological excavation, the excavators pumped plaster of paris into hollow places and encountered in the ashes numerous human and animal forms. The chemical content of the ash had apparently turned human bodies into some chemical substance that was sufficiently hard to allow the surrounding ash to retain a perfect cast of the bodies.

27-28 For the first time in this chapter Abraham enters the narrative. With a premonition that something has happened, he leaves Mamre early the next morning. This is the only chapter in the Abraham cycle in Genesis where Abraham appears but says nothing. The loquacious Abraham of ch. 18 is now taciturn. The mediator is reduced to a spectator.

The verb that is used for Lot's wife "looking (back)" *(nāḇaṭ)* to Sodom differs from the one used for Abraham's looking to Sodom *(šāqap̱)*. But the verb used here with Abraham was used earlier in connection with the three visitors he entertained (18:16). In fact, both the visitors and Abraham looked "over the face of Sodom" *(ʿal pᵉnê sᵉḏōm),* they before its destruction, he after its destruction.

Upon seeing the columns of smoke rising from the city, Abraham can conclude only that the loss of life has been total. He has no personal revelation that his nephew and his two great-nieces are alive. Nobody has lived through this conflagration. Of course, the narrator knows about the survivors (v. 29), and therefore we know it, but Abraham does not know it — at least not yet. At this point in the biblical story Lot drops out of sight (after the incident with his daughters). He is never heard from again in Genesis. This sudden departure of Lot from the narrative does not indicate that originally the Lot traditions circulated independently of the Abraham traditions. It is simply the case that Lot is not involved, and does not need to be involved, in any of the events subsequently delineated in Abraham's odyssey.

29 Perhaps at the point that Abraham is remembering Lot, God remembers Abraham.[17] Now it becomes clear why Lot is spared. An individual who does not deserve to be spared (Lot) is spared because of another (Abraham). This was precisely the issue in Abraham's dialogue with Yahweh in ch. 18. Do the righteous have a salvific effect on the guilty? Abraham receives a twofold positive answer to that query. God's response is in word and in deed. He speaks his response — "yes, I would save the city," and he demonstrates his response — Lot is salvaged from certain death. Abraham is to Lot what the hypothetical righteous remnant (50, 45, 40, 30, 20, 10; ch. 18) would have been to Sodom.

5. LOT AND HIS DAUGHTERS (19:30-38)

30 *Lot went up from Zoar and settled in the hill country, and his two daughters with him, because he was afraid to put down roots in Zoar. Thus he lived in a cave,*[1] *he and his two daughters.*

17. For God remembering someone cf. Gen. 8:1 and 30:22. For God remembering his earlier covenant cf. Exod. 2:24; 6:5; Lev. 26:42, 45.

1. Lit., "in *the* cave." According to GKC, § 126r, this is an instance of "the

31 *The older one said to the younger: "Our father is advancing in age, and there is not a man on earth to come into us,*[2] *as is done everywhere.*

32 *Come, let's get our father drunk and then lie with*[3] *him that we may preserve offspring through our father."*

33 *So they made their father drunk that*[4] *night, and the older one went in and lay with her father. He was unaware of her lying down or her getting up.*[5]

34 *Next day the older one said to the younger: "Last night I lay with father.*[6] *Let's get him drunk tonight also, and you go in and lie with him, that we may preserve offspring through our father."*

35 *That night they got their father drunk, and the younger one went in and lay with him. He was unaware of her lying down or her getting up.*

36 *Thus both daughters of Lot became pregnant by their father.*

37 *The older one bore a son whom she named Moab. He is the father of the Moabites of today.*

38 *The younger one, she also bore a son whom she named Ben-ammi. He is the father of the Ammonites of today.*

30 The smoke went up *(ʿālâ)* from burning Sodom (v. 28), and now Lot goes up *(wayyaʿal)* from Zoar. What has Lot to be afraid of? Will the divine

---

employment of the article to denote a single person/thing (primarily one that is as yet unknown . . .) as being present to the mind under given circumstances. In such cases in English the indefinite article is mostly used." But Gesenius suggests that *bamm*^{e}*ʿārâ* might mean "in the *well-known* cave."

2. *bôʾ ʿal* is unusual for describing sexual congress and is attested again only in Deut. 25:5. The usual idiom is *bôʾ ʾel.* Cf. BDB, p. 98a. In both instances where *bôʾ ʿal* occurs, it is in the context of the taboo of incest. See O. Margalith, "More Samson Legends," *VT* 36 (1986) 400 n. 7. LXX renders the following preposition, be it *ʾel* or *ʿal,* with *pros.*

3. "To lie with" is expressed in two ways in vv. 32-35: *šāḵaḇ ʿim* (v. 32), *šāḵaḇ ʾeṯ* (v. 33), *šāḵaḇ ʾeṯ* (v. 34), and *šāḵab ʿim* (v. 35). I fail to observe any difference here between the prepositions *ʿim* and *ʾeṯ.* See H. Orlinsky, "The Hebrew Root *ŠKB,*" *JBL* 63 (1944) 19-44, esp. pp. 19-22.

4. In the expression *ballay*^{e}*lâ hûʾ, hûʾ* is not an illustration of the omission of the article with the demonstrative (as maintained by GKC, § 126y). Rather, we have here an instance of shared consonants. See I. O. Lehman, "A Forgotten Principle of Biblical Textual Tradition Rediscovered," *JNES* 26 (1967) 98; W. Watson, "Shared Consonants in Northwest Semitic," *Bib* 50 (1969) 531.

5. See J. Krašovec, "Merism — Polar Expression in Biblical Hebrew," *Bib* 64 (1983) 238.

6. "My father" in MT, "our father" in LXX. Speiser (*Genesis,* p. 145) notes that the suffix "is more stylistic than proprietary."

promise not to overthrow Zoar (v. 21) be withdrawn? Is he too close for comfort to the tragic scene? Lot needed to be pulled out of Sodom by the scruff of his neck. He needs no assistance, however, in getting out of Zoar.

To that end he and his two daughters leave for the hills of Moab, where he is content to take shelter in a *cave* (as did Elijah, 1 K. 19:9). This is quite a primitive surrounding, considering the "house" he left (v. 2), or even his uncle's tent (18:1). Does the cave promise more security than the open spaces of Zoar? Having been delivered by the mercies of God (vv. 16, 19), must he now fend for himself?

31 To the best of the daughters' knowledge, the loss of life at Sodom has been total: *there is not a man on earth to come into us.* The concern of the father is for his safety, but the concern of the daughters is the loss of the possibility of motherhood. Their lifeless womb matches the lifeless situation in Sodom. Also, the husbandless daughters mirror the wifeless Lot. The older daughter's remark that "our father is advancing in age" indicates that the daughters think their father will likely remain a widower. In his old age Lot emerges as a pathetic figure. By contrast, Abraham is blessed by God in his old age (24:1) and is able to start a second family (25:1-2). Furthermore it is said of Abraham, but not of Lot, that "he died in a good old age, an old man, full of years" (25:8).[7]

The daughter's lament that *there is not a man on earth to come into us* is probably more hyperbolic than reflective of a response to a worldwide catastrophe, as in Noah's day. After all, Zoar was spared. Also, the phrase *w*^{e}*'îš 'ên bā'āreṣ* may be a local reference to "the land" (so NIV, Westermann) rather than a reference to "the world."

32 To eliminate the possibility of perpetual barrenness the older daughter suggests intercourse with their father.[8] After plying their father with wine, each will take her turn lying with him. Earlier the father was willing to use his daughters for sexual purposes without their consent. Now they will use their father for sexual purposes without his consent. The difference between the two, however, is that in the first instance sex was offered for titillation and gratification of the lust of the townsmen. The second does not emphasize the orgiastic. The daughters simply want to reproduce. Of course, this motivation does not make their behavior any less objectionable. In one sense both Lot and his daughters act out of noble motivation: he to save his guests, they to secure progeny. Both parties face dilemmas that require drastic (and to the reader, highly dubious) actions.

7. See Sternberg's discussion of "Old Age in Genesis" in *Poetics of Biblical Narrative,* pp. 349-54.

8. On the issue of incest see H. A. Hoffner, Jr., "Incest, Sodomy and Bestiality in the Ancient Near East," in *Orient and Occident,* pp. 81-90.

33-36 Unlike vv. 23ff., where the time of day is sunrise, or early in the morning (vv. 15, 27), here the emphasis is on action that takes place at night. They are already in a cave, which is quite dark. To be in a cave at night is about as dark a place as one could find.

The narrative does not discuss many aspects of this event. One of these is the daughters' plan to get their father as their sexual partner. That plan is to make him drunk, and on two successive nights at that. But where will two girls, hiding out in a cave in Moabite hill country, find enough wine — or any wine — to accomplish that? When Lot left Zoar did he carry his beverages with him? The story suggests that the territory later to be known as Moab must have been located in wine country.

The story under consideration finds two obvious biblical parallels, Gen. 38 and Ruth. In all three the story focuses on a woman who for one reason or another is unable to have children. Lot's two daughters were apparently never married, and Tamar and Ruth were widowed. In all three cases a father or father figure becomes the one by whom the family is perpetuated. And in each instance the initiative is taken by a woman who offers herself clandestinely or by guile to the "father."[9]

Of course, the story of Noah's drunkenness (9:20ff.) is also a parallel. When one relative (again the father) is intoxicated, another relative takes (sexual?) advantage of him. But the Noah story lacks two emphases of the other three — the childless woman, and a plan initiated by that woman to rectify those circumstances.

Twice these verses (vv. 33, 35) relate that Lot *was unaware* what his daughters were doing with him. This attention to his ignorance, and in particular the use of *yāḏaʿ*, "know," allows the reader to trace the theme of knowledge throughout this chapter. The Sodomites wanted to know Lot's visitors. Lot does not know what his daughters are doing to him, so deep is his drunken stupor. Noah, at least after he had slept off his hangover, "knew what his youngest son had done to him" (9:24). The narrative does not mention any response of Lot after his drunkenness ended. It focuses only on his ignorance during the act of coitus. In the earlier verses of the chapter it was clear that Lot did not know the real identity of the two men who stayed at his house. He is in the dark literally, for he is in a cave and it is night. But he is also in the dark about his guests and his daughters.

37-38 Here are two more contrasts with the earlier sections of the chapter. In vv. 1-29 the emphasis was on the loss of life. Here the events

9. All the parallels among the three stories are worked out by H. Fisch, "Ruth and the structure of covenant history," *VT* 32 (1982) 423-37. It is uncertain, however, that Fisch is correct (p. 433) when he contrasts the crudity of Lot's daughters with the more "civilized" behavior of Tamar.

describe the beginning of life. The older daughter gives birth to a son and names him *Moab.* It is an appropriate name in this context and may mean "water [i.e., seed, progeny] of the father,"[10] not necessarily "from father." The translation "from father" is based, mistakenly, on the threefold use of "through our father" (vv. 32, 34, 35), and the similar sound of *mô'āḇ* and *mē'āḇ.*[11]

The younger daughter also gives birth to a a son, whom she names *Ben-ammi,* "son of my kinsman."[12] The number two is prominent in this chapter: two messengers, two daughters, two sons with two etymologies. The time between vv. 33-35 (intercourse between daughters and father) and the birth of the children (vv. 37-38) has to be at least nine months, assuming neither of the sons was born prematurely. Everything in vv. 1-29 moved quickly: from "in the evening" (v. 1), to "dawn" (v. 15), to "sunrise" (v. 23), to "early the next morning" (v. 27). But vv. 30-38 cover three-quarters of a year, and the use of verbs like "settled" and "lived" (v. 30) and the reference to the period in which the daughters carry their child provide a slower movement in the narrative.

The text is silent on Lot's reaction. He was certainly not intoxicated for the whole period of his daughters' pregnancies. Did he respond with anger as did Noah (9:25), or did he respond as did Judah and admit that what his daughters had done was acceptable (38:26)? The absence of any evaluation by Lot, either hostile or sympathetic, is perhaps further evidence of his lackluster character, or perhaps reflects his ignorance that he was the father of Moab and Ammon.

10. M. J. Dahood ("Eblaite and Biblical Hebrew," *CBQ* 44 [1982] 13 n. 39) observes that in a bilingual text from Ebla the Eblaite equivalent of Sum. *a,* "water," is *mawu.* If one removes the case ending, *mawu* becomes *maw,* and by diphthong contraction *maw* becomes *mô.* Dahood then suggests that *mô* is a by-form of *mê,* and he presents the Ketib of Job 9:20 as evidence that *mô* means "water" in Biblical Hebrew. He gives other instances of *mô* meaning "water" in "A Sea of Troubles: Notes on Psalms 55:3-4 and 140:10-11," *CBQ* 41 (1979) 605-6.

11. The LXX may also have misled commentators here when it follows "whom she named Moab" with *légousa Ek toú patrós mou,* "saying, From my father." Targ. Pseudo-Jonathan reads similarly, "and she called his name Moab, for she had conceived of her father." It is more likely that the LXX is here expansionistic than that the MT has condensed the account, for why MT omit would words of this significance. Y. Zakovitch ("Explicit and Implicit Name-Derivations," *HAR* 4 [1980] 168-70) argues that the LXX of v. 37 is the explication of MT's implicit derivation of Moab.

12. *ʿam* here should not be translated as "people" but rather as a male relative, a "paternal kinsman." Cf. LXX *kaí ekálesen tó ónoma autoú Amman huiós toú génous mou,* "and she called his name Amman son of my people," which departs again from the MT, as it did in v. 37: it adds the name Ammon/Amman, and shifts the proper name in the MT, Ben-ammi, to the derivation of the name *(huiós toú génous mou).*

The names given to the two sons are not the final item in the narrative. Both names are followed by the line that "He is the father of the Moabites/Ammonites of today."[13] This clause subordinates the sons' names to the wider interest expressed by *of today,* a phrase which B. Long refers to as an "extension formula." Etiology is replaced by an historical, ethnological note. The narrative is now lifted out of its own historical context and projected into the time frame of the narrator. The Moabites and Ammonites exist because of the daring of two daughters of Israel and because of Lot. Indeed, Lot escaped the destruction of Sodom through no effort of his own and subsequently became the father of the Moabites and Ammonites through no effort of his own. Thus we find a third illustration of a major theme in chs. 18–19: (1) the guilty may be spared because of the innocent; (2) Lot is spared because of Abraham's covenantal relationship with God; (3) two of Israel's neighbors, both of whom caused many anxious moments for Israel, exist because of two of Abraham's progeny.

THE NEW TESTAMENT APPROPRIATION

Gen. 18:16–19:38 and Matt. 10:15; 11:20-24; Luke 10:12-15

All three Synoptic Gospels conclude the commissioning of the disciples with Jesus' words that they are to shake the dust off their feet as they leave any city that has rejected them (Matt. 10:14; Mark 6:11; Luke 9:5; 10:11). Matthew (10:15) and Luke (10:12) add the statement that it will be more tolerable for Sodom and Gomorrah on the day of judgment than for such a town.

Luke immediately adds after this verdict the woes on the Galilean cities of Chorazin, Bethsaida, and Capernaum (10:13-15) and parallels them with Tyre and Sidon. But Matthew separates the verdict statement (10:15) from the woes (11:20-24). In the threatened woes on these cities Luke does not utilize the saying on Sodom in his words to Capernaum, as does Matthew (11:23). Luke's reason for omitting this saying is clear. He has already introduced the saying about Sodom in 10:12. To introduce it again three verses later would be to create an awkward redundancy.[1]

It is Matthew who most fully compares Chorazin and Bethsaida to Tyre and Sidon (11:21-22), and Capernaum to Sodom (11:23-24). A compari-

13. See Long, *Problem of Etiological Narrative,* p. 52. See also the comments of Van Seters, *Abraham in History and Tradition,* pp. 219-21; B. S. Childs, "A Study of the Formula, 'Until This Day,' " *JBL* 82 (1963) 282.

1. See O. Linton, "Coordinated Sayings and Parables in the Synoptic Gospels, Analysis Contra Theories," *NTS* 26 (1980) 153.

son of these two subsections shows some contrast between them. First, the traditional form of the woe is used in vv. 21-22, but in vv. 23-24 Capernaum is addressed directly, with the second person singular pronoun in a position of emphasis: "and you, Capernaum." Second, allusions in vv. 23-24 — "will you be exalted to heaven?" — to OT passages such as Isa. 14:13-15 (the king of Babylon) and Ezek. 26:20 (the king of Tyre) make Capernaum's attitude all the more brazen. Third, while Chorazin and Bethsaida had been compared to Tyre and Sidon, Capernaum is juxtaposed with the infamous Sodom. Perhaps this is due to the fact that only in Matthew's Gospel does Jesus take up residence in Capernaum (4:13-15). This situation makes Jesus's statement about Capernaum standing in the shadow of Sodom all the more poignant.[2] Jesus' home is actually making Sodom look respectable!

Gen. 18:16–19:38 and Matt. 24:37-39; Luke 17:26-32

In an eschatological context Matthew and Luke speak of the coming of the Son of Man. Matthew suggests that living at that time will be like "living in the days of Noah" (24:37-39). Luke's version is similar (17:26-27), except that he adds a further parallel: "in the days of Lot" (17:28-32). In referring to the days of Noah Luke uses two pairs (eating/drinking; marrying/being given in marriage). In referring to the days of Lot he uses three pairs (eating/drinking; buying/selling; planting/building). What both comparisons have in common is that the days of normal human activity were followed by a day of great catastrophe. Luke does not emphasize the sinfulness of Sodom but the routineness of life in Sodom. The catastrophe just erupted suddenly on a certain day.

It is not clear why Luke uses Noah and Lot, while Matthew uses only Noah. On the one hand, perhaps Matthew read Gen. 6–9 as the destruction of every living being on the earth, and thus a suitable analogy for what would happen to unbelievers when the Son of Man came. On the other hand, the destruction at Sodom involved only the inhabitants of a city and its environs, an unlikely counterpart for the *parousia*.[3]

Gen. 18:16–19:38 and 2 Pet. 2:6-8; Jude 7

Both of these passages, unlike, say, Luke 17:28-32, picture Sodom and Gomorrah as hotbeds of iniquity and immorality. The evil at Sodom was inferred, of course, in Matt. 10:15; 11:23; Luke 10:12, but only in a roundabout way.

2. See J. A. Comer, "The Composition and Literary Characteristics of Matt 11:20-24," *CBQ* 39 (1977) 497-504, esp. pp. 501-2.

3. See Linton, *NTS* 26 (1980) 158.

Peter uses the phrases "filthy lives of lawless men" and "lawless deeds." Jude uses the phrases "sexual immorality" and "perversion." Peter also draws a bold contrast between "righteous" Lot, who was "distressed" and "tormented" by what he observed in Sodom, and his fellow citizens.

God's response to this moral depravity was to destroy these two cities by fire — a theme resumed in 3:7. We are somewhat surprised by the designation of Lot as "righteous."[4] Nothing in Gen. 18–19 makes the application of that adjective to Lot appropriate. What Peter is doing is using Lot as a model of one who was surrounded by evil and temptation and yet survived. If he overcame his fiery trials, cannot Peter's addressees also overcome their trials?

That Peter calls Lot "righteous" does not mean that either Peter is unaware of the pathetic side of Lot that emerges in Gen. 18–19, or that he is diminishing the value of the epithet "righteousness" by ascribing it indiscriminately to saint and sinner, to the moral and the miscreant, to the faithful and the foppish. Apart from the obvious parallels between Abraham's courtesies extended to his guests and Lot's similar courtesies to his guests, thus putting Lot in a favorable light, Peter no doubt recalls that Abraham's intercession before God for the deliverance of Sodom focused on the presence in Sodom of some righteous people. A minimum of ten *ṣaddîqîm* would have been sufficient grounds for the suspension of judgment on Sodom. But the tally comes up short by nine. Only one (and part of his family) was spared. Because Abraham made his case not on the grounds on kinship ("I have a nephew there") but on the grounds of righteousness, and because Lot is delivered from judgment, Peter has no hesitancy in applying the adjective "righteous" to Lot.[5]

Gen. 18:16–19:38 and Rev. 11:8

In Rev. 11 John has a vision of the temple, the measurements of which are taken by John himself. Prophesying by this temple are "two witnesses," also referred to as "two olive trees" and "two lampstands." Their witnessing provokes persecution, led by the "beast." The two witnesses are attacked and slain by the beast, and "their dead bodies will lie in the street of the great

4. The mention of a "just Lot" may be suggested by Wis. 10:6, which calls Lot a "virtuous man." See also 1 Clem. 11:1, which states that Lot was saved out of Sodom because of "his hospitality and piety." (1 Clement is normally dated ca. A.D. 95 or 96.) An eighth-century Jewish haggadic work similarly commends Lot for his hospitality to strangers and suggests that Lot's gracious behavior is patterned after that of Abraham (Pirqe Rabbi Eliezer 25).

5. T. D. Alexander, "Lot's Hospitality: A Clue to His Righteousness," *JBL* 104 (1985) 289-91.

city which is allegorically called Sodom and Egypt, where their Lord was crucified" (v. 8, RSV).

In this verse Sodom functions as a city, an epoch, a story, and a typological symbol.[6] For John Sodom illustrates: the rejection of God's messengers (Lot), rebellion, and the totality of God's judgment. Of these three the first is the closest in thrust to Matt. 10:15; Mark 10:15; and Luke 10:12, each of which spoke about the rejection of Jesus' disciples in their mission.

John is able to connect Sodom, where Lot was vilified, with Jerusalem, "where their Lord was crucified." Jerusalem had killed its prophets and crucified the Messiah (Matt. 28:29-32, 37; Luke 13:33-34). This is Jerusalem's kinship with Sodom.

I. ABRAHAM AND SARAH IN GERAR (20:1-18)

1. SARAH: WIFE OR SISTER? (20:1-7)

1 *From there Abraham traveled on to the Negeb region, where he settled between Kadesh and Shur. While he was a resident alien in Gerar,*[1]

2 *Abraham said regarding Sarah his wife: "She is my sister." So Abimelech, king of Gerar, sent and took Sarah.*

3 *But God came to*[2] *Abimelech in a dream one night and said to him: "You are about to die*[3] *because of the woman whom you have taken, for she is married."*[4]

4 *Abimelech, who had not approached her, said: "Lord, innocent folk would you slay?*

5 *Did not he himself say to me 'She is my sister,' and did not she herself say 'He is my brother'? With blameless heart*[5] *and clean hands I did this."*

6. See P. S. Minear, "Ontology and Ecclesiology in the Apocalypse," *NTS* 12 (1966) 94.

1. Note the paronomasia *wayyāḡār biḡrār.*

2. For *bôʾ ʾel* in texts relating to God's coming to a person in a dream or a nocturnal vision, see Gen. 31:24; Num. 22:8-9, 19-20.

3. For this rendering of the participle *mēṯ,* see W. F. Stinespring, "The Participle of the Immediate Future and Other Matters Pertaining to Correct Translation of the Old Testament," in *Translating and Understanding the Old Testament: Essays in Honor of H. G. May,* ed. H. T. Frank and W. L. Reed (Nashville: Abingdon, 1970), p. 66. See also H. Kruse, "Psalm cxxxii and the Royal Zion Festival," *VT* 33 (1983) 291 n. 52.

4. *beʿulaṯ bāʿal,* lit., "one ruled over/married by/to the lord/husband," an expression appearing again in the OT only in Deut. 22:22.

6 *God answered him in the dream: "Indeed, I am aware you did this with blameless heart. It was I myself who restrained you from sinning*[6] *against me, and did not allow*[7] *you to touch her.*

7 *So then, return the man's wife. He is a prophet*[8] *and will pray for you and you will live. But if you do not return her, know that you will certainly die, you and everyone who belongs to you."*

Most discussions of ch. 20 have been content to explore the relationships between this narrative and its parallels in 12:10-20 and 26:1ff.[9] What has gone unnoticed is the significance of ch. 20 to its immediate context. This is due primarily to the fact that source criticism attributes all of chaps. 18–19 to J, except for 19:29, and ch. 20 to E. Thus the two sections (chs. 18–19 and ch. 20) have been divorced from each other.

A quick look at these chapters reveals a number of similarities in theme and vocabulary. The most obvious parallel is that of the vulnerable female. Lot will turn over his daughters and Abraham will surrender his wife. In both cases the motive for such a move is the protection of a male — Lot's guests and Abraham himself. Both events picture a prospective (and actual) judgment of God. Related to this theme is the idea of whether God would destroy people who are innocent. Abraham makes such a point in his intercession before God (18:23-33), as does Abimelech (20:5). Central to both stories is the behavior of a man who is a *gûr,* a resident alien (19:9; 20:1). Both stories highlight Abraham's intercessory ministry (18:23-33; 20:17). The time frames of the stories move in opposite directions. The Sodom event begins in the daytime (18:1) and ends in

5. Lit., "in the integrity (or perfectness) of my heart."

6. *mēḥ*^{a}*ṭô* is written in place of the expected *mēḥ*^{a}*ṭō'*. See GKC, § 75qq, for the blending of final *he* and final *aleph* verbs in Biblical Hebrew. Note that the *aleph* is missing in the verb form *w*^{e}*niṭmēṯem* in Lev. 11:43 ("or be made unclean by them"), suggesting that the root may be *ṭmh* or *ṭmm* rather than *ṭm'*. See also F. I. Andersen and A. D. Forbes, *Spelling in the Hebrew Bible,* BibOr 41 (Rome: Biblical Institute, 1986), p. 86.

7. For the verb *nāṯan* with accusative plus infinitive meaning "to allow, permit," see BDB, 679a.

8. Any doubts about the antiquity of Heb. *nāḇî'* are now erased by the cognate word for "prophet" from Ebla, *na-ba-um.* It appears in a bilingual vocabulary with Sum. *pà,* "to speak, recite." See M. J. Dahood, "Ebla, Ugarit, and the Bible," in G. Pettinato, *The Archives of Ebla* (Garden City, NY: Doubleday, 1981), p. 278.

9. For example, see R. Polzin, " 'The Ancestress of Israel' in Danger," *Semeia* 3 (1975) 81-98; A. W. Jenks, *The Elohist and North Israelite Traditions,* SBLMS 22 (Missoula, MT: Scholars, 1977), pp. 21-22; P. D. Miscall, "Literary Unity in Old Testament Narrative," *Semeia* 15 (1979) 27-44; Culley, *Studies in the Structure of Hebrew Narrative,* pp. 33-41; Van Seters, *Abraham in History and Tradition,* pp. 167-91; G. Coats, "A Threat to the Host," in *Saga, Legend, Tale, Novella, Fable,* ed. Coats, JSOTSup 35 (Sheffield: JSOT, 1985), pp. 71-81.

the night (19:35). The Gerar event begins in the night (20:3) and ends in the day (20:8). Finally, both stories involve the activity of the patriarch in cities that lay outside the boundaries of the future land of Israel, Sodom and Gerar.

1 *From there* can refer only to the vantage point from which Abraham viewed the immolation of Sodom (19:28), or to his home at Mamre (18:1). Now relocated to the southland *(Negeb),* Abraham put down his roots — for a while at least — between Kadesh and Shur.[10] He also lived in *Gerar.* Gerar (modern Tell Abu Ḥureirah) is not located between these two places, but is some distance north of them. Some have termed the geography of v. 1 a mystery.[11] But in fact it is nothing of the sort: v. 1 is stating that Abraham's house and family remained at Gerar while he was down in the Sinai.[12]

2 This account differs in a number of ways from the similar incident in ch. 12. Here no famine drives Abraham to Gerar, as happened in 12:10ff. Nor does Abraham flatter his wife, as he did in 12:11. Of course, such an omission may have been prompted by Sarah's advancement in age from sixty-five in 12:11 to ninety in 20:2! Have the intervening twenty-five years taken their toll on Sarah's physical charms? Abraham does not prejudge the inhabitants of Gerar as immoral wife stealers, as he had the Egyptians. The impression given is that the episode in Egypt was well planned and carefully thought through. The episode in Gerar reads as a more spontaneous event. Of course, since Abraham has already perpetrated this ruse once before, no further planning was necessary.

One ought not to designate prematurely ch. 20 as a doublet of ch. 12 (i.e., two versions of the same story), simply because this is the second time Abraham has resorted to such a ruse. Obviously, the two stories have many parallels, as well as differences. Those who accept these as doublets have to explain the differences as resulting either from oral variants or the literary process of redaction. But both these approaches refuse to entertain the possibility that chs. 12 and 20 refer to two different occasions in the life of the patriarch. Who is to say that an individual, caught in a potentially dangerous situation, is not capable of stooping twice to use other people?[13] Perhaps Abraham has not learned from his previous mistakes. If one views them as two separate events, then the Scriptures are showing that the postcovenant

10. For a brief discussion of "Shur" see my comments at 16:7.

11. See Vawter, *On Genesis,* p. 245, and his support of Gunkel's contention that some detail has been omitted from the text.

12. See W. F. Albright, "Abram the Hebrew: A New Archaeological Interpretation," *BASOR* 163 (1961) 48. I follow Speiser in reading v. 1c as a temporal protasis to v. 2. "In the Negeb, Abraham ranged with his herds from Kadesh to Shur; in the course of that stay, he paid a visit to Gerar" (Speiser, *Genesis,* p. 148).

13. Kidner states (*Genesis,* pp. 137-38): "Critical scholars reckon the story a duplicate of 12:10ff., ultimately on the ground that a man does not repeat a lapse of this kind. But it is easier to be consistent in theory than under fear of death."

Abraham, for all his spiritual maturation (e.g., Gen. 15:6), is still much like the precovenant Abraham.

The entire OT is replete with examples of individuals who display continuity between precovenant and postcovenant behavior; or perhaps more accurately, the OT is replete with illustrations of individuals who, though postcovenant, live as if they were precovenant. Abraham is not alone in illustrating moments of greatness intermingled with moments of disobedience and shortsightedness. This inconsistency is also present in the NT, say, in 1 Corinthians, in which a congregation of believers, styled by Paul as "sanctified in Christ Jesus" (1 Cor. 1:1), finds itself involved in all sorts of unsanctified circumstances, from dissensions to litigation to immorality. In the case of OT instances of such Jekyl-and-Hyde behavior, it would appear that the only beacon of hope for a more consistent, God-glorifying covenant life-style is that envisioned by the provisions of promised new covenant (Jer. 31:31-34; Ezek. 36:22-32; Joel 3:1-4 [Eng. 2:28-32]). In the NT instances such behavior must been seen as an aberration, rather than as an expected, normal pattern of the justified life. Indeed, Rom. 7:13ff. is the main Pauline passage used within Lutheran and Reformed traditions to buttress the concept of the bondage of the will, even the will of the redeemed. It pictures a seething, civil war raging within the life of Paul, resulting in failure to do the good and an inability not to do the evil.

I am inclined to believe that what Paul does in the autobiographical section of Rom. 7:13ff. is to trace his unregenerate experience while under law, before Christ, not his experience under Christ. I would suggest this view primarily on the grounds that the order in chs. 6 and 7 is logical rather than psychological or historical. Paul's statements about justification and sanctification (ch. 6) raise questions about law (ch. 7), particularly whether Paul is implying that the law is evil. The natural thing to do in answering such a question is to talk about his experience under the law.

3 Earlier God had made Pharaoh aware of who Sarah really was by sending plagues. Here the means of revelation is a dream. This is the first of four instances in Genesis in which an outsider receives a dream revelation from God (cf. 31:24 — Laban; 40:5 — the Egyptian butler and baker; 41:1 — Pharaoh). Each of these dreams is a warning dream, and as such may be compared with Dan. 4:1ff.; Matt. 2:13; 27:19. The instincts and feelings tell the person one thing, but the dream prevents and/or corrects the implementation of these feelings. Thus Abimelech is informed that Sarah is not an unattached woman, available to him for sexual congress. Joseph's dream (Matt. 2:13) informs Joseph about Herod's real intentions vis-à-vis the child Jesus and provides him with directives on how to circumvent Herod's aggression.

Implicit in these accounts is the idea that God's people do not have a monopoly on revelation of the deity. The revelation of his will to all people is possible. Surely the most stunning illustration of this universality in the OT is the claim made by the biblical narrator that godly Josiah died because he did not listen to the words of Pharaoh Neco from the mouth of God (2 Chr. 35:22).[14]

Also implicit here is the idea that all peoples are obligated to the morality of the patriarchs' God about adultery, the violation of which — even if done in ignorance — brings the most damaging consequences. Whether committed by Israelite or non-Israelite, adultery is an affront to deity. Abimelech is told that he is about to die for taking Sarah. Here we are dealing with apparent adultery, whereas in ch. 12 the issue was (probably) actual adultery. Interestingly, God pronounces the sentence of judgment and then mitigates it, with his explanation given in v. 6. The explanation suggests that God was well aware that Abimelech was not guilty of adultery. His crime is simply "taking" (short of sexual congress) another man's wife.[15]

4-5 To his credit, Abimelech freely admits guilt, as do Pharaoh (Exod. 9:27; 10:16) and Balaam (Num. 22:34), both of whom are also outsiders. But in all three cases the admission of guilt is self-motivated. Abraham can pray for Abimelech (v. 7), but he does not attach culpability to him in any speech of indictment.

The passage begins with a statement by the narrator which shows that his evaluation of Abimelech was the same as Abimelech's self-evaluation. I have translated *qārab̲* literally, *approached,* but what is intended is not just "drawing near" but a sexual encounter, a nuance this verb carries elsewhere in the OT.[16] The narrator denies that Abimelech had approached Sarah in this way.

Presumably Abimelech's response to God is still part of the dream. He remonstrates with God, as did Abraham, on the issue of theodicy: *Innocent folk would you slay?* The difference between the *ṣaddîq* for whom Abraham prays (ch. 18) and the *ṣaddîq* for whom Abimelech speaks (i.e., a self-reference) is that the former are *ṣaddîq* because they have not contributed to Sodom's depravity. The latter is *ṣaddîq* not because he has sinned inadvertently but despite that sin. While Gen. 20 does not use the category of "sinning inadvertently" in the same way as Lev. 4–5, it provides an illustration of this

14. Along these same lines see the creative essay by James A. Sanders in which he traces Luke's usage (Luke 4:18-30) and development of Isa. 61:1-2: "Isaiah in Luke," in *Interpreting the Prophets,* ed. J. L. Mays and P. J. Achtemeier (Philadelphia: Fortress, 1987), pp. 75-85.

15. This term provides another vocabulary link with chs. 18–19. Lot's sons-in-law were "takers" of their wives (19:14), and Abimelech "took" Sarah. For other instances of *lāqaḥ* for "taking [a wife]" see Gen. 21:21; 24:4, 7, 38, 40, 48; Jer. 29:6 (taking a wife for another), and Gen. 4:19; 6:2; 11:29; 12:19 (taking a wife for oneself). In all these passages the verb is followed by the preposition *l^e^*. The preposition is lacking, however, in Gen. 20:2-3.

16. See Lev. 18:6, 14, 19 (illicit sex); Deut. 22:14; Isa. 8:3 (licit sex).

kind of a violation. This kind of sin may happen in one of two ways. A person may know the law and accidentally violate it (i.e., negligence), or he may act deliberately without knowing he did wrong (i.e., ignorance). Abimelech's act falls into this second category.

Abimelech queries whether God would slay *innocent folk (gôy*[17] *gam-ṣaddîq).* Unless we are dealing with a corrupt text,[18] we have here the one use in the OT of *gôy* to refer to a person or persons. Or does *gôy* possibly refer to the punishment of the king's nation because of the king's actions? Later portions of this narrative make plain that God's judgment is directed not at Abimelech per se but at the whole area of Gerar, its women, and the future population growth of Gerar. Possibly Abimelech knows, if he is indeed guilty, that not only he but his entire kingdom (*mamlaḵtî,* v. 9) stands to suffer the consequences of the king's trespass. It is unlikely that Abimelech is using the term *gôy* to refer only to himself. As titular head of his people, the king's behavior determines the future of his subjects (the *gôyîm*). The ancient versions rendered *gôy* in this passage as "people" (Targ. Onqelos: *(hʿm zk'y tqṭwl,* "will you slay people even though innocent") and as "nation" (LXX: *(éthnos agnooún kaí díkaiov apoleís;* Vulg.: *num gentem ignorantem et instam inferficies,* "will you destroy an ignorantly [sinning] and just nation?").[19]

To buttress his case Abimelech, whom the narrator just quoted, now himself becomes the quoter. He reminds God of what Abraham had led him to believe. He also incriminates Sarah with "did not she herself say 'He is my brother'?" Those words were not recorded earlier and hence are unverifiable. Is Abimelech adding to the dialogue and thus forcing Sarah to shoulder part of the blame with her husband? In any case, the king strengthens his claim to innocence by quoting both Abraham's and Sarah's description of their sibling kinship as

17. Another possible vocabulary link with chs. 18–19: Abraham is to be a powerful *gôy* (18:18) and Abimelech is an innocent *gôy.*

18. See the expanded note by Speiser, *Genesis,* p. 149. Many others agree that *gôy* should be deleted and *hagam* be read instead (e.g., *HALAT,* 1:175b; *BHS;* Westermann, *Genesis,* 2:317-18).

19. The seminal study of *gôy* is E. A. Speiser, " 'People' and 'Nation' of Israel," *JBL* 79 (1960) 157-63; see also R. E. Clements and G. J. Botterweck, *TDOT,* 2:426-33, esp. their disclaimer on p. 432 that "there is no support in the OT for the usage which emerged in Talmudic Hebrew where the sing. *goy* could denote an individual member of a non-Israelite nation." Cf. also L. Kutler, "A Structural Semantic Approach to Israelite Communal Terminology," *JANES* 14 (1982) 69-77, who says (p. 75) that *gôy* "refers to a people bound together to form a nation and is distinguished from the rest of Hebrew communal terminology by its stress on nationhood and its affinity to a geographical location." For some criticisms of Speiser's conclusion on the distinction between *ʿam* and *gôy* (e.g., for the most part the two terms are not interchangeable, and where they are, it is from a later source and probably due to poetic parallelism), see N. K. Gottwald, *The Tribes of Yahweh* (Maryknoll, NY: Orbis, 1979), pp. 509-10.

evidence against them. Here then is an instance of quoted direct speech from the past to serve as evidence for the accuracy of a claim in the present (for a parallel see David's words to the Amalekite in 2 Sam. 1:16).[20]

Thus far, Abimelech in self-defense has appealed to God's sense of justice and drawn attention to the mutual duplicity of Abraham and Sarah; now he proceeds to delineate his own innocence. He appeals both to the "heart" and to the "hands,"[21] that is, thoughts and actions. On both the inside and the outside he had no evil intention.

6 God's response is to agree with Abimelech: *I am aware* [Heb. *yāḏaʿ*, lit., "know"][22] *you did this with blameless heart.* God adds the further point that only because of his silent and restraining intervention did Abimelech's "taking" Sarah not progress to "lying with Sarah." The emphasis made here is that Abimelech is not by nature and conviction an individual of high moral principle. It is not any commitment to God that prevents him from sinning. It is the restraints and checks imposed on him by God. Interestingly, God says to Abimelech that adultery would have been a sin against God, not against the husband: "I restrained you from sinning against me." This is in line with other Genesis references that designate adultery as a sin against God (see 26:10 and 39:9b). In all three cases the specification is made by a non-Israelite (26:10) or to a non-Israelite (20:6; 39:9b).

The verb *touch* (Heb. *nāḡaʿ*) may reflect an interesting double entendre. In the first wife-sister story *nāḡaʿ* was used with man as object and meant "to afflict (with plagues)" (12:17). Here, with woman as object, it means "to approach sexually."[23] It will not be necessary for God to send any *n*ᵉ*ḡāʿîm* (plagues) on Abimelech, for Abimelech has not *nāḡaʿ* (touched) Sarah.

7 Now that he has been apprised of the actual situation, Abimelech must act on that new knowledge. He must return Sarah to Abraham. Abimelech is also informed that Abraham is a prophet and that Abraham will pray for him lest he die. This does not mean that Abimelech is guilty simply because he has taken Sarah. He has not committed adultery, and he

20. On the functions of citing a prior statement see B. S. Childs, *The Book of Exodus,* OTL (Philadelphia: Westminster, 1974), pp. 362-63; G. W. Savran, *Telling and Retelling: Quotation in Biblical Narrative* (Bloomington: Indiana University, 1988), pp. 10, 21, 22, 29, 106.

21. For other references to "clean hands" as a metaphor for sinlessness see 1 Sam. 12:5; 26:18; Ps. 24:4; 26:6; 73:13. Cf. L. A. Snidjers, "Psaume xxvi et l'innocence," *OTS* 13(1963) 112-30.

22. Cf. God who "knows" Lot and the motif of "knowing" in chs. 18–19, another vocabulary connection between chs. 18–19 and 20.

23. See Van Seters, *Abraham in History and Tradition,* p. 181. Note that in Ps. 105:15 this verb is again used with Abraham and the other patriarchs, designated there as "my anointed ones": "do not abuse my anointed ones."

is no kidnaper. But if he refuses to return her, he *will certainly die*. Later in the narrative, however, vv. 17-18 indicate that God's judgment was not only threatened but already actualized, simply because Sarah had been taken, unless one understands these later verses to say that God closed the wombs of the women of Abimelech's household not because of any sin by Abimelech but to deter him from committing the sin of adultery. Thus, vv. 6 and 7 would have to be read along with vv. 17-18. How did God restrain Abimelech from sinning (v. 6)? By sealing the wombs of women in the king's palace (vv. 17-18).

This is the first use of *prophet* in the Bible. The role of the prophet here is that of intercessor: he *will pray for you*. Abraham has already done that for Sodom, but he was not styled there as a *nāḇî'*. Abraham's duplicity apparently did not disqualify him from functioning as an interceding *nāḇî'*.

The verb for *pray* is *pālal* in the Hithpael stem, and in some 25 of 60 occurrences this verb refers to intercessory praying. Beginning with the fact that the related noun means "judgment, assessment, estimate," and that the verb in the Piel (or Pillel) means "to make assessment," Speiser proceeds to render the Hithpael of this verb as "to seek assessment (on behalf of others)." This rendering indicates one meaning of the Hithpael, to seek what the Qal (simple) stem designates.[24] The designation by God of Abraham as a *nāḇî'* to Abimelech does not need to be explained to the king, unless one understands the two parts of the sentence "he is a prophet and will pray for you" to be (a) identification ("he is a prophet") and (b) explication ("i.e., he is one who will pray for you") instead of (a) identification/cause ("he is a prophet") and (b) effect ("therefore he will pray for you").

2. ABRAHAM TAKEN TO TASK (20:8-18)

8 *Early the next morning he summoned all his courtiers. When he informed them about these matters the men were greatly disturbed.*
9 *Then Abimelech called in Abraham and said to him: "What have you*

24. See E. A. Speiser, "The Stem *PLL* in Hebrew," *JBL* 82 (1963) 301-6, esp. p. 305. See also D. R. Ap-Thomas, "Notes on some terms relating to prayer," *VT* 6 (1956) 225-41. Speiser's understanding of this root is challenged by C. Toll, "Ausdrücke für 'Kraft' im Alten Testament mit besonderer Rücksicht auf die Wurzel *BRK*," *ZAW* 94 (1982) 119-21. Toll understands the Hithpael (or Hithpallel) to mean "to seek power." The verb for Abraham's intercession *(yiṯpallēl)* also occurs with Moses (Num. 11:2; 21:7; Deut. 9:20, 26), Hannah (1 Sam. 1:10, 27; 2:1), Samuel (1 Sam. 7:5; 8:6; 12:19, 23), Elisha (2 K. 4:33; 6:17-18), Hezekiah (2 K. 19:15, 20; 20:2), Jeremiah (Jer. 42:2, 4, 20), Jonah (Jon. 2:2 [Eng. 1]; 4:2), Job (Job 42:8, 10), Nehemiah (Neh. 1:4, 6; 2:4; 4:3 [Eng. 9]), Solomon (2 Chr. 6:19-20).

done to us? And how have I offended you so that you brought upon me and my kingdom such enormous guilt?[1] *What you have done to me is unconscionable."*[2]

10 *"What possessed you*[3] *to do this?" Abimelech asked Abraham.*

11 *Abraham responded: "I assumed that there was certainly no piety*[4] *in this place, and they would have slain me because of my wife.*

12 *Furthermore, I testify*[5] *she is my sister, my father's daughter, but not my mother's daughter, and she became my wife.*[6]

13 *But when God caused me to wander*[7] *from my father's home, I said to her, 'This is the agreement*[8] *which you must make with me: every place where we go, say about*[9] *me, He is my brother.' "*

14 *Abimelech took sheep and oxen, male and female slaves, and gave them to Abraham; and he restored to him Sarah his wife.*

1. Lit., "a great sin," *(ḥᵃṭāʾâ gᵉḏōlâ).* See the commentary on v. 9.

2. Lit., "deeds that are not done you have done with me."

3. *rāʾâ kî* is rare.

4. Lit., "fear of God." On the rendering of this phrase in the LXX see E. Tov, "Compound Words in the LXX Representing Two or More Hebrew Words," *Bib* 58 (1977) 191, 195.

5. *ʾomnâ* introduces assertions of a legal nature. Cf. S. Talmon, "The New Hebrew Letter from the Seventh Century B.C. in Historical Perspective," *BASOR* 176 (1964) 34, who suggests "I testify" for *ʾomnâ* in Gen. 20:12 and Ruth 3:12. On the basis of an oral suggestion by F. M. Cross, Talmon suggests (n. 27) the possible connections between *ʾomnâ* and some of Jesus' sayings that open with the formula "Amen, I say unto you" (e.g., Matt. 5:18, 26; 6:5; 8:10; Luke 23:43; John 1:51; 3:3).

6. Or, "and so she could be[come] my wife."

7. Note the use of the pl. verb *hiṯʿû* with *ʾᵉ̆lōhîm. ʾᵉ̆lōhîm* occurs with a pl. verb here and in 31:53; 35:7; Exod. 22:8 (Eng. 9); 2 Sam. 7:23 (but sing. in the parallel verse in 1 Chr. 17:21); with a pl. participle in Ps. 58:12 (Eng. 11); in the expression "living God," Deut. 5:26; 1 Sam. 17:26, 36; Jer. 10:10; 23:36. The SP reads the sing. here: *htʿh.* Speiser (*Genesis,* p. 150) suggests that the accompanying pl. verb allows one to translate *ʾᵉ̆lōhîm* with a broader connotation, something like "Heaven, Fate, Providence." GKC, § 145d, suggests that such constructions (*ʾᵉ̆lōhîm* with pl. verb/adjective) may be a vestige of an earlier polytheistic form of expression. But if so, why were these few left untouched, while most, presumably, were modified?

8. *ḥeseḏ* cannot be translated as "mercy" here, although the idea of mercy and loyalty is involved. Cf. C. F. Whitely, "The Semantic Range of *Ḥesed,*" *Bib* 62 (1981) 524; H. F. Peacock, "Translating 'mercy', 'steadfast love', in the book of Genesis," *BT* 31 (1980) 203; G. Gerleman, "Das übervolle Mass. Ein Versuch mit *ḥaesaed,*" *VT* 28 (1978) 159; Sakenfeld, *Meaning of Ḥesed,* pp. 26-27; F. I. Andersen, "Yahweh, the Kind and Sensitive God," in *God Who Is Rich in Mercy,* Fest. D. B. Knox, ed. P. T. O'Brien and D. G. Peterson (Grand Rapids: Baker, 1987), p. 53.

9. For *ʾāmar lᵉ* = "to say about" cf. Judg. 9:54; Ps. 3:3 (Eng. 2); 41:6 (Eng. 5); 71:10; Eccl. 2:2.

15 *And Abimelech said: "My land is at your disposal.*[10] *Settle down wherever you wish."*

16 *To Sarah he said: "I herewith give*[11] *a thousand (pieces of) silver to your brother. Let that be a foil*[12] *to everybody who is with you. With respect to all that has gone on you have been vindicated."*[13]

17 *Then Abraham prayed to God,*[14] *and God restored*[15] *fertility to Abimelech, his wife, his slave girls, so that they could conceive again.*

18 *For Yahweh had rendered infertile every womb in Abimelech's household because of Sarah, Abraham's wife.*

The symmetrical outline of this chapter may be detailed as follows:

(a) the narrator introduces a problem (the potential death of Abraham), vv. 1-2
(b) God and Abimelech in dialogue, vv. 3-7
(c) Abraham and Abimelech in dialogue, vv. 8-16
(d) the narrator introduces a solution to a problem (the barrenness of the Gerarite women), vv. 17-18

Two scenes of narration (of which the first involves a very brief monologue — two words in Hebrew) are separated by two dialogue scenes, the first of which is in a nocturnal setting (v. 3), and the second of which is in a daytime setting.

10. "At your disposal" catches the nuance of Heb. *lᵉpāneyḵā,* lit., "to your face."

11. One should translate *hinnēh nāṯattî 'elep kesep* with the force of the present tense rather than the past tense. For other instances in Genesis of rendering a verb in the perfect form as a present tense, see 1:29; 9:13; 15:18; 17:20; 23:11; 48:22. Cf. also Deut. 1:8 and 2 Sam. 19:30 (Eng. 29), where *'āmartî* means not "I have said" or "I have decided" (RSV), but "I herewith declare." If *nāṯattî* is rendered as past tense, then one would have to assume that the gifts given to Abraham by Abimelech are a dowry for Sarah, as were those presented by Pharaoh to Abraham in Gen. 12:16.

12. Lit., "a covering of the eyes." See discussion of v. 16.

13. The *waw* on *wᵉnōḵāḥaṯ* introduces the conclusion after a preliminary phrase. Cf. Gen. 3:5; 40:9; Exod. 16:6; Lev. 7:16; and BDB, p. 254b. Such an understanding of the *waw* makes unnecessary the emendations to the text suggested by *BHS* (also KB, p. 380, but not in *HALAT,* p. 392) of transposing the *waw* from the beginning of *wᵉnōḵāḥaṯ* (Niphal participle, fem., from *yāḵaḥ*) to the end of *kōl.* BDB, p. 407a, cites a suggestion to repoint the participle *(nōḵāḥāṯ)* as a 2nd fem. sing. perfect *(nōḵaḥat),* but this change also seems unnecessary.

14. *'ĕlōhîm* occurs 6 times in this chapter, and twice it appears inexplicably with the definite article, here and in v. 6.

15. The use of the root *rāpā'* with Abraham's intercession reminds one of Danel's stock epithet in the Ugaritic Epic of Aqhat: *mt rpi,* "the man of healing." Danel was presumably credited with curative powers.

8 Abimelech wastes no time sharing the revelation he has received from God with his attendants. Early the next morning they are summoned to his palace to receive the tidings. Abimelech could have furtively returned Sarah to Abraham and avoided embarrassment. Who wants to admit publicly that he has been tricked? His willingness to be open and tell the truth contrasts with Abraham and his subterfuge. Also, Abraham's concern about the absence of any awe or fear of God ("piety") (*'ên yir'aṯ 'ĕlōhîm,* v. 11) in Gerar turns out to have been unwarranted, for the courtiers are *disturbed* or afraid *(wayyir'û)* when Abimelech fills them in on recent developments.

9-10 The Bible shares with other ancient Near Eastern works the concept that adultery is "the great sin" (cf. *ḥᵃṭā'â gᵉḏōlâ,* here translated *enormous guilt*).[16] Abraham's role here is reversed from that of ch. 18. There Abraham challenged God. Here Abimelech challenges Abraham. No longer an intercessor, Abraham is now a target. Abimelech's accusation that Abraham has done things he should not have done sounds like Abraham's word to God that he ought not to do what he is about to do (18:23). Abraham's act hurts not only himself but Sarah as well. Abimelech's taking Sarah jeopardizes not only himself but his kingdom as well. If a city can be saved by the presence of ten virtuous people, an empire can be dismantled by the actions of one guilty person.[17]

11 Abraham will do everything except tell the truth. He offers excuses and defends himself through uncalled-for false assumptions (v. 11), casuistry and a convoluted argument (v. 12), and an appeal to precedent (v. 13).

In v. 11 is another thematic connection with chs. 18–19. At this point Abraham behaves like Lot's sons-in-law. They did not take Lot seriously when he urged them to leave Sodom, for they assumed he was joking. Abraham is equally good at jumping to conclusions, that is, that there is *no piety* (Heb. *yir'aṯ 'ĕlōhîm,* lit., "fear of God") in Gerar. While I have translated *yir'aṯ 'ĕlōhîm* ("fear of God") as "piety," the context makes clear that it encompassed the implications that a relationship with God has for our relationships with others: in this particular case, sensitivity to and respect for the rights of outsiders.[18]

16. See J. J. Rabinowitz, "The 'Great Sin' in Ancient Egyptian Marriage Contracts," *JNES* 18 (1959) 73; W. L. Moran, "The Scandal of the 'Great Sin' at Ugarit," *JNES* 18 (1959) 280-81; J. Milgrom, *Cult and Conscience* (Leiden: Brill, 1976), pp. 132-33.

17. See H. Wheeler Robinson, *Corporate Personality in Ancient Israel* (Philadelphia: Fortress, 1964).

18. See H. W. Wolff, "The Elohistic Fragments in the Pentateuch" (tr. K. R. Crim), in W. Brueggemann and Wolff, *Vitality of Old Testament Traditions,* 2nd ed. (Atlanta: John Knox, 1982), pp. 70-71. Westermann (*Genesis,* 2:325-26) agrees with Wolff's analysis of the meaning of the phrase "fear of God" in Gen. 20 and adds, "it [viz., the expression

Abraham thought that the Gerarites would *slay (hāraḡ)* him. This verb appeared in the first section of the chapter (v. 4): "innocent folk would you slay?" Abimelech protested that he would be slain for something he did innocently. Abraham presumed he would be slain for no other reason than that he was married and an alien. The potential death of Abimelech in the first section of the chapter is replaced by the potential death of Abraham.

It is possible that Abraham's statement about Gerar is not an assumption but is based on observation. Such a view necessitates taking *'āmar* as "see" and not "say," and emending *raq,* "certainly," to *rîq/rēq,* "empty, vain, worthless"; hence, "Indeed, I have beheld worthlessness: there is no fear of God in this place." The second phrase in this verse would specify Abraham's definition of *rîq.*[19] This reading evolves Abraham's statement about Gerar from a hypothetical one to a matter-of-fact one.

12 Abraham now proceeds to share with Abimelech a bit of family biography. He reminds the king that Sarah is indeed his half-sister, for she and Abraham have the same father, but not the same mother. But Gen. 11:27ff., where one would expect to find the details of this kinship, gives no genealogy for Sarah. She is never mentioned there as the daughter of Terah. One wonders why Abraham did not volunteer this information earlier, when he first came to Gerar. Had he been honest about their situation, he would have saved Sarah and himself a lot of shame, and Abimelech a lot of guilt. Then again, the writer may have intended it as a total fabrication on Abraham's part.

In this verse a comparison may be made between Abraham, who lives with his half-sister, and Lot, who lives with his two daughters. Later OT law condemned a marriage with a (half-) sister (see Lev. 18:9, 11; 20:17; Deut. 27:22; Ezek. 22:11).[20]

13 To make matters worse, Abraham now incriminates both God and Sarah. The verb Abraham uses for *wander (tā'â)* means to wander about hopelessly and aimlessly, often in a hostile environment (see Gen. 21:14, Hagar's wandering, and 37:15, Joseph's wanderings). On two occasions (Ps.

"fear of God"] does not prescribe specifically the relationship of a person to the God of the fathers or to the God of Israel, but a religious or reverential attitude which one meets even outside Israel."

19. See M. J. Dahood, "Abraham's Reply in Genesis 20,11," *Bib* 61 (1980) 90-91. In any case the proposed emendation of *mâ rā'îṯā,* "what you have seen," to *mâ yārē'ṯā,* "what were you afraid of," is unnecessary, although it is encouraged by many scholars (see *BHS*).

20. The story in 2 Sam. 13 describes Amnon's lust for his half sister Tamar. Tamar protests premarital intercourse with Amnon and rape (vv. 12-13a) rather than possible marriage to Amnon upon David's consent (v. 13b). See P. K. McCarter, Jr., *II Samuel,* AB (Garden City, NY: Doubleday, 1984), pp. 323-24.

95:10 [see v. 7] and Jer. 50:6) the verb is connected with sheep, those who are led astray most easily and gullibly.

Abraham also informs Abimelech that he and Sarah had a standing agreement on this arrangement whenever such a ruse needed to be used. Hence Sarah is named as a consenting member in the trick. In 12:13 Abraham put this proposal to Sarah as a request: *'imrî-nā',* "say, please." Here the *-nā'* is dropped, and a request sounds more like a command.

14 In the first wife-sister story, Pharaoh gave gifts to Abraham *before* he found out who Sarah really was (12:16). Here Abimelech gives gifts to Abraham *after* he finds out Sarah's true identity. This point gives the impression that Pharaoh's gifts are a bridal price, and those of Abimelech are compensation.

This procedure is known from the Middle Assyrian laws (15th-12th centuries B.C.), one of which reads: "If in the case of a seignior's [man's] wife one not her father, nor her brother, nor her son, but another person, has caused her to take to the road, but he did not know that she was a seignior's wife, he shall (so) swear and he shall also pay two talents of lead to the woman's husband."[21] This law involves a man taking an oath and paying damages to the husband when he has taken the wife of another man on a journey. Note that, according to this law, the oath functions only to establish the fact that the man was unaware that the woman who accompanied him was married: "he did not know that she was a seignior's wife, he shall (so) swear." It is not an oath to clear him of any sexual involvement with the woman. Just to take a married woman on a trip without her husband's consent is a crime. This is the case with Abimelech. Had he taken Sarah into his palace knowing she was married, he would have committed a wrong, even if he had not slept with her.

It is obvious that Abimelech gives gifts to Abraham to compensate for his inadvertent trespass, but the absence of any oath by Abimelech calls into question whether Gen. 20:14 is an actual parallel to the Middle Assyrian law. Interestingly, the Genesis Apocryphon from Qumran (1st century B.C. or A.D.) expands the incident of Abraham/Sarah and Pharaoh (Gen. 12:10-20) with: "And the king swore an oath to me that [he had] not [touched her]. And then [they brought] Sarai to [me]. The king gave to her [mu]ch [silver and go]ld; many garments of fine linen and purple."[22] Here is both an oath and compensation, exactly the stipulations spelled out in the Middle Assyrian law cited above. It appears, however, that the author of the Genesis Apocryphon conflated the story of Abimelech in ch. 20 with that of Pharaoh in ch. 12. Evidence

21. *ANET,* p. 181, § 22.

22. Translation of J. A. Fitzmyer, *The Genesis Apocryphon of Qumran Cave I: A Commentary,* BibOr 18A, 2nd ed. (Rome: Biblical Institute, 1971), p. 67.

for this conflation is his reading of the incident in ch. 12 in which Pharaoh's gifts to Abraham come at the end of the episode (as in ch. 20) rather than at the beginning, and the addition of an oath by the king to Abraham. To be sure, Gen. 20 is quiet about Abimelech making an oath to Abraham, but the author of the Genesis Apocryphon may have inferred it from Abimelech's phrase "my heart was blameless and my hands were clean" (v. 5).[23]

For biblical law dealing with compensation to the husband or relatives for injury to a woman, see Exod. 21:22-24; 22:16-17; Deut. 22:25-29.

15 Abimelech's further invitation to Abraham to stay and settle in his territory is in marked contrast to the pharaoh who sent Abraham on his way (12:20). For one king the duplicitous Abraham became a persona non grata. For another king he became a persona grata. Of course, Abimelech knows that his physical healing and that of his fellow citizens depends on Abraham's praying for them, and hence on Abraham's goodwill. Accordingly, it is unlikely that Abimelech is about to give Abraham an order to leave.

16 In addition to all his gifts to Abraham, Abimelech gives a *thousand (pieces of) silver* to Sarah's *brother* — not husband. The biting irony is hard to miss. This presentation of money is to be *a foil* (Heb. *k^esûṯ ʿênayim,* lit., "a covering of the eyes").[24] Besides Gen. 20:16 and 32:21 (Eng. 20), the covering of parts of the body (faces/eyes) is mentioned in Exod. 23:8; 1 Sam. 12:3; Job 9:24. But none of these passages helps in the elucidation of Gen. 20:16. Most likely *k^esûṯ* is used figuratively and is to be connected with the notion of concealing any kind of sexual impropriety.[25] The eyes of any of Sarah's acquaintances will be blind to any sexual misconduct on her part.

Abimelech further absolves Sarah from any wrong in this situation. She can leave, or stay, holding her head high. I suggest that the *w^eʾeṯ kōl*

23. See M. Weinfeld, "Sarah in Abimelech's Palace (Genesis 20) — Against the Background of Assyrian Law and the Genesis Apocryphon," *Tarbiz* 52 (1982/83) 639-42 (Hebrew), repr. in *Mélanges bibliques et orientaux en l'honneur de M. Mathias Delcor,* ed. A. Caquot, S. Légasse, and M. Tardieu (Neukirchen-Vluyn: Neukirchener; Kevelaer: Butzon und Bercker 1985), pp. 431-36.

24. On whether "cover the face" of 32:21 (Eng. 20) is connected with "covering of the eyes" see B. A. Levine, *In the Presence of the Lord* (Leiden: Brill, 1974), p. 60 n. 18.

25. See C. Carmichael, "Forbidden mixtures," *VT* 32 (1982) 414-15; von Rad, *Genesis,* p. 229. Weinfeld (in *Mélanges bibliques,* p. 434 n. 20) understands the phrase to mean "ransom," and this is Abimelech's way of atoning for his guilt with Sarah (v. 16), after he has atoned for his guilt with Abraham (v. 14). The gifts of both animals/servants and silver are penance or compensation for the wrong committed. Weinfeld appeals both to the LXX ("these are for the honor/value of your face," *eis timḗn toú prosṓpou sou*) and to Targ. Onqelos ("it is for you a cover of honor,"*h' hw' lyk kswt dyqr*). Weinfeld's interpretation presupposes guilt rather than innocence on Abimelech's part, and thus the need of penance. But how would this interpretation carry over into the last three words of the verse, which Weinfeld nowhere discusses?

which precedes the verb does not mean "in the presence of everyone." That idea has just been stated by *l^e^ḵōl ʾ^a^šer ʾittāḵ, to everybody who is with you.* Rather, the phrase designates *with respect to all that has gone on* (lit., "with everything").[26]

17-18 Abraham intercedes on behalf of Abimelech before God, and as a result fertility is restored to Abimelech, his wife, and slave girls. If the word *brother* was ironic in Abimelech's mouth, then here is another instance of irony. Abraham can pray, and as a result barren Philistine women are able to conceive. Yet his own wife has not yet been able to become pregnant.[27] As if to accentuate that irony, even the verb that is used in v. 18 to describe Yahweh's closing of the wombs of Abimelech's household *(ʿāṣar)* had been earlier used by Sarah about herself and her own condition (16:2). The Philistines girls have had their fertility restored. Will Sarah's fertility also be restored?

Throughout at least sixteen of the first eighteen verses in this chapter, Abimelech appears to be the exemplary character; by contrast, Abraham' character is unappealing. Abraham first deceived Abimelech, then tried to exonerate himself. Abimelech is an innocent victim. He denounces Abraham's behavior, offers him settlement privileges, and makes a handsome payment to both Abraham and Sarah. Suddenly, and perhaps unexpectedly, those characterizations are reversed, and Abraham becomes the exemplary saint, while Abimelech is under the judgment of God, as much as was Pharaoh in ch. 12. In ch. 12 the order was: (1) taking Sarah, (2) God's judgment via plagues, (3) returning Sarah. Here the order is (1) taking Sarah, (2) returning Sarah, (3) God's judgment via sterility. The delay of God's response has the effect of unmasking Abimelech. He is more than an innocent victim. Only the restraining providence of God, rather than any moral vigor on Abimelech's part, deterred Abimelech from sleeping with Sarah.[28]

J. ISAAC AND ISHMAEL (21:1-34)

1. THE BIRTH OF ISAAC (21:1-7)

1 *Yahweh then*[1] *visited Sarah as he said he would; Yahweh did for Sarah as he promised he would.*

26. See R. Gordis, "Studies in the Esther Narrative," *JBL* 95 (1976) 54.

27. E. M. Good (*Irony in the Old Testament* [Philadelphia: Westminster, 1965], pp. 94-95) cites several instances of irony in Gen. 20, but he does not include this one.

28. See Sternberg, *Poetics of Biblical Narrative,* pp. 315-17.

1. I include "then" in the translation to capture the nuance of the unusual syntax of the opening of the verse: subject, then verb. Cf. also 22:1, *w^e^hāʾ^ĕ^lōhîm nissâ ʾeṯ ʾaḇrāhām.*

2 *Sarah conceived and bore to Abraham a son in his advanced years, at the specific time about which God had spoken to him.*

3 *Abraham named his newborn son whom Sarah had borne him Isaac.*

4 *Then Abraham circumcised his son Isaac when he was eight days old, as God*[2] *had commanded him.*

5 *Abraham was one hundred years old when Isaac his son was born to him.*

6 *And Sarah said: "God has made a joke of me; whoever hears will laugh at me."*

7 *She also said: "Would that it were told to Abraham, 'Sarah will have suckled sons,' for I have borne a son in his old age."*[3]

1 Earlier references to Sarah's forthcoming pregnancy took place either in Sarah's absence (17:19), or with Sarah as a silent spectator in the background (18:12). Here it is Abraham who becomes silent and Sarah who talks. The biblical writer's selection of the verb *visit* (Heb. *pāqaḏ*) is deliberate.[4] Three men have just come to Abraham. Two "men" have recently appeared to Lot. Now there is a third appearance, this time a visit of Yahweh to Sarah.

Yahweh's visiting a woman who subsequently gives birth finds later parallels in the stories about Hannah (1 Sam. 2:21) and Elizabeth (Luke 1:68). Although *pāqaḏ* may be used of a husband who visits his wife for sexual purposes (Judg. 15:1), it is unlikely that this is the implication of Gen. 21:1, or that we have here the torso of a myth about Isaac's divine paternity. Rather, as evidenced by 1 Sam. 2:21, we have here an instance where *visit* takes on

2. For some reason the LXX renders MT *ʾĕlōhîm* as *kýrios* in vv. 2 and 6 but as *theós* (as expected) in v. 4. Does this fluctuation represent a complex history of the Hebrew text or translation idiosyncrasies in the LXX?

3. R. Gordis ("The Structure of Biblical Poetry," in *Poets, Prophets, and Sages: Essays in Biblical Interpretation* [Bloomington: Indiana University, 1971], p. 76) suggests that Sarah's words in v. 7 are an ancient poetic fragment. He appeals for evidence to the inverted word order in stich b, the use of the poetic word *millēl,* and the 3:3 rhythm of the tristich.

(stich a) Whó would-have-sáid to-Abráham
(stich b) Given-to súck sońs has-Saráh
(stich c) For-I-have-bórn a-són in-his-óld-age

4. On the wide nuances of *pāqaḏ* in the OT, see B. Grossfeld, "The Translation of Biblical Hebrew פקד in the Targum, Peshitta, Vulgate and Septuagint," *ZAW* 96 (1984) 83-101. Grossfeld notes (p. 98) that the LXX renders *pāqaḏ* in Gen. 21:1 (and Judg. 15:1) with *episképtomai* ("to visit [in a beneficial way]"), while the Targ. uses the verb *dkr* ("remembered").

the connotation of Yahweh mercifully delivering one from an apparently hopeless situation, that is, infertility.[5]

The second half of the verse repeats substantially the first half. Speiser sees here a needless duplication, the result of J being responsible for the first part of the verse and P being responsible for the second part (the presence of P is observable in the last half of the verse with a secondary change of Elohim to Yahweh). All this speculation becomes needless, however, once it is seen that the whole verse is poetry,[6] a fact reinforced by the chiasm of subject-verb — verb-subject. Also, the two statements made by the narrator in terms of Yahweh in v. 1 balance Sarah's two statements with which this unit concludes (vv. 6-7).

2 This particular verse represents the fulfillment of God's promise to Abraham in 17:16 and 18:10-14. The *kāʿēṯ ḥayyâ* of 18:10, 14, "sometime soon," has now become *lammôʿēḏ, at the specific time.* Sarah is able to conceive only because of that earlier promise of God. God is willing to suspend judgment on Sodom because of Abraham's intercession. He opens the infertile wombs of the Philistine women because of Abraham's prayers. Sarah conceives and gives birth because Yahweh visits her. Nothing is said here about the advanced age at which Sarah gave birth. She herself indirectly picks up on that point in v. 7. But the focus is on the advanced age at which Abraham becomes a father. In only two words (*wattahar* and *wattēleḏ*) the narrative covers nine months.[7]

3 For a second time (see earlier 16:15) Abraham engages in naming. As he conferred the name Ishmael on the child he fathered by Hagar, now he confers the name *Isaac* on the child he has fathered by Sarah, and this in response to God's earlier directive (17:19). "Isaac" is God's choice for the name of this child. "Ishmael" was Abraham's choice for the name of his firstborn "Ishmael" evolves as a name only after the child's birth. "Isaac" is revealed as the name for the second child before he is even conceived. These distinctions between the names Ishmael and Isaac (when they were chosen,

5. The verb *pāqaḏ* refers to God's gracious visitation to an individual or individuals, bringing them deliverance from various types of crises, also in Exod. 4:31; Ruth 1:6; 1 Sam. 2:21; Ps. 106:4. The meanings for the Hebrew verb vary from "count" to "muster." Its Akkadian cognate, *paqādu,* suggests that its basic meaning is "hand over, deliver, assign," and so by extension "to turn one's thoughts/attention to" (as here in v. 1).

6. See W. von Soden, "Zum hebräischen Wörterbuch," *UF* 13 (1981) 160. See also the objections of Westermann, *Genesis,* 2:332.

7. Did Sarah conceive Isaac after the incident in Gerar or before? If there is a whole year from 17:21 ("Isaac, whom Sarah shall bear to you at this season next year") until Isaac's birth (21:2), and if there are nine months from 18:10 ("I will surely return to you in the spring") to the birth of Isaac (21:2), and if Isaac is born immediately after the narrative of Gen. 20 concludes, then Abraham is identifying his pregnant wife as his sister. See D. J. A. Clines, *What Does Eve Do to Help?* JSOTSup 94 (Sheffield: Sheffield Academic, 1990), pp. 75-76.

by whom they were chosen) serve to reinforce the fact that Isaac is indeed the special son, the promised son. *Isaac* means "he laughs." The subject is not identified. Who laughs: God, Abraham, or Isaac? Ishmael's name is provided with a contextual etymology (16:11); Isaac's is not.[8]

4 Unlike Moses, who ignored the circumcision of his son (Exod. 4:24-26), Abraham is careful not to bypass God's directions on this subject given to him back in 17:10ff. The text is surprisingly silent about any emotional outburst by Abraham upon the successful birth of Isaac, even though this is the child for whom he has had to wait twenty-five years, the child whose birth at times appeared to be an impossible dream. If Abraham is understandably euphoric at this moment in his life, such a feeling must not be allowed to lull the father into indifference with regard to his spiritual obligations to his son. After all, the verse ends by reminding us that this is an act that *God had commanded.* Abraham is not so much excited as obedient.

5 Abraham's earlier question of 17:17 — "can a child be born to a centenarian?" — is now answered by the narrator. Again, the focus is on Abraham's age, not Sarah's, at the birth of Isaac. He is the son *(ben)* of 100 years when his own son *(b^enô)* is born to him.

6-7 Some commentators who take *ṣ^eḥōq* of v. 6 as the laughter of joy are quick to point out that Sarah's words in v. 6a are inconsistent with her use of *yiṣḥaq* in v. 6b. In one breath it is the laughter of joy and in the next breath it is the laughter of ridicule, unless one takes *yiṣḥaq lî* of v. 6b to mean "rejoice with me" instead of "laugh at me." But even if we take both uses of the root in v. 6 to mean joyful laughter, then we have a strong contrast with earlier uses of the root where the idea was unbelief or sarcasm (17:17; 18:12, 13, 15). Source critics often cite these verses as evidence for triplicate traditions about Isaac's name: 17:17 (P); 18:12-15 (J); 21:3-7 (E). But 21:6 is entirely consistent with 17:17 and 18:12-15 if one translates *ṣ^eḥōq* as *joke.*

Furthermore, our translation *Would that it were told to Abraham* fits more smoothly with earlier references in Genesis than does the traditional "Who would have said to Abraham" (e.g., RSV, AV). In fact, God had said several times to Abraham that his wife would bear a son. Sarah was aware of that promise. What she wishes God would have said is that she would mother *sons* (or "children," Heb. *bānîm*) and not just a son *(ben).*[9]

8. On three occasions laughter is associated with the announced or actual birth of Isaac (17:17; 18:12-15; 21:6). Isaac, meaning "he laughs," might well be an instance of popular etymology. It is possible that the proper name is actually a verbal form, now lacking a divine subject, "may (God) laugh," i.e., may God look benevolently upon him. See N. Sarna, "Isaac," *EncJud,* 9:4.

9. I am following here the interpretation of I. Rabinowitz, "Sarah's wish (Gen xxi 6-7)," *VT* 29 (1979) 362-63. This interpretation necessitates that MT *mî millēl* be read

2. THE EXPULSION OF HAGAR AND ISHMAEL (21:8-21)

8 *The child grew and was weaned, and on the day Isaac was weaned Abraham put on a great feast.*[1]

9 *But Sarah spotted the son of Hagar the Egyptian, whom she had borne to Abraham, playing.*[2]

10 *She raved against*[3] *Abraham: "Drive out that slave woman with her son! No son of this slave woman*[4] *is going to share the inheritance with my son, with Isaac!"*

11 *The matter was very upsetting to Abraham on account of his son.*[5]

12 *But God said to Abraham: "Do not be upset*[6] *about the lad or about your slave woman. Whatever Sarah tells you, do it, for it is through Isaac that your descendants shall be named.*

13 *Also, the son of the slave woman I shall establish as a nation, for he too is your offspring."*

14 *Rising early in the morning, Abraham took bread and a skin of water and gave them to Hagar, putting them on her shoulder, along with the*

---

as *mî yᵉmallēl,* and that *mî* be understood not as the interrogative but as *mî* with the imperfect to express a wish. In a matter unrelated to translation, it is time to call into question the widely held opinion that *millēl* is an Aramaism (Dan. 6:22 [Eng. 21], and otherwise only in Hebrew poetry — Job 8:2; 33:3; Ps. 106:2). The root is attested as early as the 8th century B.C. in a Phoenician inscription (Karatepe): *wbl kn mtmll bymty ldnnyn,* "and there was no one speaking against the Dananians in my days." See Dahood, *Psalms,* 3:67.

1. The phrase "make/put on a feast [for] — " *(ʿāśâ mišteh [lᵉ])* is common in the OT. BDB, p. 1059b, lists some 20 occurrences. See Gen. 19:3; 26:30; 40:20, etc.

2. Both LXX *(paízonta metá Isaak toú huioú autḗs)* and Vulg. *(ludentum cum Isaac filio suo)* add "with Isaac her son." But Pesh. and Targ. Onqelos follow MT. See the commentary below.

3. Lit., "spoke to." Cf. Speiser, *Genesis,* p. 153, "turned on."

4. *ben-ʾāmâ* occurs 6 times in the OT: Gen. 21:10, 13; Exod. 23:12; Judg. 9:18; Ps. 86:16; 116:16. For a helpful discussion of this term as it bears on the narrative in Gen. 21:8ff., see F. C. Fensham, "The Son of a Handmaid in Northwest-Semitic," *VT* 19 (1969) 312-21. Jenks (*Elohist and North Israelite Traditions,* , p. 70 n. 13) notes that 8 of 16 instances of *ʾāmâ* in the Pentateuch occur in the Covenant Code, an indubitable non-E source, and other occurrences of *ʾāmâ* in pentateuchal passages are also most likely not from E. Thus, the case becomes dim for assigning a passage to E simply on the basis of the presence of the word *ʾāmâ.*

5. Some Greek versions add "Ishmael," to pinpoint which of Abraham's two sons is meant.

6. See G. I. Davies, "The uses of *rʿʿ* Qal and the meaning of Jonah IV I," *VT* 27 (1977) 106, who suggests that Gen. 21:12 is an illustration of *rāʿâ* used impersonally (he cites two others: 2 Sam. 11:25; 1 Chr. 21:7).

child.[7] *Then he sent her off, and she wandered hopelessly in the wilderness of Beer-sheba.*

15 *When the water in the skin was gone, she left*[8] *the child under one of the desert shrubs.*[9]

16 *Then she went and sat down by herself*[10] *opposite him about a bowshot*[11] *away, for she said:*[12] *"Do not let me see the child die." Sitting down opposite him, she*[13] *started to sob.*

17 *God heard the lad's cry, and the messenger of God called out to Hagar from heaven. "What ails you,*[14] *Hagar? Do not be afraid, for God has heard the lad's voice from*[15] *where he is.*

18 *Get up, lift the lad up, and steady him with your hand, for a great nation I will make of him."*

19 *Then God opened her eyes,*[16] *and she spotted a well of water. She went*

7. I follow the MT here and take *'eṯ-hayyeleḏ* as the object of *nāṯan,* which means not only "set, place" but also "entrust, give over."

8. For contextual reasons *tašlēḵ* should not be translated "threw, cast" (contra AV, RSV, Westermann).

9. For *śîḥîm* see the commentary on 2:5. In Job 30:4 *śîḥîm* are a source of food for the extremely hungry who pick and eats its leaves; and in Job 30:6-7 wild asses in the wilderness bray among them. They are larger than a plant *('ēśeḇ)* but smaller than a tree *('ēṣ).*

10. The preposition *lāh* (lit., "to her") is an ethical dative. Cf. *lāḵem* in 22:5. See GKC, § 199s.

11. *kimṭaḥ^a^wê* (preposition plus participle plus suffix) may be compared with *b^e^mōṣa'^a^ḵem* in 32:20 (Eng. 19). The term *ṭāḥâ* is a hapax legomenon, but its meaning is fairly certain from the context and its Arabic cognates. See F. E. Greenspahn, *Hapax Legomena in Biblical Hebrew,* SBLDS 74 (Chico, CA: Scholars, 1984), p. 119. The whole Hebrew phrase is lit. "making distant [or, 'at a distance'] like shooters of a bow."

12. It is unclear whether Hagar is speaking to God or to herself.

13. LXX has a masc. subject, making Ishmael the one who weeps. This reading is encouraged no doubt by the opening clause in v. 17, "God heard the lad's cry." As Speiser has pointed out (*Genesis,* pp. 155-56), however, two arguments militate against favoring the masc. of the LXX: (1) the noun *qôl,* "cry, sound, voice" is not expressly to be connected with weeping; (2) the text is unambiguously fem. in its syntax and needs no emendation — "*she* lifted *her* voice, *she* wept." As P. Trible notes, "masculine emendations cannot silence Hagar" ("The Other Woman: A Literary and Theological Study of the Hagar Narratives," in *Understanding the Word: Essays in Honor of Bernhard W. Anderson,* ed. J. T. Butler, et al., JSOTSup 37 [Sheffield: JSOT, 1985], p. 235).

14. On the idiom *mah-lāḵ,* lit., "what to you?" i.e., "what ails you?" or "what do you want?" see BDB, p. 552b, § 1a(c).

15. Note *b* here in the sense of "from." GKC, § 138e, cites this verse as an instance in which *'^a^šer* can itself express a substantial idea.

16. Cf. 2 K. 6:17 for another incident in which God opens someone's eyes (also Num. 23:31; Luke 24:31); cf. also the name of a king of Israel, Pekahiah (2 K. 15:23),

and filled the skin with water, and quenched the lad's thirst.

20 *God was with the lad as he grew up. He lived in the wilderness and the young man became a bowman.*[17]

21 *He lived in the wilderness of Paran; and his mother obtained a wife for him from the land of Egypt.*

An accepted axiom of OT literary criticism is that Gen. 21:8-21 is E's account of the expulsion of Hagar and Ishmael, and parallels 16:1-16, which is J's account along with a few editorial notes from P. The arguments to support the existence of an indubitable doublet are well known. One is the consistent use of Yahweh in ch. 16 but the use of Elohim in ch. 21. Another is the different light in which Abraham appears. In ch. 16 he is compliant (16:6), but in ch. 21 he is disturbed by Sarah's ultimatum (21:11) and is compassionate toward Hagar's physical needs (21:14). Hagar also appears in a different light. In ch. 16 she is haughty and contemptuous. In ch. 21 she is totally passive. Again, commentators have noted that twice "Ishmael" is given an etymology connected with the verb "hear" (16:11; 21:17). The most obvious evidence for a doublet is thought to lie in the confusion over Ishmael's age in the two accounts. Ch. 21 agrees with ch. 16 that at his mother's explusion Ishmael was an infant, for she carries him on her shoulder (v. 14) and later leaves (lit., "casts") him under a bush to die while she watches from some distance (vv. 15-16). Yet, according to 16:16 (Abraham is 86 years old when Ishmael is born) and 21:5 (Abraham is 100 years old when Isaac is born), Ishmael must be in his early teens when the incident in 21:8ff. takes place. Does one carry a fourteen-year-old boy on her back and thrust that teenager under a desert shrub to die? Our commentary below will call into question the above conclusion drawn from a comparison of chs. 16 and 21.

8 The first unit (vv. 1-7) ended with (potential) conflict. Sarah feared that she would now become the butt of sarcasm and sneer. That emphasis on conflict will now continue in vv. 8-21, except that Sarah shifts from the object to the subject in terms of the conflict. Also, the first unit had evolved from a moment of euphoria, the birth of a child, into a moment of grave uncertainty. Similarly, here a festive mood (a feast accompanying the weaning of the child) turns sour. We are not sure at what age a child was weaned. The child might be as old as three (2 Macc. 7:27), or even older (1 Sam. 1:22, 24). Note the

---

"Yah(weh) has opened." For a different sort of eye-opening experience, but with the same verb *(pāqāḥ),* see Gen. 3:5.

17. For this rendering of *rōḇeh qaššāṯ* I follow R. Gordis, *The Book of Job* (New York: Jewish Theological Seminary of America, 1978), p. 286. The equation of *rōḇeh* with "young man" (as in Aramaic) is not without difficulty, however. See the notes in Speiser, *Genesis,* p. 156; Skinner, *Genesis,* p. 324.

difference in time covered by v. 8a and vv. 8bff. The first three or four years of Isaac's life are summed up with *the child grew.*[18] Vv. 8bff focus on two days, the day of conflict (vv. 8b-13) and the day of banishment (v. 14).

9 The gaiety of the feast is interrupted by Sarah when she observes Ishmael *playing.* The narrator's reference to Ishmael as *the son of Hagar*[19] is not much better than Sarah's "son of this slave woman" (v. 10). Neither will call Ishmael by his name. But at least the narrator uses the mother's name. Sarah can refer to her only by the subservient position she holds.

playing. It has long been a source of curiosity as to what Ishmael was actually doing. It was serious enough to enrage Sarah, as her words in the next verse reveal. As already noted in the translation, the LXX and Vulg. added "with her son Isaac" after "playing." A number of modern translations (e.g., RSV, JB) accept this addition into the text. Even if we accept the addition, the question arises whether Ishmael was playing innocently with Isaac, or whether he was abusing him. If it is the first, then Sarah's anger is prompted only by the impropriety of her child associating with a child from a lower social class (see von Rad). In the NT Paul goes the second route with his suggestion (Gal. 4:29) that Ishmael was "persecuting" *(edíōken)* Isaac. Such abuse could have been verbal or physical/sexual.[20]

An examination of the verb used here (the Piel participle of *ṣāḥaq*) may indicate that the ancient versions unnecessarily added the prepositional phrase. The Qal of *ṣāḥaq* appears only in Genesis, and always in connection with Isaac (17:17; 18:12, 13, 15 [2 times]; 21:6). The Piel of this verb is found in 19:14; 21:9; 26:8; 39:14, 17; Exod. 32:6; Judg. 16:25. To capture the stronger sense conveyed by the Piel we translated the root as "clowning" in Gen. 19:14. In 26:8 it refers to Isaac "playing" with his wife Rebekah *(ṣāḥaq* followed by the preposition *'ēṯ).* Does this connote sexual activity (RSV "fondling"), as I am inclined to believe, or something as innocent as

18. For other instances of *gāḏal* to describe the growing up of a child, see references in BDB, p. 152a. By itself, *gāḏal* might refer to more than just the first two or three years of life. For example, when Judah's youngest son has "grown" (Gen. 38:11, 14), he is old enough to marry the sister of his deceased brother. Note also that the reference to Moses having grown up (Exod. 2:11) is made more explicit by Stephen's use of "when he was forty years old" (Acts 7:23).

19. The LXX may also betray an anti-Hagar bias at this point. Back in v. 3 the LXX rendered the active verb *yālᵉḏâ,* when Sarah was the subject, as *éteken.* But in this verse, when Hagar is the subject of *yālᵉḏâ,* the LXX employs *egéneto* as it did earlier in v. 5 for the passive *bᵉhiwwālēḏ.* See P. Walters and D. W. Gooding, *The Text of the Septuagint* (Cambridge: Cambridge University, 1973), p. 116.

20. On Paul's use of *edíōken* in Gal. 4:29 see H. Ridderbos, *The Epistle of Paul to the Churches of Galatia,* tr. H. Zylstra, NICNT (Grand Rapids: Eerdmans, 1953), p. 181; H. D. Betz, *Galatians,* Hermeneia (Philadelphia: Fortress, 1979), pp. 249-50; F. F. Bruce, *The Epistle to the Galatians,* NIGTC (Grand Rapids: Eerdmans, 1982), pp. 223-24.

"horsing around"? In 39:14, 17 the verb is followed by the preposition *b* and is used by Potiphar's wife. She says that her husband brought a Hebrew to their house *lᵉṣaḥeq bānû,* "to insult us" (RSV), "to make love to us" (Speiser), "to make sport of us" (NAB). But one could argue that Potiphar's wife is claiming: "Look! He brought us a Hebrew fellow to sport in our presence; (instead) he tried to bed me but I screamed my head off."[21] If we apply the simple meaning "playing, sporting" to 21:9, it may mean that Sarah spotted Ishmael performing athletic feats, something for which Ishmael had quite a reputation (16:12; 21:20). Such activities would be considered unacceptable by Sarah, performed as they were at the feast celebrating Isaac's weaning. Is Ishmael, in Sarah's understanding, trying to draw attention away from Isaac?

One can understand "playing" in other ways, without the additions of LXX and Vulg. For instance, Jub. 17:4 states that "Sarah saw Ishmael playing and dancing, and Abraham rejoicing with great joy, and she became jealous of Ishmael." Thus, Sarah was riled by Ishmael's enjoying himself and playing happily on an occasion when the spotlight should be exclusively on her son. "Playing" could also have a sexual sense: to play with oneself, to masturbate.[22] It has long been noted that *mᵉṣaḥēq* is a Piel participle of the verb *ṣāḥaq,* from which the name "Isaac" is formed. Thus, Sarah observes Ishmael playing/sporting and "Isaac-ing." Perhaps she sees Ishmael doing something to make himself like Isaac, setting his sights on a familial position equal to that of Isaac.[23]

10 So perturbed is Sarah that she orders Abraham to *drive out* (Heb. *gāraš*) Hagar and Ishmael. We have already met this verb, for it was used back in 3:24 and 4:14 to describe the banishment of Adam and of Cain. Because the verb can carry the idea of dismissal from a position of authority (see 1 K. 2:27), it also functions as a term in the OT for divorce.[24] This is hardly grounds, however, for interpreting Sarah's word to Abraham that he

21. See J. M. Sasson, "The Worship of the Golden Calf," in *Orient and Occident,* Fest. C. H. Gordon, ed. H. A. Hoffner, AOAT 22 (Kevelaer: Butzon und Bercker; Neukirchen-Vluyn: Neukirchener, 1973), p. 155. S. McEvenue ("A Comparison of Narrative Styles in the Hagar Stories," *Semeia* 3 [1975] 74) prefers the MT as the *lectio difficilior.* He claims that the addition deliberately destroys the subtlety intended by the text.

22. Trible mentions briefly this possibility in "Other Woman," p. 244 n. 46.

23. See Jo Ann Hackett, "Rehabilitating Hagar: Fragments of an Epic Pattern," in *Gender and Difference in Ancient Israel,* ed. Peggy L. Day (Minneapolis: Fortress, 1989), pp. 20-21.

24. See Lev. 21:7, 14; 22:13; Num. 30:10 (Eng. 9); Ezek. 44:22, all in the form of the Qal passive fem. participle, *gᵉrûšâ,* and describing the prohibition of a priest's marrying a divorcée (Lev. 21:7, 14; Ezek. 44:22), allowable food for a priest's daughter who is a divorcée (Lev. 22:13), or a divorcée's vow (Num. 30:10 [Eng. 9]).

divorce Hagar.[25] A more helpful approach is to recall that this verb *gāraš* is used several times in Exodus (6:1; 10:11; 11:1; 12:39) to describe Pharaoh's expulsion of the Hebrews from Egypt. The roles are reversed in Genesis 21 and Exodus. First a Hebrew would expel an Egyptian from her land. Then an Egyptian monarch would expel Hebrews from his land.

Sarah refers to Hagar as a *slave woman ('āmâ)* and to Ishmael as a *son of this slave woman (ben-'āmâ).* In the earlier episode Sarah — as well as the narrator and Abraham — referred to Hagar as a "maid" (*šip̱ḥâ* in 16:1, 2, 3, etc.). The shift from *šip̱ḥâ* to *'āmâ* indicates that Hagar's social position has advanced from that of ch. 16. No longer merely a servant girl, she is now, in her own eyes, for all practical purposes a second wife.[26] But for Sarah, Hagar is only a lowly slave.

Sarah's real concern now becomes clear. She is disturbed not by Ishmael's behavior (v. 9), but by the possibility that this *ben-'āmâ* is in a position, legally, to share the inheritance with Isaac. This is an altogether different explanation for the source of conflict than in ch. 16. There the controversy emerged because of Sarai's infertility and Hagar's fertility. Here the issue is inheritance.

Cuneiform law indicates that the son of a slave woman had a legal claim on his father's property.[27] If that custom forms the backdrop to this story, then Sarah is asking Abraham to commit an illegal act. This may also explain why Sarah uses the verb *gāraš,* which, as we noted, can be a term in the OT for divorce. Ishmael is not just a slave girl's boy, but the son of Abraham's second wife. Sarah is pushing for Ishmael's disinheritance, however contrary it may be to legal principles.

11 Abraham is visibly upset by his wife's ultimatum, for it involves breaking an emotional tie with his son, as well as the sabotaging of legal procedures. As the household head, he is the one who must give the order of banishment to Hagar. Sarah can request it and demand it, but she cannot issue it. The verse speaks eloquently of the affection of Abraham for Ishmael, but nowhere does the narrative speak of Abraham's affection for his wife.

25. That *gāraš* occurs a few times in the OT for divorce does not mean it is therefore a technical term for divorce. P. K. McCarter, Jr. (*II Samuel,* AB [Garden City, NY: Doubleday, 1984], p. 324), argued for *šillaḥ* as a technical term for the dismissal of a divorced wife, but as D. Pardee comments (*JNES* 49 [1990] 364) in a review: "The fact that a truly technical term [viz., for divorce in the OT] is missing . . . is not a basis for taking the expression of a concept by a general term to be a technical expression."

26. It is unlikely that *'āmâ* and *šip̱ḥâ* are synonyms. Either *'āmâ* ranks socially higher than *šip̱ḥâ* (E. Neufeld, *Ancient Hebrew Marriage Laws* [London: Longmans, Green, 1944], pp. 121-24; Fensham, *VT* 19 [1969] 318), or, as I think, *'āmâ* carries a derogatory nuance not present in *šip̱ḥâ* (A. Jepsen, "Ama^{h} und Schiphcha^{h}," *VT* 8 [1958] 293-97; Trible, "Other Woman," p. 240 n. 11).

27. See the Code of Hammurapi, §§ 170-71; *ANET,* p. 173.

12 God tells Abraham not to fret and to do whatever Sarah tells him. This second command sounds like Mary's counsel to the servants at the wedding: "Do whatever he tells you" (John 2:5). A (God/Mary) tells B (Abraham/the servants) to follow C's (Sarah's/Jesus') instructions, in spite of a reservation by both Abraham (Gen. 21:11) and Jesus (John 2:4-5).

In one point Sarah is correct, but for the wrong reason: Ishmael will not share the inheritance with Isaac, but that is not because of Sarah's pettiness, or jealousy, or skulduggery. It is because God has decreed that Abraham's line of promise will be continued through Isaac. Here is an instance of God using the wrath of a human being to accomplish his purposes. A family squabble becomes the occasion by which the sovereign purposes and programs of God are forwarded.

It is interesting that every time God refers to Ishmael he calls him a *lad* (*naʿar;* cf. vv. 12, 17 [2 times], 18, 20). But when Abraham or Hagar refer to him they call him a *child* (*yeleḏ;* cf. vv. 14, 15, 16). The latter word denotes a biological relationship. The use of the former word by God minimizes Ishmael's relationship to Abraham as son. Thus Ishmael is a *yeleḏ* to Abraham and Hagar, but he is a *naʿar* to God. It is almost as if God is siding with Sarah in calling Ishmael Abraham's *naʿar* rather than his *yeleḏ*. Thus von Rad says, "One could call vs. 12f. the 'tense moment' in the structure of the narrative, for the reader has not expected that God would be on Sarah's side, but rather on Abraham's."[28]

13 The banished child himself is to become a *nation.* Many ancient versions (LXX, Vulg., SP) insert "great" after "nation," making the promise even more impressive. Ishmael loses property but gains a nation. It may well be that such a promise to Ishmael, in the light of the legal ramifications discussed in v. 12, is to be viewed as compensation.[29] It may also be an instance of divine grace. As Cain suffered both banishment from the divine and protection by the divine, so Ishmael is both loser and winner, cut off from what should be his but promised a significant lineage. Doubtless Hagar's banishment to the desert and the hopeless situation in which she found herself would have been more bearable if Abraham had only let her in on this good news. The text gives no indication whether she overheard God's declaration to Abraham vis-à-vis Ishmael, or whether Abraham subsequently passed the news on to Hagar. Certainly God nowhere speaks to Hagar directly in this episode, as he did in ch. 16 (see esp. the promise of many descendants in

28. Von Rad, *Genesis,* p. 233. Note also that God uses the same term for Hagar (*'āmâ)* as Sarah did (v. 10). A similar unexpected disclosure appeared in ch. 20 as well. The readers' sympathies had been with Abimelech until the last two verses suggest that Abimelech is just another wife-taking pharaoh with whom God must deal.

29. See Fensham, *VT* 19 (1969) 318.

v. 10), until after her expulsion. To Abraham God said that he would make a nation *(gôy)* from Ishmael. Later God would say to Hagar that he would make a great nation *(gôy gāḏôl)* from Ishmael (v. 18). The promise she receives about her son's lineage is greater than the one Abraham receives.[30]

14 Abraham is an early riser. He rises early in the morning to send off Hagar and Ishmael, and later to start an apparently final voyage with Isaac (cf. 22:3).[31] Abraham's early rise is not dictated by eagerness to get Hagar out of the house. Either he wants to do this farewell, however reluctantly, as privately as possible, or else he wants Hagar to be able to spend at least the first part of her first day of exile in the cool of the morning.

Concerned that starvation or thirst might strike, Abraham provides Hagar with bread and some water. While a thoughtful gesture on Abraham's part, it provides little solace for mother and son as they face a life-threatening situation.

along with the child. Abraham transfers Ishmael from his guardianship to Hagar's. Only if one follows the LXX does he encounter the idea that Abraham placed Ishmael (a teenage adolescent!) on his mother's back. The Hebrew reads literally: "he took bread and a skin of water and gave (them) to Hagar, putting (them) upon her shoulder, and the child." When we recall that *nāṯan* means not only "put, place" but also "commit, entrust," then the meaning is plain. Both "bread/water" and "child" serve as direct objects of *nāṯan.* Abraham places the physical provisions on her back and entrusts their son and his welfare to Hagar's care.[32] Sarah had insisted that Hagar be banished *(gāraš),* but Abraham is not that harsh. He does not expel Hagar; *he sent her off* (*šālaḥ,* in the Piel). At times *gāraš* is paired with *šālaḥ* (Piel), suggesting an overlap in meaning between the two. Yahweh "sent forth" (*šālaḥ,* Piel) sinning man from the garden (3:23), and "drove him out" (*gāraš,* 3:24). Yahweh informs Moses that Pharaoh will send out (*šālaḥ,* Piel) Israel from Egypt, and that he will drive *(gāraš)* them out of his land (Exod. 6:1). The same two verbs occur in the same sequence when Pharaoh dismisses and expels Israel from his territory (Exod. 11:1). There is, however, a basic difference between *gāraš* and *šālaḥ* (Piel). "Whereas

30. I am aware that much ancient textual evidence (SP, LXX, Pesh., Vulg.) supports the inclusion of *gāḏôl* in v. 13 as well, but this may be a case of artificial streamlining.

31. Irvin (*Mytharion,* p. 25) says the phrase *wayyaškēm babbōqer* "is usually used to describe beginning an action. . . . Its character as a formula becomes clear from its use in cases where sleeping is not mentioned and no night has passed, for example Ex 24:4; Num 14:40; Jgs 21:4; 1 Sm 17:20; 2 Kgs 3:22."

32. See H. C. White, "The Initiation Legend of Ishmael," *ZAW* 87 (1975) 302.

33. D. Daube, *The Exodus Pattern in the Bible* (London: Faber and Faber, 1963), p. 30. For instances where the Piel of *šālaḥ* means to send away without the possibility of return, see Exod. 5:2 (Israel); Lev. 14:7, 53 (birds); Lev. 16:10 (the goat for Azazel); Deut. 22:19, 29 (divorcing one's wife); 2 Sam. 13:17 (Tamar).

the latter often refers to a friendly release, the former is invariably a hostile act."[33] Similarly, the English verbs "send off, dismiss" do not carry the harsh nuances of "expel, drive out."

Hagar's hopeless and precarious condition in the wilderness is underscored by the use of the verb *tā'â,* "wander (hopelessly)."[34] Abraham used this verb to describe his own wanderings in 20:13. The root describes straying animals (Exod. 23:4; Job 38:41; Ps. 119:176; Isa. 53:6; Jer. 50:6), persons who are lost (Gen. 37:15; Ps. 107:4; Isa. 47:15), and drunkenness (Job 12:25; Isa. 19:14; 21:4; 28:7).

15 Unable to go any further, and the water supply exhausted, Hagar leaves Ishmael under the shade of one of the desert shrubs in order to let him die as peacefully and painlessly as possible, or at least to shade him from the harsh sun. I noted above that some mistakenly translate the verb here *(šālaḵ)* as "throw, cast," further contributing to the misconception that Ishmael was indeed an infant at the time. When used with a human being as its object the verb almost always refers to lowering a dead body into its grave (2 Sam. 18:17; 2 K. 13:21; Jer. 41:9), or the lowering of a person into what will presumably be his grave (Gen. 37:24; Jer. 38:6). Obviously, carcasses are not hurled into their grave. They are deposited there with dignity.[35]

The mother's treatment of her son parallels Abraham's treatment of Hagar. Even the verbs sound alike *(šālaḥ, šālaḵ).* Abraham sent *(šālaḥ)* Hagar away, and Hagar placed *(šālaḵ)* Ishmael under a bush on the ground. The care Abraham showed in giving provisions to her is matched by her watchful observance of her son.

16 This verse is characterized by little phrases such as *by herself, opposite him, away.* The mother is powerless to stop the march of death against her son. She can watch, but that is all she can do. She is as incapable of arresting death as was Abraham in attempting to thwart Sarah.

If this mother and child have any hope at all it is God. In a sense Hagar utters one of the first prayers in the Bible: *Do not let me see the child die.* We have seen others speak to God with rationalizations (Adam), protestations (Cain), and interrogations (Abraham). The Hebrew form that is used *('al-'er'eh)* is the cohortative, one use of which is to express a wish — more often a positive rather than a negative one. Where it is negative the speaker is in some kind of distress.[36]

34. Trible ("Other Woman," p. 234) says of this verb: "In reference to physical movement, the verb *wander (t'h)* connotes uncertainty, lack or loss of direction, and even destitution." Irvin (*Mytharion,* p. 24) renders thus: "she left and got lost."

35. White, "Initiation Legend," p. 287; see also M. Cogan, "A Technical Term for Exposure," *JNES* 27 (1968) 133-35.

36. GKC, § 108c, cites 10 instances of *'al* plus cohortative: Gen. 21:16; 2 Sam. 24:14; Jer. 17:18; 18:18; Ps. 25:2; 31:2, 18 (Eng. 1, 17); 69:15 (Eng. 14); 71:1; Jon. 1:14.

17 For a second time in this incident a theophany occurs. God spoke to Abraham (v. 12), and now he speaks to Hagar. For some reason, in this chapter no one ever refers to Ishmael by name. Neither Sarah, nor Abraham, nor God, nor the narrator uses it. He is either the son of a slave girl, or a lad, or a child. So God too heard *the lad's* voice. This is the only time in Genesis, apart from 22:11 and 15, where the messenger of God/Yahweh calls out to one *from heaven.* (For Yahweh talking directly from heaven, cf. Exod. 20:22.) It is interesting that this phrase is confined to two consecutive chapters. God hears, but the messenger of God speaks, and from heaven at that. *šāmayim* is God's abode, which he shares with his messenger. Hagar does not have as intimate a revelation from God as does Abraham. God speaks with Abraham, but the messenger from heaven speaks with Hagar. The message "from heaven" in ch. 21 contrasts with Hagar's direct encounter with the messenger in ch. 16.

The angel's question *What ails you (mah-llāḵ)* is surely rhetorical, for the angel does not even give Hagar an opportunity to respond. In fact, throughout this whole narrative Hagar speaks only four words (in Hebrew): "do-not let-me-look on-the-death-of the-child." God's speeches to Abraham (vv. 12-13) and to Hagar (vv. 17-18) are both divine monologues. The angel's question is now followed by words of reassurance: *Do not be afraid, for God has heard the lad's voice.* In both of his speeches God has reassured the person caught in difficult circumstances that he is active and is in control of the situation. Abraham need not fear sending Hagar into the desert, and Hagar need not fear her circumstances there. When Abraham sent the exiled party of two off into the desert, God was with them. The use of the verb *šāmaʿ* in this verse by both the narrator and the heavenly messenger, with *ʾĕlōhîm* as the subject both times, points to the etymology of Ishmael's name: *ʾĕlōhîm* has heard *(šāmaʿ)* the voice of Ishmael *(yišmāʿēl).*

18 Only now is Hagar informed that her son has a future beyond the wilderness: *for a great nation I will make of him.* The revelation about God's plan for Ishmael is made known only after their ordeal. There is no indication that Abraham, though himself aware of this promise, had shared it with Hagar. One is reminded of Moses' request for a sign from God to confirm his call *before* he went to Pharaoh. God gives him a sign: "*after* you have brought out the people . . . you shall serve God on this mountain" (Exod. 3:12). First the ordeal, then the revelation.

19 God is concerned not only about Ishmael's future (v. 18b) but also about his present. He needs something to drink, for their supply of water is exhausted (v. 15). To that end God opens their eyes to a nearby well. In an equally harrowing situation (a cave), God supplied Elijah with "a cake baked on hot stones and a jar of water" (1 K. 19:6). Thus Ishmael receives two blessings from God — a destiny and a drink.

Hagar apparently was not able to spot the well of water until God opened her eyes. It was there all the time, but Hagar missed it. What God brings to her attention becomes the means of her son's physical survival. (The text does not refer to Hagar quenching her own thirst. The mother's concern is only for her child.) Ishmael's life-threatening ordeal in the wilderness (21:8-21) has a number of parallels with Isaac's life-threatening ordeal at Moriah (22:1-19). R. Alter has called such a fixed and parallel sequence of narrative motifs a "type-scene."[37] V. 17 supplies one of these motifs vis-à-vis 22:1-19. With the life of a child in danger God opens Hagar's eyes *(ʿêneyhā)* and she sees *(wattēre')* a well that prevents Ishmael from dying of thirst. Similarly, with the life of another child hanging in the balance, Abraham lifts up his eyes *(ʿênāyw)* and sees *(wayyar')* a ram that, as Isaac's surrogate, prevents Isaac from dying of a knife wound.

20 This unit began with a reference to Isaac's growth (*wayyiḡdal,* v. 8). Now it is Ishmael who grows up *(wayyiḡdal).* This double use of *gāḏal,* first in reference to Isaac and then to Ishmael, ties together the beginning and end of vv. 8-21. The emphases of v. 8 would lead one to think that what will follow will be data about Isaac. He is weaned, named, and honored with a feast. But from that point on it is Ishmael (though not named) who is prominent. Thus the unit divides as follows: v. 8 — Isaac; vv. 9-21 — Ishmael.

The previous distant language ("an angel of God called out to Hagar from heaven") becomes the more intimate *God was with the lad.* "From heaven" gives way to *with,* and a celestial theophany is replaced by the imminent, divine presence.

The place of Ishmael's exile became his domicile — *the wilderness.* In such an environment one could survive only by developing skills with a bow, and thus Ishmael adapted to that environment and became a *bowman (qaššāt).* At one point in his life it appeared that the closest Ishmael would ever come to bowmanship is when his mother sat about a bowshot *(qešeṯ)* from his dehydrated body (v. 16).

21 The wilderness in which Ishmael lived is identified as *Paran.* This is the main desert in the eastern Sinai peninsula. It stretches as far south as the Red Sea (Deut. 1:1) and possibly as far north as Kadesh or even Beer-sheba (Num. 13:3, 26). The narrative in Genesis suggests that Ishmael inhabited the more northerly sections of this wilderness.

That Hagar (now at last styled "mother" and not "the Egyptian" or "slave woman") *obtained a wife* for Ishmael is in line with Oriental custom in which the parents (or a parent) select a wife for their son (Gen. 24:3ff.;

37. R. Alter, *The Art of Biblical Narrative* (New York: Basic Books, 1981), pp. 181-82; Trible, "Other Woman," p. 245 n. 73.

34:4; Judg. 14:2). *from the land of Egypt.* Hagar turns to her own roots (see Gen. 21:9) to procure a bride for Ishmael. She is no less concerned to match her son with the proper person than is Abraham with Isaac (24:3): an Egyptian with an Egyptian and an Aramean with an Aramean. The text does not mention how Hagar procured Ishmael's wife or her name.

3. A CONFLICT OVER A WELL (21:22-34)

22 *Shortly thereafter Abimelech, together with Phicol,*[1] *the commander of his army, said to Abraham: "God is with you in everything you undertake.*

23 *Accordingly, swear to me by God here and now that*[2] *you will not deal falsely with me, or with my kith and kin,*[3] *but in accordance with the loyalty which I have extended to you, you shall extend (loyalty) to me and to the land in which you are staying."*

24 *And Abraham replied: "I give you my word."*

25 *Abraham, however, reproached*[4] *Abimelech about a well of water which Abimelech's servants had seized.*[5]

26 *Abimelech responded: "I do not know who has done this; moreover, you never informed me and until now I never heard about it."*

27 *Abraham then took sheep and cattle and gave them to Abimelech, and the two of them made a covenant.*

28 *Abraham also set apart seven ewe lambs from the flock by themselves.*

29 *Abimelech questioned Abraham: "What is the meaning of these seven ewe lambs which you have set by themselves?"*[6]

1. This name means "the mouth of all" or "mouthful," which M. Astour understands as a metaphorical designation of an open, bottomless abyss, i.e., the hostile water — chaos. See his *Hellenosemitica* (Leiden: Brill, 1965), pp. 125-27.

2. For *'im* after formulae of swearing see GKC, § 149c; also C. Van Leeuwen, "Die Partikel אִם," *OTS* 18 (1973) 36.

3. Lit., "with my offspring and my posterity," but "kith and kin" captures the alliteration of the Heb. *l*^{e}*nînî ûl*^{e}*neḵdî;* so also Speiser, *Genesis,* p. 159. For the same pair of words see Job 18:19; Isa. 14:22; and W. G. E. Watson, "Some Additional Word Pairs," in *Ascribe to the Lord: Biblical and Other Studies in Memory of Peter C. Craigie,* ed. L. Eslinger and G. Taylor, JSOTSup 67 (Sheffield: JSOT, 1988), p. 193.

4. It is not necessary to emend MT *w*^{e}*hôḵiaḥ* to *wayyôḵîaḥ* (SP) or *wayyôḵaḥ,* but *w*^{e}*hôḵēaḥ* is possible (not demanded, however). See J. Huesman, "The Infinitive Absolute and Waw + Perfect Problems," *Bib* 37 (1956) 413-14.

5. For the distinction between *gāzal* ("seized" here) as furtive stealing and *gānaḇ* as nonfurtive stealing, see J. Milgrom, *Cult and Conscience* (Leiden: Brill, 1976), p. 91.

6. For the 3rd fem. pl. pronominal suffix *-ānâ instead of -hen* see GKC, § 91f.

30 *He responded:*[7] *"The seven ewe lambs you will accept from me that they may be a witness that I dug this well."*

31 *Accordingly he named that site Beer-sheba when there the two of them swore to each other.*

32 *After they had made a covenant in Beer-sheba, Abimelech, along with Phicol, the commander of his army, arose and returned to Philistine country.*

33 *He planted a tamarisk in Beer-sheba and there he invoked the name of Yahweh, the eternal God.*

34 *Abraham stayed in Philistine country for many years.*

Two immediate observations emerge from a study of vv. 22-34. One concerns the unity of the section, which some scholars dispute on the basis of three apparent evidences of dual traditions: (a) twice it is said that Abraham and Abimelech "cut" a covenant (vv. 27, 32); (b) Abraham presented two different animal gifts to Abimelech: sheep and cattle (v. 27) and seven ewe lambs (v. 28); (c) at one point Beer-sheba is connected with the numeral "seven" (vv. 28-30), and at another with the noun "oath" (v. 31). Our translation of these verses has already shown that (a) and (b) are not evidences of a dual tradition. We will reserve comment on the etymology of Beer-sheba until later.

A second issue is the separation of this story about Abimelech and Abraham from the earlier one about these two (20:1-18). Does the "Shortly thereafter" (lit., "at that time") of v. 22 refer to the incident involving Hagar and Ishmael (21:8-21) or to the incident involving Abraham, Sarah, and Abimelech (20:1-18)? If it be the former, then the time lapse between 20:1-18 and 21:22-34, both of which highlight Abraham and Abimelech, would be three or four years. This period would allow time for Sarah's pregnancy (21:1-7) and the first few years of Isaac's life (21:8).

The placement of this incident after 21:8-21 presents an interesting thematic parallel. Both 21:8-21 and 21:22-34 describe a scene of conflict — conflict over a boy and over a well. Abraham is the loser in both instances. Ishmael is banished and Abraham's well is seized by another. In 21:8-21 Sarah is the one who expresses a grievance and Abraham is an innocent bystander and Ishmael's provider. But in 21:22-34 Abraham's role is switched and he becomes the one who expresses a grievance. Abimelech replaces Abraham in his role as the innocent bystander and provider. Both times Abraham gives

7. The verb "responded" is followed by the particle *kî* and is not reflected in my translation. We have here either an instance of a *kî recitativum* (i.e., a particle introducing direct speech after verbs of saying), or a *kî* that is explicative — "(they mean) that you will accept the seven ewe lambs from me." I am inclined to the former, but for the latter see A. Schoors, "The Particle *kî*," *OTS* 21 (1981) 258.

provisions or gifts to another: bread and water to Hagar and Ishmael; sheep, cattle, and ewe lambs to Abimelech. Referring to 21:22-34 as a buffer passage between 21:8-21 and 22:1-9, R. Alter says that "the tale of a dispute over a well in the desert reinforces this network of connections, for it involves obtaining a source of life in the wilderness (as explicitly happens in the Ishmael story) and it concludes with Abraham's making a covenant meant to guarantee peace and well-being for his progeny."[8]

22 Accompanied by his military commander Phicol,[9] Abimelech approaches Abraham and affirms the reality of the divine presence with the patriarch. His information is apparently based on what he observed and felt when Abraham prayed (20:17). It is standard in Genesis that a foreigner refers to God using the designation *Elohim,* as does Abimelech here (cf. 31:29; 41:38; also Exod. 8:19). This pattern does not continue, however, throughout the Pentateuch (as Exod. 5:2; 9:27, 28; 10:16-17 demonstrate).

Abimelech's statement also provides a parallel with the one made just a few verses earlier about Ishmael (v. 20). Both Abraham and Ishmael are vulnerable, for both are away from home — one in a wilderness, one in Philistine country — but God is with both.

23 In the light of the presence of Elohim in his life, Abraham's behavior should be predictable and above reproach. People with whom God dwells should not engage in false, devious practices or conduct. Nonetheless, Abimelech requests Abraham to bind himself by oath to a covenant relating to Abimelech's own person and that of his posterity primarily because he does not trust Abraham. The verb and preposition used here — *šāqar l^e* — do not mean "tell a lie" but rather "deal falsely, break a covenant," as can be seen in Ps. 44:18 (Eng. 17); Isa. 63:8.[10]

Abimelech's use of the root *šqr* and his invitation to Abraham to swear off any activity of this type are ironical. Abraham had just perpetrated on Abimelech a perfect instance of *šeqer* ("falsehood"), although the word was

8. Alter, *Art of Biblical Narrative,* p. 182.

9. It is not clear why Abimelech was joined by Phicol, the commander of the king's army, on this occasion. One of the Alalakh Tablets (54:16-18) describes a sheep sacrifice in connection with the sale of a city by Irkabtum to Ammitakum as follows: *GÚ SILÁ a-sa-ki IGI* PN *UGULA UKU.UŠ ta-bi-iḫ*: "the neck of a sacrificial lamb was cut in the presence of PN the general." See A. Draffkorn, "Was King Abba-AN of Yamḫad a Vizier for the King of Ḫattuša?" *JCS* 13 (1959) 95 n. 11; M. Weinfeld, "The Covenant of Grant in the Old Testament and in the Ancient Near East," *JAOS* 90 (1970) 197 n. 119; idem, *Deuteronomy and the Deuteronomic School* (Oxford: Clarendon, 1972), p. 102 n. 7.

10. Cf. also the Aramaic Sefire texts (I B 38; III 14, 19, 27, et passim [*KAI,* 222.B.38; 224.14, 19, 27]), in which *šqr b* is used when the treaty itself is the object of treachery, and *šqr l* when a person or god is the object of treachery. See J. A. Fitzmyer, *The Aramaic Inscriptions of Sefire,* BibOr 19 (Rome: Pontifical Biblical Institute, 1967), p. 107.

not used there, when he led the Philistine king to believe that his female companion was only his sister (20:1-17). Will their relationship in the future, asks Abimelech, be determined by *šeqer,* "falsehood," or by *ḥeseḏ,* "loyalty"?[11] I disagree with those commentators who see Abimelech speaking here from the perspective of the more superior party rather than from an inferior position.[12] On the one hand, the only evidence to support that position is the presence of Phicol at Abimelech's side and Abraham's giving of gifts. On the other hand, what Abimelech says to Abraham in v. 23 hardly seems to be argued from a position of strength. It appears that Abimelech is asking for a favor rather than imposing terms or dictating agenda.[13] In an earlier relationship with Abraham, Abimelech was clearly the superior party who treated Abraham fairly nevertheless (20:15). Now the roles are reversed. Abimelech still has the authority of the crown and some military muscle, but he also knows that a powerful God had worked through Abraham's intercession to bring healing to his people, and the impact of that intercession on Abimelech surfaces only in 21:22.

Hence, Abimelech's appeal to Abraham for *ḥeseḏ* is based solely on the *ḥeseḏ* he had extended earlier to Abraham. He argues not from his position but from precedent. By *ḥeseḏ* Abimelech means "behavior which is appropriate to a covenant relationship."[14] That God is with Abraham does not mean, however, that Abraham has a two-to-one majority over Abimelech. It means that others' expectations of him increase.

24 Apart from the introduction (v. 22a), Abimelech's covenant request took twenty-one words in Hebrew (v. 23). Abraham's response takes

11. On the use of *ḥeseḏ* in this verse cf. K. Sakenfeld, *Meaning of Ḥesed in the Hebrew Bible,* HSM 17 (Missoula, MT: Scholars, 1978), pp. 70-75; H. J. Stoebe, "Die Bedeutung des Wortes *ḥäsäd* im Alten Testament," *VT* 2 (1952) 247, 249; H. F. Peacock, "Translating 'mercy,' 'steadfast love,' in the book of Genesis," *BT* 31 (1980) 204; Andersen, "Yahweh, the Kind and Sensitive God," in *God Who Is Rich in Mercy,* pp. 53-54; S. Romerowski, "Que signifie le mot *ḥesed,*" *VT* 40 (1990) 91.

12. See Speiser, *Genesis,* p. 160: "Abimelech brings with him his army chieftain, and perhaps also his political councilor . . . to strengthen his position as the stronger party"; Vawter, *On Genesis,* p. 252: "Abimelech is the superior of the two parties to the pact"; von Rad, *Genesis,* p. 236: "Abimelech pushes Abraham to an agreement . . . the concession that Abimelech makes does not seem large."

13. D. J. McCarthy, "Three Covenants in Genesis," *CBQ* 26 (1964) 182-84, repr. with same pagination in *Institution and Narrative: Collected Essays,* AnBib 108 (Rome: Biblical Institute, 1985); Sakenfeld, *Meaning of Ḥesed,* pp. 70-75; Westermann, *Genesis,* 2:348: "The effect is grotesque . . . the Canaanite king with his commander-in-chief confronts a nomad shepherd who is utterly powerless, and more, a mere tolerated alien."

14. Sakenfeld, *Meaning of Ḥesed,* p. 72. For other incidents in the OT where present/future behavior is urged on the basis of past *ḥeseḏ* see Josh. 2:12-14; 1 Sam. 15:6; 2 Sam. 10:1-2a (= 1 Chr. 19:1-2); 1 K. 2:7.

two words: *'ānōkî 'iššāḇēa', I give you my word* (lit., "I, I swear"). Perhaps the use of the independent pronoun before the verb reinforces the certainty of Abraham's pledge. Here the emphasis is solely on Abraham's act of swearing, but a later verse (v. 31) observes that it was a mutual swearing. Also, later verses in this unit have the verb "swear" (*šb',* v. 31) as a parallel to "cut a covenant" (*kāraṯ bᵉrîṯ,* vv. 27, 32). Here one swears an oath but cuts a covenant, as in Josh. 9:15.[15] Although considered a part of the covenant ceremony, the swearing is separated from the process of "cutting a covenant."

The expression "swear a covenant" is relatively uncommon (see Deut. 4:31; 8:18), although the expressions "cut/enter into a covenant" and "swear" are often used in proximity to each other. For *šāḇa'* and *kāraṯ bᵉrîṯ* see, in addition to Gen. 21, Gen. 26:28, 31; Josh. 9:15-27; 2 K. 11:4; Ezra 10:35; Ps. 89:4, 29-36 (Eng. 28-35); 105:9. For *šāḇa'* and *bô' bᵉrîṯ* see 2 Chr. 15:11-15; Ezek. 16:8. Those instances in which *šāḇa'* is followed by the noun "oath" *('ālâ)* or by "vow" *(neḏer)* help us to understand the place of swearing in covenant rituals.[16] This oath taken by the covenant partners would presumably be some kind of a confirmatory act in the form of a self-imprecation for covenant violation — "may such-and-such happen to me if I violate my obligation." Such oaths would carry much weight in a society without items like court records and verbatim testimony.

25 Abimelech offers a covenant and Abraham offers a complaint. A well belonging to Abraham was seized by Abimelech's servants. His wife had been "taken" (20:3-4), and now his well is stolen. Abraham has already sworn to show *ḥeseḏ* to Abimelech. Accordingly, he cannot counter a criminal act by taking the law into his own hands. Here is a test case for Abraham. His only genuine option is to appeal to due process, that is, to state his grievance to Abimelech.

Interestingly, the conclusion to this issue is not mentioned. Does Abraham get his well back? Is the crisis resolved to everybody's satisfaction? We never find out. The narrative never presses on to announce a legal resolution, but only to lay the groundwork for that resolution, that is, a mutually binding covenant.

26 For some reason Abraham had kept quiet about this act of theft carried out by Abimelech's servants. Abimelech's *you never informed me* could have easily been said back in ch. 20 — "why did you not tell me that

15. Cf. the Akkadian treaty of Abba-AN from Alalakh in the 18-17th century B.C.: "Abba-AN swore an oath and cut the throat of a sheep" (see McCarthy, *CBQ* 26 [1964] 181, for the reference).

16. For *šaḇa' 'ālâ* or a variant thereof cf. Gen. 26:31; Num. 5:21; 1 Sam. 14:24, 27; Neh. 10:30; Dan. 9:11; for *šāḇa' neḏer* as a parallel to *šāḇa' šᵉḇû'â* see Num. 30:3 and Ps. 132:2.

she was your wife?" (as in 12:18). In both cases Abraham has withheld information from Abimelech, either by subterfuge (ch. 20) or by silence (ch. 21). It may be that the well was seized before Abraham first talked with Abimelech about Sarah, and hence was his reason to convince Abimelech that Sarah was his sister. "They took my well, will they take me too?" Convinced that he is surrounded by brigands, Abraham must be wary.

27-28 It is Abimelech who initiated the action, inviting Abraham to join him in a nonaggression pact (v. 23), but it is Abraham who presents a gift to Abimelech, gifts of sheep, cattle, and seven ewe lambs. The Bible has instances in which an individual in a perilous position attempts to save himself from one stronger than he with what amounts to a bribe. Compare Jacob's "gift" to Esau (32:20-21), and Ahaz's offer of cash to Tiglath-pileser for protection against Rezin and Pekah (2 K. 16:5-9). Scripture also has illustrations of a weaker power offering a gift to the stronger power in the hopes of cementing their pact as much as possible. Compare Asa's gift of silver and gold to Ben-hadad so that both nations may unite in a league against Baasha, king of Israel (1 K. 15:16ff.), and Hezekiah's gift of silver and gold to Sennacherib (2 K. 18:13ff.). In at least one instance a more powerful king (Merodach-baladan) sent a gift to a king who was much less powerful (Hezekiah; 2 K. 20:12), an action on Hezekiah's part that Isaiah did not accept with glee (2 K. 20:14ff.).

In the instances cited from Kings, the giving of gifts is a means of opening negotiations in instances of international diplomacy, hardly the point in Gen. 21. Rather than seeing Abraham's gifts as either bribes or diplomatic ways of commencing negotiations with a potentially hostile, nonsympathetic individual, one should understand them to be a gift to cement a pact of friendship. Abraham has lost a well to Abimelech's servants, but this seizure must not be allowed to put distance between Abraham and Abimelech. Abraham has no interest in terminating his friendship with Abimelech over the well.[17] One might also note the covenant between David and Jonathan; Jonathan gave his personal garments and weapons to David to symbolize the finalizing of the covenant (1 Sam. 18:3-5).[18] The explicit purpose of Abraham's gift to Abimelech, at least the seven ewe lambs, will be made clear in v. 30.

29 Abraham's actions are not self-explanatory, and hence Abimelech presses Abraham for clarification. As a matter of fact, as far as Abimelech is concerned, hardly anything Abraham does or says is self-explanatory! For whatever reason, Abimelech is not eager to accept Abraham's benevolence. The king's curiosity is naturally aroused by the fact that Abraham isolated the

17. McCarthy, *CBQ* 26 (1964) 182-83.

18. On the significance of the transfer of these items from Jonathan to David cf. P. K. McCarter, Jr., *I Samuel,* AB (Garden City, NY: Doubleday, 1980), p. 305.

seven ewe lambs from the rest of the animals and set them off by themselves (*l^{e}ḇadd^{e}hen,* in v. 28), lit., "in their separation"; *l^{e}ḇaddānâ* here in v. 29). His strange action provokes Abimelech's question, just as his earlier puzzling action provoked a question from Abimelech (20:9-10).

30 Abraham clarifies his motives and actions in the gift of the ewe lambs. In accepting them, Abimelech becomes involved in a legal transaction which binds him as a witness to the fact that Abraham is the legitimate owner of this particular well. The lambs are to be *a witness* (or "proof," *ʿēḏâ*).[19]

No sacrificial activity is involved, nor is there any covenant meal. The parties swear to the pact simply in words. In accepting the lambs Abimelech releases rights over the well and concedes ownership to the patriarch. In other words, Abimelech is challenged to accept the reliability of Abraham's word, *I dug this well,* and to side with him in any future altercation. Of course, in an incident not too far removed from this one, Abraham's earlier word to Abimelech had been anything but reliable. If Abraham can cheat on the truth about Sarah, can he do the same with the truth about a well?

31 Abimelech chooses to believe Abraham, for both of them swore an oath.[20] To the site Abraham gives the name *Beer-sheba,* "well of seven," a reference to the seven lambs. Now, the Hebrew words for "seven" and "oath" are the same *(šāḇaʿ).* For that reason many scholars see in this unit a twofold explanation of *Beer-sheba.* In part of the narrative it means "well of seven," but in other sections it means "well of oath." For example, on the basis of this duality, H. Gunkel assigned vv. 22-24, 27, and 31 ("oath") to E, and vv. 25-26, 28-30, and 32-33 ("seven") to J^b.[21] Some later scholars have emended Gunkel. For example, J. Van Seters is content to label vv. 25-26, 28-31a as pre-Yahwistic, and to connect vv. 22-24, 27, 31b-34 with the Yahwist.[22] Y. Zakovitch sees the part connecting the site with "oath" as the authentic one (vv. 22-24, 31ff.), and dismisses the part about "seven" (vv. 25-30) as an addition for the sake of precise derivation.[23] B. Long also takes

19. For another instance of *ʿēḏ/ʿēḏâ* followed by *l^e* plus object see Isa. 19:20. On the use of "witness(es)" in covenant ritual see Z. W. Falk, "Forms of testimony," *VT* 11 (1961) 88-91; M. Delcor, "Les attaches littéraires, l'origine et la signification de l'expression biblique 'Prendre à temoin le ciel et la terre,' " *VT* 16 (1966) 8-25; G. M. Tucker, "Witnesses and 'Dates' in Israelite Contracts," *CBQ* 28 (1966) 42-45; McCarthy, *CBQ* 26 (1964) 185-88. *ʿēḏâ* occurs again only in Gen. 31:52 and Josh. 24:27 (2 times). The masc. *ʿēḏ* is much more frequent.

20. For the evidence in the Near East that a covenant could also be called an oath, see G. M. Tucker, "Covenant forms and contract forms," *VT* 15 (1965) 488-90.

21. Gunkel, *Genesis,* pp. 233-36.

22. Van Seters, *Abraham in History and Tradition,* pp. 184-91.

23. Y. Zakovitch, "A Study of Precise and Partial Derivations in Biblical Etymology," *JSOT* 15 (1980) 34-35.

vv. 25-26, 28-30 (the B Block) as a secondary elaboration of vv. 22-24, 27, 31 (the A tradition).[24]

All these attempts to see dual explanations of the etymology of *Beer-sheba* arise through a translation of the Hebrew particle *kî* as "because" in v. 31. I suggest that *kî* introduces here an independent temporal clause, not a result clause.[25] Thus v. 31b does not tell why Abraham gave this place the name Beer-sheba, but when Abraham gave it this name. If *kî* is rendered "because," then v. 31b clearly conflicts with v. 31a. The *Accordingly (ʿal-kēn)* of v. 31 provides the connective between the "seven ewe lambs" of v. 30 and "Beer-sheba" of v. 31a.

Genesis frequently connects the patriarchs with activities at Beer-sheba. The work of archeologists in the Negeb, however, has cast doubt over the historical accuracy of such references. In particular, Y. Aharoni claims that his excavations at Tel Beersheba show conclusively that none of the events attributed to the patriarchs at Beer-sheba could have taken place prior to the 13th or 12th century B.C.[26] His major supporting evidence for that position was the discovery of a well on the mound at Tel Beersheba, the well that Abraham claims to have dug, which can be dated only in the era of Joshua at the very earliest. But Aharoni offers no firm evidence that the well his team discovered at Tel Beersheba has to be the same one v. 30 mentions. Indeed, a number of wells less than two miles west of Tell Beersheba have been discovered. Nor can one be certain, as is often the case, that the modern name represents the same site as the biblical name. Modern Tel Beersheba might not be the same as patriarchal Beer-sheba.[27]

32-34 The covenant now ratified and accepted by both parties, Abimelech and Phicol return home. They leave, but Abraham remains.

Abraham's first stopping place in Canaan (Shechem) was by a tree (12:6). Later he built an altar by a tree at Mamre (13:18). He lived near trees (14:13), and entertained Yahweh under a tree (18:1). Now he plants a tree. Note that the LXX *árouran* and Vulg. *nemus* ("grove") take Heb. *ʾēšel* ("tamarisk") as referring to a strip of ground (so NEB; cf. AV).[28] Gk. *ároura*

24. Long, *Problem of Etiological Narrative,* pp. 18-20.

25. For the evidence see W. J. Martin, "Beersheba," *New Bible Dictionary,* ed. J. D. Douglas (Grand Rapids: Eerdmans, 1962), p. 138.

26. Y. Aharoni, "Nothing Early and Nothing Late: Re-Writing Israel's Conquest," *BA* 39 (1976) 55-76, esp. pp. 62-65.

27. See A. R. Millard, "Methods of Studying the Patriarchal Narratives as Ancient Texts," p. 50; and J. J. Bimson, "Archaeological Data and the Dating of the Patriarchs," pp. 75-76, both in *Essays on the Patriarchal Narratives,* ed. A. R. Millard and D. J. Wiseman (Winona Lake, IN: Eisenbrauns, 1983).

28. In the light of the LXX and Vulg. translations of *ʾēšel* one may see a connection between Heb. *ʾēšel* and Akk. *ašlu,* "rope," which is used in Nuzi texts for "a strip of land." See W. von Soden, *Akkadisches Handwörterbuch,* 3 vols. (Wiesbaden: Harrassowitz, 1965-81), 1:81.

refers to an Egyptian measure approximately 100 cubits square. Thus, according to several ancient traditions Abraham did not plant a sacred tree in Beer-sheba but laid out a plot of land there. This interpretation would connect nicely with the data about Abraham in v. 34.

In Beer-sheba Abraham's life is permeated by worship. Abimelech can refer to Abraham's God as Elohim, but Abraham himself, when he calls on his God, calls upon *Yahweh. Yahweh* is further described as *the eternal God, 'ēl 'ôlām.* This appellative, *the eternal God,* appears as early as the Proto-Canaanite inscriptions of the 15th century B.C., and as late as the incantation text from Arslan Tash (7th century B.C.).[29] Scholars still hotly debate whether "El" religion is a Canaanite heritage which Israelite tribes met and absorbed after settlement in Canaan, or whether it is a direct Hebrew heritage. Although the former view is probably the more widely held one, it is interesting in this particular case that Gerar, where Abraham occasionally stays (20:1), is not a Canaanite city at all. Furthermore, the connection of *'ēl 'ôlām* with Beer-sheba, which is only a campsite and hardly a city at this time, militates against the necessary connection between the *'ēlîm* and specific localities.

Many commentators have viewed the designation *Philistine* (vv. 32, 34) as an anachronism, because external sources (i.e., Egyptian texts) attest the presence of Philistines as Philistines in Palestine only as early as 1200 B.C. But such a conclusion is unwarranted. The later Philistines, mentioned in Judges and Samuel, are bellicose and live under "lords." The Philistines of the patriarchal age are peaceful and live under a "king." If this is an anachronistic retrojection it would be most unlikely that the character of those pictured in the retrojection would clash with the later Philistines. One would expect imitation and correspondence. I suggest that the Philistines of Genesis represent the first wave of Sea Peoples from the Aegean, and that the later Philistines represent the last wave (ca. 1200 B.C.). These early Philistines would then represent some earlier Aegean group, such as the Caphtorim from Crete (Deut. 2:23).[30]

29. For data on *'ēl 'ôlām* see F. M. Cross, "Yahweh and the God of the Patriarchs," *HTR* 55 (1962) 236-41; idem, *Canaanite Myth and Hebrew Epic* (Cambridge: Harvard University, 1973), pp. 47, 48 and n. 18, 49, 50; cf. also pp. 17-19; idem, "*'ēl,*" *TDOT,* 1:245-46, 255-57; E. Jenni, "*'ōlām,*" *THAT,* 2:236-37, 239.

30. See C. H. Gordon, *The Ancient Near East,* 3rd ed. (New York: Norton, 1965), p. 121; K. A. Kitchen, *Ancient Orient and Old Testament* (Chicago: Inter-Varsity, 1966), pp. 80-81; idem, "The Philistines," in *Peoples of Old Testament Times,* ed. D. J. Wiseman (Oxford: Clarendon, 1973), pp. 56-57; E. E. Hindson, *The Philistines and the Old Testament* (Grand Rapids: Baker, 1971), pp. 93-104; Y. M. Grintz, "The Philistines of Gerar and the Philistines of the Coast," in *Studies in Memory of Moses Schorr 1874-1941,* ed. Louis Gingberg and A. Weiss (New York; Professor Moses Schorr Committee, 1944), pp. 96-112; W. S. LaSor, "Philistines," *ISBE,* 3:841-46; R. D. Barnett, *Cambridge Ancient History,* ed. I. E. S. Edwards, et al., 3rd ed. (Cambridge: Cambridge University, repr. 1980), 2:2A:271-78; W. F. Albright, ibid., pp. 507-16.

THE NEW TESTAMENT APPROPRIATION

Gen. 16; 21 and Gal. 4:21–5:1

Locked in a dispute with Galatian Christians over whether faith in Christ is sufficient for salvation, Paul turns to Gen. 16 and 21 and attempts to buttress his argument by allegorizing on Hagar and Sarah.

Abraham had two sons, Ishmael and Isaac. At least at the beginning of the allegory, each son is identified only by his mother, and the mother in turn is known only by her position in society. One is the son of a slave (*paidískē,* a term used in the LXX to describe Hagar as a *šip̱ḥâ* [Gen. 16:1-3, 5-6, 8; 25:12] and as an *'āmâ* [Gen. 21:10, 12-13]), and the other is a son of a free woman (*eleythéra,* a term not used anywhere in the LXX). That Ishmael is dubbed as one "born according to the flesh" is not inherently a pejorative statement, for elsewhere Paul talks to believers about "Abraham, our forefather according to the flesh" (Rom. 4:1). Isaac is designated as a "son of promise," presumably a reference to Gen. 17:16. Paul does not say that Ishmael was born "according to the flesh," while Isaac was born "according to the Spirit." Paul does not contrast flesh with Spirit, as elsewhere in Galatians, until v. 29; rather, he contrasts flesh with promise. This is Paul's way of contrasting the ordinary circumstances surrounding Ishmael's conception/birth with the supernatural circumstances surrounding Isaac's conception/birth.

It is, however, the mothers rather than the sons whom Paul uses. He refers to Hagar and Sarah as "two covenants."[1] Paul uses the plural of "covenant" again only in Rom. 9:4 and Eph. 2:12. As I remarked earlier, the plural of "covenant" never appears in the OT.[2] Hagar and Sarah represent two covenants that are simultaneous and not successive, and hence the possibility is eliminated that Paul is contrasting the old covenant with the new covenant. After all, Hagar and Sarah live synchronically with each other, not diachronically after one another. In speaking of Hagar and Sarah as "two covenants" he indicates clearly that he is using an allegory; Paul discerns in the narratives of Gen. 16 and 21 a secondary and hidden meaning that is beneath the primary meaning of the narrative.[3]

1. By referring to Hagar and Sarah as "two covenants," Paul demonstrates that his primary concern is not in these two women as "historical persons, but in the two worlds they represent" (H. D. Betz, *Galatians,* Hermeneia [Philadelphia: Fortress, 1979], p. 243).

2. On the significance of the pl. of "covenant" in the Pauline literature see C. Roetzel, "*Diathēkai* in Romans 9:4," *Bib* 51 (1970) 377-90.

3. Some scholars suggest that Gal. 4 is more typology than allegory (F. F. Bruce, *Epistle to the Galatians,* NIGTC [Grand Rapids: Eerdmans, 1982], p. 217: "he [viz., Paul] has in mind that form of allegory which is commonly called typology"). Others argue that

Next, Hagar is identified with Mt. Sinai and "the present Jerusalem." Sarah is identified with "the Jerusalem above"[4] (i.e., the eschatological age and the antithesis to both Mt. Sinai and "the present Jerusalem"). It is appropriate for Paul to quote here Isa. 54:1, which is a word spoken by the prophet to the present (and widowed, desolate) Jerusalem (vv. 1ff.) about the future (and fertile) Jerusalem (vv. 11-14) — precisely the correspondence Paul is making in Gal. 4.[5] Paul's concluding point and his application (introduced by "now we . . . ," v. 28) are that the Christian believers have been called to be like Isaac, and here they find their freedom.

I would strongly disagree with commentators who suggest that in this allegory Paul is contrasting Judaism with Christianity, and that he uses Hagar to represent Israelites or Jews (that would be an odd association!) and Sarah to represent Christians and the new covenant. Those who follow that approach are forced to admit that Gal. 4:21-31 is among Paul's most demeaning attacks on Judaism.[6]

The problem with this interpretation is that Paul's message and confrontation is not with Jews but with Gentiles (see 1:16; 2:2, 7; 3:8, 14; 4:8). His phrase "you who desire to be under law" (4:21) does not necessarily identify his opponents as Jews. Law may be understood here as "scripture" (3:8, 22; 4:30).

Believers, says Paul, must choose between being Ishmael people (i.e., those who live by the flesh) or Isaac people (i.e. those who live by the Spirit). One can, thank God, move from the first option to the second. But God forbid that Gentile believers should reverse that move. They would be making such a reversal whenever, say, they force circumcision on others as a mark of authentic faith. In such cases it will be Ishmael "persecuting" Isaac all over again.[7]

Gal. 4 is a mixture of typology and allegory (Betz, *Galatians,* p. 239). For a strong statement that Hagar and Sarah are not treated typologically in Gal. 4, see R. N. Longenecker, *Biblical Exegesis in the Apostolic Period* (Grand Rapids: Eerdmans, 1975), p. 127.

4. Gal. 4:26 is Paul's only use of the phrase *hē ánō Ieroysalḗm,* but it appears also in Heb. 12:22; 13:14; cf. Rev. 21:2, 10.

5. C. H. Cosgrove ("The Law Has Given Sarah No Children [Gal. 4:21-30]," *NovT* 29 [1987] 230-31) observes from Paul's use of this OT quotation that "Paul reinforces in the strongest possible terms the repeated accent in Galatians that *life* . . . is not to be found in the Torah."

6. For example, Betz (*Galatians,* p. 246) labels Gal. 4:21ff. "one of Paul's sharpest attacks upon the Jews."

7. Very helpful here is the discussion by L. Gaston, "Israel's Enemies in Pauline Theology," *NTS* 28 (1982) 400-423, esp. 400-411. On Paul's use of Ishmael's "persecuting" Isaac, see Bruce, *Galatians,* pp. 223-24; and Betz, *Galatians,* p. 250 n. 116.

K. THE BINDING OF ISAAC (22:1-24)

1. ABRAHAM IS TESTED BY GOD (22:1-19)

1 *Some time later God tested Abraham. He said to him, "Abraham!" "Yes,"*[1] *he answered.*

2 *Then he said: "Take, please,*[2] *your son, your precious one*[3] *whom you love, Isaac, and go to*[4] *the land of Moriah,*[5] *where you shall offer him up as a burnt offering on one of the peaks that I will identify for you."*

3 *Arising early that morning Abraham saddled his donkey, took two of his servants*[6] *with him, along with Isaac his son. He split kindling wood for a burnt offering, and went to the place about which God had spoken to him.*

4 *On the third day Abraham saw the place from a distance.*

5 *Abraham spoke to his servants: "Remain here by yourselves with the donkey. I and the lad will go over there; we will worship and then return to you."*

6 *Thereupon Abraham took the wood for the burnt offering and placed*

1. The traditional "Here am I" seems a bit wooden. The Hebrew is lit. "behold me." Although *hinnēh* with 1st person sing. suffix is common in the OT, it appears in the Abraham Cycle only in this chapter (vv. 1, 7, 11). BDB, p. 244, says that *hinnēh* plus pronominal suffix, "in response to a call, indicates the readiness of the person addressed to listen or obey." See C. E. L'Heureux, *Life Journey and the Old Testament* (New York: Paulist, 1986), pp. 41-80. For the translation "yes" in 22:1 see Crenshaw, *Whirlpool of Torment,* p. 19; S. D. Walters, "Wood, Sand, and Stars: Structure and Theology in Genesis 22:1-19," *TJT* 3 (1987) 301. Speiser (*Genesis,* p. 162) renders "ready."

2. On the particle *-nā'* see the commentary on v. 2.

3. *yᵉḥîḏᵉḵā* should not be taken as "your only one" but as "your precious one" (NJPS "favored one"). Cf. Prov. 4:23; Ps. 22:21 (Eng. 20); 35:17; cf. also A. Berlin, "Shared Rhetorical Features in Biblical and Sumerian Literature," *JANES* 10 (1978) 38 n. 15; F. C. Fensham, "Notes on Keret in CTA 14:90-103a," *JNWSL* 8 (1980) 41-42. But the retention of "only" also has its merits. See Walters, *TJT* 3 (1987) 303 n. b. Note LXX's rendering of *yāḥîḏ* by *agapētón,* "beloved."

4. *leḵ lᵉḵā,* lit., "go to yourself," occurs in this form only in Gen. 12:1 and 22:2; see the commentary on 12:1 (1:369 n. 1). H. Shanks ("Illuminations: Abraham Cut Off From His Past and Future by the Awkward Divine Command 'Go You!,'" *BRev* 3/1 [1987] 8-9) notes that in 12:1 the phrase cuts Abraham off from his past, while in 22:2 the phrase cuts Abraham off from his future.

5. The ancient versions disagree significantly among themselves on how to render Heb. *hammōrîyâ.* See the commentary on v. 2.

6. This chapter uses Heb. *naʿar* both for the two servants who accompanied father and son (vv. 3, 5, 19) and for Isaac (vv. 5, 12, where I have translated it "lad"). The narrator employed the first three, and Abraham himself and God's messenger employed the last two in direct speech.

it on Isaac his son. He himself carried the tinder[7] *and the knife. The two of them walked together.*

7 *Isaac said to his father Abraham: "Father!" "Yes, my son," he answered. "Here are the tinder and the wood," he said, "but where is the sheep for a burnt offering?"*

8 *Abraham replied: "God will provide for himself*[8] *the sheep for a burnt offering, my son." The two of them continued walking together.*

9 *When they reached the place about which God had spoken to him, Abraham built an altar there and arranged the wood. Then he bound Isaac his son above the altar on top of the wood.*

10 *Abraham reached and took the knife to slaughter his son.*

11 *But Yahweh's messenger called to him from heaven: "Abraham! Abraham!" "Yes," he answered.*

12 *"Do not lay a hand on the lad, or even do the least thing to him," he said, "for I now know you fear God, since you have not withheld your son, your precious one, from me."*

13 *As Abraham looked around, what should he see but another*[9] *ram snagged in a thicket by its horns! So Abraham went and took the ram, and offered it up as a burnt offering in place of his son.*

14 *So Abraham named that place Yahweh-yireh;*[10] *and even today it is said: "In Yahweh's mountain he is seen."*

15 *Yahweh's messenger called to Abraham a second time from heaven,*

16 *and said: "I swear by myself, says Yahweh, that indeed because you have acted thus, and did not withhold your son, your precious one,*

17 *I will certainly bless you, and greatly multiply your descendants as the stars of heaven and the sands of the seashore; your descendants shall take possession of their*[11] *enemies' gates.*

7. Here and in v. 7 the Hebrew has *'ēš,* "fire," but it is unlikely that Abraham carried something that was in flames already. BDB, p. 77, says of *'ēš* in Gen. 22:6, 7, "of tinder for lighting fire." On the basis of Akk. *(aban) išāti* "fire (stone)," Speiser (*Genesis,* p. 163) translates "firestone," and Westermann (*Genesis,* 2:352, 353) follows him with his "fire-(flint)."

8. Lit., "God will see for himself the sheep," if one understands *lô* as reflexive ("for himself") rather than intensive ("God himself"). The use of *yir'eh,* "will see, provide," in this verse becomes the basis for Abraham's choice of name for this site in v. 14 (Yahweh-*yireh*).

9. In the commentary below I explain my hesitation to accept the change of *'aḥar* to *'eḥāḏ*.

10. Lit., "Yahweh sees (or provides)"; cf. v. 8.

11. Lit., "his enemies" *('ōyeḇāyw). zeraʿ* ("descendant") is a collective noun, sing. in form but pl. in meaning.

18 *And all the nations of the earth shall be blessed in your descendants, all because you obeyed me."*

19 *Abraham then returned to his servants, and they set out together for Beer-sheba. Abraham remained in Beer-sheba.*

This best-known event in the life of Abraham is at the same time the most baffling, and for various reasons. Textual and literary questions are among the concerns. The consensus among source critics is that vv. 1-13 (or 14) are the work of E, and continue the Elohist's saga about Abraham, first encountered in ch. 20. Vv. 14 (or 15)-18 are marked as secondary and are attributable to the redactor of the JE materials. The primary evidence for associating the binding of Isaac story with E is the frequent use of Elohim (5 times) throughout the narrative (vv. 1, 3, 8, 9, 12). But note the use of Yahweh five times (vv. 11, 14 [twice], 15, 16), or three times if we confine ourselves to the Elohistic section. Is it not surprising that the Elohist has Abraham calling the site "Yahweh-yireh" and not "Elohim-yireh"?

Another problem focuses not on literary sources but on the historical matter of whether the story is a reflection, however dim, of an actual event which has been applied only secondarily to Abraham. Or is the story a cultic legend without any historical nucleus at all?[12] That is, can we penetrate behind the final form of the story and reconstruct the story's original form? If we can do that, then we can then trace how the story has been adapted to novel circumstances in Genesis. But such an exercise can never be finally proved or disproved; it remains hypothetical. It also rejects the canonical witness that the event is sui generis and that it involves Abraham. One looks in vain for vestiges of literary strata in this narrative that would surely have been present had it passed through various levels of retelling and reinterpretation.

It is best to see the chapter as contextually related in theme to the previous one. Abraham has lost one child, Ishmael. Now is he to lose his only other child, Isaac? Is Isaac on the altar only an extension of Ishmael in the wilderness? Is Abraham who sent off Hagar and Ishmael at Sarah's command any different from Abraham the knife wielder who acts at God's command? Is Sarah's "get rid of Ishmael" now replaced by God's "get rid of Isaac"? Can God protect and provide both for Ishmael and Isaac? Such common

12. The first of these positions is taken by H. G. Reventlow, *Opfere deinen Sohn: Ein Auslegung von Gen. 22,* Biblische Studien 53 (Neukirchen-Vluyn: Neukirchener, 1968). The second of these positions is espoused by R. Kilian, *Isaaks Opferung: Zur Überlieferungsgeschichte von Gen. 22,* SBS 44 (Stuttgart: Katholisches Bibelwerk, 1970). For his own reasons Van Seters (*Abraham in History and Tradition,* pp. 231-37) is unhappy with the conclusions of both Reventlow and Kilian.

themes, and vocabulary as well,[13] suggest associations between 21:8-21 (the dismissal of Hagar and Ishmael) and 22:1-19 (the binding of Isaac).

1 It is impossible to identify *Some time later* (see 15:1) with a specific antecedent. Is it some time after Abraham's covenant with Abimelech, or is it some time after the disappearance of Hagar and Ishmael? And how much later is it? Days? Months? Years? It is more likely years, since Isaac does not appear to be a newborn or a toddler in ch. 22. Yet Abraham's reference to Isaac as a *naʿar,* a "lad" (v. 5), suggests that Isaac is not a man who is physically in the prime of life. Then again, to one who has reached the century mark the term *naʿar* would understandably have a broad range. Early Jewish tradition (Midrash Gen. Rabbah 56:8) suggested that Isaac was 37 at the time of his binding by Abraham. This number is arrived at by subtracting the age at which Sarah gave birth to Isaac (90) from the age at which she died (127), a sudden death caused by discovering that Abraham is about to slaughter Isaac. By putting Isaac in his late 30s, Jewish tradition gives a much larger role to Isaac than Christian tradition, which has highlighted the obedience of Abraham and the faithfulness of God.

Two items in v. 1 highlight the intensity of the situation. One is the addition of the definite article to *'ĕlōhîm* (hence, lit., "the God"). This feature appears also in vv. 3, 9, but not in vv. 8, 12. In the narrator's mouth "the God" is used, but in direct discourse "God" is sufficient. The three instances in which *'ĕlōhîm* is definite describe God as "speaking" *('āmar)* to Abraham. The affixing of the article in these three instances may be the narrator's way of emphasizing that it was God, Abraham's God,[14] who was speaking to Abraham. What he was hearing came from no other source nor from his own imagination.

The second feature is the word order. Normal Hebrew syntax calls for

13. P. Trible, "The Other Woman: A Literary and Theological Study of the Hagar Narratives," in *Understanding the Word: Essays in Honour of Bernhard W. Anderson,* ed. J. T. Butler, et al., JSOTSup 37 (Sheffield: JSOT, 1985), p. 245 n. 73, notes the following parallels: (1) God opens the eyes of Hagar and she sees *(rā'â)* a well, from which she provides a drink for Ishmael (21:19); Abraham lifts up his eyes and sees *(rā'â)* a ram, which he sacrifices instead of Isaac (22:13-14). (2) In both narratives Abraham "rose early in the morning" (21:14; 22:3). (3) A messenger of God calls from heaven (21:17; 22:11), at a moment, I might add, when death seems imminent for Abraham's sons. (4) Hagar is told "fear not" and Abraham "fears" God (21:17; 22:12). (5) Both Ishmael and Isaac are called "lads" *(naʿar),* Ishmael by the narrator (21:17, 20) and by God's messenger (21:18), Isaac by his father (22:5) and by Yahweh's messenger (22:12). (6) Hagar is told to lift Ishmael up and hold him first with her "hand" (21:18); Abraham is told not to lay a "hand" on Isaac (22:12).

14. GKC, § 126e, cites *hā'ĕlōhîm* as an instance of the article's use where "terms applying to whole classes are restricted to particular individuals." The article may also imply possession, "his God." See Joüon, *Grammaire,* § 137f (I.2).

the verb to precede the subject; hence we would expect: "tested Elohim Abraham." But the placing of the subject first, as here, draws special attention to it: "the Elohim — he tested Abraham!" Since the "he" is already contained in the verb, "the Elohim" must be taken as a *casus pendens.*[15]

The text clearly makes the point that what follows is a divine testing, not a demonic temptation. This particular verb, with God as the subject, does not occur again until Exod. 15:25 (and cf. Exod. 16:4; Deut. 8:2, 16; 33:8 for references to the same time period; also Deut. 13:4 [Eng. 3]; Judg. 2:22; 3:1, 4 for other divine testings). The wilderness period, after the departure from Egypt, is a testing experience. Will the Israelites take freedom with all the insecurities that freedom brings, or will they take incarceration and the guarantee of regular meals? That is the test. Whenever a human being is the subject of this verb and God is the object, the testing is negative, uncalled for, and out of place.[16] Perhaps the closest parallel to Gen. 22:1-19 for the "divine testing" motif occurs in Exod. 20:20, right after the revelation of the Decalogue. In both instances the source of the test is *hā'ĕlōhîm,* some form of the verb *nāsâ* is used *(nissâ/nassōṯ),* and the aim of the testing is to evidence the fear of God (*yᵉrē' 'ĕlōhîm,* Gen. 22:12; *tihyeh yir'āṯô,* Exod. 20:20). The major difference between the two is that in Exod. 20:20 the people know well, via Moses, that through the revelation of his law God will test his people. How will his people respond to this God who has revealed himself in word and act? By contrast, the reader, but not Abraham, knows that what he is about to hear is a divine test.

2 The divine command *Take* is followed by the particle *-nā',* which is normally translated something like "please" or "I beg you." It might seem strange to some modern readers for God to say to Abraham "Take, please, your son" or "Take, I beg you, your son." For this reason some have assigned to *-nā'* here a strengthening function instead of the usual precative meaning.[17] But I observed in my discussion of Gen. 13:14 that *-nā',* which occurs more than sixty times in Genesis, is used only five times in the entire OT when God speaks to a person.[18] Each time God asks the individual to do something staggering, something that defies rational explanation or understanding. Here then is an inkling at least that God is fully aware of the magnitude of his test for Abraham.[19]

15. See GKC, § 143c.

16. See Exod. 17:2, 7; Num. 14:22; Deut. 6:16; Ps. 78:18, 41, 56; 95:9; 106:14. The exception is Ps. 26:2. In a few places *nissâ* carries the idea of "to have experience of, to practice, to be used to, be familiar with." Cf. M. Greenberg, "*nsh* in Exod. 20:20 and the Purpose of the Sinaitic Theophany," *JBL* 79 (1960) 273-76. Besides Exod. 20:20 cf. Deut. 28:56; 1 Sam. 17:39.

17. See J. Hoftijzer, "David and the Tekoite woman," *VT* 20 (1970) 440 n.2.

18. See Y. T. Radday, "The Spoils of Egypt," *ASTI* 12 (1983) 136-37. We need to add Isa. 7:3 to Radday's four examples (Gen. 13:14; 15:5; 22:2; Exod. 11:2).

19. See Crenshaw, *Whirlpool of Torment,* p. 14.

The intensity of the test is magnified by the three direct objects of the imperative: *your son, your precious son whom you love, Isaac.* Each of the objects hits a little closer to home, as the list moves from the general to the more intimate. This specification is precisely what we encountered when God first spoke to Abraham: "Leave your country, your homeland, your father's house" (12:1), that is, an imperative followed by a series of gradually intensifying terms.[20] This is the only time in vv. 1-19 that someone other than the narrator uses the name "Isaac." Later, when Yahweh's messenger has stayed Abraham's hand (v. 12), he repeats the first two direct objects of v. 2, "your son, your precious son," but not the third direct object, "Isaac." In fact, no one uses the name "Isaac" after his father binds him on top of the altar (v. 9). The stacking up of three direct objects after the imperative "take," each of which is preceded by the accusative indicator *'eṯ-,* slows down the reading of the verse and accentuates the solemnity of the divine imperative.[21]

Abraham is instructed to take Isaac to *the land of Moriah.* The only other OT use of this name is in 2 Chr. 3:1. There Moriah is connected with Jerusalem, specifically that part of Jerusalem where Solomon built the temple. Interestingly, 2 Chr. 3:1 makes no reference to Moriah as the place where Abraham bound Isaac on the altar. It is remembered in Chronicles as the site of a theophany to David, rather than to Abraham. The omission of any reference to Abraham in 2 Chr. 3:1 does not, however, cast a cloud of doubt over the integrity of "Moriah" in Gen. 22:2. Nor does it lend credence to the view that the use of Moriah in 2 Chr. 3:1 reflects an artificial attempt by the Chronicler to confer sacrosanctity on the temple site by associating it with Abraham's binding of Isaac. Probably the Chronicler associates the site at which Solomon built the temple with Gen. 22 because this Genesis narrative connects Moriah with "Yahweh's mountain" (v. 14), a phrase and a concept frequent in the OT (Isa. 2:2-3; 30:29; 65:25; 66:20; Mic. 4:1; Zech. 8:3). Note that the Chronicler's phrase is "the mountain Moriah," while the phrase in Gen. 22:2 is "the land of Moriah."

Unable to provide an explanation for *Moriah (mōrîyâ),* scholars have emended it to *mor'ehyâ,* "seen of Yah(weh)," or to *mar'ehyâ,* "vision of Yah(weh)," in both cases "Moriah" having something to do with *rā'â,* "to see." Other suggestions have been to read the "Land of Ḥamorim," or "land of the asses" (see v. 5), an allusion to Shechem (see Gen. 33:19; 34:2, "She-

20. Cf. NJPS on Gen. 44:16 for the same rhetorical feature: "What can we say to my lord? How can we plead, how can we prove our innocence?" The structural similarities between Gen. 12 and 22 have been underlined by Cassuto, *Genesis,* 2:310; and by Sarna, *Understanding Genesis,* p. 160.

21. See S. E. McEvenue, "The Elohist at Work," *ZAW* 96 (1984) 323.

chem the son of Ḥamor")[22] or "the land of the Amorites."[23] The ancient versions were also puzzled as they attempted to connect it with *rā'â,* "to see."[24] Two recent suggestions for the meaning of Moriah are more promising. Dahood suggests that the name means "my teacher is Yah."[25] It may be connected with Eblaite *mu-rí-gú*[ki], "my teacher is the voice." *mu-ri* (or *mori*) contains the Hiphil participle of *yārâ,* "to teach, instruct, direct." Another suggestion, which I find attractive, is that the name is Hurrian and is composed of the relative or demonstrative pronoun *me/ma* ("which is of," "this of") and *iwri* ("lord, king"); hence, "land which is the king's."[26] The Hurrian character of Jerusalem and the Jebusites is confirmed by the name "Araunah/Ornan" (from *iwri*), the Jebusite from whom David purchased the land on which to build the temple (2 Sam. 24:18-25 par. 1 Chr. 21:28-30). Thus if Moriah is a Hurrian name its connection with Jerusalem would be most suitable.

The intensity of the divine test is further demonstrated by the fact that Abraham is instructed to offer Isaac as a whole *burnt offering ('ōlâ).* Later Levitical ritual (see Lev. 1) designated this particular offering as the only one to be completely consumed (except for the hide) on the altar, and hence the appropriate and normal Greek translation for Heb. *'ōlâ* is *holokáutōma,* "holocaust." In all instances of *'ōlâ* in Gen. 22 (vv. 3, 6, 7, 8, 13), however, the LXX uses *holokárpōsin,* a rare word in the LXX, appearing again only in Gen. 8:20; Lev. 9:3; Isa. 40:16; 43:23.[27]

The test for Abraham is not primarily whether to sacrifice a beloved son, thought that is no doubt involved emotionally. The real test is whether

22. See J. Wellhausen, *Die Komposition des Hexateuchs und der historischen Bücher des Alten Testaments* (Berlin: George Reimer, 1889), p. 19.

23. See Skinner, *Genesis,* p. 329; Crenshaw, *Whirlpool of Torment,* p. 20 n. 37. This is also the reading of Pesh. and Targ. Jonathan.

24. SP *hmwr'h,* Symm. *tḗs optasías* "vision"; Vulg. *visionis;* perhaps all these reflect Heb. *hammar'eh;* see *BHS.* Pesh. suggests "land of the Amorite" (Heb. *hā'ĕmōrî*). LXX reads *hypsēlós,* which means "high" or "exalted," to render Moriah (whereas in 2 Chr. 3:1 it renders "the mountain of the Amorites" [*órei toú Amoria*]). As a noun, it would have to be translated something like "up-country" or "highland."

25. See M. Dahood, "The God *Ya* at Ebla?," *JBL* 100 (1981) 608 n. 6; idem, "Eblaite and Biblical Hebrew," *CBQ* 44 (1982) 16; J. P. Fokkelman, "On the Mount of the Lord There Is Vision," in *Signs and Wonders: Biblical Texts in Literary Focus,* ed. J. C. Exum, SBL Semeia Studies (Atlanta: Scholars, 1989), p. 52.

26. See S. Yeivin, "Marginal Glosses," *Tarbiz* 40 (1971) 396-97 (Hebrew, English summary on p. I); G. Rendsburg, "A New Look at Pentateuchal HW'," *Bib* 63 (1982) 358-59.

27. See J. A. L. Lee, *A Lexical Study of the Septuagint Version of the Pentateuch* (Chico, CA: Scholars, 1983), p. 52, who observes that *holokárpōsis* is one of the few words in the Greek of the Pentateuch that illustrates a new formation peculiar to Biblical Greek.

Abraham will sacrifice the one person who can perpetuate the promises of God, and particularly those promises that his posterity should thrive.[28]

This verse raises the ethical question about the place of child sacrifice in OT religion, and whether the God of Abraham really asked the patriarch to sacrifice his son. The classic expression of this issue is Søren Kierkegaard's *Fear and Trembling*.[29] Kierkegaard has Abraham say to Isaac as father and son climb Moriah: "Stupid boy, do you think I am your father? I am an idolater. Do you think it is God's command? No, it is my desire." Subsequent to a cry to God by Isaac, Abraham says to himself softly, "Lord God in heaven, I thank you; it is better that he believes me a monster human than that he should lose faith in you."[30] For Kierkegaard there are two Abrahams. One is the ethical Abraham for whom the moral law is universal and has a categorical claim to obedience. The other Abraham is "the knight of faith" who knows of a higher obedience than even that to universal moral law, and this may lead to the taking of the life of another, "the teleological suspension of the ethical." Thus, for Kierkegaard, Abraham is torn between his obligation to obey God and whether the command he accepts is really from God. Accordingly, he proceeds "in fear and trembling."

Kierkegaard was not, however, the first to raise a question about the propriety of God's command to Abraham in Gen. 22:2. Early Jewish tradition also made some emphatic objections. For example, the Talmud (see *Taʿan.* 4a) expands on the phrase in Jer. 19:6 about those who burned their sons as burnt offerings to Baal that God "did not command, decree, nor did it come into his mind" as follows: " 'which I did not command': this refers to the sacrifice of the son of Mesha, the king of Moab: 'nor decree it': this refers to the daughter of Jephthah: 'nor did it come into my mind': this refers to the sacrifice of Isaac, the son of Abraham."

The OT has undeniable instances of child sacrifice.[31] For example, the

28. See J. Yoder, *The Politics of Jesus* (Grand Rapids: Eerdmans, 1972), pp. 80-81 n. 3.

29. Søren Kierkegaard, *Fear and Trembling,* tr. H. V. Hong and E. H. Hong (Princeton: Princeton University, 1983). This book was first published in Danish in 1843.

30. The quotations are from pp. 10-11.

31. On child/human sacrifice in the OT see de Vaux, *Ancient Israel,* 2:441-46; idem, *Studies in Old Testament Sacrifice* (Cardiff: University of Wales, 1964), pp. 52-90; M. Weinfeld, "The Worship of Moloch and of the Queen of Heaven," *UF* 4 (1972) 133-54; M. Smith, "A Note on Burning Babies," *JAOS* 95 (1975) 477-79; A. R. W. Green, *The Role of Human Sacrifice in the Ancient Near East,* ASOR Dissertation Series 1 (Missoula, MT: Scholars, 1977), esp. ch. 9; J. Milgrom, "First-Born," *IDBS,* pp. 337-38; E. E. Carpenter, "Sacrifice, Human," *ISBE* 4:258-60; B. Levine, *Leviticus,* JPS Torah Commentary (Philadelphia: Jewish Publication Society, 1989), Excursus 7, "The Cult of Molech in Biblical Israel," pp. 258-59.

curse pronounced by Joshua on anyone who would rebuild Jericho (Josh. 6:26) is fulfilled in 1 K. 16:34 when Hiel buried two of his sons under the foundations of rebuilt Jericho, possibly to bring good luck or the blessing of the deity to his building project. Judg. 11:30ff. describes Jephthah's vowing to God a (human) sacrifice, which in this case is his daughter. The practice obtained also in neighboring Moab, whose king offered up his oldest son on the wall of a city while he was under siege (2 K. 3:27). But one cannot draw conclusions about standard Israelite ritual on the basis of the practices of a Moabite king or instances in Israel itself that border on the extraordinary, if not on the aberrant.

There is ample evidence that at times the cult of Molech flourished in Israel. Lev. 18:21 commands: "You shall not give any of your children to devote them by fire to Molech." Lev. 20:1-5 adds further regulations concerning sacrifices to Molech, including execution by human hands for such a practice (v. 2). Should the community fail to punish the perpetrator, God will do it himself (v. 3). Similarly, Deut. 18:10 fulminates against anyone who "makes his son or his daughter pass through the fire." The eighth-century Judean King Ahaz engaged in such illicit rituals (2 K. 16:3), and in the next century Josiah attempted to purge this practice as part of his reforms (2 K. 23:10). Among the prophets Mic. 6:6-7 is the clearest statement against child sacrifice. That such a practice had to be addressed by priestly tradition (Lev. 18; 20), by the Deuteronomist, by Judean royalty, and by prophets demonstrates that many in Israelite society assumed child sacrifice to be a valid way to worship God, and only the prohibitions and purgings instigated by the above groups corrected that notion. That Abraham offered no objection to God's command might also evidence the pervasiveness of the acceptability of child sacrifice as a mode of worship, sacrifice that was not perceived to be incongruous with the character of God.

Only two times in the OT is God the stimulus behind child sacrifice, Gen. 22 and Ezek. 20:25-26. In the latter passage God intends to punish his people in a most unusual way: by replacing his good laws that bring life with not-good laws that bring death, such as child sacrifice via the offering of the firstborn (see Exod. 22:28b [Eng. 29b]). Thus God will incite his apostate people to do something that elsewhere he and his spokespersons condemn.[32]

In the case of Gen. 22, if one focuses exclusively on v. 2, then God

32. On this difficult Ezekiel text see de Vaux, *Ancient Israel,* 2:444; W. Zimmerli, *Ezekiel 1,* tr. R. E. Clements, Hermeneia (Philadelphia: Fortress, 1979), pp. 411-12; M. Greenberg, *Ezekiel 1–20,* AB (Garden City, NY: Doubleday, 1983), pp. 368-70. God's hardening of Pharaoh's heart (Exod. 7ff.), God's charge to Isaiah to make the heart of his people fat (Isa. 6:9-10), God's misdirecting a prophet (1 K. 22:21ff.; Ezek. 14:9), and God's hardening of his own people (Isa. 63:17) raise the same issue as does Ezek. 20:25-26: "the incomprehensibility of the holy judge" (Zimmerli, *Ezekiel,* 1:412).

appears to be deceptive, irrational, and self-contradictory, if not cruel. If one focuses, however, on the whole narrative — the provision of the ram, the command to Abraham not to let the knife fall, and the subsequent promises to obedient Abraham — then the view of God that emerges is quite different. As de Vaux has said, "Any Israelite who heard this story would take it to mean that his race owed its existence to the mercy of God and its prosperity to the obedience of their ancestor."[33]

3 The most recent time when Abraham arose *Early that morning* was in an equally uncertain moment — sending Hagar and Ishmael away (21:15). Now it is he himself and Isaac who venture forth into the unknown. Note the similarity in sound between the beast of burden he uses (*his donkey,* Heb. *ḥᵃmōr*) and his destination (*Moriah,* Heb. *hammōrîyâ*). That Abraham cuts[34] the wood before he leaves, rather than after he arrives, is strange. Is there no wood available near Moriah, and if not, how does Abraham know that? Does this detail suggest his anxiousness to get on with the act, however difficult, and to avoid any possibility of shirking what he knows he must do when he reaches Moriah?

One also wonders why it is Abraham, rather than his servants, who saddles the donkey and splits the wood. Is not such activity more suitable for servants than for the servants' master? Indeed, throughout the narrative the servants do nothing. They are simply there. It is Abraham who splits the kindling wood, and later it is Isaac who carries it (not the donkey). Possibly in usurping the servants' duties, "Abraham aims to occupy himself with matters which presumably help him divert his thoughts from his upcoming shuddering mission . . . and temporarily postpone the execution of his horrible task."[35] Thus, one could interpret Abraham's actions in v. 3 as either a desire to move quickly and get the inevitable over as soon as possible, or an attempt to postpone the inevitable as long as possible.

The actions of Abraham early in this day are told in the following sequence: (1) saddled his donkey; (2) took two servants; (3) took Isaac; (4) split the kindling wood; (5) set out for Moriah. Why, or how, would Abraham take Isaac (3), and then split the kindling wood (4)? Would he not more likely saddle his ass, split the wood, then take his servants and Isaac with him?[36] Possibly Abraham hopes to conceal from Isaac for as long as

33. See de Vaux, *Ancient Israel,* 2:443; W. C. Kaiser, Jr., *Toward Old Testament Ethics* (Grand Rapids: Zondervan, 1983), pp. 262-64.

34. Note that "split, cut" in this verse is in the Piel *(wayᵉḇaqqaʿ).* BDB, p. 132a, says of the Piel stem of this verb: "often more complete or more violent than Qal."

35. See Y. Mazor, "Genesis 22: The Ideological Rhetoric and the Psychological Composition," *Bib* 67 (1986) 87.

36. R. Lack ("Le sacrifice d'Isaac: Analyze structurale de la couche élohiste dans Gen 22," *Bib* 56 [1975] 1-12, esp. 5-8) is bothered by the sequence of actions in this verse to the degree that he arbitrarily suggests the deletion of the phrase "he split kindling wood."

possible the real purpose of their trip to Moriah.[37] Or by saving mention of splitting the wood for the last, the author may wish to engage the reader as deeply as possible in Abraham's reticence to carry out the divine assignment.[38]

4 Not a word of conversation is recorded for the journey of three days (or two days and part of a third) from Beer-sheba to Moriah. If Abraham ever said, "if it is possible, let this cup pass from me," Scripture has not recorded it. This absence of any speech by Abraham prompts G. Coats to say of the patriarch: "He appears in superhuman, somewhat unrealistic dress. He never objects to the unreasonable, slightly insane commandment to sacrifice his son, as the Abraham of Genesis 12 or Genesis 16 most certainly would have done. To the contrary, he seems to move about his grim task with silent resignation, as if he were an automaton."[39]

In this verse we encounter the third verb in ch. 22 that has something to do with "raising, lifting up," as if to prepare Abraham — and us — for what he is about to do. He is to "offer up" (*ʿālâ,* v. 2) Isaac, he "went out" (*qûm,* v. 3) early that morning, and now he *spotted* (*nāśāʾ ʾeṯ-ʿênāyw,* lit., "lifted up his eyes") the place.

It may well be that we should take *On the third day* literally to describe how long it took Abraham to travel from Beer-sheba to Moriah, if Moriah is to be identificd with Jerusalem (an identification that is far from certain, as seen in the ancient versions and in modern writers), which is about fifty miles from Beer-sheba. It would be difficult to spot Jerusalem "from a distance" when one travels from the south because of surrounding mountains. If Moriah is Jerusalem, then Abraham and his party would have averaged sixteen or seventeen miles per day. But the expression *hayyôm haššᵉlîšî,* "the third day," is often used in the Torah to refer to some ominous event, such as the execution of Hamor and the Shechemites (Gen. 34:25), the execution of Pharaoh's baker (40:20), Joseph testing his brothers (42:18), and the day of God's descent on Mt. Sinai (Exod. 19:11, 16). It may be that one should take *On the third day* in a similar way here. The expression is used not primarily for exact chronological purposes, but as an idiom to underscore the drama in the narrative. *On the third day* may be the Hebrew equivalent of "at the eleventh hour."[40]

5 Included in Abraham's and Isaac's trek to Moriah are two servants (vv. 3, 5, 19). Abraham's *nᵉʿārîm* have already been mentioned in 14:24, and

37. See Walters, *TJT* 3 (1987) 304; J. L. Ska, "Gen. 22:1-19: Essai sur les niveaux de lecture," *Bib* 69 (1988) 330-31.

38. See Y. Mazor, "Genesis 22," *Bib* 67 (1986) 85.

39. See G. Coats, "Abraham's Sacrifice of Faith: A Form-Critical Study of Genesis 22," *Int* 27 (1973) 397.

40. The "three days" motif (as distinct from the third day motif) is explored by G. M. Landes, "The 'Three Days and Three Nights' Motif in Jonah 2:1," *JBL* 85 (1967) 446-50; H. B. Bauer, "Drei Tage," *Bib* 39 (1958) 354-58.

a single *naʿar* was spoken of in 18:7. This Hebrew word belongs to the legal-social vocabulary of the OT, and is only indirectly related to age. *naʿar* refers to any person who is under the authority and protection of his father (i.e., any young person from infancy to just before marriage), or anyone under the authority and protection of his superior or commander (i.e., any kind of servant or employee).[41]

Both uses of *naʿar* occur in Gen. 22. Abraham and God refer to Isaac as *naʿar* (vv. 5, 12). But the two who accompany father and son are also *neʿārîm.* Note that when Isaac is designated as a *naʿar* the absolute form is used *(hannaʿar),* that is, "the young person";[42] but when the others are referred to the form used is the construct with a pronominal suffix (3rd masc. sing.), that is, "his servants." Abraham can say "my son" (*benî,* vv. 7-8), but he never says "my boy" *(naʿarî).*[43] When speaking to his son Abraham uses the more affectionate term, but when speaking to others about his son he uses a less affectionate term, "the lad." If one assumes that Isaac overheard these words, the less personal "the lad" would not be lost on Isaac.

Some writers read Abraham's words to the servants ("we will worship and return to you") as an attempt by Abraham to conceal from the servants, or even from Isaac, what is about to happen. He is trying to be as diplomatic and sanguine as possible under the circumstances, and in the process he resorts to ambiguity and deception.[44] But Heb. 11:17-19 understood these words as a powerful illustration of Abraham's faith that God was able to raise up Isaac. In other words, Abraham went beyond Job's "the Lord gives and the Lord takes away" (Job 1:21) with his own "the Lord gives, the Lord takes away, and the Lord gives back."

6 The wood for the sacrifice is now placed on Isaac's shoulders, a fact that did not escape the NT writer's description of the *via dolorosa* (John

41. Studies on this word include: J. Macdonald, "The Status and Role of the *Naʿar* in Israelite Society," *JNES* 35 (1976) 147-70, who renders *naʿar* in Gen. 22, when used of Abraham's two servants, as "squire"; H. P. Stähli, *Knabe-Jüngling-Knecht: Untersuchungen zum Begriff naʿar im Alten Testament,* Beiträge zur biblischen Exegese und Theologie 7 (Frankfort am Main: Peter Lang, 1978).

42. As also with Ishmael (Gen. 21:12, 17, 18, 20).

43. The pl. form of the noun with first person pronominal suffix does occur in Job 29:5: "when my children *[neʿāray]* were about me."

44. See Crenshaw, *Whirlpool of Torment,* p. 22; Mazor (*Bib* 67 [1986] 86-87) offers the following justifications for Abraham's evasion from the truth: (1) to protect Isaac from the atrocious truth; (2) a humanistic, psychological abhorrence of taking another's life; (3) if he does not speak about it, maybe it will never happen. F. Landy ("Narrative Techniques and Symbolic Transactions in the Akedah," in *Signs and Wonders,* p. 14) makes the most blunt statement: "the most dignified of the patriarchs has to resort to a crude, and what is worse clumsy, lie (as he does in the wife-sister stories). We sense the desperateness of the improvisation."

19:17).[45] Isaac is big and strong enough to carry the wood, but young enough to ask a childlike question (v. 7c). In splitting the wood Abraham takes over the servant's work, and in carrying it Isaac takes over the donkey's work.

It is hard to say which tore more at the heart of Abraham — placing the bread and water on Hagar's shoulders, or placing the wood on Isaac's shoulders. At least Abraham has Isaac for a short while longer, for "the two of them walked together," a point made by the narrator before Isaac's question (v. 6) and after Abraham's answer (v. 8).[46]

7-8 The drama is slowed down here and solemnity is lent to the situation by the twofold use of *wayyōʾmer* in v. 7: literally, "Isaac said to Abraham his father, and he said, 'My father.' "[47]

Isaac is curious, and he does not hesitate to raise a logical question: *Where is a sheep for a burnt offering?* Isaac's question indicates that he knew what was involved in the act of worship (v. 5) in which he and his father were about to engage. Although the text has not expressly said that Isaac was informed that they were going to offer a burnt offering, the burnt offering was not only the oldest offering but the only offering mentioned in the patriarchal age (see Job 1:5). Abraham, yet some distance from his destination, can see the place (v. 4), but Isaac cannot see any sacrifice.

An honest question deserves an honest answer. Abraham does not turn on Isaac for speaking out of turn or for being presumptuous. Isaac's question consists of six words (in Hebrew), and Abraham responds with an answer of six words. Isaac begins his question with *Father.* Abraham ends his answer with *son.* We have here the same phenomenon as in v. 1 — special attention is drawn to the subject by placing it ahead of the verb: *God himself will provide. . . ."* There is no indication that Abraham replies hesitantly or mis-

45. Unlike the Synoptic writers (Matt. 27:32; Mark 15:21; Luke 23:26), John makes no mention of Simon of Cyrene carrying Jesus' cross. One could attempt harmonization by suggesting either that Jesus carried one part of the cross (all that John mentions) and Simon carried another part (the Synoptics, esp. Luke 23:26), or that Jesus carried the cross as far as his strength permitted, and only then did Simon get involved. I am more inclined to agree with R. E. Brown, *The Gospel According to John,* AB, 2 vols. (Garden City, NY: Doubleday, 1966-70), 2:916ff., that John deliberately omitted any references to Simon in order (a) to emphasize that Jesus was in control of his own destiny, even to the point of carrying his own cross unaided in a trying time; and (b) to introduce the typology of Isaac. Jer. 7:18 speaks of "the children gathering wood and the fathers kindling the fire" in preparation for engagement in pagan practices.

46. R. Gordis (*The Book of Job* [New York: Jewish Theological Seminary, 1978], p. 19) cites *yaḥdāw* in vv. 6, 8 as an instance of the repetition of a word with different connotations — "separately" (v. 6) and "together, of one mind" (v. 8). But I fail to discern this distinction here.

47. For other cases of *wayyōʾmer . . . wayyōʾmer* for dramatic effect cf. 2 Sam. 24:17; Est. 7:5; Neh. 3:34; Ezek. 10:2.

leadingly, but at least one writer defects ambiguity in Abraham's "God will provide." That answer can be reduced to either "I don't know" or "it will come out right in the end."[48] There is possible ambiguity not only in Abraham's first word to Isaac, "God will provide," but in his last words in this verse: "God will provide . . . for a burnt offering, my son." "My son" at the end of the quote may be understood as a vocative (the way Abraham wished Isaac to hear it) or in apposition to "a burnt offering" — "God will provide . . . for a burnt offering, i.e., you, my son" (the way Abraham would not want Isaac to hear it).[49] Isaac makes no response to his father's explanation. Such silence could be read as either satisfaction with Abraham's projection or bewilderment.

9 The previous mentions of Abraham's building an altar occurred much earlier in the narrative (12:7, 8; 13:18). In these three earlier events altar building took place on the heels of a divine promise. It was a response by Abraham to something God said he would do for Abraham's future. Now this altar-building ceremony threatens the fulfillment of those promises.

It should not go unnoticed that Isaac makes no attempt to deter his father. He had asked, "Where is the sheep?" but he does not ask "Why these ropes?" If Abraham displays faith that obeys, then Isaac displays faith that cooperates. If Isaac was strong and big enough to carry wood for a sacrifice, maybe he was strong and big enough to resist or subdue his father.

The verb *bound (ʿāqaḏ)* occurs only here in the OT. It is the source for the word *Aqedah,* by which Gen. 22 is identified throughout Jewish tradition. In postbiblical Hebrew the verb means "to bind the legs of an animal for sacrifice." The term in the OT priestly texts for placing sacrifices on an altar is *ʿāraḵ,* "to set up, arrange, lay out" (Lev. 1:8, 12; 6:5). Other portions of the OT use the verb *śîm,* "to put, place, set" (1 K. 18:33). *ʿāraḵ* may be used for arranging the wood on the altar before the sacrifice is placed in position (as here in Gen. 22:9; also Lev. 1:7; 1 K. 18:33; Isa. 30:33). The writer of Gen. 22 may have used *ʿāqaḏ* rather than *ʿāraḵ* or *śîm* to describe Abraham's placing his son on top of the wood for two possible reasons. First, he has just used *ʿāraḵ* to speak of Abraham arranging the wood on the altar. For variation, and to avoid the double use of *ʿāraḵ,* the writer uses first *ʿāraḵ,* then *ʿāqaḏ*. Second, *ʿāqaḏ* makes more sense — indeed, is essential — with the sacrifice of a living person.[50] In the case of the burnt offering of Lev. 1,

48. See F. Landy, "Narrative Techniques," p. 17. Westermann (*Genesis,* 2:359) describes Abraham's response as throwing "the ball back into God's court."

49. See Sternberg, *Poetics of Biblical Narrative,* p. 192; Crenshaw, *Whirlpool of Torment,* p. 23. The reading of "my son" in apposition to "burnt offering" has a long history and is not a discovery of modern exegetes. See Midrash Gen. Rabbah 56:4-5.

50. Cf. Rom. 12:1, "I appeal to you therefore, brethren, by the mercies of God to present your bodies as a living sacrifice" (RSV).

ʿārak̲ is more appropriate: the sacrificial victim was first slaughtered; then its blood was drained and disposed of; then it was sectioned; and last of all parts were placed on the altar for incineration.

10 It is interesting that the word used to describe what Abraham was about to do to Isaac is *slaughter (šāḥaṭ).* Biblical Hebrew has five verbs for "sacrifice": *šāḥaṭ, ṭāḇaḥ, zāḇaḥ,* the Hiphil of *ʿālâ,* and the Hiphil of *qāraḇ.* Only the first two may be used of the slaughter of animals for both secular and sacred purposes. The last three are confined to slaughter for sacred reasons. In addition, *šāḥaṭ* was used to describe the slaughter or sacrifice of children to false gods in pagan cults (see Isa. 57:5; Ezek. 16:21; 23:39). Its use in Gen. 22:10, then, makes Abraham's sacrifice of Isaac assume an even more dreadful aspect. Also, the use of the infinitive of *šāḥaṭ (lišḥōṭ)* after a long series of narrative forms *(wayyiqṭōl)* in the preceding verses and in this verse lends suspense to the narrative.[51]

The instrument Abraham planned to use on Isaac is a "knife" *(hammaʾᵃk̲elet̲).* Outside Gen. 22:6, 10, it is used again in the OT only in Judg. 19:29 and Prov. 30:14. Judg. 19:29 in particular is close to Gen. 22:10, for there a man uses a knife to butcher his concubine into twelve pieces. Thus a *maʾᵃk̲elet̲* is a very lethal instrument. Elsewhere the OT never indicates which instrument was used to slaughter sacrifices; perhaps the *maʾăk̲elet̲* served that purpose.

11 Yahweh's messenger is now suddenly introduced into the story as a voice from heaven. In both of the divine speeches thus far the speaker has been Elohim (vv. 1, 2). We last heard of this messenger in 16:7 and 21:17 (there, Elohim's messenger), when he came to Hagar and Ishmael in the desert. On several occasions in Torah stories the angel of Yahweh/Elohim is introduced subsequent to the start of the narrative, even if that narrative starts with something God says (as here), or if Yahweh is quoted (31:3ff.), or if he is referred to in the third person (16:1ff.; 21:1ff.). According to the next verse in the story (22:12) the messenger is almost indistinguishable from his master (see also 16:13; 21:18; 31:11, 13; Exod. 3:2, 4; Judg. 6:12, 14, 16, 20, 22, 23).[52]

The urgency with which the messenger speaks is indicated by the repetition of the name: *Abraham! Abraham!* Cf. "Moses, Moses" (Exod. 3:4),[53] "Samuel, Samuel" (1 Sam. 3:4), "Saul, Saul" (Acts 9:4). In three

51. See J. I. Lawlor, "The Test of Abraham: Gen. 22:1-19," *GTJ* 1 (1980) 23-24. On the use of the phrase at the beginning of the verse, "Abraham reached" (lit., "Abraham sent his hand") see P. Humbert, "Étendre la main," *VT* 12 (1962) 383-95.

52. See Westermann, *Genesis,* 2:360-61; Eichrodt, *Theology of the Old Testament,* 2:23-29.

53. The parallels between Gen. 22 and Exod. 3 have been drawn by N. Habel, "The Form and Significance of the Call Narratives," *ZAW* 77 (1965) 301-2.

of these instances either Yahweh's messenger (Gen. 22:11), or God (Exod. 3:4), or simply a voice (Acts 9:4; cf. 22:7; 26:14) speaks in order to stop an action the person is about to do (plunge a knife into a son, profane sacred ground with shoes, arrest Christians in Damascus).[54] The messenger's words are clearly intended to make Abraham desist from what God had earlier commanded. For another instance of Yahweh's messenger reversing the divine intention as perceived by the antagonist see Num. 22:22-35. God told Balaam to accompany Balak's princes if they approached him with the request to accompany them back to Balak (22:20); subsequently, Yahweh's messenger rebuked Balaam (22:32b), prompting Balaam to confess his sins (22:34).[55]

12 Abraham's willingness to carry through on the divine imperative is sufficient evidence that he is *committed to God* (*y^{e}rē' '$^{\breve{e}}$lōhîm,* lit., "fears God"). The story defines the meaning of *y^{e}rē' '$^{\breve{e}}$lōhîm.* It is "obedience which does not hold back even what is most precious, when God demands it, and commits to God even that future which he himself has promised."[56]

Of special interest here is that Abraham's obedience provides the messenger with undeniable data that Abraham is loyal and obedient. Did he not know that before the test was exacted? Is this phrasing similar to other biblical phrases, such as God putting a bow in the cloud to remind him of his covenant with humankind (Gen. 9), or the instruction to the Israelites at Passover to put blood on the doors for Yahweh to see (Exod. 12:23), even though the Israelites are already living by themselves in Goshen?

The Hebrew word for "provide" in v. 8 (*yir'eh,* with God as subject) and the word for "fear" in v. 12 (*y^{e}rē',* with Abraham as subject) sound quite similar. In the judgment of Abraham, God *yir'eh,* God "sees/provides." In the judgment of the messenger, Abraham *y^{e}rē'* God, Abraham "fears" God. In

54. The psalmist's cry "My God, My God, why have you forsaken me" (Ps. 22:1; cf. Matt. 27:46; Mark 15:34), although it too uses the doubling of the name as back-to-back vocatives, may be more a cry of desperation and bewilderment than of urgency.

55. Note the parallels between Gen. 22 and the Balaam-Balak incident: (1) a nocturnal revelation (stated in Num. 22; implied in Gen. 22); (2) the recipient rises early in the morning and saddles his donkey (Gen. 22:3; Num. 22:21); (3) Abraham makes a journey from Beer-sheba to Moriah, Balaam from Pethor to Moab; (4) neither individual makes this journey alone (two servants and Isaac are with Abraham; the princes of Moab are with Balaam); (5) Abraham lifted up his eyes and saw the place from a distance (v. 4); Yahweh opened Balaam's eyes and he saw Yahweh's messenger (Num. 22:31); (5) Yahweh's messenger speaks to the person with a command (Gen. 22:12; Num. 22:35). See also J. D. Safren, "Balaam and Abraham," *VT* 38 (1988) 105-13.

56. See H. W. Wolff, "The Elohistic Fragments in the Pentateuch" (tr. K. R. Crim), in W. Brueggemann and Wolff, *Vitality of Old Testament Traditions,* 2nd ed. (Atlanta: John Knox, 1982), p. 72. See also H. F. Fuhs, *TDOT,* 6:297-303, 310.

an "artful play on words"[57] the narrator transforms the theme of the story from providing to fearing.

13 In a providential way God does provide a surrogate for Isaac — *another ram.* Almost all commentators suggest emending *'aḥar,* "another," to *'eḥāḏ,* literally, the numeral one, which can be used as the indefinite article, "a." This reading has substantial textual support (many early Hebrew mss., LXX, SP), but such a reading misses the irony of the statement. For all practical purposes Isaac was to be the first ram. Now here is *another* one.[58] The sudden appearance of the ram is a total surprise to Abraham, as the expression *wᵉhinnēh,* literally, "and lo," suggests.

Earlier in the story Isaac had asked, "where is the sheep?" *(śeh),* v. 7. Abraham responded with "God will provide for himself the sheep" *(śeh),* v. 8. God does not provide a sheep, however, but a ram *('ayil).* The text does not explain why God provided an animal different from the one Abraham assumed he would provide. Abraham had earlier brought a ram to God (15:9) as one of the animals to be slain when God instituted his covenant with Abraham. On this occasion, however, God brings the ram to Abraham. S. Walters has observed that apart from Gen. 22 "burnt offering," "appear, be seen" (Niphal of *rā'â*) and "ram" occur together in only two places in the OT. These are (1) the ordination of the priests (Lev. 8–9, esp. 9:2-4) and the Day of Atonement (Lev. 16, esp. vv. 1, 3). Thus the ram is associated with priesthood and atonement.[59] Through such inner-biblical allusions, Walters suggests, the story of Abraham's offering and binding of Isaac is moved beyond simply the private religious experience of one individual and identified with "the communal worship of God's people in which divine reality appears."[60]

14 Appropriately Abraham names this place *Yahweh-yireh,* "Yahweh sees (or provides)." He does not call this site "Abraham-shama" ("Abraham obeyed"). The name does not draw any attention to Abraham's role in the story. Thus his part in the story is not memorialized; rather, it is subordinated

57. Fuhs, *TDOT,* 6:310.

58. See M. J. Dahood, "Northwest Semitic Notes on Genesis," *Bib* 55 (1974) 79. M. H. Pope ("The Timing of the Snagging of the Ram, Gen. 22:13," *BA* 49/2 [1986] 114-17) retains MT's *'aḥar* but gives to it the temporal sense "when" (as frequently in Ugaritic), i.e., immediately or virtually simultaneously with the action that follows — "Abraham lifted up his eyes and immediately saw a ram." R. L. Grimes ("Infelicitous Performances and Ritual Criticism," *Semeia* 41 [1988] 103-22, esp. 117-18) describes Abraham's sacrificing of the ram instead of Isaac as a "breach" in a child-sacrificing culture (if there ever was one).

59. The case for a connection between Gen. 22 and Lev. 16 would be strengthened if the text of Gen. 22:13 is read as *'ayil 'eḥaḏ* ("a ram"), which could be linked with Lev. 16:5, a verse telling Aaron to take two male goats for a sin offering and "one ram" *('ayil 'eḥaḏ)* for a burnt offering. I have given my reasons above in the commentary on v. 13 for retaining MT *'ayil 'aḥar.*

60. See Walters, *TJT* 3 (1987) 305-6, 309-10.

to that of Yahweh. The name highlights only the beneficent actions of Yahweh. The reader will come away from this story more impressed with God's faithfulness than with Abraham's compliance.

This emphasis is borne out by the fact that the following phrase, *and even today it is said,* lifts the event out of Abraham's time and projects it into the time of the narrator.[61] Thus the phrase gives to the entire narrative a certain timelessness. It witnesses to the gracious provisions of God.

There are some textual problems in the last few words of the verse: *b^ehar YHWH yērā'eh.* The following are possible translations of the text as it stands: "In the mountain of Yahweh he is seen"; "In the mountain of Yahweh he shall be seen"; "In the mountain of Yahweh it shall be provided." The problem here is to identify the relationship, if any, between the active of *rā'â* in *Yahweh-yireh,* "Yahweh sees," and the passive of *rā'â, yērā'eh,* "is seen."

The ancient versions do not reflect the MT. Hence LXX *En tṓ órei kýrios ṓphthē,* "in the mountain the Lord is seen," necessitates reading the first word in the MT *(b^ehar)* as *bāhār.*[62] The Vulg. reads *yir'eh* (Qal) for MT *yērā'eh* (Niphal), and thus translates "In the mountain the Lord sees" *(in monte Dominus videbilt).*

Other suggestions are that the variation of *yir'eh* and *yērā'eh* reflects the fact that the Masorah possessed two vocalizations of the place name and has preserved both variants,[63] or that the relative clause in v. 14b is so obscure that it probably did not originally belong with v. 14a. Perhaps even "Yahweh-yireh" is an explanation for a lost name.[64]

The use of the active and passive of *rā'â* may be deliberate, and if so, we should be hesitant about excising it.[65] God not only sees and provides for the needs of his servants but also shows himself to his servants. Elohim is no anonymous philanthropist. But in this incident at least, God shows himself not in any self-revelation but by his act of providing a ram in lieu of Isaac. Revelation for Abraham at Moriah was a visible manifestation of God's act.[66]

15-18 Commentators almost unanimously view these four verses as

61. See S. J. DeVries, *Yesterday, Today and Tomorrow,* p. 155.

62. Cf. Skinner, *Genesis,* p. 331.

63. See F. Zimmermann, "Some Textual Studies in Genesis," *JBL* 73 (1954) 97-98.

64. See Long, *Problem of Etiological Narrative,* pp. 28-29.

65. See S. R. Driver, *Genesis,* p. 220.

66. See S. Talmon, "Revelation in Biblical Times," *HS* 26 (1985) 53-70, esp. pp. 63-64, for a helpful exegetical study of *rā'â* and other Hebrew verbs connoting revelation that attempts to restore validity to G. E. Wright's famous but now often maligned phrase "God Who Acts" (*God Who Acts: Biblical Theology as Recital,* SBT 1/8 [London: SCM, 1952]).

secondary, for two reasons.[67] One is the suspicious introduction in v. 15 — *The angel of Yahweh called to Abraham a second time from heaven.* This sounds artificial to some, a less than smooth attempt by a later author to insert the promise theme into the Aqedah. The second reason is that the introduction of the promise theme refocuses the narrative in a different direction and therefore is not an integral part of the original story.

But these reasons are hardly correct. To have concluded the story at v. 14 would have been to produce a truncated narrative. Abraham has not withheld his only son; therefore, his descendants will be numerous (v. 17a), victorious (v. 17b), and influential (v. 18). They shall prosper because Abraham was faithful. That is the ultimate consequence of the divine testing of Abraham, not the sparing of Isaac.[68]

This section has some unique and powerful phrases. One is the use of *šēnîṯ,* "a second time" in v. 15. It may be compared with Yahweh's word that came to Jonah "a second time" (Jon. 3:1). Far from being a telltale evidence of a later addition, *šēnîṯ* serves to show that the following promises made to Abraham are the climax of the previous ordeal and of all previous ordeals.[69]

67. See, e.g., L. R. Bailey, *The Pentateuch* (Nashville: Abingdon, 1981), p. 148; J. A. Emerton, "The origin of the promises to the Patriarchs in the older sources of the book of Genesis," *VT* 32 (1982) 18. Among the Genesis commentators see Skinner, p. 331; von Rad, p. 242; Vawter, p. 259; Westermann, 2:363 ("There are only a few texts in Gen. 12 — 50 which are so easily recognizable as an addition").

68. The originality of vv. 15-18 is supported by Van Seters, *Abraham in History and Tradition,* p. 239. In addition, he departs radically from the consensus when he attributes all of 22:1-19 to the Yahwist! For other attempts to interpret vv. 15-18 as integral to the narration see G. W. Coats, "Abraham's Sacrifice of Faith: A Form-Critical Study of Genesis 22," *Int* 27 (1973) 395, who sees the reward for Abraham's obedience, as spelled out in vv. 15-18, to be entirely appropriate to the story (though in itself this does not negate the possibility that vv. 15-18 are supplemental, as Coats concedes). T. D. Alexander ("Genesis 22 and the Covenant of Circumcision," *JSOT* 25 [1983] 17-22, esp. p. 21) argues too that vv. 15-18 are not secondary on the basis that, on the analogy of God's covenant with Noah in Gen. 6 — 9, they are the oath that God confirms with Abraham by way of promise. They thus mark the necessary conclusion to and ratification of the conditional covenant announced in ch. 17. The proposal of such a connection between chs. 17 and 22, or between Gen. 6–9 and Gen. 17, 22 is ingenious but may not be convincing to many. G. Rendsburg (*The Redaction of Genesis* [Winona Lake, IN: Eisenbrauns, 1986], pp. 33-34) also argues against the secondary nature of vv. 15-18 on the basis of the redactional structuring of the Abraham Cycle. Since, in Rendsburg's analysis, the second apart (B) of the structure of the Abraham Cycle (12:1-9) begins with God's blessing, the second part from the end (B^1) of the cycle (22:1-19) must conclude with the same blessing. As Yahweh spoke twice to Abraham in B (12:17), his messenger speaks twice to Abraham in B^1 (22:11, 15). See also Sternberg, *Poetics of Biblical Narrative,* p. 55, who shows how the divine praise of vv. 15-18 is absolutely necessary.

69. See C. H. Gordon, "Build up and Climax," in *Studies in Bible and the Ancient*

While other instances of the divine oath occur in Genesis, this is the only instance in which the oath is introduced with Yahweh swearing by himself *(bî nišbaʿtî).*[70] Its import here is to lay as heavy an emphasis as possible on the following words. As if to underscore the importance of the divine promise, for *bî nišbaʿtî* would be sufficient by itself, the messenger adds, "says Yahweh" *(nᵉʾum yhwh).* Used often in the prophets, the phrase appears in the Pentateuch only here and in Num. 19:28.

The introductory *kî* in v. 17 probably does not introduce a result clause ("because you have not acted thus . . . I therefore will bless you") but rather has an emphasizing, reinforcing force: "I will *certainly/indeed* bless you." But the following four words add their emphasis through the use of the infinite absolute plus finite form of the verb: *ḇārēḵ ʾᵃḇāreḵᵉḵā wᵉharbâ ʾarbeh.*

The novel element in this catena of promises is the emphasis on conditionality — that human behavior determines God's response. These promises are uttered and shall be fulfilled *because* Abraham has done the appropriate thing. The same emphasis appears again in 26:5. Isaac receives the promises because his father was obedient to Yahweh.[71] Is it not interesting that not until God's last spoken word to Abraham — which is what 22:15-18 is — is an explicit connection made between performance and promise? Every promise to Abraham up to this point has been essentially unconditional. The postponement of the announcement of this cause and effect relationship clearly subordinates performance to promise, works to faith, and merit to grace. In addition, these promises affirm that because of Abraham's obedience, the blessing of Yahweh will extend far beyond faithful Abraham. They will extend into generations to come. Thus later Israel will partially owe its existence and the blessing of the Lord on its community to the faithful patriarch.[72]

19 Abraham now retraces his steps to Beer-sheba. Geographically, we began with Abraham at Beer-sheba (implied by 21:33); he departed (from Beer-sheba; v. 3); he sighted Moriah (v. 4); he arrived at Moriah (vv. 5-18); he departed from Moriah and arrived at Beer-sheba (v. 19). Details about the six days of travel from Beer-sheba to Moriah and back again are minimal.

Near East Presented to Samuel E. Loewenstamm, ed. Y. Avishur and J. Blau (Jerusalem: Rubinstein, 1978), p. 30.

70. For this identical phrase see Isa. 45:23; Jer. 22:5; 49:13. See further H. C. White, "The Divine Oath in Genesis," *JBL* 92 (1973) 165-79, esp. pp. 172-73, who lists the various oath formulae that precede Yahweh oaths.

71. On these two passages see W. C. Kaiser, Jr., *Toward an Old Testament Theology* (Grand Rapids: Zondervan, 1978), pp. 93-94.

72. R. W. L. Moberly ("The Earliest Commentary on the Akedah," *VT* 38 [1988] 302-23, esp. pp. 320-21) expands on this role of the promise theme in Gen. 22. Furthermore, Moberly suggests that the value of human obedience, as described in Gen. 22:15-18, is analogous to the assumptions underlying intercessory prayer.

Not even Isaac is mentioned in this verse, which simply says "Abraham returned to his servants and they set out together." The "they" of "they set out together" could easily be Abraham and his two servants. Note too that only Abraham "returned" (*wayyāšob,* sing.) to his servants. Also, the early part of the narrative (vv. 6, 8) used the expression "the two of them together" (*šᵉnēhem yaḥdāw*). But in v. 19 "the two of them" (*šᵉnēhem*) is missing. All that is present is "they set out together *[yaḥdāw]*."

The absence of Isaac from the narrative's conclusion raises the question of whether Isaac was sacrificed. The famous Jewish Bible commentator from medieval Spain, Ibn Ezra (1089-1164 A.D.), in his commentary on Gen. 22:19, quotes an opinion that Abraham actually did kill Isaac, and that Isaac was later resurrected from the dead. Such a view was more pervasive in medieval Jewish writings than at other periods, according to S. Spiegel,[73] in order to deny that the sacrifice of Isaac was in any way less than the sacrifice of Jesus, and to provide for Jewish communities suffering martyrdom an illustration of an actual sacrifice rather than simply an intended sacrifice.

The apparent absence of Isaac from the end of the narrative parallels the apparent absence of Sarah at the beginning of the narrative.[74] Thus the reader of Gen. 22 knows that Isaac was spared, and yet v. 19 seems to leave some unanswered questions. The tension between these two ideas may be deliberate. It suggests "that the intent and willingness to offer Isaac is seen as equivalent to doing it. Abraham's inner act of responsiveness to God's command is the equivalent of an outward act in which Isaac was returned to God as a sacrifice."[75] Abraham and the divine messenger anticipate Samuel's position (in the form of a rhetorical question): "Has the Lord as great delight in burnt offerings and sacrifices as in obeying the voice of the Lord? Behold, to obey is better than sacrifice, and to hearken than the fat of rams" (1 Sam. 15:22, RSV).

2. NAHOR'S FAMILY (22:20-24)

20 *Sometime later Abraham was told: "Milcah, she also has given birth to sons for Nahor your brother:*

21 *Uz his firstborn, Buz his brother, and Kemuel the ancestor of Aram;*

22 *Chesed, Hazo, Pildash, Jidlaph, and Bethuel."*

23 *Bethuel fathered Rebekah. These eight Milcah bore to Nahor, Abraham's brother.*

73. See Shalom Spiegel, *The Last Trial* (New York: Schocken, 1967); L. Jacobs, "Akedah," *EncJud,* 2:481-82; Crenshaw, *Whirlpool of Torment,* pp. 27-28.

74. See S. Brock, "Genesis 22: Where was Sarah?" *ExpTim* 96 (1984) 14-17.

75. See Walters, *TJT* 3 (1987) 320.

24 *His concubine,*[1] *whose name was Reumah, she too gave birth to Tebah, Gaham, Tahash, and Maacah.*

20-24 These verses seem to belong with Gen. 24 (see esp. v. 47); they provide the historical background for Isaac's marriage into the family of Nahor.[2] An unidentified source informs Abraham that his brother Nahor has fathered twelve sons, eight by his wife Milcah, and four by his concubine Reumah.[3] The twelve Aramean tribes are named after these sons.

Some of these names are identifiable. For example, according to some biblical texts (Jer. 25:20; Lam. 4:21), a place named *Uz* is located in Arabia, but other biblical texts suggest Aram (Gen. 10:23). *Chesed* may represent the Chaldeans of Lower Mesopotamia. This identification would suggest that the Chaldeans, who entered southern Babylonia in the early part of the 2nd millennium B.C., are an Aramean tribe. Places or tribes named *Buz* and *Hazo* were probably located in the mountainous region of northern Arabia, evidenced by the fact that in Jer. 25:23 Buz is mentioned along with Dedan and Tema, which are Arabian tribes or territories. *Gaham* appears on a sixth-century inscription from Arad as one of eight persons from whom grain is either distributed to or collected from.[4] A place named *Maacah* is located between Gilead on the south, Bashan on the east, and Mt. Hermon to the north, that is, in southern Syria.[5]

Two items tie Abraham's marriage to Nahor's marriage. First, both Abraham's marriage to his (half)-sister and Nahor's marriage to his niece (Gen. 11:29) are outlawed by later Levitical law (Lev. 18:9, 11; 20:17 and 20:20, respectively).[6] But in the patriarchal period such marriages are legitimate. Second, both Abraham and Nahor fathered children by a wife and by a concubine.

In its present context the genealogy of Nahor provides a ready illustration of one way in which God's recently recited promises to Abraham may find fulfillment. For the emphasis in this genealogy is on one of the nations of the earth (Nahor's descendants) who find blessing in Abraham's descendants.[7]

1. For a brief survey of *pileḡeš,* "concubine," see my study in *TWOT,* 2:724; and C. Rabin, "The Origin of the Hebrew Word *PĪLEGEŠ,*" *JJS* 25 (1974) 353-64.

2. See S. Sandmel, "The Haggada Within Scripture," *JBL* 80 (1961) 117.

3. On the number twelve see de Vaux, *Early History of Israel,* pp. 702-3.

4. See Y. Aharoni, "Three Hebrew Ostraca from Arad," *BASOR* 197 (1970) 35-36.

5. See B. Mazar, "Geshur and Maacah," *JBL* 80 (1961) 16-28.

6. The marriage of Nahor (uncle) to Milcah (niece) is like that of Amram (nephew) to Jochebed (aunt) in Exod. 6:20.

7. D. Sutherland ("The Organization of the Abraham Promise Narratives," *ZAW* 95 [1983] 337-43) is prepared to limit the Abraham narratives to 12:1–19:19, which are framed by two genealogies, Terah's (11:27-32) and Nahor's (22:20-24). See esp. p. 339 and his palistrophe on p. 340. But one should not see 22:20-24 as a banal conclusion to the dramatic story of 22:1-19. Rendsburg (*Redaction of Genesis,* pp. 29-30) notes evidence of the mastery of the compiler of the Abraham cycle in comparing its introduction (the genealogy of Terah, 11:17-32) with its conclusion (the genealogy of Nahor, 22:20-24). For example, in both a

The genealogy of Nahor's introduced with the same phrase as was the binding of Isaac: *wayᵉhî 'aḥᵃrê haddᵉḇārîm hā'ēlleh* (v. 1). This similarity in itself should alert us to observing some connection between the narrative and the genealogy. In the narrative Abraham did not know that he was being tested. Nor did he know that he would not have to sacrifice Isaac. In the genealogy he is unaware of his brother Nahor, whom Abraham has not seen since he has left Haran, and of Nahor's children, if any. This information is revealed now to Abraham (v. 1) some time after he has faithfully taken Isaac to Moriah's altar and returned to Beer-sheba. He who at times despaired of ever fathering a child by Sarah, and who came within a hair's breadth of executing the son God gave to him and Sarah, is now apprised of brother Nahor's fertility and the blessings of God on him as well. Such an announcement must have been for Abraham "an extra confirmation, even an eye-opener, of God's dedication."[8]

THE NEW TESTAMENT APPROPRIATION

All agree that Gen. 22 surfaces repeatedly in the NT. The question is how to interpret the NT reading of Gen. 22. Jewish tradition places more emphasis on Isaac's role than on Abraham's. In these sources, especially the Targums, Isaac is actually offered and sheds his blood, thus providing expiation for the sins of Israel.[1] Because of these emphases, some suggest that Paul, far from

---

grandchild is mentioned (Lot, 11:27; Rebekah, 22:23) who is to play a significant role in the immediately following chapters. On the introduction of Rebekah in 22:23, see N. M. Sarna, "The Anticipatory Use of Information as a Literary Feature of the Genesis Narratives," in *The Creation of Sacred Literature: Composition and Redaction of the Biblical Text,* ed. R. E. Friedman (Berkeley: University of California, 1981), pp. 78-80.

8. J. P. Fokkelman, "Time and the Structure of the Abraham Cycle," *OTS* 25 (1989) 105-6.

1. The best example of this tendency occurs in the Fragmentary Targ. (also known as Targ. Yerushalmi II): "And Abraham said: The Word of the Lord shall prepare a lamb for Himself. If not, my son, you shall be the burnt offering [22:8]. . . . Isaac answered and said to Abraham his father: Bind my hands properly that I may not struggle in the time of my pain and disturb you and render your offering unfit and be cast into the pit of destruction in the world to come. . . . In that hour the angels of heaven went out and said to each other: Let us go and see the only two just men in the world. The one slays, and the other is being slain. The slayer does not hesitate, and the one being slain stretches out his neck [22:10]. . . . You told me to offer Isaac my son, and to make him dust and ashes before you. But I departed immediately in the morning and did your word with joy and fulfilled it. Now I pray for mercy before you, O Lord God, that when the children of Isaac come to a time of distress, you may remember on their behalf the binding of Isaac their father, and loose and forgive them their sins and deliver them from all distress, so that the generations which follow him may say: In the mountain of the Temple of the Lord, Abraham offered Isaac his son [22:14]."

See also Targ. Jonathan (also known as Targ. Yerushalmi I) on Gen. 22:1: " 'Behold, I [viz., Isaac] am now thirty-seven years old, but were the Holy One, blessed be he, to ask for

inventing the relation between Isaac and Jesus, developed his soteriology at this point from rabbinic tradition.[2]

Committed to the view that the sacrificial soteriology of the NT must be studied in the light of Aqedah developments, R. J. Daly takes the following approach.[3] First, he finds "certain" references to the Aqedah in the NT:

(1) Heb. 11:17-19 is the clearest reference of all. Abraham offered Isaac his only son *(monogenḗ)*[4], believing God was able to raise him up. This idea is not expressly stated in Gen. 22, but may be inferred from 22:5, where Abraham promises to return with his son to the servants. It may have been slightly easier to believe God for this second resurrection when Abraham had already seen his own loins and Sarah's womb revived. Unlike the targumic traditions, the emphasis here is on Abraham, not Isaac. The son does not emerge as an atoning figure as he does in the Aqedah.[5]

Verse 17 speaks first of Abraham who offered up Isaac, and uses the perfect of *prosphérō (proseuḗnochen)* to describe this act, but then a few words later uses the imperfect of this verb *(prosépheren),* which ther RSV renders "he was ready to offer up." The use of the imperfect just after the perfect of the same verb is probably the author's way of stating that Abraham attempted to sacrifice Isaac but was prevented from doing so.[6] Thus Heb. 11 makes the point that Isaac did not die.

---

all my members, I would not deny them to Him.' These words were immediately heard before the Lord of the world. Immediately also, the Word of the Lord tried Abraham." Similarly the Sifre (a halakhic midrash) to Deuteronomy, compiled at the end of the 4th century A.D., speaks of "Isaac who bound himself upon the altar" (§ 32). Sources earlier than either the Targs. or the Sifre that speak of Isaac's voluntary involvement include Josephus (*Ant.* 1.13.1-4), who says that Isaac, upon hearing from Abraham that he was to be the victim, felt joy and ran to the altar (§§ 228-29, 232); and 4 Macc. 16:20 (1st century A.D.): "Isaac offered himself to be a sacrifice for the righteous. Isaac did not shrink when he saw the knife lifted against him by his father's hand." As I have indicated earlier (see p. 117 and n. 73), in Jewish medieval literature the emphasis was even more pervasive on Isaac's consent and enthusiastic participation in the Aqedah and on the expiatory nature of his actual death (e.g., "Isaac said to him: Father, have no fears. May it be His will that one quarter of my blood serve as atonement for all Israel"; see Spiegel, *Last Trial,* pp. 44ff.).

2. See I. Levi, "Le sacrifice d'Isaac et la mort de Jésus," *REJ* 64 (1912) 161-84; H. J. Schoeps, "The Sacrifice of Isaac in Paul's Theology," *JBL* 65 (1946) 385-92. G. Vermes associates Isa. 53 with Gen. 22 ("Redemption and Genesis xxii," in *Scripture and Tradition in Judaism* [Leiden: Brill, 1961], pp. 193-227).

3. See R. J. Daly, "The Soteriological Significance of the Sacrifice of Isaac," *CBQ* 39 (1977) 45-75.

4. On *monogenḗ* see my brief discussion of John 3:16 below.

5. See P. R. Davies and B. D. Chilton, "The Aqedah: A Revised Tradition History," *CBQ* 40 (1978) 529-30.

6. H. W. Attridge, *The Epistle to the Hebrews,* Hermeneia (Philadelphia: Fortress, 1989), p. 334. He calls the imperfect "conative." See also F F. Bruce, *Epistle to the Hebrews,* NICNT, rev. ed. (Grand Rapids: Eerdmans, 1990), p. 301 n. 134.

Verse 19 states that Abraham received Isaac back "figuratively speaking" (RSV, NIV, JB; *en parabolē*). Other translations of *en parabolē* include: "parabolically" (Buchanan), "as a type" (Bruce), "as a symbol" (Attridge), "in a sense" (NEB). Heb. 11, however, does not say as a type or symbol of what. Bruce's suggestion that Abraham received Isaac back "as a type," i.e., in a manner that prefigured the resurrection of Christ, is perhaps too narrow. While the phrase may embrace that possibility, it also includes the forthcoming resurrection that all faithful disciples can anticipate.[7]

(2) In Jas. 2:21-23 James evokes Abraham as an illustration of justification by works. Abraham was justified by works when he offered Isaac on the altar. NIV's "considered righteous" is an improvement over RSV's "justified by works." If James is making a case for the position that a sinner can be made right with God by works or performance, then he is in clear contradiction with Pauline thought, which declares that this is impossible. James, however, is not using "works" in the sense of works that count for one's salvation; rather, by "works" James means acts of charity and mercy, as the preceding verses (vv. 1-17) make abundantly clear. James is speaking ethically rather than forensically, morally rather than judicially. Abraham's faith in God was more than cerebral. It informed his life and his life-style (note the pl. "works," not the sing.), culminating in the offering of Isaac. For James these choices made throughout his life are a fulfillment of Gen. 15:6 (Jas. 2:23).

James's use of this verse differs from that of Paul (see Rom. 4:3; Gal. 3:6). For James Gen. 15:3 is a double commentary on the life of Abraham. First, he had faith in God ("Abraham believed God"); second, God declared Abraham righteous whenever Abraham gave expression to that faith. It is such an expression — works not as a merit for salvation but as a mark of salvation — that James is urging on his audience.[8] James illustrates the same principle with Rahab. Here are two vastly different people — a Hebrew patriarch and a Canaanite prostitute — both showing a faith that works. Thus Abraham is not unique. Once again, the emphasis in James is on Abraham, not on Isaac. Aside from Heb. 11:17-19, Jas. 2:21-23 is the only explicit reference to the offering of Isaac in the NT.

7. See Attridge, *Hebrews,* p. 335; Bruce, *Hebrews,* pp. 304-5; J. Swetnam (*Jesus and Isaac: A Study of the Epistle to the Hebrews in the Light of the Aqedah,* AnBib 94 [Rome: Biblical Institute, 1981], pp. 122-23, 128) sees in *en parabolē* a foreshadowing of a receiving from the dead that, in the thought of Hebrews, is preeminently applicable to Christ (à la Bruce). By the way, Swetnam's attempt to see influences of the Aqedah in other portions of Hebrews (2:5-18; 5:7-10; 6:13-15; 9:22) are, in my judgment, unconvincing.

8. R. B. Ward, "The Works of Abraham: James 2:14-26," *HTR* 61 (1968) 283-90; M. Dibelius and H. Greeven, *James,* Hermeneia, tr. M. A. Williams (Philadelphia: Fortress, 1976), pp. 160-66; P. Davids, *Epistle of James,* NIGTC (Grand Rapids: Eerdmans, 1982), pp. 126-32.

(3) In Rom. 8:32 Paul refers to God who "did not spare his own Son but gave him up for us all." Here the language of "not sparing" (or withholding) is close to Gen. 22:16.[9] Does Paul mean to suggest that God's handing over his Son is to be compared with Abraham handing over his son? That seems quite possible, but Paul does not make the analogy. We have to read it, imaginatively, into the text and thus I am less inclined than Daly to read Rom. 8:32 as a certain reference to the Aqedah. For a third time, if this is the case, however, the emphasis is once again on Abraham, or at least on Abraham's God. Note that many of the items listed by Paul that might separate one from Christ — tribulation, distress, persecution, famine, etc. — come straight out of the cursing-for-disobedience language of Deut. 27 and 28. For Paul such traumas are not divine judgments but part and parcel of the Christian life. For Paul the one sure evidence that God loves us and is for us is not one's pleasant circumstances but that God did not spare his own Son.

Under "probable" references Daly lists (1) John 3:16, because of its observation that God "gave his only Son"; *tón monogenḗ* is found also for Heb. *yāḥîḏ* in Aquila's Greek version (although the LXX itself reads *agapētós,* "beloved");[10] (2) Mark 1:11, because of "you are my beloved Son" (cf. Gen. 22:2);[11] (3) 1 Cor. 15:4, a reference to Christ being raised "on the third day in accordance with the scriptures," for it was on the third day that Abraham's obedience passed its climactic test;[12] (4) Rom. 4:16-25, because Abraham put his faith in God who gives life to the dead (a capacity for resurrection) and who calls things that are not as though they were (a capacity for creation). But the issue in Rom. 4 is not Abraham's offering of Isaac but Sarah's conception of Isaac. Unlike James, Paul does not here appeal to Gen. 22 to illustrate entrance into the life of faith, which is the major concern of Rom. 4.[13]

9. See N. A. Dahl, "The Atonement — An Adequate Reward for the Akedah? (Rom. 8:32)," in *Neotestamentica et Semitica,* Fest. Matthew Black, ed. E. E. Ellis and M. Wilcox (Edinburgh: T. & T. Clark, 1969), pp. 15-29. The verb *pheídomai* is used in both Rom. 8:32 and the LXX of Gen. 22:16.

10. For a further study of *monogenḗs,* see D. Moody, "God's Only Son: The Translation of John 3:16 in the Revised Standard Version," *JBL* 72 (1953) 213-19. Brown (*John,* 1:13-14) has stated: "*Monogenēs* describes a quality of Jesus, his uniqueness, not what is called in Trinitarian theology his 'procession.' It reflects Heb. *yāḥîd,* 'only, precious,' which is used in Gen xxii 2, 12, 16, of Abraham's son Isaac. . . . Isaac was Abraham's uniquely precious son, but not his only begotten."

11. See C. S. Mann, *Mark,* AB (Garden City, NY: Doubleday, 1986), p. 201, who sees in Mark 1:11 combined motifs from the soteriological ideas of Gen. 22, a messianic designation in Ps. 2, and the Servant of Isa. 42.

12. See J. E. Wood, "Isaac Typology in the New Testament," *NTS* 14 (1968) 588-89.

13. In *Handbook on the Pentateuch* (Grand Rapids: Baker, 1982), p. 112, I suggest how Paul and James view differently the function of faith in Abraham.

Daly's "possible" references include 1 Pet. 1:19-20 and John 1:29, which designate Jesus as "a lamb" and "the lamb of God," respectively. Does the binding of Isaac provide the stimulus for these depictions of Jesus as the lamb of God? Might not the Servant figure in Isaiah provide an even better antecedent, or the Passover lamb of Exodus? Not until Epistle of Barnabas 7:3 (2nd century A.D.) is Isaac clearly identified as a "type" of Christ. One major difference between the two stories prevented the NT writers from clearly connecting Christ's death with Isaac typology: In Gen. 22 the son is spared, but in the Christian story the Son is not spared.[14]

To summarize, the NT writers appropriate the story of the offering of Isaac primarily to make a point about Abraham — his faith, his works, his loving obedience. There is no evidence that Paul's theology, contra that observable in Jewish rabbinical and midrashic literature, is informed by later Jewish expansions of the biblical narrative. Other references to the Aqedah in the NT, outside Heb. 11 and Jas. 2, are at best only allusory, with words like "only" or "beloved" or "lamb" or "withhold."

L. ABRAHAM'S PURCHASE OF A FAMILY BURIAL PLOT (23:1-20)

1. THE DEATH OF SARAH (23:1-9)

1 *Sarah's life was 127 years — such were the years of Sarah's life.*[1]

14. See G. L. Carey, "The Lamb of God and Atonement Theories," *TynBul* 32 (1981) 102-3. It was the ram, not Isaac, that gave up its life, and thus in a sense the ram is the real type of Christ. Compare the poem by the Israeli poet Yehuda Amichai, "The True Hero of the Aqedah":

The angel went home.
Isaac went home
Abraham and God went home too.
But the true hero of the *Aqedah*
Was the ram.

(tr. E. A. Coffin, *Michigan Quarterly Review* 22/3 [1983] 445)

See also Walters, *TJT* 3 (1987) 324-27, esp. 326, who notes that "the link between this story and the New Testament is not some superficial resemblances between Jesus and Isaac or the ram, but the *fundamental likeness in the way God operates.*"

1. LXX and Vulg. omit the last three words of MT, *š^enê ḥayyê śārâ,* lit., "years of the life of Sarah." Many commentators, e.g., Speiser, Westermann, see this textual evidence as a sign that *š^enê* has been dislocated from the beginning of the verse, where it should precede *ḥayyê*. This change would yield the more common expression *š^enê ḥayyê,*

2 *Sarah died in Kiriath-arba, that is, Hebron, in the land of Canaan. Abraham went in to wail for Sarah and to weep for her.*[2]
3 *Then Abraham arose from mourning*[3] *before his deceased one and spoke to the Hittites:*
4 *"Although I am a resident alien*[4] *under you, sell me a burial place from*[5] *your holdings that I may inter my dead away from me."*
5 *The Hittites answered Abraham: "Please,*[6]
6 *listen to us, my lord! You are God's elect one*[7] *among us. In the choicest of our burial sites bury your dead. None of us would refuse*[8] *you his burial ground for the burial of your dead."*
7 *Abraham began to bow*[9] *before the local citizenry, the Hittites,*
8 *and pleaded with them: "If you find it in your heart*[10] *that I bury my*

"years of the life of," which appears also in 25:17; cf. similar expressions in 25:7; 47:8, 9, 28.

2. The suffix on *lib̠kōṯāh* is a dative suffix, "for her." Cf. *UT,* 125:25: *al tbkn,* "weep not for me." BDB, p. 113b, suggests "and bewail her," reading the pronominal suffix as an accusative, and then citing Gen. 37:35; 50:3; Lev. 10:6; Num. 20:29; Deut. 21:13; 34:8; Jer. 8:23 as parallels. In all of these cited cases, however, the accusative is preceded by *'eṯ*. This is not so in Gen. 23:2.

3. For *wayyāqom* in reference to arising from mourning one's dead cf. Ruth 1:6 and J. Sasson, *Ruth* (Baltimore: Johns Hopkins University, 1979), pp. 21-22.

4. Speiser, Westermann, and others take *gēr wᵉṯôšāb̠* as a hendiadys: "sojourner and settler," i.e., "resident alien" (so NAB).

5. "From your holdings" is lit. "with (or from) you" *('immāḵem).* For *'im* meaning "from," see Speiser, *Genesis,* p. 170; M. J. Dahood, "Hebrew-Ugaritic Lexicography vii," *Bib* 50 (1969) 350.

6. MT reads *lô,* "to him." If one accepts the MT here (and in v. 14), then these are the only instances in the entire OT, along with Lev. 11:1, of *lē'mōr,* "saying," being followed by a preposition. Thus with Speiser, *BHS,* et al., I read *lû,* a desiderative particle (cf. GKC, § 110e), for MT *lô*. Cf. also D. Sivan and W. Schniedewind, "Letting Your 'Yes' Be 'No' in Ancient Israel: A Study of the Asseverative *l'* and *hᵃlō',*" *JSS* 38 (1993) 222-24.

7. Heb. *nᵉśî' 'ĕlōhîm,* lit., "prince of God" (see JB "God's prince"). The common rendering "mighty prince" (AV, RSV, NIV, NEB) is also possible; see D. W. Thomas, "A Consideration of Some Unusual Ways of Expressing the Superlative in Hebrew," *VT* 3 (1953) 209-24, esp. pp. 210-19. See further the commentary below.

8. The Hebrew verb behind "refuse" is *yiḵleh* (written with *hē*). By contrast the same verb is written with *aleph* in 8:2, "and the rain stopped" *(wayyikkālē' haggešem).* On the MT's wavering between treating *kl'* as a third *aleph* verb and as a third *hē* verb, see M. Held, "A Faithful Lover in an Old Babylonian Dialogue," *JCS* 15 (1961) 19. Cf. also F. I. Andersen and A. D. Forbes, *Spelling in the Hebrew Bible,* BiBOr 41 (Rome: Biblical Institute, 1986), p. 83.

9. *qûm* is used here in an auxiliary sense. Abraham has already arisen (*wayyāqom,* v. 3).

10. For this sense of *'im-yēš ('eṯ-) napšᵉḵem,* lit., "if your desire [or soul] exists," cf. BDB, p. 661a, § 8; H. W. Wolff, *Anthropology of the Old Testament,* tr. M. Kohl (Philadelphia: Fortress, 1974), p. 16; M. I. Gruber, "Hebrew *da'ăbôn nepeš* 'dryness of

dead away from me, then listen! Intercede[11] *on my behalf with Ephron son of Zohar,*

9 *that he sell me the cave of Machpelah*[12] *which is his, and which is on the edge of his field. At the full price let him sell it to me in your presence for a burial place."*

I am well aware that those who hold to the documentary hypothesis assign the last three chapters in the Abraham narratives to three different sources: ch. 22, E; ch. 23, P; ch. 24, J. Thus the Elohist climaxes his account of Abraham with the offering of Isaac; the Priestly account climaxes with Abraham's interment of Sarah; and the Yahwist concludes with Abraham arranging for the proper selection of Isaac's wife.

Such slicing of the chapters into different sections forces a compartmentalization on the canonical shape of the text, and as a result fails to probe for any connections among the chapters. Both the preceding chapter and this one are concerned with the death of a person very close to Abraham — Isaac's potential death (ch. 22) and Sarah's actual death (ch. 23). Sarah is conspicuously absent from the events surrounding Isaac, and Isaac is not mentioned as being present with his father at Sarah's death. In both cases, then, Abraham endures the heartache alone. The trip from Beer-sheba to Moriah was a wrenching one for Abraham, but so was the trip from Beer-sheba to Hebron.

1 All that we know of Sarah's activities between the age of 90 and 127 is that she gave birth to Isaac and died thirty-seven years later.[13] Such phasing out of a biblical character occurs also with Abraham. The only events associated with Abraham during the last thirty-eight years of his life (from age 137 to 175; 25:7) are the selection of a bride for Isaac and his own remarriage.

While Genesis provides the age of each of the patriarchs at their death (Abraham — Gen. 25:7; Isaac — Gen. 35:28; Jacob — Gen. 47:28), Sarah is the only one of the matriarchs whose age at her death is recorded. Rebekah's death is not even mentioned (apart from the reference to her burial in 49:31),

---

throat': from symptom to literary convention," *VT* 37 (1987) 366; Z. Zevit, "Phoenician NBŠ/NPŠ and its Hebrew Semantic Equivalents," *MAARAV* 5-6 (1990) 340.

11. The basic meaning of *pāgaʿ* is "to meet, encounter." By extension it means to pray, speak, either to God (Jer. 27:18; 36:25) or to human beings (Ruth 1:16 and here).

12. Every time Machpelah occurs in the Bible it occurs with the definite article (23:9, 17; 25:9, etc.), which indicates that it is not a personal name. Machpelah may be connected with the Hebrew root *kpl,* meaning "double" (a double cave, or a cave in which couples were buried?). Cf., e.g., the LXX's rendering of MT's *wᵉyitten lî ʾeṯ mᵉʿāraṯ hammakpēlâ* as "give me the double cave" *(tó spélaion tó diploún).* The OT uses *hammakpēlâ* with some fluidity. In Gen. 23:9 and 25:9 it is a cave, in 23:17 it is a place, and in 49:30 it refers to a field.

13. See 17:17, 21; 21:1-7.

and Rachel's demise is only briefly noted (35:19). Cassuto explained the 127 years of Sarah's life as a round number (120) plus an even more significant number (7), and made a comparison with the number of provinces in the Persian empire that Dan. 6:2 (Eng. 1) gave as 120, but which Esth. 1:1; 8:9; 9:30 increased by seven (127).[14] It is also possible that Sarah's life span represents the maximum life span (120; see Gen. 6:3), increased by 7, the number of fullness.[15] Gen. 25:20 indicates that Isaac married Rebekah three years after his mother's death.

2 Chapter 23 shares with ch. 22 the concern to update the narrative to the narrator's time. Abraham's name for Moriah persisted into a later period (22:14), and *Kiriath-arba* had been renamed *Hebron* by the narrator's time. *Kiriath-arba* means "city of four,"[16] a tetrapolis. Cf. the name "Beer-sheba," which means "well of seven." "Four" more than likely refers to four confederated settlements of families around Hebron. Josh. 15:13 names "Arba" as the father of Anak, who was apparently the progenitor of the Anakim, the dreaded inhabitants of Canaan whom the Israelites encountered (cf. Deut. 2:10-11, 21; 9:2).

Hebron would be an excellent choice of an alternative name for Kiriath-arba if Hebrew *ḥeḇrôn* is connected with *ḫibrum* in the Mari documents. Malamat has defined *ḫibrum* as a "separate union of families closely linked together within the larger unit of the clan or tribe . . . an association of wandering families which had been drawn into closer union as a result of their nomadic status."[17] In a number of instances the renaming of places is occasioned by a change in ownership. In addition to Gen. 23 cf. Num. 32:42 (Kenath: Nobah); Deut. 3:15 (Argob: Havvothjair); Josh. 15:15-17 (Kiriath-sepher: Debir); Judg. 1:17 (Zephath: Hormah); Josh. 19:47/Judg. 18:29 (Laish: Dan); 2 Sam. 5:7-9 (the stronghold of Zion: city of David).[18] With the exception of Gen. 23, however, each of these name changes came about as a result of new ownership claimed through battle and seizure.

3-4 The occupants of Kiriath-arba are called *Hittites* (lit., "children/sons of Heth"; so Speiser/JB). Many scholars question a Hittite presence as far south in Canaan as Hebron, just as many doubt the existence of the

14. Cassuto, *Genesis,* 2:59.

15. C. J. Labuschagne, "The Life Spans of the Patriarchs," *OTS* 25 (1989) 124.

16. Kiriath as "city" may be reflected in "Judas Iscariot," which is often explained as meaning "Judas man of Kiriath"; see G. Buchanan, *ISBE,* 2:1151-52; E. P Blair, *IDB,* 2:1006-7.

17. A. Malamat, "Man and the Bible: Some Patterns of Tribal Organization and Institutions," *JAOS* 82 (1962) 145.

18. See O. Eissfeldt, "Renaming in the Old Testament," in *Words and Meanings: Essays Presented to David Winton Thomas,* ed. P. R. Ackroyd and B. Lindars (Cambridge: Cambridge University, 1968), p. 71.

Philistines in the patriarchal age (see ch. 21). Are the Hittites of Gen. 23 the same as the Hittites who established themselves as a great empire in Asia Minor throughout most of the 2nd millennium B.C.? Or are they distinct?

In favor of the former view (the Hittites of the Bible are the Hittites of the Anatolian-Syrian empire), a minority view to be sure, are the following data. (1) Each of the lists (18 altogether) of nations whom the Israelites are to drive out of Canaan includes the Hittites.[19] (2) This listing dovetails with Gen. 10:15, which identifies Heth as the son of Canaan, and with Josh. 1:4, which calls Canaan "the land of the Hittites." (3) M. R. Lehmann has suggested that the transaction in Gen. 23 between Abraham and Ephron the Hittite is best explained by two laws in the Hittite law code, a code that dates to about the mid-2nd millennium B.C.[20] This connection has been denied and challenged by some (see our commentary below), but not convincingly in our judgment. (4) More and more scholars are recognizing the presence of Hittite words behind some of the Hebrew vocabulary of the OT.[21] (5) Although his conclusions are debated by many, G. E. Mendenhall has made a strong case for the close parallelism in structure between the Sinaitic covenant (both the initial act and acts of renewal) and second-millennium B.C. Hittite political suzerainty covenants.[22] (6) It has often been observed that the names of individual Hittites in the OT seem to be Semitic in meaning: Ephron (Gen. 23), Zohar (23:8), Judith, Beeri, Basemath, Elon (26:34), Adah (36:2), Ahimelech (1 Sam. 26:6), Uriah (2 Sam. 11).[23] While the name Ahimelech

19. See, e.g., Gen. 15:20; Exod. 3:8; Deut. 7:1; Josh. 3:10; Judg. 3:5. To some this fact is totally unimpressive. For example, J. Van Seters ("The terms 'Amorite' and 'Hittite'," *VT* 22 [1972] 78-80) makes much of the fact that all references to Hittites in the Pentateuch are from P. For P, "Hittite" is a rhetorical term, largely synonymous with "Canaanite," a kind of catchall phrase for the original inhabitants of Canaan. Does this mean, then, that all the nations mentioned in pentateuchal sources are used rhetorically? If not, why are only the Hittites so used?

20. See M. R. Lehmann, "Abraham's Purchase of Machpelah and Hittite Law," *BASOR* 129 (1953) 15-18.

21. See C. Rabin, "Hittite Words in Hebrew," *Or* 32 (1963) 113-29; H. A. Hoffner, Jr., "Second Millennium Antecedents to the Hebrew *'ôb*," *JBL* 86 (1967) 385-401; idem, "Hittite *tarpiš* and Hebrew *terāphim*," *JNES* 27 (1968) 61-68; J. Ebach, "Unterweltsbeschwörung im Alten Testament, Teil II," *UF* 12 (1980) 205-20; W. Helck, "Ein sprachliches Indiz für die Herkunft der Philister," *BN* 21 (1983) 31; Y. L. Arbeitman, "The Hittite is Thy Mother: An Anatolian Approach to Genesis 23 (Ex Indo-Europea Lux)," in *Bono Homini Donum: Essays in Historical Linguistics in Memory of J. Alexander Kerns*, ed. Y. L. Arbeitman and A. R. Bomhard (Amsterdam: John Benjamins, 1981), pp. 889-1018.

22. See G. E. Mendenhall, *Law and Covenant in Israel and the Ancient Near East* (Pittsburgh: Biblical Colloquium, 1955); idem, "Covenant," *IDB*, 1:714-23.

23. See H. A. Hoffner, Jr., "Some Contributions of Hittitology to Old Testament Study," *TynBul* 20 (1969) 32.

is patently Semitic, new studies are suggesting that some of the Hittite onamastica of the OT may be analyzed as Hittite or Hurro-Hittite, including the names Ephron and Uriah.[24] (7) Ezek. 16:3, 45, "your mother was a Hittite, and your father was an Amorite," may preserve a memory in Israel's past of a distinct Hittite presence in Canaan. (8) Archeologists have found near Bethel a crater that dates to the late 1200s and is Hittite in style.[25] (9) A text from the Tell el-Amarna collection (14th century B.C.) tells of a letter from Abdu-Ḫeba (or Abdiheba), "king" of Jerusalem, to Pharaoh requesting help against those attacking his city. "Abdi" is Semitic for "servant" and "Ḫeba" is a Hittite or Hurrian goddess. Hence the name means "servant of Heba."[26]

Abraham identifies himself to his hosts as a *resident alien (gēr-wᵉṯôšāḇ),* a combination of terms found elsewhere in the OT.[27] The addition of *tôšāḇ* to *gēr* indicates even more forcefully that Abraham viewed himself as one with tenant status only before the Hebronite Hittites. Even though the text said that Abraham "sojourned" *(gûr)* in Gerar (20:1), he did not draw attention to his subordinate status before Abimelech when Sarah was alive. But after her death he is much more deferential to his hosts. Had he called himself only a *gēr* he would have been drawing attention only to his immigrant status. *tôšāḇ* adds the element of socioeconomic dependence. The irony is that Abraham, who has been promised the land both for himself and for his

24. See Arbeitman, "The Hittite is Thy Mother."

25. See J. A. Callaway and R. E. Cooley, "A Salvage Excavation at Raddana in Bireh," *BASOR* 201 (1971) 15-19; A. Kempinski, "Hittites in the Bible," *BAR* 5/4 (1979) 38-39, 43.

26. See C. J. Mullo Weir, in *Documents from Old Testament Times,* ed. D. Winton Thomas (New York: Harper & Row, 1961), p. 40.

27. See Lev. 25:23, 35, 47; Num. 35:15. The three verses in Leviticus use *ʿim* after the phrase in question to mean "under," as does Gen. 23:4. On the relation between *gēr* and *tôšāḇ,* see D. Kellermann, *TDOT,* 2:448: "Presumably *toshabh* denotes, 'from the economic standpoint, the same man that is called a *ger* when speaking of his legal status, and thus one who, without any property of his own is taken in by a fully enfranchised Israelite citizen' " (Kellermann is quoting from K. Ellinger, *Leviticus,* HAT 4 [Tübingen: Mohr (Siebeck), 1966], 293-94). In Lev. 25:23 Yahweh describes his own people as *gērîm wᵉṯôšāḇîm* to him; hence, they may not sell or alienate the land for they are but God's tenants on Yahweh's land. In Lev. 25:35, *gēr wᵉṯôšāḇ* refers to one who has mortgaged his land to another and has become a tenant on his own land. The *tôšāḇ* is seized in default of his debt and forced to work off his indebtedness. In Lev. 25:47 an Israelite could become indentured to a non-Israelite, i.e., a *gēr wᵉṯôšāḇ.* Twice in Leviticus (22:10 and 25:6) *tôšāḇ* is used alongside of *śāḵîr.* Levine (*Leviticus,* JPS Torah Commentary [Philadelphia: Jewish Publication Society, 1989], pp. 149, 170-71) suggests "hired laborer" for *śāḵîr* and "bound laborer" for *tôšāḇ.* The *tôšāḇ* was bound to reside in the home of the creditor until he paid off his debt, or else lived on the estate of his employer. On the different meanings of *gēr* in the Hexateuch, and on the LXX's different translations of the word — esp. in Gen. 23:4 — cf. T. Meek, "The Translation of *Gêr* in the Hexateuch," *JBL* 49 (1930) 172-80, esp. pp. 176, 179-80.

descendants, reduces himself to the status of a *tôšāḇ* without rights, and solicits a piece of property on which to bury his wife.

5-6 Abraham may think of himself as a *gēr-wᵉṯôšāḇ,* but to these Hittites he is *God's elect one* (Heb. *nᵉśî' 'ĕlōhîm,* lit., "prince of God"). The expression is too graphic to be a greeting of formal courtesy. Despite Abraham's self-denigration, his hosts greet him as an individual of some importance. Abraham is no marginal person. Given his contacts with people like Pharaoh (ch. 12) and Abimelech (ch. 20), one might expect that he would be considered royalty. Recall also that God promised that Abraham would be the father of kings (17:6).

This point is all the more clear in the LXX, which only here translates *nāśî'* with *basileús,* "king."[28] The normal LXX translation for *nāśî'* is *árchōn,* "leader, chieftain" (cf. Vulg. *princeps,* "prince"). In Hebrew society a *nāśî'* is an elected chieftain, one who is a presiding officer, the exact opposite of a *gēr.* Speiser connects *nāśî'* quite closely with *nāśā',* and renders the phrase here "the elect of God" (so also NAB).[29] Scholars still debate the possible connections between Heb. *nāśî',* Egyp. *nsw,* "king" (in Upper Egypt), and Sum. *ensi,* "ruler." To these two non-Hebrew words we can now add from Ebla *na-se₁₁,* "prefect."[30]

Having given Abraham a royal welcome, the residents of Hebron are quite willing to offer him space in which to bury Sarah. Perhaps they would even have given the plot to Abraham, much as Araunah offered the threshing floor to David gratis (2 Sam. 24:22). In refusing their generous offer Abraham is displaying the attitude he reflected earlier after the battle with the kings, when he did not help himself to the booty (14:22-23). This is the only instance in Genesis where a speech or address begins with some form of the verb *šāmaʿ.* This special form of address is found again only in Chronicles (1 Chr. 28:2; 2 Chr. 13:4; 15:2; 20:20; 28:11).[31]

7 Abraham addresses himself again to *the local citizenry* (Heb. *ʿam-*

28. See C. H. Gordon, "Abraham the Basileus," *Jahrbuch für kleinasiatische Forschung* 2 (1965) 227-30; M. H. Gottstein, "*nsy' 'lhm* (Gen. xxiii, 6)," *VT* 3 (1953) 298-99.

29. See Speiser, *Genesis,* p. 170; idem, "Background and Function of the Biblical *nāśī,*" *CBQ* 25 (1963) 111-17, esp. p. 116. M. H. Gottstein ("*nsy' 'lhym* [Gen. xxiii 6]," *VT* 3 [1953] 298-99) translates "one brought along by God." In his larger discussion of *nāśî'* in Ezekiel (*Theology of the Program of Restoration of Ezekiel 40–48,* HSMS 10 [Missoula, MT: Scholars, 1976], p. 162), J. Levenson says of *nāśî'* in Gen. 23:6, "from context clearly an exalted position rather than a modest secular civil office."

30. See M. J. Dahood, "Ebla, Ugarit, and the Bible," in Pettinato, *Archives of Ebla,* pp. 278-79.

31. See S. Japhet, "The Supposed common authorship of Chron. and Ezra-Neh. investigated anew," *VT* 18 (1968) 358-59.

hā'āreṣ, lit., "people of the land") in the role of a *gēr-wᵉṯôšāḇ*. Although the expression *'am-hā'āreṣ* is often a technical term designating a specific social or political class within the population of a country, here it is used in the most general manner — the local citizenry.[32]

8-9 Abraham insists on buying a burial plot for Sarah, and to that end asks the Hebronites to persuade Ephron[33] to sell him the cave of Machpelah, located near the edge of Ephron's property.[34] This feature in the story has led to the belief that the transaction between Abraham and Ephron reflects Hittite law, as I noted above. The two laws under review in the Hittite law code read as follows:

> 46: If in a village anyone holds fields under socage as inheritance — if the fields have all been given to him, he shall render the services; if the fields have been given to him only to a small part, he shall not render the services, they shall render them from his father's house. If he usurps fields of the estate-leaver or the people of the village give a field (to him), he shall render the services.
>
> 47: If anyone holds fields as a gift from the king, he shall not render the services. The king will take a loaf from (his) table and give it to him. — If anyone buys all the fields of a craftsman, he shall render the services. If he buys a great (part of) the fields he shall not render the services. If he *usurps* the fields or the people of the village give them (to him), he shall render the services.[35]

If these two laws (esp. no. 47) provide the legal background to Gen. 23, then they explain why Abraham wished to purchase only a cave, and why Ephron insisted on selling nothing or everything. Purchasing only a section of the land meant that Abraham would not have the obligation to bear levies ("render the services") on the real estate. But if Ephron can unload the whole piece of land, then his feudal obligations on it will cease.

32. See E. W. Nicholson, "The Meaning of the Expression *'am hā'āreṣ* in the Old Testament," *JSS* 10 (1965) 59-66; A. R. Hulst, *THAT,* 2:299-301; de Vaux, *Ancient Israel,* 1:70-72. N. K. Gottwald (*The Tribes of Yahweh* [Maryknoll, NY: Orbis, 1979], pp. 510 and 779 n. 513) is inclined to give to *hā'ām* in 23:7 the meaning of an *'apiru*-like band of retainers around a prominent leader.

33. Ephron is further identified as the son of Zohar. N. Sarna ("Genesis Chapter 23: The Cave of Machpelah," *HS* 23 [1982] 19) notes how rarely the OT records the father's name in the case of a non-Israelite. For another instance cf. Itamor the father of Shechem. For both Zohar and Ephron as personal names connoting a color see A. Brenner, *Colour Terms in the Old Testament,* JSOTSup 21 (Sheffield: University of Sheffield, 1982), pp. 44, 116-18, 157.

34. For burial in a cave cf. John 11:38.

35. Translation of A. Goetze, *ANET,* p. 191, §§ 46, 47.

M. R. Lehmann's explanation of Gen. 23 has met with both approval and disapproval.[36] H. Petschow, G. Tucker, and J. Van Seters suggest that Gen. 23 represents a contract known as a dialogue document (i.e., an interchange between buyer and seller), a form that occurs for the first time in the 1st millennium B.C. Hence, Gen. 23 is a late composition that cannot shed any light on the historical Abraham. But the fact that such "dialogue documents" can now be traced back to the early 2nd millennium B.C. vitiates this argument.[37]

If it is difficult to agree with Petschow, et al., that Gen. 23 is a dialogue document from Neo-Assyrian or Neo-Babylonian times (for it is only the report of a transaction, not an actual deed or contract, as we have in Jer. 32:8-15), it is equally hard to believe that Abraham was as familiar with the intricacies of Hittite jurisprudence as Lehmann's analysis would demand. What we may have instead is a "characteristic Hebrew description of the oral manoeuvering of two parties prior to agreeing on a transaction."[38] It parallels the exchange between David and Araunah over the purchase of Araunah's threshing floor (2 Sam. 24:18-25; 1 Chr. 21:22-25), even to the point that David insists on paying the full price for the property. Like Abraham before him, David believes that the property cannot legally become his unless he pays the full, legitimate price (1 Chr. 21:24). To receive the property for free could be an insidious way of the original proprietor retaining actual ownership of the land. It is probable that Abraham's request for a spot on the edge of

36. Lehmann, *BASOR* 129 (1953) 15-18. For approval see C. H. Gordon, *Ancient Near East,* p. 124; idem, *The Common Background of Greek and Hebrew Civilizations,* 2nd ed. (New York: Norton, 1965), p. 94. For disapproval see H. Petschow, "Die neubabylonische Zwiegesprächsurkunde und Genesis 23," *JCS* 19 (1965) 103-20; G. Tucker, "The Legal Background of Genesis 23," *JBL* 85 (1966) 77-84; Van Seters, *Abraham in History and Tradition,* pp. 98-100; Hoffner, *TynBul* 20 (1969) 33-37.

37. See D. J. Wiseman, "Abraham in History and Tradition," *BSac* 134 (1977) 130 n. 29; K. A. Kitchen, *Ancient Orient and Old Testament* (Chicago: Inter-Varsity, 1966), pp. 154-56; idem, *The Bible in Its World* (Downers Grove, IL: Inter-Varsity, 1978), p. 71.

38. Hoffner, *TynBul* 20 (1969) 35 n. 23. R. Westbrook has drawn attention to several passages (Gen. 23:20; 25:9-10; 49:32) that strongly suggest that the Hittites (lit., "son/children of Heth") were not just observers but actual vendors in this transaction. He parallels their role to other instances of land transfer between private individuals that takes the form of a tripartite transaction in which, in addition to the two individuals involved, the king makes a gift of the same item to the alienee. Such a gift, really a fictitious one, provides the alienee with even more extensive rights, given the fact that the buyer is now in possession of a royal gift. Such tripartite transactions are found in ancient Near Eastern literature from Elamite documents of 1600 B.C. down to documents from Ugarit. Thus, according to Westbrook, while Gen. 23 might reflect some form of a dialogue document, it is only the result of the "editing of an essentially ancient source." See Westbrook, "Purchase of the Cave of Machpelah," in *Property and the Family in Biblical Law,* JSOTSup 113 (Sheffield: JSOT, 1991), pp. 24-35.

Ephron's field is dictated more by modesty than by a desire to avoid payment of land dues. After all, how precocious can a *gēr* be? His position restricts him to minimal privileges.

2. ABRAHAM AND EPHRON (23:10-20)

10 *Ephron was present*[1] *with the Hittites. So Ephron the Hittite replied to Abraham in the hearing of the Hittites, even*[2] *of all who came in by the city gate:*

11 *"Indeed,*[3] *my lord, hear me out! The field I give*[4] *you and the cave on it I give you too. Before my own people I give it to you. Bury your deceased one!"*

1. It is difficult to know whether here *yōšēḇ* carries its normal meaning of "be present with, live/dwell among," or rather a more specialized political meaning such as "elder, ruler." Gottwald (*Tribes of Yahweh,* pp. 512ff.) has studied instances in the OT in which he claims *yōšēḇ* means "ruler, authority." He does not cite Gen. 23:10 as an instance of this upper-class political nuance for *yōšēḇ,* but Sasson (*Ruth,* p. 107) does. Abraham had earlier used a noun of the verb *yāšaḇ* to identify himself to these people: he called himself a *gēr wᵉṯôšāḇ* (v. 4). The one who was a *tôšāḇ* is now answered by one who is present *(yōšēḇ)* with his people.

2. For the *lᵉ* on *lᵉḵōl* as "indeed, even," see G. R. Driver, "Notes on Two Passages in the Odes of Solomon," *JTS* 25 (1974) 435. See also v. 17 below. Cf. BDB, p. 514b.

3. Scholars have understood MT *lō'* in several ways: as the negative "no" (Z. Zevit, "Expressing denial in Biblical Hebrew and Mishnaic Hebrew, and in Amos," *VT* 29 [1979] 506); as concealing the stative participle *lē',* "O master, my lord" (M. J. Dahood, "Phoenician-Punic Philology," *Or* 46 [1977] 469); as an emphatic *l* as in Ugaritic [expressing a wish or desire, "indeed," "if only," "would that," "please"] (F. C. Fensham, "Ugaritic and the Translation of the Old Testament," *BT* 18 [1967] 73; *BHS; CHAL,* p. 174). C. Rabin pursues a completely different direction, connecting it with a Hurrian imperative form characterized by inserting after the stem the infix *-el-* or *-ol-*. See C. Rabin, "L- with Imperative (Gen. xxiii)," *JSS* 13 (1968) 113-24. I prefer to take it as the emphatic *l*; Dahood's and Rabin's suggestions sound farfetched. It is possible that *lû* could be read as a negative (Zevit; Speiser, *Genesis,* p. 168), but Zevit's citing of Gen. 42:10 as a parallel (Joseph's brothers declare untrue his preceding statement in v. 9 that they are really spies with their "No, my lord") is not adequate. There Joseph has spoken directly to them. They heard his accusation and immediately disavowed it. Here Abraham has not spoken to Ephron but about Ephron: "intercede on my behalf with Ephron son of Zohar that he sell me the cave." Meeting Abraham for the first time, Ephron more likely would begin with a word of emphasis or entreaty than with a negation.

4. On the three uses of the perfect of *nāṯan* in this verse in a legal-commercial context R. Gordis (*The Word and the Book* [New York: Ktav, 1976], p. 98) remarks: "We suggest that the perfect serves to affirm the act in the present, being similar in psychological motivation to the perfect of prophetic certitude." The same use of the perfect of *nāṯan* appears in v. 13. See also E. F. Campbell, Jr., *Ruth,* AB (Garden City, NY: Doubleday, 1975), p. 144.

12 *Abraham bowed before the local citizenry,*[5]

13 *and spoke to Ephron in the presence of the local citizenry. "Yea,*[6] *if you would indeed*[7] *hear me, I will pay the price of the field. Accept it from me that I may bury my deceased one there."*

14 *Ephron answered Abraham: "Please,*[8]

15 *my lord, hear me out! The piece of land is valued at 400 shekels of silver — between you and me, what is that? Then bury your deceased one."*

16 *Abraham accepted Ephron's terms, and so Abraham weighed out to Ephron the silver about which he had spoken in the presence of the children of Heth, 400 shekels of silver at the current market value.*[9]

17 *So Ephron's land in Machpelah, facing Mamre — the field and its cave and all the trees anywhere within the confines of the field*[10] *— passed over legally*[11]

18 *to Abraham as his possession, in the presence of the Hittites, even of all*[12] *who came in by the city gate.*

5. See the discussion of 23:7 above.

6. McEvenue (*Narrative Style of the Priestly Writer,* p. 68 n. 58) draws attention to the colloquial nature of *'aḵ*. Excluding legal texts, it occurs only twice outside dialogue in the Pentateuch (Gen. 7:23; 27:30), and 14 times in dialogue, of which 23:13 is one.

7. See C. F. Whitley, "Some Remarks on *lû* and *lô'*," *ZAW* 87 (1975) 203: "Hebrew *lû* which is normally used to express a wish or desire with the meaning 'would that' has in a few instances the value of 'indeed, verily,' " and then he cites Gen. 23:13. It is not impossible, however, that Abraham, through his use of *lû,* is expressing a wish, a hope that Ephron will hear him out. At this stage in the dialogue it is Ephron who holds the bargaining chips. LXX and SP read *lî,* "to me."

8. I read MT *lô,* "to him," as *lû,* expressing a wish; see the discussion of 23:5 above, and Speiser, *Genesis,* p. 169.

9. Lit., "silver that passes along to the merchant" *(kesep ʿōḇēr lassōḥēr).* For another instance of *kesep* as the subject of *ʿāḇar* see 2 K. 12:5 (Eng. 4). Speiser (*Genesis,* p. 171) notes the parallel Akkadian phrase *maḫīrat illaku,* "the current rate."

10. The mention of trees does not provide further evidence that the transaction conforms to Hittite procedures, as has often been maintained. The clause "*A* sold his fields to *B* along with its *x* and with its *y* and with its everything" appears in the Alalakh texts, in Akkadian texts from Ras Shamra, and in the legal documents from Wadi Murabbaʿat. See Y. Muffs, *Studies in the Aramaic Legal Papyri from Elephantine* (Leiden: Brill, 1969), p. 20 n. 4.

11. *qûm* in vv. 17, 20, lit., "to stand," means here "legally become the property of." See Num. 30:5; Deut. 25:6; Ruth 4:5, and B. Levine, *Leviticus,* p. 176; GKC, § 111k. Four verses in this chapter have begun with *wayyāqom* (vv. 3, 7, 17, 20), two in the first part with Abraham as the subject, and two in the second half with the field as the subject.

12. Following some ancient Hebrew mss. and Targ. mss., I read MT *bᵉḵōl* as *lᵉḵōl,* which yields an exact parallel to v. 10b above.

19 *Abraham then buried Sarah his wife in the cave of the field of Machpelah, facing*[13] *Mamre, that is, Hebron, in the land of Canaan.*
20 *And so the field and the cave on it passed over legally to Abraham as a burial plot*[14] *from the Hittites.*

10-11 Ephron hears Abraham's request and does not need the message brought to him by intermediaries. He wants to make this transaction public so that not only his fellow Hittites know of his offer to Abraham, but so will anyone coming into the city (hence, *even of all*). E. A. Speiser has argued that the phrase "all those who entered at the gate of his [i.e., Ephron's] city" is an idiomatic expression for a group that has a voice in community affairs, that is, the highest city authorities, the city fathers.[15] But our translation suggests that the phrase simply designates anybody — including the city fathers — who enter the city in their daily business.[16] The number of witnesses is swelled by the addition of these passersby. Ephron will do nothing furtively. His willingness to be honest with Abraham contrasts with Abraham's earlier unwillingness to be honest with Pharaoh (ch. 12) and with Abimelech (ch. 20).

Four times Abraham has used the verb *nāṯan* (vv. 4, 9 [2 times], 13). Each time I translated this term by "sell" or "pay." Abraham wishes to buy a portion of Ephron's property from him. He is not looking for a hand-out. Ephron uses the verb *nāṯan* three times in v. 11, and here I have translated it "give."[17] Trying to obtain ownership rights to some property, Abraham is the buyer. Owning the property, Ephron will impress Abraham with his magnanimity — he is the giver.

12-13 For a second time (see v. 7) Abraham bows before his hosts. (See also 18:2; 19:1; 24:26, 52; 33:3; 43:28; 48:12 for other "bowing" inci-

13. There may be a wordplay here on "facing *[ʿal p^{e}nê]* Mamre." Abraham now faces Sarah's burial plot; earlier Abraham mourned before his wife (*mēʿal p^{e}nê,* v. 3). Cf. also his use of *mill^{e}pānāy* in v. 4, and *mill^{e}pānay* in v. 8.

14. *qeḇer* by itself means "grave, sepulchre." The expression *ʾ^{a}ḥuzzaṯ qeḇer* is confined in the OT to the patriarchs' burial site at Machpelah (23:4, 9, 20; 49:30; 50:13). Abraham uses this phrase (vv. 4, 9), as does the narrator (v. 20), but the local residents use only *qeḇer* (v. 6). In priestly literature *ʾ^{a}ḥuzzâ* (e.g., Lev. 14:34; 25:13; 24; 27:16, 22, 28) refers to land that belonged to an original owner, i.e., tenured land. But here Abraham acquires this land and becomes its new proprietor.

15. E. A. Speiser, " 'Coming' and 'Going' at the City Gate," *BASOR* 144 (1956) 20-23. Cf. also H. Reviv, "Early Elements and Late Terminology in the Descriptions of Non-Israelite Cities in the Bible," *IEJ* 27 (1977) 189-91.

16. See G. Evans, " 'Coming' and 'Going' at the City Gate — A Discussion of Professor Speiser's Paper," *BASOR* 150 (1958) 28-33; F. S. Frick, *The City in Ancient Israel,* SBLDS 36 (Missoula, MT: Scholars, 1977), pp. 118-19.

17. Speiser (*Genesis,* p. 168) also retains the sell/give nuances of *nāṯan* in Gen. 23; Westermann (*Genesis,* 2:370) renders "give/make a present."

dents.) Now somewhat exasperated, Abraham pushes the case for his purchase of the field. He no longer seeks only the cave, but has now expanded his request to include the entire field, which is really the condition for sale laid down by Ephron (v. 11). Abraham never identifies his deceased wife by name or relationship to these Hittites. In this context Sarah is only *mēṯî,* "my deceased one" (vv. 4, 13). The narrator uses her name (vv. 1, 2, 19), but not Abraham. To use her name before strangers would be meaningless. In many instances so far Abraham has been promised land (12:7; 13:14-17; 15:7, 16, 18-21; 17:8; 22:17). Yet he must negotiate with a Hittite in order to purchase a bit of it to bury his spouse.[18]

14-16 The field costs Abraham *400 shekels.* The piece of property was no bargain for Abraham; *400 shekels* would be more than a hundred pounds of silver. David paid only one-eighth that amount — 50 shekels of silver — for the purchase of the temple site from Araunah (2 Sam. 24:24). Jeremiah paid 17 shekels of silver for his cousin's field in Anathoth (Jer. 32:9). Omri paid fifteen times as much as Abraham — two talents of silver (6,000 shekels) — for the large hill of Samaria (1 K. 16:24). In another patriarchal land transaction Jacob paid 100 *qᵉśîṭâ* (value unknown) for a piece of land in Shechem (Gen. 33:19). But to Ephron 400 shekels is a paltry amount — *between you and me, what is that?* — to pay for a burial site. Ephron plays a bit on Abraham's emotions at this point through an interesting change of word order in v. 15. In v. 11 Ephron's last words to Abraham were "bury your deceased one" *(qᵉḇōr mēteḵā),* imperative-accusative. In v. 15 Ephron's last words to Abraham were "bury your deceased one" *(wᵉʾeṯ mēṯᵉḵâ qᵉḇōr)* accusative (preceded by the direct object indicator)-imperative. The shift in order in v. 15 draws attention to Abraham the widower. Surely 400 shekels is a minuscule amount for one to pay for a piece of land in which to inter one's beloved spouse. Abraham offers no resistance to the amount set by Ephron and does not attempt to persuade Ephron to lower his asking price.

One wonders if the 400 silver shekels was perhaps taken from the 1,000 pieces of silver that Abraham received from Abimelech for Sarah (20:16). Abraham persuaded God to a change of heart over Sodom's destruction, but he cannot persuade Ephron (nor does he even try) to budge from the terms of his offer.

17-18 The field and the cave are the only bit of property over which Abraham actually assumes possession. All of the promises of land to Abraham (13:17; 15:7-8), to Abraham and his descendants (13:15; 17:8), or to his descendants only (12:7; 15:18; 22:17) start here, however undramatically.[19]

18. See E. M. Good, *Irony in the Old Testament* (Philadelphia: Westminster, 1965), p. 97.

19. See McEvenue, *Narrative Style of the Priestly Writer,* p. 142 and n. 77a; B. S.

Perhaps the story of Abraham's purchase of the land serves as a model to later Israel that the taking of their land will also be costly. Nothing will come easily or automatically. Israel taking over Canaanite land will be as difficult as Abraham taking over Ephron's land. But the cost will be moral, not monetary. Abraham's descendants will gain possession of the land not by putting up a large amount of silver shekels, but by obeying Yahweh and his decrees.

19 Precious little in this chapter is given over to Sarah's death (one verse — v. 1) and burial (one verse — v. 19). Vv. 2-18 describe transactions between death and interment. The grief Abraham experienced at Sarah's death (vv. 2b-3a) does not reappear at her time of burial. Later, Abraham himself will be buried here (25:9), as will Isaac (35:27-29) and Jacob (49:30; 50:13). God has no concern about burying the patriarchs privately in an unmarked grave as he did with Moses (Deut. 34:6), for there is no danger, as there was with Moses, that after the demise of the patriarchs a cult of the dead would flourish in their memory and honor. To none of the patriarchs did the people of Israel owe immediate debt as they did to Moses.

20 This verse is a conclusion to vv. 2-19. It seems strange appearing after v. 19 — which would have been a reasonable note on which to conclude. Its placement here points out that the crucial element in this chapter is not Sarah's death, but Abraham's acquisition of land from outsiders. As such, it is a harbinger of things to come.

M. FINDING A WIFE FOR ISAAC (24:1-67)

1. ABRAHAM INSTRUCTS HIS SERVANT (24:1-9)

1 *Abraham had grown old, along in years,*[1] *and Yahweh had blessed him in everything.*

2 *Abraham said to his senior servant*[2] *of his household, who had responsibility for all his belongings: "Put your hand under my thigh,*

Childs, *Old Testament Theology in a Canonical Context* (Philadelphia: Fortress, 1985), p. 219. For a different perspective see Westermann, *Genesis,* 2:376, who argues against a theological interpretation of Gen. 23, and for an interpretation that sees in Gen. 23 information and example for landless exiles who must bury their own dead. But the inclusion of "the land of Canaan" in vv. 2, 19 argues for a theological nuance behind Gen. 23.

1. Lit., "he went in days." Cf. Gen. 18:11; Josh. 13:1; 23:1, 2; 1 K. 1:1. "Days" is used here as a spatial metaphor, something through which one moves. See S. J. DeVries, *Yesterday, Today and Tomorrow,* p. 44 n. 60.

2. Lit., "old of his house" (*z^{e}qan bêṯô*). Abraham is *zāqēn* (v. 1), his servant is *z^{e}qan* among Abraham's household servants.

3 *and I will make you swear*[3] *by Yahweh, God of the heavens and God of the earth, that you will not procure a wife for my son from the daughters of the Canaanites in whose midst I am dwelling,*

4 *but*[4] *you will go to my land, the place of my birth,*[5] *to procure a wife for my son, for Isaac."*

5 *The servant responded: "What if the woman does not wish to follow me to this land? Am I to return*[6] *your son to the land from which you came?"*

6 *But Abraham said to him: "Take my son back there? Absolutely not!*[7]

7 *Yahweh, the God of the heavens who took me from my father's house and the place of my birth, who spoke to me, and swore to me, 'I will give this land to your descendants,' he will send his messenger before you so that you may procure a wife for my son from there.*

8 *If the woman does not wish to follow you, you are free of the obligations*[8] *of this oath of mine. But under no circumstances must you take my son back*[9] *there."*

9 *So the servant put his hand under the thigh of Abraham his master and swore to him about this matter.*

Celibacy was virtually unknown in the OT. Jeremiah is the only person in the OT divinely called to this life-style (Jer. 16:2). Children, many of them, are a blessing from God, and one lives on in one's children and grandchildren.

3. The Hiphil of *šāḇa'* is used here, but the Niphal of *šāḇa'* is used in v. 9 (and in v. 7), suggesting that the causative stem of this verb is used for the imposition of an oath, and that the passive/reciprocal stem is used for the actual act of swearing.

4. *kî,* normally translated "because, for," often means "but, rather" when following a negation (e.g., Deut. 13:10; Isa. 7:8). See R. Westbrook, *Studies in Biblical and Cuneiform Law* (Paris: Gabalda, 1988), p. 99.

5. It is possible that one should read *'el 'arṣî wᵉ'el môlaḏtî* as a hendiadys, "my native land." See also v. 7.

6. *hehāšēḇ 'āšîḇ*. GKC, § 113q, gives instances of the use of the infinitive absolute with a finite verb form in order to strengthen a question.

7. Lit., "Take care lest you return my son there" Speiser (*Genesis,* p. 174) renders "on no account are you to take my son back there." *hiššāmēr (pēn)* is a frequent expression, esp. in Deuteronomy, to convey a strong warning.

8. The verb *nāqâ* means "be clean." In the derived sense it means "be free of obligation" that is imposed by a covenant. Cf. Gen. 44:9-10 and see D. R. Hillers, "*bĕrît 'ām:* 'Emancipation of the People,' " *JBL* 97 (1978) 179.

9. W. L. Holladay (*The Root Šûbh in the Old Testament* [Leiden: Brill, 1958], p. 89) lists 13 instances in which the Hiphil of *šûḇ* is followed by a human object who is accompanied by the person who is the subject yet who acts under his or her own power and will. Gen. 24 supplies 3 of these 13 (vv. 5, 6, 8).

To that end Abraham dispatches a high-ranking servant back to the land of Abraham's nativity to fetch a wife for Isaac. Not just any woman will do, and certainly no Canaanite woman will do. It is interesting that the longest chapter in Genesis is given over to discussion of marriage and not, say, to the creation of the world or the covenant with Abraham. This is a subject that has been only obliquely mentioned since Gen. 2 (or 6:1-4?).

The narrative shifts geographically from one spot to another in an ABBA pattern. There are four scenes, with the first and last the same, and the middle two the same:

(1) Canaan: Abraham and his servant (vv. 1-9)
  (2) Mesopotamia: the servant and Rebekah (vv. 10-28)
  (3) Mesopotamia: the servant and Laban (vv. 29-61)
(4) Canaan: Isaac and Rebekah (vv. 62-67)[10]

Another shift in the narrative involves the change in the two speakers in these four scenes in an ABAB pattern: man and man (vv. 1-9), man and woman (vv. 10-28), man and man (vv. 29-61), man and woman (vv. 62-67). Although dialogue scenes dominate the chapter, Rebekah's conversation is minimal and is limited to offers of refreshment (vv. 18a, 19b), a self-identification (v. 24), an offer of hospitality (v. 25), a statement of consent (v. 58b), and an inquiry (v. 65a).

1 Abraham's life is lived out between the promise of divine blessing (12:2) and the actualization of that promise (24:1). The future "I will bless" is now completed with *Yahweh had blessed.* Prospect has become reality. The fact that the statement of Yahweh's blessing on Abraham follows immediately after a reference to Abraham's advanced age pinpoints one of God's blessings to Abraham — longevity. Other manifestations of that blessing would include his material prosperity, his victory over the eastern kings, the restoration of fertility to Sarah's womb, the birth and survival of Isaac, Abraham's own survival through uncertain times, and the reception of divine promises that signal Abraham and his descendants as a light to the nations.

2 Now an event unfolds that describes one way a blessed man behaves. We do not know who this servant is that is commissioned by Abraham to get a bride for Isaac. The only servant named thus far was Eliezer (15:2), but whether he is Abraham's majordomo in ch. 24 is uncertain. It cannot be one of the two men who accompanied Abraham and Isaac to Moriah, for they are described as *n*e*'ārîm* ("[young] servants," 22:3), but this servant is *z*e*qan* (lit., "old," hence *senior*). Abraham himself cannot assume the responsibility for this trip because

10. This analysis is slightly modified from S. Bar-Efrat, "Some observations on the analysis of structure in biblical narrative," *VT* 30 (1980) 167.

his advanced age will not permit such a long excursion. Nor is Abraham willing to send Isaac himself, as Isaac will later do with Jacob (28:2). The recent ordeal at Moriah and the death of Sarah have no doubt cemented an even closer bond between father and son, making another parting even less desirable.

Abraham instructs his servant: *Put your hand under my thigh,* a prelude to the servant's act of swearing. *thigh* is undoubtedly a euphemism for genitalia, in the light of passages such as Gen. 46:26 and Exod. 1:5, where a man's children are said to come from his thigh. Holding Abraham's membrum in his hand, the servant promises to carry out Abraham's wishes. The signficance of this procedure is uncertain. It is unlikely that this act should be read as a self-imprecation by the servant, calling down sterility on himself or extirpation for his children[11] (but see my comments on v. 8 below). R. D. Freedman has suggested that taking the membrum — now circumcised as a covenant sign — into the hand is a way of invoking the presence of God at this moment between master and servant.[12] Or it may simply be a way in which the servant reassures Abraham that he will honestly and truthfully carry out his master's wish.[13]

One may discover some clue as to the significance of this act by comparing the only two episodes in the OT that connect oath taking with placing the hand under another's thigh: Gen. 24:2 and 47:29. In both cases the one who asks another to place his hand under his thigh is elderly. Abraham is "old, along in years" (24:1), and Jacob/Israel is on his deathbed (49:29); therefore neither Abraham nor Jacob can guarantee that their wishes will be faithfully carried out. The other individual, the one who places his hand on the thigh, is well known to the person requesting the oath (a servant, a son, respectively). In both cases the real concern of Abraham and Jacob is with family matters. Abraham desires the right woman for his son, and Jacob wishes to be buried with his ancestors. Finally, both stories involve a "not-here-but-there" geography (a wife not from Canaan but from Aram-Naharaim (Mesopotamia); buried not in Egypt but in Canaan). In touching the genitalia of Abraham and Jacob, the servant and Joseph are placing themselves under oath faithfully to expedite the last wishes of two elderly patriarchs on family matters. Any attempt to void those wishes will arouse the wrath of the ancestral spirits.[14]

11. Cf., e.g., Speiser, *Genesis,* p. 178. Would Jacob ever have placed his beloved son under such an ominous threat?

12. See R. D. Freedman, " 'Put Your Hand Under My Thigh,' — The Patriarchal Oath," *BAR* 2/2 (1976) 3-4, 42.

13. Note that words such as *testimony, testify, attest* have their origin in Latin *testes,* suggesting the possibility that Roman society had some kind of symbolic gesture of touching (some)one's genitals when an oath was taken.

14. See M. Malul, "More on *paḥad yiṣḥāq* (Genesis xxxi 42, 53) and the oath by

3-4 Earlier Abraham had no problems with the possibility of his wife living with an Egyptian or a Philistine, nor did he himself have any second thoughts about relations with an Egyptian maid. If Abraham knew about the two husbands-to-be of his grandnieces, both Moabites and both pitiful individuals, then that would have been stimulus enough to avoid marriage with outsiders. Or do Abraham's intentions at this point reflect a growing sensitivity to the need to perpetuate the blood line? Abraham does not instruct his servant to select a bride who believes in Yahweh. Religious qualifications of the bride or her family are not part of the agreement. Later chapters reveal that Laban, Rebekah's brother, was a practicing polytheist, who panicked when "his gods" were stolen. The concern is that Isaac's future wife be Aramean and not Canaanite. Isaac must not marry exogamously in Canaan but return to Aram-Naharaim for an endogamous bride.[15] Later in the narrative (vv. 5, 6, 8) Abraham insists that Isaac not relocate in Mesopotamia under any circumstances at all. So, the servant operates under two restrictions vis-à-vis Isaac. Isaac must avoid a local intermarriage and emigration to the land of his father. If Isaac is to inherit the land, he must not marry among those destined to disinherit the land. Nor must Isaac disinherit himself by repatriation to Mesopotamia.[16]

To that end Abraham instructs his servant to *swear by Yahweh,* who is here styled as *God of the heavens and God of the earth.* The phrase *God of the heavens* is frequent in the later portions of the OT (10 times in the Hebrew Bible, and 12 times in the Aramaic portions of Daniel and Ezra). Most often the phrase is used when Hebrews are involved with non-Hebrews. The exception to that is Gen. 24:3, 7. Andrews suggests that the entire expression may be a Hebrew adaptation of an oath formula in which the gods of heaven and the gods of earth are summoned to witness an oath.[17] Abraham's reference to Isaac as *my son* is a laconic reminder that he is now a widower, and to style Isaac as "our son" would not be appropriate.

5 Abraham's convincing his servant to undertake this mission involves the same dynamics as when God attempts to convince one of his servants to undertake a prophetic mission. First is the commission (vv. 3-4, vv. 37-38), then comes an objection (v. 5, v. 39), followed by words of reas-

---

the thigh," *VT* 35 (1985) 192-200, esp. pp. 196-98; idem, "Touching the sexual organs as an oath ceremony in an Akkadian letter," *VT* 37 (1987) 491-92.

15. On exogamy and endogamy in Hebrew marriage see O. J. Baab, "Marriage," *IDB,* 3:281-82.

16. See Sternberg, *Poetics of Biblical Narrative,* p. 134.

17. See D. K. Andrews, "Yahweh the God of the Heavens," in *Seed of Wisdom: Essays in Honour of T. J. Meek,* ed. W. S. McCullough (Toronto: University of Toronto, 1964), pp. 45-57.

surance (vv. 6-8, 40-41), and finally a confirming sign (vv. 42-48).[18] Like Moses and Jeremiah after him, the servant has questions or observations about the proceedings which he thinks may be problematic for the proceedings.

6-8 Abraham acknowledges the possible reluctance of the woman to return to Canaan with the servant. For she is being asked to do what her future father-in-law was once asked to do: uproot oneself, abandon family, and leave for a strange land; in addition, all this data is passed along by one (God, a servant) about whom the person knows little, if anything. It is not Isaac who is to forsake mother and father and cleave to his wife. It is the woman who is to forsake father and mother and cleave to her husband.

Abraham's statement that a *messenger* will precede the servant is surprising at this point. Does this claim reflect Abraham's own recent experience with an intervening messenger when Isaac was also involved (22:11)?[19] Abraham is confident here because God has already sworn to him (v. 7). And because God has sworn to Abraham, the servant can also swear to Abraham.

The woman, should she not want to go to Canaan, is to be allowed that option. The servant is not to use coercion if a polite invitation does not succeed. The emphasis is thereby placed on the obedience with which the servant expedites the mission, rather than on any success or failure he may encounter. This too sounds much like the word of Yahweh to an apprehensive prophet: "whether they listen or not" (Ezek. 2:5, 7).

If the woman chooses not to accompany the servant, the servant is free from the oath. The word Abraham uses for *oath* is *šᵉḇuʿâ.* But when the servant repeats Abraham's speech to Laban he uses *ʾālâ* ("ban," v. 41), which is related to the verb "to curse." Is it a "curse-oath" that Abraham is asking the servant to assume? Does this use indicate that the curse-oath is the heart of the covenant?[20] Perhaps it is more accurate to say that every pact (i.e., here

18. See N. Habel, "The Form and Significance of the Call Narratives," *ZAW* 77 (1965) 321-22.

19. If Gen. 22 is attributed to E and Gen. 24 to J, then this double use of the messenger motif cannot be read sequentially, as if one is the offshoot of the other. The double use of the divine messenger in chs. 22 and 24 would simply indicate the presence of the *malʾāḵ* in both the E and J stories of the patriarchs. The use of *malʾāḵ* in 24:7 as one whom God will send before Abraham's servant as the latter sets out on his mission is the closest parallel in Genesis to the vanguard motif in Exodus, i.e., the pillar of cloud and fire as an expression of divine guidance and presence. See T. W. Mann, *Divine Presence and Guidance in Israelite Traditions: The Typology of Exaltation* (Baltimore: Johns Hopkins University, 1977), p. 112.

20. See J. Milgrom, "The Concept of *Maʿal* in the Bible and the Ancient Near East," *JAOS* 96 (1976) 238 n. 11; idem, *Cult and Conscience,* p. 20 n. 64. Cf. Ezek. 17:18, "he spurned the oath [*ʾālâ*], thereby violating the covenant." See also J. Scharbert, "*ʾālāh,*" *TDOT,* 1:261-66.

between Abraham and his servant) is sealed by an oath *(šᵉḇûʿâ)* that contains an imprecation or sanction *(ʾālâ)*.[21]

9 The narrator relates briefly the servant's acceptance of Abraham's charge. He places his hand on his master's thigh and swears to him. Thus the mission is solemnized by an oath.

2. THE SERVANT MEETS REBEKAH (24:10-27)

10 *The servant took ten of his master's camels, as he went out,*[1] *with all sorts of his master's luxuries*[2] *with him, and he headed for Aram-Naharaim, for the city of Nahor.*

11 *He made the camels kneel*[3] *outside the city by a well, for it was evening, the time when women go out to draw water.*

12 *And he said: "O Yahweh, God of my master Abraham, grant me good fortune today, and so deal graciously with my master Abraham.*

13 *As I am standing by the spring, and the daughters of the townsmen are coming out to draw water,*

14 *let the girl*[4] *to whom I say, 'Please tilt*[5] *your jug that I may drink,' and she responds, 'Drink, and your camels too I will give drink to' — let her be the one you have selected*[6] *for your servant, for Isaac, and by her*[7] *I shall be convinced that you have dealt graciously with my master."*

21. Cf. H. C. Brichto, *The Problem of "Curse" In the Hebrew Bible,* JBLMS 13 (Philadelphia: Society of Biblical Literature, 1963), pp. 25-28. *bᵉrîṯ* does not appear in Gen. 24, but all three terms appear in 26:28-31: "let there be an oath *[ʾālâ]* between you and us, and let us make a covenant *[bᵉrîṯ]* with you . . . and they took oath *[wayyiššāḇᵉʿû]* with one another" (RSV).

1. LXX omits MT's *wayyēleḵ*, probably thinking it to be a scribal error, an accidental repetition of a later *wayyēleḵ* in the verse.

2. *ṭûḇ* is more concrete that *ṭôḇ* and includes items of material prosperity such as wealth or produce from the soil. Cf. Deut. 6:11; 2 K. 8:9; Neh. 9:25.

3. This is the only instance in the Hebrew Bible of the use of *bāraḵ* in the Hiphil stem.

4. The form is consistently *hannaʿᵃrā,* not *hannaʿᵃrâ,* in this chapter. *naʿᵃrā* instead of *naʿᵃrâ* supplies one of the two instances in which the *Qere pepetuum* occurs in the Pentateuch. GKC, § 17c, suggests that *naʿᵃrā* for *naʿᵃrâ* is "a survival of a system of orthography in which a final vowel was written defectively."

5. *haṭṭî* is the Hiphil imperative of *nāṭâ,* "to stretch out, spread out, bend, incline." See M. J. Dahood, " 'A Sea of Troubles,' " *CBQ* 41 (1978) 605.

6. The basic meaning of the verb is "decide, adjudicate." Followed by the preposition *lᵉ,* it also takes on the meaning "appoint, select" (see BDB, p. 407a).

7. The 3rd person sing. fem. suffix might also refer to the idea contained in the preceding sentence, i.e., "thereby." See GKC, § 135p.

15 *Scarcely had he finished speaking and there*[8] *was Rebekah (who was*
born to Bethuel, son of Milcah, the wife of Abraham's brother Nahor);
she came out with a jug on her shoulder.
16 *The girl was very good-looking,*[9] *a virgin. No man had known her. She*
went down to the spring and filled her jug. As she was returning
17 *the servant ran to meet her, and said: "Please give me a sip*[10] *of water*
from your jug."
18 *"Take a drink, sir," she replied, and quickly she lowered*[11] *her jug onto*
her hand and gave him a drink.
19 *When she let him drink all he wanted, she said: "For your camels also*
I will draw until they have drunk[12] *all they want."*
20 *Quickly she emptied*[13] *her jug into the trough, and ran back to the well*
to draw, until she had drawn enough for all his camels.
21 *The man was staring*[14] *at her all the while, waiting silently*[15] *to find*
out whether Yahweh had made his mission successful.
22 *When the camels had finished drinking, the man took a gold ring*[16]

8. See D. J. McCarthy, "The Uses of *wᵉhinnēh* in Biblical Hebrew," *Bib* 61 (1980) 337.

9. For other instances of the construct form of the adjective *ṭôḇ,* see T. Muraoka, "The status constructus of adjectives in Biblical Hebrew," *VT* 27 (1977) 378.

10. *gāmā'* is a *dislegomenon,* appearing only here and in Job 39:24, a reference to the speed of a horse whose racing feet appear to swallow the earth.

11. In *wattᵉmahhēr wattōreḏ* the main idea is introduced by the second verb, while the first verb defines the manner in which the action was taken (cf. v. 20). See GKC, § 120d.

12. On the use of the perfect to express actions or facts existing in the future in a completed state, see GKC, § 106o.

13. *'ārâ* means "be naked, bare" (Qal), "lay bare" (Piel). The way to lay bare a water jug is by removing its contents.

14. *mištā'ēh* is most likely a Hithpael of *šā'â* II, "to gaze, stare," a hapax legomenon, and a parallel form to *šā'â* (BDB, p. 981a). R. Gordis ("A Note on Genesis 24:21," in *The Word and the Book: Studies in Biblical Language and Literature* [New York: Ktav, 1976], p. 335) links *mištā'ēh* with *šā'â* I, "to destroy," which in later Hebrew develops the force of "be astonished" in the Hithpael.

15. *maḥᵃrîš,* Hiphil participle of *ḥārēš* II, "be silent, speechless." Cf. Gen. 34:5; Exod. 14:14. Gordis (*The Word and the Book,* p. 336) connects *maḥᵃrîš* with *ḥāraš* I, "engrave, plan, devise," and notes the Hiphil of this root meaning "to plan" in 1 Sam. 23:9 ("plan evil against"). Both 1 Sam. 23:9 and Gen. 24:21 use the Hiphil participle *maḥᵃrîš.* Yet *ḥārēš* II may be behind *maḥᵃrîš* in 1 Sam. 23:9 ("Saul would not pass over the evil concerning him [viz., David] in silence"). Cf. LXX B's rendering of *maḥᵃrîš* in 1 Sam. 23:9 by *parasiōpá,* "pass in silence."

16. Whenever the material from which a *nezem* is identified, it is gold. It may be worn by a woman or by a man (Judg. 8:24-26; Job 42:11), and may be worn on the nose (Gen. 24:47) or the ear (Judg. 8:24-26).

weighing half[17] *a shekel,*[18] *and two bracelets weighing ten gold shekels for her wrists.*

23 *Then he said: "Whose daughter are you? Tell me, please. Is there room enough in your father's house*[19] *for us to spend the night?"*

24 *She responded: "I am the daughter of Bethuel*[20] *the son of Milcah, whom she bore to Nahor.*

25 *And there is," she continued, "plenty of straw and feed at our place,*[21] *and also a lodging place for the night."*

26 *Thereupon the man bowed and worshiped*[22] *Yahweh,*

27 *and said: "Blessed be Yahweh, the God of my master Abraham who has not withdrawn his true kindness*[23] *from my master. Yahweh has guided me to the house of my master's brother."*

10-11 The ten camels and the luxuries the servant took with him were undoubtedly to serve as part of the *mōhar,* the bride-price (see Gen. 34:12). Abraham's ten camels as a gift may be compared with Jacob's ten bulls (32:15), Joseph's ten donkeys (45:23), Jesse's ten loaves (1 Sam. 17:17), Jeroboam's ten loaves (1 K. 14:3), Naaman's ten talents of silver (2 K. 5:5), all of which are gifts from one person to another.

The servant's destination is *Aram-Naharaim,* that is, central Mesopotamia, or the region near the Habor and Euphrates rivers. The expression *city of Nahor* may refer to either a city by that name (cf. Nahuru east of the

17. *beqaʿ* is a half-shekel, and appears again only in Exod. 38:26. The word means lit. "fraction, part" (cf. *bāqaʿ,* "to break"), and then "one part (out of two)," hence here "half a shekel." Stone weights weighing 6.1 grams and marked *beqaʿ* have been unearthed at sites throughout Israel.

18. SP inserts "which he put on her nose" *(wayyāśem ʿal-ʾappāh).* MT has the phrase later in v. 47.

19. The expression *bêṯ ʾāḇîḵ,* "(in) your father's house," provides an illustration of the omission of the preposition *b* before *bêṯ* in the construct case. See M. J. Dahood, *Proverbs and Northwest Semitic Philology* (Rome: Pontifical Biblical Institute, 1963), p. 33; also, *UT,* p. 95 and n. 3.

20. In a similar clause of identification Joseph leads with the personal pronoun, then follows with his name (*ʾănî yôsēp̄,* Gen. 45:3). Rebekah leads with her lineage ("the daughter of Bethuel"), then follows with the personal pronoun *(ʾānōḵî).* If she had used the same sequence as Joseph, then she would have implied that her name was Bath-Bethuel. Cf. F. I. Andersen, *The Hebrew Verbless Clause in the Pentateuch,* JBLMS 14 (Nashville: Abingdon, 1970), p. 42.

21. Lit., "with us" *(ʿimmānû),* as in French *chez nous.*

22. For "bowing" and "worshiping" before Yahweh, see Exod. 4:31; 12:27; Num. 22:31; 2 Chr. 29:30; Neh. 8:6.

23. *ḥeseḏ weʾĕmeṯ* is a frequently used hendiadys. See v. 49; 47:29; Exod. 34:6; Josh. 2:14; etc. The reverse expression *ʾĕmeṯ weḥeseḏ* is rare (Prov. 14:22).

Balikh River and known from the Mari texts) or to a city in which Nahor, Abraham's brother, lived.

The journey would have taken at least a month for the servant,[24] but this aspect of the story is virtually ignored — as was Abraham's three-day journey from Beer-sheba to Moriah. In. v. 10 he leaves Canaan (Beer-sheba?), and in v. 11 he is at the outskirts of Nahor. No indication is given how the servant knew where to go. Granted, the choice of roads was limited, but perhaps the text's silence on this matter witnesses to the presence of the messenger about whom Abraham had spoken to the servant. The servant has no guarantee that his mission will succeed — only that he will have divine guidance.

In earlier narratives the action commenced in the morning (20:8; 21:14; 22:3). Here it is in the evening, by a well, when the townswomen come out to draw water.[25] The scene is now set for some high drama.

12-14 There is no evidence that the servant prayed as he journeyed; he apparently waits until he is on the outskirts of Nahor to pray. His prayer shows greater concern for Abraham than for Isaac, although he does mention Isaac in v. 14. Thus he prays for the extension of *ḥeseḏ* to Abraham rather than to Isaac.

To that end the servant requests a sign from God that will guarantee that the servant is talking with Isaac's bride-to-be. No word for "sign" occurs here, but the idea is represented by the phrase *grant me good fortune today.*[26] This request is impressive in its immediacy — *today.* This is the first passage of many in Scripture where the urgency of a prayer, an appeal, or a command is qualified by "today."[27]

The boldness of the prayer is also impressive. Whatever girl offers the servant a drink is the girl he has come to find. This first sign is to be confirmed by a second, more unlikely one — this girl is to offer to give drink to the ten camels traveling with the servant. Such is the servant's way of perceiving the will of God. As a method of finding divine guidance it may be compared with

24. See Speiser, *Genesis,* p. 183.

25. For women drawing water cf. Exod. 2:16; 1 Sam. 9:11; John 4:7. Such an assignment assumedly by women provides evidence that women's primary responsibility, apart from bearing and caring for children, was taking care of assorted household tasks.

26. Lit., "let it cause to occur before me today." Cf. an identical use of the Hiphil of *qārâ* in Gen. 27:20. The servant uses the Hiphil imperative of *qārâ* while he is on the outskirts of a foreign city. M. Weinfeld ("The Tribal League at Sinai," in *Ancient Israelite Religion: Essays in Honor of Frank Moore Cross,* ed. P. D. Miller, Jr., P. D. Hanson, and S. D. McBride [Philadephia: Fortress, 1987], p. 304) points out that *qārâ* is not the conventional term for revelation in Israel but is characteristic of revelation to foreigners (Num. 23:3, 4, 15, 16).

27. See table 4, col. III in DeVries, *Yesterday, Today and Tomorrow,* pp. 254-60.

Gideon's woolen fleece (Judg. 6:36-40). He, too, put God to the test with his demand that, if Gideon was the one through whom God would work, that "that night" a fleece of wool be wet with dew, while the ground was dry. Like Abraham's servant, Gideon followed the first test by a second test which would be a greater miracle. The ground is to be wet, but the fleece dry. This second part is the equivalent of the servant's *and your camels too I will give drink to.* Lacking priest, or temple, or prophetic oracle, and hundreds of miles from home, how else shall this servant find the will of God in a strange land?[28]

15 *Scarcely had he finished speaking and there was Rebekah.* The point made here is the proximity between the prayer and the response.[29] Such alacrity of response points to Scriptures such as Isa. 65:24: "before they call I will answer."

The narrator relates Rebekah's identity and lineage before she identifies herself (v. 24). The lineage provides the name of her father *(Bethuel),* her grandmother *(Milcah),* and her grandfather *(Abraham's brother Nahor).* Thus we are given a word about Rebekah's genealogy before we are told anything about her physical appearance (v. 16a), her chastity (v. 16b), her sharing attitude (v. 18), her kindness toward animals (v. 19), and her generous hospitality (v. 25).

16 Rebekah is not only physically attractive; she is a *virgin (bᵉṯûlâ)* as well. Later, when the servant is talking to Laban, he does not use *bᵉṯûlâ* but *ʿalmâ* (v. 43), suggesting an interchangeability between these two Hebrew words.[30] It would be more appropriate for the narrator to refer to Rebekah as a *bᵉṯûlâ,* but for the servant himself to refer to her as an *ʿalmâ,* a "maiden, young woman," when talking about her to her brother Laban.

Scholars debate whether *bᵉṯûlâ* should be translated as "virgin" or as something else, say, "a girl of marriageable age."[31] One argument against taking *bᵉṯûlâ* as *virgo intacta* is that such an understanding makes the follow-

28. "The inviting of coincidence by Abraham's servant is presented as a distinct sign of the will of Providence . . . the elements of chance or surprise may be joined together in a system of human reasoning . . . the manner of using them . . . is destined at one and the same time to signify the existence of a system of divine reasoning" (Y. Amit, "The dual causality principle and its effects on biblical literature," *VT* 37 [1987] 394).

29. Cf. also 1 K. 1:42; Job 1:16; Dan. 4:31, for phrases like "while he was speaking" or "while the word was yet in his mouth."

30. G. W. Savran (*Telling and Retelling,* p. 34) calls the shift from *naʿᵃrā* in v. 14 to *ʿalmâ* in v. 43 (the quotation of v. 14) simply a stylistic substitution.

31. For *bᵉṯûlâ* meaning "virgin" cf. F. Zimmermann, "Some Textual Studies in Genesis," *JBL* 73 (1954) 98 n. 4. For other definitions cf. C. H. Gordon, "The Patriarchal Age," *JBR* 21 (1953) 240-41; C. Isbell, "Does the Gospel of Matthew Proclaim Mary's Virginity?" *BAR* 3/2 (1977) 18-19, 52; G. J. Wenham, "*Bᵉtûlāh:* 'a girl of marriageable age,' " *VT* 22 (1972) 326-48.

ing expression *(No man had known her)* redundant. But this is not necessarily the case, for the Hebrew Bible provides other instances of redundant or *idem per idem* constructions. Thus Job 24:21 refers to "the sterile female who does not bear children." One would think that "the sterile female" would be sufficient. Of course sterile women do not bear children. Cf. also Isa. 54:1, "Sing, barren one, who did not bear." Or 2 Sam. 14:5, "I am a widow and my husband is dead."[32]

A clearer indication that *b^{e}ṯûlâ* does not necessarily mean "virgin," as we use that word today, comes from verses like Joel 1:8, in which a *b^{e}ṯûlâ* mourns "the husband of her youth." Looking again then at the two phrases in v. 16, I suggest that *b^{e}ṯûlâ* designates Rebekah as a marriageable woman. The following sentence, *No man had known her,* specifies her premarital virginity.

17-20 The girl proceeds to give the servant a drink. He had asked only for a *sip* (*m^{e}ʿaṭ-mayim,* lit., "a little water"), but *she let him drink all he wanted* (*watt^{e}ḵal l^{e}hašqōṯô,* v. 19). Both the servant and the girl act quickly. He *ran to meet her (wayyārāṣ),* and *quickly (watt^{e}mahēr) she lowered her jug onto her hand.* These verbs, which emphasize speed, reinforce the quickness with which God gave the servant the sign. On her own Rebekah accepts the responsibility for fetching water to quench the thirst of ten camels, using one jug — no small task! Alter points out that Rebekah in particular is presented "as a continuous whirl of purposeful activity. In four short verses (Gen. 24:16, 18-20) she is the subject of eleven verbs of action and one of speech."[33] In her behavior she is reflecting the quick and hospitable actions of her father-in-law-to-be. Abraham, when visited by three men, "ran" from the tent door to meet them (Gen. 18:2), then "hastened" into Sarah's tent and told her to make ready "quickly" three measures of fine meal (Gen. 18:6), while he himself "ran" to the herd to fetch a calf for the meal (Gen. 18:7).[34]

21 This verse does not record what the servant did after Rebekah went back to the well to get water for the camels. Rather, it records what he did as he engaged Rebekah in conversation and watched her depart for the well. This continuous activity is expressed by two participles, *mištāʾēh (staring)* and *maḥ^{a}rîš (waiting silently).* The servant has no premonition that this girl is the one for whom he has come. Only her actions will demonstrate that. The servant thinks, presumably, that God has consented to abide by his request for two propitious signs. The text never does say, however, that God agreed to work the matter out the way the servant suggested.

32. I take these references from M. Pope, *Job,* AB, 3rd ed. (Garden City, NY: Doubleday, 1973), pp. 175-76.

33. Alter, *Art of Biblical Narrative,* pp. 53-54.

34. Sternberg, *Poetics of Biblical Narrative,* p. 138.

This is the first of three narratives in the Pentateuch where woman meets man at the well, and a marriage is eventually consummated. The other two are Gen. 29:1-14 and Exod. 2:15-21.[35] The parallels in all three are that a man visits a land other than the one in which he is living. By a well he meets a girl who comes to draw water. She runs home to tell, and shortly a marriage occurs. A feature that Gen. 24 shares with Gen. 29, but not with Exod. 2, is that the land where the woman lives is the original home of the man; and the woman he marries is a relative. Unique to Gen. 24 is the representation of the husband-to-be by proxy, and the absence of anything heroic by the servant. He does not roll away the stone at the well, as did Jacob (29:10); nor does he drive away any nasty shepherds, as did Moses (Exod. 2:17). Also, in Gen. 29:10 and Exod. 2:17 it is Jacob and Moses who do the watering of the animals. The absence of Isaac from this event (versus the actual presence of Jacob and Moses in the other incidents) and the drawing of the water by Rebekah (versus the drawing of the water by Jacob and Moses in the related narratives) highlight both the passivity of Isaac and the determination of Rebekah.

22 The servant presents two gifts to Rebekah, *a gold ring weighing half a shekel, and two bracelets weighing ten gold shekels.* Rebekah may have thought that these gifts were expressions of extravagant gratitude by the servant; she does not seem to realize that they are meant as bridal gifts.

23-24 The servant is restrained in his conversation. Although both signs have now been given, he does not say anything to the woman about the reason for his mission. He does not hoist Rebekah onto one of the camels and head back to Canaan. He simply asks her to identify herself, but by lineage or daughtership, not by name — which she does by naming not only her father but also her grandparents. Then he asks for overnight lodging *for us (lānû).*[36] He had presumed upon God, and now he will presume upon Bethuel.

25 Rebekah's effusive nature is attested by the fact that she offers not only to water the servant's camels but to feed them as well. In this respect she is like Lot, who opened his home willingly to total strangers. It would not be unheard-of for a man or a husband to offer to host strangers. It would be more unusual for a daughter to extend the same hospitality without first checking with her father.

35. See R. C. Culley, *Studies in the Structure of Hebrew Narrative* (Philadelphia: Fortress; Missoula, MT: Scholars, 1976), pp. 41-43; R. Melugin, "Muilenburg, Form Criticism, and Theological Exegesis," in *Encounter with the Text,* ed. M. J. Buss (Philadelphia: Fortress, 1979), pp. 96-99.

36. "Us" is either a polite way for the servant to refer to himself, or else he is including the camels who need not only water but shelter. Note also in v. 32, "water was brought to bathe his feet and the feet of the men with him."

26-27 Unable to restrain himself any more, the servant bows before Yahweh and thanks him for a providential leading to the house of Abraham's kinsman. The directions that Abraham had given his servant were quite general. As a result the story highlights even more the sovereign leadership of God. Abraham is as meager in his geographical directives to the servant as God was to Abraham.

Does the servant offer his doxology quietly or aloud? In favor of the latter is that in his doxology the servant does not make any reference to the girl or to the purpose of this mission. It is all cloaked in generality. He might have prayed: "Blessed be Yahweh . . . who has guided me to the woman who is to become Isaac's bride." The only information Rebekah might have gained from the prayer, if she overheard it at all, is that the servant's master and the girl's grandfather are brothers, and that this stranger affirms the kindness and loyalty of his God to the one who dispatched the servant on his mission. This is the thrust of his praise, that Yahweh has demonstrated his sure loyalty to Abraham. Finding the right bride-to-be for Isaac is only instrumental to this larger concern.[37] In retelling this incident later (v. 48), the servant emphasizes more the purpose of his journey — "to take my master's brother's daughter for his son." A more convincing argument that the servant's words are spoken aloud is that an examination of other instances of the formula "blessed be Yahweh who . . ." (e.g., Exod. 18:10; Ruth 4:14; 1 Sam. 25:32, 39; 2 Sam. 18:28; 1 K. 1:48; 10:9 [= 2 Chr. 9:8]; 2 Chr. 2:11; Zech. 11:5) shows that it is used most frequently in conversation between persons and may in fact be uttered primarily for the benefit of the hearer.[38]

3. THE SERVANT MEETS LABAN (24:28-49)

28 *The girl ran and told her mother's household about the conversation.*

29 *Rebekah had a brother whose name was Laban.*[1] *Laban ran to the man outside by the spring.*

30 *Taking note of the ring and the bracelets on his sister's wrists, and hearing these words of Rebekah his sister, "thus the man conversed with me," he went*[2] *to the man who was standing beside the camels at the spring.*

37. See K. D. Sakenfeld, *Faithfulness in Action: Loyalty in Biblical Perspective,* OBT (Philadelphia: Fortress, 1985), p. 91.

38. See W. S. Towner, " 'Blessed be Yahweh' and 'Blessed Art Thou, Yahweh': The Modulation of a Biblical Formula," *CBQ* 30 (1968) 386-99, esp. pp. 388-89.

1. On the use of a circumstantial clause to introduce a new character in a new episode, see Andersen, *Sentence in Biblical Hebrew,* p. 79.

2. For the import of an infinitive with a preposition followed by an imperfect with *waw,* see GKC, § 114r. Cf. Gen. 39:18 for the same structure.

31 *He said: "Come, blessed of Yahweh! Why do you stand outside? For I have readied*[3] *the house and a place for the camels."*

32 *The man then entered the house, and while the camels were unloaded*[4] *and given straw and food, water was brought to bathe his feet and the feet of the men with him.*

33 *With the food now having been set*[5] *before him he said: "I will not eat until I have told my mission." He said:*[6] *"Tell it, then."*

34 *He began: "I am the servant of Abraham.*[7]

35 *Yahweh has blessed my master abundantly so that he has become wealthy. He has given him sheep and cattle, silver and gold, male and female slaves, camels and asses.*

36 *Sarah, the wife of my master, has borne a son for my master in her advanced years,*[8] *and he has given him everything he has.*

37 *My master put me under oath, saying: 'You shall not procure a wife for my son from the daughters of the Canaanites in whose land I am living;*

38 *rather,*[9] *to my father's house, to my own kindred, you shall go, and procure a wife for my son.'*

39 *I said to my master: 'What if the woman will not follow me?'*

40 *He replied: 'May Yahweh, before whom I have walked, send*[10] *his messenger with you and make your mission successful so that you may*

3. "Readied" is the Piel of *pānâ,* "to turn." In the Piel it means "to turn away, put out of the way, clear," hence "make clear/ready."

4. *Pāṯaḥ* means "open" in the Qal but "loose, free, ungird" in the Piel *(wayᵉp-attaḥ).*

5. The Ketib *wyyśm* is strange, for it appears to be from a root *yśm,* which is otherwise unattested (but cf. Gen. 50:26, where the same Ketib occurs); in this context one expects the verb *śîm* (or *śûm*). Accordingly, some suggest that the verb be read (as in the Qere and SP) as *wayyuśam* or *wayyûśam,* a form which could be either the Hophal or the Qal passive of *śîm* (see GKC, § 73f). LXX reads *wayyāśem* (a Qal imperfect; see *BHS*). The Qere *wayyûśam* could also be read as a Qal passive from the metaplastic root *yśm,* which is cognate to *śîm.* See M. J. Dahood, "Qoheleth and Northwest Semitic Philology," *Bib* 43 (1962) 354 n. 6.

6. LXX, SP, and Pesh. read the verb as pl., "and they said."

7. Like Rebekah earlier (v. 24), the servant introduces himself in terms of relationship to another (*baṯ bᵉṯû'ēl 'ānōḵî* and *'eḇeḏ 'aḇrāhām 'ānōḵî,* respectively).

8. LXX and SP read a masc. pronominal suffix rather than MT's fem. suffix, hence as a reference to Abraham's advanced age, "his advanced years." Cf. 21:2.

9. On antithetical *'im lō'* see Andersen, *Sentence in Biblical Hebrew,* p. 184.

10. Here I read the verbs as precatives. If the verbs are futures then v. 41 would be superfluous, if not incongruous. See Brichto, *Problem of "Curse" in the Hebrew Bible,* p. 26 n. 5.

procure a wife for my son from my own kindred and from my father's house.

41 *Only then you shall be released from my ban, if you approach my kindred. If they do not cooperate with you, then you are released from my ban.'*

42 *When I came today to the spring, I said: 'O Yahweh, God of my master Abraham, if you really intend to*[11] *prosper my mission on which I have embarked,*

43 *while I am standing by a spring let the young girl who comes out to draw water and to whom I say, "Please give me a sip of water from your jug,"*

44 *And she says to me, "Both you drink and also*[12] *for your camels I will draw" — let her be the woman whom Yahweh has selected for my master's son.'*

45 *I had scarcely finished speaking in my mind*[13] *and there*[14] *was Rebekah coming out, her jug on her shoulder. After she went down to the spring and drew water, I said to her: 'Let me have a drink, please.'*

46 *Quickly she lowered her jug from above her and said: 'Drink, and also your camels I will water.' I drank, and also the camels she watered.*

47 *I asked her: 'Whose daughter are you?' She responded: 'The daughter of Bethuel, son of Nahor, whom Milcah bore to him.' Then I placed the ring on her nose and the bracelets on her wrists.*

48 *I then bowed down and worshiped Yahweh, and blessed Yahweh, the God of my master Abraham who has guided me on the true road to procure the daughter of my master's kinsman for his son.*

49 *And now, if you are willing to extend true kindness to my master, tell me so; and if not, tell me so that I will know where I stand."*[15]

11. On *yēš* after *'im* and before a participle to express an intention see BDB, p. 441b.

12. On the nuance of *gam . . . w^egam* see Andersen, *Sentence in Biblical Hebrew,* p. 159.

13. Or, "to myself/to my heart" (*'el-libbî*). A parallel phrase to *dibbēr 'el-lēḇ* in the sense of inward musing is *dibbēr ʿal-lēḇ* (1 Sam. 1:13), but which elsewhere means "to speak kindly" (Gen. 34:3; 50:21; Judg. 19:3; Ruth 2:13). Note the contrast between the narrator's earlier report of the servant's prayer in which the servant prayed fervently to his God (vv. 12-14), and the servant's own less emphatic report of that prayer (v. 45). Sensing the difference between the earlier words of the narrator and the later words of the character himself, the LXX added to the end of v. 44 the liturgical formula of 24:13, "and by her I shall be convinced that you have dealt graciously with my master Abraham." This addition makes the servant's own account sound more like an explicit prayer.

14. On this meaning of *hinnēh* see McCarthy, *Bib* 61 (1980) 337.

15. Lit., "so that I may turn on (the) right or on (the) left." Since the verb *pānâ*

28 The action continues apace. The servant "ran" to meet the girl (v. 17). She "quickly" lowered her jug for him to drink (v. 18). She "quickly" emptied her jar into the trough and "ran" back to the well (v. 19). Now she "runs" back to her house (indicating more than casual interest or courtesy), and shortly Laban "runs" to meet the servant (v. 29). That Rebekah returns to *her mother's household,* rather than to her father's, may indicate that Bethuel is deceased. (If so, "Bethuel" in v. 50 would have to be considered intrusive.) Then again, other texts refer to a girl returning to her mother's house, with no indication that the father is no longer living (Ruth 1:8; Cant. 3:14; 8:2). Or, this verse could be an evidence of matrilineal descent.

29 If Bethuel is still living, then it is puzzling why Rebekah's brother *Laban* goes out to meet the servant, and not her father Bethuel. Laban's prominence may reflect the element of fratriarchy.[16] If Bethuel is dead, however, Laban represents the male family head; and thus he is the one to arrange Rebekah's bride-purchase.[17]

30 The jewelry Rebekah is wearing immediately arrests Laban's attention. He must not have been accustomed to seeing her so bedecked. Perhaps Laban is wondering whether this man has other valuables with which he is willing to part. Is he covetous, or simply surprised?

It has often been noted that both v. 29b and v. 30b refer to Laban's quick move outside to see the servant. Uncomfortable with an apparent redundancy, some interpreters either delete one of the two, or else transpose v. 29b after v. 30a.[18] But these emendations are unnecessary if we understand v. 30 as the author's reflection on Laban.[19] V. 29, then, is the author's telling the narrative, and v. 30 becomes an aside, a parenthetical note.

31-32 Interesting here is Laban's use of *Yahweh.* More often than not foreigners use Elohim when speaking of God. Laban's knowledge of the servant's God makes sense only if the things Rebekah told her household

---

does not occur elsewhere with *'al* ("on"), but occurs frequently with *'el* ("to, toward"), some suggest that *'el* be read here (see, e.g., *BHS;* Westermann, *Genesis,* 2:382). As Speiser points out, the expression seems to be an idiom for "to know where one stands" (*Genesis,* p. 181). R. Coote and D. R. Ord, *The Bible's First History* (Philadelphia: Fortress, 1989), p. 135: ". . . so that I can do what I have to do."

16. See C. H. Gordon, "Fratriarchy in the Old Testament," *JBL* 54 (1935) 223-31, esp. p. 226.

17. See N. K. Gottwald, *Tribes of Yahweh,* p. 314. For the prominence of Laban as due not to the death of Bethuel but to the presence of a setting in which descent was figured through mothers, see N. Jay, "Sacrifice, descent and the Patriarchs," *VT* 38 (1988) 61-62.

18. See Van Seters, *Abraham in History and Tradition,* p. 240; Westermann, *Genesis,* 2:379, 381.

19. See Speiser, *Genesis,* p. 181.

include the servant's prayer to Yahweh (vv. 26-27). But one could argue that Laban describes the servant as one blessed by Yahweh not because Yahweh has guided the servant to the correct destination but because the servant appears with camels and gold jewelry. Whoever this stranger is, Laban knows that he is no destitute vagabond.

Laban is as free with his hospitality as his sister is. She offers water and he opens their house. Laban has also apparently done some quick housekeeping — he has *readied* (lit., "cleaned"; cf. Lev. 14:36; Isa. 40:3) his house for the servant and his camels. The camels may have been cared for in part of the house that served as a stable or in the courtyard.[20]

33 The servant's prior concern had been for a drink of water (v. 17). Now his own physical needs become secondary, and the telling of his mission becomes primary. Eating can be postponed. The eating is not recorded until v. 54.

34-36 The servant repeats what the narrator had earlier said about Abraham (v. 1), even using the same word order, for here too the subject precedes the verb (unusual in Hebrew). What the servant does that the narrator did not do is to spell out the nature of the divine blessing. It consisted of material prosperity (v. 35) and a son (v. 36). The first of these blessings has nothing to do with the servant's mission, unless the listing of Abraham's property be viewed as an attempt by the servant to fend off any objection the girl or her brother may voice. Her future father-in-law is not poor!

The second part of the blessing explains the servant's presence in Aram-Naharaim. Abraham has a son, but no daughter-in-law. Never does the servant identify Isaac by name. He is simply Abraham's *son* and one whom Sarah has borne. The servant's further addition that Sarah gave birth to her son "in her advanced years" makes Isaac an appealing candidate to become Laban's brother-in-law. His words to Laban might persuade Laban to think of Isaac as a miracle baby, and if his mother gave birth to him when she was elderly, then Isaac must still be a relatively young man. It is to the servant's credit that he ascribes Abraham's success to God. Abraham is not an independently wealthy man. The servant surrounds his discussion of Abraham with references to the real source of Abraham's circumstances: *Yahweh has blessed my master . . . he has given him everything he has.*

37-41 The servant moves his presentation from who Abraham is to what Abraham said, and in so doing makes the purpose of his mission obvious. He repeats almost verbatim what Abraham had said to him. He makes a few minor changes. For example, as we have already seen, the servant replaces Abraham's *šᵉḇûʿâ,* "oath" (v. 8), with *'ālâ, ban* (v. 41). He omits any reference

20. Stalls for animals were often apparently part of the house; see S. W. Fawcett, "Stall," *IDB,* 4:439. Westermann (*Genesis,* 2:388) thinks they were in a courtyard.

to placing his hand under Abraham's thigh. Abraham tells the servant to go to "my country [*'arṣî*], my native land [*môladtî*], to get a bride for Isaac" (v. 4). In the servant's speech *'arṣî* is replaced by *bêṯ–'āḇî, father's house,* and *môladtî* is replaced by *mišpaḥtî, my own kindred* (v. 38).[21]

One repetition and one deletion in the servant's speech call for special attention. First, the repetition. It may sound odd to the reader that the servant would so slavishly reproduce his earlier dialogue with Abraham even to the point of repeating the question he had raised with Abraham: *What if the woman will not follow me?* (v. 39).[22] This hardly sounds like the positive approach! Would it not have been wiser, perhaps, for the servant to keep his apprehensions to himself rather than blurt them out at this inopportune time?

Second, the deletion. Understandably, the servant does not repeat Abraham's insistence that under no circumstances is the servant to take Isaac to Aram-Naharaim (vv. 6, 8b). Diplomacy dictated this deletion. It would not have been the kind of remark that would give the servant rapport with Laban and entry into his house. In fact, it could have severed the conversation there and then.

The servant also deletes Abraham's earlier reference to being led out of Laban's land himself (v. 7a), and the promise of Canaan-land which Abraham received (v. 7b). In their place the servant inserts the note that Abraham is one who walked before God (*Yahweh, before whom I have walked,* v. 40a). Thus the servant has shifted his emphasis from Abraham's blessings (vv. 30-36) to Abraham's behavior. His commendable features are not only his abundant possessions but also his obedience to Yahweh.

42-49 Again, the servant makes some minor changes from the initial description when he recounts his meeting with Rebekah. In the first telling she is called a virgin (*bᵉṯûlâ,* v. 16). Here the servant calls her an *ʿalmâ, the young girl* (v. 43). The success the servant desires is first expressed by the verb *qārâ* (v. 12) and in the recounting by *ṣālaḥ* (v. 42). We discover only in the retelling that the servant prayed *inwardly* (*'el-libbî,* lit., "to my heart," v. 45). The servant also eliminates Rebekah's initial offer of provision and overnight lodging (v. 25). That offer does not need repetition, for the servant is by now a houseguest (vv. 32-33). Most interesting is a comparison between vv. 22-23 and v. 47. In the original episode the servant placed jewelry on Rebekah (v. 22), then asked "whose daughter are you?" (v. 23). But in the retelling of that the servant

21. Sternberg (*Poetics of Biblical Narrative,* p. 147) remarks: "Rebekah's guardians would obviously find it much harder to reject a proposal of marriage addressed to them as kinsmen than as Mesopotamians."

22. Although even here there is a slight change; earlier the servant had said to Abraham (v. 5), "what if the woman does not wish *[tō'ḇeh]* to follow me?" Here he simply says "what if the woman will not follow me?" On this subtle change see Sternberg, *Poetics of Biblical Narrative,* p. 148.

reverses this sequence. First he asked "whose daughter are you?" (v. 47a). Then he placed the jewelry on her nose and wrists (v. 47c), as if to suggest that "he would not commit himself as long as there remained the slightest doubt about the alignment of human wishes with divine disposition."[23]

From v. 37 on, the servant, in retelling the narrative, makes frequent use of quoted direct speech. He quotes Abraham (vv. 37-38), himself (v. 39), Abraham (vv. 40-41), himself (vv. 42-43), Rebekah (v. 44), himself (v. 45), Rebekah (v. 46), himself (v. 47), Rebekah (v. 47). It is conceivable that in v. 48 the servant could have quoted directly himself again (see v. 27). Instead, he narrates in indirect speech the doxology he uttered in v. 27. In this instance it would be unwarranted for the servant to draw attention to his piety by quoting his actual words.[24]

Now the decision is up to Laban. God has already shown "kindness" *(ḥeseḏ)* to Abraham (vv. 12, 14, 27). Will Laban also extend *ḥeseḏ* to Abraham (v. 49)? Will Laban deal with Abraham as God has dealt with Abraham? Will divine kindness be complemented by human kindness? Or will the divine leadings and the long journey all go for naught? The servant has made his case in such a convincing fashion that it will be almost impossible for Laban to turn him down and send the servant away empty-handed.

4. THE SERVANT AND REBEKAH DEPART (24:50-61)

50 *Laban and Bethuel*[1] *responded: "By Yahweh has this happened; we can neither discourage nor encourage.*[2]

51 *Rebekah is at your disposal; take her and go, so that she be a wife to your master's son, just as Yahweh has spoken."*

23. Ibid., p. 151; and G. W. Savran, *Telling and Retelling,* p. 48, who notes that the reversal of the order both flatters Laban and sets up the expectation in Laban that the one who makes the correct response will receive an appropriate gift. Laban will get a chance to make a response after the servant says what he does in v. 49.

24. See Savran, *Telling and Retelling,* p. 47. Savran again draws attention to the various ways in which the servant is self-effacing and highlights divine providence in "The Character as Narrator in Biblical Narrative," *Prooftexts* 5 (1985) 1-17. I see no significance in the fact that in v. 27 the servant used the Qal *nāḥanî,* "has guided me," while in v. 48 he uses the Hiphil *hinḥanî.* On synonymous verbal pairs, see R. J. Ratner, "Morphological Variation in Biblical Hebrew Rhetoric," *MAARAV* 8 (1992) 145-46.

1. See the commentary below for a discussion of the originality of "and Bethuel."

2. Lit., "we cannot speak to you evil or good." A. M. Honeyman ("*Merismus* in Biblical Hebrew," *JBL* 71 (1952) 14) understood the expression to mean "anything at all." This meaning is unlikely. What Laban is stating is that since Yahweh has given his decision (Rebekah is the one for Isaac), then Laban is no longer free to exercise his own decision. See W. M. Clark, "A Legal Background to the Yahwist's Use of 'Good and Evil' in Genesis 2–3," *JBL* 88 (1969) 273.

52 *When Abraham's servant heard their offer he bowed to the ground before Yahweh.*

53 *Then the servant produced objects of silver and gold, and articles of clothing, and presented them to Rebekah. Expensive presents*[3] *he presented to her brother*[4] *and her mother.*

54 *After he and his companions who were with him ate and drank, they spent the night. When they got up the next morning, he said: "Allow me to return to my master."*

55 *Her brother and mother replied: "Let the girl remain with us for a while, say, ten days;*[5] *after that you may go."*[6]

56 *But he said to them: "Do not detain me, for Yahweh has made my mission successful. Let me go so that I can return*[7] *to my master."*

57 *They responded: "Let us summon the girl and ask her."*[8]

58 *So they summoned Rebekah and asked her: "Will you go with this man?" She replied, "I will."*

59 *They said farewell to Rebekah their sister, and to her nurse,*[9] *and to Abraham's servant and his companions.*

60 *They blessed Rebekah, saying to her:*

> *"Our sister are you; become*
> *thousands of ten thousands;*[10]

3. *migdānâ* occurs again only in later literature (2 Chr. 21:3; 32:23; Ezra 1:6).

4. Here and in v. 55 some LXX mss. and Vulg. read *'āḥîhāh,* "her brother," as *'aḥeyhāh,* "her brothers," suggesting that Laban was the oldest of several brothers.

5. Lit., "days or ten." Says Speiser (*Genesis,* p. 182), "If correctly transmitted, this is the kind of idiom that makes no sense whatever when it is slavishly reproduced." Targ. Onqelos rendered "for a year" (lit., "a time in time," *'ydn b'ydn*), understanding *yāmîm* as "year."

6. *'aḥar tēlēk̲* is one of the Masorah's three *'iṭṭur Sopherim* (i.e., omission of the conjunctive *waw*) in the Pentateuch (see Gen. 18:5; Num. 31:2). On this phenomenon see A. Dotan, "Massorah," *EncJud,* 16:1410; and Gordis, *The Word and the Book,* p. 71 n. 77. Note LXX's "and after that she shall depart" *(kaí metá taúta apeleúsetai).*

7. Clauses using imperative plus cohortative *(šallᵉḥûnî wᵉ'ēlᵉk̲â)* do so to express causal sequence (Andersen, *Sentence in Biblical Hebrew,* p. 112). V. 60 provides an instance of imperative plus jussive *(hᵃyî . . . wᵉyîraš).*

8. Lit., "inquire at her mouth." For Yahweh's mouth as the object of *šā'al* cf. Josh. 9:14; Isa. 30:2.

9. LXX *tá hypárchonta autḗs* suggests *miqnāṯāh,* "her property," instead of MT *mēniqtāh,* "her nurse." *Mēniqtāh* is the fem. participle of *yānaq,* "to suck" *(mêneqeṯ)* with the 3rd fem. sing. pronominal suffix.

10. *'alp̲ê rᵉb̲āb̲â.* On the frequent parallelism of *alp* and *rbt* in Ugaritic see M. J. Dahood, *RSP,* 1:114; Gevirtz, *Patterns in the Early Poetry of Israel,* pp. 15-24; and N. K. Gottwald, *Tribes of Yahweh,* pp. 278-82.

and may your offspring possess
the gate of those who hate them."

61 *Then Rebekah and her maids mounted*[11] *the camels and followed*[12] *the man. So the servant took Rebekah and set out.*

50-51 Many writers doubt that *and Bethuel* is the original reading, since Bethuel plays no role at all in the story. Rebekah tells "her mother's house" about the arrival of the servant (v. 28). It is Laban the brother who assumes the lead in negotiations (v. 29). The servant gave costly presents to Rebekah's brother and mother only (v. 53b). And it is again brother and mother who wish to hold on to Rebekah for a while longer (v. 54). Accordingly some suggest that MT *ûḇᵉṯû'ēl, and Bethuel,* be read as a textual corruption of *ûḇēṯô,* "and his household."[13] One does not have to excise "and Bethuel" as a marginal gloss, however, if one interprets the family of Rebekah to be matrilineal. That Sarah's consent was solicited (v. 58) and the blessing of v. 60 desires her fecundity make more sense if the family is matrilineal rather than patrilineal (although the latter was more common).[14]

Laban is prepared to accept the fact that *Yahweh* is involved in this event. Because Yahweh has made his decision, Laban no longer has the privilege of making his own decision.[15] The text does not indicate whether Laban's statement is a true religious conviction or only a matter of politeness. In favor of the former notion is that Laban encourages the servant to take Rebekah. Furthermore, Laban and Bethuel make no mention of the wealth of Abraham or of the kinship between Abraham and Nahor as valid reasons for Rebekah to leave and marry Isaac. Their only reason for relinquishing her is the unmistakable hand of God throughout this whole episode. It is not the servant, Abraham, or Isaac, but rather their God, that Laban and Bethuel find persuasive. Thus even "the Mesopotamians undergo a process of discovery that brings home to them God's management of the world."[16]

11. I take MT *wattāqom . . . wattirkaḇnâ,* lit., "and she arose . . . and they rode" (see AV, RSV) to signify "they mounted" (cf. NIV, JB, NEB, NAB).

12. For *rāḵaḇ* followed by *hālaḵ 'aḥᵃrê* cf. 1 Sam. 25:42; 1 K. 13:13. That *rāḵaḇ* is followed by a verb indicating horizontal movement must mean that *rāḵaḇ* signifies vertical movement (i.e., "mount"). See W. B. Barrick, "The Meaning and Usage of RKB in Biblical Hebrew," *JBL* 101 (1982) 481-503, and esp. p. 482 for *rāḵaḇ* plus *hālaḵ* plus preposition.

13. For example, Speiser, *Genesis,* pp. 181-82; cf. Westermann, *Genesis,* 2:382, 389; *BHS.* Note that the first verb in v. 50 is sing. *(wayya'an)* but the second verb is pl. *(wayyō'mᵉrû).* The same feature (sing. verb plus compound subject plus pl. verb) occurs in v. 61 *(wattāqom . . . wattirkaḇnâ).*

14. See N. Jay, "Sacrifice, descent and the Patriarchs," *VT* 38 (1988) 62.

15. See n. 2 above.

16. Sternberg, *Poetics of Biblical Narrative,* p. 152.

52 This is the third time the servant worships God (see vv. 12-14, and v. 26). The first time the emphasis was on the content of the prayer. In the second and third instances words are absent. Petition gives way to prostration, and in these last two there is a progression from lowering one's head (v. 26) to lowering one's entire body (v. 52). Anxiety, if it was ever present at all, has now given way to adoration. Nowhere does the servant thank Laban. What he always does is offer praise to Yahweh.

53 It is important that the gifts for Rebekah and the gifts for her relatives are presented to the parties after Laban has agreed to release Rebekah. Had they been offered before Laban was asked for Rebekah, his cooperation would have been seen as motivated by greed. Had they been offered before the servant worshiped (v. 52), they would have been seen as part of a business negotiation. This is the second time Rebekah has received a gift from the servant (see v. 22), but the first time her family has received anything in the way of a dowry.

54-56 Both the servant and Rebekah's family have legitimate concerns. On the one hand, the servant wants to return posthaste with the girl to Abraham. His mission now accomplished, he is anxious to get back and break the good news to his master. In this way he is the opposite of Lot's prospective sons-in-law, who were content to linger in Sodom. The servant will not linger in Nahor. He needs to be up and on his way. On the other hand, Rebekah's family would understandably like her to stay a few more days, rather than leave immediately.

57-58 These two verses should not be read as a contradiction of v. 51. There is no inconsistency between Laban granting permission for Rebekah to go with the servant (v. 51) and Rebekah herself agreeing to go. Laban's permission concerned whether Rebekah would be allowed to leave Nahor with the servant. What is being solicited in vv. 57-58 is both Rebekah's feelings about leaving and leaving with so short a notice or waiting for a few days. She is being asked not only whether she wants to leave but also if she wants to leave now or later. Speiser has drawn attention to the fact that in Nuzi contracts the woman's consent was requested as part of the marriage procedures.[17] But both consent and the time of departure are the issues here.[18]

59 Rebekah's own decision seals the matter. There is nothing more to do except send Rebekah on her way. The *nurse* who accompanies Rebekah

17. Speiser, *Genesis,* pp. 184-85.

18. K. T. Aitken ("The Wooing of Rebekah: A Study in the Development of the Tradition," *JSOT* 30 [1984] 19, 20) suggests that the narrative served as a paradigm of the willing bride who departed the security of her parental home and left for her bridegroom's home.

is identified later as Deborah (35:8). Perhaps her anonymity in 24:59 is to balance the unnamed servant and his companions.[19] Also, the deliberate omission of ancillary characters who are not involved in the plot keeps the focus on Rebekah (as in Exod. 2:1ff. — " a man from the tribe of Levi took a woman from the tribe of Levi").

60 Rebekah's departure from her household does not leave any of the bitter taste that Jacob's clandestine and nocturnal exodus from Laban's house with Rachel and Leah (ch. 31) will leave. Rebekah does not abscond with Bethuel's household gods (if he had any), as Rachel will do. Of course, the difference is that Rachel leaves with her husband, and Rebekah leaves to find and meet her husband.

The family give two blessings to Rebekah — one, the prayer for much offspring; and two, the prayer for the victory and prosperity of those offspring over their enemies (for which see 22:17). This two-pronged blessing is very close in style and sequence to the blessing of Noah on Shem and Japheth (9:26-27).[20] The second part of this blessing also parallels 22:17b: what the messenger said about Abraham's descendants Rebekah's brothers now say about her descendants.

61 The last half of the verse is not a needless variant of the first half of the verse.[21] Rather, the last part of the verse summarizes the successful completion of the servant's mission and his leadership over the party as it sets out for Canaan. Rebekah and the servant do not walk together as did Abraham and Isaac (ch. 22). He leads. She follows. Earlier the servant was himself led (vv. 7, 26), but now he is leader. This is the sixth time in this chapter that *lāqaḥ* has been used in connection with Rebekah. In five of them (vv. 4, 7, 38, 40, 48 [and see also v. 67]) *lāqaḥ* means "to take in marriage." On each of these five occasions I translated *lāqaḥ* as "procure." Once Abraham used this verb about himself (v. 7) to refer to the time when Yahweh took him from Aram-Naharaim. Now the servant is doing for/to Rebekah what Yahweh had earlier done for/to Abraham.

19. G. A. Rendsburg ("Notes on Genesis xxxv," *VT* 34 [1984] 365) cites the mention of "nurse" in Gen. 24:59 as another example of what N. Sarna termed "the anticipatory use of information" (see N. Sarna, "The Anticipatory Use of Information as a Literary Feature of the Genesis Narratives," in *The Creation of Sacred Literature: Composition and Redaction of the Biblical Text,* ed. R. E. Friedman [Berkeley: University of California, 1981], pp. 76-82).

20. See C. Westermann, *Blessing in the Bible and the Life of the Church,* tr. Keith Crim, OBT (Philadelphia: Fortress, 1978), p. 55. Also cf. Ruth 4:11-12 for a marriage blessing involving the acquiring of children.

21. As maintained by Skinner, *Genesis,* p. 347.

5. REBEKAH MEETS ISAAC (24:62-67)

62 *Meanwhile*[1] *Isaac had gone from*[2] *Beer-lahai-roi and had settled in the area of the Negeb.*

63 *While Isaac was out roaming*[3] *in the field toward*[4] *evening, he spotted, as he looked up, camels approaching.*

1. I suggest that we have in vv. 61, 62 the use of the *yqṭl-qṭl* syntactical structure to express the synchronism of two events, and hence my reason for translating the w^{e}- at the beginning of v. 62 as "meanwhile." This device uses first the verb in the imperfect with consecutive *waw (wqṭl)* preceding the substantive (v. 61), and second the perfect form *(qṭl)* following the substantive (v. 62).

2. MT *mibbô',* "from coming (to)," is difficult to explain, for what is the meaning of "had gone from coming to"? Both LXX and SP read *b^{e}miḏbar,* "to the wilderness of," for MT *mibbô'.* If this reading is correct, then it suggests that Isaac met Rebekah near Beer-lahai-roi. Other ancient versions (Symm. and Targ. Onqelos) read *mibb^{e}'ēr,* "from Beer," instead of *mibbô'* and delete the following *b^{e}'ēr* as a dittographic corruption of *mb'r* (which I think is the most cogent possibility). BDB, p. 98b, gives to *mibbô'* the meaning "as far as," but admits the text is dubious.

3. The hapax legomenon *śûaḥ* defies explanation (see NAB, which does not even try to translate it). If it is a form of the verb *śîaḥ,* then its meaning is "pray," "meditate" (Ps. 119:15, 23, 27). Most of the ancient versions so understood it: LXX *adoleschḗsai;* Vulg. *ad meditandum;* Targ. Onqelos: *lṣl'h* (so also AV, RSV, NIV, NASB). Because of "walk" *(hālaḵ)* in v. 65 I suggest "roam" as a parallel here (cf. Pesh. "walk about," from *šûṭ*). Westermann (*Genesis,* 2:390) and H. P. Müller ("Die hebräische Wurzel שׂיח," *VT* 19 [1969] 368) agree that this is the most likely interpretation (so also JB). Scholars have made at least three other suggestions as to the meaning of *śûaḥ.* One connects it with an Arabic root meaning "to fling one's arms" (J. Blau, "Etymologisch Untersuchungen auf Grund des palästinischen Arabisch," *VT* 5 [1955] 343-44); a second connects it with a root found in the Dead Sea Scroll Manual of Discipline (1QS 7.15), repoint the *ś* to *š,* read as *šûaḥ,* and translate "Isaac went out in order to lie down outside" (P. Wernberg-Møller, "A note on *lāśûaḥ baśśāḏeh* in Genesis 24:63," *VT* 7 [1957] 414-16); a third suggestion, which I find most attractive next to "roam," is that the verb means "to dig a hole" and is a euphemism for relieving oneself. This is reflected in NEB's translation "hoping to meet them," to which it adds the footnote indicating that the verb may actually refer to relieving oneself. For this interpretation see G. R. Driver, "Problems of Interpretation in the Heptateuch," in *Mélanges bibliques, rédigés en l'honneur de André Robert,* Travaux de l'Institut Catholique de Paris 4 (Paris: Bloud et Gay, 1957), pp. 66-76, esp. 66-68; J. Ellington, "What did Isaac go out to do? (Gen. 24:63-65)," *BT* 38 (1987) 446-47; and Coote and Ord, *Bible's First History,* p. 135, "to urinate"; G. A. Rendsburg, "The Mock of Baal in 1 K. 18:27," *CBQ* 50 (1988) 417 n. 15; idem, "Hebrew *św/yḥ* and Arabic *šḫḫ,*" in *FUCUS: A Semitic/Afrasian Gathering in Remembrance of Albert Ehrmann,* ed. Y. L. Arbeitman, Current Issues in Linguistic Theory 58 (Amsterdam and Philadelphia: John Benjamins, 1988), pp. 419-30. For a summary of these various interpretations, see Frederick E. Greenspahn, *Hapax Legomena in Biblical Hebrew,* SBLDS 74 (Chico, CA: Scholars, 1984), p. 160; and *HALAT,* 4:1223.

4. For the use of the infinitive with *l^{e}* to express time see GKC, § 114f n. 1.

64 *And Rebekah, as she looked up, spotted*[5] *Isaac, and she quickly got down*[6] *from her camel.*

65 *She asked the servant: "Who is the man yonder, walking in the field in our direction?" "He*[7] *is my master," replied the servant. So she took her veil and covered herself.*

66 *The servant related to Isaac everything he had done.*

67 *Then Isaac brought her into the tent of Sarah his mother.*[8] *He married*[9] *Rebekah and she became his wife. In being in love with her*[10] *Isaac was consoled*[11] *after the death of*[12] *his mother.*

5. Both times the phrase "he/she lifted up his/her eyes/looked up" and "saw" for Isaac and Sarah *(wayyiśśā' 'ênâw wayyar' . . . wattiśśā' riḇqâ 'eṯ 'ênehā wattēre').* Westermann (*Genesis,* 2:390) remarks: "These two sentences reduce to a minimum a meeting between two peoples so as to allow what is unspoken to speak all the more forcefully." See also R. E. Whitaker, *RSP,* 3:214.

6. Lit., "fell" *(wattippōl).* For substantiation of *nāpal* in the same sense as *yāraḏ* cf. Judg. 1:14, *wattiṣnaḥ mē'al haḥ^{a}môr* with 1 Sam. 25:23, *wattēreḏ mē'al haḥ^{a}môr.*

7. For *hû'* to introduce a person, see R. J. Clifford, "Style and Purpose in Psalm 105," *Bib* 60 (1979) 423 n. 8; or as subjects of clauses that answer questions, see Andersen, *Hebrew Verbless Clause in the Pentateuch,* p. 40.

8. Most modern translations and commentators eliminate the phrase "Sarah his mother" (e.g., RSV, JB, NEB, NAB; cf. AV, NIV, RSV mg., NEB mg.), primarily because the syntax of "*the* tent of Sarah" — with the definite article on the noun in construct — is so unusual. See GKC, § 127f; *BHS;* Speiser, *Genesis,* p. 182; Westermann, *Genesis,* 2:382, 391. Yet the Hebrew Bible has examples of this syntax (one maybe as close as 17:17 if MT *h^{a}ḇaṯ* is read as *habbaṯ,*) but this emendation is questionable. For more persuasive examples of the article with the *regens* of the construct chain see 31:13, *hā'ēl bêṯ-'ēl* ("the God of Bethel"); Josh. 3:14, *hā'ārôn habb^{e}rîṯ* ("the ark of the covenant"); Jer. 25:26, *kol-hammaml^{e}ḵôṯ hā'āreṣ,* "all the kingdoms of the earth." In Num. 21:14 the phrase *hann^{e}ḥālîm 'arnôn* ("the valleys of Arnon") may show both the article on the *regens* in a construct chain and the enclitic *mem* (see M. J. Dahood, "Punic *hkbm 'l* and Isaiah 14, 13" *Or* 34 (1965) 172.

9. On *lāqaḥ* meaning "married" see the commentary above on v. 61.

10. As S. Terrien has pointed out (*Till the Heart Sings: A Biblical Theology of Manhood and Womanhood* [Philadelphia: Fortress, 1985], p. 32) it is preferable to read the verbal form here as a stative ("he was in love with her") rather than an active ("he loved her"); the stative suggests a state of duration.

11. For other instances where the subject of the verb (in the Niphal) is a bereaved mourner see Gen. 38:12; 2 Sam. 13:39; Jer. 31:15; Ezek. 31:16; 32:31; and H. Van Dyke Parunak, "A Semantic Survey of NḤM," *Bib* 56 (1975) 520. On the LXX's different translations of *nāḥam* in Genesis (9 times) see J. Cook, "The Exegesis of the Greek Genesis," in *VI Congress of the International Organization for Septuagint and Cognate Studies, 1986,* ed. C. E. Cox, SBL Septuagint and Cognate Studies (Atlanta: Scholars, 1987), p. 117.

12. Speiser (*Genesis,* p. 182) points out that the Hebrew preposition *'aḥ^{a}rê* may mean both "after" and "after the death of," as does the Akkadian preposition *arki.* See also M. J. Dahood, "Northwest Semitic Notes on Genesis," *Bib* 55 (1974) 79. Cf. also Westermann, *Genesis,* 2:382, 391.

62-67 The absence of any mention of Abraham in these verses, plus the servant's reference to Isaac as *my master* (v. 65) — a term used earlier only for Abraham — may imply that Abraham is now dead, or died shortly after the servant's return.[13] The next chapter relates that Abraham remarried and lived until the age of 175 (25:7); this reference could be an instance of rewinding the narrative tape, much as the book of Judges opens with a reference to the death of Joshua (1:1), but then 2:6-7 mention Joshua as alive and vv. 8-9 recount his death again. Since Abraham was 137 years old when Sarah died (he was ten years older than she), he would have lived thirty-eight years after Sarah's death. If the servant and Rebekah did not return until after the death of Abraham, then Isaac was consoled thirty-eight years after his mother died. Such a time span would indicate how deeply Sarah's death affected Isaac.

Interestingly, the text has no record of any conversation between the prospective spouses. Rebekah speaks to the servant, and the servant speaks to Rebekah (v. 65). The servant also converses with Isaac at length (v. 66). But bridegroom and bride exchange no conversation. The quickness with which Isaac and Rebekah are married matches the quickness with which Rebekah alighted from her camel.

Rebekah knows Isaac's identity (v. 65) before Isaac knows her identity (v. 66). Accordingly, she veils herself as the prospective bride.[14] That particular piece of clothing had not been mentioned among the articles with which Rebekah left home.

Now informed and assured that Rebekah was indeed the person for whom Abraham had sent the servant, Isaac brings her into his home, that is, his *tent,* and marries her. It was not necessary that the servant go into great detail about his odyssey to Aram-Naharaim and back in order to inform Isaac of his father's plan and directives for the servant vis-à-vis Isaac. Just as Isaac was kept uninformed of why he and his father headed for Moriah, so he is kept in the dark about Abraham's arrangement for his marriage. In both cases, when the truth dawns upon Isaac, he consents to the situation. He accepts binding from his father, and he accepts the Aramean wife brought to him from afar.

Several times in our analysis of Gen. 24 we have drawn attention to the prominent theme of divine guidance. The pivotal role of this motif in the story becomes even clearer when it is compared with the Ugaritic Epic of

13. Westermann (*Genesis,* 2:391): "It is presupposed that Abraham . . . is no longer alive."

14. For the veiling of the bride (though a different Hebrew term is used), see Cant. 4:1, 3; 6:7; for the veiling of a harlot (using the same Hebrew term as in Gen. 24:65), see Gen. 38:14, 19. See also de Vaux, *Ancient Israel,* 1:33-34.

Keret, which shares many emphases with Gen. 24. Keret's first wife has "departed," meaning either she died or she has been kidnaped.[15] The story then proceeds to narrate Keret's attempt to find a new wife (or to reclaim his stolen wife).

The Epic of Keret and Gen. 24 have at least six parallel features. (1) An individual is commissioned to leave his home (Ḫbr/Canaan) and travel to another land (Great and Little Udum/Aram-Naharaim) to find a wife (Ḥurrai/Rebekah). (2) His journey abroad completed, both the servant and Keret engage in extensive negotiations at the destination of their expedition. (3) The marriage proposal is accepted. (4) The bride departs. (5) The couple are united in marriage, and a family is promised. (6) Both stories abound with repetitions of earlier scenes.

The messenger leads the servant to the city of Nahor (at least that is what Abraham promised, v. 7, and what the servant affirms, v. 27) and El gives directions to Keret on how to find Great and Little Udum. It is at this point that we encounter a major difference in the two narratives. In the Ugaritic epic El gives Keret exact directives through a dream (lines 39-153). Keret is told to wash and rouge himself, to sacrifice to El, to take provisions for his army that will accompany him, the makeup of his troops, how long the expedition will take, what Udumites he is to capture, Pbl's — the king of Udum — attempts to dissuade Keret from persisting in taking Ḥurrai away, how Keret is to reply to Pbl, and a description of Ḥurrai's beauty.

In the remainder of the story (lines 156ff.) Keret simply acts out these directives. Little, if anything, is left to imagination and Keret's initiative. This restriction contrasts with Gen. 24, where Abraham's directives to his servant are vague and very general. God is to be trusted for the working out of the specifics. In the Keret Epic El's guidance is recognized *before* Keret leaves for Udum. In Gen. 24 God's guidance is recognized *after* the servant reaches Nahor. The reader knows how the Ugaritic story will terminate long before he reads the conclusion. In the OT event the reader shares the servant's apprehension. Will he be successful or not? Thus the biblical narrative displays a "greater freedom of human action and a more subtle relationship with the deity."[16]

15. It is not my purpose to decide between these two interpretations of the Ugaritic epic. Cf. J. Gray, *The KRT Text in the Literature of Ras Shamra,* 2nd ed. (Leiden: Brill, 1964); J. C. L. Gibson, *Canaanite Myths and Legends,* 2nd ed. (Edinburgh: T. & T. Clark, 1977), pp. 19-23, 82-102; P. C. Craigie, *Ugarit and the Old Testament* (Grand Rapids: Eerdmans, 1983), pp. 55-58; M. D. Coogan, *Stories from Ancient Canaan* (Philadelphia: Westminster, 1978), pp. 52-74.

16. See S. B. Parker, "The Historical Composition of KRT and the Cult of El," *ZAW* 89 (1977) 172 n. 54.

N. THE END OF THE ABRAHAM CYCLE (25:1-18)

1. THE DEATH OF ABRAHAM (25:1-11)

1 *Abraham married another wife, whose name was Keturah.*

2 *She bore him Zimran, Jokshan, Medan, Midian, Ishbak, and Shuah.*

3 *Jokshan fathered Sheba and Dedan. The descendants of Dedan were the Asshurim, the Letushim, and the Leummim.*

4 *The descendants of Midian were Ephah, Epher, Hanoch, Abida, and Eldaah. All of these were descendants of Keturah.*

5 *Abraham deeded*[1] *to Isaac everything he owned.*

6 *To his sons by concubines*[2] *Abraham gave gifts, and while he was still living he sent them away eastward to the land of Kedem,*[3] *away from Isaac his son.*

7 *The whole span of Abraham's life was one hundred and seventy-five years.*

8 *Then he breathed his last, dying at a ripe old age, elderly and full of days,*[4] *and was gathered to his kin.*

9 *Isaac and Ishmael his sons buried him in the cave of Machpelah, in the field of Ephron son of Zohar the Hittite which faces Mamre,*

10 *the field which Abraham had purchased from the Hittites; there he was interred along with his wife Sarah.*

11 *After the death of Abraham, God blessed Isaac his son, and Isaac settled down near Beer-lahai-roi.*

1 This is the only passage in Genesis that mentions *Keturah.* Here she is called Abraham's *wife,* but in 1 Chr. 1:32 she is identified as "Abraham's

1. Lit., "gave"; see Speiser, *Genesis,* p. 187, for this translation of *nāṯan.*

2. If one retains the pl., the reference can only be to Hagar and Keturah, neither of whom is directly styled a concubine elsewhere in Genesis. The translation "concubinage" (suggested by Speiser) takes *pîlagšîm* as an abstract. For other examples of abstract pls. see *GKC,* § 124a. Yet I see no compelling reason for interpreting *happîlagšîm* as an abstract. Abraham's sons by concubines total seven, one by Hagar and six by Keturah.

3. Or, "he sent them away . . . eastward, to the east country." The repetition of "east" in this phrase demonstrates that *'ereṣ qeḏem* is a place-name. See Westermann, *Genesis,* 2:397.

4. I follow LXX, SP, Pesh., etc., which supply "days," probably on the basis of the parallel expression in 35:29 (Isaac); 1 Chr. 29:28 (David; cf. also 23:1); 2 Chr. 24:15 (Jehoiada); Job 42:17 (Job). AV, RSV, NIV read "full of years" (see also JB), an interpretative translation of the same expression (so also Westermann, *Genesis,* 2:394, 397). MT has only "old and contented," followed by NAB, NEB.

concubine." This coidentification is comparable with Bilhah, who is called both Jacob's concubine (35:22) and Jacob's wife (30:4). By contrast, Zilpah is identified as Jacob's wife (30:9) but never as his concubine. If "by concubines" in 25:6 is a reference to Hagar and Keturah (see n. 2), then again both Hagar (16:3) and Keturah (25:1) are called "wife" in one place but "concubine" in another (25:6).[5]

The emphasis on Keturah's status as wife would suggest that Abraham married her after the death of Sarah. If the emphasis is on her status as concubine then one would think that Abraham married her while Sarah was still living, as he did with Hagar. In that case one would have to understand *married* in this verse as a pluperfect — "had married."

2 Keturah gives birth to six sons, the first time Abraham has had more than one child by the same wife or the same surrogate wife. Fertility, one of God's choicest blessings to his own, is minimally manifested with Sarah and Hagar, but maximally manifested in the life and womb of the relatively obscure Keturah.

Zimran may refer to the eponymous ancestor of an Arabian tribe, perhaps located west of Mecca on the Red Sea.[6] Jer. 25:25 lists "all the kings of Zimri" as one of the group of peoples right after "all the kings of Arabia and all the kings that dwell in the desert" that will fall to Babylon, suggesting perhaps an Arabian location for "Zimri." But the remainder of v. 25 links the kings of Zimri with "the kings of Elam and the kings of Media," territories in what is now western Iran. Thus the placement of the Zimri of Jer. 25:25 in Arabia is called into doubt.[7] *Jokshan* is probably the same as Joktan of Gen. 10:26-27, for both are listed as the father of Sheba. Also, both Joktan in Gen. 10:25ff. and Jokshan in Gen. 25:2-3 occupy significant places in these two genealogies in terms of the number of their offspring who are identified. *Medan* is unidentifiable. Is it to be connected with Badan (with the interchange of *b* and *m* in Arabic) located to the south of Tema? *Midian* is the only well-known name in the verse. The Midianites were located east of the Gulf of Aqaba. That they made moves into Moab and Edom (Gen. 36:35; Num. 22:4, 7), and even through Gilead into Palestine (Judg. 6–8), reflects their northward migrations. In the Joseph story both "Medanite" and "Midianite" appear. Traders called "Midianites" *(miḏyānîm)* drew Joseph out of the pit (Gen. 37:28). Later the "Medanites" *(mᵉḏānîm)* sold him to Potiphar (37:36).

5. On the use of *pilegeš* and *'iššâ* referring to the same woman, see my *Genesis, Chapters 1–17,* NICOT (Grand Rapids: Eerdmans, 1990), pp. 445-46.

6. Ptolemy (*Geog.* 6.7.5) mentions a Zembram in this location; cf. LXX B, "Zembran," in 1 Chr. 1:32.

7. On the reading of *zimrî* as *zimkî* in Jer. 25:25 see W. L. Holladay, *Jeremiah,* Hermeneia, 2 vols. (Philadelphia: Fortress, 1986-89), 1:671, 675.

The only difference between these two spellings (in the consonantal text) is the presence of the *yôḏ* after the *dāleṯ* in *miḏyānîm*. The closeness of these two names might suggest that their offspring "allegedly intermingled, either in reality by intermarriage or in tradition by confusion of their names."[8] *Ishbak* is unknown. *Shuah* represents the tribe of Job's friend, Bildad the "Shuhite" (Job 2:11). Akkadian sources mention a country *Sūḫu* located on the Middle Euphrates below the mouth of the Khabur River, but Gen. 25's connection of Shuah with names like Sheba and Dedan argues for a Shuah farther to the south.[9]

3 The genealogy says nothing about children of Zimran, but moves instead to a discussion of the second son's descendants. Here *Sheba* and *Dedan* (cf. Isa. 21:13; Jer. 49:8; Ezek. 27:20; 38:13) are listed as the sons of Jokshan. In Gen. 10:7 they are mentioned as the sons of Raamah. Thus in 25:3 Sheba and Dedan are grandsons of Abraham, but in 10:7 they are great-grandsons of Ham and non-Semitic. One may explain the use of different patronymics for Sheba and Dedan as due either to the use of the same name by different persons and tribes in different parts of Arabia, or more likely, the convergence of Hamitic and Semitic lines in southern Arabia.[10]

The three descendants of Dedan are the *Asshurim*, the *Letushim*, and the *Leummim*. These are the only members of the Keturah peoples that are written with the gentilic form. Does the first name indicate that the founders of the Assyrian empire (cf. *'aššûr* in 10:11 as a place name and in 10:22 as a son of Shem) stemmed from a branch of the tribe Dedan?[11] Or does *Asshurim* reflect the name of Ashur, a tribe near Egypt, mentioned in South Arabian inscriptions and a much more likely possibility, given the identifiable area of 25:2-4?[12]

4 The first son by Keturah was omitted when genealogical data were presented. Now the third son is omitted, and we are given five descendants of Midian. *Ephah* is connected with Midian in Isa. 60:6. *Abida* may be

8. See Y. T. Radday, "Humour in Names," in *On Humor and the Comic in the Hebrew Bible*, ed. Y. T. Radday and A. Brenner, JSOTSup 92 (Sheffield: Almond, 1990), pp. 69-70.

9. See M. Pope, *Job*, AB, 3rd ed. (Garden City, NY: Doubleday, 1973), p. 24; J. Hartley, *The Book of Job*, NICOT (Grand Rapids: Eerdmans, 1988), p. 86.

10. See E. E. Carpenter, "Sheba," *ISBE*, 4:456; W. S. LaSor, "Sabeans," *ISBE*, 4:255; M. D. Johnson, *The Purpose of the Biblical Genealogies*, SNTSMS 8 (Cambridge: Cambridge University, 1969), pp. 5-6.

11. See A. Poebel, "The Assyrian King List from Khorsabad," *JNES* 1 (1942) 255.

12. See J. A. Montgomery, *Arabia and the Bible* (Philadelphia: University of Pennsylvania, 1934), p. 44 and n. 25. Montgomery (p. 45) connects Letushim with a root that suggests the meaning "smiths," and Leummim he takes as a generic term meaning "hordes."

connected with a king from Maan in South Arabia, Abi-yadaʿa.[13] *Epher, Hanoch,* and *Eldaah* are mysteries.

5-6 Abraham gives all his possessions to Isaac (as was earlier mentioned in 24:36b), but the sons he had by his concubines he sends away with gifts. Abraham had once given all he had to God (ch. 22). Now the objects are changed: Abraham gives all he has to Isaac. Abraham is concerned that his sons by Keturah not be too close to his son by Sarah. This concern may reflect the same kind of concern of ch. 24 that Isaac not get too close to the locals by marrying a Canaanite.

The expression *the land of Kedem* (Heb. *'ereṣ qeḏem*) may mean "east country" or "the land of the East." References to it as a place would position it east or southeast of the Dead Sea.[14] The difference between sending the servant eastward (ch. 24) and sending his children by concubines eastward is that the latter are sent away never to return. In this respect one might also compare Abraham's actions with the sons of his concubines, especially Keturah's, and his earlier action with his concubine with wife Hagar and her son Ishmael (ch. 21). On both occasions he sent his sons by concubinage away, an action expressed by the Piel of *šālaḥ* (21:14; 25:6), thus distancing them from Isaac. On both occasions Abraham sent the sons away with provisions (water, food; gifts). Abraham apparently viewed both dismissals as permanent.

7 One hundred years of Abraham's life have passed since the first mention of a specific year (75 in 12:4). His life span of 175 years ranks him as living 5 years less than his son Isaac (35:28), but 22 years longer than his grandson Jacob (47:28) and 65 years longer than his great-grandson Joseph (50:26).

I argued above that v. 1 probably describes something Abraham did before Sarah died, even though 25:1 follows the death of Sarah. Similarly, the marriage of Isaac at the age of forty to Rebekah (25:20), and the twins that came from this marriage twenty years later (25:26), took place before Abraham died (25:8). At the birth of Isaac Abraham was 140, and at the birth of his grandchildren he was 160, and he lived fifteen years beyond that. Yet Genesis has no record of any meeting between Abraham and Jacob.

8 It is one thing to live a long life. It is another thing to live a long life that is also a happy life. This obituary notice about Abraham draws attention to the fact that Abraham died not only at an elderly age but in a frame of mind filled with inner *shalom* and satisfaction. That is the thrust of the phrase *full of days* or "contented."[15]

13. See *ANET,* p. 666.

14. See Gen. 29:1; Num. 23:7; Judg. 6:3, 33; 7:12 (in all three verses parallel with Midianites and Amalekites); Isa. 11:14; Jer. 49:28; Ezek. 25:4, 10; Job 1:3.

15. See von Rad, *Genesis,* p. 262; Wolff, *Anthropology of the Old Testament,* p. 112; J. Pedersen, *Israel: Its Life and Culture,* 4 vols. bound as 2 (repr. London: Oxford University, 1964), 1-2:327-28. Cf. also G. von Rad's statement in his *Old Testament Theology,* trans. D. M. G. Stalker, 2 vols. (New York: Harper & Row: 1962-65), 1:390,

The expression *was gathered to his kin* is found only ten times in the OT, and all of them are in the Pentateuch.[16] Here in 25:8 it is distinguished from death (v. 8a) and burial (v. 9), and accordingly suggests the reunion of the deceased with his forefathers. A fourfold process is involved here. An individual breathes his last, dies, is gathered to his kin, and is buried. Dying precedes being gathered to one's kin, and being gathered to one's kin precedes burial. Therefore, to be gathered to one's kin cannot mean to be entombed in the grave. That one is gathered to one's kin/fathers before being buried implies either a belief in a continued existence in the netherworld or that the spirit of the deceased joined the ancestors in the underworld, and that even in death family solidarity was not broken.[17] Of the six individuals in the Pentateuch of whom the phrase "gathered to his kin" is used (Abraham, 25:8; Ishmael, 25:17; Isaac, 35:29; Jacob, 49:29, 33; Moses, Num. 27:13; Deut. 32:50; and Aaron, Num. 20:24; Deut. 32:50), four of them were not buried in an ancestral grave (Abraham, Ishmael, Moses, and Aaron).[18]

9-10 Isaac and Ishmael together buried their father. Those scholars who attribute this passage to P claim that P did not share J's knowledge (ch. 16) or E's knowledge (ch. 21) of Ishmael's expulsion. Or does this verse reflect that the brothers, deeply at odds with each other, had a real or artificial reunion at the death of their father? One may compare this possible reunion with that of Esau and Jacob, between whom no love was lost and both of whom were present at their father's funeral (35:29).

11 For the second time in Genesis blessing moves from promise to fact. God had blessed (*bērak̲*, 24:1) Abraham. Now God *blessed (wayᵉb̲ārek̲) Isaac.* The narrator's terse comment about God's blessing on Isaac shortly after Abraham's death confirms the wisdom of Abraham's actions as told in v. 5. But unlike Abraham, who had to wait until the end of his life to be blessed, Isaac receives this blessing at the threshold of his adult life.

"when death drew near to one 'old and full of days' it was really a gracious fulfillment, since from the start life was regarded as something limited, meted out to man, to which there could therefore also be a condition of satiety."

16. Gen. 25:8, 17; 35:29; 49:29, 33; Num. 20:24, 26; 27:13; 31:2; Deut. 32:50. The kindred phrase "he was gathered to his fathers" or "he was buried with his fathers" appears in Genesis (15:15; 47:30) and elsewhere in the OT (e.g., Judg. 2:10).

17. See B. Alfrink, "L'expression *neʾĕsap̲ ʾel-ʿammāyw,*" *OTS* 5 (1948) 118-31; G. R. Driver, "Plurima Mortis Imago," in *Studies and Essays in Honor of Abraham A. Neuman,* ed. M. Ben-Horin, B. D. Weinryb, and S. Zeitlin (Leiden: Brill, 1962), pp. 128-43, esp. pp. 137-43; N. J. Tromp, *Primitive Conceptions of Death and the Nether World in the Old Testament,* BibOr 21 (Rome: Pontifical Biblical Institute, 1969), pp. 168-69; T. J. Lewis, *Cults of the Dead in Ancient Israel and Ugarit,* HSM 39 (Atlanta: Scholars, 1989), pp. 164-65; Westermann, *Genesis,* 2:397.

18. See G. A. Lee, "Gather," *ISBE,* 2:414.

Exactly how God blessed Isaac is perhaps clarified by v. 11b, *Isaac settled down near Beer-lahai-roi.* According to 16:14 Beer-lahai-roi is where Yahweh's messenger appeared to the distraught and pregnant Hagar, and where subsequently Ishmael was born. That Isaac settles in the place where Ishmael was born indicates that, geographically, Isaac is indeed the one son chosen by Yahweh to be blessed, and that Ishmael is to be either displaced, or more likely, replaced.

2. ISHMAEL'S DEATH AND HIS SONS (25:12-18)

12 *These are the descendants of Ishmael, Abraham's son whom Hagar the Egyptian, Sarah's slave, bore to Abraham.*

13 *These are the names of Ishmael's sons in the order of*[1] *their birth: Nebaioth (Ishmael's firstborn), Kedar, Adbeel, Mibsam,*

14 *Mishma, Dumah, Massa,*

15 *Hadad, Tema, Jetur, Naphish, and Kedemah.*

16 *These are the sons of Ishmael, their names by their villages and encampments: twelve chieftains for each of the tribal groups.*

17 *And this was the life span of Ishmael: 137 years. Then he breathed his last and died, he was gathered to his kin.*

18 *They extended from Havilah, by Shur, which faces Egypt, as far as Asshur; and he settled*[2] *close to his kindred.*

1. Lit., "these are the names of the sons of Ishmael by their names." Of the ten persons/groups with whom the formula *ʾēlleh tōlᵉḏôṯ* is used, three (Ishmael [Gen. 25:12, 13]; the second *tōlᵉḏôṯ* of Esau [Gen. 36:9ff.]; Aaron and Moses [Num. 3:1-3]) share the following introductory formulae: (1) the usual formula, "these are the descendants of *X*"; (2) a historical note ("whom Hagar the Egyptian, Sarah's slave, bore to Abraham"; "the father of the Edomites in the hill country of Seir"; "at the time when Yahweh spoke with Moses on Mount Sinai"); (3) the pleonastic "these are the names of" following "these are the descendants of." On the significance of this parallel structure in these three instances, see M. D. Johnson, *Purpose of the Biblical Genealogies,* pp. 20, 25.

2. Lit., "he fell," but for a reference to *nāp̱al* meaning "settle," see Judg. 7:12. There is, however, one difference between the phrase in Judg. 7:12 and the one here: the former is *nāp̱al bᵉ*, while the latter is *nāp̱al ʿal-pᵉnê*. Another possibility for *nāp̱al ʿal-pᵉnê* in Gen. 25:18 is "he/each made raids against." I note that both *nāp̱al bᵉ* (Josh. 11:7) and *nāp̱al ʿal* (Jer. 48:32) may mean "to attack, invade." Speiser (*Genesis*, p. 188) argues for this interpretation in Gen. 25:18 ("each made forays against his various kinsmen"). Also, *nāp̱al bᵉ* in Judg. 7:12 might also mean "invaded" (J. A. Soggin, *Judges,* tr. J. Bowden, OTL [Philadelphia: Westminster, 1981], p. 140) or at least "assembled for battle" (cf. R. G. Boling, *Judges,* AB [Garden City, NY: Doubleday, 1975], p. 143: "Midian . . . lay along the valley as numerous as locusts"). The major argument for reading *nāp̱al ʿal pᵉnê* as "settle" is the parallel phrase in Gen. 16:12 about Ishmael: *wᵉʿal pᵉnê kol ʾeḥâw yiškōn.* See also BDB, p. 657b, which suggests "settle" in Gen. 25:18 as one of the idiomatic uses of *nāp̱al.*

12-18 This is an approriate place to include some data about Ishmael's family and his death, since vv. 1-11 just recounted details of Abraham's family and death. Thus the structure of vv. 1-11 and vv. 12-18 is very similar: (1) the reference to Keturah and the unnamed wife of Ishmael (see 21:21); (2) Abraham's children and Ishmael's children (if one does not count the three gentilics of v. 3 Abraham's genealogy contains 13 personal names, and Ishmael's genealogy has 12 names); (3) the span of life each enjoyed (175 years, 137 years, respectively); (4) each breathed his last, died, and was gathered to his kin.

Also, the mention of Ishmael at the burial of his father provides an opportunity for the insertion of material about his progeny. He outlived his father by forty-eight years (cf. 16:16 with 25:17), and he lived eight years after his half-brother's marriage to Rebekah (v. 20). Was there a period of some forty years of *shalom* between Isaac and Ishmael after the demise of their father?

Ishmael's twelve sons (see the prophecy of 17:20) is surely not a fortuitous parallel to the twelve Aramean tribes (22:20-24), the twelve Edomite tribes (36:10-14), and the twelve tribes of Israel. Perhaps the number *twelve* is dictated by the fact that each tribe was responsible to take a monthly turn in the maintenance of the central place of worship.[3]

We were told in v. 11 that God blessed Isaac, but we are not told how. Here we do not find the verb "blessed" in reference to Ishmael, but we do find an ample illustration of what constitutes a blessing, twelve offspring. That Ishmael had so many children and that he enjoyed longevity are sure trademarks of the divine blessing.

The text goes into some detail in describing how these tribal groups were organized (v. 16). Such organization included division according to their *villages (ḥᵃṣērîm)* and *encampments (ṭîrōṯ),* with a *chieftain* or prince *(nāśî')* over each tribe. The word *ḥᵃṣērîm* ("villages") is used for the abode of the Avvites (Deut. 2:23) and of the sons of Kedar (Isa. 42:11). It is also used to describe a village that is not fortified (Lev. 25:31), or a settlement in the vicinity of a city (Josh. 19:8; Neh. 12:29).[4]

The term for *tribal group* is *'ummâ* (v. 16b), which occurs only three times in the OT (here; Num. 25:15; Ps. 117:1) and is to be identified with the term *ummatum* from the Mari texts. It describes a tribal unit of considerable size, and in the OT it is restricted to nomadic and non-Israelite tribes.[5] Israelites tribes are designated by either *šēḇeṭ* or *maṭṭeh.*

3. See de Vaux, *Early History of Israel,* pp. 702-3, for the proliferation of the number twelve. Also, J. Bright, *A History of Israel,* 3rd ed. (Philadelphia: Westminster, 1981), pp. 162-65; Gottwald, *Tribes of Yahweh,* pp. 352-56.

4. See A. Malamat, "Mari and the Bible: Some Patterns of Tribal Organization and Institutions," *JAOS* 82 (1962) 147.

5. Ibid., p. 144; idem, "*UMMATUM* in Old Babylonian Texts and its Ugaritic and Biblical Counterparts," *VT* 11 (1979) 527-36. If the same word is found in Ps. 117:1, then

Of the names listed in vv. 13-15, Kedar, Mibsam, Mishma, Dumah, Massa, Jetur, Tema, and Naphish are mentioned elsewhere in the Bible.[6] Nebaioth, Kedar, Abdeel, Dumah, Massa, and Teman are mentioned in Assyrian and North Arabian inscriptions.[7] The nomadic nature of these tribes is attested by the scope of their wanderings, which stretch (based on biblical and nonbiblical data) from the northern Sinai (Abdeel) to the western border of Babylonia (Kedar, Nebaioth, and Massa).

Nebaioth and *Kedar* (in reverse order) are coupled in a poem about the glory of the New Jerusalem (Isa. 60:7). Among those who will participate in that grand day are the flocks of Kedar and the rams of Nebaioth. The prophet exhorts Kedar to join in a hymn to Yahweh the Redeemer (Isa. 42:11). The female in the Song of Solomon compares her black and beautiful appearance to the tents of Kedar (Cant. 1:5). Once known for its military prowess, Kedar will one day see that reputation come to an abrupt halt (Isa. 21:16). For Jeremiah (2:10) Kedar along with Cyprus represent the extremes of east and west, and they also serve as models of non-Israelites who serve their (false) gods more faithfully than Israel serves Yahweh. Kedar is located east of Transjordan in northern Arabia. As in Isa. 60:7 Kedar and Nebaioth (Nabaiati) are listed together as places whose king and people the seventh-century B.C. King Ashurbanipal conquered.[8] In Ps. 120:7 Kedar (to the south and east of the psalmist) and Meshech (to the north and east of the Psalmist) represent again geographical extremes that still would not sufficiently remove the psalmist from opposition in his estimation. *Adbeel* and *Mibsam,* respectively, the third and fourth sons of Ishmael, appear only here and in 1 Chr. 1:29. The former name, Adbeel, is probably reflected in the personal name Idi-bi'li, who is connected with Arabia in an inscription from the latter part of the 8th century B.C. of Tiglath-pileser III.[9]

Mishma appears only here and in 1 Chr. 1:20. In 1 Chr. 4:2-26 Mibsam is identified as the grandson of Simeon and Mishma as his great grandson, and

---

we have a word that is written twice as a fem. pl. (Gen. 25:16 and Num. 25:15) and once as a masc. pl. *['ummîm]* in Ps. 117:1.

6. Kedar, Isa. 21:17; 42:11; 60:7; Jer. 49:28; Ezek. 27:21; Mibsam, 1 Chr. 1:29; 4:25; Mishma, 1 Chr. 1:30; 4:25; Dumah, Josh. 15:52; Isa. 21:11; 1 Chr. 1:30; Massa, 1 Chr. 1:30; Prov. 30:1; 31:1; Jetur, 1 Chr. 1:31; 5:19; Tema, Job 6:19; Isa. 21:14; Jer. 25:23; Naphish, 1 Chr. 5:19.

7. For further information see J. A. Montgomery, *Arabia and the Bible* (Philadelphia: University of Pennsylvania, 1934), pp. 45-47; I. Eph'al, "Ishmaelites," *EncJud,* 9:87-90; F. V. Winnett and W. L. Reed, *Ancient Records from North Arabia* (Toronto: University of Toronto, 1970); F. V. Winnett, "The Arabian Genealogies in the Book of Genesis," in *Translating and Understanding the Old Testament,* Fest. H. G. May, ed. H. T. Frank and W. L. Reed (Nashville: Abingdon, 1970), pp. 171-96.

8. See *ANET,* pp. 297-301.

9. See ibid., pp. 282-83.

this suggests the possibility of a commingling of the Simeonites and Arabians. *Dumah* is mentioned in Isa. 21:11 and 1 Chr. 1:30. Dumah is most likely connected with "Adumatu, the stronghold of the Arabs," which Sennacherib conquered in his campaigns against the Arabs and Egypt.[10] In Isa. 21:11 the LXX translates Dumah as "Idumea" (Edom). More than likely the LXX's rendering is secondary and derivative and reflects the point that at the time of the LXX's production the Arabian significance of Dumah had been forgotten. *Massa* appears here, in 1 Chr. 1:30, Prov. 30:1, and 31:1.[11] Tiglath-pileser III speaks of "the inhabitants of Mas'a, of Tema . . . the tribe of Idiba'ileans . . . whose countries [(are) far away], toward West, [heard] the fame of my rule [. . . and brought] without ex[ception] as their tribute; gold, silver . . ."[12]

Hadad as one of Ishmael's twelve sons appears only here and in 1 Chr. 1:30. The same name appears elsewhere for individuals from Edom (Gen. 36:35, 36; 1 K. 11:14-22, 25; 1 Chr. 1:50, 51). I have already mentioned the appearance of *Tema* in cuneiform inscriptions in conjunction with other Arabian localities. It also appears in a list of Arabian cities — Dadanu, Padakku, Hibra, and Jadihu — on a stelae of Nabonidus.[13] Tema is also mentioned in Isa. 21:14 along with Dedan (v. 13) and Kedar (v. 16), and they are urged to provide water and bread for Arabian refugees who have been ravaged by Syrian forces. Cf. also Job 6:19 and Jer. 25:23.

Jetur and *Naphish* are located by 1 Chr. 5:19 in Transjordan, and were attacked there by the Reubenites, Gadites, and the half-tribe of Manasseh. Jetur is the people of Ituraea, the area over which Philip, son of Herod the Great, was tetrarch (Luke 3:1). Ituraea is a region northeast of Galilee. That territory this far north was settled by people of Ishmaelite stock confirms the mobility of these Arabian tribes. *Kedemah* appears only in Gen. 25:15 and 1 Chr. 1:31. These are the twelve eponymous ancestors of the Arabians whose eastern boundary is *Havilah* (a region in North Arabia or in eastern/southeastern Arabia), and whose northern boundary is *Asshur,* by which is meant either Assyria or Syria, more likely the latter.[14]

10. See ibid., p. 291.

11. A place-name in RSV, NEB, JB, NAB, and Speiser, but in other translations "prophecy" (AV), "utterance" (NKJV), "oracle" (NIV, NRSV).

12. See *ANET,* p. 283; and see p. 284, where "Mas'ai" appears with Tema, the Sabaeans, and the Ibida'leans.

13. See ibid., p. 562.

14. On Havilah and Asshur in v. 18 see Winnett, "Arabian Genealogies," pp. 175-79, 190-91.

III. THE ISAAC/JACOB CYCLE (25:19–36:43)

A. THE BIRTH OF ESAU AND JACOB (25:19-26)

19 *This is the story*[1] *of Isaac, Abraham's son; Abraham fathered*[2] *Isaac.*
20 *Isaac was forty years of age when he married Rebekah the daughter of Bethuel the Aramean of Paddan-aram, the sister of Laban the Aramean.*
21 *Isaac entreated Yahweh on his wife's behalf*[3] *because she was barren. Yahweh accepted his entreaty,*[4] *and Rebekah his wife conceived.*
22 *But the children inside her struggled*[5] *with each other, so she said: "If this is so, why ever I . . .?"*[6] *She went to consult Yahweh.*

1. This is the eighth appearance of the formula *'ēlleh tôlᵉḏôṯ* in Genesis. If one translates the phrase literally and consistently, then the rendering will be "these are the descendants of." Another option is to render only as "these are the descendants of" when a genealogy follows, but translate as "story" or "account" when a narrative follows.

2. The use of the Hiphil of *yālaḏ* with only a brief list of immediate descendants is best paralleled by Gen. 6:9-10, and is but one of four introductions used after the *'ēlleh tôlᵉḏôṯ* formula. The other three are: (1) the use of the Hiphil of *yālaḏ* and the listing of numerous descendants (ch. 5; 11:10-27); (2) a double introductory formula (25:12-17; 36:9-14); and (3) the use of the formula "the sons of *X*" without any use of *yālaḏ* (10:2-4, 6-7, 20, 22-23, 31). See M. D. Johnson, *Purpose of the Biblical Genealogies,* p. 22.

3. *lᵉnōḵaḥ* represents the substantive *nōḵaḥ* ("front") combined with the preposition *lᵉ*. It means lit. "in front of" (30:38), or "in front of" in the sense of "on behalf of."

4. The Niphal *ye'tar,* lit., "was entreated," can mean "allowed himself to be entreated" (i.e., he accepted Abraham's entreaty). GKC, §§ 51c, 121f, calls this use a *Niphal tolerativum.* For *'āṯar* (in Niphal) plus *lᵉ* = "accept entreaty, supplication" cf. 2 Sam. 21:14; 24:25.

5. LXX *eskírtōn* (for MT *yiṯrōṣᵃṣû*) is the same word used in Luke 1:41, 44, "the leaping" of the foetus in the womb.

6. Lit., "if thus, why this, I?" I take *lāmmâ zeh 'ānōḵî* as an aposiopesis in which Rebekah suddenly breaks off her thought. See GKC, §§ 147, 159dd, 167a. Cf. G. R. Driver,

23 *Yahweh answered her:*
"Two nations are in your womb,
two peoples are drawing themselves apart while yet[7] *in your bosom;*
but one people shall be stronger than[8] *the other people,*
and the older shall serve the younger."[9]

24 *When the time of her delivery came there were*[10] *twins in her womb!*

25 *The first to emerge was ruddy*[11] *all over. He was like a hairy garment; so they named*[12] *him Esau.*

26 *His brother emerged next, grasping Esau's heel; so they named him Jacob.*[13] *Isaac was sixty years old when he fathered them.*[14]

We have read about Abraham's sons (vv. 2-4) and about Ishmael's sons (vv. 13-15), and now we come to Isaac's sons. Two is the number of sons he fathered, a total that seems insignificant compared to Ishmael's twelve children. Ishmael is more like his father than is Isaac, in terms of numerous progeny. While the story of Ishmael's children is confined to a few verses (vv. 13-18), however, the story of Isaac's children is spread over 25:19–36:43 (and beyond), with 25:19–35:29 being given to Jacob and 36:1-43 to Esau.

"Ezekiel: Linguistic and Textual Problems," *Bib* 35 (1954) 155n.7; J. Barr, "Why? in Biblical Hebrew," *JTS* 36 (1985) 19. RSV renders arbitrarily, "if it is thus, why do I live?" *(ḥāyyâ 'ānōḵî),* following Pesh. and probably influenced by 27:46. M. Rottenberg, "The Interpretation of Rebekah's Question, *'lāmmâ zeh 'ānōkî,'* " *Beth Mikra* 29 (1983/84) 218-19 (Hebrew) suggests adding a *b* to *zeh*: "Why am I here?" but this is unnecessary.

7. I prefer to read the *min* on *mimmēʿayiḵ* as a preposition of time (i.e., the separation takes place while they are still in the womb) rather than as a preposition of place (i.e., an event due to happen at the time of birth).

8. *'āmēṣ* plus preposition *min* meaning "be stronger, mightier than" occurs again in the Qal only in 1 Sam. 22:18 (= Ps. 18:18 [Eng. 17]); Ps. 142:7, both of which focus on deliverance from enemies mightier than the supplicant.

9. For a discussion of some textual problems in this verse consult R. A. Kraft, "A Note on the Oracle of Rebecca (Gen. xxv 23)," *JTS* 13 (1962) 318-20.

10. On the use of a *wᵉhinnēh* clause to report a surprise development see Andersen, *Sentence in Biblical Hebrew,* p. 95.

11. *'aḏmônî,* i.e., a play on the word "Edom." See the commentary below.

12. The pl. is used in v. 25 *(wayyiqrᵉ'û)* versus the sing. in v. 26 *(wayyiqrā).* The ancient versions attempted to give the two verses consistency. LXX, Pesh., and Vulg. read the pl. verb of v. 25 as a sing.; SP read the sing. verb of v. 26 as a pl.

13. Note the acoustical similarity between "Jacob" *(yaʿᵃqōḇ)* and "heel" *(ʿāqēḇ),* which I discuss further in the commentary below.

14. For other examples of a circumstantial clause ending a story, see 16:16; 17:24-25.

19 After the phrase *Isaac, Abraham's son,* the clause *Abraham fathered Isaac* seems redundant. Furthermore, the mention of Isaac's birth in his own genealogy is without parallel. Thus some have suggested that v. 19b may be a gloss.[15] This may not be the case, however. Left intact, the phrase may be saying that Isaac was fathered by Abraham, but he himself did not perpetuate his patrilineal descent. Unlike the situation with Abraham and Isaac, the text nowhere states that Isaac "fathered" *(yālaḏ)* Esau and Jacob. It states only that he married Rebekah, the sister of Laban.[16]

20 Later rabbinical tradition fixed the minimum age for marriage at eighteen for boys (Mishnah *Abot* 5:21). If one is not married by twenty he is cursed by God (T.B. *Sanh.* 76b). Isaac's *forty years of age* at his marriage puts him well beyond that. Still, in spite of his advanced years, he played no role in selecting his own bride. That choice was expedited by Abraham and his servant (ch. 24).

Rebekah's family as outlined here differs in only one respect from the information in ch. 24. In 24:10 her family was identified with Aram-naharaim or Mesopotamia. The equivalent to that designation here (i.e., Upper Mesopotamia) is *Paddan-aram.*[17] *Paddan* may be interpreted by the Assyr. *padanū,* "road," and hence *Paddan-aram* would mean "road of Aram."

21 Rebekah's condition is the same as her mother-in-law's had once been. Both were *barren* or sterile (*ʿaqārâ;* see 11:30). This circumstance raises interesting questions about the servant's arduous trip to Paddan-aram to procure Rebekah. The servant obeyed his master, and the master honored his God. Every test or fleece the servant placed before God in order to make sure that the girl he brought home was the right one has turned up positive. There can be no further room for doubt. This woman is indeed Isaac's wife-to-be and the future mother of his children. But now everything is called into question. Can a sterile woman actually be the one who is divinely selected to carry on the promised line? Or has the servant, or even Isaac, misread some sign? An act of God brought Sarah and Isaac together. Now it will take another act of God to overcome her barrenness.

Isaac's handling of his wife's infertility is distinguished from Abraham's handling of a similar problem. Abraham's prayers result in the opening of the wombs of Philistine women (20:17), but never did we read that Abraham prayed for Sarah when she was incapacitated. In order to

15. See F. M. Cross, *Canaanite Myth and Hebrew Epic,* pp. 303-4; Westermann, *Genesis,* 2:412.

16. N. Jay, "Sacrifice, descent and the Patriarchs," *VT* 38 (1988) 61.

17. Paddan-aram is also mentioned in 28:2-7; 31:18; 35:9, 26; 46:15. In 48:7 "Paddan" appears alone. All these passages are located in what the source critics label as the P strand of Genesis. The mention of Haran (28:10; 29:4) in conjunction with Paddan-aram argues for the location of the latter in northwestern Mesopotamia.

alleviate barrenness God visited Sarah (21:1-2) and remembered Rachel (30:22). But no verb is used with God as subject and Rebekah as object. Instead, the urgent prayer of Isaac is highlighted.[18]

The verb used to describe Isaac's praying is *ʿāṯar,* the same one used by Manoah before God in regard to the alleviation of his wife's barrenness (Judg. 13:8). The root often means to supplicate before God for the removal of an unpleasant situation, as evidenced by its frequent use in the plague accounts of Exodus (8:26 [Eng. 30]; 10:18 [both Qal]; 8:4, 5, 24, 25 [Eng. 8, 9, 18, 19]; 9:28; 10:17 [all Hiphil]). Such entreaty is what Pharaoh wishes Moses to do before Yahweh so that the plague may disappear.

22 Isaac's problem is getting Rebekah pregnant. Rebekah's problem is being pregnant. Perhaps no pregnancy that produces this much anguish is worthwhile. For inside Rebekah's womb two fetuses *struggled with each other.* The verb used here for the fetal movements is a strong one and means "to abuse, crush"; several times it parallels *ʿāšaq,* "to oppress" (1 Sam. 12:3, 4; Hos. 5:11; Amos 4:1).

First came Isaac's prayer expressed with *ʿāṯar: Isaac entreated Yahweh.* Now comes Rebekah's prayer expressed with *dāraš:*[19] why ever I . . .? God answers these prayers either with an act (v. 21b) or with an explanation (v. 23). It is interesting that the text says nothing about any techniques Sarah used in ascertaining the divine oracle, such as one finds in much of non-Israelite religion. In Akkadian literature, for instance, in terms of sheer number of texts, the largest single category deals with divinatory practices. A widely practiced technique involved the observation of the entrails of slaughtered sheep or goats, particularly the liver, and hence the name hepatoscopy (or extispicy, a more general term, because it involved divination by means of the *exta,* the vital organs). The findings of such methods were collected in manuals or handbooks in which a typical entry might use the following casuistic formulation: "If the liver has the shape of *X,* then the outcome of the situation will be *Y.*" Other techniques included libanomancy (observing the configurations of smoke rising from a censer filled with incense); lecanomancy (pouring oil into water or vice versa); belomancy (shooting arrows); psephomancy (the casting of dice); and oneiromancy (the interpretation of dreams). Astronomy probably originated as a divinatory practice. The purpose of all divination techniques is to seek a divine response to a human initiative, and that divine response is

18. M. E. Donaldson, "Kingship Theory in the Patriarchal Narratives: The Case of the Barren Wife," *JAAR* 49 (1981) 77-87, suggests that the barrenness of the patriarchs differs according to their kinship relationships with their husbands.

19. For instances of *dāraš* meaning "to consult an oracle, to inquire of Yahweh" (as Rebekah does here) cf. Judg. 6:29; 1 Sam. 9:9; 1 K. 14:5; 22:5, 8; 2 K. 1:2; 3:11; 8:8; 22:13, 18; 1 Chr. 10:13; 2 Chr. 34:21, 26; Isa. 19:3; Jer. 21:2; 37:7; Ezek. 14:3, 7.

ascertained either inductively (as in hepatoscopy) or intuitively (as in oneiromancy).[20]

By contrast, Israel never produced anything like the literary products of Mesopotamian divination. There is the attested means of learning the divine will by means of the sacred lot, the Urim and Thummim, a distinctly priestly function. The clearest passage illustrating this practice is Num. 27:21-23 in which Joshua, possibly Moses' replacement, is to stand before Eleazar, who is to "inquire for him by the judgment of the Urim before Yahweh" (v. 21). But note that this procedure never became more than a narrative element.

More frequent in Israel was inquiring of Yahweh by a prophet. The clearest example of this is found in 2 K. 8:7-15. The elements include: (1) a setting: a need described and a request that the prophet inquire of God about that need (vv. 7-9a); (2) sharing the problem with the prophet (vv. 9b); (3) the prophet delivers an oracle (vv. 10-13); (4) fulfillment of the oracle (vv. 14-15).

Rebekah's situation follows closely this pattern. There is (1) a setting that describes the need — she is barren; (2) Rebekah goes to consult Yahweh (directly, not through an intermediary); (3) an oracle is delivered (v. 23); and (4) that oracle is fulfilled (v. 24).[21]

23 God's explanation provides at least three surprises for Rebekah. (1) She is carrying two peoples in her womb. (2) These boys are already designated as the ancestor of these peoples. (3) The older son will be subordinate to the younger son, and hence will surrender his right of primogeniture.[22] It may be more than coincidence that the home of Esau is elsewhere called Seir *(śēʿîr),* but the one from Seir is to be usurped by his younger brother *(ṣāʿir).* The two words sound alike, and suggest literary artistry on the part of the author.

This revelation to Rebekah provides another in a long list of illustrations in which the younger brother replaces his older brother(s). One thinks of Isaac and Ishmael, Zerah and Perez (also twins), Joseph/Benjamin and their older brothers, Ephraim and Manasseh, David and his older brothers, Solomon and Adonijah. All of these bear witness to God's gratuitous choice in which the factor in the choice is not age but God's sovereign will.

The oracle hardly brings comfort to Rebekah. This uterine struggle is but

20. For further study of this subject see A. Caquot and M. Leibovici, eds., *La Divination* (Paris: Presses universitaires de France, 1968); A. L. Oppenheim, *Ancient Mesopotamia* (Chicago: University of Chicago, 1964), pp. 206-27; W. W. Hallo and W. K. Simpson, *The Ancient Near East: A History* (New York: Harcourt Brace Jovanovich, 1971), pp. 158-63.

21. B. O. Long, "The Effect of Divination upon Israelite Literature," *JBL* 92 (1973) 489-97, esp. p. 495. Josephus (*Ant.* 1.18.1 [§ 257]) in retelling this incident has Isaac seeking Yahweh, and substitutes Isaac for Rebekah as the recipient of the oracle in v. 23. B. H. Amaru, "Portraits of Biblical Women in Josephus' *Antiquities,*" *JJS* 39 (1988) 149.

22. The practice of passing the father's inheritance is referred to as ultimogeniture, in contrast to primogeniture.

an anticipation of a much more difficult situation. It explains her pain, but perhaps it raises more questions than ever. If only Sarah had known — but perhaps her ignorance is bliss — that it would take almost a millennium for at least the last part of the prophecy to be fulfilled. Not until the time of David do the Israelites (the younger) subjugate the Edomites (the older) — see 2 Sam. 8:12-14, especially v. 14b, "and all the Edomites became David's servants."

24 The oracle produced no queries by Rebekah. She is content with the explanation, and is now more able to endure a painful pregnancy. The end of the pregnancy proves the accuracy of the first part of the prophecy. The two nations *(gōyim)* in her womb are twins *(tōmîm).*[23]

25 The firstborn, when he emerges from the womb, is *ruddy ('aḏmônî), like a hairy garment* or mantle *('addereṯ śēʿar),* and is called *Esau (ʿēśāw).* The color *'aḏmônî* is used again only of David (1 Sam. 16:12; 17:42). It may refer either to the color of Esau's skin or to the color of his hair, although the latter is more likely.[24] It appears that this word for "red" supplies the etiology for Edom, while the word for "hairy" *(śēʿār)* supplies the etiology for Seir, Esau's eventual home. Obviously, *'aḏmônî* is closer in sound to Edom than it is to Esau. Thus one might have expected v. 25c to read: "so they named him Edom." The similarity between "hairy" *(śēʿār)* and "Esau" *(ʿēśāw)* is remote. In fact, the first two consonants are reversed: *śēʿār: ʿēśāw* (śʿ; ʿś). Precise etymology is clearly not the primary concern here. This reference to Esau's hair will become a prominent part of the later narrative when Jacob has to masquerade as Esau, "a hairy man" *('îš śāʿir),* Gen. 27:11.

26 One wordplay (v. 25) is followed by another. The second son to be born was *Jacob (yaʿᵃqōḇ),* so called because at birth he was *grasping Esau's heel (ʿāqēḇ).* Thus the older brother is named in accordance with his appearance, and the younger brother in accordance with his actions. Esau is born ruddy, and Jacob is born grabbing. Even the very infantile Jacob is acting out the oracle of Yahweh announced in v. 23. From the very moment of birth the divine plan is in evident operation.

Scholars are agreed that the name *Jacob* is an abbreviated name, of which the longer form is "Jacob-el," or *yaʿqub–alel.* The meaning would be "May El protect (him)" or "El will protect (him)." In fact, D. N. Freedman has suggested that the original, unabbreviated name of Jacob is preserved in Deut. 33:28: "Israel dwells in safety; by himself Jacob-el settles."[25]

23. The word for "twins" elsewhere in the OT is spelled with an *'aleph (tᵉ'ômîm).* Cf. 38:27; Cant. 4:5; 7:4 (Eng. 3); and GKC, § 23f.; F. I. Andersen and A. D. Forbes, *Spelling in the Hebrew Bible,* BibOr 41 (Rome: Biblical Institute, 1986), pp. 85ff., for a full listing of words from which an *'aleph* has been omitted.

24. Cf. LXX *pyrrákēs,* Vulg. *rufus.* See also Brenner, *Colour Terms in the Old Testament,* pp. 127-30.

25. D. N. Freedman, "The Original Name of Jacob," *IEJ* 13 (1963) 125-26.

The personal name *yaʿqub–alel* is widely attested outside the Bible. In Egyptian the Semitic names *Yʿqbʿr* and *Yʿqbhr* ("Har [the mountain god] shall protect"?) are borne by rulers of the Hyksos period.[26] Also, *yaʿqob-ʾEl* is a Palestinian place name in the geographical list of Thutmose III (ca. 1450 B.C.), and later recopied by Ramses II and III.

The Mesopotamian evidence is as follows. In Upper Mesopotamia the name *Ya-ah-qu-ub-El* occurs four times in the Chagar Bazar inscriptions (ca. 1800 B.C.); and *Ya-a-qu-ub-El* appears once at Qattuna on the Habur River (end of 18th century).[27] In Lower Mesopotamia the names *Ya-ah-qú-ub-El* and *Ya-qú-ub-El* appear in texts from Kish a century before Hammurapi, as does *Ya-qú-ub-El* in documents from Tell Ḥarmal (ancient Šaduppum).[28]

From the noun *ʿāqēḇ,* "heel," a Hebrew denominative verb is formed *(ʿāqaḇ)* which means "to follow closely." In Jer. 9:3 (Eng. 4) it has the connotation "to overtake, supplant," as it does in Gen. 27:36. But "follow closely" may also develop into "restrain, stop, hold back" (i.e., "guard," "protect"), as in Job 37:4: "Men stay not when his voice is heard."[29]

So then, *yaʿqub–alel* may be taken either as a prayer, "May God protect (him)," or as a statement, "God will protect (him)." If one takes *yaʿqub* as a past tense and not as an imperfect, then the meaning is "God has protected (him)."[30] This possibility would be particularly appropriate, in view of the painful and uncertain pregnancy Rebekah had to endure. Jacob has survived that ordeal.

B. ESAU SURRENDERS HIS BIRTHRIGHT (25:27-34)

27 *When the lads*[1] *grew up, Esau became a skillful hunter,*[2] *a man of the steppe, whereas Jacob was a wholesome man*[3] *who stayed around his tents.*

26. For the Egyptian evidence see S. Yeivin, "YAʿQOBʾEL," *JEA* 45 (1959) 16-18.

27. See J. Nougayrol, "Documents du Ḫabur," *Syria* 37 (1960) 207, 208 ("ia-qu-ub-DINGER").

28. See S. D. Simmons, "Early Old Babylonian Tablets from Ḥarmal and Elsewhere," *JCS* 13 (1959) 114 (no. 26, line 7); idem, *JCS* 14 (1960) 27 (no. 57, line 13).

29. Translation of M. Pope, *Job,* AB, 3rd ed. (Garden City, NY: Doubleday, 1973), pp. 278, 280.

30. In sentence names, formed either with the perfect or imperfect form of the verb, the predicate-subject type is much more frequent than the inverse. With the imperfect form the predicate-subject type is esp. frequent among the oldest proper names. See J. J. Stamm, "Names," *EncJud,* 12:803-6.

1. *naʿar* has been used earlier for Ishmael (21:12), Isaac (22:5, 12), the servants who accompanied Abraham and Isaac (22:5; cf. 14:24), and later with Joseph (37:2).

2. Lit., "a man who knew (or was experienced in) hunting."

3. The phrase *ʾîš tām* will be discussed in the commentary below. For now note

28 *Isaac loved Esau, for he was fond of game,*[4] *but Rebekah loved*[5] *Jacob.*

29 *Once, when Jacob was preparing a stew, Esau came in from the field, starving.*

30 *Esau said to Jacob: "Let me swallow, please, some of that red stuff,*[6] *for I am starving." (That is why he was called Edom.)*[7]

31 *"First*[8] *give me in exchange*[9] *your birthright," Jacob replied.*

32 *Esau responded: "I am on the verge of dying. What benefit*[10] *will a birthright be for me?"*

33 *Jacob said: "Swear to me first." So he swore to him and he exchanged his birthright with Jacob.*

---

the modern translations: "quiet" (AV, RSV, NRSV, NIV, JB, Westermann, *Genesis,* 2:411); "of quiet disposition" (Berkeley); "led a settled life" (NEB); "mild" (NJPS, NKJV, Alter, *Art of Biblical Narrative,* p. 42); "retiring" (Speiser, *Genesis,* p. 193); "naive" (Coote and Ord, *Bible's First History,* pp. 139, 142).

4. Or, "he had a taste for game"; Heb. *ṣayiḏ bᵉpîw,* lit., "for [Esau's] game was in his [viz., Isaac's] mouth."

5. "Isaac" is followed by a finite form of *'āhaḇ,* but "Rebekah" is followed by the participle of *'āhaḇ ('ōheḇeṯ),* thus making it a circumstantial clause, unless *'ōheḇeṯ* conceals an archaic suffixed perfect verb (see Andersen, *Sentence in Biblical Hebrew,* p. 128). Note the subjects are chiastically arranged in the two parts of this verse: "loved-Isaac: Rebekah-loved."

6. MT *min-hā'āḏōm hā'āḏōm* has been interpreted variously. Some (e.g., Westermann, *Genesis,* 2:416, 418) see it as an intentional repetition that Esau blurts out; others (e.g., Skinner, *Genesis,* pp. 361-62) think the repetition is awkward and revocalize the first *'dm* as *'ĕḏōm,* a cognate to Arab. *'idām,* "seasoning or condiment for bread"; still others (e.g., Brueggemann, *Genesis,* p. 218) understand the two words as homographs, one meaning "red" and the other "pottage" (cf. LXX *toú hepsématos toú pyrroú*). Brenner (*Colour Terms in the Old Testament,* p. 60) states "that anyone of the proposed emendations would rob Esau's utterance of the sense of urgency and the oblique, too-tired-to-care attitude."

7. Here is another play on "Edom," Heb. *'ĕḏôm.* The "red stuff" Esau craves is *hā'āḏōm.* Cf. v. 25 above.

8. For *kayyôm,* lit., "as the day," meaning "first," see v. 33 below, and 1 Sam. 2:16; 9:27; 1 K. 1:51 par. 2 Chr. 18:4. See BDB, p. 400b; GKC, § 35n; M. Rottenberg, "Towards the Meaning of *kayyom* in Eight of its Biblical Occurrences," *Leš* 48-49 (1983-85) 60-62 (Hebrew).

9. The root *māḵar* usually means "sell" but more likely here is "exchange," for Jacob is more a barterer than he is a buyer. Speiser (*Genesis,* p. 195) comments: "Traditionally 'sell me' does not bring out the fact that the birthright was to be battered . . . for food; in v. 33, however, 'sold' may be retained."

10. J. Barr ("Why? in Biblical Hebrew," *JTS* 36 [1985] 19) discovers only eight instances in the OT where *lammâ* means "to what purpose?" and three of these are in Genesis (25:22, 32; 27:46).

34 *Jacob then gave*[11] *him bread and lentil stew; Esau ate, drank, got up, and went out. Thus Esau spurned*[12] *his birthright.*

27 Scripture has already provided two instances of fraternal rivalry: Cain and Abel, and Ishmael and Isaac. Both times the elder brother (as in the NT parable, Luke 15:25-32) emerges in a less than desirable light. The case is no different with Esau and Jacob.

In their personalities and in their likes and dislikes, Esau and Jacob, though from the same womb, are worlds apart. Esau resembles Enkidu of the Gilgamesh Epic. Created by Aruru to relieve the populace of Uruk of Gilgamesh's tyrannical rule, Enkidu is described as "[Sha]ggy with hair is his whole body" and as a "hunter, a trapping-man."[13] Esau is the outdoors type.

By contrast, Jacob is a *wholesome man ('îš tām),* who is content to stay inside. Normally in the OT *tām* means innocence or moral integrity (i.e., "blameless"), as in Job 1:1, 8; 2:3; 9:20-22, and is connected with the verb *tāmam.* But one may argue that this would be a poor translation here for two reasons. First, Jacob is anything but blameless; second, it would provide a puzzling and meaningless contrast with Esau as an outdoorsman, a hunter. It is unlikely that *tām* is used to describe Jacob as a way of reinforcing the Bible's preference for a domesticated life-style over that of a nomadic life-style.

It may be that *tām* comes not from *tāmam* but from *tîm,* a root attested in Arabic and meaning "to be kept in ṣubjection, enslaved (by love)." Thus *'îš tām* may mean, by semantic development, "domesticated" or "homebody." This interpretation would provide a perfect contrast with Esau, who is styled *a man of the steppe ('îš śāḏeh).*[14]

I am persuaded, however, that we should give the same meaning to *'îš tām* in Gen. 25:27 as we do to *'îš tām* in Job 1:8. As Evans has pointed out,

11. The chiasm in vv. 33-34 between direct object and indirect object (birthright to Jacob, to Esau bread) is discussed by Andersen, *Sentence in Biblical Hebrew,* pp. 135-36. Because Andersen maintains the translation "sell" for *māḵar* in v. 33, he must translate *nāṯan,* "gave," in v. 34 as "sold." But the observation that *māḵar* means "exchange" (see n.8 above) makes this translation of *nāṯan* as "sell" in v. 34 unnecessary.

12. N. Sarna (*Genesis,* JPS Torah Commentary [Philadelphia: Jewish Publication Society, 1989], p. 182) remarks: "The abrupt succession of five short Hebrew verbs [viz., *wayyō'ḵal, wayyēšt^{e}, wayyāqôm, wayyēlaḵ, wayyiḇez*] effectively reproduces the chilling, sullen atmosphere in which Esau silently devours the meal."

13. *ANET,* p. 74a. T. H. Gaster compares "a man of the steppe" *('îš śāḏeh)* with *'š bšdh,* "a man who is in the field," in a magical text directed against a demon who preys on victims outdoors. See T. H. Gaster, "A Hang-Up for Hang-ups: The Second Amuletic Plaque from Arslan Tash," *BASOR* 209 (1973) 20 n. 6.

14. See G. R. Driver, "Studies in the Vocabulary of the Old Testament," *JTS* 31 (1930) 281.

only various characters in the Jacob story condemn and accuse Jacob; the narrator never articulates that point of view. Furthermore, the narrator does not hesitate to use a verb or phrase that shows his condemnation of Esau — "he spurned his birthright" — in this particular incident, but employs no corresponding verb that shows a negative evaluation of Jacob.[15]

28 Any potential problems Esau and Jacob might have with each other are fueled by two unwise parents. Parental favoritism is transparent here, with Isaac preferring Esau, and Rebekah preferring Jacob. We are not told why Rebekah was fonder of Jacob than of Esau, but later narratives (see ch. 27) focus more on that relationship than they do on Isaac's favoring Esau. Isaac prefers Esau because of his own love of venison. The absence of any motive for Rebekah's love of Jacob might suggest that "her affection is not dependent on a merely material convenience that the son may provide her, that it is a more justly grounded preference."[16]

29 Jacob is at home *preparing a stew (wayyāzeḏ nāzîḏ).*[17] The verb "prepare" *(zîḏ)* is most frequently translated in the RSV OT as "act presumptuously" (Deut. 17:13; Neh. 9:16, 29; cf. Deut. 1:43; 18:22). This passage shows the basic meaning of the verb — "to cook, prepare, seethe," which developed into "become heated, animated," and then "act presumptuously."

It may be more than coincidence that Jacob's work, described with the verb *zîḏ,* sounds in Hebrew much like Esau's work, that of a hunter *(ṣayiḏ).* This wordplay might be the author's way of saying that about all Jacob and Esau have in common is the acoustical similarity between the sounds of their activities (Jacob: *zûḏ/zîḏ;* Esau: *ṣûḏ*).

It is ironic that Esau the hunter is famished. Has he not killed any game? Is he returning empty-handed? One might translate *ʿāyēp̄* not as *starving* (see RSV, NIV, NAB, Speiser) but as "exhausted" (so NEB, JB, Westermann; cf. AV "faint"). Both hunger and exhaustion make one vulnerable to manipulation by others. I prefer "starving" over "exhausted" because in the next verse Esau requests something to eat, although one could be exhausted from exertion and hunger.

30 Esau does not ask to eat some of the *red stuff,* probably stew, that Jacob is preparing. He wants to *swallow* it or "gulp it down" (*lāʿaṭ,* a hapax legomenon). Skinner notes that this is "a coarse expression suggesting bestial voracity."[18] Speiser labels Esau "an uncouth glutton."[19]

15. C. D. Evans, "The Patriarch Jacob — An Innocent Man," *BRev* 2/1 (1986) 32-37.

16. Alter, *Art of Biblical Narrative,* p. 44.

17. GKC, § 85n, notes the rare existence in Hebrew of nouns formed with a *nun*-prefix.

18. Skinner, *Genesis,* p. 361.

19. Speiser, *Genesis,* p. 195. Alter (*Art of Biblical Narrative,* p. 44) translates felicitously, "let me cram my maw." M. Aberbach and B. Grossfeld (*Targum Onkelos to*

Esau's name was first explained in v. 25 — he was "ruddy" *('aḏmônî)* all over, like a "hairy garment" *('addereṯ śēʿār),* so they named him "Esau" *(ʿēśāw).* V. 30 expands that explanation: *let me swallow some of that red stuff* [*hā'āḏōm hā'āḏōm*] . . . *(That is why he was called Edom* [*'ĕḏôm*]).[20] Running throughout these two verses is an emphasis on redness or some shade thereof — *'aḏmônî, 'āḏōm, 'ĕḏôm.* Esau is one of two individuals in the OT whose natural appearance is described as red. Both he and David are called *'aḏmônî* (Gen. 25:25; 1 Sam. 16:12; 17:42) C. H. Gordon has provided evidence from Egypt, Crete, Ugarit, and Homer showing that men (but never women) are colored red or reddish brown when they assumed heroic or ceremonial purposes.[21]

31 Jacob is more than willing to provide food for Esau, but at a price. He will gladly serve some of this red stew to Esau in exchange for Esau's birthright. Jacob's response is swift and spontaneous; he knows what he wants, and he goes after it. Does he know, somehow, about the divine promise made to his mother while he was still inside her womb? Had Rebekah informed him of it, perhaps? Or is Jacob working out, in ignorance, the oracle Yahweh had spoken to his mother? (v. 23). Perhaps a comparison of the imperative used by Esau in v. 30 with the imperative used by Jacob in v. 31 may help us see what is behind Jacob's maneuvering. In v. 30 Esau said to Jacob, "let me swallow some of that red stuff" *(halʿîṭēnî nā,* the imperative followed by the particle of entreaty *nā'*). In v. 31 Jacob says to Esau, "first give me in exchange your birthright" (*miḵrâ,* the imperative without the particle of entreaty). In other words, there is no "please" or "I beg you" in Jacob's mouth as there was in Esau's. Jacob is the aggressive one, dictating the terms of the transaction. He speaks from a position of strength, and will use that position to get his hands on his older brother's birthright.

It would be unusual for a younger son to take the initiative and request an elder brother to surrender his birthright. Some scholars use a fifteenth-century B.C. text from Nuzi as a parallel to the Esau-Jacob exchange of vv. 31-34.

Genesis [New York: Ktav, 1982], p. 152 n. 20) note that both Targ. Onqelos and Targ. Pseudo-Jonathan tone down MT's *halʿîṭēnî* with *'ṭʿymny,* "give me some of that red stuff *to taste.*" This translation is esp. strange in Pseudo-Jonathan, given its vehement anti-Esau (v. 12, Esau is Rome) tendency. The authors suggest that these two targums to Genesis, due to the absence of a precise Aramaic equivalent of *lāʿaṭ* in their Jewish-Aramaic sources, used the Aphel of *ṭʿm* in the sense of feeding rather than simply tasting.

20. Long (*Problem of Etiological Narrative,* p. 9) considers Gen. 25:30b ("That is why he was called Edom") a gloss. Of the three reasons he lists to substantiate his point, the third is the most compelling. The explanation of the name Edom seems to be a digressive motif, for the major thrust of vv. 27-34 is the selling of the birthright.

21. C. H. Gordon, *Ancient Near East,* p. 125 n. 26; idem, *The Common Background of Greek and Hebrew Civilizations* (New York: Norton, 1965), pp. 230-31.

A man by the name of Tupkitilla transfers his inheritance rights to a grove over to his brother Kurpazah in exchange for three sheep: "On the day they divide the grove (that lies) on the road of the town of Lumti . . . , Tupkitilla shall give it to Kurpazah as his inheritance share. And Kurpazah has taken three sheep to Tupkitilla in exchange for his inheritance share."[22] Because of some differences between these two texts, other scholars have advanced the view that the texts are not parallel.[23] These differences or interpretative issues include: (1) the Nuzi text does not make clear that Tupkitilla is the elder brother and Kurpazah is the younger brother; (2) we cannot be sure that the grove that Tupkitilla sells to Kurpazah represents his entire inheritance or just a portion; (3) it is far from certain that Tupkitilla is driven into relinquishing his grove because of ravaging hunger; there is also a gross disparity between what Tupkitilla relinquishes (a grove 42 cubits on the southern side and 45 cubits on the northern side) and what he receives (three sheep). The text never mentions any hunger of Tupkitilla or suggests any motivation for selling his grove. Thompson cites instances from Nuzi texts in which the value of three sheep was three shekels of silver. A field brought in one Nuzi text (HSS 60.116) went for six shekels of silver, and earlier texts speak of a garden that sold for five and a half shekels, and another for one and a half shekels.[24] What the Nuzi text does illustrate —here is its real parallel with Gen. 25:27-34 — is that one brother could sell inherited property to another brother. This Nuzi text may also provide an illustration of a fictitious adoption, a practice that concealed the transference of land or property that could not be otherwise legally transferred to another person.[25]

32 Esau exaggerates not only his hunger but the imminence of his death as well, unless one understands his *hinnēh ʾānōḵî hôlēḵ lāmûṯ* as an

22. See C. H. Gordon, "Biblical Customs and the Nuzu Tablets," *BA* 3 (1940) 5. Later Gordon expanded on the connection of the text from Nuzi with Gen. 25:27-34 with this statement: "This [viz., Jacob's purchasing the birthright from Esau] is no longer a peculiar incident without parallel. In the Nuzu tablets, inheritance prospects are negotiable (though only from brother to brother) much as bonds and stocks are today. One Nuzu tablet records how a man in need of food sold his inheritance portions to his own brother in exchange for livestock even as the hungry Esau had sold his to Jacob for a 'mess of pottage' " (*Ancient Near East,* p. 126). For a translation of the full text into English, see H. Lewy, "The *aḫḫûtu* Documents from Nuzi," *Or* 9 (1940) 369-70.

23. Van Seters, *Abraham in History and Tradition,* pp. 92-93; T. L. Thompson, *Historicity of the Patriarchal Narratives,* pp. 280-85; M. J. Selman, "Comparative Methods and the Patriarchal Narratives," *Themelios* 3 (1977) 12; idem, "Comparative Customs and the Patriarchal Age," in *Essays on the Patriarchal Narratives,* ed. A. R. Millard and D. J. Wiseman (Winona Lake, IN: Eisenbrauns, 1983), pp. 97, 116, 123, 135-36.

24. Thompson, *Historicity of the Patriarchal Narratives,* p. 285.

25. See de Vaux, *Early History of Israel,* p. 250.

idiom of hyperbole, akin to our "I'm starving to death" or "I'm dying of thirst." When Esau first spoke about his hunger (v. 30), he used the exact phrase that the narrator had used in the previous verse: narrator (v. 29): "Esau . . . starving (*ʿēśāw . . . ʿāyēp̱*); Esau (v. 30): "I am starving" (*ʿāyēp̱ ʾānōḵî*). Here he exaggerates "I am starving" to "I am on the verge of dying." If he really believes that he is dying, then does he think a bowl of stew can arrest the inevitable? But given the choice of retaining his special status or getting something to eat, he opts for the latter.

Accordingly, Esau is prepared to sacrifice his *birthright (bᵉḵōrâ)*.[26] In Hebrew usage "the firstborn (male)" *(bᵉḵōr)* may be described additionally as "the first issue of (his) strength," which stresses the relation to the father (see Gen. 49:3; Deut. 21:17; Ps. 78:51; 105:36). Or he may be referred to as "the first to open the womb," which stresses the relation to the mother (see Exod. 13:2, 12, 15; etc.). Deut. 21:15-17 demonstrates that a father was obligated to acknowledge his firstborn son as his principal heir, and to grant him for an inheritance twice as much of his possessions as any other son(s) would receive. (Possibly in patriarchal times the grant to the firstborn was even greater than the double portion or two-thirds of Deut. 21:15-17, for 25:5 states that Abraham gave Isaac everything he had.) This is the case even in a polygamous family.

But Jacob has only half of what he needs — the *bᵉḵōrâ*. He also needs the "blessing" *(bᵉrāḵâ)*, which he later obtains deceitfully from his father (Gen. 27). The *bᵉrāḵâ* (ch. 27) was probably more crucial than the *bᵉḵōrâ* (ch. 25) because pronouncing the blessing was considered to be the act formally acknowledging the firstborn as the principal heir.[27]

33 Jacob's "First, give me in exchange" (v. 31) now becomes "First, swear to me." He wants Esau to take an oath that he is once and for all relinquishing any prerogatives he might enjoy as the firstborn. A gentleman's agreement and a handshake will not do, for Jacob knows only too well that in a saner moment Esau would deny such an agreement.

Jacob's *Swear to me* here contrasts dramatically with his "swear to me" in 47:31. In the first Jacob is in control, he is master of the situation — he will dictate the terms. In the second he is a helpless, elderly man, totally dependent on the will of somebody else to expedite his last wish.

26. For further studies on *bāḵar, bᵉḵôr, bᵉḵōrâ* see Y. Green, "The Rebellion of the *Bechorim*," *DD* 14 (1985) 77-81; D. F. Pennant, "Alliteration in Some Texts of Genesis," *Bib* 68 (1987) 390-92; N. Rubin, "The Social Significance of the Firstborn in Israel," *Beth Mikra* 33 (1987/88) 155-170 (Hebrew); D. G. Kent, "Death of the Firstborn," *Biblical Illustrator* 14/3 (1988) 76-78; T. Lewis and R. K. Harrison, "First-Born," "Firstling," *ISBE,* 2:308; J. M. Wilson and R. K. Harrison, "Birthright," *ISBE,* 1:515-16; M. Tsevat, *"bᵉḵôr," TDOT,* 2:121-27.

27. See B. Levine, "Firstborn," *EncJud,* 6:1308.

34 Esau capitulates and Jacob capitalizes. His brother's birthright in hand, Jacob assumes the position of firstborn once held by Esau. The narrative judges only Esau overtly. He *spurned (yiḇez* from *bāzâ)* his birthright. But what about Jacob, who spurned his brother? What about the attitude that says: "I will give you something only if you give me something first"? As I indicated above, the author or narrator of 25:27-34 never condemns Jacob for his modus operandi. But he indicts Esau for spurning his birthright. The basic meaning of *bāzâ* is "to despise, regard with contempt." It may describe how one person views another person (with disdain) — 1 Sam. 10:27; 17:42; 2 Sam. 6:6), how one treats the name of Yahweh (Mal. 1:6), the words of Yahweh (Num. 15:31 and 2 Sam. 12:9), and the curse-oath in the covenant with Yahweh (Ezek. 16:59; 17:16, 18, 19: "to flout"). In Esau's case *bāzâ* should be translated with *spurned* or "repudiated."

The food that Jacob prepared for Esau is *bread and lentil stew (n^e^zîḏ ʿ^a^ḏāšîm).* The latter phrase defines what Esau earlier had called "that red stuff" (v. 30). But why would Jacob prepare lentils that Esau would refer to as "that red stuff"? Are lentils, when cooked, reddish? Noticing that *'āḏōm* ("red") are *dām* ("blood") are similar in sound, D. Daube suggested that Esau thought Jacob was preparing a blood-broth that, if imbibed, would be a source of life and potency to Esau.[28] Or at least Jacob prepared the lentils in such a way to make Esau think he was preparing a blood soup. Daube's intriguing suggestion has two problems. One, he narrowly restricts the meaning of *'āḏōm* to red, that is blood-red. In only a few instances in the OT does *'āḏōm* mean "blood-red." Cf., for example, 2 K. 3:22, "the Moabites saw the water opposite them as red as blood" *('^a^ḏummîm kaddām).* Second, it is doubtful that there is any etymological connection between *'āḏōm* and *dām.*

When lentils are cooked they are not red but a faded brown or yellow, or a yellowish brown. This suggests that *'āḏōm,* which I have translated "red (stuff)," is "an expanded 'blanket' term which is inclusive of many more chromatic shades than those we attribute to our modern 'red.' "[29] This color would include orange, yellowish orange, or yellowish brown. Thus there is no real discontinuity between the *'āḏōm* that Esau begged for and the dish of *ʿ^a^ḏāšîm* that Jacob prepared.

28. D. Daube, *Studies in Biblical Law* (Cambridge: Cambridge University, 1947), pp. 191-200, esp. pp. 193-95.

29. Brenner, *Colour Terms in the Old Testament,* p. 61.

THE NEW TESTAMENT APPROPRIATION

a. Gen. 25:21, 23 and Rom. 9:10-13

Paul's shocking thesis stated here and elsewhere is that "not all who are descended [physically] from Israel belong to Israel [spiritually]." Pedigree is not an automatic criterion of acceptance with God. Before he states this premise he anticipates an objection that the premise might raise: "Does this mean the word of God has failed?" (v. 6a).

Paul then proceeds to give two illustrations of his premise, and for these he goes back to Genesis. Both Isaac and Ishmael are sons of Abraham (vv. 7-8), but Ishmael is not among the elect. Both Jacob and Esau are sons of Isaac, but Esau is not among the elect (vv. 10-13). These two brothers had the same father, the same mother, and came from the same act of sexual intercourse or the same seminal emission (*koítē,* v. 10), although Paul ignores the tradition that affirms fetal enmity between Jacob and Esau (Gen. 25:22). They had not done anything, good or bad, when Jacob became the recipient of God's gracious election. In God's mouth "Jacob I loved" (Mal. 1:2; Rom. 9:13) means "Jacob I have chosen." In the narrator's mouth Rebekah's "Jacob I loved" (Gen. 25:28) means "I like him better than Esau." In God's mouth "Esau have I hated" (Mal. 1:2; Rom. 9:13) means "Esau I have not chosen."

This answer in turn, Paul knows, will produce a second objection. The first objection to his thesis centered on the question of God's fairness (v. 6a). Now the question focuses on God's justice (v. 14). Is God arbitrary, capricious, unpredictable, whimsical?

To answer that objection Paul now turns to Exodus for evidence, just as he turned to Genesis for support of his thesis in vv. 6-13. God showed mercy on the Israelites while at the same time he showed judgment on Egypt and its pharaoh by hardening his heart. Because Yahweh made that distinction between those who receive mercy and who receive judgment, shall we conclude, infers Paul, that the God of the Exodus was unjust? The obvious answer is of course not! The pharaoh — Israel's great enemy — existed only in order that God could exercise his mercy toward Israel. Unlike Esau and Ishmael who were not even chosen, Pharaoh was chosen, yet not for his own sake but solely as an instrument of God's grace to Israel.

Just as Jewish election depends solely on God's grace (vv. 6-23), so does Gentile election (vv. 24-26). Yet the second group will never replace the first group, for God will never abandon his people totally (vv. 27-29). In so appealing to Genesis and Exodus history, Paul has driven home one truth: election (Jewish or Gentile) depends on God's mercy. Certainly it is not fortuitous that nine of the twelve occurrences of "mercy" in Romans are in chs. 9–11 (9:15 [2 times], 16, 18, 23; 11:30, 31 [2 times], 32). The remaining three are 12:1, 8; 15:9.[1]

b. Gen. 25:29-34 and Heb. 12:16

Following his exhortation to pursue "peace and the sanctification without which no one will see the Lord" (v. 14), the writer of the Epistle to the Hebrews follows with three clauses — each introduced with "lest" — that justify the exhortation (AV): (1) "lest any man fail of the grace of God; (2) lest any root of bitterness springing up trouble you; (3) lest there be any fornicator or profane person, like Esau."

The third "lest" clause is v. 16: "Lest there be any fornicator, or profane person, as Esau, who for one morsel of meat sold his birthright" (AV). Because the OT has no explicit reference to immoral behavior by Esau, it is hard to know whether "fornicator" is to be understood literally or metaphorically.[2] In nonbiblical Jewish literature Esau was accused of being a womanizer and one who not infrequently engaged in immoral trysts with married women (Gen. Rabbah 65:1; Jub. 25:1, 8). More than likely Heb. 12:16 reflects that tradition.

The incident to which the writer of Hebrews clearly alludes illustrates a misplaced sense of values more than it does sexual immorality. To prostitute oneself, as in Esau's case, means to be bereft of any spiritual values, to put the needs of the immediate moment ahead of any other considerations, to put feeling ahead of conscience, to give away much ("sold his birthright") and receive back little in return ("for a single meal"). This, says the writer to the Hebrews, is what Esau did, but what those who pursue peace and sanctification will avoid. Note that Heb. 12:16 describes Esau as both *pórnos* and *bébēlos* ("profane" [AV]; "irreligious" [RSV]; "degrade religion" [JB]; "worldly-minded" [NEB]); "defiled" [Buchanan]; "unclean" [Attridge]). In the LXX *bébēlos* is associated with cultic matters (e.g., Lev. 10:10; Ezek. 4:14; 21:25; 22:26; 44:23). But in the NT it is always an ethical/religious term, applied either to people (1 Tim. 1:9; Heb. 12:16) or to things (1 Tim. 4:7; 6:20; 2 Tim. 2:16).

1. To the commentaries on Romans add L. Gaston, "Israel's Enemies in Pauline Theology," *NTS* 28 (1982) 400-423, esp. 413-14; J. W. Aageson, "Typology, Correspondence, and the Application of Scripture in Romans 9–11," *JSNT* 31 (1987) 51-72, esp. pp. 55-56; idem, "Scripture and Structure in the Development of the Argument in Romans 9–11," *CBQ* 48 (1986) 265-89, esp. pp. 268-70; M. A. Getty, "Paul and the Salvation of Israel: A Perspective on Romans 9–11," *CBQ* 50 (1988) 456-69, esp. 464-65.

2. Cf. F. F. Bruce, *Epistle to the Hebrews,* NICNT (Grand Rapids: Eerdmans, 1964), p. 366, who argues for the literal; and G. W. Buchanan, *To the Hebrews,* AB (Garden City, NY: Doubleday, 1972), p. 220, who argues for the metaphorical (i.e., *pórnos* meaning "apostate"). In agreement with Buchanan and noting that fornication was a metaphor for or component of idolatry in the OT, H. W. Attridge argues for metaphorical connotations of *pórnos* (*Epistle to the Hebrews,* Hermeneia [Philadelphia: Fortress, 1989], p. 369).

C. ISAAC AND ABIMELECH (26:1-35)

1. A FAMINE OF FOOD AND TRUTH (26:1-11)

1. *There was a famine in the country, besides*[1] *the earlier famine that occurred in Abraham's time, and so Isaac went down to Abimelech, the Philistines' king in Gerar.*
2. *Yahweh appeared to him, saying: "Do not go down to Egypt; camp*[2] *in the country about which I will speak to you.*
3. *Remain as an immigrant*[3] *for a while in this country, and I will be with you and bless you; for to you and to your seed I will give all these lands, and thus fulfill the oath I swore to Abraham your father.*
4. *I will make your descendants as numerous as the stars of the heavens, and give them all these lands, and in your descendants shall all the nations of the earth be blessed,*
5. *all because Abraham obeyed me,*[4] *keeping my mandate (my commandments, my laws, my instructions)."*[5]
6. *So Isaac settled in Gerar.*
7. *When the men of the place inquired about his wife he responded: "She is my sister," for he was hesitant to say "My wife," thinking,*[6] *"The men of this place might kill me because of Rebekah, for she is so good-looking."*
8. *Once, after he had been there a long time, Abimelech, king of the Philistines, looked*[7] *through a window, and spotted*[8] *Isaac fondling*[9]

1. On *millᵉḇaḏ* BDB, p. 94b, remarks "chiefly P and late," but here it is in a unit normally attributed to J.

2. Speiser (*Genesis,* p. 201) observes that in some instances in Genesis *šāḵan,* "to stay, dwell," carries the idiomatic nuance of "to camp."

3. In the OT whenever a person left Canaan/Israel to become a *gēr* it was to escape either from hunger (Gen. 12:10; 26:3; 47:4; 2 K. 8:1) or from war (2 Sam. 4:3) as opposed to permanent relocation.

4. *ʿēqeḇ ʾᵃšer šāmaʿ ʾaḇrāhām bᵉqōlî* is parallel to 22:18, *ʿēqeḇ ʾᵃšer šāmaʿtā bᵉqōlî.*

5. My use of parentheses is to show that the three nouns *miṣwōṯay, ḥuqqôṯay* and *tôrōṯāy* are explications of the basic term in this list, *mišmartî.*

6. Here is an illustration of a virtual quotation without an explicit verb of speaking or thinking. See R. Gordis, *Poets, Prophets, and Sages: Essays in Biblical Interpretation* (Bloomington: Indiana University, 1971), p. 120 (repr. of "Quotations in Biblical, Oriental, and Rabbinic Literature," *HUCA* 22 [1949] 181).

7. The same verb *(šāqap)* is used in 18:16 and 19:28 for the messenger's and Lot's "look" toward Sodom.

8. On surprise clauses introduced by *wayyar' wᵉhinnēh* see Andersen, *Sentence in Biblical Hebrew,* pp. 94-95.

9. Both the name "Isaac" *(yiṣḥāq)* and the participle "fondling" *(mᵉṣaḥēq)* are

Rebekah his wife.

9. *He summoned Isaac and said: "Surely*[10] *she is your wife! How is it*[11] *that you said 'She is my sister'?" Isaac responded to him: "I so spoke lest I might lose my life on her account."*

10. *Abimelech said: "See what you have done to us! One of the people might easily*[12] *have lain with your wife and you would have brought upon us retribution."*

11. *Then Abimelech charged all the people: "Anyone who touches this man or his wife shall be put to death."*

This is the one chapter in Genesis that is given over completely to the activities of Isaac. Scholars have frequently observed that ch. 26 looks speciously intrusive between 25:19-34 and 27:1ff. That is, Isaac's own problems come between the account of Jacob's exploitation of his brother (25:19-34) and the account of his deception of his father (27:1ff.), two events that probably were sequential. There are at least two apparent reasons for the placement of this chapter in this position. First, as Michael Fishbane has observed, ch. 26 plays the same role in the Jacob narrative as does ch. 34, and that role is one of an interlude. Both chapters involve not Jacob, but a member of his family — either a father or children — who is involved in some duplicity. Ch. 26 is the second unit and ch. 34 the second from the last unit in the symmetrical design in which the story is cast.[13]

Second, this chapter provides a pungent illustration of a reversal of fortunes for Isaac. Both chs. 26 and 27 are laced with the theme of deception. The difference is that Isaac is the deceiver in ch. 26 but the deceived in ch. 27. The villain becomes a victim, and nemesis is at work in his life as much as it is in the life of his younger son.

Another problem in the broad interpretation of vv. 1-11 is the relationship of this story about the "wife-sister" motif to the two stories of similar theme that have already occurred (12:10-20, 20:1-18). Twice Abraham lied about his wife's true identity when sojourning in a foreign country, and now it is Isaac's turn to prevaricate. Because of the many parallels among the three stories many scholars suggest that all three narratives are either oral or literary variants of a single

---

from the same root, *ṣḥq;* the narrator is no doubt engaging in wordplay. Isaac was "Isaac-ing" with Rebekah.

10. See N. Snaith, "The meaning of the Hebrew *'ak,*" *VT* 14 (1964) 222.

11. See S. E. Loewenstamm, "Die ugaritische Partikel *iky,*" *Or* 53 (1984) 256.

12. *kim'aṭ,* lit. "like a little," hence here "almost" or "easily" of unrealized action. Cf. BDB, p. 590a.

13. See Fishbane, *Text and Texture,* pp. 42, 46-48; Rendsburg, *Redaction of Genesis,* pp. 56-59.

tradition. Most scholars have taken them as literary variants and have attempted therefore to untangle the redactional process by determining which of the three accounts represents the most original form of the tale, and which of the stories are compositional variants or literary conflations.[14] But an increasing number of scholars think that these three episodes are not interdependent and variants of each other, but that, although sharing some common motifs, the episodes are each unique and probably contemporaneous.[15]

Most commentators[16] give this third story in Genesis about wife-as-sister little historical credibility or theological significance, for two reasons: its significant differences from the first two stories in chs. 12 and 20, and the mention of Abimelech and his commander Phicol (v. 26) in both the Abraham story (ch. 20) and the Isaac story a generation later (ch. 26). Such negative criticism, however, avoids the fact that 26:1 refers clearly to the first incident (ch. 12), and Abimelech's annoyance with Isaac, as expressed in vv. 10-11, makes most sense if Abimelech (or his namesake) has already had (or almost had) contact with a Hebrew's wife. Thus ch. 26 refers to the incident in ch. 12 and presupposes the incident in ch. 20.[17]

1 How paradoxical it is that this chapter opens with a reference to a *famine* in the land of Canaan. The previous chapter concluded with the information that in return for his brother's birthright Jacob had served Esau a meal consisting of bread and lentil stew. No famine there! Jacob has more than enough to provide for Esau, but now Canaan is losing its fertility. One famished individual foreshadows a nation of famished families.

Going to Egypt (see v. 2) during a famine in Canaan could keep a person from starvation. Abraham knew that, and Joseph would later discover it. But it is highly questionable whether a flight to the much nearer Philistine *Gerar,* a city bordering on the patriarchs' homeland, would provide the same respite.[18] At God's bidding Elijah fled from famine ravished Israel to the

14. See Culley, *Studies in the Structure of Hebrew Narrative,* pp. 33-41; Van Seters, *Abraham in History and Tradition,* pp. 167-91; K. Koch, *The Growth of the Biblical Tradition: The Form-Critical Method,* tr. S. M. Cupitt (New York: Scribner's, 1969), pp. 111-32.

15. D. L. Petersen, "A Thrice-Told Tale: Genre, Theme, and Motif," *BRev* 18 (1973) 30-43; S. Niditch, *Underdogs and Tricksters: A Prelude To Biblical Folklore* (San Francisco: Harper & Row, 1987), pp. 23-69; T. L. Thompson, *The Origin Tradition of Ancient Israel: I. The Literary Formation of Genesis and Exodus 1–23,* JSOTSup 55 (Sheffield: JSOT, 1987), pp. 51-59; T. D. Alexander, "The Wife/Sister Incidents of Genesis: Oral Variants?" *IBS* 11 (1989) 2-22; idem, "Are the wife/sister incidents of Genesis literary compositional variants?" *VT* 42 (1992) 145-53; J. Ronning, "The Naming of Isaac: The Role of the Wife/Sister Episodes in the Redaction of Genesis," *WTJ* 53 (1991) 1-27.

16. For example, Noth (*History of Pentateuchal Traditions,* pp. 263-64) describes 26:1ff. as the most profane of the three accounts.

17. See Kidner, *Genesis,* pp. 152-53.

18. Van Seters (*Abraham in History and Tradition,* p. 177) also notes that for Isaac

Phoenician city of Zarephath near Sidon (1 K. 17:8-24), a city that was already feeling the effects of the drought and famine. It would appear from v. 8 here ("after he had been there [Gerar] a long time") that Gerar escaped the famine, in spite of its geographical proximity to the catastrophe, or that the famine was local and did not spread to cities in neighboring countries.

The Abimelech of ch. 20 cannot be the same *Abimelech* of ch. 26, if one takes the years and figures of Genesis seriously. The adult and married Abimelech of ch. 20 enters the Abraham story before Abraham reaches the age of 100. The Abimelech of ch. 26 comes much later, after Abraham's death at the age of 175. Isaac is now 60 (25:26) and his two boys have grown up. Hence the Abimelech of ch. 20 and the Abimelech of ch. 26 are separated by at least seventy-five years, and we must be dealing with two individuals with the same name. The same must be the case with *Phicol* (21:22; 26:26). This is probably an instance of dynastic or royal names borne by a number of individuals such as one finds in the English monarchy with Henry, George, or Edward. Note that the title of Ps. 34 is "A Psalm of David, when he feigned madness before Abimelech"; yet 1 Sam. 21:10-15 identifies the king as Achish. These texts are not necessarily contradictory; they may show that among earlier and later Philistine kings Abimelech was a favorite throne name to assume alongside one's own name.

2 If v. 2 follows v. 1 chronologically, then *Yahweh appeared* to Isaac while he was in Gerar, spoke to him there, and forbade further migration to Egypt. This interpretation would also indicate that Gerar and its environs were to be included in the "lands" Yahweh would give to Isaac's descendants (see v. 3). But v. 1 may be the story of vv. 2-11 in capsule form, with the particulars spelled out in vv. 2-11.

It is understandable why Isaac needs to be told not to move as far as Egypt. For one thing, that is exactly what his father had done in a similar circumstance (ch. 12). For another, Egypt represents a guarantee of safety, far enough away from the horrors of a famine. Isaac is certainly not foolish enough to court disaster by staying too close to the area of famine. "Remember Lot's wife" must not become "Remember Isaac"! As Isaac will discover, God is able to preserve his own even in the midst or on the edges of a life-threatening famine.

It is worthwhile to compare God's prohibition to Adam, "you shall not eat," the Hebrew of which reflects one way of expressing a prohibition — *lō'* with the imperfect — with his prohibition here to Isaac, *Do not go down*

---

to go to Gerar "would be of no help at all," and takes this as an evidence that Gerar in 26:1 is simply taken from the Gerar mentioned in 20:2 in which there was no mention of famine. Thompson (*Origin Tradition,* p. 55) rejects Van Seters's reasoning, and interprets famine in these stories as having only a narrative function, and unlike real famines does not need "to be circumvented by good geographic sense."

to Egypt — *'al* with the jussive — a second way of expressing a prohibition in Biblical Hebrew. The first form has a much stronger force. The second is more of an entreaty, a supplication, an exhortation.[19] On this one occasion alone Yahweh urges Isaac not to travel to Egypt.

Three verbs are used in vv. 1-6 to describe Isaac's relationship to Gerar: *camp* (*šāḵan,* v. 2b), *remain as an immigrant* (*gûr,* v. 3a),[20] and *settled* (*yāšaḇ,* v. 6). The first of these three is normally translated as "dwell," but the context here suggests something like "camp."

3-5 In the Abraham story God's "I will bless you" (12:2) preceded "Yahweh blessed him" (24:1). First the promise, then the fact. In Isaac's case this order is reversed. "God blessed Isaac" (25:11) precedes God's "I will bless you" (26:3). The first blessing for Isaac is in a context of bereavement — the loss of a father. The second blessing for Isaac is in the context of adversity — a famine.[21]

Verses 3-5 alternate between the future and the past: v. 3a — future; v. 3b — past; v. 4 — future; v. 5 — past. The passing of Abraham does not require another covenant, for a covenant lasts for more than one generation. What is called for is the perpetuation and fulfillment of the covenant announced to its original recipient.

A reminder to Isaac that in his *descendants shall all the nations of the earth be blessed* (for which cf. 12:3; 18:18; 22:18) is most appropriate while Isaac is at Philistine Gerar. By his conduct Isaac nearly brought not blessing but judgment on one of these nations. A faithful Abraham (v. 5) means a blessed Isaac (vv. 3-4). Will not, then, a faithful Isaac be the mediator of divine blessing to Abimelech?

These verses also provide the first instance in the patriarchal narratives of the promise from God: *I will be with you.*[22] This promise makes Isaac's behavior even more unconscionable; the promise of divine companionship is not adequate to deter Isaac from engaging in duplicity. To have the assurance of God's presence with one is fine, but when Isaac imagines his life to be in danger (v. 7), he resorts to an ethic of the end justifies the means.

19. See GKC, §§ 107o, 109c-e; J. Bright, "The Apodictic Prohibition: Some Observations," *JBL* 92 (1973) 185-204.

20. In the opposite order these two verbs appear in Ps. 15:1: "who shall sojourn [*gûr*] in your tent? Who shall dwell [*šāḵan*] on your holy hill?" In Gen. 20:2, 3 *šāḵan/gûr* is temporary, whereas *gûr/šāḵan* in Ps. 15:1 is permanent.

21. See Kidner, *Genesis,* p. 153.

22. See H. D. Preuss, ". . . ich will mit dir sein!" *ZAW* 80 (1968) 139-73. In v. 3 the promise of the divine presence is followed by the preposition *'im,* but later in v. 24 that same promise is followed by the preposition *'eṯ*. See also G. W. Coats, "I Will Be With You," *LTQ* 7 (1972) 77-85, who focuses on the "I-will-be-with-you" implications of the names Yahweh and Immanuel.

Verses 3-5 sound much like 22:16-17, "Because you [Abraham] have done this . . . I will indeed bless you." Here the blessing of God promised to Isaac and his descendants is tied causally to Abraham's unswerving loyalty to God; thus the blessing is a divine response to appropriate behavior. This situation presents another dimension to the promise themes in the patriarchal narratives, most of which are announced unconditionally,[23] but in 26:3-5 the promise is made to Isaac because of what God said to Abraham ("and thus fulfill the oath I swore to Abraham," v. 3)[24] and because of Abraham's exemplary behavior ("all because Abraham obeyed me," v. 4). So Yahweh begins by speaking to Isaac about himself (vv. 2-4 have eight verbs in the 1st person sing. with Yahweh as subject [v. 2, one; v. 3, five; v. 4, two]).

Yahweh concludes the revelational content of this theophany by talking to Isaac about Abraham (v. 5). Yahweh's evaluation of Abraham's life is that the patriarch *obeyed me, keeping my mandate (wayyišmōr mišmartî),*[25] which is broken down into three constituent parts: *my commandments, my laws, my instructions.* Both the verb and the nouns following the verb are close to the sequence one finds in passages like Deut. 11:1 and the Deuteronomistic 1 K. 2:3. In living by Torah, Abraham models the quality of response to God that should characterize the people Israel.[26]

If God blessed the second generation because of the piety of the first generation, he will also bless the third generation because of the piety of the first generation. Abraham's spiritual legacy to Jacob will be no less than Abraham's legacy to Isaac. Now the question is this: will Isaac's moral demeanor be such that he will be a catalyst for the transmission of divine blessing to his children?

6 Isaac now takes up temporary abode in Gerar. That move would have never happened if not for the famine. Much as the early church in Acts was scattered through persecution and thus went throughout the world to spread its faith, Isaac too has left his Jerusalem and moved to his Samaria.

23. W. C. Kaiser, Jr. (*Toward an Old Testament Theology,* pp. 92-94) notes that where conditionality is present in the divine promises it is attached not to the promise itself but to the participants who received the promise.

24. Only four texts in Genesis mention God swearing an oath (22:16; 24:7; 26:3; 50:24). In the last three the divine swearing is clearly in reference to the promise of land, whereas in 22:16 the reference is to the promise of descendants.

25. On the nuance of *šāmar* meaning "to guard against violation" see B. A. Levine, *Leviticus,* JPS Torah Commentary (Philadelphia: Jewish Publication Society, 1989), pp. 55, 205 n. 34.

26. On the Jewish tradition that Abraham observed *tôrâ* before God revealed it to Moses, and that the pl. *tôrōṯāy* suggested "two Torahs," the oral and the written, see R. W. L. Moberly, "The Earliest Commentary on the Akedah," *VT* 38 (1988) 55 n. 16; and J. L. Kugel, *In Potiphar's House* (San Francisco: Harper, 1990), p. 121 n. 12.

Almost every time in Genesis that a Hebrew leaves his homeland, it is because of a stressful situation such as famine (Abraham, Isaac, Jacob, and Joseph) or problems at home (Jacob).[27] The verb I have translated *settled* is used frequently in Genesis to describe a person's relocation in a new place after he has left his home (4:16; 13:18; 19:30; 20:1; 21:20, 21; 25:11).

7 A conversation between Isaac and the townsmen of Gerar turns to a discussion of Rebekah. The Gerarites simply and politely inquire about her. The text does not indicate any menace in their inquiry, but Isaac seems to feel threatened. To prevent losing his wife and perhaps his life he resorts to deception and tells the group that she is his sister. Here he mimics his father (chs. 12, 20). The shortage of food in the land is an appropriate context for the shortage of truth in Isaac. The famine caused by a food shortage he leaves behind, but the famine of truth, caused by a preference for expediency over conviction, persists at Gerar.

8 That Isaac was at Gerar *a long time* demonstrates that the danger to Rebekah was more imagined than real.[28] Sarah, Rebekah's mother-in-law, was indeed "taken" (12:5; 20:3) into the house of another, but Rebekah was not. Thus Isaac's act is repugnant in that it was not only deceitful but also unnecessary.

Quite by accident Abimelech discovers the real relationship between Rebekah and Isaac. One day, peering through a palace window, he observes *Isaac fondling Rebekah*. The way in which Abimelech discovers the true relationship between Isaac and Rebekah contrasts with the pharaoh of ch. 12 and the Abimelech of ch. 20, both of whom learned of Sarah's identity by a divine revelation (plagues and a dream, respectively). This Abimelech accidentally stumbles onto the truth.

This verse may be the only time in the OT where the Piel of *ṣāḥaq* (7 times in all) might take on the connotation of sexual play or foreplay. The remaining six passages (19:14; 21:9; 39:14, 17; Exod. 32:6; Judg. 16:25) make good sense if the verb is translated something like "play, sport, amuse, entertain."[29] Isaac's indiscretions are further heightened by the fact that he behaves intimately with his wife in public. Some translators render *meṣaḥēq* in a nonsexual sense (NEB "laughing together"; Coote and Ord, "laughing with"; Sasson, "bantering, horsing-around"). Among the ancient

27. See n. 3 above.

28. See Culley, *Studies in the Structure of Hebrew Narrative*, p. 39.

29. Many scholars attach a sexual connotation to the Piel of *ṣāḥaq* in Gen. 39:14, 17 and Exod. 32:6, but this interpretation can be disputed, as I will show later in my remarks on Gen. 39. See J. M. Sasson, "The Worship of the Golden Calf," in *Orient and Occident*, Fest. Cyrus H. Gordon, ed. H. A. Hoffner, Jr., AOAT 22 (Kevelaer: Butzon und Bercker; Neukirchen-Vluyn: Neukirchener, 1973), pp. 154-57.

versions Targ. Onqelos, which reads *yṣḥq mḥyyk yt rbqh 'yttyh,* "Isaac was jesting with Rebekah his wife," supports this rendering of *m^{e}ṣaḥēq.* If Isaac was simply engaging in a bit of playful conversation with Rebekah, however, how did the king ascertain that the man and woman were in fact husband and wife?

Earlier it was Sarah who was incensed when she saw Ishmael "playing" with Isaac (21:9). Now it is Abimelech who sees Isaac "playing" with Rebekah. Both incidents involving two people playing with each other produce antagonism in a third person, an observer, who happens to chance upon the event.

9 Understandably, Abimelech has unanswered questions by his guest's lack of honesty and summons Isaac to explain his actions (cf. 12:18; 20:9). It is Abimelech, the Philistine king, who is the defender of truthfulness. Why, he wonders, would Isaac stoop to this level? Abimelech here is like the later prophets, who so often pointed out and denounced the people's sins; an Abimelech before Isaac is not far from a Nathan before David. In the first royalty is the accuser; in the second royalty is the accused.

This verse includes two quotations. First Abimelech quotes the earlier words of Isaac to Isaac (cf. v. 7 with v. 9, "she is my sister") without any change in the words. This is one of the four basic patterns of quotations in the OT: *X* quotes *Y* to *Y.* In most cases the purpose of such quotations is *X* wanting to know why *Y* said the things he did (e.g., Josh. 9:22; Judg. 18:4). The second quotation in this verse is one in which Isaac quotes his earlier words (or thoughts) to Abimelech (cf. v. 7 with v. 9). This is another pattern of quotations in the OT; this time *X* quotes *X* to *Y.* Note that in quoting his own thoughts, Isaac, for purposes of tact, significantly modifies his statement. The earlier "The men of this place might kill me because of Rebekah, for she is so good-looking" becomes in quotation *I so spoke lest I might lose my life on her account.*[30]

10 This scene, with Isaac, the accused, standing before Abimelech, the plaintiff, has a later parallel when Jacob, the accused, stands before Laban, the plaintiff (31:26-31). Isaac answers his interrogator only indirectly, while Jacob responds directly to his interrogator. Isaac answers with the first person ("I . . .) and Jacob answers with the first and second person ("I . . . you . . .").

Abimelech's first question (v. 9) was concerned with motive. His second question (lit., "what is this you have done to us?"; cf. 12:18; 20:9) is rhetorical and hence the equivalent of a declarative accusation.[31] Isaac has

30. Savran, *Telling and Retelling,* pp. 25, 29, 30, 34, 49.

31. Cf. Gen. 29:25 (Jacob to Laban); Exod. 14:11 (Israelites to Moses); Numbers 23:11 (Balak to Balaam); Ephraimites to Gideon (Judg. 8:1); men of Judah to Samson (Judg. 15:11). Judg. 20:12 reflects the same device, but the idiom is a bit different there.

missed the fact that in attempting to spare his own life he was risking the lives of everybody else. A whole city was put in jeopardy because one man wanted to escape jeopardy. That Abimelech understood this fact is clear when he says: *and you would have brought upon us retribution.* The translation of this last word *('āšām)* by "guilt" (so RSV, NIV, JB, NAB; AV "guiltiness"; cf. NEB) is too weak. Here is an instance where a biblical term for bad (or good) behavior also connotes the respective punishment (or reward).[32] It is not just the potential immoral behavior of the Gerarites that concerned Abimelech but the consequences of that behavior.

A number of other texts and incidents scattered throughout the OT regard Israel as Yahweh's holy people. If any outsider tries to harm them, or exceeds the punishment that the Lord intends for Israel, then the outsider experiences *'āšām,* i.e., he incurs guilt. Thus Jer. 2:3 says (RSV): "Israel was holy to the Lord. . . . All who ate of it became guilty" *(ye'šāmû).* The predatory nations who have devoured Israel as a wolf devours a sheep try to evade responsibility for this carnage by saying, "we are not guilty [*lō' ne'šām*], for they have sinned against the Lord" (Jer. 50:7). In the next chapter the Lord says of the land of the Chaldeans that it is "full of guilt" *['arṣām mālᵉ'â 'āšām]* (Jer. 51:5). Ezek. 25:12 speaks similarly of Edom, which has acted vengefully against Judah and as a result has become guilty *(wayye'šᵉmû 'āšôm).* Cf. also 2 Chr. 28:8-15, esp. vv. 10 and 13; Zech. 11:5.[33]

11 Abimelech issues a command that demonstrates his moral sensitivity: *Anyone who touches[34] this man or his wife shall be put to death.*[35] The verb "touch" here is a double entendre. To touch Isaac means to abuse him physically, to injure him. To touch Rebekah means to abuse her sexually (cf. 20:6). Nobody is to touch *(nāga')* Rebekah as Isaac has touched (i.e., fondled) *(ṣāḥaq)* her. Biddle has pointed out that approximately sixty texts in the OT use *nāga'* as a technical term to describe contact with things holy/unholy that

In questions such as one finds in Gen. 3:13; 4:10; Josh. 7:19 the indictment is there, "what have you done?" but there is no "to us" or "to me." G. W. Ramsey, "Speech-Forms in Hebrew Law and Prophetic Oracles," *JBL* 96 (1977) 50; Niditch, *Underdogs and Tricksters,* p. 39.

32. J. Milgrom calls this a "consequential *asham*" (*Cult and Conscience,* pp. 5, 132).

33. M. E. Biddle, "The 'Endangered Ancestress' and Blessing for the Nations," *JBL* 109 (1990) 606-7.

34. In all three of the wife/sister episodes the verb *nāga'* appears. In 12:17 it refers to the plagues with which Yahweh "afflicted" Pharaoh and his house. In 20:7 it refers to the fact that God did not permit Abimelech to "touch" Sarah, i.e., to engage in any sexual act with her. Perhaps *nāga'* in 26:11 combines both of these nuances — "whoever afflicts/injures Abraham and attempts to engage in sexual activity with Rebekah. . . ."

35. The form of the apodictic directive is much like Exod. 19:12, "whoever touches the mountain shall be put to death."

results in *'āšām.*[36] For Abimelech or any of his people to touch *(nāg̱aʿ)* either Isaac or Sarah would result in *'āšām* for himself and his subjects, and this would be a fulfillment of God's promise to Abraham in 12:3 that God will bless/curse any who bless/abuse Abraham and his descendants.

The word of warning for violation of this command *(shall be put to death)* is much like God's word to the first Abimelech — "you shall surely die" (20:7). The difference between the two is that God uses the Qal of *mûṯ* (i.e., an active form, with God presumably the agent of the action), and Abimelech uses the Hophal of *mûṯ* (i.e., a passive form, with man presumably the agent).[37] Abimelech's order apparently carried weight, for later he and his officers said to Isaac "we have not touched you" (v. 29). Interestingly, Abimelech's decree covers both Isaac and Sarah. Sarah deserves protection, but Abimelech is also merciful to a two-faced deceiver like Isaac.

2. ENVY THAT LEADS TO QUARRELING (26:12-22)

12 *Isaac planted seed in that region and reaped in the same year a hundredfold.*[1] *Because Yahweh blessed him,*

13 *the man grew richer and richer until he was exceedingly rich.*[2]

14 *He acquired flocks and herds, and many servants,*[3] *with the result that the Philistines were envious of him.*

15 *All the wells that his father's servants had dug in Abraham's time the Philistines stopped up*[4] *and filled with dirt.*

36. Biddle, *JBL* 109 (1990) 608.

37. In Genesis–Numbers the Qal of *mûṯ* preceded by the infinitive absolute refers to death "as directly the work of God"; similarly, the Hophal of *mûṯ* preceded by the infinitive absolute refers to execution by human hands. This distinction does not carry over into the rest of the OT, however. Note, for example, that *môṯ tāmûṯ/yāmûṯ* refers to something God does directly (2 K. 1:4, 6, 16; Ezek. 3:18; 33:8, 14) or something one person does to another (1 Sam. 14:44; 22:16; 1 K. 2:37, 42; Jer. 26:8). See my earlier discussion of Gen. 2:17 in *Genesis, Chapters 1–17,* NICOT (Grand Rapids: Eerdmans, 1990), pp. 173-74. I note that Targ. Onqelos translates the two instances of *môṯ tāmût* in Genesis (2:17; 20:7) quite literally: *mmt tmwt.* But it translates *môṯ yûmāṯ* of 26:11 as *'ytqṭl' ytqṭyl,* using the ʿIthpaal of *qṭl* for *mût,* perhaps to indicate some kind of a violent death.

1. MT *šᵉʿārîm* ("measures, proportions") need not be emended to *śᵉʿōrîm* ("barley") as in LXX. The noun occurs only here in the OT and is better understood as a mathematical factor than an unknown standard of measure.

2. Note the three uses of *gāḏal* in this verse: "grew richer" (imperfect with *waw* consecutive, *wayyiḡdal*); "and richer" (participle, *gāḏēl*); "he was very rich" (perfect, *gāḏal*).

3. *ʿᵃḇuddâ* is a broken pl. used collectively, only here and in Job 1:3.

4. Vv. 15 and 18 are the only instances of the Piel of *sāṯam* in the Hebrew Bible.

16 *Then Abimelech said to Isaac, "Go away from us, for you are too strong*[5] *for us."*

17 *Isaac departed from there and encamped by the Wadi Gerar, and settled there.*

18 *Isaac reopened the wells which his father's servants*[6] *had dug in Abraham's time and which the Philistines had stopped up after Abraham's death; he gave them the identical names his father had given them.*

19 *But when Isaac's servants dug by the wadi and discovered springing water*[7] *in their well,*

20 *the shepherds of Gerar made a complaint against Isaac's shepherds saying, "The water is ours!" So the well was called Esek, because they challenged him there.*

21 *They dug another well, and they quarreled over that one too;*[8] *so it was called Sitnah.*

22 *Moving from there, he dug another well; but they did not quarrel over this one. It was called Rehoboth, for he said, "This time Yahweh has allowed us larger space, and we shall be fruitful in the land."*

12 A convenient way for Abimelech to have avoided the possibility that any of his townsmen might "touch" Isaac or Rebekah was simply to send the two

---

The meaning "to stop up (a well, a spring)" for the Qal of this root is found in 2 K. 3:19, 25. The pronominal suffix on *sāṯam* in vv. 15 and 18 (and on *mālē'* in v. 15) is masc. *(-m),* even though the antecedent "wells" *(bᵉ'ērōṯ)* is feminine. See GKC, §§ 60h, 130o.

5. The connection between "bone" *('eṣem)* with a root meaning of "power" or "might" and the verb *'āṣam* in 26:16 is noticed by W. Brueggemann, "Of the Same Flesh and Bone (GN 2,23a)," *CBQ* 32 (1970) 534. The juxtaposition of *'āṣam* with *rāḇâ* elsewhere (e.g., Exod. 1:7; Isa. 31:1; 47:9; Jer. 5:6) suggests that Isaac's strength is in his greater numbers of personnel. Note J. W. Olley's translation of Isa. 53:12 in " 'The Many': How Is Isa. 53:12a To Be Understood?" *Bib* 68 (1987) 330-356: "Therefore I will give to him of the many (*rabbîm* [RSV, "the great"]), and with numerous (*'ăṣûmîm* [RSV, "the strong"]), he shall share the spoil."

6. MT *hāpᵉrû bîmê 'aḇrāhām 'āḇîw,* lit., "they dug in the days of Abraham his father." LXX, Vulg., and SP have "the servants of Abraham his father dug"; cf. v. 15. Most likely *'aḇᵉḏê 'āḇîw,* "the servants of his father," was inadvertently omitted in the MT. Cf. *BHS;* Speiser, *Genesis,* pp. 201-2.

7. Heb. *mayim ḥayyîm,* lit., "water of life, living water," refers to fresh running water, which was of course highly prized in the ancient Near East. See *TDOT,* 4:333. Cf. this expression in the NT in John 4:10, 11; 7:38.

8. The inclusion of the particle *gām* ("too, also") between the verb *wayyārîḇû* and the prepositional phrase *'ālêhā* makes clear that the subject of *wayyārîḇû* in v. 21 is the same as the subject of *wayyārîḇû* in v. 20, i.e., the shepherds of Gerar. Otherwise, the subject of *wayyārîḇû* in v. 21 could be both the shepherds of Gerar and Isaac's servants.

away, as Pharaoh did with Abraham and Sarah (12:19b). If the potential problem is removed the temptation is removed. Instead, Abimelech is more like the earlier Abimelech who allowed Abraham to settle in his territory (20:15). Isaac, too, is allowed to remain in Gerar and practice agriculture.

Isaac's reaping[9] of *a hundredfold* is to be contrasted with the famine in Canaan that precipitated this whole affair. A wasteland is only a few miles away, but here is Isaac, now a farmer, harvesting a bountiful crop.[10]

13-14 The reason for Isaac's success is the blessing of God (and the courtesy of Abimelech). These blessings are certainly not the divine response to model obedience by the patriarch.

Of course, whenever an outsider moves in and becomes very prosperous in someone else's backyard, the natives feel resentment — *the Philistines were envious of him.* That Isaac would lie to them is bad enough. That he would subsequently prosper beyond them is worse again. The Gerarites are envious of his success at farming. Perhaps the effects of the famine from which Isaac fled are beginning to spill over into Philistine territory, but here is Isaac enjoying his Goshen in Gerar. His prosperity is twofold: he is a successful farmer (v. 12) and a prosperous herdsman (v. 14). In the process he manages to accumulate a sizable workforce ("many servants").

15 In an attempt to arrest Isaac's phenomenal gains the Philistines *filled with dirt* the wells that Abraham had dug a generation earlier. This action will put an end to Isaac's success! The residents of Gerar might have "seized" the wells (as in 21:25) and thus have been able to use them for themselves. A well filled with dirt is useful to nobody. But because they do not have the human resources (see v. 16), they resort to vandalism rather than thievery. It is from these essential wells that Isaac must water his crops and provide his flocks and animals with water. Stopping them up and filling them with dirt would make Isaac's ability to tend his crops and herds tenuous in an area where the annual rainfall was meager.[11]

16 Interestingly, it is Isaac's prosperity, and not his lying and deception, that makes him persona non grata to Abimelech. It is when Yahweh blesses Isaac that Isaac becomes obnoxious to Abimelech. Thus he orders

9. The use of the verb *māṣā'* in the sense of "reap, acquire, secure," with a crop as object, is unique in the OT. In v. 19 "springing water" is the object of *māṣā'*.

10. Isaac's reaping of a hundredfold may be compared with the yield of the hundredfold (and sixty and thirty) in the parable of Jesus (Matt. 13:23). The NT number is taken nonsymbolically by K. D. White, "The Parable of the Sower," *JTS* 15 (1964) 302, but eschatologically by J. Jeremias, "Pälastinakundliches zum Gleichnis vom Säemann," *NTS* 13 (1966) 53.

11. T. L. Thompson ("The Background of the Patriarchs: A Reply to William Dever and Malcolm Clark," *JSOT* 9 [1978] 25) notes that the annual rainfall in this area in the Early Bronze Age "falls below 300 mm."

Isaac out of Gerar as the later pharaoh would do with Moses (Exod. 10:28). Although Abimelech uses the imperative *Go away from us,* suggesting he speaks from a position of authority, his addition of the subordinate phrase *for you are too strong for us* makes his words more of a request, a plea, than an ultimatum. The presence of a strong and potentially threatening force of outsiders at Gerar may be compared with the later situation in Egypt, when multiplying numbers of Israelites threatened the pharaoh (Exod. 1:9-10). In describing the multiplication of Israelites in Egypt, Exod. 1:7 uses the same verb *(wayyaʿaṣmû)* about Israel that Abimelech uses about Isaac *(ʿāṣamtā).* Although Exodus speaks clearly of the large numbers of Israelites who resided and eventually left Egypt, Gen. 26 has spoken only of Isaac, who went to Gerar to escape the famine in Canaan. V. 19 does tell us that Isaac was accompanied by his servants who helped dig wells. Would these be sufficient for Abimelech to say that Isaac has become too strong and numerous for him and his people? It is unlikely that Isaac was the only individual who would have fled to bordering countries to escape famine in his homeland. Perhaps Isaac is but one representative of a large migratory group (hence Abimelech's fear), and clogging the wells with dirt may have been the local citizens' way of discouraging other migratory groups from entering their area.[12]

17-18 Isaac does not flee directly from Gerar to his homeland. Rather, he voluntarily and amicably relocates. His first stop is at the Wadi Gerar,[13] a water course running between hills, and whose water amounts may vary from a swift-flowing and deep stream to a completely dry bed of river mud, depending on the amount of rainfall.

To his credit Isaac does not respond with anger against those who plugged his father's wells. Instead, he quietly goes about the business of redigging and reopening these wells. That Isaac named these wells using the names his father had already given to them would be one way in which Isaac would claim ownership over them (cf. 21:25). It is clear that Isaac knew not only the names of the wells that his father had earlier dug but also where to find them. This would be no easy task for one who is now in the process of relocating, as an outsider, in the area of Wadi Gerar.[14]

12. See V. H. Matthews, "The Wells of Gerar," *BA* 49 (1986) 123. I. Cornelius ("Genesis XXVI and Mari: The Dispute over Water and the Socio-Economic Way of Life of the Patriarchs," *JNWSL* 12 [1984] 53-61) cites a text from Mari (ARM II:28) analogous to the situation in Gen. 25:12-22. It is a dispute over water (but with irrigation rather than wells) in which one party appeals to his king to intercede on his behalf against another party and requests that ownership of the watering place be returned to him.

13. See Y. Aharoni, "The Land of Gerar," *IEJ* 6 (1956) 26-32.

14. Matthews ("Wells of Gerar," p. 123) notes that "one of the essential pieces of information that is carefully passed on from one generation of pastoralists to the next is the location and quality of environmental resources."

19-22 In addition to reopening wells (v. 18), and perhaps because the older wells were dry or starting to run dry, Isaac's servants dig three new ones, and to each Isaac gives a name, two of which are negative — (*Esek,* "challenge"; *Sitnah,* "opposition," from the same root as the Hebrew word for "Satan"), one of which is positive (*Rehoboth,* "open spaces").[15]

The discovering and digging of these wells also produced a verbal altercation (*rîḇ: made a complaint against,* v. 20; *quarreled,* v. 21)[16] between the shepherds of Isaac and those of Gerar. This quarrel reminds us of the strife (also the verb *rîḇ*) that broke out between Abraham's and Lot's herdsmen over territorial rights for pasturage (13:2ff.).

The shepherds of Gerar filled in Abraham's wells, but they make legal claim to Isaac's new wells as their own (v. 20). Isaac's wells are so valuable because they contain not just water, but *springing water,* that is, a spring that provides a constant supply of running water.

3. THE OATH BETWEEN ISAAC AND ABIMELECH (26:23-33)

23 *He went up*[1] *from there to Beer-sheba.*

24 *Yahweh appeared to him that night, saying:*
"I am the God of Abraham your father.

15. *ʿēśeq* occurs only here, as does the verb *ʿāśaq, śiṭnâ* occurs twice, here and Ezra 4:6 (a reference to lodging "a complaint" against the residents of Judah and Jerusalem). On *reḥōḇôṯ* see J. M. Sasson, "Reḥōvōt ʿÎr," *RB* 90 (1983) 95. Cf. the expression *reḥōḇôṯ hannāhār,* "wide spaces at the river," in Gen. 36:37. On the form of the etiologies here, see Long, *Problem of Etiological Narrative,* pp. 46-47.

16. On the use of *rîb* in Gen. 26, see B. Gemser, "The *rîb*- or controversy-pattern in Hebrew Mentality," *Wisdom in Israel and in the Ancient Near East,* Fest. H. H. Rowley, ed. M. Noth and D. Winton Thomas, VTSup 3 (Leiden: Brill, 1955), p. 120. J. Limburg ("The Root *rîb* and the Prophetic Lawsuit Speeches," *JBL* 88 [1969] 294-95) notes that of the three uses of *rîḇ* here (vv. 20, 21, 22), only the first one introduces direct speech. I have followed Gemser in translating *rîḇ* in v. 20 as "make a complaint against" (i.e., an oral complaint made by the aggrieved party against the party held responsible for the grievance), but have used "quarreled" in vv. 21, 22, with the shepherds of Gerar as the subject of the verb all three times. See also M. De Roche, "Yahweh's *rîb* Against Israel: A Reassessment of the So-Called 'Prophetic Lawsuit' in the Preexilic Prophets," *JBL* 102 (1983) 567, who notes the ability of the two parties to arrive at a solution without recourse to a third party.

1. G. R. Driver ("On *ʿlh* 'went up country' and *yrd* 'went down country,'" *ZAW* 69 [1957] 74) notes that *ʿālâ,* which usually means "to go up," actually refers to a descent in altitude in this verse: Rehoboth (325 meters) is 85 meters higher than Beer-sheba (240 meters). He points out three other places where *ʿālâ* seems to refer to descents (1 Sam. 24:13; 28:19; 1 K. 24:1). In all four of these instances the journey is in a northerly direction, and thus at times *ʿālâ* may mean "go northward, go up country."

Fear not, for I am with you.
I will bless you and multiply your descendants,
for the sake of Abraham my servant."

25 *He built an altar there and called on Yahweh's name and pitched his tent there. His servants started to dig*[2] *a well there.*

26 *In the meantime Abimelech, along with Ahuzzath his adviser*[3] *and Phicol the chief of his army, had come to him from Gerar.*

27 *Isaac asked them: "Why*[4] *have you come to me, since you despise me and drove me away from you?"*

28 *They responded: "We certainly see that Yahweh is with you, so we thought that there ought to be*[5] *a sworn oath between us, between us*[6] *and you. Let us make a treaty with you:*[7]

29 *that*[8] *you will not harm us just as we have not abused you,*[9] *and just*

2. Speiser (*Genesis,* p. 201) notes the two verbs for digging a well in this chapter: *ḥāpar* and *kārâ* (only v. 25). The first designates excavation that is completed. The second designates excavation that is in process.

3. Lit., "friend"; functionally, "adviser." Note that Hushai, who assumed an important role during Absalom's rebellion, is both David's servant (2 Sam. 15:34; 16:19) and David's "friend" (2 Sam. 15:37; 16:16), indicating that the friendship between David and Hushai differs from the friendship between David and Jonathan. Among a list of David's high officials, 1 K. 4:5 mentions Zabud, who was "priest and king's friend." See A. van Selms, "The Origin of the Title 'The King's Friend,'" *JNES* 16 (1957) 118-23.

4. In Genesis twenty-three questions begin with *lammâ* and only two with *maddûaʿ* (26:27; 40:7). In seven cases *maddûaʿ* is used with the verb *bôʾ* (Gen. 26:27; Judg. 11:7; 1 Sam. 20:27; 2 Sam. 3:7; 24:21; 2 K. 9:11; Isa. 50:2), while *lammâ* (which is used almost twice as many times) is followed by *bôʾ* only in 2 Sam. 14:32; 2 Chr. 32:4; Dan. 10:20. Judg. 11:7 is esp. close to Gen. 26:27 because both use a question introduced by *maddûaʿ*, then the verb *bô,* plus the verb *śānēʾ*, "despise." See J. Barr, "Why? in Biblical Hebrew," *JTS* 36 (1985) 25.

5. I render *t^{e}hî* "there ought to be" to catch the force of the inclusion of the particle *nāʾ* in Abimelech's words. He offers a suggestion; he does not make a demand.

6. Heb. *bênôṯênû bênênû*. GKC, § 103p n. 1, suggests that the first term means "between us" in the inclusive sense, i.e., both parties; the second refers to one of the two parties, "us." It is more likely that *bênôṯênû* has a stylistic function only, however; it is used to avoid a double use of *bênênû*. See J. Barr, "Some Notes on *ben* 'between' in Classical Hebrew," *JSS* 23 (1978) 12-22, esp. pp. 15, 19. The ancient versions apparently thought *bênênû* was redundant, so they omitted it. See *BHS*.

7. The expression "let us make [lit., cut] a treaty with [*ʿim*] you" is the one used when the subject of the verb is a suppliant. Cf. Hos. 12:2 (Eng. 1); 2 Chr. 23:3.

8. On the use of *ʾim* as an emphatic negative in adjurations see BDB, p. 50a, § b.2.

9. Because the Qal of *nāgaʿ* is never followed by a direct object, but by some preposition (e.g., *ʾel* in 20:6; *b^{e}* in 26:11), *n^{e}gaʿ^{a}nûḵā* must be an instance of a pronominal suffix used as an indirect object. See H. L. Ginsberg, "Lexicographical Notes," *ZAW* 51 (1933) 308.

as we have done nothing but good[10] *for you, and let you depart in peace. You are now the blessed of Yahweh."*

30 *He put on a feast for them, and they ate and drank.*

31 *Early next morning they took an oath with each other. Then Isaac sent them on their way and they parted from him in peace.*

32 *On that very day*[11] *Isaac's servants came to him and informed him about the well they had been digging, and they announced to him: "We have found water!"*

33 *He called it Shibah. Therefore the name of the city is Beer-sheba even still.*

23 Genesis 25:11b had earmarked *Beer-sheba* as the home of Isaac. The famine now presumably over, Isaac is able to return home.

24 Isaac's first experience upon returning to Beer-sheba is to receive a theophany from Yahweh. Furthermore, it is a nocturnal revelation — *that night.* Isaac's experience here parallels that of his son Jacob, who, upon returning from a stay at Paddan-aram, is confronted at night by God (32:22ff.).[12] Both theophanies come on the heels of highly questionable behavior by the patriarchs (Isaac with Abimelech, Jacob with Laban), but the content of both revelations is nothing but unmitigated promise. Unlike either his father or his son, however, Isaac does not receive a new name.

What Isaac does receive is: (1) a revelation of his father's God; (2) the promise of divine presence; (3) the promise of blessing and seed. The last two of these three elements may also be found in the theophany recorded in the earlier part of this chapter (vv. 2-4). For there we find too the promise of divine presence (v. 3), of blessing (v. 3), and of multiplication of seed (v. 4). Both times the point is made that Isaac is so honored because of Abraham (vv. 5, 24b). God is not initiating anything with Isaac. He is perpetuating what he started with Abraham.

In the first and last lines of the theophany Abraham occupies a prominent position. First Yahweh says to Isaac that he is the "God of Abraham your father," and then Yahweh concludes by calling Abraham "my servant." This first expression — "the God of your/my/his father" — is frequent in Genesis and in the Mosaic period (Exod. 3:6; 15:2; 18:4), but it never appears in the post-Mosaic period. The other formula close to this one is "the (Lord) God of your/our/their fathers" (pl.). This occurs a few times in Exodus (3:13, 15, 16; 4:5), more often in Deuteronomy (1:11, 21; 4:1; 6:3; 12:1; 27:3; 29:24

10. With *raq ṭôḇ* ("only good, nothing other than good") cf. *raq raʿ* (Gen. 6:5, "only evil, nothing other than evil").

11. This section began with a similar time-marker — "on that very night," v. 24.

12. For other manifestations of deity to a patriarch at night cf. Gen. 15:5ff; 28:10ff.

[Eng. 25]). Other uses of the plural formula are scattered throughout the OT (e.g., Josh. 18:3; Judg. 2:12; 2 K. 21:22; Ezra 7:27; 8:28; 10:11), with most appearing in 1 and 2 Chronicles. The use of the plural "fathers" is appropriate in these contexts because the audience for most of these references is the nation of Israel, who is called on to serve the God of their fathers, i.e., the patriarchs of Genesis.

The expression "the (Lord) God of my father" (sing.) is used by Yahweh (Gen. 26:24; 28:13; 46:3; Exod. 3:6), by a patriarch (Gen. 31:5, 42, 53; 32:10 [Eng. 9]; 49:25; 50:17), by the narrator (46:1), by an outsider (Laban, 31:29), and by a servant of a patriarch (24:13, 27, 42, 48). Other phrases include "the God of your father Abraham" (26:24), or "the God of his father Issac" (46:1), or "the God of your father Abraham and the God of Isaac" (28:13), or "I am the God of your father, the God of Abraham, the God of Isaac, the God of Jacob" (Exod. 3:6). But the absence of a reference like "I am the God of your father Terah" indicates that with Abraham a new era of biblical history commences. One is to distinguish the God of Abraham from the gods of the father Terah (Josh. 24:2). That Yahweh would identify himself to Isaac as "the God of Abraham your Father" attests to the existence of a personal relationship between Yahweh and the patriarch.[13]

25 Isaac's response is to build *an altar.* In so doing he follows the example of his father (12:7, 8; 13:18; 22:9) and anticipates his son (33:20; 35:7). These actions seem to be spontaneous rather than mandated, for only once (35:1) is a patriarch expressly told by God to build an altar. And only once (ch. 22) are we told that a patriarch made sacrifices on an altar. But the expression *and called on Yahweh's name* makes it clear that the *altar* was a place of worship, a place to commune with God. But life is more than worshiping at altars. While Isaac is building an altar his servants are excavating a new well. Both kinds of labor projects are necessary.

26 First it was Isaac who visited Abimelech in Gerar. Now it is Abimelech, accompanied by two of his chief advisers, who visits Isaac in Beer-sheba.[14] The roles of guest and host have shifted.

The reason for Abimelech's visit is clear. He realizes that God has blessed Isaac with both material power (vv. 13-14) and manpower (vv. 14,

13. For the expression "God of your father Abraham" cf. 28:13; 32:10. Cf. also J. P. Hyatt, "Yahweh as the God of My Father," *VT* 5 (1955) 130-36; M. Haran, "The Religion of the Patriarchs," *ASTI* 4 (1965) 35-37; A. Alt, "The God of the Fathers," in *Essays on Old Testament History and Religion,* tr. R. A. Wilson (Garden City, NY: Doubleday, 1967), pp. 3-100; Cross, *Canaanite Myth and Hebrew Epic,* pp. 4-43; N. Sarna, *Genesis,* JPS Torah Commentary (Philadelphia: Jewish Publication Society, 1989), pp. 396-97. *'ānōḵî* is the first word in the first line of this blessing and the last word in the second line of the blessing: "I (am) . . . I (am)." This is a revelation of Yahweh about Yahweh to Isaac, and not a revelation by Yahweh about Isaac to Isaac.

16). Beer-sheba is not far from Gerar, and in any future dispute Isaac and his entourage are too close for comfort. Accordingly, Abimelech seeks a more solid footing for security purposes, viz., a covenant of peace.

Abimelech does not travel alone to meet with Isaac. He brings with him *Ahuzzath,* his main civilian officer, and *Phicol,* his main military officer (cf. the Phicol who accompanied Abimelech in the latter's negotiations with Abraham, 21:22). No reason is given why they accompany their king. If they are there to make Abimelech's position seem more impressive (i.e., there is strength in numbers and in appearances), they do not succeed — Isaac is not intimidated. Indeed, neither Ahuzzath nor Phicol does anything or says anything (except by implication — vv. 28, 29). They are just there, silent observers of the pact between Abimelech and Isaac. Whatever the (foreign) etymology of Phicol may be,[15] in Hebrew it means "mouthful"; yet he utters not even a syllable![16]

27 Isaac is anything but a gracious host. He becomes belligerent with Abimelech and his two officers and accuses them of hating him *(you despise me)* and ordering him out of Gerar *(and drove me away from you).* It never occurs to Isaac that maybe Abimelech had justifiable grounds for doing what he did, given both Isaac's behavior in Gerar and his new circumstances there. Isaac is as rough on his visitors as the incognito Joseph is on his brothers when they seek him out in Egypt for grain (e.g., 42:9).

28-29 Abimelech begins the conversation more diplomatically than Isaac. He starts with a testimony to the effect that he indeed knows *that Yahweh is with* Isaac (cf. 21:22). Abimelech's confession may be compared with that of Jethro (Exod. 18:10-11), Rahab (Josh. 2:9-11), or Namaan (2 K. 5:15), all recognitions by Gentiles of the power and presence of Yahweh with his people. There is no evidence, however, that Abimelech became a follower of Yahweh.

This acknowledgment now made, Abimelech asks Isaac to enter into a *treaty (bᵉrîṯ)* and to make it binding by swearing (*wayyiššāḇᵉʿû,* v. 31) a solemn *oath.*[17] Isaac's relationship with Abimelech now provides three par-

14. Cf. the three "men" who came to Abraham at Mamre (18:1).

15. The suggestions range from Egyptian (M. Noth, *History of Pentateuchal Traditions,* p. 155 n. 443; W. F. Albright, "Egypt and the Early History of the Negeb," *JPOS* 4 [1924] 138-39) to Anatolian (J. D. Ray, "Two etymologies: Ziklag and Phicol," *VT* 36 [1986] 355-59). See above, p. 86 n. 1.

16. Y. T. Radday, "Humour in Names," in *On Humour and the Comic in the Hebrew Bible,* ed. Y. T. Radday and A. Brenner, JSOTSup 92 (Sheffield: Almond, 1990), pp. 64-65. On Ahuzzath, see J. D. Safren, "Ahuzzath and the Pact of Beer Sheba," *ZAW* 101 (1989) 184-98.

17. *ʾālâ* may not be an oath itself but rather an adjuration, a challenge to the parties involved to swear an oath. See G. R. Driver's comments in his review of Brichto, *The Problem of "Curse" in the Hebrew Bible,* in *JSS* 10 (1965) 94.

allels with Abraham's relationship with the earlier Abimelech. The first parallel is the wife-sister deception (20:2-18 and 26:1-16); the second is the dispute over wells (21:25-26 and 26:15-22); the third is the treaty with the Philistine king (21:27-34 and 26:28-31).

The very existence of these parallels has suggested to some scholars that these stories about Abraham are suspicious, and have been applied artificially to Abraham by being extrapolated from an earlier Isaac cycle; other scholars have suggested the reverse, that is, the stories about Isaac in ch. 26 have been borrowed from the Abraham cycle in order to give Isaac a measure of dignity and to reinforce the relationship between Abraham and Isaac and the relationship between Abraham and Jacob.[18] Here is another example of the way in which many modern scholars understand parallels. First, parallels cast a cloud of doubt over the historicity of one of the two sources; second, the parallels indicate literary dependence, one way or the other. Why is it not possible to think that ch. 26 describes a renewal between Isaac and Abimelech of the treaty between Abraham and (the earlier) Abimelech? This explanation seems most appropriate at this juncture.

Again, as in 21:23-24, it appears that the Philistine king is making a plea rather than dictating terms. He is presenting his case from a position not of strength but of vulnerability. Speaking for his two officers and for all the Gerarites (notice how often the king uses "we" and "us"), Abimelech appeals to past cordial relationships between Isaac and himself and his citizenry as the basis for his hope that Isaac will now extend *šālôm* to him (v. 29). But Abimelech's appeal is based on more than the relationship that already exists between himself and Isaac. He makes his appeal the way he does because of the observable relationship that exists between Isaac and his God — "you are now the blessed of Yahweh." This must be a reference back to v. 12, which ascribes Isaac's prosperity to the fact that Yahweh had blessed him. The bumper harvest (v. 12) made Isaac a wealthy individual (v. 13), and this prosperity produced envy among the Philistines (v. 14). Give Abimelech credit for knowing the real source of Isaac's prosperity: it is due to divine blessing, not agricultural skills.

30 The festive meal precedes the actual swearing of the oath. It is much like the meal that Jacob and Laban observed when they took their oath (31:46, 54), except that there the meal (v. 54) comes after the swearing (v. 53). This meal is not simply a courtesy extended by Isaac to Abimelech as host to visitor. It is, rather, an integral element of the covenant-making process, in which, in a sense, the individual offering the meal admits the other individual

18. For the former, see, e.g., Noth, *History of Pentateuchal Traditions,* pp. 104ff. For the latter, see Westermann, *Genesis,* 2:424; Van Seters, *Abraham in History and Tradition,* pp. 167-71; Coats, *Genesis,* p. 191.

to his family circle.[19] The counterpart to Isaac's meal given to and shared with Abimelech (i.e., a visible sign of covenant making) is Abraham's gift of animals to Abimelech (21:28).

31 Isaac and his guests rise early in the morning.[20] He and his visitors swear *an oath,* and they are on their way. Isaac's early anxieties (v. 27) have dissipated. In v. 28 Abimelech requested a "sworn oath" *('ālâ)* between himself and Isaac and a "treaty" *(b^erîṯ).* That wish is honored in v. 31 as both Isaac and Abimelech swear an oath to each other, an action that is this time conveyed by the verb *šāḇaʿ*. (For other instances of *šāḇaʿ* in covenants between two people see Gen. 21:23, 24, 31; 31:53b.) This use suggests that the verb *šāḇaʿ* covers the demands of an *'ālâ* and a *b^erîṯ*. McCarthy suggests that the presence of *šāḇaʿ* after these two nouns "serves to affirm and record the fact that a covenant has been completed. It sums up the result of the action. It seems doubtful that in addition to this it is intended to present a separate action or at least a separate element in the total action."[21] Interestingly, both the "sent away" of v. 27 and the *sent away* of v. 31 are the Piel of *šālaḥ*. The same verb and the same stem of that verb are used, but the different nuance requires a different English translation to capture the mood.[22] In v. 27 the subject of the verb was Abimelech, and the object was Isaac. In v. 31 Isaac is the subject of the verb, and Abimelech (and his party) is the object. Abimelech "drove" Isaac from Gerar; Isaac "sends" Abimelech back to Gerar in peace.

32 Isaac's servants are adroit at finding water. They have already done it three times (vv. 19-20, 21, 22), and now they accomplish it a fourth time. They make their discovery *On that very day* Isaac concludes his pact with Abimelech. The text does not say that the discovery of water should be read as a sign of divine approval on the Abimelech-Isaac reciprocal treaty, but such an interpretation is not impossible.

The verse resumes the information provided at the end of v. 25. The start of excavation of the well (expressed in v. 25 by the verb *kārâ*) preceded the Abimelech-Isaac meeting. The discovery of water at that well now excavated (expressed by the verb *ḥāpar*) follows the meeting.

33 In response to his servant's announcement, Isaac names (re-

19. W. McCree, "The Covenant Meal in the OT," *JBL* 45 (1926) 120-28; D. J. McCarthy, "Three Covenants in Genesis," *CBQ* 26 (1964) 184-85.

20. BDB, p. 1014b, observes that *šāḵam* is followed by *babbōqer* 30 times in the OT. In Genesis the phrase appears with Abraham (19:27; 21:14; 22:3); with Abimelech (20:8); with Abimelech and Isaac (26:31); with Jacob (28:18); with Laban (32:1 [Eng. 31:55]).

21. D. J. McCarthy, "Covenant-relationships," in *Institution and Narrative,* AnBib 108 (Rome: Biblical Institute, 1985), p. 58.

22. Cf. also the Piel of *šālaḥ* in v. 29. "It is true," says Abimelech, "that we sent you away, but we sent you away in peace [*b^ešālôm*]." Now Isaac sends them on their way *b^ešālôm* too.

names?) the city *Shibah.* This word (Heb. *šiḇʿâ*) is most likely the feminine form of the numeral "seven" (masc. *šeḇaʿ;* fem. *šiḇʿâ*), which is frequent in the Hebrew Bible.[23] This suggests that Isaac is simply reaffirming the name given to this site by Abraham (21:31), and there is therefore no reason for the repeated emphasis on "seven" as there was in ch. 21. Thus Isaac follows his father at two points: in making an alliance of peaceful coexistence with a Philistine King, and in naming a city.

If one does not accept *šbʿh* as the numeral "seven," then one has three ways of integrating the etymology of Beer-sheba in ch. 21 with that given here in ch. 26. (1) One can opt for one of the other readings, especially LXX; then "seven" has nothing to do with the name at all, and Beer-sheba means (in both places) "well of oath."[24] (2) One may resort to literary sources and attribute the story in ch. 21 to sources E and J^b, and that in ch. 26 to J^R.[25] (3) Instead of appealing to sources, one may appeal to an earlier tradition of the story in which Beer-sheba was connected with "oath," and a later tradition in which the name was connected for more explicit purposes with "seven."[26]

even still. Isaac's actions had an impact. Long after his day people still labeled this site as Isaac had named it. Whenever the formula "until this day/even still" occurs in an etiological usage, the pattern usually is: reference to some event that includes a keyword (e.g., "why did you bring *trouble* on us? May Yahweh *trouble* you [Josh. 7:25]), then the etymological etiology: "Therefore until this day the name of that place is called the Valley of Achor/Trouble" (Josh. 7:26). This second section of the pattern is introduced by the adverb "therefore" *(ʿal kēn),* followed by the verb "called" *(qārāʾ),* either as a frequentative perfect (the subject of which is general or impersonal), or as a *waw*-consecutive imperfect. Finally the formula "until this day" modifies the verb ("is called until this day)."[27] The basic difference between this pattern and what we find in Gen. 26:33 is twofold. The verb *qārāʾ* does not appear in v. 33. Instead, we have a verbless clause. Accordingly, and this

23. Some of the ancient versions read something other than "seven" for *šiḇʿâ,* LXX *hórkos* suggests *šᵉḇuʿâ,* "oath." Pesh. and Vulg. *(abundantiam)* read the Hebrew word as *śiḇʿâ,* "abundance," which is certainly a possible reading, and would follow nicely after v. 32. Isaac calls the name of the place where water was found "Well of Abundance." See Long, *Problem of Etiological Narrative,* pp. 34-36.

24. So Speiser, *Genesis,* p. 202.

25. So Gunkel, *Genesis,* pp. 233-36.

26. See Y. Zakovitch, "A Study of Precise and Partial Derivations in Biblical Etymology," *JSOT* 15 (1980) 34-36.

27. For the thrust of "even still" in v. 33 see B. S. Childs, "A Study Of The Formula, 'Until This Day,' " *JBL* 82 (1963) 282; D. J. McCarthy, "The Theology of Leadership in Joshua 1–9," *Bib* 52 (1971) 167-68.

is the second difference, the formula "until this day/even still" does not modify a verb but a noun. Thus it is not the etiology of Beer-sheba that is highlighted in v. 33 (i.e., the verse does not explain why people in general even now call Beer-sheba by that name); rather, it simply states the extension and perpetuation of the name Beer-sheba for this particular site from the time of the patriarch to the time of the narrator.

4. ESAU'S HITTITE WIVES (26:34-35)

34 *When Esau was forty years old, he married Judith, daughter of Beeri the Hittite, and Basemath, daughter of Elon the Hittite.*[1]
35 *They were a source of bitterness*[2] *to Isaac and to Rebekah.*

That Esau married these two woman at the age of *forty* means that Isaac is exactly one hundred when he gets two daughters-in-law (25:26b). It is interesting to compare Abraham and Isaac when each reaches the century mark. Abraham fathers Isaac (21:6), and Isaac obtains two Hittite daughters-in-law.

Why is the account of Esau's wives placed here? Could it be because of the similarity in sound between *Beeri* and the Hebrew word for "well" *(beʾēr),* a word that is prominent in the preceding narrative? Does its placement here "soften the bad impression created by the ruthless and unscrupulous conduct portrayed of Rebekah and Jacob in chapter 27"?[3] Or is Esau's relationship with Judith and Basemath to be contrasted with Isaac's relationship with Abimelech? Alliances of a political nature with outsiders are condoned, but marital alliances with outsiders bring grief to the husband's parents. Sarna has suggested that the placement of these two verses here reinforces the unworthiness of Esau to be his father's heir. Esau's errors are threefold. He has contracted the marriage himself, thus bypassing his parents; he married exogamously rather than endogamously; he has gone against the honor of his clan group by intermarrying with the native women.[4] Thus in several important

1. LXX, SP, Pesh. read "Hivite" *(haḥiwwî)* instead of MT *haḥittî.*

2. Lit., "a bitterness of spirit." *rûaḥ* and *mārar* occur again near each other (but not in juxtaposition as in Gen. 26:35) in Ezek. 3:14, *wāʾēlēḵ mar baḥᵃmaṯ rûḥî,* "and I went, bitter, my spirit raging." On the use of *mōraṯ* in Gen. 26:35 (clearly a situation of distress) to help translate *mar* in Ezek. 3:14 (bitter? strengthened?) see D. Pardee, "The Semitic Root *mrr* and the Etymology of Ugaritic *mr(r)* ‖ *brk,*" *UF* 10 (1978) 260 n. 69. On *(bᵉ)mar rûaḥ* in Sir. 4:6 and 7:11 see O. Sander, "*napšāʾ* = 'syrischer Sprachgebrauch," *ZAW* 87 (1975) 82-83.

3. See Vawter, *On Genesis,* p. 297.

4. Sarna, *Genesis,* p. 189. Sarna's suggestion is along the lines of Vawter's.

ways the marriage of Isaac to Rebekah (ch. 24) contrasts with the marriage of Esau to Judith and Basemath.[5]

Chapters 26 and 27 provide several contrasts. In ch. 26 Isaac and Rebekah weep (v. 35). But in ch. 27 Esau weeps. If in ch. 26 a son by his conduct embitters a mother, in ch. 27 a mother by her conduct embitters a son. The difference between the two incidents is that in ch. 26 the mother (Rebekah) is fully aware of her son's (Esau) activities, whereas in ch. 27 the son (Esau) is unaware of his mother's (Rebekah) involvement in and contribution to his distress.

D. JACOB RECEIVES BLESSING THROUGH DECEPTION (27:1-45)

1. ISAAC PREPARES TO BLESS ESAU (27:1-5a)

1 *Isaac, now elderly and with failing eyesight,*[1] *summoned Esau his older son and said to him, "Son!" He responded: "Yes!"*[2]

2 *And he said: "Look, I am so elderly, and do not know the day of my death.*

3 *So now take your weapons, bring*[3] *your bow as well, then go out into the field, and hunt me some game,*[4]

4 *and prepare for me a delicacy*[5] *which I relish, and bring it to me to*

5. However much a source of grief Esau's choice of wives may have been to his parents, each of the daughters-in-law bears a beautiful name. Judith, like Judah, is probably connected with the Hophal of *yāḏâ,* "to praise," thus "praised one." Basemath is connected with *bōśem,* "spice, balsam" and translates as "perfume."

1. Lit., "and his eyes became too faint/were too dim to see."

2. Lit., "Behold me." Some form of the formula "*X* said to him, '*Y!*' and *Y* said 'Here I am' " appears in the context of divine revelation (Gen. 22:1; 31:11; 46:2; Exod. 3:4); in conversations between a father and a son (Gen. 27:1, 18); Samuel's answers to both Eli and Yahweh (1 Sam. 3:4, 5, 6, 8, 16), a priest to his king (1 Sam. 22:12); the Amalekite to Saul (2 Sam. 1:7); the prophet to Yahweh (Isa. 6:8). Jenks (*The Elohist and North Israelite Traditions,* p. 25) notes that the formula was "a regularly used reply in ordinary speech, especially between persons related by intimacy or respect (father-son, king-subject)."

3. The imperative "bring" is obtained by repointing MT *tely*^{e}*ḵā* to *tōlîḵ,* the Hiphil imperative of *hālaḵ,* "to go." Cf. M. J. Dahood, "Poetry versus a Hapax in Genesis 27,3," *Bib* 58 (1977) 422-23. If MT is retained, then the noun *t*^{e}*lî* is a *hapax legomenon* from *tālâ,* "to suspend, hang," and hence something like "quiver" (so Westermann, *Genesis,* 2:434).

4. The anomalous Ketib *ṣêḏâ* (cf. Qere *ṣāyiḏ*) may represent the noun plus the suffixed *â,* the archaic accusative ending (Dahood, *Bib* 58 [1977] 423).

5. *maṭʿām,* which occurs only in this chapter of Genesis (vv. 4, 7, 9, 14, 17, 31) and in Prov. 23:3, 6.

eat, so that I may bless you before I die."[6]

5a *Rebekah overheard what Isaac was chatting about with his son Esau.*

Chapter 27 represents the third round of battle and manipulation between Jacob and Esau. The first was at birth (25:21-28). The second was over a birthright (25:29-34). Now the third is over a blessing.

The whole chapter is divided into scenes involving two personalities in each: (1) Isaac and Esau (vv. 1-4); (2) Rebekah and Jacob (vv. 5-17); (3) Isaac and Jacob (vv. 18-29); (4) Isaac and Esau (vv. 30-40); (5) Rebekah and Jacob (vv. 41-45); (6) Rebekah and Isaac (v. 46). Thus Isaac appears in four scenes, Rebekah in three scenes, Jacob also in three scenes, and Esau but twice. Hence Isaac is most prominent and Esau is least prominent.

1 Advancing age and diminishing physical faculties moves Isaac to arrange a meal with his son Esau at which time he might pass the family blessing on to his older son (v. 4b). Isaac's health is like that of Jacob, who lost most of his eyesight in his later years (Gen. 48:10), as did Eli the priest (1 Sam. 3:2), but unlike Moses, who retained his vision until the day of his death (Deut. 34:7). (The same root used for the "failing" or "dimming" of the eyes in Gen. 27:1 *(kāhâ)* is used in 1 Sam. 3:2; Deut. 34:7; Job 17:7, but not in Gen. 48:10 [which uses *kāḇēḏ*].)

Isaac is still of the opinion that his older son Esau will receive the blessing, in spite of the oracle about "the older serving the younger" (25:23). This variance is not an indication of different sources, for source critics attribute both 25:21-26a and 27:1-45 to J. Perhaps Isaac is still unaware of the divine oracle (forty years later?), or he has misunderstood it, or he has forgotten it. Failing eyesight and advanced years may be coupled with failing memory. Sternberg notes that for Isaac, in contrast to his father Abraham (24:1), old age "goes neither with admirable character nor with happiness and success but with failing powers all around, notably spiritual as well as physical decay."[7]

2 Genesis does not record Abraham's transmitting the blessing to Isaac, but Isaac must prepare to pass the blessing to his elder son. His advanced years tell him to take care of this strategic family matter before death makes any action impossible. Indeed, the clause *and do not know the day of my death* may be more than just a truism. It may be a recognized formula that accompanies a solemn and final disposition, and thus a phrase with sociojuridical overtones.[8] Isaac is like his mother, who also claims "I have grown old"

6. Lit., "so that my soul [my being] may bless you before I die." The same phrase appears in vv. 19, 25, 31. Cf. Wolff, *Anthropology of the Old Testament,* p. 24.

7. Sternberg, *Poetics of Biblical Narrative,* p. 350.

8. See E. A. Speiser, "I Know Not The Day Of My Death," *JBL* 74 (1955) 252-56 (repr. in *Oriental and Biblical Studies,* pp. 89-96).

(18:12), proceeds to do something she regrets, and then denies it. In this chapter Isaac does not know two things: the day of his death, and the identity of Jacob when he pretends to be Esau.

3-4 If Isaac's eyesight and memory are failing, his appetite is not. He instructs Esau to employ his hunting and culinary skills one more time.[9] Here Esau is hunting to kill game; later in the narrative he will be hunting to kill Jacob (v. 41).

It is not unusual to have the consumption of food and drink as an accompaniment to blessing. For example, the Ugaritic texts provide references to El taking "a cup in one hand, a flagon in the other," and then blessing his servant.[10]

5a Like her mother-in-law (18:10), Rebekah overhears (accidentally? deliberately?) a conversation between her husband and someone else, and what she hears spurs her into action. The first half of v. 5 ought to go with the events of vv. 1-4 because *overheard* is a participle *(šōmaʿaṯ),* thus demonstrating that v. 5a is a circumstantial clause that goes with what precedes.[11]

9. W. G. E. Watson ("The Falcon Episode in the Aqhat Tale," *JNWSL* 5 [1977] 75) cites Ugaritic passages that seem to suggest that a youth had to undergo an initiation rite into manhood that involved the hunting and bagging of game.

10. See D. Pardee, "An Emendation in the Ugaritic Aqht Text," *JNES* 36 (1977) 53-56, who provides the following illustrations from Ugarit of the consumption of (food and) drink as an accompaniment to blessing:

(1) Keret 2.16-18:

Thereafter the assembly of the gods arrives.
Baal speaks up:
"Do not depart, O Latpan, merciful Il,
You must bless noble Kirta,
Must (bless) the goodly lad of Il."
Il takes a cup in one hand,
a flagon in the other,
He does indeed bless his servant,
Does bless noble Kirta,
Does (bless) the goodly lad of Il.

(2) 2 Aqhat 1.35:

Il takes a cup in one hand
A flagon in the other,
He does indeed bless his servant,
Does bless Danil, man of rp'
Does (bless) the hero, man of hrnm."

11. For examples of a circumstantial clause ending an episode or paragraph see Andersen, *Sentence in Biblical Hebrew,* p. 81.

2. REBEKAH INCITES JACOB TO DECEIVE ISAAC (27:5b-17)

5b *After Esau had gone out into the field to hunt some game for his father,*[1]

6 *Rebekah said to her son Jacob: "I just overheard*[2] *your father speaking with Esau your brother,*

7 *'Fetch me some game and prepare a delicacy that I may eat it, and that I may bless you in Yahweh's presence*[3] *before I die.'*

8 *Now, my son, pay attention to me*[4] *as I give you instructions.*

9 *Go to the flock and get me two choice kids. With them I will prepare a delicacy for your father, just the way he likes it.*

10 *Then bring it to your father to eat, that he may bless you before he dies."*

11 *Jacob said to his mother: "My brother Esau is a hairy man, but I am a smooth-skinned man.*[5]

12 *What if my father feels*[6] *me? In his estimate*[7] *I will be making fun of*

1. Following LXX (i.e., *le'āḇîw*) instead of MT *lᵉhāḇî',* lit., "to bring" (cf. AV, NIV, NEB). In the Hiphil *bô'* is a transitive verb and demands an object. Where it means "bring near, back," the verb is followed by a prepositional phrase, rather than standing alone (cf. v. 10, *wᵉhēḇē'ṯā lᵉ'āḇîḵā,* "and bring it [back] to your father," and v. 7, *hāḇî'â lî* "fetch me some game").

2. For *šāma'* meaning "overhear" (vv. 5, 6) see 18:10.

3. Lit., "before Yahweh." I see no reason to accept Speiser's suggestion (*Genesis,* p. 209) that we have here an idiomatic usage of *lip̱nê,* "approval." It is unlikely that *lip̱nê* has an idiomatic usage, then two words later has its normal sense, "before."

4. Here (and in v. 13) *šāma' bᵉqōlî* has its common meaning "pay attention to [or 'obey'] me" (lit., "hear my voice"). Thus within a few verses we see different nuances of *šāma' bᵉ:* in vv. 5 and 6, of Rebekah about Isaac's words, as "overhear"; and in v. 8 of Jacob about Rebekah's words, as "obey" or "pay attention to."

5. For this root see K.-D. Schunk, *"chālaq* I," *TDOT,* 4:444-47, who notes that the basic meaning of the root is "be smooth/smoothness." From this basic meaning it developed the meaning "be slippery/slipperiness" (Jer. 23:12), and the metaphorical meanings "to flatter/flattery" (Prov. 6:24; 29:5; Isa. 30:10); "be empty (Ezek. 12:24); "be bare" (Josh. 11:17; 12:7). S. Gevirtz ("Of Patriarchs and Puns: Joseph at the Fountain, Jacob at the Ford," *HUCA* 46 [1975] 48) observes the geopolitical wordplay when one compares Gen. 27:11 and Josh. 11:16-17. Jacob has just called Esau *'îš śā'ir* and himself *'îš ḥālāq.* Josh. 11:16-17 states that "Joshua took all that country . . . from Mount Halak [*hāhār heḥālāq*] toward Seir [*śē'ir*]." See also Z. Kallai, "The southern border of the land of Israel — pattern and application," *VT* 37 (1987) 445.

6. The Qal of *māšaš* occurs only here and in v. 22. Otherwise it is in the Piel or Hiphil. The same verb appears again in the Jacob cycle (in the Piel) in 31:34, 37. Laban "felt" all about the tent looking for his missing household gods. In both cases the act of feeling/touching by Laban/Isaac fails to uncover the duplicity of Jacob/Rachel. See Fishbane, *Text and Texture,* p. 51.

7. Lit., "in his eyes." The narrator is obviously making a wordplay here; the

him,[8] *and I shall bring on myself a curse instead of a blessing."*

13 *His mother replied: "Upon me (be) any curse,*[9] *my son; just pay attention to me, and go and get (them) for me."*

14 *So Jacob went and got them and brought them to his mother; and his mother prepared a delicacy, just the way his father liked.*

15 *Rebekah then took the best clothes of Esau her son, her older son, with her in the house, and dressed Jacob, her younger son.*

16 *And with the skins of the kids she covered up his hands, and the hairless parts of his neck.*

17 *Then she placed the delicacy and the bread which she had prepared in the hand of Jacob her son.*

5b-10 Esau's departure for the open fields in chase of game provides the opportunity for Rebekah to launch her act of duplicity. Rebekah is careful to identify Isaac and Esau in relation to Jacob and not to herself. Thus Isaac is *your father* (not "my husband") and Esau is *your brother* (not "my son").

Rebekah is only somewhat accurate in her reporting to Jacob of Isaac's words to Esau. She makes a minor adjustment to Isaac's "that my *nep̄eš* may bless you" to "that I may bless you." More than likely the two phrases are two ways of saying the same thing. Accordingly, I have translated both the same.[10] She also adds *in Yahweh's presence (lip̄nê YHWH).*[11] One would suspect that the addition of this particular phrase would make Jacob even

---

narrative began with a man whose eyes were beginning to fail him (v. 1). Jacob is perhaps weighing his father's eyes against his mother's voice.

8. Heb. *mᵉṯaʿtēʿa* is variously rendered: "frivolous" (Speiser); "making sport" (NAB, Vawter); "mocking" (RSV, Westermann, BDB); "a trickster" (NJPS, Brichto, *Problem of "Curse" in the Hebrew Bible,* p. 197; cf. NEB, NIV "tricking"); "deceiver" (AV, S. R. Driver); "make fun of" *(HALAT).* The root is a *dislegomenon* in Biblical Hebrew, appearing again only in 2 Chr. 36:16, where it is used along with the verbs *lāʿaḇ,* "mock, ridicule," and *bāzâ,* "despise."

9. Lit., "your curse." Speiser (*Genesis,* p. 209) observes that the literal translation "your curse" would be ambiguous.

10. Two translations of v. 4 ("so that I may bless you") suggest that Isaac's own words are much stronger than Rebekah's version of them. Coote and Ord (*Bible's First History,* p. 146) render v. 4, "so I can give you a robust blessing"; C. W. Mitchell (*The Meaning of BRK "To Bless" in the Old Testament,* SBLDS 95 [Atlanta: Scholars, 1987], p. 82) has "so that I may wholeheartedly bless you."

11. Note also that "before I die" in Isaac's speech is *bᵉṭerem ʾāmûṯ.* In Sarah's renarration "before I die" is *lip̄nê môṯî.* This construction allows for the double use of *lip̄nê: before* Yahweh, *before* I die. For the idea that *lip̄nê YHWH* is a phrase with a technical legal connotation in treaty contexts see D. C. T. Sheriffs, "The Phrases *ina IGI DN* and *lipĕnēy Yhwh* in Treaty and Covenant Contexts," *JNWSL* 7 (1979) 55-68.

more hesitant about participating in his mother's ruse. If this blessing is to be with Yahweh's blessing and in Yahweh's presence, why should Jacob attempt to sabotage it?[12]

Rebekah uses still other devices to help convince Jacob of her plan. First, she quotes direct speech rather than using indirect speech, thus making Jacob's hearing of Isaac's words to Esau as precise as possible (in his mind, anyway). Second, her use of the participle *m*^{e}*ḏabbēr,* "speaking," underscores the urgency of the situation. Jacob must act now or forever lose his oppportunity to obtain the blessing. Third, Rebekah deletes almost all of Isaac's words in v. 3 about hunting, an activity Jacob never found pleasurable.[13]

Rebekah is persistent. Just as she overheard Isaac *(šāmaʿ b*^{e}*),* Jacob is now to *pay attention* (*šāmaʿ b*^{e}*,* vv. 8, 13, 43) to her. Furthermore, Rebekah does not make a suggestion to Jacob — she issues an order. Isaac converses with Esau, but Rebekah imposes on Jacob.[14] Her suggestion is that Jacob copy his brother's physical features and that she copy Esau's culinary skills. Jacob is to feel like Esau and Rebekah is to cook like Esau.

11-12 Jacob had earlier been described as an *ʾîš tām* ("an innocent man," 25:27), and Esau as an *ʾîš śāḏeh* ("a man of the steppe," 25:27). Now we discover another difference between the two. The *ʾîš tām* is also an *ʾîš ḥālāq* (lit., "a smooth man"), and the *ʾîš śāḏeh* is also an *ʾîš śāʿir* (lit., "a hairy man"). Here is a problem, thinks Jacob, with which his mother has not reckoned. True, his father is blind, but Isaac still retains a sense of touch. What will slip by his eyes will not slip through his fingers.

Furthermore, Jacob knows that such deceitfulness would once and for all disqualify him from any kind of paternal blessing and inheritance. Such a ploy would produce only a *curse (q*^{e}*lālâ).*[15] To confound matters even more, such behavior would make it appear that Jacob *is making fun of* Isaac, in that he would be ridiculing his own father. Jacob is clearly less concerned with the rightness, the morality, of his mother's suggestion than he is with what happens to him if his disguise is discovered and his impersonation revealed.

13 Not to be thwarted, Rebekah offers to take any blame that will occur if Jacob's true identity becomes known and the ploy falls apart. In so speaking to her son, she becomes the first person to offer herself as the recipient of a curse

12. On the addition of "in Yahweh's presence" in Sarah's version, see Sternberg, *Poetics of Biblical Narrative,* pp. 391-93.

13. Savran, *Telling and Retelling,* pp. 41-42.

14. Cf. the two Piel participles: Isaac is speaking (*m*^{e}*ḏabbēr,* v. 6) with Esau; Rebekah gives instructions (*m*^{e}*ṣawwâ,* v. 8).

15. Brichto (*Problem of "Curse" in the Hebrew Bible,* p. 197) calls this an ambiguous use of *q*^{e}*lālâ*. That is, does *q*^{e}*lālâ* in vv. 12 and 13 refer to misfortune, or to the invocation of misfortune? Or both (which is more likely)?

for someone else.[16] She promises that Jacob would receive all the benefits of the blessing, but none of the punishments of the curse, should one be forthcoming. This is the reason why Calvin refers to Rebekah's "hasty zeal."[17]

14 Rebekah easily answered Jacob's objections and silenced him. He who is later capable of wrestling with God wrestles little with his mother or with his conscience. He did what he was told to do. His compliance is immediate.

15-17 If Jacob is smooth, then his mother is a smooth operator. His skin is like her imagination. First of all, Rebekah's scours through Esau's closets and helps herself to some of his choice clothes, and then puts them on Jacob. That she has access to Esau's clothes means that Esau and his wives must be living with his parents.[18] If Esau has made life bitter for Rebekah by marriage (26:34-35), Rebekah will make life bitter for Esau by manipulation (27:1ff.). Both son and mother are involved in the no-win game of one-upmanship.

Now dressed like Esau, Jacob must be costumed to feel like Esau as well. To that end Rebekah covers the exposed parts of Jacob's skin — his hands and his neck. Nothing is said about facial coverings, for presumably here the differences between the two brothers are minimal, or else Rebekah is counting on no facial contact. Rebekah must believe that her husband is extremely incapacitated, for he will not be able, she thinks, to distinguish between human hair and goatskins. She really thinks she can pull the wool over Isaac's eyes.

3. JACOB DECEIVES ISAAC (27:18-29)

18 *He came[1] to his father and said, "Father!" "Yes?" he answered. "Which one of my sons are you?"[2]*

16. See C. G. Allen, "On Me Be the Curse, My Son," in *Encounter with the Text,* ed. M. J. Buss (Philadelphia: Fortress; Missoula, MT: Scholars, 1979), pp. 159-72.

17. J. Calvin, *Commentaries on the First Book of Moses Called Genesis,* tr. J. King, 2 vols. (Grand Rapids: Eerdmans, repr. 1948), 2:87. Calvin remarks that Sarah "burns with such hasty zeal . . . no one will deny that this zeal, although preposterous, proceeds from special reverence for the word of God."

18. Or is J (ch. 27) unaware of Esau's marriages (26:34-35, P)?

1. I see no reason to accept LXX and Vulg. "and he brought (them)" *(wayyāḇē')* over MT *wayyāḇō'. wayyāḇē'* does appear in v. 25.

2. The lit. translation "who are you, my son?" would make no sense at all, for Isaac does not need an introduction to his son. Isaac's question *mî 'attâ bᵉnî* may be compared with Naomi's question to Ruth after Ruth has returned from her second visit with Boaz: *mî 'at bittî* (3:16). The thrust of Naomi's question is not "How did you fare, my daughter?" (RSV), but rather "Is that you, daughter?" In each case the identity of one (the son and daughter-in-law, respectively) is hidden from another (the father and mother-in-law) because visual recognition is impossible (due, respectively, to blindness and the darkness of the night). Thus Isaac's question has the force of "Who is it, son? Are you Esau or Jacob?" See B. Rebera, "Translating Ruth 3:16," *BT* 38 (1987) 234-37.

19 *Jacob answered his father: "I am Esau, your firstborn. I have done as you requested of me. Now, sit up,*[3] *eat some of my game, so that you might bless me."*

20 *Isaac asked his son: "How did you find it so quickly, my son?" "Yahweh your God made it come*[4] *before me," he replied.*

21 *Isaac said to Jacob: "Come closer,*[5] *my son, that I may learn by touching whether you are my son Esau."*

22 *So Jacob moved closer to Isaac his father. When he touched him he said: "The voice is Jacob's voice, but the hands are Esau's hands."*

23 *He failed to identify him because his hands were like the hands of Esau his brother — hairy. Accordingly, he was on the verge of blessing him.*[6]

24 *Again he asked: "You*[7] *are my son Esau?" And he replied: "I am."*

25 *So he said: "Serve me, and let me eat some of my son's game, so that I may bless you." He served it to him, and he ate; then he brought him wine, and he drank.*

26 *Then Isaac his father said to him: "Come closer, my son, and kiss me."*

27 *When he approached and kissed him, (Isaac)*[8] *caught the smell of his clothes. Then he blessed him:*

3. Lit., "arise now, sit down" *(qûm-nā' šeḇâ),* which sounds contradictory. This is an instance of coordinate commands in apposition in which the first verb is almost "semantically empty, functioning merely as a hortatory particle" (Andersen, *Sentence in Biblical Hebrew,* pp. 56-57).

4. For another use of *qārâ* in the context of the chase of game see M. J. Dahood, "The Hapax *ḥārak̲* in Proverbs 12,27," *Bib* 63 (1982) 60-62. The Hiphil of *qārâ* was used in 24:12 by the servant as he set out on a long mission to find a bride for Isaac. In both cases *qārâ* (Hiphil) indicates the opposite of an accidental event, i.e., a providential occurrence planned and executed by Yahweh.

5. The verb *nāgaš* appears 6 times in vv. 21-27. The Qal imperative is used twice (vv. 21, 26), the Qal imperfect twice (vv. 22, 27), the Hiphil imperative once (v. 25), and the Hiphil imperfect once (v. 25).

6. The imperfect of *bārak̲* here can only be an ingressive imperfect (i.e., action that is about to take place). Otherwise, the text has Isaac blessing Jacob twice (vv. 23, 27). See Speiser, *Genesis,* p. 209; Fokkelman, *Narrative Art in Genesis,* p. 103.

7. SP adds the interrogative indicator *ha-* to the pronoun to bring it into conformity with the parallel question in v. 21.

8. I put Isaac in parentheses to indicate that the subject of the verb changes without any indication in the Hebrew text. If *wayyāraḥ* has a transitive sense, the subject can only be Isaac. Jacob could also be the subject of the verb if it has the sense: "Jacob gave forth the scent of his clothes." See P. A. H. de Boer, "*wmrḥwq yryḥ mlḥmh* — Job 39:25," in *Words and Meanings: Essays Presented to David Winton Thomas,* ed. P. R. Ackroyd (Cambridge: Cambridge University, 1968), pp. 37-38. For other references to clothes giving off an odor, in this case a spicy scent, see Cant. 4:11; Ps. 45:9 (Eng. 8).

"See, the smell of my son
is like the smell of a field
that Yahweh has blessed.
28 *May God give you*
of the dew of the heavens
and of the fatness[9] *of the earth —*
abundance of grain and wine.
29 *May peoples serve you*
and populations[10]*bow down*[11] *to you.*
Be master over your brothers,
and may your mother's sons[12] *bow down*[13] *to you.*
Who curses you be cursed,
who blesses you be blessed."

18-19 It may be surprising that Isaac even had to ask which of his sons was now standing before him. For he had just sent Esau on an errand and instructed him to return with some game. Since Esau had been gone so short a time, however, Isaac is caught off guard.

Jacob proceeds to utter two lies. First, he claims to be Esau, and for good

9. I repoint MT *ûmišmannê* to *ûmiššamnê,* also in v. 39. For this vocalization see H. L. Ginsberg, *The Ugarit Texts* (Jerusalem: Vaad Halashon, 1936), p. 63; and M. Held, "The YQTL-QTL (QTL-YQTL) Sequence of Identical Verbs in Biblical Hebrew and in Ugaritic," in *Studies and Essays in Honor of Abraham A. Neuman,* ed. M. Ben-Horin, et al. (Leiden: Brill, 1962), p. 284 n. 3. Cf. GKC, § 20m; BDB, p. 1032a. Another possibility is to repoint MT to *miššammî* (*šēmen* plus genitive ending), "oil of" — "May God give you of the dew of heaven and the oil of earth." See M. J. Dahood in a review article in *Or* 39 (1970) 376; idem, "Ugaritic-Hebrew Parallel Pairs," in *RSP,* 1:84.

10. For other instances of "people(s)" *(ʿam)* and populations *(lᵉʾōm)* as a fixed pair in Biblical Hebrew, see the references in Gevirtz, *Patterns in the Early Poetry of Israel,* pp. 40-41, and p. 41 n. 16. Gevirtz also provides instances of the verbs "serve" *(ʿāḇaḏ)* and "bow down" *(ḥāwâ)* (p. 41 and n. 17) together in this order (or in the reverse order — *ḥāwâ//ʿāḇaḏ* [p. 41 n. 18]).

11. Most Hebraists are now agreed that the stem of the frequently used *hištaḥᵃwâ* is the Ishtaphal (Št) of *ḥwy,* which means either "to gather" (so S. Kreuzer, "Zur Bedeutung und Etymologie von *hištaḥᵃwah/yštḥwy,*" *VT* 35 [1985] 54-60), or "to bow down" (so H. D. Preuss, *"ḥwh," TDOT,* 4:249-56; E. Yamauchi, *"ḥāwâ," TWOT,* 1:267-69). Cf. J. A. Emerton, "The Etymology of HIŠTAḤᴬWĀH," *OTS* 20 (1977) 41-55, who advocates a return to the older explanation that the form in question is a Hithpalel of *šāḥâ,* "bow down."

12. With the Hebrew pair "brother(s)//mother's son(s)" cf. the instances of *aḫ//bn um* in Ugaritic texts cited in M. Dahood, "Ugaritic-Hebrew Parallel Pairs," in *RSP,* 1:103.

13. Note that in the poetic pattern here the second verb in a sequence of four is repeated as the fourth: "serve," "bow down," "be master," "bow down." See J. S. Kselman, "The ABCB Pattern: Further Examples," *VT* 32 (1982) 224-29.

measure he adds *your firstborn.* This phrase will remind Isaac why father and son are getting together on this occasion. Second, he claims to have captured the game and now wants to share that with Isaac. He also reminds his father that he is there for his father's blessing, not just for some food and a chat.

20 Isaac knows that Esau is an excellent hunter, but not so good that he could *find it so quickly.* The low point in Jacob's conversation with his father is his statement that he is back so quickly because God[14] just put the game in front of him. Here is an appeal to deity in order to cover up duplicity. It is important that Jacob implements his strategem rapidly. He has to be gone before Esau returns.

But this statement merely exacerbates Jacob's dishonesty. Jacob's digging a deeper hole for himself by making a false claim vis-à-vis divinity may be compared with a situation mentioned in Leviticus in connection with the guilt/reparation offering. Lev. 6:3 addresses one type of trespass that calls for the guilt/reparation offering — an individual finds lost property and then lies about finding it. That lie is sufficient to incur guilt. The trespasser, however, compounds his guilt by "swearing falsely," i.e., "I swear to God, I'm telling you the truth."

One may profitably relate Jacob seeking his father's blessing through a ruse (ch. 27) and his open and determined seeking of God's blessing (ch. 32). Without the latter, the former is meaningless. Throughout much of his early life, Jacob has all the trappings of one who is declared the family beneficiary (i.e., the birthright and the paternal blessing), but he does not have the blessing of God. In this respect he is like King Saul, who retained all the symbols of royalty, except for the most crucial one — the divine anointing.

21 Now for the second time (cf. v. 18, and v. 24 to follow) Isaac asks the identity of his son in front of him. The question is not settled by Jacob's appeal to his father's God. Isaac wants to make sure and thus requests his son to "come closer" (and cf. v. 26). Given the prominence of the verb *nāgaš* in this section (see n. 5 above), one would think that Jacob wants to get no nearer to Isaac than is absolutely necessary.

22-24 Isaac's bewilderment is now even more intense. It is Esau whom he feels, but it is Jacob whom he hears. Here was an oversight in Rebekah's machinations. She made sure that Jacob felt and smelled like Esau. But she had suggested nothing about voice imitation, possibly because as twins their voices were quite similar. This omission explains why Isaac inquires a third time (v. 24).

14. Almost all commentators attribute all (or most) of ch. 24 to J. But how does one account for the presence of *'ĕlōhîm* in a J narrative? L. Schmidt ("Jakob erschleicht sich den väterlichen Segen. Literarkritik und Redaktion von Genesis 27,1-45," *ZAW* 100 [1988] 159-83) attributes vv. 14b-22 and 29-34 to E, but not v. 28.

25 Convinced now that it is indeed Esau before him, Isaac shares a meal with the one he is to bless. Isaac had requested only some game to eat. To put the finishing touches on the meal, however, Jacob adds a little wine.

26 Isaac's request that his son kiss him may be one last attempt by Isaac to resolve any lingering doubts.

27-29 The blessing of Isaac on Jacob has three parts: (1) a statement of what Jacob is, v. 27; (2) a statement of what he will receive, v. 28; (3) a statement about his relationship with others (v. 29). In the end it is the odor of Jacob's clothes and covered skin that seals the matter for Isaac and paves the way for the pronouncement of this threefold blessing.

The essence of the part of the blessing found in v. 28 is agricultural fertility. This future fertility is described with the poetic pair, *the dew of the heavens* and *the fatness of the earth.*[15] Interestingly, the same two phrases are used for Esau later in the chapter, but in reverse order (see v. 39). The reversed phrases represent a reversal of the blessings.

This blessing of fertility is further spelled out as an *abundance of grain* [*dāg̲ān*] *and wine* [*tîrōš*]. That Dagan is a Canaanite (Philistine) deity is well known. Tirosh is also now recognized as the name of a Canaanite god,[16] a kind of Bacchus from which the Hebrews obtained the term *tîrōš,* their poetic word for "wine."

Parts of v. 28 are much like some lines from an Ugaritic text: *ṭl šmm šmn arṣ rbb rkb ʿrpt,* "dew of heaven, fat of earth, rain of the Rider of clouds."[17] In the light of the similarity of the phraseology and the identification of Dagon and Tirosh, Dahood is prepared to translate v. 28 as follows: "May God give you of the dew of Heaven and of the oil of Earth and of the spray of Dagan and Tirosh."[18] That is, the God of Jacob will provide Jacob with all the ingredients of fertility that were thought to be given by the Canaanite gods Heaven, Earth, Dagan, and Tirosh.

15. For "oil, fat of the land" as a metaphorical expression for rain see H. J. Zobel, "Der bildliche Gebrauch von *šmn* im Ugaritischen und Hebräischen," *ZAW* 82 (1970) 209-16.

16. See M. C. Astour, "Some New Divine Names From Ugarit," *JAOS* 86 (1966) 284; A. Cooper, "Divine Names and Epithets in the Ugaritic Texts," in *RSP,* 3:428. In a review article Albright (*BASOR* 139 [1955] 18) observes the presence of the name *ʿAbdi-ti-ir-ši* in an Ugaritic text (*PRU,* III, 16.257, iv:8) and connects it with *ᵐAbdi-TIR-ši,* a king of Hazor in Galilee who dispatched one of the Amarna Letters to Pharaoh. The name translates as "Servant of the God(dess) Tiršu."

17. See *UT,* ʿnt II:39-40 (*CTA,* 3.II.39-40). Translation of C. H. Gordon, *Ugarit and Minoan Crete* (New York: Norton, 1966), p. 52.

18. M. J. Dahood, review of *Ugaritica V* in *Or* 39 (1970) 376. For a translation that does not appeal to the presence of Canaanite deities in the verse see R. E. Whitaker, "Ugaritic Formulae," in *RSP,* 3:215.

The last part of Isaac's blessing over Jacob shifts from agricultural fertility (v. 28) to political supremacy (v. 29). Peoples will *serve* and *bow down* to Jacob. Closer to home, his *brothers* and *mother's sons* are also to come under his authority. Now, to be sure, nowhere does Genesis state that Isaac and Rebekah had other children besides Esau and Jacob. But Genesis does refer to Jacob's brothers (see 27:37; 31:46); also, the association of the terms "brother(s)" and "mother's sons" was a standard feature of OT verse, and thus "brothers"/"mother's sons" may be poetic craft rather than a reference to Jacob's blood brothers.[19]

The last part of the promise about curse/blessing is very close to Num. 24:9 with regard to nations, except that the lines are reversed. "Cursing" comes first in Gen. 27:29; "blessing" comes first in Num. 24:9. In form, Gen. 27:29 is much closer to Num. 24:9, for in both texts the active participles are in the plural and the passive participles are in the singular, a construction known as the distributive singular — "Those who curse you, cursed be every one of them; those who bless you, blessed be every one of them."[20]

Isaac has unknowingly spoken the truth. He does not know he has been tricked, but neither does he know that he has spoken prophetically. The last two parts of the prophecy find fulfillment within the very narrative. For who is it that qualifies for "who curses you"? Esau. And who is it that qualifies for "who blesses you"? Isaac. To all of this blessing Jacob makes no response. He exits quietly, as recorded in the next verse ("had left his father's presence").

Speiser has claimed this incident in Gen. 27, Isaac's last blessing, as a parallel to a few Nuzi tablets (HSS ix:34; v:48; AASOR xvi:56) that focus on (a) the validity and irrevocability of a deathbed blessing, and (b) the father's authority to bestow the family inheritance on a son other than the oldest son.[21] Subsequent study of these texts suggests that they describe not a final disposition but an administrative transfer of authority (HSS ix:34); not the power of the father to reverse the natural order but the father's obligation to make it transparent that he has adopted the son in question as heir (HSS v:48); not the legally binding oral statement made to a son by a dying father but a claim, upheld by witnesses, that the deceased father

19. For references see Gevirtz, *Patterns in the Early Poetry of Israel,* pp. 42-43; and n. 10 above.

20. See GKC, § 145l; J. Milgrom, *Numbers,* JPS Torah Commentary (Philadelphia: Jewish Publication Society, 1990), p. 205. On the order "curse . . . blessing" in Gen. 27:29 and "blessing . . . curse" in Num. 24:9, i.e., an inverted quotation, see the examples collected by P. C. Beentjes, "Inverted Quotations in the Bible: A Neglected Stylistic Pattern," *Bib* 63 (1982) 506-23, esp. 509-10.

21. See, e.g., *Genesis,* pp. 212-13; idem, "I Know Not the Day of My Death," *JBL* 74 (1955) 252-56.

promised his son a wife but failed to give her to his son while he was still living (AASOR xvi:56).[22] Even if Speiser's interpretation of the Nuzi tablets be upheld, how could Gen. 27 be anchored in Hurrian law if in this story "the father would never make the transfer willingly, and must be bamboozled into it."[23]

4. ESAU SEEKS HIS FATHER'S BLESSING (27:30-40)

30 *No sooner*[1] *had Isaac blessed Jacob, and no sooner*[2] *had Jacob left Isaac his father, than Esau his brother returned from his hunt.*

31 *He too prepared a delicacy, and carrying it to his father, he said: "Let my father sit up and eat of his son's game, that*[3] *you may then bless me."*

32 *Isaac his father responded: "Who are you?" "I am your son, your firstborn, Esau!" he answered.*

33 *Isaac was exceedingly distraught*[4] *and said: "Who was it then*[5] *that hunted game and brought it to me? I finished eating it*[6] *just before you came, and I blessed him. Now,*[7] *blessed shall he remain!"*

22. See T. L. Thompson, *Historicity of the Patriarchal Narratives,* pp. 285-93.

23. Sternberg, *Poetics of Biblical Narrative,* p. 183.

1. Lit., "and it came to pass when" (with temporal force for *ka'ašer).* For *wayehî ka'ašer* see Gen. 12:11; 20:13; 24:22, 52, and many other instances.

2. Here is a case of *'aḵ* as an adverb of time ("only just," "scarcely," "no sooner"). For its use in this sense before an infinitive absolute and a finite cognate verb form (as in Gen. 27: *yāṣō' yāṣā')* cf. Judg. 7:19: *'aḵ hāqēm hēqîmû.* GKC, § 164b n. 1, notes that the presence of *'aḵ* and the infinitive absolute emphasize the rapid succession of events referred to in these first two clauses of v. 30.

3. The use of *ba'aḇûr* for "(so) that" in "(so) that you may bless me" (vv. 4, 19, 31) and the use of *lema'an* for "(so) that" (in v. 25) demonstrates the interchangeability of subordinating conjunctions.

4. I prefer the nuance of anger rather than panic or terror for *ḥāraḏ* (cf. the common translation "tremble" in AV, RSV, NIV, etc.). Isaac would more likely be angry than fearful after he discovers that his son has deceived him, although it is quite conceivable for somebody to tremble from anger. See G. R. Driver, "Hebrew Homonyms," in *Hebräische Wortforschung,* Fest. Walter Baumgartner, ed. B. Hartmann, et al., VTSup 16 (Leiden: Brill, 1967), pp. 54-55. Cf. A. Baumann, *"ḥāraḏ," TDOT,* 5:166-70.

5. The inclusion of both the enclitic particle *'ēpô'* and the personal pronoun *hû'* immediately after the interrogative makes the question vivid. See GKC, § 150l.

6. MT *'ōḵal mikkōl,* lit., "I ate of everything." Some (e.g., *BHS;* Westermann, *Genesis,* 2:434) suggest reading *'āḵōl* (infinitive absolute, "to eat") for *mikkōl,* but the sense would be the same (cf. Speiser, *Genesis,* p. 210).

7. Andersen (*Sentence in Biblical Hebrew,* p. 166) explains the *gam* (without the *we*) as an emphasizing *gam.*

34 *On hearing his father's words, Esau burst*[8] *into long and bitter*[9] *groans. "Bless me, even me also, father," he said.*

35 *He replied: "Your brother came fraudulently and has taken away your blessing."*

36 *Esau said: "Is it because*[10] *they name him Jacob that he should be at my heel twice?*[11] *My birthright*[12] *he took away, and now he has taken away my blessing!*[13] *Have*[14] *you reserved*[15] *a blessing for me?" he said.*

37 *Isaac answered Esau: "As master I have already appointed him over you; and all his kinsmen I have handed over to him as slaves; also, with grain and wine have I sustained him. What then am I able to do for you, my son?"*

38 *Esau said to his father. "Only one blessing have you, father?*[16] *Bless me, even me also, father." (Isaac remained silent.)*[17] *Esau wept aloud.*

39 *Isaac his father answered and said:*

8. The narrator may be making a wordplay between "Isaac" *(yiṣḥāq)* and Esau's "crying" *(yiṣʿaq).*

9. Esau's sobs, which are described as "bitter" *(mārâ),* recall the earlier emotions he brought upon his parents — "a source of embitterment" *(mōraṯ rûaḥ),* 26:35.

10. *h*ᵃ*ḵî* introduces an interrogative nominal clause having a *kî*-clause as subject. See GKC, § 150e; R. Gordis, *The Word and the Book: Studies in Biblical Language and Literature* (New York: Ktav, 1976), p. 164 n. 9.

11. For *zeh* as a particle that stresses a quantity or a number, see S. Talmon, "The New Hebrew Letter from the Seventh Century B.C. in Historical Perspective," *BASOR* 176 (1964) 34 and n. 23; and GKC, § 136d, for instances of *zeh* before words denoting numbers.

12. The sequence *b*ᵉ*ḵōrāṯî lāqāḥ . . . lāqaḥ bir*ᵉ*ḵāṯî* is an example of "semantic-sonant chiasmus," a literary device involving chiasm and assonance. See J. S. Kselman, "Semantic-Sonant Chiasmus in Biblical Poetry," *Bib* 58 (1977) 220.

13. B. Levine (*In the Presence of the Lord,* p. 17 n. 39) urges "estate, grant" as the proper translation of *bir*ᵉ*ḵāṯî*. While this rendering is possible here, in the next clause it is unlikely that Esau would say, "Have you reserved a grant/estate for me?"

14. *h*ᵃ*lō'* normally introduces questions that will be answered in the affirmative (see GKC, § 150e), but sometimes a negative answer follows this particle. See H. A. Brongers, "Some Remarks on the Biblical Particle *h*ᵃ*lō',*" *OTS* 21 (1981) 179.

15. *'āṣal l*ᵉ has the meaning "reserve, withdraw" in Num. 11:17 and Eccl. 2:10. See J. Milgrom, *Numbers,* JPS Torah Commentary (Philadelphia: Jewish Publication Society, 1990), p. 87.

16. On this expression see J. Joosten, "The Syntax of *habərākāh 'aḥat hī' ləkā 'ābī* GEN. 27:38aa)," JSS 36 (1991) 207-21, esp. 215-17.

17. This clause is not present in the MT but is in the LXX: *katanychthéntos dé Isaak,* which in Hebrew would be *wayyiddōm yiṣḥāq;* cf. Lev. 10:3; Ps. 30:13 (Eng. 12). Speiser (*Genesis,* p. 210) remarks: "Although LXX is not supported in this instance by other versions, it is improbable that this highly effective remark was made up by the translators. It is brief enough to have been skipped accidentally by a scribe."

"Away from[18] *the fatness of the earth be your home,*
and away from the dew of the heavens above.
40 *By your sword you shall live*
and your brother you shall serve.
But when you become restless,[19]
you shall throw off his yoke from your neck."

It is now Isaac's and Esau's turn to be in the limelight. In these eleven verses (vv. 30-40) "father," with third or first person pronominal suffix, appears twelve times (or thirteen times if one adds "my father" to the end of v. 36, as does LXX). This is the fourth of six scenes in the chapter, all of which feature only two individuals together (vv. 1-4, Isaac and Esau; vv. 5-17, Rebekah and Jacob; vv. 18-29, Isaac and Jacob; vv. 30-40, Isaac and Esau; vv. 41-45, Rebekah and Jacob; v. 46, Isaac and Rebekah). Isaac meets alone with his favorite son twice (vv. 1-4; vv. 30-40), and Rebekah meets alone with her favorite son twice (vv. 15-17; 41-45).[20]

18. In this line and the following line the preposition *min* may have a partitive force: "Some of the fatness of the earth," or it may have a privative force: "Away from the fatness of the earth." Dahood opts for the latter with his strong translation, "Alas, without the oil of earth will be your dwelling; yes, without the dew of the heavens above" ("Northwest Semitic Notes on Genesis," *Bib* 55 [1974] 79).

19. The meaning of Heb. *tārîḏ* is uncertain, and the ancient versions seem to reflect a different *Vorlage:* SP *tʾdr,* perhaps reflecting *tĕʾāḏēr,* "you shall be glorious"; LXX *kathélēs,* perhaps reflecting *tōrîḏ,* "you shall bring down"; see Skinner, *Genesis,* p. 373; *BHS*. The form of the verb reflects the root *rûḏ,* "to wander," which seems to occur a few other times in the OT, but each occurrence is problematic (BDB, p. 923b). In Jer. 2:31 the people renounce their relationship to God by saying *raḏnû,* which RSV translates "we are free" but AV "we are lords" (AV probably reflects *rāḏaḏ;* cf. LXX). In Hos. 12:1 (Eng. 11:12) the prophet says that Judah *ʿōḏ rāḏ ʿim-ʾēl,* "yet ruleth with God" (AV), "still known by God" (RSV, emending *rd* to some form of *ydʿ*), or "still wanders with the holy gods" (F. I. Andersen and D. N. Freedman, *Hosea,* AB [Garden City, NY: Doubleday, 1980), pp. 593, 602-3). Ps. 55:3 (Eng. 2) reads: *ʾārîḏ bᵉśîḥî,* "I mourn in my complaint" (AV), "I am overcome by my trouble" (RSV). Dahood (*Psalms,* 2:31) claims the MT is unexplainable and emends the text. The root may appear in Judg. 11:37, "that I may go and wander on the hills and bewail my virginity." This translation involves taking *yāraḏtî* as a by-form of *rûḏ* (see R. G. Boling, *Judges,* AB [Garden City, NY: Doubleday, 1975], p. 209). I see no need to emend the text in Gen. 27:40 or in any other place that *rûḏ* occurs. The modern translations are close to each other ("when you become restless" [NKJV]; "when you become restive" [NAB]; "when you grow restive" [Speiser, NEB, NJPS]); "when you win your freedom" (JB), "when you break loose" (RSV, NRSV), "when thou shalt have dominion" (KJV), and "when you shall tear yourself free" (Westermann) are stronger. I am inclined to agree with Holladay's connection of Heb. *rûḏ* with Arab. *rāda,* "walk about, prowl" (W. L. Holladay, *Jeremiah,* Hermeneia, 2 vols. [Philadelphia: Fortress, 1986-89], 1:55).

20. See Fokkelmann, *Narrative Art in Genesis,* p. 102; and Fishbane, *Text and Texture,* pp. 49-50.

30 Not to be glossed over is the emphasis in this verse that Jacob *left (yāṣāʾ)* his father just before Esau arrived on the scene. The two brothers almost met, but not quite. This is a reversal of 25:25, where Esau "came forth" *(yāṣāʾ)* before Jacob.

31 This verse picks up from v. 4. Esau has bagged his game and now returns from the hunt to share it with his father. His anticipation is that a blessing will be forthcoming. Esau has resolutely obeyed his father, just as Jacob has resolutely obeyed his mother.

Still before us is the key word in this chapter — "bless(ing)." The root *brk* occurs no less than 22 times in this chapter, 17 times as a verb and 5 times as a noun.[21] Every time the Piel stem of *bāraḵ* is used, except for the Qal passive participle in vv. 29, 33.[22]

32-34 Isaac's distress is matched by Esau's. *Isaac was exceedingly distraught (wayyeḥᵉraḏ yiṣḥāq ḥᵃrāḏâ gᵉḏōlâ ʿaḏ-mᵉʾōḏ)* and *Esau burst into long and bitter groans (wayyiṣʿaq ṣᵉʿāqâ gᵉḏōlâ ûmārâ ʿaḏ-mᵉʾōḏ).*[23] In both cases a verb (in the Qal stem) is followed by a cognate accusative, which is qualified with the adjective "great," which in turn is qualified with the adverbial phrase "very."

Upon discovering that he has been tricked, Isaac makes no attempt to rescind his earlier blessing on Jacob.[24] Abrogation is not an option for Isaac, for the essence of an oracle is that it is irrevocable.[25] Isaac says here, "What I have said, I have said." The text has no indication that Isaac's insistence on maintaining the original pronouncement is stimulated by a sudden insight into the divine will or by a recall of a forgotten divine word. But he has pronounced the blessing "in Yahweh's presence" (v. 7), which might have suggested to Isaac that Yahweh approved of Jacob as the recipient of the blessing. In addition, there was probably no socially acceptable legal procedure for rescinding a paternal blessing.[26]

21. Verb: vv. 4, 7, 10, 19, 23, 25, 27 (twice), 29 (twice), 30, 31, 33 (twice), 34, 38, 41. Noun: vv. 29, 35, 36, 38, 41.

22. The Qal of *bāraḵ* — apart from the Qal passive participle *bārûḵ* — is rare.

23. Esau's "long and bitter groans" emphasize the emotional dimension, i.e., the stress, hurt, desperation in which he now finds himself. When *ṣāʿaq* is followed by an adverbial accusative (in the form of a cognate accusative) nondirected cries are normally involved. See R. N. Boyce, *The Cry to God in the Old Testament,* SBLDS 103 (Atlanta: Scholars, 1988), p. 9 n. 7, 21.

24. See T. L. Thompson, *Historicity of the Patriarchal Narratives,* pp. 285-93.

25. Jephthah's vow is similar (Judg. 11:30-35). Even if he hastily worded the vow ("anything coming out of the doors of my house to meet me . . . I will offer it up as a burnt offering"), he must not retract a vow made to Yahweh. Cf. Num. 30:3 (Eng. 2): "when a man vows a vow to the Lord, or swears an oath to bind himself by a pledge, he shall do according to all that proceeds out of his mouth."

26. See A. .C. Thiselton, "The Supposed Power of Words in the Biblical Writings," *JTS* 25 (1972) 294: "A convention for withdrawing a performative utterance did not exist;

35 Isaac admits openly that Jacob took Esau's blessing *fraudulently (mirmâ)*. This word is often associated in the OT with deceptive speech (e.g., Gen. 34:13; Ps. 24:4). The use of the verb *rāmâ,* "to deceive" (from which the noun *mirmâ* is formed) in Gen. 29:25 is interesting. After Jacob discovers that the woman with whom he has spent the night is not Rachel but Leah, he protests to Laban: "Why then have you deceived me?" *(rimmîṯānî)*. Laban responds that it is not a local custom to marry off the younger before the firstborn (v. 26). In Gen. 27 Jacob, the younger son, obtains the blessing by impersonating the older/firstborn son and thus tricking Isaac. In Gen. 29 deception *(rāmâ)* again takes place, but this time Jacob is tricked into spending the night with the older/firstborn daughter rather than with Rachel.[27]

36 Here is a second play on the name *Jacob,* the first being 25:26. Esau is fully aware of the significance of Jacob's name, the "heel-grabber, the overreacher."[28] Apparently Esau is more concerned by the loss of the blessing than by the loss of the birthright. Nowhere did he protest the relinquishment of the latter. He also never said to Isaac: "Have you only one birthright?" He is stretching the point to say that Jacob *took away* his birthright. What about Esau's own culpability at that point, Jacob's opportunism notwithstanding?

37-38 Isaac informs Esau that he has already blessed Jacob. As if to emphasize this fact, in Isaac's speech the direct object comes three times

---

hence the original performative utterance remains effectively in force"; also C. W. Mitchell, *Meaning of BRK "To Bless" in the Old Testament,* p. 83.

27. See Fishbane, *Text and Texture,* p. 55. Interestingly Targ. Onqelos read v. 35 as: "Your brother came with wisdom [*bḥwkmh*] and received [*wqbyl*] your blessing." This is an attempt by the Targ. to soften Isaac's criticism of Jacob, esp. in an age where Jacob represented the Jewish people and Esau the Roman world. See M. Aberbach and B. Grossfeld, *Targum Onkelos to Genesis* (New York: Ktav, 1982), p. 165 nn. 11-12. See also the comment of R. Yohanan in Gen. Rabbah 67:4: "[He came] with the wisdom of his knowledge of the Torah" (J. Neusner, *Genesis Rabbah: The Judaic Commentary to the Book of Genesis,* 3 vols. [Atlanta: Scholars, 1985], 2:413).

28. It is interesting to notice that the Ugaritic texts also use the root *ʿqb* in this metaphorical way. In the Aqhat Epic El addresses Anat and says: *dṯ ydṯ mʿqbk:* "who hinders thee will be crushed" (Ginsberg, *ANET,* p. 142b). A more literal rendering is: "verily trampled be he-who-grasps-your-heel." See B. Margalit, "Lexicographical Notes on the Aqht Epic (Part I: KTU 1.17-18)," *UF* 15 (1983) 95-96. Margalit's translation of Gen. 27:36 is: "Not for naught is his name 'Yaʿqob'; this is the second time that he has foiled me ([*wa-*]*yaʿqᵉḇēnî,* lit. 'grasped-my-heel')." The LXX also, by its translation, connects 25:26 and 27:36 rather than seeing two different meanings in *ʿqb* in the two passages. The LXX renders 25:26 as "his hand holding Esau's heel" *(tēs ptérnēs),* and 27:36 as "he was justly named Jacob for he has now kicked me on the heel [*eptérniken,* from *pternizō*] for a second time." See T. Muraoka, "Towards a Septuagint Lexicon," in *VI Congress of the International Organization for Septuagint and Cognate Studies,* ed. C. E. Cox (Atlanta: Scholars, 1987), pp. 265-68, 273.

before the verb: "master I have appointed him"; "his kinsmen I have handed over"; "with grain and wine have I sustained him." The focus is more on who Jacob is, or what he has, than it is on what Isaac has done. Furthermore, the father's speech suggests that his blessing on Jacob has been total and exhaustive. There is nothing left for Esau to claim. In blessing Jacob, Isaac has deprived himself. In the face of Esau's persistence, Isaac's only response is to remain taciturn. As a result, Esau weeps a second time.

Isaac's original blessing differs slightly from the blessing he gives here. In the first account Isaac blessed Jacob with the words: "May God give you of the dew of the heavens and of the fatness of the earth." Here that sequence is reversed: *the fatness of the earth . . . the dew of the heavens.* Noting the inversion of this sequence, Gevirtz raises the possibility that by reversing the parallelism the author/Isaac may have intended to reverse the blessing as well (v. 28).[29] When Isaac first spoke to Jacob he said: "Be master over your kin" (*hĕwēh gᵉḇîr lᵉʼaḥeyḵā,* v. 29). Here Isaac says to Esau: "As master I have already appointed him over you" *(gᵉḇîr śamtîw lāḵ).* Thus the reiteration of the blessing reinforces Esau's personal subservience to Jacob.

39-40 If v. 39 is part of Isaac's response *(wayyaʿan)* to Esau's plea of v. 38 ("Bless me, even me also, father"), then it is not the kind of response that Esau was hoping for, or even the kind of words that would fall into the category of a *bᵉrāḵâ.* If anything, it is a *qᵉlālâ,* a curse. For Esau is not to enjoy the degree of agricultural fertility that is coming to his brother. He will receive neither his father's blessing, nor heaven's dew, nor earth's fatness.

In addition, Esau is consigned to living like a predator: *By your sword you shall live*[30] (i.e., an existence by war and plunder). But the possession of this sword will not give him domination over his brother — Jacob will never be among his victims.

Jacob's hegemony over Esau is not to be permanent. At some undisclosed point in the future, when Esau *becomes restless,* he will throw off the *yoke* of Jacob. Here we have the paradox of an Isaac who does not know which son is really Esau, but who knows about Esau's future. His eyesight may be failing, but his prophetic insight is as sharp as ever. The descendants of Esau (Edomites) make a move for independence as early as the reign of Solomon (1 K. 11:14-22), and sporadically thereafter. The total independence of Edom from Judah came as a result of a revolt against Jehoram king of Judah (2 K. 8:20-22; 2 Chr. 21:8-10).

29. Gevirtz, *Patterns in the Early Poetry of Israel,* pp. 35-40.

30. Westermann, *Genesis,* 2:443: "The Israelite farmer takes a negative view of a life-style which others regard as particularly noble; but it is not contested that other tribes can live from rapine and raids, as in the case of Ishmael."

5. REBEKAH URGES JACOB TO FLEE (27:41-45)

41 *Esau nursed a grudge*[1] *against his brother Jacob because of the blessing with which his father had blessed him. He mused with himself:*[2] *"When the days for mourning for my father draw near I will kill Jacob my brother."*

42 *When Rebekah was informed of*[3] *the intentions of Esau her older son, she summoned Jacob her younger son and said to him: "Esau is intending to execute his wrath*[4] *by killing you.*

43 *Now, then, my son, pay attention to me. Flee by yourself to Laban my brother in Haran,*

44 *and stay with him a while, until your brother's anger subsides.*[5]

45 *When*[6] *your brother's fury turns away from you, and he forgets what*

1. Heb. *wayyiśṭōm,* from *śṭm,* apparently a by-form of *śṭn,* the root from which "Satan" derives. This verb appears five more times in the OT: Gen. 49:23; 50:15; Job 16:9; 30:21; Ps. 55:4 (Eng. 3). Of these texts, the one closest in meaning to Gen. 27:41 is Gen. 50:15, in which Joseph's brothers wonder whether Joseph will feel resentment or nurse a grudge toward them for their earlier mistreatment of him. In the other four passages *śāṭam* means more than "nurse a grudge"; rather, it carries the idea of "attack, rage against, assault."

2. Lit., "said in his heart" *(wayyō'mer belibbô).* M. Niehoff ("Do Biblical Characters Talk to Themselves? Narrative Modes of Representing Inner Speech in Early Biblical Fiction," *JBL* 111 [1992] 580) remarks that this phrase "does not represent an intense debate within himself [viz., Esau]. This expression rather introduces a momentous awareness of an unforeseen opportunity and indicates . . . an uncontrolled flush of the evil inclination."

3. Here is an instance in which a pl. noun or phrase *(diḇrê 'ēśāw)* is governed, as an object, by the passive 3rd person sing. used impersonally *(wayyuggaḏ).* For other uses of this construction see Num. 28:17; 32:5; Deut. 20:8; 2 Sam. 21:11; Job 30:15; Ps. 87:42; Jer. 50:20; Ezek. 46:23. Cf. GKC, § 121a, b; T. Booij, "Some observations on Psalm lxxxvii," *VT* 37 (1987) 19; Milgrom, *Numbers,* p. 328.

4. See H. Van Dyke Parunak, "A Semantic Survey of NḤM," *Bib* 56 (1975) 522, 528, who notes that the basic meaning of *nāḥam* in the Hithpael is "release emotional tension, either by performing a declared action (i.e., "execute wrath" [Gen. 27:42 and Ezek. 5:13]), or by retracting a declared action (such as blessing [Num. 23:19] or punishment [Deut. 32:36]). In the latter case only Yahweh is the subject. In the former case the subject may be either a human (Gen. 27:42) or Yahweh (Ezek. 5:13).

5. Of the nineteen instances in the OT where "anger" is the subject of *šûḇ* (Qal), Gen. 27:44 and 45 are the only two where the anger is not God's anger. See W. L. Holladay, *The Root Šûbh in the Old Testament* (Leiden: Brill, 1958), pp. 77-78. In v. 44 Rebekah uses *ḥēmâ (ḥamaṯ 'āḥîḵā)* for "anger" and in v. 45 *'ap ('ap-'āḥîḵā)* for "anger." To distinguish the two I have rendered the first by "anger" and the second by "fury."

6. Before verbal nouns (Gen. 33:3; 43:25; etc.) *'aḏ* does not mean "until" but "at the time of, when, while, so long as." See G. R. Driver, "Forgotten Hebrew Idioms," *ZAW* 78 (1966) 5-6.

you have done to him, then I will send[7] *and fetch you from there. Must I lose both of you in one day?"*

41 Esau plots a crime parallel to that of Cain — fratricide. He is, however, unlike Cain, who acted in a fit of uncontrollable passion; Esau is more like Absalom, who planned his revenge against his half-brother Amnon for two years (2 Sam. 13:23). Esau is enraged, but not impulsive.

42-45 Rebekah learned of her husband's intentions by eavesdropping *(šāmaʿ bᵉ).* She learns of Esau's intentions by being told *(wayyuggaḏ)* by somebody, apparently someone close to Esau. It is interesting to speculate on how this informant became aware of Esau's revenge, since it was all plotted *bᵉlibbô,* "in his heart" (*He mused with himself* is lit., "He said in his heart").

Rebekah continues to emerge as a quick thinker, the mistress of all emergencies. She will send Jacob to live for a while[8] with her brother Laban in far-off Haran. Esau will go after game in the field, but he will not hunt down Jacob in Paddan-aram. She also assures Jacob that time heals all hurts. The day will come when Esau's seething will dissipate, and the scenario with Jacob and Esau will become only part of Esau's distant past. As subsequent chapters in Genesis reveal, Jacob is not at all sure, even twenty years later, of his mother's favorable forecast. Jacob knows too well that memories, especially painful memories, die only too slowly, if at all.

Nevertheless, Rebekah is actually unrealistic. She tells Jacob that he need stay away only *a while* (*yāmîm ʾaḥāḏîm,* "a few days"), and by then Esau will have cooled down and become more rational. But *yāmîm* ("days") turned into *šānîm* ("years"), though in one way Rebekah was correct, for Jacob's tenure with Laban and his daughters seemed only to be *yāmîm ʾaḥāḏîm* (29:20).

In persuading Jacob to leave promptly, Rebekah's final line to him is: *Must I lose both of you in one day?* Jacob will be murdered if he stays around, and Esau will be executed for slaying his brother (cf. Gen. 4:14; 2 Sam. 14:6-7).[9]

7. *šālaḥ* is used here to indicate that the agent "takes" by means of someone else (or others). For this use of *šālaḥ* (with *lāqaḥ*) see T. Booij, "The role of darkness in Psalm cv 28," *VT* 39 (1989) 210.

8. A "while" *(yāmîm ʾaḥāḏîm)* will turn out to be twenty years (29:18, 30; 31:38)!

9. On blood revenge see de Vaux, *Ancient Israel,* 1:10-12; B. K. Waltke, "Avenger," *ISBE,* 1:372; M. Greenberg, "Avenger of Blood," *IDB,* 1:321. Greenberg refers to the fictitious case of the Tekoite woman (2 Sam. 14:6-7) who describes her plight to David vis-à-vis her two sons, one of whom killed the other. Justice requires that the surviving son be handed over to the family, but she seeks an exceptional ruling from David. Gen. 27:45 and 2 Sam. 14:6-7 show that blood redemption could be carried out within a family as well. Thus in 27:45 Rebekah is understandably fearful.

THE NEW TESTAMENT APPROPRIATION

a. Gen. 27:28-29, 39-40 and Heb. 11:20

The writer of Hebrews cites only one instance of faith from Isaac's life (but two different episodes): Isaac's blessing on Jacob (Gen. 27:28-29) and on Esau (Gen. 27:39-40). These were utterances done "in faith." Nothing is mentioned in Hebrews about Jacob's method of obtaining the paternal blessing. What is mentioned is that both blessings were in connection with the future of each son, and thus Isaac's faith reverberates the essence of faith spoken of in Heb. 11:1 — "faith is the evidence of things not seen." If we take the terms literally, Gen. 27 introduces Isaac's words to Jacob as a "blessing" (v. 27), but introduces Isaac's words to Esau as an "answer" (v. 39). The letter to the Hebrews styles both oracles as an act of blessing *(eulógēsen).*

b. Gen. 27:34, 38 and Heb. 12:17

Esau, who has already been likened to one who had a sexual vice and a profane life for selling his birthright (Heb. 12:16), is now held up as one who was unable to repent. He wanted to obtain the blessing, but he was "rejected" by God. This language is stronger than that used in Gen. 27. The Greek word translated "rejected" *(apodokimázō)* was used by the Greek orators for officials who were disqualified.[1] Although he sought it with tears, he has no second chance for repentance (cf. Heb. 6:4ff. for a parallel). The antecedent of "it" in "sought it with tears" may be either "blessing" or "repentance." The context suggests the latter.[2] The repentance that Esau sought was not directed to God, or even to his father, but within himself. He could not move

1. See J. Moffatt, *The Epistle to the Hebrews,* ICC (Edinburgh: T. & T. Clark, 1924), p. 212.

2. Against F. F. Bruce, *Epistle to the Hebrews,* NICNT, rev. ed. (Grand Rapids: Eerdmans, 1990), p. 351. Agreeing with Bruce is B. F. Westcott, *Epistle to the Hebrews* (Grand Rapids: Eerdmans, repr. 1965), p. 409. For scholars arguing for "repentance" as the antecedent of "it" cf. E. Riggenbach, *Der Brief an die Hebräer* (Leipzig: A. Deichert, 1913), p. 407; C. Spicq, *L'Epitre aux Hebreux,* 2 vols. (Paris: Gabalda, 1952-53) 2:402; Moffat, *Hebrews,* p. 212 (*autḗn* refers to *metanóias,* not to *eulogías* [which would require *metanoías . . .euren* to be taken as a parenthesis, a construction that is wrecked on the antithesis between *heúren* and *ekzētḗsas*]); G. W. Buchanan, *To the Hebrews,* AB (Garden City, NY: Doubleday, 1972), p. 220; H. W. Attridge, *Epistle to the Hebrews,* Hermeneia (Philadelphia: Fortress, 1989), p. 370 ("The proximity of the latter term [viz., *metanoías*] . . . strongly support[s] the latter alternative [viz., the antecedent of 'it' is repentance]"). Only D. Hagner (*Hebrews,* New International Biblical Commentary [Peabody, MA: Hendrickson, 1983], p. 223) argues that the antecedent could be both "blessing" and "repentance." Futility in one means futility in the other.

himself to change. Esau illustrates, says the author of Heb. 12:27, that repentance after apostasy is an impossibility. Beware, says the writer to his audience, that any of you be like tragic Esau: the consequences of his actions could not be reversed by a subsequent repentance. Esau's faithlessness is irremediable.[3]

E. JACOB MEETS GOD AT BETHEL (27:46–28:22)

1. A DEPARTED JACOB AND A DEVIANT ESAU (27:46–28:9)

27:46 *Rebekah said to Isaac: "I am very frustrated with my life*[1] *because of the Hittite women. If Jacob were to marry a Hittite woman like these, native daughters,*[2] *why should I go on living?"*[3]

28:1 *Thereupon Isaac sent for Jacob, greeted him with a blessing, and charged him:*[4] *"You shall not marry a Canaanite woman!*

2 *Up,*[5] *go to Paddan*[6]*-aram, to the house of Bethuel, your mother's father, and select a wife for yourself from among the daughters of your uncle Laban.*

3 *May El Shaddai bless you, make you fruitful and numerous, so that you may become an assembly of peoples.*

4 *May he pass on to you the blessing of Abraham, to you and to your descendants with you, so that you take possession of the land in which you sojourn, which God gave to Abraham."*

5 *Then Isaac sent Jacob away, and he went to Paddan-aram, to Laban*

3. See P. R. Jones, "A Superior Life: Hebrews 12:3–13:25," *RevExp* 82 (1985) 395-96.

1. The basic meaning of *qûṣ* is "loathe, abhor" (Lev. 20:23), but sometimes the verb conveys also the sense of extreme frustration or dislike (Num. 21:5; Isa. 7:6). It is frequently followed by the preposition *b^e*, whether the object is a person (Lev. 20:23; 1 K. 11:25) or a thing (Gen. 27:46; Num. 21:5; Prov. 3:11).

2. Lit., "from the daughters of the land" *(mibb^{e}nôṯ hā'āreṣ).*

3. Lit., "why to me [is] life?" See J. Barr, "Why? in Biblical Hewbrew," *JTS* 36 (1985) 19, for *lāmmâ* meaning "to what purpose?"

4. The note of urgency in the verb *ṣāwâ* is indicated by the fact that it does not occur in the Qal stem but always in the intensive Piel (or Pual).

5. Where coordinate commands are in apposition, the first imperative functions almost as an exclamation. See Andersen, *Sentence in Biblical Hebrew,* pp. 56-57.

6. Both "Paddan" and "house" have the locative suffix *â*. For the locative form in the construct case cf. also vv. 5, 6, 7; 43:17, 24; 44:14; 47:14; Exod. 8:20; for a nonbiblical example, see Y. Aharoni, "The Use of Hieratic Numbers in Hebrew Ostraca and the Shekel Weights," *BASOR* 184 (1966) 14-15.

the son of Bethuel the Aramean, the brother of Rebekah, who is the mother of Jacob and Esau.

6 *Esau observed that Isaac had blessed Jacob when he sent*[7] *him away to Paddan-aram to obtain from there a wife for himself, and that he had charged him, when he blessed him, "You shall not marry a Canaanite woman,"*

7 *and that Jacob had obeyed his parents and had gone to Paddan-aram.*

8 *Esau, realizing how contemptible the Canaanite women were to Isaac his father,*

9 *went to Ishmael and obtained Mahalath, daughter of Abraham's son Ishmael and sister of Nebaioth, in addition to*[8] *the wives he already had.*

27:46 Evidence for multiple sources behind the patriarchal stories is as impressive here as anywhere. The critical consensus is that 27:1-45 is from J and 27:46–28:9 is from P. The most blatant reason for this splintering of the narrative is the apparent contradiction involved with the chronology.[9] Ch. 27 pictures Isaac as an elderly man with failing eyesight (v. 1), whose death may be imminent (v. 2), who will soon be mourned (v. 41). Now we know that Isaac was sixty when his sons were born (25:26), and that he was one hundred when Esau married his Hittite wives (26:34). But eighty years come between this marriage and Isaac's death (33:28)! Although blind and near death, does Isaac live for eighty more years? If one suggests that 27:1 describes Isaac's deteriorating physical condition many years after the event of 26:34, say twenty-five or fifty years later, then we are faced with the oddity of a father sending a seventy-five-year-old or a hundred-year-old son away to another country to get a bride from his mother's brother. Furthermore, would Rebekah fret over the possibility of one son doing what the other son had done twenty-five years previously? Rebekah's concern, as voiced in 27:46, makes sense only if it comes shortly after Esau's marriages (26:34).

7. J. Huesman ("The Infinitive Absolute and the Waw and Perfect Problem" *Bib* 37 [1956] 414) emends MT *w^{e}šillaḥ* to *w^{e}šālōaḥ* or *w^{e}šallēaḥ*. Cf. *BHS,* which suggests reading *wayyišlaḥ*, i.e., the imperfect with *waw* consecutive, the more expected verbal form. Huesman's revocalization of the text from a perfect to an infinitive absolute would illustrate the infinitive absolute indicating a finite action in past time (for which see Huesman, "Finite Uses of the Infinitive Absolute," *Bib* 37 [1956] 284-95). MT may stand as is, however, if one takes *bērak̲* . . . *w^{e}šallaḥ* as simple *waw* with the perfect on the latter because of two verbs in a closely related series.

8. For *ʿal* with the meaning "in addition to" see R. J. Williams, *Hebrew Syntax: An Outline,* 2nd ed. (Toronto: University of Toronto, 1976), p. 52, § 292.

9. See the concise statement of the problem by S. R. Driver, *Genesis,* p. 262.

To the matter of chronology we may add the two apparently different reasons given in chs. 27 and 28 for Jacob's departure. In ch. 27 Jacob prepares to leave home to escape revenge by Esau. In ch. 28 Jacob leaves home to get a wife from his own people. This second criterion for distinguishing J and P accounts is not critical, however. Rebekah's first plot is to get Esau's blessing away from Esau, and she accomplishes that in ch. 27:1-45. Her second plot is to get Jacob away from Esau (27:46–28:9). If first Rebekah took advantage of her husband's debilitating physical condition, then here she plays on her husband's sense of disgust with Esau's earlier marriages. In effect, she says: "You do not want a third Hittite daughter-in-law do you, Isaac?" Fishbane says correctly: "Rebekah's supplication of Isaac in 27:46 to preserve endogamy transforms the motivation in 28:1-9 for Jacob's departure from one in flat contradiction to 27:1-45 (fear of Esau's revenge) to one supplementary to it."[10]

28:1-4 Isaac is persuaded by his wife's logic. He summons Jacob to him, and discreetly says nothing about the way his son took advantage of him and deceived him. On the contrary, he blesses Jacob, forbids him from marrying a Canaanite girl, and sends him to Paddan-aram to obtain a wife. This procedure is familiar to Isaac, for he is certainly able to recall when his father sent a servant to Paddan-aram to seek a bride for him (Gen. 24). But the two situations do differ. V. 2 makes clear that Isaac desires Jacob to marry the daughter of Rebekah's brother. That means that Jacob will marry his first cousin and that his maternal uncle will be his father-in-law. But one needs to distinguish first cousins, which are parallel cousins (children of same sex siblings [probably the case with Isaac and Rebekah], either matrilaterally or patrilaterally), from cross-cousins (children of opposite sex siblings [the case with Jacob and Leah/Rachel]). The latter form of marriage, while strange in Western culture, is frequent in other societies. A cross-cousin is an ideal mate if one wants to marry a close relative who is nonetheless outside one's tribal unit. Oden remarks that such a marriage "is a most elegant solution to the typical problem of marriage that is at once neither too exogamous nor too endogamous."[11]

Isaac's order that Jacob take a wife from the daughters of his uncle Laban creates an avuncular marriage alliance. Again, many societies witness to the prominence of the relationship between nephew and maternal uncle. The portrayal in Gen. 29ff. of the up-and-down relationship between Laban and Jacob is an accurate presentation of the behavior in such a relationship, as noted by anthropologists.[12]

10. Fishbane, *Text and Texture,* p. 49; see also Fokkelman, *Narrative Art in Genesis,* pp. 105-6.

11. R. A. Oden, Jr., *The Bible Without Theology* (San Francisco: Harper & Row, 1987), pp. 120-23.

12. Ibid., pp. 123-27.

Rebekah's reminder to Isaac (27:46) that Esau had married *Hittite* women, and Isaac's ultimatum to Jacob not to marry *Canaanite* women (28:1), are not in conflict. Nor do these two verses demonstrate that in P terms like "Hittite" and "Canaanite" are void of any historical significance.[13] Given Esau's Hittite marriages, Isaac desires to scuttle the possibility of any Canaanite marriages for Jacob. It also presents further evidence for a Hittite enclave in Canaan, so that Hittite women could also be called *native daughters* (lit., "daughters of the land").

To Isaac's credit, the blessing he gives to his son is the blessing of *Abraham.* This is the only time Isaac mentions his father. The God of Abraham was with Isaac (26:24), and now the blessing of Abraham is to be with Jacob. Isaac recognizes his role as that of a link in a chain, a transmitter.

5 Jacob leaves for Paddan-aram. The irony is that Rebekah is anxious to save Jacob, but she never sees him again. Rebekah's death is nowhere recorded in Genesis, nor is any subsequent meeting between mother and favored son.

6-9 Only after he has observed Jacob's faithful implementation of his father's charge[14] does it dawn on Esau how repugnant his marriages with Hittite women (26:34) were to his parents. The grief these nuptial arrangements brought on the parents never reached the son. This point provides further evidence of continuity with the narrative of 27:1-45. Given his insensitivity here, Esau merits neither the birthright nor the blessing. His marital liaisons have disqualified him from both, and confirm the correctness of the divine choice of Jacob over Esau.

In an attempt to redeem himself and please his parents, Esau makes one last move. He marries *Mahalath,* the daughter of his paternal uncle Ishmael, the son of Abraham by Hagar (i.e., Esau's parallel cousin). In 36:3 Mahalath is called Basemath. According to 26:34 Esau was also married to another Basemath, the daughter of Elon the Hittite (who is called Adah in 36:2)! Is Basemath a nickname ("fragrant perfume") that was given to both Adah and Mahalath? Or should we understand "Mahalath, the daughter of Ishmael" (28:9) to be the same person as "Basemath, daughter of Ishmael" (36:3)?[15] One could account for the difference in the name of Ishmael's daughter who married Esau by attributing each to different traditions. But the fact that 26:34 and 28:9 (both P) list Esau's wives as Judith, Basemath, and

13. As argued by J. Van Seters, "The Terms 'Amorite' and 'Hittite,' " *VT* 22 (1972) 64-81, esp. p. 79.

14. On the distinction between quotations spoken by characters and those spoken by the narrator (end of v. 6: "you shall not marry a Canaanite woman"), see Savran, *Telling and Retelling,* pp. 13, 20, 24.

15. See N. J. Opperwall, *ISBE,* 1:436.

Mahalath, while 36:2-3 list his wives as Adah, Oholibamah, and Basemath, would at least mean that one must distinguish P from the Toledoth source, with each representing a different stage of the tradition.[16]

In this last-minute ploy by Esau to redeem himself, to some degree at least, before his father dies, he fails. The marriage goes unnoticed by Isaac. Esau may now have three wives (two Hittite, one Ishmaelite), but he also has three family members (father, mother, brother) who have succeeded in marginalizing him. Jacob has the birthright in hand, thus voiding Esau's palce as firstborn. Jacob also has his father's blessing, thanks to Rebekah's machinations and Isaac's unretractable blessing. What Esau has is three wives, and a limited blessing from his father that amounts almost to a curse (subservience to Jacob), which one day will be mitigated (27:40b). While Esau can only stay home and mourn his losses, Jacob, the blessed and the holder of the birthright, is off to Paddan-aram in search of a bride.

2. JACOB MEETS GOD AT BETHEL (28:10-22)

10 *Jacob left Beer-sheba and headed for Haran.*

11 *He struck upon*[1] *a certain place*[2] *and lodged there, as the sun had already set.*[3] *Taking one of the stones of that place, he put it at his head place,*[4] *and stretched out on that place.*

16. See M. D. Johnson, *Purpose of the Biblical Genealogies,* p. 16. R. R. Wilson (*Genealogy and History in the Biblical World,* pp. 174-76) opines that the names found in 26:34 and 28:9 were originally part of the Esau narratives before Esau was linked with Edom. By contrast, the wives mentioned in 36:2-3 represent names that were originally part of an old Edomite tribal tradition. Gen. 36:1-5 is then an attempt to harmonize these two traditions. Note that in both places the ethnic designation of Esau's wives is the same: (1) Judith, the Hittite; Basemath, the Hivite (LXX, SP); Mahalath, the daughter of Ishmael; (2) Adah, the Hittite; Oholibamah, the Hivite; Basemath, the daughter of Ishmael.

1. This is the thrust of *pāḡaʿ bᵉ* in this context; its meanings range from "meet, encounter" to "attack." *pāḡaʿ bᵉ* occurs only one more time in the Jacob cycle, but at an interesting point, 32:2 (Eng. 1), which is also a prelude to a theophany involving *mal'āḵîm,* "messengers." On this root, see my study in *TWOT,* 2:715; J. F. A. Sawyer, "Types of Prayer in the Old Testament: Some Semantic Observations on *Hitpallel, Hithannen,* etc.," *Semitics* 7 (1980) 131-43; R. L. Hubbard, "The Hebrew Root *PGᶜ* as a Legal Term," *JETS* 27 (1984) 129-33.

2. GKC, § 126r, gives instances where the definite article denotes a single thing that is yet unknown, and in English should be rendered with the indefinite article. Cf. also P. Joüon, *Grammaire de l'Hébreu biblique* (Rome: Pontifical Biblical Institute, 1947), § 137n.

3. Especially in ancient times, when artificial illumination was scarce, it would not be unheard-of for individuals to go to bed at sunset. See Gen. 15:12. Cf. J. C. de Moor, "Problematical Passages in the Legend of Kirtu (I)," *UF* 14 (1982) 165.

4. Lit., "what (is at) his heads." The same word occurs in v. 18. See BDB, p. 912, which

12 *He had a dream: a stairway*[5] *was set on the ground, with its top reaching to heaven; and messengers of God were going up and going down on it.*

13 *And lo! Yahweh, standing beside him,*[6] *said: "I, Yahweh, am the God of your grandfather Abraham and the God of Isaac; the ground on which you are stretched out, to you I will give it, and to your descendants.*

14 *Your descendants shall be as the dust on the ground, and you shall spread out west and east, north and south; and in you shall all the earth's families be blessed, and in your offspring.*

15 *Surely*[7] *I am with you; I will protect you wherever you go, and will return you to this land. I will not abandon you until I have done what I promised you."*

16 *When Jacob awoke from his sleep, he said: "Surely, Yahweh is in this place, and I, I was unaware of it."*

17 *Frightened, he said: "How*[8] *frightening is this place. This can only be*[9] *God's abode, and that*[10] *— the gateway of heaven!"*

18 *Early the next morning Jacob took the stone that he had placed at his head place, set it up as a pillar, and poured oil on its top.*

19 *He named that place Bethel, whereas Luz was the name of that city previously.*[11]

20 *Jacob then made a vow: "If God stays with me, and protects me on this trip which I am undertaking, and gives me bread to eat and clothing to wear,*

---

says of *mᵉraʾᵃšōṯ* "place at the head, head place." In addition to v. 18 see 1 Sam. 19:13, 16; 26:7; 1 K. 19:6. The stone more likely served as protection for his head rather than as a pillow. Cf. 1 Sam. 26:7, where Saul sleeps in the trench with his spear stuck in the ground "at his head."

5. *sullām* is a hapax legomenon in Biblical Hebrew; I discuss it in the commentary below.

6. *ʿālāyw* by itself could also be translated "on top of it," i.e., the *sullām.* But see the commentary below on v. 13 for further discussion.

7. Speiser (*Genesis,* p. 217) renders *wᵉhinnēh* here by "remember."

8. See Williams, *Hebrew Syntax,* p. 25, § 127, for *mâ* as the exclamatory "how!"

9. *ʾên zeh kî ʾim,* lit., "naught (is) this except. . . ." Note Andersen's translation of this verse (*Sentence In Biblical Hebrew,* p. 113): "this is nothing but the house of God and this is (nothing but) the gate of heaven"; i.e., a single negation *(ʾên)* does double duty by modifying a conjunctive sentence as a whole.

10. The double use of the demonstrative *zeh* carries a distributive sense (Speiser, *Genesis,* p. 218).

11. LXX mistakenly read *kaí Oulamlous ḗn ónoma tḗ pólei tó próteron,* "but the first name of this city was Oulamlouz." This mistake arose as a result of reading *ʾûlām* as the noun "hall" instead of as the adverb "at first, previously." See M. G. Glenn, "The Word *lûz* in Genesis 28:19, in the LXX, and in Midrash," *JQR* 59 (1968) 73-75.

21 *and I return*[12] *safely to my father's house, and if Yahweh shall be my God,*

22 *then this stone which I have erected as a pillar shall be God's abode. Of everything you give to me, a tenth I will tithe to you."*

Jacob has already a good bit of his life behind him. Even before he deceived his father by imitating Esau he was forty years old (26:34). Some have even suggested that the Jacob of ch. 28 who heads toward Haran is in his seventies! Whatever Jacob's age, Genesis has not yet recorded any instance where Yahweh has revealed himself or spoken to Jacob. The reader encounters a good bit of biographical data on Jacob before Jacob encounters Yahweh. Thus this cycle is unlike the Abraham cycle, which tells us little about Abraham before Yahweh became a part of his life. Jacob follows the direction he does ostensibly to find a wife. But first he finds God. The immediate purpose of his mission is for a while subordinated to another purpose of that mission. Jacob's expectations of encountering Yahweh somewhere between Beer-sheba and Haran were about as great as Saul's expectations of meeting the Christ somewhere between Jerusalem and Damascus.

10 Unlike vv. 2 and 5, which identified not only Jacob's destination but also the individual whom he was to seek out and the relationship of that individual to Jacob's family, v. 10 is as brief as possible. There is no need to retell the names of Jacob's relatives at Haran. What is crucial here is not whom he will meet at Haran, but whom he will meet before he reaches Haran. The trip ahead of Jacob is a formidable one; from Beer-sheba to Haran is a distance of several hundred miles. In ch. 29 Jacob arrives in Haran. Thus in a journey that must have lasted a considerable time, the biblical narrative focuses on only two days, and on only one place at which Jacob slept.

11 Jacob "happens upon" or *strikes upon a certain place*. The verb chosen carries a different nuance than a bland "he came." It emphasizes the randomness with which Jacob chose this place to pass the night. The place of lodging represents simply the end of daylight hours for Jacob. It was certainly not a predetermined resting place. Three times this verse uses the word *māqôm* ("place," "spot") for the site at which Jacob lodged. No name is yet attached to this area by Jacob or the narrator. It is not yet "Bethel" or "Luz," just *a certain place* (*māqôm,* from *qûm,* "rise, stand up"). Each of the three times, however, *māqôm* is qualified with the definite article *ha-*. Jacob happens upon "the" place *(bammāqôm,* not *b*^{e}*māqôm).* I suggested above (n. 2) that the use of the article with *māqôm* may be to stress the unfamiliarity (to Jacob) of the site. Since it is used with the article first by

12. LXX read the verb as a Hiphil: *kaí apostrépsē me,* "and if he returns me" (i.e., *w*^{e}*h*^{ĕ}*šîḇanî* instead of MT *w*^{e}*šaḇtî*).

the narrator, this construction may be the narrator's way of hinting that this was more than an outdoor resting spot — it is *the* place, i.e., a holy place.[13] The extremities of Jacob's itinerary are clearly spelled out in v. 10. In between the start of his journey at Beer-sheba and the end of his journey at Haran, God chooses to encounter him at an anonymous "place." Jacob now *stretched out (šāḵaḇ b^{e})* at a *place.*

12 In vv. 10-11, and including the first Hebrew word of v. 12, no less than eight narrative *waw*-consecutive verb forms occur, relating where Jacob went, what he did, and what experience he encountered. Now suddenly in vv. 12 and 13 the *waw* consecutives are replaced by no less than five participles: *muṣṣāḇ* (Hophal), "was set"; *maggîaʿ* (Hiphil), "reaching"; *ʿōlîm, yōr^{e}ḏîm* (Qal), "going up, going down"; *niṣṣāḇ* (Niphal), "standing." These participles are made even more pungent by the threefold use of the exclamatory *hinnēh* — two times in v. 12 and once in v. 13. The chain of participles bluntly shifts the narrative from the past to the present. The switch in verbal form also moves the story beyond what the narrator saw Jacob doing (vv. 10-12a) to what Jacob himself saw (vv. 12a-13a).[14]

Jacob's dream involves a *stairway* stretching from the earth up into the sky, and on which heavenly beings ascend and descend. Many have objected to the traditional rendering "ladder" (so AV, RSV), for a ladder is not a place for two-way traffic (unless one assumes that all the angels went up together and then descended together — but on a ladder?). This is, however, more of a modern, rationalistic concern than a linguistic observation. If we wish to be completely modern and rationalistic, then we need to isolate the issue in terms not of "ladder" versus "stairway," but why angels would need either one!

The Hebrew word here is *sullām,* which occurs only here in the Hebrew Bible. Many commentators have connected *sullām* with the verb *sālal,* "heap up," and accordingly suggest for the noun something like "ramp" or "stairlike pavement."[15] More likely is the suggestion that Heb. *sullām* is to be connected (through metathesis) with Akk. *simmiltu,* "stairway."[16]

13. Westermann, *Genesis,* 2:453-54.

14. Fokkelman (*Narrative Art in Genesis,* pp. 51-52) captures this change in syntax and the threefold use of *hinnēh* with "there, a ladder! oh, angels! and look, the Lord himself!" and says that *hinnēh* here "goes with a lifted arm, an open mouth." See also Andersen, *Sentence in Biblical Hebrew,* p. 95: each clause has the structure *w^{e}hinnēh* plus subject (noun) plus predicate (participial phrase).

15. See, e.g., von Rad, *Genesis,* p. 284; Speiser, *Genesis,* p. 218; Brueggemann, *Genesis,* p. 243. LXX *klímax* and Vulg. *scala* are ambiguous — both can mean "ladder" or "stairway."

16. See H. Hoffner, Jr., "Second Millennium Antecedents to the Hebrew *'ÔB,*" *JBL* 86 (1967) 397 n. 30; A. R. Millard, "The Celestial Ladder and the Gate of Heaven

It is uncertain whether Egyptian or Babylonian literature provides the background imagery for *sullām* here, though the latter carries wider acceptance.[17] (Actually, one need not appeal to either possibility.) This interpretation posits a parallel between Jacob's "ladder" and the stairways of the ziggurat in Mesopotamia.[18] But as H. Hoffner has pointed out, the parallel is not without its difficulties, for while priests used ziggurat stairways for climbing to the summit of the temple tower for worship, the deities did not use the stairways for descent to the ground level (as in the Jacob story).[19]

One cannot help but be struck by the parallel between the stairway in this dream, a stairway whose top reaches the sky, and the tower of Babel, whose top also extended into the heavens (11:4).[20] But the similarity stops here. Unlike the Babel tower, Jacob's stairway is not a product of human delusions of grandeur. It is a way by which God will make himself known to Jacob. Messengers, not pride, go up and down this structure.

There is much movement in this narrative. Jacob is traveling, and so are the messengers. He is heading east; they are ascending and descending. Jacob strikes upon *(pāg̱aʿ)* a certain site, and a stairway reaches *(nāg̱aʿ)* the sky. Two rhyming verbs describe somebody/something reaching somewhere.

13 This verse does not claim that Yahweh was standing on top of the stairway ("above it," AV, RSV, NIV),[21] but that Yahweh was standing at Jacob's side ("beside him," NEB, NAB; cf. "over him," JB). By itself the combination of the preposition and pronominal suffix in *ʿālāyw* could be interpreted either way. While *nāṣaḇ* (Niphal) followed by *ʿal* may indicate

---

(Genesis xxviii.12, 17)," *ExpTim* 78 (1966/67) 86-87; H. R. Cohen, *Biblical Hapax Legomena in the Light of Akkadian and Ugaritic,* SBLDS 37 (Missoula, MT: Scholars, 1978), pp. 34, 108. Cf. Westermann, *Genesis,* 2:454, who connects *sullām* to both *sālal* and Akk. *simmiltu.* The connection of Hebrew *sullām* with Akk. *simmiltu,* if correct, means that the Hebrew word is a metathesis of the Akkadian one (Hebrew reversing the consonants *l* and *m*). In his treatment of hapax legomena, F. Greenspahn (*Hapax Legomena in Biblical Hebrew,* SBLDS [Chico, CA: Scholars, 1984], p. 176) cautions that "reliance on metathesis . . . reduces the probability of a proposed cognate relationship." He confines *sullām* to his list of "Non-absolute Hapax Legomena" (p. 195) rather than to his list of "Absolute Hapax Legomena" (which he discusses at length).

17. For the former see J. G. Griffiths, "The Celestial Ladder and the Gate of Heaven (Genesis xxviii,12 and 17)," *ExpTim* 76 (1964/65) 229-30. For the latter see Millard, *ExpTim* 78 (1966/67) 86-87.

18. See Speiser, *Genesis,* pp. 218, 219.

19. Hoffner, *JBL* 86 (1967) 397-98.

20. Cf. *werōʾšô ḇaššāmayim* (11:4) with *werōʾšô maggîaʿ haššāmāyemâ* (28:12).

21. This interpretation has wide support among the ancient versions (LXX, Vulg., Pesh.); Targ. Onqelos's *ʿylwwhy* could be either "over him" or "over it," though the former is more likely.

"to stand on top of something" (see Exod. 17:9; 33:21; 34:2; and in the Hiphil, "put something on top of something — 2 Sam. 18:17), in many more instances it means "to stand beside" or "to stand over" (e.g., Exod. 7:15; Num. 23:6, 17; 1 Sam. 19:20; 22:9; etc.). *niṣṣāḇ ʿālāyw* means that the subject of the sentence rises above the person or the thing by which it stands. Hence in Gen. 18:1, 2 Abraham sat while three men stood by (over) him *(niṣṣāḇîm ʿālāyw)*. Similarly, Abraham's servant stands near *(niṣṣāḇ ʿal)* the well (24:13, 43).[22] Particulary instructive is 1 Sam. 19:20, where Samuel was "standing over" *(niṣṣāḇ ʿal)* the prophets. "To stand over" here means to stand in a position of authority, to preside over. Cf. also Ruth 2:5-6, where the expression *hanniṣṣāḇ ʿal haqqôṣᵉrîm* refers to the one in charge of the reapers, i.e., the foreman, the overseer.

Thus here in 28:13 Yahweh and Jacob are near each other, and because of this propinquity Yahweh can "say" *(ʾāmar)* to Jacob, rather than "call" *(qārāʾ)* to him as we have it in 22:11, 15: "and Yahweh's messenger called [*wayyiqrāʾ*] to him from heaven." Furthermore, that Jacob says a few verses later (v. 16), "Surely, Yahweh is in this place," presupposes Yahweh's immediate presence in the place, rather than in heaven at the top of the stairway.

What does Yahweh say when he does speak? Perhaps surprisingly to the reader, he does not say one word to rebuke Jacob for his behavior toward his father and brother. Far from fulminating against Jacob, Yahweh bestows on Jacob a catena of unconditional promises. In this respect, Jacob joins Isaac and Abraham in that all three are relatively free from censure by God for patently scandalous behavior. This absence of rebuke contrasts vividly with the primeval stories where Adam and Eve, Cain, Noah's contemporaries, and the tower builders enjoy no such exemption. On the contrary, the hand of divine judgment falls on them heavily. In the patriarchal stories it is non-Hebrews (the pharaohs and the Abimelechs who unsuspectingly took patriarchal wives as their own) who pay a heavy price for unethical acts.[23]

It may well be, however, that we do have in the opening part of God's speech at least an indirect censure. Yahweh reveals himself to Jacob as the God of his grandfather and the God of his father. He is the God of the first generation. He is the God of the second generation. Will he be the God of the third generation? The phrase *the God of Isaac* would be particularly poignant to Jacob's ears. For Jacob now lies before the one who says in essence: I am the God of the one whom you deceived and of whom you took advantage.

22. See C. Houtman, "What did Jacob see in his dream at Bethel? Some remarks on Genesis xxviii 10-22," *VT* 27 (1977) 348.

23. Apart from Onan's death (Gen. 38:9), the first instance of divine judgment against the patriarchs or the patriarchs' descendants occurs in the story of the golden calf (Exod. 32), Israel's first post-Sinai covenant transgression.

Jacob could supplant Esau. He could deceive Isaac. But what will he do with Yahweh? Can Jacob *ʿāqab̲* (supplant, cheat) Yahweh?

14 Yahweh promises Jacob land (v. 13c), numerous[24] and scattered descendants, plus spiritual blessing through both Jacob and his offspring.[25] This last promise is particularly intriguing. God has chosen Jacob and Jacob's family as the means whereby God will mediate his blessing to the world. In spite of Jacob's behavior he is a link in the chain. Thus far in the Jacob story the emphasis has been on Jacob's "getting" the blessing. Here the emphasis shifts to "being" the blessing. *berāk̲â* is not something to be sought at all costs. It is, rather, something to be bestowed.

This is the fifth text in Genesis (cf. 12:3; 18:18; 22:18; 26:4) to refer to a patriarch (and/or his offspring) as the means of worldwide blessing. In 18:18; 22:18; and 26:4 "the nations of the earth" *(gôyê hā'āreṣ)* are the beneficiaries. In 12:3 and 28:14 the "families of the earth" *(mišpeḥōt̲ hā'ad̲āmâ)* are the beneficiaries. The reason for *hā'ad̲āmâ* in 28:14 (and 12:3) over *hā'āreṣ* is because *hā'āreṣ* has already been used in v. 13 to specify the land of Canaan, that narrow strip of land to be occupied by Jacob's progeny (in 12:1 *hā'āreṣ* refers to Abraham's birthplace). To remove any doubt that the blessing envisaged by v. 14c is a universal blessing, and not a blessing on Jacobites in Canaan, the narrator chooses *hā'ad̲āmâ* over *hā'āreṣ*.[26] But if one attaches universality to *'ad̲āmâ* in v. 14, how does one explain that in the very next verse *'ad̲āmâ* clearly has a local referencce, where it is modified by the demonstrative *zō't̲* — "I will return you to this land"? Is the force of the demonstrative in v. 15 sufficient to say that *'ad̲āmâ* in v. 14 has a universal meaning, while in v. 15 it has a localized meaning? Perhaps the use of *'ad̲āmâ* may, on occasion, represent "a unity extending across the border of nations."[27]

In some ways this particular promise is even more dramatic than in Abraham's case. When Abraham first receives the promise as the catalyst in blessing for the nations (12:3), he is married but childless. When Jacob receives the same promise he is not only childless but also unmarried. Here is a promise about numerous descendants by whom the nations will be blessed; yet, Jacob has not produced one descendant or even one blessing.

15 The catalogue of unconditional promises continues. Vv. 13-14

24. Only eight times in the OT does "dust" imply a great number: Gen. 13:16; 28:14; Num. 23:10; 1 K. 20:10; 2 Chr. 1:9; Job 27:16; Ps. 78:27; Zech. 9:3.

25. The inclusion of the phrase "your offspring/descendants" in vv. 13, 14 (twice) would be particularly meaningful to an unmarried person in flight from a wounded brother and in flight to Haran to obtain a wife, thence to start his family. Yahweh announces indirectly ahead of time the success of Jacob's journey to Haran to procure a bride.

26. See Fokkelman, *Narrative Art in Genesis,* p. 60 n. 35.

27. J. G. Plöger, *"'adhāmāh," TDOT,* 1:92.

cited words of Yahweh that involved both Jacob and his descendants — what Yahweh would do for and through him and them. But here the only object of the verb is Jacob himself. Six times Yahweh is the subject: "I am . . . I will protect . . . I will return . . . I will not abandon . . . I have done . . . I promised"; and six times Jacob is the object.

This emphasis on Yahweh, the giver of promises, and Jacob the receiver of promises, makes all the more clear that Jacob is the recipient of God's unconditional guarantee of involvement in, protection over, and guiding of his life. Should anything happen to Jacob, should Yahweh leave him or withdraw his protection, all the earlier promises involving Jacob's descendants would be aborted. Thus it is the divine "I ams/wills/haves" of v. 15 that serve as guarantee for the multiplication of Jacob's offspring and their possession of the land as well as the blessing of the earth's families (vv. 13-14).

Just as God speaks to Jacob about descendants before Jacob has any, so he speaks to Jacob about "returning you to this land"[28] even before Jacob has left the land. Thus Jacob will not need to find his own way back. His parents prompted his departure from Canaan; Yahweh will determine and direct his return to Canaan.

The last part of the verse does not mean that once God has wrung from Jacob's life what he wants, he will *abandon (ʿāzab̲)* him.[29] Jacob is of more significance than momentary usefulness to God. The point at which God does "abandon" Jacob is recorded in 49:33, when he breathes his last. At this point (ch. 28), Jacob is the one who is leaving or abandoning his home. To this one who leaves his home God says that he will not *ʿāzab̲* him. Jacob may have to turn his back on his home, but God will not turn his back on Jacob.

16 Upon awakening, Jacob does not take long to realize the significance of his dream.[30] Dreams of this nature do not just happen. Jacob thought he had this place, this *māqôm,* all to himself. How wrong he was! He is as shocked to discover the reality of the divine presence with him as his father was when he discovered that Jacob had been in front of him. Isaac might have said: "Surely Jacob was in this spot, and I, I did not know it." Jacob, once the source of shock and surprise, is now the object of shock and surprise.

28. W. L. Holladay (*The Root Šûbh in the Old Testament* [Leiden: Brill, 1958], pp. 87-88) lists 25 references where the Hiphil of *šûb̲* means motion back to a point of departure with God a subject and human beings as object. The only other example of this use of *šûb̲* in Genesis is 48:21. About half of these 25 references are to God bringing his people back from exile.

29. A. P. Ross, "Jacob's Vision: The Founding of Bethel," *BSac* 142 (1985) 231.

30. S. Terrien (*The Elusive Presence* [San Francisco: Harper & Row, 1978], pp. 84-85) remarks that there is on Jacob's part "the awareness of divine proximity without any mediating intrusion."

Jacob seems particularly shamed (he reproaches himself) that he was oblivious to Yahweh's presence. This is brought out by the use of the independent pronoun *'ānōḵî.* The *I* is already present in the first person verb *yāḏā'tî* (lit., "I know"). Jacob's *'ānōḵî* in v. 16 parallels Yahweh's *'ānōḵî* in v. 15. Is Jacob's understanding of God's mobility being stretched? Sure, Yahweh is to be found at holy sites such as Beer-sheba, but is he also to be found at anonymous *meqōmôṯ* (places)? Jacob's comprehension of God and his presence is the opposite of Samson's: Jacob was unaware that Yahweh was with him in that place; Samson was unaware that Yahweh was not with him (Judg. 16:20). Ignorance of or presumption on the presence of God is inexcusable.

17 The first phrase, *Frightened, he said,* does not make clear whether the source of Jacob's fear is the unexpected presence of God or his ignorance of that fact. But this ambiguity is cleared up by Jacob's words, which seem, according to J. S. Kselman, to contain a tricolon of poetry:

How frightening is this place!
This can only be God's abode,
and that — the gateway to heaven.[31]

Jacob's life is laced with fear. First, when God draws near he is frightened (28:17). Second, Jacob gives as his reason for stealing away from Laban in the night that he was afraid of Laban (31:31). Third, he is afraid of his brother, apprehensive of what Esau may do in the way of retaliation (32:7, 11). Afraid of God, afraid of one's employer/father-in-law, and afraid of one's brother!

Now it is true that Jacob says *How frightening is this place,* not "how frightened am I." His fear is beyond him and outside him. It is the *place (māqôm)* that provokes the fear.[32] But Jacob need not say "how frightened am I," for the narrator has already said he was *frightened (wayyîrā').* This is not, to be sure,

31. See J. S. Kselman, "The Recovery of Poetic Fragments from the Pentateuchal Priestly Source," *JBL* 97 (1978) 161-62. The juxtaposition of *bêṯ* and *ša'ar* is formulaic in Hebrew and Ugaritic, and lends weight to the possibility of a poetic tricolon in v. 17. Cf. M. Dahood and T. Penar, "Ugaritic-Hebrew Parallel Pairs," in *RSP,* 1:158.

32. S. J. DeVries (*The Achievements of Biblical Religion* [Lanham, MD: University Press of America, 1983], p. 69) remarks on v. 17: "In Israel's early epiphanic tradition, God displays his numinous power and presence not in particular shrines and rituals, but freely and sovereignly, always in terms of personal endearment and commitment." Thus the narrator has so far deliberately not used the name Bethel in his story. Had he begun his narrative with something like "Jacob came to Bethel, but he did not recognize it as such," then DeVries's point would not apply to Gen. 28. What gives Bethel its significance is not hallowed tradition, but Yahweh's revelation to Jacob on this particular occasion. See Fokkelmann, *Narrative Art in Genesis,* pp. 63-64.

the first instance of fright in Genesis. Adam experiences it (3:10), as did Abraham (15:1), Sarah (18:15), Lot (19:30), Abimelech's servants (20:8), Hagar (21:17), and Isaac (26:7). What is unusual is that when Yahweh encountered Abraham or Isaac the result was never shock or terror (with the possible exception of 15:12b).[33] They took theophanies in stride. Perhaps the best parallel to the emotions conveyed by this verse is that found in 3:10. Adam, after his sin of disobedience, hears God walking in the garden and is afraid. Jacob, after his scenario involving his brother and father, sees God standing by him and is afraid. Yet, in neither instance did God issue one word of rebuke.

It has been standard to interpret this Bethel narrative as a fusion of J and E. Thus J is found in vv. 10, 11a, 13-16, 19, 21b; E is found in vv. 11b-12, 17-18, 20-21a, 22. One of the main reasons for so dividing the text is the presence of "Yahweh" in those verses attributed to J (vv. 13, 16, 21b), while "El/Elohim" appears in those verses attributed to E (vv. 12, 17, 20, 22). Furthermore, vv. 16 and 17 are cited as an instance of repetition arising from the duplication of the story. That is, there are two explanations of Jacob's response after the theophany: J's in v. 16, and E's in v. 17.[34] But this may be a case of the presence of seeming repetitions when in fact there are none. Instead of reading vv. 16 and 17 as mutually exclusive, one may read them as a "progression in Jacob's reaction from surprise and awe to fear, and together prepare the ground for the cultic action and naming of the place as Bethel, 'house of God,' which follow."[35]

18 Early in the morning, Jacob takes the stone which has been at his head, and raises it as a *pillar (maṣṣēḇâ)*. A *maṣṣēḇâ* designates something which is upright, normally an upright stone.[36] In the days of the patriarchs and Moses such a practice was licit (Gen. 28:18, 22; 31:13, 45; 35:14, 20; Exod. 24:4). No pejorative overtones were attached to the erection of pillars.

33. Sarna (*Understanding Genesis,* p. 193) draws attention to "the emphatic expressions of wonderment that the dream-vision occasions, the only such example in all of the patriarchal narratives."

34. Thus S. J. DeVries (*Yesterday, Today and Tomorrow,* p. 349 n. 12) states that v. 16 (J) represents "the personalistic, historically oriented conception," while v. 17 (E) represents "the cultic."

35. R. N. Whybray, *The Making of the Pentateuch,* JSOTSup 53 (Sheffield: Sheffield Academic, 1987), p. 84. See also R. Rendtorff, "Jakob in Bethel. Beobachtungen zum Aufbau und zur Quellenfrage in Gen 28,10-22," *ZAW* 94 (1982) 511-23, who raises serious questions about splitting Gen. 28:10-22 into J and E versions. Rendtorff's own position is that 28:10-22 represents a single story that underwent editorial expansion. In the process, however, Rendtorff fragments the text even more. He distinguishes no less than five stages covering the original story and the subsequent expansion: v. 10; vv. 11-13a, 16-19a; 13ab-15; 20-22.

36. On *maṣṣēḇâ* see de Vaux, *Ancient Israel,* 2:285-86; idem, *Early History of Israel,* pp. 285-86; E. Stockton, "Sacred Pillars in the Bible," *AusBR* 20 (1972) 16-32.

Such pillars might (1) recall a meeting with God, or serve as a visible symbol of the divine presence (Gen. 28:18, 22; 31:13; 35:14); (2) establish a boundary and witness to a parity treaty (31:45); (3) stand as a monument at the tomb of a loved one (35:20; cf. 2 Sam. 18:18).

Later the *maṣṣēḇâ* was considered illicit. They were part of the Canaanite cultic apparatus which needed to be dismantled (Exod. 23:24; 34:13; Deut. 7:5; 12:3; 16:22). The pillars were also associated with lapses by God's people into pagan and syncretistic cults (1 K. 14:23; 2 K. 17:10). Significantly, *maṣṣēḇâ* is at times linked with *pesel,* "a sculptured idol" (Lev. 26:1; Deut. 7:5; 12:3; Mic. 5:13). Hosea is not as disturbed by *maṣṣēḇâ* (Hos. 3:4-5) as is Micah (Mic. 5:13).

Perhaps the reason for the allowable becoming the disallowable is that the stone itself, formerly only a symbol, was theologically transformed into an idol. That Jacob erected a pillar on several occasions without divine rebuke attests to the antiquity of the patriarchal narratives. It is unlikely that later biblical writers would credit to their forefathers a once-legitimate practice that in their own day had become dishonorable and pagan.

It is interesting that Jacob raises a *pillar (maṣṣēḇâ)* and not an "altar" *(mizbēaḥ),* as did his grandfather. *maṣṣēḇâ* is a noun built off the root *nṣb.* This root has already appeared twice in this chapter: a stairway "was set" *(muṣṣāḇ)* on the ground (v. 12); Yahweh "stood" *(niṣṣāḇ)* beside Jacob (v. 13). Perhaps we are to understand through these linguistic repetitions that the stone raised by Jacob is a symbol of the stairway set on the ground. This possibility is heightened by the parallel mention of the pillar's *top* (*rō'š,* lit., "head"), which Jacob anoints in an act of consecration,[37] and the stairway's *top* (*rō'š,* v. 12), which reaches the sky. Both the pillar and the stairway have a "head."[38]

19 First Jacob poured oil *(šemen);* now he gives a name *(šēm)* to the site: *Bethel.* For the first time we are informed that this place already has a name: *Luz.* Heb. *lûz* means "nut, almond, hazelnut" or a "nut-tree" itself. The place name may originally have been "Lauz, Loz," later vocalized Luz, and would mean "place of refuge," which is exactly the function of Bethel for Jacob at this point.

It is the narrator, not Jacob, who draws attention to the prior name of Bethel. This observation should explain that there is no real problem in Abraham's

37. The verb here for pouring oil is *yāṣaq* (also in 35:14, where again Jacob sets up a pillar and pours oil on it), one that is used elsewhere for anointing something/someone with oil (Exod. 29:7; Lev. 8:12; Num. 5:15; 1 Sam. 10:1). But in 31:13, which refers back to 28:18, the verb is *māšaḥ,* "anoint," the verb for the sacred ceremony of anointing and consecration.

38. See Fokkelman, *Narrative Art in Genesis,* pp. 66-67.

associations with Bethel *qua* Bethel, i.e., "Bethel" is anachronistic there (12:8; 13:3). The narrator in both places (chs. 12, 28) uses the adopted name for this site.

The insignificance of the name *Luz* is highlighted by the use of chiasm in this verse, which reads literally: "the *name* of that place *Bethel . . . Luz,* the *name* of the city" *(šēm-hammāqôm hahû' bêṯ-'ēl . . . lûz šēm-hā'îr).* In the first clause "name" precedes the proper name; in the second clause "name" follows the proper noun. Normally the sequence is *šēm* followed by a name (cf. *šēm . . . lûz* in Judg. 1:23). There are only three instances in the Pentateuch (Gen. 17:15; here; and Exod. 15:3) where the sequence is reversed, with *šēm* as predicate following the subject.[39] We now discover that Jacob's *māqôm* is somebody's (the Canaanites'?) Luz.

The story is filled with incidents of transformation. A stone becomes a pillar. A *māqôm* becomes Bethel. A man running away from home runs into God. He who is later himself renamed (Jacob becomes Israel) plays a role in the Luz to Bethel shift. And the -el of Bethel (reflecting the Canaanite El?) becomes the personal God of Jacob.

It is interesting that Jacob names this site *Bethel.* For what happens to *maṣṣēbâ* ("pillar") in later biblical history (licit to illicit) also happens to Bethel. An originally thoroughly legitimate shrine becomes a place deserving of destruction. It is here that the schismatic Jeroboam I started his rival cult to challenge that in Jerusalem (1 K. 12:26-33). The altar built there by Jeroboam is condemned in no uncertain language (1 K. 13:1-5). Its idolatrous practices prompted the rebukes of both Amos (3:14; 4:4; 5:5-6; 7:13) and Hosea (4:15; 5:8; 10:5). In fact, Hosea does not call it Bethel but "Beth-aven,"[40] meaning "house of nothingness/wickedness." The altar at Bethel was destroyed as part of Josiah's reform measures (2 K. 23:15).

20-21 It is now Jacob's turn to move from name calling to vow taking. God has spoken in the dream to Jacob, and that divine speech is recorded in vv. 13-15. In his vow Jacob ignores the very distant aspects of the divine speech (i.e., vv. 13-14), but picks up on the more immediate aspects of the divine promise (i.e., v. 15). To that end Jacob focuses on the promise of divine companionship (cf. v. 20 and v. 15a), and the promise of certain return to the land (cf. v. 21 and v. 15b).[41] His vow underscores how utterly dependent Jacob is upon his God. He who so easily and callously manipulated his brother and father is now pictured as one who is completely beyond his own resources

39. See Andersen, *Hebrew Verbless Clause in the Pentateuch,* p. 41.

40. For an attempt to connect Beth-aven/Beth-awen with Beth'aben ("House of the Stone Pillar"), possibly the location of the Bethel sanctuary in Gen. 28, see N. Na'aman, "Beth-Aven, Bethel and Early Israelite Sanctuaries," *ZDPV* 103 (1987) 13-21.

41. For *šālôm* as the *conclusio* of successful negotiations see D. J. Wiseman, " 'Is it Peace?' Covenant and Diplomacy," *VT* 32 (1982) 325.

and at the mercy of another. What Esau once was to Jacob, Jacob now is to God. In contrast to what he did with Esau, Jacob cannot manipulate God.

Most translations of the OT render the last half of v. 21 as "then Yahweh shall be my God." This translation assumes that in Jacob's vow vv. 20-21a form the protasis and vv. 21b-22 form the apodosis. If God goes with him, returns him to the land, and gives him sustenance, *then* Yahweh shall be his God. For grammatical and theological reasons, however, we are inclined to believe that v. 21b should be read as the last clause in the protasis, and that the apodosis (main clause) be confined to v. 22.

First, the grammatical reasons. The verbs *protects, gives* (v. 20), and *returns* (v. 21a) are all *waw* plus perfect, as is *shall be* (w^e*hāyâ)* in v. 21b. But v. 22a uses the imperfect: *yihyeh, shall be.* This change in verb form suggests a shift from protasis (vv. 20-21) to apodosis (v. 22). Furthermore, in vv. 20 and 21 the verbs come first in their clauses, but in v. 22 the verb follows a lengthy subject in the form of a *casus pendens.* Finally, the subject of these five verbs in vv. 20-21 is God four times and Jacob once (God 5 times if one follows LXX), whereas the subject of the verb in v. 22 is "this stone."[42]

Second, the theological reasons. It is difficult to envision the possibility of Jacob "choosing" Yahweh as his God, for the context of the Jacob story thus far is Yahweh's choosing of Jacob. In this story, God does not sit idly by, waiting to discover if he has Jacob's trust. Read as "and if Yahweh shall be my God," the statement becomes a further part of Jacob's imploring of God. By his actions Jacob recognizes that God has a right to look elsewhere. Maybe Jacob has disqualified himself — but is there a second chance? Jacob is throwing himself on God's mercy, not calculating whether to accept God.[43]

A study of other vows throughout the OT shows that they are, unlike promissory oaths, conditional.[44] For example, after the Canaanite king of Arad has attacked Israel, Israel made this vow to Yahweh: "If you will deliver these people into our hands, we will totally destroy their cities" (Num. 21:2). Jephthah's vow to Yahweh goes as follows: "If you give the Ammonites into

42. See Fokkelman, *Narrative Art in Genesis,* p. 75. Note the gender incongruity between "this stone" (*hā'eḇen hazzō'ṯ,* fem.) and "shall be" (*yihyeh,* masc.). The narrator's preference for a masc. verb was dictated by his equation of "stone" (fem.) with what this stone was to become: God's "abode" (*bêṯ,* masc.).

43. For a discussion of biblical vows in general and Gen. 28:20-22 in particular cf. L. R. Fisher, "Two Projects at Claremont," *UF* 3 (1971) 27-31; S. Parker, "The Vow in Ugaritic and Israelite Narrative Literature," *UF* 11 (1979) 693-700, esp. pp. 698-99; T. W. Cartledge, *Vows in the Hebrew Bible and the Ancient Near East,* JSOTSup 147 (Sheffield: Sheffield Academic Press, 1992), pp. 166-75.

44. J. Milgrom, "Excursus 66," in *Numbers,* JPS Torah Commentary (Philadelphia: Jewish Publication Society, 1990), pp. 488-90; W. Richter, "Das Gelübde als theologische Rahmung der Jakobsüberlieferung," *BZ* 11 (1967) 21-52.

my hands, whatever comes out of the door of my house to meet me when I return in triumph from the Ammonites will be Yahweh's, and I will sacrifice it as a burnt offering" (Judg. 11:30-31). Hannah's vow states, "If you will only look upon your servants misery and remember me, and not forget your servant but give her a son, then I will give him to Yahweh for all the days of his life, and no razor shall ever be used on his head" (1 Sam. 1:11). Absalom vowed, "If Yahweh takes me back to Jerusalem, I will worship Yahweh in Hebron" (2 Sam. 15:8). All these vows, including that of Jacob, were taken in a time of crisis. This explains the reason for the presence of exhortations to the people of Israel not to forget their vows, to carry through on their vows (Num. 30:2; Deut. 23:21; Eccl. 5:5-6 [Eng. 4-5]). Taken under some form of duress, a vow could be forgotten once the duress had subsided or disappeared.

22 Thus far in the vow, Jacob has spoken about God as "he." Here he addresses God directly: "Of everything *you* give to me, a tenth I will tithe to you."[45] As with Abraham and Melchizedek (Gen. 14:20), *a tenth* is a token of Jacob's relationship with God. Here is evidence that Jacob is serious about his relationship with God — he commits himself to tithing. He also expresses awareness of the source of his provisions — "of everything you give to me." Earlier (v. 13) Yahweh promised to give the ground on which he was sleeping to him and his descendants. Later (v. 20) Jacob is hopeful that God will give him bread to eat and clothing to wear. V. 22 contains the third use of *nāṯan* in this episode. It is interesting that the two individuals in Genesis in whose life tithing is mentioned, Abraham and Jacob, are in those instances connected with Jerusalem (ch. 14) and Bethel (ch. 28), the southern and northern royal sanctuaries. To those individuals living later in the southern kingdom, their model for tithing would be Abraham. To those individuals living later in the northern kingdom, their model for tithing would be Jacob.[46]

THE NEW TESTAMENT APPROPRIATION

Gen. 28:12 and John 1:51

John has been describing the calling of various individuals to discipleship with Jesus: Andrew and Peter (1:35-42), Philip (1:43), Nathaniel (1:45-50).

45. Fokkelman, *Narrative Art in Genesis,* p. 81: "Jacob frees himself from the formally solemn tone [v. 12, using the 3rd person sing.], also discernable in the vow, which now seems too cool and impersonal to him, and he addresses himself straight to God — as a suppliant might who has an urgent prayer to make, or a panegyrist who sings of God's acts of deliverance." For other instances of the shift from talking *about* God to talking *to* God, see Exod. 15:1-5, 6ff.; Ps. 23:1-3, 4ff.; Jon. 2:2a, 2bff.

46. Milgrom, "Excursus 46," in *Numbers,* pp. 432-33.

On the heels of these events Jesus states: "Truly, truly, I say to you, you will see heaven opened, and the angels of God ascending and descending upon the Son of man" (1:51).

This last verse calls for some comment. First, the "you" in "I say to you" and in "you will see" is a plural "you," indicating that Jesus is addressing not only Nathaniel, but at least Andrew, Peter, and Philip as well and perhaps others. Second, the reference to "angels ascending and descending upon the Son of man" guarantees that this reference alludes to Jacob's dream of the stairway with angels ascending and descending at Bethel.

Although scholars have suggested many different interpretations of this verse,[1] all agree on its general meaning. Jesus is now the nexus between God and humankind. This Johannine language is the Fourth Gospel's counterpart to the priestly imagery attached to Christ in the Epistle to the Hebrews (4:14–5:10; 7:1–10:18). A stairway and a priest (Latin *pontifex,* "bridge-builder") join together two entities separated from each other.[2]

Perhaps there is also a hint about the real thrust of this passage in the fact that Jesus is speaking to Israelite (not Judean) Jews at this point. Speaking to them he recalls Jacob's vision at Bethel, which is in Samaria (part of Israel, not Judah). It is well known that the Samaritans identified Bethel with Mt. Gerizim.[3] This may be another instance of Samaritan sympathies in the Fourth Gospel.

The Samaritan connection of Bethel with Mt. Gerizim may also add to the significance of the Samaritan woman's question to Jesus: "Our fathers worshiped on this mountain; and you say that in Jerusalem is the place where men ought to worship" (John 4:20). The Jacob story (Gen. 28:16-18) may have been read to support an alternate site to Jerusalem as the legitimate place of worship, and Jacob himself perhaps seen as a justification for Samaritan traditions regarding Mt. Gerizim.[4]

1. The more cogent explanations are explored by R. E. Brown, *The Gospel According to John,* AB, 2 vols. (Garden City, NY: Doubleday, 1966-70), 1:90-91.

2. Targ. Neofiti supplies an instance of the rabbinic exegesis of Jacob's dream in which Jacob is joined to his heavenly archetype by the stairway, and accordingly the suggestion has been made that in John 1:51 the author is not appealing directly to the OT but to contemporary Jewish exegesis of Gen. 28:12. See B. Lindars, "The Place of the Old Testament in the Formation of New Testament Theology," *NTS* 23 (1976) 61.

3. See C. H. H. Scobie, "The Origins and Development of Samaritan Christianity," *NTS* 19 (1973) 406.

4. See J. H. Neyrey, "Jacob Traditions and the Interpretation of John 4:10-26," *CBQ* 41 (1979) 426-29.

F. JACOB MEETS LABAN AND RACHEL (29:1-35)

1. JACOB ARRIVES IN HARAN (29:1-8)

1 *After resuming his journey,*[1] *Jacob reached the land of the Easterners.*

2 *There in front of him*[2] *he spotted a well in the field, and three flocks of sheep huddled beside it, for from that well the flocks were watered.*[3] *The stone covering the well's mouth was enormous.*[4]

3 *When the shepherds*[5] *converged they, together, could roll the stone away from the well's mouth and water the sheep; then they would reposition the stone over the well's mouth in its usual place.*

4 *Jacob said to them: "My brothers, from where do you come?" "From Haran*[6] *we are," they replied.*

5 *Then he asked them: "Do you know Laban son of Nahor?" "We do,"*[7] *they replied.*

1. Lit., "lifted up his feet." A. B. Ehrlich (*Randglossen zur Hebräischen Bibel* [1901; repr. Hildesheim: Olms, 1968], 1:52) provides examples of *nāśā'* in idiomatic word combinations for which he claims the sense "to put into action" *(in Aktion setzen).*

2. Lit., "he looked, and behold, a well," an instance of the *rā'â* plus *hinnēh* clause. The insertion of *hinnēh* in such clauses "acts like a camera shutter to freeze the 'sight' which is seen" (W. M. Clark, "The Righteousness of Noah," *VT* 21 [1971] 268).

3. *yašqû* is an example of a 3rd pl. of a verb used impersonally, and hence equal to a passive. See GKC, § 144f.

4. *g*^{e}*ḏālâ* ("enormous") cannot be an attributive (as in NAB, NEB, "a large/huge stone"), for it lacks the definite article. SP does read "an enormous stone" by deleting the definite article from "stone."

5. MT reads "flocks" *(ha'*^{a}*ḏārîm)* here and again in v. 8. The reading "shepherds" *(hārō'îm)* is obtained from the SP rendering of vv. 3 and 8 and the LXX of v. 8. One advantage of this reading is that it provides an antecedent for "to them" in the next verse. One may retain the MT if one reads *w*^{e}*gāl*^{a}*lû* as a 3rd pl. impersonal used as a passive, like *yašqû* in the previous verse (see Westermann, *Genesis,* 2:461: "When all the flocks had gathered there, they would roll the stone away . . . water the sheep"; without rejecting MT he assumes "shepherds" to be the subject of the verbs). In any case the four verbs of v. 3 should be taken as iteratives (a verb form suggesting repeated action). Cf. H. Y. Priebatsch, "Der Weg des semitischen Perfekts," *UF* 10 (1978) 343.

6. For the identification of the predicate in a response clause, see Andersen, *Hebrew Verbless Clause in the Pentateuch,* pp. 21, 122 n. 10.

7. "Since Hebrew lacks a word for 'yes,' it can only express affirmation by restating the question in positive terms" (Speiser, *Genesis,* p. 222). See also GKC, § 150n. This idiom occurs also in the shepherds' response in v. 6. Perhaps instead of saying "Hebrew lacks a word for 'yes,'" it would be more accurate to say Biblical Hebrew has no way precisely to say "yes." See also E. L. Greenstein, "The Syntax of Saying 'Yes' in Biblical Hebrew," *JANES* 19 (1989) 51-59, esp. pp. 52, 54. Greenstein notes that in Akkadian too "yes" may be conveyed by the respondent's repetition of the verb from the question with

6 *"Is he well?" he inquired. "Yes, he is," they answered, "and here comes Rachel his daughter with the sheep."*

7 *Then he said: "It is still broad daylight. It is not yet*[8] *time to gather in the animals. Water the sheep and go on pasturing them."*

8 *"We cannot," they replied, "until all the shepherds have converged to roll away the stone from the front of the well; only then can we water the sheep."*

1 That the home of Nahor may be described as among *the Easterners* shows that *bᵉnê qeḏem* (lit., "sons of the East") may refer to Arameans along the northern Euphrates. In other places in Scripture (Isa. 11:14) the same term designates Israel's enemies on the east, or south and southeast, as opposed to their enemies on the west and southwest, i.e., the Philistines. In Judg. 6:3, 33; 7:12 the expression is a summarizing appositive for the Midianites and the Amalekites (not a distinct third group). In Ezek. 25:4, 10 the "sons of the East" represent a desert group that will overun Ammon and Moab. Cf. also 1 K. 5:10 (Eng. 4:30); Job 1:3; Jer. 49:28. More than any other book in the OT, Genesis emphasizes the east (see 3:24; 4:16; 10:30; 11:2; 13:11; 25:6) as a direction of some significance. Movement to the east in Genesis is in the context of judgment (4:16) or vanity (11:2; 13:11) or alienation (25:6). The same is true with Jacob. The journey to the east is filled with heartaches and is far from ideal. It is not until Jacob journeys to the west (i.e., his return to Canaan) that peace comes. The reference to "the East" is thus a general one and is flexible. Haran is obviously much more north than east of Canaan, but it is still east of the Euphrates.

2-3 Jacob sees a well in a field[9] around which three flocks of sheep are huddled. Over this well is a very large stone. "Cisterns — and sometimes also wells — are . . . covered in by a broad and thick flat stone with a round hole cut in the middle, which in its turn is often covered with a heavy stone, which it requires two or three men to roll away, and which is removed only at particular times."[10]

---

conversion to the appropriate grammatical form. He quotes from the Gilgamesh Epic (XII:153) this line in the dialogue between Gilgamesh and Enkidu: (Q): *ša eṭimmašu pāqida lā īšū tāmur?* (A): *ātamar.* (Q): "Him whose spirit has no one attending it have you seen?" (A): "I have seen."

8. G. E. Whitney, "Lō' ('not') as 'Not yet' in the Hebrew Bible," *HS* 29 (1988) 44-45.

9. The well in Gen. 24 was located "outside the city" (24:11). The emphasis on the well in Gen. 29 being "in the field" provides a setting for the Jacob-Laban confrontation that will "unfold against a background of pastoral activity, with close attention to the economics and ethics of sheep and cattle herding" (Alter, *Art of Biblical Narrative,* p. 55).

10. Quoted in S. R. Driver, *Genesis,* p. 269.

In adjacent narratives a stone *('eḇen)* becomes a pivotal part of the story. In the preceding narrative, the stone that first was situated at Jacob's head (28:11) is raised as a commemorative pillar before God (28:18). In this narrative the stone at the well becomes the means by which Jacob meets Rachel.

4-6 These three verses provide illustration of the fulfillment of God's recent promise to Jacob, "I will be with you" (28:15), for the text should be read as a providential leadership of Jacob in his wanderings. It is no coincidence that he stumbles upon some individuals who know Laban well, anymore than it is coincidence that Ruth happens to glean in the fields of Boaz. Furthermore, the seemingly chance meeting of Jacob and Rachel is not serendipitous.

Is he well? (Heb. *h^ašālôm lô,* lit., "Is peace to him?"), the third of Jacob's three questions. In the previous narrative Jacob was concerned about his own *šālôm* (28:21). Here his concern is directed toward his uncle's *šālôm.* One need not read into the word *šālôm* all the rich nuances it carries elsewhere in the Bible.[11] Jacob's question to the shepherds about Laban's *šālôm* is simply polite inquiry about the state of Laban's well-being. One may compare it with Gen. 43:26ff., where Joseph inquires about the *šālôm* of his brothers, then to his brother about their father. In both instances, chs. 29 and 43, *A* inquires about the *šālôm* of *B* from *C.*[12]

Unlike Gen. 24, which featured lengthier and more formal dialogue when Abraham's servant first met Sarah by the well (24:15ff.), Jacob's meeting with the shepherds around this well is marked by the quick exhange of short questions and answers: v. 4 — first question, first answer; v. 5 — second question, second answer; v. 6 — third question, third answer. Such a format, according to Alter, is "an appropriate prelude to Jacob's quick-paced story of vigorously pursued actions, deceptions, and confrontations."[13]

7-8 Jacob shows no immediate interest in Rachel. His concern is rather for the sheep. In his judgment they have been folded for the night too early, and as a result the shepherds are not working as hard or as long as they should be. "Back to work," he urges. This may have been a subterfuge by Jacob in the hopes of attaining a few minutes alone with Rachel at the well.[14] Get rid of the unwanted company — the shepherds!

11. See W. Brueggemann, *Biblical Reflections on Shalom: Living Toward a Vision* (Philadelphia: United Church, 1976).

12. For the expression *šā'al l^ešālôm* ("to greet") cf. Gen. 43:27; Exod. 18:7; Judg. 18:15; 1 Sam. 10:4; 17:22; 25:5; 30:21; 2 Sam. 8:10; 11:7; 1 Chr. 18:10. See D. J. Harris, *The Biblical Concept of Peace* (Grand Rapids: Baker, 1970), p. 75; H. H. Schmid, *Šālôm "Frieden" im Alten Orient und im Alten Testament,* Stuttgarter Bibelstudien 51 (Stuttgart: Katholisches Bibelwerk, 1971), pp. 47-48.

13. Alter, *Art of Biblical Narrative,* p. 55.

14. See von Rad, *Genesis,* p. 288, who refers to Benno Jacob; see also Sarna, *Genesis,* p. 202.

2. JACOB MEETS RACHEL AND LABAN (29:9-14)

9 *While he was still speaking with them,*[1] *Rachel came*[2] *on the scene with her father's sheep, for she was a shepherdess.*[3]

10 *As soon as Jacob saw Rachel, the daughter of his uncle Laban, with the sheep of his uncle Laban, he went up, rolled away the stone from the well's mouth, and watered the sheep of his uncle Laban.*

11 *Then Jacob kissed Rachel and wept aloud.*[4]

12 *Jacob told her that he was her father's relative,*[5] *Rebekah's son; and at that she ran to tell her father.*

13 *When Laban heard the report*[6] *about Jacob, his sister's son, he ran out to meet him; he embraced him, and kissed him, and led him into his house. He shared with Laban everything that had happened.*

14 *Laban said to him: "Indeed, you are my bone and my flesh."*[7] *And he stayed with him for an entire month.*

In several ways Jacob's first encounter with Rachel and Laban parallels the encounter of Abraham's servant with Rebekah (24:10-33) and Moses' encounter with the daughters of Jethro (Exod. 2:15-21). (1) The hero (or his representative) goes to a distant land. (2) He stops at a well. (3) A girl (or girls) comes to the same well to draw water. (4) The hero draws water for them, or she for him. (5) The girl (or girls) returns home and reports the meeting to a brother or father. (6) The man is brought to the girl's house. (7) Subsequently a marriage takes place between the man at the well (or the

1. On the use of a participle that lays stress on the fact that the first action still continues on the occurrence of the second (always introduced by *wᵉ*), see GKC, § 116u.

2. The fem. perfect verb *bā'â* of v. 9 should be distinguished from the fem. participle *bā'â* in v. 6, for the 3rd fem. perfect and the fem. participle of *bô'* are written the same. Following the participle *mᵉḏabbēr* and *wᵉrāḥēl, bā'â* in v. 9 must be a perfect. See the examples cited in GKC, § 116u.

3. LXX adds "of her father's sheep."

4. Lit., "raised his voice and wept." See 27:38.

5. For the force of a pronoun following a noun in a nominal clause see J. Hoftijzer, "The Nominal Clause Reconsidered," *VT* 23 (1973) 488-89.

6. LXX reads *ónoma,* apparently reflecting Heb. *šēm,* instead of MT *šēma'*.

7. W. G. E. Watson ("Some Additional Wordpairs," in *Ascribe to the Lord,* Fest. P. C. Craigie, ed. L. Eslinger and G. Taylor, JSOTSup 67 (Sheffield: JSOT, 1988), pp. 185-87) notes the collocation *'ṣm wbśr,* always with a pronominal suffix, in Gen. 29:14; Judg. 9:2; 2 Sam. 5:1; 19:13, 14; 1 Chr. 11:1; Ps. 102:6; *'ṣm//bśr* in Gen. 2:23; Job 2:5; 4:14-15; Ezek. 24:4; Prov. 14:30; Lam. 3:4; Mic. 3:2-3. Regardless of sequence, the expression denotes, according to Watson, kinship (Gen. 2:23), food (Exod. 12:46), or one's physical body (Job 33:21).

man whom he represents) and the girl (or one of the girls) at the well.[8] The two Genesis stories contain the further parallels that the strange land is in fact the land of the father (or his ancestors), and that the girl who comes to draw water is a cousin or the daughter of a cousin of the groom-to-be.

9-10 Jacob does what the shepherds will not or cannot do individually. In a feat of herculean strength he rolls away the stone from the well's opening. That Jacob is able single-handedly to roll the stone away must be attributed to the earlier promise Yahweh had made to the patriarch: "I will be with you" (28:15). The reality of that divine presence with Jacob confers on him the ability to perform a brute physical act, the likes of which he has not done previously nor will he again. Jacob acts Samsonesque only on this one occasion. The shepherds' curiosity might have been aroused at this point, as the Philistines' curiosity would be in Samson's day (Judg. 16), for v. 9 makes clear that the shepherds were present to observe Jacob's feat of strength. They did not suddenly egress after Rachel arrived.

Jacob says nothing. He simply performs. His mother Rebekah is not there to tell him what to do; he is on his own now. When alone, he is apparently capable of shedding his passivity and becoming master of the situation. No longer in his mother's shadow, he manages to upstage the shepherds. It is likely that such responsibilities were a part of his past. Esau could hunt the wild game; Jacob would be responsible for the domesticated animals.

his uncle. Three times v. 10 describes Laban as *'ᵃḥî 'immô* (lit., "brother of his mother"). Jacob earlier referred to the shepherds around the well as "my brothers" (*'aḥay,* v. 4). Jacob introduced himself to Rachel as her father's "relative" (*'ᵃḥî 'aḇîhā,* lit., "brother of her father," v. 12). Laban will shortly refer to Jacob as his "relative" (*'āḥî 'attâ,* lit., "my brother [are] you," v. 15). Though *'āḥ* can have various connotations, as reflected in the translations here ("brother," "relative"),[9] its unusual prominence in this unit is interesting, for the story is about one brother (Jacob) who is fleeing another (Esau) but who is about to gain another "brother" (Laban). To the modern reader of this narrative, the threefold mention of Laban as "the brother of his mother" by Jacob may seem clumsy and unnecessary. But this is a good case of "how a redundant family attribution implies motive."[10] Jacob responds as he does to his mother's side of the family because he recalls both his mother's

8. See Culley, *Studies in the Structure of Hebrew Narrative,* pp. 41-43.

9. See H. Ringgren, *"'āch," TDOT,* 1:188-93.

10. Sternberg, *Poetics of Biblical Narrative,* p. 538 n. 15. See also R. A. Oden, Jr., *The Bible Without Theology* (San Francisco: Harper & Row, 1987), p. 124, who notes that the three references to Laban in this verse as the brother of Jacob's mother underscores the avunculate relationship between Jacob and Laban, a relationship of significance in many traditional narratives.

former assistance in obtaining the blessing from Isaac and her insistence that Jacob flee to her brother in Haran (27:43).

11 Jacob's kissing of Rachel, followed by his weeping aloud, strikes the modern, Western reader of Scripture as strange. Rachel does not ask why he is crying, nor does he offer her an explanation. But Jacob's crying may be brought on by the successful termination of his journey. He is now in the right place and he has met the right person. The providential leading of God again becomes obvious. Earlier, the same expression (lit., "lifted up his voice and wept") was used of Esau (27:38). But Esau's weeping stems from grief and disappointment, whereas Jacob's weeping reflects his gratitude. This is one of the rare instances in a biblical narrative of a man kissing a woman. In the OT kissing (as a sign of greeting or blessing) normally involves two men. For a man kissing a woman, see Gen. 31:28 and 32:1 (Eng. 31:55; Laban and his daughters); 1 K. 19:20 (Elisha and his mother); Cant. 1:2 (the beloved and her lover).[11]

12-13 Rachel bears the news about Jacob's arrival to Laban, her father, and this brings Jacob and Laban together. Laban is even more demonstrative than Jacob. Jacob kissed Rachel (*wayyiššaq,* Qal), while Laban "embraced" and "kissed" Jacob (*wayᵉnaššeq,* Piel).[12]

14 Laban's only recorded words to Jacob are: *Indeed, you are my bone and my flesh.* This expression is a formula that occurs first in Gen. 2:23 and again in Judg. 9:2; 2 Sam. 5:1 (par. 1 Chr. 11:1); and 2 Sam. 19:13. While each of these passages includes, by this formula, the possibility of blood ties, the larger context would suggest that a reciprocal covenant oath is involved as well. Laban is not only celebrating family connections, but is instituting, albeit in an incipient stage, a bond between nephew and uncle. Of course, Laban will be the head, while Jacob will be the junior partner.[13]

The sparse dialogue in vv. 1-14 is mostly between Jacob and the shepherds (vv. 4-9a). Jacob and Rachel do not talk to one other in direct discourse, nor do Rachel and Laban, nor does Jacob with Laban. Laban's own words are minimal (four words in Hebrew).[14] But while words are few,

11. In Prov. 7:13 it is reversed. There it is the personified "Dame Folly" who kisses any simple man who wanders into her house.

12. The other instances of the Piel of *nāšaq* are Gen. 31:28; 32:1 (Eng. 31:55); 45:15. In the first two Laban kisses his daughters in a final parting, with the understanding that they probably will not meet again. In 45:15 Joseph kisses his brothers and weeps over them shortly after he has identified himself to them. Both situations are fraught with emotion.

13. See D. Daube and R. Yaron, "Jacob's Reception by Laban," *JSS* 1 (1956) 60-61; W. Brueggemann, "Of the Same Flesh and Bone (Gn 2,23a)" *CBQ* 32 (1970) 537-38.

14. I cannot agree with Fokkelman's interpretation (*Narrative Art in Genesis,* p. 126) that *'aḵ* is, in Laban's mouth, an expression of disappointment, rather than a particle of emphasis — "you do not bring riches; oh well, yet you are my flesh and blood." For *'aḵ* as a particle for emphasis, see Andersen, *Sentence in Biblical Hebrew,* p. 177.

enthusiasm is abundant. Rachel *ran* (Heb. *rûṣ*) to tell Laban, and Laban *ran out* (Heb. *rûṣ*) to meet Jacob.

The concluding note in v. 14 that Jacob stayed with Laban *for an entire month* does not conflict with later references that he remained twenty years with Laban (31:41).[15] V. 14b does not imply that Jacob headed back to Canaan at the end of the month. It simply indicates that at the end of that month Laban proposed that Jacob's position be regularized by Laban paying Jacob a wage, and that Jacob should not be expected to work for Laban for free just because he is kin.[16]

3. JACOB SERVES SEVEN YEARS FOR RACHEL (29:15-20)

15 *Laban then said to him, "Because[1] you are my relative, does that mean you should serve me for nothing?[2] Tell me what your wage should be."*

16 *Now Laban had two daughters; the older was called Leah, the younger Rachel.*

17 *Leah had tender eyes, but Rachel was shapely and attractive.*[3]

18 *Jacob loved Rachel, and thus responded: "I will serve you seven years for Rachel your younger daughter."*

19 *Laban replied: "It is better to give her to you rather than to an outsider. Stay with me."*

20 *So Jacob served for Rachel seven years, yet they seemed to him but a few days because of his love for her.*

15 Laban informs Jacob that it is not the custom to marry off the younger daughter before an older daughter, *after* he has indirectly said Jacob may

15. As argued by Noth, *History of Pentateuchal Traditions,* pp. 88-89.

16. See R. N. Whybray, *The Making of the Pentateuch,* JSOTSup 53 (Sheffield: Sheffield Academic, 1987), p. 194.

1. On *h^{a}ḵî,* see my remarks at 27:36; cf. R. Gordis, *The Word and the Book* (New York: Ktav, 1976), p. 164 n. 9, who renders *h^{a}ḵî* as an interrogative and a conjunction: "is it because you are my brother, that you must serve me for nothing?" Cf. also A. Schoors, "The Particle *kî,*" *OTS* 21 (1981) 260.

2. *ḥinnām,* "for nothing," is related to the verb *ḥānan* "show favor, be gracious," and the noun *ḥēn,* "favor, grace." Laban does not expect Jacob to work for his uncle merely as a favor. The same connection between "grace" and "free" is found in words like *gratis* or *gratuitously*.

3. On the predicative use of an adjectival construct, see T. Muraoka, "The status constructus of adjectives in Biblical Hebrew," *VT* 27 (1977) 380 n. 15. For *tō'ar* and *mar'eh* constituting a word pair whose components appear together in parallelism, see Y. Avishur, *Stylistic Studies of Word-Pairs in Biblical and Ancient Semitic Languages,* AOAT 210 (Neukirchen-Vluyn: Neukirchener, 1984), pp. 215, 219, 644, 730.

marry Rachel. Here he offers Jacob remuneration for his work, but only *after* he has worked a month for him (v. 14).

D. Daube and R. Yaron have forwarded a novel interpretation of this verse.[4] They have suggested that the verse is not made up of an assertion — "you are my relative" — followed by a question — "why should you serve . . . ?" Rather, it is made up of two questions: (1) "Are you my relative?" (2) "Why should you serve . . . ?" They understand the first question to mean "you are not my relative"; Laban is thereby severing family ties with Jacob, thus reducing Jacob to a hireling who can now receive wages. Heb. *h^a^ḵî* may introduce a legitimate question (i.e., the questioner does not know the answer; 2 Sam. 9:1), or it may introduce a rhetorical question (i.e., the questioner is quite certain of the answer; Job 6:22 ["no!"]; 2 Sam. 23:19 ["yes!"]).[5] Gen. 29:15 seems to fit into this second category, with the question of Laban demanding a yes answer (as in 27:36). Contra Daube and Yaron, I would argue that Laban is claiming that Jacob, as a relative, should not receive wages. But given his sanguine nature, Laban is prepared to waive this technicality, and compensate Jacob adequately for his labor, even to the point of allowing Jacob to determine his own wage. In the process, however, Jacob's nephew-uncle relationship with Laban will be subordinated to that of an employee-employer relationship, giving Laban (so he hopes) the upper hand in this relationship.

16-17 Jacob is not interested in monetary wages. What he is really after is the hand of Rachel in marriage. Laban has two daughters, Leah and Rachel. One is *older (hagg^e^ḏōlâ),* and the other is *younger (haqq^e^ṭannâ).* This family matches that of Jacob, for Jacob is a younger brother *(haqqāṭān)* and Esau is an older brother (*haggāḏōl,* 27:15, 42). Here, then, the younger brother *(qāṭān)* is in love with the younger sister *(q^e^ṭannâ).* Just as Esau, an older brother, stands between Jacob and the blessing, here an older sister stands between Jacob and his true love.

The traditional rendering "Leah's eyes were weak" (RSV, NIV; cf. NEB, JB) is in need of reexamination. The adjective *raḵ* means "weak"[6] only in a few places, particularly Gen. 33:13 ("frail" children) and Deut. 20:8 ("softhearted, timid" paralleling "fearful," *yārēʾ*). More often it describes something that is tender (flocks, Gen. 18:7), gentle (a king's reign, 2 Sam. 3:39), soft (speech, Prov. 15:1; Job 40:27 [Eng. 41:3]), delicate (a woman,

4. See D. Daube and R. Yaron, *JSS* 1 (1956) 61-62; Sarna, *Genesis,* p. 203.

5. See GKC, § 150d, e.

6. Understanding the Hebrew to mean "weak," and following the custom of saying nothing disparaging about the patriarchs and matriarchs of Israel, Gen. Rabbah 70:16 chose to translate *raḵ* as "lovely" *(y'yn).* It adds, further, that Leah's eyes were "weak" on account of her weeping over the possibility that, as the elder sister, she would have to marry Esau, the older brother.

Deut. 28:56; Isa. 47:1), and young (an inexperienced lad, 1 Chr. 22:5; 29:1; 2 Chr. 13:7). In the last three references *raḵ* is parallel with *naʿar,* "inexperienced, youthful." Leah may be older, but her eyes are the beautiful eyes of a person who looks much younger.

In an earlier story involving Abraham's servant and Rebekah, attention was drawn right at the outset of the meeting to Rebekah's beauty (24:16). Notice is made of her charms before there is any dialogue. Here it is reversed. There is dialogue between Jacob and Rachel (v. 12), then Leah and Rachel are introduced, then attention is drawn to Rachel's pulchritude. Such a positioning stresses that Rachel's beauty is indeed what attracts Jacob to Rachel. Jacob did not put out a fleece before Yahweh, as Abraham's servant did. He is attracted by Rachel's physical appearance.[7]

18 Here is an instance of love at first sight (cf. Mark 10:21). The text does not say whether Rachel reciprocated.

Unlike his grandfather's servant who came to this same territory earlier for the same purpose, but with ten camels and gifts, Jacob arrives empty-handed. Accordingly, he is not prepared to offer Laban a monetary sum as the bride price. He has nothing to offer. In the place of a sum of money Jacob is willing to pledge himself to seven years of service for Laban.[8]

Here then is Jacob's response to Laban's earlier question: "should you serve [*ʿāḇaḏ*] me for nothing?" (v. 15). Jacob says he will "serve" seven years (v. 18) for Rachel, and he "served" seven years (v. 20). Earlier in the Jacob narrative Jacob was designated the object, not the subject, of this verb (25:23). Service was something he was supposed to receive (from Esau). Now the object of *ʿāḇaḏ* becomes the subject of *ʿāḇaḏ*. No reason is given why Jacob chose *seven years.* But it seems as if he is in no hurry to go home. Why should he? Why precipitate an unnecessarily early meeting with Esau? Let Esau wait for as long as possible.

19 Laban is as concerned, or at least seems as concerned, about whom his daughter marries as Isaac was about whom his son would marry (28:2). Rachel is not consulted for her opinion. A daughter is "given"[9] by her father to her husband-to-be. That Laban says *It is better to give her to you,* and not "it is better to give Rachel to you," may be intentionally ambiguous; he thereby lays the groundwork for his forthcoming act of deception.

20 The Hebrew narrative offers no details about the seven years of Jacob's service. The only comment is on how quickly the years passed for

7. Cf. Alter, *Art of Biblical Narrative,* p. 56, who contrasts Rachel's beauty as part of her objective identity with Rebekah's beauty as a "casual element in Jacob's special attachment to her."

8. David's providing a hundred Philistine foreskins to Saul for the hand of Michal in marriage (1 Sam. 18:21-25) is another case of a nonmonetary bride price.

9. Cf. the words in the marriage ritual: "Who giveth this woman to this man?"

Jacob. They seemed like only *a few days (yāmîm ’*^{a}*ḥāḏîm).* Rebekah used the same Hebrew expression when she told Jacob to stay with Laban "a few days" (27:44). Time will not always pass so swiftly for Jacob. Later on, when he prepares to meet Esau, surely a few days will feel like seven years.

4. JACOB IS DECEIVED BY LABAN (29:21-30)

21 *Then Jacob said to Laban: "Let me have*[1] *my wife, for my time is completed, that I may go in to her."*

22 *Laban gathered all the local people and put on a feast.*

23 *At nightfall he took Leah his daughter and brought her to Jacob, and he went in to her.*

24 *Laban gave her Zilpah his maid to be Leah his daughter's maid.*[2]

25 *Morning came, and there was Leah!*[3] *Jacob said to Laban: "What have you done to me? Was it not for Rachel I served you?*[4] *Why did you trick*[5] *me?"*

26 *Laban replied: "It is not customary in our place to marry off a younger daughter before the firstborn.*

27 *Finish up the bridal week*[6] *of this one, and the other as well will be*

1. *hāḇâ* may function as an interjection ("[come] now!" 11:3, 4, 7) or as an imperative of *yāhaḇ* ("give") with an accusative (30:1; 47:15). If *hāḇâ* is an interjection here, Jacob says to Laban, "Now then! my wife."

2. On the use of the pronominal suffixes and apparent redundant expressions in this verse, and in vv. 28, 29, see J. Blau, "Redundant Pronominal Suffixes Denoting Intrinsic Possession," *JANES* 11 (1979) 34 n. 14. Thus v. 24 reads lit., "Laban gave to her Zilpah his maid, to Leah his daughter a maid"; v. 28: "and he gave to him Rachel his daughter, to him for a wife (with *lô l*^{e}*’iššâ* constituting a separate syntagmeme); v. 29: "and Laban gave to Rachel his daughter Bilhah his maid, to her as a maid."

3. J. Blau ("Adverbia als psychologische und grammatische Subjekte/Praedikate im Bibelhebraeisch," *VT* 9 [1959] 134 n. 2) says that *w*^{e}*hinnēh hiw’ lē’â* is an adverbial sentence, the subject of which is usually *hāyâ.*

4. Speiser (*Genesis,* p. 225) notes that the prepositional phrase (in Laban's mouth) in 29:19 — "stay with me," *ʿimmāḏî* — suggests "under my authority." The narrator has Laban use *ʿimmāḏî* again (v. 27) when speaking to Jacob. But here in v. 25 Jacob himself uses the phrase *ʿimmāḵ.* Now Biblical Hebrew does not attest *ʿimmāḏ-* with any suffix except the 1st person. But Laban's failure to use *ʿimmî* may suggest that he had something in mind by service that Jacob did not (i.e., Jacob would work under Laban, not with Laban).

5. In 25:20 Laban was called an "Aramean" *(ha’*^{a}*rammî).* Here Jacob says "Why did you trick me?" *(rimmîṯānî).* Connected with Laban's ethnic background and his deceit of Jacob are words involving the consonants *r-m-m.* If *yaʿ*^{a}*qōḇ* (Jacob) is an *ʿāqēḇ* (heel), the *’*^{a}*rammî* is one skilled at *rimmâ* (deceiving).

6. Lit., "Finish up the period of seven [days? years?] for this one."

given to you,[7] *in return for another seven years of service with me."*
28 *Jacob consented.*[8] *He finished the bridal week for Leah,*[9] *and then Laban gave him Rachel his daughter to be his wife.*
29 *And Laban gave Rachel his daughter Bilhah his maid to be her maid.*
30 *He then went in to Rachel also; besides, he loved Rachel, not Leah.*[10] *He remained seven additional years in Laban's service.*

21 The reader may be somewhat surprised that Jacob refers to Rachel as *my wife,* rather than "your daughter." His relationship to Rachel must be akin to Joseph's relationship to Mary in the NT. The couple are husband and wife, but the marriage has not yet been physically consummated.[11] This is clear from Jacob's words to Laban. He does not say, "let me have Rachel so that I may take her as my wife." He says: *Let me have my wife . . . that I may go in to her,* i.e., have sexual intercourse with her. Jacob's expressed desire is not for marriage but for sexual congress on the heels of marriage.

It may not be accidental that Jacob uses *hāḇâ* for Laban "giving" Rachel to him, and that Laban uses *nāṯan.* By using *hāḇâ,* which we saw may function as an interjection — "Now then! my wife" — Jacob's words are raised above a request to a demand.

22 No record is given of Laban's response to Jacob. The silence is certainly indicative of sinister plans on Laban's part. Had he said "Okay, I will give her to you," then his ruse would have been aborted from the start. So instead of a vocal commitment, Laban ignores Jacob and gathers the townspeople to a nuptial feast.

23-25 After the feast Laban conducts Leah, not Rachel, to Jacob, and the two enjoy a night of sexual intimacy. Only in the morning does Jacob

7. *nitt^{e}nâ* may be read as a 1st person pl. cohortative in the Qal stem (see S. Mandelkern, *Veteris Testamenti Concordantiae* [Tel Aviv: Schocken, 1971], p. 784, col. 3), or as a 3rd fem. sing. perfect in the Niphal stem. The presence of *'eṯ* does not present problems for reading the verb as a Niphal, for we have already seen examples in Genesis of *'eṯ* with the subject of passive verbs (4:18; 17:5; 21:5; 27:42). Many of the ancient versions (LXX, SP, Vulg., Pesh.) read it as a first person sing., "and I will give."

8. Lit., "And Jacob did so."

9. I have inserted the proper name Leah here, and Laban in the next clause, for sense. The Hebrew simply says, "he finished the bridal week of this one, and he gave to him Rachel."

10. The traditional translation "he loved her more than Leah" is unconvincing if for no other reason than that the next verse says that Leah was "unloved" *(ś^{e}nû'â),* and it is impossible to make *ś^{e}nû'â* mean "loved less." The preposition *min* in *millē'â* is used not in a comparative sense but in an excluding sense. See Fokkelmann, *Narrative Art in Genesis,* p. 129 n. 10.

11. On legal matters vis-à-vis the betrothed wife, see Deut. 20:17; 22:23-24.

discover the identity of his nocturnal bed-partner. Jacob, once the subject of deceit, now becomes the object of deceit. The perpetrator of subterfuge becomes its victim. The nemesis is made all the more pungent by the fact that Jacob is caught in the same device he himself had once used. He pretended to be Esau in front of Isaac. Leah pretends to be Rachel next to Jacob. While Jacob's ruse was pretending to be his older brother, Leah's ruse is pretending to be her younger sister. Jacob is deceived as he deceived his father.

The story raises many issues. How does Leah feel about being led to Jacob's bed by her father? Does she voluntarily accept the role of surrogate wife? What does this incident do to her own reputation? Is she content to be reduced to a means to an end? That Laban gave his handmaid to Leah (v. 24) suggests that Leah was unaware that she was being used. That is, Laban follows the frequent practice of presenting one's daughter with a gift at the time of her marriage.[12]

In one sense the note about Laban giving Zilpah to be Leah's maid may appear to contribute nothing to the drama of this event. That is, the narrative reads smoothly from vv. 21-23 straight into v. 25 (bypassing v. 24). Thus, at the end of v. 23 Jacob cohabits, unsuspectingly, with Leah; at the beginning of v. 25 comes the shocking revelation. This does not imply that v. 24 is a later addition.[13] While intrusive, v. 24 functions as a retardation device of the narrator to increase the tension regarding Jacob's reaction to this ruse.[14]

The most obvious question is, How is Laban able to pull off this deceit? Most commentators have been content with the explanation that Leah was heavily veiled (which brides were; cf. 24:65) and that inside the wedding chamber at night was complete darkness.[15] Lovestruck perhaps to the point of being blinded by love, Jacob was unaware of the incognito Leah. This explanation is correct but incomplete. The veil and the darkness would surely not themselves be sufficient to camouflage both Leah and her voice.

The suggestion is as old as Josephus that Jacob was "deluded by wine and the dark."[16] This is the second time in Genesis that *ṣᵉʿîrâ,* "younger," and *bᵉḵîrâ,* "firstborn," have been used together. The same terms were used to describe Lot's two daughters. They too deceived their father, made him

12. For other instances of a bride receiving a gift from her family, cf. Caleb's daughter, who, after being given in marriage to Othniel, asked her father to give her springs of water (Josh. 15:19; Judg. 1:15), and Pharaoh's giving of Gezer to his daughter as a dowry (1 K. 9:16).

13. Contra Westermann, *Genesis,* 2:467.

14. Sarna, *Genesis,* p. 205; Sternberg, *Poetics of Biblical Narrative,* p. 243.

15. For example, R. Patai, *Sex and Family in the Bible and the Middle East* (Garden City, NY: Doubleday, 1959), pp. 64-65.

16. Josephus *Ant.* 1.19.6 (§ 301).

drunk, and then had intercourse with him.[17] Here in Gen. 29 is another "younger" daughter and "firstborn" daughter, and again inebriation is a part of the story. For Laban's duplicity follows his "feast" (*mišteh,* from *šāṯâ,* "to drink"), i.e., a drinking banquet.

26 Only after the fact, when a bewildered Jacob presses him, does Laban rationalize his deception of Jacob. He informs Jacob that it is not the custom in Paddan-Aram to marry off a younger sister before an older sister. Perhaps in Canaan a Jacob can usurp an Esau, but that will not happen in Laban's homeland.

Even if Laban is legally correct, why did he not inform Jacob of that custom before the feast? Would not such a disclosure have prevented any such furor as has erupted here? Is it possible that Laban was actually surprised by Jacob's protest? Does he believe for technical reasons that Jacob must first marry Leah, whether he wants to or not, and then he may have Rachel? Note that the expression Laban uses to justify himself and his substitution is, "It is not customary in our place . . ." *(lōʾ yēʿāśeh ḵēn).* This expression refers to serious violations of custom that threaten the fabric of society and is tantamount to rebuke. Thus Abimelech uses this phrase with Abraham after Abraham deceives him (20:9). Likewise, the sons of Jacob use this phrase after they hear about their sister's violation (34:7). Tamar, daughter of David, attempted to dissuade her half-brother Amnon from forcing himself on her by appealing to the force of this expression (2 Sam. 13:12).[18]

In explaining his course of action to Jacob, Laban does not use the same words to differentiate between the two sisters, as the narrator had done earlier (v. 16). In the narrator's mouth Leah is *haggᵉḏōlâ,* "the older" (lit., "the greater"), and Rachel is *haqqᵉṭannâ,* "the younger" (lit., "the smaller"). In Laban's mouth Leah is *habbᵉḵîrâ,* "the firstborn," and Rachel is *haṣṣᵉʿîrâ,* "the younger." Laban's choice of vocabulary enables the narrator to link ch. 29 with chs. 25 and 27, esp. ch. 25, in which Jacob the younger (*ṣāʿîr,* 25:23) has taken the birthright *(bᵉḵōrâ)* from Esau, the firstborn (*raḇ,* 25:23; *gāḏôl,* 27:15). Jacob, the *ṣāʿîr,* who supplanted his brother (who was *gāḏôl*), wished to marry a sister who was *qᵉṭannâ/ṣᵉʿîrâ.* Instead, Laban explains that he must overrule that desire, and give to Jacob his daughter who is *gᵉḏôlâ/bᵉḵîrâ.*

17. See J. A. Diamond, "The deception of Jacob: a new perspective on an ancient solution to the problem," *VT* 34 (1984) 211-13; C. Carmichael, *Women, Law and the Genesis Traditions* (Edinburgh: University of Edinburgh, 1979), p. 99 n. 22.

18. Gen. 34:7 and 2 Sam. 13:12 are parallel in that not only do both use the phrase *lōʾ yēʿāśeh ḵēn,* but both Jacob's sons and Tamar refer to such a forbidden act as a *nᵉḇālâ,* "sacrilege."

27 This verse makes clear that Laban's stratagem occurred on the first night of the feast.[19] This is indicated by Laban's suggestion that Jacob *Finish up the bridal week of this one* (Leah). Laban did not wait until the end of the feast to carry out his plan. When Laban moved, he moved quickly.

Laban has no problems with one man being married to two sisters simultaneously. Nor do the patriarchal narratives. But later biblical law condemns such a practice (Lev. 18:18), thus indicating that the patriarchal traditions of Jacob and his wives antedate the book of Leviticus.[20]

28-30 Jacob offers no further protest. He accepts Laban's request of seven more years of service if he is to marry Rachel. At the end of the bridal week Rachel is given to Jacob. This is an act of trust by Laban. Might not Jacob abscond with Rachel after seven years and a week under Laban's roof? What is there to guarantee Jacob's commitment to a promise made in excruciating circumstances? It is a testimony to Jacob's character that he fulfills his duty to Laban chronologically, even though his employment tenure with Laban is doubled due to Laban's ability to switch his daughters, causing great distress for Jacob (and probably for Rachel too).

Between vv. 20 and 30 fourteen years elapse: seven pre-Rachel years, seven post-Rachel years. Essentially nothing is recorded about this long period, unless one reads the narrative in 29:31ff. (the birth of Jacob's children) as synchronous with 29:30, the seven additional years for which Jacob served Laban. In fact, this is the more likely reading; yet, taking 29:31ff. as sequential to 29:30 is not impossible. V. 31 suggests that Rachel was unable to conceive for an extended period of time, and not just for the first year of marriage. Then again, Leah surely was not barren herself for seven years. About the seven years of courtship nothing at all is said. Perhaps the first seven years of marriage were stormy, for Jacob cannot split his affection evenly between Rachel and Leah. He is clearly in love with Rachel. If Laban has become the Jacob in this event, Jacob is becoming like his mother and father, each of whom loved one son more than the other (25:28). Parental favoritism is now replaced with marital favoritism. The former led to friction in Isaac's family. Will the latter produce friction in Jacob's family?

19. For other references to a seven-day period of elaborate feasting see Judg. 14:12-18; 1 K. 8:65-66; Esth. 1:5. The first of these three concerns a wedding feast (Samson's).

20. R. A. Oden, Jr. (*The Bible Without Theology* [San Francisco: Harper & Row, 1987), pp. 110ff.) chides biblical commentators for giving such an answer that considers only the historical growth of biblical traditions, without asking whether such an "incorrect" marriage plays any role in structuring the biblical narratives. But while Oden goes on to make an interesting case for the pervasive practice of cross-cousin marriage, he does not address the issue here — a man married to two of his cross-cousins simultaneously.

5. JACOB'S FOUR SONS BY LEAH (29:31-35)

31 *When Yahweh saw that Leah was unloved, he opened her womb,*[1] *while Rachel remained barren.*

32 *Leah conceived and gave birth to a son whom she named Reuben; for she said: "It means*[2] *Yahweh has seen my distress; it means my husband will love me!"*

33 *Again she conceived and gave birth to a son. She said: "Now that Yahweh has heard that I was unloved,*[3] *he has given me also this one." So she named him Simeon.*

34 *Again she conceived and gave birth to a son. She said: "Certainly now my husband will attach himself to me, since I have borne him three sons." Thus he was named*[4] *Levi.*

35 *Again she conceived and gave birth to a son. She said: "This time I will praise Yahweh." Thus she named him Judah. Then she ceased bearing.*

31 This is the first reference to Yahweh's activity since he spoke to Jacob at Bethel. Jacob has continued beyond Bethel to Haran; met some shepherds, Rachel, and Laban; has married Leah and Rachel; and has worked seven years for his father-in-law. Did Yahweh remain behind at Bethel, near the stairway? On the contrary, as Jacob continued his journey, Yahweh went with him as he said he would (28:15). Deity has not been involved in the story for seven years at least. Now, seven years plus a week later, two marriages later, and one embarrassing scenario later, Yahweh reenters the scene.

It is he, not Laban, who observes that Leah is *unloved.* The Hebrew word is *śᵉnûʾâ,* literally, "hated."[5] The preceding verse has defined what hate

1. Y. Avishur ("Studies in Stylistic Features Common to the Phoenician Inscriptions and the Bible," *UF* 8 [1976] 14) shows the parallel between *wayyiptaḥ ʾeṯ raḥmāh . . . wattēleḏ bēn* of vv. 31, 32 and a Phoenician text (*KAI,* 27.22): *lypth [rḥ]my wtld,* "may he open her womb that she may give birth."

2. The last two *kî*s in this verse are probably not causal ("since") and asseverative ("surely"), but explicatives or recitatives ("it means . . . it means"). The same may be said of the first *kî* in v. 33. See B. Childs, *The Book of Exodus,* OTL (Philadelphia: Westminster, 1974), p. 312; Speiser, *Genesis,* p. 230; A. Schoors, "The Particle *kî,*" *OTS* 21 (1981) 256-58.

3. The nominal clause *śᵉnûʾâ ʾānōḵî* may be rendered as "I (was) unloved" or "I (am) unloved."

4. Some versions of the LXX, SP, and the Palestinian Targ. read the 3rd fem., *tiqrāʾ,* against MT 3rd masc., *qārāʾ* ("he called"). I prefer to retain MT *qārāʾ,* understood as an active perfect rendered as past and passive; for this phenomenon see H. C. Brichto, "Kin, Cult, Land and Afterlife — A Biblical Complex," *HUCA* 44 (1973) 15.

5. On the use of the tradition in Genesis about Jacob's two wives, one loved, one unloved, in the formulation of the law in Deut. 21:15-17 ("If a man has two wives, the

means: "Jacob loved Rachel, not Leah." "Hate" is used here as it is in Deut. 21:15 and Matt. 6:24. The use of *ś^{e}nû'â* also shows that in Hebrew a word, especially a verb, "may be used to describe not merely its own actions, but also the omission or prevention of an opposite action."[6]

As Yahweh chose the second-born over the firstborn (i.e., the unlikely one) in Jacob's and Esau's case, he now chooses the unloved Leah over the loved Rachel (i.e., the unlikely one). He permits Leah, the hated one, to mother first. This is the second instance of womb opening Yahweh has brought about, the first being that of the Philistine women in Abimelech's kingdom (20:17-18). There may be some irony in the fact that the first two of three consonants in "womb" *(reḥem)* and "Rachel" *(rāḥēl)* are the same. But it is not Rachel's *reḥem* that is opened — it is Leah's.

Verse 31 speaks about Yahweh's action with Leah: "he opened her womb." Jacob is not mentioned in any of the acts of conception in vv. 31-35, although he is obviously the father of Leah's four children listed in these verses. Jacob did not love Leah, but after she and he were married, he made no attempt to divorce her (cf. Deut. 22:13ff., a law about a husband who, after having intercourse with his wife, hates her and wishes to dissociate himself from her). Perhaps divorce was not even an option for Jacob. If it had been, Laban's switching Leah for Rachel would not have made sense if Jacob could simply divorce Leah. Furthermore, if Jacob went beyond verbal protest, he might have lost Rachel too.

32 Assuming that Leah's pregnancies are contemporary with the second seven years of Jacob's services under Laban, we may understand that the first four years of these seven involve Leah having children. Leah may not have Rachel's curvacious body, but then Rachel does not have Leah's fruitful womb. What one has, the other lacks. One sister is childless, the other sister is the one who is reproducing. Interestingly, Leah never covets Rachel's body, but Rachel does covet Leah's womb (see 30:1). In fact, it cannot be fortuitous that the seven additional years Jacob agrees to serve Laban for Rachel parallel the seven children (six sons, one daughter) he fathers by Leah. Leah mothers one child for each of the seven years Jacob put in for Rachel.

Leah's firstborn is *Reuben.* She apparently makes a wordplay using two clauses which supply a popular or folk etymology for Reuben. In *Yahweh has seen my distress* (Heb. *rā'â YHWH b^{eʿ}onyî*) one detects, rather far apart, the consonants *r-b-n.* In the clause *my husband will love me* (Heb. *ye'^{ĕ}hāḇanî*) the cluster *b-n* may be identified with the *b-n* sequence in Reuben. By itself

---

one loved and the other hated . . ."), see C. Carmichael, *The Laws of Deuteronomy* (Ithaca, NY: Cornell University, 1974), pp. 58-62.

6. See R. Gordis, "Some Hitherto Unrecognized Meanings of the Verb *SHUB,*" *JBL* 52 (1933) 153-54.

Reuben (Heb. *rᵉʾûḇēn*) makes perfectly good sense: "See, a son!"[7] In this light, the phrases from Leah's mouth after Reuben's birth may be read as affirmations by Leah, not as etymological explanations.

The first part of Leah's statement is correct: *Yahweh has seen my distress.* The same noun was used for Hagar's situation: "Yahweh has given heed to your distress" (16:11). In both instances one wife/concubine (Leah/Hagar) plays a subordinate role to another wife (Rachel/Sarah). The result of Yahweh's involvement in the plight is that the subordinate woman gives birth to a child. Both times the name given to the child is followed by a phrase that highlights a verb in the child's name: Yahweh *has seen;* Yahweh *has given heed.* Leah's second phrase — *my husband will love me* — is not as accurate. Leah is not the last woman to discover that her pregnancy is not a guarantee of a spouse's support and love.

Reuben's birth differs from the following three births in one respect. In the other three the name is given to the child after Leah makes a comment. In Reuben's case the name is given to the child before she makes a comment.[8] Is this a way of highlighting Reuben as the firstborn? Here is the firstborn (Leah) mothering the firstborn (Reuben).

33 The name of the second child, *Simeon* (Heb. *šimʿôn*), is connected with the verb *has heard* (Heb. *šāmaʿ*). As with Reuben's birth, Simeon's birth is linked with an unsavory experience, followed by a happy rectification of that chagrin. In naming the child Leah focuses not on an unpleasant circumstance but on Yahweh who overcame that circumstance. She will not name her first child "My distress," nor will she name the second child "Unloved one."

First (v. 31), Yahweh "saw" that Leah was unloved. Leah now says that Yahweh *heard* that she was unloved. Heard from whom? Or does "hear"

7. For the literal and interpreted meaning of Jacob's sons, see M. Calloway, *Sing, O Barren One: A Study in Comparative Midrash,* SBLDS 91 (Atlanta: Scholars, 1986), p. 27.

8. Both B. O. Long (*Problem of Etiological Narrative*) and J. Fichtner ("Die etymologische Atiologie in der Namengebung der geschichtlichen Bucher des Alten Testaments," *VT* 6 [1956] 372-96) distinguish between etiologies in which the name precedes the etiology (Form I), and those in which the name follows the etiology (Form II). All the etiologies in 29:31-35 are Form I: (1) the act of naming is narrated in the historical tense by the use of *waw*-conversive prefix form of the verb *qārāʾ;* (2) the etymological explanation with affix verb form follows the name giving itself. Thus v. 32 has (1) "and she named him" *(wattiqrāʾ),* and (2) "for she said" *(kî ʾāmᵉrâ).* What distinguishes vv. 33-35 from v. 32 is that in the former a short statement providing the motivation for the name (e.g., v. 33, "now that Yahweh has heard that I was unloved") precedes (1) and contains a wordplay. Vv. 33 and 34 come close to Form II because of the presence of *ʿal kēn,* the formula introducing Form II etiologies (on which see Long, *Problem of Etiological Narrative,* pp. 54-55).

mean "take heed to, take action on"? There is a bold contrast between the use of "love" in v. 32 *(ʾāhaḇ)* and *unloved (śᵉnûʾâ)* in v. 33. Reuben's birth has not caused a change in Jacob's feelings about Leah. Interestingly, Jacob takes no part in naming the children.

34 Leah names her third child *Levi* (Heb. *lēwî*), for she hopes that her husband *will attach himself* (Heb. *yillāweh*)[9] to her. She has not yet given up on Jacob. Jacob is giving his seed to Leah, but he is not giving his affection to her. One wonders why, given her fecundity, Jacob continues to cohabit with Leah, since he does not love her. He could continue to be married to her without continuing to cohabit with her. The last phrase in v. 35, *she ceased bearing,* may mean that Jacob ceased from sexual activity with Leah, but only after the birth of the fourth child, and then resumed again (according to 30:16ff.).

35 Only with the birth of her fourth son does Leah say nothing about her lamentable situation. She names this child *Judah* (Heb. *yᵉhûḏâ*), and says *I will praise* [*ʾôḏeh*] *Yahweh.* W. F. Albright understood *Judah* as a Hophal jussive of *yāḏâ,* with the divine-name element *-ʾel* (El) represented by the *-â* ending. Thus Judah (perhaps originally Jehudael or Jehudeel) means "may God be praised."[10] Similarly, A. R. Millard suggests that the name is an abbreviation for Jehudjah ("may Yah be praised"), which is the explanation offered in v. 35.[11]

The birth of these last two sons is not without import. Levi, we remember, is the ancestor of the Levitical priests. Moses and Aaron are sons of Levites. From Judah issues the principal line of the monarchy. Two of the major OT institutions — priesthood and kingship — have their origin in an unwanted and unplanned marriage.

9. *lāwâ* (Niphal), "to attach," followed by the preposition *ʿim* refers to attachment between equals (Ps. 83:9 [Eng. 8]); followed by the preposition *ʾel* or *ʿal,* it refers to attachment between nonequals, with one subordinated to the other (Num. 18:2, 4; Isa. 14:1; 56:3; Jer. 50:5; Zech. 2:15). Interestingly, Leah uses *lāwâ ʾel.*

10. W. F. Albright, "The Names 'Israel' and 'Judah' with an Excursus on the Etymology of *Todah* and *Torah,*" *JBL* 46 (1927) 168-78. According to him *yᵉhûḏâ* was probably abbreviated from an original *yᵉhûḏᵉʾēl.* He accounts for the *-â* ending on *yᵉhûḏâ* by arguing that the *qāmeṣ* "is simply the pretonic lengthening of the traditional short *a* vowel, which originated in the influence of the weak largyngeal *ʾalef* upon the preceding *šewă,* giving it an *a* coloring. . . . When hypocoristica were formed from composite names of this type, the clipped imperfects retained the *a* coloring, which was lengthened to *qāmeṣ* under the tone" (pp. 173-74).

11. See A. R. Millard, "The Meaning of the Name Judah," *ZAW* 86 (1974) 216-18. For support Millard appeals to the alternative ways of writing other personal names that end in *-â* and that clearly refer to the same person: *mîḵâ* (2 Chr. 34:20) with *mîḵāyâ* (2 K. 22:12).

G. JACOB GAINS CHILDREN AND FLOCKS (30:1-43)

1. JACOB'S CHILDREN BY BILHAH (30:1-8)

1 *When Rachel saw that she had borne Jacob no children, she became envious of*[1] *her sister. She said to Jacob: "Give me children, or*[2] *I shall die!"*[3]

2 *Jacob, angry with*[4] *Rachel, responded: "Can I take the place of God, who had denied you the fruit of the womb?"*

3 *She said: "Here is my maid Bilhah.*[5] *Go in to her, and let her give birth on my knees, so that I at least may have descendants*[6] *through her!"*

4 *So she gave him her maid Bilhah as concubine,*[7] *and Jacob went in to her.*

5 *Bilhah conceived and bore Jacob a son.*

6 *Rachel said: "God has vindicated me; indeed, he has heard my plea and given me a son." Whereupon she named him Dan.*

7 *Bilhah, Rachel's maid, conceived again and bore a second son to Jacob.*

8 *Rachel said: "I have been entangled in a desperate contest*[8] *with my sister; moreover, I emerged victorious."*[9] *So she named him Naphtali.*

1. For *qānā'* (Piel) *b^e* meaning "to be envious," with a person as the object of that envy, cf. Gen. 37:11; Ps. 37:1; 73:3; Prov. 3:31; 23:17; 24:1, 19.

2. On the use of ellipsis in a clause introduced by *w^e'im 'ayin,* see C. Van Leeuwen, "Die Partikel *'im,*" *OTS* 18 (1973) 30.

3. "Or I shall die" is not an imperfect form of the verb, but a nominal clause consisting of a participle followed by the independent personal pronoun. Such a construction highlights the contrastive nature of v. 1a with v. 1b. See J. Hoftijzer, "The nominal clause reconsidered," *VT* 23 (1973) 501-2.

4. For *hārâ b^e* referring to being angry with a relative cf. Gen. 44:18 (although the brothers do not yet recognize Joseph as their younger brother); 1 Sam. 17:28 (older brother with a younger brother); 1 Sam. 20:30 (father with a son).

5. The etymology of Bilhah is uncertain, but in the Bible non-Israelites have names beginning with Bil-: Bilhan, Gen. 36:27, representing a Horite clan; Balaam (which in Hebrew is Bilam), Num. 22:5; Bildad the Shuhite, Job 2:11. Bil is the Akkadian pronunciation of Baal, but it is not clear if that is the element in these Bil-names.

6. Lit., "I shall be built up." Cf. 16:2; Jer. 31:4.

7. Heb. *'iššâ,* which may be "wife" or "concubine" (as in 16:3).

8. *naptûlê 'ĕlōhîm niptaltî* is notoriously difficult; see the discussion below.

9. Lit., "I have prevailed" *(yāḵōltî).* The same verb is used later in the Jacob narrative after Jacob's own wrestling match: "and you have prevailed" (*wattûḵāl,* 32:29 [Eng. 28]).

1 How the Philistines felt about Isaac's possessions (*qānā',* 26:14) and how Joseph's brothers felt about his dreams (*qānā',* 37:11) parallels how barren Rachel felt about fruitful Leah: *she became envious (qānā').* No mention had been made earlier that Leah envied Rachel's lovely and shapely body, which attracted Jacob. Now, however, Rachel envies Leah's womb. Her inability to bear children she cannot attribute to Jacob, for he has already fathered four children. *Give me children.* Rachel's use of the interjection or imperative *hāḇâ* to Jacob recalls Jacob's use of the same word to Laban in his request for Rachel (29:21). But unlike Jacob's use of *hāḇâ* to introduce a legitimate request (he had completed his seven years of service for Rachel's hand in marriage), Rachel's use of *hāḇâ* introduces an anguished cry. It is ironic that Rachel, who believes she will die if she mothers no children and who is not satisfied with adopted children, dies while trying to mother a second child (35:16-19).[10]

2 Jacob and Rachel do not use finite forms of the verb when they talk to each other. She started (v. 1) with an imperative or interjection ("give") and moved to a nominal clause ("I shall die" is lit. "dying I"). He responded with his own nominal clause, *Can I take the place of God?* (lit., "in place of God[11] I?"). Jacob's question shows that not all clauses which have an interrogative morpheme are functionally interrogative. A rhetorical question, such as Jacob's, is functionally not a request of any kind.[12] Here it is really a rebuke. It is not Jacob who has the power to open and close the womb. He can impregnate, but he cannot play God. Other seemingly insurmountable obstacles he was able to overcome, but not this one.

3 Apparently unable to have her own natural children, Rachel hands over her maid Bilhah to Jacob in the hope that Bilhah will produce adoptive children for Rachel. The expression *let her give birth on my knees* most likely refers to adoption. The same is true of 50:23, "the children of Makir, son of Manasseh, were born on the knees of Joseph."[13] But the use of *knees* by Rachel

10. See A. Brenner, "Female social behaviour: two descriptive patterns within the 'birth of the hero' paradigm," *VT* 36 (1986) 263. This example of irony is sad rather than funny; see idem, "On the Semantic Field of Humour, Laughter, and the Comic in the Old Testament," in *On Humour and the Comic in the Bible,* ed. Y. T. Radday and A. Brenner, JSOTSup 92 (Sheffield: Almond, 1990), p. 41 n. 9.

11. While some evidence points to the traditions about the birth and naming of Jacob's sons being a composite narrative, the presence of *'ĕlōhîm* in v. 2 should not lead one automatically to ascribe v. 2 to E (so, e.g., Jenks, *The Elohist and North Israelite Traditions,* p. 36). Thus Westermann (*Genesis,* 2:4-14), deeply commited to the existence of multiple sources behind Genesis, remarks: "even the Yahwist must use אלהים." For another instance of *haṯaḥaṯ 'ĕlōhîm* with the 1st sing. independent personal pronoun, see 50:19 (Joseph speaking to his brothers).

12. For example, "my brother's keeper I?" (4:9) is not a request. Cf. also 18:17.

13. Cf. Exod. 1:16 and Job 3:12. Cf. also de Vaux, *Ancient Israel,* 1:42-43. For birth on somebody's knees as a symbolic act of adoption (outside the OT) see Diodorus

is special, for the Hebrew word for "knee" *(bereḵ)* is related to the verb "to bless" *(bāraḵ)*. Jacob has the blessing *(b^e rāḵâ)*, and Rachel has the knees *(birkay)*. But Rachel desires, naturally, a little bit of *b^e rāḵâ* on her *birkayim*.

4-6 Jacob raises no question about Rachel's suggestion. He complies and Bilhah becomes pregnant. It seems that everybody except Rachel is able to conceive a child! To add to the hurt, every other wife and concubine of Jacob is bearing him a *son,* not just a child. The preference for sons over daughters in the patriarchal period is indicated by the fact that Dinah is the only child of Jacob whose name the mother does not explain (v. 21).

Rachel, not Bilhah, names the child, for it is Rachel's via adoption. Bilhah functioned only as a surrogate mother. The child is called *Dan,* which is connected with *has vindicated me (dānannî)*. In such a context, the verb *dîn* signifies justice for an individual who finds herself in a heretofore hopeless and helpless state.[14]

7-8 Again Bilhah conceives a child, and this one Rachel names *Naphtali,* which is connected with *I have been entangled in a desperate contest (naptûlê*[15] *'ĕlōhîm*[16] *niptaltî)*. Rachel's experience of wrestling *(pāṯal)* is par-

---

Siculus 4.39; J. Friedrich, "Churritische Märchen und Sagen in hethitischer sprache," *ZA,* N.F. 15 (1950) 221, lines 245ff. An older study of the custom may be found in B. Stade, "Auf jemandes knien gebären," *ZAW* 6 (1886) 143-56.

14. D. Daube, *The Exodus Pattern in the Bible* (London: Faber and Faber, 1963), p. 35. C. Rabin ("Etymological Miscellanea," *Scripta Hierosolymitana* 8 [1961] 389) rejects the connection of *dānannî* with *dîn.* Instead, he connects it with the Arabic root *danâ,* "to be close," and renders the verse "God has been close to me and hath harkened to my voice." While his comments are directed more to *dān yāḏîn ʿammô* in 49:16 ("Dan shall judge his people"), J. A. Emerton ("Some Difficult Words in Genesis 49," in *Words and Meanings: Essays Presented to David Winton Thomas,* ed. P. Ackroyd and B. Lindars [Cambridge: Cambridge University, 1968], pp. 88-91) connects *dîn* (at least in 49:10) with Akk. *danānu,* "to be strong." But in 30:6, translating *dîn* as "God has strengthened me" does not fit well. I see no good reason for not translating *dîn* here with its common meaning "pass a favorable judgment on behalf of, vindicate." See A. Globe, "The Muster of the Tribes in Judges 5:11e-18," *ZAW* 87 (1975) 179.

15. *naptûlê* (from *naptûlîm*) represents one of the few instances of a *naqṭāl* noun in the OT (i.e., one that begins with a prefixed *nun*). GKC, § 85n, cites only this one in Gen. 30:8 and *nāzîḏ* (from *zîḏ*), "boiled pottage" (Gen. 25:29, 34). See also R. Gordis, *The Word and the Book* (New York: Ktav, 1976), p. 320.

16. My translation takes *'ĕlōhîm* not as "God" but as an intensifying epithet. See also Speiser, *Genesis,* pp. 229, 230-31, who renders a "fateful contest" for *naptûlê 'ĕlōhîm* in order to preserve the numinous, supernatural force of *'ĕlōhîm.* See also Westermann, *Genesis,* 2:474, who says that *'ĕlōhîm* must be understood adjectivally. D. W. Thomas ("A Consideration of Some Unusual Ways of Expressing the Superlative in Hebrew," *VT* 3 [1953] 218) does state, however: "In the O.T. it is, I believe, difficult, if not impossible, to point to any unambiguous example of the use of the divine name as an intensifying epithet and nothing more." He also notes (p. 214) that *'ĕlōhîm* occurs in 30:8 in a context that is too obscure to permit definite conclusions about its function there. Among the

allel to Jacob's forthcoming experience of wrestling (*'ābaq,* 32:25, 26 [Eng. 24, 25]). The basic meaning behind the verb *pātal* is "to be crafty, wily" (Ps. 18:27 [Eng. 26]; Job 5:13). In Prov. 8:8 the word means "twisted" and is parallel with *'eqqēš,* "crooked." Thus the related noun *pātîl* comes to refer to a cord or rope, which is formed by twisting together strands.

The phrase *naptûlê 'ĕlōhîm* could be translated as "divine wrestling match" or "God's fight" (JB), which takes *'ĕlōhîm* as "God." Thus Fokkelman renders, "twists of God I have twisted (in the fight) with Leah, but I have prevailed."[17] That is, Rachel's struggle with Leah has actually been a struggle with God and for his favor, for Rachel knows well that it is God who has closed her womb and opened Leah's. F. I. Andersen offers another way of reading *'ĕlōhîm* as "God" here: "I wrestled (with) God/With my sister I did succeed."[18]

In addition to Rachel's wrestling paralleling Jacob's wrestling, chs. 30 and 32 have another motif in common. Rachel wrestled and prevailed *(yākōltî,* "I emerged victorious"). Jacob also fought with Elohim, and he too prevailed *(tûkāl,* 32:29 [Eng. 28]). The "man," however, did not prevail *(yākōl,* 32:26 [Eng. 25]) against Jacob.

2. JACOB'S CHILDREN BY ZILPAH (30:9-13)

9 *When Leah saw that she had ceased bearing, she took her maid Zilpah and gave her to Jacob as concubine.*[1]

10 *Zilpah, Leah's maid, bore Jacob a son.*

11 *Leah said: "Fortune has come!"*[2] *So she named him Gad.*

12 *Zilpah, Leah's maid, bore Jacob a second son.*

---

modern English translations, most read *'ĕlōhîm* as an adjective: "great wrestlings" (KJV, NKJV); "mighty wrestlings" (RSV); "a great struggle" (NIV); "a fine trick" (NEB); "a fateful struggle" (NAB); "a fateful contest" (NJPS). Only JB reads it as a noun: "I have fought God's fight with my sister."

17. Fokkelmann, *Narrative Art in Genesis,* p. 135.

18. F. I. Andersen, "Note on Gen 30:8," *JBL* 88 (1969) 200. He understands the first word *naptûlê* as a Niphal infinitive absolute of *pātal* (which in the sing. would normally be *hippātōl* or *niptōl*). He then reads *naptôlî* (with the terminal *-î* as an archaism) for MT *naptûlê.* W. L. Moran ("The Hebrew Language in Its Northwest Semitic Background," in *The Bible and the Ancient Near East: Essays in Honor of William Foxwell Albright,* ed. G. E. Wright [Garden City, NY: Doubleday, 1965], p. 70) made a similar suggestion by repointing *naptûlê* to *niptôlî.*

1. As noted in v. 4 above, *'iššâ* can mean either wife or concubine.

2. The Ketib *bāgad* is supported by Vulg. and LXX. The Qere *bā' gād,* which is followed here, was accepted as early as Symm., Targ. Onqelos, and Targ. Pseudo-Jonathan. Cf. *BHS*; and F. I. Andersen and A. D. Forbes, *Spelling in the Hebrew Bible,* BibOr 41 (Rome: Biblical Institute, 1986), p. 86.

13 *Leah said: "My blessedness has come!*[3] *Now the women*[4] *will count me blessed."*[5] *So she named him Asher.*

Jacob fathers his seventh and eighth children by Leah's maid Zilpah. Again, as in the previous verses, a catch phrase in the adoptive mother's mouth is then connected with the proper name. The first of these two children is called *Gad* (Heb. *gāḏ*), because Leah said *Luck has come!* (Heb. *bā' gāḏ,* "luck has come," or *bāgāḏ,* "with luck").[6] The second child is called *Asher* (Heb. *'āšēr*), because *the women will count me blessed* (Heb. *'iššᵉrûnî*).[7] One may compare Leah's words with Mary's words in her NT canticle: "from now on all generations will call me blessed" (Luke 1:48). The major difference between the two is that Leah speaks of "the women" (LXX A "all the women," *pásai hai gynaíkes*), while Mary speaks of "all generations" *(pásai hai geneaí).* This emphasis on "all generations" calling Mary blessed implies an unusual respect for Mary as the mother of the Lord.[8] The event being celebrated in this song is significant for "all generations," an emphasis that provides some preparation for Luke 1:50 and 55.[9] All women will deem Leah fortunate because of the child Asher whom she brings forth. But all generations will deem Mary fortunate because of the child she will bring forth, a child who will bring salvation to all the nations.

3. *bᵉ'ošrî* represents *bā' 'ošrî,* as in Symm. and Targ. Onqelos. Cf. W. G. E. Watson, "More on Shared Consonants," *Bib* 52 (1971) 46; *BHS.*

4. Lit., "daughters." As Gordis has pointed out (*Poets, Prophets, and Sages* [Bloomington: Indiana University, 1971], p. 395 n. 113), *baṯ* is not always restricted to the specific family relationship (he cites Gen. 30:13; Isa. 32:9; Prov. 31:29); in places one should translate *baṯ* as "women" or "girls."

5. GKC, § 106n, cites *'iššᵉrûnî* of v. 13 as the perfect used to express a fact that is imminent, and therefore, to the imagination of the speaker, already accomplished. See also J. W. Watts, *A Survey of Syntax in the Hebrew Old Testament* (Grand Rapids: Eerdmans, 1964), p. 39.

6. J. Tigay ("Israelite Religion," in *Ancient Israelite Religion: Essays in Honor of Frank Moore Cross,* ed. P. D. Miller, Jr., P. Hanson, and S. D. McBride [Philadelphia: Fortress, 1987], pp. 163, 167, 185 n. 39) provides extrabiblical references to *gaḏ,* which was sometimes personified as the genius or fortune of an individual (i.e., a semidivine being or spirit). Cf. the personal name Gaddiel in Num. 13:10. See also J. Teixidor, *The Pagan God: Popular Religion in the Greco-Roman Near East* (Princeton: Princeton University, 1977), pp. 159-60. In contrast, *gāḏ* in Gen. 30:11 is only a common name. Cf. O. Eissfeldt, "Gut Glück!' in Semitischer Namengebung," *JBL* 82 (1963) 195-200, esp. 199-200.

7. On *'āšar, 'ešer, 'āšār,* and *'ōšer* see G. Bertram and F. Hauck, *"makários," TDNT,* 4:364-70; H. Cazelles, *"'ašrê," TDOT,* 1:445-48.

8. See J. A. Fitzmyer, *The Gospel According to Luke,* AB, 2 vols. (Garden City, NY: Doubleday, 1981-85), 1:367; R. E. Brown, *The Birth of the Messiah* (Garden City, NY: Doubleday, 1977), p. 360 n. 62.

9. See R. C. Tannehill, "The Magnificat as Poem," *JBL* 93 (1974) 272.

3. LEAH BEARS MORE CHILDREN TO JACOB (30:14-21)

14 *One day, at the time of the wheat harvest, Reuben chanced upon some mandrakes in the field and he brought them to Leah his mother. Rachel said to Leah: "Please give me some of your son's mandrakes."*

15 *She said to her:*[1] *"Was your taking*[2] *my husband not enough,*[3] *and would you also take my son's mandrakes?" Rachel responded: "Alright,*[4] *he may sleep with*[5] *you for the night in exchange for your son's mandrakes."*

16 *That evening, when Jacob returned from the field, Leah went out to meet him: "You must come in with me because I have hired you with my son's mandrakes." Thus he slept with her that night.*

17 *God heard Leah, and she conceived, and bore Jacob a fifth son.*

18 *Leah said: "God has given me my wage for having let my husband have my maid." So she named him Issachar.*[6]

19 *Leah conceived again and bore to Jacob a sixth son.*

20 *Leah said: "God has given me, even me, a valuable gift. Now my husband will exalt me, for I have borne him six sons." So she named him Zebulun.*

21 *Afterward she bore a daughter, and named her Dinah.*

14-16 During the time of wheat harvest (March or April) Reuben, Leah's firstborn, finds some mandrakes out in the fields. *Mandrakes* (Heb. *dûḏā'îm*) grow all over Israel. There is no stalk, but large leaves fan out from the root at ground level. In the midst of these leaves appear violet flowers and yellow fruit. This fruit, which looks like a tomato, ripens in March and April, and emits a very distinct odor (see Cant. 7:14 [Eng. 13]).[7]

1. LXX has *Leia,* "Leah," apparently reading Heb. *l'h* instead of MT *lh,* "to her."

2. *qaḥtēḵ* illustrates the use of the infinitive construct as the nominative of the subject (lit., "not a little [is] your taking my husband"). See GKC, § 114a.

3. For *me'aṯ* with the interrogative see Num. 16:9-10, 13; Josh. 22:17-18; Isa. 7:13; Ezek. 34:18.

4. For *lāḵēn* used to introduce the reaction of somebody to the words of another person, see B. Jongeling, "*Lāḵēn* dans l'Ancien Testament," *OTS* 21 (1981) 193.

5. H. M. Orlinsky ("The Hebrew Root *ŠKB,*" *JBL* 63 [1944] 21) shows that *šāḵaḇ 'im* describes both a legal sexual act (Gen. 30:15, 16; 2 Sam. 11:11) and an illicit one (Deut. 27:20-23), and that both *šāḵaḇ 'im* (Gen. 30:15, 16) and *šāḵaḇ 'eṯ* (Lev. 15:18, 24) may describe a licit sexual act between man and wife. This suggests that the two expressions are interchangeable.

6. The Ketib of Issachar is *yiśśa(ś)ḵār,* with a second quiescent second *ś,* for which see GKC, § 17c; J. M. Sasson, "Love's Roots: On the Redaction of Genesis 30:14-24," in *Love and Death in the Ancient Near East: Essays in Honor of Marvin H. Pope,* ed. J. H. Marks and R. M. Good (Guilford, CT: Four Quarters, 1987), p. 206 n. f.

7. See H. N. and A. L. Moldenke, *Plants of the Bible* (Waltham, MA: Chronica Botanice, 1952) pp. 137-39, no. 132.

Its relationship to *dôḏ,* "lover," and *dôḏîm,* "love," has evoked legends about the aphrodisiac properties of the fruit so that even to the present a popular name for the fruit of the herb is "love apples."[8] Rachel seems to believe that the possession of these will bring about fertility. Vv. 22-24 make it clear, however, that Rachel's ability to bear a child are due to God, not to the mandrakes.

Jacob has yet to say a word. Returning from the field he finds that he has been hired by Leah to sleep with her that night. First he was hired by Laban, and now he is hired by a woman who has already borne him four children. He raises no questions about Leah's arrangement with Rachel. The narrator emphasizes Leah's right to spend the night with Jacob by using the infinitive absolute before the cognate verb: *śāḵōr śᵉḵartîḵā,* "hiring, I have hired you."

He consents and sleeps with Leah for the night. That Leah *hired (śāḵar)* Jacob rather than "bought" him indicates that this is a temporary arrangement.[9]

The account of Esau giving the birthright to Jacob has some similarities to Leah giving the mandrakes to Rachel.[10] Both start with a son (Esau, Reuben) returning from the field. In both a situation has reached a desperate point: Esau's hunger and Rachel's infertility. The donor (Jacob, Leah) receive something substantial in return for their gift (soup, mandrakes). Jacob receives the birthright and Leah is allowed to have intercourse with Jacob. Perhaps Jacob is unable to reprimand Leah for exploiting her bargaining power because he himself had once done the same.

17-18 The fifth son Leah bares to Jacob she calls *Issachar* (Qere *yiśśāḵār;* Ketib *yiśśā(ś)ḵār*). The repetition of the *s* in the MT supports the Ketib. The Ketib is then divided into *yš śkr* ("man of [or who is] [my] reward"),[11] or "man of hire." Leah states that God has given her Issachar as *my wage (śāḵār)* in return for Leah giving her maid to Jacob. This idea reminds us of Ps. 127:3, "sons are a heritage from Yahweh, the fruit of the womb a reward [*śāḵār*]."

19-20 Leah gives birth to a sixth son and names him *Zebulun*

8. M. H. Pope, *Song of Songs,* AB (Garden City, NY: Doubleday, 1977), pp. 647-50.

9. See Daube, *Studies in Biblical Law,* pp. 16-24. Daube observes the distinction in Roman law between A hiring B to C *(locatio conductio rei)* and A hiring A to B *(locatio conductio operarum).* Rachel hiring Jacob to Leah illustrates the first. Jacob indenturing himself to Laban for seven years illustrates the second. See also Daube's comments on the rabbinic interpretation of "he may sleep with you for the night" in "The Night of Death," *HTR* 61 (1968) 629-32.

10. See S. Ben-Reuven, "Buying Mandrakes as Retribution for Buying the Birthright," *Beth Mikra* 28 (1982/83) 230-31 (Hebrew).

11. See C. D. Isbell, "Initial 'Alef-Yod Interchange and Selected Biblical Passages," *JNES* 37 (1978) 229. Isbell correctly notes the expression *yēš śāḵār* in 2 Chr. 15:7, "there is a reward," and this may indeed be the meaning of Issachar.

(zᵉḇulûn). Her explanation is that *God has given me, even me, a valuable gift (zᵉḇāḏanî ʾĕlōhîm ʾōṯî zēḇeḏ ṭôḇ),* and *my husband will exalt me (yizbᵉlēnî ʾîšî)*. Zebulun is based on the root *zbl,* not on the root *zbd.*[12] As a verb, *zāḇal* occurs only here in the Hebrew Bible. On the basis of the use of the root elsewhere in the OT (1 K. 8:13 par. 2 Chr. 6:2; Ps. 49:15 [Eng. 14]; Isa. 63:15; Hab. 3:11), all of which have to do with an "exalted abode,"[13] and on the basis of the use of the root in Ugaritic ("prince, royalty"), one may posit a meaning such as "exalt, elevate."[14]

21 Unlike the sons, *Dinah* is given no etymology. Although some commentators regard this brief mention as unoriginal or as an afterthought, it seems more likely that it is preparatory for ch. 34.[15] The inclusion of Dinah also means that Leah's children reach the optimal number of seven.[16]

4. RACHEL GIVES BIRTH TO JOSEPH (30:22-24)

22 *God remembered Rachel. He heard her and opened her womb.*

23 *She conceived*[1] *and gave birth to a son, saying: "God has removed my reproach."*

12. But if one accepts two etymologies for Zebulun (*zaḇaḏ,* "give, endow, bestow"; *zāḇal,* "exalt"), then they are the result of a blending of two literary traditions or were produced by two different writers altogether, with an approximate etymology followed by a precise etymology. See Y. Zakovitch, "A Study of Precise and Partial Derivations in Biblical Etymology," *JSOT* 15 (1980) 31-32. There are instances of personal names in (and outside) the OT formed from the verb *zāḇaḏ,* for example, Zabdiel ("gift of God/El," not "God/El is my gift"), the father of one of David's officers (1 Chr. 27:2), or an overseer in Nehemiah's time (Neh. 11:17). See S. C. Layton, *Archaic Features of Canaanite Personal Names in the Hebrew Bible,* HSM 47 (Atlanta: Scholars, 1990), pp. 142-45. Barr ("Etymology and the Old Testament," *OTS* 19 [1974] 26) cites the use of the roots *zbd* and *zbl* in Gen. 30:20 to suggest that etymology was a play on word similarity, rather than a serious analysis of root meanings; thus *zbd* and *zbl* were close enough for their one consonant difference not to matter.

13. Ps. 49:15 (Eng. 14) is a *crux interpretum* that many commentators consider hopelessly corrupt (see, e.g., A. A. Anderson, *Psalms,* NCBC, 2 vols. [Grand Rapids: Eerdmans, repr. 1981], 1:379). Cf. J. Gamberoni, *"zᵉbhul," TDOT,* 4:29-31; R. B. Coote, "Sibyl: 'Oracle,'" *JNWSL* 5 (1977) 7 n. 28; P. Bordeuil, *"mizzĕbul lô:* à propos de Psaume 49:15," in *Ascribe to the Lord,* Fest. P. Craigie, ed. L. Eslinger and G. Taylor, JSOTSup 67 (Sheffield: JSOT, 1988), pp. 95-98.

14. See M. Held, "The Root *ZBL/SBL* in Akkadian, Ugaritic and Biblical Hebrew," *JAOS* 88 (1968) 90-91.

15. Cf. von Rad, *Genesis,* p. 295, who calls it an afterthought; Skinner, *Genesis,* p. 389, who thinks that an interpolator added it "with a view to ch. 34"; Westermann, *Genesis,* 2:476, who attributes it to a glossator, perhaps in preparation for ch. 34.

16. Sasson, "Love's Roots," p. 206 n. i.

1. In the LXX a participle (here, *syllaboúsa*) is frequently used where two Hebrew

24 *She named him Joseph, and said: "Yahweh shall add*[2] *to me another son."*

God remembered Noah (8:1) and now he remembers Rachel.[3] He heeded Rachel, as he had Leah (v. 17), and he opened her womb, as he had Leah's (29:31). Rachel names the child *Joseph (yôsēp̱).* She precedes the naming with *God has removed* [*'āsap̱*] *my reproach.* She follows the naming with *Yahweh shall add* [*yōsēp̱*] *to me another son.*

Most writers have suggested a double etymology for *Joseph* on the basis of Rachel's comments.[4] Her words in v. 23b are attributed to E (note the use of *'ĕlōhîm*), which connects Joseph with *'āsap̱,* "to gather, remove." Hence the name means "he has removed" or "he will remove." Rachel's words in v. 24b are attributed to J (note the use of Yahweh), which connects Joseph with *yāsap̱,* "he will add" or "may he add."[5] But one need not resort to this explanation; the structure here is parallel to that of vv. 19-20: (a) conception; (b) birth of a son; (c) an initial comment by the mother that contains one word that is close in sound to the name; (d) the naming of the child; (e) an explanation of the meaning of the name. Thus, while Rachel's use of *'āsap̱* in v. 23 and *yāsap̱* in v. 24 undeniably involves a pun, one need not conclude that vv. 23-24 arc rival etymologies for the name Joseph.

In using a pun, Rachel addresses both the shame of her present condition — "God has removed my reproach"[6] — which God has now rectified,

verbs in successive coordinate clauses describe the same activity. See A. Aejmelaeus, "*Participium coniunctum* as a criterion of translation technique," *VT* 32 (1982) 390.

2. The verb may equally well be translated as an optative: "May Yahweh add to me another son."

3. B. S. Childs (*Memory and Tradition in Israel,* SBT 1/37 [Naperville, IL: Allenson, 1962], p. 41) observes that the phrase "God remembers," which employs a finite verb in the 3rd person, had its original context within the structure of a hymn in which the object of God's remembrance is his covenant people. Especially in the early prose narratives, as in Gen. 30:22, the object of God's memory is occasionally a single individual.

4. E.g., Westermann, *Genesis,* 2:476; Speiser, *Genesis,* p. 232; Sarna, *Genesis,* p. 210; Jenks, *The Elohist and North Israelite Traditions,* p. 36.

5. Y. Zakovitch (*JSOT* 15 [1980] 32) accepts the duplicate derivation but does not trace that to E and J. In fact, he suggests that the original account is that in v. 23b. Cf. also E. C. B. MacLaurin, "Joseph and Asaph," *VT* 25 (1975) 30. For MacLaurin v. 24b has to be anachronistic, for it contains the tetragrammaton, which according to Exod. 6:2 was first revealed to Moses.

6. The only other place in the OT where *ḥerpâ* ("reproach") is used by a woman/women to describe a condition of shame or reproach brought on by barrenness is Isa. 4:1 (also with the verb *'āsap̱*). Due to the loss of males in wartime the female population greatly outnumbers the male population. Accordingly, says the prophet, "seven women shall take hold of one man in that day, saying, '. . . take away our reproach,'" (*'ĕsōp̱ ḥerpāṯēnû*).

and her hope for the future — "Yahweh shall add/may Yahweh add to me another son." Any mention of the mandrakes is conspicuously absent from Rachel's words. Instead, both of her sentences focus exclusively on her perception of the work of God in her life and her womb.

5. JACOB'S POSSESSIONS MULTIPLY (30:25-43)

25 *After Rachel had given birth to Joseph, Jacob said to Laban: "Allow me to leave*[1] *and go to my own homeland.*

26 *Give me*[2] *my wives, and my children, for whom*[3] *I have served you, that I may leave. You are fully aware of the service I have rendered you."*

27 *Laban said: "If you will permit me,*[4] *I have grown rich,*[5] *for Yahweh*[6]

1. D. Daube (*The Exodus Pattern in the Bible* [London: Faber and Faber, 1963], pp. 29 n. 11, 34, 64, 79) points to the frequent use of *šillaḥ,* "to dismiss, let leave," as legal terminology in the Exodus story, and points to the similarity of the Israelites and Jacob that they be allowed to leave and return to their homeland.

2. The Palestinian Targ. supplies *lî.* This is admittedly meager textual evidence to support an original reading of "to me"; yet all modern verisons read "give to me" or "let me have." "Me" must be inserted in English; "give my wives and my children" would be awkward.

3. The pronominal suffix in *bāhēn* (here and in v. 37) is fem. but has masc. antecedents. Cf. Ruth 1:13; Job 24:5. The choice of the fem. is probably due to the fact that Jacob served fourteen years for his wives (although the pl. of *'iššâ* has a masc. form: *nāšîm*), not for his children, and thus the antecedent of *bāhēn* is Leah and Rachel.

4. Lit., "if, pray, I have found favor in your eyes"; for the idiomatic rendering of this phrase as "if you will permit me" (cf. NJPS "if you will indulge me") as an introduction to the speaker's forthcoming words, see Ehrlich, *Randglossen,* 1:148. The expression is used normally by a subordinate to or about one in authority over him or in a more powerful position (thus Jacob to Esau, 32:6 [Eng. 5]; 33:8, 10, 15; Joseph to Potiphar, 39:4; David to Saul, 1 Sam. 16:22; David to Achish, 1 Sam. 27:5; Joab to David, 2 Sam. 14:22; Ziba to David, 2 Sam. 16:4; Hadad to Pharaoh, 1 K. 11:19). It is used by a woman to or about a man (Deut. 24:1; Ruth 2:2, 10, 13; 1 Sam. 1:18; Est. 5:8; 7:3), but never by a man to or about a woman. It is unusual for a father-in-law, employer, or uncle to use this expression when he speaks to his son-in-law, employee, or nephew, respectively (but cf. Gen. 47:29, where Jacob uses this phrase when he talks to Joseph).

5. Some translations have "I have learned by divination" (e.g., RSV, NIV, NAB; cf. JB); so also many commentators, e.g., Speiser, *Genesis,* pp. 234, 236; von Rad, *Genesis,* pp. 297, 300; Westermann, *Genesis,* 2:478. Cf. AV "I have learned by experience." See the commentary below. Targ. Onqelos read the verb as "I have divined/learned by divination" and, to avoid the idea that Yahweh would guide Laban while he practiced the forbidden rites of divination, substituted "I have learned through testing" *(nsyty).*

6. Most ancient versions read "Elohim" instead of "Yahweh"; the former is expected from a foreigner and non-Yahwist. But there is no good reason to change "Yahweh" to "Elohim." Laban will be able to make a stronger case by using the name of Jacob's God.

has blessed me[7] *because of you.*

28 *Name*[8] *your wage before me," he said, "and I will pay."*

29 *He answered: "You, you know how I served you, and furthermore how your livestock fared with me.*

30 *However little you had before I came, now it has increased*[9] *abundantly, since Yahweh has blessed you wherever I turned.*[10] *And now I, I myself, must provide for my own household."*

31 *"What should I pay you?" Laban said. Jacob answered: "You need pay me nothing at all. If you do for me this one thing, I shall again*[11] *pasture and guard*[12] *your flock.*

32 *Let me go*[13] *through your entire flock today, and remove from there*

7. For the imperfect with *waw (wayᵉḇārᵃḵēnî),* see GKC, § 111h n. 2 (it arises from the "pregnant brevity of expression: *I have observed and* have come to the conclusion, *the Lord hath blessed me*"), § 120f ("the natural complement of the first verb is . . . added immediately after in the form of an historical statement. . . . *I have divined, and the Lord hath blessed me*").

8. MT *nāqᵉḇâ* is a Qal energic imperative of *nāqaḇ,* hence "name" (RSV, NIV, JB), "appoint" (AV). A repointing to *niqbâ* produces a Niphal precative perfect of *qāḇâ.* See M. J. Dahood, "The Ugaritic Parallel Pair *qra//qba* in Isaiah 62,2," *Bib* 58 (1977) 527-28. Thus v. 28 reads "let your wages be stated before me" instead of "name/designate your wages." But retaining MT presents no problem, reading the verbal form as an imperative of *nāqaḇ,* meaning "designate," as in Num. 1:17. Cf. B. A. Levine, *Numbers 1–20,* AB (New York: Doubleday, 1993), p. 139.

9. The basic meaning of *pāraṣ* is "to break." The shades of meaning range from "break out, burst out" (*pāraṣ ʿal,* Gen. 38:29); "break down" (Isa. 5:5); "break into" (*pāraṣ ʾet,* 2 Chr. 24:7); "break up, break in pieces," 2 Chr. 20:37); "break open" (Job 28:4); to here, "break over" *(pāraṣ lᵉ),* i.e., "break over (limits), increase." God used the verb earlier in a promise to Jacob at Bethel (Gen. 28:14).

10. Lit., "to/according to my foot" *(lᵉraḡlî).* BDB, p. 919, renders "at one's foot, i.e., at every step." For another understanding of this idiom, "God blessed you because of me," see M. Weinfeld, *Deuteronomy 1–11,* AB (New York: Doubleday, 1991), pp. 360, 444. In this case *lᵉraḡlî* of v. 30 functions like *biḡlāleḵā* of v. 27.

11. For *šûḇ* as an auxiliary verb and translated as "again" to repeat the action of the accompanying verb, see W. L. Holladay, *The Root Šûbh in the Old Testament* (Leiden: Brill, 1958), pp. 66-72.

12. For *šāmar* used with a the shepherd guarding or tending sheep see 1 Sam. 17:20, 28; Hos. 12:13 (Eng. 12). The sheep are entrusted to the custody and care of the shepherd.

13. MT reads as a 1st person imperfect *(ʾeʿĕḇōr),* "I will pass through" (so AV; cf. RSV, NEB, JB). Vulg., followed by some modern translations (e.g., NIV, NAB), reads as an imperative *(ʿᵃḇōr).* This reading balances the second imperative in the sentence, "remove" *(hāsēr).* V. 35 may be thought to confirm this interpretation, for the subject of "remove" in v. 35 is Laban. See A. Gai, "The Reduction of the Tense (and Other Categories) of the Consequent Verb in North-West Semitic," *Or* 51 (1982) 255, who suggests, convincingly, retention of the MT. Gai reads *hāsēr* as a Hiphil infinitive absolute of *sûr* (written the same as the Hiphil imperative), and believes this to be an instance of an infinitive having the value of a conjugated verb, and following another fully conjugated

every speckled and spotted animal, that is,[14] *every black lamb, and the spotted and speckled among the goats; such shall be my wage.*

33 *In the future,*[15] *whenever you go over*[16] *these wages of mine, my righteousness will answer*[17] *for me: any unspeckled and unspotted among the goats, and any not black among the lambs with me may be counted as stolen."*

34 *"Agreed," said Laban, "Let it indeed*[18] *be as you suggest."*

35 *He removed that day the he-goats that were striped and spotted and all the she-goats that were speckled and spotted, all those with some white on them, as well as the lambs that were black, and put them in charge of his sons.*

36 *And he put a three days' distance*[19] *between himself and Jacob. Jacob, meanwhile, tended the remainder of Laban's flock.*

37 *Then Jacob took fresh shoots of poplar, almond, and plane trees, and peeled*[20] *in them white stripes, exposing the white of the shoots.*

38 *He set upright the rods he had peeled in the watering troughs*[21] *— the*

---

verb whose tense it assumes. Gai cites Gen. 41:43, Judg. 7:19 (past); Gen. 30:32; Jer. 32:44 (future); Isa. 37:30 (imperative) for illustration of this phenomenon.

14. The *waw* is a *waw explicativum. śeh* ("animal") includes both *keśāḇîm* ("lambs") and *ʿizzîm* ("goats").

15. *māḥār* means "tomorrow" more often than not; but here it means "later, in the future," a deferred *hayyôm.* See DeVries, *Yesterday, Today and Tomorrow,* pp. 282-84, esp. 283 n. 5; Weinfeld, *Deuteronomy 1–11,* p. 347.

16. The phrase *bôʾ ʿal* with the meaning of "go over, check" is unique to this verse. Elsewhere the phrase refers to sexual activity (Gen. 19:31; Deut. 25:5); in a military sense, "to advance against" (Gen. 34:27; Deut. 28:2; 2 K. 7:6; Isa. 10:28); to enter a room that contains a dead body (Lev. 21:11; Num. 6:6); to bring judgment (Josh. 23:15).

17. On the force of the LXX *epaukoúō* for "answer" see J. Barr, "The Meaning of *epakouō* and Cognates in the LXX," *JTS* 31 (1980) 68.

18. See C. F. Whitely, "Some Remarks on *lû* and *loʾ*," *ZAW* 87 (1975) 203. *lû* is normally used to express a wish or a desire ("would that"), but in a few places it means "verily, indeed." See also *UT,* p. 76, § 9.16.

19. On *dereḵ* meaning "distance" see A. Hurvitz, *A Linguistic Study of the Relationship Between the Priestly Source and the Book of Ezekiel* (Paris: Gabalda, 1982), p. 94 n. 119.

20. *pāṣal* occurs only here and in v. 38 in the entire OT. It has shown up in Ugaritic in the phrase *adm banšt npẓl,* "the man from the infirmity is peeled"; see F. Saracino, "Ras Ibn Hani 78/20 and some Old Testament connections," *VT* 32 (1982) 341. This text appears to be a ritual of exorcism in which Baal was sought to drive out demon-flies that were the cause of impotency. This last line of the ritual might refer to some gesture of peeling some objects, thus inducing the revival of sexual potency. R. Yaron (*Introduction to the Law of the Aramaic Papyri* [Oxford: Clarendon, 1961], p. 90) connects the verb with Aram. *paṣṣel,* "to clean."

21. *rᵒhāṭîm* is used again in v. 41 and in Exod. 2:16 to refer to gutters or troughs into

watering troughs[22] *to which the flocks came to drink — in front of the flocks. When they were in heat*[23] *as they came to drink,*

39 *the flocks mated by the rods and they brought forth streaked, speckled, and spotted young.*

40 *The lambs Jacob kept separate, and he set the flock in the direction of the streaked and all the black in Laban's flock. Thus he produced for himself special flocks, which he did not mingle with Laban's flocks.*

41 *Whenever the stronger*[24] *animals were in heat,*[25] *Jacob would set the rods in the troughs in full view of the flock so that they mated*[26] *by the rods.*

42 *But with the feebler animals he would not place*[27] *them there. So it was that the feeble ones went to Laban, and the stronger ones to Jacob.*

43 *Thus the man became exceedingly prosperous, and he owned large flocks, maidservants, manservants, camels, and asses.*

25-26 Rachel's successful delivery of Joseph signals to Jacob that it is time for him and his retinue to head back to Canaan. He does not inform Laban that he is leaving; rather, he asks Laban for permission to leave and also asks that his wives and children be given to him. Three times in v. 26 Jacob uses the root *ʿbd* ("I have served you," *ʿāḇaḏtî;* "the service," *ʿăḇōḏāṯî;* "I have

---

which or through which the water flows for watering the flocks. In Cant. 7:6, which compares the lady's hair to the action of moving water, it means "tresses" (Pope, *Song of Songs,* p. 630).

22. GKC, § 95f, describes *šiqăṯôṯ* as an abnormal formation from the sg. *šōqeṯ.*

23. For the verb form *wayyēḥamnâ* (from *ḥāmam*) as an illustration of an archaic *yiqṭōlnâ* 3rd fem. pl. (with preformative *y-*) see GKC, § 47k; R. Gordis, *The Word and the Book* (New York: Ktav, 1976), p. 267 n. 9; R. Ratner, "Does a *t-* preformative third person plural verbal form exist in Biblical Hebrew?" *VT* 38 (1988) 87.

24. "Stronger" in v. 41 is the Pual participle (fem. pl.) of *qāšar (hamquššārôṯ),* while "stronger" in v. 42 is the Qal passive participle (masc. pl.) of *qāšar (haqqešurîm).* The basic meaning of *qāšar* is "bind, conspire, knit together." The passive participle means "well-knit," i.e., vigorous or stronger.

25. Verses 38 and 39 use the verb *ḥāmam* for "to be in heat, mate," while v. 41 twice uses the verb *yāḥam* for "to be in heat, mate." These verbs overlap in meaning; the only difference between them is that the former can also have a broader sense ("be warm"), while the latter occurs exclusively in the OT to mean either "be in heat" (30:41 [twice]; 31:10) or "conceive" (as a result or consequence of being in heat) (Ps. 51:7 [Eng. 5]). On the latter see G. Fohrer, "Twofold aspects of Hebrew Words," in *Words and Meanings: Essays Presented to David Winton Thomas* (Cambridge: Cambridge University, 1968), p. 101.

26. On the unusual 3rd fem. pl. pronominal suffix *-ēnâ* on *leyaḥhemēnâ* see GKC, § 91f.

27. The frequentative nature of Jacob's actions in vv. 41 and 42 is expressed by the use of *wehāyâ* plus perfect and *waw (weśām)* plus imperfect and *waw (û . . . lō' yāśîm).* See GKC, § 112ee.

rendered you," *ʿaḇadtîḵā*) to remind Laban that he has served his father-in-law. When has Jacob fulfilled his terms of the arrangement?

27-28 Laban responds graciously with *If you will permit me . . .* (lit., "if I have found favor in your eyes"). Fourteen years earlier Leah's eyes were mentioned; now Jacob's eyes are mentioned. Laban readily admits that he has grown rich and that he is blessed of Yahweh because of Jacob. This is one instance of a fulfillment of God's word to Abraham in 12:3, "and in you all the nations of the earth shall be blessed."

I have grown rich. As noted above, Heb. *niḥaštî* has often been translated as "I have learned by divination." Passages such as Gen. 44:5, 15 demonstrate that "to divine" is a legitimate translation of this verb. There is one major problem with that rendering here. Divination is a device by which one gains knowledge about the future, not about the past.[28] Laban could have pinpointed Jacob as the cause of his blessing only through some such medium as a dream or a vision, neither of which is covered by *nāḥaš.* The translation *I have grown rich* is obtained by taking *niḥaštî* as cognate with Akk. *naḫāšu,* "to flourish, prosper."[29] To be blessed by Yahweh means to be enriched. Thus Laban is, to a degree, Deuteronomic in his theology; that is, he attributes his material prosperity to Jacob's God. His statement is un-Deuteronomic in the sense that his prosperity, by his own admission, is not a divine reward for his own virtue but is due solely to the presence of Jacob in his home.[30]

29-30 Jacob had asked for his wives and children. Laban ignored that request and instead focused on wages (v. 28). Jacob repeats what Laban has just said. Indeed, Laban has grown properous because of Jacob and Yahweh. By playing off *m*ᵉ*ʿaṭ (however little)* against *rōḇ (abundantly),* Jacob emphasizes his own indispensable role in Laban's reversal from rags to riches.

31-34 Jacob requests no wages, except the following. Jacob (or Laban) is to remove from Laban's flocks dark-colored sheep and variegated goats (v. 32).[31] In the Mediterranean world the sheep are normally white and

28. See G. Ch. Aalders, *Genesis,* 2:122.

29. See the lengthy note in J. J. Finkelstein, "An Old Babylonian Herding Contract and Genesis 31:38f," *JAOS* 88 (1968) 34 n. 19.

30. The concept of God blessing A because of B (and not because of any virtue in A) is found also in Deut. 9:1-5. There Yahweh reminds his people through Moses that he is not giving them the land because of their own righteousness but because of the wickedness of the nations already living there, and because of the promises he made to Abraham, Isaac, and Jacob. For such an un-Deuteronomic concept in Deuteronomy, see J. Gammie, "The Theology of Retribution in the Book of Deuteronomy," *CBQ* 32 (1970) 11.

31. For a discussion of the color *ḥûm* ("black, dark brown") and the terms *nāqōḏ*

the goats black. Thus Jacob is requesting the irregular, abnormal parts of Laban's flock.

If Laban discovers, subsequently, any monochrome goats or white sheep/lambs among Jacob's flocks, he can be sure that Jacob stole them (v. 33). Although the root *gnb* ("steal")[32] was not used in chs. 25 and 27, in a sense Jacob did steal the birthright and blessing from Esau. But what he did with Esau, he claims he will not do with Laban — *my righteousness* [or integrity, honesty; Heb. *ṣ*ᵉ*ḏāqâ*] *will answer for me.* If Laban had only known Jacob's earlier capabilities for dishonesty, perhaps he would not have been so quick to accept Jacob's integrity. With Esau and Isaac Jacob was anything but *ṣeḏeq.* Perhaps the only reason Laban consents (v. 34) is because of Jacob's willingness to accept so little.[33] At most it would amount to twenty percent of the flocks. Before Jacob came Laban had only a little *(m*ᵉ*ʿaṭ).* Now Jacob is content himself to leave with a pittance.

35-36 To guarantee further as small a share as possible for Jacob, Laban isolated those irregular animals chosen by Jacob from the monochromes and left them with his own sons. Jacob has only the monochrome members of the flock to tend, and they will produce few, if any, irregulars. Thus Laban thinks he has limited Jacob's acquisitions. This move by Laban will work ultimately for Jacob's advantage, for it will allow Jacob to carry out his crossbreeding in relative privacy, without Laban or his shepherds spying or checking on him.

The first of those animals that Laban isolated are described as he-goats and she-goats that were speckled and spotted, and had some white *(lāḇān)*[34] on them. "White," which is the meaning of Laban's name, is promiment in vv. 35, 37. Jacob takes shoots of poplar *(liḇneh),* that is, white poplar (v. 37). In these he peels "white stripes" *(p*ᵉ*ṣālôṯ l*ᵉ*ḇānôṯ,* v. 37), thus exposing the white *(hallāḇān)* of the shoots, v. 37. Here in v. 35 Laban ("the white one") removes at a safe distance from Jacob those animals of his that are not totally white, not totally *lāḇān.*

37-40 If he is to increase his flock, Jacob's challenge is to get monochrome animals to produce spotted young. To that end, Jacob took shoots

("speckled"), *ṭālû'* ("spotted") see Brenner, *Colour Terms in the Old Testament,* pp. 121-23, 169. Brenner (p. 169) quotes approvingly from David Kimḥi, a medieval Bible commentator and grammarian, who states that the difference between *nāqōḏ* and *ṭālû'* is in the size of the stain referred to.

32. For another reference to finding stolen material in the possession of a thief, which implies a search of some kind, see Exod. 22:3 (Eng. 4). See B. S. Jackson, *Theft in Early Jewish Law* (Oxford: Clarendon, 1972), p. 216.

33. Westermann, *Genesis,* 2:482: "This clear and controllable offer . . . would appeal to the avaricious Laban."

34. On *lāḇān,* see Brenner, *Colour Terms in the Old Testament,* pp. 83-85.

of various trees and peeled them in such a way that there were white stripes on them, and these he placed in the watering troughs. After the monochrome goats came to drink they mated and brought forth spotted kids (surprise of surprises!). Further, he bred variegated flocks with monochrome flocks (v. 40) to increase his flocks even more.

How does Jacob manage to succeed? Do one-colored animals produce bicolored young simply by looking at a bicolored object in their mating time? This interpretation borders on sympathetic magic. Jacob's rods function much as do Rachel's mandrakes. It is not the mandrakes that produce fertility, and it is not Jacob's white rods that produce the right kind of offspring for Jacob — although perhaps that is what Jacob wanted Laban to think. It is God who opened Sarah's womb, and in 31:10-12 Jacob testifies that it was God, not magic, that brought about the desired results.

The flock tended by Jacob had only monochrome animals in respect of phenotype. As regards genotype, however, a third were pure monochromes (homozygotes) and two-thirds were heterozygotes (who contained the gene of spottedness). By crossing the heterozygotes among themselves, Jacob would produce, according to the laws of heredity, twenty-five percent spotted sheep.[35] Thus he multiplies his flock. Jacob has displayed ingenuity; he has not practiced deception.

41-43 Verses 41-42 describe not a new breeding method different from that described in vv. 37-39. Rather, these two verses imply that Jacob applied the breeding method of vv. 37-39 selectively.[36] The *stronger animals* are the heterozygotes. The *feebler animals* are the homozygotes. Jacob crossbred only the former. How he could distinguish one from the other is made clear in 31:12 — the heterozygotes are excessively potent and conceive earlier than the homozygotes. Jacob's knowledge of zoology is far from primitive. But perhaps such knowledge has been given him by God, just as his son's capacity to interpret dreams was a gift from God.

In the incident at Bethel (ch. 28), one of Yahweh's promises to Jacob was "you shall expand/spread out [*pāraṣtā*] to the west and to the east" (v. 14). The narrator uses that same verb in this chapter (v. 43): "thus the man became exceedingly prosperous [*wayyip̄rōṣ*]. His possessions are now expanded to include not only large flocks but maidservants, manservants, camels, and asses. The promise in Bethel of *pāraṣ* to Jacob is first fulfilled some years later in Haran.

35. See J. Feliks, "Biology," *EncJud,* 4:1024-27.
36. See Fokkelman, *Narrative Art in Genesis,* p. 145.

H. JACOB'S FLIGHT FROM LABAN (31:1-54)

1. JACOB AND HIS WIVES RESOLVE TO LEAVE LABAN (31:1-16)

1 *Now (Jacob)*[1] *heard that Laban's sons were saying: "Jacob has taken everything which was our father's; and from what should be our father's, he has amassed all this wealth."*[2]

2 *Jacob observed for some while that Laban's feelings*[3] *toward him were different*[4] *than they previously*[5] *had been.*

3 *Then Yahweh said to Jacob: "Return to your father's land, your birthplace, and I will be with you."*

4 *So Jacob sent for and called Rachel and Leah out into the field with his flock.*

5 *He said to them: "I have observed*[6] *that your father's feelings toward me are different than they previously had been; but my father's God has been with me.*

6 *You, you know that I served your father with every last bit of my energy.*

1. I supply "Jacob" for sense only. It is not in the Hebrew, which simply states "Now he heard."

2. *kāḇōḏ* has the meaning "abundance, riches, wealth" here and in Ps. 49:17, 18 (Eng. 16, 17); Isa. 10:3; 22:24; 61:6; Nah. 2:10 (Eng. 9). The Qal of *kāḇēḏ* means "to be rich, wealthy" in Gen. 13:2, "And Abram was very rich"; and the Piel means "pay, enrich" in Num. 22:17, "I will pay you well/reward you richly," i.e., a euphemism for monetary rewards. S. Gevirtz ("West-Semitic curses and the problem of the origins of Hebrew law," *VT* 11 [1961] 142 n. 5) points to this meaning for *kbd* (D stem) in the Akkadian of Ugarit: *ù* ^{m}*Ša-wì-it-te-nu me-at KUG.GI LUGAL EN-šu uk-tab-bi-id,* "And Š. paid the king, his lord, one hundred (shekels of) gold" (*PRU,* III, no. 16.251, lines 10-12). The much more frequent meaning of *kāḇōḏ* is "honor, glory, splendor," usually used with reference to God.

3. Lit., "faces."

4. Both here and in v. 5 SP reads *'ēnām* (lit., "there is not for them") for MT *'ênennû* (lit., "there is not for it/him"). The problem in the MT is that *'ênennû* is sing. while *p*^{e}*nê* is pl. The SP reading *'ēnâm* removes the inconsistency between gender disagreement. Cf. R. Weiss, "On Ligatures in the Hebrew Bible *(nu = m),*" *JBL* 82 (1963) 190. See also v. 5.

5. *kiṯmôl šilšôm,* lit., "as yesterday (and) the day before/the third day." See BDB, p. 1070a.

6. Jacob's use of the participle followed by the independent personal pronoun *(rō'eh 'ānōḵî)* draws attention both to Jacob's repeated observation of Laban's continuing change of attitude vis-à-vis Jacob and to the action noted by the verb. A. Caquot ("Cinq observations sur le Psaume 45," in *Ascribe to the Lord,* Fest. P. C. Craigie, ed. L. Eslinger and G. Taylor, JSOTSup 67 [Sheffield: JSOT, 1988], p. 256) translates "I see well that. . . ."

7 *Yet your father, he cheated me*[7] *and changed*[8] *my wages ten times;*[9] *still, God did not permit him to harm me.*

8 *If he said, 'The speckled shall be your wages,' then the entire flock would bear*[10] *speckled young. And if he said, 'The striped shall be your wages,' then the entire flock would bear striped young.*

9 *Thus God salvaged*[11] *your*[12] *father's livestock and gave it to me.*

10 *Once, during the flock's mating season, I had a dream*[13] *in which I saw he-goats that were striped, speckled, and mottled mounting*[14] *the flock.*

11 *A messenger of God said to me in the dream, 'Jacob!' 'Yes,' I answered.*

12 *He said, 'Observe well that all the he-goats mounting the flock are striped, speckled, and mottled, for I have seen all the things Laban has been doing to you.*

13 *I am the God of*[15] *Bethel where you anointed a pillar and where you*

7. *tālal,* "mock, deceive, cheat," appears 9 times in the OT (Gen. 31:7; Exod. 8:25 [Eng. 21]; Judg. 16:10, 13, 15 [Delilah to Samson]; Job 13:9 [twice]; Isa. 44:20; Jer. 9:4). The verb means to deceive in the sense of failing to deal with another person in a serious and straightforward manner.

8. The verbal form is *heḥĕlip̱*. SP emends to a Hiphil imperfect, *wayyaḥªlēp̱*. J. Heusman ("The Infinitive Absolute and the Waw + Perfect Problem," *Bib* 37 [1956] 414) repoints it as a Hiphil infinitive absolute *(haḏhªlēp̱),* thus rejecting S. R. Driver's understanding of *wᵉheḥᵉlip* as an instance of the weak *waw* and the perfect as an advancement of the narrative by accretion rather than by development (S. R. Driver, *Treatise on the Use of the Tenses in Hebrew,* 3rd ed. [Oxford: Clarendon, 1892], pp. 158-59, §§ 131-32). For the perfect with *waw* after a perfect (i.e., a frequentative perfect) see GKC, § 112h.

9. *mōnîm* demonstrates that a participial noun may indicate an action or a state of a verb, rather than a person involved in that action. See P. Wernberg-Møller, "Observations on the Hebrew Participle," *ZAW* 71 (1959) 54-67.

10. For the frequentative perfect, with *waw (wᵉyālᵉḏû),* see S. R. Driver, *Treatise on the Use of Tenses,* p. 152, § 123b; and for the imperfect found in the protasis in reference to past time ("if he said," *'im kōh yō'mar*), p. 177, § 136d, obs.

11. On the pair *nāṣal* and *nāṯan,* "salvaged . . . gave," see C. J. Labuschagne, "The *našû-nadānu* Formula and its Biblical Equivalents," in *Travels in the World of the OT,* Fest. M. A. Beek, ed. M. S. H. G. Heerma van Voss (Assen: Van Gorcum, 1974), pp. 176-80; J. C. Greenfield, "*našu-nadānu* and its Congeners," in *Essays on the Ancient Near East in Memory of J. J. Finkelstein,* ed. Maria de Jong Ellis (Hamden, CT: Archon, 1977), pp. 87-91; idem, "Aramaic Studies and the Bible," *Congress Volume: Vienna, 1980,* VTSup 32 (Leiden: Brill, 1981) 129.

12. *'ªḇîḵem* (masc. pronominal suffix) should certainly be read as *'ªḇîḵen* (fem. pronominal suffix), as in v. 5, since Jacob is speaking to Leah and Rachel.

13. *wā'ēre' baḥªlôm,* lit., "and I saw in the dream."

14. See S. M. Paul, "Two cognate Semitic terms for mating and copulation," *VT* 32 (1982) 492.

15. For the presence of the definite article in the construct chain see M. J. Dahood, "Northwest Semitic Notes on Genesis," *Bib* 55 (1974) 79-80. Cf. also F. M. Cross,

made a vow to me. Now then, arise, leave this land and return to the land of your birth.' "

14 *Rachel and Leah answered him: "Have we still a patrimony*[16] *in our father's estate?*

15 *Are we not regarded by him as foreign women?*[17] *Not only has he sold us, but the money due us he has devoured!*

16 *All the wealth which God has taken away from our father is rightfully ours and our children's. Therefore, do just as God has told you."*

1-3 Jacob hears that Laban's sons resent his success. In their estimation their father has remunerated Jacob excessively, and as a result there will not be anything left for them. This is the second reference to Laban's sons. In 30:35 they are mature enough to be placed in charge of their father's flocks, and here in 31:1 they are old enough to be rivals to Jacob, to see themselves as those whose future material security is in doubt due to Jacob's large gains. These two references imply, then, that it is incorrect to think that for a good while after Jacob reached Haran and Laban's house, Laban had only daughters.

Jacob also notices that he is falling out of Laban's graces. In such a situation, what is a persona non grata to do? Later, when he sees God's face (32:31 [Eng. 30]), he wonders why he still is living. Here he sees Laban's face, and it clearly shows disfavor toward Jacob. Unlike v. 1, however, which stated the concern of the brothers and quoted their actual words, v. 2 simply comments on Jacob's observation of Laban's shifting disposition but supplies no reason for the shift. It is presumably due to Laban's awareness of Jacob's prosperity, something Laban had tried his best to check.

Still, it is not fright or intuition that drives Jacob back to Canaan, but a directive from Yahweh. Jacob is to return to his homeland. Particularly

---

Canaanite Myth and Hebrew Epic (Cambridge: Harvard University, 1973), pp. 46-47, who argues against "the god Bethel."

16. Lit., "portion and inheritance" *(ḥēleq wᵉnaḥᵃlâ),* which is a hendiadys. "Patrimony" would capture the meaning. The two words appear together in 2 Sam. 20:1 and 1 K. 12:16, both of which describe a revolt against one in authority. See also Deut. 10:9; 12:12. For the significance of the Akkadian cognate to Hebrew *naḥᵃlâ* (i.e., *niḫlatu* ("property handed over, transferred" [*CAD* N/2:219]) and the Ugaritic cognate *nḥlt* ("estate"), see B. A. Levine, *Numbers 1–20,* AB (New York: Doubleday, 199), pp. 449-50.

17. For *noḵrî,* "foreign(er)," to designate one "outside the family," see S. M. Paul, *Studies in the Book of the Covenant in the Light of Cuneiform and Biblical Law,* VTSup 18 (Leiden: Brill, 1970), p. 54 n. 6. For other places where this word refers to one who is not recognized as a member of a family, see Exod. 21:8; Job 19:15; Ps. 69:9 (Eng. 8; see P. Humbert, "Les Adjectifs *zār* et *nŏkrī* et 'la femme étrangère' des Proverbes bibliques," in *Opuscules d'un Hébraïsant* [Neuchâtel: Secrétariat de l'Université, 1958], pp. 111-18); and possibly Ruth 2:10 (J. M. Sasson, *Ruth* [Baltimore: Johns Hopkins University, 1979], p. 51).

reassuring to him is the promise of God's presence with him. Yes, Leah and Rachel and the children will go with him, but most importantly Yahweh will accompany him. This is the same promise Jacob received when he was fleeing Canaan (28:15a). Whether leaving his home or returning to it, Jacob does not travel alone. Laban's relationship with Jacob was degenerating to a level where the face of Laban was no longer with Jacob as before *(pᵉnê . . . 'ênennû 'immô* (v. 2). But in the next verse (v. 3) Yahweh makes clear that his relationship with Jacob has neither changed nor degenerated: "I will be with you" *('immāk). 'immô* (with a negative) tells us about Laban and Jacob. *'immāk* (a positive) tells us about Yahweh and Jacob.

4-9 Jacob shares his recent perceptions about Laban (v. 2) and his religious experiences (v. 3; cf. v. 13b) with his wives. All this is done in the field, away from either Laban or his sons. He does not tell them about their brothers' hard feelings, but only about their father's change of heart. In talking to Leah and Rachel about Laban, Jacob never uses his name but consistently refers to him as *your father* (vv. 5, 6, 7, 9). It may not be accidental that there is a contrast not only between Laban's brutal treatment of Jacob and Yahweh's gracious treatment of Jacob, but also between "your father" and "Return to your father's land" and "my father's God." One father is repugnant; the other father is inviting.

Jacob reminds his wives (1) of his years of devoted service to Laban (v. 6); (2) of the fact that their father has at least ten times[18] acted like a "Jacob" (v. 7);[19] (3) of God's overruling of Laban's machinations (vv. 8-9).[20] Jacob's explanation of the size of his own flocks to his wives does not contradict that told in the previous chapter (i.e., in ch. 30 Jacob prospered because he was crafty and adept at sympathetic magic; in ch. 31 Jacob was blessed by God).[21] Jacob's explanation here represents his sobered reflections on the happenings of the last several years. With hindsight, he is able to put the increment of his flocks in proper perspective.

18. "Ten times" is probably a round number. Cf. v. 41; Num. 14:22; Job 19:3.

19. The contrast between Jacob's loyal service to Laban and Laban's duplicity to Jacob in return is highlighted by the chiasm in vv. 6 and 7: "with every last bit of energy I served your father [*'aḇāḏtî 'eṯ 'ᵃḇîḵen*]. . . "your father has cheated me [*wa'ᵃḇîḵen hēṯel bî*]." In v. 6 *'ᵃḇîḵen* is direct object, and in v. 7 it is subject of the following verb.

20. Note the use of *nāṯan* in vv. 7, 9. With respect to Laban God "did not permit" *(lō' nāṯan)* him to harm Jacob. With respect to Jacob God "gave" *(nāṯan)*. Through the double use of *nāṯan* the narrator may reinforce that Yahweh oversees the life of both Laban and Jacob, by restraining the first and prospering the second.

21. This is one reason why some writers attribute the account in 30:25ff. to J and that in 31:4ff. to E; see, e.g., Jenks, *The Elohist and North Israelite Traditions,* p. 36: "Whereas J portrays Jacob simply as a clever and fortunate adversary to Laban, E justifies Jacob's actions as obedience to divine revelation."

10-13 Jacob relates to his wives his dream from God. The dream is apparently subsequent to or near the end of the events in ch. 30, not previous to them, or even concurrent with them, since ch. 30 said nothing about a dream. The data in vv. 12-13a are novel. Jacob's responsibilities are threefold: observe (v. 12), listen and remember (v. 13a), and leave Haran and return to his native land (v. 13b). Only now does Jacob share with his wives how he obtained so many animals. He is making clear to them that he did not dupe Laban out of his flocks by magic or trickery. Had he done so, then Leah and Rachel might have been sympathetic toward Laban. Rather, God is responsible for Jacob's prosperity.

Verse 13b reflects v. 3. V. 3 emphasized returning; v. 13 emphasizes leaving and returning. V. 3 had one imperative; v. 13b contains three imperatives. Jacob concludes his sharing of the dream by telling Leah and Rachel of God's self-identification to Jacob *(I am the God of Bethel),* God's recall of Jacob's earlier acts at Bethel *(where you anointed a pillar and where you made a vow to me),* and of God's commands to Jacob not to settle permanently in Haran *(arise, leave this land and return to the land of your birth).* Jacob apparently feels that this dream will help persuade his wives to leave their father and join him in a permanent move back to his country.[22]

14-16 If Jacob thinks he needs to convince his wives, he is wrong. They already believe him and are prepared to support him, not because of what Laban has done to Jacob, but because of what Laban has done to them. He has shortchanged his own daughters. Their complaint that Laban *sold* them and *devoured*[23] what was due them indicates that in early Israelite society the father enjoyed the fruits of the bride price only for a while. The money, in whole or in part, was to revert to the daughter at the time of succession, or if she were impoverished by her husband's death. Laban's sons have displaced Laban's daughters. Financially they are abandoned. Because Jacob "paid" for his wives with service instead of money, they feel they are entitled to the equivalent of his service in money.[24]

Another possibility for understanding Leah's and Rachel's bitterness is that it was fueled by Laban's failure to let the bride payment become part

22. See Fokkelman, *Narrative Art in Genesis,* pp. 156-57.

23. With the Hebrew phrase *wayyōḵal gam 'āḵôl 'eṯ kaspēnû,* "the money due us he has devoured," one might compare the recurrent phrase at Nuzi *akalu kaspa,* "to eat the money." Laban has used up the bride payment instead of holding it for his daughters. See references in T. L. Thompson, *Historicity of the Patriarchal Narratives,* pp. 274, 275 and 274 n. 341. For Thompson this phrase in 31:15 proves that Jacob's marriage was not an *errebu* marriage, i.e., one that provided a man who did not have a son with a male heir through the adoption of the son-in-law. For in an *errebu* marriage a bride price was not paid.

24. See M. Burrows, "The Complaint of Laban's Daughters," *JAOS* 57 (1937) 259-76.

of the dowry. Van Seters points to a Neo-Assyrian text from the late 7th century B.C. that treats marriage as a purchase transaction. The mother purchased a bride for her son for 16 shekels of silver.[25] Note that in 31:15 Laban's daughters complain that he has *sold* them *(m^e^k̲ārānû),* much as one might sell slaves. But Gen. 31 makes no explicit reference to Jacob paying any amount for Rachel and Leah, and one should not place too much weight on the use of *māk̲ar* here, for Rachel and Leah are speaking only analogously, and "a protest of indignant women is no evidence of legal custom."[26]

2. THE FLIGHT FROM LABAN'S HOME (31:17-21)

17 *Thereupon*[1] *Jacob put his children*[2] *and his wives*[3] *on camels.*

18 *And he led out all of his livestock and all of his property that he had acquired, livestock in his possession that he had acquired*[4] *in Paddan-aram, to go to Isaac his father in the land of Canaan.*

19 *With Laban gone to shear his sheep, Rachel stole*[5] *her father's household gods.*

20 *Jacob had deceived Laban*[6] *the Aramean by not*[7] *telling him of his flight.*

25. J. Van Seters, *Abraham in History and Tradition* (New Haven: Yale University, 1975), pp. 81-84.

26. See G. R. Driver and J. C. Miles, *The Babylonian Laws,* 2nd ed., 2 vols. (Oxford: Clarendon, 1956), 1:263 n. 4.

1. This is an instance of *qûm* (*wayyāqom,* lit., "and he arose") used as an auxiliary verb. See also v. 21, *wayyāqom wayyaʿ^a^b̲ōr,* which I rendered "Once across the river."

2. Lit., "his sons" (*bānāyw*), with no specific reference to Dinah his daughter.

3. LXX reverses the order: "his wives and his children."

4. LXX omits *ʾ^a^šer rāk̲āš miqnēh qinyānô,* probably because the eye of the translator skipped from the *ʾ^a^šer rāk̲aš* ("that he had acquired") down to the *ʾ^a^šer rāk̲aš* in the middle of the verse, thus omitting four words.

5. Due to the respect and veneration in which the matriarch was held, Targ. Onqelos toned down MT's "stole" to "took" *(nsybt).* Similarly in the next verse, Targ. Onqelos reads MT's "Jacob deceived Laban" (also *gānab̲,* as in v. 19, lit., "Jacob stole the heart of Laban") as "Jacob concealed [*ksy*] from Laban."

6. For MT's "Jacob stole the heart of Laban" LXX reads "and Jacob hid the matter from Laban" *(ékrypsen dé Iakōb Laban),* which is close to Targ. Onqelos (see above, n. 5). This is an instance of the LXX reducing two or more words in Hebrew ("stole the-heart-of") to one word in Greek ("hid") that comprised all the elements expressed by a number of words in the MT. See E. Tov, *The Text-Critical Use of the Septuagint in Biblical Research* (Jerusalem: Simor, 1981), p. 86. See also M. Niehoff, "Do Biblical Characters Talk to Themselves? Narrative Modes of Representing Inner Speech in Early Biblical Fiction," *JBL* 111 (1992) 585-87.

7. On *b^e^lî* as an adverb of negation, see BDB, p. 115b: "with finite verb rare and only once in prose, Gen. 31:20 (E)."

21 *He fled, he and all that he had. Once across the river, he headed for*[8] *the hills of Gilead.*

17-18 With his wives' approval of his planned departure from Laban, Jacob assembles his family (v. 17) and his livestock (v. 18). The *livestock* which Jacob takes are not animals that he has swindled from Laban. They are livestock he has *acquired (rāḵaš)* legitimately, says the narrator. The way the narrator makes this point is by his repeated use of the third person pronominal suffix: "his children," "his wives," "his livestock," "his property," "his possession." To make his point even more obvious, the narrator twice uses the expression *that he acquired ('ašer rāḵaš).*

19 Laban's absence from home to attend to sheepshearing (cf. 38:12ff.; 1 Sam. 25:2ff.; 2 Sam. 13:23) provides Rachel with the opportunity to abscond with her father's *household gods (tᵉrāpîm).* It is something she does on her own initiative; she informs neither her sister nor her husband about her theft.

The Hebrew verb for *stole* here is *gānaḇ,* which appears seven times in this narrative (vv. 19, 20, 26, 27, 30, 32, 39). Two verbs in the OT denote misappropriation of property, *gānaḇ* and *gāzal.* Scholars have suggested, as early as tannaitic sources, that *gānaḇ* refers to a furtive act, and *gāzal* to a nonfurtive act.[9] Thus one might render the first as "steal," and the second as "rob." While *gānaḇ* is used seven times in ch. 31, *gāzal* is used only once (v. 31, by Jacob against Laban) and means "to take away by force." But some OT texts do not observe this neat distinction between the two verbs. A key text is Lev. 5:20-26 (Eng. 6:1-7), which deals with the expiation of false oaths involving three kinds of deceit, all of which cause loss of property to another: (1) misappropriation of what was entrusted to one's safekeeping or of a pledge; (2) robbery (?) *(bᵉgāzēl);* and (3) fraud. Does *gāzēl* in this case refer clearly to robbery by open force? An argument against understanding *gāzēl* as robbery for force or violence is that the other two illustrations used, misappropriation and fraud, are offenses of deceit, thus suggesting the same for *gāzēl.*

8. Lit., "he set his face," which is a phrase used idiomatically inside and outside the OT to denote movement toward a specific location. See U. Cassuto, *Biblical and Oriental Studies,* tr. I. Abrahams, 2 vols. (Jerusalem: Magnes, 1973-75), 2:22; S. Layton, "Biblical Hebrew 'to Set the Face' in Light of Akkadian and Ugaritic," *UF* 17 (1986) 175. For an NT example cf. Luke 9:51, where Jesus "set his face to go to Jerusalem."

9. Mishnah *Baba Qamma* ch. 7 provides examples of *gānaḇ,* and chs. 9 and 10 examples of *gāzal.* For a modern advocate of that position, see J. Milgrom, *Cult and Conscience* (Leiden: Brill, 1976), pp. 89-102. For entries in theological wordbooks and dictionaries that disagree with this position, see V. Hamp, *"gānabh," TDOT,* 3:41-42; J. Schüpphaus, *"gāzal," TDOT,* 2:456-58; James E. Smith, *"gānab," TWOT,* 1:168. For *gānaḇ* as something done secretly see Josh. 7:11; 2 Sam. 19:4; 2 K. 11:2 par. 2 Chr. 22:11; Prov. 9:7.

B. S. Jackson made a different distinction to the effect that, in the earlier literature at least, *gānaḇ* is used primarily of the act of an individual, a member of the community. *gāzal* is used primarily of the act of, or action against, an outsider, and is often committed by a group.[10] Thus in Judg. 9:25 the men of Shechem repudiated Abimelech's rule by ambushing and robbing *(gāzal)* all who traveled in the hills. Similarly Judg. 21:23 speaks of the Benjamites who raided their neighbors to capture or steal (*gāzal;* RSV "carry off") brides. This distinction explains, for Jackson, why Laban uses *gānaḇ* and Jacob uses *gāzal.* Laban, wishing to retain Jacob as part of the household, uses the term appropriate to an offense committed by a community member. Jacob, however, wishes to leave the community, become an outsider, and assert his independence.[11] A problem with Jackson's distinction between the two verbs is that in a number of texts *gānaḇ* is also used for theft by an outsider (Gen. 44:8, the theft of Joseph's cup by those who are outsiders to Egyptian society; 2 Sam. 21:12, the removal of the corpses of Saul and his sons from Bethshan [controlled by the Philistines] by the men of Jabesh-gilead). A simpler explanation is that Laban accuses Jacob of *gānaḇ* because as a client Jacob could get the better of Laban only by stealth. Laban, as the family head, could simply exercise his power and commit *gāzal.*[12]

Rachel's theft of her father's gods (and here one can have no doubt that *gānaḇ* means theft by stealth) is the first in a number of incidents involving the theft of sacred property. One is reminded of Benjamin who is accused of stealing Joseph's divining cup (Gen. 44:1-13); of the Danites' theft of Micah's graven image and other paraphernalia (Judg. 18:18); and of Achan's pilfering of the objects devoted for destruction (Josh. 7:1). In each of these incidents the suspect is sought and his possessions searched thoroughly.

The story in Gen. 31 never comments on Rachel's ability to steal *her father's household gods.* From a Hebrew perspective, of course, one might ask: "Can one steal gods?" "Is the destiny of a god at the beck and whim of a mortal?" The ancient reader would not miss the sarcasm in this story, for here is a new crime — "godnapping"!

Rachel steals her father's *household gods,* or teraphim *tᵉrāp̄îm,* as the narrator refers to them (vv. 19, 34, 35). But Laban himself refers to them as "my gods" (v. 30), as does Jacob (v. 32). Thus they are clearly household gods, rather than temple gods, probably small and obviously portable in the Genesis narrative, for Rachel is able to conceal them inside her camel's saddle (v. 34) and to sit on them. By contrast, the teraphim used by Michal to conceal David's departure from Saul's house were larger and could be made to look

10. B. S. Jackson, *Theft in Early Jewish Law* (Oxford: Clarendon, 1972), p. 6.
11. Ibid., pp. 7-8.
12. See Milgrom, *Cult and Conscience,* p. 91.

humanlike after they were modified (Michal put goat's hair at the head of the teraphim; see 1 Sam. 19:13, 16). That the text says simply that Michal "took" the teraphim implies that they were readily available in and to the royal household, and no stigma was attached to having them in one's possession. Similarly in the book of Judges we read of Micah from Ephraim who had teraphim in his house along with other iconic or religious objects (Judg. 17:5; 18:14, 17, 20), especially the ephod, both of which were used for some form of divining by the Levitical priest. Other texts, however, condemn the presence and use of the teraphim (see 1 Sam. 15:23; 2 K. 23:24; Ezek. 21:26 [Eng. 21]; Hos. 3:4; Zech. 10:2).

The meaning and origin of the word *t^erāp̱îm* are uncertain. Modern scholars offer four possibilities. (1) "Old rags," based on a Semitic root *trp.*[13] But the existence of a Proto-Semitic root *trp* is uncertain. (2) "Interpreters," based on a metathesized form from an original *ptrym* (*p-t-r* for *t-r-p*).[14] In their original function they were mantic devices consulted in connection with dream interpretation. But it is highly speculative to suggest that *ptrym* appeared in an early text where *trpym* now stands, especially when no textual evidence supports that reading. (3) "Demon, spirit," connected with Hittite *tarpiš,* a spirit that may be either protective or malevolent.[15] But nowhere in the OT is *t^erāp̱îm* parallel to an expression designating demons. (4) "Healers, protectors," from *rāp̱ā',* "to heal," with a *t*-preformative.[16] This suggestion is as old as the LXX, which connected it with the verb *therapeuō,* "to heal." The teraphim are the ancestors who provide healing and well-being for their living descendants. The third and fourth options seem most likely, but none is convincing.

13. An Ugaritic cognate may occur in a poem about Baal and Anat: *ṯṯkḥ ttrp šmm,* "the heavens will wear away and will sag." See W. F. Albright, "Are the Ephod and the Teraphim Mentioned in Ugaritic Literature?" *BASOR* 83 (1941) 39-42.

14. Such metathesis was intentional and was an expression of a religious perspective that viewed such objects as obnoxious. See C. J. Labuschagne, "Teraphim — A New Proposal," *VT* 16 (1966) 115-17.

15. See H. A. Hoffner, Jr., "Hittite *Tarpiš* and Hebrew *Terāphîm,*" *JNES* 27 (1968) 61-68. According to Hoffner, Hittite proper names and common nouns lose their consonantal case when they are borrowed into Ugaritic. Thus Hittite *tarpiš* in West Semitic becomes *tarpi,* the nominative sing. of which would be *tarpu.* In Hebrew such a form would be *terep* (sing.) and *t^erāpîm* (pl.). But if, according to Hoffner, Hittite *tarpiš* is to be equated with Akk. *šēdu,* then these two words are already represented in the OT by *šēḏîm,* "demons" (Deut. 32:17). It is unlikely there would be two Hebrew equivalents for *tarpiš* and *šēdu.*

16. See W. E. Barnes, "Teraphim," *JTS* 30 (1929) 177-79; S. S. Smith, "What Were the Teraphim?" *JTS* 33 (1932) 32; P. R. Ackroyd, "Teraphim," *ExpTim* 62 (1950-51) 378-79; H. Rouillard and J. Tropper, "*trpym,* rituels de guérison et culte des ancêtres d'après 1 Samuel xix 11-17 et les textes parallèles d'Assur et de Nuzi," *VT* 37 (1987) 340-61, esp. pp. 358-59 for an explanation of the omission of the final *'aleph* in the writing of *terāpîm* (from *rāp̱ā'*). For an in-depth analysis of most of these proposals, see K. van

Why would Rachel steal her father's household gods? Some scholars appeal to a Nuzi document, part of which reads:

> Tablet of adoption, whereby Nashwa, son of Arshenni, has adopted Wullu, son of Puhishenni. So long as Nashwa is alive, Wullu will give him food and clothing, and when Nashwa is dead, Wullu will give him burial. If there be a son of Nashwa, he shall divide (the estate) equally with Wullu, and the gods of Nashwa the son of Nashwa shall take. But if there be no son of Nashwa then Wullu shall take also the gods of Nushwa. Also he has given his daughter Nuhuia to Wullu to wife; if Wullu shall take another wife he shall vacate the lands and houses of Nashwa. Whoever infringes (the agreement) shall pay in full one mina of silver and one of gold.[17]

Because this tablet explains that the gods constituted the title to the chief inheritance portion and headship of the family, some scholars suggest that Rachel stole the gods in order to guarantee that privilege for her husband.[18] Jacob would officially be presumptive heir.

Other scholars, notably M. Greenberg, have challenged this interpretation of Gen. 31:19.[19] Greenberg suggests that the above text, and others like it, connect possession of household gods not with inheritance or entitlement to inheritance, but with the determination of who is to carry on as head of the family unit. Furthermore, possession of symbolic objects was not sufficient to establish a claim on the office that the objects symbolized. Jacob would have to substantiate that Laban had bequeathed the gods to him. Finally, if it is indeed Rachel's intention to secure for Jacob a position of chief heir and paterfamilias, then how will this all be implemented, now that she is leaving her father's home and moving to a foreign country, apparently for good? A

---

der Toorn, "The Nature of the Biblical Teraphim in the Light of Cuneiform Evidence," *CBQ* 52 (1990) 203-22.

17. See C. J. Gadd, "Tablets from Kirkuk," *RA* 23 (1926) 126-27; cf. *ANET,* pp. 219-20.

18. See C. H. Gordon, "The Story of Jacob and Laban in the Light of the Nuzi Tablets," *BASOR* 66 (1937) 25-27; idem, "Biblical Customs and the Nuzu Tablets," *BA* 3 (1940) 5-6; S. Smith, "What were the Teraphim?" *JTS* 33 (1932) 33-36; A. E. Draffkorn, "Ilāni/Elohim," *JBL* 76 (1957) 216-24, esp. pp. 219-23; Ackroyd, *ExpTim* 62 (1950-51) 378-80. Or possibly to guarantee that privilege for her son Joseph over any of her sister Leah's children (K. Spanier, "Rachel's theft of the teraphim: her struggle for family primacy," *VT* 42 [1992] 404-12).

19. M. Greenberg, "Another Look at Rachel's Theft of the Teraphim," *JBL* 81 (1962) 239-48. See also Van Seters, *Abraham in History and Tradition,* pp. 93-94; T. L. Thompson, *Historicity of the Patriarchal Narratives,* pp. 272-78; de Vaux, *Early History of Israel,* pp. 251-53; M. J. Selman, "Comparative Customs and the Patriarchal Age," in *Essays on the Patriarchal Narratives,* ed. A. R. Millard and D. J. Wiseman (Winona Lake, IN: Eisenbrauns, 1983), pp. 103, 117-18. For a contrary view on the connection of Hittite *tarpiš* with Heb.

simpler explanation is that Rachel possibly stole the hearth gods for protection on her journey to Canaan.[20]

But Gunkel's (and Greenberg's) explanation of the motives for Rachel's theft (i.e., religious reasons) does not exhaust the possibilities. For example, Rachel could have stolen her father's teraphim for their monetary value, motivated by greed, or out of spite, motivated by vindictiveness. The latter motive would explain why Rachel, rather than Leah, stole the gods. Earlier it was Rachel, the object of Jacob's desire, whom Laban stole from Jacob, then imposing seven additional years of service on Jacob for Rachel. Now the tables are turned: it is Rachel who steals from Laban the objects of his desire.[21] But the text represses any mention or explanation of Rachel's motives. What it does comment on is simply the circumstances that made possible her act of thievery: Laban is out shearing sheep.

The publication of cuneiform texts (Late Bronze Age) from Emar has again opened the question about possible connections between heirship and access to the family's gods.[22] The Emar texts are legal documents, four of them wills. In the first text Unara, the daughter of Zikri-Dagan, is given permission by her father "to call upon my gods and my dead (family ancestors?)." This privilege is not extended to her three brothers (or sons?). In the second text Mazazu says of his daughter Al–ubhātī (his only child): "she may call upon my gods and my dead. Now then, I have given my estates, my possessions (and) property, everything of mine to my daughter Al-ḫātī."

There are, to be sure, some distinctions between the Emar documents and Gen. 31, as they are between the Nuzi texts and Gen. 31. It is unlikely that Rachel, in the heat of the moment, thought logically through the implications of her act. True, the gods of her father may not assist Jacob in Canaan when Laban dies in Mesopotamia; but did Rachel think that far ahead? Hers is a quickly hatched scheme which is not without its gaping faults and oversights.

20-21 *Jacob had deceived Laban* (lit., "Jacob stole Laban's heart").

---

t^erāpîm, see F. Josephson, "Anatolien *tarpali-,* etc.," in *Florilegium anatolicum: Mélanges offerts à Emmanuel Laroche* (Paris: E. de Boccard, 1979), pp. 177-84.

20. N. Jay ("Sacrifice, descent and the Patriarchs," *VT* 38 [1988] 65-66) traces the theft to Rachel's claim to legimate herself to Joseph as a "mother's son." Jacob is not paterfamilias but a mere husband in a system of descent through women. Gunkel (*Genesis,* pp. 344ff.) was the first modern commentator to suggest this explanation, and he is followed by Greenberg (who appeals to a parallel in Josephus).

21. See E. Fuchs, "'For I Have the Way of Women': Deception, Gender, and Ideology in Biblical Narrative," *Reasoning with the Foxes: Female Wit in a World of Male Power,* ed. J. C. Exum and J. W. H. Bos, Semeia 42 (Atlanta: Scholars, 1988), pp. 74, 77.

22. See J. Huehnergard, Jr., "Five Tablets from the Vicinity of Emar," *RA* 77 (1983) 11-43, esp. 28; idem, "Biblical Notes on Some New Akkadian Texts from Emar (Syria)," *CBQ* 47 (1985) 428-34, esp. 428-31.

Rachel stole Laban's gods, and Jacob stole Laban's heart. Twice *gānab̲* is used, in v. 20 with Rachel, and in v. 21 with Jacob. Laban had deceived *(rāmâ)* Jacob (29:25), but Jacob "stole Laban's heart." We have already noted the similarity in sound (29:25) between "deceive" and "Aramean." It is appropriate to style Laban here as an Aramean just after he himself has been duped.

In v. 19 *gānab̲* is used in its literal sense: "Rachel stole her father's household gods." When the verb is used with Jacob in v. 20 it is used figuratively: "he stole Laban's heart." Rachel perpetrated an actual theft, while Jacob's theft is an act of self-defense and reasonable. Hers is unexplained and appears to be arbitrary. The juxtapositioning of the two acts of thievery in this way creates the impression that Jacob's deception is not as serious as Rachel's.[23]

3. LABAN OVERTAKES JACOB AND HIS PARTY (31:22-35)

22 *Laban was informed on the third day that Jacob had fled.*

23 *Taking his kinsmen along with him, he pursued him for seven days until he overtook[1] him in the hill country of Gilead.*

24 *But God came[2] to Laban the Aramean in a night dream and warned him: "Refrain from threatening Jacob with any harm."*

25 *When Laban overtook Jacob, Jacob's tents were pitched in the hill country; Laban encamped with his kinsman[3] in the hill country of Gilead.*

26 *"What do you mean," protested Laban, "by[4] deceiving me and dragging away my daughters like captives of the sword?[5]*

23. See Fuchs, "For I Have the Way of Women," pp. 74-75.

1. The usual meaning for *dāb̲aq* (Qal) is "cleave," as in 2:24, and thus "cause to cleave" in the Hiphil. The root *nāśag* is used in v. 25 for "overtake." On the possibility of Aramaisms here see J. C. Greenfield, "Aramaic Studies and the Bible," *Congress Volume: Vienna, 1980,* VTSup 32 (Leiden: Brill, 1981), p. 130. BDB, p. 180, cites Gen. 31:23; Judg. 18:22; 20:42 as the only instances where the Hiphil of *dāb̲aq* means "overtake." I note that Targ. Onqelos translates both *wayyad̲bēq* of v. 23 and *wayyaśśēg̲* of v. 25 as *w'dbyq.*

2. Other instances of where God comes to somebody *(bôʾ ʾel)* in the night (in a dream or vision) are Gen. 24:3 and Num. 22:8-9, 19-20.

3. Because the text has Jacob "pitching his tents" and Laban "pitching his kinsmen" (same verb), most emend *ʾeḥāyw,* "his kinsmen," to *ʾohᵒlô,* "his tent" (see, e.g., *BHS*). But the text may stand as it is with subject, verb, and prepositional phrase (see NJPS), but accusative omitted (BDB, p. 1075b).

4. The *waw* in *wattignōb* is an instance of where *waw* on an imperfect after *ʿāśâ* is explanatory. See S. R. Driver, *Treatise on the Use of Tenses,* p. 83, § 76a; A. B. Davidson, *Hebrew Syntax,* 3rd ed. (Edinburgh: T. & T. Clark, 1901), p. 71, § 47.

5. Note that the order of the consonants in "sword" *(ḥrb,* v. 26) is reversed in "sneak away" *(brḥ,* v. 27). *šᵉb̲uyôt̲* is the Qal passive fem. pl. participle (in construct) of *šāb̲â,* "take captive," hence "captives," or "prisoners."

27 *Why did you sneak away*[6] *and steal from me, and not*[7] *tell me? And so*[8] *I could have sent you on your way with festive singing,*[9] *with tambourine and lyre.*

28 *You did not even allow me*[10] *to kiss my grandsons*[11] *and daughters farewell! What you have done was foolish.*[12]

29 *It is in my power*[13] *to harm every one of you; but last night the God of your father warned me: 'Refrain from threatening Jacob with any harm.'*

6. Or, "why did you run away furtively?" In *naḥbēʾṯā liḇrōaḥ,* the second verb (an infinitive introduced with *lᵉ*) expresses the principal idea, while the first indicates the manner, and so may be rendered as an adverb. See Williams, *Hebrew Syntax,* p. 41, § 226; Davidson, *Hebrew Syntax,* pp. 8-9, § 82.

7. LXX seems to have read *wᵉlûʾ* for MT *wᵉlōʾ,* hence: "for if you had told me I would have sent you on your way."

8. The *waw* on *wāʾᵃšallēḥᵃḵā* is best rendered as "and so" or "so that" introducing a consecutive clause after an interrogative sentence. Cf. GKC, § 111m; S. R. Driver, *Treatise on the Use of Tenses,* pp. 80-81, § 74a. This rendering is preferable to emending the MT in favor of LXX earlier in the verse (see n. 7).

9. Lit., "with joy and with songs" *(bᵉśimḥâ ûḇᵉširîm).* The two words appear together again in Ps. 137:3 (RSV): "our captors required of us songs [*diḇrê šîr*], and our tormentors, mirth [*śimḥâ*]"; and in Isa. 30:29 (RSV): "you shall have a song [*haššîr*] as in the night . . . and gladness of heart [*wᵉśimḥaṯ lēḇāḇ*]." D. N. Freedman ("The Structure of Psalm 137," in *Near Eastern Studies in Honor of William Foxwell Albright,* ed. H. Goedicke [Baltimore: Johns Hopkins University, 1971], p. 192) notes that "the terms are complimentary and should be combined. . . . Reading them together, we arrive at the following verse: 'words of a song of joy, i.e., joyous lyrics.' " For an alternate interpretation of *šîr* and *śimḥâ* in Ps. 137:3, see F. Renfroe, "Persiflage in Psalm 137," in *Ascribe to the Lord,* Fest. P. C. Craigie, ed. L. Eslinger and G. Taylor, JSOTSup 67 (Sheffield: JSOT, 1988), pp. 518-19.

10. The verb is *nāṭaš,* which in Biblical Hebrew usually means "leave, forsake, abandon," while here "you did not allow (or let) me" is demanded. In Aramaic *šbq* means both "to leave" and "to allow," and Targ. Onqelos and Pesh. use it in 31:28. See J. C. Greenfield, "Aramaic Studies and the Bible," *Congress Volume: Vienna, 1980,* VTSup 32 (Leiden: Brill, 1981), p. 129.

11. Lit., "sons," but surely grandsons or grandchildren is meant.

12. MT *hiskaltā ʿᵃśô,* lit., "you have acted foolishly to do." On the form of the infinitive *ʿᵃśô,* see GKC, § 75n. The normal infinitive construct of *ʿāśâ* would be *ʿᵃśôṯ* (e.g., Gen. 2:24). *ʿᵃśô* is an illustration of the infinitive construct of a third *hē* verb ending in *ô.* The Hiphil of *sāḵal* appears only here and in 1 Sam. 26:21, where Saul says about himself: "I have played the fool" *(hiskaltî).*

13. On the possibilities for *yeš-lᵉʾēl yāḏî* cf. Skinner, *Genesis,* p. 398; W. G. E. Watson, "Reclustering Hebrew *l'lyd,*" *Bib* 58 (1977) 213-15; S. Kogut, "The Biblical Expression *yēš/ʾên lᵉʾēl yaḏ:* The Interpretations and Development of a Mistake," *Tarbiz* 57 (1987/88) 435-44 (Hebrew).

30 *Granted that you left*[14] *because you were homesick*[15] *for your father's house, but why*[16] *did you steal my gods?"*

31 *Jacob answered Laban: "I was frightened because I thought that you might forcibly take*[17] *from me your daughters.*

32 *With whomever*[18] *you find the gods, he shall not live! In full view of our kinsmen identify*[19] *anything that is yours, and take it." Jacob was unaware that Rachel had stolen them.*

33 *Laban entered Jacob's tent and Leah's tent, plus the tent of the two maidservants, but he did not find anything. Leaving Leah's tent, he entered Rachel's tent.*

34 *Now Rachel had taken*[20] *the gods, placed them*[21] *inside*[22] *a camel saddle,*[23] *and sat on top of them. Laban searched through the rest of her tent, but found nothing.*

35 *She then said to her father: "Let not my lord be provoked that I cannot rise in your presence, for a woman's period is upon me."*[24] *He searched, but still did not find the gods.*

14. An infinitive absolute used before its own verb (here, *hālōḵ hālaḵtā)* may express concession. See Davidson, *Hebrew Syntax,* p. 118, § 86a.

15. "To be homesick" is *niḵsōp niḵsaptâ,* a Niphal infinitive and perfect from Heb. *kāsap̱,* which may be related to Heb. *kesep̱,* "silver," i.e., "to grow pale (the color of silver) with longing." See BDB, pp. 493-94; and G. L. Archer, *TWOT,* 1:450. *kāsap̱* (Niphal) plus *lᵉ* occurs again only in Ps. 84:3 (Eng. 2): "my soul longs . . . for the courts of the Lord."

16. A question from the accuser to the accused party may begin either with *lāmmâ* (31:27, 30; 1 Sam. 26:15) or with *maddûaʿ* (2 Sam. 16:10; Jer. 26:9).

17. This is the only time that the stronger verb *gāzal* is used in this narrative. For example, in the immediately preceding verse, Laban uses the verb *gānaḇ,* "steal," as does the narrator in the following verse.

18. For *'ᵃšer* with the unusual sense of a relative pronoun, see GKC, § 138f. To avoid a death sentence on Rachel, Targ. Onqelos reads: "the place where you will find the gods . . . shall not remain in existence."

19. The Hiphil of *nāḵar* means to observe something with a view to recognition. For other places where the Hiphil imperative of *nāḵar* is used in a similar context, see 37:32; 38:25.

20. For imperfect with *waw* consecutive having a pluperfect sense, see GKC, § 111q; Andersen, *Sentence in Biblical Hebrew,* p. 85.

21. The suffix on "placed them" and "on top of them," referring back to the gods/teraphim, is pl., although in 1 Sam. 19:13, 16 only one teraphim is intended. See GKC, § 124h; Davidson, *Hebrew Syntax,* p. 45, § 31.

22. Note the consonantal chiasm between "placed inside" *(śmm)* and "searched" *(mšš).*

23. *kar,* "basket-saddle" occurs only here. BDB, p. 468a, remarks, "the basket-saddle of the camel, a sort of palankeen bound upon the saddle proper."

24. Lit., "the way of women is upon me." For *dereḵ* in this sense, see BDB, p. 203, § 4b.

22 Laban discovers that Jacob and his daughters have left three days after the fact. This is the second reference to a space of three days' journey between Jacob and Laban. Laban instituted the first (30:36), and Jacob instituted the second. Laban is absent because he has gone to shear his sheep. This was an important time of the year for a shepherd. It required a lot of people and a lot of time, depending on the size of the flocks. One text from Mari on this subject says that 150 men are too few and that for shearing, 300 or 400 men are needed for a period of three days. Another Mari text states that shearing will continue for more than five days because of rain and lack of personnel, and may last for ten or twelve days.[25] This kind of data explains how Jacob could be gone for three days before Laban is aware of it.

23 Abram took his "retainers" with him (14:14) when he went after Lot. Laban musters his *kinsmen* (i.e., relatives and close neighbors) when he goes after Jacob. *seven days* is probably to be understood nonliterally, for the distance from Haran to Gilead is "*c.* 350 miles as the crow flies,"[26] which would require that Jacob's party travel an average distance of 35 to 40 miles per day, a pace very high, if not impossible, for a party consisting of the husband, two wives, two concubines, twelve children, camels, and much livestock. In any case, Laban and his party catch up to Jacob and his party.

24 During one night of this pursuit, Laban has a dream in which God tells him not to harm Jacob. This is much like Abimelech's experience in 20:3. An outsider is duped by a Hebrew. The outsider is enraged and intent on settling the score. Before he can retaliate, God speaks to him in a nocturnal dream, and deters him from reciprocation.

That Laban is forbidden *from threatening Jacob with any harm* (lit., "lest you speak with Jacob from good unto evil") does not mean that Laban is not allowed to speak "any word at all" against Jacob.[27] Silence is not imposed on him. Rather, even if he feels that he has a legitimate grievance, Laban is not to prosecute and take (legal) action against Jacob.[28] "God has corked the bottle of his aggressiveness."[29]

25 Elsewhere in Genesis the verb used for "pitching" tents is *nāṭâ* (12:8; 26:25; 33:19; 35:21). Here the verb *tāqaʿ* is used. In some places the verb means "thrust, drive (a weapon into a person)" (Judg. 3:21; 4:21; 2 Sam.

25. See R. Frankena, "Some Remarks on the Semitic Background of Chapters xxix–xxxi of the Book of Genesis," *OTS* 17 (1972) 57.

26. Skinner, *Genesis,* p. 397. Sarna (*Genesis,* p. 217) suggests 400 miles (640 km.).

27. Against A. M. Honeyman, "*Merismus* in Biblical Hebrew," *JBL* 71 (1952) 12, who renders "not any word at all."

28. See W. M. Clark, "A Legal Background to the Yahwist's Use of 'Good and Evil' in Genesis 2–3," *JBL* 88 (1969) 269.

29. Fokkelman, *Narrative Art in Genesis,* p. 166.

18:14), and so by extension is used here of pitching a tent by driving its pegs into the ground. The most frequent use of *tāqaʿ* is "blow (a trumpet)" (cf. Num. 10:4) as a prelude to battle or to sound an alarm. Thus, *tāqaʿ* occurs in contexts of war or violence, and it is appropriate in Gen. 31:25 where the possibility of violence is aborted only by divine intervention.

26 Laban now moves from the role of paterfamilias to that of plaintiff.[30] His first accusation is that Jacob has duped him, and the second is that he has carried off his daughters like captives. This second charge is not exaggerated; it is untrue. Vv. 14-16 point out that the daughters have gone along with Jacob voluntarily. To make Jacob's "crime" even more heinous, Laban refers to Leah and Rachel as *my daughters* rather than "your wives." Jacob now stands accused of fraud, breach of trust, and kidnapping. The verb Laban uses to describe what Jacob did with his daughters, *dragging away* (*wattᵉnahēg* [Piel]), is the same one used earlier of Jacob when he led his livestock clandestinely away from Laban's home (*wayyinhag* [Qal], 31:18). If these two passages may be connected through the double use of *nāhag* in the Piel[31] and Qal stems, then the point of v. 26 would be that Laban is furious because Jacob took his daughters as captives much as one would drag off cattle. Little does Laban know at this point how wrong he is. The reader knows well that Leah and Rachel were not compelled to accompany Jacob — they left voluntarily and enthusiastically (vv. 14-16).

27-28 Laban pictures himself both as victim (v. 26) and as a hurt but understanding father (vv. 27-28). Why would Laban consent to let Jacob and his daughters depart, when up to this time he has done everything he can to detain them? It is unlikely that his expression of beneficence is genuine. But it makes his case more appealing to his listening kinsmen, and perhaps to his daughters. His spate of questions directed at Jacob might engender some sympathy from them, especially when he points out that he was denied even the privilege of kissing his daughters and his grandchildren good-bye, and when he accuses Jacob of folly in the presence of his wives.

festive singing, with tambourine and lyre. The Bible offers no other evidence that music played a role in the send-off activities when children left their parents' home, but Luke 15:25 shows that music could play a part in welcome-home activities after the prolonged departure of a child.

30. L. B. Kutler ("Features of the Battle Challenge in Biblical Hebrew, Akkadian, and Ugaritic," *UF* 19 [1987] 96, 99) demonstrates that the scene describing the meeting of Laban with Jacob at Gilead has the four standard parts of a battle challenge in Near Eastern literature: (1) an act is committed or omitted; (2) factions assemble to confront each other; (3) a challenge is declared; (4) battle ensues or is avoided.

31. The Piel of *nāhag* means, in a negative sense, to drive or lead into exile (Deut. 4:27; 28:37), and in a positive sense, to lead, guide: Ps. 48:15 (Eng. 14); 78:52 (through a wilderness); Isa. 49:10; 63:14. All of the above instances of *nāhag* have Yahweh/God as the subject.

29 Laban just mentioned that what Jacob had done *(ʿᵃśô)* was foolish. Laban now says he has power "to do" *(laʿᵃśôṯ)* Jacob harm. By *harm every one of you* (note here the plural: Laban indicts the whole party, not just Jacob), Laban may mean anything from "kill you" to "imprison you" to "take my daughters away from you." The only power standing above the paterfamilias is God. Only he can restrain Laban from exercising his authority. When Laban shares with Jacob and his party what God said to him in a dream, he faithfully reproduces God's words. The only difference between the original divine announcement (v. 24) and Laban's repetition of it (v. 29) is that the *pen tᵉḏabbēr* (conjunction plus imperfect form of the verb) of v. 24 becomes in v. 29 *middabbēr* (preposition plus infinitive), which likely has no great significance. Thus Laban gives priority to his respect for the God of Jacob over the rightful exercise of his own prerogatives in this situation.

30 Laban can understand why Jacob would want to return home — he is *homesick,* not having seen his father in twenty years.[32] But he pretends not to understand why Jacob would abscond with his gods. Laban assumes that Jacob is the thief; perhaps he has discerned some of Jacob's character. He does not know that Rachel has stolen them. Indeed, Jacob does not know that Rachel has stolen them.

Laban's first accusation against Jacob — his departure with Laban's daughters — was rather lengthy (vv. 26-28). Laban's second accusation — *why*[33] *did you steal my gods?* — is confined to four words in Hebrew. The brevity with which this charge is spoken might suggest that for Laban it is the less evil of Jacob's two acts, an addendum to Laban's charges. Additionally, the pact between Jacob and Laban (vv. 43-54) says nothing about the gods, but much about Laban's daughters. Nonetheless, it is more likely that Laban's second charge against Jacob is the more serious one.[34] Laban respected Jacob's God, but Jacob has not respected Laban's gods.

31-32 Jacob begins his defense with a justification for his actions (v. 31b). He does not deny Laban's charges. He did what he did because he thought Laban would forcibly take his wives from him.[35] The use of the fear motive to justify a course of action is as ancient as Gen. 3:10. In his earlier conversation with his wives, Jacob drew attention to the directive from God to leave, and to his frustrations of maltreatment by Laban in return for faithful

32. Sarna (*Genesis,* p. 218) remarks: "For devastating psychological effect, Laban cynically reinforces his feigned magnanimity with a beguiling show of empathy." But must we judge every word and action of Laban with distrust?

33. On the preference for *lāmmâ* in "why" questions asked in rapid succession, see J. Barr, "Why? in Biblical Hebrew," *JTS* 36 (1985) 29-31.

34. See T. L. Thompson, *The Origin Tradition of Ancient Israel,* JSOTSup 55 (Sheffield: JSOT, 1987), p. 108; von Rad, *Genesis,* pp. 309-10.

35. Cf. 1 Sam. 25:44, where Saul takes Michal from David.

service (31:4-13). But he never shared with them, as he does with Laban himself, the possibility that Laban would put a wedge between Jacob and his wives. It is possible that Jacob has fabricated this idea on the spot, in order to give a quick response to Laban's questions and to put his departure in as good a light as possible.

I have suggested above on 31:19 that it is too much of a generalization to say that in Biblical Hebrew *gānab̲* means "to steal" and *gāzal* (the verb Jacob uses here for Laban "forcibly taking away" Leah and Rachel) means "to rob," the first done secretly, the second done by open force. Now it cannot be denied that on many occasions *gāzal* does indeed mean "to rob (by open force)," especially in prophetic literature. But that is not true in all cases. For example, in Gen. 21:25 Abraham lodges a complaint with Abimelech to the effect that the king's servants had seized or robbed *(gāzal)* a well belonging to Abraham. Now it is clear in this case that the individuals against whom Abraham makes his grievance are not armed robbers, but royal officials. And it is most unlikely that any act of violence ensured in the takeover. What happened was the illegal expropriation of property which Abraham could not thwart. Abraham is a victim of the abuse of power, and lost his property in the process. I suggest that that same nuance of *gāzal* is present in 31:31. Jacob was fearful (and whether he is being honest or deceitful here does not matter) that Laban would abuse his authority, given the fact that Laban might have some right to reclaim his daughters (not reclaim Jacob's wives), especially if Jacob was guilty of some criminal act.[36]

In v. 32 Jacob addresses Laban's second accusation — the theft of the gods. He invites Laban to search their camp and to *identify* anything that is his.[37] Of course, in Laban's opinion, much that Jacob has is rightfully Laban's — all those polychromed herds and flocks. But those are not his concern here; now he wants to find his gods.

Unknowingly, Jacob places Rachel in danger with his words: *With whomever you find the gods, he shall not live.* The sentence is much like that of Joseph about his cup: "with whomever of your servants it is found, let him die" (44:9). From this oath several scholars have concluded that for the theft of sancta the death penalty was imposed.[38] We need to remember, however,

36. See R. Westbrook, *Studies in Biblical and Cuneiform Law* (Paris: Gabalda, 1988), pp. 23-38, esp. pp. 26, 36.

37. The Hiphil of *nāk̲ar* can mean "recognize" in a nontechnical sense (e.g., 27:23; 42:7, 8). But it can also have the technical sense of "making a statement to the other party about a fact of legal relevance" (31:32; 37:32, 33; 38:25, 26). See Daube, *Studies in Biblical Law,* pp. 5-6, 206.

38. See Daube, *Studies in Biblical Law,* pp. 94, 210ff.; Jackson, *Theft in Early Jewish Law,* pp. 164-67. But Daube and Jackson read the intent of the verse differently. For Jackson the serious factor is the sacred nature of the stolen property. For Daube the

that "drawing legal ruling from possible hyperbole in narrative speech is a precarious enterprise."[39]

33-34 Laban begins his search in all the logical, but wrong, places — Jacob's tent (does he start here because he suspects his son-in-law the most?), Leah's tent, the maidservants' tent, and finally Rachel's tent (as the suspense grows). The word used for *searched* is *māšaš,* which was used earlier of Isaac's "touching, feeling" of Jacob (disguised as Esau, 27:21, 22). He who was once touched, searched by his father, now has his tent and Rachel's tent touched, searched by his father-in-law. The gods, we now discover, were small, for Rachel hides them in her *camel saddle* and sits on them. One can steal gods, hide gods, and sit on gods, ideas at which orthodox Yahwism would shudder.

35 With a little bit of respect *(Let not my lord be provoked that I cannot rise in your presence),* Rachel manages to fool her father.[40] Her menstrual period has sapped her strength and therefore she cannot even rise to greet her father. Again we may imagine the ancient Hebrew hearing this story. Not only can one sit on gods, but such gods can be rendered unclean if they are stained by Rachel's blood. The gods, so crucial to Laban, are reduced to "sanitary towels,"[41] or at least a soft cushion on which to rest her body, now weakened by the loss of blood. Note that in the pericope dealing with a woman's menstrual flow (Lev. 15:19-33), anybody (i.e., any male) who touches anything on which the woman sits becomes unclean (15:23). While such regulations were obviously of no relevance to Laban, still Rachel's explanation of her situation to Laban is one that her father would be unlikely to question.[42] Thus the reader comes to the end of this unit and shares Laban's ignorance. Neither he nor we know whether Rachel's claim is true or fabricated.

---

theft is more serious and subject to stiffer penalties when the thief is caught *in flagranti,* and this is what Jacob is permitting and encouraging. See also Westbrook, *Studies in Biblical and Cuneiform Law,* pp. 123-24. A. Phillips' remark (*Ancient Israel's Criminal Law* [Oxford: Blackwell, 1970], p. 141 n. 68) that v. 32 merely illustrates the absolute, uncontested power of the head of the clan in patriarchal times, and his ability arbitrarily to set penalties, regardless of the offense, is wide of the mark.

39. J. Milgrom, "The Concept of Maʿal in the Bible and in the Ancient Near East," *JAOS* 96 (1976) 246 n. 67.

40. One may compare Rachel's deception of her father with Michal's deception of her father, Saul (1 Sam. 19:11-17). But unlike the case of Rachel, it is clear in the narrative that Michal acted out of loyalty to her husband and concern for his safety (1 Sam. 19:11).

41. See Fokkelman, *Narrative Art in Genesis,* p. 170.

42. See N. Steinberg, "Israelite Tricksters, Their Analogues and Cross-Cultural Study," in *Reasoning with the Foxes: Female Wit in a World of Male Power,* ed. J. C. Exum and J. W. H. Bos, Semeia 42 (Atlanta: Scholars, 1988) 7; M. Bal, "Tricky Thematics," in ibid., 151: "A woman would simply have checked, a man would not dream of trying."

4. JACOB'S APOLOGIA (31:36-42)

36 *Jacob, incensed, rejected the charge of Laban:*[1] *"What is my crime,*
what is my offense[2] *that you should dog me?*[3]
37 *Now that you have searched through*[4] *all my things, have you found*
anything of your belongings? If so, produce them in front of my kinsmen
and yours. Let them choose between the two of us.
38 *In the twenty years that I was under you your ewes*[5] *and your she-goats*
never miscarried,[6] *nor on rams from your flock did I ever feast.*
39 *Torn animals*[7] *I never brought you; I made restitution for*[8] *whatever you*
held me responsible for,[9] *whether it was stolen*[10] *by day or by night.*
40 *Thus were my circumstances.*[11] *By day scorching heat ravaged me and*
frost at night,[12] *while sleep fled*[13] *from my eyes.*
41 *Of*[14] *the twenty years I spent in your household, I served fourteen years*

1. Or "disputed/quarreled with Laban" *(rîḇ b^{e});* see the commentary below.

2. On the use of a question repeated in apposition, see Andersen, *Sentence in Biblical Hebrew,* p. 38.

3. *dālaq* has the meaning "hotly pursue" in Gen. 31:36 (Speiser renders "hound") and 1 Sam. 17:53 (both followed by *'aḥ^{a}rê*); also in Ps. 10:2; Lam. 4:19.

4. The narrator used *māšaš* (Piel) in v. 34 for Laban's search for his gods in Rachel's tent.

5. The Hebrew word for "your ewes" is *r^{e}ḥeleyḵā,* i.e., "your rachels."

6. For *šāḵal* used with animals aborting or miscarrying see Job 21:10.

7. For *ṭ^{e}rēpâ/ṭārap* see Gen. 37:33; 44:28; Lev. 7:24; 17:15; 22:8. The root *ṭrp* always describes the rapaciousness of wild beasts or people who resemble such beasts.

8. The translation of *'ānōḵî '^{a}ḥaṭṭennâ* is debated, and will be discussed below. The imperfect is frequentative. See S. R. Driver, *Treatise on the Use of Tenses,* p. 34, § 30a.

9. "To hold responsible for" is lit. "require/seek from the hand." This expression has an Akkadian equivalent: *ina qāti bu'û* (*CAD,* B:364-65), which means "to hold someone accountable, responsible." Cf. S. M. Paul, "Unrecognized Biblical Legal Idioms in the Light of Comparative Akkadian Expressions," *RB* 86 (1979) 237-39. The idiom *bāqaš mîyāḏ* occurs in Gen. 31:39; 43:9; 1 Sam. 20:16; 2 Sam. 4:11; Ezek. 3:18, 20; 33:8.

10. On the passive participle with an *-î* ending *(g^{e}nuḇ^{e}ṯî)* see GKC, § 901, who understands *-î* as the remains of early case endings. One might also read: "whether I was robbed by day or by night." On the use of inflected participles (i.e., used with the suffixes usually attached to perfect verbs), possibly under the influence of Aramaic (and Gen. 31 is set in an Aramaic-speaking milieu), see G. A. Rendsburg, "Morphological Evidence for Regional Dialects in Ancient Hebrew," in *Linguistics and Biblical Hebrew,* ed. W. R. Bodine (Winona Lake, IN: Eisenbrauns, 1992), pp. 82-84.

11. Lit., "(Thus) I was."

12. Note the chiasm: day: scorching heat::frost: night.

13. The idea of sleep fleeing from somebody (*nāḏar* plus *šēnâ*) occurs only here and in Est. 6:1; and in Job 7:14 without *šēnâ.*

14. *zeh* is not a demonstrative pronoun here, but an enclitic, an undefined particle

for your two daughters, and six years for your flock, while you altered my wages ten times.

42 *If my father's god, the God of Abraham and the Dreaded One of Isaac,*[15] *had not been with me, surely by now you would have sent me away*[16] *empty-handed. But my affliction and my labor God saw; and last night he pronounced judgment."*

36 Jacob now takes the offensive and addresses himself to the question of the stolen gods and Laban's frantic and embarrassing search for them. We have translated *yāreḇ* (from *rîḇ*) as *rejected the charge of.* This is the third narrative in Genesis in which this root occurs. In 13:7-8 the herdsmen of Abraham and Lot engage in a *rîḇ* over grazing land. In 26:20-22 there is a *rîḇ* between Isaac and the men of Gerar for possession of wells. In all three of these cases the contending parties settle their differences without appealing to a third party. That is the reason why it is inappropriate to refer to these as "lawsuits," in which irreconcilable differences force the parties involved into third-party arbitration. Here the dispute and its solution is entirely bilateral. Laban rejects Jacob's suggestion that their respective kinsmen decide (v. 37b), and the two of them resolve their own differences.[17]

Jacob defends his own integrity with the counterclaim *What is my crime, what is my offense?*[18] According to Mabee, the word *crime* (Heb. *pešaʿ*) suggests a property crime, and *offense* (Heb. *ḥaṭṭāʾṯ*) suggests a legal offense.[19] If the original meaning of *ḥāṭāʾ* is "to miss, fail," then here one may view *ḥaṭṭāʾṯ* as failure, a lack of perfection and acceptability in expediting a duty.

Jacob then asks Laban for clarification and substantiation as to how, if at all, Jacob has not fulfilled the claims of a relation. Thus it is better to translate the Hebrew word here as "offense" rather than "sin." Jacob's question to Laban

---

that frequently precedes numbers (also in v. 38). See GKC, § 136d; Williams, *Hebrew Syntax,* p. 24, § 118.

15. For *paḥaḏ yiṣḥāq* see the commentary below on v. 42.

16. *šillaḥtānî* is an illustration of the use of the perfect whose realization in the past is only hypothetical. See GKC, §106p; Davidson, *Hebrew Syntax,* p. 179, § 131.

17. See M. DeRoche, "Yahweh's *rîb* Against Israel: A Reassessment of the So-called 'Prophetic Lawsuit' in the Preexilic Prophets," *JBL* 102 (1983) 567.

18. G. W. Coats ("Self-Abasement and Insult Formulas," *JBL* 89 [1970] 14-15, 22, 24) cites Gen. 31:36 as an illustration of a self-abasement formula comprised of two parts: (a) a nominal sentence introduced by an interrogative particle, and (b) a verbal sentence connected to the nominal sentence by a *kî* (although 31:36 should be *aab,* rather than *ab*). The *kî* clause that follows ("that you should dog me") is not an expression of self-abasement but a request for information, unless Jacob is implying something like, " 'what is my offense?' (It does not merit your pursuit)" (p. 22).

19. See C. Mabee, "Jacob and Laban. The Structure of judicial proceedings (Gene-

is like David's question to Jonathan vis-à-vis Saul: "what is my guilt [*ʿᵃwōnî*], and what is my offense [*ḥaṭṭāʾṯî*] before your father that [*kî*] he seeks my life" (1 Sam. 20:1). All perceived unscrupulous behavior by a subordinate is "offense" in the eyes of the superior. See also Gen. 40:1, where the butler and baker "offended" *(ḥāṭᵉʾû)* the king of Egypt. The first term Jacob uses, *pišʿî, my crime,* has the basic meaning of "breach." Jacob's use of *pišʿî* would challenge Laban to provide empirical evidence that Jacob is guilty of behavior that has fractured the peaceful relation between the two parties.[20] Of neither breach nor offense is he culpable. Laban believes Jacob is guilty until proved innocent, while Jacob believes he is innocent until proved guilty.

37 As we saw above, Jacob is willing to turn this confrontation into a legitimate lawsuit, with their kinsmen being the third party who will adjudicate between the two litigants. *Let them choose between us.* They will establish guilt or innocence.[21] In so speaking, Jacob is distancing himself from Laban. Earlier (v. 32) he had said to Laban: "In full view of our kinsmen [*ʾaḥênû*] identify anything that is yours." Now he divides that one composite group into two subgroups: "produce them in front of my kinsmen [*ʾaḥay*] and yours [*ʾaḥeyḵâ*]." The alienation between son-in-law and father-in-law is growing. Laban does not respond to Jacob's suggestion.

38 Jacob moves from the present (vv. 36-37) to the past (vv. 38-41), and then back to the present (v. 42). He has, he believes, an unblemished track record. In the last twenty years he has served Laban faithfully and done nothing to raise suspicion in his father-in-law. It is of interest that Jacob begins his autobiography with a reference to Laban's *ewes (rᵉḥēleyḵā),* which is the plural of the same word that is Rachel's name *(rāḥēl).* For twenty years Jacob has indeed cared for Laban's "Rachels," all his "rachels" and his one "Rachel." To draw attention to the care with which he handled his job, a claim designed to bring satisfaction to any normal employer, Jacob begins with nouns and follows with verbs in the negative (an inversion of the usual Hebrew word order of verb-noun): *your ewes and she-goats never miscarried, nor on rams from your flock did I ever feast. . . . Torn animals I never brought you* (v. 39).

39 Jacob claims, further, that he *made restitution* to Laban for any of his flock attacked and ravaged by wild animals. The thrust of *ʾānōḵî ʾᵃḥaṭṭennâ*

---

sis xxxi 25-42)," *VT* 30 (1980) 203 n. 32. Mabee takes this distinction from R. Knierim, *Die Hauptbegriffe für Sünde im Alten Testament* (Mohn: Gütersloh, 1965).

20. E. Lipiński, "Sin," *EncJud,* 14:1587-88; K. Koch, *"ḥāṭāʾ," TDOT,* 4:309-19, esp. p. 311; H. Seebass, *"pāšaʿ," TWAT,* 6:791-810, esp. 795; R. Youngblood, "A New Look at Three OT Roots for 'Sin,'" in *Biblical and Near Eastern Studies,* Fest. W. S. LaSor, ed. G. A. Tuttle (Grand Rapids: Eerdmans, 1978), pp. 201-5.

21. The Hiphil of *yāḵaḥ* (here translated "choose") not only means "chide, reprove," but has legal connotations as well: "conduct a legal case, mediate a legal dispute." See R. R. Wilson, "An interpretation of Ezekiel's dumbness," *VT* 22 (1972) 99-100.

is debated. The verb might be read as the Piel of *ḥāṭā'*, "to sin."[22] One of the unique facts about the verb *ḥāṭā'* is that the Piel refers to the undoing and removal of the condition conveyed by the Qal. Thus *ḥāṭā'* in the Piel does not mean "commit sin" but "remove sin," that is, "purify." Now if the original meaning of *ḥāṭā'* is "to miss" (an archery term, among other nuances), then the Piel means "to make up for those misses (or losses)," that is, to make restitution.

What is unique about the Piel of *ḥāṭā'* in this verse, if that is the verb involved, is that it is the only OT occurrence of it in a profane usage. All others are in the sacral or cultic sphere. Several attempts to explain the verbal form have been offered. B. Levine translates "I shall make restitution for it" and suggests a parallel with the denominative *kipper*.[23] J. J. Finkelstein explains the verb by connecting it with the Akkadian words *ḫīṭum, ḫīṭīṭum,* "loss, damage," and translates "make good a loss."[24]

It may well be that the form in question has nothing to do with the root *ḥṭ'*, but rather reflects the root *ḥwṭ/ḥyṭ,* which in turn is to be connected with the Akkadian verb *ḫiāṭu,* "repay, pay back": "but I paid you for it."[25] This meaning is reflected in LXX *apotinnýō.*

you held me responsible for. As a shepherd Jacob assumed liability[26]

22. N. Zohar ("Repentance and Purification: The Significance and Semantics of חטאת in the Pentateuch," *JBL* 107 [1988] 616) reads the verb as *ḥāṭā',* which he renders "I made substitution for it," understanding the basic meaning of *ḥāṭā'* as "replace, displace, transfer." But both Zohar's interpretation and his seeing *ḥāṭā'* in this verse are problematic. First, from where would Jacob, a hired hand, possess or obtain animals to take the place of those killed? It is more likely that in such a situation Laban deducted the cost of the animal losses from Jacob's wages (see 31:41b). Second, if the verb in question is *ḥāṭā',* how is one to explain the absence of the final *aleph* in *'ᵃḥaṭṭennâ?* Cf. J. Milgrom, "The *Modus Operandi* of the *Ḥaṭṭā't:* A Rejoinder," *JBL* 109 (1990) 112. E. Jenni (*Das hebräische Pi'el* [Zurich: EVZ, 1968], p. 267) identifies the form in question as an "estimative-declarative Piel" of the verb *ḥāṭā',* "I owned up to anything that went wrong," but neither does Jenni explain the absence of the *aleph.*

23. B. Levine, *In the Presence of the Lord,* p. 102 n. 123.

24. J. J. Finkelstein, "An Old Babylonian Herding Contract and Genesis 31:38f.," *JAOS* 88 (1968) 30.

25. See A. van Selms, "CTA 32: A Prophetic Liturgy," *UF* 3 (1971) 234-48, esp. 244f.; O. Loretz, "Hebräisch *ḥwṭ* 'bezahlen, erstatten' in Gen. 31,39," *ZAW* 87 (1975) 207-8; M. Dietrich, O. Loretz, and J. Sanmartín, "Lexikalische und literarische Probleme in RS 1.2 = CTA 32 und RS 17.100 = CTA Appendice I," *UF* 7 (1975) 152-53; S. E. Loewenstamm, *"'anōḵî 'ăḥaṭṭennāh," ZAW* 90 (1978) 410; idem, *"'ānōkî 'ăhaṭṭennâ," Leš* 29 (1965) 69-70 (Hebrew), translated in *Comparative Studies in Biblical and Ancient Oriental Literature,* AOAT 24 (Neukirchen-Vluyn: Neukirchener, 1980), pp. 225-27; J. Milgrom, *Leviticus 1–16,* AB (New York: Doubleday, 1991), p. 1084.

26. Cf. the Code of Hammurapi, § 263: "if he [the shepherd] has lost [the ox] or sheep which was committed to him, he shall make good ox for [ox], sheep for [sheep] to their owner" (*ANET,* p. 177).

for animals stolen either in the daytime or at night.[27] A shepherd would be expected to provide protection against theft, as Exod. 22:9-13 (also, 1 Sam. 17:34-36) makes clear; but he would not be expected necessarily to provide protection against a raid.

40-41 Jacob endured all kinds of extremes of weather in the line of duty, from scorching heat that *ravaged ('āḵal)*[28] him, to cold temperatures at night; even *sleep fled from* Jacob, just as Jacob fled from Laban. The changeable weather Jacob has lived through is akin to the changeable Laban with whom he has lived. At times Laban can be solicitous and at other times he can be duplicitous.

The repetition of *twenty years* (see v. 38) is not evidence of two traditions behind the story. In the excitement of the moment, rallying all the facts possible to defend his record, Jacob will more than likely repeat himself in such an animated speech. The repetition also indicates how much Laban is chafing under the raw deal and blatant accusations he has received from Laban. At an earlier stage in his life, Jacob was able to telescope large segments of time into a transitory moment. Thus the seven years for which he served for Rachel were but "a few days" (29:20). There is no "few days" here — only twenty long years of arduous toil.

42 Jacob appeals to God just as Laban had done earlier (v. 29). Only God could put a halt to Laban's revenge, and he did. Jacob takes that one step further. Only God could overrule Laban's slyness, and he has. If the kinsmen of the two will not make a decision or "choose" between Laban and Jacob (*yôḵîḥû,* v. 37), then God will and has made that choice — *he pronounced judgment (yôḵaḥ,* v. 42). God has intervened in Laban's life much more than Laban knows. Laban, originally the plaintiff, has become the criminal. Jacob, originally the criminal, has become the plaintiff.

Of special interest here is Jacob's reference to God as *the Dreaded One of Isaac (paḥaḏ yiṣḥāq).* Because most ancient versions translated this expression as "the Fear of Isaac," that translation has found its way into most of our modern versions. Doubt that *paḥaḏ* has anything to do with fear has led scholars to look elsewhere. L. Kopf connected it with an Arabic word and translated "the Refuge of Isaac."[29] Much more well received has been

27. For shepherds whose responsibility for the flock continues during the night, cf. Luke 2:8: "there were shepherds out in the field, keeping watch over their flock by night."

28. Three authors call attention to the Ugaritic expression *bakit* in the Aqhat Epic, used by Danel as he makes the rounds of his parched territory, and compare it with *'āḵal* in Gen. 31:40 to describe the effect of drought and cold on a person. See J. Gray, *Legacy of Canaan,* VTSup 5 (Leiden: Brill, 1965), p. 119 n. 6 ("in the blasted land"); U. Cassuto, *Biblical and Oriental Studies,* tr. I. Abrahams, 2 vols. (Jerusalem: Magnes, 1973-75), 2:196-98 ("in his parched field"); J. C. L. Gibson, *Canaanite Myths and Legends,* rev. ed. (Edinburgh: T. & T. Clark, 1977), p. 116 ("in the blighted land").

29. L. Kopf, "Arabische Etymologien und Parallelen zum Bibelwörterbuch," *VT* 9 (1959) 257.

Albright's connection of *paḥaḏ* with Aramaic and Hebrew cognates meaning "family, clan, tribe, a tribe of closest kin," and with Ugar. *pḫd,* "flock," suggesting the translation "the Kinsman of Isaac".[30] Some convincing phonetic arguments have called this equation into question.[31] A third suggestion is that of A. Lemaire, who takes *paḥaḏ* as an ancestral deity and renders: "If the God of my father, Paḥad, had not been with me."[32] This, for Lemaire, is the primitive reading of the text, with Pahad being the ancestral deity of the sons of Jacob. A fourth suggestion is to understand *paḥaḏ* as an Aramaic word for "thigh."[33] The thigh, a euphemism for the genitals, symbolizes both Isaac's creative power and his family and ancestral spirits. But this interpretation dissociates the phrase from the coordinate phrase *the God of Abraham.* The best support for the traditional rendering is supplied by the Ebla texts. A personal name found there is *li-pá-ad,* "Dread is powerful."[34] The meaning of "dread" for Heb. *paḥaḏ* is borne out by Job 4:14: "Terror [*paḥaḏ*] seized me, and trembling, all my members shuddered [*hiphîḏ*]."[35] Note also Job 39:16b, speaking about the alleged cruelty of the ostrich to its young, which should be translated something like "though her labor is in vain, she is without fear [i.e., concern; Heb. *bᵉlî pāḥaḏ*]," or "that her labor is in vain she has no fear."[36]

It may well be that the personal name Zelophehad (*ṣᵉlop̄ḥāḏ,* Num. 26:33; 27:1ff.; 36:1ff.; Josh. 17:3) is connected with the name Jacob uses for divinity in v. 42. Zelophehad may mean "fear [is his] shadow/protector." Two phenomena open the door to relating the two. First, according to Josh. 17:3, Zelophehad is the son of Hepher, who is the son of Gilead; in Gen. 31:21 the

30. W. F. Albright, *From the Stone Age to Christianity,* 2nd ed. (Garden City, NY: Doubleday, 1957), p. 248 n. 71; O. Eissfeldt, "El and Yahweh," *JSS* 1 (1956) 32; M. Dahood, *Ugaritic-Hebrew Philology,* BibOr 17 (Rome: Pontifical Biblical Institute, 1965), p. 69, no. 2035; G. R. Driver, "Hebrew Homonyms," in *Hebräische Wortforschung,* Fest. W. Baumgartner, ed. B. Hartmann, et al., VTSup 16 (Leiden: Brill, 1967), p. 64.

31. See D. Hillers, "Paḥad Yiṣḥāq," *JBL* 91 (1972) 90-92.

32. A. Lemaire, "Les Benê Jacob. Essai d'interprétation historique d'une tradition patriarcale," *RB* 85 (1978) 323-27; idem, "A propos de *paḥad* dans l'onomastique ouest-sémitique," *VT* 35 (1985) 500-501.

33. See M. Malul, "More on *paḥad yiṣḥaq* (Genesis xxxi 42, 53) and the oath by the thigh," *VT* 35 (1985) 192-200. Cf. Job 40:17, a reference to Behemoth's "thighs" *(paḥᵃḏāw).*

34. See M. J. Dahood, "The Ebla Tablets and Old Testament Theology," *TD* 27 (1979) 308-9; here he revises his earlier suggestion of "cabal" or "pack (of dogs)" (*Ugaritic-Hebrew Philology,* p. 69).

35. Translation of M. Pope, *Job,* AB, 3rd ed. (Garden City, NY: Doubleday, 1973), p. 34.

36. Gen. 31:42 and Job 39:16b share three vocabulary words: terms from the root *pḥḏ* ("the Dreaded One of..."/"she has no fear"); the adverb *rēqām* ("empty-handed") and the related noun (in an adverbial phrase) *rîq* ("in vain"); and the noun *yᵉḡîaʿ,* "labor, toil" ("my labor God saw"/"though her labor be in vain."

action between Laban and Jacob takes place at Gilead, which Jacob later (v. 47) names "Galeed." Second, the incident in Numbers regarding Zelophehad involves his five daughters; a major part of the incident in Gen. 31 involves Laban's two daughters.[37]

If one understands *paḥaḏ yiṣḥāq* as "the Dreaded One of Isaac,"[38] does it mean "the One whom Isaac dreads," or "the One of Isaac who inspires dread"? Two points argue for the latter. First, whenever *paḥaḏ* is used in a compound, it always refers to the cause or source of dread, rather then the object of dread. Thus we find "fear of the Jews" (Est. 8:17), "fear of Mordecai" (Est. 9:3), "dread of Yahweh" (1 Sam. 11:7), "fear of God" (Ps. 36:2 [Eng. 1]), "dread of the enemies" (Ps. 64:12 [Eng. 11]), "terror of the night" (Ps. 91:5), "dread of evil" (Prov. 1:33).[39] Second, Jacob's choice of this name for divinity ("the One of Isaac who inspires dread") fits better with the context of the narrative. In using this name, Jacob is no doubt referring to the fact that the only reason Laban did not physically harm Jacob was because the God of Jacob's father spoke to Laban and issued a restraining order (v. 29). That revelation was deterrent enough.

Jacob is not aware that the gods of his father-in-law are with him too. What he does know is that the God of Abraham and the Dreaded One of Isaac is with him.

5. COVENANT NEGOTIATION (31:43-54)

43 *Laban replied to Jacob: "The daughters are mine, the grandchildren are mine, and flocks are mine; everything you can see is mine.*[1] *For these my daughters what can I do today, or for the grandchildren they have borne?*

44 *Come, then, let us make a pact, you and I, that there*[2] *may be*[3] *a witness*

37. E. Puech, "La crainte d'Isaac en Genèse xxxi et 53," *VT* 34 (1984) 356-57.

38. Cross, *Canaanite Myth and Hebrew Epic,* p. 269.

39. See Sarna, *Genesis,* p. 366 n. 17, for the references. In two of these Psalm references (64:12 [Eng. 11] and 91:5) Dahood (*Psalms,* 2:104, 331) connects *paḥaḏ* with Ugar. *pḫd,* "flock."

1. On conjoined verbless clauses, see Andersen, *Sentence in Biblical Hebrew,* p. 100.

2. If *bᵉrîṯ,* "covenant," is the understood subject of *hāyâ,* the sentence would read "and it shall be a witness." Because *bᵉrîṯ* is fem. and *hāyâ* is masc., an impersonal subject is assigned to *hāyâ* instead. G. R. Driver observes, however, that a fem. often has a masc. complement if separated from the latter ("Hebrew Studies," *JRAS* 71 [1948] 164-76, quoted in D. J. McCarthy, "Three Covenants in Genesis," *CBQ* 26 [1964] 179 n. 3). The LXX adds "behold, there is no one with us; behold, God is a witness between me and you," just after *wᵉhāyâ lᵉʿēḏ bēnî ûbêneḵā,* as in v. 50, suggesting either that the LXX has

between you and me."

45 *Jacob then took a stone and built*[4] *a pillar.*[5]

46 *Jacob said to his kinsmen: "Collect some stones." So they got stones and made a mound, and shared a meal by the mound.*

47 *Laban called it Jegar-sahadutha*[6] *but Jacob called it Galeed.*[7]

48 *"This mound," Laban said, "is witnessing,*[8] *as of today, between me and you." That is why it was named Galeed—*

49 *and Mizpah*[9] *as well, for he said: "May Yahweh*[10] *watch*[11] *between you and me when we are separated from each other.*

---

artificially made v. 44 parallel with v. 50, or that it preserves the original of v. 44, the clause in question having been accidentally deleted from v. 44 in transmission. Another credible suggestion for this verse is to take *ʿēḏ* as Aram. *ʿāḏ,* "pact": "Let us make a covenant . . . let there be a pact." See F. O. Garcia-Treto, "Genesis 31,44 and 'Gilead,'" *ZAW* 79 (1967) 14-15. Garcia-Treto accounts for the *lᵉ* on *lᵉʿēḏ* as an artificial addition by later redactors who, baffled by the Aram. *ʿāḏ,* needed to give the text some sense of syntactical propriety to their secondary reading. Cross (*Canaanite Myth and Hebrew Epic,* p. 269) also accepts this repointing and translates, "Come now, let us make a covenant, and let it be a treaty between you and me."

3. For the perfect with *waw* after a jussive or, as here, cohortative, see S. R. Driver, *Treatise on the Use of Tenses,* p. 127, § 113.2.b; Davidson, *Hebrew Syntax,* p. 81 § 55a.

4. For *rûm* meaning "build" see Y. Avishur, "RWM (RMM) — 'Build' in Ugaritic and the Bible (and *hpryḥ* — "Build' in the Bible and Tosephta)" *Leš* 45 (1980/81) 270-99 (Hebrew). In v. 51 the verb *yārâ,* "throw up, raise," is used.

5. The similarity (for pun's sake?) between *maṣṣēḇâ* and *miṣpâ* (Mizpah, v. 49) may illustrate the interchange of the voiced and voiceless bilabial plosives *b* and *p* in Biblical Hebrew. See S. Gevirtz, "On Hebrew *šebeṭ* = 'JUDGE,'" in *The Bible World,* Fest. C. H. Gordon, ed. Gary Rendsburg, et al. (New York: Ktav, 1980), p. 63.

6. Aramaic for "mound of witness."

7. Hebrew for "mound of witness" or "(the) mound (is) witness," or originally "mound of the treaty (between Laban and Jacob)." This interpretation assumes that the Masoretes mispointed *ʿāḏ* to read *ʿēḏ,* "witness" (see n. 2). *gilʿāḏ,* then, would show the primary etymology ("mound of the treaty"), while *gilʿēḏ* would show the secondary etymology, "mound of witness."

8. *ʿēḏ* is a participle rather than a noun, unless v. 48 be the one verbless clause in the Pentateuch with unemcumbered subject:predicate sequence. See F. I. Andersen, *The Hebrew Verbless Clause in the Pentateuch,* JBLMS 14 (Nashville: Abingdon, 1970), pp. 17, 43, 56 no. 39.

9. Lit., "and the Mizpah as well."

10. LXX reads "God." The differences between the LXX and the MT of vv. 44-53 are so many (see n. 2 above) that the LXX may depend on a Hebrew *Vorlage* different from that of the MT. See H. Seebass, "LXX und MT in Gen 31,44-53," *BN* 34 (1986) 30-38.

11. Mizpah is Heb. *miṣpâ,* "watchtower"; "may he watch" is Heb. *yiṣep.* For MT *miṣpâ* SP reads *miṣbâ.*

50 *Should you mistreat my daughters, or take wives other than*[12] *my daughters, even though nobody is with us, take note*[13] *— God will be witnessing between me and you."*

51 *Laban said further to Jacob: "Here is the mound and here is*[14] *the pillar I have thrown up between me and you.*

52 *Let this mound be a witness,*[15] *and the pillar a witness, that I am not to pass by this mound in your direction, nor*[16] *are you to pass by this mound or this pillar in my direction with malicious intentions.*

53 *May the God of Abraham and the god of Nahor (the gods of their fathers) maintain justice*[17] *between us." Jacob took the oath by the Dreaded One of Isaac his father.*

54 *Jacob then offered a sacrifice in the highland, and invited his kinsmen to share a meal. So they ate together and passed the night on the highland.*

Many commentators see in vv. 43-54 two interwoven accounts (J and E) of the covenant between Jacob and Laban. There are two names (Gilead, Mizpah). There are two monuments (a mound and a pillar). There are two meals (vv. 46, 54). The easiest way to divide the unit is to assign vv. 43-50 to J and vv. 51-54 to E.[18] The unity of the pericope may be maintained if we understand

12. For *ʿal* with the sense "besides, other than" cf. Exod. 20:3, "you shall have no other gods besides me" *(ʿal pānāy)*. See also Gen. 28:9 "in addition to his wives" *(ʿal nāšâyw)*.

13. On the suggested emendation of *rᵉʾēh* to *rōʾeh*, "watching" (see *BHK;* Westermann, *Genesis,* 2:489), cf. N. H. Snaith, "Genesis xxxi 50," *VT* 14 (1964) 373. The verse illustrates the category of crimes without witnesses, for which see P. Borati, *Re-Establishing Justice, Legal Terms, Concepts and Procedures in the Hebrew Bible,* trans. M. J. Smith, JSOTSup 105 (Sheffield: Sheffield Academic, 1994), p. 273.

14. The repetition of *hinnēh* serves "to paint two pictures, by drawing attention to two items in succession" (Andersen, *Sentence in Biblical Hebrew,* p. 115).

15. Both of these opening verbless clauses are to be read as wishes, in which the predicate ("witness") precedes the subject ("mound," "pillar"), rather than a statement of fact. Cf., e.g., the sequence subject:predicate in v. 48 *(haggal hazzeh ʿēḏ)* with the sequence predicate:subject in v. 52 *(ʿēḏ haggal hazzeh)*. See Williams, *Hebrew Syntax,* p. 92, § 551; p. 99, § 580.

16. On the negative oath introduced by *ʾim . . . wᵉʾim* ("that I am not . . . nor are you to . . .") see GKC, § 149c; Andersen, *Sentence in Biblical Hebrew,* p. 116; also H. W. Gilmer, *The If-You Form in Israelite Law,* SBLDS 15 (Missoula, MT: Scholars, 1975), pp. 30-31.

17. LXX and SP read a sing. verb *(yišpōṯ)* rather than the pl. in MT *(yišpᵉṭû)*.

18. So Speiser, *Genesis,* p. 248. Others are more detailed. Thus Skinner (*Genesis,* pp. 399-400) assigns vv. 44, 46, 48, 51-53a to J; and vv. 45, 49, 50, 53b, 54 to E. D. J. McCarthy (*CBQ* 26 [1964] 179) assigns vv. 46, 51-53a to J; and vv. 44-45, 49-50, 53b-54 to E. Jenks (*The Elohist and North Israelite Traditions,* p. 37) feels that vv. 43-54 are the

the story as one that tries to explain the origin of the compound place name Mizpah of Gilead. This requires two monuments, one to represent Mizpah (a *maṣṣēḇâ*) and the other to represent Gilead (a *gal*).[19] Also, the frequent appearance of items in twos throughout the narrative might be the narrator's way of saying that in the proposal he is about to make, Laban "tacitly acknowledges Jacob as contituting a separate, independent social entity of equal status."[20] Other points will be made on the relevant verses below.

43 Laban casts a pathetic shadow of himself in v. 43. First, he begins with a statement that is grandiose and false. He still believes he has legitimate control over his daughters and grandchildren. His claim directly contradicts both Jacob's earlier statement ("God salvaged your father's livestock and gave it to me," v. 9, also vv. 38ff.), and his daughters' earlier statement ("All the wealth that God has taken away from our father is rightfully ours and our children's," v. 16). Laban's claim to proprietorship over his daughters and grandchildren is essentially only a "juridical fiction"[21] and a cry of frustration. He follows his (false) claim with a weak-kneed question suggesting he still has their welfare at heart.

44 It is Laban's idea, not Jacob's, to make a pact. Is this a final attempt by Laban to maintain some visible means of control over his family? Jacob already made one "pact" with Laban (the agreement about wages for service) which Laban did not honor. Why should Jacob think Laban has changed? Why should Jacob want to "cut" a covenant with Laban, when on several occasions Laban has tried to cut Jacob out of what was rightfully his? The kinsmen of the two were witnesses enough for Jacob (v. 37). Laban wants another kind of a witness. He wants an oath, not just spectators.

For this pact he wishes to make with Jacob, Laban proposes two different witnesses that will give the pact abiding validity. The first of these is the covenant itself (here, v. 44), and the second is the mound and the pillar (v. 52). These two witnesses do not contradict each other, but balance each other. If the second focuses on the almost indestructible nature of the witness, the first (in v. 44) preserves information (either in writing or in memory) about the pact and its terms, should the agreement ever be distorted.[22] It is understandable why Laban's first proposal for witnesses to this event should be the pact itself.

45-46 Jacob responds to Laban only with action (v. 45). He ignores

---

only ones in the chapter that cannot be linked with certainty to E, although the signs of a double recension are indubitable.

19. See F. V. Winnett, "Re-examining the Foundations," *JBL* 84 (1965) 8; M. Ottoson, *Gilead: Tradition and History* (Lund: Gleerup, 1969), pp. 41-46. For a brief evaluation of Ottoson's literary analysis of 31:44-54, see the review article of A. Cody in *Bib* 51 (1970) 270.

20. Sarna, *Genesis,* p. 221.

21. Fokkelmann, *Narrative Art in Genesis,* p. 184; Van Seters, *Abraham in History and Tradition,* pp. 79-80.

22. McCarthy, *CBQ* 26 (1964) 186.

Laban conversationally. Laban had said: "let us make a pact." Jacob first builds a pillar (v. 45) then responds not to Laban but to his kinsmen (v. 46): "Collect some stones." (Jacob has only two words in this whole episode: *liqṭû ʾaḇānîm.*) Jacob is giving Laban the silent treatment. He builds a *pillar* (or memorial stone or stele, *maṣṣēḇâ*) from one stone, and a *mound (gāl)* from several stones. Jacob has experience in erecting a *maṣṣēḇâ* (see 28:18, 22; 31:13) with "stones" (see 28:11, 18; 29:2, 3, 8, 10). For Jacob the erecting of the stele is a way of memorializing God's goodness to him (in both ch. 28 and 31). Laban may view the stele as some kind of a platform on which the deity may stand and "watch" for any treaty violations. Later biblical references (Exod. 23:24; 34:13; Lev. 26:1; Deut. 7:5; 12:3; 16:22; Hos. 10:1; Mic. 5:12 [Eng. 13]) threaten or mandate the destruction of a *maṣṣēḇâ,* which was linked with idolatrous practices.

47 Laban first names the site in his own Aramaic tongue: *Jegar-sahadutha.*[23] Jacob follows with a Hebrew name: *Galeed.*[24] Jacob is bilingual (he has lived in an Aramaic-speaking country and an Aramaic-speaking home for 20 years) and is able to translate Laban's phrase into Hebrew (or "Judaic/Judean" to use the OT term; see Isa. 36:11, 13). This is the only instance in which translation is involved between Abrahamites and Labanites, suggesting two languages sufficiently similar to each other to permit conversation, as in the case with Abraham and the Philistines.

48-50 Only with v. 50 does it become clear why Laban is so concerned to establish this pact with Jacob. The pact will be an incentive to Jacob not to mistreat Laban's daughters (he still cannot say "your wives") or to take additional wives.[25] Laban, who time and time again has mistreated Jacob, now solicits a promise from Jacob that he will not mistreat Leah and Rachel. The irony of his request escapes Laban.

23. Gen. 31:47; Jer. 10:11; Dan. 2:4–7:28; Ezra 4:8–6:8; 7:12-26 constitute the Aramaic parts of the OT. According to *BHS* the Aramaic portions of the OT occupy about 22 pages (plus the phrase in Gen. 31:47 and Jer. 10:11) out of a total of 1574 pages. Aramaic may have been the more important of the two languages (by the 8th century B.C. it had become the lingua franca of the ancient Near East), but Hebrew was the more indigenous of the two in ancient Palestine. See J. A. Fitzmyer, "The Study of the Aramaic Background of the New Testament," in *A Wandering Aramean: Collected Aramaic Essays,* SBLMS 25 (Missoula, MT: Scholars, 1979), p. 6. On Laban's Aramaic word for "witness," see M. Wagner, *Die lexikalischen und grammatikalischen Aramaismen im alttestamentlichen Hebräisch,* BZAW 96 (Berlin: de Gruyter, 1966), p. 109.

24. See W. Weinberg, "Language Consciousness in the OT," *ZAW* 92 (1980) 187-88; D. I. Block, "The Role of Language in Ancient Israelite Perceptions of National Identity," *JBL* 103 (1984) 328, 338 n. 74.

25. Clauses that contain provisions forbidding a man from taking an additional wife/wives may be found in texts from Old Assyrian documents and Nuzi texts to Neo-Babylonian times. See references in R. Yaron, *Introduction to the Law of the Aramaic Papyri* (Oxford: Clarendon, 1961), p. 60 and n. 4; Van Seters, *Abraham in History and Tradition,* p. 84.

The inclusion of *as of today* in the proposed oath further illustrates biblical oral contracts including date formulae in order to indicate the consummation and perpetual validity of a transaction.[26] Laban is careful and proposes a strictly defined arrangement. To make the arrangement even more binding, Laban invokes God as a sentry, a watchman.[27] A sentry is one who is constantly on the lookout for trouble, and who raises his voice at the first sign of assault or disturbance. Of course, Laban thinks that Jacob is liable to break the pact. God will have to keep Jacob under observation!

51 I do not understand this verse (Laban erected the cairn and stele) to conflict with v. 45 (Jacob erected them), although many scholars make this apparent conflict a major point in support of two traditions in these verses. Rather, he falsely claims for himself (as in v. 43a) what is Jacob's.[28] Perhaps because he has helped in construction, he believes he is entitled to ownership. The women and children are his; the monuments are his. He is wrong on both counts.

52-53 Laban is suspicious of what Jacob may do to his daughters (hence his comment in v. 50). He is also suspicious of what Jacob may do to him (hence his comment in v. 52). Again Laban invokes deity. God will "watch" (*ṣāp̄â,* v. 49) and now he will *maintain justice (šāp̄aṭ).* Each is to commit himself to a nonaggression pact against the other.[29] The unspoken assumption is that Jacob has the greater potential for belligerence, for in v. 53b he is the only one to take the oath.

54 First Jacob offers a sacrifice, then he shares a meal with his kinsmen. A meal subsequent to the sacrifice would normally mean that the meal consisted of the animals that were just offered. The same order of sacrifice, then meal, occurs in Exod. 18:12 (Moses and Jethro), where again *zeḇaḥ* ("sacrifice") is followed by *le'ĕḵōl leḥem* (lit., "to eat bread"), as here (although this text does not mention the making of a covenant or pact between Moses and Jethro, as in Gen. 31).[30]

26. See G. Tucker, "Witnesses and 'Dates' in Israelite Contracts," *CBQ* 28 (1966) 42-45, esp. p. 44; S. J. DeVries, *Yesterday, Today and Tomorrow* (Grand Rapids: Eerdmans, 1975), pp. 156-57.

27. The verb that Laban uses for God watching for treaty violations on the part of either Jacob or Laban *(yiṣep)* is used in participial form *(ṣōp̄eh/ṣōp̄îm)* to describe prophets whom God has appointed to watch for covenant violations by or dangers to God's people (Jer. 6:17; Ezek. 3:17; 33:7; Hos. 9:8).

28. With Fokkelman, *Narrative Art in Genesis,* pp. 189-90.

29. B. Mazar connects this treaty with life between Aram and Israel before the beginning of David's war against Aram-zobath ("The Historical Background of the Book of Genesis," *JNES* 28 [1969] 79), for it presupposes a time of peace and civility between the Hebrews and the Arameans when each will honor the frontiers of the other.

30. That a covenant can be ratified by eating a common meal is attested in Gen. 26:26-30 (Abimelech and Isaac). One might also detect this custom in Exod. 24:9-11 ("they beheld God, and ate and drank"). Thus Childs (*Book of Exodus,* OTL [Philadelphia:

But Jacob's invitation to his kinsmen *to share a meal (le'ᵉkōl leḥem)* must be connected with his words back in 28:20, "and give me bread to eat" *(leḥem le'ᵉkōl).* God has fulfilled the desires of Jacob's heart physically. He does have bread to eat. Now Jacob needs to see the desires of his heart fulfilled in wanting to return home. So far he has traveled from Haran to the highland area of Gilead/Galeed. *Gilead* is used in several ways in the OT, referring in the narrowest sense to a city (Hos. 6:8), and in the broadest sense to all of the land east of the Jordan, from the Yarmuk River in the north (which flows into the Jordan just south of the Sea of Galilee) to the northern end of the Dead Sea in the south (Judg. 20:1). This region is mountainous and rocky, hence the mention (vv. 21, 54) that Jacob was in the *highland* of Gilead.[31]

I. ENCOUNTERS, HUMAN AND DIVINE (32:1-33 [Eng. 31:55–32:32])

1. MEETING ANGELS AT MAHANAIM (32:1-3 [Eng. 31:55–32:2])

1 (31:55) *Rising early the next morning, Laban kissed his grandchildren and his daughters, and blessed them. Then he returned to his own place.*

2 (1) *Jacob then continued*[1] *on his journey,*[2] *but messengers of God encountered him.*

3 (2) *Upon seeing them, Jacob said: "God's encampment is this." So he named that place Mahanaim.*[3]

Westminster, 1974], p. 507) remarks: "The final description 'they ate and drank' places the whole account into the context of a covenant meal." While accepting the presence of a covenant meal in Gen. 26:26-30 and in 31:43-50, E. W. Nicholson (*God and His People: Covenant and Theology in the Old Testament* [Oxford: Clarendon, 1986], pp. 123-33) fails to see the same in Exod. 24:9-11. What he does see there is simply a celebratory meal, the activity of the people of God eating and drinking before their God. K. van der Toorn ("Ordeal procedures in the Psalms and the Passover meal," *VT* 38 [1988] 443) links ceremonial eating and drinking of consecrated food with ordeals.

31. For photographs of these highlands of Gilead, see Y. Aharoni, "Gilead," *EncJud,* 7:570; W. S. LaSor, "Gilead," *ISBE,* 2:469.

1. Note the chiasm of subject and verb in vv. 1 and 2 (lit.): "rose Laban — Jacob went." The inversion of subject and predicate in v. 2 evidences a change in subject matter.

2. Between the first and second half of the verse LXX inserts *(kaí anablépsas eíden parembolḗn theoú parembeblēkyían,* "and having looked up, he saw the camp of God encamped."

3. Lit., "two camps." *maḥᵃnayim* is the dual of *maḥᵃneh.*

1 (31:55) Laban appears anxious to end this meeting with Jacob, and so rises early in the morning. He gives a kiss and a farewell blessing to his grandsons and daughters, but not to Jacob. Laban appears to ignore him. This last encounter between Jacob and Laban contrasts vividly with their first meeting, when Laban "ran to meet him, and embraced him, and kissed him" (29:13).

2 (1) Jacob unexpectedly confronts *messengers* or angels (Heb. *mal'āḵîm) of God.* This event recalls his earlier departure from Isaac, Rebekah, and Esau, after which he had a dream involving "angels of God." Departure from Laban is followed by a meeting with angels.

The verb *encountered (pāḡaʿ bᵉ)* also occurred in the Bethel event to describe a place Jacob "struck upon" (28:11). *pāḡaʿ bᵉ* may mean "meet for hostile purposes," that is, "harm, attack" (cf. Josh. 2:16; Judg. 8:21; 15:12; 18:25; 1 Sam. 22:17, 18; 2 Sam. 1:15), or "intercede, entreat" (Job 21:15; Jer. 7:16; 27:18). In Ruth 1:16 *pāḡaʿ bᵉ* means "entreat, pressure" but in Ruth 2:22 it means "be molested, abused." The neutral sense "meet" is normally expressed by the verb with the accusative indicator *'ēt* (Exod. 5:20; 23:4; 1 Sam. 10:5). Perhaps *pāḡaʿ bᵉ* here in 32:2 stresses the notion of unexpectedness. His dream (ch. 28) was unexpected, and now the meeting with the *mal'āḵîm* is equally surprising.

3 (2) After seeing (in a vision? in a dream? face to face?) the angels, Jacob says, *God's encampment is this. So he named that place Mahanaim.* Both of these actions recall similar actions in ch. 28. Jacob's "God's encampment is *this*" matches "*this* is God's abode" and "*that* the gateway to heaven" (28:17). Even the name formula is the same: "and he called the name of that place Bethel/Mahanaim."[4] Finally, while the expression *mal'aḵ hā'ᵉlōhîm,* "angel of God," is common in the OT, the expression *mal'ᵃḵê 'ᵉlōhîm* is limited to 28:12 and 32:2.

What is missing from 32:1-3 is any speech from God or his representatives like that at Bethel (28:13-15). The divine messengers encounter Jacob but say nothing. They are just there, silent. Also absent is any statement about Jacob's anxiety (cf. 28:17) or any speech by Jacob. He observes, but he does not panic.

It is not readily clear why Jacob should name this site *Mahanaim* ("two camps"). Why did he not call it "Mahaneh-elohim" (1 Chr. 12:22; cf. Judg. 18:12, "on this account that place is called Mahaneh-dan ['camp of Dan']"), or "Mahanim" ("camps")?[5] Is the dual a reference to Jacob's camp and God's camp, or to Jacob's camp and Esau's camp? Does the "two

4. See Long, *Problem of Etiological Narrative,* pp. 39-40.

5. LXX *(Parembolaí)* and Vulg. *(castra)* read the word as a regular pl.; Greek and Latin lack a distinct dual form.

camps" of v. 3 balance the "two camps" *(šᵉnê maḥᵃnôṯ)* of v. 8 (Eng. 7)?[6] In the beginning of the narrative the dual of the name is given no significance,[7] for Jacob says *God's encampment is this,* not "God's encampments are these."

Mahanaim is located east of the Jordan, on the border between the territories of the half-tribe of Manasseh and of the tribe of Gad (Josh. 13:26, 30).[8] For a while it served as the captial of Ishbosheth, Saul's son (2 Sam. 2:8), as well as a temporary capital for David after Absalom's coup (2 Sam. 17:24, 27). Solomon later made it a district center (1 K. 4:14).

2. JACOB PREPARES TO MEET ESAU (32:4-13 [Eng. 3-12])

4 (3) *Jacob sent messengers ahead to his brother Esau to the land of Seir, the country of Edom,*

5 (4) *and he commanded them to say: "Thus shall you say, 'To my lord Esau,*[1] *thus says your servant Jacob: I have been staying with Laban and have been detained*[2] *until now.*

6. To distinguish between *maḥᵃnayim* and *šᵉnê maḥᵃnôṯ* one might translate the first as "twin/double camps" and the second as "two camps."

7. See C. Houtman, "Jacob at Mahanaim. Some remarks on Genesis xxxii 2-3," *VT* 28 (1979) 40-41, 42; P. D. Miller, Jr., *The Divine Warrior in Early Israel,* HSM 5 (Cambridge: Harvard University, 1973), p. 132. For other instances of place names in the OT that are formed as duals, see most notably *yᵉrûšāla(y)im* (Jerusalem) and *miṣrayim* (Egypt); and cf. C. Fontinoy, "Les noms des lieux en *-ayim* dans la Bible," *UF* 3 (1971) 33-40. On the use of the dual again in the expression *kimḥōlaṯ hammaḥᵃnāyim,* Cant. 7:1 (Eng. 6:13, "in the dance of the two camps"), see M. H. Pope, *Song of Songs,* AB (Garden City, NY: Doubleday, 1977), pp. 603-14.

8. R. Boling and G. E. Wright (*Joshua,* AB [Garden City, NY: Doubleday, 1982], p. 345) suggest that the name Mahanaim reflects "twin sites on opposite sides of a dogleg bend" in the Jabbok River, the northernmost (on the south bank) being Tulul ed-Dahab, ancient Penuel, and the site of Jacob's encounter with a man in vv. 23ff. The southernmost (on the north bank) would be Tulul el-Gharbiyeh. See also Y. Aharoni, *Land of the Bible,* tr. and ed. A. F. Rainey, 2nd ed. (Philadelphia: Westminster, 1979), p. 34.

1. Speiser (*Genesis,* p. 254) notes that the expression "to my lord Esau" is part of the message the messengers are to deliver to Esau, not part of the mesage Jacob delivers to his messengers, although the punctuation in his translation (p. 252) does not show this clearly. D. Pardee ("An Overview of Ancient Hebrew Epistolography," *JBL* 97 [1978] 333) cites the opening greetings in letters from Arad (no. 18: *'l 'dny 'lyšb,* "to my lord Elyashib") and from Lachish (nos. 2 and 6: *'l 'dny y'wš,* "to my lord Ya'ush"). These greetings are close to the greeting of the message Jacob wants brought to Esau: *la'ḏōnî lᵉʿēśāw*.

2. MT *wā'ēḥar* represents a contraction of *wā'e'ᵉḥar.* Cf. GKC, § 64h; BDB, p. 29a. This is the only instance of the Qal of *'āḥar* in the OT.

6 (5) *I own cattle*[3] *and donkeys and flocks, menservants and maidservants. I am sending this report to my lord in the hope of gaining your favor.' "*[4]

7 (6) *When the messengers returned to Jacob, they said: "We reached your brother Esau. He is now on his way*[5] *to meet you, accompanied by four hundred men."*[6]

8 (7) *Jacob was beside himself with fear.*[7] *In his anxiety*[8] *he divided the people with him, plus his flocks, herds, and camels,*[9] *into two camps.*

9 (8) *"If Esau should attack one*[10] *camp and overrun it," he reasoned, "the other camp may yet be left for escape."*

10 (9) *Then Jacob prayed: "O God of my grandfather Abraham, and God of my father Isaac, O Yahweh who told me, 'Return to the land of your birth and I will treat you well!'*

11 (10) *I am undeserving*[11] *of every kindness which you have faithfully per-*

3. All the nouns in v. 6a are collectives. See GKC, § 123b.

4. Lit., "And I am sending (in order) to tell to my lord (in order) to find mercy/favor in your eyes." One may compare the expression *wā'ešl*ᵉ*ḥâ l*ᵉ*haggîḏ* ("I am sending [in order] to tell") with Lachish Letter III:1-2: "Thy slave Hosha'yahu has sent to [*šlḥ l*] tell [*hg(d)*] my lord Ya'ush." H. Torczyner (*Lachish,* vol. I [London: Oxford University, 1938], p. 52) cites 2 Sam. 11:22 as a parallel to Lachish *šlḥ lhgd* ("so the messenger went and told David all that Joab had sent him for"), but Gen. 32:6 is even closer.

5. It is not uncommon for the pronoun to be omitted when it is the subject of a participle, or when the subject has just been mentioned. Cf. Williams, *Hebrew Syntax,* p. 100, § 587; Davidson, *Hebrew Syntax,* p. 134, § 100a.

6. I see no significance in the change of sequence of *w*ᵉ*'arba' mē'ôṯ 'îš 'immô* in v. 7 to *w*ᵉ*'immô 'arba' mē'ôṯ* in 33:1. See Andersen, *Hebrew Verbless Clause in the Pentateuch,* p. 50.

7. Lit., "And Jacob was greatly afraid."

8. *wayyēṣer lô* illustrates the 3rd person sing. used impersonally: "it became straight/narrow for him," i.e., "he was anxious, he was in straits/distress."

9. LXX omits "camels." MT is suspect here because "camels" lacks the sign of the accusative *('eṯ),* present before "flocks" and "herds."

10. SP reads *hā'eḥāḏ* (masc.) for MT *hā'aḥaṯ* (fem.). Though most nouns denoting place vary in gender, according to GKC, § 122l n. 1, *maḥ*ᵃ*neh* is fem. "only when it is collective, denoting the persons in a camp." Cf. Job 28:6, which illustrates an instance of a noun being referred to first as fem. (the pronominal suffix on *'*ᵃ*ḇāneyhā*), then as masc. *(lô).* S. Gevirtz ("Asher in the Blessing of Jacob," *VT* 37 [1987] 162, 163) considers this a stylistic device whereby gender discrepancies in successive verses, or within a verse itself, were deliberately contrived. Thus in v. 8 "camps" is fem. *(maḥ*ᵃ*nôṯ),* as is "one camp" in v. 9a *(hammaḥ*ᵃ*neh 'aḥaṯ).* The remainder of v. 9, however, treats *maḥ*ᵃ*neh* as masc.: "the other camp [the adjective *hanniš'ār* is masc.] may yet be (*w*ᵉ*hāyâ* is 3rd person masc. sing.] left for escape." Also the suffix on *w*ᵉ*hikkāhû* ("overrun it") is masc.

11. Lit., "I am little." *qāṭōn min* means "be too insignificant for, unworthy of." *qāṭōntî* illustrates the use of the perfect to represent a state that extends its influence into the present. See GKC, § 106g.

formed for your servant. With only my staff have I crossed this Jordan, and now I have grown into two camps.

12 (11) *Rescue me, I pray, from the hand of my brother Esau. Otherwise I fear*[12] *that when he comes he will attack me (mother with children too).*

13 (12) *For you yourself said: 'I will treat you exceedingly well, and will make your descendants like the sands of the sea, too numerous to be counted.' "*

4 (3) Jacob had encountered angels or messengers *(mal'āḵîm)* of God (vv. 2-3). Now he sends his own *messengers (mal'āḵîm)* to Esau. To round off the emphasis in this chapter on "messengers," we note Hosea's comment (12:5 [Eng. 4]) that Jacob "strove with the angel" *(mal'āḵ),* a reference to Gen. 32:22-32.

The purpose for the messengers' mission is to attempt to mollify Esau. The brothers have had no contact for over twenty years. Jacob's assumption is that Esau has not for one minute forgotten or forgiven Jacob. Time heals some wounds, reasons Jacob, but exacerbates others. Jacob's apprehensions turn out to be misapprehensions, as the narrative will indicate. He need no more live in anxiety of Esau than Joseph's brothers need live in anxiety of what Joseph will do to them with their father now gone (50:15). Neither Esau nor Joseph is bent on reprisal, but neither Jacob nor Joseph's brothers could have known beforehand that the brother would not be intent on retaliation. Thus in both cases it was natural and understandable for Jacob and Joseph's brothers to feel anxious and uncertain about their own well-being.

The narrator describes the destination of the messengers as *the land of Seir, the country of Edom.* Three of these words, or words similar to them, have been used earlier in Genesis to describe some feature of Esau. The place name *Seir (śēʿîr)* recalls earlier references to Esau being hairy, both at birth (*śēʿar,* 25:25), and later in life (*śāʿir,* 27:11). The reference to the *country (śᵉḏēh)* of Edom recalls earlier references to Esau as a "man of the field" (*ʾîš śāḏeh,* 25:27) and one who hunted in the field (*haśśāḏeh,* 25:29). The reference to *Edom (ʾĕḏôm)* recalls redness earlier associated with Esau, both his appearance at birth (*ʾaḏmônî,* 25:25) and his attraction to the "red stuff" (*ʾāḏōm,* 25:30) that Jacob was preparing. The three words recall three sources of tension between the brothers — birth, birthright, and blessing.[13]

5-6 (4-5) Jacob gives to his representatives a message to pass on to

12. According to Andersen, *Hebrew Verbless Clause in the Pentateuch,* pp. 47-48, when the predicate of a verbless clause is a participle the sequence is subject:predicate in declarative clauses. Since here we have predicate:subject, this suggests to Andersen that *yārēʾ* be read as an infinitive absolute rather than as a participle.

13. Sarna, *Genesis,* p. 4.

Esau. At the very beginning of the message Jacob identifies himself to Esau as *your servant.* The speech within the speech begins with *To my lord Esau, thus speaks your servant Jacob,* rather than with "I have been staying with Laban" (as in RSV). The double use of the verb *say* may be compared with a first-millennium B.C. Phoenician letter from Saqqara: *'mr l'ḥty 'ršt 'mr 'ḥtk bšʿ*, "say to my sister *'rst* [Arishut]: 'your sister *bšʿ* [Bashu] said. . . .' "[14] Other texts have subsequently come to light with the pattern "A said, say to B (and to C)," indicating that 32:5 reflects an actual epistolary message formula.[15]

Jacob is able to telescope more than twenty years into six words (in Hebrew; or four words if one counts two words joined by a *maqqēp̄,* the Hebrew hyphen, as one): *ʿim-lāḇān gartî wāʾēḥar ʿaḏ–ayāttâ* (lit., "with-Laban I-have-been-staying and-I-have-been-detained until-now"). Jacob is careful to emphasize the reason for the delay of his return, and he cautiously avoids any reference to the alacrity of his departure in the first place.

In the message Jacob rattles off all of his possessions, which, he suggests, are Esau's for the taking. We have translated these items as plurals —*donkeys, flocks, menservants, maidservants.* In the Hebrew they are actually all singular (used as collectives?). This may be another subtle move (avoiding plurals) by Jacob to give Esau enough information to arouse his interest, but not exhaustive information to give his hand away.

Jacob states his purpose in sending the message: *in the hope of gaining* (lit., "finding") *your favor.* Noah was the first person in Scripture who "found favor" *(māṣāʾ ḥēn)* in the eyes of another (6:8). For Noah, however, this is an accomplished fact. For Jacob it is an objective. Lot "found favor with the messengers" (19:19). Akin to 32:6 is 47:29, where Jacob speaks to Joseph: "If I have found good will in your eyes."[16]

One should not surmise that by using *ḥēn* Jacob considers himself an inferior to Esau. In using this word, Jacob is appealing to the generosity, the goodwill, of Esau, that the rift between them might be healed.[17]

14. See D. Pardee, *Handbook of Ancient Hebrew Letters,* SBL Sources for Biblical Study 15 (Chico, CA: Scholars, 1982), p. 121.

15. See J. C. Greenfield, "Notes on the Phoenician Letter from Saqqara," *Or* 53 (1984) 242-43. Thus the text on one of the two pithoi discovered at Kuntillet ʿAjrud in northern Sinai reads *'mr 'mryw 'mrl 'dny h*[*mlk*]: "A said, say to my lord the [king]." The inscription dates from shortly before or after 800 B.C. according to J. A. Emerton, "New Light on Israelite Religion: The Implications of the Inscriptions from Kuntillet ʿAjrud," *ZAW* 94 (1982) 3.

16. *māṣāʾ ḥēn* appears frequently in the Jacob narrative; once by Laban to Jacob (30:27); four times by Jacob to Esau (32:6; 33:8, 10, 15); once by Shechem to Jacob and his sons (34:11). In speaking of Jacob and his relations with God, Hos. 12:5 (Eng. 4) uses the verbs *ḥānan (wayyiṯḥannen)* and *māṣāʾ (yimṣāʾennû):* "and sought his favor . . . he met/found."

17. See W. L. Reed, "Some Implications of *ḤĒN* for Old Testament Religion," *JBL* 73 (1954) 39.

7 (6) The messengers return with a brief announcement. They have met Esau (whom they identify as "your brother," not "your lord"), who is now on his way with *four hundred men* to meet Jacob. Jacob's grandfather assembled 318 men for a rescue mission (14:14). Jacob's brother has gathered 400 men on what Jacob believes is a search-and-destroy mission. The messengers bring back no word from Esau; they say not a word about the reason for Esau's entourage. Perhaps Jacob jumps to a conclusion and cuts the messengers off prematurely. He has interpreted the words of the messengers as conveying a threat.

But the messengers' words, *He* [Esau] *is now on his way to meet you* (Heb. *hōlēḵ liqrā'ṯᵉḵā*) are ambiguous: on his way to meet you in order to kill you or harm you? on his way to meet you in order to greet you and heal the estrangement between you? The construction the messengers use, the verb *hālaḵ* and the infinitive of *qārā'* with prefixed preposition *lᵉ*, is used elsewhere in the OT to describe a situation fraught with danger (e.g., 1 K. 20:27; 2 K. 23:29). In such cases "go to meet" means to confront (militarily). At other times, however, the phrase has nothing to do with hostility. Thus Rebekah, coming to see and meet her husband-to-be for the first time, asks: "who is the man yonder, walking in the field to meet us?" (Gen. 24:65, RSV; cf. also Josh. 9:11; 2 K. 8:8, 9; 9:18). Clearly, then, one must consider the context to determine the connotation of the expression. No doubt Jacob's perception of the situation is affected by the *four hundred men* accompanying Esau.

8-9 (7-8) Jacob devises a survival plan. He divides his group into *two camps.* If one is overwhelmed, the other may survive. But if Esau intends to attack Jacob, why does he let the messengers return to Jacob? Perhaps Esau is trying to manipulate Jacob psychologically. Even a forewarned Jacob will be no match for Esau. Or does Esau act toward Jacob as Joseph, at that point incognito (42:18ff.; 44:2ff.), later does to his brothers? That is, he creates the circumstances that establish a maximum amount of guilt in Jacob.

In splitting his family into two camps, Jacob creates cleavage among his own for the second time. For Jacob's family has already been divided into two camps: one represented by Esau and Isaac, the other by Jacob and Rebekah.

10-13 (9-12) First Jacob acts (vv. 8-9), then he prays (vv. 10-13). His prayer is composed of seven parts:[18] (1) the address, "O God of my father . . . O Yahweh"; (2) description, "who told me . . . I will treat you well"; (3) self-deprecation, "I am undeserving . . . for your servant"; (4) detail,

18. The divisions are those suggested by M. Greenberg, *Biblical Prose Prayer* (Berkeley: University of California, 1983), p. 10.

"With only my staff . . . into two camps"; (5) petition, "Rescue me[19] from . . . my brother Esau"; (6) description of distress, "Otherwise I fear . . . children too"; (7) motivation, "For you yourself said . . . too numerous to be counted."

The prayer begins (v. 10) and ends (v. 13) by focusing on God. It does so by having Jacob quote God: "who told me . . . you yourself said." In the previous verses Jacob had quoted himself (vv. 5-6).

Jacob has a number of reasons for believing that he has some claim upon God. First, the God he invokes is the family God: *O God of my grandfather Abraham, and God of my father Isaac.* Second, Jacob is doing only what God told him to do — returning to his land. Third, Jacob has the promise from God that God would treat him well and prosper him. Twice Jacob refers to this promise, in the middle of the prayer and at the end, by use of the Hiphil of *yāṭaḇ* (*wᵉʾêṭîḇâ,* v. 10; *hêṭēḇ ʾêṭîḇ,* v. 13). Jacob has grasped the intention of God's promise, but his choice of language differs slightly from the original wording of the promise. V. 10b ostensibly refers back to 31:3 — "return to your fathers' land, your birthplace, and I will be with you" *(wᵉʾehyeh ʿimmāḵ).* Jacob has revised "I will be with you," a statement of divine presence, into "I will treat you well," a statement of divine treatment. Nowhere earlier in the story of Jacob had the Hiphil of *yāṭaḇ* been used by anybody.

Jacob's fourth reason for a claim on God is Jacob's own position. He is undeserving of God's kindness *(haḥᵃsāḏîm).*[20] He desires that those kindnesses continue, for God's "loyalty manifest in family and flocks is meaningless if it is suddenly to be cut off."[21] He is also undeserving of Esau's kindness, but he is careful not to mention that. The expression *I am undeserving* is literally "I am little" *(qāṭōntî).* The adjective of this root was used back in 27:15, 42 to describe Jacob as Rebekah's "younger son" *(bᵉnāh haqqāṭān).* To be "little" describes one who lacks legal credentials to make a claim for himself, or a person who is totally dependent on another for his welfare. Jacob certainly has no claim against Esau. Accordingly, he can only appeal to Yahweh's fidelity.[22] Esau, so to speak, is now holding all the cards. Jacob is suggesting to God that God, if he acts, has the power to prevent a potential massacre.

In this prayer Jacob has combined his own circumstances and God's

19. The verbal form *haṣṣîlēnî* (Hiphil imperative of *nāṣal* with 1st person sing. pronominal suffix) occurs frequently in the Psalms: 7:2 (Eng. 1); 25:20; 31:3, 16 (Eng. 2, 15); 39:9 (Eng. 8); 51:16 (Eng. 14); 59:2 (Eng. 1); 59:3 (Eng. 2); 69:15 (Eng. 14); 144:7, 11.

20. *ḥeseḏ* appears in the OT in the sing. 227 times but the pl. only 18 times. See H.-J. Zobel, *TDOT,* 5:450. Zobel suggests that of these 18 uses of the pls. of *ḥeseḏ* only those in Gen. 32:11 (Eng. 10) and Ps. 89:2, 50 (Eng. 1, 49) are from preexilic OT sources.

21. K. D. Sakenfeld, *Faithfulness in Action: Loyalty in Biblical Perspective,* OBT (Philadelphia: Fortress, 1985), p. 86.

22. See W. Brueggemann, "Amos' Intercessory Formula," *VT* 19 (1969) 386-87.

circumstances into one petition. As such, Jacob's prayer is "a model of rhetoric — a principle of which is to persuade the one appealed to that his interests and one's own coincide."[23]

3. GOING TO MEET ESAU (32:14-22)

14 (13) *After spending the night there, he selected from what was available the following gifts for his brother Esau:*

15 (14) *two hundred she-goats, twenty he-goats, two hundred ewes, twenty rams,*

16 (15) *thirty milch camels*[1] *and their young,*[2] *forty cows, ten calves, twenty she-asses, and ten foals.*[3]

17 (16) *He put them in charge of his servants, in separate droves, and he told his servants: "Precede me, but keep a space between each of the droves."*

18 (17) *He instructed the leader: "When Esau my brother runs into you, if he asks, 'Whom do you represent? Where are you going? To whom do these animals in front of you belong?' —*

19 (18) *then*[4] *you shall respond: 'They belong to your servant Jacob, and are sent as a gift to my lord Esau; he himself is right behind us.' "*

20 (19) *Likewise he instructed the second and third in command, in fact all who followed behind the droves: "You are to speak in the same fashion to Esau when you reach him.*[5]

21 (20) *Be certain to add, 'Your servant Jacob is right behind us.' " For Jacob reasoned: "I may be able to propitiate*[6] *him with gifts that precede me.*

23. Greenberg, *Biblical Prose Prayer,* p. 14.

1. *g^{e}mallîm* is construed as masc. in 24:63 *(g^{e}mallîm bā'îm),* and as fem. here *(g^{e}mallîm mênîqô<u>t</u>).* See GKC, § 122d.

2. For *b^{e}nêhem* (masc.) instead of *b^{e}nêhen* (fem.) referring to a feminine antecedent, see GKC, § 135o, for instances of masc. suffixes used to refer to fem. substantives.

3. The sequence in v. 16 seems to be in pairs of young and old. For *pārô<u>t</u>* . . . *pārîm* ("cows . . . calves") and *'^{a}<u>t</u>ōnō<u>t</u>* . . . *'^{a}yārim* ("she-asses . . . foals") cf. Akk. *būrātu* . . . *būrū* and *atānū* . . . *mūrū.* See H. L. Ginsberg, "Abram's 'Damascene' Steward," *BASOR* 200 (1970) 35.

4. On the resumptive use of *waw,* introducing an apodosis, see Williams, *Hebrew Syntax,*p. 72, § 440.

5. MT *b^{e}mōṣa'^{a}<u>k</u>em* need not be emended to an infinitive (*b^{e}moṣ'^{a}<u>k</u>em,* as argued by GKC, §§ 74h, 93q). What we have here is a preposition plus a participle plus a suffix. For the attachment of a preposition to a participle cf. *k^{e}mēšî<u>b</u>* in Gen. 38:29.

6. *'^{a}<u>k</u>app^{e}râ pānāyw* (lit., "I will cover his face") is an intriguing idiom and will be discussed below.

Then, later, when I face him,[7] *perhaps he will forgive me."*
22 (21) *So the gifts went on ahead of him, while he remained that night in camp.*[8]

14-16 (13-15) Throughout this incident *minḥâ* (vv. 14, 19, 21, 22) should be rendered as *gift* rather than as "tribute." In the OT *minḥâ* means both "gift, present" (here in Gen. 32; 43:11; 1 K. 10:25) and "tribute" (2 Sam. 8:2; 1 K. 5:1 [Eng. 4:21]; 2 K. 17:4). As gift, *minḥâ* is given voluntarily. As tribute, *minḥâ* is exacted.[9] Jacob is not providing any tribute Esau has imposed on him; rather, he is acting independently, trying as much as possible to win Esau's good graces. Jacob is not appealing to Esau as vassal/servant to suzerain/lord primarily, but to Esau's goodwill. The gift is a substantial one: it consists of five hundred and fifty animals, four hundred and ninety of which are female.

17-22 (16-21) Sending ahead gifts to a person who has been wronged is not without sequel in the OT. It appears again in the Nabal-Abigail-David incident (1 Sam. 25). David sent ten of his men to relay good wishes to and collect "protection money" from the well-to-do Nabal. Nabal refused to comply, and almost brought tragedy on himself, had not his wife, Abigail, brought gifts to David to appease him (1 Sam. 25:19). Abigail's present is a *b^erāḵâ* (1 Sam. 25:27), and Jacob's is a *minḥâ.* One significant difference between a *minḥâ* and a *b^erāḵâ* is that the former is given to another only by one who is in some sense subservient (Jacob to Esau, the worshiper to God). God will give a *b^erāḵâ,* but never a *minḥâ.* Note also that both Esau (Gen. 32:7 [Eng. 6]) and David (1 Sam. 25:13) come with 400 men.

Jacob hardly emerges in this event as the epitome of bravery. Always he is in the rear, behind something or somebody. In v. 17 he tells his servants, *Precede me* (*ʿiḇrû l^epānay,* lit., "go ahead of my face"). They are to say to Esau: *Jacob himself is right behind us* (*'aḥ^arênû,* vv. 19, 21). The gifts are sent on *ahead of him* (*ʿal-pānāyw,* lit., "on his face," v. 22). First come the animals, then

7. Lit., "I see his face" *('ereh pānāw).* The expression is used elsewhere in the context of coming from afar to see someone: Jacob to Esau (33:10); of the brothers to Joseph (43:3, 5; 44:23, 26); Jacob to Joseph (46:30; 48:11); Moses to Pharaoh (Exod. 10;29); Abner to David (2 Sam. 3:13); Absalom to David (2 Sam. 14:24, 28, 32).

8. M. Anbar ("La 'reprise,' " *VT* 38 [1988] 395) cites the phrase *w^ehû' lān ballay^elâ hahû' bammaḥaneh* in 32:22b as an original resumptive repetition of the phrase *wayyālen šām ballay^elâ hahû)* in 32:14a. The repetition shows that Jacob did not actually spend the night in the camp and fall asleep until first he had arranged the gifts for Esau into separate droves and given instructions to his selected leaders.

9. B. Levine (*Leviticus,* JPS Torah Commentary [Philadelphia: Jewish Publication Society, 1991], p. 10) connects *minḥâ* with the verb *nāḥâ,* "to lead, conduct," and interprets *minḥâ* as "what was set before, brought to somebody." For *minḥâ* as compensation and gift, see P. Bovasti, *Re-establishing Justice. Legal Terms, Concepts and Procedures in the Hebrew Bible,* trans. M. J. Smith, JSOTSup 105 (Sheffield: Sheffield Academic, 1994), pp. 137-39.

his representatives, and lastly Jacob. Jacob will do everything except "face up" to Esau. Five times in vv. 21-22 some form of the Hebrew word for "face" *(pāneh)* is used: (1) "I may cover his face" (here translated *propitiate him*); (2) "gifts that go before my face" *(gifts that precede me);* (3) "when I see his face" *when I face him);* (4) "he will raise my face" *(he will forgive me);* (5) "the gifts went on ahead of his face" *(the gifts went on ahead of him).* This focus on *face* has a twofold effect. First, it highlights a Jacob who would rather die than face his brother. Second, it prepares us for the following incident (vv. 23-33) at "Peniel," which means "the face of God."

Jacob's purpose in sending the gift is that he might *propitiate* Esau (Heb. *'ᵃḵappᵉrâ pānāyw,* v. 21). This expression is interesting because it is the only time in the OT that *pāneh,* "face," is a direct object of *kippēr* (lit., "cover"). Its Akkadian counterpart is *kuppuru panê,* "wipe the face," that is, "wipe (the anger from) the face."[10] Heb. *'ᵃḵappᵉrâ pānê* is an abbreviated idiom, to be compared with *lᵉhaḇ'îšēnî,* "by making me odious" (Gen. 34:30). The word "odious" is to be understood as "to cause (the odor) to be foul," as can be seen in the full idiom in Exod. 5:21, *hiḇ'aštem 'eṯ-rêḥēnû bᵉʿênê parʿōh,* "you have made our odor foul in the eyes of Pharaoh."[11]

The OT has other examples of the removal of wrath by "covering." Thus Prov. 16:14 counsels that "a king's wrath is a messenger of death, but a wise man may appease it" *(yᵉḵappᵉrennâ).*[12] When Phinehas executed an Israelite man and a Midianite woman, he turned back God's wrath from Israel (Num. 25:4, 11), and also "covered" *(wayᵉḵappēr)* the people of Israel (Num. 25:13). Thus, it becomes clear that Jacob is saying:" "that I may wipe off (the wrath) from his countenance by means of the gifts which precede me."

4. JACOB AT PENIEL (32:23-33 [Eng. 22-32])

23 (22) *During that*[1] *night he got up, took his two wives, his two maidservants, and his eleven children, and crossed*[2] *the ford of the Jabbok.*

10. See J. Milgrom, "Atonement in the OT," *IDBSup,* p. 81; idem, "Kipper," *EncJud,* 10:1042; idem, *Leviticus 1–16,* p. 1084.

11. See B. Levine, *In the Presence of the Lord,* p. 60 n. 18.

12. For *kpr* in Gen. 32:21; Exod. 21:30; and Prov. 16:14 meaning ransom for purposes of placating or mollifying, see A. Schenker, "*kōper* et expiation," *Bib* 63 (1982) 32-46, esp. pp. 34-37; D. Judisch, "Propitiation in the Language and Typology of the Old Testament," *CTQ* 48 (1984) 223-24.

1. Demonstrative adjectives that follow their substantives normally exhibit concord of determination, but there are exceptions. Three times in Genesis (19:33; 30:16; 32:23 [Eng. 22]), the article on "that" is missing in the phrase "in/during that night."

2. *ʿāḇar* is in the Qal stem in v. 23 (Eng. 22). In v. 24 (Eng. 23) it occurs twice in the Hiphil stem. In the Qal the meaning is "cross," and in the Hiphil "send across/take over."

24 (23) *After he had taken them over the stream, he sent over all*[3] *his belongings.*

25 (24) *So Jacob was left alone. A man wrestled with him until the break of dawn.*[4]

26 (25) *When he saw he could not prevail, he struck his hip socket, so that Jacob's hip socket was dislocated as he wrestled*[5] *with him.*

27 (26) *He said: "Release me, for dawn has broken." He replied: "I will not release you unless*[6] *you bless me."*

28 (27) *"What is your name?" he asked. "Jacob," he answered.*

29 (28) *He said: "Not as Jacob shall you be addressed,*[7] *but as Israel, because you have struggled with God,*[8] *and with men have you succeeded."*[9]

30 (29) *Jacob inquired: "Tell me your name, please!" He replied: "Why*[10] *is it that you inquire about my name?" He, then, bade him farewell.*[11]

31 (30) *Jacob named the place Peniel,*[12] *"Because I have seen God*[13] *face-to-*

3. On the addition of "all" see the note in *BHS.*

4. *ʿaḏ ʿᵃlôṯ haššāḥar* may also be read as "at dawn." Cf. Exod. 12:10b: "anything that remains until morning [*ʿad-bōqer*] you shall burn"; Judg. 16:3: "But Samson lay till midnight" *(ʿad ḥᵃṣî hallayᵉlâ). ʿad* permits either "until" or "at." At issue here is the length of the contest between Jacob and the man.

5. Both in the preceding verse and here Targ. Onqelos translates "wrestle" *(ʾāḇaq)* with "contend" *(ʾštdl),* which indicates verbal strife rather than physical conflict. This is an attempt by the Targ. to avoid the idea of a mortal wrestling with an angel of God.

6. *kî ʾim* means "unless" after a clause containing or implying a negative, but this is not always the case, as the *kî ʾim* of the next verse indicates. Andersen (*Sentence in Biblical Hebrew,* p. 174) says of *kî ʾim* that "it is used to mark the exclusive condition that cancels a general rule."

7. For *yēʾāmēr* as an iterative past/future see Isa. 19:18; 32:15; 61:6; 62:4; Jer. 7:32; Hos. 2:2.

8. The *wa-* on *wattûḵal* may be understood as a postpositive *waw.* See F. I. Andersen, "Notes on Genesis 30,8," *JBL* 88 (1969) 200. For instances in Ugaritic where, following an adverbial phrase, a *yqṭl* form may be preceded by a *waw,* see *UT,* § 13.34.

9. Targ. Onqelos again attempts to tone down the episode with its rendering of the last part of v. 29 (Eng. 28) as "for you are great [or 'a prince'] before the Lord and among men, therefore you have prevailed" *(rb ʾt qdm yy wʿm gbryʾ wykylt').* Thus the Targ. connected *śarîṯā* ("you have struggled") with *śar* ("prince, great one"), and replaced *ʿim* ("with") by *qdm* ("before"). See further the commentary below.

10. See J. Barr, "Why? in Biblical Hebrew," *JTS* 36 (1985) 1-33, esp. p. 32, for the relatively few times God, or one of his angels, asks a "why" question in narrative. In prophetic literature, by contrast, "why" questions from God are prominent.

11. Speiser (*Genesis,* p. 255) prefers this translation of *wayᵉḇāreḵ ʾōṯô šām* to "and he blessed him there," since the blessing has already been given in the preceding verse with the name change. Cf. NJPS, "and he took leave of him there."

12. MT *pᵉnîʾēl,* lit., "the face of El." Cf. SP, Symm., Pesh., and Vulg., which read *pᵉnûʾēl,* as in v. 32 (Eng. 31) and elsewhere in the OT. LXX has *eídos theoú.* Most commentators consider Peniel to be a variant used here to make the wordplay clearer (see von Rad, *Genesis,* p. 323; Westermann, *Genesis,* 2:519).

13. For a third time in this episode Targ. Onqelos avoids anthropomorphism (see

face, and yet[14] *my life has been preserved."*

32 (31) *The sun shone on him as he left Penuel*[15] *— and he was limping because of his hip.*[16]

33 (32) *Accordingly, to this very day, the children of Israel do not eat the sciatic muscle*[17] *that is on the hip socket, since he struck Jacob's hip socket, on the sciatic muscle.*

This famous, but enigmatic, story about Jacob is spread over three sections. Vv. 23-26 (Eng. 22-25) are narrative, describing Jacob's and his entourage's crossing of the Jabbok, and Jacob's wrestling with a man. Vv. 27-30 (Eng. 26-29) are dialogue between Jacob and the man, and they climax in the renaming of Jacob to Israel. Vv. 31-33 (Eng. 30-32) are etymology, explaining the origin of the name Peniel and a certain dietary restriction.

23-24 (22-23) Sometime during the night Jacob sends his wives, his maidservants, and his eleven children (where is Dinah?) across the *Jabbok.* This river in eastern Canaan flows through deep-cut canyons into the Jordan about 23 miles north of the Dead Sea. It is approximately 50 miles long and descends from its source at 1900 feet above sea level to about 115 feet below sea level where it meets the Jordan. This fact explains the many deep-cut canyons. As such it provides an impressive locale for the event that is about to take place. It is shallow enough to ford.

The events throughout this chapter occur at *night.* Distressed at Esau's coming with 400 men, Jacob passes the "night" (v. 13) to consider strategy. It is during the "night" (v. 21) that he sends his gift on to Esau. And now, he himself gets up in the *night.* Anxiety may have produced insomnia. He is too afraid to be able to sleep. It was, we recall, in the night that God first revealed himself to Jacob (28:10-22).

There is no indication about the reason for Jacob's nocturnal departure from the camp. Is this a further attempt to put distance between himself and Esau? Is it an acceptance of having to face the inevitable? His earlier instructions to his servants were that they were to tell Esau that "Jacob is behind

---

nn. 5 and 9 above) by reading "an angel of the Lord" *(ml'k' dyy)* to describe what Jacob says he saw.

14. S. R. Driver, *Treatise on the Use of Tenses,* p. 81, §74b: "where the two ideas are in reality contrasted we may with advantage make the contrast more perspicuous by rendering [the *waw* on the imperfect] *and yet.*"

15. Penuel is an alternate form of Peniel, with *pᵉnû-* reflecting the old nominative case ending. Penuel as a name may be compared with the personal name Bethuel, or with Jemuel (Gen. 46:10). See GKC, § 90k.

16. On participial circumstantial clauses, see Andersen, *Sentence in Biblical Hebrew,* p. 82.

17. LXX *neúron;* Vulg. *nervum* ("nerve, tendon, muscle").

us." This mandates that Jacob accompany the appeasement gift and its bearers, if only at a retiring distance.

But how much of a distance? One can read vv. 23-24 in two ways. First, Jacob himself crosses the river ("crossed" in v. 23 is sing., not pl.). Second, Jacob sends his entourage across, but he himself does not cross (possibly v. 24). The second interpretation suggests that the distance between Jacob and his party included at least the Jabbok, and that Jacob fought with the man on the north side of the Jabbok. But if Jacob has crossed the river with his caravan and subsequently put a distance between himself and them, then Jacob fought with the man on the south side of the Jabbok. This interpretation seems more likely and indicates that the man who encountered Jacob is no river demon who tries to stop Jacob from fording the river. There are no obstacles in the river crossing.[18] Indeed, taken together, vv. 23-24 might suggest that Jacob crisscrossed the Jabbok several times.

25 (24) Jacob is momentarily left alone, separated from his party. Earlier he had told his servants (v. 18 [Eng. 17]) to arrange the animals in separate droves *(ʿēḏer ʿēḏer lᵉḇaddô),* with a space between each drove. Now, it is not the droves that are "alone" *(lᵉḇaddô),* but Jacob that is *alone (lᵉḇaddô).*[19] The space is not between drove and drove, but between Jacob and his party.

Alone, Jacob is suddenly locked in a wrestling match with a *man.* Undoubtedly, there is an acoustical similarity in *Jacob (yaʿᵃqōḇ), Jabbok (yabbōq),* and *wrestled (yēʾāḇēq).* The consonantal pattern is *yʿqb/ybq/yʾbq.* Vv. 25 and 26 (Eng. 24, 25) are the only two places where this denominative verb *ʾbq* occurs in the OT (and both are Niphal).[20] The noun from which the verb is built is *ʾāḇāq,* "dust," suggesting perhaps that when one wrestles on the ground he gets dirty or dusty. It is more than likely that we are to see a connection between *ʾbq* here and *ḥāḇaq* in 33:4. In ch. 32 a man wrestles *(ʾāḇaq)* Jacob (embrace for fighting). In ch. 33 Esau embraces *(ḥāḇaq)* Jacob (embrace for greeting). Two verbs that rhyme are chosen to describe the start of Jacob's encounters.

Jacob's assailant is identified simply as a "man" *(ʾîš).* Jacob will later

18. See R. Barthes, "The Struggle with the Angel: Textual Analysis of Genesis 32:23-33," in *Structural Analysis and Biblical Exegesis,* PTMS 3, tr. A. M. Johnson, Jr. (Pittsburgh: Pickwick, 1974), pp. 24-25; H. A. McKay, "Jacob Makes It Across the Jabbok: An Attempt to Solve the Success/Failure Ambivalence in Israel's Self-consciousness," *JSOT* 38 (1987) 5.

19. The verb *yūṯar* in the Niphal, followed by *lᵉḇaḏ* and pronominal suffix, occurs only here and in 1 K. 19:10, 14.

20. The narrator could have used the verb *pāṯal* for "wrestle," for this verb was used earlier in the Jacob stories in connection with the birth of Naphtali (30:8), but that term would not have allowed him the verbal play with Jacob that he achieved with *ʾāḇaq.*

identify the man as Elohim/God (v. 31), and Hos. 12:5 (Eng. 4) identifies him as an angel *(mal'aḵ)*. The narrator's use of the term *'îš* provides another illustration of the inability of mortals to ascertain the divinity of a supernatural visitor until this visitor performs some wonder. This idea is present in Gen. 18–19, which begins with three men standing in front of Abraham; in Judg. 6 where Yahweh's angel sat under an oak tree, and shortly engaged Gideon in conversation; and especially in Judg. 13, where Manoah and his wife take Yahweh's angel to be a man of God. Thus it is not unusual or unheard-of in the OT for supernatural beings to assume human form.

26 (25) Jacob was no easy conquest for the man. Jacob's herculean strength was observed in 29:10 when he rolled away the stone from the well. Against Jacob the man *could not prevail (lō' yāḵōl),* but with men *('ᵃnāšîm)* Jacob prevailed (*tûḵāl,* v. 29 [Eng. 28]). What the man could not do, or did not do, Jacob did.

In the first half of the verse the text does not clearly identify the subject of the verbs it uses: "when he saw he could not prevail [the man? Jacob?] he struck [the man? Jacob?] his hip socket [the man's? Jacob's?]." The latter part of the verse identifies retroactively the subject and object in the first half of the verse ("Jacob's hip socket was dislocated"). The same ambiguity in identifying the actors occurs in the next two verses ("he said. . . . He replied . . . unless you bless me. . . . 'What is your name?' he asked"). Who is speaking to whom? Only the phrase " 'Jacob,' he answered," clarifies the identity of the two participants.[21]

To avoid a resounding defeat, the man *struck his* [Jacob's] *hip socket.* There is no "Yahweh sought to kill him" as in Exod. 4:24, an incident similar in many ways to this one. The Hebrew for *struck* is *nāḡaʿ bᵉ*. In many instances it is sufficient to translate it simply as "touch" (Gen. 3:3 being the first instance of *nāḡaʿ bᵉ* meaning "to lay a finger on"). Other passages suggest something more violent than touching. The Satan's request that God "touch" all that Job has (Job 1:11; 2:5) is more than minimal physical contact. One catastrophe that happens to Job is that the wind "struck" *(nāḡaʿ bᵉ)* the four corners of his house, that is, flattened it (Job 1:19). Cf. also Josh. 9:19 and 1 Sam. 6:9 in which *nāḡaʿ bᵉ* means "strike, harm."[22] For the idea of a supernatural being touching *(nāḡaʿ bᵉ)* a mortal being cf. Isa. 6:7, "he touched my mouth," and Jer. 1:9, "Yahweh . . . touched my mouth." It is difficult, if not impossible,

21. S. A. Geller ("The Struggle at the Jabbok: The Uses of Enigma in a Biblical Narrative," *JANES* 14 [1982] 37-60) believes ambiguity and enigma to be the fundamental characteristics in the cryptic narration of the Jabbok incident.

22. In Gen. 20:6 and Prov. 6:29 *nāḡaʿ bᵉ* is used of touching in sexual relations. For the use of *nāḡaʿ bᵉ* meaning "to touch, to come into contact with the holy," see J. Milgrom, "Sancta contagion and altar/city asylum," *Congress Volume: Vienna, 1980,* ed. J. A. Emerton, VTSup 32 (Leiden: Brill, 1981), pp. 278-310.

to decide whether in Gen. 32:26 *nāga' b^e* should be rendered "struck" or "touched."

The words for *his hip socket* are *kap y^erēkô* (lit., "hollow of his thigh"). *kap* normally refers to the palm of the hand or the sole of the foot. Here it means *socket* or "hollow."[23] Its presence here provides another instance of the selection of words with similar sounds or consonants. I noted above the clustering of *qb/bq/bq,* to which one may now add *kp.* Several other texts in Genesis involve the *thigh.* Abraham had his servant place his hand under his thigh (24:2, 9; cf. 47:29), which may be instances of "thigh" meaning genitals. Exod. 1:5 refers to the seventy offspring who came forth from "the thigh of Jacob." Since *kap* has the connotation of hollowness (as in a vessel or pan, or pouch), and *yārēk* may have the meaning of genitals, it is possible that the phrase *kap y^erēkô* refers to the scrotum, the hollow pouch of skin holding the testicles, rather than to the hip socket. Thus the situation would be that two men are engaged in combat, and at some point in the contest one combatant touches/strikes the scrotum of the other combatant. This situation would then be comparable to that envisioned in the law of Deut. 25:11-12 in which two men are wrestling *(yinnāṣû).* The wife of the losing combatant disadvantages the winning combatant by "seizing him by the private parts" (RSV).[24]

Given the other references to "thigh" in the patriarchal traditions, it is inconceivable that any later Israelite would have missed the national import of this verse. Jacob, the ancestor of Israel, had his thigh struck, and it was from that thigh that Israel came forth (Exod. 1:3).[25]

The touching of Jacob's thigh results in the thigh's being *dislocated*

23. See BDB, p. 497a. Gen. 32 is the only place in the OT where *kap* is used with *yārēk.*

24. See L. Eslinger, "The case of an immodest lady wrestler in Deuteronomy xxv 11-12," *VT* 31 (1981) 273-74, 277-81; V. H. Matthews, "Jacob the Trickster and Heir of the Covenant: A Literary Interpretation," *Perkins Religious Studies* 12 (1985) 192-93. I would add that in Num. 5:23 "thigh" is a euphemism for the sexual organs, and the phrase "causing her thigh to sag" refers to the woman's inability to conceive children. For other interpreters who also believe that *kap y^erēkô* designates the area of the genitals, see S. Gevirtz, "Of Patriarchs and Puns: Joseph at the Fountain, Jacob at the Ford," *HUCA* 46 (1975) 52-53; S. H. Smith, " 'Heel' and 'thigh': the concept of sexuality in the Jacob-Esau narratives," *VT* 40 (1990) 466-69.

25. Gen. Rabbah 72:3 already interpreted the phrase "touch/strike the thigh" symbolically as an attack on and persecution of Jacob's descendants by Hadrian.

26. If *wattēqa'* is not from *yāqa',* but from *nāqa'* (which is unlikely), then we would have the sequence *nāga' . . . nāqa'.* One finds *yāqa'* and *nāqa'* adjacent to each other in Ezek. 23:18: "my soul was estranged/alienated [*wattēqa'* from *yāqa'*] from her just as my soul was estranged/alienated [*naq^e'â* from *nāqa'*] from her sister." *nāqa'* appears to be a by-form of *yāqa'.*

(wattēqaʿ). In the Hiphil stem *yāqaʿ*[26] designates some kind of public ritual act of execution on living bodies (Num. 25:4; 2 Sam. 21:6, 9, 13). In the Qal stem (as here) the meaning is "separation, alienation, dislocation."[27]

27 (26) We do not know why the man struck Jacob on the hip socket. Neither do we know why the man requests Jacob to "release" him because dawn is beginning to break.[28] Gunkel's commentary popularized the notion that this is a vestige of the *Ur*-form of the story. In the narrative's earlier tradition the man who fought with Jacob was a nocturnal demon (or a river spirit) who loses his power at daylight. Even if that is the case, and this narrative represents the final stage of a multilayered tradition, then what function, if any, would the emphasis on dawn play in the final form of the narrative? It appears that the *dawn,* as well as the place of the incident (the Jabbok River in the Transjordan area), are foils for the character of Jacob.[29] The dawn is that part of day that is half light and half darkness. The Transjordan represents territory that is both holy and unholy. Jacob the person mixes within himself traits of both godliness and profaneness, a combination that Paul in the NT would refer to as "carnality" (1 Cor. 3:1ff., AV).

It is possible that the "man's" need to leave before morning is prompted by his desire to hide his true identity from Jacob. Already Jacob has passed one night in his life close to somebody, a somebody whose true identity he learns only in the morning. Might not "and in the morning, behold, it was Leah" now become "and in the morning, behold, it was Elohim"? If Jacob can take the form of Esau, why cannot Elohim take the form of a man *(ʾîš)*? It is in Jacob's best interests than he not see God, a sure sentence of death.

Jacob is a model of physical tenacity. He refuses, despite having been injured, to release the antagonist unless the antagonist blesses him. This request provides a clue that the real nature of the man is dawning on Jacob as day breaks, for the inferior would solicit a blessing from the superior. But why does Jacob request a blessing, and of what should the blessing consist? Jacob is insisting on something that he cannot provide for himself. He received Isaac's blessing by duplicity, but he can receive this blessing only by clinging. It would appear that what Jacob desires in such a blessing is the strength of his assailant. Perhaps he will need such strength in facing

27. See R. Polzin, "*HWQYʿ* and Covenantal Institutions in Early Israel," *HTR* 62 (1969) 227-40.

28. Gen. Rabbah 78:2 expands considerably the dialogue between the angel and Jacob. The angel wishes to be released so he may rejoin his fellow angels for the time of giving praise to God, lest he lose his position. Jacob reminds the angel that the angels who came to Abraham took their leave from him by giving him a blessing.

29. See Geller, *JANES* 14 (1982) 55.

Esau and his four hundred men. Thus it is not certain that Jacob's request is an act of piety.[30]

28 (27) The man does not honor, immediately at least, Jacob's demand for a blessing. Instead, he asks Jacob his name. This request compares with Moses' question to God: "If they ask me, 'What is his name?' what shall I say to them?" (Exod. 3:13). An even closer parallel is Luke 8:30, "Jesus then asked him, 'What is your name?' And he said 'Legion.' "

In neither Gen. 32 nor Luke 8 are we to infer from the question that the questioner is ignorant about the identity of his opponent. To raise that possibility is to miss the point of either story. There is no parallel in Gen. 32 between Jacob, who does not know who the man is, and the man, who does not know who Jacob is. In disclosing his name Jacob is doing more than sharing information. He is making a confession about the appropriateness of his name. Only now would Jacob agree with Esau that Jacob is the perfect name for him (27:36). The acknowledgment of the old name, and its unfortunate suitability, paves the way for a new name.

29 (28) Jacob now learns that he shall no longer be called *Jacob*. No longer will the stigma of heel and supplanter be attached to him. Biblical Hebrew uses the idiom "they shall say no more" (*lō' yō'mᵉrû 'ôḏ,* Jer. 3:16; 23:7; 31:29) or "it shall be said no more" (*lō' yē'āmēr 'ôḏ,* Jer. 16:14) to indicate a spiritual metamorphosis of some kind.[31] Close to the Jeremiah passages is Ezek. 18:3, "this proverb shall no more be used by you" *(lāḵem 'ôḏ mᵉšōl hammāšāl hazzeh).* Cf. also Ezek. 12:23, "and they shall no more use it as a proverb" *(wᵉlō' yimšᵉlû 'ōṯô 'ôḏ).* In several of these passages we have the full formula *lō' yō'mᵉrû 'ôḏ . . . kî 'im* (Jer. 23:7, 8; 31:29, 30), or *lō' yē'āmēr 'ôḏ . . . kî 'im* (Jer. 7:32; 16:14, 15).

Particularly close to Gen. 32:29 (Eng. 28) is Jer. 3:16-17: "they shall no more say [*yō'mᵉrû*] . . . but it shall be called [*yiqrᵉ'û*]." We find this interplay of *'āmar* and *qārā'* also in Jer. 7:32 ("it will no more be called [*wᵉlō' yē'āmēr 'ôḏ*] Tophet") and Jer. 19:6 ("this place shall no more be called [*wᵉlō' yiqqārē' . . . 'ôḏ*] Tophet"). Note that in Gen. 32:29 (Eng. 28) the text reads: *Not as Jacob shall you be addressed (lō' yē'āmēr 'ôḏ).* In a subsequent reference (35:10) the text reads "Not as Jacob shall you be addressed" *(lō' yiqqārē' 'ôḏ).* The passage describing Abram's name change to Abraham (17:5) uses the formula *wᵉlō' yiqqārē' 'ôḏ,* but lacks any following *kî 'im.*

30. Von Rad, *Genesis,* p. 321. S. Terrien (*The Elusive Presence* [New York: Harper & Row, 1978], p. 88) explains Jacob's words as follows: "Because he needed a renewal of his being in order to face the ordeal of the next day." Similarly O. Eissfeldt, *"Non Dimittam Te, Nisi Benedixeris Mihi,"* in *Mélanges Bibliques rédigés en l'honneur de André Robert* (Paris: Bloud et Gay, 1957), p. 78.

31. See M. Weinfeld, "Jeremiah and the Spiritual Metamorphosis of Israel," *ZAW* 88 (1976) 19.

Instead, it uses *waw* plus the perfect of *hāyâ* (17:5). Both 17:5 and 32:29 (Eng. 28) conclude with a *kî* clause explaining the significance of the new name.

The new name given to Jacob is *Israel,* and the explanation following is that Jacob has *struggled with God, and with men have you succeeded.* There is a play on sound here in *yiśrā'ēl* ("Israel") and *śarîṯā* ("you have struggled"). The original meaning of *Israel* is much debated ("God rules"? "God heals"? "God judges"?),[32] as is the relationship between *yiśrā'ēl* and the verb *śārâ,* ("struggled"?). Uncertainty about the meaning of *śārâ* is engendered by the fact that it occurs only one other time in the OT, Hos. 12:4 (Eng. 3), Hosea's reference to Jacob, "he strove with [*śārâ 'eṯ*] God."[33] The ancient versions disagreed on the meaning of *śārîṯā* in Gen. 32:29 (Eng. 28). LXX, Vulg., and Pesh. derive it from *šrr* (Aramaic), "be strong." Aquila and Symm. derive it from *śārar,* "to rule." As already noted, Targ. Onqelos attempts to eliminate the idea of a mortal engaged in combat with God: "for you are great [or: 'a prince,' reading *śar* for *śārîṯā*] before the Lord and among men, therefore you have prevailed."

It seems that in Gen. 32 one must interpret *Israel* as "El will rule (or strive)," or "Let El rule," rather than as "he has striven with El." For one thing, it is very unusual for the theophoric element in a personal name to serve as anything but subject. Up to this point in Jacob's life Jacob may well have been called "Israjacob," "Jacob shall rule" or "let Jacob rule." In every confrontation he has emerged as the victor: over Esau, over Isaac, over Laban, and even more startlingly over this "man." The man says as much to Jacob: "you have struggled [*śarîṯā*] with God, and with men you have succeeded [*wattûkāl*]." Note the chiasm in v. 29b: verb: prepositional phrase::preposi-

32. For the first, see M. Noth, *Die israelitischen Personennamen im Rahmen der gemeinsemitischen Namengebung* (Hildesheim: Olms, 1966), pp. 207-8. For the second, see W. F. Albright, "The Names 'Israel' and 'Judah' with an Excursus on the Etymology of *Tôdâh* and *Tôrâh,*" *JBL* 46 (1927) 154-68. For the third, see R. Coote, "The Meaning of the Name Israel," *HTR* 65 (1972) 137-46.

33. On the Hosea passage cf. H. L. Ginsberg, "Hosea's Ephraim, More Fool than Knave," *JBL* 80 (1961) 339-47; P. R. Ackroyd, "Hosea and Jacob," *VT* 13 (1963) 245-59; W. L. Holladay, "Chiasmus, the key to Hosea xii 3-6," *VT* 16 (1966) 53-64; E. M. Good, "Hosea and the Jacob Tradition," *VT* 16 (1966) 137-51; F. I. Andersen and D. N. Freedman, *Hosea,* AB (Garden City, NY: Doubleday, 1980), pp. 593ff.; W. D. Whitt, "The Jacob Traditions in Hosea and Their Relation to Genesis," *ZAW* 103 (1991) 18-43. The verb might also appear in Hos. 12:5a (Eng. 4a), "he strove with the angel," if it were pointed as *wayyiśśer* (see KB, p. 930). MT *wayyāśar* suggests the verb *śārar,* "to rule, exercise authority over." Thus the two parts of the two verses read: "he strove with God" (12:4b [Eng. 3b]); "he lorded it over the angel" (12:5a [Eng. 4a]). *śārâ* could be a by-form of *śārar,* for verbs that are third *hē* and geminates are close to each other (e.g., *qlh-qll,* "treat lightly"; *rbh-rbb,* "multiply"; *rdh-rdd,* "rule").

tional phrase: verb. The change in sequence possibly reinforces the change of name that has just been disclosed to Jacob.

Note, however, that the reason for the name change is clear: *because you have struggled with God, and with men have you succeeded.*[34] The explanation for the name change focuses on what Jacob has done: he has struggled with God; he has succeeded with men. The explanation says nothing directly about any repentance by Jacob, or even about any shedding of distasteful character traits. The new name does not carry any guarantees that from this point on Jacob is transformed. What it highlights is Jacob's success in wrestling with God and his success with people. Accordingly, one is led to conclude that the change of name from *Jacob* to *Israel* focuses on Jacob's assertiveness, his ability to cling to his stronger assailant despite his injury, his insistent desire for his opponent's blessing.[35]

30 (29) Jacob's question is like and unlike the one that the man had earlier asked him. The man had said to Jacob: "What is your name?" (*mah-ššᵉmeḵā,* v. 28 [Eng. 27]). Jacob's question is phrased a bit differently: *Tell me your name, please* [*haggîḏ-nāʾ šᵉmeḵā*]. In asking Jacob his name, the man need not add "please" as Jacob did when he asks his question. The man's question is introduced as a statement ("he said . . ."). Jacob's request is introduced as an inquiry and a statement (lit., "Jacob inquired and he said . . .").

The man's question is: *Why is it that you inquire about my name?* It is a question to which Jacob is not given the opportunity to respond, or perhaps he chooses not to respond. The scene is much like the one between the angel of Yahweh and Samson's father Manoah: "And Manoah said to the angel of Yahweh, 'What[36] is your name, so that . . . we may honor you?' And the angel of Yahweh said to him, 'Why do you ask my name, seeing it is wonderful?' "

34. The more traditional translation is: "you have struggled with God and with men, and have prevailed." The LXX varies somewhat: *hóti eníschysas metá theoú kaí metá anthrṓpōn dynatós* ("Since you have been strong against God, so you will triumph over men"), as does Vulg.: *quoniam si contra Deum fortis fuisti, quanto magis contra homines praevalebis* ("Because you have been strong against God, in the same amnner you will prevail against men with great strength."). In both LXX and Vulg., Jacob's exhibition of strength against God is a token of his success against humankind. In the traditional translation the phrase "with God and with men" could be understood as a hendiadys, "you have struggled with everybody, God and men, and have prevailed." For the hendiadys "gods and men" spoken by the olive tree and the vine in Jotham's fable, see Judg. 9:9, 13.

35. See F. Lindström, *God and the Origin of Evil,* tr. F. H. Cryer, ConBOT 21 (Lund: Gleerup, 1983), pp. 30-35; F. C. Holmgren, "Holding Your Own Against God! Genesis 32:22-32 (In the Context of Genesis 31–33)," *Int* 44 (1990) 5-17.

36. Manoah uses *mî* instead of *māh:* "Who . . . your name?" Noting the wrong use of the pronoun by Manoah, R. G. Boling (*Judges,* AB [Garden City, NY: Doubleday, 1975], p. 222) suggests that Manoah was momentarily reduced to stuttering, then recovered: "Who? . . . Your name?"

(Judg. 13:17-18). Both the man (Gen. 32) and the angel (Judg. 13) ask the same question: *lāmmâ zeh tiš'al lišmî.* In both instances the silence, the hesitancy, of the other being, begins to produce within Jacob/Manoah a realization of the supernatural status of that being. One wonders if "Why is it that you inquire about my name?" is another way of asking, "Jacob, don't you realize who I am?"

The text contains no evidence that Jacob desires to know the name of his adversary so that he might exercise power over him. This interpretation is based solely on parallels drawn from primitive religion in which demons and numens played a large part. Jacob's question is nothing more than a request for information from and identification of his adversary. This request is a formal element in the theophanies of the OT (see, e.g., Judg. 13:6, 18). A feature of those theophanies seems to be that only with the disappearance of the deity does the protagonist realize he or she has had contact with the divine. Cf. Judg. 6:22; 13:21; Luke 24:31.[37]

The man turns down one of Jacob's requests — "What is your name?" — but grants Jacob's other request — "I will not release you unless you bless me." The verse concludes with the cryptic *wayᵉḇāreḵ 'ōṯô šām* (lit., "he blessed him there," which I translated *He, then, bade him farewell*). The blessing is the new name itself, and this is followed by a parting blessing.

31 (30) Jacob does not receive a direct answer to his question about the man's name, but that does not stop him from naming the place where this wrestling match occurred. He calls it *Peniel,* that is, "the face of El." Jacob tones down his language when the significance of what recently happened dawns on him. He refers to that event by saying, *I have seen God face-to-face,* a statement all the more remarkable given that it happened during the night at the bottom of a dark gorge. Until now, the narrative has focused only on Jacob struggling with a man, not with him seeing divinity. Jacob does not give to this place any name that recalls his struggling with God. The emphasis here on seeing God recalls 32:2-3 (Eng. 1-2), "but messengers of God encountered him. Upon seeing them. . . ." The reference to the visual act also anticipates 33:10: "I see your face as one sees the face of God." The expression *face-to-face* need not be confined to literal visual perception. In an idiomatic fashion it refers "to the direct, nonmediated (i.e., immediate) character of a manifestation of presence. It describes a 'person-to-person' encounter, without the help or hindrance of an intermediary."[38]

37. Lindström, *God and the Origin of Evil,* pp. 29-30; J. O. Lewis, "Gen 32:23-33, Seeing a Hidden God," SBLASP, 1972, 1:453; R. Martin-Achard, "An Exegete Confronting Genesis 32:23-33," in *Structural Analysis and Biblical Exegesis,* p. 54.

38. Terrien, *Elusive Presence,* p. 91; also P. Dhorme, "L'emploi métaphorique des noms de parties du corps en hébreu et en akkadien," *RB* 30 (1921) 374-99; A. R. Johnson,

This is the third occasion on which Jacob memorializes a site by giving it his own name; cf. "Bethel" (28:19) and "Mahanaim" (32:2). All of them involved Jacob and a *mal'āḵ* or *mal'āḵîm,* "angel(s)."

When Jacob adds *now my life has been preserved,* he does not mean that he is happily surprised that he has seen God and is still alive. Jacob is not saying: "By all logical considerations, I should be dead by now." It is true that God says that "a man shall not see me and live" (Exod. 33:20) (a concept that admits exceptions throughout the OT), but that is hardly Jacob's concern. Such an interpretation misses the thrust of the double use of the root *nṣl* in this chapter. Earlier Jacob had prayed "Preserve me [*haṣṣîlēnî*] from my brother" (v. 12). Now he says: *my life has been preserved (wattinnāṣēl napšî).* In other words, Jacob's recognition that none other than God himself stands before him gives to Jacob the assurance that Esau shall not destroy him. Jacob's earlier prayer for deliverance is now answered by God in this encounter.[39] Jacob shall be "preserved" from Esau, for God has "preserved" him. In this verse Jacob moves, in his own words, from a proclamation of revelation ("I have seen God face-to-face") to a statement of testimony ("and yet my life has been preserved"), that is, he shifts from awe to relief.

32 (31) Jacob's encounter with the man has progressed from *laylâ* ("night," v. 23) to *šaḥar* ("dawn," vv. 25, 27) to *šemeš* ("daylight," lit., "sun"). Jacob's exclamation *I have seen God face-to-face* is mentioned before the rising of the sun, indicating that it is not the displacement of the darkness by the sun that permits Jacob to identify his antagonist.

As Jacob departs Penuel (the more common name for Peniel), he leaves with two things he did not bring with him to the Jabbok River. He has a new name and a new limp. The new name will forever remind Jacob of his new destiny. The new limp will forever remind him that in Elohim Jacob met for the first time one who can overpower him.

The word for *limping* is *ṣōlēaʿ,* which occurs but a few times in the OT. The radicals *ṣlʿ* may indeed cover two different verbs, *ṣālaʿ* I ("to stray") and *ṣālaʿ* II ("to stumble, halt").[40] In his famous words to the Baal prophets Elijah uses the root *pāsaḥ:* "How long will you go limping [*pōsᵉḥîm*] with two different opinions?" (1 K. 18:21). *ṣālaʿ* is probably used in Gen. 32 rather than *pāsaḥ* to produce a fine alliteration with the verb *nāṣal.* Note the *ṣ-l* sequence in *wattinnāṣēl* (v. 31) and in *ṣōlēaʿ* (v. 32). On the one hand, being lamed is a small price to pay for seeing God. On the other hand, such a limp

---

"Aspects of the Use of the Term *pānîm* in the Old Testament," in *Festschrift Otto Eissfeldt zum 60. Geburtstag,* ed. H. J. Fück (Halle an der Saale: Niemeyer, 1947), pp. 155-59.

39. A. P. Ross, "Jacob at the Jabbok, Israel at Peniel," *BSac* 142 (1985) 349.

40. See G. R. Driver, "Theological and Philological Problems in the Old Testament," *JTS* 47 (1946) 161-63.

would constitute a *mûm,* a defect, that would disqualify him from service to God according to later biblical teaching (e.g., Lev. 21:18).[41]

33 (32) Jacob's new limp has an aftereffect, as does his new name. If his new name means some changes in his own behavioral patterns, then his new limp means a change in the dietary patterns of his offspring. Because of what the man did to Jacob and where he struck him, Jacob's offspring do not eat *the sciatic muscle (gîḏ hannāšeh).* The sciatic nerve runs down the back of the leg. Heb. *gîḏ* occurs in Job 40:17 in the expression *gîḏê paḥᵃḏāw,* "the sinews of his thighs."[42] Job 10:11 and Ezek. 37:6 demonstrate that *gîḏ* refers to the tendons and other connective tissues which, along with the bones, provide the framework for the skin.[43]

The origin and meaning of the Hebrew word *nāšeh* are more difficult to determine than that of *gîḏ.* The former occurs only here in the Hebrew Bible. Gevirtz suggested that *nāšeh* was related to Akk. *nīšū,* "people, life," Ugar. *nš,* "man," and Heb. *'ᵉnôš,* "man." Thus the expression *gîḏ hannāšeh* denotes the *membrum virile,* "the male sinew," the "life(-producing) sinew," and the food taboo of v. 33(32) has specific reference to the male genitalia.[44] I am more inclined to agree with those who connect *nāšeh* with Ugar. *'anš* in the expression *'anš dt ẓrh,* "the small muscles of her back."[45]

This dietary prohibition is provided with the editorial expansion[46] that the Israelites[47] do not eat this part of the body *to this very day.*[48] After 32:33

41. Geller, *JANES* 14 (1982) 56 n. 54.

42. Cf. M. Pope, *Job,* AB, 3rd ed. (Garden City, NY: Doubleday, 1973), p. 317, who renders it "the thews of his thighs"; Vulg. *nervi testiculorum.*

43. See J. A. Wharton, "Sinew," *IDB,* 4:379.

44. Gevirtz, *HUCA* 46 (1975) 53. For Gevirtz here is the pun in this episode. The expression *gîḏ hannāšeh* is a pun on the names of the tribes of Gad *(gāḏ)* and Manasseh *(mᵉnaššeh),* for the Jabbok River served as a common border for the tribe of Gad and the half-tribe of Manasseh (Deut. 3:13-17; Josh. 13:14-21). S. H. Smith (" 'heel' and 'Thigh': the concept of sexuality in the Jacob-Esau narratives," *VT* 40 [1990] 468) agrees with Gevirtz's understanding of *nāšeh.* Gevirtz's reading is suggestive but speculative.

45. *KTU,* 1.3.III.32. This meaning was originally proposed by A. Goetze, "The Tenses of Ugaritic," *JAOS* 58 (1938) 298 n. 165, who rendered the phrase "and the muscles (?) of his back." See also J. C. de Moor, "The Anatomy of the Back," *UF* 12 (1980) 426. J. C. L. Gibson (*Canaanite Myths and Legends,* 2nd ed. [Edinburgh: T. & T. Clark, 1978], p. 141) has this entry in his glossary: *"ảnš* broken pl. 'muscles [Hebr. *nāšeh*]." Both Heb. *nāšeh* and Ugar. *anš* may derive from Hittite *anašša,* a body part, of both humans and animals, between the back and the anus.

46. See J. Weingreen, "Rabbinic-Type Glosses in the Old Testament," *JSS* 2 (1957) 149-62, esp. pp. 150-51.

47. The only other reference to the nation Israel in Genesis is 36:31.

48. See B. S. Childs, "A Study of the Formula, 'Until This Day,' " *JBL* 82 (1963) 288; idem, "The etiological tale re-examined," *VT* 24 (1974) 394. The formula "accordingly X does not do Y to this day" is rare. Cf. 1 Sam. 5:5.

nothing is said in the Jacob story (or even in the remainder of the OT) about this particular cultic abstinence.[49] Mention of Jacob's name change to Israel does resurface, however, in 35:10. What follows in ch. 33 is not a discourse on the sciatic muscle but a test case of how transforming the Jacob-to-Israel shift is. The tradition about the thigh sinew is clearly subordinated to the acquistion of Jacob's new name, and thus the food taboo may be read as secondarily added to the main thrust of the story, i.e., Jacob's change of name to Israel. Yet v. 33 is more than simply a postscript. The double reference to the hip socket in the verse balances the double reference to the hip socket with which the narrative began (v. 26 [Eng. 25]). The etiology of v. 33 (Eng. 32) balances the etiology of v. 31 (Eng. 30), and sandwiched between the two etiologies is narrative (v. 32 [Eng. 31]). Finally, Geller has noted that v. 33 (Eng. 32) with its internal chiasm of *sciatic muscle . . . hip socket . . . hip socket . . . sciatic muscle* gives a sense of summary and completion to vv. 31-33 (Eng. 30-32).[50]

J. JACOB IS RECONCILED WITH ESAU (33:1-20)

1 *Jacob looked up and saw Esau coming, and with him four hundred men. He divided*[1] *his children among Leah, Rachel, and the two maidservants,*

2 *putting the maidservants and their children first, Leah and her children next,*[2] *and Rachel and Joseph last.*

3 *But he himself went on ahead of them,*[3] *bowing to the ground seven times until he reached his brother.*

4 *Esau, however, ran to meet him, embraced him, and flinging himself on his neck,*[4] *kissed him*[5] *as he wept.*[6]

49. But cf. Mishnah *Ḥullin* 7, which expands on this alimentary taboo.

50. Geller, *JANES* 14 (1982) 40.

1. *ḥāṣâ* was used earlier in 32:8 (Eng. 7) to describe Jacob's dividing of his retinue when first apprised of the fact that Esau was coming to meet him with 400 men. In 32:8 (Eng. 7) the verb is followed by the preposition *l*^{e} *(lišnê maḥ*^{a}*nôṯ),* and here by *ʿal (ʿal lēʾâ),* giving the two meanings "divide into" and "divide among."

2. MT *ʾaḥ*^{a}*rōnîm . . . ʾaḥ*^{a}*rōnîm* ("next . . . last") is read by LXX as *opísō . . . eschátous.* Skinner (*Genesis,* pp. 412-13) and *BHS* suggest *ʾaḥ*^{a}*rêhem,* "after them," for the first *ʾaḥ*^{a}*rōnîm*, thus assuming the first to be a mistake (dittography).

3. For *ʿāḇar lip̱nê* meaning "go/pass on before so-and-so," cf. v. 14 below and Gen. 32:17 (Eng. 18), 22 (Eng. 21); Exod. 17:5.

4. The Qere and many mss. read the pl. *ṣawwāʾrāyw* (which BDB, p. 848, calls a pl. of intensity); the Ketib is sing., *ṣawwāʾrāw.* R. Gordis ("On Methodology in Biblical

5 *Looking around,*[7] *Esau spotted the women and the children. "Who are these with you?" he asked. Jacob answered: "They are the children with whom God has favored your servant."*

6 *Then the maidservants approached, they and their children, and bowed.*

7 *Likewise Leah and her children approached, and bowed; lastly, Joseph and Rachel*[8] *approached*[9] *and bowed.*

8 *Then Esau said: "What*[10] *were you up to with all that company I came across?" He responded: "It was for the purpose of gaining my lord's favor."*

9 *Esau replied: "I have an abundance, my brother; keep what is yours."*

Exegesis," in *The Word and the Book* [New York: Ktav, 1976], p. 6 n. 13) cites this word in Gen. 33:4 as an instance where a marginal notation was used to help fix the pronunciation before the invention of the vocalic system in the case, as here, of the reading of pl. suffixes written defectively.

5. Each of the consonants in *wayyiššāqēhû,* "and he kissed him," has a dot over it. This Masoretic notation, called *puncta extraordinaria* (see GKC, § 5n), occurs on entire words also in 37:12; Num. 3:39; 21:30; 29:15; Deut. 29:28; 2 Sam. 19:20; Isa. 44:9; Ezek. 41:20; 46:22; Ps. 27:13. Are they marks of erasure? Do they point to a doubtful reading? Are they a mnemonic device? Do they serve to guard against omission by later copyists who might be tempted to eliminate the word for some reason? See C. Levias, "Masorah," *Jewish Encylopedia* (New York: Funk and Wagnalls, 1904), 8:368; A. Dotan, "Masorah," *EncJud,* 16:1407-8. S. Lieberman (*Hellenism in Jewish Palestine* [New York: Jewish Theological Seminary of America, 1962], pp. 44-46) quotes the early rabbis who took such dots to be signs calling for special interpretation. Thus either Esau did not kiss Jacob sincerely, or Esau, who once hated Jacob, on this occasion kissed Jacob sincerely. See E. Tov (*Textual Criticism of the Hebrew Bible* [Assen and Maastricht: Van Gorcum; Minneapolis: Fortress, 1992], pp. 55–57), who argues that dots represent the erasure of letters.

6. MT has the pl., *wayyiḇkû,* "and they wept," which is supported by LXX's inclusion of "the two of them." More than likely we have here a case of dittography. The last word of v. 4 ends with a *waw (wayyiḇkû),* and the first word of v. 5 begins with a *waw (wayyiśśā').* Hence I read the sing., *wayyēḇk,* with *BHS* and Speiser, *Genesis,* p. 259. Note, however, that both LXX *(amphóteroi)* and Targ. Onqelos *(wbkw)* have the pl.

7. Lit., "and he raised/lifted his eyes."

8. LXX reverses the order: "Rachel and Joseph," probably to conform to the order of the personal names in v. 2.

9. The verb is pointed as a Niphal perfect (*niggaš,* lit., "were brought"), which is strange after the Qal imperfect of this verb in the first part of the sentence *(wattiggaš).* In the case of *nāḡaš* a Qal perfect and participle are expressed by the Niphal. See *HALAT,* p. 633, and Exod. 34:22; Deut. 20:2; 21:15; Isa. 29:13.

10. Davidson (*Hebrew Syntax,* p. 7, § 8) notes that *mî* may be used (instead of the expected *mâ*) of things when the idea of a person is involved. For *mî* = "what," see Judg. 13:17, *mî šᵉmeḵā,* "what is your name?" and Mic. 1:5, *mî p̱eša' ya'ᵃqōḇ . . . ûmî bāmôṯ yᵉhûḏâ,* "what is Jacob's crime . . . and what [is the crime of] Judah's heights?" See P. B. Dirksen, "Song of Songs iii 6-7," *VT* 39 (1989) 220-21.

10 *Jacob said: "No, I beg you! If I have gained your favor, then accept this gift from me; just to see your face is like seeing God's face,*[11] *now that you have treated me so favorably.*

11 *Accept, please, the present*[12] *brought*[13] *to you, because God has favored me, and I have more than enough." When he pleaded with him, he accepted.*

12 *Then he said: "Let us break camp and be on our way; I will accompany you."*

13 *But he said to him: "As my lord can observe, the children are frail. Furthermore, the flocks and herds nursing*[14] *deeply concern me;*[15] *if*[16] *pushed too fast,*[17] *even for a day, the entire flock would die.*

14 *Let my lord go on ahead of his servant, please, while I move more slowly*[18] *and gently*[19] *at the pace of the livestock*[20] *in front of me, and at the pace of the children. I will join my lord at Seir."*

11. Targ. Onqelos avoids even the suggestion that one could in fact see God's face with the rendering "as the sight of the face of the great ones" *(kḥyzw ʾpy rbrbal).*

12. Lit., "blessing" *(b^{e}rāḵâ).* For the significance of Jacob's shift from *minḥâ* ("gift") in v. 10 to *b^{e}rāḵâ* ("present") in v. 11,, see the commentary below on v. 11. Speiser (*Genesis,* p. 260) renders *b^{e}rāḵâ* as "bounty."

13. LXX, SP, and Vulg. read "I have brought" *(hēḇēʾṯî).* MT is a 3rd fem. Hophal perfect.

14. Lit., "the flocks and herds are giving suck upon me." Speiser (*Genesis,* p. 260) renders "upon me" idiomatically as "much to my encumbrance." For the coupling of the fem. participle with *bāqār,* cf. Job 1:14: *habbāqār hāyû hōr^{e}šōṯ,* "the oxen were plowing."

15. For the preposition *ʿal* to express what rests heavily on a person or is a burden/concern to a person, see BDB, p. 753, § II.1.b.

16. A conditional clause may be introduced simply by a *waw,* in which case it is attached to the perfect both in the protasis *(ûḏ^{e}pāqûm)* and in the apodosis *(wāmēṯû).* See Davidson, *Hebrew Syntax,* pp. 180-81, § 132; J. W. Watts, *A Survey of Syntax in the Hebrew Old Testament* (Grand Rapids: Eerdmans, 1964), pp. 134-35.

17. MT *ûḏ^{e}pāqûm* is a 3rd pl. Qal perfect with pronominal suffix. Some scholars (e.g., Skinner, *Genesis,* p. 414; BDB, p. 200) emend to a 1st perfect *(ûḏ^{e}paqtîm)* "if I push them," on the basis of LXX, SP, Pesh.; see also *BHS. dāp̱aq* occurs only twice again in the OT, both times to describe knocking on doors: once a persistent, threatening banging against the door by the Gibeonite riffraff (Judg. 19:22, Hithpael), and the other a less boisterous knocking on the door by the man at his beloved's house (Cant. 5:2, Qal). Only in Gen. 33:13 is the verb used of the driving of animals, a meaning the same root has in Arabic.

18. "I move more slowly" is the Hithpael of *nāhal* (which occurs only here), which BDB, p. 625, renders: "I will proceed, journey on, by stages (i.e. deliberately, with family and cattle)."

19. *ʾaṭ* is a substantive ("gentleness"), but it is used only adverbially (2 Sam. 18:5; 1 K. 21:27; Job 15:11; Isa. 8:6).

20. *m^{e}lāʾḵâ,* otherwise "work, service," has the meaning "property" in Exod. 22:7, 10 (property of a neighbor); 1 Sam. 15:9; 2 Chr. 17:13; and here, where it refers to possessions of herds and flocks.

15 *Esau replied: "Let me leave with*[21] *you some of the men who are with me." But Jacob queried: "Why? Please indulge me in this, my lord."*[22]

16 *So Esau started on his trek home to Seir that day.*

17 *Jacob journeyed to Succoth, where he built himself a home; and for his livestock he made booths. That is why the place was called Succoth.*[23]

18 *Having come from Paddan-aram, Jacob arrived safely*[24] *in the city of Shechem, which is in the land of Canaan; and he camped on the city's edge.*

19 *He purchased the portion of the field on which he pitched his tent from the sons of Hamor, the father of Shechem, for one hundred kesitahs.*[25]

20 *He erected an altar there, and called it El-Elohe-Israel.*[26]

1-2 Having already contended with one *'îš* ("man"), Jacob now has to face *four hundred* of them *('arbaʿ mē'ôṯ 'îš)*. The inclusion of Esau brings the total to 401. This total recalls the 401 prophets (400 + Micaiah) consulted by Ahab about potential military campaigns (1 K. 22:1ff.). The messengers of Jacob have moved more quickly than has Esau's entourage. In 32:7 (Eng. 6) it is reported that Jacob's advance party has returned to Jacob with news that Esau is on the way with 400 men. Jacob has had time to arrange his group into two sections, send them across the river, dispatch a second group to Esau with a conciliatory gift, spend most of the night battling with a supernatural being, and lastly leave Peniel with a noticeable limp.

Verses 1-2 describe the limping Jacob's further maneuvers the morning after he has divided his property, sent a deputation of servants and animals to Esau, ferried his family and the remainder of his property across the Jabbok, and wrestled with the "man." In 32:8 (Eng. 7) Jacob's dividing of his family and flocks is purely a military maneuver in an effort to save 50 percent of

21. This verse uses two different words for "with" *(ʿim . . . 'eṯ): ʿimmᵉḵā* ("with you"), *'ittî* ("with me").

22. Lit., "let me find favor in the eyes of my lord."

23. Lit., "booths, huts, sheds."

24. LXX, Pesh., and Vulg. read *šālēm,* "safely," as the name of a city, "to Salem." SP read *šālôm,* "peace(fully)." See n. 38 below.

25. It is impossible to determine the value of this coin or weight unit. According to Gen. Rabbah 79:7, *qᵉśîṭâ* refers to precious stones, sheep, and selas (i.e., coins). M. Aberbach and B. Grossfeld (*Targum Onkelos to Genesis* [New York: Ktav, 1982], p. 6) call attention to a similar word, *ksyrth,* used in the 2nd century A.D. in Aramaic to denote pearls as well as sheep. Targ. Onqelos, LXX, and Vulg. all render *qᵉśîṭâ* with "sheep/lambs," possibly because coins stamped with images of sheep/lambs were in use from the time of the translation of the LXX down to the talmudic age.

26. Lit., "El, the God of Israel" or "El (is) the God of Israel."

Jacob's family and herds, in the case of attack by Esau and his retinue. No corresponding military strategy is at work in 33:1-2. Jacob simply divides his family into three groups of wives and children in the inverse order of his affection for them: concubines, Leah, Rachel.

3 Here is an evidence of some genuine change in Jacob's style of operation. The pre-Peniel Jacob was insistent that he stay "behind" his party (32:17, 19, 21). Now the post-Peniel Jacob will be at the vanguard of his party. Jacob's "pass on before me" (*ʿiḇrû lᵉpānay,* 32:17 [Eng. 16]) shifts to *But he himself went on ahead of them (wᵉhûʾ ʿāḇar lip̄nêhem).* The inclusion of the independent personal pronoun before the verb accentuates Jacob's radical shift of position — from rearguard to vanguard.[27]

In addition to a shift in positions for Jacob, there is also a shift in subject and object of the verb "bow down." Earlier portions of the Jacob narrative indicated that nations would "bow down" before him (27:29). That is reversed here — it is Jacob who bows down before the ancestor of the Edomites.

4 Esau *raced to meet* Jacob. Esau can race; Jacob can only limp. This verse picks up 32:7 (Eng. 6) with its "to meet you" *(liqrāʾṯᵉḵā).* Esau moves quickly *to meet him (liqrāʾṯô).* Nobody, neither Jacob nor the reader, yet knows Esau's intentions. Will Esau meet him to scold him, attack him, kill him? Jacob is at Esau's mercy. How can a limping man evade a running man?

Instead of spewing anger on Jacob, Esau *embraced him.* We have already drawn attention to the phonetic similarity between "wrestle" of ch. 32 *(ʾāḇaq)* and "embrace" of ch. 33 *(ḥāḇaq).* Both verbs imply physical contact, but for significantly different purposes.

Esau's flinging himself on Jacob's neck and weeping parallels Joseph's behavior when he first saw Benjamin (45:14) and his father Jacob (46:29). For embracing followed by kissing, cf. 29:13; for kissing followed by embracing, cf. 48:10.

One may compare Esau's meeting with Jacob, after the latter has engaged in combat with a divine assailant, with Aaron's meeting his brother Moses after Yahweh almost killed Moses (Exod. 4:24-27). In Exod. 4:24 Yahweh "met" *(wayyip̄gᵉšēhû)* Moses, and in Exod. 4:27 Aaron "met" (also *wayyip̄gᵉšēhû)* Moses on the mountain of God. While Esau did not "meet" Jacob, he did "meet" *(pāḡāštî,* Gen. 33:8) the deputation Jacob had sent on ahead. Then the deity

27. S. A. Geller ("The Struggle at the Jabbok: The Uses of Enigma in a Biblical Narrative," *JANES* 14 [1982] 43) diagrams the disposition of the actors in ch. 32 and 33 as follows:

ch. 32: ESAU deputations family // JACOB
Jabbok
——→ ←————————————

ch. 33: ESAU JACOB concubines Leah Rachel
——→ ←————————————

initiates a struggle during the night (explicitly in Genesis, implicitly in Exodus). The struggle takes place while Jacob and Moses are on return journeys to Canaan and Egypt, respectively. In the midst of this struggle the man touches *(wayyigga')* Jacob's thigh (Gen. 32:26 [Eng. 25]), and Zipporah touched *(wattagga')* the feet of either Moses or Gershom (Exod. 4:25). Following this struggle, the older brother (Esau, Aaron) takes the initiative to go and meet the younger brother (Gen. 33:4; Exod. 4:27, *liqrā'ṯô, liqra'ṯ mōšeh,* respectively). In both cases, after the reunion the older brother kisses his younger brother *(wayyiššāqēhû, wayyiššaq lô).* In both instances, then, the sequel to a severe encounter with God in which the human combatant is both wounded and transformed is the forging of a new relationship with one's brother.[28]

Esau's actions toward Jacob on his homecoming are also similar to those of the father toward his homecoming son in the parable of Jesus (Luke 15:11-32). Both Esau and the father fell on the neck and kissed their brother/son.[29] On both occasions the kiss is possibly not just a display of joyous feelings but an indication of forgiveness (cf. 2 Sam. 14:33).

5-7 The last time Esau saw Jacob, Jacob was single and healthy. Nowhere in the narrative does Esau make inquiry about his limp. But he does ask about the party accompanying Jacob. Esau asked about both the women and the children with Jacob. In his reply Jacob speaks only of the children. He says nothing to identify his maidservants or his wives. Perhaps he feels that mentioning them would only resurrect in Esau's mind Jacob's departure some twenty years ago from Canaan to get a wife from Paddan-aram, and Esau's involvement in that event. The more the past remains entombed, the better for Jacob.

Jacob telescopes a fairly involved history of his children into a crisp *they are the children with whom God has favored your servant.* He is not about to unload lengthy, autobiographical facts on Esau. Nor will he make a fool of himself by sharing with his brother how he was duped into polygamy. Not a word about that wedding night! Jacob's choice of the verb *ḥānan* in v. 5 and again in v. 11 ("favor") may be deliberate. A few verses later Jacob will make clear to Esau that he desires Esau's favor (*ḥēn,* vv. 8, 10). Jacob's hope is that his brother will treat him in the present moment exactly as God has treated him in the past.

The wives', children's, and maidservants' conduct have been carefully orchestrated by Jacob. Not counting Jacob, sixteen people approach Esau, in three successive groups of six, eight, and two, and bow before him. Each

28. B. P. Robinson, "Zipporah to the rescue: a contextual study of Exodus iv 24-26," *VT* 36 (1986) 451-52.

29. Gen. 33:4 (LXX): *prosépesen epí tón tráchēlon autoú, kaí éklausan amphóteroi;* Luke 15:20: *epépesen epí tón tráchēlon autoú kaí katephílēsen autón.*

group includes male and female: two females and four males in the first; two females and six males in the second; one female and one male in the third. They all act like automatons. They approach, genuflect, make room for another group, but say nothing. Jacob's reservation of *Joseph and Rachel* until last indicates Jacob's fondness for these two, and hence his extra caution. The Niphal in v. 7b (*approached,* lit., "were brought") may indicate that Jacob escorted them to Esau (but see n. 9 above).

8 When asked about the purpose of the party that Jacob had sent on ahead to meet Esau, Jacob elaborates on his original explanation he gave to his servants. Originally he described it as a "gift" (32:19 [Eng. 18]). He now amplifies that explanation with *It was for the purpose of gaining my lord's favor.* Again, there is a similarity in sound between *company (maḥ^{a}neh)* and *favor (ḥēn),* with the *ḥ-n* sequence in both. The purpose of the *maḥ^{a}neh* was to find *ḥēn.* Two verses later (v. 10), Jacob calls what he has sent with the company to Esau his gift *(minḥāṯî),* another word with the *ḥ-n* sequence. Indeed, the proliferation of words with the consonants *ḥ-n* in Gen. 32 and 33 is one factor that binds the accounts in the two chapters together.[30]

Not only is the post-Peniel Jacob courageous ("he himself went on ahead of them"), but he is honest as well. Up until this point candor has not been one of Jacob's more distinctive traits. Now it is. He is forthright with Esau about his intention to buy Esau's forgiveness. He hopes that a generous gift would mollify any belligerent moves by Esau.

9 Esau is able to call Jacob *my brother.* Jacob cannot yet reciprocate. In relation to Esau, Jacob's label for himself is "your servant" (vv. 5, 14). For Esau himself, Jacob's designation is "my lord" (vv. 8, 13, 14 [twice], 15). Now that they are reunited, Esau desires a fraternal relationship, but Jacob is unable to move beyond a formal relationship.

Only the restraining intervention of God kept Laban from retaliation against Jacob (31:24, 29). Esau is apparently in no need of a similar divine check. His own good nature acts as a check on him. Since his rage and hate of ch. 27, Esau himself has undergone his own transformation. No longer is he controlled by vile passions.

Esau first rejects his brother's gift, not because he is suspicious of it or of him, but because he already has more than he needs of everything. This situation is ironic. He lost out on the first son's double portion. But missing that two-thirds share did not reduce him to a pauper. Esau, in turning down Jacob's gift, may well have paraphrased his grandfather with "I will not take anything that is yours, lest you say 'I have made Esau rich' " (see 14:23).

10-11 Jacob ties together his meeting with God in ch. 32 with his

30. See S. L. McKenzie, "The Jacob Tradition in Hosea xii 4-5," *VT* 36 (1986) 315-16.

meeting with Esau in ch. 33 by *just to see your face is like seeing God's face.* "Peni-el" (face of God) has been followed by "Peni-esau" (face of Esau). Reconciliation with God is now capped off with reconciliation with a brother. For one of vassal status (like Jacob) comparing a superior to a divine being cf. 1 Sam. 29:9; 2 Sam. 14:17, 20; 19:28 (Eng. 27). On a different level cf. Acts 6:15, "they saw his face as it had been the face of an angel." Of course, Jacob is not saying that Esau has undergone a metamorphosis, or that he exudes a divine luminesence. The surprise in ch. 32 is that Jacob saw God, and yet his life was spared. The surprise in ch. 33 is that Jacob has seen Esau, and yet his life is spared. God's mercy to Jacob is conveyed by the verb *nāṣal* (Gen. 32:31 [Eng. 30]); Esau's mercy to Jacob is conveyed by the verb *rāṣâ* (33:10).

Jacob is as insistent with Esau as he was with the man at Peniel. His "I will not let you go unless you bless me" now becomes, in effect, "I will not let you go unless you accept my gift." Jacob's shift in terms from *minḥâ* (lit., "gift") in v. 10 to *b*^{e}*rāḵâ* (lit., "blessing") in v. 11 is not just for variety of expression. Jacob, who earlier had stolen the blessing from Esau (ch. 27), would now return a blessing to Esau. This is his way of attempting to make amends, without suggesting as much.[31] Jacob never does come right out and say: "Forgive me for what I did to you years ago."

Esau does not specify the source of his wealth, but Jacob does: *because God has favored me.* This insertion would perhaps discourage Esau from harming Jacob, if he was predisposed to do so. Would Esau lay a hand on one whom God has so prospered? Jacob's reference to God as *'ĕlōhîm* (vv. 5, 10, 11) is strange in a narrative commonly attributed to J, but this use may be due to the fact that Jacob converses with an "outsider," Esau from Seir (even if the outsider is his own brother).

12 Esau, ever conciliatory, offers to escort Jacob on the remainder of his journey back home. It is now time for the kind of companionship reflected in "they went both of them together" (22:6). Two can walk together if they are in agreement (Amos 3:3).

Esau will not only escort Jacob; he will actually lead him on the way home. *I will accompany you* is literally "I will go in front of you" *(w*^{e}*'ēl*^{e}*ḵâ l*^{e}*negdeḵā).* This Hebrew expression is close to *k*^{e}*negdô* of 2:19, a phrase describing Eve's complementary relationship to Adam.

13-14 Earlier, Esau rejected Jacob's offer of a gift, but later he relented. Jacob now rejects Esau's offer of companionship, and he persists in

31. Sarna (*Genesis,* p. 230) suggests the same with his comment: "By a change of terminology . . . Jacob signals to Esau that the present is in a way a reparation for the purloining of the paternal blessing twenty years earlier." Both BDB, p. 139, and *HALAT,* p. 155, list Gen. 33:11; Josh. 15:19; Judg. 1:15; 1 Sam. 25:27; 30:26; 2 K. 5:15 as places where *b*^{e}*rāḵâ* means "gift/present connected with (wish of) blessing."

that refusal. His reason for declining is that the children are frail, and that among the livestock are many newborns. Both of these factors would slow Jacob's movement with his party to a snail's pace. Hence, Esau should go ahead by himself to Seir. Jacob will catch up with him there eventually. Earlier Jacob had gone on ahead of his party (*ʿāḇar lip̄nêhem,* v. 3). Now he urges Esau to go on ahead of him *(yaʿaḇār lip̄nê ʿaḇdô).* In ch. 32 Jacob preferred a position of being "behind," then in 33:3 he shifted to a position of "in front of," now he returns to following in 33:14.

It would appear that the second excuse Jacob makes to Esau is more open to substantiation than is his first. Esau can plainly see whether there are a number of sucking newborns in Jacob's herds. It is not as clear why Jacob should suddenly refer to his children as *frail (rakkîm).* They seem to have weathered the journey thus far with no ill effects. If anybody is *raḵ,* it should be Jacob after his wrestling with a divine being and then limping as he traveled.

All of Jacob's concerns voiced at this point may be another subterfuge to distance himself once more from Esau. Does Jacob really intend to join Esau at *Seir,* Esau's domain? To be sure, he had no qualms about earlier sending a party ahead of him to Seir (32:3). Will he himself go? Earlier (see my comments on v. 3 and n. 27) I argued for evidence of a shift from a cunning Jacob to an upright Israel as a result of the Peniel episode. Such evidence should not be gainsaid. These two verses, especially v. 14, however, indicate that post-Peniel Jacob is not above making false promises and offering misleading expectations to Esau. "Though he became Israel, he is not 'upright' Israel but, throughout chs. 32–33, 'uptight' Israel."[32]

15 Esau's second offer to Jacob is to leave behind an escort to accompany Jacob. With a host of nursing animals and frail children, Jacob should be able to use some extra manpower. And if Jacob and his entourage are attacked, who will protect them? Esau is clearly concerned about his brother's safety. At almost every point in this story, Esau emerges as the more appealing, more humane, and more virtuous of the two brothers.

Jacob's response to the second offer is different from his response to the first offer. To the first offer Jacob presented logical counterarguments. To sidestep the second offer he appeals to Esau's sense of favor *(ḥēn).* That Esau has even welcomed Jacob back without reprisal is favor enough. It is asking

32. This last phrase is that of E. M. Good, "Deception and Women: A Response," in *Reasoning with the Foxes: Female Wit in a World of Male Power,* ed. J. C. Exum and J. W. H. Bos, Semeia 42 (Atlanta: Scholars, 1988), p. 129. Westermann (*Genesis,* 2:526-27) is one of the few commentators who states that he sees nothing reprehensible or dishonest about Jacob's words to Esau. While I agree that it is not necessary that reconciliation mandates that Esau and Jacob live adjacent to each other, each pursuing the same life-style, I do not see how Westermann can state that Esau knows quite well that nothing Jacob says in v. 14 is meant to be taken seriously. V. 15 seems to indicate Esau took Jacob quite literally.

too much, says Jacob, for Esau both to welcome Jacob back home and to lend a percentage of his men to protect the well-being of Jacob and his party. It is easier on this occasion for Jacob to give than to receive. He insists that Esau accept his gift (v. 11b), but he cannot accept Esau's generous offer of assistance. With Esau's men traveling with him, Jacob must journey to Seir rather than to Succoth (v. 17).

This is only the second — and it is the last — conversation between Esau and Jacob mentioned in Genesis. On the first occasion (25:29-34) Esau failed to perceive Jacob's capacity for exploitation. On the second occasion he fails to perceive Jacob's hesitancy and lack of excitement about going to Seir. In both cases, Jacob succeeds in deceiving Esau. Of course, it is unlikely in Gen. 33 that Jacob will come right out and say to Esau "No, I'm not going with you. Seir is not my home." Why risk infuriating Esau?

16-17 Esau and Jacob now part ways permanently, to be reunited briefly only at the burial of their father (35:29). The different directions in which the brothers move is underscored by the difference of word order in these two verses. With Esau the order is verb-subject. With Jacob in v. 17 the order is subject-verb, thus calling special attention to the subject "Jacob." One could almost read the beginning of v. 17: "on the other hand, Jacob, he. . . ."

Jacob's first stop is at a site he names *Succoth,* because there he made booths *(sukkōṯ)* for his livestock.[33] This is the fourth instance on which Jacob gives a name to a place: Bethel, Mahanaim, Peniel, and Succoth. In the first three of these events, the name grew out of an experience Jacob had with God or with one of his messengers. In this one deity is not a factor in the choice of a name. It also appears that the etymology is considerably removed from any transparent connection with the narrative that has preceded (again, unlike the previous three etymologies).

Succoth is a town east of the Jordan in the territory of Gad (Josh. 13:27, assigned to the Gadites from the original kingdom of Sihon). Elders from this town refused assistance to Gideon in his pursuit of the Midianites, for which omission he took revenge on them (Judg. 8:5-7, 14-16). In Solomon's time it was a southern site in the Jordan plain where bronze vessels for the temple were cast (1 K. 7:46; 2 Chr. 4:17). If Succoth is to be identified with modern Tell Deir-alla,[34] then Jacob, instead of heading south to Seir, went north about two miles from the Jabbok River.

33. See Long, *Problem of Etiological Narrative,* pp. 11-12.

34. See H. J. Franken, "The excavation at Deir ʿAllā in Jordan with 16 Plates," *VT* 10 (1960) 386-93; idem, "The excavations at Deir ʿAlla in Jordan, 2nd Season: With 23 Plates," *VT* 11 (1961) 361-72; idem, "The excavations at Deir ʿAlla in Jordan, 3rd season," *VT* 12 (1962) 378-82; idem, "Excavations at Deir ʿAlla, season 1964: With X Plates," *VT* 14 (1964) 417-22.

18-20 Jacob's itinerary takes him from Succoth, across the Jordan somewhere (not recorded), and on to Shechem. He is now back in Cisjordan for the first time in over twenty years. He encamps on the outskirts of Shechem, a place that appeared for the first time in the OT as a city through which Abram passed on his way to Bethel and the Negev (12:6). The difference between Abram and Jacob is that Abram was only a transient in Shechem, while Jacob claimed it as his domicile, at least for a while (v. 19). Such references as 33:18-20 (and 48:22) indicate that Shechem's central role in Israel's religion (see, e.g., Josh. 24) had its roots in pre-Mosaic, patriarchal traditions, especially those about Jacob.[35] The residents of Shechem are identified as *the sons of Hamor,* that is, "the sons [or children] of the ass." On the basis of analogous material from Mari, this designation must refer to members of a community in covenant, whose closeness with each other has been formalized by the ritual slaughter of an ass.[36] It is less likely that the name *Hamor* reflects the practice of Near Easterners giving children animal names.

Jacob's first act is to purchase a piece of land from the Hamorites *for one hundred kesitahs.* In acquiring land from strangers, Jacob follows his grandfather (Gen. 23). The *qᵉśîṭâ* is an unknown unit of weight, and thus we cannot be sure how much Jacob paid for the purchase of real estate.

There is, however, no doubt about what Jacob does with the land, once it is legally his. He builds an altar on it, and thus again follows in the train of his grandfather (12:7, 8; 13:18; 22:9) and of his father (26:25). Jacob erects another altar in 35:7. In all of these the verb used for altar construction is *bānâ.* The one exception is 33:20, which uses *nāṣaḇ.* Because *nāṣaḇ* is used elsewhere in the Jacob narratives to describe the building of a pillar (rather than an altar), some have suggested that originally v. 20 read: "he set/raised a pillar there." This reading would necessitate changing *mizbēaḥ wayyiqrā' lô* (masc.) to *maṣṣēḇâ wayyiqrā' lāh* (fem.).[37]

The use of *nāṣaḇ* here recalls its double occurrence in 28:12-13, where Jacob saw a stairway "set" on the ground, and Yahweh "standing" beside him. This is one tie between ch. 28 and ch. 33. In addition, ch. 33 answers

35. Both D. N. Freedman ("Who Is Like Thee Among the Gods?' The Religion of Early Israel," in *Ancient Israelite Religion,* Fest. F. M. Cross, ed. P. D. Miller, Jr., et al. [Philadelphia: Fortress, 1987], pp. 321, 322, 324) and J. Gray ("Israel in the Song of Deborah," in *Ascribe to the Lord,* Fest. P. C. Craigie, ed. L. Eslinger and G. Taylor, JSOTSup 67 [Sheffield: JSOT, 1988], pp. 452-53) believe that the reference to "Israel" (listed last in towns from south to north) in the stele of Merneptah, together with data such as one finds in Gen. 33:18-20, argue for the existence of an ancient community whose cult center was Shechem.

36. See G. R. H. Wright, "Shechem and League Shrines," *VT* 21 (1971) 575 and n. 1.

37. See the critical apparatus in *BHS;* and Westermann, *Genesis,* 2:529.

two questions raised by ch. 28. First, in his vow at Bethel, Jacob had raised before God the issue of whether he would return to his father's house "in peace" (*bešālôm,* 28:21). That is now answered with *Jacob arrived safely* [*šālēm*][38] in the city of Shechem.

Second, at Bethel Jacob had promised "if God will be with me . . . then Yahweh shall be my God" (28:20-21). The altar Jacob erects at Shechem he calls *El-Elohe-Israel,* "El (is) the God of Israel (i.e., Jacob)."[39] Here Jacob, via his new name, fulfills that commitment he made first at Bethel many years earlier. God is indeed his God. God is indeed the God of (the patriarch) Israel.

THE NEW TESTAMENT APPROPRIATION

Gen. 33:19 and John 4:5, 6, 12; Acts 7:16

John informs us that Jesus rested at a Samaritan city called Sychar,[1] which is "near the field Jacob gave to his son Joseph" (John 4:5). The field Jacob passed on to Joseph is most certainly the one Jacob purchased from the Hamorites (Gen. 33:19). It was in this field that Joseph was buried (Josh. 24:32). Nowhere does Genesis record that Jacob dug a well, much less that he handed it on to his children (though he did dig a field). The only well Jacob is associated with in Genesis is the well in Haran (29:1-10), the top of which he removed when Rachel approached with Laban's flock.[2] It may well be that

38. Cf. the opening line of Lachish Letter VI: "May Yahweh cause my Lord to see this time safely," vocalizing the last word as *šālēm,* rather than as *šālōm* (cf. *ANET,* p. 322, "in good health"). In addition to some of the ancient versions (see n. 24 above) that read *šālēm* as a place name ("Salem"), some modern commentators also opt for this reading (Westermann, *Genesis,* 2:528). However, Westermann's argument that *šālēm* is never used of people with the meaning "safe(ly), intact" is called into question by its use in Lachish Letter VI. Moreover, to what or with what can one connect "Salem, the city of Shechem"? Such a place is unknown from the time of even the Elohist or Yahwist, to which this part of v. 18 is usually attributed. For the translation "safely" see G. Gerleman, *"šâlōm," THAT,* 2:926; W. Eisenbeis, *Die Wurzel šlm im Alten Testament,* BZAW 113 (Berlin: de Gruyter, 1969), pp. 69, 335.

39. See M. Pope, *El in the Ugaritic Texts,* VTSup 2 (Leiden: Brill, 1955), p. 15; Cross, *Canaanite Myth and Hebrew Epic,* pp. 46 n. 13, 49.

1. R. E. Brown (*The Gospel According to John,* AB, 2 vols. [Garden City, NY: Doubleday, 1966-70], 1:169) argues for "Shechem" instead of Sychar, although the ms. evidence for Shechem is meager.

2. The Palestinian Targ. has a comment that may illuminate John 4:15: "Five signs were performed to our father Jacob . . . the fifth sign: after our father Jacob had lifted the stone from the mouth of the well, the well rose to its surface and overflowed and was

the references to Jacob's well find their locus in the traveling well tradition of Jewish literature. Thus one reference (Pirqe Rabbi Eliezer 35) states that "Jacob was seventy-seven years old when he went forth from his father's house, and the well went with him." At one point, says the tradition, Jacob left this well at Bethel.[3] To return to John 4, I suggest that John uses the woman's question "are you greater than our father Jacob?" to insinuate that indeed Jesus does supplant Jacob, as Jacob once supplanted Esau.

Acts 7:16 is interesting in that it states that it was Abraham (!) who bought the field in Shechem from the sons of Hamor. Either Stephen has his facts confused, or else he has telescoped the two accounts of purchases of land in Canaan (Gen. 23, 33), just as he telescoped the two calls of Abraham in v. 2, and the two divine messages in v. 7.[4]

K. THE HUMBLING OF DINAH (34:1-31)

1. DINAH IS VIOLATED (34:1-7)

1 *And Dinah, daughter of Leah, whom the latter bore to Jacob, went out to be seen*[1] *among the women of the land.*

2 *When Shechem, son of Hamor the Hivite,*[2] *leader of the region,*[3] *saw*

---

overflowing twenty years: all the days that our fathers dwelt in Haran." See J. R. Díaz, "Palestinian Targum and New Testament," *NovT* 6 (1963) 76-77.

3. See J. H. Neyrey, "Jacob Traditions and the Interpretation of John 4:10-26," *CBQ* 41 (1979) 421-22.

4. See F. F. Bruce, *Book of Acts,* rev. ed., NICOT (Grand Rapids: Eerdmans, 1988), p. 137 n. 35.

1. The infinitive of the Qal stem is neutral (GKC, § 114k) and may be translated passively or actively. See C. H. Gordon, *Homer and Bible* (repr. Ventnor, NJ: Ventnor, 1967), p. 42 n. 84. Note, e.g., Josh. 2:15: "and the gate was to be shut" *(lisgôr).*

2. LXX reads "Horite," but this is not sufficient reason for emending the MT. According to MT Hivites are located in Shechem (34:2), Gibeonite cities (Josh. 9:7; 11:19), the Beqa (Josh. 11:3; Judg. 3:3; 2 Sam. 4:7), and possibly in Edom (Gen. 36:2). This last reference has supplied the major evidence for the close association of Hivites with Horites (Hurrians), possibly even suggesting that the two terms are interchangeable. One suggestion has been to derive "Hivite" from *quwe* or *qawe,* the name used in Assyrian inscriptions from the mid-9th century B.C. for the kingdom of Kizzuwadna, a region within the Hittite sphere of influence in the mid-14th century, and also a region in which Hurrians were well established. See J. Blenkinsopp, "The Prophetic Reproach," *JBL* 90 (1971) 275 n. 38.

3. As argued by F. S. Frick, *The City in Ancient Israel,* SBLDS 36 (Missoula, MT: Scholars, 1977), p. 37, *hāʾāreṣ* might well here mean "city."

her, he seized her and lay with her[4] *illicitly.*[5]

3 *Because*[6] *he was so strongly attracted to Dinah,*[7] *daughter of Jacob, and loved the maiden, he attempted to woo her.*[8]

4 *So Shechem spoke to his father Hamor: "Get me this girl for a wife."*

5 *Meanwhile, Jacob had heard that*[9] *Shechem had defiled his daughter Dinah; because his sons were out with his livestock in the fields, Jacob said nothing*[10] *until they returned.*

6 *Hamor, the father of Shechem, came to Jacob to discuss the matter with him,*

4. MT *'ōṯāh* may be the direct object indicator plus pronominal suffix (i.e., "he lay her"), rather than LXX *met' autḗs,* which presupposes *'ittāh,* "with her." For other instances where the MT has vocalized the object of *šāḵaḇ* to suggest a direct object of a transitive verb, see Lev. 15:24; 2 Sam. 13:14. See, however, n. 21.

5. The basic meaning of *'ānâ* (Piel) is "to afflict a dependent" (Gen. 15:13; 16:6; 31:50). In some instances *'ānâ* carries the technical meaning "to take a woman without the correct formalities" (Deut. 21:14; 22:24, 29) rather than that of force or compulsion. Note that in v. 31 her brothers give as the reason for their revenge that Shechem had treated her as a harlot. Note also that Amnon "humbled" *('ānâ)* Tamar (2 Sam. 13:12, 14, 22, 32) in taking her without, as she says, "speaking to the king" (v. 13), in other words, without following due procedure. It is this disgrace that rankles Absalom, not the use of force per se. See D. Daube, *The Exodus Pattern in the Bible* (London: Faber and Faber, 1963), p. 65 n. 6. What Shechem has done to Dinah is not rape her, but humble or shame her. For the idea that *'ānâ* (Piel) does not by itself connote rape, but rather the shaming or humbling of a woman through sexual intercourse, see L. M. Bechtel, "What If Dinah Is Not Raped? (Genesis 34)," *JSOT* 62 (1994) 19-36, esp. pp. 23-31. See also M. Weinfeld, *Deuteronomy and the Deuteronomic School* (repr. Winona Lake, IN: Eisenbrauns, p. 286: "When used in connection with women the verb *'nh* appears, then, to connote sexual intercourse in general rather than rape, and it is to be rendered accordingly in such verses as Gen. 34:2; Judg. 19:24; 2 Sam. 13:12; Ezek. 22:10-11."

6. The threefold repetition of clauses beginning with *waw* consecutive on imperfect verbs in this verse *(wattiḏbaq . . . wayye'ĕhaḇ . . . wayyeḏabbēr)* is a way of underscoring the intensity of Shechem's attraction to Dinah. Cf. Andersen, *Sentence in Biblical Hebrew,* p. 42.

7. Lit., "and his soul clung to Dinah." *dāḇaq be* frequently occurs as an expression to denote loyal or deep affection. See, e.g., Gen. 2:24; Ruth 1:14; Josh. 23:12; 2 Sam. 20:2.

8. Lit., "he spoke upon the heart of the girl"; cf. BDB, p. 181, which takes this idiom to mean "speak kindly, comfort." Here, and in Judg. 19:3 and Hos. 2:16, the expression means to persuade or woo a woman. In 2 Sam. 19:8; 2 Chr. 30:22; 32:6 the expression refers to encouragement a king gives to his people. In Gen. 50:21; Ruth 2:13; and Isa. 40:2 it means to comfort or relieve. See G. Fischer, "Die Redewendung *dbr 'l lb* im AT — Ein Betrag zum Verständnis von Jes 40,2," *Bib* 65 (1984) 244-50.

9. *weya'aqōḇ šāma' kî* is an instance of a circumstantial clause with a perfect verb. It serves as a flashback and is rendered into English with a pluperfect. See Andersen, *Sentence in Biblical Hebrew,* p. 85.

10. GKC, § 112ss, cites *wehеḥĕriš* as a use of the *we* with perfect to denote "a longer or constant continuance in a past state."

7 *just as Jacob's sons were returning from the fields. When they heard the news, they were shocked*[11] *and furious. What he had done by lying with Jacob's daughter was in Israel a wanton sin.*[12] *Such behavior ought not be done.*[13]

1 This is the only place in the Jacob story where an event involving Dinah is related. We saw in 29:21 that the recording of Dinah's birth was limited to one brief verse, and even there no etymology was provided with her name, in contrast to her brothers, each of whom were given etymologies. We also noted the absence of Dinah when Jacob sent his "eleven" children across the Jabbok (32:23 [Eng. 22]). Where she is mentioned obliquely (33:7, 13), Dinah is included among Jacob's "children" (*yᵉlāḏîm,* masc.).

Before Dinah is identified as the "daughter of Jacob" (v. 3), she is first identified as *daughter of Leah.* This is only one of seven instances in which the OT traces lineage through a woman.[14] Dinah's connections with Leah occur only in this verse. Hereafter she is "daughter of Jacob" (v. 3), "his daughter" (v. 5), "Jacob's daughter" (vv. 7, 19), "their sister" (vv. 13, 27), "our sister" (v. 31).[15]

to be seen among the women of the land. If we translate the infinitive construct *lir'ôt* as active, then v. 1 would imply that Dinah simply visited in other people's houses, that Dinah was not confined to her house. Such freedom was enjoyed by Rebekah, who drew water from the well for her father (24:16), and by Rachel, who tended her father's sheep (29:6), and presumably by Dinah too. The combination *rā'â bᵉ* is rare (cf. 1 Sam. 16:1), however, and nowhere else is the infinitive construct of this verb followed by the preposition *bᵉ*. This construction suggests that "visit" for *lir'ôṯ bᵉ* is unlikely. I suggest the passive *to be seen among*. The active sense is possible only if one understands *bᵉ* partitively, that is, "to see *some* of the women."[16]

2 The villain in this first part of the story is Shechem ben Hamor, the Hivite (or Horite). We find this Hivite (in MT)-Horite (in LXX) alternation

11. The Hithpael of *'āṣaḇ* ("hurt, pain, grieve") occurs again only in Gen. 6:6 to describe God's inner feelings as he reflected on worldwide evil in the days of Noah.

12. *nᵉḇālâ* is traditionally translated as "folly" (so AV, RSV). See the commentary below on v. 7.

13. Lit., "and such is not done" or "and thus it is not done." *wᵉḵēn lō' yē'āśeh* is an obligative imperfect, to be translated by "ought to." Cf. Gen. 20:9: "things that ought not to be done"; Williams, *Hebrew Syntax,* p. 31, § 172.

14. Gen. 34:1; 2 Sam. 3:3, 4 (twice); 2 Chr. 24:26 (twice); Esth. 9:29.

15. See Sternberg, *Poetics of Biblical Narrative,* pp. 461-63.

16. Gen. Rabbah 80:1 connected Dinah's going out to be seen *(wattēṣē' . . . lir'ôṯ)* with Leah's going out to meet Jacob and inviting him to sleep with her (*wattēṣē' lē'â liqrā'ṯô,* 30:16), citing this proverb: "as the mother, so her daughter (Ezek. 16:44)." Thus, when used with a woman, "go out" was associated with "whoring." See also Bechtel, *JSOT* 62 (1994) 31-32.

again in Josh. 9:7. Most scholars are inclined to retain the reading *Hivite,* a point that would demonstrate that Hivite territory consisted of a number of separate and dispersed enclaves.[17] It should also be pointed out that the Greek versions of Aquila and Symm. support the Hebrew text. W. F. Albright is one of the few who prefers "Shechem, son of Hammor the Horite," on the basis of the tradition that Shechem was founded by a Horite donkey driver.[18]

Hamor is identified as the *leader (nᵉśîʾ)* of the Shechem community. We have already encountered this term in reference to the twelve *nᵉśîʾîm* of the Ishmaelites (25:13-16). Understood literally, the word has a passive sense, "lifted up" (by or in the community). It is used frequently in Ezekiel, where it has the meaning "king,"[19] but most certainly does not mean that in Gen. 34:2, or in another old source, Exod. 22:27 (Eng. 28): "You shall not revile God, nor curse a ruler [*nāśîʾ*] of your people." Hamor is a chief or leader chosen either by the Hivites in Shechem or by a subdivision of the Shechem Hivites.

Shechem is anything but a sexually restrained individual. In v. 1 *rāʾâ* was used with Dinah *(lirʾôṯ).* In v. 2 *rāʾâ* is used with Shechem *(wayyarʾ).* But the two verses use this verb in quite different contexts. The use of the same word in close proximity but with a different meaning is a literary device by which the author uses the semantic shift to transfer the action from a broad scene to a more specific, narrow one.[20]

The sequence *(he) saw her* [*wayyarʾ ʾōṯāh*] . . . he seized her [*wayyiqqaḥ ʾōṯāh*] recalls the same sequence in the episode concerning the sons of God and the daughters of men (*wayyirʾû . . . wayyiqḥû lāhem,* 6:2). The same order occurs with Eve and the forbidden fruit in the Garden (*wattēreʾ . . . wattiqqaḥ,* 3:6). First comes the desire, then the action when that lust is not checked.

The last part of the verse reads literally "he lay with her and humbled her" *(wayyiškaḇ ʾōṯāh wayʿannehā).* My translation *he lay with her illicitly* understands these two verbs as a hendiadys. Other instances of *šāḵaḇ ʾōṯāh* are Lev. 15:18, 24; Num. 5:13; 2 Sam. 13:14; Ezek. 23:8. We need not emend *ʾōṯāh* in these passages, once it is understood that *ʾōṯ* is not only the indicator of the direct object but also has the meaning "with" (e.g., Josh. 10:25; 14:12; 2 Sam. 24:24).[21] Then again *šāḵaḇ ʾōṯāh* might be used because of the nearby *wayyarʾ ʾōṯāh* and *wayyiqqaḥ ʾōṯāh.*

17. See M. Haran, "The Gibeonites, the Nethinim, and the sons of Solomon's servants," *VT* 11 (1961) 159-60; R. North, "The Hivites," *Bib* 54 (1973) 52-56.

18. W. F. Albright, "From the Patriarchs to Moses: II. Moses out of Egypt," *BA* 36 (1973) 50.

19. See the summarizing statement of M. Haran, "The Law Code of Ezekiel XL–XLVIII and its Relation to the Priestly School," *HUCA* 50 (1979) 57 n. 24.

20. B. S. Childs (*Book of Exodus,* OTL [Philadelphia: Fortress, 1974], p. 29) provides illustrations of this device from Exod. 2.

21. Cf. BDB, pp. 85b, 1012a (although BDB believes the text was originally *ʾittâ*); H. M. Orlinsky, "The Hebrew Root *ŠKB,*" *JBL* 64 (1944) 23-27.

3 It is true that in the marriage relationship the Bible mandates the husband's separation from his parents and "clinging to his wife" (*wᵉḏāḇaq bᵉʾištô,* 2:24). But when 34:3 speaks of Shechem being *so strongly attracted to Dinah* (lit., "his soul clung to Dinah," *wattiḏbaq napšô bᵉḏînâ;* here is a case of *nep̱eš* meaning "longing, desiring, yearning"), it speaks of something quite different. In Gen. 2 *dāḇaq* comes after marriage. In Gen. 34 *dāḇaq* comes after intercourse outside of marriage. In Gen. 2 *dāḇaq* follows genuine *agape.* In Gen. 34 *dāḇaq* follows unrestrained *eros,* which develops into genuine *agape* for Dinah (see also v. 8),[22] as sort of an aftereffect on the rapist.

In an attempt to win the hand of Dinah in marriage, Shechem tries *to woo Dinah.* In v. 2 Shechem was physically overpowering. In v. 3 Shechem tries to be verbally persuasive and overpowering, as if that will do any good after his violation of Dinah. The expression at the end of the verse reads literally "he spoke upon the heart of the girl." The expression occurs ten times in the OT, always in less than ideal situations, where there is a sense of guilt or repentance, where A attempts to persuade B of his feelings.[23]

It is interesting to note that the LXX renders Heb. *naʿᵃrâ,* here translated *maiden,* as *parthénos,* even after Dinah has had sexual congress. This use shows that *parthénos* may refer to a marriageable young woman, rather than to a *virgo intacta.* In fact, *parthénos* is derived from *par* ("past") and *then/thēn* ("growing"), that is, a young woman who has ceased to grow. She is, therefore, adult and marriageable.

4 Shechem is like Samson. Both see a foreign girl they would like to marry, inform their father of that fact, and then request their father to obtain the hand of the girl in marriage. Shechem's *Get me this girl for a wife* is close to Samson's "Get[24] her for me as my wife" (Judg. 14:2). Shechem's request may be more selfish than Samson's, for in Gen. 34 the order is "get for me this girl," with the indirect object preceding the direct object. In Samson's case the direct object "her" precedes the indirect object "for me."

It should not go unnoticed that Shechem's directive to his father to *get* Dinah for his wife uses the same verb (*qaḥ,* lit., "take") as the narrator used in v. 2 to describe Shechem's "seizing" Dinah *(wayyiqqaḥ ʾōṯāh).* Shechem asks Hamor to do with Dinah what Shechem has already done with Dinah — take her. Of course, in v. 2 *lāqaḥ* means "to take by force," while in v. 4 *lāqaḥ* means "to take in marriage."

22. Referring to this event as a "paradox of an *agapē* which permeates *eros,*" S. Terrien (*Till the Heart Sings* [Philadelphia: Fortress, 1985], pp. 34-35) wonders whether Shechem's delight and love for Dinah could be sustained "without a reciprocity of passionate devotion [by Dinah]." By contrast, M. M. Caspi ("The Story of the Rape of Dinah, the Narrator and the Reader," *HS* 26 [1985] 33) suggests that the verbs of v. 3 almost mitigate Shechem's actions of v. 2 by softening the grimness of the rape (if it was a rape).

23. See Gen. 34:3; 50:21; Judg. 19:3; Ruth 2:13; 1 Sam. 1:13; 2 Sam. 19:8; 2 Chr. 30:22; 32:6; Isa. 40:2; Hos. 2:16. See Fischer, *Bib* 65 (1984) 244-50.

Another difference between the narrator's words and Shechem's own words is how they label Dinah. Shechem refers to her as a *girl (yaldâ).* The narrator refers to her as a *maiden (na'ᵃrâ).* The second term has more dignity attached to it.

5 Again the narrator uses a word different from ones he used previously to describe Shechem's action with Dinah. His earlier verbs describing Shechem's action with Dinah were literally "took," "lay with," and "abused." Here the narrator says that Shechem *defiled (ṭāmē')* Dinah. Although not a frequent use of the verb, *ṭāmē'* is sometimes used for the violation of chastity. See, for example, the ordeal of the suspected adulteress (Num. 5:13, 14, 27-29), and especially Ezekiel (18:6; 22:11; 23:13, 17; 33:26). In the OT this verb might describe a person who has contacted impurity through such things as skin diseases, bodily emissions, or touching something dead. It is usually translated "unclean," but it does not mean sinful, though it does mean exclusion from the camp until cleanness is restored. Through being subjected to such an indignity by an outsider, Dinah is relegated to the status of an outcast.

Through some means, news of Dinah's rape reaches Jacob quickly. He keeps the matter to himself for a while, only because his sons are out tending his livestock in the fields. Jacob will not personally seek redress for the physical agony and emotional trauma that has been inflicted on his daughter. Nothing is said about Jacob's feelings. Was he as shocked and incensed as his sons (v. 7)? Recall Jacob's reaction upon hearing of Joseph's "death." He tore his clothes, put sackcloth on his waist, mourned for Joseph for a long time, and refused to be comforted by his other children (37:34, 35) — none of that here. David, when informed that his daughter had been raped, at least became agitated and angry (2 Sam. 13:21) — not Jacob. Yet David is not more appealing than Jacob, for he institutes no punitive measures against Amnon for the latter's violation of Tamar.

6 Hamor faces great difficulties. He must try to convince Jacob that Shechem, who just violated Dinah, would now like to marry her. That is a proposal over which most fathers would not have to muse terribly long! Jacob is in the position of the father whose virgin daughter has been seduced by a man (Exod. 22:16-17). Will he become the rogue's father-in-law, or not?

7 Jacob's sons are not nearly as restrained as their father. After they return from the fields they discover, through some unidentified means, the tragedy that has befallen their sister. That they did not find out about this until they returned home indicates that Jacob made no attempt to send word to them, or get in touch with them, about Dinah's condition.[25] They are indignant

24. The pl. imperative *(qᵉḥû)* is strange since the quote is introduced with "Samson said to his father."

25. The Hebrew of v. 7 does permit the reading: "And the sons of Jacob came in from the field when they heard." The reading I have followed provides a potent contrast

and beside themselves with rage, and rightly so. Their feelings about the situation are conveyed by a verb (*yiṯʿaṣṣeḇû,* here translated *shocked*) which earlier described God's innermost feelings as he viewed the chaos of Noah's day (*yiṯʿaṣṣēḇ,* 6:6). A noun from the same root described the pain to be experienced by fallen woman (3:16) and by fallen man (3:17). The pain in Gen. 34 is literally Dinah's, but her brothers share it.

a wanton sin. The narrator uses the word *neḇālâ* to describe Shechem's violation of Dinah, a word choice that shows the narrator's evaluation of Shechem's behavior. The noun appears thirteen times in the OT, eight of which involve sexual crimes (Gen. 34:7; Deut. 22:21; Judg. 19:23, 24; 20:6, 10; 2 Sam. 13:12; Jer. 29:23). This noun is used in other contexts to describe, for example, Achan's breach of the ban on Jericho (Josh. 7:15), and Nabal's behavior (1 Sam. 25:5). On one occasion it is something God may do (Job 42:8), or threaten to do, to Job's "comforters" for their attempt to defend God. *neḇālâ* is something a person "does" (*ʿāśâ*; see Deut. 22:21; 2 Sam. 13:12; Jer. 29:23; etc.). The word covers any kind of "serious disorderly and unruly action resulting in the break-up of an existing relationship whether between tribes, within the family, in a business arrangement, in marriage or with God."[26] Shechem's actions will produce only disharmony between Shechemites and Jacobites, for Shechem has done what *ought not be done.* His crime is a violation not so much of sacral law as of accepted ethic ("it is not done so in Israel"). Shechem has not only destroyed and dishonored the sanctity of a family, but he has frontally challenged a nation's modus operandi in matters sexual. "Israel" as a nation does not exist in the time of Jacob, and thus the reference to "Israel" must be anachronistic — unless "Israel" is a reference to Jacob. Shechem's offense is by extension an offense against Jacob.[27]

2. HAMOR AND SHECHEM MAKE THEIR CASE (34:8-12)

8 *Hamor appealed to them: "Shechem my son*[1] *— his heart is set on your daughter. Please give her to him as a wife.*

---

between the father who heard, but with absence of feeling, and the sons who heard, with the presence of feeling.

26. See A. Phillips, "*Nebalah,*" *VT* 25 (1975) 237-41. The quote is from p. 241. Cf. also W. M. W. Roth, "NBL," *VT* 10 (1960) 394-409; J. Jensen, "Does *porneia* mean Fornication? A Critique of Bruce Malina," *NT* 20 (1978) 167-70. See Sternberg, *Poetics of Biblical Narrative,* p. 452.

27. See Sternberg, *Poetics of Biblical Narrative,* p. 453.

1. "Shechem my son — " is an instance of *casus pendens* with pronominal resumption, here used "to announce a fresh topic, especially at the beginning of a speech." See Andersen, *Sentence in Biblical Hebrew,* p. 92.

9 *Intermarry with us;*[2] *your daughters, give to us; and our daughters,*[3] *take for yourselves.*[4]

10 *With us you can live.*[5] *The land shall be available to you. Settle and trade in it, and acquire property here."*

11 *Shechem too appealed to her father*[6] *and brothers: "Do me this favor,*[7] *and whatever you demand of me I will pay.*

12 *Regardless of how high you set*[8] *the bridal price,*[9] *I will pay whatever you demand of me; only give me the maiden as a wife."*

8 Hamor builds his case first by sharing his son's feelings toward Dinah (v. 8), and then by making Jacob and his sons a generous offer (vv. 9-10). The narrator had used the verb *dāḇaq* in v. 3 to express the clinging of Shechem's "soul"[10] to Dinah. Hamor uses the verb *ḥāšaq* (b^{e}), which is used elsewhere of a man's love for a woman (Deut. 21:11), Yahweh's love for Israel (Deut. 7:7; 10:15), and of a person's love for Yahweh (Ps. 91:14). An expression denoting an intimate relationship based on loyalty and trust is put in the mouth of Hamor, indicating that, as far as Hamor is concerned, Shechem's feelings for Dinah are genuine and honorable. Also, Hamor accentuates his son by placing him at the beginning of the sentence syntactically as a *casus*

2. "With us" in v. 9 is *'ōṯānû,* but "with us" in v. 10 is *'ittānû.* Cf. GKC, § 117w; *BHS;* Westermann, *Genesis,* 2:534, all of whom emend *'ōṯānû* to *'ittānû.* But observe that GKC, § 54f, does cite places where the Hithpael takes an accusative.

3. "your daughters," the object of "give," is inexplicably not preceded by *'eṯ,* the accusative indicator, whereas "our daughters," the object of "take," is. Cf. vv. 16, 21, in which "give our daughters" does include the accusative indicator *'eṯ.* Even in prose the *nota accusativi* is not invariably necessary (GKC, § 117a).

4. The provisions for intermarriage are stated three different ways in this episode. First, Hamor uses two clauses that are conjoined (v. 9); Jacob's sons then use two clauses that are chiastic (v. 16); finally, Hamor uses a conjunctive sentence (v. 21). See Andersen, *Sentence in Biblical Hebrew,* p. 132.

5. The beginnings of vv. 4 and 5 are chiastically arranged: *w^{e}hiṯhatt^{e}nû 'ōṯānû . . . w^{e}'ittānû tēšēḇû.*

6. Unusual *'āḇîh* should be written *'āḇîhā.*

7. Lit., "let me find mercy in your eyes." *māṣā' ḥēn* occurs frequently in narratives involving Jacob (30:27; 32:6; 33:8, 10, 15; 34:11; cf. Hos. 12:5 [Eng. 4]).

8. Lit., "increase greatly the marriage price and gift upon me." Dahood suggests for *'ālay* "to my debit" (*Ugaritic-Hebrew Philology,* p. 31).

9. I take *mōhar ûmattān,* lit., "bride price and gift," as a hendiadys. Thus Shechem offers one payment, not two, for Dinah. Speiser (*Genesis,* p. 265) compares the similar hendiadys in Akk. *biltu u mandatte,* "tribute and payment," i.e., payment of tribute.

10. On *nepeš* meaning "desire" see H. W. Wolff, *Anthropology of the Old Testament,* tr. M. Kohl (Philadelphia: Fortress, 1974), pp. 15-17. Here is a case (Gen. 34:3, 8), says Wolff, where "the organ with its specific impulses recedes behind the whole man and his corresponding behaviour."

pendens: "As for Shechem my son, his soul is attached to your daughter." Hamor is also careful to address both Jacob and his sons. One might have expected Hamor to say: "Shechem has his heart set on your daughter, and your sister." *your daughter* is *bitt^e^ḵem* (with the masc. pl. pronominal suffix). Dinah is the daughter of Jacob and the "daughter" of her brothers. Thus Hamor accentuates Jacob's sons as well as his own son. Hamor's choice of the word *daughter* for Dinah, instead of Shechem's earlier "girl" (v. 3), and his use of *b^e^ḇitteḵem* instead of *b^e^ḇitt^e^ḵā,* is his way of addressing the whole family in the most respectful way possible.

9-10 Hamor's suggestion is that Jacob and his children *intermarry* with the Shechemites. The Hebrew verb for *intermarry* is *hiṯḥattēn,* a denominative verb of *ḥāṯān,* "son-in-law," and *ḥōṯēn,* "father-in-law."[11] The verb thus means "to offer oneself as a son-in-law/father-in-law." Jacob will be the father-in-law of Hamor's children and Hamor will be the father-in-law of Jacob's children. One might have expected Hamor to say: "your *sons,* give to us," instead of "your *daughters,* give to us." Jacob has twelve sons, but only one daughter. To what can Hamor be referring when he talks about *b^e^nōṯêḵem?*

Hamor follows his proposal of intermarriage with (1) an offer of peaceful co-settlement; (2) access to and mobility throughout Shechem's territory; (3) the possibility of purchasing land.

Two of the verbs used by Hamor call for special comment. The one in v. 10 I have translated *trade* is *sāḥar.* It is used again in v. 21 and in 42:34. The participle of the verb appears in 23:16 and 37:28. In the first three of these texts (34:10, 21; 42:34) the verb is followed by a direct object. Because the participial forms in 23:16 and 37:29 are best rendered as "traders, merchants," it might seem advisable to translate the finite verb forms of this stem as "trade."[12] The ancient versions also support "trade" for Heb. *sāḥar* (cf. LXX *emporeúomai*). But Speiser has used etymology, syntax (the verb takes an accusative),[13] context, and related languages (e.g., Akkadian[14] and the

11. See BDB, p. 368b.

12. See W. F. Albright, "Some Remarks on the Meaning of *SḤR* in Genesis," *BASOR* 164 (1961) 28; C. H. Gordon, "Abraham and the Merchants of Ura," *JNES* 17 (1958) 28-31, esp. p. 29.

13. For example, with respect to 34:10, the word *ûs^e^ḥārûhā* (in which *-hā* is the direct object), if *sāḥar* means "trade," would translate, "and you may trade the land," which no translator I know advocates. But if *sāḥar* means "to move around (in)," then the direct object would fit better, "and you may move around in it." See T. L. Thompson, *Historicity of the Patriarchal Narratives,* pp. 183-84.

14. The Akkadian cognate *saḫārum* means "to turn, circle, traverse." Also, Akkadian used *tamkārum* for "trader, merchant," rather than a noun formed from the verb *saḫārum.*

Aramaic Qumran Genesis Apocryphon)[15] to provide strong evidence for the translation "move around."[16]

But Speiser's arguments have some weaknesses. That English must add the preposition "in" in "trade in it," whereas the Hebrew makes use of the accusative, shows merely that English has a different idiom. Also, the verbs preceding (*yāšab̠,* "settle") and following (*'āḥaz,* "acquire property") *sāḥar* make "trade" a more preferable translation for *sāḥar* than "move around." Comparative philology should not be as critical in determining the meaning of *sāḥar* as the contextual evidence.[17] Finally, Speiser uses the Genesis Apocryphon to provide evidence for *sāḥar* meaning "move around," but makes no use of late Hebrew and Jewish Aramaic in which *sāḥar* means "to trade."[18]

It may be possible to steer a middle route between these options by suggesting that in 34:10 Jacob was indeed offered trading privileges by Shechem. This offer does not mean that one should conceive primarily of Jacob, or his grandfather, as merchants. But Jacob and Abraham were individuals of some means, and as a result, shared some of the characteristics of merchants.[19]

The second verb of interest is *hē'āḥᵃzû,* a Niphal plural imperative (lit., "be seized, be taken hold of"), here translated *acquire property.* This form of the verb is used again for taking possession of land in Gen. 47:27; Num. 32:30; Josh. 22:9, 19. One recalls that *'āḥaz* was used of Jacob in 25:26 when, at birth, he seized/grabbed Esau's heel. That the same verb appears near the end of the Jacob narrative, but this time with the meaning "acquire property," may provide a clue about the thrust of *'āḥaz* in 25:26: it is an action by which Jacob shows his intentions to take control of Esau's position of power and prominence.[20]

While Hamor's offer to Jacob and his sons seems generous, it noticeably lacks any reference to his son's humiliation of Dinah. He offers no apologies. Indeed, his invitation contains no hint that Shechem had acted reprehensibly with Dinah.

15. 1QapGen 21:15: *w'zlt 'nh 'brm lmsḥr wlmḥzh 'r'*, "So I, Abram, set out to go around and look at the land" (text and translation of J. A. Fitzmyer, *Genesis Apocryphon of Qumran Cave I,* BibOr 18A, 2nd ed. [Rome: Biblical Institute, 1971], pp. 68-69).

16. See E. A. Speiser, "The Verb *SḤR* in Genesis and Early Hebrew Movements," *BASOR* 164 (1961) 23-28; de Vaux, *Early History of Israel,* pp. 228-29; Fitzmyer, *Genesis Apocryphon,* p. 152.

17. A. F. Rainey, "Merchants at Ugarit and the Patriarchal Narratives," *Christian News from Israel* 14/2 (1963) 21.

18. J. Levy, *Wörterbuch über die Talmudim und Midraschim* (Darmstadt: Wissenschaftliche Buchgesellschaft, 1963), 3:498.

19. F. B. Knutson, "Political and Foreign Affairs," in *RSP,* 2:114-19.

20. S. H. Smith, " 'Heel' and 'thigh': The concept of sexuality in the Jacob-Esau narratives," *VT* 40 (1990) 464.

11-12 Shechem had requested his father to make the official contact with Jacob (v. 4). It would be out of place for Shechem to do this himself. But he does accompany his father, and he speaks as soon as he has the opportunity. Hamor's speech focused on how good it would be for both families if the marriage could be arranged. His son's speech focuses on what this marriage would mean for Jacob and his sons financially. He may be able to provide some of the money they will need to acquire property.

Shechem agrees to meet any price they may ask for Dinah. He will pay anything to get the *maiden.* Note that when Shechem spoke to his father about Dinah he called her a "girl" (*yaldâ,* v. 4). But when he speaks about her to her father and brothers he calls her a *maiden (naʿarâ).* We understand immediately his purpose in using a word with more dignity attached to it.

I suggested above that the phrase *mōhar ûmattān* is a hendiadys, *bridal price.* This is the only place in the OT where *mattān* refers to a wedding gift. (For its only other occurrences see Num. 18:11; Prov. 18:16; 19:6; 21:14.) Those who would see two distinct concepts here understand *mōhar*[21] to be a gift from the groom (or groom's family) to the bride's father, and the *mattān* to be a gift to the bride. Comparison may be made with Akk. *nudunnū,* a gift from the husband to his wife.[22] But this interpretation is unlikely here, because Shechem is not interested in enriching both Jacob (and his sons) and Dinah. His primary concern is to lure Jacob and his sons to consent to Dinah's marriage to Shechem by making them a financial offer they cannot resist.

3. JACOB'S SONS MAKE A PROPOSAL (34:13-17)

13 *The sons of Jacob replied to Shechem and his father Hamor with duplicity,*[1] *thus speaking*[2] *because*[3] *he had defiled Dinah their sister.*

21. Deut. 22:29 fixes the *mōhar* at fifty silver shekels. In the incident in Gen. 34:12, the bride's family may set the *mōhar* as high as they choose, making it in effect a punishment or fine on Shechem for shaming Dinah.

22. See Andersen and Freedman, *Hosea,* AB, pp. 273-75.

1. Targ. Onqelos reads "with wisdom" *(bḥwkm')* for MT *bᵉmirmâ.* The same change was made in 27:35: "your brother came with wisdom" (MT "with deceit").

2. The function of and placement of *wayyᵉḏabbērû* is admittedly difficult to explain. It is possible to follow the Pesh. and place *wayyᵉḏabbērû* before *bᵉmirmâ,* rather than leave it after *bᵉmirmâ* (so Westermann, *Genesis,* 2:534). Another suggestion is to translate *wayyᵉḏabbērû* as "they turned their backs, refused," i.e., Jacob's sons made a pretense of refusing Hamor's and Shechem's request. See G. R. Driver, "Studies in the Vocabulary of the Old Testament. II," *JTS* 32 (1931) 250-51.

3. For the causal use of *'ᵃšer* see Williams, *Hebrew Syntax,* p. 77, § 468 ("because in that . . ."). It is also possible to render the clause: "and they spoke to him who had defiled Dinah their sister."

14 *So they said to them:*[4] *"We could not do such a thing, and give our sister to an uncircumcised man; that would be a disgrace for us.*
15 *We will agree*[5] *with you on one condition*[6] *only, that you become like us and every male be circumcised by you.*[7]
16 *Then we will give you our daughters, and your daughters take for ourselves;*[8] *we will settle among you, and be one kindred.*
17 *But if you do not comply with our terms as regards circumcision, we will take our daughter and go."*[9]

13 For a second time the word *mirmâ* occurs in the Jacob cycle. It was used first by Isaac in telling Esau what Jacob did: "Your brother came fraudulently [*b^{e}mirmâ*] and has taken away your blessing" (27:35). In 29:25 Jacob uses the related verb: "Why did you trick [*rimmîṯānî*] me?"

The choice of the verb *replied (wayyaʿ^{a}nû)* must be deliberate. The story began with Shechem violating *(wayʿannehā)* Dinah (v. 2). Both verbs contain the same radicals. Shechem violates Dinah (*ʿānâ* II). The brothers now reply to Shechem (*ʿānâ* I).

Jacob's sons may be compared with Absalom. Both have had a sister (Dinah, Tamar) that has been violated. Both times (Gen. 34:2; 2 Sam. 13:14) the same verbs are used to describe the violation, but in reverse order (Gen. 34:2: *šāḵaḇ-ʿānâ;* 2 Sam. 13:14: *ʿānâ-šāḵaḇ*). The sons of Jacob resort to a stratagem, while Absalom takes two years to plan his vendetta.[10] Jacob and David do not get involved. What separates the Dinah incident from the Tamar incident is that the latter uses the verb *ḥāzaq,* "force, overpower" (2 Sam. 13:11), and Tamar protests clearly to her half-brother (2 Sam. 13:12).

14-17 If the LXX of v. 14a reflects the original reading of the text (see n. 3 above), then one of the main reasons for perceiving a J and E account of the Dinah incident (as argued, e.g., by Westermann) is removed. Much has

4. LXX reads: "Simeon and Levi, brothers of Dinah, said to them," suggesting that only two of Dinah's brothers were involved in plotting revenge.

5. *nē'ôṯ* is either an imperfect Qal of putative *'wt* (GKC, § 72h) "consent, agree," or an imperfect Niphal of *'ûṯ* (Mandelkern, *Concordance,* p. 25b; BDB, p. 22).

6. GKC, § 119p, calls the *b^{e}* in *b^{e}zō'ṯ* the *beth pretii,* i.e., the price being considered as the means of acquiring something.

7. See R. Althann, "*mwl,* 'Circumcise' with the *lamedh* of Agency," *Bib* 62 (1981) 239.

8. The perfect verbs and direct objects are arranged chiastically: *w^{e}nāṯannû 'eṯ b^{e}nōṯênû . . . w^{e}'eṯ b^{e}nōṯêḵem niqqaḥ.*

9. LXX renders the MT's two perfects with *waw* by a participle and a main verb: *labóntes tás thygatéras hēmṓn apeleusómetha.*

10. See H. Hagan, "Deception as Motif and Theme in 2 Sam. 9–20; 1 Kgs. 1–2," *Bib* 60 (1979) 310-11.

been made of the inconsistency between the "sons of Jacob" (vv. 14ff.) who suggest the deceptive plan, and the fact that only Simeon and Levi are actually involved in its implementation (vv. 25ff.). Perhaps the plan is Simeon's and Levi's from the start.

The sons' stratagem is their claim that they will give Dinah to Shechem for marriage on the condition that every male Hamorite be circumcised. In so doing they will become like the sons of Jacob.[11] There is no indication that Jacob is privy to this ruse, that he is even consulted for an opinion, that he has any say in the matter, or that he approved. He is reduced to silence, passivity, and noninvolvement.

Surprising also is the brother's claim that they have *daughters (b^enōṯênû)* to give to Shechem and his people. To be sure, the sons distinguish between *our daughters* (*b^enōṯênû,* v. 16) and *our daughter* (*bittēnû,* v. 17). To what do they refer when they speak of "our daughters"? Is this part of the deception? And why do they refer to Dinah as "our sister" *(ʾ^ahōṯēnû)* in v. 14, but as "our daughter" *(bittēnû)* in v. 17? Why play with words? If Shechem may call Dinah *yaldâ* in one breath but *naʿ^arâ* in another, may her brothers call her *baṯ* in one breath but *ʾ^ahôṯ* in another?

Obviously *circumcision,* as proposed herein, has nothing in common with the circumcision emphasis we encountered in Gen. 17. Here circumcision is not a sign of the covenant. Rather it has the primitive significance of initiation into marriage and into the communal life of a tribe.[12] There is no indication here that the Hamorites are asked to convert from one religion to another.[13] Assimilation is by marriage (cf. Ruth),[14] not by conversion. It is no wonder that later biblical laws inveigh against Hamor's proposal. His suggestion was that Jacob's sons "intermarry" (*hiṯḥatt^enû,* v. 9) with his people. Cf. Deut. 7:3, a warning to Israelites about to settle in Canaan: "You shall not make marriages with them" *(w^elōʾ hiṯḥattēn bām).*

In concluding their proposal, Jacob's sons make clear that in their judgment, they are arguing from a position of strength (v. 17). Only later in the narrative (v. 26) do we learn that throughout all these negotiations Dinah has been kept in Shechem's house. She was not allowed to rejoin her family

11. Compare *tihyû ḵāmōnû* here with *hāyâ k^eʾaḥaḏ mimmennû* (3:22), in which *hāyâ k^e* connotes the idea of entering a new relationship or assuming an additional identity.

12. De Vaux, *Ancient Israel,* 1:47. De Vaux observes that the Hebrew words for bridegroom, son-in-law, and father-in-law all derive from the root *ḥtn,* which in Arabic means "to circumcise."

13. See J. Milgrom, "Religious Conversion and the Revolt Model for the Formation of Israel," *JBL* 101 (1982) 169-76, esp. p. 173.

14. Ruth's marriage to an Israelite precedes her words to Naomi: "your God shall be my God." As Milgrom states (ibid.), if Ruth had settled among Israelites as an unattached person, her words "your God shall be my God" would have fallen on deaf ears.

after she was humbled. Perhaps Shechem and Hamor have kept Dinah at their residence as a bargaining chip. The brothers may be more easily persuaded to give their sister (v. 14) to Shechem and Hamor if the latter already have her under lock and key. Her brothers, however, are undaunted by this situation. If Shechem took Dinah from her house by force (*wayyiqqaḥ ʾōṯāh,* v. 1), the brothers are now prepared, if necessary, to take Dinah (by force) from Shechem's house (*welaquḥnû ʾeṯ bittēnû,* v. 17).[15]

4. THE MALES OF SHECHEM ARE CIRCUMCISED (34:18-24)

18 *Their proposal seemed fair to Hamor and to Shechem the son of Hamor.*

19 *The young man lost no time in doing this, so infatuated was he with Jacob's daughter; moreover, he was the most honored member of his household.*

20 *So Hamor, and Shechem his son, went to their city gate, and addressed their fellow townsmen as follows:*

21 *"These men, they are*[1] *friendly*[2] *with us. Let them settle*[3] *in the land and trade in it; there is adequate space*[4] *in the land for them. Their daughters we can take for ourselves in marriage, and our daughters give to them.*

22 *But the men will consent to settle with us and be one kindred only on this condition, that every male be circumcised by us*[5] *as they themselves are circumcised.*

23 *Would not their livestock and property*[6] *— all their animals — then be ours? Let us cooperate with them, so that they might settle with us."*[7]

15. For the view that Dinah is now in Shechem's house of her own accord, see D. N. Fewell and D. M. Gunn, "Tipping the Balance: Sternberg's Reader and the Rape of Dinah," *JBL* 110 (1991) 200.

1. In nonverbal clauses a demonstrative functioning as a copula follows the predicate. See Davidson, *Hebrew Syntax,* p. 149, § 106d; Williams, *Hebrew Syntax,* p. 99, § 579.

2. Compare *šelēmîm hēm* with *šlm hʾ* in line 4 of the Nora Stone. See F. M. Cross, "An Interpretation of the Nora Stone," *BASOR* 208 (1972) 16.

3. By eliminating the *we* on *weyēšeḇû* SP and LXX read: "these men are friends; they will settle with us."

4. Lit., "broad of (two) hands" or "broad on both sides." Cf. Judg. 18:10; Isa. 22:18; Ps. 104:24; Neh. 7:4. Perhaps we are to imagine Hamor and Shechem holding up their two hands and spreading them apart as much as possible.

5. See R. Althann, "*mwl,* 'Circumcise' with the *lamedh* of Agency," *Bib* 62 (1979) 239.

6. That *miqnēhem weqinyānām wekol-behemtām* be understood as a hendiadys (so Speiser, *Genesis,* p. 265) is strengthened by LXX's rendering of *hēm* by *éstai* (sing.).

7. Vulg. adds "and we would become one kindred."

24 *All of the able-bodied men*[8] *in the city*[9] *agreed with Hamor and with Shechem his son, and every male — every able-bodied man in the city*[10] *— was circumcised.*

18-19 Shechem and Hamor respond quickly and positively to the proposal. While the sons had addressed Shechem and Hamor (each "you" in vv. 15-17 is pl.), it was Shechem who was singled out. Thus v. 19 focuses on Shechem's circumcision, not on Hamor's. Shechem is, interestingly, identified by the narrator as *the young man (hanna'ar).* A *na'ar* is seeking as wife a *na'ᵃrâ.*

Shechem's feelings for Dinah have shifted from *dāḇaq* ("clinging") to *'āhaḇ* ("loving") to *ḥāpaṣ (infatuated).*[11] Thus at two points in the narrative (vv. 3, 19), the narrator makes clear that he agrees with Hamor's understanding (v. 8) of Shechem's feelings toward Dinah. She is not the victim of impetuous and unbridled sexual impulses, to be discarded once sexual congress is completed. Shechem is romantically attracted to Dinah. The father says so, as does the narrator.

Shechem first circumcises himself, then turns to the circumcision of his townsmen (vv. 20ff.), much as Abraham attended to his own circumcision and then to that of his nuclear family (Gen. 17). His right to urge this circumcision on them is validated by his stature in the community. He is *the most honored member (nikbāḏ mikkōl)* of that community. Shechem may be held in high honor by his fellow townsman, but he is not so held by Dinah's brothers. He had done everything that is the opposite of honorable in their eyes.

20-23 The text emphasizes that it was *Hamor* who approached the town council, with Shechem accompanying him, but both of them addressed that assembly. This point is brought out by the two verbs in v. 20, the first of which is singular *(wayyāḇō'),* the second of which is plural *(wayᵉḏabbᵉrû).*

Nowhere in their speech do father and son indicate to the council members the real reason why they want all male Hamorites to be circumcised. They say not one word about Shechem's passion for Dinah, his violation of her, or about Jacob's sons' ultimatum of what the price was for Dinah's hand in marriage. Instead, Hamor and Shechem concentrate exclusively on the material gains intermarriage will provide their people. There will be more

8. Lit., "all those who go out at the gate." See the commentary below.

9. *'îrô* provides an instance of the use of the pronominal suffix instead of the article. Cf. Gen. 33:10.

10. For the repetition of "every able-bodied man in this city" LXX substitutes "the flesh of their foreskin," apparently reading the second "every able-bodied man in the city" as dittography of the phrase in the first part of the verse. *BHK* suggests this preferred reading, but *BHS* does not.

11. Other translations of *ḥāpaṣ bᵉ* may be "favor" (1 Sam. 18:22; 2 Sam. 20:11), "delight in" (2 Sam. 24:3), "prefer" (2 Sam. 22:20). Cf. Ps. 1:2, *bᵉṯôraṯ YHWH ḥeṗṣô,* "in Yahweh's Torah is his delight/preoccupation."

women than ever to choose from, to say nothing of the collegiality[12] the Jacobites will bring to their city, along with their abundant livestock. Thus we have two cycles of duplicity going on simultaneously. Jacob's sons are deceiving Shechem and Hamor, who in turn are deceiving their own villagers. The deceivers are themselves being deceived. This scenario of double deception we may recall from earlier days in Jacob's life, where the perpetrator of deceit was also the victim of deceit.

A comparison of the conversation between Jacob's sons and Hamor with that between Hamor (and Shechem) and their own people reveals the following differences. First, Hamor made this proposal to Jacob's sons: "Your daughters, give [*nāṯan*] to us; and our daughters, take [*lāqaḥ*] for yourselves" (v. 9). In speaking later to their own people about that proposal, Hamor and Shechem say: "their daughters we can take [*lāqaḥ*] for ourselves in marriage, and our daughters give [*nāṯan*] to them" (v. 21). Thus the major difference between these verses is that Hamor (and Shechem) shift the subject of the verbs *nāṯan* and *lāqaḥ*. In v. 9 it is Jacob's sons who are the givers, while in v. 21 it is the residents of Shechem who are the givers; in v. 9 Jacob's sons are the takers, while in v. 21 the men of Shechem are the takers. This shift would create the impression among the Shechemites that Shechem's and Hamor's proposal will work much to their advantage. Also, the replacement of two verbs in the first person plural and second person plural, respectively (*titt^{e}nû/tiqḥû,* v. 9), with two verbs in the first person plural (*niqqaḥ/nittēn,* v. 21) makes it appear that the Shechemites will be in charge throughout these negotiations. They will be both takers and givers.

A second difference is found in a comparison of Hamor's account of the privileges he will extend to Jacob's family in return for Dinah's hand in marriage (v. 10) and his passing that bit of information on to the townsmen (v. 21). The original offer was that Jacob's family could settle *(š^{e}ḇû),* trade *(s^{e}ḥārûhā),* and acquire property *(hē'āḥ^{a}zû)* in Shechem's territory. In retelling this to their own people, Shechem and Hamor repeat the first two verbs (*yēš^{e}ḇû, yisḥ^{a}rû* v. 21) but not "acquire property." Thus a threefold invitation is diminished to a twofold invitation in the retelling. A few verses later, the twofold invitation is reduced to one verb, "so that they might settle [*yēš^{e}ḇû*] with us" (v. 23). One of the reasons why Hamor and Shechem are able to make these modifications (either through deletion or expansion) is that the agreement between the sons of Jacob and Hamor and Shechem is simply a verbal one. A written document would not have permitted Hamor and Shechem

12. Hamor and Shechem refer to Jacob's family as *šālēm* (v. 21), "friend(ly), ally." Related terms like *šôlēm* (Ps. 7:5) and *šālûm* (2 Sam. 20:19), and Akk. *šalamum* mean "ally," one bound by treaty or covenant. See J. H. Tigay, "Psalm 75 and Ancient Near Eastern Treaties," *JBL* 89 (1970) 182-84; B. A. Levine, *In the Presence of the Lord* (Leiden: Brill, 1974), p. 36 n. 90.

the liberty to make any adjustments in the arrangements in order to make their proposal as convincing and palatable as possible to their townsmen.[13]

24 The emphasis here is that it was all the *able-bodied men in the city* who agreed to be circumcised. They would be the individuals counted on to launch a counteroffensive against the sons of Jacob when the latter attempt to eliminate the men of Shechem. Simeon and Levi are fully aware of that. Their circumcision, however, will incapacitate them just long enough for Simeon and Levi to strike with deadly effectiveness.

The expression *All of the able-bodied men in the city* is literally "all who go out at the gate of his city" (*kōl-yōṣ*^{e}*'ê šaʿar ʿîrô).* Speiser has made a convincing case that the phrase is a technical one referring to those male members of a community who are capable of bearing arms.[14] Thus to go out at the gate of one's city means to represent one's community in battle.[15] In several OT texts *yāṣā'* means "go out to battle, march" (cf. Deut. 28:25; Judg. 2:15; 2 K. 18:7; Prov. 30:27).[16] Compare also line 2 of the Phoenician inscription of Milk-yathon, king of Kition, and Idalion, son of Baʿalram: "I conquered those who came out [in battle] [*hyṣ'm*] and their allies."[17]

5. THE SONS OF JACOB RETALIATE (34:25-31)

25 *On the third day, while they were still in pain, Simeon and Levi, two of Jacob's sons, and Dinah's brothers, each took his sword, and advanced upon*[1] *the city unintimidated,*[2] *and massacred every male.*

13. M. M. Caspi, "The Story of the Rape of Dinah," *HS 26 (1985) 38.*

14. Speiser, *Genesis,* p. 265; idem, " 'Coming' and 'Going' at the City Gate," in *Oriental and Biblical Studies,* pp. 83-88.

15. The corresponding phrase "all those who went in at the gate of the city" (23:10, 18) does not, however, necessarily represent the other one of two groups that together represented the source of urban authority, i.e., the body of elders, as maintained by Speiser. The term in Gen. 23 may refer to all the citizens, not just to the elders. See G. Evans, " 'Coming' and 'Going' at the City Gate — A Discussion of Prof. Speiser's Paper," *BASOR* 150 (1958) 33; F. S. Frick, *The City in Ancient Israel,* SBLDS 36 (Missoula, MT: Scholars, 1977), p. 118.

16. In Prov. 30:27 the LXX's rendering of *wayyēṣē'* by *ekstrateúei* suggested to some the emendation *wayyiṣbā'*. This change is unnecessary once one recognizes that *yāṣā'* may mean "march."

17. See G. A. Cooke, *Text-Book of North-Semitic Inscriptions* (Oxford: Clarendon, 1903), pp. 76-77. Cooke provides two more illustrations in the OT where *yāṣā'* means "march out into battle": 1 Sam. 8:20; 2 Sam. 11:1.

1. The combination *bô' ʿal* is not common. Cf. v. 27. In fact, Westermann (*Genesis,* 2:534) wishes to read *ʿal,* but see BDB, p. 98b, for the idiom *bô' ʿal* meaning "to come upon, fall or light upon [of enemy], attack."

2. The noun is related to *bāṭaḥ,* "to trust," but may have the force of an adjective

26 *Hamor and Shechem his son they massacred by the sword. Then they removed Dinah from Shechem's house and left.*

27 *The other sons of Jacob, when they came upon the slain,*[3] *looted the city because they had defiled their sister.*

28 *Their flocks and cattle and asses, whether*[4] *in the city or in the country, they seized.*

29 *All their possessions, their children and their wives they captured, they looted whatever*[5] *was in the homes.*[6]

30 *Jacob said to Simeon and Levi: "You have brought trouble on me by making me a stench*[7] *to the occupants of the land, the Canaanites and the Perizzites. With so few men*[8] *I have, should they unite against*[9] *me and strike, I would be decimated, I and my family."*

31 *But they responded: "Like a whore should he treat*[10] *our sister?"*

25-26 For other references in Genesis to *the third day* cf. 22:4; 31:22; 40:20; 42:18. The third day after the circumcision is the day on which the pain from the operation would be the most intense. The fever that would develop as a result of the operation would only make the condition of the recently circum-

---

or adverb. Westermann translates "boldly" and Speiser "unopposed." GKC, § 118q, has "unawares."

3. H. Gunkel seems to have been the first to suggest emending *ḥ^a^lālîm* ("slain") to *ḥōlîm* ("sick"). See also *BHS;* Westermann, *Genesis,* 2:534. Gunkel suggested this change as a better balance to *kō'ăḇîm* ("in pain") of v. 25. But those in pain have already been "massacred" (*wayyahar^e^gû,* v. 25).

4. *w^e^* . . . *w^e^*- illustrates 2 *waws* used coordinately ("whether . . . or"; "both . . . and"). Cf. Num. 9:14; Josh. 9:23; Isa. 38:15; Jer. 13:14; BDB, p. 253a.

5. The *waw* on *w^e^'eṯ* is strange. Is it patterned after the first word of the verse?

6. *bāyiṯ* is used collectively. Cf. LXX *en taís oikíais.*

7. *l^e^haḇ'îšēnî* is an instance of an abbreviated idiom with the word for odor, "stench" understood. The full idiom is found in Exod. 5:21: *hiḇ'aštem 'et rêḥēnû,* "you have caused our odor to be foul in Pharaoh's eyes." See B. A. Levine, *In the Presence of the Lord* (Leiden: Brill, 1974), p. 60 n. 18. See also P. R. Ackroyd, "The Hebrew Root *b'š,*" *JTS* 2 (1951) 31-36, esp. p. 33; he argues for "be ashamed" rather than "stink."

8. *m^e^ṯê mispār* is lit. "people of number," i.e., few men. The expression may be compared with *mēṭê milḥāmâ,* "the dead of war" (Isa. 22:2). Short vowels are reduced to *shewa* (*muṭay* becomes *m^e^ṭê*), but *ṣere* is retained like a naturally long vowel (thus *mēṯê milḥāmâ,* not *m^e^ṯê milḥāmâ*). The expression *m^e^ṯê mispar* is a rare instance in Biblical Hebrew of a genitive expressed by measure or number. Cf. GKC, § 128n; Williams, *Hebrew Syntax,* p. 12, § 48.

9. *'āsap* (Niphal) by itself may mean "to assemble for war, confrontation" without being followed by the preposition *'al* (as here). See Josh. 10:5; Judg. 6:33; 9:6; 10:17; 20:11 (followed by *'el*).

10. On the use of the imperfect in interrogative sentences, see GKC, § 107t.

cised more intolerable.[11] The men of Shechem would be least able to retaliate. In fact, retaliation would be ruled out. Accordingly, the sons of Jacob bide their time, and strike with a passion when counter-resistance is expected to be minimal.

Interestingly, only two of Jacob's sons are associated with involvement in the massacre — *Simeon and Levi.* What about the remaining ten, or even their four full brothers by Leah (Reuben, Judah, Issachar, and Zebulon)? Dinah is as much a sister to them, especially these last four, as she is to Simeon and Levi. Those who have subjected this chapter to historical analysis (and reconstruction) have concurred that the names Simeon and Levi have been inserted secondarily into the narrative, perhaps in order to supply an explanation for the condemnation of the tribes of Simeon and Levi in Gen. 49:5-7.[12] Those who excise these names maintain that they thereby solve the problem of an otherwise unknown bellicose (and secular) tribe of Levi. An examination of the function of the later Levites regarding the tabernacle, however, shows that the Levites were responsible for guarding the tabernacle and its sancta, especially against encroachment.[13] Such a presentation accords well with Levi's (and Simeon's) sacking of Shechem in Gen. 34. Also apropos is the reference to the Levite's slaughtering of 3,000 of their own people involved in the golden calf debacle (Exod. 32:25-29).[14]

It may seem odd that two sons of Jacob were able to *massacre every male (wayyaharᵉgû kol-zāḵār)* of Shechem. Of course, the same issue arose in ch. 14. How could Abraham and 318 servants go up against the armies of four of the mightiest rulers of the day? Or Gideon's 300 versus the Midianites? How is Samson able to kill 1,000 Philistines? In the case of Gen. 34, the only way for two brothers to face a numerically superior opponent is to engage in deceit. Before the enemy can be killed, it must be incapacitated and its ability to launch a counterattack wiped out.[15]

The death of two men (here, Hamor and Shechem) in which a woman is involved appears again with Tamar (Er and Onan, Gen. 38), Rizpah (Ishbo-

11. F. C. Fensham, "Gen XXXIV and Mari," *JNWSL* 4 (1975) 89.

12. See A. de Pury, "Genèse xxxvi et l'histoire," *RB* 71 (1969) 5-49; S. Lehming, "Zur Überlieferungsgeschichte von Gen. 34," *ZAW* 70 (1958) 228-50.

13. See J. Milgrom, *Studies in Levitical Terminology* (Berkeley: University of California, 1970), esp. p. 48.

14. Note *'îš ḥarbô* in Gen. 34:25 and Exod. 32:27, a phrase to describe the actions of both the ancestor Levi and the tribe of Levi.

15. Gen. Rabbah 80:10 asserts that Jacob eventually came and fought with his sons: "Now our father, Jacob, had not wanted his sons to do this. But once they had done it, he said, 'Now shall I leave my sons to fall into the hand of the nations of the world?' What did he do? He took his sword and bow and stood at the gate of Shechem. He said, 'If the nations of the world come to make war against them, I shall do battle against them.' "

sheth and Abner, 2 Sam. 3), Bathsheba (Uriah and Bathsheba's child, 2 Sam. 11, 12), Tamar (Amnon and Absalom, 2 Sam. 13–19), Abishag (Adonijah and Joab, 1 K. 2).[16] For Blenkinsopp,[17] the abundance of such incidents is evidence of the pervasiveness of the motif of the woman who brings death in the literature of ancient Israel.

Only with the end of v. 26 does the reader discover that throughout this whole ordeal Dinah has been held in the house of Shechem. The chiastic arrangement of the two verbs *yāṣā'* and *lāqaḥ* in vv. 1-2 and 26 provides a fine conclusion to the opening of this chapter (vv. 1-2), and something of a closure to the incident as far as Dinah, Levi, Simeon are concerned. The narrative began with Dinah going out (*wattēṣē',* v. 1), and subsequently being taken by Shechem (*wayyiqqaḥ,* v. 2). In v. 26 the brothers remove *(wayyiqḥû)* Dinah from Shechem's house, and leave *(wayyēṣē'û).*

27-29 Killing is followed by pillaging. Levi's and Simeon's brothers finished off what the two of them started. The city is plundered. Animals, children, and wives are seized and captured. The narrator uses wordplay with the verb *lāqaḥ.* The story began with Shechem "seizing" Dinah (*wayyiqqaḥ 'ōṯāh,* v. 2). Now Jacob's sons *seized* (*lāqāḥû,* v. 28) the city's livestock. They also *removed* (*wayyiqḥû,* v. 26) Dinah from Shechem's house. Twice Dinah has been the object of *lāqaḥ:* taken once for sexual activity (Piel), and taken a second time for rescue (Qal).

Two verses are devoted to the act of slaughter, carried out by Simeon and Levi (vv. 25-26). Three verses are devoted to the act of plundering, carried out by Jacob's other sons (vv. 27-29). But the number of Hebrew words in these two sections are almost the same: thirty-six words to describe the killing; thirty-seven words to describe the looting. That the narrator devotes the same length of description to both acts may suggest that he evaluates equally the massacre and the looting. Thus the narrator may be distancing himself from Jacob, who is terribly distressed about the slaughtering but says nothing to the looters (v. 30). Also, the narrator has described Simeon's and Levi's actions as more bold and daring than that of their brothers. The actions of both groups of brothers are introduced by *bô' 'al* (lit., "came upon," vv. 25, 27). But Simeon and Levi came upon a living enemy, albeit one in pain. Their brothers came upon the slaughtered, like vultures landing on lifeless corpses. Earlier it was the Hivites of Shechem whom Hamor managed to persuade with the possibility that one day they could lay claim to the livestock and property of Jacob's sons. Now it is Jacob's sons

16. See D. M. Gunn, "Traditional Composition in the 'Succession Narrative,'" *VT* 26 (1976) 223.

17. J. Blenkinsopp, "Theme and motif in the succession history (2 Sam. xi 2ff) and the Yahwist corpus," *Volume du Congrès: Genève, 1965,* VTSup 15 (Leiden: Brill, 1966), pp. 44-57.

who lay claim to the flocks and cattle of the Hivites. The actions of Simeon and Levi result in a redress for the defilement brought on the victim Dinah. The actions of their brothers result in a sizeable expansion of their flocks. These contrasts between Simeon and Levi and their brothers may be the narrator's way of picturing Simeon and Levi as individuals of conscience and integrity, the later fulmination of their father notwithstanding.[18]

30 Jacob addresses only Simeon and Levi, not his other sons. It is the execution of the men of Shechem, rather than the plundering of the city and its surviving occupants, that has infuriated Jacob. Hence words of rebuke are reserved only for Simeon and Levi. The reason for this rebuke ought to be clear: Simeon and Levi have betrayed an arrangement they first negotiated with Hamor and Shechem, who in turn negotiated this agreement with their own townsmen. But Jacob does not explicitly chide them for being dishonest or deceptive. Rather, Jacob now fears that he and his family may become the object of punitive action by other united groups. His concerns are tactical and strategic, rather than ethical (as in 49:5-7).[19] He is without the resources to oppose a united force; Jacob has been reduced to a position of vulnerability.[20]

In ch. 33 Jacob lived in dread of Esau's 400 men. In ch. 34 Esau's 400 men are replaced by *Canaanites and Perizzites,* as those who contribute to Jacob's apprehensions. It is ironic to hear Jacob venting his disgust over Simeon's and Levi's failure to honor their word, especially in terms of its potential consequence for Jacob, for he had done exactly that on more than one occasion. One need only recall events as recent as those in ch. 33, where Jacob gave Esau his word that he would follow Esau to Seir, only to take off for Succoth and Shechem. Why might the sons be rebuked for backing out of a commitment, while it is permissible for the father to back out of his commitment? Why is Jacob's subterfuge in ch. 33 acceptable, while his sons' subterfuge in ch. 34 is not? Jacob's answer would be that his subterfuge, if it

18. See Sternberg, *Poetics of Biblical Narrative,* pp. 471-72, for this suggestive presentation of the contrast between the individuals in vv. 25-26 and those in vv. 27-29. By contrast, Bechtel (*JSOT* 62 [1994] 34) perceives no redeeming features in the two brothers: "Ironically if there is rape in this story, it is Simeon and Levi who 'rape' the Shechemites."

19. See Gottwald, *Tribes of Yahweh,* p. 520.

20. The verb Jacob uses for "brought trouble" is *ʿāḵar.* It can refer to someone or something that is taboo or an outcast (here and Josh. 6:18), or to someone who causes trouble (Josh. 7:35; Judg. 11:25; 1 Sam. 14:29; 1 Chr. 2:7). The use of this verb by Ahab to Elijah (1 K. 18:1) may include both meanings: the prophet is both a troubler in Israel and an outcast in that he has hidden from the king. See A. J. Hauser and R. Gregory, *From Carmel to Horeb: Elijah in Crisis,* JSOTSup 85 (Sheffield; Almond, 1990), pp. 32, 86 n. 23. D. Jobling (*The Sense of Biblical Narrative,* JSOTSup 7 [Sheffield: University of Sheffield, 1978], pp. 70, 87 n. 6) suggests that *ʿāḵar* means "put in cultic jeopardy" in Josh. 6:18; 7:25; Judg. 11:35; and 1 Chr. 2:7, and possibly also in Gen. 34:30 and 1 Sam. 14:29.

did backfire, would bring only the wrath of Esau, who is his brother, after all. Furthermore, Jacob's own ruse followed reconciliation with Esau. Here there has not been, nor can there be, any reconciliation. In addition, it is not just one individual who looms as a potential adversary but large groups of peoples, Canaanites and Perizzites.

31 Simeon and Levi have the last word. Jacob is unable to respond to their rhetorical question: *Like a whore should he treat our sister?* So revolted are they that Simeon and Levi cannot say "Should Shechem treat . . . ?" To repeat his name is cause for nausea. They simply say, "Should he[21] . . . ?" Jacob's silence is token acceptance of the legitimacy of their conduct, as portrayed by the narrator.

This chapter has six conversation scenes: (1) Shechem to Hamor (v. 4); (2) Hamor to the sons of Jacob (vv. 8-12); (3) the sons of Jacob to Hamor and Shechem (vv. 14-17); (4) Hamor and Shechem to their townsmen (vv. 21-23); (5) Jacob to Simeon and Levi (v. 30); (6) Simeon and Levi to Jacob (v. 31).[22] The first and last of these six conversations is a son (or sons) speaking to a father. In neither case does the son(s) speak mildly. Shechem gives his father a command. Simeon and Levi give to their father what amounts to a scolding. They speak as coarsely to him as Joab did to sentimental and ineffectual David (2 Sam. 19:5-7). It is almost as if they say to Jacob in the light of his own words in the previous verse: "Father, damn the consequences."[23] Accordingly they are very careful in their last reference to Dinah to call her *our sister* rather than "your daughter."

Throughout all of this violence and vendetta, not one word has been heard from Dinah! She is abused, avenged, spoken about, delivered, but she never talks. If in 30:21 she was denied an etymology for her name, in ch. 34 she is denied an opportunity to speak.

It is interesting that works from the Hellenistic and Roman periods praise the activity of Simeon and Levi. For example, Philo praises Simeon and Levi as "the hearers and pupils of sound sense" who overthrew the Shechemites, who were "still occupied in the pleasure-loving, passion-loving toil of the uncircumcised."[24] Philo also speaks of Simeon and Levi as "the

21. That the verb *ya'aśeh,* "should he treat," has no explicitly stated subject opens up the possibility that the subject could be someone other than Shechem. Perhaps Jacob? Sternberg (*Poetics of Biblical Narrative,* p. 475) raises this possibility.

22. The interrelationship of the second, third, and fourth speeches is creatively handled by A. Berlin, *Poetics and Interpretation of Biblical Narrative* (Sheffield: Almond, 1983), pp. 76-78.

23. So Sternberg, *Poetics of Biblical Narrative,* p. 474. For another reading of vv. 30 and 31 that places Jacob in a more favorable light and Simeon and Levi in a less attractive light, see Fewell and Gunn, *JBL* 110 (1991) 206-7.

24. Philo *Migration of Abraham* 224.

champions who stand ready to repel such profane and impure ways of thinking."[25] Other sources such as the Testament of Levi, Jubilees, and Judith praise Simeon and Levi for their zeal and compare them to Phinehas (Num. 25:6-15).[26] In all these cases Simeon's and Levi's behavior assumes paradigmatic significance when the issue is guarding Israel's purity at all costs.[27]

L. FROM SHECHEM TO MAMRE VIA BETHEL (35:1-29)

1. BURYING SOME GODS (35:1-4)

1 *God said to Jacob: "Go up now*[1] *to Bethel.*[2] *Settle there and erect an altar to the God who appeared to you while you were fleeing from Esau your brother."*

2 *So Jacob addressed his household and any others who were with him: "Get rid of the foreign gods,*[3] *cleanse yourselves, then put on a change of clothes.*[4]

3 *We will go up to Bethel, and I*[5] *will erect an altar there to the God who answered*[6] *me in my moment of dire need, and who has been with me wherever I have gone."*

25. Philo *On the Change of Names* 200.

26. T. Levi 6:3; Jub. 30:18; Jdt. 9:4.

27. R. Pummer, "Genesis 34 in Jewish Writings of the Hellenistic and Roman Periods," *HTR* 75 (1982) 177-88.

1. Lit., "arise, go up." See Andersen, *Sentence in Biblical Hebrew,* pp. 56-57, who cites many illustrations of the juxtapositioning of two imperatives in which the first imperative assumes the role of an exclamation.

2. LXX reads "to the place of Bethel" *(eis tón tópon Baithēl),* which is likely an artificial addition.

3. Targ. Onqelos reads: "get rid of the idols of the nations" *(ṭʿwt ʿmmyʾ)* for MT *ʾ^{e}lōhê hannēḵār,* thus avoiding even the possibility that pagan idols are divine. See also the same reading in v. 4.

4. The Hiphil of *ḥālap̱* is used here for changing garments *(haḥ^{a}lîp̱û),* but Gen. 41:14 and 2 Sam. 12:20 used the Piel of *ḥālap̱* for the same *(y^{e}ḥallēp̱)* — unless the Piels of Gen. 41:14 and 2 Sam. 12:20 be repointed as Hiphils *(yāḥ^{a}lēp̱),* as argued by G. R. Driver, "Theological and Philological Problems in the Old Testament," *JTS* 47 (1946) 165, who maintains that the Hiphil and Piel of this verb must carry different nuances. But cf. A. Guillaume, "A Reply to Professor Driver," *JTS* 49 (1948) 56-57.

5. LXX: "we will erect," in order to maintain consistency with the first two verbs, which are 1st person pl. *(nāqûmâ, naʿ^{a}leh).* The only other instance of such harmonization in the LXX of Genesis is 2:18, where "I shall make" is *poiḗsōmen.*

6. Or, "who heard me" *(hāʿōneh ʾōṯî).* LXX renders Heb. *ʿānâ* as *epakoúō,* "hear" or, better, "answer." See J. Barr, "The Meaning of *epakoúō* and Cognates in the LXX,"

4 *They handed over to Jacob all the foreign gods they had, and the rings in their ears. Jacob buried them under the terebinth near*[7] *Shechem.*[8]

1 Jacob's life has been one of "rising and going." Such a directive came from his mother (27:43), from his father (28:2), and from the "God of Bethel" (31:13). It is now the God of Bethel who summons Jacob back to Bethel.[9] There is now no need for God to "encounter" Jacob (*pāgaʿ,* 32:2 [Eng. 1]), or to "wrestle" (*ʾāḇaq,* 32:25 [Eng. 24]) with him. Just "speaking" *(wayyōʾmer)* is sufficient. God's command that Jacob *Go up to Bethel*[10] is topographically accurate, for Bethel is approximately a thousand feet more above sea level than Shechem.

It is not uncommon for the patriarchs to build altars (12:7, 8, 13:18; 22:9; 26:5; 33:20). This verse is unique in that it is the one instance in which God tells a patriarch to build an altar. On all other occasions such construction is a spontaneous or responsive action. Interestingly, God's word to Jacob is a reminder of his distant past, rather than of his immediate past. It is not Jacob's reconciliation with Esau that is recalled (ch. 33), but his earlier flight in terror from Esau (28:10ff.).

2-4 Before leaving Shechem, Jacob instructs his family and entourage to *Get rid of the foreign gods, cleanse* [or wash] *yourselves, then put on a*

JTS 31 (1980) 68. While one might expect *epakoúō* to mean "hear," in the LXX it is frequently better rendered as "answer." This is not an illustration of the often-alleged antianthropomorphism of the LXX, i.e., God "hears" prayer rather than "answering" it. It simply demonstrates that *epakoúō* actually meant "answer" and was therefore a literal translation of *ʿānâ.* Note, however, the antianthropomorphism of Targ. Onqelos: "who accepted my prayer [*dqbyl ṣlwty*] on the day of my distress."

7. For this meaning of *ʿim* see M. Dietrich and O. Loretz, "Von hebräisch *ʿim/lpny* (Ps. 72:5) zu ugaritisch *ʿm* 'vor,' " in *Ascribe to the Lord,* Fest. P. C. Craigie, ed. L. Eslinger and G. Taylor, JSOTSup 67 (Sheffield: Sheffield Academic, 1988), pp. 109-16.

8. LXX adds "and destroyed them until this day" *(kaí apṓlesen autá héōs tḗs sḗmeron hēméras).* The LXX wants to make clear that Jacob, in burying the foreign gods, was in effect destroying their usefulness, not simply concealing them in a place where he could later retrieve them if necessary (as Rachel had done earlier with her father's gods).

9. *qûm bᵉraḥ* (27:43); *qûm lēḵ* (28:2); *qûm ṣēʾ* (31:13); *qûm ʿᵃlēh* (35:1).

10. It is well known that the ancient sanctity of Bethel is anchored in the period of the patriarchs (12:8; 28:10-22; 31:13; 35:1ff.; Hos. 12:5 [Eng. 4]), but in a later period there emerged a struggle against the cult conducted in Bethel (1 K. 12:29-33), reflected in the preaching of Amos (3:14; 4:4; 5:5; 7:10, 13), and possibly Hosea (4:15; 5:8; 10:5), and in the reforms of Josiah (2 K. 23:4, 15, 19). Thus Bethel is a holy city whose cult is an abomination, and such ambivalence toward Bethel illustrates that Bethel was a "subject of polemic" in the OT. See Y. Amit, "Hidden polemic in the conquest of Dan: Judges xvii–xviii," *VT* 40 (1990) 16-17. H. M. Barstad (*The Religious Polemics of Amos,* VTSup 34 [Leiden: Brill, 1984], pp. 50-51) takes the position that Amos was the only prophet who systematically condemned the cult of Bethel.

change of clothes. Jacob, the object of three imperatives in the first half of v. 1 *(qûm, ʿ^{a}lēh, šeḇ),* becomes the subject of three imperatives in v. 2 *(hāsîrû, hiṭṭah^{a}rû, haḥ^{a}lîp̄û).*

Commentators have been intrigued by Jacob's insistence that the people surrender their gods to Jacob, and that he buried them under a terebinth or oak tree in Shechem. He does not grind them to powder, as did Moses with the golden calf, but rather he buries them. Undoubtedly this is the most crucial of his directives, indicated by the fact that v. 4 recounts only what Jacob did with the gods. Nothing is said subsequently about purification or garment changes.

What is the significance of burying the gods? Is it a black magic ritual of interment of guardian figurines?[11] Is it a preparatory rite in holy war to activate the "terror of God" against the enemy, and thus not a real burial, but a laying aside of religious figurines?[12] Or is it a forsaking of the father gods?[13]

The best parallel to Jacob's actions seems to be that of Joshua, who (also at Shechem) commanded the elders to "put away the gods [*w^{e}hāsîrû ʾeṯ-ʾ^{ĕ}lōhîm*] that your fathers served" (Josh. 24:14).[14] The presence of such "other gods" will be a barrier preventing legitimate service of Yahweh. The language of Jacob also matches that of Samuel, who calls Israel to the ancient covenant ritual of renouncing foreign gods (*hāsîrû ʾeṯ-ʾ^{ĕ}lōhê hannēḵār,* 1 Sam. 7:3ff.).

A similar situation is probably in view in Gen. 35. Exactly who or what these *strange gods* are is unclear, but they must include the teraphim Rachel stole from her father's house (ch. 31). The parody on such gods continues from ch. 31 into ch. 35. Such gods may be stolen, sat on, stained with menstrual blood, and now *buried.* The verb used for the gods' burial (and for the burial of the jewelry)[15] is *ṭāman* (see Exod. 2:12), rather than the more common *qāḇar.* This verb choice may have no special significance; however, when we recall that *ṭāman* is often used to convey the idea of capturing by hiding a concealed trap (esp. in the Psalms), the choice of the verb may be deliberate. Job 3:16 uses the root to refer to a miscarriage, literally, "a hidden abortion" *(nēp̄el ṭāmûn);* perhaps some such connotation is present here? Or *qāḇar* may have been avoided lest the idea be conveyed that the gods were given a (decent) burial.

It is to Jacob's credit that he himself is responsible for suggesting the

11. See B. Nielsen, "The Burial of Foreign Gods," *ST* 8 (1954/55) 103-22.

12. See O. Keel, "Das Vergraben der 'Fremden Gotter,'" *VT* 23 (1973) 305-36.

13. See O. Eissfeldt, "El and Yahweh," *JSS* 1 (1956) 36.

14. See V. Maag, "Sichembund und Vätergötter," in *Hebräische Wortforschung,* Fest. W. Baumgartner, ed. B. Hartmann, et al., VTSup 16 (Leiden: Brill, 1967), p. 217. Cf. also Josh. 24:23: *hāsîrû ʾeṯ-ʾ^{ĕ}lōhê hannēḵār,* the same expression one finds in Gen. 35:2.

15. It is unlikely that the reference here is to normal jewelry, but rather to ornaments that carried some kind of religious significance, possibly with iconic impressions on them. Note that Targ. Onqelos renders *n^{e}zāmîm* ("rings") by *qdšyʾ,* "holy objects."

extirpation of the gods. That was not a part of God's directive to Jacob in the previous verse. He intuitively senses that the continued presence of these gods is irreconcilable with the new life he has found in Yahweh. The whole incident must be read as an illustration of Jacob's religious maturation.

Jacob also exhorts the people: *cleanse yourselves, then put on a change of clothes.* Here we see Jacob the preacher or exhorter. One of the features of East Mediterranean epic literature is the homecoming (the *nóstos*), one part of which is the washing and changing of clothes by the hero before, or just after, he returns home.[16] By themselves, these admonitions in 35:2b might be so interpreted, but their attachment to the command to expunge the gods reinforces their cultic thrust. It is appropriate that Jacob, who has recently had his name changed, now encourages a change of clothes. Both changes speak of moral transformation. Cf. in Eden the change from clothes of fig leaves (3:7) to clothes of skin (3:21).

Nonetheless, Jacob seems to have difficulty recalling his past, especially as it involved Esau, while talking to his family. God's word to Jacob was to go to Bethel and "erect an altar to the God who appeared to you while you were fleeing Esau your brother" (v. 1). Jacob's own version of that command to his family is: "I will erect an altar there to the God who answered me in my moment of dire need" (v. 3). Thus "while you were fleeing Esau your brother" in God's mouth becomes "in my moment of dire need" in Jacob's mouth. A clearly definable, identifiable expression gives way to a more general, ambiguous one.

2. JACOB REACHES BETHEL (35:5-8)

5 *As they set out, a terror*[1] *from God fell*[2] *upon the cities round about them, so that they did not pursue Jacob's sons.*

16. See G. Rendsburg, "Notes on Genesis xxxv," *VT* 34 (1984) 361-64. For other uses of the Hithpael of *ṭāhēr* ("cleanse, purify") in ritual contexts, see Lev. 14:19, 28; Num. 8:7; Neh. 13:22; Isa. 66:17. Jacob's directives to his entourage about purifying themselves and changing their clothes has analogies with Exod. 19:10-15; Josh. 3:5; 7:13; Num. 11:18. Assuming that the Hithpael of *qāḏaš* in such narratives refers to a ritual bath of purification, and thus is equivalent to the Hithpael of *ṭahar*, what the above incidents have in common is bathing and washing/changing of clothes (at least in Gen. 35 and Exod. 19) that take place the day before one encounters the presence of God. See J. Milgrom, *Leviticus 1–16,* AB (New York: Doubleday, 1991), pp. 963-66.

1. The verb from which *ḥittâ* derives *(ḥāṯaṯ)* is common enough, but the noun *ḥittâ* is a hapax legomenon. The related substantive *ḥaṯ* is found in Gen. 9:2 and Job 41:25 (Eng. 33). It is possible that the expression *ḥittaṯ ʾĕlōhîm* is an instance of the expression of an adjective by a divine epithet — "a divine terror." See Williams, *Hebrew Syntax,* p. 18, § 81.

2. Lit., "was" *(wayᵉhî).*

6 *Thus Jacob reached Luz (that is, Bethel) in the land of Canaan, along with all the following*[3] *who were with him.*

7 *There he built an altar and named the place El-Bethel,*[4] *for it was there that God had revealed himself*[5] *to him when he was fleeing from his brother.*

8 *Deborah, Rebekah's nurse, died; and she was buried under the oak below Bethel, and it is named Allon-bacuth.*[6]

5 Throughout his life Jacob has had to contend with his own fears — fear of God (28:17), fear of Laban (31:31), fear of Esau (32:8, 12 [Eng. 7, 11]). Nobody has been in fear of him. Angry, yes; fearful, no. On Jacob's travels from Shechem to Bethel, that all changes. A *terror from God (ḥittaṯ ʾᵉlōhîm)* overshadows Jacob's entourage and immobolizes any potential opposition. What happened to Dinah (ch. 34) will not happen to her brothers. The only parallel in Genesis to such a "fear from God" is that which overcame Abram when he received the covenant promise (*ʾêmâ ḥᵃšēḵâ gᵉḏōlâ,* "a deep, dark dread," 15:12). The unmistakable presence of God with his people, with the resulting paralysis of enemy nations, appears again in the second half of Moses' song of praise by the Sea (Exod. 15:14-16). These nations — Philistia, Edom, Moab, Canaan — are struck with "terror and dread" (*ʾêmāṯâ wāpaḥaḏ,* v. 16), and thus stilled.

6-7 Jacob is still known by his old name, as *Luz* still retains its former name. It is appropriate that we encounter again at Bethel the word *māqôm, the place.* In the first Bethel narrative *māqôm* appeared four times: 28:11 (twice), 17, 19. Jacob has now returned to the *māqôm.*

3. *hāʿām,* lit., "the people," is a collective sing. for "retainers, followers," See BDB, p. 766b, § 2c.

4. LXX and Vulg. read simply "Bethel."

5. MT *niglû . . . hāʾᵉlōhîm* could be translated "for there the gods [or angels? or divine beings?] revealed themselves to him." SP, LXX, Vulg., Targ., and Pesh. read *niglâ* (3rd masc. sing. Niphal perfect), which is the form one would expect when *ʾᵉlōhîm* refers to the one God (even though it is technically a pl. form). See GKC, § 145h, i. I prefer the translation "God had revealed himself" for two reasons. First, I am inclined to believe that *ʾᵉlōhîm* must have the same meaning in v. 7 as it does in v. 1 and v. 5, even though *ʾᵉlōhîm* in v. 7 has the definite article prefixed to it. Second, in the episode to which v. 7 refers, there is no evidence or suggestion that the messengers/angels revealed themselves to Jacob. R. Rendtorff ("The Concept of Revelation in Ancient Israel," in *Revelation and History,* ed. W. Pannenberg, tr. D. Granskou [New York: Macmillan, 1968], p. 49 n. 17) is surprised by the Niphal of *gālâ* in v. 7 instead of the Niphal of *rāʾâ,* which Rendtorff believes is the term used for divine revelations that bear a cult-etiological character. But *gālâ* and *rāʾâ* are used as synonymous expressions in parallelism (9:21-23; Isa. 47:3; Ezek. 16:36-37; 21:19), are employed as alternatives in passages dealing with secular and sexual themes (Lev. 20:11, 17), and in contexts that describe revelation (1 Sam. 3:21; Isa. 40:5; cf. Num. 24:3-4, 16-17). See S. Talmon, "Revelation in Biblical Times," *HS* 26 (1985) 58.

6. Lit., "oak of weeping (or tears)."

Once there, he renames it. No longer is he content with revisiting; he includes renaming. *Bethel* now becomes *El-Bethel.* "House of El" becomes "El of the House of El."[7] This name is also appropriate, for the next section of the chapter (vv. 9ff.) draws attention to Jacob's own name change. Thus, in v. 7 he changes a name; in v. 10 his name is changed.

No reason for the new name is provided.[8] However, it seems best to link the new name with Jacob's vow in 28:20ff., especially v. 21b, "Yahweh shall be my God." His earlier vow was conditional, with "if God will be with me and bring me back safely." God has done that. Jacob's memories of two experiences at Bethel (chs. 28 and 35) will recall for a long time to come the God Jacob encountered there, rather than recall Bethel as a divine residence, a holy site. Jacob has gone from Bethel to El-Bethel. He has renamed this place "The God of the House of God" rather than simply "The House of God."

8 A curious note follows about the death of Deborah, Rebekah's nurse (see 24:59), and her burial at an oak tree near Bethel. Many commentators are puzzled by the presence of this material here,[9] but two factors account for its inclusion at this point.

The first factor concerns Rebekah. The last we heard of her was 27:46, well over twenty years before this scene. Without exception Genesis tells us about each patriarch's death and burial (Abraham, 25:7-11; Isaac, 35:29; Jacob, 49:33). Genesis also tells us about the death and burial of each patriarch's favorite wife (Sarah, 23:1-20; Rachel, 35:19). The exception is Rebekah, apart from the summarizing statement in 49:31. Presumably she died and was buried before Jacob returned from Aram-naharaim, for there is no reference to Jacob being reunited with Rebekah. Rebekah is gone, though survived by her nurse, but only until Jacob arrives. He not only does not get to see his mother, but he is forced to become undertaker for his late mother's nurse. Thus, one of Jacob's first experiences after coming back home is confronting death. By including the name Rebekah, the author helps his reader recall her character, she who instigated the deception of Isaac. Her punishment (implied at least) is that she will never get to see her son again.[10]

There is a second reason for its placement here. Deborah's being *buried* [*wattiqqāḇēr*] *under the oak tree*[11] [*'allôn*] parallels Jacob's burying *(way-*

7. See Cross, *Canaanite Myth and Hebrew Epic,* pp. 46-47, who reads *'ēl bêṯ 'ēl* as "the god of Bethel" rather than "the god Bethel." The latter translation is favored by O. Eissfeldt, "Der Gott Bethel," *Archiv für Religion und Wissenschaft* 28 (1930) 1-30; J. P. Hyatt, "The Deity Bethel and the Old Testament," *JAOS* 59 (1939) 81-98.

8. See Long, *Problem of Etiological Narrative,* p. 29.

9. See, e.g., Coats, *Genesis,* p. 238; Speiser, *Genesis,* p. 270; Skinner, *Genesis,* p. 425; cf. von Rad, *Genesis,* p. 338; Westermann, *Genesis,* 2:552; also the remarks by Long, *Problem of Etiological Narrative,* pp. 47-48.

10. See G. Rendsburg, "Notes on Genesis xxxv," *VT* 34 (1984) 364-65.

11. O. Margalith ("Samson's riddle and Samson's magic looks," *VT* 36 [1986]

yiṭmōn) the false gods under a terebinth *('ēlâ),* earlier in the chapter. For the gods' burial the root *ṭāman* is used. For Deborah's burial, the more usual root *qāḇar* is used. The opening unit in the Jacob cycle (25:19-34) contains, among its emphases, the birth of two people, Esau and Jacob. The concluding unit in the Jacob cycle (35:1-22) contains, among its emphases, the death of two people, Deborah and Rachel.[12]

Jacob's life after the events at Peniel is filled with hardship: the trauma of facing Esau again, the violation of Dinah, the death of his late mother's nurse, the death of Rachel in childbirth. In the remainder of his life he will face more tragic and distressing situations.

3. JACOB IS INDEED ISRAEL (35:9-15)

9 *God appeared to Jacob again upon his return from Paddan-aram, and blessed him.*

10 *God said to him:*
"You whose name is Jacob,
Your name shall no longer be called Jacob,
But Israel shall be your name."
Thus he was named Israel.[1]

11 *God said to him:*
"I am El Shaddai.
Be abundantly fruitful.[2]
A nation, indeed,[3] *a host of tribes,*
shall stem from you,[4]
and kings shall spring from your loins.

12 *The land I formerly gave to Abraham and Isaac*
I now give to you,
and to your future descendants
will I give this land."

---

228 n. 4) suggests that the reference in v. 8 to Deborah (which means "bee"), the nurse being buried under the oak/tree of weeping, is reminiscent of Cretan Zeus, who was nursed in infancy by Melissa/Melitta, the daughter of Melisseus, who was a bee-god. Also, the reference to Deborah's being buried under the oak *(taḥaṯ hā'allôn)* recalls the judge Deborah, who presided under the palm (*taḥaṯ tōmer,* Judg. 4:5).

12. M. Fishbane, *Text and Texture* (New York: Schocken, 1979), p. 42.

1. LXX omits this phrase.

2. On the use of *pᵉrēh ûrᵉḇēh* as a hendiadys in conjunctive sentences, see Andersen, *Sentence in Biblical Hebrew,* p. 117.

3. I parse the *û* on *ûqᵉhal* as an emphatic.

4. *mimmekkā* is a nominalized prepositional phrase meaning "those from you," i.e., "your offspring." See M. J. Dahood, "Hebrew-Ugaritic Lexicography XII," *Bib* 55 (1974) 389; idem, "Hebrew Lexicography," *Or* 45 (1976) 353.

13 *Then God departed from him, from*[5] *the place where he spoke with him.*

14 *Jacob raised a pillar on the spot where God had spoken with him, a pillar of stone, and upon which he made a libation, and poured out oil.*

15 *Jacob named the site Bethel, because God had spoken with him there.*

9 *God appeared to Jacob again.* It is difficult to determine what *again* refers to here. It could refer to "God said to Jacob" (v. 1) while he was at Shechem. More likely, the reference is to the earlier theophany at Bethel (28:10ff.). That being the case, we note that here Jacob is not overcome by dread, as he was in 28:10ff. As a matter of fact, Jacob says nothing at all this time, something that is not normal for him. Jacob's lack of dread is all the more significant, for this theophany is introduced with *God appeared* [*wayyērā',* Niphal, lit., "showed himself"] *to Jacob,* rather than with the more modest "God said to Jacob" of v. 1.

In addition to showing himself, God *blessed* Jacob, something he had already done in 32:30 (Eng. 29). The essence of that blessing follows in vv. 10ff. God's first appearance to Jacob at Bethel is described with the Niphal of *gālâ* (v. 7). His second appearance to Jacob at Bethel is described with the Niphal of *rā'â.* God's first appearance is to be read in the context of Jacob "fleeing" (*bāraḥ,* v. 7). God's second appearance is to be read in the context of Jacob being *blessed* (*bāraḵ,* v. 9).[6]

10 The blessing God pronounces over Jacob recalls Jacob's encounter with God at Peniel (v. 10) and at Bethel (vv. 11-12). Thus vv. 10-12 are treated in reverse order in terms of their chronological sequence in the Jacob narrative. First is a flashback to 32:29 (Eng. 28; Peniel), then to the promises of 28:13-15 (Bethel). For a second time we read that God announces to Jacob the patriarch's name change from *Jacob* to *Israel.* Must we read this only as P's account of Jacob's name change (which took place at Bethel), in contradistinction to 32:23-33 (Eng. 22-32), which is J's account of the same event (only he places it where the Jabbok and Jordan rivers meet)? Apart from geography, the accounts have other differences. The account in ch. 35 is much briefer. For example, no question is addressed to Jacob — "what is your name?" No meaning of the

5. Note the first "from" which is *min,* and this second "from" which is *b.* It is not out of place here, contra Speiser, *Genesis,* p. 271. Cf. M. J. Dahood, "Northwest Semitic Notes on Genesis," *Bib* 55 (1974) 80.

6. See W. Gross, "Jakob, der Mann des Segens. Zu Traditionsgeschichte und Theologie der priesterschriftlichen Jakobsüberlieferungen," *Bib* 49 (1968) 321-44. Gross has pointed out (pp. 329-32, 341-42) a high number of similarities in the style of Gen. 17 and 35:9ff. Thus both begin with God appearing (*wayyērā',* Niphal of *rā'â*) to Abraham and Jacob (17:1; 35:9). Both conclude with God departing from the patriarch (*wayyaʿal 'ĕlōhîm mēʿal,* 17:22; *wayyaʿal mēʿālâw 'ĕlōhîm,* 35:13). See also S. E. McEvenue, *The Narrative Style of the Priestly Writer,* AnBib 50 (Rome: Biblical Institute, 1971), pp. 146, 165-66.

name is provided in ch. 35, as there was in ch. 32. There is no dialogue here, as there was in ch. 32. There is no reference in ch. 35 to the dietary prohibition that formed from the Peniel incident (a strange omission, given P's penchant for cultic matters). Finally, God who appears to Jacob (ch. 35) replaces a man who wrestles with Jacob (ch. 32). Perhaps the repeated bestowal of the new name *Israel* both before Jacob is reconciled with Esau (ch. 32) and after he is reconciled with Esau (ch. 33) suggests that reconciliation with his estranged brother is a necessary prelude to his becoming truly "Israel."[7]

This is the first word that God speaks to Jacob after he arrives in Bethel, back home, so to speak. How appropriate it is on this occasion for God to act (v. 9) and speak (v. 10). Jacob is reminded that he returns to Canaan not as Jacob but as Israel. He is not only to bury the foreign gods, but he is to bury what has become for all practical purposes a foreign nature — a Jacob nature. He who earlier instructed the people to change their garments must live up to his own change of name. The reason, then, for the truncated version in ch. 35 is that it is a reminder and not an alternative account. Only the major point (i.e., the name change) bears repeating.

11 The imperative *Be abundantly fruitful* (*pᵉrēh ûrᵉḇēh,* lit., "be fruitful and multiply," here taken as a hendiadys) recalls several earlier and later texts in Genesis.[8] Such commands or promises were addressed to childless couples (Adam and Eve, 1:22, 28; the sons of Noah and their wives, 9:1, 7), to a father awaiting a son divinely promised (Abraham, 17:6), or to an unmarried man (Ishmael, 17:20; Isaac speaking to Jacob, 28:3 — no doubt the referent here in 35:11). But in between the "may El Shaddai make you fruitful and multiply you" of 28:3 and the imperatives of those verbs in 35:11, Jacob has cohabited with four women and fathered thirteen children. How much more fruitful and numerous must one become? (It is ironic that the recording of his beloved wife's passing is only a few verses away — v. 19.)

The last half of v. 11 answers what God has in mind by fruitfulness and multiplication. It is not more sons or daughters. Rather, God is thinking in terms of a *nation (gôy),* which is composed of *a host of tribes (qᵉhal gôyim). gôyim* is not the usual word to refer to "tribes," but see Ezek. 2:3 for a parallel.[9] And among Jacob's progeny will be *kings* (cf. 17:6b).

The phrase *future descendants* cannot refer to Jacob's living children.

7. See M. Fishbane, "Composition and Structure in the Jacob Cycle (Gen. 25:19–35:22)," *JJS* 26 (1975) 28; idem, *Text and Texture* (New York: Schocken, 1979), p. 52. M. Weinfeld ("Historical facts behind the Israelite settlement pattern," *VT* 38 [1988] 328) sees Jacob's name change that transpired in Bethel (according to 35:10) as an attempt by priestly circles not to accept the fact that Peniel was the site of the revelation to Jacob, thus downplaying the sanctity of any land east of the Jordan.

8. See 1:22, 28; 9:1, 7; 17:20; 28:3; 47:27; 48:4; also Exod. 1:7.

9. See M. Greenberg, *Ezekiel 1–20,* AB (Garden City, NY: Doubleday, 1983), p. 63.

It refers to the children they will beget, and to their children's children. They will possess the land to which Jacob has recently returned. In the first Bethel theophany the promises of God were, in order, land (28:13) and multiple descendants (28:14); in ch. 35 the order of those promises is reversed: multiple descendants (v. 11) and land (v. 12).

13 In several ways ch. 35 parallels ch. 17: El Shaddai is the name used for the deity; a reference to a name change; and a reference to kings among the patriarch's seed. Even the formula used to conclude the revelation is the same. Cf. 17:22, "God went up from Abraham," with "God went up from him" (*ʿālâ mēʿal* both times, meaning essentially "disappear"). Only one more time, and that a good bit later, will God address Jacob (46:2-4).

14-15 The first structure Jacob built at Bethel was an altar (vv. 1, 7).[10] The second structure he raises is a *pillar (wayyaṣṣēḇ . . . maṣṣēḇâ).* This construction also recalls his earlier actions at Bethel, except in ch. 28 the verb *śîm* (28:18) was used, but here it is *nāṣaḇ* (cf. v. 20 also). The root *nṣb* did appear in ch. 28, but there it described the position of Yahweh relating to the stairway (28:13), or the placing of the stairway on the ground (28:12). The anointing of the pillar with oil also recalls Jacob's earlier visit to Bethel (28:18); both times the verb *yāṣaq* is used. Not mentioned in Jacob's first visit to Bethel is pouring a *libation* or drink offering on the pillar (this is the only time that *nāsaḵ* or *neseḵ* appears in Genesis). Perhaps the threefold use of "where God/he spoke with him" in vv. 13, 14, 15 is meant to parallel the three oracles of God to Jacob in vv. 10, 11, 12.[11]

4. BIRTH, DEATH, AND INCEST (35:16-22a)

16 *Then they left[1] Bethel,[2] but while they were still a good distance[3] away from Ephrath, Rachel started into labor,[4] and she was in much pain.[5]*

10. On the tradition in Jub. 32:16 vis-à-vis Jacob's attempt to also build a temple after his return to Bethel, and the divine command to desist from that project, see J. Schwartz, "Jubilees, Bethel and the Temple of Jacob," *HUCA* 56 (1985) 63-85.

11. See Fokkelman, *Narrative Art in Genesis,* p. 234.

1. Here the Qal imperfect of *nāsaʿ* is spelled *wayyisʿû.* In v. 5 the Qal imperfect was spelled *wayyissāʿû,* as if it were a Niphal.

2. LXX inserts v. 21 here, "he pitched his tent beyond the tower of Gader."

3. On the meaning of *kiḇraṯ hāʾāreṣ* see E. Vogt, "Benjamin geboren 'eine Meile' von Ephrata," *Bib* 56 (1975) 30-36, who suggests a mile. The phrase is, lit., "a distance of the land." See 2 K. 5:19.

4. *wattēleḏ* cannot mean "gave birth to" (its usual sense) but must mean "started labor." This is the inchoative aspect of the verb (Speiser, *Genesis,* p. 273).

5. "She was in much pain" (lit., "she made hard in her bearing") is Piel *(wattᵉqaš).* But "when her pain was most severe" (v. 17) is Hiphil *(bᵉhaqšōṯāh).* The Piel and Hiphil

17 *When her pain was most severe, her midwife said to her: "Do not be apprehensive,*[6] *for you are having a son this time too."*

18 *With her last breath,*[7] *for she was on the verge of dying, she named him Ben-oni;*[8] *his father, however, named him Benjamin.*[9]

19 *Rachel died; and she was buried on the way to Ephrath, that is, Bethlehem.*[10]

20 *Jacob set up a pillar on her grave,*[11] *the pillar that is on Rachel's grave to this day.*

21 *Israel continued his journey and pitched his tent beyond Migdal-eder.*[12]

22a *After Israel settled in that region, Reuben went and lay with Bilhah, his father's concubine. And Israel found out about it.*[13]

---

of the same verb are not variants of E and J (contra Skinner, *Genesis,* p. 426); rather, the form used in v. 17 illustrates the elative use of the Hiphil (Speiser, *Genesis,* p. 273).

6. Or, "fear not, do not be afraid" *('al tîr*^{e}*'î).*

7. Lit., "when her soul went out." The same expression occurs in Cant. 5:6, but there more with the idea "my soul sank," i.e., dispiritment, not death. For the idea of the departure of the soul from the body see Jer. 15:9 (which uses the verb *nāpaḥ*).

8. Lit., "son of my affliction/sorrow," "son of my strength/vigor," or "son of wailing/mourning." The problem of how best to translate Ben-oni is the precise meaning of -oni *('ônî).* One might derive it from *'āwen,* "trouble, affliction" (in which case it would be the only instance in the OT of a name type *ben* plus noun plus 1st person suffix). Another possibility is to associate *'ônî* with *'ôn,* "vigor, strength," but why then would Jacob suggest a name change? A third possibility is to connect *'ônî* (the absolute form of a *quṭl* noun third *yodh*) with Ugar. *un,* "mourning" and Heb. *'ānâ,* "to mourn" (cf. Deut. 26:14; Hos. 9:14). See C. Rabin, "Etymological Miscellanea," *Scripta Hierosolymitana* 8 (1961) 386-87; T. J. Lewis, *Cults of the Dead in Ancient Israel and Ugarit,* HSM 39 (Atlanta: Scholars, 1989), p. 103.

9. Lit., "son of (my) right (hand)," i.e., "son of good fortune."

10. Both v. 19 and v. 20 illustrate the use of apposition instead of a relative clause. See Andersen, *Sentence in Biblical Hebrew,* pp. 58-59.

11. 2 Sam. 18:18 records that Absalom erected a stele for himself since he had no son to perpetuate his name. B. Peckham ("Phoenicia and the Religion of Israel: The Epigraphic Evidence," in *Ancient Israelite Religion,* Fest. F. M. Cross, ed. P. D. Miller, et al. [Philadelphia: Fortress, 1987], p. 90 n. 23) provides instances of Phoenician steles erected by children for their parents, by a man for himself and his wife, and by individuals for themselves.

12. Migdal-eder means lit. "tower of the flock," and could be an ancient name for the Jebusite citadel that became the city of David. The same name appears in Mic. 4:8 in parallel with "hill of the daughter Zion." Possibly a place name with Migdal as its first component refers to small urban settlements that were grouped around a nuclear citadel: Migdal-Penuel (Judg. 8:9, 17); Migdal-El (Josh. 19:38); Migdal-Gad (Josh. 15:37). See F. S. Frick, *The City in Ancient Israel,* SBLDS 36 (Missoula, MT: Scholars, 1977), pp. 47-48, 70 n. 144.

13. LXX adds "it appeared grievous before him." For instances in the MT of a section division in the middle of a verse, rather than at the end of a verse, see E. Tov, *Textual Criticism of the Hebrew Bible* (Minneapolis: Fortress; Aassen/Mastricht: Van Gorcum, 1992), pp. 53-54; and S. Talmon, "Pisqah Be'emṣa' Pasuq and 11QPs^{a}," *Textus* 5 (1966) 11-21.

16-18 Jacob, who has just been reminded of his new name, is about to receive a new son. Jacob and his party are between *Bethel* and *Ephrath, still a good distance away from Ephrath,* when Rachel starts heavy labor. Until this point, we were not even informed that Rachel was pregnant. Her pregnancy surprises the reader.

Rachel's labor pain is conveyed (vv. 16b, 17a) by the verb *qāšâ.* Her painful experience in carrying the child approximates that of her mother-in-law, who was at the point of wishing for death as a release from the pain of two struggling lives she was carrying within her (25:22). In neither of these two instances is the pain experienced by Rebekah and Rachel described by the root *ʿāṣaḇ,* the one used for Eve back in 3:16, 17, but both Rebekah and Rachel did bring forth their children in much pain.

It is interesting that it is Rachel's *midwife* (the functional counterpart of Rebekah's nurse, v. 8?), rather than Jacob, who consoles and encourages Rachel. Jacob is present but apparently not to comfort his pregnant wife. It appears that the midwife knows of Rachel's wish expressed in 30:24, and believes that God is now bringing that prayer to fruition. Twice in the OT when a woman is dying in childbirth, she is comforted by her female attendant(s) with the assurance that she is giving birth to a son — here and 1 Sam. 4:20. Given the absence of any account in biblical literature in which the birth of a daughter is so announced, one may infer that the assurance a mother was giving birth to a male child was the supreme consolation to a woman dying in childbirth.[14]

From the start of his life *Benjamin* has two distinctions. He is the only child of Jacob born in Canaan, not in Mesopotamia.[15] Second, he is the only child of Jacob who is named by the father, rather than by the mother.

His mother, on her deathbed, names him *Ben-oni,* but Jacob proposes *Benjamin,* and the latter name prevails. Just as Jacob became Israel (vv. 9-10), Ben-oni becomes Benjamin. The significance of these two names is debated. If *Ben-oni* means "son of my *mis*fortune," then *Benjamin,* taking a clue from Arab. *yamin,* means "son of *good* fortune."[16] Another suggestion is that *-'ôn* means not "misfortune" or "strength" but "sin, wickedness" (thus Ben-oni means "son of my wickedness"), and *yāmîn* means "oath" (thus Benjamin means "son of the oath").[17] In so naming her child, Rachel believes her death

14. See S. B. Parker, "The Birth Announcement," in *Ascribe to the Lord,* Fest. P. C. Craigie, ed. L. Eslinger and G. Taylor, JSOTSup 67 (Sheffield: JSOT, 1988), p. 144.

15. See J. Muilenburg, "The Birth of Benjamin," *JBL* 75 (1956) 194-201; J. A. Soggin, "Die Geburt Benjamins, Genesis xxxv 16-20 (21)," *VT* 11 (1961) 432-40.

16. See F. Zimmermann, "Some Textual Studies in Genesis," *JBL* 73 (1954) 100-101.

17. See D. Cohen, "But His Father Called Him Benjamin," *Beth Mikra* 23 (1978) 239-41 (Hebrew).

is punishment for stealing her father's gods and then lying about them. In thus naming his child, Jacob draws attention to the earlier oath he made (31:32) that whoever stole Laban's gods should die. A third suggestion is to read SP's *binyāmîm,* that is, "son of days," instead of MT *binyāmîn.*[18] Rachel will die, but Benjamin will be granted a long life, so hopes Jacob. But the most promising explanation for the name Ben-oni is "son of wailing/mourning," with which "son of good fortune" provides a contrast (see n. 8 above).

The ambiguity that causes disagreement among scholars about how best to translate Ben-oni may suggest that the narrator wants to say that Jacob too found the meaning of Ben-oni ambiguous. Accordingly, his giving the child the name Benjamin is his attempt to resolve that ambiguity.[19] Instances in the Bible where one name is given to a child, then rescinded and replaced by a different name are rare. One thinks of John the Baptist: relatives and neighbors suggested that he be named after his father, itself a rare custom. They wanted to name him "little Zechariah" (Luke 1:59). His mother resisted this name and insisted that he be called John (1:60), which her husband subsequently confirmed (1:63). Another possible example of a mother and father giving opposite names to their child may be found in Isa. 7:14 and 8:3, if Immanuel, the name given to the child by his mother (7:14), and Maher-shalal-hash-baz, the name given to the child by his father (8:3), are in fact two names for the same child.[20]

If either Rachel or Jacob feels that her impending death is sin-related (the second suggestion above), neither of them gives any indication to that effect in the name pronouncement. Jacob has yet to relate any of his troubles or misfortunes to previous actions, and it is unlikely that he would start here. By this time, Rachel is no longer a young bride, and thus her death cannot be taken as premature (contra the third suggestion above). The normal explanation (much like the first suggestion, without going the way of Arabic cognates) is most appealing. The right side represents in biblical thought images of fortune, goodness, and strength.[21] Given his own new name, and a new series of promises from God he has just received (vv. 9-12), Jacob would naturally think in these categories.

Many writers have made a connection between *Benjamin,* "son of the right (or south)," in the OT and the "sons of [written ideographically and

18. See J. Shaanan, "And His Father Called Him Benjamin (or Benjamim?)," *Beth Mikra* 24 (1978) 106 (Hebrew).

19. P. D. Miscall, *1 Samuel: A Literary Reading* (Bloomington: Indiana University, 1986), p. 29.

20. This interesting and plausible explanation is advanced by H. M. Wolf, "A Solution to the Immanuel Prophecy in Isa 7:14–8:22," *JBL* 91 (1972) 449-56. See esp. p. 455.

21. The right-handed–left-handed prejudice is illustrated in Lat. *dexter-sinister.*

with the pl. sign] of Yamina (south)" and the "sons of Shimal (north)," two tribes mentioned in the Mari texts (18-17th century B.C.).[22] I would support those who see in Benjamin and Binu-Yamina (or Marē-Yaṃina) a similarity of name only, with no further association. Such a semantic parallel between a Hebrew personal or tribal name and a cuneiform text from the 18-17th century B.C. provides another instance of links between patriarchal names and similar names in the first two or three centuries of the 2nd millennium B.C.

19-21 No sooner has Jacob finished with one funeral (Rebekah's nurse) than he is involved with a second one — Rachel's. Here is one more grief in an ever-mounting catalogue of griefs for Jacob. A son is gained; a wife is lost. What is the source of fruitfulness, tribes, and kings promised to Jacob (v. 11) with Rachel deceased? It is ironic that Rachel, who earlier had proclaimed she would die if she had no children (30:1), and who gave to her firstborn the name Joseph, implying a yearning for another son (30:22-24), dies at the birth of this avidly looked-for second son.[23]

To memorialize Rachel, Jacob raises a *pillar* over her grave. This is the third time Jacob has attempted to commemorate some event or person, either glorious (28:18; 35:14) or tragic (35:20), by raising a pillar. Two episodes in Jacob's life outlast Jacob, and continue to exist *to this day* (i.e., the narrator's day). These are the prohibition about eating (32:33 [Eng. 32]), and Rachel's stele (35:20).

Some writers have claimed a gross inconsistency between the connection of *Ephrath* with *Bethlehem* (v. 19) and 1 Sam. 10:2, which tells us that Rachel's tomb was in the territory of Benjamin. Reference is made also to Jer. 31:15, where Rachel's weeping for her children can be heard in Ramah of Benjamin. Ramah is on the boundary between Israel and Judah, approximately five miles north of Jerusalem and twelve miles north of Bethlehem. But it is possible that the place name Ramah in Jer. 31:15 should be read instead as "height" — "a voice on the height may be heard."[24] Is the editorial note of v. 19 a mistake, then, a confusion of a Judean Ephrath for a Benjaminite Ephrath? Matt. 2:18 clearly situates Rachel's tomb near Bethlehem (in agreement with Gen. 35:19), and that

22. See G. Dossin, "Benjaminites dans les textes de Mari," in *Mélanges Syriens offerts à Monsieur René Dussaud* (Paris: Geuthner, 1939), 2:982-96; cf. von Rad, *Genesis,* p. 341; de Vaux, *Early History of Israel,* p. 641.

23. On the presence of irony in v. 19, albeit certainly not in any humorous way, see A. Brenner, "Female social behaviour: two descriptive patterns within the 'birth of the hero' paradigm," *VT* 36 (1986) 263; idem, "On the Semantic Field of Humour, Laughter and the Comic in the Old Testament," in *On Humour and the Comic in the Hebrew Bible,* ed. Y. T. Radday and A. Brenner, JSOTSup 92 (Sheffield: Sheffield Academic, 1990), p. 41 n. 9.

24. See W. Holladay, *Jeremiah,* Hermeneia, 2 vols. (Philadelphia/Minneapolis: Fortress, 1986-89), 2:186-87.

is why Matthew can associate Rachel's weeping in Ramah with the slaughter of infants in Bethlehem. See also Jub. 32:34 for the same connection.

One needs to note that Gen. 35 does not state that Rachel died and was buried in Ephrath. Rather, it was while they were "still a good distance away from" (v. 16) and "on the way to" (v. 19) Ephrath that she died. These phrases could refer to a site south of Jerusalem. Furthermore, 1 Sam. 10:2 refers to Rachel's tomb on the border of Benjamin. If this is Benjamin's south border, then it could be a place south of Jerusalem (Josh. 15:8; 18:15-17). In any case, the issue is complicated, and no problem-free solution is currently available to make Gen. 35:19 agree with 1 Sam. 10:2.

22a Jacob must now face another disturbing experience. Behind his father's back, Reuben has intercourse with Bilhah, his father's concubine, maidservant of the late Rachel, and mother of Reuben's half-brothers Dan and Naphtali.[25] Jacob's sons get quite angry when their sister is violated, but they express no concern when their father's concubine is taken by one of their brothers. Of course, Reuben did not rape Bilhah. Both times Jacob restrains himself and does not seek revenge. Such refusal to strike back is due either to impotence or to a desire on Jacob's part not to meet violence and sexual indulgence with recrimination and more violence.

Reuben's actions are not simply sexually motivated.[26] The OT provides examples of a deceased king's wives becoming the wives of his successor (2 Sam. 12:8). Closer to this passage are those narratives in which a man went into the concubines of another. Ishbosheth was disturbed when Abner went into the late Saul's concubine Rizpah, not because of moral reasons but because he interpreted Abner's action as a subtle move to grab the throne (2 Sam. 3:7). The same idea is operating when Ahithophel urges Absalom to take possession of his father's ten concubines (2 Sam. 16:20-22). Through this move Absalom is making clear his intentions to usurp his father's royal authority. Once he has reasserted himself, David will have nothing to do with these concubines (2 Sam. 20:3). Solomon so interpreted Adonijah's request for Abishag (1 K. 2:22). Is Reuben simply engaging in sexual play? Or, more likely, is he attempting to usurp his father and take control of the family? Jacob's lack of response to Shechem over the Dinah incident clearly cost Jacob any credibility with his family. What will Jacob do here?

Carmichael has suggested that Deut. 23:1a (Eng. 22:30a) is legal com-

25. Later rabbinical tradition considered the story of Reuben's sleeping with his father's concubine offensive enough to fall into the category of biblical material that during the synagogal Torah reading may be read but not translated *(nqr'yn w'ynn mtrgmyn)*. See M. L. Klein, "Not to be Translated in Public — *l' mtrgm bṣ'bwr'*," *JJS* 39 (1988) 80-83, 91.

26. See G. C. Nichol, "Genesis xxix.32 and xxxv.22a: Reuben's Reversal," *JTS* 31 (1980) 536-39.

mentary on the Reuben-Bilhah-Jacob affair: "a man shall not take his father's wife."[27] The expression "father's wife" refers to one's step-mother, and it is marriage with a step-mother that is prohibited (at least in the first half of the verse). Of course, in Gen. 35:22a we have not a marriage with a step-mother but the seduction of a father's concubine, while the father is still living, thus calling into question Carmichael's contention that Deut. 23:1a (Eng. 22:30a) has been influenced by the patriarchal narratives.[28]

5. JACOB'S FAMILY (35:22b-29)

22b *Jacob's sons numbered twelve.*

23 *The sons of Leah: the firstborn of Jacob — Reuben; and Simeon, Levi, Judah, Issachar, and Zebulon.*

24 *The sons of Rachel: Joseph and Benjamin.*

25 *The sons of Bilhah, Rachel's maid: Dan and Naphtali.*

26 *The sons of Zilpah, Leah's maid: Gad and Asher. These are the sons of Jacob born to him in Paddan-aram.*[1]

27 *Jacob came to Isaac his father at Mamre, in Kiriath-arba (that is, Hebron),*[2] *where Abraham and Isaac had sojourned.*

28 *Isaac was 180 years old.*

29 *Then Isaac breathed his last and died; he was gathered to his kin, at a ripe old age. Esau and Jacob his sons buried him.*

22b-26 Verses 16-18 detailed the birth of Jacob's last born son. V. 22a spoke of the debauchery of Jacob's firstborn son. This information about two of Jacob's sons is followed by a summarizing statement about all his sons. Dinah is again conspicuous by her absence. The order of the sons is not chronological, such as we found in Gen. 29–30. Rather, the names are organized around Jacob's wives: Leah (v. 23), Rachel (v. 24), Bilhah (v. 25), and Zilpah (v. 27). Leah heads the list, and Leah's maidservant ends the list. Rachel and Rachel's maidservant are in the middle. This is the exact order we find for Jacob's sons (Joseph excepted, of course) in Exod. 1:1-4, "These are the names of the sons of Israel, who came to Egypt with Jacob. . . ." We find a different order of the son's listing by their

27. See C. Carmichael, *The Laws of Deuteronomy* (Ithaca: Cornell University, 1974) pp. 170-71.

28. See A. Phillips, "Uncovering the father's skirt," *VT* 30 (1980) 40-41.

1. This is an instance of a summary statement at the end of a piece functioning as a concluding title or colophon. See Andersen, *Sentence in Biblical Hebrew,* p. 54.

2. I assume *BHS heḇrôn* is a misprint for *ḥeḇrôn* (see *BHK*).

mothers in 46:8ff. The sequence there is Leah's sons (vv. 8-15), Zilpah's sons (vv. 16-18), Rachel's sons (vv. 19-22), and Bilhah's sons (vv. 23-25). Always the sons of Leah are in the primary position, be it in Gen. 35, 46, or Exod. 1.[3]

That v. 26b refers to these twelve sons as boys *born in Paddan-aram* presents a problem for understanding Benjamin's birth. We just read (vv. 16-18) that Benjamin was born near Ephrath in Canaan, after he had left Paddan-aram (v. 9). Thus either the genealogy in vv. 22a-26 is from a source (P) that was unaware of the account of Benjamin's birth outside Paddan-aram (E), or the genealogy sacrifices literality for compactness.[4]

27-29 The Jacob story rounds off with a notice about Isaac's death. In ch. 35 Jacob has faced three family-related deaths: his mother's nurse (v. 8), Rachel's (v. 19), and now his father's. Then as now, the passing of a loved one brings together members of a scattered family. Jacob comes from Ephrath or thereabouts, and Esau travels from Seir (33:16). They meet at *Hebron,* known also as *Mamre* or *Kiriath-arba* (see 13:18 and 23:2). Jacob shares two names in this chapter; so does Benjamin; and so does Hebron. Twice an editorial gloss has been inserted for purposes of name clarification (vv. 19, 27).

Isaac is *180 years old* when he dies. This is interesting. According to 25:26 Isaac was 60 years old when Esau and Jacob were born. Also, according to 26:34 Isaac was 100 years old when Esau married. In ch. 27 we read that Isaac was "elderly and with failing eyesight." He thinks his death is imminent (27:2, 4), and so does Rebekah (27:10). Yet, on the basis of 35:28 it appears that Isaac lived 80 years more, if the event in ch. 27 follows immediately upon Esau's marriages. Again, this information might suggest that the tradition in 35:27-29 (P) is not cognizant of the tradition about the aged Isaac, near death at 100, of ch. 27 (J).[5] Or, the coupling of 35:28 and ch. 27 gives a new meaning to 27:2: "I do not know the day of my death." If he lived for another eighty years or so, he certainly did not know when he would die! In such a case, to paraphrase Mark Twain, the account of Isaac's fast-approaching demise is greatly exaggerated. He was wrong about which son was which, and he was equally wrong about how much longer he would live.

In many ways the account of Isaac's death parallels that of his father

3. On the various listings of Jacob's sons in the OT see J. M. Sasson, "A Genealogical 'Convention' in Biblical Chronography?" *ZAW* 90 (1978) 179-84; W. M. W. Roth, *Numerical Sayings in the Old Testament: A Form-Critical Study,* VTSup 13 (Leiden: Brill, 1965), pp. 12-13.

4. See Skinner, *Genesis,* p. 427; Speiser, *Genesis,* p. 273; Westermann, *Genesis,* 2:549, 556; cf. Coats, *Genesis,* pp. 243-44. Noting the accumulating evidence that the preposition b^e may at times mean "from," one might translate the phrase in v. 26b as "born to him (who came) from Paddan-aram."

5. Cf. Skinner, *Genesis,* p. 428; Speiser, *Genesis,* pp. 274-75; Westermann, *Genesis,* 2:557.

(25:7-11). The ages of both at their death are given (25:7; 35:28). In 25:8 Abraham's death is reported by *wayyigwaʿ wayyāmot̲ ʾab̲rāhām*. In 35:29 Isaac's death is reported by *wayyigwaʿ yiṣḥāq wayyāmot̲*. Gen. 25:8 uses the expression *zāqēn wᵉśāb̲ēʿa* for Abraham, while 35:29 uses *zāqēn ûśᵉb̲aʿ* for Isaac. Both are "gathered to their kin" (25:8 and 35:29). Both had two sons bury them (Isaac and Ishmael, 25:9; Esau and Jacob, 35:29). Both times "they buried him" *(wayyiqbᵉrû ʾōt̲ô)* is used (25:9; 35:29). Finally, Mamre appears in 25:9 and 35:27.[6]

M. ESAUITES AND EDOMITES (36:1-43)

1. ESAU'S IMMEDIATE FAMILY (36:1-8)

1 *These are the descendants of Esau, he who is Edom.*[1]

2 *Esau took his wives from among the Canaanite women: Adah, daughter of Elon the Hittite; Oholibamah, daughter of Anah son of*[2] *Zibeon the Hivite,*[3]

3 *and Basemath,*[4] *Ishmael's daughter, and sister of Nebaioth.*

4 *Adah bore to Esau Eliphaz; Basemath bore Reuel;*

5 *and Oholibamah bore Jeush, Jalam, and Korah. These are the sons of Esau who were born to him in the land of Canaan.*

6 *Esau took his wives, his sons, his daughters, and every household member,*[5] *plus his livestock, his work animals, and all the property he*

6. These parallels have been observed by most commentators, but see esp. G. Rendsburg, *The Redaction of Genesis* (Winona Lake, IN: Eisenbrauns, 1986), p. 75.

1. See Andersen, *Sentence in Biblical Hebrew,* p. 30, for a verbless clause in which an alternative proper name for a person/place is given; also, pp. 58-59 for the use of apposition instead of a relative clause.

2. The reading "son of" *(ben)* follows LXX, SP, and Pesh. against MT *bat̲,* "daughter of." Vulg. supports MT. See also vv. 14, 39 below. One reason for opting for the reading *ben* is that later (v. 20) Anah is listed as one of the sons of Seir. But that reference presents its own problem, for then in v. 2 Anah and Zibeon are son and father, while in v. 20 they are brothers.

3. In v. 20 Zibeon "the Hivite" is a "Horite." For "Hivite" as a spelling variant for "Hurrian" see R. North, "The Hivites," *Bib* 54 (1973) 56.

4. SP reads Mahalath (cf. 28:9) instead of Basemath, in an attempt to harmonize 28:9 with 36:3. See J. W. Wevers, *Text History of the Greek Genesis* (Göttingen: Vandenhoeck & Ruprecht, 1974), p. 146.

5. For this interesting use of *nep̲eš* designating persons and translated by *sōma* in the LXX, see D. Lys, "L'arrière-plan et les connotations vétérotestamentaires de *sarx* et de *soma* (étude préliminaire)," *VT* 36 (1986) 198.

had acquired in the land of Canaan, and went to the land of Seir,[6] *away from his brother.*

7 *Their possessions had become too numerous for them to dwell*[7] *together; and the land in which they were sojourning could not support them because of their livestock.*

8 *So Esau settled in the hill country of Seir. Esau is Edom.*

Chapter 36 is one of the longest in Genesis, and it is given over exclusively to genealogy — Esau's family and lists of Edomite leaders. Illustrative of the Bible's interest in the development and history of other nations is the inclusion of forty-three verses that trace meticulously the proliferation and history of the Edomites.

But it is only Esau's descendants who are so thoroughly documented. To a lesser degree Ishmael's descendants had also been noted (25:12-18). Closer examination of the biblical texts reveals that the report of Abraham's death (25:7-11) is followed first by "these are the descendants of Ishmael, an older brother" (25:13-18), then by "these are the descendants of Isaac, a younger brother" (25:19ff.). Similarly, the report of Isaac's death (35:27-29) is followed first by *These are the descendants of Esau,* an older brother (36:1-43), then by "these are the descendants of Jacob," a younger brother (37:2ff.). In both cases, the death of a patriarch is followed first by a *tōlᵉḏôṯ* formula that applies to a family that is outside the covenant promise, then by a *tōlᵉḏôṯ* formula that applies to a family who receives the covenant promise. Just as the Ishmael genealogy serves as a bridge between the Abraham-Isaac narratives, the Esau genealogy serves as a bridge between the Isaac-Jacob narratives.

1-5 Jacob fathered thirteen children by two wives and two concubines, and Esau fathered five children by three wives. His first wife is *Adah,* who is identified as the *daughter of Elon the Hittite.* Lamech's wife was also known by this name (4:19). His second wife is *Oholibamah,* the *daughter of Anah,* who is the son of Zibeon, a *Hivite* (i.e., a Hurrian living in Palestine). His third wife is *Basemath,* the daughter of Ishmael and the sister of Nebaioth.

6. MT reads simply, "and he went to a land." Targs. Onqelos and Jonathan read "he went to another land." SP and LXX read "he went from the land of Canaan." Pesh. reads "to the land of Seir." These are all attempts to fill in what is obviously a defective Hebrew text. D. Steinmetz (*From Father to Son: Kinship, Conflict, and Continuity in Genesis* [Louisville: Westminster/John Knox, 1991], pp. 182 n. 54 and 200 n. 45) asserts that the omission of any specific place name in 36:6 has the effect of generalizing the narrative, and is to be contrasted with other texts in Genesis which state that *X* went to place *Y* (4:16; 25:6; 29:1).

7. For *min* with the infinitive *(miššeḇeṯ)* for an "absolute comparative (elative), expressing a quality of too high a degree" see Williams, *Hebrew Syntax,* p. 55, § 318.

It is of interest that vv. 2-3 subsume Hittite, Hivite, and Ishmaelite under the general rubric of *Canaanite*. In the references to these three women as wives the order is: Adah, Oholibamah, Basemath (vv. 2-3). In the references to these women as mothers the order is: Adah, Basemath, Oholibamah (vv. 4-5).

This mention of Esau's three wives needs to be considered with earlier references to his three wives: (1) Judith, daughter of Beeri the Hittite (26:34); (2) Basemath, the daughter of Elon the Hittite (26:34); (3) Mahalath, the daughter of Ishmael, sister of Nebaioth (28:9). There are two problems here. The first problem is the paralleling of Judith/Basemath/Mahalath with Adah/Oholibamah/Basemath; only one of the names appears in both lists (Basemath). The second problem is the shift in family relationships. In 36:3 Basemath is identified as the daughter of Ishmael and as the sister of Nebaioth, but in 28:9 Mahalath is so designated. In 36:2 Adah is introduced as the daughter of Elon the Hittite, but in 26:34 Basemath is introduced as Elon's daughter. In 36:3 Basemath is Ishmael's daughter, but in 26:34 she is Elon's daughter. The only thing both lists of wives' names have in common is the order of ethnic designation: (1) Judith/Adah (Hittite); (2) Basemeth/ Oholibamah (Hivite, if SP's and LXX's reading of "Hivite" is preferred in 26:34b); (3) Mahalath/Basemath (Ishmaelite).

What evaluations or explanations may be made for these two different set of names for the wives of Esau? One possibility is attempted harmonization (e.g., Basemath of 26:34 and Adah of 36:2 are the same, for both have the same father; and the same would be said of Mahalath of 28:9 and the Basemath of 36:3).[8] But what is one to do with Judith (26:34) and Oholibamah (36:2) who have different fathers? A second possibility is that the differences are due to the fact that the lists have suffered in transmission.[9] A third approach reads 36:1-5 as an attempt by the editor to harmonize the data of 36:9ff. with the data of 26:34 and 28:9, a fact which produced genealogical fluidity.[10] A fourth possibility is that the problem defies solution, and is akin to an attempt to unscramble an omelette (Gordon's analogy).[11]

6-8 It is not clear whether these three verses describe a separation that took place between Esau and Jacob after the death of their father, a kind of a final separation, or whether they refer to a separation between the two that had taken place much earlier. Certainly this is not the first mention of Esau's location in *Seir.* Gen. 32:4 (Eng. 3) tells that Jacob sent messengers to Esau in the land of Seir. And after Jacob is reconciled with Esau, Esau returns to Seir (33:16).

8. See Stigers, *Genesis,* p. 216.

9. See Kidner, *Genesis,* p. 177.

10. See R. R. Wilson, *Genealogy and History in the Biblical World* (New Haven: Yale University, 1977), pp. 174-76.

11. See C. H. Gordon, *The Ancient Near East,* 3rd ed. (New York: Norton, 1965), p. 126 n. 30.

Their parting is not in hostility, such as we read about in chs. 27–28, unless one reads hostility into the words *away from his brother.* Their problem is the same as that experienced by Abraham and Lot (cf. ch. 13). The flocks of each are so great that there is not enough land for Esau and Jacob to work side by side. Esau settles in Seir; Jacob remains in Canaan.

Although Esau is outside the covenant promise, God's blessing extends to him in two ways: children (vv. 4-5)[12] and prosperity (vv. 6-7). At some points Esau appears in a better light than Jacob. He departs from Canaan with an amiable, commonsense view of things, not in anger or resentment.

Esau

2. ESAU'S SONS AND GRANDSONS (36:9-14)

9 *These are*[1] *the descendants of Esau, ancestor of Edom, in the hill country of Seir.*

10 *These are the names of Esau's sons: Eliphaz, son of Esau's wife Adah; Reuel, son of Esau's wife Basemath.*

11 *The sons of Eliphaz were: Teman, Omar, Zepho, Gatam, and Kenaz.*

12 *Eliphaz, Esau's son, had a concubine Timna, and she bore Amalek to Eliphaz. These are the grandsons of Adah, Esau's wife.*

13 *These are the sons of Reuel: Nahath, Zerah, Shammah, and Mizzah. These were the grandsons of Basemath, Esau's wife.*

14 *These were the sons of Oholibamah, Esau's wife, daughter of Anah son of*[2] *Zibeon, whom she bore to Esau: Jeush, Jalam, and Korah.*

These six verses repeat the information given in vv. 1-5 about the names of Esau's three wives and his five sons. Two new pieces of data are supplied. First, unlike v. 1, which identified Esau with Edom, v. 9 identifies Esau as the *ancestor* (lit., "father") *of Edom.* Second, the family of Esau is traced to

12. Among Esau's family members, along with wives and sons and other household members, are daughters. None of them is named. They appear only as an anonymous group, in contradistinction to the sons, who were named in vv. 4, 5. The absence of any reference to Esau's daughters-in-law or grandchildren in v. 6 has led N. P. Lemche (*Early Israel,* VTSup 37 [Leiden: Brill, 1985], p. 253) to suggest that this is evidence of a nuclear family that was also neolocal, i.e., the newly married formed their own households. But such relatives could be included under the general term "other household members."

1. The translation "these *are* the descendants (or [grand]sons) of" indicates a nominal sentence (vv. 9a, 10a, 12b, 13a). The translation "these *were* the descendants (or [grand]sons) of" indicates a verbal sentence (vv. 11a, 13b, 14a). Only the former (the nominal sentence) is, technically, a title.

2. As in v. 2 above, LXX, SP, and Pesh. read "son of" *(ben)* for MT "daughter of" *(baṯ).* See also v. 39 below.

the third generation through the progeny of two of his sons. Through *Eliphaz* Esau realizes six grandsons (or five if one discounts the bastard child Amalek, mothered by Timna, Eliphaz's concubine). Through *Reuel* Esau realizes four grandsons. There is no reference to grandchildren through Oholibamah's three children. One son by one mother fathers six children. One son by another mother fathers four children. Three sons by yet a third mother father no children. The most fertile wife has no grandchildren.

It is strange that reference to Oholibamah's children (the second generation) is delayed (v. 14) until the names of the third generation through Eliphaz and Reuel have been listed (vv. 11-13). This sequence permits the grouping of and placing on the same level of ten (or nine) third-generation Esauites with three second-generation Esauites.

Including Amalek among Esau's legitimate offspring, the total number of Esau's descendants (through the third generation) is fifteen: five sons and ten grandsons. Because we have already met the twelve sons of Ishmael (25:12-16), the twelve sons of Jacob (35:22b-26), and the twelve sons of Nahor (22:20-24), some[3] have suggested that 36:10-14 originally described a twelve-tribe amphictyony among the Edomites. A major challenge to this proposal is that nowhere in ch. 36 is there a list containing precisely twelve names, as in the other three lists. To arrive at a twelve-member genealogy for Esau, one must first count three of Esau's sons by Oholibamah as one. Then one must reduce Esau's grandsons to nine (to get the combination 9 + 3) by excluding Amalek. Furthermore, two names would have to be deleted from vv. 15-19, which refer to fourteen major divisions of Edomites, and one name would need to be added to vv. 40-43, which mention eleven names.[4]

Only a few of these names are known elsewhere. *Teman* could be a district or a clan, with the eponym being Esau's grandson. In Amos 1:12 it is obviously a town, possibly a leading city, if not the capital, of Edom.[5] Elsewhere it is a target for judgment speeches by the prophets (Jer. 49:20; Ezek. 25:13; Obad. 9). *Kenaz,* the fifth son of Eliphaz, was the name of a people (Kenizzites) whose land would be taken away and given to Abraham (Gen. 15:19), but elsewhere the Judahite Caleb is called a Kenizzite (Num. 32:12; Josh. 14:6, 14). The Kenizzites were apparently originally an Edomite clan that later affiliated itself with the tribe of Judah.[6]

Eliphaz's son by his concubine Timna is *Amalek.* The nomadic tribe

3. For example, M. Noth, *Das System der zwölf Stämme Israels* (Darmstadt: Wissenschaftliche Buchgesellschaft, 1966), pp. 42-45, 159.

4. R. R. Wilson, *Genealogy and History in the Biblical World,* p. 171 n. 82.

5. R. de Vaux, "Téman, ville ou région d'Edom?" *RB* 76 (1969) 379-85.

6. J. Milgrom, *Numbers,* JPS Torah Commentary (Philadelphia: Jewish Publication Society, 1990), excursus 31, pp. 391-92.

that bears his name appears frequently in the OT (Exod. 17:8-16; Num. 14:39-45; Deut. 25:17-19; 1 Sam. 15). His genealogy implies his special status as a nomad as distinct from the sedentary Edomites.[7] The name of *Zerah,* the second son of Reuel, may be reflected in the Edomite settlement at Uḏruḥ/Ḏarḥ, an agricultural settlement in the 7th/6th century B.C.[8]

3. CLANS FROM ESAU (36:15-19)

15 *These are the clans of Esau's sons. The descendants of Eliphaz, Esau's firstborn: the clans of Teman, Omar, Zepho, Kenaz,*

16 *Korah, Gatam, and Amalek. These are the clans of Eliphaz in the land of Edom; they are descended from Adah.*

17 *These are the descendants of Reuel, Esau's son: the clans of Nahath, Zerah, Shammah, and Mizzah. These are the clans of Eliphaz in the land of Edom; they are descended from Basemath, Esau's wife.*

18 *These are the descendants of Oholibamah, Esau's wife: the clans of Jeush, Jalam, and Korah. These are the clans of Oholibamah, daughter of Anah, Esau's wife.*

19 *These are the sons of Esau (that is, Edom) together with their clans.*

In many ways vv. 15-19 presents the same list of Esau's progeny as did vv. 9-14, suggesting to some scholars that P is the source for vv. 9-14 and J the source for vv. 15-19. There are indeed some differences between the two lists. First, vv. 15-19 are simply a list of Esau's descendants through the third generation. Second, for some unknown reason, the order of two of Eliphaz's sons is changed. In vv. 9-14 Gatam is the fourth son and Kenaz is the fifth. In vv. 15-16 Gatam is the sixth and Kenaz is fourth. Third, vv. 15-19 list Korah as one of the clans of Eliphaz.[1] This inclusion boosts to seven the number of Eliphaz's sons, whereas vv. 9-14 list only six.[2] Adah's seven children to Eliphaz may be compared with Leah's seven children to Jacob.

7. S. Abramsky, "Amalekites," *EncJud,* 2:790. M. Görg ("Ein Gott Amalek?" *BN* 40 [1987] 14-15) proposes, on slender Egyptian evidence, that the tribal name Amalek could have originally been the name of a deity.

8. E. A. Knauf and S. Maáni, "On the Phonemes of Fringe Canaanite: The Cases of Zerah-Uḏruḥ and Kamâšḫaltâ, "*UF* 19 (1987) 91-93.

1. SP alone omits any reference to the clan of Korah. The double mention of Korah (vv. 16, 18) probably implies a time in Edomite history when a portion of the Korahites split from the Oholibamah group and joined themselves to the Eliphaz confederation. See Sarna, *Genesis,* p. 250.

2. See J. M. Sasson, "A Genealogical 'Convention' in Biblical Chronography?" *ZAW* 90 (1978) 179.

Thus there are two Korahs in these genealogies, one who is a fifth son of Esau by Oholibamah, and one who is a fifth clan of Eliphaz. A fourth distinction is that the concluding verse in this unit (v. 19) summarizes not only the data of vv. 9-14 ("these are the sons of Esau"), but also the data of vv. 15-19 ("together with their clans"). The verse serves as a colophon both to the writer's interest about Esau's family tree and about political structures emanating from that family tree. In other words, to read vv. 15-19 as simply a duplicate of vv. 9-14 misses the distinct purpose of the later unit.

The most obviously unique element about vv. 15-19 is that the progeny of Esau are introduced not as "the sons of Esau (or their father)," except as an introductory formula, but rather as *the clan of ('allûp̄)*, or "the clan leader." This title appears eighteen times in vv. 15-19, fourteen times in the singular, four in the plural. Traditional translations of this word have been "chiefs" or "dukes" (cf. Vulg. *dux*), but "clan(s)" appears more accurate. Its uses in vv. 15-19 (and in vv. 20-30, 40-43) are to be understood, more likely, as a reference to a group rather than a person (and cf. Zech. 9:7, "a clan in Judah"; also Zech. 12:5, 6).[3]

The antiquity of the term is attested by its use in Exod. 15:15, where it is parallel with *'êlê* ("leaders of") and *yōšᵉḇê* ("inhabitants of"). It appears also in the Ras Shamra texts as a title applied to the clan leaders of Hittites, Hurrians, and other foreign neighbors of Ugarit.[4]

4. THE GENEALOGY OF SEIR (36:20-30)

20 *These are the sons of Seir the Horite, rulers*[1] *of the land: Lotan, Shobal, Zibeon, Anah,*

21 *Dishon, Ezer, and Dishan. These are the Horite clans of the sons of Seir, in the land of Edom.*

3. On *'elep̄/'allûp̄* see the seminal study of G. Mendenhall, "The Census Lists of Numbers 1 and 26," *JBL* 77 (1968) 52-66. Cf. Gottwald, *Tribes of Yahweh,* pp. 270-78, who distinguishes two senses of *'elep̄:* a military unit and a social unit. Observe, however, that at least in the early texts *'elep̄* stands clearly for the entire clan and not just the fighting force (1 Sam. 23:23; Mic. 5:1). See further remarks on *'elep̄/'allûp̄* by D. W. Patten, "The Two Major Censuses in the Book of Numbers," *Proceedings of the Second Seminar of Catastrophism and Ancient History* (Los Angeles: C & AH Press, 1985), pp. 19-29; J. Milgrom, "Priestly Terminology and the Political and Social Structure of Pre-monarchic Israel," *JQR* 69 (1978) 79-81; idem, *Numbers,* JPS Torah Commentary (Philadelphia: Jewish Publication Society, 1990), pp. 7, 336-39. J. W. Wenham ("Large Numbers in the Old Testament," *TynBul* 18 [1967] 24-32) revocalizes in a number of places *'elep̄* to *'allûp̄,* and interprets the latter as a term for an officer or for a professional, fully armed soldier.

4. See J. Gray, *Legacy of Canaan,* VTSup 5 (Leiden: Brill, 1957), pp. 189, 190.

1. For *yōšᵉḇê* as "rulers," rather than the traditional "inhabitants" (RSV, NEB; cf. AV, NIV, JB, NAB), see Gottwald, *Tribes of Yahweh,* pp. 519-34, esp. pp. 520-21.

22 *Lotan's sons were Hori and Hemam; and Lotan's sister was Timna.*

23 *These are the sons of Shobal: Alvan, Manahath, Ebal, Shepho, and Onam.*

24 *These are the sons of Zibeon: Aiah and Anah. (He is the Anah who discovered lakes in the wilderness while he was pasturing the asses of Zibeon his father.)*

25 *These are the children*[2] *of Anah: Dishon and Oholibamah daughter of Anah.*

26 *These are the sons of Dishon:*[3] *Hemdan, Eshban, Ithran, and Cheran.*

27 *These are the sons of Ezer: Bilhan, Zaavan, and Akan.*

28 *These are the sons of Dishan: Uz amd Aran.*

29 *These are the Horite clans: the clans Lotan, Shobal, Zibeon, Anah,*

30 *Dishon, Ezer, and Dishan. These are the Horite clans, clan by clan, in the land of Seir.*

Two genealogies of Esau's sons (vv. 9-14, 15-19) are now followed by a genealogy of *the sons of Seir the Horite.* According to Deut. 2:12 the Horites (= Hurrians?)[4] were the original occupants of Edom but were later dispossessed and destroyed by the descendants of Esau. What Israelites did to Canaanites, Esauites did to Horites. Thus Gen. 36 is moving backward from the conquerors (vv. 9-19) to the conquered (vv. 20-30).

Seven sons of Seir are listed as *rulers* [*yōšᵉḇê*] *of the land:* Lotan, Shobal, Zibeon, Anah, Dishon, Ezer, and Dishan. Between them they father twenty children, for a total of twenty-seven names in this list (twenty-eight if one counts Lotan's sister Timna). Like the genealogies of Esau in vv. 1-19, this genealogy of Seir is traced through three generations. The genealogy is framed by references to the second generation (vv. 20, 21 and vv. 29-30). In between these framing devices is data about the third generation (vv. 22-28).

An otherwise unbroken list is interrupted only by the gloss on Anah, that it was he *who discovered lakes* [*hayyēmim,* lit., "waters"] *in the wilderness while*

2. MT *bᵉnê.* "Children of" rather than "sons of" is necessitated by the inclusion of Oholibamah.

3. MT mistakenly reads "Dishan." I follow SP and Pesh., which read "Dishon," as in 1 Chr. 1:41.

4. Believing Heb. *ḥōrî* to be ambivalent, Speiser ("Horite," *IDB,* 2:645, 664) suggested that *ḥōrî* was left in that form only when it designated pre-Edomites (with *ḥōrî* meaning "cave" and the Horites being pre-Edomite cave dwellers). *ḥōrî* was changed to "Hivite" in every case where *ḥōrî* meant Hurrians. See also R. North, "The Hivites," *Bib* 54 (1973) 58-62; J. R. Bartlett, "The Land of Seir and the Brotherhood of Edom," *JTS* 20 (1969) 1-20.

he was pasturing the asses of Zibeon his father (v. 24b). The best translation of *hayyēmim* is still uncertain. Even the ancient versions disagreed with each other significantly. The different versions of the LXX simply transliterated the Hebrew word as *Iamein,* which appears to be a homophone of the Hebrew word for "water, lakes." Vulg. rendered it with *aquae calidae,* "thermal springs" (cf. RSV, NIV, JB "hot springs"). Pesh. used "water" (so NAB). SP translated with "the Emim" (the giantlike early inhabitants of Palestine — Deut. 2:10). This rendering is close to "giants" or "mighty ones" *(gwbry')* of Targ. Onqelos. Even "mules" (so AV, NEB) is suggested by Targ. Pseudo-Jonathan's *pwrnyta* (and see Palestinian Talmud *Ber.* 8.6.12b; T. B. *Pes.* 54a; Gen. Rabbah 82:14).

More recent suggestions are as divided. They include: (1) "water," with the transposition of *hymm* to *hmym;*[5] (2) "fish";[6] (3) a "geyser" which was attributed to a demon, and hence the sketchy reference;[7] (4) a "mirage," that is, not something Anah really saw, but something he thought he saw — namely, lakes.[8] This last suggestion, if correct, would provide an analogy to a scenario in the Jacob story. Isaac thought he was touching, talking to, and blessing Esau. Now in a chapter mostly about Esau's descendants we read of Anah who thought what he saw was a lake. In both cases, what one sees is not what one gets.

W. J. Horwitz has forwarded the suggestion, on the basis of 36:20-30, that originally there were two six-tribe Horite amphictyonies.[9] Two facts cast immediate suspicion on this proposal. One is the highly subjective selection of names from the second and third generations of the Horites. The first league comprises, in this reconstruction, six of Seir's seven sons. The second league comprises two of Seir's sons and four grandsons through Dishon. But why select these grandsons and none of the others? A second flaw in Horwitz's proposal is that it posits Anah as a member of both leagues, a highly unlikely situation.

5. KINGS OF EDOM (36:31-39)

31 *These are the kings who reigned in the land of Edom prior to any king reigning for the Israelites.*

32 *Bela,*[1] *son of Beor, became king in Edom, and the name of his city was Dinhabah.*

5. See Speiser, *Genesis,* pp. 279-80; cf. Westermann, *Genesis,* 2:559, 560, 564.

6. See G. R. Driver, "Genesis xxxvi 24: Mules or Fishes," *VT* 25 (1975) 109-10.

7. See B. Z. Luria, "He is the Anah who Found the *yēmim* in the Wilderness (Gen. 36:24)," *Beth Mikra* 30 (1984/85) 262-68 (Hebrew).

8. See A. F. L. Beeston, "What did Anah See?" *VT* 24 (1974) 109-10.

9. See W. J. Horwitz, "Were There Twelve Horite Tribes?" *CBQ* 35 (1973) 69-71.

1. LXX reads the personal name *bela'* as *balak.* Since, however, *'ayin* is never transcribed in Genesis by *k* but always by *g* or not at all, the reading *balak* cannot be

33 *When Bela died, Jobab,*[2] *son of Zerah, from Bozrah, succeeded him as king.*

34 *When Jobab died, Husham, from the land of the Temanites, succeeded him as king.*

35 *When Husham died, Hadad, son of Bedad, succeeded him as king. He was the one who defeated the Midianites in the land of Moab. The name of his city was Avith.*

36 *When Hadad died, Samlah from Masrekah succeeded him as king.*

37 *When Samlah died, Shaul from Rehoboth-on-the-River succeeded him as king.*

38 *When Shaul died, Baal-hanan, son of Achbor, succeeded him as king.*

39 *When Baal-hanan, son of Achbor died, Hadad*[3] *succeeded him as king; the name of his city was Pau. (His wife's name was Mehetabel, daughter of Matred, who was the son*[4] *of Mezahab.)*

These nine verses represent a king list, tracing *the kings* of Edom over eight generations, beginning with Bela and ending with Hadad. These kings are introduced in v. 31 as those *who reigned in the land of Edom prior to any king reigning for* [l^e] *the Israelites.* This sentence may be interpreted in two ways. It may mean that these kings reigned in Edom before any Israelite king reigned in Israel (i.e., pre-Saul).[5] Or, it may mean that these kings reigned in Edom before any Israelite king reigned over Edom (i.e., David). Regardless, the dating data of v. 31 would indicate that this particular king list is either a

---

original. The LXX's "Balak son of Beor" comes from an erroneous connection of "Balak son of Beor" here with "Balaam son of Beor" in Num. 22:5, the well-known Moabite king. See Wevers, *Text History of the Greek Genesis,* p. 214.

2. LXX adds to Job 42:17 these words: "Now these were the kings that reigned in Edom . . . first Balak, the son of Beor . . . and after Balak, Jobab who is called Job; and after him Asom." M. Pope (*Job,* AB, 3rd ed. [Garden City, NY: Doubleday, 1973], p. 354) evaluates these traditions as "garbled and of dubious value."

3. MT reads "Hadar," but 1 Chr. 1:50, SP, Pesh., and many ancient mss. support "Hadad." Cf., e.g., LXX *'Arad* with *r* and *d* transposed. See Wevers, *Text History of the Greek Genesis,* p. 216; and J. R. Bartlett, "An Adversary Against Solomon, Hadad the Edomite," *ZAW* 88 (1976) 206.

4. Reading "son of" with LXX and Pesh. against MT "daughter of" (cf. 36:2, 14 above).

5. Note LXX's rendering of *liḇnê yiśrā'ēl* as "in Israel"; according to *BHS* LXX must have read *byśr'l* rather than *lbny yśr'l.* Since the verb *mālaḵ* ("reign") is not used elsewhere with the preposition *l* in a locative sense (1 Chr. 1:43 is based on Gen. 36:31), it may be best to understand the *l* here as introducing a genitive (see GKC, § 129c; so Skinner, *Genesis,* p. 434; i.e., "a king of the Israelites reigned (over Edom)." Westermann (*Genesis,* 2:565) rejects this interpretation.

post-Saul or post-David composition inserted into the genealogies of Esau and Seir.[6] Its only connection with the former is its Edomite content.

What is most interesting about the king list is that it reflects an elective kingship rather than a dynastic one. If that is the case, then it is the only evidence of a nondynastic monarchy in the national states of the ancient Near East, with the exception of the election of Saul in which there was no provision for a son to inherit the father's throne.

The evidence that this is an elective kingship emerges from the following. First, although the eight kings follow each other in orderly succession, never is any king a son of his predecessor. For example, Jobab, the second king, is not the son of Bela (the first king), but of Zerah. Second, in each instance the place of origin (and capital city?) is different. Thus Bela is from Dinhabah, but Jobab is from Bozrah.

The existence of such an elective, nondynastic monarchy, one of sufficient import to be included by some writer with Israel's sacred traditions, is strange alongside the monarchical systems existent in Israel. Whether we are comparing the several minor dynasties of northern Israel, or the major dynasty of the Davidides of southern Judah, the Israelite system never produced a parallel to that of its Edomite cousins.

One may question whether this is a legitimate list of eight nationally recognized Edomite kings. For one thing, the lists of cities mentions both Edomite and Moabite cities.[7] More importantly, we know that *king* was often used in the OT for a tribal sheikh (cf. Judg. 8:5, 12, "the kings of Midian"; 1 Sam. 14:47, "the kings of Zobah"; 1 K. 20:24, the kings who followed Benhadad, king of Damascus). Second, in Ugaritic "king" *(mlk)* alternates with the term "judge" *(špṭ)*.[8] These "kings" may have indeed been charismatic individuals who, like the judges, assumed their office without regard to heredity.

6. E. A. Knauf ("Alter und Herkunft der edomitischen Königsliste Gen. 36,31-39," *ZAW* 97 [1985] 245-53) suggests the end of the 6th or beginning of the 5th century B.C. primarily because he thinks that the list presupposes that the Edomite kingdom has long been extinct. This argument does not seem convincing.

7. See J. R. Barlett, "The Edomite King-List of Genesis xxxvi.31-39 and 1 Chr. i.43-50," *JTS* 16 (1965) 301-14; de Vaux, *Early History of Israel,* pp. 517-18.

8. See G. Buccellati, *Cities and Nations of Ancient Syria* (Rome: Instituto Di Studi Del Vicino Oriente, Universita Di Roma, 1967), pp. 125-27. If we understand "king" in these verses as a reference to petty tribal kings who controlled local grazing lands rather than national leaders of a monarchy, then the possibility is raised that some of these individuals at least are contemporaneous or overlap (as with the judges). If that is the case, then the author(s) of Gen. 36 has transformed an Edomite list of local chieftains/kings into a list that traces Edomite national leaders through eight representatives (although not dynastic). See further Sarna, "Excursus 28: The Edomite King List," in *Genesis,* pp. 408-10.

Indeed, eight generations back from the time of Saul and David would bring us to the period of the 13th century B.C., enhancing the possibility that the Edomite kings and Israelite judges were contemporaries and entered into their respective offices on the same basis. The redactional gloss in v. 35 about Hadad's defeat of the Midianites recalls Gideon's triumphs over the same nomadic peoples.

It may be only coincidence that the first male name in Gen. 36, apart from Esau, is his son by Adah, *Eliphaz*. This name means "my God is fine gold."[9] The last name in this Edomite king list is Mezahab ("goldwater").[10] The chapter is almost ringed by "gold" names.

One wonders if the inclusion of this Edomite king list may suggest that the promise to Abraham of kings from his loins (17:16) finds its fulfillment, partially at least, through non-Israelite Abrahamic kings.[11] Jacob also was promised that kings would spring from him (35:11). Esau, who received no such promise, is now associated indirectly with eight kings.

6. THE CLANS OF ESAU (36:40-43)

40 *These are the names of Esau's clans by families and dwellings — by their names: the clans Timna, Alva, Jetheth,*[1]

41 *Oholibamah, Elah, Pinon,*

42 *Kenaz, Teman, Mibzar,*

43 *Magdiel, Iram. These are Edom's clans, by their settlements in the territories they held.*[2] *This is Esau, father of Edom.*

9. On "Eliphaz" see M. J. Dahood, "Eblaite and Biblical Hebrew," *CBQ* 44 (1982) 14. W. Kornfeld ("Die Edomiterlisten (Gn 36; 1 C 1) im Lichte des altarabischen Numensmateriales," in *Mélanges bibliques et orientaux en l'honneur de M. Mathias Delcor,* ed. A. Caquot, S. Légasse, and M. Tardieu [Kevelaer: Butzon & Bercker; Neukirchen-Vluyn: Neukirchener, 1985], p. 231) associates the latter part of the name with an Arabic root meaning "to be(come) frightened."

10. For another interpretation of Mezahab, cf. J. A. Emerton in a review article in *VT* 34 (1984) 493.

11. See J. D. Levenson, "The Davidic Covenant and Its Modern Interpreters," *CBQ* 41 (1979) 217.

1. See D. N. Freedman, "A Second Mesha Inscription," *BASOR* 175 (Oct. 1964) 50-51.

2. "In the territories they held" is *b*^{e}*ereṣ ʾ*^{a}*ḥuzzāṯām.* We have already seen the use of *ʾ*^{a}*ḥuzzâ* in Gen. 12–36 to refer to one's territory, but its occurrence here at the last appearance of Esau in Genesis may be deliberate. The same root was used in the first appearance of Esau in Genesis where the newborn Jacob's hand took hold *(ʾōḥezeṯ)* of Esau's heel (25:26). See Sarna, *Genesis,* p. 253.

This final list in Esau's genealogy names eleven clans descended from Esau. Seven of these names appear for the first time in the chapter (Alva, Jetheth, Elah, Pinon, Mibzar, Magdiel, and Iram). Four of the names have appeared already in the chapter. *Timna* (v. 40) we met earlier as a concubine of Eliphaz (v. 12), and as a sister of Lotan, son of Seir (v. 22). *Oholibamah* (v. 41) was mentioned earlier as the daughter of Anah and wife of Esau (vv. 2, 14, 18). *Kenaz* and *Teman* (v. 42) appeared earlier as sons one and five of Eliphaz (v. 11), and clans one and four of Esau through Eliphaz (v. 15).

The major problem with this eleven name list of the clans of Esau is its relationship, if any, to the fourteen names in vv. 15-19, each of which also represents a clan of Esau. As we have seen, only two names (Teman and Kenaz) are common to vv. 15-19 and 40-43. Three solutions are possible. One, vv. 40-43 are an ad hoc creation without any historical value. Two, the list in vv. 40-43 is a list of later chieftains of Edom than those mentioned in vv. 15-19. Three, the names in vv. 15-19 are genealogically arranged, while those in vv. 40-43 are geographically arranged. Vv. 40-43 do refer to Esau's clans by *families (l^{e}mišp^{e}ḥōṯām)* and by *dwellings (limqōmōṯām).* The *names* that follow *(bišmōṯām)* might refer to the names of the dwellings rather than of the chieftains.[3]

3. A. Malamat ("*UMMATUM* in Old Babylonian Texts and Its Ugaritic and Biblical Counterparts," *UF* 11 [1979] 529, 533) connects the character and structure of 36:40ff. with a tablet from Tell al-Rimah (between the Tigis and the upper Khabur [Habor]) that dates to the first half of the 18th century B.C. It contains a list of artisans who were recruited from various villages and townships for royal service, either administrative or military. Included is their place of origin and their tribal or family affiliation. The general structure is (1) personal name; (2) the Sumerogram SI.LÁ (which Malamat renders "registered" or "supplied with provisions") followed by a toponym; (3) the term *ummatum* together with a personal name. This structure, says Malamat, is exactly what one finds in Gen. 36:40ff., albeit in reverse order.

IV. THE JOSEPH STORY (37:1–50:26)

A. JOSEPH IS SOLD INTO SLAVERY (37:1-36)

1. JOSEPH RUNS AFOUL OF HIS BROTHERS (37:1-11)

1 *Jacob settled in the land in which his father had sojourned, the land of Canaan.*

2 *This is the story of Jacob. Joseph, now seventeen years old, was shepherding*[1] *the flocks with his brothers, an assistant*[2] *with the sons of Bilhah and Zilpah, his father's wives. He maligned*[3] *them to their father.*

3 *Israel loved Joseph more than any of his sons, for he was the child of his advanced age; and that is why he made*[4] *him a long colorful tunic.*

4 *His brothers, observing that him*[5] *their father loved more than any of*

1. *hāyâ* may be used with a participle in an independent clause to express the idea of duration. See Davidson, *Hebrew Syntax,* p. 136, § 100. H. Donner ("Psalm 122" in *Text and Context: Old Testament and Semitic Studies for F. C. Fensham,* ed. W. Claasen, JSOTSup 48 [Sheffield: Sheffield Academic, 1988], p. 82) lists 26 instances in the OT of the arrangement subject plus perfect of *hāyâ* plus participle as complement.

2. It would be possible to translate *w*^{e}*hûʾ naʿar,* "he (was) yet a lad," but passages such as Exod. 33:11 and 1 Sam. 20:35 show that *naʿar* may also mean "assistant, helper."

3. Lit., Joseph brought a "bad report about them." The definite article does not appear on *rāʿâ* because it has predicative force and is not just a descriptive epithet. See G. R. Driver, "A Lost Colloquialism in the Old Testament (1 Samuel 25:6)," *JTS* 8 (1957) 272 n. 2; and Davidson, *Hebrew Syntax,* p. 45, § 32, Rem. 1, who observes that *rāʿâ,* an adjective, is an accusative of condition and functions as a predicate. GKC, § 126z, suggests that the adjective is not determined here because the substantive is determined by a suffix, and so the attribute is less closely attached.

4. There is no need to emend *w*^{e}*ʿāśâ* to *wayyaʿaś* (SP; Westermann, *Genesis,* 3:34) or to *wayya*^{ʿa}*śeh* (cf. Skinner, *Genesis,* p. 444; *BHS*). See GKC, § 112h; Speiser, *Genesis,* p. 289; S. R. Driver, *Treatise on the Use of Tenses,* p. 162 n. 1.

5. The direct object is placed before both verb and subject for special emphasis.

his brothers,[6] *despised him with the result that they could not*[7] *speak to him*[8] *amicably.*

5 *Once Joseph had a dream which he shared with his brothers, and this but added to their hate for him.*[9]

6 *He said to them: "Listen*[10] *to this dream I had:*

7 *There*[11] *we were, binding*[12] *sheaves in the field, when my sheaf*[13] *rose up and stood erect, and then your sheaves surrounded*[14] *and bowed down to my sheaf."*

6. SP, LXX, and some Hebrew mss. read "any of his sons." I see no reason to change MT (contra *BHS;* JB; NAB; Speiser, *Genesis,* p. 290). Note how NIV and NEB (and Westermann) avoid the problem by translating "any of them." The appearance of *'eḥāyw* as the second word of the verse cannot mean that *l*ᵉ*'eḥāyw* is an erroneous dittography instead of *bānāyw.*

7. Targ. Onqelos renders "could not" by "did not wish to" *(wl' ṣbn)* to indicate that the brothers were able to speak to Joseph but chose not to.

8. On the basis of LXX both *BHK* and *BHS* emend, needlessly, *dabb*ᵉ*rô* to *dabbēr lô,* and thus miss the use of the suffix with dative force (see GKC, § 115c; cf. Skinner, *Genesis,* p. 444; Westermann, *Genesis,* 3:37). See M. J. Dahood, "The Dative Suffix in Job 33,13," *Bib* 63 (1982) 258.

9. LXX omits this last clause (i.e., v. 5b), though it retains the identical clause in v. 8b (where it is less intrusive). Cf. Skinner, *Genesis,* p. 445; Westermann, *Genesis,* 3:34; *BHS.*

10. See S. E. Loewenstamm, "The Address 'Listen' in the Ugaritic Epic and the Bible," in *The Bible World,* Fest. C. H. Gordon, ed. G. Rendsburg, et al. (New York: Ktav, 1980), p. 129, who draws attention to the departure from a normal, stylistic rule involving "listen" in v. 5b. Loewenstamm remarks: "In standard style this passage would read: *šm' n' ('ḥy) ḥlwm ḥlmty,* 'Hear (my brothers) a dream I dreamed' and thus lose much of its natural charm."

11. "There," "when," and "then" in this verse are attempts to avoid the insipid "behold" for *hinnēh.* On the different nuances of *w*ᵉ*hinnēh* in this verse, see D. J. McCarthy, "The Uses of *w*ᵉ*hinnēh* in Biblical Hebrew," *Bib* 64 (1980) 335-36.

12. All other occurrences of this root *('lm)* are Niphal and suggest the meaning "to be dumb, silent" (Ps. 31:19; 39:3; Isa. 53:7; Ezek. 3:26; 24:27). Here alone the sense is "to bind," in the Piel. Unlike BDB (pp. 47-48), which detects only one *'ālam* in Biblical Hebrew, *HALAT,* 1:55, distinguishes between *'lm* I ("be dumb, silent") and *'lm* II ("bind"), a denominative verb from *'*ᵃ*lummâ,* "sheaf." In the case of Ezekiel (3:26; 24:27), God renders the prophet dumb/silent by binding his tongue to the roof of his mouth.

13. For possible connections between Joseph's sheaf *('*ᵃ*lummâ)* and the law about the sheaf left behind in the field (*'ōmer,* Deut. 24:19-22), cf. C. M. Carmichael, "The Law of the Forgotten Sheaf," *SBLASP,* 1981, pp. 35-37.

14. *hinnēh* followed by the imperfect is admittedly rare. But Andersen (*Sentence in Biblical Hebrew,* p. 95) is incorrect when he says that this third clause in v. 7 is the only place in the entire OT where *hinnēh* is followed by an imperfect verb. Cf. 1 Sam. 21:15: *hinnēh tir'û.*

8 *His brothers responded to him: "Do you really intend to rule over us,*[15] *to be master over us?"*[16] *All talk about his dream*[17] *but added to their hate for him.*

9 *Then he had another dream that he shared with his brothers:*[18] *"I had another dream. There*[19] *the sun, the moon, and eleven stars were bowing down*[20] *to me."*

10 *When he shared it with his father, in addition to his brothers,*[21] *his father rebuked him. "What is the meaning of this dream of yours?" he asked. "Am I and your mother and your brothers to come and bow to the ground before you?"*

11 *His brothers resented him, but his father pondered the matter.*[22]

1 The Joseph story begins with a fleeting reference to Jacob settling in the land which his late father (see 35:28-29) had claimed as home. For Isaac *Canaan* was a land for sojourning *(gûr).* For Jacob it was a place of settlement *(yāšaḇ).* Perhaps Jacob has seen the last of his many trials and setbacks. Perhaps he is now ready for an eventless retirement in Canaan. If he is thinking that, then he is about to be rudely awakened.

2 Although everything in 37:2b and following is titled as *the story*

15. GKC, § 113q: "The infinitive absolute is used to strengthen a question, and especially in impassioned or indignant questions."

16. In most disjunctive questions, the first clause is introduced by *hᵃ* and the second clause by *'im,* which is parallel to and synonymous with *hᵃ;* thus the brothers' remarks in v. 8 include an instance of synonymous parallelism. See Andersen, *Sentence in Biblical Hebrew,* pp. 38, 147.

17. Although the word is pl. in form *(ḥᵃlōmōṯāyw),* it needs to be read as a sing., since Joseph has related only one dream. Cf. GKC, § 124e (who does not cite this passage); M. Greenberg, *Ezekiel 1–20,* AB (Garden City, NY: Doubleday, 1983), p. 41 (who does refer to this passage).

18. LXX reads "and with his father and his brothers," as in v. 10a.

19. "There" translates *hinnēh* (lit., "behold"), as above in v. 7 (see n. 11 above).

20. Is there any significance in the fact that the activities of the principals in the first dream are conveyed by finite verb forms ("rose up, surrounded, bowed down" ["were binding" is a Piel participle]), while the activities of the principals in dream two are conveyed by a participle ("bowed down")? *hinnēh . . . mᵉ'allᵉmîm* in v. 7 parallels *wᵉhinnēh . . . mištaḥᵃwîm* in v. 9. In both cases the participle is construed verbally.

21. That Joseph has already shared the second dream with his brothers (v. 9) suggests that it may be best to delete v. 10a, with LXX (so Skinner, *Genesis,* p. 445; Speiser, *Genesis,* p. 290). Or perhaps Joseph shares the dream first with his brothers (v. 9), then with his father (v. 10).

22. *šāmar 'eṯ-haddāḇār,* lit., "kept (or guarded) the word." Here *šāmar* may have the nuance of "kept in mind, held in memory," thus overlapping with *zāḵar,* "remember" (cf. the Sabbath commandment in Exod. 20:8, which uses *zāḵar,* and Deut. 5:12, which uses *šāmar*). In the first half of the verse the subject ("his brothers") follows the verb, but in the second half of the verse the subject ("his father") precedes the verb, thus emphasizing the difference between the reactions of the brothers and the father. See Williams, *Hebrew Syntax,* p. 96, § 573.

of Jacob (37:2a), it is obvious that the data is preponderantly about *Joseph.* Bits and pieces appear about Simeon, Judah, and Benjamin, but only as they relate to Joseph. Seventeen years have passed since 30:23-24, the birth and naming of Joseph. No special reference has been made to him from that moment to this, except for the genealogical notice in 35:24. His life has been relatively obscure until this point.

His chore is *shepherding the flocks with his brothers, an assistant with ths sons of Bilhah and Zilpah.* One might understand *brothers* as just the sons of Bilhah and Zilpah, but more likely it includes all his brothers. Neither Bilhah's sons (Dan and Naphtali) nor Zilpah's sons (Gad and Asher) figures prominently in the Joseph story, but they are Joseph's colaborers. The syntax of the Hebrew allows for the translation "Joseph was shepherding his brothers," if *'eṯ* is understood as the sign of the accusative rather than as the preposition "with." So understood, this verse would provide an excellent introduction to the Joseph story in the form of anticipatory paranomasia. What Joseph is doing during his teen life is exactly what he will be doing in his adult life — caring and providing for those who are dependent on him.[23] But in what sense might a younger brother *shepherd* his older half-brothers? In several instances *rā'â 'eṯ* means "to rule over." For example, in 2 Sam. 5:2 (par. 1 Chr. 11:2), "you will shepherd my people Israel," *rā'â 'eṯ* clearly means "rule." The same nuance for *rā'â 'eṯ* appears in 2 Sam. 7:7 (par. 1 Chr. 17:6), "whom I appointed to shepherd my people Israel."[24] Note that later (v. 8) Joseph's brothers wondered aloud if Joseph intended to rule over them *(mālaḵ)* and be master over them *(māšal).*

For some undisclosed reason, Joseph *maligned* his brothers to Jacob. To describe Joseph's malignment of his brothers the narrator uses *dibbâ rā'â.* In Ps. 31:14; Jer. 20:10; and Ezek. 36:3 *dibbâ* is the whispering of hostile people (see also Prov. 10:18; 25:10). The closest parallel to its use in Gen. 37:2 is Num. 13:32; 14:36, 37 to refer to the bad report of the land that the returning spies spread *(yāṣā')* throughout the camp. *dibbāṯām rā'â* of Gen. 37:2 is close to *dibbaṯ hā'āreṣ rā'â* of Num. 14:37.[25]

23. See D. L. Christensen, "Anticipatory Paronomasia in Jonah 3:7-8 and Genesis 37:2," *RB* 90 (1983) 262-63.

24. P. K. McCarter, Jr. (*II Samuel,* AB [Garden City, NY: Doubleday, 1984], p. 132) observes "that only in these two passages is the verb *ra'â* [*sic*], 'shepherd,' used in the sense of 'rule' in Samuel-Kings." For the idiom elsewhere see Ps. 78:72; Jer. 3:15; 23:2, 4; Ezek. 34:2, 3, 8, 10, 23.

25. R. Gordis (*The Word and the Book* [New York: Ktav, 1976], pp. 348-49) suggests that the verb *dāḇaḇ* ("speak") and the noun *dibbâ* (cf. Akk. *dabâbu,* "speak, charge") have a cognate *ṭōb, ṭbb,* which he detects in Hos. 14:3 (*w^eqaḥ ṭôḇ:* "accept our speech"). He supports this view by observing that Targ. Onqelos renders *dibbāṯām* in Gen. 37:2 by *ṭyb',* Pesh. by *ṭ'bhwn.*

3 It is somewhat surprising to find a reference to Joseph as *the child of his* [i.e., Jacob's] *advanced age.*[26] Joseph is but the penultimate son of Jacob. If there is a son of Jacob's advanced age, then it would technically be Benjamin, the last born. Of course, Joseph's birth to Jacob by Rachel is the only instance of a birthing incident involving Rachel that has a happy ending. In Joseph's birth Jacob gained a son. In Benjamin's birth he gained a son but lost a wife.

Jacob's love for Joseph is a doting love. Surely he was aware of the potential for friction in a family where parental favoritism was blatant. He knew personally the schism that results from such tactics. Nevertheless, he proceeds to make clear to all his preferential concern for Joseph.

To that end he engages his tailoring skills (a reflection of Jacob as an *'îš tām,* 25:27?), and makes a special article of clothing for Joseph, *a long colorful tunic.* The Hebrew phrase for this covering is *kᵉṯōneṯ passîm.* There is no problem with the translation of *kᵉṯōneṯ;* the use of "coat" or "long robe" or *tunic* is quite acceptable, for this word describes a garment worn by a man or by a woman. The problem is encountered with *passîm,* which occurs only here (37:3, 23, 32, with *passîm* preceded by the definite article in vv. 23 and 32), and in 2 Sam. 13:18, 19 (the only other instance of the phrase *kᵉṯōneṯ [hap]passîm*).

The source of AV "coat of many colors" is LXX *chitṓna poikílon,* "a multicolored frock," and Vulg. *tunicam polymitam.* The source behind RSV "a long robe with sleeves" is Aquila's rendering of *passîm* by *astrágalōn,* "(a frock) reaching to the ankles)."

Support for this second reading may be found in two areas. One way is to connect *passîm* with postbiblical *pas,* which means the "flat of the hand" (i.e., the palm) and "the flat of the foot" (i.e., the sole). *pas* as "palm" appears in the Aramaic of Daniel (Dan. 5:5, 24). Thus a *kᵉṯōneṯ passîm* would be a covering extending to the palms and soles. Furthermore, 2 Sam. 13:18 (LXX) renders *kᵉṯōneṯ passîm* as *chitṓn karpōtós,* "a frock with sleeves extending to the wrists."

Another attempt has been made to connect Heb. *passîm* with *'epes,* "end, extremity," and with *'opsāyim,* "ankles" (cf. Ezek. 47:3). Thus, a *kᵉṯōneṯ passîm* is a garment extending to the extremities of one's body (hands and feet).[27] Support for the equation of *pas* and *'epes* may be found in the place

26. Targ. Onqelos reads "for he was a wise son to him" *(br ḥkym hw' lyh)* instead of "a child of his advanced age." This reading may be due to the fact that those who produced this targum were quite aware that Joseph had a younger brother Benjamin who also was described as *yeleḏ zᵉqunîm* (44:20), and thus they chose another description for the older of the two brothers; or it may be an apologetic attempt by the targumists to defend Jacob against charges of unjustified favoritism. See M. Aberbach and B. Grossfeld, *Targum Onkelos to Genesis* (New York: Ktav, 1982), p. 215 n. 1.

27. See McCarter, *II Samuel,* p. 325.

name Ephes-dammim (1 Sam. 17:1), which is called Pas-dammim in 1 Chr. 11:13.

Those who appeal to cognate languages for elucidation of *passîm* have been less than convincing in their proposals. For example, G. Mendenhall appeals to Ugaritic, and in particular to the Baal-Yamm conflict in which Yamm's messengers say to the assembled pantheon:

> Deliver, O gods, the one whom you obey,
> whom the multitudes obey;
> Deliver Baʿal and his *ʿanan,*
> The son of Dagon, I shall succeed to his *paz* [or *pa<u>d</u>*].[28]

Scholars have translated the last two lines quite differently: (1) "Give up Baal [and his *partisans*]; Dagon's Son, so that I may inherit his *gold*";[29] (2) "Give Baal [to me *to lord over*], Dagon's son whose *spoil* I'll possess";[30] (3) "Give up Baal [and his *lackeys*], the son of Dagon that I may possess his *gold.*"[31]

Mendenhall avoids either "gold" or "spoil" for *pa<u>d</u>,* and prefers to connect it with Akk. *melammū* and *puluḫtu,* that glory surrounding the deity which provokes fear or awe. For Mendenhall, then, the robe given to Joseph is to be associated with social or political status. The "dazzling" robe marks Joseph as a superior to his brothers. As appealing as Mendenhall's suggestion is, it falls principally on the ground that the equation of Heb. *pas* with Ugar. *pa<u>d</u>* is most unlikely due to the lack of correspondence between Heb. *s* and Ugar. *<u>d</u>,* to say nothing of the uncertain nature surrounding the actual meaning of *pa<u>d</u>.*

Speiser links *kᵉ<u>t</u>ōne<u>t</u> passîm* with Akk. *kitu pišannu,* a ceremonial robe draped about statues of goddesses and studded with gold ornaments.[32] This background may provide some basis for the translation "coat of many colors." Also possibly related is Phoenician *ps,* "tablet, piece," suggesting a garment made of pieces of material sewn together. Finally, we note the possible connection with Akk. *paspasu,* "brightly colored bird."

28. G. Mendenhall, *The Tenth Generation* (Baltimore: Johns Hopkins University, 1973), pp. 54-55, referring to *UT,* 137:18-19, 34-35. The Ugaritic consonant *<u>d</u>* (which Mendenhall transliterates as *z*) is equivalent to Hebrew *z,* not *s.*

29. See C. H. Gordon, *Ugarit and Minoan Crete* (New York: Norton, 1966), p. 44.

30. See H. L. Ginsberg, *ANET,* p. 130.

31. See J. C. L. Gibson, *Canaanite Myths and Legends,* rev. ed. (Edinburgh: T. & T. Clark, 1978), p. 41.

32. See Speiser, *Genesis,* p. 290. See A. L. Oppenheim, "The Golden Garments of the Gods," *JNES* 8 (1949) 172-93 ("*pišannu* was reserved — in the Neo-Babylonian period — exclusively for the clothing of images. It is often made of linen, but dyed wool . . . is used for its decoration," p. 179).

Ancient Mediterranean art provides us with ample illustrations of richly colored clothing. One thinks of the clay figures from Ur, some of which were "human figures clad in a garment composed of a pointed hat and a long robe painted with scales."[33] The Beni-hasan tomb painting (ca. 1800 B.C.) picturing thirty-seven Semites, all dressed in bright, colorful garments, on their way to Egypt is worthy of consideration here.[34]

A mural fresco from the palace of Zimri-Lim at Mari (ca. 18th century B.C.) reveals a garment made of small rectangular panels of multicolored cloth sewn together into a wide strip and wound around the body like a sari. The next distinctive men's garment style after this was a sari-like robe edged with fur (16th-15th century B.C.).[35] The parallel between the Mari garment and Joseph's *k^e^ṯōneṯ passîm* argues, indirectly at least, for an early date for the Joseph story.

4 The brothers' resentment is traditionally understood as directed against Joseph. But why take out their wrath on him? He had not placed an order for the garment. In no way had he been solicitous of his father's time and gifts. Hebrew syntax would allow for the possibility that the *him* the brothers despised and with whom they could not speak peaceably could be Jacob their father. His doting over Joseph was as offensive to them as was his gift to Joseph of the robe. It is not unknown for Jacob's sons to speak rather harshly to their father when they disagree with him (see 34:31).

So far in the narrative, everything that Joseph has done (v. 2) and what he has received (v. 3) serve only to alienate him from his brothers. His sharing of his dreams will broaden the chasm between brother and brothers. As Sternberg remarks, "God's future agent and mouthpiece in Egypt could hardly make a worse impression on his first appearance: spoiled brat, talebearer, braggart."[36]

5-8 Joseph has a dream that he feels compelled to share with his brothers. The brothers were annoyed both by his compulsion to share the dream (v. 5b) and by its contents (v. 8b). Joseph is a blabbermouth, and a megalomaniac to boot, so conclude his brothers. Thus the narrator records the brothers' contempt for Joseph not only after (v. 8) but also before (v. 5) he narrates the dream (vv. 6b, 7). The use of the verbal form *wayyôsip̱û* for *added*

33. H. W. F. Saggs, *The Greatness that was Babylon* (London: Sidgwick and Sidgwick, 1962), p. 314; E. C. B. MacLaurin, "Joseph and Asaph," *VT* 25 (1975) 33-34.

34. For a black-and-white reproduction see *ANEP,* no. 3; for a color reproduction see Y. Yadin, *The Art of Warfare in Biblical Lands,* tr. M. Pearlman, 2 vols. (New York: McGraw-Hill, 1963), 1:166-67; J. D. Douglas, et al., eds., *Illustrated Bible Dictionary,* 3 vols. (Wheaton: InterVarsity, 1980), 1:421.

35. See W. F. Albright, "From the Patriarchs to Moses: I. From Abraham to Joseph," *BA* 36 (1973) 31-32.

36. Sternberg, *Poetics of Biblical Narrative,* p. 98.

in the clause "but added to their hate for him" in vv. 5 and 8 is a play on the name Joseph *(yôsēp̱)*.

He invites his brothers to *Listen to this dream I had.* As he and his brothers were binding sheaves in a field, his sheaf *stood erect,*[37] and the sheaves of his brothers genuflected before his sheaf. Joseph makes no attempt to interpret, analyze, or apply his dream.[38] He is narrator, not commentator. Perhaps the brother's curt response (v. 8) cut off anything further Joseph might have had to say.

This is the first dream recorded in Genesis in which the voice of God does not speak, thus removing it from the category of a theophany. The absence of any specific divine speech or revelation in the dream accentuates its ambiguity. Is the dream an exhibition of hubris or is it a prophecy? Heretofore the dream has been the medium for a divine announcement, be it to an outsider (20:3; 31:24), or to one within the chosen family (28:12; 31:11). At this point the dream of the baker and cupbearer of Pharaoh (ch. 40) and the two dreams of Pharaoh (ch. 41) resemble those of Joseph, rather than those of Jacob, Abimelech, or Laban.

The text is silent on the issue of Joseph's motivation in sharing this dream. If it is told out of arrogance, Gen. 37 does not bother to make that point. The brothers are upset with Joseph, but the narrator is not. More than likely, the dream, and its recounting, is to be understood as an unsuspecting prophecy uttered by Joseph. God has a plan for his life, a destiny in his future, and Joseph spontaneously shares the enthusiasm that revelation spawns. How little could he know at this point in his life the exactness with which the particulars of that dream would be fulfilled among his family. A sheaf is something to eat, or something from which food is processed. Food, or the lack of it, will play a large part later in the Joseph narrative.

The brothers have no doubt about the meaning of Joseph's dream. At some future point they will become Joseph's subordinates and subjects, and he their superior. They express their disgust through the use of the verbs *mālaḵ* and *māšal.*[39] I am inclined to see these two verbs as essentially synonymous;

37. The same verb is used to describe the stairway set in the ground (*muṣṣāḇ,* 28:12) that Jacob saw in his dream, as well as Yahweh standing (*niṣṣāḇ,* 28:13) beside him.

38. A. L. Oppenheim (*The Interpretation of Dreams in the Ancient Near East* [Philadelphia: American Philosophical Society, 1956], p. 206) draws attention to symbolic dreams in which interpretations can be dispensed with, for they are self-explanatory. Cf. also J. S. Cooper's comments on the dream of Sargon in "Sargon and Joseph: Dreams Come True," in *Biblical and Related Studies Presented to Samuel Iwry,* ed. A. Kort and S. Morschauser (Winona Lake, IN: Eisenbrauns, 1985), p. 35.

39. *māšal bᵉ* was used in 3:16 to describe one person ruling over another. On whether the brothers' questions may be understood as a conscious allusion to the historical preeminence of the house of Joseph in the northern kingdom of Israel, see D. B. Redford, *A Study of the Biblical Story of Joseph,* VTSup 20 (Leiden: Brill, 1970), p. 71 n. 2.

but Ibn Ezra, the medieval Jewish commentator, was the first to suggest that *mālaḵ* refers to appointed kingship, while *māšal* refers to the usurpation of power by a tyrant.

9-11 At some later point Joseph has a second dream and manages to exacerbate the situation by telling this one to his brothers, too. The *sun* and *moon* (i.e., his parents) and *eleven stars* (i.e., his brothers) *were bowing down* before him. This verse indicates that Benjamin is born by this time, for there are twelve brothers involved, and therefore the dream cannot have occurred before 35:18.

It is surprising that Jacob would retort with *Am I and your mother . . . to come and bow to the ground before you?* Joseph's mother Rachel has been dead since 35:19. To some this reference indicates that Gen. 37 may be from a tradition different from that of ch. 35, one that is unaware of Rachel's demise.[40] Or, more likely, with the passing of Rachel, Leah has become the stepmother of Benjamin and Joseph.[41]

Jacob has already bowed before his brother (33:3). Must he now bow before his son as well? Jacob's maidservants and children have bowed before Esau (33:6). Must they now bow before their brother?

Jacob censures his son for his impertinence. He is not only rebuking his son in a moral sense, however; he is also unleashing an angry protest. Both ideas are conveyed by the verb used in v. 10a *(gāʿar)*.[42] Jacob rebukes his son, but he does not "hate" Joseph as did his other sons. On the contrary, something bids him exercise restraint. There may be more in this dream than he can perceive at the moment. As with Mary, who, when she was confronted with a situation half-plausible and half-incredulous, pondered it in her heart (Luke 2:19, 51),[43]

40. See, e.g., von Rad, *Genesis,* p. 352.

41. See Sarna, *Genesis,* p. 257; and Sternberg, *Poetics of Biblical Narrative,* p. 292, who notes that both of Joseph's dreams have one participant too many: his mother (the moon) Rachel in the first, and Benjamin in the second, for only ten brothers, not eleven, came to buy grain from Joseph.

42. See A. A. Macintosh, "A consideration of Hebrew *gʿr,*" *VT* 19 (1969) 471-79, esp. p. 474. R. E. Longacre (*Joseph: A Study of Divine Providence: A Text Theoretical and Textlinguistic Analysis of Genesis 37 and 39–48* [Winona Lake, IN: Eisenbrauns, 1989], p. 71) states that in the Joseph story a common pattern with verbs of speech and sensation is to start with a specific verb that is followed by a form of the verb *ʾāmar.* Gen. 37:10 is the first: *wayyigʿar . . . wayyōʾmer. wayyōʾmer* identifies the speech act as one of rebuke. See also 37:9, 21, 33; 39:8; 40:9, 18; 43:19-20, 27.

43. Luke 2:19: *pánta synetḗrei tá rhḗmata,* "she preserved all these words/things,"; Luke 2:51: *dietḗrei pánta tá rhḗmata,* "she carefully kept all these words/things"; Gen. 37:11 (LXX): *ho dé patḗr autoú dietḗrēsen tó rhḗma.* The verb used in Gen. 37:11 LXX is the same as that in Luke 2:51. For a slightly different interpretation of Jacob's response, see A. Berlin, *Poetics and Interpretation of Biblical Narrative* (Sheffield: Almond, 1983), pp. 48-49.

so too Jacob will not jump to conclusions but will give the matter more serious reflection. Jacob's contrast in mood with his sons is reflected in the chiastic structure of v. 11 (verb-subject [sons]::subject [father]-verb).

No less than three reasons have surfaced for the anger of Joseph's brothers against him: (1) his maligning some of them (v. 2); (2) the obvious favoritism lavished on him by his father (vv. 3-4); (3) his insistence on sharing his seemingly pompous dreams (vv. 5-12). These three actions do not necessarily indicate three different traditions behind the Joseph story, each of which had its own explanation of the origin of hostility between brothers and brother. Rather, the three instances illustrate the escalation of the deeply entrenched animosity against Joseph. From the beginning there is no love lost between Isaac and Ishmael. That fraternal acrimony continues to the Jacob-Esau relationship and is perpetuated in Joseph's alienation from his brothers.

2. JOSEPH GOES IN SEARCH OF HIS BROTHERS (37:12-17)

12 *Once, when his brothers had gone to pasture their father's flock*[1] *at Shechem,*

13 *Israel said to Joseph: "Your brothers, you are aware,*[2] *are pasturing (the flocks) at Shechem. Come, let me send you to them." "I am ready to go,"*[3] *answered Joseph.*

14 *"Go then," he continued, "and see how well your brothers and the flocks are doing, then report back to me." With that he sent him off from the valley of Hebron and he headed for Shechem.*

1. The dots over *'et* provide another illustration in Genesis of what is know as "extraordinary points" in the apparatus of the Masorah (see 16:5; 18:9; 19:33; 33:4). The oldest list of these passages with extraordinary points is in the Sifre (a halakhic midrash to Numbers and Deuteronomy, compiled near the end of the 4th century A.D.) on Num. 9:10. It places dots over "their father's flocks," suggesting that these words are not original. Thus the passage read: "his brothers had gone to feed (themselves)," and this reading dovetails with v. 13: "your brothers . . . are pasturing/feeding." Later authorities, wanting to restrict as much as possible the indication of spurious words in the Bible, placed dots only over the sign of the accusative. Cf. C. D. Ginsburg, *Introduction to the Massoretico-Critical Edition of the Hebrew Bible* (repr. New York: Ktav, 1966), pp. 318-34, esp. pp. 325-26.

2. Translating *hᵃlō'* with declarative force, rather than with interrogative force. Davidson (*Hebrew Syntax,* p. 167, § 123, Rem. 2) cites 37:13, where *hᵃlō'* implies an affirmative response and here equals *hinnēh.*

3. The literal "here I am" *(hinnēnî)* is banal. I prefer "I am ready," with Westermann, *Genesis,* 3:33; and Speiser, *Genesis, p. 288.*

15 *A man chanced upon him*[4] *as he was wandering about in the fields, and the man asked him: "What are you looking for?"*[5]

16 *"My brothers I am looking for,"*[6] *he replied. "Could you tell me where they are pasturing?"*

17 *The man said: "They left this place; in fact I heard them say,*[7] *'Let us go on to Dothan.' "*[8] *So Joseph pursued his brothers and overtook*[9] *them in Dothan.*

This unit contains a number of problems. First, Jacob sends Joseph to inquire about how well *(r^{e}'ēh 'eṯ-š^{e}lôm)* his brothers and the flocks are getting along. But we know from an earlier reference that his brothers are not even able to speak amicably with him (*w^{e}lō' yāḵ^{e}lû dabb^{e}rô l^{e}šālōm,* v. 4). Why would Jacob, if he is aware of his sons' hatred for Joseph, send Joseph to visit his brothers? He would surely know what his sons would do to Joseph if, in their father's absence, they got their hands on him. One must conclude that Jacob is unaware of the simmering rage of the brothers toward Joseph, that the brothers have not in any way, either through language or conduct, conveyed to their father the rancor they feel toward Joseph.

Second, why send Joseph to Shechem where Jacob, and especially his family because of the Dinah incident, have become persona non grata? (Cf. Gen. 34.) Have bygones become bygones? Are Shechemites and Jacobites now able to live together and work together peaceably? Perhaps the reason Jacob dispatches Joseph to inquire about the welfare of his sons and flocks in Shechem is his recall of the incident there involving his daughter, two of

4. Lit., "found him." Speiser's rendering is "came upon him."

5. On the word pair *bāqaš/māṣā',* used here in vv. 15-17, cf. M. V. Fox and B. Porten, "Unsought Discoveries: Qoheleth 7:23–8:1a," *HS* 19 (1978) 26-38.

6. The order object-subject-verb is usual in nominal sentences with participial predicate. See Davidson, *Hebrew Syntax,* p. 156, § 111, Rem. 1.

7. G. R. Driver ("Ezekiel: Linguistic and Textual Problems," *Bib* 35 [1954] 303) supplies instances of *'ōm^{e}rîm* as the pl. participle used indefinitely. It is LXX, SP, and the Palestinian Targ. that supply the pronominal suffix as the antecedent for the participle by reading *š^{e}ma'tîm* for MT *šāma'tî.* Driver's understanding of the participle allows the MT to stand as is. A parallel use of the same participle may be found in Ezek. 8:12: "Do you see, son of man, what the elders of the house of Israel are doing into the dark . . . for they say [*'ōm^{e}rîm*], 'Yahweh does not see us.' "

8. Note the two spellings of "Dothan" — *dōṯāyn* and *dōṯān.* The second spelling may illustrate the older orthography for the *ay* diphthong in which the *yodh* was unexpressed. See R. Gordis, *The Biblical Text in the Making: A Study of the Kethibh-Qere* (Philadelphia: Dropsie College, 1937), p. 100; idem, *Koheleth: The Man and His World,* 3rd ed. (New York: Schocken, 1968), p. 239.

9. Lit., "and found them in Dothan." Speiser (*Genesis,* p. 288) renders "caught up with them."

his sons, Shechem, and Shechem's townsmen. The brothers *are pasturing* (*lirʿôṯ,* v. 12; *rōʿîm,* vv. 13, 16) at Shechem. In a few texts *rāʿâ* takes on a sexual nuance (Cant. 2:16; 6:2, 3). Should we see any relationship between the brothers of Joseph pasturing in Shechem and the earlier incident in Gen. 34 in which Shechem "pastured" among Jacob's "garden"? It is unlikely that Joseph's question in v. 16c as to the whereabouts of his shepherding brothers is, as often suggested, a parallel to the question of the beloved about or to her lover: "Tell me, my true love, where do you pasture?" (Cant. 1:7). In the case of Joseph, it is clear why he should raise this question. In Canticles, by contrast, it is not at all clear why the beloved asks this question.

The third and most perplexing issue here is how one is to account for the distance from home the sons are pasturing their father's flock, and the distance Joseph needs to travel to meet them. Joseph leaves from the valley of Hebron (v. 14), travels north to Shechem (v. 15), approximately 50 miles, and beyond Shechem to Dothan (v. 17) approximately 13 more miles. The distance from Hebron to Dothan is then about 65 miles. This is no little excursion to the next pastureland on which Jacob sends Joseph.

Attempts to make sense of these geographical sites have gone in several directions. One suggestion is to emend the text, arbitrarily we may add, from *ʿēmeq ḥeḇrôn* to *ʿēmeq rᵉḥāḇōn,* a site probably to be associated with Tell es-Sarim in the valley of Bethshan.[10] A journey from Bethshan to Dothan would be considerably shorter and much more logical. Another suggestion is to explain the extensive journey as due to the collation of two traditions of the Joseph story. Thus, to the literary critics it is the northern Elohist who features these northern localities in contrast to the southern shrines favored by the Yahwist.[11] The juxtapositioning of a southern site by a northern one would parallel Judah's invovlement in this story (vv. 25-27, J) with Reuben's involvement (vv. 21-24, E), providing another illustration of J/E elements in ch. 37.

As the text stands, Jacob's sons must be removed some distance from their father. Otherwise, Jacob sending Joseph to inquire about the welfare of his sons and flocks would make no sense. If the sons are close enough to home to return nightly or regularly, Joseph's mission would have been unnecessary.

Archaéology has confirmed that both of these Canaanite towns — *Shechem and Dothan* — were occupied in the time of Joseph (i.e., the Middle Bronze Age).[12] This evidence lends plausibility to the geographical referents

10. See H. Seebass, "Der israelitische Name der Bucht von *Bēsān* und der Name Beth Schean," *ZDPV* 95 (1979) 166-72.

11. See R. North, "Can Geography Save J from Rendtorff?" *Bib* 63 (1982) 48.

12. On Shechem, see G. E. Wright, *Shechem: Biography of a Biblical City* (New York: McGraw-Hill, 1965). On Dothan, see J. L. Free, "The Excavation of Dothan," *BA* 19 (1956) 43-48.

of the Joseph story. Apart from Gen. 37:17 the only other OT reference to Dothan is in 2 K. 6:13.

An unidentified man discovers the wandering Joseph and redirects him from Shechem to Dothan (vv. 15-17). Whoever he is, he is introduced first only as *a man* (*'îš*, v. 15a), but afterward is twice referred to as *the man* (*hā'îš*, vv. 15b, 17a). By contrast, Joseph is identified only with the pronominal suffix *him* (in "chanced upon him" and "asked him").[13] The chance encounter with this anonymous man provides a transition from Joseph's association with his father to Joseph's association with his brothers, from an environment of love, acceptance, and maybe even doting, to one of hostility and rejection.[14] Joseph has this man to thank, or curse, for pointing him toward Dothan.

3. THE BROTHERS CONSPIRE TO KILL JOSEPH (37:18-24)

18 *They saw him some distance off; and before he reached them they conspired[1] to put him to death.*

19 *"Here comes that master dreamer,"[2] they said to each other.*

20 *"Come on, let us kill him and throw him[3] into one of the cisterns. We can say that a wild beast devoured him. We shall see then what is to become[4] of his dreams."*

13. See Longacre, *Joseph*, pp. 152, 156-57, who suggests that when the narrator of the Joseph story desires to represent someone in a position where he is dominated by somebody else, he does so by using pronominal suffixes attached to the verb as objects.

14. See W. L. Humphreys, *Joseph and His Family: A Literary Study* (Columbia, S.C.: University of South Carolina, 1988), p. 103.

1. *nāḵal* is used sparingly in the OT: Num. 25:18 (Piel); Ps. 105:25 (Hithpael, as in Gen. 37:18); Mal. 1:14 (Qal). The Hebrew root is to be connected with Akk. *nakālu*, "be crafty, cunning." RSV translates the Hithpael of *nāḵal* in Ps. 105:25 as "to deal craftily with," and finds the root also in Prov. 13:15, "the intelligence of a good man breeds charm, but the conduct of the faithless, craftiness" (*nēḵel* for MT *'êṯān kol*). BDB, p. 647, translates the Hithpael in Gen. 37:18 as "they knavishly planned." For a verb in the Hithpael (a reflexive conjugation) taking an accusative, see GKC, § 117w; Davidson, *Hebrew Syntax*, p. 106, § 73f, Rem. 4. Targ. Onqelos softens the expression, which reflects on the brothers' harshness, by reading "they thought about him" (*wḥšybw 'lwhy*).

2. *baʿal haḥᵃlōmōṯ hallāzeh* illustrates the genitive of attribute or quality common with some nouns such as *'îš/'iššâ, ben/baṯ,* and *baʿal*. See illustrations listed by GKC, § 128s, u; Davidson, *Hebrew Syntax*, p. 33, § 24d, Rem. 3. Westermann (*Genesis*, 3:33) renders "this dream-addict." Another possibility would be "this dream-lord."

3. On conjoined cohortative clauses that are serial, see Andersen, *Sentence in Biblical Hebrew*, p. 111.

4. For *mah-* followed by the imperfect of *hāyâ*, "what is to become of . . .," see Ezek. 15:2, and M. Greenberg, *Ezekiel 1–20*, AB (Garden City, NY: Doubleday, 1983), p. 264; also R. Gordis, *The Word and the Book* (New York: Ktav, 1976), p. 257.

21 *When Reuben*[5] *overheard this, he tried to snatch*[6] *him from their hands. Said he: "We must not take his life."*[7]

22 *Reuben added:*[8] *"Do not shed blood.*[9] *Rather, throw him into this cistern in the wilderness, but do not harm him"*[10] *— he intended to snatch him*[11] *from their clutches and to restore him to his father.*

23 *So when Joseph reached*[12] *his brothers, they stripped Joseph of his coat,*[13] *the long, colorful tunic which he was wearing,*

5. Speiser (*Genesis,* p. 291) effectively refutes the necessity of reading "Judah" instead of "Reuben" in v. 21a, as advocated by *BHS.* First, the reading "Judah" is totally arbitrary in v. 21, and without support from the ancient versions. Second, the alleged duplication in v. 22 of v. 21 disappears when the imperfect verb *(wayyaṣṣilēhû)* is read as carrying a conative sense (see n. 6 below).

6. The verb may justifiably be read as a conative: "he tried to snatch him." Indeed, such a rendering provides a more satisfactory smoothness between v. 21 and v. 22. For this reading of the imperfect, see P. P. Saydon, "The Conative Imperfect in Hebrew," *VT* 12 (1962) 125.

7. Lit., "Let us not smite him as to life." *nep̱eš,* in this instance the second object, is an accusative of specification. Cf. GKC, § 117l̄l; Davidson, *Hebrew Syntax,* p. 100, § 71; Williams, *Hebrew Syntax,* p. 12, § 57, who reads "let us not wound him mortally."

8. Lit., "And Reuben said to them," *wayyō'mer 'elēhem rᵉ'ûḇēn.* Cf. NJPS "And Reuben went on. . . ." The LXX deletes the first three words of the MT, but this is not necessary. When two or more *wayyō'mer*s ("and he said") follow each other, it may indicate that the speaker is "scrutinizing the effect of his words before he continues." See E. I. Lowenthal, *The Joseph Narrative in Genesis* (New York: Ktav, 1973), p. 25.

9. J. Bright ("The Apodictic Prohibition: Some Observations," *JBL* 92 [1973] 187) differentiates between the *'al* prohibitive (as in Gen. 37:22) and the *lō'* prohibitive as follows: "Whereas the *'al* prohibitive expresses a specific command for a specific occasion, the *lō'* prohibitive expresses a categorical prohibition of binding validity both for the present and the future." In the Pentateuch, the *lō'* prohibitive is always in the mouth of God or Moses, except for two times with Isaac (Gen. 28:1, 6), and four times with Pharaoh (Exod. 5:7, 8, 9; 8:24 [Eng. 28]).

10. For *šālaḥ yaḏ bᵉ* (lit., "stretch out a hand to") in the sense "to harm, to smite," see the Aramaic Sefire treaty, I B, lines 24-25, 34; II B, line 6; cf. H. Tawil, "Two Notes on the Treaty Terminology of the Sefire Inscriptions," *CBQ* 42 (1980) 33; P. Humbert, "Entendre la main," *VT* 12 (1962) 383-95; J. A. Fitzmyer, *The Aramaic Inscriptions of Sefîre,* BibOr 19 (Rome: Pontifical Biblical Institute, 1967), p. 66. The idiom occurs 21 times in the OT (references in Humbert, p. 386), of which Gen. 37:22 is the first, and the only one in Genesis. In 22:12 the idiom is *šālaḵ yāḏ 'el.*

11. For *lᵉma'an* with infinitive to express purpose, see Williams, *Hebrew Syntax,* p. 61, § 367; p. 86, § 520.

12. *ka'ᵃšer bā'* is an illustration of the infinitive construct with preposition having the meaning of a finite verb.

13. There is no need to delete "of his coat" with the LXX. For the presence of a double accusative after a verb, see GKC, § 117cc; and M. Ben-Asher, "Causative *Hip̱'il* Verbs with Double Objects in Biblical Hebrew," *HAR* 2 (1978) 11-19, esp. pp. 12-13.

24 *and seizing him, they threw him into the cistern, which was empty and without water.*[14]

18 The brothers lose no time in venting their feelings against Joseph. Away from the safety of home, he is fair game for their animosity. They are not expecting Joseph, but when he appears on the horizon, they quickly conspire to kill him. The unique coat he is wearing allows them to spot him some distance off. The following verses (vv. 19-22) relate the details of the brothers' plan to kill him (and Reuben's plan to circumvent that killing).

19-20 I translate *baʿal haḥᵃlōmôṯ* (lit., "master of dreams") as *master dreamer* to indicate that in the mouths of his brothers such a designation is blatantly sarcastic. Heb. *baʿal* need not contain such a nuance; it may be simply a noun of relation.[15] The whole expression would then be equivalent to "dreamer." I feel, however, that to translate the expression simply as "dreamer" misses the irony of the brothers' phrase. Heaped on Joseph as a scornful phrase, the expression will later be an appropriate title for Joseph (chs. 40 and 41), who will emerge as master and interpreter of the dreams of others. Note von Rad's understanding of this phrase along the same lines: "the one empowered to prophetic dreams."[16]

Their original plan is to throw Joseph's corpse into one of the cisterns near Dothan. Perhaps the translation *throw* for *šālaḵ* in vv. 20, 22, 24 is inaccurate. The brothers will not "toss" Joseph into a cistern. When used with a person as its object, *šālaḵ* almost always refers to the placing of a dead body in a grave (e.g., 2 Sam. 18:17; 2 K. 13:21; Jer. 41:9) or to the placing of a living body into what is assumed will be its grave (e.g., Gen. 21:15; 37:24; Jer. 38:6).[17] But note that, with the possible exception of Gen. 21:15 and 2 K. 13:21, all these verses refer to the hurried and careless placement of individuals (e.g., Absalom, 2 Sam. 18:17; Jeremiah, Jer. 38:6) who are held in contempt by those who place them.

The brothers are infuriated not only by Joseph's tattling on some of them to their father (v. 2b), nor only by his possession of a special garment (v. 4), but especially by his grandiose dreams (vv. 7, 9; cf. vv. 19, 20). They identify Joseph not as a favorite of their father, nor as a bearer of tales, but as a "master dreamer." It is his dreams that their plan will sabotage.

The explanation they devise to cover their own crime — and Jacob will certainly ask about Joseph — is that *a wild beast devoured him.* The

14. On the use of the redundant repetition of the same concept by means of the negation of an antonym, see Andersen, *Sentence in Biblical Hebrew,* p. 43. The dryness of the well is thus doubly emphasized.

15. See n. 2 above.

16. Von Rad, *Genesis* p. 353.

17. See H. C. White, "The Initiation Legend of Ishmael," *ZAW* 87 (1975) 287.

Hebrew for *wild beast* is *ḥayyâ rāʿâ* (lit., "evil beast"). In v. 2b we read that Joseph brought tales *(dibbāṯām rāʿâ)* to his father about several of his brothers. Thus *rāʿâ* occurs twice in this chapter; first Joseph is the author or source of the *rāʿâ,* then he is the victim of the *rāʿâ.* Joseph, himself despicable as far as his brothers are concerned, will meet a rapacious beast, at least in the story the brothers will hatch. Joseph, who dreamed of himself "standing" before his prostrated brothers (*qûm,* v. 7), is now to be thrown (or lowered, *šālaḵ*) by his brothers into his grave.

21-22 For reasons unclear to us, *Reuben* comes to Joseph's defense with an alternate plan. He urges that Joseph not be killed, but that he be thrown into one of the cisterns alive. There Joseph will die of starvation or exposure (or at least that is what Reuben wants his brothers to believe). This stratagem will help Reuben to gain some time and eventually be able to implement his plan. Perhaps it will also help salve the conscience of the brothers. They did not kill their young brother; they merely placed him in a *cistern.* Cisterns were shaped like a bottle, with a small opening in the top, and often covered with a stone. They were hewn deep in the rock, and the narrow vertical shaft near the top was for letting down pitchers. In most cases they would be waterproofed with plaster made from burnt and slaked lime.[18] Joseph's chances of escaping from a cistern are minimal. Nonetheless, the brothers will be innocent of outright murder and of shedding blood. History's first perpetrator of fratricide had to listen to the blood of his fallen brother crying from the ground (4:10). They do not want to have to listen to the blood of their brother crying from the ground, or so Reuben insinuates with his counterproposal.

Reuben plans to return to the cistern clandestinely after the brothers have left. He will lift Joseph out of his confinement and return him to Jacob. But what would the brothers do with Reuben? If he foils their plan and thwarts their malice, will they not despise him as much as they do Joseph? Will he too become a target for revenge? Reuben is willing to take such a risk.

We know that Reuben has been out of favor with his father ever since the scandalous affair with Bilhah (35:22). Is Reuben's magnanimity to Joseph an attempt to rebuild some broken communication with his father? That he is Joseph's savior should pave the way for reconciliation with Jacob. It is more likely that he is here exercising the role of the oldest brother, the one who is most answerable to his father for the well-being of his beloved Joseph.

In the OT *šālaḥ yaḏ bᵉ* often means to harm someone physically. Cf. David's repeated commitment that he will not "harm" Yahweh's anointed (1 Sam. 24:7 [Eng. 6]; 26:23; 2 Sam. 1:14 [with *lᵉ* instead of *bᵉ*]). In several places the idiom *šālaḥ yaḏ* (with various prepositions following) means just the

18. See R. W. Hamilton, "Water-works," *IDB,* 4:813; A. C. Dickie and D. W. Harvey, "Cistern," *ISBE,* 1:702-4.

opposite of "harm," that is, the thrust is "to protect" by extending the hand. Comparable is the Akk. *qāta tarāṣu,* "to stretch out the hand, to protect."[19] In the OT see Ps. 138:7 (with *ʿal*); 18:17 (Eng. 16); 144:7 (both with *min*). Perhaps Reuben is encouraging his brothers not to stretch out their hand against Joseph (i.e., harm him), so that he may stretch out his hand to Joseph (i.e., deliver him).

Reuben may attempt to modify the brothers' plan to get rid of Joseph in one other way. Not only does he advise against killing Joseph and placing his body in somebody's domestic cistern somewhere in Dothan, but he urges that Joseph be placed alive in a cistern *in the wilderness* (v. 22). By *wilderness* Reuben is referring to the largely unpopulated pasturelands that would ring the perimeter of Dothan. On the one hand, this locale may appeal to the brothers in that any calls for help by Joseph would go unheeded. On the other hand, perhaps Reuben can successfully retrieve Joseph from a cistern that is far enough away from the watchful eyes of his brothers.

23-24 Joseph is roughly handled by his brothers. He is stripped[20] of his coat, thus increasing the chances of death by exposure, and he is cast into a dried-up cistern, thus increasing the chances of death by thirst. The deep, dark, vacuous atmosphere into which Joseph is plunged is intensified by the parallel phrases describing the well: *empty and without water.* The first term, *rēq,* would have been sufficient. The second expression, *ʾên bô māyim,* is redundant but adds to the chilling effect.

Joseph's cistern may provide an early parallel for the famine that wipes out Canaan later in the Joseph story. The *habbôr rēq* ("the empty well") anticipates the "seven empty ears" (*šeḇaʿ haššibbᵒlîm hārēqôṯ,* 41:27) which represent the seven famine years. And what Reuben desires to be to Joseph, Joseph will be to his brothers.

4. JOSEPH IS SOLD TO EGYPT-BOUND TRADERS (37:25-30)

25 *While they were sitting down, eating their meal, they lifted up their eyes and looked: and there was*[1] *a caravan of Ishmaelites coming from*

19. See H. Tawil, "Some Literary Elements in the Opening Sections of the Hadad, Zakir . . . Inscriptions," *Or* 43 (1974) 44.

20. In priestly texts, *pāšaṭ* (Hiphil) is used of the skinning or flaying of a sacrifice (e.g., Lev. 1:6). Its figurative use, i.e., "stripping/removing (clothes)," is found here and in Num. 20:26, 28.

1. For a *wᵉhinnēh* clause after the verb *rāʾâ* to report a surprised development to one of the participants in an event, see Andersen, *Sentence in Biblical Hebrew,* pp. 94-95, who cites fifteen uses of this idiom in Genesis. See also A. Niccacci, *The Syntax of the Verb in Classical Hebrew Prose,* tr. W. G. E. Watson, JSOTSup 86 (Sheffield: Sheffield Academic, 1990), pp. 100-101.

Gilead. Their camels were carrying spicery, balm, and myrrh to be taken down[2] *to Egypt.*

26 *Judah said to his brothers: "How would we be ahead*[3] *by killing our brother and covering up*[4] *his blood?*

27 *Come, let us sell him to the Ishmaelites, and thus our own hand would not be upon him.*[5] *After all, he is our brother, our own flesh." His brothers consented.*[6]

28 *When certain Midianite merchants passed by, they*[7] *pulled up*[8] *Joseph from the cistern, and sold Joseph to the Ishmaelites for twenty pieces of silver,*[9] *and they brought Joseph to Egypt.*

29 *Reuben returned to the cistern, and Joseph was not there!*[10] *He tore his clothes,*

2. Lit., "going in order to bring down (to)," *hōlᵉḵîm lᵉhôrîḏ*.

3. The range in meaning of Heb. *beṣaʿ* includes "bribe" (Exod. 18:21), "legitimate gain" (Job 22:3; Mal. 3:14), "unjust gain" (Judg. 5:19; Mic. 4:13), "profit" (with a selfish suggestion), here and in Mal. 3:14, and respectively rendered by the LXX as *ti chrḗsimon* and *ti pléon* (R. Bergmeier, "Das Streben nach Gewinn — des Volkes *ʿāwôn*," *ZAW* 81 [1969] 95). The verb *bāṣaʿ* means "to cut off"; hence, the noun means lit. "a portion, something cut off."

4. In *nahᵃrōg . . . wᵉkissînû* the second verb illustrates the use of the perfect with *waw* continuing an imperfect when it is contingent or dependent on the first verb. See Davidson, *Hebrew Syntax*, p. 79, § 53b.

5. Judah's expression *wᵉyaḏēnû ʾal tᵉhî ḇô* is close to the earlier one of Reuben, *wᵉyaḏ ʾal tišlᵉḥû ḇô* (v. 22). Both times emphasis falls on the subject "hand" by its placement ahead of the verbal predicate.

6. Lit., "listened" *(wayyišmᵉʿû)*. Cf. NJPS "agreed." Note, however, that in v. 21 *wayyišmaʿ* was used of Reuben, and there it meant clearly "listened (and disagreed)." In v. 27 it appears to mean "listened (and agreed)."

7. The subject of the verb could be either the Midianite merchants or Joseph's brothers (understood). See the commentary below.

8. "They pulled up" is, lit., "they drew [Qal of *māšaḵ*] and lifted out [Hiphil of *ʿālâ*]." Cf. the same phrase with Jeremiah in Jer. 38:13: *wayyimšᵉḵû . . . wayyaʿᵃlû ʾōṯô min*.

9. The LXX rendering of *kesep̱* is *chrysoús,* a measure of value and weight in the 3rd century B.C. equal to 20 silver drachmae. The translators may have avoided using *drachmē,* for 20 drachmae would be abnormally low. J. A. L. Lee (*A Lexical Study of the Septuagint Version of the Pentateuch,* SBL Septuagint and Cognate Studies 14 [Chico, CA: Scholars, 1983], pp. 64-65) cites a Greek text from the 3rd century B.C. in which 300 drachmae are paid for a girl slave. By using *chrysoús,* the translators give the impression that Joseph was sold for about 400 drachmae.

10. The *hinnēh* in *wᵉhinnēh ʾên yôsēp̱ babbôr* may either introduce a surprise clause (indicated by my punctuation of the clause with an exclamation point) or be causal ("and because Joseph was not in the cistern, he tore his clothes"). See D. J. McCarthy, "The Uses of *wᵉhinnēh* in Biblical Hebrew," *Bib* 61 (1980) 334.

30 *and returned to his brothers, saying: "The boy has disappeared!*[11] *What am I going to do!"*[12]

25-27 The brothers' treatment of Joseph has not diminished their appetite. While he is trapped in a cistern from which there is no possible escape, they sit down and eat. A group of passing caravaneers (Midianites/Ishmaelites) on their way to Egypt[13] gives Judah another idea of what to do with Joseph. He suggests that they sell Joseph to these traders. Judah thus joins Reuben in having second thoughts about the outright murder of Joseph.

Judah's motives, however, are not as noble as those of Reuben. Judah is primarily concerned that he and his brothers not shed innocent blood (v. 26). His apprehension is that spilled blood cries out from the ground for vengeance when one attempts to cover it (Gen. 4:10; Job 16:18; Isa. 26:21; Ezek. 24:7, 8).[14] For even then blood retains some of its power, and in the case of the deceased Abel it cries out for vindication. By contrast, Job desires that his blood may remain uncovered so that he might have an antemortem vindication. The same idea occurs in Rev. 6:10, where the martyrs cry out to the Lord for their blood to be avenged. There is no indication that Judah really desires to rescue his brother, as there was with Reuben. Joseph could be retrieved from a cistern, but he cannot be retrieved once he is sold to strangers headed for a foreign land. In fact, Judah, if he simply wants to get rid of Joseph, might offer him to the Ishmaelites for free. His proposal, however, is to exchange Joseph for a payment in silver. Both later biblical law and cuneiform law prohibit what Judah and his brothers did to Joseph.[15] It is a crime that is considered a capital offense.

11. Lit., "the boy, he [is] not." Following a defined subject, *'ên* takes a pronominal suffix referring to the subject (hence *'ênennû*).

12. Lit., "and I, where shall I go?" The isolated subject is *'^{a}nî,* and it is repeated in the predicate clause, where again it serves as the subject. GKC, § 116p, cites *bā'* in v. 30 as an instance of a participle in a deliberative question. Although depicted as speaking to his brothers, Reuben is really speaking to himself and therefore does not expect his brothers to answer his question, and they do not. See M. Niehoff, "Do Biblical Characters Talk to Themselves? Narrative Modes of Representing Inner Speech in Early Biblical Fiction," *JBL* 111 (1992) 587-89.

13. The resins and gums that the Ishmaelite caravans carry *(n^{e}ḵō'ṯ, ṣ^{e}rî, lōṭ)* are the same commodities that Jacob will later send with his sons, along with other items, on another caravan to Egypt (43:11). The ironic connection of Joseph's brothers with the Ishmaelite traders is noted by Alter, *Art of Biblical Narrative,* p. 172.

14. Excluding Gen. 4:10, all these verses use some form of the noun "blood" and the Piel of *kāsâ* (*t^{e}ḵassî,* Job 16:18; *t^{e}ḵasseh,* Isa. 26:21; *l^{e}ḵassôṯ,* Ezek. 24:7; or the Niphal, *hikkāsôṯ,* Ezek. 24:8). The parallel expression in Gen. 37:25 is *kissînû 'eṯ dāmô* (verb in the Piel followed by an accusative). See S. E. Balentine, "A Description of the Semantic Field of Hebrew Words for 'Hide,'" *VT* 30 (1980) 137-53.

15. For the biblical laws see Exod. 21:16; Deut. 24:7. For the cuneiform law see

28 Joseph is sold for *twenty pieces of silver* to these traders. This was the average price for a male slave in Old Babylonian times (early 2nd millennium B.C.). The price gradually goes higher. At Nuzi (mid-2nd millennium) it was thirty shekels (for both male and female). At Ugarit (mid- to late 2nd millennium) it was forty shekels. In Neo-Babylonian times (1st millennium) it was fifty shekels. In Persian times (late 1st millennium) the price was ninety to one hundred and twenty shekels.[16] These are, of course, the general standards from which there were many departures. Joseph's sale for twenty shekels fits perfectly with the amount a man was to give to the sanctuary if he vows himself or one of his male relatives between the ages of five and twenty (Joseph is seventeen) to the Lord (Lev. 27:5).[17]

It is widely assumed that this section of Gen. 37 presents the clearest evidence for a conflation of two accounts of the Joseph story. Scholars use three points to substantiate that position. First, here Judah is Joseph's mediator (vv. 26-27, J), rather than Reuben (vv. 21-22, E). Second, the text shifts back and forth on who actually took Joseph — Midianites (E) or Ishmaelites (J). Third, if the verses under consideration are from one source, then Reuben heard Judah's proposal to sell Joseph and was present when Joseph was actually sold. Why, then, is he shocked (vv. 29-30) when he returns to find the well empty? These three observations have led to the conclusion that in 37:25ff. we have the following two strands: J, vv. 25-27, 28b; E, vv. 28a, 29-30.[18] This breakdown explains, so it is assumed, all the inconsistencies within the text of 37:25-30.

Let us examine another possibility that does not follow the J-E analysis. Judah is not convinced that Reuben's suggestion is an improvement over the original plan. The brothers have two ways to kill Joseph — immediately or gradually, the brothers' way or Judah's way. Of course, Judah is not aware of

---

Hammurapi's Code, § 14 (*ANET,* p. 166). Note that in these two verses *gānaḇ* ("steal") and *māḵar* ("sell") are used together. In Gen. 37:27, 28 Joseph is "sold" *(māḵar),* but in 40:15 Joseph himself says "stolen" *(gānaḇ).* Some think that "Midianites" in v. 28 is a gloss, inserted to remove the problem of the brothers committing a crime punishable by death.

16. The figures are from I. Mendelsohn, *Slavery in the Ancient Near East* (New York: Oxford, 1949), pp. 117-18. See also K. C. Hanson, "Slavery," *ISBE,* 4:541, who notes the inflation in price throughout the OT from 20 shekels (Gen. 37:28), to 30 in the Covenant Code (Exod. 21:32), to 50 even later (2 K. 15:20).

17. See G. J. Wenham, "Leviticus 27:2-8 and the Price of Slaves," *ZAW* 90 (1978) 264-65; idem, *Book of Leviticus,* NICOT (Grand Rapids: Eerdmans, 1979), p. 338, who suggests that the rationale for the scale in Lev. 27:2-8 is that it represents the price of slaves of different age and sex in Israel.

18. See Jenks, *The Elohist and North Israelite Traditions,* pp. 28-29. Speiser (*Genesis,* p. 291) speaks for many when he says of v. 28: "This single verse alone provides a good basis for a constructive documentary analysis of the Pentateuch." Similarly D. B. Redford (*A Study of the Biblical Story of Joseph [Genesis 37–50],* VTSup 20 [Leiden: Brill, 1970], p. 145) says: "Generations of Bible students have utilized this discrepancy as a show piece for demonstrating the validity of the Documentary Hypothesis."

Reuben's intentions. Accordingly, he suggests a less hostile proposal — do not kill our brother in any way; rather, sell him to some barterers.

These traders are identified as *Midianites* and *Ishmaelites.* Judg. 8:22-28 state clearly that Midianite and Ishmaelite are overlapping, identical terms.[19] In other words, the two names were used interchangeably to refer to North Arabian caravaneers who branched off through Gilead (v. 25) from the main transport route on the way to Egypt. This would be but one episode of pastoral groups repeatedly journeying from Northern Arabia and southern Canaan to Egypt, bringing their products of incense to sell at the Pharaoh's court.[20] That Judg. 8:24 in particular equates Ishmaelites with Midianites suggests that in Gideon's time at least "Midianites" represented a confederation of tribal groups.[21] The interchange of "Ishmaelites" and "Midianites" in Gen. 37 suggests that at one time the Ishmaelites were the most prominent confederation of nomads in southern Palestine, and that their name might be attached to and linked with other groups. This would mean that "Ishmaelite" in Gen. 37 is not primarily an ethnic designation but is a catchall term for nomadic travelers. Thus "Ishmaelite" is the more generic term (Bedouin nomad), while "Midianite" is the more specific and ethnic term.

Does the text provide any evidence for this theory? Why identify this new group first by a more general term (v. 25), and then subsequently re-identify them by a different and more specific term (v. 28a)? To answer the first question, I would point to the phrase *'ōrᵉḥaṯ yišmᵉʿē'lîm* in v. 25, which I have translated "a caravan of Ishmaelites." One might also render it "an Ishmaelite [i.e., nomadic] caravan," implying a general name for this group. Who constitutes this ambiguous group of caravaneers is made clear by v. 28a: *'ᵃnāšîm miḏyānîm sōḥᵃrîm,* "Midianite men, merchants."

To answer the second question, note that vv. 18-24 follow the same progression of description as vv. 25-28. First, Joseph (v. 18) and the Ishmaelite caravan (v. 25) are observed approaching the brothers from a distance. Second, Joseph (vv. 19-22) and the caravaneers (vv. 26-27) are talked about by the brothers before either meets the brothers. Third, when Joseph and the Ishmaelites do meet the brothers, the brothers go into action, stripping Joseph and casting

19. See K. A. Kitchen, *Ancient Orient and Old Testament* (Chicago: Inter-Varsity, 1966), pp. 119-20; S. Talmon, "The Presentation of Synchroneity and Simultaneity in Biblical Narratives," *Scripta Hierosolymitana* 27 (1978) 18-19; M. Anbar, "Changement des noms des tribus nomades dans la relation, d'un même événement," *Bib* 49 (1968) 221-32. The incisive contribution of Judg. 8:22-28 to the Ishmaelite/Midianite issue in Gen. 37 was observed as early as Gunkel's 1st ed. of *Genesis* in 1901 (here I refer to the 6th ed., p. 409).

20. See A. Musil, *The Northern Ḥeǧâz* (New York: AMS, 1926), pp. 282-83; P. E. Newberry, *Beni Hasan* I (London: K. Paul, Trench, Trübner, 1893), pp. 69, 72, plates xxviii, xxx, xxxi, xxxviii; A. A. Saleh, "An Open Question on Intermediaries in the Incense Trade during Pharaonic Times," *Or* 42 (1973) 378.

21. R. Boling, *Judges,* AB (Garden City, NY: Doubleday, 1975), p. 160.

him into a cistern (vv. 23-24), and eventually selling Joseph to the Ishmaelites (v. 28). The last unit, vv. 25-30, describes the group that the brothers saw on the horizon, and for this distant sighting it uses the more general term. From afar they appeared to be a group of Bedouin nomads. When this group subsequently comes into closer view they are identified as Midianites.[22]

This interpretation raises considerably the possibility that the subject of "pulled up" and "sold" in v. 28 is the brothers. As these Ishmaelite caravaneers (i.e., Midianite merchants as they come into focus) pass by, Joseph's brothers pull him up from the cistern and sell him to these passers-by.[23]

29-30 That Reuben was dumbfounded to find the well empty indicates that he was not present when the transaction with the Midianites/Ishmaelites was carried out. Perhaps as the oldest brother he went to guard the sheep that the brothers were pasturing as these strangers passed by. After they depart, he is free to leave the flock unattended or turn that responsibility over to one of his brothers, return to his brothers, and check on Joseph in the well.

It is true that Joseph later identifies himself to the brothers as the one they "sold" into Egypt (45:4), but earlier in his Egyptian confinement he told his cell mate that he was "stolen" from the land of the Hebrews (40:15). Does this variation reflect one tradition in which Joseph was sold by his brothers to Ishmaelites (J), and a second tradition in which Joseph was stolen by Midianites (E)? Why two words to describe what happened to Joseph— "sold"and "stolen"? It is quite probable that Joseph deliberately adjusted the story as he narrated it in ch. 40, for he was attempting to curry the cupbearer's favor. He knows the cupbearer is his only path to freedom. To have mentioned that he was sold by his brothers would make the cupbearer suspicious, rather than trusting. By saying he was stolen, Joseph is underscoring that what happened to him was something over which he had no control, and which he, in his judgment, had done nothing to deserve.

Enough has been said to indicate that recourse to a J-E hypothesis, or to an original story with later redactional expansions,[24] is not the only option in order to make sense of Gen. 37. The older study of Rudolph, and more recent narrative readings by Sandmel, Coats, Greenstein, Berlin, and White, argue convincingly for the literary unity of Gen. 37.[25]

22. Longacre, *Joseph,* p. 31.

23. Ibid., p. 155. He suggests that if the Midianites of v. 28a are a separate and new group of participants, then we would "expect that Hebrew participant introduction and integration . . . would introduce them *not once* but twice and in the process would name them as the unambiguous subject of the verbs."

24. See Redford, *Study of the Biblical Story of Joseph,* p. 141. There is, according to Redford, a "Judah version" of the conspiracy story that is an expansion of a "Reuben version," which is earlier.

25. W. Rudolph, "Die Josefsgeschichte," in P. Volz and W. Rudolph, *Der Elohist als Erzähler — Ein Irrweg der Pentateuchkritik?* BZAW 63 (Giessen: Töpelmann, 1933), pp.

5. JACOB IS DECEIVED (37:31-36)

31 *They took Joseph's tunic, slaughtered a goat, and dipped the tunic in its blood.*

32 *They had the long, colorful tunic sent*[1] *back to their father, and said: "This we found.*[2] *Examine*[3] *it. Is it your son's*[4] *tunic or not?"*[5]

33 *He examined it and said: "My son's tunic! An evil beast has devoured him;*[6] *Joseph has surely been ripped to pieces."*[7]

143-83; S. Sandmel, "The Haggada within Scripture," *JBL* 80 (1961) 112; G. W. Coats, *From Canaan to Egypt: Structural and Theological Context for the Joseph Story,* CBQMS 4 (Washington, D.C.: Catholic Biblical Association, 1975), pp. 16-19; E. L. Greenstein, "An Equivocal Reading of the Sale of Joseph" in *Literary Interpretations of Biblical Narratives,* vol. 2, ed. K. R. R. Gros Louis, et al. (Nashville: Abingdon, 1982), pp. 114-25; A. Berlin, *Poetics and Interpretation of Biblical Narrative* (Sheffield: Almond, 1983), pp. 114-21; H. C. White, "Reuben and Judah: Duplicates or Complements?" in *Understanding the Word,* Fest. B. W. Anderson, ed. James T. Butler, et al., JSOTSup 37 (Sheffield: JSOT, 1985), pp. 73-97.

1. MT *wayᵉšallᵉḥû* (Piel) *'eṯ-kᵉṯōneṯ happassîm wayyāḇî'û* (Hiphil), lit., "and they sent the long, colorful tunic and they brought," sounds contradictory or nonsensical. The second verb may be emended to *wayyāḇō'û,* "and they came" (Gunkel, *Genesis,* p. 355; cf. also *BHS*), but I think this is unnecessary. The text makes sense as it stands: "they sent . . . had it brought," i.e., a hendiadys. Nor is it necessary to suggest that behind *wayᵉšallᵉḥû* is an otherwise unattested Hebrew verb that is the equivalent of Aram. *telaḥ,* "tear, rend" (F. V. Winnett, "A Brief Comment on Genesis 37:32," *Bulletin of the Canadian Society of Biblical Studies* 12 [1947] 13). Against Westermann (*Genesis,* 3:43), I would argue that the brothers did not themselves send the tunic to their father. For one thing, there is another instance later in the Joseph narrative where the brothers first sent messengers (50:15ff.), then later came themselves (50:18ff.). For another, as Alter points out (*Art of Biblical Narrative,* p. 4), the indirection of the brothers' approach to their father is emphasized by the fact that when the brothers say to Jacob "this we found" *(zō'ṯ māṣā'nû), zō'ṯ* precedes the brothers literally and syntactically.

2. LXX adds "in the field."

3. *nāḵar,* "to recognize, identify," occurs at other key places in the Joseph narrative: 38:26; 42:7, 8.

4. Palestinian Targ. adds "Joseph."

5. On disjunctive questions expressed by *hᵃ . . . 'im lō'* see GKC, § 150i; and Williams, *Hebrew Syntax,* p. 91, § 544.

6. Most of the Targumim insert a negative particle before the verb: "*neither* the beast of the field has devoured him." See M. L. Klein, "Converse Translation: A Targumic Technique," *Bib* 57 (1976) 522-23, who advances an explanation for the addition. This interpretation is based on a reading of 37:35 (Jacob refused to be consoled) in which one is consoled for the dead but not for the living who are missing, and on the rabbinic conviction that Jacob was endowed with prophetic knowledge that Joseph was alive.

7. For the infinitive absolute before a Qal passive see GKC, § 113w. Cf. also S. J. P. K. Riekert, "The Strict Patterns of the Paranomastic and Co-ordinated Infinitives Absolute in Genesis," *JNWSL* 7 (1979) 70; B. K. Waltke and M. O'Connor, *An Introduction to Biblical Hebrew Syntax* (Winona Lake, IN: Eisenbrauns, 1990), pp. 375 n. 31, 584. Targ. Onqelos uses the verb *qṭl* ("kill") for MT *ṭārap,* since Heb. *ṭārap̱* refers to meat of an improperly killed animal, thus all the more disgusting in association with Joseph.

34 *Jacob tore his clothes, put sackcloth on his loins, and mourned for his son many days.*

35 *All his sons and daughters tried*[8] *to console him, but he refused to be consoled,*[9] *saying: "No, I will go down to my son in the underworld*[10] *mourning."*[11] *Thus did his father bewail him.*[12]

36 *And the Midianites*[13] *sold him in Egypt to Potiphar, Pharaoh's courtier and chief steward.*

31 The long, colorful tunic Jacob had given to Joseph is not something Joseph chooses to wear only on special occasions. It may be that he wears it on this occasion because that is all he had to wear. He might know that wearing it on a long journey to visit his brothers and flaunting it (from the brother's perspective) before them will only intensify their antagonism. Wearing it in Dothan is like waving a red flag in front of a bull. The brothers' design was only to cast him into a pit and then fabricate the story that a "wild beast" had killed him. That Joseph is wearing this particular tunic gives them the opportunity to make their story even more plausible. They slaughtered a goat (something they would have liked to do to Joseph too!), and smeared the tunic with bloodstains. It is ironic that Jacob, who earlier deceived Isaac with *ʿōrōṯ hāʿizzîm* ("skin of the kids") in 27:16, is now deceived by a garment dipped in the blood of a goat *(ś^{e}ʿîr ʿizzîm).*

32 The brothers deliver the tunic back to Jacob in Hebron, about 65 miles to the south (did they take their flocks with them?). Understandably they do not say: "Is this Joseph's tunic or not?" or: "Is this our brother's tunic or not?" Their question, *Is it your son's tunic or not?* distances them from Joseph. They are careful not to say too much. The power of suggestion is greater than the power of explanation. They will let Jacob draw his own conclusion.

33 It never dawns on Jacob that his sons are to blame for Joseph's tragic demise. In fact, quite by coincidence, he draws the conclusion which his sons were prepared to give (v. 20) but which he himself inferred first.

8. LXX *synḗchthēsan de* presupposes *wayyiqah^{a}lû,* "and they came together," for MT *wayyāqumû.*

9. See H. Van Dyke Parunak, "A Semantic Survey of *NḤM,*" *Bib* 56 (1975) 520, for other uses of *nāḥam* where the subject of the verb is a bereaved mourner (Gen. 24:67; 38:12; 2 Sam. 13:39; Jer. 31:15; Ezek. 31:16; 32:31).

10. Lit., "to Sheol" *(š^{e}'ōlâ).* See the commentary below.

11. "Mourning" *('āḇēl)* is an accusative of condition/state, placed after a verb to describe some kind of a condition (GKC, § 118n; Davidson, *Hebrew Syntax,* p. 100, § 70; Waltke and O'Connor, *Biblical Hebrew Syntax,* p. 171 and n. 18).

12. For *bāḵâ* followed by an accusative see the references in BDB, p. 113, § 4.

13. MT has *hamm^{e}ḏānîm* (Medanites) instead of *hammiḏyānîm* (Midianites).

Jacob concludes that an *evil beast (ḥayyâ rāʿâ)* has killed Joseph. According to Ezek. 5:17; 14:15, 21; 33:27, "evil beasts" are one of four of God's agents of punishment, along with sword, famine, and pestilence. The idea is also implicit in Jer. 15:3 (where God appoints the sword, dogs, birds, and beasts as destroyers), in Lev. 26:22 ("I will let loose the wild beasts among you"), and in Hos. 2:14 (Eng. 12: "the beasts of the field shall devour them"). This fact may explain the mixture of terror and grief that Jacob now experiences. Joseph may have met this tragic end because of a divine judgment, due either to Joseph's sin or Jacob's sin.

Jacob's explanation is identical to the sons' devised explanation, even down to subject and verb, and that only makes their case stronger. At this point, however, Jacob's speech shifts from prose to "formal verse, a neat semantic parallelism that scans with three beats in each hemistich: *ḥayáh raʿáh ʾakhláthu / taróf toráf Yoséf.*"[14] Jacob pronounces, metrically, that Joseph is dead.

34 Jacob's display of remorse is much greater than that of Reuben. Reuben simply "tore his clothes" (*wayyiqraʿ ʾeṯ-beḡāḏāyw,* v. 29). Jacob *tore his clothes (wayyiqraʿ . . . śimlōṯāyw), put sackcloth on his loins, and mourned* (durative Hithpael of *ʾāḇal*) for *many days.* The Hithpael of *ʾāḇal* is used of mourning rites that may be funerary (1 Sam. 6:19; 2 Sam. 19:2; Amos 8:10), penitential (Exod. 33:4; Num. 14:29; Ezra 10:6), or supplicatory (Neh. 1:4; Dan. 10:2). One wonders if the verb here may include all three of these nuances, although the first appears the most obvious.

How long *many days* is we are not sure. In the Ugaritic legend, Aqhat wept for Danel for six or seven years, but this text is cultic. Later in Genesis the situation is reversed, and it is Joseph who mourns for Jacob seven days (50:10; cf. 1 Sam. 31:13). There were thirty days of mourning for Aaron (Num. 20:29) and for Moses (Deut. 34:8).[15] Joseph himself was mourned for seventy days (Gen. 50:3). While tearing the clothes is a normal mourning custom, it is especially appropriate here for Jacob to *tear (qāraʿ)* his clothes, grieving as he is over a son who has been *ripped to pieces (ṭārap̱)* by a wild animal.

35 The reference to Jacob's sons and *daughters* is surprising. Dinah is the only daughter mentioned thus far. Perhaps daughters-in-law are included in this reference. His children are skilled at putting on a facade. They attempt to comfort their father, all the time restraining their glee at the demise of Joseph, and just after they deceived their father about Joseph's alleged horrible death. Deceivers become (pseudo-) comforters.

14. See Alter, *Art of Biblical Narrative,* p. 4.

15. See E. F. de Ward, "Mourning Customs in 1, 2 Samuel," *JSS* 23 (1972) 1-27, 145-66.

Jacob rejected their condolences. Instead, he proclaims *I will go down* [*'ērēḏ*] *to my son in the underworld* [Sheol] *mourning.* Indeed, later Joseph would go down (*'ērēḏ* again), not to Sheol but to Egypt, where he will rejoin Joseph (46:3-4). Jacob's statement may be compared with that in the Ugaritic text of Baal and Mot. The kindly god Latipan,[16] informed that Baal is dead, engages in various mourning rites and then proclaims: "After Baal I would go down into the earth."[17] Jacob has no concept of a heaven for the faithful. What he does believe in is an *underworld* where life is far from pleasant for all its occupants. If the connection of Gen. 37:35 with the above Ugaritic text can be maintained, then the verse may not imply that Jacob will mourn for Joseph the rest of his life until he himself goes down to Sheol. Rather, v. 35 would suggest that Jacob will make a ritual descent into the underworld.[18]

36 While Jacob is mourning for Joseph, the Midianites sold Joseph in Egypt to Potiphar, one of the pharaoh's officials. The subjects of vv. 35b and 36a are placed side by side in the Hebrew text (*'āḇîw wᵉhammᵉḏānîm,* lit., *his father and the Midianites*). The effect created by this juxtapositioning

16. Latipan, meaning "gentle, kindly," is a title of El.

17. *aṯr b'l 'ard b'arṣ* (*UT,* 62:7-8; *CTA,* 5.6.24-25). The translation is that of J. C. L. Gibson, *Canaanite Myths and Legends,* 2nd ed. (Edinburgh: T. & T. Clark, 1978), p. 74 (tablet 5, col. vi, lines 24-25). Gordon splits the line with "Woe, to the multitudes of Athar-Baal! Let us go down into the earth" (*Ugarit and Minoan Crete* [New York: Norton, 1966], p. 81). One may compare this Ugaritic text with another, *KTU,* 1.161, a lamentation over the dead King Niqmaddu on the occasion of the accession of Ammurapi III. In this ritual, descent into the underworld is acted out through recitation. The goddess Shapash is to locate the summoned deceased kings and the Rephaim. The relevant lines (20-22) read: *aṯr [b]'lk l ksh aṯr b'lk arṣ rd arṣ rd* ("After your lord, from the throne; after your lord to the netherworld descend. To the netherword descend"; translation of B. A. Levine and J. M. de Tarragon, "Dead Kings and Raphaim: The Patrons of the Ugaritic Dynasty," *JAOS* 104 [1984] 650). In the myth descent into the underworld is accomplished by a goddess (Anat). In the liturgy descent into the underworld is accomplished by recitation. Both *atr. b'l. ard. barṣ* of the first text and *aṯr b'lk arṣ rd* of the second remind one of Jacob's intention to descend *(yāraḏ)* to his son (see Levine and Tarragon, p. 658). Levine and Tarragon note that both the myth from Ugarit and Gen. 37:35 have a double entendre. Both El and Jacob wish to make the descent in order to locate and retrieve the dead. Also, both El and Jacob so identify with Baal and Joseph that they desire to join them in the underworld. H. Hoffner, Jr. ("A Prayer of Muršili II about His Stepmother," *JAOS* 103 [1983] 187-92) discusses the prayer of the Hittite king who has removed his stepmother from power for killing his own wife and thus forcing the widowed king to experience the agony of daily trips to the dark netherworld. This Hittite text supplies confirming evidence that Jacob's descent to Sheol was not a thing to take place at the end of his life, but would be a daily experience for the rest of his life (Hoffner, p. 190).

18. See T. J. Lewis, *Cults of the Dead in Ancient Israel and Ugarit,* HSM 39 (Atlanta: Scholars, 1989), pp. 43, 118, 173.

of the subjects, separated only by a *waw* ("and"), is to stress the simultaneous action of the two subjects on Joseph. This is the reason why I retain the translation of *waw* as *And* (a literal reading of the Hebrew parataxis; so also AV) instead of the more common "Meanwhile" (so RSV, NIV, NEB, JB, NAB). Alter states: "In this cunningly additive syntax, on the same unbroken narrative continuum in which Jacob is mourning his supposedly devoured son, Midianites are selling the living lad."[19]

the Midianites. It may well be that "Medanites" is simply an alternative writing for "Midianites."[20] Note that in Gen. 25:2 Medan *(mᵉḏān)* and Midian *(miḏyān)* are brothers. Medianites are mentioned only in 25:2 and 37:36. It is interesting to note that elsewhere in the Hebrew Bible (Prov. 6:19; 10:12), *mᵉḏānîm* (the same cluster of consonants in Gen. 37:36) has the meaning "discord, quarrels." Prov. 6:19 is instructive: among the seven things that God hates are a false witness breathing out lies, and one "who sows discord [*mᵉḏānîm*] among brothers" (RSV). At the heart of the trouble in Gen. 37 is discord among brothers, *mᵉḏānîm.*[21]

THE NEW TESTAMENT APPROPRIATION

Discussion of the NT reading of the Joseph narrative follows the commentary on ch. 50.

B. JUDAH AND TAMAR (38:1-30)

1. TAMAR, THE CHILDLESS WIDOW (38:1-11)

1 *About that time*[1] *Judah went down from his brothers and pitched his tent near*[2] *a certain Adullamite whose name*[3] *was Hirah.*

19. Alter, *Art of Biblical Narrative,* p. 5.

20. So Speiser and others. See n. 13 above.

21. See Y. T. Radday, "Humour in Names," in *On Humour and the Comic in the Hebrew Bible,* ed. Radday and A. Brenner, JSOTSup (Sheffield: Sheffield Academic, 1990), pp. 69-70.

1. On *bāʿēṯ hahiwʾ* see S. J. DeVries, *Yesterday, Today and Tomorrow,* index, s.v. "Hebrew words and phrases," p. 363. DeVries notes that when this particular phrase is used, "the intent is little more than to equate in time a second event with a first" (p. 340). Applied to 38:1, this means that the marriage of Judah must be equated in time with the selling of Joseph and his descent into Egypt (37:36).

2. For *ʿaḏ* with the force of *ʾel,* "to," cf. 1 Sam. 9:9. Note that later in the chapter, *nāṭâ* is followed by the preposition *ʾel* (v. 16). Thus v. 1 has *wayyēṭ ʿaḏ;* v. 16, *wayyēṭ ʿēlêhā.*

3. MT reads *ûšᵉmô,* "and his name." The masc. is probably used impersonally. LXX reads "and her name was Hirah."

2 *There Judah met the daughter of a Canaanite named Shua, married her, and cohabited*[4] *with her.*

3 *She conceived and bore a son, and named*[5] *him Er.*

4 *Again she conceived and bore a son, and named him Onan.*

5 *She bore still another son, and named him Shelah; she was*[6] *in Chezib when she bore him.*

6 *Judah took a wife for Er his firstborn, and her name was Tamar.*

7 *Er, Judah's firstborn, displeased*[7] *Yahweh, with the result*[8] *that Yahweh*[9] *killed him.*

8 *Then Judah said to Onan: "Cohabit with your sister-in-law, levirate*[10] *her, namely,*[11] *raise up offspring for your brother."*

9 *Onan knew, however, that the offspring would not be his. Accordingly, whenever he cohabited*[12] *with his sister-in-law he wasted his semen on the ground,*[13] *to avoid contributing*[14] *offspring for his brother.*

10 *What he did displeased Yahweh, with the result that he killed him as well.*

11 *Then Judah said to his daughter-in-law: "Stay as a widow in your father's house*[15] *until Shelah my son grows older"—for he thought*

4. Lit., "and he went in to her" *(wayyābō' 'ēleyhā).* Cf. also vv. 8, 9.

5. MT reads "and he named him Er"; SP, Targ. Jonathan, and 12 Hebrew mss. read "and she named him Er," as in vv. 4, 5. See J. A. Emerton, "Some problems in Genesis XXXVIII," *VT* 25 (1975) 339.

6. MT reads *wᵉhāyâ,* "and he was." LXX reads *autḗ dé ḗn,* "and she was." J. Huesman ("The Infinitive Absolute and the *Waw* + Perfect Problem," *Bib* 37 [1956] 415) emends to *wᵉhāyōh,* lit., "and to be" (infinitive absolute), and understands the infinitive absolute to indicate a finite action in past time. Accordingly, Huesman would translate: "and she called his name Shelah. She was in Chezib when she bore him." This translation explains LXX "and she was" without having to emend the consonantal text of MT *wᵉhāyâ* to *wᵉhî',* "and she . . ." (as suggested by Skinner, *Genesis,* p. 451; Westermann, *Genesis,* 3:48; GKC, § 112uu; Emerton, *VT* 25 [1975] 339).

7. Lit. "(he was) wicked/evil in the eyes of Yahweh." See also v. 10.

8. The *waw* on *wayᵉmiṯēhû* links a cause-and-effect statement.

9. LXX reads "and God killed him."

10. Or, "do the duty of a brother-in-law" *(wᵉyabbēm).* See the commentary below.

11. An instance of a *waw explicativum*, on which see GKC, § 154a, n. 1.b.

12. On the use of the perfect after *'im* as a frequentative perfect consecutive in the apodosis, see GKC, § 112gg. Cf. also LXX *hótan eisḗrcheto.*

13. Lit., "whenever he went in to the wife of his brother, that he spoiled toward the earth." See BDB, p. 1008; *HALAT,* 4:1363.

14. The only other place in the Hebrew Bible where the infinitive construct of *nāṯan* is *nᵉṯan* (and not *tēṯ*) is Num. 20:21. See GKC, § 66i, who labels this form the strong formation of the infinitive construct.

15. On the accusative of place see GKC, § 118d, g.

that he too might die like his brothers. So Tamar went to live in her father's house.

All commentators agree that ch. 38 clearly interrupts the flow of the Joseph story: 39:1 picks up where 37:36 left off. Why the insertion of the story about Judah, his sons, and his daughter-in-law into the Joseph story at all? And why its insertion between chs. 37 and 39?

To answer the first question, I suggest that the biblical author/redactor, with the tradition about Judah and his family in hand, had no other place for this story. It could not precede the Joseph story, for it would be chronologically out of place. In ch. 37 Judah is single, young, working for his father, living at home, pasturing his father's flocks near Dothan. In ch. 38 Judah is older, now married, and has three sons. Thus ch. 38 must follow the opening of the Joseph story. But It would be odd for the tradition to come after the end of the Joseph story — to have a story about Judah in Canaan appearing after the Joseph story in which Judah goes to Egypt for famine relief and spends the rest of his life there.[16]

Why is the narrative inserted between chs. 37 and 38, and not elsewhere in the Joseph story? I suggest that this is the only logical place for it to appear. Obviously ch. 39 does not pick up where 38:30 left off, but where 37:36 left off. This is even more clear if one reads 39:1 as "Joseph had been taken down to Egypt." In the thirteen-year period between Joseph's being sold to caravaneers and his exaltation in the pharaoh's service (cf. Joseph's age of 17 in 37:2 and and 30 in 41:46) falls Judah's marriage, the birth of his three sons, and the fathering of two (grand)children to his daughter-in-law.

In addition, I note a number of intentional literary parallels between chs. 37 and 38, and between chs. 38 and 39, which would be lost if ch. 38 had been placed elsewhere.[17] Such parallels include linguistic and thematic overlaps. In the linguistic group we call attention to the following. (1) When Jacob was presented with Joseph's bloodied tunic, his sons instructed him to "examine it" (*hakker-nā',* 37:32); then the text says "and he examined it" (*wayyakkîrāh,* 37:33). Holding Judah's items in her hands, Tamar says to Judah: "identify them" (*hakker-nā',* 38:25b); and Judah "identified them" (*wayyakkēr,* 38:26). Two back-to-back uses of the Hiphil imperative of *nāḵar* (37:32; 38:25) and of the Hiphil imperfect of *nāḵar* (37:33; 38:26) unite these two chapters. (2) In 37:31 we read that the brothers dipped the coat in the blood of a goat *(śᵉʿîr ʿizzîm).* In 38:17 Judah promises to give Tamar a kid from his flock *(gᵉḏî ʿizzîm)* as payment for her services as a harlot. It may be noted that the play on *nāḵar* and

16. See Redford, *Study of the Biblical Story of Joseph,* p. 17.

17. I draw some of these parallels from the scintillating study of Gen. 38 by Alter, *Art of Biblical Narrative,* pp. 3-12. See also U. Cassuto, "The Story of Tamar and Judah," in *Biblical and Oriental Studies,* tr. I. Abrahams, 2 vols. (Jerusalem: Magnes, 1973-75), 1:29-40.

'izzîm in chs. 37 and 38 was observed as early as Jewish rabbinic literature: "The Holy One, Praised be He, said to Judah, 'You deceived your father with a kid. By your life Tamar will deceive you with a kid'. . . . The Holy One, Praised be He, said to Judah, 'You said to your father, *hakker-nā'*. By your life Tamar will say to you, *hakker-nā'*."[18] (3) Ch. 38 begins by telling us that Judah "went down" *(wayyēreḏ)* from his brothers. Ch. 39 opens by reminding us that Joseph "had been taken down" *(hûraḏ)* to Egypt. In one Judah "goes down" *(yrd)* from the hill country to Adullam, and in the other Joseph "goes down" *(yrd)* from Canaan to Egypt. (4) Finally, the two chapters contrast a Jacob who refused to be consoled (*lᵉhiṯnaḥēm,* 37:35) over Joseph, and a Judah who was consoled (*wayyinnāḥem,* 38:12) over his wife's death.

In addition to these linguistic parallels, I note the following thematic parallels and contrasts. (1) Ch. 38 highlights Tamar's deception of Judah by disguising herself as a harlot. This theme of deception parallels ch. 37, where the sons deceive Jacob through the bloodied coat, and ch. 39, where Potiphar's wife attempts to deceive her husband about Joseph. In chs. 37 and 38 the deception is perpetrated by a relative (sons, daughter-in-law). (2) In all three chapters evidence is presented by one party (the bloodied coat, ch. 37; Judah's seal, cord, and staff, ch. 38; Joseph's coat, ch. 39) to another party to establish either facticity (ch. 37) or culpability (chs. 38, 39). (3) Tamar the seductress balances Potiphar's wife the seductress, and the seduced Judah contrasts with the chaste Joseph. (4) Jacob's grief over the alleged death of one son (37:34, 35) contrasts with the absence of any grief displayed by Judah over the death of two sons. (5) In ch. 37 Joseph has a dream which provokes this question: Shall you rule over us? and the rest of the Joseph story shows Joseph, so to speak, ruling over his brethren. In ch. 38 the focus is on Judah out of whose line will come the kings who will rule over God's people. (6) In both chs. 37 and 38 we observe fraternal rivalry.[19] Onan feels about Er as Joseph's brothers feel about him. (7) In both episodes the law of primogeniture is set aside. A younger son (Joseph) is his brother's salvation, and a younger son (Perez) continues the messianic line (Ruth 4:18; Matt. 1:3).

1 While Joseph is being sold to the Egyptian-bound Midianites, Judah leaves his brothers, journeys to Adullam, and pitches his tent adjacent to a person named Hirah. Adullam (cf. Josh. 15:35; 1 Sam. 22:1; Mic. 1:15) is most likely to be identified with Tell esh-Sheikh Madhkur in the Shephelah, southwest of Bethlehem and northwest of Hebron. One may compare Judah's accidental encounter with this stranger (who may or may not have introduced him to his future wife) to Joseph's running into a stranger at Shechem who

18. Gen. Rabbah 84:11-12.

19. See J. Goldin, "The Youngest Son or Where does Genesis 38 Belong," *JBL* 96 (1977) 27-44.

directs him to his brothers (37:15-17). Judah had flocks at Timnah (v. 12), which is 4 miles northeast of Adullam.

2 Judah's marriage to a Canaanite[20] girl contrasts boldly with his great-grandfather's concern that Isaac not marry a Canaanite (24:3) and with Isaac's concern that Jacob avoid a Canaanite spouse (28:1). One gets the distinct impression that ever since the Dinah incident (ch. 34) Jacob has less and less control over the behavior of his family.

Only the name of Judah's father-in-law is given: *Shua.* His wife remains anonymous. Their relationship to each other is conveyed by six verbs: three for him (he meets her, marries her, and has intercourse with her, v. 2), and three for her (she conceives, bears a son, and names the child, v. 3). Judah and his wife relate sexually, but the text says nothing else about their relations.

3 The firstborn is named *Er.* The commentaries and dictionaries give Er (Heb. *ʿēr*) the meaning "watchful" or "watcher" by relating it to *ʿûr* II, "to be awake."[21] Sarna notes that a midrash and Targ. Jonathan link the name with *ʿărîrî,* "childless."[22] This meaning of the name would reflect the context of ch. 38 quite well — a firstborn who dies without progeny.

4 *Onan,* the second born, is often explained in connection with the word *ʾôn,* "strength, vigor, wealth," hence, "vigorous one" or "healthy one."[23] It is unlikely that the name derives from *ʾāwen,* "trouble, sorrow" (with *ān* as an Aramaic ending?),[24] with the meaning being "one of trouble, sorrow," something Onan brought to his family.

20. Aberbach and Grossfeld (*Targum Onkelos to Genesis,* p. 221 n. 1) draw attention to the fact that the majority of the versions of Targ. Onqelos read "merchant" *(tgrʾ)* for *kĕnaʿănî,* a meaning the translators claim for *kĕnaʿănî* in Job 40:30; Prov. 31:24; Isa. 23:8; Zech. 14:21. It is more likely that the rabbis gave "Canaanite" its nonethnic meaning because they were well aware of the Torah's prohibition of marriage to a Canaanite. Yet nowhere do the rabbis try to make Tamar an Israelite. For example, Targ. Pseudo-Jonathan claims that Tamar was a non-Israelite and that Judah made her a proselyte. See J. A. Emerton, "An examination of recent structuralist interpretations of Genesis XXXVIII," *VT* 26 (1976) 90-91.

21. See, e.g., *IDB,* 2:124; *ISBE,* 2:126; M. Noth, *Die israelitischen Personennamen im Rahmen der gemeinsemitischen Namengebung* (Hildeshiem: Olms, repr. 1980), p. 228; W. F. Albright ("The Egyptian Empire in Asia in the Twenty-First Century B.C.," *JPOS* 8 [1928] 238) identifies the name as the Qal participle of *ʿûr,* "wakeful, watchful, alert, vigilant."

22. Sarna, *Genesis,* p. 265. See also C. H. Bowman and R. B. Coote, "A Narrative Incantation for Snake Bite," *UF* 12 (1980) 138. C. Carmichael connects it with *ʿayir,* "male ass," in Jacob's blessing on Judah, Gen. 49:11 (*VT* 32 [1982] 400). G. Rendsburg connects Er *(ʿēr)* with *naʿar,* the lad of David and Bathsheba in 2 Sam. 12:16 (*VT* 36 [1986] 443).

23. See, e.g., *IDB,* 3:602; *ISBE,* 3:604; Noth, *Die israelitischen Personennamen,* p. 225.

24. Emerton (*VT* 26 [1976] 91-92) provides evidence from ancient sources, specifically Jub. 41:1-2 and T. Judah 10:1-2, 6, that Tamar was regarded as an Aramean from Mesopotamia, possibly in imitation of Tamar the daughter of David who was half Aramean (2 Sam. 3:3; 13:1; 15:8), and in imitation of Jacob and Isaac, who married Aramean wives. Both Targ. Jonathan and Gen. Rabbah 85:5 relate Onan to the Hebrew word for "grief, sorrow."

5 The three verbs for Judah (v. 2) and the three verbs for his wife (v. 3) are now followed by the birth of their third child, *Shelah.* The grouping of three is maintained by a subsequent reference to Timnah (v. 12): 3 verbs, 3 children, 3 localities. At some undesignated point Judah has moved from Adullam (v. 1) to Chezib (v. 5). More than likely *Chezib* (a name that appears nowhere else in the OT in this form) is to be equated with Achzib (Josh. 15:44; Mic. 1:14), another city somewhere in the central Shephelah.[25]

6 Judah feels quite free to select his own wife, but he does not extend that privilege to Er. We do not know Tamar's family or background, but possibly she is, like her mother-in-law, a Canaanite and comes somewhere from the region of Adullam and Chezib. Her name means "date palm." Personal names containing the names of animals and plants are not uncommon in the Bible.[26]

7 Like many of the other firstborn in the Bible (Cain, Ishmael, Esau, Reuben, etc.), Er is set aside by God. He was killed because he *displeased Yahweh,* either by something evil he did or because he was reprehensible.[27] The text does not give even a hint of what that sin was, and the reason for the omission is that Er's sin, and its identification, is not central to the movement of the story. But it must have been a grave sin. Not since the days of Noah and Sodom and Gomorrah has God taken the life of one who displeased him, and there it was groups who were annihilated. Er is the first individual in Scripture whom Yahweh kills *(wayᵉmiṯēhû).*[28]

8 The text does not record that Judah displayed any remorse over

25. C. A. Ben-Mordecai ("Chezib," *JBL* 58 [1939] 283-86) rejects *kᵉzîḇ* as a place name, and renders instead "(Shelah) was born in a caul," the caul being the thin membrane that may encircle the head and face of the newborn at birth. He also connects *kᵉzîḇ* with *kāzāḇ,* "lying, falsehood." (Cf. Albright's editorial comment on this suggestion [p. 286], which he says is plausible if one follows MT, but he thinks LXX is preferable.) NEB also seeks to eliminate Chezib as a place name: "and she ceased to bear children when she had given birth to him"; for criticisms of such a rendering, see Emerton, *VT* 25 (1975) 340-41.

26. For illustrations see J. J. Stamm, "Hebräische Frauennamen," in *Hebräische Wortforschung,* Fest. W. Baumgartner, ed. B. Hartmann, et al., VTSup 16 (Leiden: Brill, 1967), pp. 328-30; D. Stuart, "Names, Proper," *ISBE,* 3:487. P. Bird ("The Harlot as Heroine: Narrative Art and Social Presupposition in Three Old Testament Texts," *Semeia* 46 [1989] 134 n. 11) designates Tāmār/palm a fertility symbol. See also W. D. Reyburn, "Totemism," *IDBSup,* p. 912. For the place name Baʿal-Tamar (Judg. 20:33), located in hill country outside the normal palm groves area, see B. Rosen, "Early Israelite cultic centers in the hill country," *VT* 38 (1988) 116.

27. Note the reversal of consonants in the name Er *(ʿr)* and the word used to describe his character/activities, "evil" *rʿ).*

28. Within vv. 1-11, vv. 1-6 highlight the beginning of life with verbs like "conceived," "bore," and "named." Vv. 7-11 highlight the termination of life with verbs like "killed" and "wasted." See J. W. H. Bos, "Out of the Shadows: Genesis 38; Judges 4:17-22; Ruth 3," *Semeia* 42 (1988) 42.

Er's death. Instead, his sole concern is that his deceased firstborn not lack offspring. To prevent that, he instructs Onan, the second born, to *cohabit with* (Heb. *bōʾ ʾel,* lit., "go in to") Tamar (the same verb later used of Judah with Tamar in v. 18). Note that Judah does not say to Onan, "marry her," just "go in to her," or "have sex with her." The father appeals to Onan's sense of sympathy by referring to the late Er as *your brother* rather than as "my son." Judah's concern is plainly with his dead son, not with his living daughter-in-law. He refers to Tamar only by relationship *(your sister-in-law),* never by name. Only the narrator calls her Tamar (vv. 6, 11, 13). Judah hears her name (v. 24) but never employs it himself. Thus, unlike Deut. 25:5-10, which addresses both the brother-in-law's duties and marriage for the childless wife, Gen. 38:8 speaks only of the first of these. Tamar remains Onan's sister-in law; she does not become his wife. This point makes clear that Tamar's legitimate entitlement extends only to a male son, not to marriage.[29]

Onan's responsibility is to fulfill his part in what is known as levirate marriage.[30] He is to *levirate,* or perform the duty of a brother-in-law to *(wᵉyabbēm),* Tamar. Later biblical law spells out the particulars of the levirate in Deut. 25:5-10, in which the root *ybm* (cf. *yāḇām,* "brother-in-law") appears six times (twice as a verb, vv. 5, 7; four times as a noun, vv. 5, 7 [twice], 9). These six occurrences of *ybm* account for all but two uses of the root in the OT (here and Ruth 1:15).

The law states that if brothers live together, and if one of them is married but dies without children, one of the surviving brothers is to marry or take her as wife and father a child with her. The child born of this levirate relationship (*levir* is Latin for "brother-in-law") carries on the name of his deceased father and eventually inherits the family estate. Here Judah is clever enough to mention only producing a child for the brother. For obvious reasons he says nothing about the inheritance this child will one day receive. The brother-in-law can apparently decline this obligation, but not without having to endure public humiliation and disgrace. The widow with whom he is supposed to have intercourse removes his shoe and spits in his face. In fact, this is the only OT law that brings such disgrace on one who fails to observe it.[31] Ruth's marriage to Boaz is levirate, though it departs significantly from the legislation of Deut. 25:5-10. Levirate marriage existed as

29. See G. W. Coats, "Widow's Rights: A Crux in the Structure of Gen. 38," *CBQ* 34 (1972) 463. For a contrary view, see E. W. Davies, "Inheritance rights and the Hebrew levirate marriage. Part 1," *VT* 31 (1981) 143.

30. Among the many studies on levirate marriage consult the following and their bibliographies: D. A. Leggett, *The Levirate and Goel Institutions in the Old Testament* (Cherry Hill, NJ: Mack, 1974); E. W. Davies, *VT* 31 (1981) 138-44, 257-68.

31. C. M. Carmichael, "A Ceremonial Crux: Removing a Man's Sandal as a Female Gesture of Contempt," *JBL* 96 (1977) 321-36.

an institution even into Jesus' day (Matt. 22:23-30; Mark 12:18-25; Luke 20:27-35).

9-10 The *levir* in this case is to be *Onan,* the second born. But he refuses to accept his responsibility. Instead, he practices coitus interruptus with Tamar; that is, instead of impregnating her, *he wasted his semen on the ground* (lit., "he spoiled [it] groundward").[32] This is clearly a reference to withdrawal to prevent conception, rather than a reference to masturbation.[33] Thus the etymological connection of "onanism" (in the sense of masturbation) with Onan's name is misleading.[34]

What Onan did, or refused to do, was so serious a breach of duty that it cost him his life. His action of wasting his semen is compounded by a series of sins. First, Onan refused to carry out his levirate responsibilities. The method he used to evade these responsibilities is wasting his seed. Second, he persistently failed to expedite these responsibilities. V. 9 does not isolate one incident by Onan, but refers to repeated offenses by him. The syntax of v. 9 does not refer to one time "when" Onan had sex with Tamar, but to *whenever* he had sex with her.[35] Third, Onan put his own interests ahead of Tamar and Tamar's future child. Num. 27:8-11 states that if a man dies without a son, then his inheritance is to pass to his daughter; if he has no daughter, then the inheritance is to pass to his brothers. Onan apparently does not want to father a son who will prevent him from receiving his deceased brother's inheritance.[36] Fourth, what makes Onan's sin so offensive is that he appears to undertake his responsibility, but he fakes it. He does not say, "No, I will not have sex with my sister-in-law." Tamar does not remove Onan's shoe and expectorate in his face. Onan does sleep with Tamar, begins intercourse, but then withdraws. Such subterfuge does not escape Yahweh's notice.[37]

11 Because *Shelah,* Judah's third son, is too young to have intercourse with Tamar, Judah sends Tamar off to her own *father's house* where she may bide her time. The OT provides little evidence that a widow, on the death of

32. Note the two Piels here — what Onan was supposed to do (*yabbēm,* v. 8), and what he actually did (*šiḥēṯ,* v. 9).

33. Cf. E. Ullendorff, "The Bawdy Bible," *BSOAS* 42 (1979) 434.

34. If one defines masturbation as self-gratification via self-stimulation, then plainly Onan's act is not masturbation. If masturbation is defined as incompleted coitus as a birth control technique, then the noun would be applicable here. Ullendorf (ibid.) provides references from talmudic literature (T.B. *Nid.* 13ab; *Yebam.* 34b) that distinguish clearly between masturbation and coitus interruptus.

35. See GKC, § 159o, which discusses the consecutive perfect after the conditional particle *'im* used in a frequentative sense; see also n. 12 above.

36. See E. W. Davies, *VT* 31 (1981) 257-58.

37. See T. Thompson and D. Thompson, "Some legal problems in the book of Ruth," *VT* 18 (1968) 93-94.

her husband, returned to her father's house (cf. Lev. 22:13, which says that a priest's daughter, if a widow or a divorcée without children, may return to her father's house; cf. also Ruth 1:8). This is one of four ways in which a widow might establish economic security. A widow might also be married to her brother-in-law (Deut. 25:5-10), or remarry (1 Sam. 25:39-42; 2 Sam. 11:26ff.; 1 Tim. 5:14), or remain celibate and attempt to support herself.[38] Judah promises to bring Tamar and Shelah together when the latter is a bit older. Thus Tamar, to whom Shelah is promised, is regarded as betrothed to Shelah. This makes Judah's intercourse with Tamar later on adultery.[39]

Judah's concern is not with Tamar but with his surviving son (v. 11b). Perhaps, thinks Judah, the fate of Er and Onan will overcome Shelah as well.[40] Judah is in danger of becoming like Er his firstborn — married, but with no male descendants. Judah does what he thinks is necessary to prevent that possibility. He declares Shelah ineligible, and he dismisses Tamar. She obeys quietly. Thus the reader knows, but Tamar does not know, the reason why she is being sent back to her father's house, or at least the real reason why she is being sent back. For this fleeting moment the reader is given entry into Judah's secret thoughts.[41]

2. TAMAR DECEIVES JUDAH (38:12-19)

12 *Much later, Judah's wife, the daughter of Shua, died. When the mourning period was over, he went up to his sheepshearers at Timnah, accompanied by his friend*[1] *Hirah the Adullamite.*

13 *When Tamar was told: "Your father-in-law is now*[2] *on his way to Timnah to shear his sheep,"*

38. D. E. Holwerda and N. J. Opperwall-Galluch, "Widow," *ISBE,* 4:1060. F. H. Cryer ("David's rise to power and the death of Abner: an analysis of 1 Samuel xxvi 14-16 and its redaction-critical implications," *VT* 35 [1985] 388 n. 9) argues that Zeruiah returned to live in her father's house after the death of her husband, à la Tamar, with her children assuming her name, and thus the use of the matronymic instead of the patronynmic to designate Joab, Abishai, and Asahel (e.g., 1 Chr. 2:16).

39. See A. Phillips, "Another example of family law," *VT* 30 (1980) 243.

40. The expression used about Judah to introduce his concerns about the well-being of Shelah: "for he thought that . . ." *(kî 'āmar pen . . .)* is the same as that used a few chapters later (42:4) about Jacob to introduce his concerns about the well-being of Benjamin.

41. For the irony in this narrative based on the discrepancy of knowledge between the characters, and between some characters and the reader, see J. L. Ska, "L'Ironie de Tamar (Gen. 38)," *ZAW* 100 (1988) 261-63.

1. LXX *poimḗn autoú,* "his shepherd," presupposes Heb. *rō'ēhû* instead of MT *rē'ēhû,* "his friend."

2. For *hinnēh* to express vivid immediacy, see Waltke and O'Connor, *Biblical Hebrew Syntax,* p. 675.

14 *She removed her widow's garb, put on[3] a veil, perfumed herself,[4] and positioned herself seductively at Enaim,[5] which is on the way to Timnah; for she saw that even though Shelah had grown up, she had not been given to him[6] in marriage.*

15 *Seeing her, Judah assumed she was a prostitute, even though[7] she had veiled her face.*

16 *So he went over to her at the roadside, and said: "Come, let me have sex with you,"[8] for he did not recognize her as his daughter-in-law. She said: "What will you pay[9] me so that[10] you may have sex with me?"*

17 *He said: "I,[11] I will send you a kid from the flock." She said, "Provided[12] you leave a pledge[13] until you deliver it."*

18 *He said: "What pledge shall I leave with you?" She said: "Your seal, and cord, and the staff you carry." So he gave them to her, had sex with her, and she conceived by him.*

3. SP and Targ. Onqelos read *wattiṯkas* (Hithpael), "she covered herself" (so also *BHS;* Westermann, 3:48). For *watt^ekas b^e* cf. 1 Sam. 19:13. For the form *watt^eḵas* see Exod. 8:2; 16:3; Num. 16:33; Ps. 106:17.

4. The meaning of *ʿlp* is debated. Thus AV, RSV, NAB translate the Hithpael here as "wrapped herself" (cf. also NIV, JB), but NEB has "perfumed herself." We agree with the latter translation on the basis of Ugar. *ǵlp,* "dye, perfume," and Arab. *ǵalafa,* "to smear, perfume oneself." See M. J. Dahood, "Northwest Semitic Notes on Genesis," *Bib* 55 (1974) 80; idem, review in *Bib* 53 (1972) 578-79.

5. *b^epeṯaḥ ʿênayim* offers many possibilities, which will be discussed in the commentary below.

6. LXX reads, "and he had not given her to him."

7. Is *kî* causal ("because") or concessive ("even though")? I translate the latter for reasons I state in the commentary below. Cf. also NEB. For the concessive meaning of *kî* see T. C. Vriezen, "Einige Notizen zur Uebersetzung des Bindeswort *kî,*" *BZAW* 77 (1958) 266-273; A. Schoors, "The particle *kî,*" *OTS* 21 (1981) 271-73. But neither of these studies cites Gen. 38:15 as an example. See also J. Muilenburg, "The Linguistic and Rhetorical Usage of the Particle *kî* in the Old Testament," *HUCA* 32 (1961) 147.

8. Lit., and again in vv. 16, 18, "let me go into you"; "so that you may go into me"; "he went into her."

9. Lit., "give." For "giving" *(nāṯan)* payment to a prostitute cf. Hos. 2:7 (Eng. 5).

10. R. Gordis (*The Word and the Book* [New York: Ktav, 1976], p. 211 n. 5) gives the meaning "if" to *kî* at this point: "if you have sex with me."

11. On the use of the independent pronoun in response to a preceeding statement or request, see Davidson, *Hebrew Syntax,* p. 151, § 107, Rem. 1.

12. Lit., "if you give me a pledge." For the suppression or ellipsis of the apodosis in a conditional sentence, see GKC, § 159dd; and C. Van Leeuwen, "Die Partikel *'im,*" *OTS* 18 (1973) 33.

13. With Heb. *ʿērāḇôn* (and Ugar. *ʿrbn*) cf. Gk. *arrabṓn,* Latin *arrabo,* and French *les arrhes,* "pledge, deposit." See C. H. Gordon, *Common Background of Greek and Hebrew Civilizations,* 2nd ed. (New York: Norton, 1965), p. 37.

19 *She left there, removed her veil, and again put on her widow's garb.*

12 Judah's experiences parallel those of his father. Both lose a son or sons (Er and Onan, Joseph — so Jacob believes), and both lose their wives. Nothing was said about any mourning period by Judah for either Er or Onan, but for his wife — who plays no part in the story — there is a time of grief. When this period is over Judah heads to Timnah to oversee his sheepshearers. Passages like 1 Sam. 25:2-8 and 2 Sam. 13:23-24 make it clear that the period for sheepshearing was a major feast in later Judah. In fact, in 1 Sam. 25:8 David refers to the time he sent his men to Nabal's sheepshearers as a *yôm ṭōḇ* (lit., "good day"), which is an expression meaning a feast day (so RSV), a time for more than the usual feasting and drinking (Esth. 8:17; 9:19, 22). As the owner of the flocks it is imperative that Judah be there to oversee the proceedings. This is true of Laban (31:19), Nabal (1 Sam. 25:8), and Absalom (2 Sam. 13:23-24).[14]

Two locations are possible for *Timnah* (which means "allotted portion"). One is on the border of Judah, a bit over four miles northwest of Beth-shemesh, and identified with Tell el-Batashi (see Josh. 15:10 and 19:43, which places Timnah in the territory of Dan). It became famous as a center of Philistine occupation in the days of Samson (Judg. 14:1, 2, 5). Another possibility, and probably a preferable one, is Khirbet Tibneh, about two miles south-southwest of Beth-shemesh (cf. Josh. 15:57).[15]

Tamar bides her time until Judah's wife is dead. For one thing she has no interest in ruining and defaming the marriage of her in-laws. For another thing, she knows that Judah is more sexually vulnerable now that he is a widower. But why does she make her move at sheepshearing time? Hos. 4:13-14 details the aberrant practice of sacred prostitution at feast times in Israel, and Hos. 9:1-2 comments on ritual fornication on threshing floors in the hopes of producing a bumper crop. If this is an accurate description of what accompanied the observance of feast days, then it might explain why Tamar chose this opportune moment to seduce Judah.[16]

13-14 Tamar is told about her father-in-law's journey to Timnah and what the journey's purpose was. The Hebrew for *father-in-law (ḥām)* occurs only four times in the OT (Gen. 38:13, 25; 1 Sam. 4:19, 21), and it always signifies the husband's father, never the wife's father (which is *ḥōṯēn* [see,

14. See J. C. Greenfield, " 'Les bain des brebis': Another Example and a Query," *Or* 29 (1960) 101.

15. V. R. Gold, "Timnah," *IDB,* 4:649; G. L. Kelm and W. S. LaSor, "Timnah," *ISBE,* 4:855-56.

16. See M. C. Astour, "Tamar the Hierodule," *JBL* 85 (1966) 192-93; Kidner, *Genesis,* p. 188; S. D. Mathewson, "An Exegetical Study of Genesis 38," *BSac* 146 (1989) 378.

e.g., Exod. 18]). It is clear that Tamar will employ her strategem before the sheepshearing, not after. Ruth approaches Boaz (Ruth 3) after Boaz has completed his work. Tamar approaches Judah on his way to work. Who gave Tamar the particulars about Judah's itinerary we do not know. She owes this bit of information about her father-in-law's movements to an anonymous informer.

Tamar removes her widow's garments, veils herself (to conceal her identity from Judah), perfumes herself (to attract Judah), and positions herself *b^e^peṯaḥ ʿênayim* (lit., "at [the] opening of [the] eyes"). The NEB and JB, following Targs., Pesh., and Vulg., understood the phrase as a parting of the road, a crossroads ("where the road forks in two directions"). Other versions (e.g., RSV, NIV, NAB, NJPS), following the LXX, take *ʿênayim* as a place name ("at the gate [or entrance] to Enaim"). We know of no Enaim from the OT, though a site in the Shephelah is known as Enam, *ʿênām* (Josh. 15:34), and perhaps the two refer to the same place. This equation of Enam of Josh. 15:34 with Enaim of Gen. 38:14 was made as early as the Babylonian Talmud (*Sota* 10a). The existence of a place name *ʿênayim* may be deduced from the Ebla geographical atlas, where the name of one of the cities in Syria-Palestine is written with Sumerian logograms IGI.IGI^{ki}. The meaning would be something like "twin springs" (IGI is Sumerian for "eye, spring").[17]

Ira Robinson has suggested that the phrase *b^e^peṯaḥ ʿênayim* here ought to be compared with the phrase *k^e^sûṯ ʿênayim* in 20:16, literally, "a covering of the eyes."[18] When the truth of Sarah's identity is revealed to Abimelech after he had almost committed adultery with her, Abimelech gives to Abraham a thousand shekels of silver, which is to serve as "a covering of the eyes" to Sarah. That is, the money will vindicate Sarah publicly from any suspicion of irregular sexual behavior, and be a compensation for any embarrassment she has had to live with. If *k^e^sûṯ ʿênayim* signifies vindication from suspicion of harlotry, *p^e^ṯaḥ ʿênayim* may signify the opposite — to pose in such a way to cause one to stop, look, and open his eyes. Thus *b^e^peṯaḥ ʿênayim* may be a double entendre: Enaim is not only the place where Tamar met Judah, but also her sexual invitation to Judah.

In this setting the name *b^e^peṯaḥ ʿênayim* (lit., "opening of the eyes") is particularly appropriate and ironic. At "Opening of the Eyes," even though he has sexual congress with her, Judah's eyes are closed as to the identity of his daughter-in-law, and thus he fails to recognize his partner.[19]

17. See M. J. Dahood, "Ebla, Ugarit, and the Bible," in G. Pettinato, *Archives of Ebla* (Garden City, NY: Doubleday, 1981), pp. 280-81.

18. See I. Robinson, "*bĕpetaḥ ʿênayim* in Genesis 38:14," *JBL* 96 (1977) 569.

19. J. W. H. Bos, "Out of the Shadows," *Semeia* 42 (1988) 42; E. M. Good, "Deception and Women: A Response," *Semeia* 42 (1988) 116-17.

Tamar is aware that Shelah is no longer a youth. Judah's earlier argument that Tamar live with her father "until Shelah grows older" (*ʿaḏ-yigdal šēlâ,* v. 11) no longer applies, for now *Shelah had grown up* (*kî gāḏal šēlâ,* v. 14). But Judah had not fulfilled his promise to Tamar. Judah's failure to inform Tamar that Shelah is now eligible for marriage (end of v. 14) may be explained in two ways. On the one hand, it could be an unconscionable oversight on Judah's part. On the other hand, it could well be that Judah never intended to bring Shelah and Tamar together, and therefore his earlier statement that she return to her father's house until Shelah comes of age was nothing but a ruse. If that is the case, then the trick Tamar played against Judah is a response to the trick Judah played against Tamar, rather than the initiative of trickery.[20] What happens to Judah, then, parallels what happened earlier to his father Jacob: the perpetrator of deceit is now the victim of deceit.

15 The narrator tells us that Judah *assumed* (Heb. *ḥāšaḇ,* lit., "thought")[21] that the incognito Tamar was a *zônâ,* a common prostitute. Part of Tamar's subterfuge was to "put on a veil" (*watteḵas baṣṣāʿîp̱,* v. 14), that is, "cover her face" (*kisseṯâ pāneyhā,* v. 15, here translated *she had veiled her face*).[22]

Most translations understand v. 15b as causal: "Judah assumed she was a whore, *since* [so JB, NAB; cf. AV "because"; RSV, NIV "for"] she had veiled her face." But there is little evidence that prostitutes in Canaan wore veils. Two references, Hos. 2:4 (Eng. 2) and Cant. 1:7, might support this idea. In the first text, Hosea's wife Gomer is exhorted "to remove her harlotry (or promiscuity, *zenûneyhā*) from her face." This is more likely a reference to makeup rather than to veils.[23] We do know that prostitutes painted their faces, especially around the eyes (Jer. 4:30; Ezek. 23:40). The second text is Cant. 1:7, which M. Pope translates: "Tell me, my true love, Where do you pasture? Where do you fold at noon? Lest I be as one veiled [*keʿōṭeyâ*] Among your comrades' flocks."[24] Pope suggests that the beloved in the Song is concerned that she will appear to be a (veiled) prostitute, if

20. M. Bal, "Tricky Thematics," *Semeia* 42 (1988) 148-49.

21. For another instance of *ḥāšaḇ* followed by two accusatives in which the preposition *le* is prefixed to the second accusative, cf. 1 Sam. 1:13: *wayyaḥšeḇehā ʿēlî lešikkōrâ.* Eli assumed Hannah was drunk; she was not. Judah assumed this person was a prostitute; she was not.

22. For "covering the face" *(kāsâ pānîm)* cf. Isa. 6:2; Jer. 51:51; Ezek. 12:6, 12; Ps. 44:16 (Eng. 15); 69:8 (Eng. 7); Job 9:24; 15:27; 23:17; Prov. 24:31.

23. See F. I. Andersen and D. N. Freedman, *Hosea,* AB (Garden City, NY: Doubleday, 1980), pp. 224-25.

24. M. Pope, *Song of Songs,* AB (Garden City, NY: Doubleday, 1977), p. 291. Cf. also NIV, AV mg., RSV mg.

she has to wander around looking for her beloved.[25] This is not, however, the only possible interpretation of Cant. 1:7. For example, the veil might be a sign of mourning (e.g., 2 Sam. 15:30), not harlotry. Several ancient versions (Pesh., Vulg., Symm.) suggest the reading "Lest I be a wanderer" (reading *keṭōʿîm,* i.e., transposing the ʿ and *ṭ*). The NEB reads "lest I be left off picking lice"![26]

Later on (v. 21) Tamar will be referred to as a "cult prostitute" *(qeḏēšâ).* The Middle Assyrian laws state that free Asssyrian women, their daughters, and concubines must veil themselves when they go out on the street. In addition, a married "sacred prostitute" must veil herself when she goes outside. Those who must not be veiled when they are outside are (1) an unmarried sacred prostitute (*qadiltu* [= *qadištu*]); (2) a harlot *(ḫarīmtu);* and (3) female slaves.[27] Those who must be veiled in public were married women and women of the upper classes, whether married or not. Also a concubine was to be veiled when traveling with the chief wife in any public area. Thus Assyrian law, at least, would argue that harlots were not veiled. Furthermore, the law states that anybody who sees a prostitute or an ordinary slave girl veiled in a public place must turn her over to the authorities or be subject to a heavy penalty.[28] Of course, these laws say nothing about Israelite society or culture. Even the code of the Babylonians has no reference to veiling as either required for some or illegal for others. But note that the Hebrew prophet (Isa. 47:1-3) warns the "daughter of Babylon" (i.e., the high-born women), among other things, to put off their veils in the light of the coming judgment of Yahweh against them.

One might compare Tamar's veiling herself with Rebekah's taking a veil and covering herself (24:65) as Isaac drew near. Both veilings are done at the approach of a man (Isaac, Judah), and both precede sexual activity, although the former is clearly in the context of a marriage, the veiling of a bride. I propose that Tamar's wearing of the veil was not to make Judah think

25. Ibid., pp. 330-31. R. E. Murphy (*The Song of Songs,* Hermeneia [Minneapolis: Fortress, 1990], pp. 130-31) understands the covering to be simply a disguise the woman will have to use as she seeks for her companion in order to avoid identification by her companions.

26. See G. R. Driver, "Lice in the Old Testament," *PEQ* 160 (1974) 159-60; J. A. Emerton, review in *VT* 34 (1984) 502.

27. Middle Assyrian law § 40; see the translation of T. Meek, *ANET,* p. 183b; cf. M. C. Astour, "Tamar the Hierodule," *JBL* 96 (1977) 187. On what harlot clothing Tamar may have worn, besides the veil, see C. M. Carmichael, "Forbidden Mixtures," *VT* 32 (1982) 408-9, and his interesting quotation of Jdt. 16:8. The appropriate cuneiform texts are cited also by P. Bird, "The Harlot as Heroine," *Semeia* 46 (1989) 134 n. 5.

28. See G. R. Driver, *The Assyrian Laws* (Oxford: Clarendon, 1935), pp. 129-31. See also *"ḫarimtu"* ("prostitute"), *CAD,* Ḫ:101b.

she was a prostitute. Rather, it was intended to prevent him from recognizing her.[29] It is not the veil but Tamar's positioning herself at Enaim (v. 14) that made her appear to be a prostitute.[30]

Tamar's taking advantage of Judah for a more noble purpose is not without parallel in the OT. One may think of Esther's exploitation of Ahasuerus's sexual desires for the achievement of her praiseworthy aims, that is, the deliverance of her people.[31] Or one may think of Naomi, the childless widow, playing on Boaz's predictable appreciation of Ruth's beauty. Here then is an instance where the end justifies the means.

16 This chapter began (v. 1) by telling us that Judah pitched his tent near *(wayyēṭ ʿaḏ)* Hirah the Adullamite. Now he goes over beside *(wayyēṭ ʾel)* the harlot. Thus the verb *nāṭâ* (lit., "turn") is used twice: once for turning aside for lodging, once for turning aside for sex. Judah offers no preliminary conversation. He comes directly to the point: *Come, let me have sex with you.*

Her response is as quick as his request: *What will you pay me so that you may have sex with me?* She does nothing to dissuade him, of course, for that is her reason for being at Enaim. Nor does she even set the price for her favors. She leaves that to Judah. In this way Judah becomes even more responsible for his behavior.

Verse 15 ended with a *kî* clause — "even though [*kî*] she had veiled her face." V. 16b is composed of three *kî* clauses — "*for* he did not recognize her *as* his daughter-in-law. . . . *so that* you may have sex with me." Thus vv. 15 and 16 are bound together by *kî . . . kî . . . kî . . . kî. . . .*

17-18 He offers a *kid from the flock,* exactly what Samson took when he went to visit his wife (Judg. 15:1). The only other OT source containing data about a harlot's fees is Prov. 6:26, which mentions a loaf of bread as a prostitute's price, and this is significantly less than being involved with an adulteress who demands luxury in return for her services. That price is of considerably less value than a kid from the flock. Either Judah is very generous, or Prov. 6:26 is well below the average rate for a rendezvous with a prostitute.

Because he does not have the animal with him he agrees, at Tamar's insistence, to leave behind a *pledge.* Judah decides on the fee (v. 16b), but Tamar decides on the pledge (v. 18). He is to leave with her his *seal (ḥōṯām),* his *cord (pāṯîl),* and his *staff (maṭṭeh).*

29. See Driver, *Assyrian Laws,* p. 134. Gen. Rabbah 75:8 says of Judah: "He paid no attention to her. When she covered her face, he thought, '*If she were a whore, would she have covered her face?*'" (J. Neusner, *Genesis Rabbah,* 3 vols. [Atlanta: Scholars, 1985], 3:212).

30. On the prostitute's habitat (e.g., the public square, Lipit-Ishtar Code § 27) see Bird, *Semeia* 46 (1989) 134 n. 6.

31. See S. Talmon, " 'Wisdom' in the book of Esther," *VT* 13 (1963) 451.

The giving and taking of pledges was common in Israel, with laws specifying procedure (cf. Exod. 22:25 [Eng. 26]; Deut. 24:6, 10-13). Wisdom literature warns a third party against becoming surety for another's outstanding pledge, especially a stranger's, apparently because of the likelihood of default (Prov. 6:1-5; 11:15; 17:18; 22:26). A pledge to a prostitute is unique to Gen. 38:17-18, except possibly for a passage like Amos 2:7-8, which refers to "pledged garments" that the clients (here, father and son), unable to pay cash, deposit with the prostitute (here *hanna*ʿ*ᵃrâ,* lit., "the girl") until they can pay.[32]

The *seal* was made of metal or stone and worn on a *cord* around the neck. In other instances the seal might be a stamp-seal as part of a ring (e.g., Jer. 22:24; Hag. 2:23). References such as Exod. 28:11, 21, 36; 39:6, 14, 30 suggest that much artistic skill was used in the making of seals. The *staff* is another means of identification.[33] W. W. Hallo has argued that Judah's seal, cord, and staff were, in fact, a cylinder seal, a bracelet, and a pin-mount respectively.[34] We must see, in reading the narrative, that Tamar does not request these items primarily as promissory notes, though she implies that to Judah. Rather, her real purpose is to possess these items, for they will function as signatures, a proof of the father's identity.[35]

19 Her deception now perfectly implemented, Tamar leaves and is then able to remove her veil and dress herself again in her widow's garb. Presumably she returns to her father's house. Wherever Tamar goes after having sexual intercourse with Judah must be a place where it is safe to remove her disguise.

32. See M. J. Dahood, "To pawn one's flock," *Bib* 42 (1961) 361-65. Dahood also appeals to his translations of Prov. 27:13 (= 20:16), "take his garment when a stranger has pledged it, and pawn it for a harlot" (following Aquila and Theodotion); and Prov. 23:27-28; he renders v. 28: "she [the harlot] lies in wait like a robber, and cloaks from men she snatches" (by revocalizing MT). No modern versions of Proverbs accept these readings. His translation and interpretation of Amos 2:7, 8 (e.g. "a man and his father go into *harlots*") differs significantly from that of F. I. Andersen and D. N. Freedman, *Amos,* AB (New York: Doubleday, 1989), pp. 307, 318-21.

33. See Speiser's fine note on these terms, *Genesis,* pp. 298-99; also O. Tufnell, "Seals and Scarabs," *IDB,* 4:254-59. T. Lambdin ("Egyptian Loan Words in the Old Testament," *JAOS* 73 [1953] 151) argues that the Hebrew word for "seal" *(ḥōṯām)* is of Egyptian origin.

34. W. W. Hallo, "As the Seal upon Thy Heart," *BRev* 1/1 (1985) 20-27.

35. See N. Furman, "His Story versus Her Story: Male Genealogy and Female Strategy in the Jacob Cycle," in *Feminist Perspectives on Biblical Scholarship,* ed. A. Y. Collins (Chico, CA: Scholars, 1985), pp. 111-12. Note also the comment of Vawter, *On Genesis,* p. 398: "What Judah does is surrender his ID card, which he expects to be quickly redeemed, but which Tamar retains for her own purposes."

3. TAMAR IS EXONERATED (38:20-26)

20 *Judah sent the kid from the flock by his friend the Adullamite to reclaim the pledge from the woman, but he was unable to find her.*

21 *So he inquired of the men of the place:*[1] *"Where is that*[2] *cult prostitute,*[3] *who was by the roadside in Enaim?" They replied: "There never has been a cult prostitute here!"*

22 *Accordingly, he returned to Judah and told him: "I was unable to find her; and moreover, the men of the place claimed there never was a cult prostitute there!"*

23 *"Let her have*[4] *the things," said Judah, "otherwise, we*[5] *shall become a laughingstock. I sent this kid, (you know that),*[6] *but you never found her."*

24 *About*[7] *three months*[8] *later, Judah was told, "Tamar your daughter-in-law has played the harlot; moreover, she is pregnant because of her harlotry." "Take her out*[9] *and let her be burned," said Judah.*

1. MT has "her place." With *BHS,* I follow SP, LXX, Pesh., and the Palestinian Targ., which read "the place." See also v. 22, which reads *hammāqôm,* "the place." Speiser notes (*Genesis,* p. 298) that the definite article in Hebrew at times has the force of the personal pronoun in English, and vice versa.

2. For the absence of the article on the demonstrative since it is already to some extent determined by its meaning, see GKC, § 126y.

3. Modern English versions render *haqq*^e^*ḏēšâ* as "cult prostitute" (NJPS), "temple prostitute" (NEB, NAB, NRSV), "prostitute" (JB, Westermann), "harlot" (AV, NKJV, RSV), "shrine prostitute" (NIV), "sacred prostitute" (R. Coote and D. Ord, *The Bible's First History* [Philadelphia: Fortress, 1989], 179), "votary" (Speiser), "ritual prostitute" (M. Bal, *Lethal Love* [Bloomington: Indiana University, 1987], p. 101).

4. Lit., "let her take it," i.e., "let her keep it." Tamar cannot take the pledge, for she already has it. Accordingly *lāqaḥ* here means "have, keep." See R. Gordis, *The Word and the Book* (New York: Ktav, 1976), p. 219.

5. Pesh. reads "lest I be a laughingstock." MT's use of the 1st person pl. indicts both Hirah and Judah.

6. "You know that" is my free translation of the particle *hinnēh.*

7. For the temporal use of *min* ("when, after, about") in *k*^e^*mišlōš,* see GKC, § 119y n. 3; Williams, *Hebrew Syntax,* p. 55, § 316. The omission of the *dagesh* in the *š* of *k*^e^*mišlōš* (one expects *k*^e^*miššᵉlōš*) is explained in GKC, § 20m.

8. Only here in the OT is *ḥōḏeš* treated as fem. (see BDB, p. 294a), but SP reads the more normal *šᵉlōšeṯ* (fem.) rather than MT *šᵉlōš* (masc.). Cf. GKC, § 97c. The basic rule for Biblical Hebrew is that numerals connected with masc. nouns take the fem. form, while numerals connected with fem. nouns take the masc. form.

9. For the Hiphil of *yāṣā'* meaning "to bring out" one guilty of adultery cf. Deut. 22:21, 24.

25 *As she*[10] *was being taken out,*[11] *she sent a message to her father-in-law: "It is by a man to whom these items belong that I am pregnant." She said, "Identify, please, whose seal, cord,*[12] *and staff these are."*

26 *Judah identified them, and said: "She is in the right, not I,*[13] *for I did not give her to my son Shelah." And never again*[14] *was he intimate with her.*

20 Judah dispatches Hirah *(the Adullamite)* to deliver the kid to Tamar and thus redeem the pledge. It is not only that Judah is an honest customer who pays his debts. He really wants to get back the articles he has deposited with Tamar. Interestingly, Hirah is sent to *the woman (hā'iššâ),* not to "the prostitute." This is the only time in the narrative that Tamar is so styled. She is a nameless woman. Her namelessness is the narrative's way of emphasizing Judah's casual relationship with Tamar. She was simply a woman with whom he had a tryst.

The verb "sent" *(šālaḥ)* is prominent in this section. First, Judah sent *(wayyišlaḥ)* the Adullamite with the kid from the flock to Tamar (v. 20). Later, Judah reminds Hirah that he had sent him with a kid to Tamar (*šālaḥtî,* v. 23). On her way to execution, Tamar sent *(šāl*^{e}*ḥâ)* a message to Judah (v. 25). Also, the verb "find" *(māṣā')* occurs three times in this section: *m*^{e}*ṣā'āh* (v. 20); *m*^{e}*ṣā'ṯîhā* (v. 22); *m*^{e}*ṣā'ṯāh* (v. 23).

21-22 In asking the townsmen about Tamar's whereabouts, Hirah does

10. On the use of two forms for "she" *(hiw'; hî')* near each other, see GKC, § 321.

11. With reference to a past state of affairs, the participle describes circumstances simultaneous with the principal event. See Waltke and O'Connor, *Biblical Hebrew Syntax,* p. 625; Davidson, *Hebrew Syntax,* pp. 188-89, § 141; GKC, § 116v.

12. *ḥōṯām* ("seal") and *pāṯîl* ("cord") of v. 18 have now become *ḥōṯemeṯ* and *p*^{e}*ṯîlîm,* respectively. Perhaps the change from "cord" in v. 18 to "cords" in v. 25 reflects that one cord was made by two strings tied or twisted (*pāṯal,* "wind, twist") together. The shift from *ḥōṯām* to *ḥōṯemeṯ* illustrates that biblical writers used unmarked substantive forms in close proximity to marked, but synonymous, forms, i.e., one with a *-ṯ*. On this feature, see R. J. Ratner, "Morphological Variation in Biblical Hebrew Rhetoric," *MAARAV* 8 (1992) 146-47 (under the general heading "synonymous nominal pairs"). Another change is that all three nouns are preceded by the definite article here, whereas in v. 18 they all had pronominal suffixes. Cf. v. 18 and v. 25 in NEB, which catches the different nuances (v. 18: "your seal and its cord"; v. 25: "the engraving on the seal, the pattern of the cord").

13. According to Waltke and O'Connor (*Biblical Hebrew Syntax,* p. 265): "In a *comparison of exclusion* the subject alone possesses the quality connoted by the adjective or stative verb, to the exclusion of the thing compared." Targ. Onqelos and Targ. Pseudo-Jonathan avoid having Judah, the main ancestor of the Jews, make an unfavorable comparison of himself to a Canaanite by reading: "She is in the right; by me she is pregnant" *(zk'h mny m'dy').* For a parallel to Judah's words see Saul's words to David in 1 Sam. 24:18 (Eng. 17): the one who speaks is the accuser but he recognizes that the accused is innocent and therefore the speaker is guilty; the syntagm *ṣdq min* also occurs in both texts.

14. *yāsap* (lit., "add") may be used to prepare us for a return shortly to the story about *yôsēp̱* (Joseph).

not say: "Where is the prostitute [*zônâ*]?" Instead, he asks: *Where is the cult prostitute* [*q^e^ḏēšâ*]?[15] They respond that there never has been a *q^e^ḏēšâ* in their locality. Why does Gen. 38 refer to Tamar by two words, *prostitute* (v. 15) and *cult prostitute?* The purpose is certainly not to elevate Judah's behavior from sleeping with street prostitutes to engaging in ritual fornication with a woman ("a holy one") who is a temple servant and devotee. Note that the narrator reports that Judah thought she was a prostitute (v. 15), but when he relates the conversation of Canaanites with each other (v. 21), he puts in their mouths the designation "cult prostitute." In other words, what the narrator called a "prostitute" was in the local idiom a "cult prostitute." Vv. 21-22 are told, then, from the point of view of Hirah and the Enaimites.[16] Furthermore, a passage like Deut. 23:18-19 (Eng. 17-18), which collocates *q^e^ḏēšâ and zônâ,* suggests that the terms are related but not necessarily synonymous. The two terms are also parallel in Hos. 4:14.

It is unlikely that Hirah would suppose that the woman who made herself available nowhere near any temple was a cult prostitute.[17] Thus it is dubious that Tamar ever intended to pass herself off as anything more than a prostitute. There would certainly be no reason to laugh at a person (see Judah's concern in v. 23 about being ridiculed) who had engaged in sexual congress with a hierodule of the Canaanite cult. In order to be as polite as possible to the townspeople, Hirah used a euphemism. In private or plain speech Tamar is a prostitute. In public or polite speech Tamar is a "cult prostitute."[18]

15. In ch. 38 LXX translates both *zônâ* and *q^e^ḏēšâ* by *pórnē,* "harlot," apparently taking the two words as synonyms in this context. Elsewhere LXX uses *pórnē* to translate *q^e^ḏēšâ* only in Deut. 23:17 (MT 18). The latter verse says that there shall be no *q^e^ḏēšâ* from among the Israelite women, and no *qāḏēš* from among the Israelite men. The LXX translates this verse twice. The first translation renders *q^e^ḏēšâ* as *pornē* ("prostitute") and *qāḏēš* as *porneúōn* ("fornicator"). The second translation, probably an indication that the translators were uncertain of the correct rendering, renders *q^e^ḏēšâ* as *telesphóros* ("female who is associated with a cult") and *qāḏēš* as *teleskóōenos* ("male who is associated with a cult"). In the only other use of *qeḏēšâ* in the OT besides Gen. 38 and Deut. 23, Hos. 4:14 mentions those who make sacrifice with the *q^e^ḏēšôṯ,* and the LXX renders the pl. of *zōnâ* and *q^e^ḏešâ* as *meta tōn pornōn* (with the prostitutes") and *meta tōn tetelesménōn* ("with the initiates"), respectively. For studies of *q^e^ḏēšâ* and cultic prostitution, see E. J. Fisher, "Cultic Prostitution in the Ancient Near East? A Reassessment," *BTB* 6 (1976) 225-36; E. M. Yamauchi, "Cultic Prostitution," in *Orient and Occident,* Fest. C. H. Gordon, ed. H. A. Hoffner, Jr. (Neukirchen-Vluyn: Neukirchener, 1973), pp. 213-222; M. I. Gruber, "Hebrew *qĕdēšāh* and Her Canaanite and Akkadian Cognates," *UF* 18 (1986) 133-48; R. Harris, "Woman in the Ancient Near East," *IDBSup,* pp. 960-63.

16. See A. Berlin, *Poetics and Interpretation of Biblical Narrative* (Sheffield: Almond, 1983), pp. 60-61.

17. This point is made by H. L. Ginsberg, "Lexicographical Notes," *Hebräische Wortforschung,* Fest. W. Baumgartner, ed. B. Hartmann, et al., VTSup 16 (Leiden: Brill, 1967), p. 75 n. 2.

18. See P. Bird, "The Harlot as Heroine," *Semeia* 46 (1989) 126, who notes that

23 Judah would rather leave the pledged items with Tamar than conduct an all-out search for them. At this point their recovery would be more of a loss than a gain. It is clear that Judah's main concern is that he not become the butt of jokes, a *laughingstock (lāḇûz)* because a street prostitute has outwitted him and taken advantage of him. *bûz* usually connotes something like "scorn, shame, contempt," but here it means "a laughingstock." Judah's continued search among the townsmen for "the prostitute" and the pledged items she holds would only broadcast how she had tricked him. It is not wise to advertise one's follies. Judah is also concerned that Hirah know that Judah is not trying to get something for nothing (v. 23c). He feels constrained to remind Hirah that he did send him with payment to the woman.

This attempt at self-exoneration by Judah is really paving the way for Tamar's forthcoming exoneration. Judah's lack of contrition or repentance over his scandalous behavior is predictable. He is concerned only about the maintenance of his own reputation.

24-26 In many ways the development of this story is similar to the David-Bathsheba liaison (2 Sam. 11). Both focus on an illicit sexual relationship from which a child is born. Both have a period of quietness (3 months here, an unspecified time in 2 Sam. 11) in which the man involved doubtless hopes that the incident is forgotten (Judah) or covered up (David). Both men express righteous indignation when informed of the misconduct of another: *Take her out and let her be burned;* "the man who has done this deserves to die" (2 Sam. 12:5). Both Judah and David are trapped into admitting their culpability. Finally, when confronted with the truth, both men made public acknowledgments: *She is in the right, not I* (v. 25); "I have sinned against the Lord" (2 Sam. 12:13).[19]

We never find out who the informers are in this story. Tamar "was told" (*wayyuggaḏ,* v. 13) that Judah had gone to Timnah to oversee the sheepshearing. Now Judah is *informed (wayyuggaḏ)* of Tamar's sexual adventures and her resulting pregnancy. Who told Tamar about Judah, and who told Judah about Tamar?

Believing that he is authorized to take legal action against a daughter-in-law who has prostituted herself, Judah's response is to order somebody to bring (*hôṣî'ûhā,* Hiphil pl. imperative) Tamar out of the city and burn her. He believes

---

the OT often uses euphemisms for both sexual acts and sex organs. Thus words for foot or hand may be used for the phallus. Bird's nonbiblical illustration of this is the use of "courtesan" for the cruder expression "whore." See also T. Hamill, "The Bible and the Imagination: A Modest Sounding of Its Harlot's Evaluation," *ITQ* 52 (1986) 107, who speaks of Hirah's replacing "an ugly word with a holy word."

19. Some intriguing and hardly coincidental parallels between the Judah/Tamar story in Gen. 38 and the story of David's family in 2 Sam. 11ff. are observed by G. A. Rendsburg, "David and his circle in Genesis xxxviii," *VT* 36 (1986) 438-46.

completely the oral report he receives, and he is apparently unwilling to suspend judgment until he has access to more facts. If Judah had been told only of Tamar's harlotry, he would have had to reach the conclusion he did on the basis of the word of another, and perhaps would have been more hesitant to assume guilt and order sanctions. It is the report of her pregnancy, now at least three months along, that decides the issue. Judah is able to substantiate Tamar's adultery by circumstantial evidence, i.e., her pregnancy during his absence.

Judah's prescribed penalty for Tamar is *let her be burned,* a form of execution that may well be intended to reflect Tamar's alleged display of unbridled sexual passion. The connection between burning and sexual indiscretions is amply illustrated by Prov. 6:27-29, which compares adultery with taking fire into one's bosom or walking on hot coals and the inevitable result that occurs.[20] Only two instances in OT law call for burning: (1) incest with one's mother-in-law (Lev. 20:14, which is similar to the Code of Hammurapi, § 157: "If a seignior has lain in the bosom of his mother after [the death of] his father, they shall burn both of them");[21] (2) prostitution by a priest's daughter (Lev. 21:9). One may compare Lev. 21:9 with the Code of Hammurapi, § 110, which mandates burning for a cult prostitute *(nadītum)* or "divine lady" (*ēntum,* a priestess?) who enters a tavern for a drink.[22] It would appear, then, from a consideration of Gen. 38:24; Lev. 20:14; and 21:9 that death by fire in the OT bore a special relationship to illicit sexual behavior.

This verse is also anomalous in other ways. This is the only place in the OT where one individual had the power to order the execution of another for adultery. Furthermore, the penalty for adultery in the OT is stoning by the community, not burning (Lev. 20:10; Deut. 22:21). Nor does it appear that harlotry was a punishable offense in Israelite society. If any later law applies here, it is Lev. 20:12, which calls for the death penalty for both parties if a man lies with his daughter-in-law. Judah is unlikely to invoke that measure! Of course, Judah's insistence that Tamar be burned is simply an outburst of indignation, a spontaneous reaction, and hardly a reflection of actual juridical enforcement for sins relating to sexual behavior.

Some have argued that v. 25 indicates that in patriarchal times it was the paterfamilias who ordered the execution of an adulteress, hence Judah's promptness at adjudicating the case.[23] But to call Judah the paterfamilias in this case is irrelevant, for Tamar is now a widow, not a married woman, and she is not even living in Judah's house but in the house of her own father.[24]

20. See C. Carmichael, "Biblical Laws of Talion," *HAR* 9 (1985) 118-19.

21. See *ANET,* p. 172.

22. See *ANET,* p. 170.

23. See A. Phillips, *Ancient Israel's Law Code* (Oxford: Blackwell, 1970), p. 117 n. 34.

24. See B. S. Jackson, *Essays in Jewish and Comparative Legal History* (Leiden: Brill, 1975), p. 60.

Rather, it would appear that Judah is acting on behalf of his young son Shelah to whom Tamar is betrothed but not married. Thus her premarital infidelity is treated as an injury to the interests of her inchoate husband who is still a minor and is therefore represented by Judah.[25]

Tamar does not defend herself immediately; she waits until she is *being taken out (mûṣēʾṯ).* Then she produces evidences that will identify the other partner in her sexual liaison. Earlier Judah referred to her as "the woman" (*hāʾiššâ,* v. 20). Now she refers to him as *a man (ʾîš).* It is a man to whom belongs the engraving on the seal, the pattern of the cord, and the staff (see NEB) who is the father of the child she is carrying. Here is one of the few instances in the OT where material exhibits are introduced as evidence when an accusation of impropriety has been made. One thinks of the "tokens of virginity" that a girl's parents are to present if their daughter is accused by her husband of not having been a virgin when he married her (Deut. 22:13-21), or of the presentation of the remains of mangled animals in actions for breach of trust (Exod. 22:13).

Judah is asked to *Identify (hakker)* the three items (v. 25), and he *recognized (wayyakkēr)* them (v. 26).[26] In a roundabout way Judah admits his involvement. He does not say: "This is my seal, cord, and staff," although that is assumed. He talks about Tamar rather than about himself. She is, he admits, totally justified in taking matters into her own hands: *She is in the right, not I.*[27] Withholding Shelah from Tamar was unconscionable on Judah's part.[28] Jub. 41:23-26 takes Judah's acknowledgment further than the OT: "And Judah acknowledged that the deed which he had done was evil, for he had lain with his daughter-in-law, and he esteemed it hateful in his eyes, and he acknowledged that he had transgressed and gone astray . . . and he began to lament and supplicate before the Lord because of his transgression . . . and he received forgiveness because he turned from his sin and from his ig-

25. See R. Westbrook, "Adultery in Ancient Near Eastern Law," *RB* 97 (1990) 546, 572. Westbrook makes a convincing case (contra Weinfeld and others) against the idea that in OT law adultery was an offense against God, whereas in other Near Eastern systems it was a private wrong against the husband.

26. See Daube, *Studies in Biblical Law,* p. 6, for the legal connotations of *nāḵar;* also H. McKeating, "Justice and Truth in Israel's Legal Practice: An Inquiry," *Church Quarterly* 3 (1970) 51-56.

27. Cf. Saul's similar admission to David: *ṣaddîq ʾattâ mimmennî* (1 Sam. 24:18 [Eng. 17]).

28. Middle Assyrian law § 43 deals with a case where a woman's husband suddenly died or disappeared. The law stipulates that the father can give her one of his remaining sons on the condition that the son is at least ten years old. To some degree, then, in the context of the levirate obligation Judah's refusal may have been valid and legitimate. That he refused to give Shelah to her after the son had grown up may reflect the fear that Shelah too might be slain, and hence the hereditary line be threatened with extinction. Cf. E. W. Davies, "Inheritance Rights," *VT* 31 (1981) 261.

norance."[29] The author of Jubilees proceeds to state that Judah's case is an exception, and God will not forgive any Israelite who violates the Torah by having intercourse with one's daughter-in-law or mother-in-law.

The text records that Judah never again had sexual relations with Tamar (note the shift from *bô',* lit., "went in to," of v. 18 to *l^eḏa'tâ,* lit., "knew," of v. 26). This statement does not necessarily imply that he could have married her if he wanted to. On the contrary, it would appear that, while "Tamar's connexion with Judah was legitimate for the purpose of obtaining offspring for her husband, it became illegitimate when it had achieved its purpose."[30] But both Hittite law and later Middle Assyrian law know of the custom of levirate marriage, and in both of the law codes marriage of a father-in-law to his widowed daughter-in-law is condoned.[31] That practice could be reflected in v. 26b — Judah chose not to exercise his prerogative. Then again it may reflect Judah's attempt to avoid any conscious violation of incest laws.

The statement that *And never again was he intimate with her* (lit., "did he know her") may have more than a legal, historical referent. Throughout most of the narrative Judah has not really known Tamar. She is a brother's wife (v. 8), a daughter-in-law (v. 11), a widow (v. 11), a prostitute (v. 15), and a woman (v. 20). Most conspicuously he did not "know" Tamar as Tamar when he thought he was consorting with a prostitute. "Judah did not know Tamar; now that he knows her, the need for further knowledge is over."[32]

4. THE BIRTH OF PEREZ AND ZERAH (38:27-30)

27 *When she was ready to give birth,*[1] *there were*[2] *twins in her womb!*

28 *While she was birthing, one extended his hand; and the midwife took and tied on his hand*[3] *a red string*[4] *to indicate that this one appeared first.*

29. R. H. Charles, *The Apocrypha and Pseudepigrapha of the Old Testament,* 2 vols. (Oxford: Clarendon, 1913), 2:72; P. Perkins, "Women in the Bible and Its World," *Int* 42 (1988) 38.

30. See H. H. Rowley, *The Servant of the Lord and Other Essays on the Old Testament* (London: Lutterworth, 1952), p. 184.

31. See Hittite law § 193 in *ANET,* p. 196; Middle Assyrian law § 33 in *ANET,* p. 182.

32. See J. W. H. Bos, "Out of the Shadows," *Semeia* 42 (1988) 47.

1. Lit., "it happened in the time of her birthing."

2. Lit., "and behold, twins in her womb."

3. One might read "wrist" for *yāḏô.*

4. On *šānî* see A. Brenner, *Colour Terms in the Old Testament,* JSOTSup 21 (Sheffield: JSOT, 1982), pp. 143-44; following B. Landsberger, she connects *šānî* with

29 *But just as he was about to draw back*[5] *his hand, his brother came out,*[6] *and she said: "What a breach you have made for yourself!"*[7] *Accordingly, his name*[8] *was Perez.*[9]

30 *Afterward his brother came out, with the red string on his hand. Accordingly his name was Zerah.*[10]

27 Tamar's condition is like that of Rebekah (25:22-23). Rebekah's two nations equal Tamar's twins. In both cases there is some jostling among the twins while they are still in the womb of their mother (cf. Gen. 25:22-26 with 38:28-30).[11] Perhaps the two children of Judah and Tamar are to be seen as compensation for the two sons (Er and Onan) whom Judah lost at the begin-

---

Akk. *šanu, šinītu,* "colorful, dyed (textile)," while rejecting Ugaritic and Arabic etymologies. The Hebrew term refers to red color obtained from the female bodies of certain insects and then used for dyeing woven fabrics, cloth, or leather. It was used with string (Gen. 38:28, 30), cord (Josh. 2:18, 21), and cloth (Num. 4:8; 2 Sam. 1:24; Prov. 31:21). Gen. 38:28, 30 have no word for "string"; *šānî* is lit. "a red/scarlet thing." Cf. also C. L. Wickwire, "Scarlet," *IDB,* 4:233-234; P. L. Garber, "Color; Colors," *ISBE,* 1:732.

5. For *k* (as a temporal preposition) with the participle to express imminent action cf. 40:10 (*k^e^pōraḥaṯ,* translated below as "Just as it was on the point of budding"). See T. J. Meek, "Translating the Hebrew Bible," *JBL* 79 (1960) 329. For the participle after prepositions instead of the infinitive cf. P. Wernberg-Møller, "Observations on the Hebrew Participle," *ZAW* 71 (1959) 61-62. In any case the proposed emendation *(BHS)* of *k^e^mēšîḇ* to *kah^a^šîḇô* or *k^e^mô hēšîḇ* (i.e., to a Hiphil infinitive construct or perfect) is unnecessary. For other references to the temporal *k^e^* see Th. Booij, "Some observations on Psalm lxxxvii," *VT* 37 (1987) 21; J. Milgrom, *Numbers,* JPS Torah Commentary (Philadelphia: Jewish Publication Society, 1990), p. 308 n. 3. For *šûḇ* in the Hiphil refering to the bringing back of one's hand, see W. L. Holladay, *The Root Šûbh in the Old Testament* (Leiden: Brill, 1958), p. 98.

6. *yāṣā'* is used three times in this section (vv. 28, 29, 30) of childbirth, and frequently so elsewhere. When used of stillbirth it appears in conjunction with *mûṯ,* "die" (Num. 12:12; Job 3:11). When used by itself it refers to a live birth. This leads to the possibility, indeed the probability, that *yāṣā'* in Exod. 21:22 refers to a premature birth rather than to a miscarriage. See B. S. Jackson, *Essays in Jewish And Comparative Legal History* (Leiden: Brill, 1975), p. 95.

7. SP reads "for us."

8. Most ancient versions (LXX, Pesh., SP) read "and she called," both here and in v. 30. The MT has "and he called."

9. Perez (Heb. *pāreṣ*) means "breach."

10. Zerah means "shining forth" or "dawning." There seems to be no connection between the name Zerah and *šānî,* "red string," other than the unlikely connection of Zerah with *zeḥorita,* the Aramaic word for *šānî* (*EncJud,* 16:996). For a connection of Zerah with an Arabic verb meaning "move from one place to another," see A. Guillaume, "Paranomasia in the Old Testament," *JSS* 9 (1964) 285.

11. Twins fighting each other prenatally is a theme that is not unique to the Bible. See O. Margalith, "More Samson Legends," *VT* 36 (1986) 402.

ning of the narrative. The phrase with which v. 27 begins is another (indirect) time marker in the story. Tamar was three months into her pregnancy (v. 24) when Judah's involvement with his daughter-in-law broke out into the open. Between vv. 24-26 and v. 27 six more months have elapsed, for Tamar is now near the end of her pregnancy. The narrative has nothing to report about this period.

It is not without significance that Judah plays no more part in the narrative after v. 26.[12] Tamar gives birth, and the midwife (or Tamar) names the two children. The midwife probably does the naming, although this is a prerogative of parents or of God. One cannot imagine Tamar offering commentary (v. 29) while she is in the middle of a painful delivery of twins, although it is not unheard-of for the mother to give a name to her newborn child (e.g., Gen. 29:32ff.). But we cannot tell in those instances the chronological gap between birthing and naming. The midwife seems to displace any role Judah might have played in the winding down of the narrative.

28 As the first child emerges from Tamar's womb, the midwife ties a *red string* around his hand to identify him as the firstborn. For another instance of tying *(qāšar)* a red cord to something as a means of identification cf. Josh. 2:18, 21 *(tiqwaṯ* [*ḥûṭ*] *haššānî).* The midwife apparently knows that Tamar is carrying twins. Otherwise, it would not have been necessary to distinguish the firstborn by attaching an identification symbol to his hand or wrist.

29 While the first son is emerging from his mother's womb, the second born pushes him aside, so to speak, and comes forth in his place. This prompts the midwife to exclaim: *What a breach you have made for yourself (mah-pāraṣtā ʿāleyḵā pāreṣ)!*"[13] Here is another example in Genesis of one family member manipulating himself into a position ahead of a sibling. To be precise, it is the story of Perez the son of Judah "the forward pusher son of the self-pusher, the grandson of him who was pushed into the blessing of succession."[14] But Perez will not try to outfox Zerah later in life, as Jacob

12. Unless one accepts the MT of vv. 29, 30, and identifies him as the unnamed subject of the verb (see n. 8 above).

13. An Arabic etymology for *prṣ* allows Guillaume (*JSS* 9 [1964] 284-85) to propose: "How have you arrived first. Priority is yours." Guillaume also connects "Zerah" with an Arabic root meaning "to move from one place to another," a word nowhere attested in the OT. In the case of the former, i.e., the etymology of *prṣ,* Guillaume fails to mention the Arabic root *frṣ,* "to divide," a meaning that would be close to Ugar. *prṣ,* "an opening in a wall," and Akk. *parāṣu,* "to cut, divide, detach." See J. J. Glück, "The Verb PRṢ in the Bible and in the Qumran Literature," *RevQ* 5 (1964) 123-27. Note how Targ. Onqelos freely renders the midwife's words to Perez: "What great power do you possess to have such strength," i.e., an allusion to the strength of the Messiah to be descended from Perez.

14. See J. Goldin, *JBL* 96 (1977) 43.

did with Esau. There is no logical or biological explanation for Perez's usurpation over Zerah, any more than there was for Jacob's over Esau. The decisions are God's. The selections are gratuitous.

30 When the firstborn comes forth, he is named *Zerah,* the exact meaning of which is obscure. There may be some connection with the concept of "bright color."[15] Isa. 60:1 uses the verb *zārah̩* and Isa. 60:3 uses the noun *zerah̩* to refer to the brilliant rising of the sun. Num. 26:20 identifies three subsequent clans of Judah as "Shelanites, Perezites, and Zerahites." (Gen. 36:13, 33 had listed Zerah as an Edomite clan with the same name.) Zerah and his clan are linked by Joshua (7:1, 17, 18, 24) with the plain of Achor, which is in the northeastern part of Judah's territory (see Josh. 15:7). Both sons, then, become catalysts in the expansion of Judahite groups.

One must also take note of the ten-generation genealogy (matching the ten years in Moab [1:4?]) with which Ruth concludes (Ruth 4:18-22). This linear genealogy begins with Perez and concludes with David. From where, asks the book of Ruth, did Israel's greatest king come? David's roots are in a marriage between a son of Jacob and his daughter-in-law, who played the role of a *zônâ* at one point, and in a birthing incident in which, for some mysterious reason, the second born outmaneuvered his older brother. The first and last names in this genealogy — Perez, David — illustrate the same principle, viz., the divine selection of a younger brother over an older one.[16]

Equally interesting as the Davidic genealogy is that of Christ (Matt. 1:1-17). Tamar is the first of several women in the genealogy of Christ (v. 3a), and her son Perez is a link in the chain that produces David's greater son (v. 3b). In this genealogy Tamar is included with Rahab (v. 5), Ruth (v. 6), Bathsheba (here mentioned only as "the wife of Uriah," v. 6), and Mary (v. 16). These are the only five ancestresses of Jesus that Matthew includes. Absent from the genealogy are, for example, the mothers of Israel, Sarah, Rebekah, Rachel, and Leah. Is there a connecting link among the women

15. See Brenner, *Colour Terms in the Old Testament,* p. 157; she discusses Zerah under the category of "indirect colour connotations." She rejects the idea that the name Zerah reflects an authentic etymological link, via wordplay, with *šānî* and *'ĕḏôm* (as proposed by R. Gradwohl, *Die Farben im Alten Testament,* BZAW 83 [Berlin: de Gruyter, 1963], 73ff.).

16. Cf. E. F. Campbell Jr., *Ruth,* AB (Garden City, NY: Doubleday, 1975), pp. 172-73; R. L. Hubbard, Jr., *Book of Ruth,* NICOT (Grand Rapids: Eerdmans, 1988), pp. 280-85. In his commentary on Ruth 4:12 ("and may your house be like the house of Perez whom Tamar bore to Judah"), Hubbard (p. 261) points out that both Tamar and Ruth were at first prevented from providing heirs (in Tamar's case by Judah's hesitancy to bring Shelah and Tamar together; in Ruth's case by the relative's hesitancy to marry her), but that subsequently both these foreign women perpetuated a family line threatened with extinction.

included, or is there anything that Tamar, Rahab, Ruth, and Bathsheba share with Mary?[17] Or might each of the four women preceding Mary in the genealogy represent a different value for Matthew?[18]

In responding to these questions, scholars have advanced various proposals to explain Matthew's citation of these four women. First, some have argued that these four were sinners, and thus Matthew has included them to provide an illustration of Jesus' power to save sinners, and to show that God's purpose for the Davidic line was achieved despite human sin.[19] Given that Matt. 1:2ff. includes the names of males whose sins were well known, and that verses like Gen. 38:26 herald Tamar's righteousness, it is unlikely that the inclusion of these women would be a productive way to highlight the saving/restoring ministry of Jesus.

Second, is it possible that Matthew's choice of these women reflects an interest in the salvation of non-Jews?[20] Tamar was a Canaanite, as was Rahab; Ruth was a Moabite; and Bathsheba was originally the wife of Uriah the Hittite. One can have no doubt that these women who were foreigners prepare the way for the inclusion of Gentile Christians for Matthew's audience (cf. Matt. 28:19), but they do not prepare in any way for Mary, who is not a foreigner.

A third suggestion is that the inclusion of these women reflects an intra-Jewish debate over the Messiah's ancestry.[21] On the one hand, advocates of a priestly Messiah pressed their point by underscoring the irregularities in the line of David, i.e., foreign blood and sinful women. On the other hand, the Pharisees defended these irregularities. By including these women, Matthew revealed his disposition to agree with the Pharisees, and therefore affirmed Jesus as son of David.

A fourth suggestion, and one one I find most plausible, is that each of these four women had a highly irregular and potentially scandalous marital union.[22] Nevertheless, these unions were, by God's providence, links in the

17. For the inclusion of women in genealogies outside the Bible, see G. Mussies, "Parallels to Matthew's Version of the Pedigree of Jesus," *NovT* 28 (1986) 38-39. For the presence of women in OT genealogies, see Gen. 11:29; 22:20-24; 35:22-26; 1 Chr. 2:18-21, 24, 34, 46-49; 7:24.

18. See R. D. Pattison, "God/Father: Tradition and Interpretation," *RefR* 42 (1989) 189-206, esp. 198-203, 206 n. 31.

19. This interpretation is as old as Jerome (*In Matt.* 9) and was perpetuated by Thomas Aquinas (*Summa theologicae* 3.31.3 ad 5).

20. A recent advocate of this view is J. M. Jones, "Subverting the Textuality of Davidic Messianism: Matthew's Presentation of the Genealogy and the Davidic Title," *CBQ* 56 (1994) 256-72 ("This Messiah . . . admits into the community of heaven those who are not of the house of Israel" [p. 271]).

21. See M. D. Johnson, *The Purpose of the Biblical Genealogies* (Cambridge: Cambridge University, 1969), pp. 131-38.

22. This view is advanced by R. E. Brown, *The Birth of the Messiah* (Garden City,

chain to the Messiah. Accordingly, each of them prepares the way for Mary, whose marital situation is also peculiar, given the fact that she is pregnant but has not yet had sexual relations with her betrothed husband Joseph. Thus the inclusion of the likes of Tamar in this family tree on one hand foreshadows the circumstances of the birth of Christ, and on the other hand blunts any attack on Mary. "God had worked his will in the midst of whispers of scandal."[23]

C. JOSEPH IN POTIPHAR'S HOUSE (39:1-23)

1. JOSEPH IN CHARGE OF POTIPHAR'S HOUSE (39:1-6)

1 *When Joseph had been taken*[1] *down to Egypt, Potiphar (a courtier of Pharaoh, his chief steward, an Egyptian) purchased him from the Ishmaelites who had brought him there.*

2 *Yahweh was with Joseph, and so he was*[2] *a success,*[3] *and was assigned to his Egyptian master's household.*

3 *When his master saw that Yahweh was with him, and that Yahweh brought success to everything that he did with his hand,*[4]

NY: Doubleday, 1977), pp. 71-73; idem, "Matthew's Genealogy of Jesus Christ: A Challenging Advent Homily," *Worship* 60 (1986) 482-90, esp. 488-89 (repr. in *A Coming Christ in Advent* [Collegeville, MN: Liturgical, 1988], pp. 16-26). See also T. Zahn, *Das Evangelium des Matthäus,* 4th ed. (Leipzig: Diechert, 1922), pp. 63-67; and E. Schweizer, *The Good News According to Matthew,* tr. D. E. Green (Atlanta: John Knox, 1975), p. 25.

23. See T. H. Graves, "Matthew 1:1-17," *RevExp* 86 (1989) 600. See also C. T. Davis, "The Fulfillment of Creation: A Study of Matthew's Genealogy," *JAAR* 41 (1973) 520-35; he believes the emphasis on outsiders in this genealogy is not on Tamar/Rahab/ Ruth/Bathsheba (whose name is not used), but rather Tamar/Rahab/Ruth/Uriah (whose name is used). Thus "Judah's great name as ancestor of the Messiah rests on the righteousness of Tamar" (p. 527).

1. The verb *hûraḏ* must be translated as a pluperfect, referring as it does to a previously completed action. Thus the information in v. 1 is retrospective, "recovered information" (Niccacci), and prepares one for the following narrative. Cf. GKC, § 142b; A. Niccacci, *The Syntax of the Verb in Classical Hebrew,* tr. W. G. E. Watson, JSOTSup 86 (Sheffield: Sheffield Academic, 1990), p. 36.

2. For *wayᵉhî* to express logical succession, see Waltke and O'Connor, *Biblical Hebrew Syntax,* pp. 547-48.

3. Lit., "a man of success" *('îš maṣlîaḥ).* H. Tawil ("Hebrew *hṣlḥ/ṣlḥ,* Akkadian *ešēru/šūšuru:* A Lexicographical Note," *JBL* 95 [1976] 405-13) describes the semantic development of *ṣālaḥ* as "to proceed/pass/to go (with speed) to advance progress prosper succeed" (p. 407).

4. Tawil (ibid., p. 407 and nn. 17 and 18) compares Heb. *hṣlḥ bmʿśh/byd,* "to be/cause to be successful in one's undertaking" with Akk. *ina šipir/lipit qāti/idi ešēru/šūšuru.* One of Tawil's examples is: *ana ilāni rubûti utninma suppêya išmûma ušēsirū qātēya,* "I prayed to the great gods, so they heard my prayers and caused my undertaking to succeed."

4 *he took a liking to Joseph,*[5] *with the result that he became his personal attendant.*[6] *He put him in charge of*[7] *his household, and all his possessions*[8] *he gave into his care.*

5 *From the moment he put him in charge of his household and all his possessions, Yahweh blessed the household of the Egyptian on account of Joseph; in fact, Yahweh's blessing was*[9] *on anything of his indoors or outdoors.*[10]

6 *And because he had left*[11] *everything of his in Joseph's care, he gave no thought to him*[12] *but only to the food he consumed.*[13] *Joseph was handsome in figure*[14] *and handsome in features.*

5. Lit., "Joseph found favor in his eyes," on which see Speiser, *Genesis,* p. 303 ("he took a fancy to Joseph").

6. Lit., "he served him." On the LXX rendering of this see P. Katz, "Two Kindred Corruptions in the Septuagint," *VT* 1 (1951) 260-62. Elsewhere in Genesis and the Pentateuch (Gen. 40:4; Exod. 24:13; Num. 11:28 *šāraṯ* is rendered by *parístasthai,* but here by *euaresteín,* "to walk" (which renders "walked [with God]" in Gen. 5:22, 24; 6:9; 17:1; 24:20; 48:15). See also J. Cook, "The Exegesis of the Greek Genesis," in *VI Congress of the International Organization for Septuagint and Cognate Studies,* ed. C. E. Cox (Atlanta: Scholars, 1987), pp. 117-18.

7. For the Hiphil of *pāqaḏ* meaning "to appoint somebody or something in, over, or with somebody or something," see G. André, *Determining the Destiny: PQD in the Old Testament,* ConBOT 16 (Uppsala: Gleerup, 1980), pp. 222-23.

8. Because v. 5 has *kol-'ᵃšer yeš-lô* (lit., "all which he had"), some ancient versions insert *'ᵃšer* into *kol-yeš-lô* (lit., "all he had") of v. 4. See *BHS.* But this change is not necessary, for *'ᵃšer* may be omitted in nominal sentences. See Davidson, *Hebrew Syntax,* p. 191, § 143; GKC, § 155d.

9. There is disagreement here between a masc. verb *(wayᵉhî)* and a fem. subject *(birkaṯ),* but "when the verb precedes, the third masculine singular of the verb is often used regardless of the gender or number of the subject" (Williams, *Hebrew Syntax,* p. 41, § 228).

10. Lit., "in the house and in the field," i.e., a merism. A. M. Honeyman ("*Merismus* in Biblical Hebrew," *JBL* 71 [1952] 15) translates this phrase "in all parts of his property."

11. Sarna (*Genesis,* p. 272) notes that *'āzaḇ bᵉyaḏ,* instead of *nāṯan bᵉyaḏ* as in vv. 4 and 8, means "to abandon to the power of," with a negative connotation (Neh. 9:28; Ps. 37:33), and thus perhaps the use of *'āzaḇ bᵉyaḏ* is a literary device hinting at the impending evil. Then again, one could possibly recognize in Gen. 39:6 and Ps. 37:33 the verb *'āzaḇ* II, "to put," and connect it with Ugar. *'db,* "to put" (M. Dahood, *Psalms,* AB, 3 vols. [Garden City, NY: Doubleday, 1965-70), 1:231). See also O. Loretz, "Ugaritische und hebräische Lexikographie," *UF* 13 (1981) 131.

12. BDB (p. 86, § 1b) lists *'ēṯ* in *wᵉlō' yāḏ' 'ittô mᵉ'ûmâ* as the only instance in the OT where this preposition means "beside" ("he knew not *with* him, *beside* him, aught [i.e. Joseph managed everything]").

13. S. R. Driver (*Treatise on the Use of Tenses,* p. 36, § 31) notes that "while the impf. multiplies an action, the participle prolongs it."

14. The expression *yᵉpēh-ṯō'ar* is an epexegetical genitive. Thus "handsome of figure/form" means "handsome as to/with regard to figure/form." See Williams, *Hebrew Syntax,* p. 11, § 46; Waltke and O'Connor, *Biblical Hebrew Syntax,* p. 151. In such cases the construct is an adjective.

1 This verse resumes the narrative of Joseph from 37:36. At the end of ch. 37 Joseph is "sold" *(maḵᵉrû 'ōṯô),* and here he is *purchased (wayyiqnēhû).* This semantic shift reinforces the shift in the story from the brothers and the Midianites to Joseph and Potiphar.[15] In particular, the sixfold use of Joseph's name in this unit (vv. 1, 2, 4, 5, 6 [twice]) reestablishes his prominence and centrality in the narrative. We are also reminded about Potiphar's titles and relationship with the (unnamed) pharaoh. He is the pharaoh's *courtier (sārîs)* and his *chief steward* (*śar haṭṭabbāḥîm,* lit., "chief of the butchers"). The title *sārîs* is hardly to be translated "eunuch" (as it is elsewhere in the OT), since Potiphar is married. In fact, Hebrew *sārîs* is most likely a loanword from Akk. *ša-rēš-šarri* or *ša-rēši,* "he who belongs to the king." In 2nd-millennium B.C. texts it means "courtier, officer," as in the Joseph story. In 1st-millennium B.C. texts (i.e., post-Joseph) it assumes the narrower meaning "eunuch."[16] Perhaps an equivalent phrase to *śar haṭṭabbāḥîm* is *raḇ haṭṭabbāḥîm,* found seven times in 2 K. 25:8-20 (Nebuzaradan, "captain of the bodyguard" of Nebuchadnezzar) and seventeen times in Jer. 39–42.[17]

There is a consensus on the meaning of *Potiphar* (or Potiphera, 41:45, 50; 46:20).[18] It is the Egyp. *Pœ-dj-pꜣ-rʿ,* "he whom (the god) Re has given." The earliest attestation of that name in Egyptian texts is from the Twenty-First Dynasty (11th and 10th centuries B.C.).[19] We cannot document Egyptian names of the type *Pꜣ-dj*-X (name of a deity) from the first half of the 2nd millennium B.C.

Both of Potiphar's titles in v. 1 were found back in 37:36. A third

15. See Sternberg, *Poetics of Biblical Narrative,* pp. 414-15.

16. Cf. K. A. Kitchen, *Ancient Orient and Old Testament* (Chicago: Inter-Varsity, 1966), pp. 165-66; G. E. Kadish, "Eunuchs in Ancient Egypt," in *Studies in Honor of John A. Wilson,* ed. G. E. Kadish, SAOC 35 (Chicago: University of Chicago, 1969), pp. 55-62. D. G. Burke ("Eunuch," *ISBE,* 2:201) notes that *sārîs* occurs 47 times in the OT, 28 of which the RSV translates "eunuch." Elsewhere it uses phrases like "(military) officer," "(political) official," or "chamberlain." NEB retains "eunuch" throughout. Note, however, that REB reads here: "Potiphar, one of Pharaoh's court officials."

17. The LXX always renders *ṭabbāḥîm* as *archimágeiros,* "head slaughterer, butcher, cook" (G. W. H. Lampe, *Patristic Greek Lexicon* [Oxford: Clarendon, 1961], p. 240), but Redford (*Biblical Story of Joseph,* p. 56) renders it, against LXX, as "guards, police." Both J. A. Montgomery (*Critical and Exegetical Commentary on the Books of Kings,* ICC [Edinburgh: T. & T. Clark, 1951], p. 562) and W. L. Holladay (*Jeremiah,* Hermeneia, 2 vols. [Philadelphia/Minneapolis: Fortress, 1986-89], 2:292-93) render the term "provost-marshall" in 2 Kings and Jeremiah.

18. Cf. Y. M. Grintz, "Potiphar — The Chief Cook," *Leš* 30 (1965-66) 12-17 (Hebrew), who disagrees. He distinguishes between the two and connects Potiphar with *pꜣ wdpw wr,* "the chief cook," and thus the Egyptian equivalent of *śar haṭṭabbāḥîm.* Redford (*Study of the Biblical Story of Joseph,* p. 228 n. 2) calls this interpretation "highly ingenious, but quite unconvincing."

19. See J. Vergote, *Joseph en Égypte* (Louvain: Publications Universitaires, 1959), pp. 147-48.

qualification is added to Potiphar in 39:1. He is referred to as *an Egyptian* (*'îš miṣrî,* lit., "a man of Egypt"). V. 2 is content to describe him as *hammiṣrî* (lit., "the Egyptian"). The reference to Potiphar in v. 1 as an *'îš miṣrî* balances the reference to Joseph in v. 2 as an *'îš maṣlîaḥ* (lit., "a man who succeeds").

2 Three uses of *wayᵉhî* punctuate this verse: Yahweh *was,* he (Joseph) *was,* he (Joseph) *was.*[20] The first of these three occurrences sounds a key theme that explains, or encapsulates the theology of, the Joseph story: *Yahweh was with him.* The phrase recalls the promise of Yahweh's presence with the patriarchs (26:3; 28:15; 31:3, all with the preposition *'im,* and 26:24, with the preposition *'eṯ*). V. 2a, however, is not a promise, but a fact (and comparable to third-person statements such as are found in 21:22; 26:28). Outside vv. 21 and 23 (and excluding Jacob's word in 49:18), this is the only time the name "Yahweh" occurs in the Joseph narrative. Of the seven uses of the tetragrammaton in ch. 39 (vv. 2, 3 [twice], 5 [twice], 21, 23), four of them occur in the phrase "Yahweh was with Joseph" (vv. 2, 3, 21, 23). The presence of Yahweh uniquely in ch. 39 is not to be explained by appeal to the presence of variant literary traditions.[21] Rather, the name Yahweh occurs here at what is the most uncertain moment in the life of Joseph. His future hangs in the balance. He is alone in Egypt, separated from family, vulnerable, with a cloud over his future. Or is he alone? Only the narrator, never any of the characters, uses the name Yahweh. Thus, it is the narrator who tells us, no less than five times, that in a very precarious situation, Joseph is not really alone. Yahweh is with him.[22]

There is no doubt about Yahweh's presence with Joseph from this point on in the narrative. Was that presence with Joseph when his brothers were disputing how to dispose of him? Was that presence with Joseph when he was mired in the pit? Was that presence with him when he joined the Ishmaelites as an involuntary passenger to Egypt? We, the readers, know it was, although the phrase is not there. Joseph probably needed a while longer to realize that God was with him.

3-4 The narrator has just stated that Joseph is succeeding admirably (*'îš maṣlîaḥ,* v. 2) because Yahweh is with him. Now Potiphar finds that out for himself (v. 3). *Yahweh brought success* [*maṣlîaḥ,* and see 39:23b] *to everything that he* [Joseph] *did with his hand.* The use of participles (*'ōśeh, maṣlîaḥ*)

20. *wayᵉhî* appears more times in this chapter than in the rest of the entire Joseph story — 15 times: vv. 2 (3 times), 5 (2 times), 6, 7, 10, 11, 13, 15, 18, 19, 20, 21. Longacre (*Joseph,* p. 32) calls attention to "the elaborate paragraph setting in v. 2 where three clauses build on the verb *hāyâ,* 'to be' (a descriptive rather than an event verb)."

21. "The alleged reasons for the curious employment of divine names in the Joseph story advanced by apologists of the Documentary Hypothesis are weak in the extreme" (Redford, *Study of the Biblical Story of Joseph,* p. 130 n. 2).

22. See Longacre, *Joseph,* p. 45. Westermann (*Genesis,* 3:62) refers to 39:2-6, 21-23 as "the theological introit to the Joseph story as a whole."

suggests that such prosperity became a pattern. Here we have the interesting back-to-back use of the Hiphil of *ṣālaḥ,* used first intransitively (v. 2), then transitively (v. 3). According to the narrator, Potiphar, a non-Yahwist, does not appear to be uninformed about the source of Joseph's success. There is no attempt to place Joseph on a pedestal or to single him out for acclaim. The source of Joseph's success is patently Yahweh's presence with him. Some have claimed that Joseph's responsibilities of being *in charge of his household* (*ʿal-bêṯô,* lit., "over his house") correspond to those of the Egyptian steward (Egyp. *ỉmy-r pr*).[23] Scholars now generally deny this connection, principally because nowhere is Joseph given titles or duties that were characteristic of the Egyptian vizierate. If an Egyptian analogue be sought to parallel the privileges and responsibilities of Joseph, then that equivalent is most likely either *ỉmry-r3 pr wr n nb t3.wy,* "chief steward in the palace," or *ḥry pr,* "household steward."[24] It is not necessary to give some specialized meaning to *bayiṯ,* "house," in the expression *ʿal bêṯô* of v. 4, or *beḇēṯô* of v. 5, such as "royal estates."[25] There is no good reason for not applying the normal use of Hebrew *bayiṯ,* i.e., "house(hold)," and that in ch. 39 one sees a Joseph who was a private steward, a role that carries with it primarily domestic responsibilities.[26]

It is interesting that the narrator attributes Joseph's promotion to his master's *observing* [Heb. *rāʾâ,* lit., "see"] *that Yahweh was with* Joseph. On what basis Potiphar knew or saw that Yahweh was with Joseph is not clear. At no point are Joseph's work habits or fruitful output cited as the reasons for his promotion. Yahweh is with him and Yahweh is bringing him success. Joseph may be over Potiphar's household, but he is under Yahweh's blessing and guidance.

5 Yahweh prospers *(ṣālaḥ)* Joseph (vv. 2-3), but he blesses *(bāraḵ)* Potiphar and his household because of his good treatment of Joseph. This verse must be read as fulfillment of 12:3a, "I will bless those who bless you."

23. R. de Vaux, "Titres et functionnaíres égyptiens à la cour de David et de Salomon," *RB* 48 (1939) 400-403.

24. For the former, see W. A. Ward, "The Egyptian Office of Joseph," *JSS* 5 (1960) 146-47; D. B. Redford, "Studies in Relations between Palestine and Egypt During the First Millennium B.C. I. The Taxation System of Solomon," in *Studies in the Ancient Palestinian World,* ed. J. W. Wevers and D. B. Redford (Toronto: University of Toronto, 1972), p. 143 n. 5. For the latter, see S. Morenz, "Joseph in Ägypten," *TLZ* 84 (1959) 412 and n. 25b.

25. T. N. D. Mettinger, *Solomonic State Officials: A Study of the Civil Government Officials of the Israelite Monarchy,* ConBOT 5 (Lund: Gleerup, 1971), pp. 73-79.

26. S. C. Layton ("The Steward in Ancient Israel: A Study of Hebrew *[ʾăšer] ʿal-habbayit* in Its Near Eastern Setting," *JBL* 109 [1990] 645-48) presents convincing evidence to reject foreign influence on the Hebrew phrase, esp. Egyptian influence allegedly reflected in the Joseph story. See also the expression in the parable of Jesus (Matt. 24:45 par. Luke 12:42): "the faithful and wise servant [Luke "manager/steward," *oikonómos*] whom the master has put in charge *[katéstēsen]* over his household *[epi tēs therapeías].*"

Just as Yahweh blessed Laban because of Jacob (30:27, 30), he now blesses Potiphar because of Joseph.[27] Perhaps it is more accurate to say he blessed Laban and Potiphar through the presence of Jacob and Joseph, respectively.

6 The only thing Potiphar does not delegate to Joseph is the preparation of his food, perhaps because of a general Egyptian concern that non-Egyptians were unaware of how properly to prepare food (see 43:32), or more likely, because of ritual separation at mealtimes. There is an interesting rabbinic tradition (see Gen. Rabbah 86:6) to the effect that the phrase "the food he consumed" is a euphemism, a reference to Potiphar's wife. Note how in Exod. 2:20 Jethro's word to his daughters to invite Moses to his home so he can "eat bread" is followed by the note in the next verse (v. 21) that Moses married one of his daughters.

The concluding note about Joseph's physical charms prepares us for the incident involving Potiphar's wife. Apparently Potiphar's leaving everything in Joseph's care includes Potiphar's wife. A young unmarried man *handsome in figure and handsome in features* who is left alone with a wife who has been virtually abandoned by her husband spells potential trouble, and is a "signal of warning in the midst of blessing that Joseph may suffer from one endowment too many."[28]

The completeness of Joseph's dedication to Potiphar, the completeness of Potiphar's trust in Joseph, and the completeness of Yahweh's blessing on the household are underscored in this unit by the fivefold repetition of *kol* (lit., "all"): Yahweh brought success to "everything" Joseph touched (v. 3); Potiphar places Joseph over "all" his possessions (vv. 4-5); Yahweh's blessing is on "anything" of Potiphar's (v. 5b); Potiphar left "everything" in Joseph's care (v. 6).

2. JOSEPH REJECTS THE ADVANCES OF POTIPHAR'S WIFE (39:7-12)

7 *Now after these things, his master's wife looked up at[1] Joseph, and said: "Lie[2] with me."*

8 *But he refused and said to his master's wife, "Behold,[3] my master gives*

27. See H. W. Wolff, in W. Brueggemann and Wolff, *The Vitality of Old Testament Traditions,* tr. W. A. Benware, et al., 2nd ed. (Atlanta: John Knox, 1982), pp. 59-60.

28. See Alter, *Art of Biblical Narrative,* p. 108.

1. Lit., "raised her eyes to."

2. The lengthened 2nd masc. imperative of *šāḵaḇ* occurs only here and in v. 12. The usual form is *šᵉḵaḇ* (1 Sam. 3:5, 6, 9; 2 Sam. 13:5; Ezek. 4:4).

3. J. Blau (*Grammar of Biblical Hebrew* [Wiesbaden: Harrassowitz, 1976], p. 105, § 103.2) notes that "*hēn* may express a conclusion *a minori ad maius,* by dint of a following interrogation introduced by *wə'ēḵ* 'and how,' as Gen 39,8-9."

no thought to me regarding anything in the house, and has left everything in my care.[4]

9 *He exercises no more authority in this house than I do;*[5] *he has withheld*
from me nothing except you, for you are his wife. How, then, could I
do so great a wrong, and thus sin[6] *against God?"*

10 *Although*[7] *she spoke to Joseph day after day,*[8] *he would not consent*
to lie beside her, or with her.[9]

11 *One such day,*[10] *when he went to the house to carry out his royal*
functions,[11] *and none of the household servants was in the house,*

12 *she grabbed him by his garment and said: "Lie with me!" But leaving*
the garment in her hand, he fled and went outdoors.

7 Potiphar's wife does more looking[12] than talking. Her propositioning of Joseph is terse. She says only two words to him: *šik^{e}ḇâ ʿimmî, Lie with me* (v. 7b), which she later repeats (v. 12). By contrast, Joseph's rejection of her

4. Lit., "and everything which is his he has placed/given into my hand."

5. Lit., "He is not greater in this house than I." Targ. Onqelos tones down Joseph's language by having Joseph compare himself to other household servants — "there is none that is greater (in autonomy) in this house than I."

6. *w^{e}ḥāṭa'ṯî* illustrates a use of the perfect with *waw* that continues the imperfect *('e'ĕśeh)* on which it is contingent. In this case the *w^{e}qāṭal* form is consequential. Cf. Davidson, *Hebrew Syntax,* p. 79, § 53b; Waltke and O'Connor, *Biblical Hebrew Syntax,* p. 528.

7. For the preposition *k^e* with an infinitive functioning as a concessive, see Williams, *Hebrew Syntax,* p. 47, § 258.

8. Heb. *yôm yôm,* lit., "day day." This construction should be distinguished from *yôm wāyôm,* which is more common in later works such as Chronicles. The asyndetic formulation is earlier than the syndetic one. See G. Rendsburg, "Late Biblical Hebrew and the Date of 'P,' " *JANES* 12 (1980) 68-69. Only the asyndetic formulation is present in Ugaritic. See also GKC, § 123c, for the use of repetition in a distributive sense.

9. Some ancient versions (e.g., LXX) delete this last phrase as needlessly repetitious, but this is specious reasoning. See the commentary below on v. 10.

10. Lit., "according to this day" *(k^{e}hayyôm hazzeh).* Cf. A. M. Honeyman, "The occasion of Joseph's temptations," *VT* 2 (1952) 85-87, who rejects for this phrase the translation "about this time" (AV), "on this particular day" (BDB, p. 400, § 7h), and "on a certain day" (Vulg., Gunkel), preferring instead "as usual." S. J. DeVries (*Yesterday, Today and Tomorrow* [Grand Rapids: Eerdmans, 1975], p. 52 n. 77) comes closer to BDB ("it actually refers to the past, seen as present in the narrator's imagination").

11. *m^{e}la'ḵtô,* lit., "his work," can have the nuance "royal functions," as in Dan. 8:27; Esth. 3:9; 9:3. See J. Milgrom, *Studies in Levitical Terminology* (Berkeley: University of California, 1970), p. 80 n. 295.

12. Speiser (*Genesis,* p. 303) points out that the identical idiom ("raise one's eyes at") appears in Akkadian in the Gilgamesh Epic to describe Ishtar's designs on Gilgamesh (Tablet VI, line 6): *ana du-un-udki ša ^{ilu}Gilgamiš i-na it-taši ru-bu-tu ^{ilu}Ištar.*

advances is much lengthier (vv. 8-9). The *these things* with which the verse begins refers back to Potiphar's entrusting Joseph with the supervision of his household.[13]

8-9 Joseph repeats to Potiphar's wife essentially what the narrator had already said to the reader (v. 6). He reminds her of the total confidence Potiphar has in him (v. 8), and therefore the wide-ranging authority he has delegated to Joseph (v. 9). *he has withheld from me nothing except you.* About the only thing Potiphar has not left in Joseph's care is the preparation of his food (v. 6). Joseph does not repeat that exception; instead he substitutes Potiphar's wife for the food as being off-limits to him, and understandably so. For Joseph to capitulate to her invitation would, for one thing, be a serious breach of the trust that his employer has placed in him. With God's help, Joseph is succeeding in all that he is doing (*ʿōśeh,* v. 3b). But there are some things that Joseph will not do (*ʾeʿĕśeh,* v. 9).

Joseph first states that he must turn down her proposition because he is committed to fulfilling Potiphar's expectations. Joseph's rejection of the woman's advances out of respect for the husband parallels the sanctions listed in Proverbs (esp. chs. 6 and 7) against adultery. Wisdom literature does not outlaw adultery because God disallows it or because it is a capital offense, the penalty for which is stoning (Lev. 20:10; Deut. 22:22). The sanctions in Prov. 6 include: self-destruction (v. 32); wounds, loss of respect, and public disgrace (v. 33); a husband bent on revenge (v. 34); no way to buy oneself out of trouble (v. 35). Prov. 7:23 comes the closest — perhaps — to connecting adultery and the death penalty: "he does not know that it will cost him his life." In short, the sanctions are not historical but rational.[14] Proverbs does not warn against adultery because God's Torah forbids it, but because the adulterer can expect that vengeance will be sought by the husband, leaving the adulterer in a disagraced, humilitated condition. Avoid adultery lest you arouse the passion of the husband.

Joseph's last stated reason for rejecting the proposal of Potiphar's wife is that it is *so great a wrong (hārāʿâ haggᵉḏōlâ),* a *sin against God.* Adultery is an offense against both spouse and deity. It is a sin against God because it is a violation of the boundaries he has placed on sexual expression. The reason

13. Gen. Rabbah 87:4 identifies "these things" as Joseph's unspoken thoughts, in the form of a self-commendation, about his recent elevation, for which God must bring him down a peg or two ("By your life, I shall sick a she-bear against you [and we'll see what reflections you have then]").

14. See J. Hempel, "Ethics in the OT," *IDB,* 2:157; V. Hamilton, "The Ethics of the Old Testament," in *Christian Ethics,* ed. L. Hynson and L. Scott (Anderson, IN: Warner, 1983), pp. 9-30, esp. pp. 24-25; H. McKeating, "Sanctions against Adultery in Ancient Israelite Society, with Some Reflections on Methodology in the Study of Old Testament Ethics," *JSOT* 11 (1979) 57-72, esp. p. 63.

why punishment from God is appropriate for this particular violation is that adultery, unlike other trespasses such as murder or theft, is typically committed in secret and may leave no physical traces.[15]

10 The first few words of v. 10 indicate that Potiphar's wife spoke to Joseph day after day,[16] even though, as already mentioned, her words to him in the narrative are limited to just two in Hebrew ("lie with-me"), repeated twice (vv. 7, 12). By contrast, Joseph's protestations are elaborate (vv. 8, 9). His lengthy statement of refusal to cooperate is sandwiched between her twice-repeated command. But this command is clearly only a tiny part of her larger, lengthier conversation with Joseph.

The narrator uses *to lie beside her* in place of Potiphar's wife's "Lie with me." Joseph will give a wide berth to temptation. Not only will he not sleep with her, he will not even lie by her side, if possible.[17] As noted above, *or with her* should not be deleted as an editorial gloss. It confirms just how far Joseph is prepared to go to avoid being caught in a morally compromising position. For if Joseph "could not be stormed [v. 7] he might be coaxed."[18]

11 The thrust of *One such day (k^ehayyôm hazzeh)* is something like "as his custom was" or "as usual." "The narrator, besides explaining the daily routine of Pharaoh's household, makes it plain that at this critical juncture Joseph was guilty of no reckless or provocative action, but was attending normally to his regular business."[19] Not all commentators agree, however. For instance, the Babylonian Talmud (*Sota* 36b) records a dispute among the rabbis as to what was meant by "to do his work" *(laʿaśôṯ mᵉlaʾḵtô)*. One took the phrase literally: Joseph went into the house on this particular day, as he did on almost any other day, to examine Potiphar's acounts. Given his high position in the household, such skilled work would be the nature of the responsibility assigned to Joseph, rather than servile labor. Another took the position that "to do his work" was a euphemism for "satisfy his desires,"

15. See R. Westbrook, "Adultery in Ancient Near Eastern Law," *RB* 97 (1990) 566-69.

16. Note that the Testament of Joseph (part of the Testament of the Twelve Patriarchs, originally a Jewish composition as early as the 1st or 2nd century B.C.) makes much of Joseph's repeated refusal, in spite of continued badgering from the woman that included everything from threatened suicide to exposure of her body (T. Joseph 2:1–9:5; translation by H. C. Kee in J. H. Charlesworth, ed., *Old Testament Pseudepigrapha,* 2 vols. [Garden City, NY: Doubleday, 1983-85], 1:819-20). Jub. 39:5-8 has Joseph claiming that Potiphar's wife "begged him for one year."

17. The LXX always renders *šāḵaḇ ʾēṯ/ʿim* with *koimán meta,* but here in v. 10 it renders *šāḵaḇ ʾēṣel* with *katheúdein (met' autḗs),* a verb that never has sexual connotations. Cf. H. M. Orlinsky, "The Hebrew Root *škb,*" *JBL* 63 (1944) 34-36.

18. Kidner, *Genesis,* p. 190. Orlinsky (*JBL* 63 [1944] 34 n. 19) provides textual reasons for rejecting the phrase as a post-LXX gloss.

19. Honeyman, *VT* 2 (1952) 86-87.

thus giving a different perspective on Joseph's character. Targ. Onqelos follows the former interpretation with its "to examine his accounts" *(lmbdq bktby),* but this could be an instance where the translator "has gone out of his way to scotch what was already a very popular, but to his mind calumnious, reading of the phrase . . . he [the translator] has substituted a more specific act that is safely beyond all possibility of double-entendre."[20]

12 Potiphar's wife now becomes insistent, not just inviting. She moves from seductress to aggressor. She grabs Joseph by his garment, evidently trying to force him down onto her bed or couch, or at least pull him to her. Joseph manages to free himself and run away, half-naked. That *he left the garment in her hand (wayyaʿ^{a}zōḇ . . . b^{e}yāḏāh)* recalls the narrator's words about everything Potiphar had "left in Joseph's care" (*wayyaʿ^{a}zōḇ . . . b^{e}yaḏ yôsēp̱,* lit., "he left in the hand of Joseph," v. 6). Here are two uses of the phrase "to leave in the hand" with different nuances. The first, v. 6, reflects Potiphar's confidence in Joseph. The second, v. 11, reflects Joseph's fidelity to Potiphar.

Thus for a second time Joseph loses a piece of clothing. First it was a *k^{e}ṯōneṯ passîm,* a long, colorful tunic (ch. 37), and now it is his garment, *beḡeḏ.* Yet a third reference (and a third word) for some article of clothing in the Joseph story appears in 45:22: Joseph gives his brothers garments *(śimlâ)* to take back to their home. *śimlâ* is also used in 41:14 to refer to Joseph's change of clothes before he appears before Pharaoh. The word used for the article of clothing by which Potiphar's wife grabbed Joseph *(beḡeḏ)* is the same as that used in the previous chapter to describe the clothing that Tamar first removed (v. 14), then put back on (v. 19), i.e., the widow's garb *(biḡḏê 'alm^{e}nûṯāh).*

Appearing about two hundred times, *beḡeḏ* is the most widely used term for a garment in the OT.[21] It appears that it could refer both to an outer garment (2 K. 7:15) and an inner garment (Ezek. 26:16). According to the end of v. 12 Joseph left all of his *beḡeḏ* with Potiphar's wife, which means he left behind either his outer garment or one of his undergarments. V. 12 states that Potiphar's wife grabbed Joseph "by his garment" *(b^{e}ḇiḡḏô).* One finds the same form of this word in Exod. 21:8 *(b^{e}ḇiḡḏô ḇāh),* where the expression refers to man who broke faith with his female slave and tried to sell her because she did not please him. By using *beḡeḏ* at this point, the narrator may be implying something about Joseph's own emotional involvement in this story. He is on the verge of acting faithlessly to his master. Also, it is interesting to note that the homonymous Hebrew verb *bāḡaḏ* is sometimes used for marital unfaithfulness (Jer. 3:7-8, 20; Mal. 2:14).[22]

20. J. L. Kugel, *In Potiphar's House* (San Francisco: Harper, 1990), p. 95.

21. See J. M. Myers, "Dress and Ornaments," *IDB,* 1:869-71; L. G. Running, "Garments," *ISBE,* 2:401-7.

22. Kugel, *In Potiphar's House,* pp. 96-98; Sarna, *Genesis,* p. 274.

3. JOSEPH IS ACCUSED OF ATTEMPTED RAPE (39:13-18)

13 *When she saw that he had left his garment in her hand as he fled outdoors,*

14 *she called for her household servants and said to them: "See here, he brought us a Hebrew fellow to sport*[1] *in our presence; (instead) he came to lie with me,*[2] *but I screamed my head off.*[3]

15 *When he heard me screaming for help*[4] *he left his garment near me and fled and went outdoors."*

16 *She set his garment near her until his master returned home.*

17 *She related to him an identical story.*[5] *"The Hebrew slave, whom you brought to us to sport in my presence, (instead) came to me.*[6]

1. *l^eṣaḥeq* is a Piel infinitive of the verb *ṣāḥaq,* "to laugh." Note the various translations of the verb in 39:14: "to insult" (RSV, NRSV, JB, Redford, *Study of the Biblical Story of Joseph,* p. 78); "to bring insult" (REB); "to mock" (AV, NKJV); "to make a fool of" (NJB); "to make a toy of" (BDB, p. 850); "to make a mockery of" (NEB); "to sport with" (Westermann, *Genesis,* 3:59); "to make fun of someone" (*HALAT,* 3:955b); "to dally with" (NJPS); "to make love to" (Speiser, *Genesis,* pp. 302, 303); "to make sexual advances on" (Coote and Ord, *Bible's First History,* p. 182); "to play games with" (Sternberg, *Poetics of Biblical Narrative,* p. 423).

2. The LXX reads: *eisḗlthen prós mē légōn koimḗthēti met' emoú,* "he came to me saying, 'lie with me,' " for which the Hebrew equivalent would be *bā' 'ēlî lē'mōr šiḵḇî ʿimmî.* One can account for the Greek rendering in two ways, either of which is plausible, though the first is more likely. First, *lē'môr* could have been accidentally omitted from the text because of its appearance earlier in the verse (haplography), in which case the imperative became the received *liškaḇ.* One might capture the nuance of the MT (as reflected in LXX) with "he came to me with the demand to lie with me." See H. M. Orlinsky, "Critical Notes on Gen 39:14, 17; Jud 11:37," *JBL* 61 (1942) 87-90. A second possibility is to understand the "l" on *liškaḇ* as an abbreviation for *lē'mōr* in the *Vorlage.* See P. Katz, "*katapaúsai* as a Corruption of *katalýsai* in the Septuagint," *JBL* 65 (1946) 324; L. C. Allen, *Greek Chronicles, Part II: Textual Criticism,* VTSup 27 (Leiden: Brill, 1974), p. 86.

3. Lit., "I called in a loud voice" or "I called loudly." For the cry of a woman who is being sexually violated cf. Deut. 22:24-27; 2 Sam 13:19.

4. Lit., "When he heard me as I lifted up my voice and called" (and see v. 18). U. Cassuto (*Biblical and Oriental Studies,* tr. I. Abrahams, 2 vols. [Jerusalem: Magnes, 1973-75], 2:75-76) compares this Hebrew expression with Ugar. *wyšu gh wyṣḥ,* "and he lifted up his voice and cried" (for which Judg. 9:7 is an even closer parallel than Gen. 39:15).

5. Lit., "according to these words." The phrase is rendered "the same story" by Speiser (*Genesis,* p. 302); "her story" by Westermann (*Genesis,* p. 59); "the whole story" by Coote and Ord (*Bible's First History,* p. 182). One could also render the expression "something like the following words" (J. M. Sasson, "The Worship of the Golden Calf," in *Orient and Occident,* Fest. C. H. Gordon, ed. H. A. Hoffner, Jr. [Neukirchen-Vluyn: Neukirchener, 1973], p. 155, n. 16).

6. Cf. the commentary above on 38:16, where the same expression occurs and clearly denotes sexual activity. Also note that the majority of LXX mss. add: "and he said

18 *When I screamed for help, he left his garment near me and fled outdoors."*

13-15 Potiphar's wife now seizes on her opportunity to get revenge for Joseph's rejection of her advances. She does not have Joseph, but she does have Joseph's garment. Passion will be replaced by prevarication. She shouts for her servants, none of whom are at present in the house (v. 11b). She fabricates the story that Joseph tried to rape her.[7] Only her screaming scared him away and prevented him from abusing her.

Several things call for special note in her speech to the servants. First, she repeats what the narrator has already said about what Joseph did and what she did, but she reverses the order. The narrator first tells us that Joseph left his shirt in her hand and fled outdoors (v. 13). Then he informs us of Potiphar's wife shouting for help (v. 14a). When Potiphar's wife tells the story, she first draws attention to her screaming (v. 14b). Then she tells of Joseph's leaving his shirt behind in his rapid departure (v. 15). The effect created by this reversal is to underscore the blatant nature of her lie.

A second item of interest here is the slight change made by Potiphar's wife when she tells the servants what Joseph did with his shirt. The narrator said (v. 13) that Joseph left it in her hand *(b^e^yāḏāh)*. She claims that Joseph left the shirt *near me* (*'eṣlî*, v. 15). The narrator will focus in the next verse on how she kept the shirt "near her" (*'eṣlāh*, v. 16). She will make the same claim to her husband (v. 18). Among the ancient versions, SP reads "in my hand" in v. 15 for "near me"; this change loses an important part of the story's dynamics. The significance of the shift from *b^e^yāḏāh* to *'eṣlî* is another way by which Potiphar's wife will shift the blame to Joseph. She must make it appear that Joseph was the initiator, indicated by the fact that he was the one who undressed himself — she did not try to undress him. Joseph's shirt in her hand would indicate that she had removed his clothing.[8]

A third item of interest is her indirect reference to her husband as *he* (v. 14) in the phrase *he brought us (hēḇî' lānû)*. If she is attaching primary

to me, 'I will sleep with you.' " Codex Alexandrinus adds: "and he said to me, 'Sleep with me.' " For textual notes and an attempt to restore a lost reading in vv. 14 and 17 cf. Orlinsky, *JBL* 61 (1942) 87-90. Orlinsky's proposal is to restore "and he said, 'lie with me' " after *l^e^ṣaḥeq bî* at the end of the sentence (following Alexandrinus), which he believes fell out accidentally.

7. The absence of a cry from a woman engaged in sexual activity in a populated area leads to the conclusion, according to Deuteronomic law, that she has engaged in consensual sex (Deut. 22:23-24). The absence of such a cry when a married/engaged person is raped in an unpopulated area is not incriminating evidence against her, for there would be nobody to hear the cry (Deut. 22:25-27).

8. See Skinner, *Genesis,* pp. 458-59; Alter, *Art of Biblical Narrative,* p. 110.

blame to Joseph, she is attaching secondary blame to her own husband. After all, it is Potiphar who brought Joseph into the household. Thus Potiphar's wife expresses contempt for Potiphar by referring to him only as *he* rather than as "Potiphar" or "my husband."[9]

Once again we encounter the verb *ṣāḥaq* (v. 14), made famous in the Isaac stories (17:17; 18:12, 15 [twice]; 21:6, 9; 26:8), and occurring once in the Lot stories (19:14). According to the text, Potiphar's wife claims that her husband brought Joseph into their household *to sport in our presence* (*lᵉṣaḥeq bānû,* v. 14), and later *to sport in my presence* (*lᵉṣaḥeq bî,* v. 17). What is she suggesting? That Potiphar brought Joseph into the household "to make sport" of them (NIV, NAB)? "to insult" them (RSV, JB)? "to mock" them (AV; cf. NEB)? "to make love" to them (Speiser)?

Speiser's interpretation is dubious simply because sexual abuse is covered by *bā' 'ēlay liškaḇ 'immî* ("he came to lie with me," v. 14) and by *bā' 'ēlay* ("he came to me," v. 17), not by *lᵉṣaḥeq bānû/bî.* The "mock" and "insult" translations suffer from a lack of evidence that *ṣāḥaq,* in either the Qal or the Piel stem, has such a meaning. Of all the instances where *ṣāḥaq* occurs, the closest in form to the references here is 19:14 — all three use *ṣāḥaq* in the Piel, followed by the preposition *bᵉ*. I suggested for 19:14 "clowning" — "horsing around," to use a colloquialism. It seems best to use an equivalent in 39:14, 17.[10] Potiphar's wife claims that what Joseph had in mind by *ṣāḥaq* was considerably different than what Potiphar had in mind by *ṣāḥaq*. Joseph was introduced to Potiphar's family to sport with them, to play games with them.

16-18 The text records no response by the servants when Potiphar's wife accuses Joseph of having sexual designs on her. They are merely listeners, witnesses who will support her story when she, the victim, relates the story about the villain (Joseph) to her husband. She is careful to set *(wattannaḥ)* the shirt beside her — the same verbal form used in 8:4 for the ark "coming to rest" on one of the mountains of Ararat (except that the Hiphil is used in 39:16, the Qal in 8:4). We do not know how long she had to wait until Potiphar came home. But she is content to wait. Her opportunity to reveal the "real" Joseph will come. When Potiphar does return to (*bō' 'el,* v. 16) his home, she will inform him of how Joseph tried to come on (*bō' 'el,* v. 17) to her. She

9. Speiser (*Genesis,* p. 303) prefers to read *'îšî,* "my husband," for *'îš* in v. 14, since *'îš 'iḇrî* (lit., "a Hebrew man") is a peculiar expression in the context (cf. *hā'eḇeḏ hā'iḇrî,* "the Hebrew slave," in v. 17). But such a change spoils the strategic juxtaposition of *'îš 'iḇrî* in the wife's speech to her servants and *hā'eḇeḏ hā'iḇrî* in the wife's speech to her husband.

10. See Sasson, "Worship of the Golden Calf," p. 155, who notes that Speiser's translation "to make love to us" "reduces the sarcasm to a mass orgy."

will be careful to tell him that she scared Joseph off by screaming (*kahᵃrîmî qôlî,* v. 18), but will be equally careful to say nothing about "looking up" (*wattiśśāʾ . . . ʾeṯ-ʿēneyhā,* v. 7) toward Joseph.

In relating Joseph's alleged misconduct to her servants, she identified Joseph as "a Hebrew fellow" (v. 14). In speaking to her husband, she identifies Joseph as *the Hebrew slave* (v. 17). Joseph has been shifted from an *ʾîš* to an *ʿeḇeḏ*. The change is certainly deliberate. To be sexually attacked by an *ʾîš* is bad enough. To be sexually attacked by a foreign slave makes her accusation all the more damning. In choosing this term, she is putting Joseph in as despicable a light as possible. It should also demand as swift a redress as possible from Potiphar, the master who has been betrayed by his servant.

She does not let Potiphar escape blame. V. 17 allows two readings. One is the way we have it, setting off the middle phrase with commas: "The Hebrew slave, whom you brought to us to sport in my presence, (instead) came to me." The verse also allows this reading: "The Hebrew slave came to me, the one you brought to us to sport in my presence." This second reading indicts Potiphar more than the first one, suggesting that he is to blame for arranging the circumstances that allowed this scenario to take place. It was he who brought Joseph to his wife for "sport." Potiphar's wife is not only seductress and prevaricator, but she is a "subtle mistress of syntactic equivocation."[11] Not only may her words to Potiphar about Potiphar be read in one of two ways, but so may her words about Joseph. *came to me (bāʾ ʾēlay)* may be taken either literally ("he approached me") or as a euphemism ("he wanted sex with me"). Thus her words shade into an ambivalence, making room for more than one interpretation.[12] But Potiphar's wife is interested only in suggesting to her husband that Joseph's behavior, in Potiphar's absence, has been indiscreet and uncalled-for, and to accomplish that she resorts to fiction and fabrication.[13]

4. JOSEPH IS PLACED IN PRISON (39:19-23)

19 *When his master heard the words his wife related to him, "Such and such your slave did to me," he was incensed.*[1]

11. Alter, *Art of Biblical Narrative,* p. 110.

12. See Sternberg, *Poetics of Biblical Narrative,* p. 426; W. L. Humphreys, *Joseph and His Family: A Literary Study* (Columbia, SC: University of South Carolina, 1988), p. 72.

13. N. Furman ("His Story Versus Her Story: Male Genealogy and Female Strategy in the Jacob Cycle," *Semeia* 46 [1989] 141-49) attempts to rehabilitate Potiphar's wife by suggesting that she, like Tamar, used a piece of clothing — normally markers of filial love — to insert herself into a patriarchal hierarchy (though Furman admits that her interpretation may be "warped, skewed by my feminist and critical concerns" [p. 149]).

1. Lit., "and his nose burned/turned red."

20 *So Joseph's master took him[2] and placed him in the round house,[3] the place[4] in which the king's prisoners[5] were incarcerated, and Joseph remained in the round house.*

21 *But Yahweh was with Joseph. He extended kindness[6] to him, and disposed[7] the chief jailer[8] in his favor.*

2. For other uses of *lāqaḥ,* "took," in the sense of police action taken against an alleged criminal, see Deut. 19:12; 1 Sam. 20:31; Jer. 36:26.

3. *bêṯ hassōhar,* "the house of roundess," the name of a prison, occurs only in 39:20 (twice) 21, 22, 23; 40:3, 5. In 39:20 (twice) the LXX renders *bêṯ hassōhar* by *ochýrōma,* which in its earliest use meant "fortification" and later (3rd century B.C.) also "fortress, prison." A fortress would naturally have been often used as a prison. *ochýroma* also translates *habbayiṯ* in 40:14 and *habbôr* in 41:14, both terms for a place of incarceration. See J. A. L. Lee, *A Lexical Study of the Septuagint Version of the Pentateuch* (Chico, CA: Scholars, 1983), p. 68.

4. For the construct before *'ᵃšer* see GKC, § 130c; Waltke and O'Connor, *Biblical Hebrew Syntax,* pp. 156, 645; Williams, *Hebrew Syntax,* p. 81, § 489.

5. I follow Qere *'ᵃsîrê* rather than Ketib *'ᵃsûrê,* as in v. 22, though the sense is nearly the same. Cf. BDB, p. 63. For a possible explanation of Ketib-Qere involving the variation *y/w* see J. Barr, "A New Look at *Ketibh-Qere,*" *OTS* 21 (1981) 27-28. Note that in Judg. 16:21, 25 the Qere and Ketib of *'sr* are reversed. There the Ketib is *hā'ᵃsirîm* and the Qere is *ha'ᵃsûrîm.* This shows that it is wrong to suggest that the Qere readings represent corrections of the Ketib. Otherwise, why would the Ketib in one instance serve as the Qere in another, and vice versa? Cf. R. Gordis, *The Word and the Book* (New York: Ktav, 1976), p. 33. The difference between *'āsûr* (the *qāṭûl* formation) and *'āsîr* (the *qāṭîl* formation) is that the former refers to the entry into a changed or modifed state, while the latter refers to the state itself. Joseph joins those who already are *'ᵃsîrîm.* See Waltke and O'Connor, *Biblical Hebrew Syntax,* p. 620. Note also that the noun "prisoners" *('ᵃsûre/'ᵃsîrê)* and the verb "incarcerated" *('ᵃsûrîm)* are from the same root.

6. *ḥeseḏ* here refers to God's help in a time of need, God doing what in this situation is necessary to make matters develop for Joseph's well-being (K. Sakenfeld, *Faithfulness in Action,* OBT [Philadelphia: Fortress, 1985], pp. 90-91).

7. "and he disposed . . . in his favor" is lit. "and he gave his favor/grace *(wayyittēn ḥannô)* in the eyes of. . . ." The expression *nāṯan ḥēn bᵉʿênê* occurs here and in Exod. 3:21; 11:3; 12:36. The Exodus passages all speak of Yahweh giving favor in the sight of the Egyptians, or causing the Egyptians to act favorably to Israel. The same expression is found in an Aramaic inscription dating from the 5th to 4th century B.C.: Yeḥawmilk, the king of Byblos, says, "May the mistress, the lady of Byblos, give him favor [*wttn lw . . . ḥn*] in the sight of [*lʿn*] the gods and in the sight of the people." See M. L. Barré, "The Royal Blessing in the Karatepe Inscription," *MAARAV* 3/2 (1982) 180; J. W. Watts, "*Ḥnt:* An Ugaritic Formula of Intercession," *UF* 21 (1989) 447 n. 32. For the force of the pronominal suffix on *ḥannô* ("he gave his favor" means "he gave him favor") see Davidson, *Hebrew Syntax,* p. 3, § 3, Rem. 2.

8. Here and in v. 22 and v. 23 the Hebrew for "chief jailer" is *śar bêṯ hassōhar.* In v. 21 the LXX renders this phrase as *toú archidesmophýlakos,* but in v. 22 and v. 23 by *archidesmophýlach tó desmōtḗrion* (*toú desmōtēpíou,* v. 23). By itself, *archidesmophýlach* means *śar bêt hassōhar,* the officer in charge of the prison. The addition of *desmōtērion* (a symomym for *ochýrōma*) is to be explained as an attempt by the LXX translators to

22 *The chief jailer placed in Joseph's hands all the prisoners who were in the round house, and all that was done*[9] *there was his doing.*

23 *Since Yahweh was with him the chief jailer did not oversee*[10] *anything that was in his hands. Whatever he undertook, Yahweh brought success.*

19-20 Potiphar is gullible. He immediately accepts the story his wife tells him. But why shouldn't he? For what reason ought he to suspect his wife of lying? One would think, however, that if Potiphar is certain that Joseph tried to rape his wife in his absence, then he would immediately order Joseph's execution. Perhaps Potiphar's decree that Joseph be incarcerated, not executed, is a sign that he is not totally convinced about the authenticity of his wife's story. Putting Joseph in jail will give Potiphar more time to probe the accuracy of the charges brought against his trusted and trustful overseer. That the narrator does not describe in v. 1 at whom or why Potiphar was incensed (the expression *wayyiḥar 'appô* stands by itself and is not followed by a preposition such as *b*ᵉ or *'el* with direct object) is perhaps his way of indicating that Potiphar is not completely convinced of his spouse's accusation, and therefore he is not as gullible as first appears.

21-23 Joseph moves from one confinement (a hole in the ground, ch. 37) to another confinement (a jail). Within ch. 39 itself he moves from one house (Potiphar's) to another house (a *round house, bêṯ hassōhar*).[11]

In vv. 19-23 a number of items stand out. One is the threefold use of *nāṯan* with three different subjects: (1) Potiphar *placed* (*wayyittᵉnēhû,* v. 20) Joseph in jail; (2) but Yahweh *disposed* (*wayyittēn,* v. 21) the chief jailer in his favor;

---

represent the Hebrew text in front of them as literally as possible. See Z. Talshir, "Double Translations in the Septuagint," in *VI Congress of the International Organization for Septuagint and Cognate Studies,* ed. C. E. Cox (Atlanta: Scholars, 1986), p. 34.

9. For participles used as predicates in a durative sense, and denoting actions of an indefinite subject, see Davidson, *Hebrew Syntax,* p. 152, § 108c; Th. Booij, "Some Observations on Psalm lxxxvii," *VT* 37 (1984) 21.

10. "Oversee" in the sense of supervise is the Hebrew verb *rā'â,* "to see." Interestingly the LXX renders *'ên . . . rō'eh* by *ouk ēn . . . ginōskōn.* There are a handful of places in the Hebrew Bible where *ginōskein/gignōskein* translates Heb. *rā'â* (Gen. 39:23; Exod. 22:10; 33:13; Num. 11:23; Judg. 2:7). In addition to *rā'â* meaning "to see," it also takes on the meaning of "come to see" or "to see so as to know," and may be used in parallelism with *yāḏa'* (Deut. 33:9; 1 Sam. 26:12; cf. Isa. 6:9). See P. Walters and D. W. Gooding, *The Text of the Septuagint* (Cambridge: Cambridge University, 1973), p. 204; T. J. Lewis, *Cults of the Dead in Ancient Israel and Ugarit,* HSM 39 (Atlanta: Scholars, 1989), pp. 108-9.

11. The possible Egyptian background to this unique Hebrew phrase (only in Gen. 39:20-23 and 40:3, 5) is explored by Vergote, *Joseph en Égypte,* pp. 25-28. Redford (*Study of the Biblical Story of Joseph,* pp. 47-48) finds wanting all attempts connecting *sōhar* with a *Vorlage* in Egyptian.

(3) and the jailer *placed* (*wayyittēn,* v. 22) the prisoners in Joseph's charge. Second, these verses contrast the chief jailer's eyes (v. 21) with the woman's eyes (v. 7).[12] Both the woman and the jailer looked at Joseph and liked what they saw: she saw a male figure to satisfy her sexual lust; he saw a reliable, model prisoner who could be trusted with responsibilities. Third, these verses establish a relationship between the chief jailer and Joseph that resembles the relationship that formerly existed between Joseph and Potiphar. This trusting relationship is indicated by phrases like *The chief jailer placed in Joseph's hands* . . . (v. 22), and *the chief jailer did not oversee anything that was in his hands* (v. 23). These phrases recall Potiphar's willingness to relinquish control to Joseph (v. 6). Potiphar "took a liking to Joseph" (lit., "Joseph found grace in his eyes," v. 4). Yahweh *disposed the chief jailer in his favor* (lit., "he gave him grace in the eyes of the chief jailer," v. 22). Fifth, Yahweh was a constant presence with Joseph — before he was accused (v. 2), and after he was jailed (v. 23). The result of that presence was that Yahweh *brought succcess* or prospered *(maṣlîaḥ)* every undertaking of Joseph (vv. 3, 23).

It has been common among commentators to discuss the similarities between the story in Gen. 39 and the late thirteenth-century B.C. Tale of Two Brothers. There are certainly parallels between ch. 39 and the first part of the Egyptian story. In both, a married woman (wife of Potiphar, wife of Anubis, respectively) attempts to seduce a virtuous youth (Joseph, Bata [her brother-in-law]). When the woman fails to achieve her goals, she maligns the youth before her husband (Potiphar, Anubis). Both young men, when tempted, immediately leave the premises. Joseph "fled outdoors" and Bata ran "like a leopard." And for a while at least, both young men are held responsible by the woman's husband for sexually abusing his spouse. One major difference between the two is that in the Egyptian story we know what happened to Anubis's wife when the truth came out: Anubis "reached his house, and killed his wife, and threw her out to the dogs." Gen. 39 says nothing about any penalty for Potiphar's wife bearing a false witness, perhaps because Gen. 39 is more interested in Joseph's destiny than in the destiny of Potiphar's wife.[13]

Beyond these parallels the two stories have little in common. When one reads the Tale of Two Brothers in its entirety, it becomes clear that the two brothers are actually thinly disguised deities, and the story abounds with wild fantasies and imaginations.[14] It contrasts vividly with the real-life situation of Gen. 39.

12. See n. 7 above, and 39:7.

13. See Sarna, *Understanding Genesis,* p. 216.

14. For the full text see M. Lichtheim, *Ancient Egyptian Literature,* 3 vols. (Berkeley: University of California, 1973-80), 2:203-11. Cf. also *ANET,* pp. 23-25; W. K. Simpson, ed., *The Literature of Ancient Egypt,* rev. ed. (New Haven: Yale University, 1973), pp. 92-107.

In extrabiblical literature a much better parallel to the Joseph story than the Tale of Two Brothers is the autobiography of Idrimi, the youngest son of a king of Alalakh in the early 15th century B.C.[15] Many of the motifs in the Joseph story are present there: (1) a forced separation from his family after a quarrel with older brothers; (2) a long sojourn in a foreign land (to the land of the Bedouin [Sutu], then to the land of Canaan, then seven years among the Habiru, then to Ugarit); (3) a series of oracles (= Joseph's dreams?) while living with the Habiru in which the storm-god (Baal) became favorable to him; (4) exaltation of the hero; (5) final reconciliation with his older brothers. These parallels between the Joseph story and Idrimi's inscription may be purely coincidental, or they may lend credence to the view that the Joseph story was in the process of formation as early as the 15th century B.C.[16]

D. JOSEPH INTERPRETS HIS JAILMATES' DREAMS (40:1-23)

1. PHARAOH'S SERVANTS IN DISTRESS (40:1-8)

1 *Some time later, the cupbearer of the king of Egypt, as well as the baker,*[1] *offended*[2] *their master, the king of Egypt.*

2 *Pharaoh was angry with*[3] *his two courtiers, with the head cupbearer and with the head baker.*

3 *He placed them in ward*[4] *at the house of the chief steward,*[5] *in the*

15. The first translation of this inscription was done by S. Smith, *The Statue of Idri-mi* (London: British Institute of Archaeology in Ankara, 1949). The translation cited here is that of A. L. Oppenheim in *ANET,* pp. 557-58.

16. See W. F. Albright, "Some Important Recent Discoveries: Alphabetic Origins and the Idrimi Statue," *BASOR* 118 (1950) 14-20; idem, "From the Patriarchs to Moses: I. From Abraham to Joseph," *BA* 36 (1973) 28-29.

1. Not more than one construct can stand before the same genitive. Thus Biblical Hebrew states "the cupbearer and the baker of the king of Egypt" as *mašqēh meleḵ miṣrayim wᵉhā'ōpeh.* See Davidson, *Hebrew Syntax,* p. 36, § 27b.

2. Lit., "sinned against" *(ḥāṭā' lᵉ).* K. Koch (*"ḥāṭā',"* *TDOT,* 4:311) states, "in the early historical books, *chāṭā'* means to commit an offense against someone with whom one stands in an institutionalized community relationship. . . . Such conduct includes . . . rebellion against one's king (Gen. 40:1; 1 S. 24:12 [Eng. v. 11]; 26:21)."

3. *qāṣap ʿal* is used to describe human anger here, in 41:10, and in Exod. 16:20; Lev. 10:16; Num. 31:14; 1 Sam. 29:4; 2 K. 13:9; Jer. 37:15. It is used only in preexilic texts (see J. Milgrom, *Leviticus 1–16,* AB [New York: Doubleday, 1991], pp. 609-10).

4. The translation "in ward" for *bᵉmišmar* in vv. 3 and 7, and for *bᵉmišmār* in v. 4, derives from the basic meaning of the verb *šāmar,* "to guard," on which see J. Mil-

round house where Joseph was confined.

4 *The chief steward assigned Joseph to wait on them. After they had been in ward for a lengthy period,*[6]

5 *each of the two had a dream*[7] *the same night, each dream having its own significance — the cupbearer and the baker who were employed by the king of Egypt, were confined in the round house.*

6 *When Joseph approached them in the morning he observed that they were disturbed.*[8]

7 *He inquired of Pharaoh's courtiers who were with him in ward in his master's house: "Why are you so dejected*[9] *today?"*[10]

8 *They said to him: "We have had a dream,*[11] *but there is no interpreter for it." Joseph spoke to them: "Do not interpretations belong to God? Please tell them to me."*

---

grom, *Numbers,* JPS Torah Commentary (Philadelphia: Jewish Publication Society, 1990), p. 312 n. 50.

5. The absence of the *dagesh* in the *ṭ* in *haṭabbāḥim* is strange (cf. v. 4, where it is present, *haṭṭabbāḥîm*).

6. "A lengthy period" is *yāmîm,* the pl. of *yôm,* "day." GKC, § 139h, states, "The simple plural of words denoting time sometimes includes also the idea of *a few, some;* thus *yāmîm a few days,* Gen. 24:55, 40:4 (here even of a longer period = *for some time*)."

7. Lit., "they both had a dream, each his own dream." On the distributive use of *'îš,* see Williams, *Hebrew Syntax,* p. 26, § 131.

8. *zō'ᵃpîm* is variously rendered: "distraught" (NJPS), "troubled" (Westermann), "dejected" (Speiser). The main meaning of the root is "disturb," e.g., of the sea (Jon. 1:15), then mentally: "disturbed, upset, out of sorts"; with Gen. 40:6 cf. Dan. 1:10. LXX renders *zō'ᵃpîm* in Gen. 40:6 as *tetaragménoi,* "troubled, terrified, unsettled" (the same word used in Luke 24:38 for the disciples' reaction to Jesus' appearance to them). See J. A. Montgomery, *Critical and Exegetical Commentary on the Book of Daniel,* ICC (Edinburgh: T. & T. Clark, 1927), p. 133; *HALAT,* 1:266; L. Kopf, "Arabische Etymologien und Parallelen zum Bibelwörterbuch," *VT* 9 (1959) 254.

9. Lit., "why are your faces evil?" D. W. Young ("With Snakes and Dates: A Sacred Marriage Drama at Ugarit," *UF* 9 [1977] 312; idem, "The Ugaritic Myth of the God Ḥōrān and the Mare," *UF* 11 [1979] 846) links the Hebrew phrase *pᵉnêḵem ra'îm* in Gen. 40:7 with the Ugaritic phrase *bḥrn pnm trġn,* which he renders "Ḥōrān's face is loathsome" rather than "Ḥōrān looked sad." In Genesis the idiom refers to the mood reflected in the faces of the king's ministers.

10. On the use of *hayyôm,* "today," and the noun-clause question of v. 7b, see S. J. DeVries, *Yesterday, Today and Tomorrow* (Grand Rapids: Eerdmans, 1975), p. 158.

11. The use of *ḥālamuû* (a perfect form) in v. 8 versus *wayyaḥalmû* (an imperfect with *waw* consecutive) in v. 5 is an illustration of the same event being described with different verbal forms. An imperfect form with *waw* consecutive is used in narrative (v. 5), while a perfect form of the same verb is used in v. 8 for a report (Pharaoh's ministers are speaking to Joseph). See A. Niccacci, *The Syntax of the Verb in Classical Hebrew Prose,* tr. W. G. E. Watson, JSOTSup 86 (Sheffield: JSOT, 1990), p. 42.

1-4 Gen. 39 said nothing about what, if anything, happened to Potiphar's wife for her false charges against Joseph. Gen. 40 is silent about the nature of the cupbearer's and the baker's offense against their pharaoh. In both cases, specifics would be much too ancillary to and detracting from the major thrust of the story, which is the destiny and promotion of Joseph. But a parallel theme in chs. 39 and 40 unites these chapters. Both chapters deal with an offense (imagined in ch. 39; real in ch. 40) against a superior or a superior's wife that lands the (alleged) criminal in prison. The pharaoh's employees *offended their master* (lit., "sinned against their master," *ḥāṭᵉʾû laʾᵃḏōnêhem,* 40:1), but Joseph was unwilling "to stand condemned before God" (lit., "to sin against God," *wᵉḥāṭāʾṯî lēʾlōhîm,* 39:9).

As interesting as the absence of specifics on the retainers' crimes is the absence of the name of Potiphar. He is referred to only by title. Presumably the *chief steward* of vv. 3 and 4 is the same as "Potiphar, the chief steward" of ch. 39. The prison in which the chief butler and baker are detained would be a room attached to Potiphar's house (40:3, which specifically identifies the place of detention as "the house of the chief steward"). Confinement is probably no more than house arrest, but prison is prison, and it is bad enough that Joseph refers to it as a "dungeon" (*bôr,* v. 15).

Potiphar assigns Joseph *to wait on* (*wayᵉšāreṯ,* v. 4) these two men. This is the same verb used back in 39:4 to describe Joseph's relationship to Potiphar (lit., "and he [Joseph] served him [Potiphar]"). According to some scholars, here is one valid criterion for separating ch. 39 (J) from ch. 40 (E). In 39:19-23 Joseph is in prison, but he is given by the chief jailer authority over the other prisoners.[12] By contrast, in ch. 40 he has no authority over any prisoners; in fact, he is a servant to two of them.[13] This is a misreading of the text. Nowhere does ch. 40 disagree with ch. 39. Joseph still maintains a position of authority in prison. When, however, the chief cupbearer and baker enter the scene, his responsibility is expanded to include meeting the needs and waiting upon these new coprisoners,[14] both of whom had earlier been responsible for putting wine (the cupbearer) and bread (the baker) on Pharaoh's table. What he did for Potiphar, and may continue to do for Potiphar, he now does for the cupbearer and baker. Certainly Joseph's responsibilities to Potiphar included anything but menial, tedious, chorelike activities. The same would be true of his responsibilities to these two.

12. On the Egyptian titles for various positions held by prison personnel see K. A. Kitchen, "A Recently Published Egyptian Papyrus and its Bearing on the Joseph Story," *TynBul* 1/2 (1956-57) 1-2.

13. For example, Speiser, *Genesis,* p. 308; von Rad, *Genesis,* p. 369.

14. See G. W. Coats, *From Canaan to Egypt: Structural and Theological Context for the Joseph Story,* CBQMS 4 (Washington, D.C.: Catholic Biblical Association, 1975), p. 23.

Furthermore, 40:3b, 15 clearly state that Joseph was in prison, exactly in accord with 39:19-23.

5-8 At some point in their confinement, the two officials of Pharaoh had dreams on the same night. They are more disturbed by their dreams than they are by their incarceration. This is clear to Joseph, for he could easily see by their faces that they *were disturbed* (*zōʿᵃp̱îm,* v. 6). Since part of Joseph's responsibilities was to wait on them, he inquires about their state. Joseph must not share the same sleeping quarters with the cupbearer and baker, for he *approached them.* And when he does, he sees immediately that something is wrong.

The chief problem that gnaws at them is not the dream itself, but the absence of a dream *interpreter.*[15] Confined to prison, they are shut off from Pharaoh's oneiromancers who may be able to assist them in this desperate moment. Few would have their insights and explanations prized as highly as those of the king's professional dream interpreters. A dream without an accompanying interpretation is like a diagnosis without a prognosis.

Almost automatically Joseph bears witness of his faith to the two. *God* (Elohim) is the dream interpreter (v. 8b). For appropriate emphasis on "God," *ʾᵉlōhîm* ("God") precedes *piṯrōnîm* ("interpretations") in the Hebrew phrase. The theme of providence emerges in two ways in Joseph's life and in his own testimony. One is Joseph's ability to interpret the happenings in his life and in that of his family as illustrative of God's control and use of otherwise inscrutable events (45:5-8; 50:20). The second is Joseph's conviction about God's control every time he interprets a dream (40:8; 41:16, 25, 28, 32). Apart from what Joseph's words say about Joseph's perception of his belief in his God's ability to reveal the interpretation of another's dream, his words to the cupbearer and the baker also demonstrate Joseph's use of appropriate protocol by one who would be a dream interpreter when he first speaks to the dreamer.[16] Thus in a frightening, uncertain situation, for the cupbearer and butler at least, Joseph displays both faith in his God and modesty in his own abilities on one hand, and sensitivity on the other hand.

15. The verb *pāṯar,* "to interpret," occurs 9 times in the OT, and all of them are in Gen. 40–41 (40:8, 16, 22; 41:8, 12 [twice], 13, 15 [twice]). The related noun *piṯrôn,* "interpretation," occurs 5 times in the OT, and all are in Gen. 40–41 as well (40:5, 8, 12, 18; 41:11). Now in a bilingual vocabulary from Ebla the Semitic equivalent of Sum. *nì-tur-du$_{11}$-ga,* "to speak softly," is *pá-tá-ru$_x$,* "to interpret." See M. J. Dahood, "Ebla, Ugarit, and the Bible," in G. Pettinato, *Archives of Ebla* (Garden City, NY: Doubleday, 1981), p. 279. This observation broadens Redford's position (*Study of the Biblical Story of Joseph,* p. 58) that *ptr* is common in postbiblical Hebrew and Aramaic.

16. A. L. Oppenheim (*The Interpretation of Dreams in the Ancient Near East* [Philadelphia: American Philosophical Society, 1956], pp. 204-5) refers to Joseph's words to the courtiers as "a customary formula in which the professional interpreter of dreams grants permission to a person to report to him a dream for elucidation."

Both the cupbearer and the baker (and Joseph) assume that what is revealed in a dream may subsequently be actualized in historical fact. Thus dreams are to be regarded as omens or presages, which often are understood only by other visionaries. Such revelatory dreams in the OT fall into one of two categories: those that are primarily auditory (Gen. 20:3, 6; 31:24; 1 K. 3:5; Matt. 1:20; 2:13, 19, 22), and those that are primarily visual experiences (Gen. 28;12; 31:10ff.; 37:5ff.; 40:9ff., 16ff., 41:1ff.; Judg. 7:13; Dan. 2:31ff.; 4:10ff.; 7:1ff.). This second type of dream often causes consternation in the recipient (Gen. 40:7; 41:8; Judg. 7:13; Dan. 2:1ff.; 4:2ff.; 7:14ff.). A dream in which someone speaks is self-interpreting. A dream in which nobody speaks can be unnerving.[17]

Some scholars have drawn attention to the fact that a second reason (see my discussion above on v. 4) for attributing ch. 40 (and ch. 41) to E, but ch. 39 to J, is the distribution of divine names. It is evident that *YHWH* occurs repeatedly in ch. 39 (7 times), and *'ĕlōhîm* only once (v. 9). By contrast, *YHWH* never appears in ch. 40 or ch. 41, but *'ĕlōhîm* appears in 40:8 and 9 times in ch. 41 (vv. 16, 25, 28, 32 [twice], 38, 39, 51, 52).[18]

A closer examination of chs. 39–41 reveals, however, that every time *YHWH* occurs in these chapters, it is used by the narrator. Every time *'ĕlōhîm* occurs, it is used in direct speech by Joseph when speaking to an Egyptian (to Potiphar's wife, ch. 39; to the cupbearer and baker, ch. 40; to Pharaoh, ch. 41; to Joseph's Egyptian wife, ch. 41); or it is used by Pharaoh speaking to his servants about Joseph (41:38, 39). All this suggests that more may be at play than simply J-E traditions. If the context is some word about God's blessing of or presence with Joseph, then *YHWH* is the choice. If the context is a conversation involving Joseph and a non-Hebrew, then the choice is *'ĕlōhîm.*

2. THE CUPBEARER'S DREAM AND ITS INTERPRETATION (40:9-15)

9 *Then the chief cupbearer told his dream to Joseph. "In my dream," he said to him, "a vine was in front of me,*

10 *and on the vine were three branches. Just as it was on the point of budding,*[1] *its blossoms shot up;*[2] *its clusters*[3] *ripened*[4] into grapes.

17. See T. H. Gaster, "Dreams," *EncJud,* 6:208-9; J. H. Stek, "Dream," *ISBE,* 1:991-92.

18. See Jenks, *The Elohist and North Israelite Traditions,* p. 29.

1. Contra, e.g., *BHS, kᵉpōrahaṯ* need not be emended. For *k* prefixed to the participle to express imminent action, see T. J. Meek, "Translating the Hebrew Bible," *JBL* 79 (1960) 329. See P. Wernberg-Møller, "Observations on the Hebrew Participle," *ZAW* 71 (1959) 56 n. 9, for "like (or as if) budding."

2. *niṣṣāh* ("its blossoms") is masc., but *ʿālᵉṯâ* ("shot up") is feminine. Skinner

11 *With Pharaoh's cup in my hand, I took the grapes, pressed*[5] *them into Pharaoh's cup, and placed the cup in Pharaoh's palm."*

12 *Joseph said to him: "This is its interpretation. The three branches are three days;*

13 *within three days*[6] *Pharaoh will summon you*[7] and restore you to your position. You will be handing Pharaoh's cup into his hand as you used to do[8] when you were his cupbearer.

14 *So*[9] *if you still recall my being with you, when all is well with you, do me the kindness, please,*[10] *of mentioning*[11] *me to Pharaoh, to get me released*[12] *from this house.*

(*Genesis,* p. 462) takes *niṣṣāh* as accusative, rather than as nominative: "it (the vine) shot up in blossom." BDB, p. 655, and *BHS* suggest changing *niṣṣaṯāh.* Cf. *pinnāh* for *pinnāṯāh* in Prov. 7:8.

3. *'eškōl* may now be connected with Eblaite *aš-kà-lum* and *aš-qa-i-lu.* See Dahood, "Ebla, Ugarit, and the Bible," in Pettinato, *Archives of Ebla,* p. 279.

4. This is the only instance of *bāšal* in the Hiphil ("ripened, brought to ripeness"). In the Qal it means "to boil, cook" (intransitive) and in the Piel "to boil, cook" (transitive).

5. For *śāḥaṭ* and Akk. *šaḫātu,* "to press (grapes)," see H. Cohen, *Biblical Hapax Legomena in the Light of Akkadian and Ugaritic,* SBLDS 37 (Missoula, MT: Scholars, 1978), p. 35.

6. Cf. "in seven days" (Gen. 7:4), "in three years" (Isa. 16:14), "within two years" (Jer. 28:3), for similar expressions of time. The expression *b^{e}‘ôḏ š^{e}lōšeṯ yāmîm,* part of Joseph's prediction, must be connected with *bayyôm hašš^{e}lîšî yôm,* v. 20 ("on the third day"), the day on which Joseph's prediction came through. Thus *b^{e}‘ôḏ* must take on the meaning "toward the end of." See G. R. Driver, "Once Again Abbreviations," *Textus* 4 (1964) 86-87. Targ. Onqelos removed all doubt by reading *bswp tlth ywmyn,* "at the end of three days."

7. Lit., "will lift your head." See also v. 20.

8. For *kammišāṭ* meaning "after the manner, custom, fashion (of)" cf. Exod. 21:9; Judg. 18:7; 1 K. 18:28, and BDB, p. 1049.

9. *kî 'im,* which normally opens the apodosis clause, and is here in the protasis clause, is difficult. GKC, § 163d, suggested that a negative lead-in sentence be supplied, "[I desire nothing] except that you remember me." This suggestion is revived by C. Van Leeuwen, "Die Partikel *'im,*" *OTS* 18 (1973) 45, "[Ich begehre nichts] ausser dass. . . ." The problem is that *kî 'im* means "except," but may that legitimately extend into "except that"?

10. The Hebrew particle of entreaty and exhortation is most frequently joined to the imperative, but it may also be joined to the precative perfect, as here *(w^{e}‘āśîṯā-nā')*. Cf. GKC, § 105b n. 1.

11. *hizkîr* in the forensic sense broadens to "make known, mention." See B. S. Childs, *Memory and Tradition in Israel,* SBT 1/37 (Naperville, IL: Allenson, 1962), p. 15.

12. For LXX *exágō,* popularly used in third-century B.C. Greek for "release from prison," see J. A. L. Lee, *A Lexical Study of the Septuagint Version of the Pentateuch* (Chico, CA: Scholars, 1983), p. 67.

15 *For I was kidnapped*[13] *from the land of the Hebrews, and I have not done anything that they should put*[14] *me in the dungeon."*

9-11 The cupbearer begins his explanation to Joseph with *In my dream (baḥ^{a}lômî).* This phrase may be compared with the opening formula *ina šuttiya,* "in my dream," which occurs in a number of the Mari prophetic texts.[15] The Mari letters that report dream revelations normally follow the pattern: "the writer's presentation of the . . . dreamer; the opening formula of the dreamer: "(I saw) in my dream" . . . ; the content of the dream which is based on a visual or, more often, on an auditory experience (e.g., hearing the voice of the god); finally, comments of the writer of the letter."[16]

The cupbearer sees a vine with three branches, which are filled with blossoms and clusters of grapes that quickly ripen. The asyndetic construction of v. 10 emphasizes the rapidity with which the cupbearer says all this took place. He squeezes the grapes into the pharaoh's cup and then gives the cup to the pharaoh to drink. There is no time in the dream for the grape juice to ferment.

It is a dream involving things of three. The vine has three branches. Then three verbs are used in v. 10 to describe the growth of the vine and the branches. The vine budded, blossoms shot up, and clusters ripened. Three times in v. 11 the cupbearer mentions Pharaoh rather than the more distant "king of Egypt" (v. 1). Finally, in v. 11 the cupbearer uses the word "cup" three times, plus three first person singular verbs to describe his activities in his dream ("I took"; "I pressed"; "I placed").

12-13 The text gives no indication that Joseph prays for an explanation from God, or that he seeks wisdom from above. His answer is automatic, instinctive, and unqualified. *The three branches are three days.* Within three days Pharaoh *will summon* his cupbearer and restore him to his former position. This is the first of three uses of the phrase (lit.) *lift up the head of* in this chapter (see vv. 19, 20). To "lift up the head (of a person)" means

13. See Jackson, *Theft in Early Jewish Law,* pp. 3, 8. For *gānaḇ* meaning "to kidnap" in narrative texts cf. 2 K. 11:2 (par. 2 Chr. 22:11). On the significance of passive infinitives in Biblical Hebrew see R. M. Frank's review of J. M. Solá-Solé, *L'Infinitif sémitique,* in *CBQ* 26 (1964) 128 n. 6.

14. On the use of the perfect with modal force *(śāmû)* see Davidson, *Hebrew Syntax,* p. 59, § 59c.

15. See J. F. Craghan, "The *ARM X* 'Prophetic' Texts: Their Media, Style, and Structure," *JANES* 6 (1974) 43-45; M. Weinfeld, "Ancient Near Eastern patterns in prophetic literature," *VT* 27 (1977) 185-86.

16. A. Malamat, "A Forerunner of Biblical Prophecy: The Mari Documents," in *Ancient Israelite Religion,* Fest. F. M. Cross, ed. P. D. Miller, Jr., P. D. Hanson, S. D. McBride (Philadelphia: Fortress, 1987), p. 45.

"to take up the case (of a person)," of which the result may be favorable (Gen. 40:13, 21; 2 K. 25:27; Jer. 52:31) or unfavorable (Gen. 40:22).[17] Speiser prefers to give the phrase in v. 13 the more specific meaning of "pardon."[18] But this is by no means certain. It is just as likely that "lift the head" means "summon."[19]

14 The propitious time to request a favor from someone is at the moment one has brought to that person an encouraging announcement. The cupbearer must be elated (although the text says nothing of his reaction to the interpretation) — if he can believe Joseph — that his imprisonment will be brief, and that he will shortly be reassigned by the pharaoh to his old position.

Joseph does not command. He requests. And his request is tempered with modesty: *So if you still recall my being* [z^e*k̲artanî*] *with you.* The cupbearer will see the pharaoh in three days. Is it possible that in three days he might forget all about Joseph? Joseph's request is that the cupbearer be kind enough *(ḥesed̲)*[20] to mention *(hizkartanî)* him to the pharaoh. Just as the cupbearer is unable to interpret his own dream, Joseph is unable to make his own defense before the pharaoh. Each needs the help of the other. "These pleas draw us closer to the man."[21]

15 To underscore further his innocence, Joseph appeals to data about which the cupbearer would be ignorant. In v. 14 his appeal is to present action; in v. 15 his appeal is to past action. He claims that he was *kidnapped from the land of the Hebrews.*[22] This is the means by which Joseph identifies himself to the cupbearer as an outsider. He might have done so earlier, had he said to the official:

17. On *nāśā' pānîm* cf. E. A. Speiser, "Census and Ritual Expiation in Mari and Israel," *BASOR* 149 (1958) 20-24; I. L. Seeligmann, "Zur Terminologie für das Gerichtsverfahren im Wortsatz des biblischen Hebräisch," in *Hebräische Wortforschung,* Fest. W. Baumgartner, ed. B. Hartmann, et al., VTSup 16 (Leiden: Brill, 1967), pp. 270-72; A. Phillips, *Ancient Israel's Criminal Law* (Oxford: Blackwell, 1970), p. 27; and G. R. Driver's comments in a review of this book (and phrase) in *JTS* 23 (1972) 161.

18. Speiser, *Genesis,* pp. 305, 308.

19. See T. J. Meek, "A New Bible Translation," *JBL* 82 (1963) 271. A. L. Oppenheim ("Idiomatic Accadian [Lexicographical Researches]," *JAOS* 61 [1941] 252-53) cites numerous cuneiform texts where *rêša našû* means "to cite, to summon" as well as other nuances such as "to examine."

20. Cf. K. D. Sakenfeld, *The Meaning of Ḥesed in the Hebrew Bible,* HSM 17 (Missoula, MT: Scholars, 1978), pp. 46-48; F. I. Andersen, "Yahweh, the Kind and Sensitive God," in *God Who Is Rich in Mercy,* Fest. D. Knox, ed. P. T. O'Brien and D. G. Peterson (Grand Rapids: Baker, 1987), pp. 56-57.

21. W. L. Humphreys, *Joseph and His Family* (Columbia, SC: University of South Carolina, 1988), p. 88.

22. See D. B. Redford, "The 'Land of the Hebrews' in Gen. XL 15," *VT* 15 (1965) 529-32, who comments on the expression as a means of designating Palestine to an Egyptian, as opposed to an expression like "land of Canaan." Redford observes that "Hebrew" appears for the first time in very late Egyptian texts.

"Do not to *Yahweh* belong interpretations?" (v. 8b). Until now Joseph has kept a low profile. He makes clear his roots by identifying his birthplace rather than by identifying his God. It is not clear how much meaning this geographical phrase would have to an Egyptian courtier, but it is sufficient to mark Joseph as an alien. Certainly this point produces a greater sense of wonderment and obligation on the cupbearer. He has been helped out of a difficult situation by a foreigner — who owes him nothing, who worships some God different from his, and who has a knowledge of mysteries far surpassing his own.

Joseph's next statement is a disclaimer that he has done anything to merit confinement. To reinforce the ugliness of the unwarranted treatment he is receiving, he shifts from calling his place of confinement "this house" (*habbayiṯ hazzeh,* v. 14) to calling it *the dungeon* (lit., "the pit," *habbôr*) — the word used to describe the well into which his brothers first placed him (37:20, 22, 24, 28, 29).

3. THE BAKER'S DREAM AND ITS INTERPRETATION (40:16-23)

16 *When the chief baker saw how well he had interpreted, he said to Joseph: "In my dream too there were three baskets of white bread*[1] *on my head.*

17 *In the top basket were all kinds of baked goods*[2] *for Pharaoh which a baker makes, but the birds*[3] *kept pecking*[4] *at them right out of the basket on my head."*

1. The translation of *ḥōrî* is debated. NAB, NIV mg., and Speiser, *Genesis,* pp. 306, 307, translate as "wicker" by connecting the word with *ḥôr,* "hole," i.e., perforated. RSV, JB, *CHAL,* p. 116, translate as "cakes." The translation "white" (so AV, NEB) comes about by connecting *ḥôrî* with *ḥāwar,* "be white" (see BDB, p. 301). This rendering is now favored by the discovery in an administrative text from Ebla that deals with cereals of *lú ḫa-rí,* "baker of white bread." See M. J. Dahood, *Bib* 62 (1981) 273-74; idem, "Eblaite *ḫa-rí* and Genesis 40,16," *BN* 13 (1980) 14-16; idem, "Eblaite and Biblical Hebrew," *CBQ* 44 (1982) 22. An Egyptian text dealing with the interpretation of dreams states: "If a man see himself in a dream, white bread being given to him — good: it means things at which his face will light up" (*ANET,* p. 495b).

2. *ma'ᵃḵal* is lit. "food." The kind of food that would be associated with a baker would be baked goods or pastries.

3. *hā'ôp̱,* sing. and defined, lit., "the bird," here and in v. 19, is a collective (see BDB, p. 733).

4. Lit., "eating" (*'ōḵēl,* a participle). When the subject of this verb is a nonhuman, it is normally some kind of rapacious animal such as "wild beasts" (Gen. 37:20, 23, Hos. 2:14 [Eng. 12]), or "dogs" (1 K. 13:28; 14:11; 16:4; 21:23, 24). See also *wᵉ'āḵal* in v. 19.

18 *Joseph answered: "This is its interpretation. The three baskets are three days.*

19 *Within three days Pharaoh will summon you*[5] *and hang you*[6] *on a stake.*[7] *The birds will peck your flesh off you."*

20 *Indeed, on the third day — for it was Pharaoh's birthday*[8] *— he threw a banquet for all his servants, and summoned the chief cupbearer and the chief butler, with his servants looking on.*

21 *He restored the chief cupbearer to his cup bearing, and he placed the cup into Pharaoh's palm.*

22 *But*[9] the chief baker he hanged — just as Joseph had interpreted for them.

23 *The chief cupbearer ignored*[10] Joseph; he forgot[11] him.[12]

5. As *BHS* suggests, *mēʿāleyḵā* may be a faulty anticipation of the same word at the end of the sentence. Vulg. and two Hebrew mss. eliminate it. See G. R. Driver, *JTS* 23 (1972) 161; Westermann, *Genesis,* 3:72, 77.

6. See NAB and Speiser, *Genesis,* p. 307, who argues against the common translation of *tālâ* as "hang" (AV, RSV, NIV, NEB, JB), for one does not hang a beheaded person. Cf. Westermann, *Genesis,* 3:77-78, who argues that "it is quite impossible" that "lift up your head" refers to beheading; thus he translates *tālâ* as "hang." Cf. von Rad, *Genesis,* p. 372; Sarna, *Genesis,* pp. 279-80.

7. Targ. Onqelos normally renders *'ēṣ* ("tree") by *'yln'*. But here and in Deut. 21:22, 23, where *'ēṣ* refers to a gallows or a stake, it uses *ṣlyb'*.

8. For *'eṯ* after passive infinitives see GKC, § 121b; and Davidson, *Hebrew Syntax,* p. 112, § 79 *(hulleḏeṯ 'eṯ parʿōh). hulleḏeṯ* is a Hophal infinitive construct of *yālaḏ,* and the expression would translate lit. as "on the day of Pharaoh's having been caused to be born." See Waltke and O'Connor, *Biblical Hebrew Syntax,* pp. 448, 601; F. I. Andersen, "Passive and Ergative in Hebrew," in *Near Eastern Studies in Honor of William Foxwell Albright,* ed. H. Goedicke (Baltimore: Johns Hopkins University, 1971), p. 11; H.-P. Müller, "Ergativelemente im akkadischen und althebräischen Verbalsystem," *Bib* 66 (1985) 410.

9. On the disjunctive *waw,* see Waltke and O'Connor, *Biblical Hebrew Syntax,* pp. 650-51.

10. Lit., "he did not remember" *(wᵉlō' zāḵar).* Cf. NJPS, "did not think of"; Speiser, "gave no thought to"; Westermann, "gave no further thought to."

11. After noting that *šāḵaḥ* is the most frequently used antonym of *zāḵar, B. S. Childs (Memory and Tradition in Israel,* SBT 1/37 [Naperville, IL: Allenson, 1962], p. 18) remarks, "forgetting is not a psychological act of having a thought pass from one's consciousness, but an outward act of worshipping other gods (Deut. 8:19), of forsaking someone (Isa. 49:14), of not keeping the commandments (Deut. 8:11)."

12. Targ. Yerushalmi endows this verse with a prophetic content not native to the verse itself: "Because Joseph forsook God's mercy and trusted the director of food . . . he did not remember Joseph but forgot him till the time was reached before the Lord for [his] redemption." See J. Weingreen, *From Bible to Mishna* (New York: Holmes & Meier, 1976), pp. 3, 27 n. 10.

16-17 It is only Joseph's happy, but as yet unconfirmed, interpretation of the head cupbearer's dream that prods the head baker into sharing his dream. He appears to be expecting from Joseph an equally good interpretation of his dream. In that dream he has three baskets stacked on top of each other, with the most delicious baked goods packed in the top basket. That he is not able to shoo the birds away, as did Abram (15:11), seems generally self-explanatory; that is, the dream seems to bode ill for the baker.

18-19 Joseph is as quick with his second interpretation as he was with his first. The meaning of the dream is that the baker will first be summoned by Pharaoh, who will then have the baker hanged. *Summon* (lit., "lift up your head," if "from you" is deleted, a possibility noted above) means "to summon for the purpose of taking up your case" (as in v. 13), only to give an unfavorable verdict, death by impalement, followed by exposure of his corpse to carrion birds, which feed off the impaled cadaver. Such a gruesome fate for the baker must indicate that his offense against Pharaoh (v. 1) was grave. But just as the text is silent about either the cupbearer's euphoria or the baker's sense of hopelessness, it is also silent about why one of the two dreamers is exonerated and restored, while the other is condemend to death. Both of them had offended their lord. The reason for the absence of such psychological and explanatory data is dictated by the purpose of the narrative. It is a narrative about Joseph and his God-given ability to interpret dreams of foreigners. One gets the impression that the presence of God with Joseph, spoken of eloquently in the previous chapter, is still a reality.

20-22 Joseph's knowledge of the future turns out to be correct. The chief cupbearer is restored to his position, and the chief baker is executed. On the day celebrating the birthday of the pharaoh (v. 20), one man keeps his life and one man loses his life. Joseph is given insight about his own future (ch. 37) and the future of others (ch. 40). There is no indication, at least not yet, that anybody informed the pharaoh of Joseph's accurate prognostications.

23 Apparently, in being restored to his position, the cupbearer forgets the favor Joseph had requested of him. Indeed, the narrator emphasizes the cupbearer's ignoring of Joseph by using two verbs that essentially say the same thing — *ignored* and *forgot* — either one of which would have sufficed to underscore the cupbearer's neglect.

For sharing his sense of divine destiny Joseph finds himself sold by his brothers to some caravaneers going to Egypt (ch. 37). For refusing to compromise his moral standards and sense of duty to his superiors, he is falsely accused and cast into prison (ch. 38). In spite of the fact that he helps a fellow prisoner, that prisoner refuses or forgets to reciprocate when he has the chance to help Joseph. Here is a chain of three aggravating setbacks for Joseph.

E. JOSEPH ASSUMES HIGH OFFICE IN EGYPT (41:1-57)

1. PHARAOH'S TWO DREAMS (41:1-8)

1 *Two full years*[1] *later, Pharaoh was having a dream: he*[2] *was standing*[3]
beside[4] *the Nile,*[5]

2 *when from the Nile came up seven cows, well formed and fat-fleshed,*
and grazed in the reed beds.[6]

3 *On their heels were seven other cows, ugly and lean-fleshed,*[7] *coming*

1. A period of time and its contents are expressed by being placed in apposition: *šenāṯayim yāmîm.* See GKC, § 131d; Williams, *Hebrew Syntax,* p. 15, § 68. The Hebrew translates lit. as "two years of days." Cf. 2 Sam. 13:23; 14:28; Jer. 28:3, 11.

2. Following most translations, I have not translated *w^{e}hinnēh* at the beginning of this nominal clause. Perhaps one could include *w^{e}hinnēh,* where it introduces the contents of a dream, under D. J. McCarthy's "excited perception" use of *w^{e}hinnēh* ("The uses of *w^{e}hinnēh* in Biblical Hebrew," *Bib* 61 [1980] 332-33). McCarthy notes that "here we are concerned with special cases where the emotional tone is so strong that we cannot treat the sentence as a simple statement of fact." Note also the study of B. O. Long, "Reports of Visions Among the Prophets," *JBL* 95 (1976) 353-65, in which he suggests that reports of visions consist of three basic elements: (1) announcement of vision; (2) transition *(w^{e}hinnēh);* and (3) vision sequence. He finds a precise translation for *w^{e}hinnēh* in such places impossible. See too W. Richter, "Traum und Traumbedeutung im AT: Ihre Form und Verwendung," *BZ* 7 (1963) 202-20.

3. GKC, § 116s, provides instances where the personal pronoun, normally used as the subject of a participial clause, is omitted.

4. GKC, § 119cc, "*ʿal-* is used after verbs of *standing* and *going* to express a towering *over* some one or something . . . e.g., Gn. 41:1, etc., *Pharaoh . . . stood* עַל־הַיְאֹר *by the Nile* (above the water level)."

5. On the Egyptian background of *y^{e}ʾôr* for "Nile" see T. O. Lambdin, "Egyptian Loan Words in the Old Testament," *JAOS* 73 (1953) 151. The Egyptian word for the river Nile was *ʾtrw,* but later spellings without the *t,* hence *ʾrw,* are frequent.

6. For this translation see M. J. Dahood, "Northwest Semitic Notes on Genesis," *Bib* 55 (1974) 80; Lambdin, *JAOS* 73 (1953) 146; Vergote, *Joseph en Égypte,* pp. 59-66 ("fourré de papyrus," from Egyp. *ȝhy,* "papyrus thicket"). See the Ugaritic references for this root discussed in B. Couroyer's review of Vergote in *RB* 66 (1959) 588; and Aram. *ʾḥwh* ("its vegetation") in J. A. Fitzmyer, *Aramaic Inscriptions of Sefîre,* BibOr 19 (Rome: Pontifical Biblical Institute, 1967), p. 47. Cf. also, W. L. Michel, *Job in the Light of Northwest Semitic,* BibOr 42 (Rome: Biblical Institute, 1987), 1:189-190.

7. In vv. 3 and 4 the Hebrew word is *daqqôṯ* (to describe the thin cows); and *daqqôṯ* is also used in vv. 6 and 7 (to describe the thin ears of grain). In vv. 19 and 20, however, *raqqôṯ* is used for the thin cows. Vv. 23 and 24 use *daqqôṯ* again for the thin ears. V. 27 uses *raqqôṯ* for the thin cows and *rēqôṯ* for the thin ears. Thus MT is as follows:

cows	**ears of grain**
v. 3, *daqqôṯ*	v. 6, *daqqôṯ*
v. 4, *daqqôṯ*	v. 7, *daqqôṯ*

up from the Nile; they stood on the bank of the Nile beside the cows.
4 *The ugly lean-fleshed cows consumed the seven well-formed, fat cows. Then Pharaoh awoke.*
5 *He fell asleep and dreamed a second time. Seven ears of grain were growing*[8] *on a single stalk — fat and healthy ones.*
6 *Seven ears of grain, lean and shrivelled by the east wind,*[9] *were sprouting behind them.*
7 *The lean ears swallowed up the seven fat and full ears. Then Pharaoh awoke. It was a dream!*
8 *Next morning, his spirit*[10] *perturbed,*[11] *he had all Egypt's cleverest magicians*[12] *summoned. He shared with them his dream,*[13] *but there was none to interpret them*[14] *for Pharaoh.*

---

cows	**ears of grain**
v. 19, *raqqôṯ*	v. 23, *daqqôṯ*
v. 20, *raqqôṯ*	v. 24, *daqqôṯ*
v. 27, *raqqôṯ*	v. 27, *rēqôṯ*

Following *BHS,* Westermann (*Genesis,* 3:84) suggests that *daqqôṯ* be read as *raqqôṯ* in vv. 3 and 4 for consistency' sake, i.e., all references to the "gaunt" cows have *raqqôṯ*.

8. "Growing" (the 7 ears of grain) is the same word for "coming up" (the gaunt cows) in v. 3 (*ʿōlôṯ*). "Ear of grain" (*šibbōleṯ*) (fem.) is written as a masc. in the pl. absolute (*šibb°lîm*) and in the pl. construct (*šibb°lê,* Zech. 4:12).

9. *aš*^{e}*ḏûpōṯ qāḏîm* illustrates the genitive of agency with a passive. See Waltke and O'Connor, *Biblical Hebrew Syntax,* pp. 616-17.

10. For H. M. Orlinsky ("The Plain Meaning of *Rûaḥ* in Gen. 1.2," *JQR* 48 [1957] 172-82) Gen. 41:8 contains the first place in the Bible where *rûaḥ* should be translated "spirit."

11. *pāʿam* occurs once with the meaning "thrust, impel" (Judg. 13:25, Samson and Yahweh's Spirit) in the Qal; three times with the meaning "be disturbed" in the Niphal (Gen. 41:8; Ps. 77:5; Dan. 2:3); once in the Hithpael with the same meaning as the Niphal (Dan. 2:1).

12. There are not two classes of persons involved here, for no distinction is made between the two groups in the following narrative. See R. N. Whybray, *The Intellectual Tradition in the Old Testament,* BZAW 135 (Berlin: Töpelmann, 1974), p. 15.

13. Lit., "his dream" (sing.), *ḥ*^{a}*lōmô.* SP reads as a pl., which is followed by many commentators, but one may make sense of the MT; see n. 14.

14. *'ôṯām,* "them" (pl.), refers back to "dream" (sing.). *BHS* proposes to follow LXX, which reads *autó* (sing.), and the MT of v. 15, which has *'ōṯô* (sing.). But perhaps the incongruity between the sing. *ḥ*^{a}*lōmŏ* and the pl. *'ôṯām* is intentional. Note the difference between the end of v. 4 ("Then Pharaoh awoke") and the end of v. 7 ("Then Pharaoh awoke. It was a dream"). The word "dream" (sing.) is used only once — to the pharaoh it was one dream. But to his dream interpreters it was two dreams; they can neither interpret nor count correctly. See Sternberg, *Poetics of Biblical Narrative,* p. 398.

Joseph has been languishing in prison for *two full years.* The butler has been dead for two years. The cupbearer has been back in the pharaoh's good graces for the same length of time. It is not difficult to believe that for two whole years the pharaoh had dreams, but that none of them caused him the distress that this one did: *his spirit* [was] *perturbed* (*wattippāʿem rûḥô,* v. 8). This same expression is used with Nebuchadnezzar and his baffling dream (Dan. 2:1, Hithpael; 2:3, Niphal), as well as by the anguished psalmist in Ps. 77:5 (Eng. 4): "I am so troubled that I cannot speak" (RSV) or "I am bewildered, yet I will not speak."[15] The latter reference provides the only instance in the OT in which the subject of the verb is not *rûaḥ.*[16]

Pharaoh has two dreams, as Joseph did in ch. 37, or better, one dream with two parts. Both parts have formal similarities. Six times in 41:1-8 the interjection *hinnēh* (lit., "behold") is used (vv. 1, 2, 3, 5, 6, 7; see n. 2 above). The section is also rife with participles in the narrator's mouth (*ḥōlēm, ʿōmēḏ,* v. 1; *ʿōlōṯ,* v. 2; *ʿōlôṯ,* v. 3; *ʿōlôṯ,* v. 5; *ṣōmᵉḥôṯ,* v. 6; *pôṯēr,* v. 8).[17]

In the first dream the pharaoh sees seven filled-out or (lit.) *fat-fleshed* cows coming up from the Nile and grazing in the reed beds by the river. They are followed by seven emaciated or (lit.) *lean-fleshed* cows, who proceed to devour the fatter cows. In the second part of the dream the pharaoh sees seven lush[18] ears of grain sprouting from a single stalk. Sprouting near them were seven blighted ears of grain, which swallowed their much healthier counterparts. No reason is given as to why one set of cows is so frail, but we are informed that the shrivelled ears of grain are in such a condition because of *the east wind,* the sirocco,[19] the autumn/spring withering wind that blows into Egypt from the south. Nor are we told why seven ears of grain escaped the effects of this wind, and why seven others fell prey. Of course, both dreams have the element of the fantastic: Cows do not eat cows; ears of grain do not consume ears of grain.

15. Translation of H.-J. Kraus, *Psalms,* tr. H. C. Oswald, Continental Commentary, 2 vols. (Minneapolis: Augsburg, 1988-89), 2:112.

16. In this one case (Ps. 77:5 [Eng. 4]) M. J. Dahood (*Psalms,* AB, 3 vols. [New York: Doubleday, 1965-73]), 2:227) is inclined to believe that the verb in question derives from *p'm,* "foot," and is thus a denominative from the name of parts of the body, hence, "I pace the floor and do not recline."

17. Cf. Joseph's use of participles in his dream telling (37:7: *mᵉʾallᵉmîm, qāmâ, niṣṣāḇâ,* 37:9: *mištaḥᵃwîm*). As in the visions of the prophets (Long, *JBL* 95 [1976] 356), the vision sequence usually begins with participial clauses.

18. This is the only place the OT uses the adjective *bārîʾ,* "fat," for something other than the animate sphere (either human [Judg. 3:17] or nonhuman [Gen. 41:2, 4; 1 K. 5:3; Ezek. 34:3, 20; Zech. 11:16]), thus making its application to something inanimate (ears of grain) a figurative one. See Sternberg, *Poetics of Biblical Narrative,* pp. 19, 20, 397, 535 n. 25.

19. See R. B. Y. Scott, "Meteorological Phenomena and Terminology in the Old Testament," *ZAW* 64 (1952) 11-25, esp. 20.

The phenomenon of duplicate dreams is well attested in ancient Near Eastern literature. In the Gilgamesh Epic, Gilgamesh tells two dreams to his mother. In the first he saw a star in the heavens which he could neither lift nor drive away. The more he looked on it the more he was attracted to it as to a woman. His mother interprets the dream. Without using the name Enkidu, she simply says: "[A stout com]rade who rescues [a friend is come to thee]. [He is the mightiest in the land]; strength he has. . . . [This is the mean]ing of thy dream."[20] Then Gilgamesh shares with his mother a second dream. This time he saw an odd-shaped axe to which he "was drawn . . . as though to a woman." Again, his mother interprets the dream to him. "The axe which thou sawest is a man. . . . He is the mightiest in the land . . . so mighty his strength."[21]

Another example of duplicate dreams is provided by Gudea, *ensi* of Lagash and a contemporary of Ur-Nammu (last part of the 3rd millennium B.C.). He came to prominence just after the liberation from the Gutian yoke. The main achievement of his reign was the erection of a temple in honor of Lagash's city-god Ningursu. His two cylinders (in Sumerian) record the events surrounding the building of this temple. Gudea states that he went into the temple with the intention of dreaming "in the god's abode" and of thus gaining knowledge of the divine will. By dream he learns that he is to rebuild Ningursu's temple, and how each step in its construction is to be taken in order to placate the gods.[22] Of course, the incubation dreams of Gudea are quite different in origin from those of the pharaoh.

The actual occasion of the first dream is a lack of water in the rivers that threatens the land with famine (after the manner of Pharaoh). In the dream Gudea saw a man whose stature was so great that it equalled the heavens and the earth. Beside the man was the divine eagle, with lions by his hands. Gudea also saw a woman holding in her hand a pure reed and carrying a tablet on which was a star of the heavens. Next, Gudea saw a second man, warriorlike, carrying a slab of lapis lazuli on which he drew the plan of a temple. A cushion was placed before Gudea, upon which was a mold with a brick in it. By the cushion an ass was laying on the ground.

Gudea turns to Nina, daughter of Enki (the god of wisdom), for the

20. *ANET,* p. 76.

21. *ANET,* pp. 76-77; see also J. S. Cooper, "Gilgamesh Dreams of Enkidu: The Evolution and Dilution of Narrative," in *Essays on the Ancient Near East in Memory of Jacob Joel Finkelstein,* ed. Maria de Jong Ellis (Hamden, CT: Archon, 1977), pp. 39-44; J. H. Tigay, *Evolution of the Gilgamesh Epic* (Philadelphia: University of Pennsylvania, 1982), pp. 82-93.

22. See A. Falkenstein, *Die Inschriften Gudeas von Lagaš: I. Einleitung,* AnOr 30 (Rome: Pontifical Biblical Institute, 1966); S. N. Kramer, *Sumerians* (Chicago: University of Chicago, 1963), pp. 137-40.

interpretation. She interprets through the mouth of her chief priest. The man whose stature was so great is Ningirsu. The woman who held the reed and carried the tablet was the goddess Nisaba. The star she carried was the pure star of the temple's construction. The second warriorlike man was the god Nidub, and the plan of the temple which he drew was the plan of Eninnu. The brick was the sacred brick of Eninnu; and the ass was Gudea himself.

Gudea then has a second dream, the purpose of which is to assure him that the first dream had no other meaning, that he has heard correctly, and that he now needs to get started on Ningursu's temple.

Finally, we may note in one of the prophecy texts from Mari, a letter from Addu-duri which she writes to Zimri-Lim: "In my dream I entered the temple of Bēlet-ekallim, and Belet-ekallim was not in residence nor the statues before her present. . . . This dream of mine was in the evening watch. Again (I dreamed) and Dada, the priest of Ištar-pišrā, was on duty in the gate of Bēlet-ekallim, and an eery voice kept crying this over: 'Come back, O Dagan. Come back, O Dagan.' "[23]

Like the above, Pharaoh's dreams are symbolic ones. It is only natural that he should turn to his *magicians* for explication. He knows enough to be disturbed, but not enough to be his own interpreter. The Hebrew word for *magicians, ḥarṭummîm,* is found only in this chapter of Genesis, in Exod. 7-9 (7 times), and in Dan. 1:20; 2:2 (the Aramaic equivalent is also found in Dan. 2:10, 27; 4:4, 6 [Eng. 7, 9]; 5:11). It has no satisfactory Hebrew etymology.[24] More than likely it is a Hebrew loanword from Egyp. *ḥry–udhb ḥry-tp,* with the meaning "chief lector priest."[25]

It would seem that Pharaoh's dreams, like those of Joseph himself, are not all that obtuse. Certainly the meaning of Joseph's dreams was immediately clear to his brothers and to his father. They did not need interpretation first. Perhaps Pharaoh's magicians feigned ignorance (which would not endear them to their ruler) rather than bring such ominous information before him. In that case they are placing a higher premium on diplomacy than on honesty. It is more

23. Translation of W. L. Moran, *Bib* 50 (1969) 38-39.

24. Cf. BDB, p. 355, which tries to connect the word with *ḥereṭ* ("graving tool, stylus") plus *m* to get the meaning "engraver, writer."

25. See Vergote, *Joseph en Égypte,* pp. 66-94; Redford, *Study of the Biblical Story of Joseph,* pp. 203-4; H.-P. Müller, *"ḥarṭōm," TDOT,* 5:176-79; *ANET,* p. 215 n. 16; K. A. Kitchen, "Joseph," *ISBE,* 2:1128. A dissenting voice is raised by Lambdin, *JAOS* 73 (1953) 150-51, on the grounds that Egyp. *t* (in *ḥry-tp*) should be represented in Hebrew by *t,* not *ṭ,* and that the *m* of Heb. *ḥarṭummîm (ḥarṭōm)* is not the anticipated equivalent of Egyp. *p.* Accordingly, Lambdin suggests that the Egyptian prototype of Heb. *ḥarṭōm* would be something like *ḥr-db(ꜣ).* On the possible connection between cuneiform *ḫarṭibi,* "dream interpreter" (appearing in a list of prisoners taken from Egypt), and Heb. *ḥarṭōm* see *CAD, Ḫ:*166b.

likely that his oneiromancers did employ all of their skills to attempt an interpretation of his dream, but they could not convince Pharaoh of the rightness of their interpretations. Thus the door of opportunity is left open for Joseph.

2. THE CUPBEARER REMEMBERS JOSEPH (41:9-13)

9 *Then the chief cupbearer spoke with Pharaoh: "My offenses*[1] *I now make known.*[2]

10 *Once, when Pharaoh*[3] *was angry with his servants, he placed me*[4] *in ward in the house of the chief steward, me*[5] *along with the chief baker.*

11 *We both dreamed*[6] *the same night, I and he. Each of our dreams had its own interpretation.*

12 *There, with us, was a Hebrew lad,*[7] *a servant of the chief steward.*

1. *ḥ^{a}ṭāʾay,* "my offenses," is from the same root as *ḥāṭ^{e}ʾû* in 40:1, "the cupbearer . . . and the baker offended their lord."

2. Joseph used *zāḵar* in 40:14 in speaking to the cupbearer *(z^{e}ḵartanî)* regarding his wish to be brought to Pharaoh's attention, esp. because of Joseph's unjust incarceration. The writer notes in 40:23, however, that the cupbearer in fact did not remember Joseph *(lōʾ zāḵar).* These two references use the Qal of *zāḵar,* but 41:9 uses the Hiphil *(mazkîr),* within a forensic setting. The OT provides six examples of the formula "to cause to remember sin" *(hizkîr ʿāwōn,* Num. 5:15; 1 K. 17:18; Ezek. 21:28, 29 [Eng. 23, 24]; 29:16; *hizkîr ḥēṭʾ,* Gen. 41:9) in which the sense of the expression is either accusing or making sin known. See B. S. Childs, *Memory and Tradition in Israel,* SBT 1/37 (Naperville, IL: Allenson, 1962), pp. 14-15.

3. In a circumstantial clause, the subject is prominent and therefore precedes the verbal predicate. For other instances of a circumstantial clause that is verbal but has the subject first, see Gen. 18:13; 24:31, 56; 26:27.

4. SP reads "them" *(ʾōṯām),* agreeing with "servants."

5. The direct object *ʾōṯî* is repeated, although it is mentioned expressly in an earlier part of the sentence. More common is the repetition of a pronominal subject before the second subject, e.g., "and he went up [*wayyaʿal*] . . . , he [*hûʾ*] and his friend Hirah" (Gen. 28:12).

6. *Waw* with the cohortative referring to the past is rare (cf. 43:21, *wanniptᵉḥâ,* "and we opened"). Davidson (*Hebrew Syntax,* p. 78, § 51, Rem. 7) says of this form that "in some cases a certain force or liveliness may still appear," and then he renders *wannaḥalmâ* as "and why! we dreamed."

7. In 37:2 *naʿar* is applied to seventeen-year-old Joseph, already a man in Near Eastern terms. In 43:8; 44:22, 31-34 it is used of Benjamin. If, however, *naʿar* be pressed for the meaning "lad" or "adolescent," then it is somewhat surprising to notice later in the chapter that Pharaoh says of Joseph, "a man [*ʾîš*] in whom is the Spirit of God." He calls him an *ʾîš,* not a *naʿar.* Two verses later (v. 40) Pharaoh places this *ʾîš/naʿar* over his house, second in command only to Pharaoh. Thus the possibility presents itself that *naʿar* in 41:12 means more than "lad." J. McDonald ("The Status and Role of the Naʿar in Israelite Society," *JNES* 35 [1976] 152-53, 157, 164) suggests a military understanding of the term. Joseph was a foreign *naʿar,* i.e., a mercenary who functioned as his commander's servant.

When we told him, he interpreted our dreams for us, interpreting to each according to his dream.

13 *And it happened exactly as he told us:*[8] *Me he had restored to my position; him he hanged."*

9 The chief cupbearer, while waiting on his superior, overhears Pharaoh's conversation with his magicians and their inability to provide him with satisfactory dream interpretation. It is difficult to know, as in the case of the magicians' ignorance, whether the cupbearer deliberately forgot Joseph and now seizes on an opportune moment to remember him (and thus ingratiate himself further with the pharaoh), or whether he actually did forget about Joseph until this particular scene jogged his memory. That the cupbearer would clearly have the pharaoh understand it as an unintentional oversight is indicated by his use of *ḥᵃṭā'ay* (lit., "my [inadvertent] offenses").[9] The cupbearer's use of the plural may indicate a reference to his offense against Pharaoh (40:1) and his subsequent offense against Joseph in forgetting him.

make known. The cupbearer's use of the verb *zāḵar (mazkîr)* recalls Joseph's earlier request to him that he "mention" Joseph (*hizkartanî,* 40:14) to the pharaoh.

10-13 In sharing his experience of two years ago with the pharaoh,[10] the cupbearer begins by repeating the verb that was used in 40:2 to describe Pharaoh's anger *(qāṣap).* He does not repeat how troubled (40:6, 7) they were by such dreams, nor does he repeat their confession of ignorance to Joseph (40:8). It also seems as if the cupbearer wants to create the impression that they took the initiative in sharing the dreams, when in fact Joseph did that (40:8b). Nor does he share Joseph's witness that he has no innate dream-interpretation skills, nor anything about Joseph's readiness to attribute such insight as he might have to divine sources.

The point is that what Joseph predicted came true. He was restored to his position, and his colleague was executed. For relaying such information to the pharaoh about Joseph, the cupbearer is implying to his lord that his

8. Lit., "and it was [the case] that as he interpreted for us, so it was." For the construction *ka'ᵃšer* plus protasis . . . *kēn* plus apodosis, see Waltke and O'Connor, *Biblical Hebrew Syntax,* p. 461.

9. I see no particular significance to the placement of the object "my offenses" before the participle *(mazkîr),* as if the cupbearer wishes to highlight the mention of his offenses. The same order as *'eṯ-ḥᵃṭā'ay 'ᵃnî mazkîr* is found in 37:16, *'et-'aḥay 'ānōḵî mᵉḇaqqēš,* "I am seeking my brothers" (37:2).

10. The cupbearer is careful not to speak to or about Pharaoh in the second person (i.e., he does not say, "Once, when you were angry . . . you placed me"). His address to Pharaoh is in the third person and adheres to court formalities and protocol. He continues the use of the third person when speaking to Pharaoh in v. 13.

agitation over his dream may be alleviated through the availability of the oneiromancer Joseph, although he never calls him by that title. Also, the cupbearer may be hoping to salve his conscience over his neglect of Joseph; or perhaps he is simply trying to curry favor with Pharaoh.

3. JOSEPH IS BROUGHT BEFORE PHARAOH (41:14-16)

14 *Then Pharaoh called for Joseph, and they quickly got him*[1] *from the dungeon. He shaved himself,*[2] *changed*[3] *his clothes, and came before Pharaoh.*

15 *Pharaoh said to Joseph: "I have had a dream, but there is no interpreter for it. But I heard it said of you*[4] *that you understand the language of dreams."*[5]

16 *Joseph answered Pharaoh: "It is not I. God will provide*[6] *a favorable answer for Pharaoh."*

1. LXX reads *exḗgagon,* apparently reflecting *wayyôṣî'uhû* (so *BHK*), rather than MT *wayᵉrîṣuhû* (lit., "made him run"). One need not emend, however. In Gen. 41:14 the Hiphil of *rûṣ* means "to remove, get out quickly" while in 1 Sam. 17:17 and 2 Chr. 35:13 the same stem means "to bring quickly" *HALAT,* 4:1127).

2. It is not necessary to change to a passive, as *BHS* proposes *(wayyiggalaḥ).* The Qal of *gālaḥ* carries a reflexive meaning. See R. Gordis, *The Word and the Book* (New York: Ktav, 1976), pp. 122, 134 n. 11.

3. The use of *ḥālup̱* in the Piel *(wayᵉhallēp̱)* for the changing of garments *(śimlâ),* but there in the Hiphil *(wᵉhahᵃlîpû).* Cf. E. Jenni, *Das hebräische Piʿel* (Zurich: EVZ, 1968), pp. 68-69.

4. For *šāmaʿ ʿal,* in which the preposition *ʿal* carries the meaning "of, concerning, regarding," see Waltke and O'Connor, *Biblical Hebrew Syntax,* p. 218; J. Arambarri, *Der Wortstamm "hören" im Alten Testament* (Stuttgart: Katholisches Bibelwerk, 1990), p. 174. Of the relatively few places where *šāmaʿ ʿal* occurs in the OT, only Isa. 37:9 shares with Gen. 41:15 *šāmaʿ ʿal . . . lēʾmōr.*

5. Lit., "(that) you understand/hear a dream so as to interpret it." For object clauses without an introductory conjunction, esp. after a preceding clause with "said" in it, see GKC, § 157a.

6. For MT *bilʿāḏāy ʾᵉ̆lōhîm yaʿᵃneh* Pesh., SP, and LXX read: "Apart from God, one will not be answered" *(bilʿᵃḏê ʾᵉ̆lōhîm lōʾ yēʿāneh).* As it stands the MT reads, "It is not I. God will answer the peace of Pharaoh." M. H. Lichtenstein ("Idiom, Rhetoric and the Text of Genesis 41:16," *JANES* 19 [1989] 85-94) argues for the SP and LXX over the MT, but must insert the interrogative particle *mî,* "who," which, he believes, has been lost through haplography: "Except for God, who can pronounce Pharaoh's well-being?" Targ. Onqelos goes its own way, and attempts to tone down God's direct invovlement in Pharaoh's *šālôm,* "Joseph answered . . . 'Not from my wisdom [*lʾ mn ḥwkmty*], but from before the Lord shall Pharaoh's peace be restored [*mn qdm yy yṯṭb šlmh dprʿh*].' "

14 Understandably, Pharaoh takes immediate action. Joseph is to be brought before Pharaoh as quickly as possible.[7] In preparation for his first royal audience Joseph shaves and doffs his prison garb. He does this, of course, to make himself more presentable to the head of state. We know that Semites preferred to be bearded, whereas the Egyptians were clean shaven.[8] Joseph will look more like an Egyptian than a Hebrew, even if he is a "Hebrew lad" (v. 12).

15 The Pharaoh states his predicament. He has had a dream but there is no one to interpret it for him. Although Joseph might assume that the pharaoh has consulted with his professionals in this area, the pharaoh does not draw attention to that. He does not tell Joseph the source of his information about Joseph. How is a mighty Pharaoh to know of the talents of an incarcerated Hebrew slave? Joseph knows how Pharaoh knows, but he makes no inquiry and does not bring up the cupbearer, whom he has not seen in two years.

16 Joseph is not at all reticent to talk about God in the presence of the pharaoh (who was considered to be a god incarnate, although Joseph addresses the pharaoh in the third person, as did the cupbearer in v. 10). First, Joseph begins with a modest denial. He himself is not the answer to the pharaoh's riddles. Second, he identifies the only source and cure for Pharaoh's apprehensions — God. Third, Joseph plays something of the prophet. Not only will God answer Pharaoh, but that answer will be about Pharaoh's peace or prosperity *(ʾeṯ-šᵉlôm parʿōh).* Here is one true prophet whose prophecies of "shalom" are not empty promises of "peace, peace, when there is no peace" (Jer. 6:14; Ezek. 13:10). So confident is Joseph in his God that it never occurs to him that the pharaoh will have to live with a dream hanging over him, but about whose significance he will be unenlightened. Joseph has this conviction even before he has even an inkling of what the pharaoh dreamt.

4. PHARAOH TELLS HIS DREAMS (41:17-24)

17 *Then Pharaoh said to Joseph: "In my dream there I was, standing on the bank of the Nile,*[1]

18 *when from the Nile came up seven cows, fat-fleshed and well formed, and they grazed in the reed beds.*

7. The six imperfects with *waw* in this verse intensify the alacrity of the action: *wayyišlaḥ . . . wayyiqrāʾ . . . wayᵉrîṣuhû . . . wayᵉgallaḥ wayᵉḥallēp . . . wayyāḇōʾ.*

8. See C. H. Gordon, *The Ancient Near East,* 3rd ed. (New York: Norton, 1965), p. 138.

1. See J. Blau, "Adverbia als psychologische und grammatische Subjekte/Praedikate im Bibelhebraeisch," *VT* 9 (1959) 130, who notes that, grammatically, in these words to Joseph, "I" is the subject, "standing" is the predicate, and "in my dream" has adverbial force, answering the question, Where? Psychologically and logically, however, "in my dream" is the subject, and "there I was, standing on the bank of the Nile" is the predicate.

19 *Behind them seven other cows came up, scrawny,*[2] *very ugly, and thin-fleshed. Never have I seen such repulsive beings*[3] *like these in all the land of Egypt!*

20 *The seven thin and ugly cows consumed the first seven fat cows.*

21 *But when they had swallowed them,*[4] *one could not tell they had swallowed them, for they were as ugly as before. Then I woke up.*

22 *In my dream I saw seven ears of grain growing on a single stalk — full and healthy.*

23 *Seven ears of grain, blighted,*[5] *thin, and shrivelled by the east wind were sprouting behind them.*

24 *The thin ears swallowed up the seven healthy ears. I have spoken with the magicians, but there is none to give me any information."*

The alacrity with which Joseph is brought to Pharaoh is matched only by the alacrity with which Pharaoh plunges into the narration of his dream. Joseph, so long the antagonist, is suddenly catapulted into the position of protagonist. There are no introductions, no recapitulations of Joseph's beneficence to Pharaoh's servants, no examination of Joseph's qualifications or credentials.

Nebuchadnezzar was willing to toy with his magicians and with Daniel. He insisted that they reveal to him not only the dream's interpretation but first the dream's contents (Dan. 2). Not so with Pharaoh. He blurts it out, and provides recapitulation (vv. 17-19a, 20, 22-24), commentary (v. 19b), and novel information (v. 21). It all sounds more like a nightmare than a dream. The worst features of Pharaoh's problems are the helpless magicians. Among them there is no interpreter (*pōṯēr,* v. 8) or one to provide information (*maggîḏ,* v. 24).[6]

2. This is the only time in the OT that *dal* ("low, weak, poor, thin") refers to nonhumans (elsewhere the poor, the weak, the helpless). Thus Gen. 41:19 is its exclusive use for describing physical appearance. Otherwise, the emphasis is on one's financial and political circumstances; *dal* describes an individual with meager resources. Cognates are Ugar. *dl,* "poor," and Akk. *dallu,* "small, inferior." See H.-J. Fabry, *"dal," TDOT,* 3:208-30, esp. p. 217.

3. Lit. "I have not seen like these/their likes in all the land of Egypt for badness." The preposition in *lārōaʿ* is the *lamedh* of specification meaning "with respect to." See Williams, *Hebrew Syntax,* p. 49, § 273.

4. Lit., "when they came into their belly." By contrast, "swallowed" in v. 21 is expressed by the verb *bālaʿ,* and the subject of the verb is inanimate.

5. The hapax legomenon *ṣᵉnumôṯ* is usually explained as related to postbiblical Heb. *ṣᵉnûmâ* ("dried bread") and Syr. *ṣûnāmāʾ* ("stone"); see F. E. Greenspahn, *Hapax Legomena in Biblical Hebrew,* SBLDS 74 (Chico, CA: Scholars, 1984), p. 154. LXX, Vulg., and Pesh. omit it; it does not occur in the parallel account in v. 6.

6. The Hiphil of *nāgaḏ* carries the nuance of explaining something that is otherwise incomprehensible in Judg. 14:12 (the challenge by Samson to the other men to explain his riddle) and in 1 K. 10:3 (Solomon's explanation of the queen of Sheba's words and questions).

When one compares the narrator's telling of Pharaoh's dream (vv. 1-7) with Pharaoh's own retelling of his dream later (vv. 17-24), differences emerge that make it appear that Pharaoh's anxiety is growing both over the dream itself and over the failure of his magicians to interpret it to his satisfaction. All this concern is expressed by one who would be considered divine by his people. For example, the narrator described the second set of cows as "ugly and lean-fleshed" (*rāʿôṯ mar'eh w^{e}ḏaqqôṯ bāśār,* v. 3). Pharaoh describes these same cows as *scrawny, very ugly, and thin-fleshed* (*dallôṯ w^{e}rāʿôṯ tō'ar m^{e}'ōḏ bāśār,* v. 19). Numerous changes in v. 19 from v. 3 are apparent: the inclusion of the word *dallôṯ;* the substitution of *tō'ar* for *mar'eh;* the addition of *m^{e}'ōḏ;* the use of *raqqôṯ bāśār* for *daqqôṯ bāśār.* Or again, just as Pharaoh led off his description of the second set of cows with a word not found in the original telling *(dallôṯ,* v. 19), so he leads off his description of the second set of ears of grain with a word not found in the original telling *(ṣ^{e}numôṯ,* "blighted," v. 23). It is in Pharaoh's description of the apparently negative elements of his dream that the departure from the first telling is most marked. Finally, Pharaoh's observational words about the unparalleled grotestqueness of the second set of bovine creatures (v. 19b) and his puzzlement over why this second set of creatures displayed no observable differences once they had eaten the first set of bovines (v. 21) accentuate the mortality and the finiteness of the dreamer, the pharaoh-god.[7]

5. JOSEPH INTERPRETS PHARAOH'S DREAMS (41:25-32)

25 *Joseph said to Pharaoh: "Pharaoh's dreams are one and the same:*[1] *What he is on the verge of doing*[2] *God has told Pharaoh.*

7. For further comparisons between telling and retelling in Gen. 41 see Humphreys, *Joseph and His Family,* p. 74; Sternberg, *Poetics of Biblical Narrative,* pp. 398-400. The LXX also demonstrates differences between vv. 1-7 and 17-24. Thus in v. 2 LXX renders MT *wattirʿeynâ* by *kai ebóskonto,* but in v. 18 by *kaí enémonto.* In v. 3 *w^{e}hinnēh . . . '^{a}ḥērôṯ* is rendered by *állai dé,* but in v. 19 by *kaí idoú . . . héterai.* In v. 3 *'aḥ^{a}rêhen* is rendered by *metá taútas,* but in v. 19 by *opísō autṓn.* But both *y^{e}p̱ôṯ mar'eh ûḇ^{e}rî'ōṯ bāśār* of v. 2 and *b^{e}rî'ôṯ bāśār wîp̱ôṯ tō'ar* of v. 18 are rendered by LXX as *kalaí tṓ eídei kaí eklektaí taís sarxín.* These similarities and differences in MT and LXX suggest to E. Tov that the LXX had a *Vorlage* different from MT ("The Nature and Background of Harmonizations in Biblical Manuscripts," *JSOT* 31 [1985] 3-29, esp. 20-21).

1. One might also translate, "Pharaoh's dream is one," but this rendering overlooks the pronoun *hû'* in the expression *ḥ^{a}lôm parʿōh 'eḥāḏ hû',* a verbless clause with pleonastic pronoun ("the dream of Pharaoh, one it [is]"). The thrust of Joseph's words is an explicit contrastive emphasis. Pharaoh has had one dream, not two. See S. A. Geller, "Cleft Sentences with Pleonastic Pronoun: A Syntactic Construction of Biblical Hebrew and Some of Its Literary Uses," *JANES* 20 (1991) 19-20, and 20 n. 21.

2. *ʿōśeh* (cf. v. 28) illustrates the *futurum instans* participle, reflected in English

26 *The seven healthy cows*[3] *are seven years and the seven healthy ears of grain are seven years — one and the same dream.*

27 *The seven thin ugly cows coming up behind them are seven years, as are the seven thin,*[4] *wind-shrivelled ears of grain; they represent*[5] *seven years of famine.*

28 *This*[6] *is just the thing I told Pharaoh: What God is on the verge of doing he has shown Pharaoh.*

29 *Seven years are about to come, ones of great abundance in all the land of Egypt.*

30 *On their heels will follow*[7] *seven years of famine, when all the abundance in the land of Egypt will be forgotten. When the famine has decimated the land,*

31 *not a trace of the abundance will be recognizable*[8] *because of the famine that follows it, for it will be that utterly severe.*[9]

32 *As for*[10] *Pharaoh having had the same dream twice, it means that*[11] *the matter has been confirmed by God, and God will soon*[12] *carry it out."*

---

by "I am about to/on the verge of/going to," denoting certainty, often with immanency. See GKC, § 116d; Waltke and O'Connor, *Biblical Hebrew Syntax,* p. 627.

3. The absence of the definite article on *pārōṯ,* which is qualified with *haṭṭōḇōṯ,* is strange. GKC, § 120x, suggests that the preceding cardinal number is equivalent to a determinant. LXX and SP do have the definite article.

4. *rēqôṯ* is used only here; *raqqôṯ* occurs in vv. 19, 20, 27 (see p. 484 n. 7 above). It originates from the verb *rûq* (or *rîq*), unlike *raqqôṯ,* which originates from *rāqaq.* LXX, SP, and Pesh. read *haddaqqôṯ.*

5. The masc. is here used for the 3rd fem. pl. imperfect *(wᵉšeḇa' hašibb°lîm hārēqôṯ . . . yihyû).* See Williams, *Hebrew Syntax,* p. 42, § 234; A. Sperber, *Historical Grammar of Biblical Hebrew* (Leiden: Brill, 1966), pp. 80-81.

6. On the rare introductory use of *hû'* in a verbless clause, see Andersen, *Hebrew Verbless Clause in the Pentateuch,* pp. 40, 53.

7. "And will arise . . . after them." On the use of the perfect with *waw* consecutive to announce future events *(wᵉqāmû),* see GKC, § 112x.

8. Lit., "The abundance will be unknown."

9. For the use of the intensifying adverb *mᵉ'ōḏ* with the adjective *kāḇēḏ,* see Waltke and O'Connor, *Biblical Hebrew Syntax,* p. 668 ("oppressively severe").

10. For *'al* indicating specification ("concerning, as to, with regard to") see Williams, *Hebrew Syntax,* p. 51, § 289.

11. For this function of *kî* in v. 32 see A. Schoors, "The Particle *kî,*" *OTS* 21 (1981) 259.

12. Commenting on *ûmᵉmahēr,* Andersen (*Hebrew Verbless Clause in the Pentateuch,* p. 48) notes that it introduces the only independent participial clause in the Pentateuch that begins with *waw* and participle. The normally expected *hinnēh* as an auxiliary predicator in independent participial clauses (see Gen. 31:5; Exod. 14:3; 26:5; 36:5; Num. 10:29) is

25 Joseph discerns the significance of Pharaoh's dreams as swiftly as he discerned those of the cupbearer and the baker. There is one significant difference between Joseph's interpretation of Pharaoh's dreams and Daniel's interpretation of Nebuchadnezzar's dream (Dan. 2). Daniel shares the situation with fellow exiles (2:17), with the encouragement that they together seek God in prayer for an answer (2:18). This is followed by the disclosure that God revealed nocturnally to Daniel both the dream's contents and its interpretation (2:19), for which Daniel thanked God (2:20-23). To be sure, Joseph acknowledges that interpretations come from God (Gen. 40:8; 41:16), but nowhere does the text state that Joseph sought God's guidance, that he prayed for wisdom, or that God first disclosed privately to Joseph the interpretation.

Joseph makes clear to Pharaoh that his dream deals with something God is about to do. No reason is given why God is going to do this, but Pharaoh needs to know that he and his empire are to be the objects of a mighty act of Joseph's God. Interestingly, Joseph uses *hā'ĕlōhîm* (lit., "the God," i.e., the usual way of referring to God in the OT) in speaking to Pharaoh (vv. 25, 28, 32 [twice]), but Pharaoh uses *'ĕlōhîm* (i.e., "God" without the definite article) in speaking about Joseph (v. 38) or speaking to Joseph (v. 39). Joseph's use of the article before *'ĕlōhîm* makes his reference to *'ĕlōhîm* a specific one, God. The absence of the article berore *'ĕlōhîm* makes Pharaoh's refence to *'ĕlōhîm* a general, all-inclusive one.

26-31 Joseph's interpretation has two parts to it. First, Joseph interprets the significance of the number *seven* (vv. 26-27a). The seven healthy cows and ears of grain represent seven years (v. 26), as do the seven unappealing cows and ears of grain (v. 27a). Second, Joseph turns to the interpretation of the number *seven* (vv. 27b-31). The seven years represented by the healthy cows and ears forecast seven years of fertility and abundance for Egypt. The seven years represented by the emaciated cows and ears forecast seven years of famine for Egypt.

Joseph clearly places much greater emphasis on the years of famine than on the years of plenty. This emphasis is indicated in two ways. First, in defining the healthy cows and ears, he speaks only of the significance of the numeral seven, and says nothing about the significance of the physical appearance of the objects (v. 26). But in defining the sickly cows and ears, he not only speaks of the significance of the numeral seven (v. 27a), but continues to identify these badly formed objects with seven years of famine (v. 27b).

---

missing here; according to Andersen, "the explanation probably lies in the survival (masquerading as the participle) of *wm-mhr,* that is, the conjunction has enclitic *mem,* and the 'perfect' verb is used as a consecutive future." See also G. A. Rendsburg, "Eblaite *U-MA* and Hebrew *WM-,*" in *Eblaitica: Essays on the Ebla Archives and Eblaite Language,* ed. C. H. Gordon, et al., 3 vols. (Winona Lake, IN: Eisenbrauns, 1987-92), 1:33, 35, 38, 39.

Second, in vv. 29-31 Joseph devotes but one sentence to the years of plenty (v. 29), but five sentences to the years of famine (vv. 30-31).[13] Vv. 30b, 31a, b, c represent four identical statements of elaboration on the seven years of famine (v. 30a). Joseph makes his case and loudly sounds the alarm by this bounty of dramatic sentences.

The concept of a seven-year famine is no hyperbole. Biblical tradition is aware of it, for this is one of the choices of punishment placed before David when he took the census (2 Sam. 24:13).[14] At least one relatively late Egyptian text (from the Ptolemaic period, end of 2nd century B.C.) contains a tradition of seven lean years in Egypt due to the Nile being low. Although a late text, it is set in the reign of Djoser of the Third Dynasty (ca. 2700 B.C.).[15] Indubitably earlier Egyptians texts speak of times when "the entire Upper Egypt was dying because of hunger, with every man eating his (own) children."[16]

The literature from Ugarit, specifically the Epic of Aqhat and "The Good and Gracious Gods" (also known as "Shaḥar and Shalim"), provides another illustration. The latter is most likely a ritual to bring to an end a succession of seven lean years and pave the way for seven prosperous years.[17] Cuneiform literature supplies instances of the same motif. In the Epic of Gilgamesh Ishtar solicits Anu her father to give her the "Bull of Heaven" to seek revenge on Gilgamesh for rejecting her proposal of marriage. Anu replies to Ishtar:

> If thou dost desire of me the Bull of Heaven,
> [There will be] in the land of Uruk seven years of (barren) husks.
> Hast thou gathered [grain against the (years of barren)] husks?
> Hast thou grown grass [for the beasts]?[18]

The seven- (or six-) year famine appears also in the Atrahasis Epic as one scheme hatched by Enlil to get rid of mankind, who was too numerous and too boisterous.[19]

13. Pointed out by Westermann, *Genesis,* 3:91.

14. The parallel account (1 Chr. 21:12) reads "three years," as does the LXX in 2 Sam. 24:13. Most text critics believe that Chronicles preserves the original reading, in view of the logic of the descending order of "three years: three months: three days."

15. See J. Wilson, "The Tradition of Seven Lean Years in Egypt," *ANET,* pp. 31-32.

16. See J. Vandier, *La famine dans l'Égypte ancienne* (Cairo, 1936), p. 105.

17. See C. H. Gordon, "Sabbatical Cycle or Seasonal Pattern?" *Or* 22 (1953) 79-81; idem, *Common Background of Greek and Hebrew Civilizations,* 2nd ed. (New York: Norton, 1965), pp. 171-78.

18. *ANET,* p. 85.

19. See W. G. Lambert and A. R. Millard, *Atra-Ḫasīs: The Babylonian Story of the Flood* (Oxford: Clarendon, 1969), pp. 109-15.

32 To round out his interpretation, Joseph informs Pharaoh that the significance of duplicate dreams, and not just one, is God's way of affirming to Pharaoh the certainty (*confirmed,* Heb. *nāḵôn*)[20] of the events to follow and their imminence (*soon,* Heb. *m^emahēr*). The participles that proliferated throughout the dream and its interpretation are now carried over into Joseph's prophecy.

Joseph, who has been in prison for two years, has interpreted two dreams for Pharaoh. In so doing, he has fulfilled the role of both oneiromancer and prophet. His own life patterns that of Egypt to some extent. He has been in his own famine for two years. Prosperity and promotion will soon replace that.

6. JOSEPH'S COUNSEL TO PHARAOH (41:33-36)

33 *"Let Pharaoh now seek out*[1] *an intelligent and wise man that*[2] *he may set him over the land of Egypt.*

34 *Pharaoh should appoint overseers*[3] *over the land and let him divide into five districts*[4] *the land during the seven years of abundance.*

20. As used here, *nāḵôn* is identical with Akk. *kīnu,* which is used in connection with reliable dreams in Babylonia: *šunāt šarri kînā,* "the dreams of the king are reliable." See M. Weinfeld, "Ancient Near Eastern patterns in prophetic literature," *VT* 27 (1977) 185.

1. Or, "let him look out for," *yēre'.* On the use of the jussive to express advice or a recommendation, see Davidson, *Hebrew Syntax,* p. 89, § 63b; J. W. Watts, *Survey of Syntax in the Hebrew Old Testament* (Grand Rapids: Eerdmans, 1964), p. 83.

2. An instance of *waw* with the jussive as the final clause.

3. On the use of *pāqîḏ/p^eqîḏîm* in the OT as a person/persons appointed in, over, or with somebody or something, see G. André, *Determining the Destiny: PQD in the Old Testament,* ConBOT 16 (Uppsala: Gleerup, 1980), p. 230. The LXX translates *p^eqîḏîm* by *topárchēs,* a word not found before the 3rd century B.C. It was a technical term of the Ptolemaic administration serving as the title of an official who was in charge of a *topos,* a subdivision of the nome. See J. A. L. Lee, *A Lexical Study of the Septuagint Version of the Pentateuch* (Chico, CA: Scholars, 1983), p. 98.

4. Lit., "take one-fifth" *(w^eḥimmēš).* Speiser (*Genesis,* p. 313) points out that the Qal passive participle of the root *ḥmš* means "armed, equipped, prepared" in Exod. 13:18; Josh. 1:14; 4:12; Judg. 7:11. This leads him to translate the denominative verb *ḥimmēš* as "organize." But there is no good reason for eliminating all indication of "fiveness" from this verb, whether one renders it as "divide into five districts," or "take [as a tax] the fifth part of the land." The OT illustrates the use of other denominative numeral verbs in the Piel in the sense of dividing or partitioning. Thus we have *šillēš,* "divide into three parts" (Deut. 19:3); *šiššâ,* "divide into six parts" (Ezek. 45:13); *'aśśēr,* "give a tenth" (Gen. 28:22). Also arguing against Speiser's rendering is the fact that in all the instances he cites, the root in question is used of a group of men prepared for war, and not, as here in Gen.

35 *They should gather all the food of these coming, prosperous years, stockpiling the grain under Pharaoh's authority,*[5] *as food in the cities, and let them protect it.*[6]

36 *The food will serve as official grainstores*[7] *for the land against the seven years of famine that are coming on the land of Egypt, with the result that the land will not perish*[8] *in the famine."*

Joseph is both a foreteller (vv. 25-32) and a forthteller (vv. 33-36). He speaks to the future and to the present. He suggests, always speaking to the pharaoh in the third person, that he appoint an *intelligent (nāḇôn) and wise (ḥāḵām) man* over the land of Egypt. Later, Pharaoh uses these two words to describe Joseph himself (v. 39). They also appear together in Deut. 4:6; Hos. 14:10 (Eng. 9); Prov. 10:13; 14:33; 16:21. The "intelligent and wise man" is one who is "capable of planning and carrying through important economic measures."[9]

It is not apparent that Joseph is pointing to himself here, that is, "an intelligent and wise man — myself!" By using *ḥāḵām,* however, the narrator may be implying a bit of sarcasm. Pharaoh has already consulted with the best of Egypt's *ḥᵃḵāmîm* ("cleverest" magicians, v. 8), and they failed him miserably. Let the pharaoh not make the same mistake twice!

41:34, of the economic reorganization of a land. See Waltke and O'Connor, *Biblical Hebrew Syntax,* p. 414; Humphreys, *Joseph and His Family,* p. 146, 152 n. 25. The suggestion of A. Sperber (*Historical Grammar of Biblical Hebrew* [Leiden: Brill, 1966], p. 638) to revocalize as an infinitive *(wᵉḥammēš)* and render "mobilize, inventorize" is not attractive, nor is the revocalization necessary.

5. Lit., "under the hand of Pharaoh." For the preposition *taḥat,* either followed by *yaḏ,* as here, or with *yaḏ* omitted (Num. 5:19), meaning "authority, control," see Williams, *Hebrew Syntax,* p. 59, § 350; Waltke and O'Connor, *Biblical Hebrew Syntax,* p. 220.

6. I see no reason either to insert a verb such as *wᵉyittᵉnû* (so *BHS* and Westermann) to make sense of this clause, or to take the *waw* on *wᵉšāmārû* as epexegetical. On Codex Alexandrinus's unusual rendering of Heb. *šāmar* by *synágein* (most LXX mss. have the expected *phylśsein*), see G. R. Driver, "Ezekiel: Linguistic and Textual Problems," *Bib* 35 (1954) 303-4.

7. *piqqāḏôn* occurs here and in Lev. 5:21, 23 (Eng. 6:2, 4) with the meaning "deposit." Derived from *pāqaḏ,* "to visit, appoint" *piqqāḏôn* in Lev. 5 means that which is entrusted (i.e., property), left with another, deposited for safekeeping, and is to be restored if the owner is deceived. I take my translation "official grainstores" from Coote and Ord, *Bible's First History,* p. 182. A *piqqāḏôn* is that over which an individual is a *pāqîḏ.*

8. Lit., "not be cut off" *(wᵉlō' ṯikkārēṯ . . . bārā'āḇ).* The reference is to the people of Egypt who would starve to death because of the famine. Cf. Gen. 9:11: *wᵉlō'-yikkārēṯ kol-bāśār 'ôḏ mimmê hammabbûl,* "that never again shall all flesh be cut off by the waters of a flood."

9. Westermann, *Genesis,* 3:92.

The second part of Joseph's plan is that this individual will have a cadre of overseers throughout the land who, during the years of prosperity, will oversee the storing of grain in granaries. The store city would be a site where storage houses were built for stockpiling government supplies of various kinds. In the OT they are always mentioned in connection with royal activity.[10] Knowing the unpredictable behavior of people who are facing starvation and trying to cope with survival, Joseph urges that such supplies be protected from public access and possible looting.

Some scholars have suggested that this part of ch. 41 has some literary problems. In v. 33 Joseph recommends the appointment of a single official over Egypt. But in v. 34 he suggests a group of overseers. In v. 34b Joseph urges that Pharaoh "take one-fifth of" (the literal translation of *ḥmš*) the harvest, whereas the very next verse urges the exacting of the entire harvest. These points, and others later on in the chapter, have suggested to some literary critics that ch. 41 is primarily Elohistic (only *'ĕlōhîm* is used), but these few jarring details suggest the intrusion of another source, most likely the Yahwist.[11] Such analysis is hardly correct. Joseph first suggests the appointment of one person (v. 33), who will be supported by a vast network of employees spread throughout the country (v. 34). As noted above, *ḥmš* here means *divide into five parts.* Thus v. 34 does not conflict with v. 35.

perish. It is interesting that the verb Joseph uses to describe Egypt's future, if the pharaoh disregards his advice, is the Niphal of *kāraṯ*. We are familiar with this verb in this stem, especially in cultic literature like Leviticus and Numbers, where it describes a person being "cut off" from the community for some kind of violation of community standards.[12] It has been used twice in Genesis (9:11; 17:14; both P according to the documentarians) to describe a potential exclusion from the community for either moral sins (9:11) or cultic sins (17:14). Joseph does not say that Egypt will "die (of starvation)," but rather Egypt "will be cut off." The consequence for rejecting Joseph's counsel is judgment. This moves Joseph's words to Pharaoh out of the category of option and into the category of mandate.

10. See Gen. 41:35, 48 (in Egypt); Exod. 1:11 (in Egypt); 1 K. 9:19 and 2 Chr. 8:4, 6 (Solomonic); 2 Chr. 16:4 (in Naphtali, associated with Baasha); 2 Chr. 17:12 (Judean, built by Jehoshaphat); 2 Chr. 32:28 (associated with Hezekiah). Cf. F. S. Frick, *The City in Ancient Israel,* SBLDS 36 (Missoula, MT: Scholars, 1977), pp. 136, 168 n. 312.

11. See, e.g., von Rad, *Genesis,* p. 377; Skinner, *Genesis,* pp. 468-69; Coote and Ord, *Bible's First History,* pp. 182-85.

12. See D. J. Wold, "The Kareth Penalty in P: Rationale and Cases," *SBLASP, 1979,* 1:1-45.

7. JOSEPH: FROM PRISON TO PRIME MINISTER (41:37-46)

37 *Pharaoh and all his officials found the suggestion acceptable.*[1]

38 *Pharaoh said to his officials: "Could one be found like this one here, an individual in whom is God's*[2] *Spirit?"*

39 *Then Pharaoh said to Joseph: "Because*[3] *God has revealed*[4] *to you all this, there could be nobody as intelligent and wise as you.*

40 *You shall be over my palace, and all my people shall follow your word.*[5] *Only in respect to the throne*[6] *shall I outrank*[7] *you."*

41 *Pharaoh said further to Joseph: "See, I have placed you*[8] *over all the land of Egypt."*

42 *Then Pharaoh removed his signet ring from his hand and placed it on Joseph's hand. He had him clothed with fine linen garments, and put a gold*[9] *chain around his neck.*

1. Lit., "the word was good in Pharaoh's eyes and in the eyes of all his servants."

2. Only NEB avoids capitalization for Pharaoh's *rûaḥ ʾĕlōhîm* in translation by reading "one who has the spirit of a god in him," though NEB does offer "God" in a footnote. See also NEB's translation of v. 39, "Since a god has made all this known to you." Interestingly, the REB, a revision of the NEB, capitalizes "God" in both vv. 38 and 39. Targ. Onqelos even places the tetragrammaton in Pharaoh's mouth: *gbr drwḥ nbwʾh mn qdm yy byh,* "a man in whom the spirit of prophecy from before Yahweh dwells."

3. See W. J. P. Boyd, "Notes on the Secondary Meanings of *ʾḥr*," *JTS* 12 (1961) 54, who notes that in the seventy-one passages where the construct form *ʾaḥărê* serves as a conjunction, in only eight of them is the force causal (cf. with Gen. 41:39, Gen. 46:30; Josh. 7:8; Judg. 11:36; 19:23; 2 Sam. 1:10; 19:31; Jer. 31:18). Davidson (*Hebrew Syntax,* p. 195, § 145, Rem. 1) renders *ʾaḥărê* in this verse as "seeing that."

4. Lit., "Because God has made known to you." Waltke and O'Connor (*Biblical Hebrew Syntax,* p. 445) suggest a modal sense of the Hiphil here *(hôḏîaʿ):* "Since God let you know all this . . ." (i.e., the Hiphil denotes permission).

5. Lit., "all my people shall kiss (?) [you] on your mouth." See the commentary below.

6. *hakkissēʾ* illustrates an accusative of specification to express means; cf. Dahood's translation, "only the throne will be greater than you," for which he appeals to Eblaite ("Eblaite and Biblical Hebrew," *CBQ* 44 [1982] 23). On the accusative of specification, cf. GKC, § 118h; Williams, *Hebrew Syntax,* p. 12, § 57; J. Milgrom, *Numbers,* JPS Torah Commentary (Philadelphia: Jewish Publication Society, 1990), p. 312 n. 19.

7. Lit., "shall I be greater than you" *(ʾegdal mimmekkā).*

8. The LXX inserts the equivalent of *hayyôm* after the verb ("I have placed you today"), and thus Pharaoh's declaration of appointment is similar to another declaration of appointment, in Ps. 2:7: *ʾănî hayyôm yĕliḏtîḵā,* "I, today, have fathered you." See S. J. DeVries, *Yesterday, Today and Tomorrow* (Grand Rapids: Eerdmans, 1975), pp. 158-59.

9. MT *hazzāhāḇ,* SP *zāhāḇ.* Waltke and O'Connor (*Biblical Hebrew Syntax,* p. 246) cite *rĕḇiḏ hazzāhāḇ* as an instance of the generic article with measurements and measured units. Cf. Cant. 1:13, *ṣĕrôr hammōr,* "a bag of myrrh." The expression in 41:42 is lit. "the chain of the gold," i.e., a chain of gold.

43 *He had him ride*[10] *in the chariot of his second-in-command,*[11] *and they cried out*[12] *before him, "Abrek."*[13] *Thus he placed*[14] *him over all the land of Egypt.*

44 *Pharaoh again said to Joseph: "Although I am Pharaoh, without your approval*[15] *no one shall raise hand or foot in all the land of Egypt."*

45 *Pharaoh gave Joseph the name Zaphenath-paneah. And he gave him as wife Asenath, daughter of Potiphera, priest*[16] *of On.*[17] *Thus Joseph rose over*[18] *the land of Egypt.*

10. The primary meaning of *rāḵaḇ* is "ride" or "mount." "Drive" is a secondary meaning. The sequence *rāḵaḇ* (Hiphil) plus accusative of person plus *b* with a chariot occurs in 2 K. 10:16. Cf. S. Mowinckel, "Drive and/or Ride in O.T.," *VT* 12 (1962) 278-99.

11. Rather than RSV "his second chariot." *mirkeḇeṯ* is a construct form. See 1 Sam. 23:17; 2 Chr. 28:7; Est. 10:3.

12. LXX, Pesh., and SP read "and he cried out," and so, according to these versions, it is Pharaoh or a herald who cries *'aḇrēḵ*.

13. An obscure word. See the commentary below.

14. *nāṯôn* has been cited as one of several illustrations of the finite use of the infinitive absolute. See J. Huesman, "Finite Uses of the Infinitive Absolute," *Bib* 37 (1956) 284. The use of the infinitive absolute in preference to a finite construction may be to emphasize the notion expressed (R. M. Frank, *CBQ* 26 [1964] 130) — "even to the point of placing. . . ." A. Gai ("The Reduction of the Tense [and Other Categories] of the Consequent Verb in North-west Semitic," *Or* 51 [1982] 255) explains *nāṯôn* in terms of verb reduction. I am inclined to interpret *wᵉnāṯôn* as an instance of a finite verb in the prefix tense, implying a past event *(wayyarkēḇ),* continued by an infinitive absolute. Cf. other examples of this in Judg. 7:19; Jer. 37:21; 2 Chr. 7:3; and see GKC, § 113z; Sperber, *Historical Grammar of Biblical Hebrew,* p. 73.

15. *bil'āḏeyḵā,* "apart from you, without you." See BDB, p. 116.

16. Targ. Onqelos read "the prince of On" *(rb' d'wn)* to avoid the idea that Joseph married the daughter of a pagan priest. Onqelos made the same change in Exod. 2:16; 18:1 where Reuel/Jethro in the MT is *kōhēn miḏyān,* "priest of Midian," but in Onqelos is *rb' dmdyn,* thus circumventing any possibility that Moses married the daughter of an idolatrous Midianite priest.

17. For *kōhēn* in the construct before a place name cf. "priest of Midian" (Exod. 2:16; 3:1); "priest of Bethel" (Amos 7:10); and on a seal from the mid-8th century B.C. from Samaria "priest of Dor" (for which see N. Avigad, "The Priest of Dor," *IEJ* 25 [1975] 101-5).

18. The phrase *yāṣā' 'al* occurs only in Gen. 19:23; 41:45; 2 K. 24:12; Esth. 1:17; Ps. 81:6; Zech. 5:3. The phrase *wayyēṣē' yôsēp 'al 'ereṣ miṣrāyīm* is omitted by LXX, a reading that Westermann (*Genesis,* 3:84) follows, presumably because he feels it is a variant of v. 46b. But once one recognizes that *yāṣā' 'al* carries the meaning "rise over (in authority)" (cf. Targ. Onqelos's "Joseph emerged as ruler over all the land of Egypt"; NJPS, "Thus Joseph emerged in charge of"; NEB, "And Joseph's authority extended over"), one may view v. 45b not as a variant of v. 46b but as a summarizing statement of Joseph's inauguration. See P. A. H. de Boer, "Psalm 81:6a: Observations on Transition and Meaning of One Hebrew Line," in *In the Shelter of Elyon,* Fest. G. W. Ahlström, ed. W. B. Barrick and J. R. Spencer, JSOTSup 31 (Sheffield: JSOT, 1984), pp. 68-70.

46 *Joseph was thirty years old when he stood before Pharaoh, king of Egypt. Joseph left Pharaoh's presence and traversed*[19] *the land of Egypt.*

37 Joseph as handsome male was good in the eyes of Potiphar's wife. Joseph as administrator is good in the eyes of Pharaoh (the lit. translation of *wayyîṭaḇ haddāḇār beʿênê parʿōh, Pharaoh . . . found the suggestion acceptable*). Nowhere does Pharaoh make a response to Joseph's interpretation of his dream(s). One might have expected a statement from him in between Joseph's interpretation (vv. 25-32) and Joseph's counsel (vv. 33-36). It appears that he is as impressed, if not more, with Joseph's counsel (vv. 33-36) as with his interpretations (vv. 25-32), and the advancement in political office he bestows on Joseph is stimulated by Joseph's suggestion to reorganize the Egyptian bureaucracy. To Joseph's credit his contribution is both the intepretation of Pharaoh's dream, including the revelation of a forthcoming and frightening seven-year famine, and then some practical counsel on how to prepare for those seven years and thus avoid mass starvation and death throughout the land. Joseph is dream interpreter, sage, and counselor.

38 Pharaoh suggests that it is most unlikely, should a nationwide search for a viable candidate for this ad hoc position be launched, that a more qualified occupant for that office than Joseph could be found. The Spirit of God that hovered over the watery mass (1:2) rests upon and abides in Joseph.[20]

It is likely that the expression *God's Spirit* in the pharaoh's speech should be read as a theological statement on pneumatology. It demonstrates that Pharaoh, via his rhetorical declaration, understood Joseph's skills: Joseph has no intrinsic ability that would explain his effective insight and counsel. For Pharaoh, Joseph is one who has been divinely equippped and gifted. That Pharaoh's exclamation follows Joseph's counsel rather than his interpretation of the dream implies that Pharaoh identifies God's Spirit more with the former than with the latter. Therefore in Pharaoh's mouth the expression "God's Spirit" refers to "outstanding ability in the areas of political economy and statesmanship."[21] Pharaoh's words about Joseph remind one of what Belshazzar would later say about Daniel (Dan. 5:14).

39-40 Pharaoh tells Joseph: *You shall be over my palace* (*bêṯî,* lit., "my house"). This is the third "house" in which Joseph has been placed. He has gone from Potiphar's house, to the jailhouse, to Pharaoh's house. Only

19. Perhaps *wayyaʿaḇōr* should be read instead of MT *wayyaʿeḇōr* (see *BHS*), the more normal form of the Qal imperfect.

20. Cf. B. T. Dahlberg, "On recognizing the unity of Genesis," *TD* 24 (1976) 360-67, who identifies a number of themes enunciated in primeval history, then developed in patriarchal history, and sounded again in the Joseph story.

21. Westermann, *Genesis,* 3:93.

one thing is withheld from Joseph's possession — Pharaoh's *throne.* Thus Joseph's relation with Pharaoh parallels his relation with Potiphar. Potiphar placed Joseph over his house, with one exception — his food (the narrator's version); his wife (Joseph's version).

The position designated by the phrase *over my palace* is uncertain. Nearly all scholars think that Joseph became vizier (i.e., prime minister), although he is given neither the duties of the vizierate nor a title that is an indubitable Hebrew equivalent of the Egyptian vizier *(tȝty).* That Joseph was placed over the pharaoh's house may mean that he was given control over the estates of the king. The Egyptian counterpart to this would be *ʾimy-r pr wr n nb tȝ.wy,* "Great Steward of the Lord of the Two Lands," or *ḥry-tp ʿȝ m pr nsw,* "Great Chief in the Palace."[22]

and all my people shall follow your word. This clause is much discussed. A literal translation is: "and on your mouth all my people shall kiss (you)" *(wᵉʿal-pîḵā yiššaq kol-ʿammî).* First, let us look at the some of the ancient versions. The LXX rendered *yiššaq* with *hypakoúsetai,* which would correspond to Heb. *yaqšēḇ* (Hiphil), meaning "give heed, obey." Hence, "all my people shall be obedient to your mouth." The Pesh. read *yiššāpēṭ,* "shall be judged." The Targ. rendered *yiššaq* by the Ithpeel of *zûn,* "be supported, managed" — "by your words all my people will be supported [or sustained, girded]," or in a secondary sense, "when you speak, all my people shall maintain silence [i.e., seal their lips, or be obedient]."[23] Of these ancient versions, the LXX seems the most likely.

Some modern scholars have looked to the Egyptian language for clarification. One Egyptian idiom for "eat" was "to kiss one's food." So understood, the phrase would be read as "according to your word shall my people eat."[24] Others have appealed to the Egyptian idiom *sn-tȝ,* literally, "kiss the earth," meaning "render homage." So understood, the phrase would be read "according to your commands shall all my people kiss (the earth in submission)."[25]

22. See W. A. Ward, "The Egyptian Office of Joseph," *JSS* 5 (1960) 146-47; idem, "Egyptian Titles in Genesis 39–50," *BSac* 114 (1957) 40-59. I follow Ward closely throughout this section. See also H. J. Katzenstein, "The Royal Steward," *IEJ* 10 (1960) 150; S. C. Layton, "The Steward in Ancient Israel: A Study of Hebrew *(ʾăšer) ʿal-habbayit* in Its Near Eastern Setting," *JBL* 109 (1990) 634-35, who distinguish between a private steward and a royal steward. The latter would be concerned with matters of state administration.

23. See J. M. Cohen, "An unrecognized connotation of *nšq peh* with special reference to three biblical occurrences," *VT* 32 (1982) 416-20.

24. See N. Adcock, "Genesis xli.40," *ExpTim* 67 (1956) 383; F. C. Fensham, "Genesis xli.40," *ExpTim* 68 (1957) 284-85.

25. See K. A. Kitchen, "The Term *Nšq* in Genesis xli.40," *ExpTim* 69 (1957) 30; J. Vergote, *Joseph en Égypte,* pp. 96-97.

Redford avoids Egyptian analogies altogether and identifies *yiššaq* with *šûq:* "and in accordance with your command shall my people order themselves."[26] Perhaps the simplest and most convincing explanation is to emend MT *yiššaq* to *yāšōq* (from *nāšaq* II, "yield, submit to").[27]

41 This verse extends Joseph's powers. In addition to being placed over the palace (v. 40), he is placed *over all the land of Egypt.* The Egyptian counterpart for this expression is *ḥry-tp n tꜣ dr.f,* "Chief of the Entire Land," an epithet applied to viziers and to lesser officials as well.[28] Note that the imperfect verbal forms of v. 40 *(tihyeh, yiššaq, 'egdal)* are now replaced by a perfect form of the verb *(nāṯattî).*

42 This verse describes Joseph's investiture with the symbols of his position: the transferring of the king's *signet ring* to Joseph, Joseph's being clothed in *fine linen (šēš),*[29] and the placement of a *gold chain* or collar around his neck. The *signet ring* that Pharaoh gives to Joseph is most likely his scarab ring, which bears his personal seal. The title that goes with the royal seal is "Royal Seal Bearer," held first only by the vizier, then later conferred on others.[30] Note that with *fine linen,* clothing once again enters into the Joseph story, recalling Joseph's coat, which his brothers removed from him (ch. 37), and his shirt, part of which Potiphar's wife ripped off him (ch. 39).

Throughout these ceremonies Joseph says nothing. We noted Pharaoh's silence while Joseph was predicting abundance followed by famine (vv. 25-36). Now it is Joseph's turn to be taciturn while Pharaoh is speaking. Joseph makes no attempt to reject Pharaoh's elevation of him. He is consenting, cooperative, and eager to assume his new responsibilities.[31]

26. D. B. Redford, *A Study of the Biblical Story of Joseph,* p. 166. S. D. Sperling ("Genesis 41:40: A New Interpretation," *JANES* 10 [1978] 113-19) arbitrarily emends *yiššaq* to *yāšaḇ,* lit., "sit," hence "at your command all my people shall sit" (i.e., obey).

27. Speiser, *Genesis,* pp. 313-14; *HALAT,* 3:690; K. Baltzer, *Die Biographie der Propheten* (Neukirchen-Vluyn: Neukirchener, 1975), pp. 150-51 and 151 n. 523.

28. See Ward, *JSS* 5 (1960) 148.

29. See T. O. Lambdin, "Egyptian Loan Words in the Old Testament," *JAOS* 73 (1953) 155; A. Hurvitz, "The Usage of *šš* and *buṣ* in the Bible and its Implication for the Date of P," *HTR* 60 (1967) 117-21. Note that the southern Pharaoh gave Joseph "garments of fine linen" *(šēš),* but the northern Persian king gave Mordecai "a mantle of fine linen" (*bûṣ,* Esth. 8:15). Ezek. 27:7 states explicitly that *šēš* was imported from Egypt. As Hurvitz points out, the distribution of *šēš* and *bûṣ* (the latter restricted to later biblical writings: Chronicles, Esther, and Ezekiel) may be explained in both chronological (preexilic and postexilic, respectively) and geographical (Egypt and Mesopotamia-Syria, respectively) terms.

30. See W. A. Ward, *BSac* 114 (1957) 49; idem, *JSS* 5 (1960) 145-46.

31. Sarna (*Genesis,* p. 286) notes that the threefold use of "Pharaoh said to Joseph" in vv. 39, 41, and 44 "probably indicates that the king pauses after each statment to ascertain the young man's reaction." See also G. W. Savran, *Telling and Retelling* (Bloomington: Indiana University, 1988), p. 127 n. 10.

43 For a second time Joseph goes for a ride. The first was to Egypt (ch. 37); the second is throughout Egypt. The first was as kidnapped victim; the second is as exalted hero. The most intriguing part of this verse is the word used by the runners before the chariot (or the pharaoh) as Joseph rides over the land: *Abrek ('aḇrēḵ)*. Three different interpretations of this term are genuine possibilities. Dahood has appealed to Eblaite *'àgarakum* and its variant *'àbarakum*, "superintendent."[32] Close to this possibility is the suggested association of Heb. *'aḇrēḵ* with Akk. *abarakku*, "chief steward of a private or royal household."[33] This Akkadian word is a technical title from Neo-Assyrian texts, a strange source to explicate a hapax legomenon in the Joseph story!

The third suggestion is to turn to the Egyptian language. In the early years of this century W. Spiegelberg connected *'aḇrēḵ* with Egyp. *ìb-r.k*, "Attention! Make way for!" (reflected in NEB and JB mg.).[34] Vergote suggested more recently a connection with Egyp. *ì.brk*, "do homage,"[35] that is, taking it as an imperative with prothetic *i* from the Semitic verb *bāraḵ*, "to kneel." Spiegelberg's suggestion is better philologically because a prothetic *aleph* is not characteristic of third radical verbs in Egyptian.[36] Vergote's suggestion is preferred contextually because it is an explicit command to do something, rather than a vague summons, "Attention!"[37]

Among the ancient authorities, both Aquila and Jerome *(genuflecterent)* anticipated Vergote's "do homage, bow." But other ancient readings go in quite different directions. For example, the LXX reads *kaí ekḗryxen émprosthen autoú kḗryx*, "and a herald made proclamation before him," on the assumption that a

32. M. J. Dahood, "Eblaite and Biblical Hebrew," *CBQ* 44 (1982) 23; idem, "Ebla, Ugarit, and the Bible," in Pettinato, *Archives of Ebla*, p. 281. C. H. Gordon ("Eblaite and Northwest Semitic," in *Eblaitica: Essays on the Ebla Archives and Eblaite Language*, ed. C. H. Gordon, et al., 3 vols. [Winona Lake, IN: Eisenbrauns, 1987-92], 2:129) also argues that *'Aḇrēḵ* is an honorific title given to Joseph and is of Mesopotamian origin. Elsewhere, Dahood (*Psalms*, 2:31) understands *'aḇrēḵ* as an Aphel causative. The normal prefix for the causative in Ugaritic is *shin*. Dahood, virtually alone, claims that in some instances the prefix in Ugaritic for a causative may be *aleph*.

33. See J. S. Croatto, "*'Abrek* 'Intendant' dans Gen XLI 41, 43," *VT* 16 (1966) 113-15; W. W. Hallo, "Genesis and Ancient Near Eastern Literature," in *The Torah: A Modern Commentary*, Vol. I: *Genesis*, ed. G. Plaut (New York: Union of American Hebrew Congregations, 1974), p. xxxii; E. Lipiński, "North Semitic Texts," in *Near Eastern Religious Texts Relating to the Old Testament*, ed. W. Beyerlin, tr. J. Bowden, OTL (Philadelphia: Westminster, 1978), p. 241 n. o.

34. First suggested by him in "Correspondences du temps des rois-prêtre," *Notices et extraits des manuscrits de La Bibliothéque Nationale* 24 (1895) 261.

35. Vergote, *Joseph en Égypte*, pp. 135-41; also Redford, *Study of the Biblical Story of Joseph*, pp. 226-28.

36. See Lambdin, *JAOS* 73 (1953) 146.

37. See K. A. Kitchen, review of Vergote in *JEA* 47 (1961) 161 n. 4.

person calling out before the chariot must be a herald. Jub. 40:7 saw in the *'br* of *'aḇrēḵ* the Hebrew word *'abbîr,* and rendered it, "and (a herald) proclaimed before him "Êl 'Êl wa 'Abîrĕr' ['God, God, the Mighty One of God']."[38] Like the LXX, Jub. 40:7 is a guess, but unlike the LXX, which represents a guess based on the context of the sentence, Jub. 40:7 is a guess based on the general framework of the Joseph story. Targ. Onqelos offers yet a third guess with its reading, "and they proclaimed before him, 'This one is father of the king' " *(dyn 'b' lmlk'),* which G. Vermes cites as a case of haggadah in the Targum.[39]

44 Pharaoh spoke first to his officials (v. 38), then to Joseph (vv. 39-40), a second time to Joseph (v. 41), and now a third time to Joseph. The three speeches to Joseph are those of intention (v. 38), implementation (vv. 39-40), and confirmation (v. 44). From this point on *no one shall raise hand or foot* without Joseph's permission. Joseph already knows what it means to have someone lift up his hand against him (his brothers). He also knows what it means to have somebody lift up their eyes against him (Potiphar's wife, 39:7). Now nobody will even be able to lay claim to property[40] or do anything or go anywhere.[41]

45 To formalize Joseph's introduction to his new position, he is given an Egyptian name, *Zaphenath-paneah,* and an Egyptian wife — *Asenath, daughter of Potiphera, priest of On.* Thus, he has a new job, a new name, a new wife. Again, Joseph does not object to any of these procedures, but then he is hardly in a position to do so. Nor does the narrator have any scruples about recording the name change and marriage. But never after this point does the Joseph story mention Joseph's Egyptian name or his Egyptian wife.

The meaning of Joseph's new name is debated. Note the following suggestions for Egyptian equivalents: (1) *Ḏd-p3-ntr-iw.f–aynḫ,* "God speaks and he lives," or, "The god has said: he will live" (Steindorff, Redford sympa-

38. R. H. Charles, *The Apocrypha and Pseudepigrapha of the Old Testament,* 2 vols. (Oxford: Clarendon, 1913), 2:71 and n. 7. Charles notes that the title in Jub. 40:7 is that of a great magician. Cf. the statement made about Simon Magus in Acts 8:10, "This man is that power of God which is called Great."

39. G. Vermes, *Post-Biblical Jewish Studies* (Leiden: Brill, 1975), pp. 63-64, 129-30. In trying to render *'aḇrēḵ,* says Vermes, Targ. Onqelos was "completely foxed" (p. 130) in its separation of *'aḇrēḵ* into two syllables, *'aḇ* ("father") and *rēḵ* (*rex,* "king"), and in its connection of *'aḇrēḵ* with 45:8, "He [God] has made me a father to Pharaoh."

40. See Z. W. Falk, "Hebrew Legal Terms: II," *JSS* 12 (1967) 243-44. This is Falk's understanding of the idiom. Noting that "or foot" is omitted in the LXX, Falk refers to Egyptian texts in which "strike," for which Hebrew "lifting up the hand" seems to be a synonym, is a way of representing claim to a property. MT's "or foot" in v. 44 need not be deleted, in spite of LXX, in the light of verses like Ps. 60:10 (Eng. 8) and 108:10 (Eng. 9), which describe God's taking possession of Edom by saying "Upon Edom I cast my shoe."

41. This broader interpretation, i.e., carry on any activity whatsoever, is advanced by S. Morenz, "Joseph in Aegypten," *TLZ* 84 (1959) 408. Again, Targ. Onqelos provides an interpretive reading with "no man shall lift up his hand to bear arms or his foot to ride a horse."

thetic);[42] (2) *P3-s-nty–aym.f-n3 iḫ(t),* "the man who knows things" (Vergote);[43] (3) *P3–aasnt-n-p3–aynḫ,* "the sustainer of life" (Albright);[44] (4) *Ḏf3-n-t3-pw–aynḫ,* "sustenance of the land is the living (or, is this living one)" (Yahuda);[45] (5) *(Yōsēp̱) ḏd-n.f('I)p–aynḫ,* "(Joseph) who is called Ip–ayanekh" (Kitchen).[46] Steindorff's proposal has enjoyed the widest acceptance. That the narrator does not interpret Joseph's name means that Joseph's Egyptian name — whatever the best translation — assumes no significant role in the narrative. Its inclusion does, however, give the event "an air of authenticity."[47]

There is more of a consensus about the meanings of *Asenath,* Joseph's wife, and *Potiphera,* Joseph's father-in-law. *Asenath* is Egyp. *Ns-nt,* "belonging to (the goddess) Neith" or "may she belong to Neith." No reason is known why Pharaoh selects this particular woman for Joseph's bride. *Potiphera* is the same in form as Potiphar, but they are not the same person. Potiphera equals Egyp. *P3-di-p3-rʿ,* "he whom Re has given." Of these three Egyptian names only the last one has been found in Egyptian records. *On* is better knows as Heliopolis ("sun city"; cf. Jer. 43:13), which is situated on the Nile in Lower Egypt just seven miles northeast of Cairo.

46 We first encountered Joseph at the age of seventeen (37:2). In 41:2 we read of Joseph being released from prison "two years later." It is unlikely that this is two years after his seventeenth birthday, for now he is *thirty years old.* Between his being sold and his being promoted thirteen years have elapsed — thirteen years of nightmare, hardship, setback, and frustration.

The story of Joseph in Gen. 41 shares with Dan. 2 and the nonbiblical story of Ahiqar[48] a basic ordering of motifs: (1) a person of lower status is called before a person of higher status to answer a question or solve a problem;

42. G. Steindorff, "Der Name Josephs Saphenat-Paʿneach," *ZÄS* 27 (1898) 41ff.; idem, "Weiteres zu Genesis 41, 45," *ZÄS* 30 (1892) 50ff.; Redford, *Study of the Biblical Story of Joseph,* pp. 230-31.

43. Vergote, *Joseph en Égypte,* p. 142.

44. W. F. Albright, "Historical and Mythical Elements in the Joseph Story," *JBL* 37 (1918) 132.

45. A. S. Yahuda, *The Language of the Pentateuch in Its Relation to Egyptian* (Oxford: Oxford University, 1933), pp. 31-35.

46. K. A. Kitchen, "Joseph," *ISBE,* 2:1129.

47. Redford, *Study of the Biblical Story of Joseph,* p. 231. Among the ancient versions and writers Jacob's Egyptian name is either simply transliterated (LXX; Jub. 40:10) or translated (Josephus *Ant.* 2.6.1 [§ 91]: "Discoverer of Secrets"; Pesh. and some verisons of Targ. Onqelos, "the man to whom mysteries are revealed"; Vulg., "savior of the world"). See Vermes, *Post-Biblical Jewish Studies,* pp. 65, 130; B. Kedar-Kopfstein, "The Interpretative Element in Transliteration," *Textus* 8 (1973) 68.

48. For a full translation of the various versions of Ahiqar, see Charles, *Apocrypha and Pseudepigrapha of the Old Testament,* 2:724-84. See a partial translation in *ANET,* pp. 427-30.

(2) the person of higher status states the question/problem that nobody is able to solve; (3) a person of lower status does solve the question/problem; (4) the person of lower status is rewarded in some way by the person of higher status for solving the question/problem.[49] What distinguishes the two biblical stories from their nonbiblical typological counterpart is that the latter emphasizes Ahiqar's reliance on his own ability and ingenuity in talking before and to Sennacherib, king of Babylon. By contrast, Gen. 41 and Dan. 2 attribute Joseph's and Daniel's ability to interpret and solve the enigma to the assistance of God (Gen. 41:16, Joseph's self-disclaimer and his faith in God's revelation of a forthcoming answer; Dan. 2:17, 18, Daniel's request for God's help; 2:19, a revelation to Daniel; 2:20-23, Daniel's praise of God).

8. YEARS OF PLENTY AND FAMINE (41:47-57)

47 *The land overproduced*[1] *during the seven years of plenty,*[2]

48 *and he collected all the food of the seven years*[3] *that the land of Egypt was experiencing, and stored the food in the cities, storing in each city the crops of the fields surrounding it.*

49 *Joseph garnered grain in great measure, like sands of the sea, until he ceased keeping entries, for it was beyond measure.*

50 *Before the start of*[4] *the famine, Joseph became the father of*[5] *two sons,*

49. See S. Niditch and R. Doran, "The Success Story of the Wise Courtier: A Formal Approach," *JBL* 96 (1977) 179-93, esp. 185-87 for Gen. 41.

1. BDB, p. 888a, suggests for *wattaʿaś . . . liqmāṣîm,* "yielded by handfuls." In its only other occurrences (Lev. 2:2; 5:12; 6:8 [Eng. 15]), *qōmeṣ* designates a minute quantity, just enough to fill the palm of the hand (cf. Lev. 9:17). Targ. Onqelos attributed this same minimal understanding to *liqmāṣîm* in Gen. 41:47 — would it be impressive for the land of Egypt to produce grain by handfuls? — and accordingly read: "the inhabitants of the land gathered grain for the granaries." On LXX *drágmata* see H. G. Liddell, R. Scott, and H. S. Jones, *Greek-English Lexicon,* 9th ed. (Oxford: Clarendon, repr. 1966), p. 447b.

2. The narrator is no doubt making a wordplay with *šeḇaʿ* ("seven") and *śāḇāʿ* ("abundance").

3. LXX and SP add "of plenty" *(haśśāḇāʿ).* See v. 53, where *šeḇaʿ š^{e}nê haśśāḇāʿ* ("seven years of plenty") does occur. The omission of *haśśāḇāʿ* in v. 28 is due to haplography (the consonants of "seven" and "plenty" are the same: (*šbʿ* and *śbʿ,* respectively).

4. Lit., "the year of" *(š^{e}naṯ).* Most instances where *šānâ* is qualified genitivally are dates or cultic terms (S. J. DeVries, *Yesterday, Today and Tomorrow* [Grand Rapids: Eerdmans, 1975], p. 47 n. 66).

5. In place of MT sing. *yullaḏ,* SP, LXX, and Vulg. have the pl. *yull^{e}ḏû.* The same construction occurs in 10:25, *ûl^{e}ʿēḇer yullaḏ š^{e}nê ḇānîm.* The Hebrew Bible has many instances of disagreement in number between the verb and the substantive that belongs to it (see Sperber, *Historical Grammar of Biblical Hebrew,* p. 89).

which Asenath daughter of Potiphera, priest of On, bore to him.[6]
51 *Joseph named the firstborn Manasseh, meaning,*[7] *"God has made me forget*[8] *entirely all my suffering and my family."*
52 *The second he named Ephraim, meaning, "God caused me to be fruitful in the land of my affliction."*
53 *When the seven years of plenty that Egypt experienced*[9] *came to an end,*
54 *the seven years of famine commenced,*[10] *just as Joseph had predicted.*[11] *There was famine everywhere, but in all the land of Egypt there was food.*
55 *When all the land of Egypt felt the famine, and the people cried to Pharaoh for food, Pharaoh would say to the Egyptians: "Go to Joseph. Whatever he tells you, do."*
56 *When the famine had spread nationwide, Joseph opened all the granaries,*[12] *and began to sell*[13] *grain*[14] *to the Egyptians, for the famine was becoming intense throughout the land of Egypt.*

6. On the existence of numerical sayings in epic or narrative texts, see W. M. W. Roth, *Numerical Sayings in the Old Testament,* VTSup 12 (Leiden: Brill, 1965), pp. 11, 13.

7. See R. Gordis, "Virtual quotations in Job, Sumer, and Qumran," *VT* 31 (1981) 412, who notes the use of *kî* as a formula with the naming of children that means "for he said" (Gen. 4:24; Exod. 18:4; 1 Sam. 1:20). See also A. Schoors, "The Particle *kî,*" *OTS* 21 (1981) 257-58, who identifies the explicative function of *kî* in sentences providing the etiology of a proper name (i.e., "saying").

8. The only instance of the Piel of *nāšāh,* and the only instance of a *pataḥ* in the first syllable of a Piel perfect. One would expect *niššānî* instead of the vocalization *naššanî.* See GKC, § 52m., and *BHS.* Possibly the unusual pointing of *naššanî* is occasioned by the vocalization of the proper name Manasseh *(mᵉnaššeh).*

9. Many Heb. mss and SP read a pl. *(hāyû).* MT understands the phrase "the seven years of plenty" as a single entity and thus uses a sing. verb.

10. For *ḥālal* (Hiphil) plus preposition *lᵉ* (here *wattᵉḥilleynâ . . . lāḇô',* "began to come"); cf. Gen. 6:1; 10:8; 11:6; and *HALAT,* 1:307.

11. Lit., "had said" *('āmar).* Cf. NJPS "had foretold."

12. MT reads "Joseph opened up everything which was in them" *(kol-'ᵃšer bāhem).* LXX and Pesh. read "he opened up all the storehouses of grain." Both the reading of these ancient versions and Targ. Onqelos's "Joseph opened all the granaries in which there was grain" are attempts to make sense of a probably defective text.

13. LXX *kaí epṓlei* suggests action that is still continuing. Cf. P. P. Saydon, "The inceptive imperfect in Hebrew and the verb *hēḥēl,* 'to begin,'" *Bib* 35 (1954) 45, who cites *wayyišbōr* as a rare *wayyiqṭōl* with inceptive meaning.

14. *bar* ("grain") may have dropped out because of the ending of the previous word, *wayyišbōr.*

57 *The whole world came*[15] *to Egypt to make purchases, to Joseph,*[16] *for famine had gripped the entire world.*

47-49 Joseph's interpretations and prognostications are now demonstrated to be accurate. Years of average production are replaced by seven abundant years. Joseph, who has done quite a bit of talking thus far in the chapter, now begins to do some work. He oversees the storing of surplus food that comes from bountiful harvests. During the coming famine the only problem will be food; the issue of adequate water never emerges. While one expects most famines to be caused by drought brought on by little or no rainfall, the OT only infrequently mentions the absence of rain in connection with famines (1 K. 18:1ff.; Hag. 1:10-11). Other causes of famine would be disease on plants and crops (Amos 4:9); insect invasion (Joel 2:1ff.); or even human-precipitated famines, usually brought on by the devastation left behind by warfare (2 K. 6:24-29). Even Egypt, which was watered by the seasonal inundation of the Nile, did not have immunity from famines.[17]

That Joseph gathered grain *like sands of the sea* from the fields surrounding the cities[18] reminds one of God's promises to the patriarchs that their descendants would be like "sand on the seashore" (22:17; 32:13 [Eng. 12]). So great were the crops that the harvested grain was *beyond measure* (*'ên mispār,* lit., "there was no counting"). This phrase parallels phrases like *wᵉ'ên-pōṯēr* ("there was none to interpret," v. 8), *ûpōṯēr 'ên 'ōṯô* ("there is no interpreter for it," v. 15) earlier in the chapter. It also recalls statements to the patriarchs to the effect that their descendants would be so great that "they could not be numbered" (15:5; 16:10; 32:13 [Eng. 12]).

Joseph's duties here probably parallel those carried out by Pharaoh's official known as "Overseer of the Granaries of Pharaoh" or "Overseer of the Granaries of Upper and Lower Egypt."[19] One Egyptian text identifies the holder of this position as Panhesi (Phineas), which means "the Nubian." Here is an extrabiblical illustration of a foreigner holding this position, as did Joseph.

15. A fem. sing. subject *('ereṣ)* here has a masc. pl. verb *(bā'û).* See GKC, § 145e, who cites this passage as an illustration of fem. nouns as collective terms denoting masc. persons. See also Waltke and O'Connor, *Biblical Hebrew Syntax,* p. 109.

16. Hebrew syntax permits the connection of a phrase with distant verbs. See M. Greenberg, *Ezekiel 1–20,* AB (Garden City, NY: Doubleday, 1983), p. 311. The sentence reads lit., "The whole world came to Egypt to buy to Joseph." See also D. Pardee, "The Preposition in Ugaritic," *UF* 7 (1975) 334 n. 24, who argues against C. H. Gordon (*UT,* pp. 92-93, § 10.1) that *'el* here assumes the meaning "from" ("to buy from Joseph").

17. See G. Hasel, "Famine," *ISBE,* 2:281-83.

18. For fields associated with cities, i.e., agricultural cities, cf. Lev. 25:31; Deut. 28:3; Josh. 21:12.

19. W. A. Ward, "The Egyptian Office of Joseph," *JSS* 5 (1960) 146.

50-52 Egypt is fruitful; so is Asenath. Egypt brings forth bountiful crops; Asenath mothers two sons to Joseph — Manasseh and Ephraim. Joseph, recently the receiver of an Egyptian name, bestows on his offspring Hebrew names. Asenath, unlike Rachel (30:24) and Leah (29:32), does not name the fruit of her womb.

Joseph's experiences are going in the opposite direction of Egypt's. Egypt has been experiencing prosperity; but famine and leanness are ahead. Joseph has been experiencing famine and leanness since he was seventeen; but he is now entering years of fruitfulness and prosperity. The birth of Manasseh ("one who causes to forget") closes the door on all the harsh treatment he has been exposed to over the last thirteen years.[20] It no longer has a hold on him. In the birth of Manasseh he is freed from that emotional bondage and trauma. Despair gives way to revitalization.

The first part of Joseph's explanation for choosing the name Manasseh is self-explanatory — *God has made me forget entirely all my suffering* (which could refer to earlier sufferings at the hands of his brothers back in Canaan, or less likely to his more recent sufferings in Egypt). But why add the phrase *and my family?* Why would Joseph give a name to a child that commemorates the fact that God has caused him to forget his family, both siblings and a father? With Sarna, I suggest that we understand both phrases as a hendiadys, "my suffering in my father's home," thus making it even clearer that the reference is to mistreatment to which Joseph had been subjected by members of his own family back in Canaan.[21]

In naming his second child *Ephraim* he reminds himself that God can turn buffeting into blessing. The place of affliction can become the place of fruitfulness. The fruitfulness to which Joseph alludes refers to more than simply the birth of a son. It must include the opportunity to be the vehicle in the survival of Egypt. If the name of Joseph's first son (Manasseh) focuses on a God who preserves, the name of Joseph's second son (Ephraim) focuses on a God who blesses.[22]

If the chapter had ended with the account of the birth of Joseph's two sons, with the names and the reasons given for those names to each by their father, then the impression might have been created that Joseph was inclined

20. I see no reason to accept the changes in v. 51 proposed by F. Zimmermann, "Some Textual Studies in Genesis," *JBL* 73 (1954) 101. He would emend MT *ʿᵃmālî,* "my sufferings," by breaking it into two words, *ʿal* and *lî,* and translating, "God has put me out of memory with all my kinsmen."

21. Sarna, *Genesis,* p. 289. I prefer this explanation to that advanced by N. P. Lemche (*Early Israel,* VTSup 37 [Leiden: Brill, 1985], pp. 252-53): Joseph, by marrying an Egyptian, has broken with his lineage, and the newly created family represents the origins of a new lineage.

22. See Westermann, *Genesis,* 3:97.

to settle down permanently in Egypt and to forget and ignore his family back in Canaan. Joseph seems to make no attempt to get word back to his family, especially to his father, about his circumstances. In fact, there is an interesting statement in Midrash Tanḥuma, *Vayyesheb* 8: "When Joseph found himself thus [promoted to supervisor of Potiphar's house] he began to eat and drink and curl his hair and said: 'Blessed is the Lord who has caused me to forget my father's house.' Said God to him: 'Your father is grieving for you in sackcloth and ashes and you are eating and drinking and curling your hair! Now your mistress will pair herself with you and will make your life miserable.' "Although clearly out of chronological sequence, the statement about Joseph's smugness is close to Gen. 41:51.[23]

Yet the chapter does not conclude with the naming of Manasseh and Ephraim. The following verses, 53-57, esp. v. 57, indirectly bring Joseph's family back into the picture.[24]

53-57 The extensiveness of the famine is underscored by the repeated use of *kol* (lit., "all") in this section. It was used once by the narrator in v. 47, twice by Joseph (v. 51), and eight times by the narrator in vv. 54-57 (twice in each verse). Most of the Egyptians are apparently not aware that grain distribution is now in Joseph's hand. V. 55 tells us that the people sought out Pharaoh, not Joseph. Interestingly, Pharaoh refers to Joseph by his Hebrew name, not by his Egyptian name. He says to the crowds: *Go to Joseph.* He does not say: "Go to Zaphenath-paneah." This is another indication that Joseph's second name plays no significant role in the narrative (unless the narrator is putting words in Pharaoh's mouth to maintain Joseph's identity).

The effects of the famine spread beyond Egypt to surrounding countries (v. 57). We do not know how they became aware of Egypt's stored-up supply of surplus grain. But the news spread. This note prepares us for the visit of Joseph's brothers to Egypt in search of food (ch. 42). Also, that the famine threatens not only Egypt and nearby Canaan but also the whole earth *(kol-hā'āreṣ)* permits the famine of the Joseph story to function as a counterpart to the flood in primeval history. Joseph is an antitype of Noah, building storehouses just as Noah built his ark.[25] The storehouses of Joseph, however, are for the survival of the masses. The ark of Noah was for the survival of one man and his family.

23. Midrash Tanḥuma is a fourth-century A.D. midrashic collection on the Pentateuch attributed to Tanḥum bar Abba, a Palestinian preacher. See J. L. Kugel, *In Potiphar's House* (San Francisco: Harper, 1990), p. 91 n. 18.

24. See Longacre, *Joseph,* p. 49.

25. See B. T. Dahlberg, "On recognizing the unity of Genesis," *TD* 24 (1976) 364.

F. JOSEPH'S BROTHERS JOURNEY TO EGYPT (42:1-38)

1. JACOB SENDS TEN SONS TO EGYPT (42:1-5)

1 *When Jacob learned*[1] *that there was grain in Egypt, Jacob said to his sons: "Why are you standing around looking at each other?"*[2]

2 *He said:*[3] *"Look, I have heard that there is grain. Go down there and procure for us provisions so that we might live and not die."*[4]

3 *So Joseph's brothers, ten of them,*[5] *went down to procure grain from*[6] *Egypt.*

4 *But Benjamin, Joseph's brother, Jacob did not send with his brothers, for he thought*[7] *tragedy might befall*[8] *him.*

5 *Thus the sons of Israel came to procure provisions along with others, for there was famine in the land of Canaan.*

1 In 34:31 Jacob's sons were upset with Jacob for his unwillingness to do anything about what happened to Dinah. Now Jacob is perturbed with his sons for doing nothing about the famine spreading over Canaan. He says to them: *tiṯrā'û,* which I have translated *Why are you standing around looking at each other* (most modern versions translate similarly; see AV, RSV, NIV, NEB, JB, NAB, NJPS). The verb presents some problems. The translation "stare" or "look" is obtained by taking the verb as a Hithpael of *rā'â.* The problem with this reading is that the Hithpael of *rā'â* occurs elsewhere only with the meaning "to meet in combat" or "face one another in battle" (2 K. 14:8, 11 par. 2 Chr. 25:17, 21). It is likely, however, that the literal meaning of the verb, "to look/stare at each other," subsequently took on the meaning

1. Lit., "saw" *(wayyar').*

2. MT *tiṯrā'û* is difficult; see the commentary below.

3. Not present in LXX. Its inclusion in the MT indicates that his question in v. 1 went unheeded by his sons.

4. For the jussive/cohortative after an imperative, see GKC, § 109g; Waltke and O'Connor, *Biblical Hebrew Syntax,* p. 578.

5. For instances of the word order: substantive, then numeral *('ᵃḥê yôsēp̄ ʿᵃśārâ)* see M. Tsevat, "Three Bulls or One? A Reappraisal of 1 Samuel 1,24," *Bib* 68 (1987) 100 n. 8.

6. Fifty Heb. mss. read "*in* Egypt," as does Vulg.

7. *'āmar,* lit., "say." Speiser (*Genesis,* p. 321) notes that *'āmar pen,* "he said: 'lest . . .' " is a Hebrew way to express indirect discourse. For *'āmar* meaning "think (to oneself)" see Gen. 20:11; Exod. 3:3; 12:33; etc.).

8. Lit., "meet him" *(yiqrā'ennû).* Cf. 44:29; Exod. 1:10; Deut. 31:29; 1 Sam. 28:10; etc., where *qārā'* points to unpleasant events ahead.

"face one another in combat"; thus there is no real problem with reading the verb as a Hithpael of *rāʾâ* with reciprocal force.[9]

The LXX seems to have been uncertain of the verb, as indicated by its translation *rhathyméō,* "linger, dally, rest" (probably presupposing Heb. *teʾaḥarû).*[10] This is the only time in the Hebrew canon that LXX uses *rhathymeín;*[11] elsewhere it uses synonyms. In 34:19 it translates *ʾēḥar* (Piel of *ʾḥr,* "delay") by *chronízō,* and in 43:10 it translates *hiṯmahmāhnû* (Hithpalpel of *mhh,* "delay") by *bradýnō.* In Sir. 35:11 the Hebrew does have *ʾl ttʾḥr,* which in the LXX (32:11) is *mḗ rhathýmei.* The LXX either had before it a text of 42:1 that had *teʾaḥarû,* or else construed it in that manner.[12]

Other ancient versions, particularly the Pesh. (*lʾ tdḥlwn,* "do not fear") and SP (*lmh ttyrʾw,* "why are you afraid?"),[13] might be supporting evidence for seeing in the Hebrew form under discussion an infixed *-t-* form of *yrʾ*.[14]

2 Through some means, Jacob has heard that there is stockpiled grain in Egypt. He has "seen" (v. 1)[15] and *heard* (v. 2) about the surplus food. His sons seem to be ignorant (or at least they feign ignorance, not wanting to make the same journey they earlier forced on their younger brother) about the grain in Egypt. If they are genuinely ignorant of this fact, then Jacob becomes their deliverer in Canaan, just as Joseph becomes their deliverer in Egypt. But they may be pretending to be uninformed because of their association of Egypt with what they did to Joseph, even though that took place twenty years earlier (when Joseph was 17; he was 30 when the famine began, and it has lasted 7 years).

3 Jacob's sons (v. 1) are now *Joseph's brothers.* This shift in designation prepares us for the eventual meeting of long separated brothers. They do not protest, complain, or even talk. They passively, silently, obey their father. As father, Jacob retains authority over even married, grown sons. He speaks and mandates; they obey and cooperate.

9. For the Hithpael with reciprocal nuance, see GKC, § 54f; Waltke and O'Connor, *Biblical Hebrew Syntax,* p. 431.

10. Cf. *BHS,* and *HALAT,* 4:1083.

11. Although Hatch and Redpath (*Concordance to the Septuagint* [Grand Rapids: Baker, repr. 1983], 2:1247) note its use in Judg. 1:16 in some LXX mss.

12. See J. Barr, "Doubts about Homophony in the Septuagint," *Textus* 12 (1985) 55-56. Barr's explanation of the LXX reading of the Hebrew of 42:1 is preferable to that of E. Tov, "Loan-Words, Homophony and Transliterations in the Septuagint," *Bib* 60 (1979) 225, who explains the LXX of Gen. 42:1 as a case of homophony, i.e., sound resemblance, the choice of Greek equivalents that sound like their Hebrew counterpart but differ in meaning. In *tiṯrāʾû* and *rhathymeíte* only two consonants align with each other *rh* and *t/th,* and they are in reverse order.

13. See S. R. Isenberg, "On the Jewish-Palestinian Origins of the Peshitta to the Pentateuch," *JBL* 90 (1971) 81.

14. See M. J. Dahood, *Or* 45 (1976) 334.

15. See n. 1 above.

4 Jacob keeps his youngest, *Benjamin,* at home. What Joseph once was to Jacob, Benjamin is now. He is less concerned that the ten sons' lives will be in danger than he is that Benjamin's would. Thus they seem expendable, but nothing must ever happen to Benjamin. He must not meet with any kind of *tragedy ('āsôn).* Jacob voices the same concern, even using the same word, in v. 38 and in 44:29. In this context *'āsôn* refers to Benjamin's (possible) death (see esp. v. 38) or at least a very serious, life-threatening injury (cf. Exod. 21:23a).[16]

5 The narrative leaves no room for any description of the journey from Canaan to Egypt. V. 3 — they left; v. 5 — they arrived! Just as the brothers did not talk at home, they do not talk after leaving home. Again, no specific names are listed. The men come as a group: *the sons of Israel.* They were first described as "sons of Jacob," then as "brothers of Joseph," and now as *sons of Israel.* The *others* with whom they travel include representatives of the "whole earth" (41:57).

This unit begins (v. 1) and ends (v. 5) by identifying Joseph's brothers in relationship to their father: they are "his sons" (i.e., of Jacob) and "the sons of Israel." In between they are identified in relationship to Joseph: "Joseph's brothers" (v. 3); "Joseph's brother, his brothers" (v. 4). If "Jacob" represents the private side of Jacob, i.e., a suffering and feeling human being, and if "Israel" represents the public side of the patriarch, i.e., his office and dignity, then this duality might explain the switch from "Jacob" in v. 1 to "Israel" in v. 5. "Jacob is a name fitting to describe the measures taken by a man to obtain food for

16. See B. S. Jackson, "The problem of Exod. XXI 22-25 (Ius talionis)," *VT* 23 (1973) 274-75; S. E. Loewenstamm, "Exodus XXI 22-25," *VT* 27 (1977) 358; A. Phillips, *Ancient Israel's Criminal Law,* pp. 88-89. *'āsôn* occurs only in these three Genesis passages (42:4, 38; 44:29) and once in Exodus, in the law about harming a pregnant woman (Exod. 21:22, 23). The word refers to a major calamity that could happen in a person's life, and more than likely that major calamity would be death. But Gen. 42:4 does not demonstrate conclusively that *'āsôn* means death. Its subsequent use in v. 38 and in 44:29 make clear that in v. 4 Jacob's fear is that Benjamin *might* die. Interestingly, the LXX translates *'āsôn* in the three Genesis passages by *malakía,* "weakness, sickness," but in Exod. 21:22, 23 uses *exeikonisménon,* "formed," and applies the word not to the mother but to the fetus (on which see S. Isser, "Two Traditions: The Law of Exodus 21:22-23 Revisited," *CBQ* 52 [1990] 30-45). R. Westbrook further clarifies the meaning of *'āsôn* by suggesting that it refers to a disaster for which nobody can be blamed. Jacob accepts the evidence the brothers have brought to him about the brutal death of Joseph (37:33). Westbrook believes, however, that this is only a formal declaration of acceptance by Jacob. As one sees from 44:28, Jacob did not really believe, or at least he had nagging doubts about, the brothers' account. Now Jacob fears that another *'āsôn* will happen to Benjamin as happened to Joseph, i.e., another disaster for which nobody can be blamed. See R. Westbrook, "Lex Talionis and Exodus 21,22-25," *RB* 93 (1986) 56-57; idem, *Studies in Biblical and Cuneiform Law* (Paris: Gabalda, 1988), p. 69 n. 131.

himself and his family . . . the reference to 'the sons of Israel' in v. 5 is a reminder of the dignity and historical importance of the one whose sons come to buy grain at this juncture in the nation's history."[17]

2. THE FIRST INTERVIEW WITH JOSEPH (42:6-17)

6 *Joseph was the administrator*[1] *of the land; it was he who dispensed provisions to the entire population. Joseph's brothers came and bowed down to him, their faces to the ground.*

7 *Joseph saw his brothers and recognized them. But he pretended not to recognize them.*[2] *He spoke sternly*[3] *to them: "Where have you come from?" They responded: "From the land of Canaan, to procure food."*

8 *Joseph recognized his brothers but they did not recognize him.*[4]

9 *Whereupon Joseph recalled that he had dreamed about them, and he said to them: "You are spies!*[5] *The weakness*[6] *of the land you have come to see."*[7]

10 *They replied: "No,*[8] *my lord. On the contrary,*[9] *your servants have come to procure food!*

17. Longacre, *Joseph,* p. 150.

1. Lit., "And Joseph, he [was] the governor." The use of the resumptive pronoun in a nominal sentence where the predicate is definite *(haššallîṭ)* throws emphasis on the subject at the beginning of the sentence. Cf. Davidson, *Hebrew Syntax,* p. 149, § 106d.

2. That is, Joseph acted as a stranger to his brothers, he pretended to be a stranger. On this use of the Hithpael *(wayyiṯnakkēr)* to express an act of pretending, see J. Blau, *Grammar of Biblical Hebrew* (Wiesbaden: Harrassowitz, 1976), p. 52, § 25.3.

3. Lit., "harsh things" *(qāšôṯ).* One may compare *wayᵉḏabbēr 'ittām qāšôṯ* with *ḥāzᵉqû 'ālay diḇrêḵem* (Mal. 3:13). GKC, § 122q, cites this passage as an illustration of fem. abstract nouns used adverbially. See also Waltke and O'Connor, *Biblical Hebrew Syntax,* p. 104.

4. Joseph's recognition of his brothers is expressed by a preterite plus noun *(wayyakkēr yôsēp),* while their failure to recognize him is expressed by a perfect *(hikkiruhû),* thus forming a narrative antithetical sentence.

5. On clauses with a participial *(mᵉraggᵉlîm)* as predicate, see Andersen, *Hebrew Verbless Clause in the Pentateuch,* pp. 34, 61 (indefinite noun plus pronoun).

6. Lit., "the nakedness of the land," also in v. 12. Targ. Onqelos renders "the vulnerable parts of the land" *(bydqh d'r').*

7. The order of the Hebrew words is *lir'ôṯ 'ṯ-'erwaṯ hā'āreṣ bā'ṯem,* lit., "to-see the-nakedness-of-the-land you-have-come"; the placement of the infinitive construct with *lᵉ (lir'ôṯ)* before the governing verb gives special emphasis to the infinitive. Cf. GKC, § 114g.

8. Z. Zevit ("A Misunderstanding at Bethel, Amos vii 12-17," *VT* 25 [1975] 789 n. 26) cites *lō'* in 43:10 as a way to express absolute denial. Here *lō'* is being used elliptically for a negative sentence (Blau, *Grammar of Biblical Hebrew,* p. 92, § 81.1). Y. Hoffmann ("Did Amos regard himself as a *nāḇî'?*" VT 27 [1977] 209-10) argued

11 *All of us, we are*[10] *sons of the same man, we are honest. Your servants have never been and are not now spies!"*[11]

12 *He said to them: "Not so!*[12] *The land in its weakness you have indeed come to see."*

13 *They said: "Your servants are twelve. We are brothers, sons of the same man in the land of Canaan; the youngest is now with our father, and the other one is gone."*[13]

14 *Joseph said to them: "It is just as I told you: you are spies.*

15 *You shall be tested in this way:*[14] *as sure as Pharaoh lives, you shall not*[15] *leave this place unless your youngest brother comes here!*

16 *Send one of you and let him bring back your brother. The rest of you will be confined*[16] *here. Thus shall your words be tested as to whether there is truth in you. Otherwise, as Pharaoh lives, you are spies."*

17 *He locked them up in the guardhouse for three days.*

6 This unit opens by reminding us that Joseph holds two positions. His political position is *administrator* [*šallîṭ*] *of the land.*[17] This word is used again only in

---

subsequently that by itself *lō'* never expressed absolute denial. Zevit's rejoinder ("Expressing denial in Biblical Hebrew and Mishnaic Hebrew, and in Amos," *VT* 29 [1979] 506) provides evidence, to the contrary, that *lō'* may be used to express absolute denial. Closest to the brothers' use of *lō' 'ᵃḏōnî* is Ephron's use of *lō' 'ᵃḏōnî* to Abraham; Ephron begins his counterproposition with, "No, my lord, hear me" (23:11).

9. A legitimate rendering of *waw,* esp. after a negative statement (GKC, § 163a). Some ancient versions omit *waw* (LXX, SP, Pesh.).

10. A shortened form of the pronoun. See GKC, § 32d.

11. *hāyû* illustrates the use of a *qāṭal* as a present perfect (Blau, *Grammar of Biblical Hebrew,* p. 86, § 61).

12. For the emphatic negative *lō' kî,* where the *kî* accentuates the negative, see J. Muilenburg, "The Linguistic and Rhetorical Usages of the Particle *ki* in the Old Testament," *HUCA* 32 (1961) 140.

13. Lit., "and he is not." For *'ênennû* see GKC, § 152m ("he is no longer alive").

14. For *bᵉzō'ṯ* meaning "in this way/this is how" cf. Gen. 34:15, 22; Exod. 7:17; Lev. 16:3; Num. 16:28 (J. Milgrom, *Leviticus 1–16,* AB [New York: Doubleday, 1991], p. 1015; B. A. Levine, *Numbers 1–20,* AB [New York: Doubleday, 1993], p. 428).

15. When the oath is negative ("you shall not leave this place"), the second part of the oath may be introduced by *'im.* Cf. C. L. Seow, *Grammar for Biblical Hebrew* (Nashville: Abingdon, 1987), pp. 233-34.

16. Lit., "and you shall be bound" (*wᵉ'attem hē'āsᵉrû,* a Niphal imperative).

17. S. A. Geller ("Cleft Sentences with Pleonastic Pronoun: A Syntactic Construction of Biblical Hebrew and Some of Its Literary Uses," *JANES* 20 [1991] 26-27) identifies the pronoun *hû'* in *wᵉyôsēp hû' haššallîṭ* as a hinge device — "as for (the aforementioned) Joseph. . . ." The sentence is both resumptive topically and functions as an introductory circumstantial clause, setting the scene for 42:7ff.

Eccl. 7:19; 8:8; 10:5.[18] In Ezek. 16:30 the feminine *šalleṭeṯ* describes a brazen harlot.[19] Joseph's economic position is *he who dispensed provisions (hammašbîr).* The brothers *bowed down to him,* showing respect for his political authority. The double identification of Joseph as *haššallîṭ* and *hammašbîr* recall Joseph's two earlier dreams, the one in which the sun, moon, and eleven stars bowed before him (his position of authority), and the other in which the brothers' sheaves bowed before his sheaf (his position of provider).[20]

7 Once again the verb *nāḵar* appears, first in the Hiphil *(recognized),* then in the Hithpael *(pretended not to recognize),*[21] then back to the Hiphil in v. 8. This verb was crucial in the binding of chs. 37 and 38 (37:32, 33; 38:25, 26). True, some twenty years have passed, but Joseph immediately recognizes his brothers. However, he chooses not to reveal himself to his brothers. One can only imagine how difficult it would be for Joseph to restrain himself, to control his emotions, at this point. What is he thinking on the inside? Is he relieved and ecstatic to know his family is alive? Does the brothers' unannounced and unexpected appearance open the floodgates of a lot of bitter memories?

Joseph asks only about their origin.[22] They answer that question, then elaborate with an explanation for their visit. Joseph would not need to ask what foreigners are doing in Egypt at this time.

8 There are many reasons why the brothers would not recognize Joseph: They assume he is dead; he is probably clean shaven; he speaks to them in Egyptian through an interpreter (v. 23); he is wearing the trappings of his Egyptian office; he has an Egyptian name (41:45). What is true at the physical level is also true at the spiritual level. Their failure to recognize Joseph here but emulates their failure to recognize the Joseph that God was preparing him to be in ch. 37. The brothers are lacking in both recognition (ch. 42) and insight (ch. 37).

The first part of v. 8 essentially repeats the first part of v. 7: Joseph

18. It is a pl. noun in Eccl. 7:19 ("Wisdom is stronger for the wise than ten *rulers* who are in the city"); an adjective in Eccl. 8:8 ("No one *has control* over the life"); a sing. noun in Eccl. 10:5 ("an error that issues from the presence of the *ruler*"), where *haššallît* is parallel to *hammôšēl* ("ruler") of v. 4. (The translations are those of J. L. Crenshaw, *Ecclesiastes,* OTL [Philadelphia: Westminster, 1987], pp. 140, 149, 168, respectively.) The adjectival use of the word occurs in Biblical Aramaic: "that the Most High has dominion over humanity's kingdom" (Dan. 4:14 [Eng. 17]).

19. See M. Greenberg, *Ezekiel 1–20,* AB (Garden City, NY: Doubleday, 1983), p. 284: "*šlṭt* is probably an Aramaism, a revival of an early usage (Gen 42:6)."

20. See Alter, *Art of Biblical Narrative,* p. 163.

21. In an attempt to remove the impression that Joseph is being dishonest and unfeeling, Targ. Onqelos translates *wayyiṯnakkēr* as "he considered what he should say to them" *(wḥšyb m' dymlyl 'ymhwn).*

22. For instances where a speaker asks a question whose answer he already knows, cf. Gen. 3:9-10; 4:9; 2 Sam. 20:9; 2 K. 5:25.

recognized (*wayyakkirēm,* v. 7; *wayyakkēr,* v. 8) his brothers. The point about the recognition in v. 7 is that he recognized them even before they spoke (v. 7b). The point about the recognition statement in v. 8 is to contrast Joseph's discernment with his brothers' lack of discernment.

9 Joseph accuses his brothers of being *spies,* knowing all the while that his charge is false. His accusation then becomes a bit more specific. They have come to see the *weakness of the land.* That is, he suggests that they want to spy on Egypt's weakness from a strategic point of view. Joseph's use of the phrase *ʿerwaṯ hāʾāreṣ* (lit., "the nakedness of the land") may be a subtle play back to ch. 37, when his brothers stripped him of his cloak and placed him, nude or semi-nude, in a cistern. Ham, we recall, saw the nakedness of his father (9:22), and paid for it dearly. For "*X* to see the nakedness of *Y*" normally refers to some kind of incest taboo (Lev. 20:17). Perhaps Joseph is suggesting here in ch. 42 that in so treating him the brothers have been guilty of incest violence.[23]

This is Joseph's first accusation that his brothers are spies, and it will be followed by no less than four repetitions of the same crime — vv. 12, 14, 15, 20. As Westermann notes, "the constant repetition of the accusation is meant to unnerve the accused and break down his resistance."[24] Yet more is at stake here than just evening the score. V. 9a makes clear that the stimulus for Joseph's course of action in vv. 9bff. is not his recall of earlier mistreatment. By beginning as it does, v. 9a syntactically connects everything that follows with Joseph's dreams.[25] It is true that earlier Joseph had named his son Manasseh and had connected that name with God causing him to forget all his hardship back in his father's house (41:51, 52). The hardship of the past is forgotten. The dreams of the past are now recalled.

Accusations of spying are found throughout Scripture. A later Pharaoh may suspect the Israelites of spying and fears they will join forces with the enemy (Exod. 1:9-10). Hanun, king of the Ammonites, suspects David is putting on a false front when David offers his condolences at the death of Hanun's father (2 Sam. 10:3). Joab urges the death of Abner, for he thinks Abner approached David to get his hands on privileged information (2 Sam. 3:25). In all of these incidents the insinuation of spying is a pretext. Ironically, in charging his brothers with lying Joseph himself becomes a liar.

10-11 The brothers offer an immediate disclaimer — *No, my lord.* For once they are telling the truth! Compare their words to Jacob back in ch. 37, where they told a bald lie. Here in v. 11b they repeat their denial. In between denying what they are not (vv. 10a, 11b), the brothers affirm what

23. See Alter, *Art of Biblical Narrative,* p. 164.

24. Westermann, *Genesis,* 3:108.

25. See J. S. Ackerman, "Joseph, Judah, and Jacob" in *Genesis,* ed. Harold Bloom (New York: Chelsea House, 1986), pp. 88-89.

they are. They do so through an asyndetic (i.e., no *waw,* "and," separates the clauses) series of counterstatements (vv. 10b, 11): *your servants have come to procure food! All of us, we are sons of the same man; we are honest men. Your servants have never been. . . .* The use of asyndeton creates a feeling of rapidity. Quickly the brothers defend their integrity.

First, they affirm they are a family, and then they describe themselves as *honest* or "forthright" *(kēnîm).* This is the only chapter in the OT in which the plural of this word occurs. The only other possible use of its application to a person is Job 9:35: Job says about God, "I shall speak and not fear him, though not-honest [*lō' ḵēn*] I am in his opinion."[26] The spirit of the brothers' words reminds one of Job's affirmation of his own innocence, as he lists fourteen possible transgressions from which he has kept himself free (Job 31).

When Joseph calls his brothers spies and claims that they are there only for espionage purposes, he is correct, but he does not know he is correct. They claim they are being truthful with Joseph. When they deny any intention of spying they are truthful. But when they pass themselves off as "honest" individuals, the reader is at least surprised. Honest? What about the explanation they offered to Jacob about Joseph's coat that they supposedly found? That was hardly an illustration of honesty. They are correct about their family roots, and they are correct about the reason for their visit to Egypt, but they are wrong in describing their character.

12 Joseph is persistent. When he repeats what he says is their main reason for coming, he varies slightly from what he said earlier: v. 9 (lit.): "to see the weakness of the land you have come"; v. 12: "the weakness of the land you have come to see" *(abc/bca).* The first focuses on the motivation of their visit to Egypt. The second focuses on the object of their spying.

13 "The brothers fall all over themselves to explain their origin."[27] They have given Joseph accurate information (vv. 7b, 10b). They have given Joseph inaccurate information (v. 11, "honest men are we"). They have given Joseph repeated information (vv. 11a, 13a). Now they offer unsolicited information: *the youngest is now with our father, and the other one is gone (wᵉhā'eḥāḏ 'ênennû).* The Targs. expand the last word to "and the other, we do not know what ultimately became of him," or "and one of us, from the time he left us, we do not know what ultimately became of him."[28] Here again the brothers speak truthfully. They are completely ignorant of where

26. This is the translation of W. L. Michel, *Job in the Light of Northwest Semitic,* BibOr 42 (Rome: Biblical Institute, 1987), 1:202, though the renderings of this verse are legion (see 1:233 nn. 214, 215).

27. Coats, *From Canaan to Egypt,* p. 34.

28. See M. L. Klein, "Converse Translation: A Targumic Technique," *Bib* 57 (1976) 520-21.

Joseph is, or even if he is alive. Of course, the brothers are not foolish enough to explain their contribution to the disappearance of one of the twelve.

14 Joseph appears to ignore his brothers' claims of innocence, and he repeats his accusation of v. 9. Either Joseph is suddenly losing control of the situation, or this is a subtle move to increase the pressure on the brothers even more. It is almost as if Joseph has not heard what the brothers claimed for themselves in v. 13. At least there is no logical connection between their "and the other one is gone" (end of v. 13) and his "It is just as I told you" (beginning of v. 14). He is able to use his own earlier words (v. 9) to consolidate his accusation, even though the brothers have said nothing that would substantiate that accusation.

15-16 To determine the level of their truthfulness Joseph devises a test. Here he uses the Niphal of *bāḥan* twice: they are to be tested: *You shall be tested in this way* (v. 15), and their words are to *be tested* (v. 16). The very idea of testing recalls God's testing (Heb. *nāsâ,* Piel) of Abraham in ch. 22. One involves taking a son; the other involves taking a brother (or son, if viewed from Jacob's perspective). What is distinctive of *bāḥan* is the metallurgical connotation. Jeremiah is sent to a people who are bronze and silver (Jer. 6:27-30). His job is to "know and assay [*bāḥan*] their ways" (Jer. 6:27). In referring to the wilderness wandering, the psalmist says, "thou, O God, hast tested [*bāḥan*] us; thou hast tried us as silver is tried" (Ps. 66:10). So *bāḥan* means to test in the sense of determining or finding out the value of something. That is what Joseph is doing.

The test includes an oath. He begins with *as sure as Pharaoh lives,*[29] thus making contact with the powerful sanctity of Pharaoh. The oath begins by concentrating on life in a context of death (perhaps Joseph's because of the brothers; Egypt's and the world's because of famine). Joseph's ultimatum is that the brothers will not be allowed to leave Egypt unless they can produce their younger brother. It will be the duty of an undesignated brother to go back to Canaan and bring Benjamin down to Egypt. The remaining nine will be detained in Egypt. If the brother returns with Benjamin, than Joseph will know that these men are not spies.

Joseph's plan has a loophole, which is obvious to us and certainly must have been obvious to Joseph. How would the appearance of Benjamin in Egypt suddenly erase all suspicion about the brother's purpose for coming to Egypt? True, it would substantiate the word of the ten about a young brother back in Canaan, but how does this establish a motive for entering Egypt? Joseph's test is clearly a smokescreen for seeing Benjamin. Earlier the brothers described

29. The LXX rendering is interesting: *nḗ tḗn hygíeian Pharaō,* "by the health of Pharaoh." See M. Greenberg, "The Hebrew Oath Particle *ḤAY/ḤĒ,*" *JBL* 76 (1957) 36, thus giving Heb. *ḥê* a nominal sense.

themselves as "honest" *(kēnîm).* Joseph cannot bring himself to use that word objectively about his brothers (although he does use it hypothetically in v. 19), but he does use *truth ('ěmeṯ)* to describe what he is attempting to ascertain.

17 To show that he is serious, Joseph has his brothers incarcerated *for three days,* a time substantially less than his own imprisonment, which lasted years. The adding of a jail sentence to the test is Joseph's way of convincing his brothers that he really thinks they are spies. The mention of three days in the context of a test reminds one of the place of the third day in the test to which Abraham was subjected (Gen. 22:4). Joseph incarcerates his brothers for three days in a *guardhouse (mišmār),* the same term used of his confinement earlier (translated "in ward" in 40:3, 4, 7).

3. THE BROTHERS LEAVE, SIMEON STAYS (42:18-26)

18 *On the third day Joseph said to them: "Do this, and you shall live.*[1] *God I fear.*

19 *If you are honest, let but one*[2] *of your brothers be detained in your place of custody, while the rest of you go and bring provisions for your hungry*[3] *households.*

20 *Your youngest brother you must bring back to me. Thus your words shall be verified,*[4] *and you will not die." They consented.*[5]

21 *Then they said to one another: "Alas,*[6] *we are being punished on account*

1. For a consequential imperative after a first imperative see GKC, § 110f. In such a case, the first imperative contains an implicit condition, while the second imperative declares the consequence for the fulfilling of that condition ("if you do this, you shall live"). See also Williams, *Hebrew Syntax,* p. 35, § 190.

2. Cf. *'ᵃḥîḵem 'eḥāḏ* here with *'ᵃḥîḵem hā'eḥāḏ* in v. 33, and see GKC, § 134d. Some attributive adjectives, especially numerals, are definite in themselves and therefore do not always take the definite article.

3. *raʿᵃḇôn,* again only in v. 33 and in Ps. 37:19, is cognate with Ugar. *rǵbn.* See M. J. Dahood, "Hebrew-Ugaritic Lexicography X," *Bib* 53 (1972) 391-92. For the construction *šeḇer raʿᵃḇôn bottêḵem,* lit. "rations (needful) for the hunger of your houses," see Davidson, *Hebrew Syntax,* p. 31, § 23. The genitive may be either genitive of the subject or genitive of the object.

4. Or, "be confirmed" *(wᵉyē'āmᵉnû).*

5. The lit. reading "and they did so" is obviously out of place, for no activity immediately follows. The sense is "they agreed to do it."

6. See N. Kilwing, "*'bl* 'ja, gewiss' — 'nein, vielmehr'?" *BN* 11 (1980) 23-28, who notes that *'ᵃḇāl* here and in 2 Sam. 14:5 and 2 K. 4:14 has an overtone of sorrow or regret. Waltke and O'Connor (*Biblical Hebrew Syntax,* p. 672) see the particle marking a reversal in expectations or beliefs ("we believed wrongly that we had gotten away with disposing of our brother").

of our brother. We saw the distress of his soul[7] *when he besought*[8] *us, and we would not hear. That is why this distress has overtaken*[9] *us."*

22 *Reuben broke in:*[10] *"Did not I say to you 'Do not harm the lad,' and you would not listen? Now comes the reckoning for his blood."*[11]

23 *As for them,*[12] *they were not aware that Joseph understood, for there was an*[13] *intermediary*[14] *between them.*

24 *He turned away from them and wept. When he was able to speak to them again,*[15] *he had Simeon taken from them and had him placed in fetters before their eyes.*

25 *Then Joseph gave orders to fill*[16] *their containers with grain, and to*

7. M. J. Dahood ("The Conjunction *wn* and Negative *'î* in Hebrew," *UF* 14 [1982] 52) attempts to uncover a parallel to *ṣāraṯ napšô* by repointing MT *wᵉnōṣēr napšᵉḵā* in Prov. 24:12 into *wan ṣar napšᵉḵā,* "Indeed He knows the anguish of your soul." With *ṣāraṯ napšô* cf. *bᵉṣar rûḥî,* "in the anguish of my spirit" (Job 7:11).

8. The Hithpael of *ḥānan* means "to seek favor *(ḥēn).*" See D. R. Ap-Thomas, "Some Aspects of the Root *ḥnn* in the Old Testament," *JSS* 2 (1957) 135-36. The verb is used in this stem about a dozen times when the subject is in real distress. Cf. also Deut. 3:23; 2 K. 1:13; Ps. 30:9, etc.

9. Lit., "has come upon us" *(bā'â 'ēlênû).*

10. Lit., "answered" *(wayyaʿan).*

11. Lit., "and also his blood, behold, it is required." For other connections of *dāraš* ("seek, require") and *dam* ("blood") see Gen. 9:5; Ps. 9:13 (Eng. 12); Ezek. 34:10; and the commentary below.

12. For a redundant independent pronoun placed before a verb in a parenthetical comment, see Seow, *Grammar for Biblical Hebrew,* p. 95.

13. Although definite *(hammēlîṣ),* the article here denotes a single person unknown to the brothers and therefore not capable of being defined. Accordingly, the indefinite article is required in English. See GKC, § 126r.

14. See H. N. Richardson, "Some notes on *lîṣ* and its derivatives," *VT* 5 (1955) 167; M. H. Pope, *Job,* AB, 3rd ed. (Garden City, NY: Doubleday, 1973), p. 125. Richardson denies that the word *mēlîṣ* means "interpreter" in the strict sense of the word; rather, it designates some official intermediary or go-between. See also S. Gevirtz, "Phoenician *wšbrt mlṣm* and Job 33:23," *MAARAV* 5-6 (1990) 158.

15. Lit., "turning back to them, he spoke to them." LXX omits "he spoke to them," perhaps because no speech of Joseph is recorded. I take my translation from Speiser, *Genesis,* p. 322, who suggests that the first verb *(wayyāšāḇ)* is used adverbially in a hendiadys construction. For the collocation and contrast of the two verbs of motion in this sentence, *sāḇaḇ* ("move in a circle, surround" and *šûḇ* ("return"), see W. L. Holladay, *The Root Šûbh in the Old Testament* (Leiden: Brill, 1958), p. 54, who notes that *šûḇ* "emphasizes motion in the opposite direction, while *sābhabh* emphasizes a change in direction without including any subsequent motion for a distance."

16. It is not necessary to emend *wayᵉmal'û* to *lᵉmallē'* (contra *BHK* and *BHS*). A pointing of the *waw* as a simple *waw,* instead of *waw* consecutive with the imperfect, demonstrates the use of the simple *waw* with the imperfect with jussive force following a verb of commanding. See T. J. Meek, "Translating the Hebrew Bible," *JBL* 79 (1960) 330.

return each man's money[17] *into his sack, and to give them provisions for their journey. It was done*[18] *for them.*

26 *They loaded their provisions on their asses and left.*

18 Joseph's two plans to deal with his brothers parallel his brothers' two plans to deal with him (ch. 37). They first place Joseph in a pit, then change their mind and sell him to the Ishmaelites. Joseph's first plan is to put all the brothers in custody and allow one to go and return with Benjamin. He then changes his plans, and permits all the brothers to go, keeping behind Simeon.

Joseph urges them: *Do this, and you shall live,* a phrase that sounds very Deuteronomic (Deut. 6:24; Lev. 18:5; cf. Luke 10:28b). That is, proper actions produce proper results; appropriate behavior brings its benefits. In the MT the demonstrative precedes the imperative: "This do!" *zō'ṯ ʿᵃśû* here recalls the brothers' *zō'ṯ māṣā'nû* ("This we found," 37:32) to their father. This position gives the demonstrative special emphasis. Joseph guarantees his promise with the addendum *God I fear.* If we are to understand by this phrase that Joseph is claiming that his word is reliable,[19] then a powerful contrast is set up. Here stands one (Joseph) whose word is reliable (for he fears God) before a group (Joseph's brothers) whose word may be quite unreliable and who fear Joseph. Their future, or lack thereof, is in his hands.

19-20 Joseph does not yet designate which of the brothers should stay behind in Egypt, just as he did not suggest in the original plan which brother should go after Benjamin. In delineating the reason for their release, Joseph draws attention first to their mission of mercy to their homeland (v. 19b), and only second to their mission of fetching Benjamin (v. 20a). Joseph is subtly reconstructing the circumstances of his brothers' crime against himself.[20] The test he puts to his brothers is not directed against Benjamin

17. Lit., "silver pieces" *(kᵉsāp̱îm),* a pl. to indicate composition (Williams, *Hebrew Syntax,* p. 7, § 9.

18. Some ancient versions read the verb as a pl. (Pesh. and Vulg.), i.e., "these things were done for them." I take the verb impersonally.

19. See H. W. Wolff, in W. Brueggemann and Wolff, *The Vitality of Old Testament Traditions,* tr. K. R. Crim, et al., 2nd ed. (Atlanta: John Knox, 1982), p. 73, who explores "fear-of-God" passages throughout Genesis–Exodus. Cf. also W. Eichrodt, *Theology of the Old Testament,* OTL, 2 vols., tr. J. A. Baker (Philadelphia: Westminster, 1961-67), 2:273 ("Men shrink from injustice in view of the majesty of the divine lawgiver, who alone is to be feared . . . a similar attitude to the holiness of the law is assumed to exist also among the pious heathen").

20. See J. Milgrom, *Cult and Conscience* (Leiden: Brill, 1976), p. 5 n. 17; Alter, *Art of Biblical Narrative,* p. 166. This involves Joseph perpetrating on his brothers a reversal (they confined him in a pit; he will confine them in a guardhouse) and a repetition (they separated one brother from the rest; he will separate one brother from the rest) of what they did earlier to him.

but against Simeon. The real question addressed to the brothers is not: "Are you willing to bring Benjamin back?" Rather it is: "are you willing to leave Simeon behind?" Will they abandon one brother (Simeon) as they once abandoned another brother (Joseph)?

Perhaps we might have expected Joseph to say: "Thus your words shall be verified and he [i.e., the brother left behind] shall not die." If they leave and do not return, they are will be out of trouble. Joseph will not hunt them down in Canaan. They will have more than enough grain, but one less brother. By saying "you will not die" instead of "he [Simeon] will not die," Joseph is underscoring the involvement of all the brothers, minus Benjamin, in this event. This statement will also serve as a stimulus to the brothers to be as convincing as possible once they see their father Jacob. If they can get him to capitulate and allow Benjamin to go, the death threat hanging over their heads will be lifted. That would be extremely comforting for the brothers, especially if they will need to make several trips to Egypt to procure provisions during a famine of undeterminable length.

Joseph had first suggested that only one brother return to Canaan and that the other nine stay behind, detained in Egypt (v. 16). Now, for several reasons, he reverses that proposal: only one brother is to be detained in Egypt; the other nine are to return to Canaan. First, nine voices might have a better chance of persuading Jacob to release Benjamin. Second, how could one son carry enough grain back to Canaan's "hungry households"? Joseph is genuinely concerned that a sufficient portion of grain provisions be transported to the needy in Canaan; such is his concern for his family's well-being. Third, Joseph must have reflected on the possibility that the nonreturn of nine of his sons could prove fatal to Jacob; such is the measure of his concern for the well-being of his father.[21]

21 The brothers' belief in a theology of retribution now comes into play. They are being punished with respect to one of their own for what they did to one of their own. It is an eye for an eye, a tooth for a tooth, a brother for a brother. They ignored their brother's *ṣārâ (distress),* and now they are the object of *ṣārâ.*

Only here are we told that Joseph did not passively accept the brutal treatment from his brothers. Ch. 37 records no response by Joseph, but twenty years later the brothers remind each other of how callous and indifferent they were when Joseph *besought (hiṯḥanᵉnô)* them. The Hithpael of *ḥānan* is used when the subject is in real distress (e.g., Deut. 3:23; 2 K. 1:13).

22 Reuben has a good memory, but he is not very helpful. The text says literally, "Reuben answered [*wayyaʿan*] them." I have translated the verb as *broke in,* but if we retain "answer," then where is the question? (although

21. See Sternberg, *Poetics of Biblical Narrative,* p. 290.

ʿānâ does not always require a previous question). Might it be that the brothers are indirectly putting blame on Reuben, their oldest sibling? Or does the verb mean something like, "Don't look at me"? It was, after all, Reuben who had first suggested that Joseph be cast into a pit (Gen. 37:22). Is it appropriate that Reuben be cast into another kind of pit?

He reminds his brothers that he spoke to them on Joseph's behalf. His *Do not harm* [*ḥāṭāʾ bᵉ;* cf. Joseph's *ḥāṭāʾ lᵉ,* 39:9] *the lad* is not an exact recall of his words in 37:21-22. There he did not use the verb *ḥāṭāʾ*. His phrases were "let us not take his life, shed no blood, cast him into the pit, lay no hand upon him." Reuben attempts to isolate himself from group responsibility by replacing their *wᵉlōʾ šāmāʿnû,* "we would not hear" (v. 21) with his own *wᵉlōʾ šᵉmaʿtem, and you would not listen.* That Reuben refers to Joseph as a *yeleḏ,* old enough to travel alone (see ch. 37), may be a device to stir his brothers to compassion.[22]

Reuben's *now comes the reckoning for his blood* recalls those passages in the OT in which Yahweh seeks or requires[23] *(dāraš, bqš)* the blood of the murdered, for this blood has been removed from beyond his control (Gen. 9:5; Ps. 9:13 [Eng. 12]; Ezek. 3:18, 20; 33:6, 8). When a person took the life of another, he in essence gained control of the blood of the victim (see 2 Sam. 4:11, "should I not now demand his blood from your hand?").[24]

The ploy used by Reuben to remove himself as a possible candidate for the brother who will remain behind in Egypt is to remind his brothers of how previously he had attempted to restrain them from harming Joseph. Should one who earlier had spoken on behalf of his brother now be the brother left behind in Egypt? Reuben's self-vindication or self-justification by quoting his earlier words is similar to Balaam's self-defense against Balak (Num. 23:6; 24:12-13) by quoting his earlier counsel that he could speak only what Yahweh told him (Num. 22:18).[25] Both Reuben and Balaam, in quoting their previous speech, are simply trying to convince the brothers and Balak that they themselves have committed no crime for which they should be punished.

23 All of this fraternal confession takes place in Joseph's presence, but the brothers think nothing of him, assuming the "Egyptian" viceroy in front of them is not bilingual. After all, *there was an intermediary* [*hammēlîṣ,* the *intermediary*] *between them.* This is the only place in Genesis where a third person is needed for two peoples speaking different languages. There

22. See H. C. Brichto, *Toward a Grammar of Biblical Poetics* (Oxford: Oxford University, 1992), p. 283 n. 6.

23. See also n. 11 above.

24. See A. Phillips, *Ancient Israel's Criminal Law* (Oxford: Blackwell, 1970), p. 86.

25. See G. W. Savran, *Telling and Retelling* (Bloomington: Indiana University, 1988), pp. 66-67.

was no mention of an interpreter when Abraham was with Pharaoh (ch. 12) or with the Philistine Abimelech (ch. 21), or when Isaac was with Abimelech (ch. 26), or when Jacob was with Laban in Mesopotamia (chs. 29–31). Joseph is maintaining his incognito role.

For the third straight verse some form of the verb *šāmaʿ* is used, here in participle form. The group confessed "we would not listen [hear]" (v. 21). Reuben indicted them with "you would not listen [hear]" (v. 22). But Joseph *understood* (lit., "heard," *šōmēaʿ*) everything.

24 There is a limit on how much role playing Joseph can maintain. At some point he will have to remove his mask. His brothers have just admitted their guilt in Joseph's disappearance, and thus have removed their mask. They have been honest about themselves. Will Joseph be honest about himself?

Once he regains his composure Joseph takes Simeon from the group and has him put in chains in front of his brothers. This action will impress on the brothers how serious Joseph is. We are not certain why he picked Simeon. Is he genuinely moved by Reuben's attempt to save him, as recorded either in the original account (ch. 37) or in Reuben's quoting of earlier words here, and thus his reason for binding the second born? In one respect, Simeon, the second-born son of Leah, is an ideal choice to detain, while the remaining nine brothers return to Canaan to bring down to Egypt Benjamin, the second-born son of Rachel.[26]

25-26 Joseph orders his subordinates to fill his brothers' containers with grain, to give them provisions for their journey, and, most surprisingly, to return the money they brought to purchase the grain into each man's sack. The reappearance of *kesep̱,* "money, silver," recalls the twenty shekels of *kesep̱* (37:28) that the brothers received for the sale of Joseph. Of the three orders that Joseph gives the first is to meet their future needs *(to fill their containers with grain).* The third is to meet their immediate needs *(to give them provisions for their journey).* Both of these directives could be carried out publicly, in full sight of the brothers. The second order *(to return each man's money into his sack)* would have to be carried out in clandestine fashion.

Either Joseph is deliberately precipitating a perfect trap (he knows that he can now prove they are dishonest),[27] or else he is acting naively, unaware that what he does out of love for his brothers will cause a great emotional trauma to his brothers. It is difficult to tell if Joseph, in so acting, is being

26. See Sternberg, *Poetics of Biblical Narrative,* p. 291.

27. Although thievery of a few coins would be considered a much lesser crime than spying.

28. Westermann, *Genesis,* 3:111.

punitive (Gunkel) or redemptive (von Rad), or a curious combination of both, neither of which is yet clearly sorted out in Joseph's mind (Westermann).[28] Sternberg raises the possibility that Joseph is here engaging in role-duplication that forces the brothers to face their past.[29] That is, Joseph recalls a time when his brothers placed a higher premium on money than they did on Jospeh's life. They had no qualms about being enriched at his expense. Here Joseph creates a parallel circumstance to that situation. Now it is Simeon's life that is on the line. Will they gladly accept the money and conveniently ignore Simeon, or will the well-being and release of Simeon be uppermost in their minds and control their behavior and choices?

We do not read when the brothers gave Joseph their money, but that Joseph possessed it is shown by the fact that he gave orders to return it *(lᵉhāšîḇ)*. First he turns back to them (*wayyāšāḇ* (v. 24), then he turns their money back to them (v. 25). Apparently the Canaanite shekel was good for making purchases in Egypt. Compare 1 Sam. 13:21 and 1 K. 10:29 where the *kesep̱* shekel was used for individual transactions with foreign countries.

4. THE SONS RETURN TO JACOB (42:27-38)

27 *At the night encampment*[1], *when one of them opened his sack*[2] *to give his ass some fodder, he spotted his money at the mouth of his bag.*[3]

28 *"My money has been returned,"*[4] *he exclaimed to his brothers. "Here it is in my bag!" Their hearts stopped,*[5] *and they turned tremblingly to*

29. Sternberg, *Poetics of Biblical Narrative,* pp. 293-94.

1. Cf. Exod. 4:24 for another incident that had its start with an individual spending the night at a *mālôn,* a night that turns out to have unexpected developments (the brothers find the money in their sacks; Moses is assailed by Yahweh).

2. LXX uses *mársippos* (= Heb. *'amtaḥaṯ*) for MT *śaq* in v. 27a as well as for *'amtaḥaṯ* in v. 27b. But LXX does have a tendency to harmonize.

3. *'amtaḥaṯ* is used only in the Joseph story (Gen. 42–44) in the OT. Most likely it is to be connected with Assyrian *mataḫu,* "lift up, carry," hence, "a burden, pack." See J. C. Greenfield, "The Etymology of *'amtaḥaṯ,*" *ZAW* 77 (1965) 90-92.

4. LXX and Vulg. add "to me."

5. Lit., "their heart went out." Gen. 35:18 supplies another illustration of a part of the human constitution used with *yāṣā'* (*bᵉṣ'ēṯ napšāh,* "with her last breath"), as does Ps. 146:4 *(tēṣē' rûḥô),* although it is easier to understand one's breath or spirit "going out" than it is one's heart. Thus the use of the verb *yāṣā'* in v. 28 with "heart" must be a figurative use of the verb (BDB, p. 423e). LXX was apparently puzzled over this phrase, for it rendered "and their heart was astonished/wonder-struck" *(kaí exéstē hē kardía autō̃n).* Hatch and Redpath (*Concordance to the Septuagint,* pp. 496-97) list 29 different Greek verbs used throughout the LXX to translate *yāṣā',* and Gen. 42:28 is the only time it uses *existánō* (a later form of *exístēmi*). Targ. Onqelos read "the knowledge of their hearts went

one another,[6] *saying: "What is this that God has done to us?"*

29 *When they got back to Jacob their father in the land of Canaan, they told him everything that had happened*[7] *to them:*

30 *"The man who is lord of*[8] *the country spoke sternly with us, and placed us in custody*[9] *as if we were spying out the land.*

31 *But we said to him: 'We are honest. We are not spies!*[10]

32 *There are twelve of us brothers, sons of the same father; the one is gone, and the youngest is now with our father in the land of Canaan.'*

33 *But the man who is lord of the country said back to us: 'This is how I shall know whether you are honest. Of your brothers, leave one with me, and take provisions*[11] *for your hungry households and go.*

34 *Bring your youngest brother to me. Then I shall know that you are not spies but honest. Your brother I will restore to you, and in the land you will be free to move about.' "*

35 *When they were emptying their sacks,*[12] *each one's*[13] *money bag was*

---

out" *(wnpq mdʿ lybhwn),* thus understanding the phrase as one of bewilderment over their inability to make sense of the current circumstances.

6. Lit., "And they trembled, each to his brother." See Waltke and O'Connor, *Biblical Hebrew Syntax,* p. 193 n. 19. E. I. Lowenthal (*The Joseph Narrative in Genesis* [New York: Ktav, 1973], p. 74) renders this phrase "they exchanged terrified glances at each other," following G. R. Driver's discussion of the verb *ḥāraḏ* in "Hebrew Homonyms," *Hebräische Wortforschung,* Fest. W. Baumgartner, ed. B. Hartmann, et al., VTSup 16 (Leiden: Brill, 1967), pp. 54-56, although Driver does not discuss this passage, and "exchange terrified glances" is not one of his four proposed translations for *ḥāraḏ*.

7. For the article with the participle governing an object in the accusative case cf. Deut. 13:6 and Ezek. 43:17. Here is a case of a participle, itself a direct object, being followed by a direct object. As such, the participle is equivalent to a relative clause ("everything that had happened to them"). See Waltke and O'Connor, *Biblical Hebrew Syntax,* pp. 616, 621.

8. For a pl. used to designate one individual *(ʾᵃḏōnê)* see GKC, § 124i.

9. Following LXX, which adds *en phylakḗ,* i.e., Heb. *bᵉmišmār.* For *nāṯan* plus *bᵉmišmar,* see 40:3. MT, however, might be self-explanatory if one understands the preposition *kᵉ* on *kimᵉraggᵉlîm* as indicating virtually a second object. See Davidson, *Hebrew Syntax,* p. 111, § 78, Rem. 8.

10. For the positive-negative parallelism involving the pairing of nominal and verbal clauses, see A. Berlin, *Dynamics of Biblical Parallelism* (Bloomington: Indiana University, 1985), pp. 56-57.

11. Following LXX and Pesh., which reflect the addition of *šeḇer.*

12. For *wayᵉhî* followed by a noun clause *(hēm mᵉrîqîm śaqqêhem)* to indicate an initial "when" clause, which in turn is followed by the apodosis introduced by *wᵉhinnēh,* cf. 2 K. 2:11; GKC, §§ 111g, 116n.

13. "Each one's" is expressed distributively by *ʾîš* (Davidson, *Hebrew Syntax,* p. 13, § 11d).

in his sack! The money bags both they and their father saw, and they were afraid.[14]

36 *Then Jacob their father said to them:*[15]

"Me have you made childless.[16]
Joseph is gone[17] *and Simeon is gone;*
Benjamin would you take?
Upon me are all these things."[18]

37 *Reuben said to his father: "My two sons you may put to death*[19] *if I fail to bring him back*[20] *to you. Place him in my care and I will return him to you."*

38 *But he replied: "My son shall not go down with you,*[21] *for his brother is dead and he alone remains.*[22] *Should*[23] *tragedy meet him on the trip you are to make, you would bring down my white head to the underworld in grief."*

14. Note the similarity in sound between *wayyir'û* ("they saw") and *wayyîrā'û* ("they were afraid").

15. Alter (*Art of Biblical Narrative,* p. 139) notes that Jacob expresses his feelings "with the dramatic heightening of scannable verse," using "semantically parallel hemistichs, placing himself and his suffering . . . at the beginning and the end of the poem."

16. The verb *šāḵal* (or *šāḵōl*) in the Piel often refers to the murder of a child or a person (Gen. 27:45; Deut. 32:35; 1 Sam. 15:33; Jer. 15:7; Ezek. 14:15), thus suggesting in 42:36 that Jacob is tacitly accusing his sons of Joseph's murder.

17. See M. L. Klein, "Converse Translation: A Targumic Technique," *Bib* 57 (1976) 521, who notes the tendency in some of the Targs. to render *'ênennû,* here and elsewhere, as "I do not know what ultimately became of him." That is, the rendering is ambiguous and leaves the question undecided whether Joseph is dead or still alive.

18. The form *kullānâ* is strange since there is no fem. antecedent. Cf. N. H. Sarna, "Epic Substratum in the Prose of Job," *JBL* 76 (1957) 18 n. 35. Davidson (*Hebrew Syntax,* p. 2, § 1, Rem. 2) notes that the fem. pronominal suffix is usual when the suffix refers back to some action or circumstance just mentioned.

19. For the use of an imperfect *(tāmîṯ)* to express permission, see Williams, *Hebrew Syntax,* p. 31, § 170; Waltke and O'Connor, *Biblical Hebrew Syntax,* p. 508.

20. Reuben's "If I fail to bring him back" *('ᵃḇî'ennû,* an imperfect) and later Judah's "if I fail to bring him back" (*hᵃḇî'ōṯîw,* a perfect, 43:9) demonstrate that the simple perfect and the imperfect may be identical in use. See J. A. Hughes, "Another Look at the Hebrew Tenses," *JNES* 29 (1970) 23.

21. It is the pl. "you" *('immāḵem).*

22. Pesh. adds "for his mother." That is, of the late Rachel's two sons, only Benjamin is alive.

23. The equivalent of a conditional sentence exists when one has the perfect plus *waw* in both the protasis and apodosis *(ûqᵉrā'āhû, wᵉhôraḏtem).* On *qāṭal* forms that are conditional, see Davidson, *Hebrew Syntax,* pp. 180-81, § 132a; J. L. Kugel, *Idea of Biblical Poetry* (New Haven: Yale University, 1981), p. 32.

27-28 The journey from Egypt back to Canaan is a long journey, making it necessary for Jacob's sons to stop overnight on the way. Moses, traveling in the opposite direction, also had to break his journey (Exod. 4:21-26). Sometime during the evening one of the brothers, who remains unidentified, opens his bag to feed his donkey. In spite of the fact that they are bearing precious food supplies back to Canaan for their consumption, they must provide food for the animals as well as for themselves. Upon opening his bag of grain, this anonymous brother discovers the money on top of the grain inside his bag.

Understandably, the brothers are distraught *(their hearts stopped),* and with a quiver on their lips they can but mutter to one another: *What is this that God has done to us?* No one in the group suggests that the brother who found the money in his sack is a cheat. The reader knows that it is Joseph who has done this. What they attribute to God has been perpetrated by Joseph. Without their knowledge, Joseph has been the vehicle God is using to bring these brothers to face reality. Joseph is not himself God, as he asserts in 50:19, but he is God's instrument. Earlier the brothers associated the demand that they bring Benjamin to Egypt with their earlier harsh treatment of Joseph (vv. 21, 22). Here they link implicitly the unexpected discovery of the money in their bags with the money they earlier received for their sale of Joseph.[24] The brothers' "what is this God has done to us" is not the same but is close to the expression "what is this you have done?" (3:13; 4:10; 12:18; 20:9; 26:10) in which the offended party calls the offending person to an explanation and justification for his or her misdeed.[25] Whether the formula is "what is this you have done?" or "what is this God has done to us?" no answer to the question is needed, for guilt is apparent.

When the brothers are talking a second time to Joseph they say: "when we came to the lodging place *we* opened *our* sacks, and there was every man's money" (43:21). It is not necessary to say that this is a contradiction — one brother opened his sack and found the money (ch. 42); all of them opened their sacks and found the money (ch. 43). What the narrator is doing in ch. 42 is describing the experience of a group as that of an individual. One brother did open his sack and find the money. It was not necessary for the narrator to describe that subsequently the remaining brothers opened their sacks and found money too. Such an addition of the obvious would be pedantic.[26]

24. See H. C. White, *Narration and Discourse in the Book of Genesis* (Cambridge: Cambridge University, 1991), p. 263; J. S. Ackermann, "Joseph, Judah, and Jacob," in *Genesis,* ed. H. Bloom (New York: Chelsea House, 1986), p. 92.

25. See W. Berg, "Nochmals: Ein Sündenfall Abrahams — der este — Gen 12,10-20," *BN* 21 (1983) 12; M. E. Biddle, "The 'Endangered Ancestress' and Blessing for the Nations," *JBL* 109 (1990) 604.

26. So C. Westermann, *Genesis,* 3:112.

Or, one might suggest that initially only one brother opened his sack and found the money, as ch. 42 maintains. Only one sack would be necessary to feed the animals, however many donkeys were with them. Spotting the money in one sack, the brothers would be hesitant to look into each of their sacks, even if curiosity urged them on. In fact, it is most likely that the brothers drew the conclusion that money was in their sacks too. But they were afraid to look lest they see the incriminating evidence. Then, when they reached their father, they all opened their sacks, and alas, their worst fears were realized. What we then have in 43:21 is the brothers compressing what is described in 42:27-38 and 42:35 into one event.

A more obvious source of contradiction might be seen in the fact that the brothers discover their money in their sacks when they stop for the night (vv. 27-28); later, they make the same discovery in Jacob's presence after arriving in Canaan (v. 35). This tension has suggested to many commentators the intrusion of J (vv. 27-28) in a chapter that is substantially credited to E.[27] Most of them write this contradiction off as clumsy editing by the redactor, who was willing, out of respect for the sanctity of his sources, to juxtapose two contradictory traditions. R. Alter has offered a suggestion as to why the Hebrew writer appropriated both traditions. Each tradition feeds a respective emphasis (one a moral-pyschological axis, the other a theological-historical axis) that reverberates throughout the Joseph narrative.[28] The latter emphasizes the inscrutable workings of God (v. 28). The former emphasizes the process by which the brothers come, reluctantly and painfully, to accept their guilt (v. 35). It is possible, still, to make sense of the logic of the story without resorting either to clumsy or to artful editing. In the two verses under consideration, only one unidentified brother discovers the money, with the remainder of the brothers taking it to be an inexplicable fluke in which they recognized God is involved and which gives them a sense of fraternal solidarity ("to us"). Upon returning home to Jacob, all of them opened their bags and discovered it was no fluke. All of them had money in their coin bags.[29]

I have suggested above an interpretation that allows for understanding vv. 27-35 as a united pericope. May not the repetition of a motif like finding

27. See Redford, *Study of the Biblical Story of Joseph,* pp. 149-58, for a full bibliography on positions commentators have taken regarding the literary strands behind Gen. 42–44. The consensus is to assign 42:1-26, 28b-38 to E, and 42:27-28a; 43:1 — 44:34 to J. According to Jenks, *The Elohist and North Israelite Traditions* p. 30, three reasons exist for ascribing the bulk of ch. 42 to E: (1) the use of *'ĕlôhîm* in v. 28b; (2) the depiction of Joseph, like Abraham before him, as one who "fears God" (v. 18); (3) the prominence of Reuben (vv. 22, 37). But cf. R. N. Whybray, "The Joseph story and pentateuchal criticism," *VT* 18 (1968) 522-28.

28. See Alter, *Art of Biblical Narrative,* pp. 137-40.

29. See Savran, *Telling and Retelling,* p. 128 n. 16.

the money be a means for heightening tension?[30] We know the money is in their sacks, but we do not know if they know the money is in their sacks.

29-34 The brothers, now back in Canaan, share with Jacob their recent experience in Egypt. They repeat their meeting with Joseph (*the man who is lord of the country,* vv. 30, 33). The original dialogue of Joseph and his brothers (vv. 6-22) differs in several ways from the brothers' renarration of it. First, in the original dialogue they tell why they have come to Egypt (vv. 7b, 10), the size of their family (v. 11a), their self-characterization (v. 11b), their denial of spying (v. 11c). In speaking to Jacob, they do not repeat to him the reason they told Joseph they went to Egypt. Also, they reverse "sons of one man . . . we are honest men" (v. 11) to *Honest men we are . . . sons of the same father* (vv. 31-32) (with Jacob shifting from "one man" to "the same father").

Second, they reverse their comments about Joseph and Benjamin. "The youngest is now with our father, and the other one is gone" (v. 13) becomes *the one is gone, and the youngest is now with our father* (v. 32). In speaking to Joseph, Joseph ("the other one") is mentioned last. In speaking to Jacob, Benjamin *(the youngest)* is mentioned last.

Third, the brothers soften Joseph's "let one of your brothers be detained in your place of custody" (v. 19) into *leave one* [of your brothers] *with me* (v. 33). The stronger *yēʾāsēr* ("be detained/bound") is modified with the weaker *hannîḥû* ("leave").

Fourth, the brothers replace Joseph's "thus your words shall be verified, and you will not die" (v. 20) with *Your brother I will return to you, and in the land you will be free to move about* (v. 34). They say nothing about Joseph's threat, but expand on (or invent!) the benefit that will come from returning with Benjamin.

Fifth, although only a change of word order, the brothers rearrange Joseph's "go, bring provisions for your hungry household" (v. 19) into *provisions for your hungry households take and go* (v. 33). Their shift of *raʿᵃḇôn bottêḵem* (lit., "the hunger of your houses") to the start of the sentence draws special attention to the plight in which Jacob and his family find themselves, thus giving Jacob little room to argue. His back is against the wall. Why take chances with an Egyptian philanthropist?

Sixth, the brothers did not tell Jacob *everything that had happened to them* (v. 29). For example, they say nothing about being imprisoned for three days (v. 17), or that Simeon remains in jail (v. 24). They mention only one charge of spying (v. 30), whereas Joseph had repeatedly accused them of spying (vv. 9, 12, 14, 16). The most obvious omission in their speech is the discovery of the money on the way from Egypt to Canaan (v. 27). Their silence is understandable. Their protestation that they are honest men would hardly be given credibility by Jacob

30. See Coats, *From Canaan to Egypt,* pp. 36, 66.

if they shared this item with him. Also missing is any additional reference to Reuben's reproach of his brothers (v. 22). To have shared that would have been an admission of complicity in Joseph's demise. They report only on the dialogue between themselves and Joseph, not on the dialogue among themselves.

One may note that Joseph's insistence on evidence in order that he might *know* whether these men are innocent follows the lines of earlier patriarchal stories. Abraham wanted some sign by which he would *know* that he would possess the land (15:8). Abraham's servant wished a sign from God so that he might *know* that Yahweh was faithful (24:14). In later times Gideon wished confirmation from God so that he might *know* whether he was the one by whom Israel would be delivered (Judg. 6:37), and he devised a test. The Philistine priests need to determine whether the presence of the ark is the cause of their troubles, or is the ark's presence and the plague's outbreak a coincidence? They devise a test (1 Sam. 6:9) in which they will *know* one way or the other.[31]

35 Upon completion of their story the brothers empty their sacks, and there is money, contained in pouches *(ṣᵉrōrōṯ)* in the sacks! Jacob's response (v. 36) may well have followed v. 34, but it makes more sense after the opening of the bags. The father is sympathetic with his sons' speech through v. 34. It was not their fault that Simeon was detained. What other option did they have? Jacob had sent them to Egypt in the first place (vv. 1, 2), although the brothers do not resurrect that fact — unlike the wife of Potiphar, who, in order to mitigate her guilt, pointedly reminded her husband that he had brought Joseph into their house (39:17). By delaying Jacob's response until after both the defense speech of the brothers (vv. 29-34) and the revelation of the money in each of their coin bags (v. 35), the narrative makes two points. First, however nearly successful the brothers may have been in persuading their father that they were innocent victims of circumstances beyond their control, the discovery of the money in their sacks drastically undercuts their credibility. Second, each time (chs. 37 and 42) Jacob's sons have left home, they have returned to their father minus a brother (Joseph, Simeon), but with extra silver in their possession. For Jacob this can hardly be a coincidence, hence his following outburst.[32]

36 Jacob names three of his children: Joseph, Simeon (both of whom have disappeared), and Benjamin (who might disappear). He judges his remaining nine sons with *Me have you made childless (šikkaltem).*[33] He allows his sons no time to explain the presence of the money pouches in their sacks.

31. For an illustration of this motif in Ugaritic literature see M. Dijkstra, "*KTU* 1.6 (= *CTA* 6) .III.1 FF and the so-called *Zeichenbeweis* (proof by a token)," *VT* 35 (1985) 105-9.

32. See Savran, *Telling and Retelling,* p. 44; Sternberg, *Poetics of Biblical Narrative,* p. 298.

33. See n. 16 above.

This is the first time Jacob accuses his sons. There was not even a hint in ch. 37 that he suspected foul play on their part. Indeed, in ch. 37 he suspects no foul play at all to account for the remnants of Joseph. He has been savagely mauled and devoured by a wild beat. The deep rift that existed between Joseph and his brothers is paralleled by the deep rift that is now coming between Jacob and nine of his sons.

37 Reuben's offer of his two sons[34] if he fails to bring back Benjamin from Egypt is hardly therapeutic. His invitation to Jacob to execute his grandsons is not what Jacob relishes. He has lost, he thinks, two sons. How would the loss of two grandsons ameliorate that? In some ways Reuben parallels Lot. Neither can live with the alternative that now confronts him. Lot would rather give the townsmen his two virgin daughters than his guests (19:8). Reuben would rather have Jacob put to death his own two sons rather than see his father having to survive the anguish of living without his beloved Benjamin. Thus both make an overstatement.[35] Whatever the reason for making this offer (he is the oldest son? he wishes to redeem himself with Jacob for his sin with Bilhah, 35:22? he wishes to prevent Benjamin meeting the same end as Joseph? [note Reuben's use of the verb *lahᵃšîḇô* in 37:22 to return Joseph to Jacob, and his use of the same verb in 42:37 to return Benjamin to Jacob, *'ᵃšîḇennû*]), Reuben's offer is magnanimous (as well as foolish). He declares that if he does not bring Benjamin back safe and sound, he is to be held liable, whatever the cause of his failure.[36] He is willing to lose two of his four sons if he is unable to rescue one of Jacob's eleven sons.

38 Jacob resolutely rejects the son's proposal. It is not to Reuben he speaks, but to all the sons *(with you, ʿimmāḵem).* His phrase about Benjamin, *he alone remains (wᵉhû' lᵉḇaddô niš'ār),* is strange. Jacob must mean that Benjamin is the only son of Rachel who is still living.[37] Is Jacob's cryptic phrase inadvertent or deliberate? Is this a backhanded slap at the sons of Leah, Bilhah, and Zilpah? Reuben may be willing to sacrifice his two sons (v. 37), but Jacob is unwilling to sacrifice his son. Jacob is in control. He refers to Benjamin as *My son,* not as "your brother." And he refers to Joseph as *his* [i.e., Benjamin's] *brother,* not as "your brother." Jacob is not against them returning to Egypt. He would like more grain, and he would like Simeon back. But he is more agitated about the possible loss of Benjamin than he is excited about the potential restoration of Simeon. Life without Benjamin would *bring*

34. Since, according to Gen. 46:9 (and cf. Exod. 6:14; Num. 26:5, 6; 1 Chr. 5:3), Reuben had four sons (Enoch, Pallu, Hezron, and Carmi), "my two sons" must mean either "any two of my sons," or less likely, the only two sons born at the time of 42:37.

35. See Lowenthal, *Joseph Narrative in Genesis,* p. 77.

36. For this concept of absolute responsibility, see D. Daube, *Studies in Biblical Law* (Cambridge: Cambridge University, 1947), pp. 12-13.

37. See n. 22 above.

down my white head to the underworld in grief. It is difficult to ascertain whether the Hebrew *š*^{e}*'ôl* should be rendered "grave" or "netherworld." A translation like NIV almost always translates it as "grave" or "death," with a footnote that the Hebrew is "Sheol." Since the word in its 65 occurrences in the OT never takes the definite article, however, it often is a proper name denoting the netherworld, which, in essence, was an extension of the grave.

Because Sheol is so often pictured in the OT in a decidedly negative fashion and is frequently cited as the destiny of the wicked (Num. 16:30, 33; 1 K. 2:6, 9, etc.), it would be proper to infer that Sheol is the ultimate and final abode of the wicked. Gen. 37:35; 42:38 (both spoken by Jacob); and 44:29, 31 (Judah's quoting Jacob to Joseph) are among the rare passages that speak of a righteous person descending to Sheol. It is likely that in these Genesis passages, all involving Jacob, one should consider Sheol as denoting the state or condition of death into which the dejected Jacob will enter, without the sphere of that existence being any more definitely defined than that to which one "descends," much like our equally vague "the great beyond" or "afterworld."[38] It is impossible to determine from these three Genesis references whether the residence of a godly person in Sheol is permanent or temporary. That question can be answered only by an investigation of all OT references to death, Sheol, resurrection, and the like.[39]

G. THE BROTHERS RETURN TO EGYPT WITH BENJAMIN (43:1-34)

1. A RIFT BETWEEN FATHER AND SONS (43:1-10)

1 *The famine in the land remained intense.*[1]

2 *So when they had consumed*[2] *the provisions which they brought back*

38. See A. Heidel, *Gilgamesh Epic and Old Testament Parallels* (Chicago: University of Chicago, 1946), pp. 186-87.

39. For further study, see N. J. Tromp, *Primitive Conceptions of Death and the Nether World in the Old Testament,* BibOr 21 (Rome: Pontifical Biblical Institute, 1969); L. R. Bailey, *Biblical Perspectives on Death,* OBT (Philadelphia: Fortress, 1979); D. Alexander, "The Old Testament view of life after death," *Themelios* 11 (1986) 41-46; J. Barr, *The Garden of Eden and the Hope of Immortality* (Minneapolis: Fortress, 1993), pp. 28-34.

1. For *kāḇēḏ* used with famine in Genesis, see 12:10; 41:31; 43:1; 47:4, 13. For the sequence subject *(hārāʿāḇ)*-predicate *(kāḇēḏ)* as a means of commencing a new paragraph in the narrative, cf. M. Eskhult, *Studies in Verbal Aspect and Narrative Technique in Biblical Hebrew Prose,* Studia Semitica Upsaliensia 12 (Stockholm: Almqvist & Wiksell, 1990), pp. 37-38, 40.

2. *killû l*^{e}*'ĕḵōl* illustrates that the infinitive construct is often preceded by the preposition *l*^{e} even when serving as an object. See Blau, *Grammar of Biblical Hebrew,* § 96.1.

from Egypt, their father said to them: "Return and procure for us a little more corn."

3 *But Judah said to him: "The man adamantly warned us:*[3] *'You shall not appear before me unless*[4] *your brother is with you.'*

4 *If you*[5] *will send our brother with us, we will go down and get provisions for you.*

5 *But if you do not send our brother with us, we will not go down, for the man said*[6] *to us: 'You shall not appear before me unless your brother is with you.'"*

6 *Israel said: "Why have you hurt me so badly as to tell*[7] *the man that you had a brother?"*

7 *They replied: "The man asked expressly*[8] *about us and our family:*[9] *'Is your father still living? Do you have another brother?' We responded to these questions of his. How could we possibly*[10] *know that he would say:*[11] *'Bring your brother down here'?"*

3. The infinitive absolute before the perfect form of the verb lends intensity to the verb. For the expression *hāʿēḏ hēʿîḏ* cf. 1 Sam. 8:9; 1 K. 2:42; etc. Cf. GKC, § 113n; Waltke and O'Connor, *Biblical Hebrew Syntax,* p. 588 n. 33. For *ʿûḏ* (Hiphil) plus *bᵉ* meaning "to warn" or "solemnly declare" cf. Exod. 19:21, 23; Deut. 4:26; 8:19; 30:19; 31:28; 32:46.

4. For *biltî* to introduce an exceptive clause see GKC, § 163c. Williams (*Hebrew Syntax,* p. 69, § 422) notes that *biltî* is limitative, usually after a negative.

5. *yēš* may be employed to introduce the pronominal subject *(yeškā)* of a participle *(mᵉšallēaḥ),* esp. after *'im* when the clause expresses intention. Cf. Gen. 24:42 for this construction, and Williams, *Hebrew Syntax,* p. 79, § 479. The same construction with the negative particle *'ên* occurs in the following verse (43:5).

6. For the sequence subject-predicate in dialogue as opposed to the same sequence in narration (see n. 1 above), see Eskhult, *Studies,* pp. 37ff. In dialogue this sequence does not, as in narration, signal a situation that affects the main course of the narrative.

7. One might also understand the infinitive construct as a gerund in this case — "by telling" *(lᵉhaggîḏ).* See Blau, *Grammar of Biblical Hebrew,* § 96.3.

8. Another illustration of the infinitive absolute plus the perfect to lend intensity to the verb (see n. 3 above).

9. See H. Jackson, "Joseph and His Brother's Beds," *JQR* 72 (1982) 205, for Gen. Rabbah's interesting rendition of "wooden beds" for the MT phrase (91:10: "Said R. Abba, 'He was even able to tell us what sort of wood our beds were made of' "). According to Jackson, R. Abba understood *šāʾal* not as "ask" but as "consult an oracle, divine," and he translates R. Abba's exposition of 43:7 as "the man practiced divination concerning us: he even told us about the wood of our beds."

10. For the use of the infinitive absolute to strengthen a question *(hᵃyāḏôaʿ nēḏaʿ)* see GKC, § 113q. For a comparison with a similar construction in Jer. 13:12 *(hᵃyāḏōaʿ lōʾ nēḏaʿ),* see W. L. Holladay; *Jeremiah,* Hermeneia, 2 vols. (Philadelphia/Minneapolis: Fortress, 1986-89), 1:403-4.

11. The imperfect *(yōʾmar)* may refer to the future from a past point of view. Cf. GKC, § 107k; Williams, *Hebrew Syntax,* p. 31, § 167.

8 *Then Judah urged Israel his father: "Let the lad go with me,*[12] *that we may be off and on our way if any of us is to live and not die — we, and you, and*[13] *our little ones.*

9 *I myself will be surety for him. You can hold me responsible for him.*[14] *If I fail to return him, and set him*[15] *before you, I shall stand condemned before you*[16] *forever.*

10 *Had we not delayed,*[17] *we could certainly*[18] *have been there and back twice*[19] *by now!"*

1 The *land* here can only be the land of Canaan. The famine is now severe *(kāḇēḏ),* a situation conveyed in 41:56, 57 by *ḥāzaq.* The reversal of the order of the subject and verb (*ḥāzaq hārāʿāḇ* in 41:57b and *wᵉhārāʿāḇ kāḇēḏ* in 43:1 draws special attention to the famine.

2 The brothers and Jacob do to their food (*killû, consume* or finish it) what the famine threatens to do the land (*killâ,* "devastate" or finish it, ravage it, 41:30). Jacob casually requests his sons to return to Egypt to get *a little more corn,* as if Egypt is a tad down the road, a place where one can make a quick trip to purchase odds and ends. Has he forgotten the ultimatum of "the man" in Egypt and the terms he laid down for a return visit to Egypt? If he remembered them, then he has consciously ignored them for one reason or other. If he really did forget them, then the brothers must have brought home an ample supply of provisions, large enough to last for a good while, long enough for Jacob to forget that conversation with his sons. Then again,

12. Pesh. has "with us," and is possibly influenced by the following first pl. verbs.

13. The threefold use of *gam (gam ʾᵃnaḥnû gam ʾattâ gam ṭappēnû)* illustrates polysyndeton (the repetition of conjunctions before every word), the opposite of asyndeton (no conjunctions separating words). Judah thus gives special emphasis to three different peoples spread over three generations whose lives may be in jeopardy.

14. Lit., "of/from my hand you shall require him."

15. *hᵃḇîʾōṯîw* ("I fail to return him") and *wᵉhiṣṣagtîw* ("and set him before you") are two instances of future perfects in the protasis of a conditional sentence. See Davidson, *Hebrew Syntax,* p. 62, § 41c; p. 177, § 130b; J. A. Hughes, "Another Look at the Hebrew Tenses," *JNES* 29 (1970) 23-24.

16. Or "I shall incur the blame of sinning against you"; or "May I be counted as having sinned against you" *(wᵉḥāṭāʾṯî lᵉḵā).*

17. Negative hypothetical clauses are introduced by *lûlēʾ*. In such cases the perfect is used in both the protasis *(hiṯmahmāhᵉnû)* and the apodosis *(šaḇnû).*

18. *kî* with *ʿattâ* introduces a climactic affirmation or gives force to predication; see J. Muilenburg, "The Linguistic and Rhetorical Usages of the Particle *kî* in the Old Testament," *HUCA* 32 (1961) 138; Williams, *Hebrew Syntax,* p. 73, § 449.

19. The demonstrative *zeh* before *paʿᵃmāyim* is an enclitic, employed as an undeclined particle for emphasis before a numerical expression. See Williams, *Hebrew Syntax,* p. 24, § 118.

perhaps he hopes his sons have a short memory, and that they will take off for Egypt without Benjamin.

3-5 Judah now steps forward as the spokesman for the group. He reminds his father of the guidelines established for them by *The man* (Joseph) in 42:15ff. They will not even see Joseph again unless their younger brother is with them. Nowhere in 42:15ff. does Joseph say as much to his brothers. Judah may be offering a loose paraphrase of Joseph's words in 42:18-20 to convince his father of the extremity of the situation. Or Judah's words could be a deliberate embellishment. Or perhaps they are exact remarks of Joseph to his brothers to which we, the readers, do not have access.[20] The man in Egypt is in control. The game will have to be played by his rules.

Judah's words to Jacob obviously presuppose a previous visit to Egypt by the brothers, and presumably that is the journey described in ch. 42. The problem with this explanation is that many source critics attribute ch. 42 to E and ch. 43 to J. The implication of this division is that Judah's words as recorded in ch. 43 refer to a trip to Egypt other than that referred to in ch. 42. The major reasons for tracing chs. 42 and 43 to E and J respectively are as follows. Judah is paramount in this section, whereas Reuben was preeminent in ch. 42 (v. 37). Judah is alleged to be prominent in J and Reuben in E. Again, Jacob is called "Israel" in ch. 43 (vv. 6, 8, 11), and that name is an indicator of E. Finally, Simeon's imprisonment in Egypt (ch. 42, E) does not resurface or appear as a motive for the brother's return to Egypt — but what about vv. 14b and 23b? It appears to us that reading ch. 43 as a sequel to ch. 42 has less problems than reading it as a juxtaposition to ch. 42, and such an interpretation makes unnecessary the invention of an earlier but unmentioned trip by the brothers to Egypt.[21]

Judah will not usurp his father. The brothers will not grab Benjamin and run. Joseph's word is final in Egypt; Jacob's word is final in Canaan. Still, Judah's speech lacks logical finesse (and maybe deliberately so). In effect he says to his father: "I would rather stay here in Canaan with you and with Benjamin, and eventually die of starvation, than return to Egypt without Benjamin and take my chances." If they stay in Canaan they have no chance for survival at all. If they travel to Egypt, with or without Benjamin, their

20. Savran (*Telling and Retelling,* p. 35; also p. 128 n. 16) observes that if Judah's words to Jacob are a paraphrase of Joseph's earlier words, they are verifiable. If they represent a fanciful embellishment, they are unverifiable. If they represent accurate, verbatim words of Joseph that were not included by the narrator in ch. 42, they are unverifiable but believable.

21. Westermann (*Genesis,* 3:118-20) offers compelling arguments in support of the unity of chs. 42 and 43, that is, reading 43 as succession to 42, not as juxtaposition with 42.

chance for survival rises. The onus is now put on Jacob. Will he consign his family to starvation, and lose Benjamin anyway? Or is he willing to release Benjamin and take his chances? Vv. 11ff. will answer that question.

6 Jacob (here called *Israel*) does not realize how badly his sons have *hurt* (Hiphil of *rāʿaʿ*) him. He rebukes his sons for saying too much, for being so forthright. Even if asked, could they not have blurred the truth? Who better than Jacob knows how not to be completely honest?

It is not apparent why the patriarch is suddenly called *Israel* in this chapter. Westermann's hesitant suggestion that originally 43:6, 8, 11 had "Jacob" and that "Israel" represents a deliberate alteration of the text is unconvincing.[22] He admits that there is no discernible motive for such an alteration. I suggested in my comments to ch. 42, following Longacre, that "Jacob" represents the suffering, human, feeling side of the patriarch, while "Israel" is used to underscore the office and the dignity of the patriarch. While in ch. 43 we do see the hurting side of Jacob (v. 6), he emerges as the clan head who gives directions to his sons about a second visit to Egypt, and commits their journey to the protection of God almighty, El Shaddai. It is as "Israel" that he thus functions in ch. 43.[23]

7 Once again, as in v. 3, the brothers give a paraphrase of their previous dialogue with Joseph. Ch. 42 did not record any questions of Joseph like: "Is your father still living?" or "Do you have another brother?" On the contrary, they seem to be the ones volunteering familial data. Either the brothers are inventing these imaginary questions of Joseph, in order to let themselves escape with impunity, or else the dialogue as recorded in ch. 42 is not complete.

The double use of an infinitive absolute in this verse before a finite verb (*šāʾôl šāʾal,* “"he asked expressly," and *h^{a}yāḏôaʿ,* "how could we possibly know") parallels the double use of an infinitive absolute before a finite verb in Lev. 10:16, 18: "Moses insistently inquired [*dārōš dāraš*] about the goat of the sin/purification offering . . . you certainly ought to have eaten it [*ʾāḵôl tōʾḵ^{e}lû*] in the sacred precinct." According to the brothers, Joseph asked several pointed questions that caught them off guard. Moses was equally penetrating with his questions about the proper eating of the sacrifice.[24]

8-10 It is interesting that Judah should refer to Benjamin as *a lad (naʿar).* Benjamin is no child. Joseph is at least thirty-seven, and Benjamin can only be a few years younger than he at most. One item that qualifies Benjamin as a *naʿar* is his unmarried status, not his specific age, which is

22. See ibid., 3:119.

23. See Longacre, *Joseph,* p. 150.

24. See J. Milgrom, *Leviticus 1–16,* AB (New York: Doubleday, 1991), p. 625.

irrelevant; but that is most unlikely the reason for Judah's use of *naʿar* for Benjamin.[25] It is Benjamin's relative youthfulness, rather than celibacy, that Judah emphasizes with his choice of *naʿar.* This term must surely play on Jacob's emotions. Benjamin is still young, hence vulnerable (see, e.g., Isa. 13:18; 40:30, which stress the vulnerability of the *naʿar*). This is the only time in the OT where a brother refers to one of his own brothers as a *naʿar,* and coupled with the brothers' earlier use of "your brother" (vv. 3, 7) and "our brother" (vv. 4, 5), this statement cements Judah's fraternal bond with Benjamin. Jacob can trust Benjamin with Judah.

Better than Jacob, Judah knows that they have no alternative. He succinctly reminds his father that if he persists in his refusal to relinquish Benjamin they will *all* die, three generations of them — *we, you, and our little ones.* To cement his plea, Judah offers to *be surety* for Benjamin in case anything happens to Benjamin. The Hebrew verb is *ʿāraḇ* II,[26] which is often used in Proverbs to urge cautiousness and hardheaded assessment of financial risks when one assumes the debts of another, particularly one whom you do not know well (Prov. 6:1; 11:15; 17:18; 20:16; 22:26: 27:13).

Judah's *You can hold me responsible* is literally "of my hand you shall require him." This idiom is close to one used in several passages in Ezekiel which liken the prophet to a sentry. If the prophet does not warn the wicked, Yahweh will require the blood of the wicked at the prophet's hand (Ezek. 3:18, 20; 33:8). All use the phrase *mîyaḏ bāqaš* to convey the sense of personal responsibility. Judah's proposal differs from that of Reuben. The latter was willing to put the lives of two of his sons on the line (42:37). Judah is prepared to place his own life on the line.[27] For a brief moment Judah drops his diplomatic, compassionate language and in essence rebukes his father for procrastinating and not acting more swiftly, possibly engaging in a bit of sarcastic hyperbole (v. 10).

25. In 41:12 Joseph himself was called a "Hebrew *naʿar;*" see my comment there. Cf. also its use with Joseph in 37:2, when he is 17 years old.

26. G. R. Driver (*The Assyrian Laws* [Oxford: Clarendon, 1935], p. 144 n. i) draws attention to Old and Middle Assyrian tablets stating that the debtors, if they fail to pay what they owe, "shall enter the house" *(ana bīt . . . ērubu)* of their creditors, or that the property belonging to the debtor "shall enter the house" *(a bīt . . . ērab)* of the creditor, or simply that the debtor "shall enter" if he does not pay his debt. This use of the Akkadian verb *ērubu,* and the noun "pledge" derived from it *(erubadu)* is the source for Hebrew *ʿāraḇ* II and *ʿērāḇôn.*

27. There are some differences as well as between Judah's word to Jacob in v. 8 and Judah's earlier words to Jacob (vv. 4-5). There he used the Piel of *šālaḥ* for "sending" Benjamin *(mᵉšallēaḥ).* Here he uses the Qal of *šālaḥ (šilḥâ),* softest in tone. Finally, he changes "our brother" to "the lad."

2. ISRAEL GRANTS PERMISSION FOR BENJAMIN TO LEAVE (43:11-14)

11 *Israel their father said to them: "If this is the way it must be, then do this: take in your vessels from the best products*[1] *of the land, and bring down for the man a gift — some balm, some honey, gum, myrrh, pistachio nuts,*[2] *and almonds.*[3]

12 *Twice as much money*[4] *take with you. The money which was returned in the mouth of your bags you must return.*[5] *Perhaps it was a mistake.*

13 *And your brother take. Up and*[6] *on your way to the man.*

1. For *zimrâ* (in the expression *mizzimraṯ hā'āreṣ*), S. E. Loewenstamm suggests that the phrase may point to the existence of songs (*zimrâ* is from *zāmar,* "to sing," rather than from "to be strong") that mention the choicest products of the land in their praise ("The Lord is my strength and my glory," *VT* 19 [1969] 467 n. 2). BDB, pp. 271 and 272, distinguishes between *zimrâ,* "song," and *zimrâ,* "choice products," in 43:11, which it labels a hapax legomenon. Loewenstamm rejects the idea that Heb. *zimrâ* represents two different Proto-Semitic roots, *zmr,* "sing," and *ḏmr,* "strength, protection" (contra F. M. Cross, Jr., and D. N. Freedman, "The Song of Miriam," *JNES* 14 [1955] 241, 243 n. b). Y. Avishur ("The 'Duties of the Son' in the 'Story of Aqhat' and Ezekiel's Prophecy on Idolatry (ch. 8)," *UF* 17 [1986] 52-53) translates the phrase as "take some of the perfumes of the land."

2. On *boṭnîm,* "pistachio nuts," see H. R. Cohen, *Biblical Hapax Legomena in the Light of Akkadian and Ugaritic,* SBLDS 37 (Missoula, MT: Scholars, 1978), pp. 35-36, who connects the Hebrew word with Akk. *buṭnu, buṭṭutu.* See also W. F. Albright, "Some Comments on the 'Amman Citadel Inscription," *BASOR* 200 (1970) 37-40.

3. On *šᵉqēḏîm* cf. M. J. Dahood, "Qoheleth and Recent Discoveries," *Bib* 39 (1958) 312, who points out that the Hebrew root is now attested in Ugar. *ṯqd.* See *UT,* 2 Aqht (= *CTA,* 17) VI:20, *wy'n aqht ġzr adr ṯqdm,* "And Aqhat the hero replied: 'Cut almond trees.' " In an earlier article ("Some Aphel Causatives in Ugaritic," *Bib* 38 [1957] 64) Dahood observed that the almond tree is native to Western Asia but was unknown in ancient Egypt. Thus "it was only natural for a Hebrew to presume that Palestinian almonds would be prized in Egypt." Unfortunately, the reading of the key word, *ṯqdm,* is disputed: *UT* reads *'qbm* and *CTA* and *KTU* read *ṯqbm.*

4. This is actually a case of apposition, *keseᵽ mišneh,* "money, double," unless one reads *keseᵽ* as a construct ("money of double amount"). See GKC, § 131e. In v. 15 *mišneh* precedes *keseᵽ,* on which see Waltke and O'Connor, *Biblical Hebrew Syntax,* p. 286.

5. For *šûḇ* in the Hiphil with the meaning of restoring property or an inanimate object cf. D. Daube, *The Exodus Pattern in the Bible* (London: Faber and Faber, 1963), p. 83 and n. 6; W. L. Holladay, *The Root Šûbh in the Old Testament* (Leiden: Brill, 1958), pp. 90-91. For the presence of a modal imperfect ("you must return") in hortatory/persuasive discourse, see R. E. Longacre, "Discourse Perspective on the Hebrew Verb: Affirmation and Restatement," in *Linguistics and Biblical Hebrew,* ed. W. R. Bodine (Winona Lake, IN: Eisenbrauns, 1992), pp. 186-87.

6. With a few Heb. mss., SP, and Pesh. read *wᵉšûḇû* for MT *šûḇû.* The *waw* ("and") prefixed to *šûḇû* was perhaps inadvertently omitted because of the concluding *waw* on the preceding word *(wᵉqûmû).*

14 *May El Shaddai be merciful to you in the man's presence, and may he send back your other*[7] *brother with you, and Benjamin too. But if*[8] *I am to be bereaved,*[9] *bereaved I shall be."*[10]

11 *Israel* (i.e., Jacob) has no other option — he must let his sons return to Egypt for more food. In order to make the brothers' return to Egypt as smooth as possible, Jacob suggests that they take with them as presents some of the choicest products of the land. It seems strange to be talking about the best products of the land in a time of famine. Whence come these products? There is a shortage of corn (v. 2), but nuts and some resinous materials seem readily available. The brothers' traveling down to Egypt recalls an earlier group (the Ishmaelites) traveling down to Egypt with much the same products (gum, balm, and myrrh). Missing from that first caravan was the honey and the nuts.

Jacob's suggestion that they take a *minḥâ,* a gift, to Jospeh recalls Jacob's earlier sending of a *minḥâ* to his estranged brother Esau (32:14-22 [Eng. 13-21]; 33:8-11). The gift or present that Jacob sent to Esau was clearly intended to appease his brother, a means of winning or buying forgiveness and reconciliation. No such ulterior motives appear here. Rather, Jacob's actions reflect appropriate etiquette and protocol when visiting the headquarters of a foreign dignitary (i.e., "the man," v. 13).

12 The double amount of money the sons are to take with them back to Egypt represents the return of the money that was in their sacks plus something extra for the purchase of more corn. Perhaps the money in the sack got there by somebody's *mistake (mišgeh)*[11] — the brothers' mistake, or the man's mistake

7. LXX and SP read *hā'eḥāḏ* (lit., "the one") for MT *'aḥēr,* "other." Citing Judg. 11:1 as a parallel, M. Margalit (" 'From Another Place' — Esther 4:14, "*Beth Mikra* 31 [1985/86] 6-9 [Hebrew]) suggests that *'aḥēr* was sometimes used to avoid mentioning an obvious and well-known name. The LXX and SP represent an attempt to normalize Hebrew grammar, but some attributive adjectives like *'aḥēr* are intrinsically definite.

8. For conditional sentences introduced by *ka'ᵃšer,* see Davidson, *Hebrew Syntax,* p. 179, § 130, Rem. 4.

9. Jacob used this verb, *šāḵal,* in 42:36, where it appeared in the Piel with the meaning "make childless." For the use of the perfect *(šāḵōltî)* to express actions or facts as existing in the future in a completed state, see GKC, § 106o. It is thus a proleptic perfect.

10. See M. L. Klein, "Converse Translation: A Targumic Technique," *Bib* 57 (1976) 523-24, who notes that with the exception of Targ. Jonathan, all the Palestinian Targs. produce the converse translation, "Just as I have not been bereaved of Joseph, so shall I not be bereaved of Simeon nor of Benjamin." This converse translation reflects the rabbinic tradition that the patriarchs were endowed with prophetic powers (cf., e.g., Gen. Rabbah 84:19).

11. BDB, p. 993, lists *mišgeh* as a hapax legomenon, but the verb from which it is derived, *šāgâ / šāgag,* is used frequently (cf. Lev. 4–5) to refer to inadvertent sin. See J. Milgrom, "The cultic ŚᵉgĀgĀ and its influence in Psalms and Job," *JQR* 58 (1967) 115-25.

(and if Jacob intends it to be Joseph's, then he is trying to convince himself that "the man" is negligent but still trustworthy). Jacob, formerly adept at taking something away from somebody by stealth, now insists that his sons keep nothing that is not legitimately theirs. Jacob is clearly in charge of making arrangements for the journey to Egypt. His words to his sons are filled with imperatives, a total of seven in this unit: three in v. 11 ("do, take, bring down"), one in v. 12 ("take"), three in v. 13 ("take, up, on your way").[12]

13 Jacob mentions taking the money back (v. 12) before he mentions taking Benjamin back (v. 13). The order indicates what is most difficult for Jacob. He has no problems sending the money. Releasing Benjamin is something else. The inevitable is contained at the end of Jacob's parting words. Note Jacob's laconic reference to Benjamin as *your brother,* not "Benjamin" or even "my son," which he used in 42:38.

14 Jacob did not invoke deity when he first sent his sons to Egypt (42:2). But he is in a dilemma now over not just food but family. Neither Simeon's absence nor Benjamin's departure weighed heavy on his heart that first time. Now, however, the problem is complicated and complex. It is fitting, therefore, that Jacob invokes *El Shaddai* (see 17:1; 28:3; 35:11; 49:25 [perhaps]; Exod. 6:3).[13] In each of these passages that do refer to El Shaddai, he is a deity who is blessing, making promises and covenants, and revealing himself. How appropriate it is, then, for Jacob to use the name El Shaddai when he is in the circumstances he is in, and appealing to a God of mercy. His hope and prayer is that El Shaddai *be merciful (yittēn raḥ^{a}mîm)*[14] to them. What Jacob means by *be merciful* is spelled out in his next phrase: *and may he* [the man? El Shaddai?] *send back your other brother with you, and Benjamin.* Jacob is more interested in his sons than in more corn, and his sympathies are more with Benjamin than with Simeon, whom he simply calls *your other brother.*

Jacob has no guarantee El Shaddai will do anything. His *if I am to be bereaved, bereaved I shall be* is the same construction as Esther's "if I perish, I perish" (Est. 4:16), *ka'^{a}šer* followed by two first person perfect verb forms.[15]

12. See the analysis of this section by Longacre, *Joseph,* p. 124. He labels vv. 11-14 a "hortatory coordinate paragraph."

13. According to source analysis, all these texts are in P, except for this one (which is J). Thus the text must have originally had Jacob using the tetragrammaton Yahweh; then, centuries later, an editor contemporary with P or subsequent to P replaced Yahweh with El Shaddai for reasons completely unknown.

14. Cf. Deut. 13:18; Jer. 42:12 for the formula *nāṯan raḥ^{a}mîm l^{e}* with deity as subject. In Gen. 43:14 the preposition plus suffix precede the pl. noun.

15. On linguistic and thematic parallels between Esther and the Joseph story see S. B. Berg, *The Book of Esther: Motifs, Themes, and Structure,* SBLDS 44 (Missoula, MT: Scholars, 1979), pp. 123-42.

It is a statement of resignation, of a willingness to accept the worst possible scenario. He does believe, however, that El Shaddai will be the one to make the final decision about the destiny of Benjamin. Neither Judah nor "the man" has that authority.

3. THE BROTHERS RETURN TO EGYPT (43:15-25)

15 *So the men took this gift, and double the amount of money*[1] *they took with them, and Benjamin. They set out and went down to Egypt, where they presented themselves before Joseph.*

16 *When Joseph saw with them*[2] *Benjamin, he said to*[3] *his steward:*[4] *"Bring the men into the house, and have a beast slaughtered*[5] *and prepared, for with me the men are to dine at noon."*

17 *The man did as Joseph said, and the man brought the men into Joseph's house.*[6]

1. On *mišneh keseP̱* (versus *mišnēh kesep̱,* i.e., the construct, read by 25 Heb. mss.) see GKC, § 131p-q, who describes the phrase as a "case of apposition in a wider sense" ("a double amount in money").

2. LXX, Vulg., and SP read "when Joseph saw them [*'ōṯām*] and [*wᵉ'eṯ*] Benjamin."

3. For a nominal clause introduced by *la'ᵃšer,* see BDB, p. 82a; GKC, § 138e; J. W. Watts, *Survey of Syntax in the Hebrew Old Testament* (Grand Rapids: Eerdmans, 1964), p. 125; Waltke and O'Connor, *Biblical Hebrew Syntax,* pp. 334, 335.

4. Lit., "to him who was over his house" *(la'ᵃšer ʿal-bêṯô).* Cf. S. C. Layton, "The Steward in Ancient Israel: A Study of Hebrew *('ăšer) ʿal-habbayit* in Its Near Eastern Setting," *JBL* 109 (1990) 633-49, who distinguishes between a private steward (the unnamed steward over Joseph's household) and a royal steward (Joseph over Pharaoh's palace).

5. Lit., "and slaughter a slaughter" *(ûṭᵉḇōaḥ ṭeḇaḥ).* For the verb *ṭāḇaḥ* used with slaughtering or butchering animals for food, cf. Exod. 21:37; Deut. 28:31; 1 Sam. 25:11; Prov. 9:2. The verb appears with a cognate accusative here and in 1 Sam. 25:11 *(ṭāḇaḥ ṭiḇḥâ). ṭāḇaḥ* is used always in the OT with profane slaughter (as is Ugar. *ṭbḥ*), whereas the verbs *zāḇaḥ* and *šāḥaṭ* are used for sacred slaughter. See J. Milgrom, "Profane Slaughter and a Formulaic Key to the Composition of Deuteronomy," *HUCA* 47 (1976) 14; idem, "Ethics and Ritual: The Foundations of the Biblical Dietary Laws," in *Religion and Law,* ed. B. Firmage, B. G. Weiss, and J. W. Welch (Winona Lake, IN: Eisenbrauns, 1990), p. 173.

6. The expression *bêṯâ yôsēp̱* shows that the locative or directional ending *-â* may intervene between a bound form and its genitive. See GKC, § 90c; Williams, *Hebrew Syntax,* p. 14, § 62; Waltke and O'Connor, *Biblical Hebrew Syntax,* p. 185. J. Hoftijzer (*A Search for Method: A Study in the Syntactic Use of the H-Locale in Classical Hebrew* [Leiden: Brill, 1981], p. 19 n. 36) states that there is a distinct difference in function between *bêṯ,* "house," with the directional *-â* when it is preceded by the article (as in v. 16, *habbāyᵉṯâ*) and when it is not (as in v. 17, where *bêṯâ* is in the construct state). "*hbyth* always has a local-terminative function and *byth* a locative function."

18 *The men became apprehensive*[7] *when they were taken into Joseph's house. They said: "Because of the money put back*[8] *in our bags the first time we were brought here; he wants to overpower us and seize us,*[9] *and take us into slavery along with our donkeys."*

19 *So they approached Joseph's steward and spoke to him at the entrance of the house.*

20 *"If you please,"*[10] *they said, "we came down once before for the sole purpose*[11] *of purchasing corn.*

21 *When we arrived at the lodging spot and opened*[12] *our bags, there was each man's money at the top of his bag, our money in its full weight. We have brought it back*[13] *with us.*

22 *And more silver we have brought with us to purchase corn. We do not know who placed our money in our bags."*

23 *He replied: "Rest assured,*[14] *do not be startled. Your God and*[15] *the God of your father*[16] *must have put a treasure*[17] *in your bags. I received your money." Then he brought out to them Simeon.*

7. Lit., "were afraid." Sperber (*Historical Grammar of Biblical Hebrew,* p. 638) takes *wayyîr^{e}'û* from *rā'â,* "to see," and reads the second *yodh* as a *mater lectionis* — "and when the men saw that they were brought into Joseph's house."

8. SP reads *hammûšāḇ* (Hophal participle), as in v. 12, instead of MT *haššāḇ* (Qal participle). For the relative participle used for action completed in the past, see Waltke and O'Connor, *Biblical Hebrew Syntax,* p. 623.

9. Lit., "that they may roll themselves over us and throw themselves on us." See P. P. Saydon, "Assonance in Hebrew as a Means of Expressing Emphasis (II)," *Bib* 36 (1955) 289-90.

10. On the formula *bî 'ᵃḏōnî* (43:20; 44:18) see J. Hoftijzer, "David and the Tekoite woman," *VT* 20 (1970) 427 and n. 2. *bî* is best explained as a contraction of *b^{e}'î,* from the root *b'h,* "ask, entreat," hence "Please, I beg." See R. Gordis, "Personal Names in Ruth — A Note on Biblical Etymologies," *Judaism* 35 (1986) 299 n. 3. BDB, p. 106, connects it with a verb *bāyay* (only Job 34:36), "entreat."

11. So translated to capture the effect of the infinitive absolute followed by the perfect *(yārōḏ yāraḏnû).* See GKC, § 113l-q.

12. For the pseudo-cohortative with *waw- (wanniptᵉḥâ)* to refer to past time, see Waltke and O'Connor, *Biblical Hebrew Syntax,* p. 577.

13. *nāšeḇ* instead of the expected *nāšîḇ* for the 1st pl. Hiphil imperfect (1 Sam. 6:4; 1 K. 12:9; 2 Chr. 10:9; Neh. 5:12); the *waw* conversive draws the accent off the final syllable to the penultimate syllable, hence reducing the vowel in the final syllable.

14. Lit., "peace to you." Cf. S. E. Loewenstamm, "Ugaritic Formulas of Greeting," *BASOR* 194 (1969) 52-53.

15. The *waw* may be explicative: "your God, i.e., your father's God."

16. LXX and SP read "God of your fathers." G. R. Driver ("Once Again Abbreviations," *Textus* 4 [1964] 80) accounts for the different readings by seeing in MT the omission of a medial letter or letters by way of abbreviation.

17. *maṭmôn,* "(hidden) treasure," derives from the verb *ṭāman,* "hide, conceal."

24 *The man brought the men into Joseph's house;*[18] *he gave them water to wash their feet, and he gave their donkeys fodder.*

25 *They made ready the present for Joseph's arrival at noon, for they had heard that they were to dine*[19] *there.*

15 Jacob's offspring, until now identified as "sons" of Jacob/Israel or "brothers," are from this point on styled simply as *the men (hā'ᵃnāšîm).* Kinship terms cease. It is the men going to see the man. The use of this term by Joseph in the following verse is understandable. But its use first by the narrator in v. 15 is perhaps surprising.

Jacob knows what it means, from previous experience, for a person in a vulnerable position to send or take a *gift (minḥâ)* to one who appears to be in control of the situation. He had his own *minḥâ* sent to Esau (32:14, 19, 21, 22 [Eng. vv. 13, 18, 20, 21]; 33:10, 11). Esau accepted reluctantly Jacob's *minḥâ* (33:11b). In ch. 43 no further word is said about the present the brothers brought apart from the narrator's few words in vv. 25, 26; we do not know if Joseph ever accepted it.

Benjamin does not speak throughout this ordeal. Does he willingly join his brothers on their trip back to Egypt, or does he share his father's reservations? The postponement of *Benjamin* to the last of three accusatives accentuates the heart-wrenching agony of the release: *the men took this gift, and double the amount of money they took with them,* and *Benjamin.* "The 'and Benjamin' hangs like the resigned sigh of a father trapped between the need to live and the possibility of a life made utterly empty through another loss."[20]

16-17 Again, as in ch. 42, Joseph and his brothers encounter each other. V. 16 almost seems to suggest that Joseph was waiting and watching for them, so sure he was that they would return — with Benjamin. At least, he saw them before they saw him. Upon sighting them, he instructs his steward[21] to usher the brothers into his house and to prepare a noon meal at which the men will join Joseph as his invited guests. Joseph's actions parallel those of the father in Jesus' parable who, on the return of his delinquent son,

18. The LXX omitted this whole clause, most likely because v. 17 already stated that the men were brought into Joseph's house. This deletion misses the ingressive thrust of the causative of *bô'* in v. 17 and the terminative thrust of the same in v. 24 (Speiser, *Genesis,* p. 328).

19. Lit., "eat bread" *(yō'ḵᵉlû lāḥem).* Only *yō'ḵᵉlû* was used by Joseph back in v. 16.

20. Humphreys, *Joseph and His Family,* p. 45.

21. The steward, or "the one over his/Joseph's house," is in this unit three times simply called "the man" (vv. 17 [twice], 24). In the preceding chapter Joseph was "the man" (42:30, 35), as well as earlier in ch. 43 (vv. 3, 5, 6, 7).

gave orders "to bring the fatted calf and kill it" (Luke 15:23). Here is a group of eleven men who have endured years of famine in which all food, including meat, has been in short supply, and now they are to be guests at a banquet. It is Joseph who gives the orders, just as Israel did in the preceding section. The steward's obedience to those orders parallels the brothers' obedience to their fathers' imperatives. Thus the first part of v. 17 emphasizes the obedience of the steward. The second part of the verse tells how he obeyed and expedited his responsibilities.

18 The invitation to the meal produces in the brothers apprehension rather than gratitude. It is a trick, a lure, they think. The man's purpose in inviting them into his house is to entrap them. They will be at his mercy, and he will be free to do with them as he pleases, even reducing them to servitude if he so chooses. This will be the man's way of punishing them for absconding with his money. "For the guilty, even hospitality can seem ominous."[22] It never dawns on the brothers that Joseph has enough authority to have them arrested on the spot without having to resort to a dinner invitation. It does not take much imagination to see that what the brothers fear might happen to them at the hands of Joseph — *he wants to overpower us and seize us, and take us into slavery* — is precisely what they once did to Joseph. In addition, the brothers must have been surprised or alarmed by this cordial treatment, when on their first visit they had been treated roughly and accused of spying (42:7ff.).

19 In hopes of averting disaster, the brothers approach Joseph's steward and speak to him *at the entrance to the house.* They want to state their case while they are still outdoors. As in v. 15, which also refers to the activities of the brothers, a motion or positional verb ("approached, set out") precedes another verb ("spoke, went down"). In such cases the first verb essentially modifies the second ("setting out, they went down; approaching, they said").[23]

20-22 The brothers speak as a chorus. They tell of their first trip to Egypt (v. 20), their return to Canaan on which they found the money in their sacks at a lodging spot (v. 21), their second trip to Egypt to procure food (v. 22a), and lastly their claim of innocence with regard to the money (v. 22b), using the verb *placed,* not "returned," as they (42:28), as well as the narrator (42:25), had earlier. For smoothness one might have expected v. 22b to precede v. 22a, and thus follow immediately on v. 21. The sequence shows that the brothers' concern is not to give geographical data about their journeys but to proclaim their innocence. Of course, they are volunteering information that has not been solicited. No accusations have been made against them; they

22. Humphreys, *Joseph and His Family,* p. 83.
23. For this phenomenon in the Joseph story, see Longacre, *Joseph,* p. 72.

are not in the dock or under scrutiny. It is of interest that the brothers say much about their past and their character, but they say nothing about Benjamin. There are no introductions, no "here is our youngest brother whom your supervisor insisted we bring back if we were ever to see him again." It should be noted that nothing the brothers say in vv. 20-21, 22b involves Benjamin. He was not on that first visit. He stopped at no lodging spot. He had no bag of corn into which somebody slipped money.

23 We know from this verse that Joseph has already informed his steward about his brothers and the restored money. Probably it was this same steward to whom Joseph gave the order in the first place to replace the money in the brothers' grain bags (42:25). It is most unlikely that the steward is himself making up this explanation about how the money got into their bags. He is passing along the answer Joseph instructed him to give. Joseph's later disclaimer "am I in the place of God?" (50:19) might not be wide of the mark as an affirmation here. That is, while the steward states that it is God who has put the treasure in their bags, we know that it was Joseph who gave orders that the silver be returned to the sacks (42:25). What we know, the brothers do not know. "Its [viz., the steward's response] dark ambiguity touches the innermost mystery of the whole Joseph story: God's concealed guidance."[24]

The steward claims that *God . . . must have put a treasure* [*maṭmôn*] *into your bags.* He avoids using the word *kesep,* "money." The word he does use (see Job 3:21; Prov. 2:4; Isa. 45:3; Jer. 41:8) is more dramatic. It refers specifically to buried treasure, as can be seen with the verb *ṭāman,* "to bury" (Gen. 35:4; Exod. 2:12). It was treasure, but they did not have to excavate far to find it. It was at the "mouth" of their bags.

The brothers must still be outside or near the entrance of Joseph's house, for the steward *brought out* Simeon to them. One might have expected the recording of a happy reunion scene between Simeon and his brothers, but none is related. Simeon's release was tied to the appearance of Benjamin in Egypt. That requirement now met, Simeon is given his freedom. If the brothers are elated to see him alive and free, then the narrator does not record that jubilation. Earlier, when the brothers first returned from Egypt, they never mentioned Simeon by name to Jacob. They only quoted Joseph's terms for his release (42:33). At the beginning of ch. 43 the brothers appear in no particular hurry to return to Egypt to liberate Simeon, for they do not return to Egypt until their rations are used up (43:1, 2). Yes, Simeon is free now. Yes, they are off the hook as suspected thieves. But doxology may be premature. They are still in Joseph's house, or the house's courtyard. Only when they leave Egypt will they be able to breathe easily.

24. See von Rad, *Genesis,* p. 388.

24-25 The brothers are now conducted into Joseph's house and treated as guests. Their donkeys are fed, and they are given water with which to wash their feet. The mention of *their feet (raḡlêhem)* here recalls Joseph's repeated charge in ch. 42 that his brothers were really "spies" *(m^e^ragg^e^lîm).* Those Joseph once suspected were in his country traveling around on foot as spies now have their feet washed.

All the reassurance given to them by the steward has not allayed their fears. They are not about to dispose of the present they have brought for Joseph. The presentation to Joseph of some choice food products from Canaan can only improve their standing with "the man."

4. JOSEPH AND BENJAMIN MEET (43:26-34)

26 *When Joseph entered the house, they brought*[1] *inside*[2] *to him the gift in their possession, and they bowed before him*[3] *to the ground.*

27 *After greeting them,*[4] *he asked: "How is your elderly*[5] *father of whom you spoke? Is he still alive?"*

28 *They replied: "Your servant our father is well and still alive." And they bowed*[6] *and prostrated themselves.*[7]

29 *When he looked up and saw Benjamin his brother, his mother's son,*[8]

1. In *wayyāḇî'û* the *'aleph* has a *mappiq,* a dot inside a Hebrew letter that indicates that the letter is to be regarded as a full consonant; cf. GKC, § 14d. Only four instances of *mappiq* with *aleph* occur in the Hebrew Bible: Gen. 43:26, Lev. 23:17; Ezra 8:18; Job 33:21.

2. Only Vulg. among the ancient versions deletes *habbāy^e^ṯâ,* a reading followed by Westermann, *Genesis,* 3:118. The second appearance of "house" indicates that the brothers were not yet inside.

3. LXX and Vulg. add *'appayim,* "(their) faces."

4. Lit., "he asked about their peace," or "he asked regarding them concerning peace." On "to ask the peace" as a technical and diplomatic phrase see D. J. Wiseman, "'Is it peace?' — Covenant and diplomacy," *VT* 32 (1982) 322. This expression means that Joseph has nonhostile intentions toward these men, and that he is prepared to negotiate. See also E. F. Sutcliffe, "A note on *'al, l^e^* and *from,*" *VT* 5 (1955) 439, for a discussion of the phrase; and Y. Avishur, "Studies of Stylistic Features Common to the Phoenician Inscriptions and the Bible," *UF* 8 (1976) 19-20.

5. For a substantive *(hazzāqēn)* used with the force of an adjective ("your father, the elderly one") see Williams, *Hebrew Syntax,* p. 15, § 67.

6. *qāḏaḏ* is used frequently with *yištaḥû* (on which see p. 219 n. 11) in worship of deity (Gen. 24:26, 48; Exod. 4:31; 34:8; Num. 22:31) or in homage to individuals of rank (here; 1 Sam. 24:9; 28:14; 1 K. 1:16, 31).

7. LXX and SP add: "and he [Joseph] said: 'Blessed is that man by God.'"

8. For the practice of forming a hendiadys from pairs of words employed in synonymous parallelism see the examples cited in M. Held, "Philological Notes on the

he said: "Is this your youngest brother of whom you spoke to me?"
And he said: "May God be gracious[9] *to you, my son."*
30 *Joseph exited hastily*[10] *because he was deeply moved*[11] *for his brother, and was on the verge of*[12] *tears. He went into his room*[13] *and wept there.*
31 *Then he washed his face, returned, and now self-controlled*[14] *he ordered: "Bring on*[15] *the meal."*
32 *They served him by himself, and them by themselves, and the Egyptians*

Mari Covenant Rituals," *BASOR* 200 (1970) 37. He notes in the Mari text under discussion the expression *hayarum mar atānim,* "a donkey foal, the young of a she-ass," as a hendiadys. For *'aḥ* parallel with *ben-'ēm* cf. Deut. 13:7; Judg. 8:19.

9. On *yoḥnᵉḵā* rather than the expected *yᵉḥonᵉḵā* (here and in Isa. 30:19) see GKC, § 67n, who observes this rare instance of a verb with identical second and third radicals *(ḥnn)* in which the *o* vowel is thrown back to the preformative. For *ḥānan* in a formula of greeting, see J. Milgrom, *Numbers,* JPS Torah Commentary (Philadelphia: Jewish Publication Society, 1990), p. 361, who renders 43:29, "May God be gracious to you, my boy!"

10. See E. Vogt, "Einige hebräische Wortbedeutungen," *Bib* 48 (1967) 66, who comments on *mhr* as a verb of going, sometimes without the expected or understood accompanying verb. But here is an instance of *mhr* used in tandem with another verb *(wayᵉḇaqqēš),* with *mhr* modifying the second verb. Thus Longacre (*Joseph,* p. 71) renders this verse: "And Joseph hurried (for his emotions were stirred concerning his brothers). And he looked [for a place] to cry."

11. Lit., "his compassion (or emotion) boiled over." The same phrase occurs in 1 K. 3:26, except there it has the preposition *'al* instead of *'el.* Waltke and O'Connor (*Biblical Hebrew Syntax,* p. 386) call *wᵉniḵmerû* an ingressive stative ("grew hot").

12. For this nuance for *wayᵉḇaqqēš,* see Sarna, *Genesis,* p. 302.

13. Targ. Onqelos reads "bedroom" *(byt mškb'),* thinking perhaps it would be the one place in his residence where Joseph could have complete privacy.

14. For *'āp̱aq* (only in the Hithpael) cf. Akk. *epēqu,* "be strong." The verb appears seven times in the OT. In a few of these at least the meaning is clearly "control, restrain one's feelings, pull oneself together" (Gen. 43:31; Est. 5:10; Isa. 64:11). The meaning in the other texts is less clear. I shall discuss the occurrence of the root in Gen. 45:1 later. Scholars have interpreted 1 Sam. 13:12b (Saul's words of explanation to Samuel why he offered the sacrifice) in two ways. On the one hand, if *'āp̱aq* has the same meaning here as in Gen. 43:31, then Saul is telling Samuel that he, in distressful circumstances, pulled himself together and offered the sacrifice. For this understanding see D. J. McCarthy, "Hero and Anti-Hero in 1 Sam. 13,2–14,46," in *Institution and Narrative: Collected Essays,* AnBib 108 (Rome: Biblical Institute, 1985), p. 252 and n. 6. On the other hand, R. Gordis (*The Word and the Book* [New York: Ktav, 1976], pp. 186, 187) suggests that *'āp̱aq* means not only "get control of oneself" but "lose control of oneself," and he renders 1 Sam. 13:12b, "I could not control myself any longer," or "I lost control of myself" (cf. NIV "I felt compelled to offer").

15. See M. Greenberg, *Ezekiel 1–20,* AB (Garden City, NY: Doubleday, 1983), p. 175, who calls this the authoritative (royal) imperative.

who dined with him by themselves, because Egyptians could not[16] *eat a meal with Hebrews. It is anathema to the Egyptians.*[17]

33 *They were seated at his direction,*[18] *the firstborn by his seniority and the youngest by his youth. The men looked at each other in astonishment.*

34 *He passed*[19] *a portion*[20] *from what was before him to them, but Benjamin's portion was several times*[21] *larger than the portions of all the others. And they feasted and drank with him.*

26 Joseph returns to his house after an unexplained absence, as Potiphar returned to his house after an absence on business (39:16b). His brothers silently follow him into his home, ready with the presentation of their gift, and do homage before him. The *gift* is never mentioned again. Joseph is more interested in their family than in their gift. They must not speak until they are spoken to.

16. *yûḵᵉlû* illustrates the use of the frequentative or habitual use of the imperfect. See Williams, *Hebrew Syntax,* p. 31, § 168.

17. The MT is lit.: "It is anathema to Egypt." It is simple enough to read *lammiṣrîm* for *lᵉmiṣrāyim* (so *BHS*). Targ. Onqelos both explains the reason for the segregation of foreigners from Egyptians and avoids any notion that the Hebrews were an abomination to any non-Hebrews by freely rendering this final clause, "for the Hebrews eat the cattle that the Egyptians worship."

18. Or, "in front of him" *(lᵉpānāyw).* See Speiser, *Genesis,* p. 329, who observes that if we translate "in front of him" then the arrangement of the brothers in order of their ages would be either a coincidence or the result of previous instructions by Joseph that had not been recorded. Accordingly Speiser attaches to the phrase the meaning "at the direction of, by the will of."

19. LXX and Pesh. read pl., "they passed" *(wayyiśśʾû),* for MT sing. *(wayyiśśāʾ),* an interpretation that implies that the brothers served themselves.

20. On *maśʾōṯ* in Ezek. 20:40 see Greenberg, *Ezekiel 1–20,* p. 375. The noun comes from *nāśāʾ,* "bear, offer [gift]." B. Levine (*In the Presence of the Lord* [Leiden: Brill, 1974], p. 17 n. 40) observes that the noun means both "tax levy" or "tribute" (Amos 5:11; Est. 2:18) and "ration, allotment" (Gen. 43:34; 2 Sam. 11:8; Jer. 40:5). He goes on to say that this noun "reflects the graphics of both the politico-economic and cultic situations, whereby a gift is presented by lifting it up, or where a tax is 'carried away' from persons (*Hipʿil* of *nāśāʾ*)."

21. Lit., "five hands" *(ḥāmēš yāḏôṯ).* For *yāḏ* meaning "shares" or "portions," see G. Robinson, "The Meaning of *yād* in Isaiah 56:5," *ZAW* 88 (1976) 283; and E. W. Davies, "The Meaning of *pî šᵉnayim* in Deuteronomy xxi 17," *VT* 36 (1986) 343. "Five" as a stylistic device is common in the Joseph story (41:34; 43:34; 45:6, 11, 22; 47:2, 24). R. Gordis (*Poets, Prophets, and Sages* [Bloomington: Indiana University, 1971], p. 101 n. 5) draws attention to the importance of five as a round number in rabbinic literature and the NT, and suggests that the use of "five" in the Joseph story may be due to Egyptian influence. He does not provide any substantiation for that suggestion, however. Cf. *ANET,* p. 28a, which reports Ta-net-Amon's several fivefold gifts.

27-28 Joseph first inquires about their well-being; then about their father's state of health. Jacob is here qualified as *elderly (hazzāqēn).* Joseph's immediate reference to the brothers' father shows to them that he has forgotten none of the family history they shared with him on their first visit to Egypt (42:11-13).[22] Joseph's question *Is he still alive?* is more than polite conversation. In times of natural catastrophes the highest casualties are among the very young and very old. Has Jacob been able to tolerate the effects brought on by famine? If the reference in v. 26 to the brothers bowing before Joseph (and also 42;6) recalls the emphasis on bowing in Joseph's earlier dreams (37:7, 9, 10), so does the frequent use of the word *šālôm* in both Joseph's inquiry and their response recall something from ch. 37. There, because they saw their father doting on Joseph, the brothers could not speak peaceably to Joseph (37:4). A few verses later (37:14) Jacob sent Joseph to see if it was well *('eṯ-šālôm)* with his brothers and with their flocks. Earlier the brothers could not speak to each other in peace, but now when they speak to each other there is "a veritable burst of *šālôms.*"[23]

Using a polite form of address, the brothers identify Jacob to Joseph as *your servant.* But how can this be when they are miles apart, live in different countries, speak different languages, and have never met? This title is a gesture by the brothers to identify themselves as those favorably disposed toward and dependent on Joseph. Even their father assumes that posture.

29 Joseph must *look up,* for he is staring down at the party kneeling in front of him. Upon surveying the group he spots a stranger, one who was not there on the previous trip. This one must be Benjamin, but to make sure, he asks the group: *Is this your youngest brother?* So, before Benjamin becomes an addressee, he is a topic. This is Joseph's way of being as casual as possible, which is part of his subterfuge. When Joseph asked his first question (v. 27b), he gave his brothers time to respond. When he asks his second question, he allows no time for a response. Instead, he moves directly from the question to a blessing: *May God*[24] *be gracious to you, my son.* This blessing must have raised some eyebrows among Benjamin's brothers. Why has "the man" never said anything like that to any of them? Joseph's reference to Benjamin as *my son* does not mean that Benjamin was still quite young, or that they differed substantially in age. This is part of Joseph's disguise and role playing. He is

22. At no point does Joseph make any inquiry about their mother. While the brothers earlier identified themselves to Joseph as "sons of one man," they did not, naturally, add "and the sons of several mothers." The Joseph story is about men and their invovlement with each other. Even their sister Dinah never surfaces in the narrative.

23. Humphreys, *Joseph and His Family,* p. 95.

24. The order of the Hebrew (*'ĕlōhîm yoḥneḵā benî,* "God be-gracious-to-you my-son") allows Lowenthal (*Joseph Narrative in Genesis,* p. 86)) to say that Joseph's "first word to his brother Benjamin is 'God.' "

wearing enough of a mask to appear as an elder statesman of Egypt addressing a Hebrew *naʿar* (43:8). His position of authority permits the use of such a vocative when speaking to a person of lower status.

30-31 Joseph's feelings — *he was deeply moved* — are naturally for his full brother, not for his half-brothers. Weeping will give away his subterfuge. People in power do not normally weep publicly, although they may make others weep. We wonder what explanation, if any, Joseph offered for leaving the room. What, if anything, is passing through the brothers' minds at this moment? A few minutes later he returns, face washed and emotions under control. The real Joseph can remain cloaked for a while longer. These two verses, along with v. 29, are an illustration of what Longacre calls a "stimulus-response" paragraph. Joseph sees Benjamin and makes a few remarks (v. 29, the stimulus). Joseph's response to the stimulation of seeing Benjamin is to withdraw from the room, wash his face, and return to the group only when he has his emotions in control. Longacre notes that such stimulus-response paragraphs are rare in the Joseph story, and "they seem to feature in especially dramatic parts of the story."[25]

32 The meal is served to three different groups: Joseph, the brothers, and Joseph's Egyptian colleagues. But they cannot be that far apart, for Joseph is close enough to them to "pass" food to them (v. 34). Still, cultic taboos forbade Egyptians eating with Hebrews.[26] They will sell and share food with Hebrews, but will not share a table with Hebrews. For a second time Joseph is separated from his brothers at meal time (see 37:25 for the first). But he is no helpless occupant of an empty cistern this time. At the first meal separation he was the victim. Here he is the victor. At least he does not deprive his brothers of food, as they once deprived him.

33 This verse seems as though it ought to precede v. 32. The seating (v. 33) normally comes before the serving (v. 32). Joseph is careful to arrange the brothers in the order of their ages. The verse concludes with *the men looked at each other in astonishment.* Why astonishment? Is it because of the royal carpet that has been rolled out for them? Or, more likely, is it because Joseph was able to seat the brothers by age without consulting them? Such a perfect seating plan would hardly be accidental. The phrase "*the men* looked at each other in astonishment" may include not only the brothers, who are taken aback with Joseph's knowledge of their birth order, but also the Egyptians present at the meal, who are surprised by Joseph's hospitality extended to these foreigners.

34 Joseph is hinting about his identity to his brothers without saying as much. For example, he sees to it that Benjamin's portion of food is sub-

25. Longacre, *Joseph,* p. 204.
26. See Redford, *Study of the Biblical Story of Joseph,* p. 235.

stantially larger than that of his brothers. Joseph received the extra coat; Benjamin receives the extra portion. The brothers certainly observe this, but under the circumstances can show no reaction. The extra portions given to Benjamin may be compared with the rich provisions offered to the Hebrew youths in the Persian court (Dan. 1:5) for the purpose of increasing their beauty or maintaining their attractiveness and wholesome appearance, and especially with the portions *(mānôṯ)* that Hegai, keeper of the women of Vashti's harem, offered to Esther (Est. 2:9). In the case of both Benjamin and Esther, the extra portions have a symbolic function rather than an actual benefit. Obviously, Benjamin will not eat five times as much as his brothers; and the basic needs of all the women in Vashti's harem would not have been neglected. Both extra provisons are signs of favor.[27]

This is more than a meal. It is closer to a banquet — lots of food and plenty of drink to wash it down. The chapter concludes with *And they feasted and drank with him.* The Hebrew reads literally, "they drank and got drunk with him." Spirits are abundant and spirits are high. Speiser observes that the phrase depicts "a convivial, but not necessarily indecorous, occasion."[28]

H. BENJAMIN — A THIEF? (44:1-34)

1. JOSEPH'S GOBLET PUT IN BENJAMIN'S SACK (44:1-5)

1 *Then [Joseph]*[1] *ordered his steward: "Fill the men's bags with corn, as much as they are able to carry, and put each man's money in the mouth of his sack.*

2 *And my goblet,*[2] *the silver goblet,*[3] *put in the mouth of the youngest one's bag, together with the money for his rations." And he did what Joseph told him.*

27. M. V. Fox, *Character and Ideology in the Book of Esther* (Columbia, SC: University of South Carolina, 1991), pp. 31-32.

28. Speiser, *Genesis,* p. 329.

1. Added by LXX.

2. Heb. *gāḇîaʿ* (used only in Exod. 25:31-34; 37:17-20 for the golden cups of the candlestick, and in Jer. 35:5) may be connected with Eblaite *lú ga-bí,* "man of the cup." See M. J. Dahood, "Eblaite and Biblical Hebrew," *CBQ* 44 (1982) 8 n. 18, 23. L. Koehler ("Hebräische Etymologien," *JBL* 59 [1940] 36) links it with Egyp. *ḳbḥ.w,* "libation vessel."

3. On *geḇîʿî geḇîaʿ hakkesep̱,* the use of apposition when a pronominal suffix refers to a noun in a chain that cannot be suffixed, see Waltke and O'Connor, *Biblical Hebrew Syntax,* p. 304.

3 *At the first light of morning, the men were sent off,*[4] *they and their donkeys.*

4 *After they had barely left*[5] *the city,*[6] *Joseph said to his steward: "Up, pursue the men. When*[7] *you have overtaken them, say to them: 'Why have you returned evil for good?*

5 *Is*[8] *it not the one from which*[9] *my master drinks and moreover the one in which he practices divination?*[10] *You have done a detestable thing.' "*

1 Sometime after the completion of the meal Joseph orders his steward to fill the mens' sacks with corn, and for a second time, to put their money back into the sacks. A number of modern commentators[11] would delete *and put each man's money in the mouth of his sack* (v. 1) and "together with the money for his rations" (v. 2) as intrusive phrases, for the restored money is not mentioned again in the chapter. The brothers are accused of taking Joseph's goblet, but not of absconding with their money which was payment for more

4. Synchronism or simultaneous action is indicated by two perfects with the subject preceding: *habbōqer 'ôr* [lit., "the morning grew light"] *wᵉhā'ᵃnāšîm šullᵉḥû.* See Williams, *Hebrew Syntax,* p. 42, § 235.

5. Lit., "they, they left the city. They had not caused themselves to be far [i.e., 'had not gone far']." One can understand the use of the perfect in *lō' hirḥîqû* as an attributive or circumstantial clause referring to the past ("not having gone far"); so Davidson, *Hebrew Syntax,* p. 63, § 41, Rem. 3. Or one might say that *lō' hirḥîqû* is a subordinate verbal clause in which the subject of the second verb *(hirḥîqû)* is the same as that of the first verb *(yāṣᵉ'û);* so GKC, § 156f. For the Hiphil *(hirḥîqû)* used intransitively, see R. Gordis, *The Word and the Book* (New York: Ktav, 1976), p. 136 n. 7.

6. For the accusative particle *'eṯ* after *yāṣā'* see N. Kinberg, "Notes on the Shift from Accusative Constructions to Prepositional Phrases in Hebrew and Arabic," *BSOAS* 44 (1981) 9. For the separative use of the accusative *'eṯ,* cf. Williams, *Hebrew Syntax,* p. 12, § 55 ("only after *yāṣā*'").

7. The equivalent to a subordinate, conditional sentence occurs when both the protasis *(wᵉhiśśaḡtam)* and the apodosis *(wᵉ'āmartā)* have *waw* plus perfect. Cf. Davidson, *Hebrew Syntax,* p. 180, § 132a.

8. LXX inserts at the beginning of v. 5, "Why have you stolen my silver goblet?" The addition is probably not original. See the commentary on v. 5. Some (e.g., Westermann, *Genesis,* 3:130; J. Barr, "Why? in Biblical Hebrew," *JTS* 36 [1985] 29 n. 11) accept LXX as the correct text.

9. For *šāṯâ bᵉ* meaning "to drink from" see GKC, § 119m n. 1, and *HALAT,* 4:1538. The latter refers to a cuneiform text from Mari (ARM, 10:129.11): *ina kās išattu,* "the cup from which he drank" (see W. von Soden, *Akkadische Handwörterbuch,* 3 vols. [Wiesbaden: Harrassowitz, 1965-81], 3:1202b).

10. Wanting to dissociate Joseph from any participation in forbidden religious activity, Targ. Onqelos freely rendered this part of the verse: "and he, moreover, carefully tests with it" *(whw' bdq' mbdyq byh).*

11. For example, Speiser, *Genesis,* p. 333; Westermann, *Genesis,* 3:130.

food. I suggest that the money does not resurface in the narrative because it is overshadowed by the stolen goblet. Joseph has no desire to indict his brothers a second time on being money thieves. The restored money is, accordingly, inconsequential.

2 It is now Benjamin's turn to be victimized. Joseph instructs his steward to place Joseph's *silver goblet* at the mouth of Benjamin's bag. It is not enough that the brothers have run off with *kesep̱* owed to Joseph for the food; one of them has run off with Joseph's *gᵉḇîaʿ hakkesep̱*. It would be easy for one of the brothers to slip the goblet into his bag. They have just finished a feast with Joseph; perhaps the goblet was temptingly placed on the eating table. At least it had to be displayed or stored in a place where the guests had access to it or could observe it, and thus later they could be charged with theft. It is unlikely that they would have had the chance to burglarize Joseph's house while they are his guests. It could be hid under one's coat or shirt, then slipped unobtrusively into the food bags. Joseph's *goblet (gāḇîaʿ)* is made of silver, but in Jer. 35:5 *gāḇîaʿ* is a common ceramic pitcher, about 8 or 10 inches in height, for holding either wine or water. That is, it is more likely (in Jer. 35) a serving vessel than a bowl from which one drinks.[12] But in Gen. 44 and Exod. 25, 37 the *gāḇîaʿ* is a cup rather than a pitcher.

3-4 All seems well. The brothers leave Egypt early in the morning. They have been fed. They have more corn to take back with them to Canaan. Simeon has been released. Benjamin is with them and unharmed. Joseph orders his steward to chase the brothers down and to charge them with being ungrateful (v. 4b)[13] and with being thieves (v. 5). It must by now be clear to the unnamed steward that Joseph is up to something, for Joseph had already informed the steward about his brothers (43:23). Joseph's first order to put the money back into their sacks (42:25) would have, accordingly, aroused no suspicion. As far as the steward was concerned, that was simply a display of magnanimity. But one does not clandestinely place a treasured vessel into the bag of another, send him on his way, overtake him, and accuse him of thievery. If he did not state it verbally, the steward at least inwardly questioned the propriety of Joseph's directive. Why is his superior going to all these lengths in order to place trumped-up charges against these Hebrews, who are his brothers? It is possible that the steward

12. See A. M. Honeyman, "The Pottery Vessels of the Old Testament," *PEQ* 71 (1939) 80; J. L. Kelso, *The Ceramic Vocabulary of the Old Testament,* BASOR Supplementary Studies nos. 5-6 (New Haven: American Schools of Oriental Research, 1948), p. 17; idem, "Pottery," *IDB,* 3:851. For a contrary view, i.e., that *gāḇîaʿ* means "drinking bowl" in Jer. 35:5, see *HALAT,* 1:166.

13. For the phrase *šallēm rāʿâ taḥaṯ ṭôḇâ* ("repaying evil for good") see Ps. 35:12; 38:21 (Eng. 20).

may have interpreted, at least initially, Joseph's instructions to place his goblet in Benjamin's bag as a "parting mark of favor,"[14] much like the larger portions of food Joseph assigned to Benjamin (43:34) when he was wining and dining his brothers.

5 What makes the cup in Benjamin's sack so valuable is that it is Joseph's own cup, and *the one in which he practices divination (naḥēš yᵉnaḥēš).*[15] The force here of the infinitive absolute *(naḥēš)* before the verb is uncertain; usually it lends extra emphasis to the verb.[16]

Drinking goblets can be replaced more easily than divination goblets. The form of divination referred to here is oleomancy (pouring oil into water) or hydromancy (pouring water into oil), or the more general term lecanomancy (observing the actions of liquids in some kind of a container). When water and oil are mixed, configurations form which are then studied and interpreted by the diviner. Do the movements portend peace/war, success/failure, progeny/no progeny, recovered health/prolonged sickness, etc.? So important was divination in Mesopotamia that divinatory texts developed into the largest single category of Akkadian literature in terms of sheer number of texts.[17]

Eating with Hebrews was anathema for the Egyptians. Attempting to ascertain the will of deity by studying the movements of oil and water was not. The first of these was an "abomination" for the Egyptians (43:32b). The second of these was an abomination for the Hebrews (Lev. 19:26; Num. 23:23; Deut. 18:10).[18] Only later did the Hebrews "become Egyptian" in their attitude to eating with others. Recall the Samaritan woman's surprise that Jesus would even drink water with her (John 4:9). But neither the Egyptians nor anybody in antiquity ever "became Hebrew" in their repudiation of divination techniques.

14. Sternberg, *Poetics of Biblical Narrative,* p. 303.

15. The verb *niḥēš* (Piel) is most likely connected with the verb *lāḥaš,* "to whisper, pronounce an incantation," in conjunction with the use of goblets or cups. See B. Levine, *Leviticus,* JPS Torah Commentary (Philadelphia: Jewish Publication Society, 1991), pp. 133, 208 n. 32 (under Lev. 19:26).

16. See GKC, § 113n. The same construction occurs in v. 15.

17. See W. W. Hallo and W. K. Simpson, *The Ancient Near East: A History* (New York: Harcourt, Brace, Jovanovich, 1971), pp. 158-63. Hallo observes that in Mesopotamia lecanomancy (divination from observing liquids), because it was cheaper than extispicy (divination from animal entrails), was used more by private citizens than by the king.

18. See Y. Kaufmann, *Religion of Israel,* tr. and ed. M. Greenberg (New York: Schocken, repr. 1972), pp. 87-91; and J. Milgrom, "Balaam: Diviner or Sorcerer?"(excursus 59), in *Numbers,* JPS Torah Commentary (Philadelphia: Jewish Publication Society, 1990), pp. 471-73.

2. THE GOBLET IS FOUND IN BENJAMIN'S BAG (44:6-17)

6 *When he overtook them he repeated*[1] *to them these words.*

7 *But they protested:*[2] *"How can my lord say such things. May it be (reckoned) a desecration*[3] *to your servants if they have done anything like this!*

8 *Look, the money*[4] *which we found in the mouth of our bags we even brought back to you from the land of Canaan. Why, then, would we steal from your master's house silver or gold?*

9 *If any*[5] *of your servants is found to have it, he shall die;*[6] *and as for the rest of us, we shall become my lord's slaves."*

10 *He replied: "What you have proposed is proper*[7]*; only he with whom it is found shall become my slave. The rest of you shall go free."*

11 *Each*[8] *of them quickly lowered his bag to the ground, and each opened his bag.*

12 *He searched, beginning*[9] *from the eldest and ending with the youngest. And the goblet was found in Benjamin's bag.*

13 *Thereupon they tore their clothing, each loaded*[10] *his donkey, and returned to the city.*

1. Lit., "he said/spoke" *(way^eḏabbēr).*

2. Lit., "they said" *(wayyō'm^erû).* Cf. Speiser's "they remonstrated."

3. For an explanation of *ḥālîlâ* see the commentary below on v. 7.

4. Reading *hakkesep̱* with LXX, SP, and Pesh., rather than MT *kesep̱.*

5. For the rare use of *'^ašer* as an indefinite pronoun, see Waltke and O'Connor, *Biblical Hebrew Syntax,* p. 334 n. 13.

6. On the use of *waw* plus perfect *(wāmēṯ)* in the apodosis of a conditonal sentence after the protasis starting with *'^ašer* and the imperfect *(yimmāṣē),* see GKC, § 112ii. SP reads *yûmaṯ,* "he shall be put to death." Cf. also Targ. Onqelos, "let him be put to death" *(ytqṭl),* which moves v. 9 beyond curse to actual punishment for thievery (but see D. Daube, *Studies in Biblical Law* [New York: Ktav, repr. 1969], p. 236).

7. Lit., "also now it shall be according to your words."

8. In vv. 11 and 13 *'îš* (lit., "man," here translated "each") takes both sing. and pl. verbs. On the distributive use of *'îš* see GKC, § 139b, c.

9. See P. P. Saydon, "The Inceptive Imperfect and the Verb *hēḥēl* 'to begin,' " *Bib* 35 (1954) 48, in which *hēḥēl* denotes "with a certain degree of emphasis the commencement of a single action, the accomplishment of which is, in some cases, also recorded." For the perfect with participial force, see Davidson, *Hebrew Syntax,* p. 63, § 41, Rem. 3.

10. Although appearing almost exclusively in later OT books (Neh. 4:11 [Eng. 17]; 13:15; Zech. 12:3; and cf. Ps. 68:20 [Eng. 19]; Isa. 46:1, 3), the root *'ms* occurs in earlier Phoenician and Ugaritic texts. For the former see the Eshmunazar inscription (*KAI,* 14.5-6, 21): *w'l l' y'msn bmškb z,* "and may he not *carry me away* from this resting place." For the latter see *UT,* 62:I:10-12 (*CTA,* 6.I.10-12): *gm tṣḥ lnrt ilm špš 'ms m'ly aliyn b'l,* "loudly she calls unto the gods' Torch Shapsh, *lift* Puissant Baal, I pray, Onto me." Translations are those of Y. Avishur, "Word Pairs Common to Phoenician and Biblical Hebrew," *UF* 7 (1975) 27.

14 *When Judah and his brothers reached Joseph's house, he was still there. They fell on the ground before him.*

15 *Joseph said to them: "What is this you have done? Are you not aware that a man like myself practices divination?"*[11]

16 *Judah said: "What can we say*[12] *to my lord? How*[13] *can we speak! How can we justify ourselves!*[14] *God has found your servants' misdeeds. We are my lord's slaves, both we and the one in whose possession the goblet was found."*

17 *He replied: "It would be a desecration for me to do this; the one in whose possession the goblet was found shall be my slave; the rest of you may go back without incident*[15] *to your father."*

6 Thus far in the Joseph story and elsewhere in Genesis (e.g., ch. 24), we have encountered many instances of recapitulation. For example, Joseph sets out the terms about Simeon and Benjamin to the brothers (43:18-20). Shortly thereafter, upon arrival back in Canaan, the brothers repeat that speech to their father (43:33-34). So we have a speech within a speech. Here is one of the few places where the original directives (or in this case, a charge of theft) are not repeated. All that is recorded is the steward's expediting of Joseph's criminal charges.

7 The brothers deny their participation in such an act of theft (v. 7a), and in effect take an oath to that end (v. 7b). Most translations[16] render *ḥālîlâ lᵉ* something like "far be it from. . . ." It appears, however, that *ḥālîlâ lᵉ* is usually used to introduce an oath, and is found in the third person (here and Job 34:10), but most often in the first person (e.g., 44:17; Josh. 22:29; 24:16; 1 Sam. 2:30; 12:23; 14:45; 22:15; 26:11; 2 Sam. 20:20; 23:17; 1 Chr. 11:19; Job 27:5).[17] *ḥālîlâ* is a substantive meaning *desecration,* and the form *ḥālîlâ*

11. As in v. 5, Targ. Onqelos reads "makes careful tests" for MT "practices divination."

12. On the placement of a *dagesh forte* in the *nun* after *mah* (3 times in v. 16), see GKC, § 37b, c.

13. "How" is a legitimate translation of *mah* (see Num. 23:8; 1 Sam. 10:27; Job 19:28), esp. in exclamatory sentences. See Williams, *Hebrew Syntax,* p. 24, § 126; Waltke and O'Connor, *Biblical Hebrew Syntax,* p. 326.

14. *niṣṭaddāq* is the Hithpael of *ṣāḏaq* ("to be just, righteous"), and it is the only time in the OT that the verb appears in this stem. With the Hithpael, if the first radical is a sibilant, the *ṯ* of the prefix *hiṯ-* follows it, instead of preceding it. If the first radical is *ṣ* (as in *ṣāḏaq*) the *ṯ* shifts to *ṭ* by partial assimilation. See GKC, § 54b. On self-justification or self-vindication as something contemptible, cf. Luke 10:29; 16:15; 18:8, 14; 20:20.

15. Lit., "for/in peace" (peacefully), *lᵉšālôm.* Speiser renders "without hindrance."

16. Speiser, Westermann, NJPS, NKJV, RSV, NRSV, NAB, NIV.

17. See J. Milgrom, "The Priestly Doctrine of Repentance," *RB* 82 (1975) 189 n. 11. Cf. also M. R. Lehmann, "Biblical Oaths," *ZAW* 81 (1969) 82-83. He connects

*l*ᵉ . . . *'im/m* . . . is an elliptical oath formula (hence I placed "reckoned" in parentheses in my translation of v. 7), referring specifically to oath violation.

8 The third way in which the brothers deny complicity in the theft is by appealing to their own previous conduct. Would those who earlier returned the money found in their bags be so foolish to steal something valuable and sacred from the steward's master? According to the Midrash (Gen. Rabbah 92:7) Rabbi Ishmael (2nd century A.D.) remarked: "this is one of the ten instancs of *qal wa-ḥomer* [i.e., the argument from the minor to the major] in the Torah [i.e., the Bible]." The other nine are Exod. 6:12; Num. 12:14; Deut. 31:27; 1 Sam. 23:3; Jer. 12:5 (twice); Ezek. 15:5; Prov. 11:31; Esth. 9:12.[18]

9 In three ways the brothers have attempted to refute the steward's charge: by denial (v. 7a), by oath (v. 7b), and by appeal to earlier behavior (v. 8). Now comes a fourth response. If the goblet *is found (yimmāṣē')* with any of the brothers, that brother *shall die (wāmēṯ),* that is, be executed, and the rest of the brothers will become slaves of the steward. This is the ultimate appeal from the brothers, who are now cast in the role of defendants. Although they do not explicitly request a hearing, it is clear they are making such an appeal.[19]

The brothers are asserting more than they should. They suggest that mere possession of the goblet is sufficient evidence to establish guilt. This emphasis on possession of the stolen matter as a sufficient evidentiary test is found in laws like Exod. 21:16, "Whoever steals a man, whether he sells him or is found in possession of him [*w*ᵉ*nimṣā' ḇ*ᵉ*yāḏô*], shall be put to death"; or Exod. 22:3 (Eng. 4), "If the stolen beast is found alive in his possession [*himmaṣē' timmāṣē' ḇ*ᵉ*yāḏô*] . . . he shall pay double." Besides these legal parallels, one thinks of the narrative parallel involving Jacob and Laban. Charged with stealing Laban's teraphim, Jacob retorts: "Any one with whom you find [*timṣā'*] your gods shall not live" (Gen. 31:32). As Daube states: "In both these cases . . . the crime is aggravated not only by the fact that it concerns holy objects [teraphim, a divining goblet] but also by being *manifestum:* the thief is pursued very soon after he has committed the crime and the pursuer searches his home."[20]

ḥālîlâ with Akk. *elêlu/ullulu,* "erase," and translates *ḥālîlâ* as "erasure," i.e., "may there be erasure unto me (from God) if I break the oath," or more freely: "may I be erased, eliminated, if I break the oath."

18. Modern logicians would call v. 8 an a fortiori argument. The construction here in which the first part of the defense is introduced by *hēn* ("look"), and the following part of the defense by an interrogation introduced by *w*ᵉ*'êḵ* ("why, then"), is the same as that of Joseph's words of defense in 39:8, 9.

19. See M. B. Dick, "The Legal Metaphor in Job 31," *CBQ* 41 (1979) 45, and pp. 41ff., for his discussion of the defendant in ancient Near Eastern civil law.

20. Daube, *Studies in Biblical Law,* p. 101 n. 28.

Note that the brothers themselves decide on the harshest sentence: *he shall die.* They do not say "he deserves to die"; they do not appeal to divine judgment. The thief is to be executed for committing a capital offense. That Jacob orders the death of the person who stole Laban's teraphim, or that Joseph's brothers suggest the death penalty for the one guilty of stealing Joseph's goblet, cannot be used as proof for the existence of a special category of theft — stealing sancta. Indeed, v. 5 would suggest (the words that Joseph instructs his steward with which to charge his recently departed brothers) that the men would not even know it was Joseph's own cup or that it was used for sacred purposes. Jacob's sentence merely illustrates the total power of the paterfamilias. Joseph's brothers are so certain of their innocence that they can afford this extravagant offer.[21] It is a demonstration of their confidence in and conviction about their innocence. At one point Jacob's proposed sentence is different from that of Joseph's brothers. Jacob admitted liability of the actual theft. The brothers were prepared to admit communal liability. But one can be generous with proposals when one is convinced that little is at stake.

10 The steward responds. He begins by agreeing legally with the brothers. Their self-sentence is most appropriate in these circumstances. But then he proceeds to modify their proposal in two ways. First, the thief himself should not be killed, but enslaved. Second, the rest of the brothers should not be enslaved, but freed *(n^e^qîyim).* The basic meaning of *nāqâ* (see 24:8, 41) is "be clean, pure." Here it takes on the derived sense of "free from servitude."[22] It is ironic that the accused suggest a severer penalty and the accuser suggests a lighter penalty.

This difference on suggested penalty may be due to more than mercy on the steward's part. A unique feature of Egyptian law (in contrast to cuneiform law) is that both witnesses and the accused were allowed to propose their own punishment for perjury or the crime in the form of an oath (as in v. 9). The steward knows that if the cup is found in Benjamin's sack (or anybody's sack for that matter) their suggested punishment will be binding, and thus Benjamin will be condemned to death. To circumvent that possibility, the steward deliberately ignores or mishears them and accepts only that portion of their self-imposed sentence that will be acceptable to Joseph.[23]

11 The eleven brothers quickly take their bags off their donkeys and

21. See Jackson, *Theft in Early Jewish Law,* pp. 63, 110; Phillips, *Ancient Israel's Law Code,* p. 141, esp. n. 68; Milgrom, *Cult and Conscience,* p. 91.

22. See D. R. Hillers, "*Bĕrît ʿām:* 'Emancipation of the People,'" *JBL* 97 (1978) 179.

23. For this interpretation see R. Westbrook, *Studies in Biblical and Cuneiform Law* (Paris: Gabalda, 1988), pp. 128r31; also J. A. Wilson, "The Oath in Ancient Egypt," *JNES* 7 (1948) 129-56.

place them on the ground. It is something they do on their own initiative, without being requested to do so. They have nothing to hide, they believe. They stop short of the actual investigative process. Their responsibility is simply to expose, or make available for search, the bags, one of which is suspected of containing the stolen goblet.

12 The steward proceeds to search *(ḥāpaš)* the bags of the men. This is the same verb used in 31:35 to describe Laban's search of Jacob's tents for his teraphim. In both of these cases the person who has the stolen items (Rachel knowingly, Benjamin unknowingly) is the last to be investigated by the pursuer. Laban starts in Jacob's tent, moves to Leah's tent, then to the tents of Bilhah and Zilpah, and lastly searches in Rachel's tent (31:33). Joseph's steward starts with the oldest (Reuben) and ends with the youngest (Benjamin). Laban investigates Rachel's tent last probably because he suspects her the least. The steward searches Benjamin's sack last to give the appearance that he suspects Benjamin the least.

This is the second time that the brothers have been arranged by age. The first was at Joseph's table in Egypt (43:33). The way in which the eldest and the youngest are designated in each incident is different. In 43:33 Reuben in *habbᵉḵōr,* but in 44:12 he is *haggāḏôl.*[24] In 43:33 Benjamin is *haṣṣā'îr,* but in 44:12 he is *haqqāṭōn.* The suspense of the situation is brought out in the Hebrew text by its emphasis on the goblet rather than on the steward. Instead of "and he found the goblet in Benjamin's bag," the text says, *and the goblet was found in Benjamin's bag.*

13 Surprisingly, the brothers say nothing to Benjamin, or at least the narrator has not recorded any words. Perhaps they are too stunned to say anything. They tear their clothes to indicate their chagrin, as had their father earlier (37:34) when his sons informed him that Joseph was dead. They no more suspect they are victims of fraud than did their father suspect foul play when he was given the bloodied coat. In neither case is an alternative explanation explored. To their credit they do not at this moment abandon Benjamin, their guilty thieving brother, and head for Canaan as quickly as possible with their new supplies. Instead, they choose to return to Egypt. The brothers' solidarity with their vulnerable, young, guilty brother will not be overlooked by Joseph.

14 The emphasis in this verse is not so much on the return of the brothers to Egypt as on the return of one brother — Judah. The text says: *When Judah and his brothers reached Joseph's house.* The verb *reached* is

24. Longacre (*Joseph,* p. 96; also p. 102) calls 44:12 a "skillful insertion of a narrative comment paragraph at a point of maximum tension" (text: "and he searched" [a preterite]; antithetical paragraph: thesis: "with the oldest he began" [noun plus perfect]; antithesis: "and with the youngest he finished" [noun plus perfect]).

singular *(wayyāḇō')*.[25] The spotlight is not on Reuben but on Judah, for earlier it was Judah who had offered himself as surety for Benjamin (43:8, 9). He will shortly emerge as the spokesman for the group (vv. 18-34). Sternberg notes that the shift in designation for Joseph's brothers from "the men" to "Judah and his brothers" "augurs well both as a reminder of the newly dominant figure and as a hint of solidarity with the brother who has gone surety as well as with the one in obvious trouble."[26]

This is the third time the brothers are admitted to Joseph's presence. The first two (42:6; 43:26) are marked with the formal bowing before one in authority. This time they are more desperate than courteous. They fall *(wayyippᵉlû),* before Joseph.[27]

15 Joseph does not repeat the charge of his steward, but instead accuses them in general terms[28] with the question, *What is this you have done?* Then he upbraids them with the intriguing clause, *Are you not aware that a man like myself practices divination?* The brothers seem to be aware of nothing. In 43:7b they said to Jacob, "How could we possibly know that he would say: 'Bring your brother down here'?"

Joseph's rhetorical question may be interpreted in one of two ways. He may have implied, "Why did you steal my cup? Don't you know I need it for divining?" Or he may have implied, "Did you think you could get away with stealing my cup? You know I am a master of divination and would have found you out, one way or the other." I prefer the second interpretation, for it underscores the utter helplessness of the brothers. They are foreigners in Egypt. They are thieves, or at least one of them is. They are at the mercy of a man who can track them anywhere with his divinatory power.

16 *Judah* speaks for all the brothers, because it was he who most recently was willing to become surety for Benjamin (43:8-10). Judah's proposal is that all of them, including the guilty Benjamin, become Joseph's *slaves*. This is a less severe penalty than the brothers jointly suggested (v. 9). Judah says nothing this time about the execution of the actual thief. At the same time it is still a more severe penalty than that suggested by the steward (v. 10) or by Joseph (v. 17). One is guilty, but all are liable, says Judah. Their willingness to become enslaved to Joseph apparently means they are prepared not to see Jacob again.

Judah's most revealing statement is: *God has found your servants'*

25. When the first of two parallel subjects is sing., the verb often agrees with the first subject and therefore takes a sing. form. But note that the following verb is pl. *(wayyippᵉlû)*. See Blau, *Grammar of Biblical Hebrew,*, p. 88.

26. Sternberg, *Poetics of Biblical Narrative,* p. 305.

27. In 42:6 the brothers came *(bô')* and bowed *(hištaḥᵃwû)* before Joseph. In 44:14 the brothers reached *(bô')* Joseph's house, and fell *(nāpal)* to the ground before him.

28. Note that Joseph uses the pl. "you" *(ʿᵃśîṯem, yᵉḏaʿtem)*.

misdeeds. In a context where so much emphasis has been placed on "finding" a stolen goblet, or "finding" the one who has in his possession a stolen goblet, greater emphasis is given to God "finding" the misdeeds of the brothers. By this statement Judah does not imply that they are all guilty of thievery. Judah knows that he is not! He took no cup. Indeed, Judah does not even concede, or at least draw attention to, the fact that the cup was stolen. What he does say is: "we are my lord's slaves, both we and the one in whose possession the goblet was found." This is God's way, says Judah, of visiting their past misdeeds upon them. They withheld mercy from Joseph (42:21). Now God will withhold mercy from them. They deserve what is happening to them even if they are not guilty of this particular crime. Here is a graphic illustration of the Bible's emphasis on God's justice.[29] The wrongs one does will be repaid, someway, somehow, somewhere.

17 Joseph uses the same oath formula in denying Judah's proposal that the brothers used in v. 7 to deny their involvement in this crime: *It would be a desecration for me to do this.*[30] To enslave the innocent with the guilty, or to condone guilt by association, would be a violation of divine law. Joseph, therefore, supports his steward's proposal. Only the one in possession of the goblet shall be enslaved. The rest are free to return home. The steward's *n^eqîyim* ("go free," v. 10) Joseph replaces with *l^ešālôm* (lit., "for peace," here translated *without incident*). He had used this same word earlier when inquiring about their "welfare" and the "welfare" of their father (43:27).

Joseph's willingness to associate guilt with the person with whom the goblet was found is a case of "substantive irrationality."[31] Mere possession of the corpus delicti is sufficient for an indictment. That is, Joseph's decision is ad hoc. He does not arrive at this position on the basis of rules, but rather on the grounds of how well his sentence will suit his purposes and interests.

Joseph is trusting that the brothers will not accept his counterproposal without protest. They were willing to leave Simeon behind and return to Canaan. Will they now leave Benjamin behind and return to Canaan? Of course, in the first instance Joseph had attached a proviso — "If you want Simeon released and if you want more corn, you must go and bring back your youngest brother." Here Joseph is offering a permanent separation. He does not say: "If you want to see your youngest brother again, go and bring back your father." On the surface, Joseph wants the case closed. Happily, in v. 18 Judah steps forward and offers evidence why Joseph's ruling is unacceptable to them.

29. See Daube, *Studies in Biblical Law,* pp. 248-55; Sternberg, *Poetics of Biblical Narrative,* p. 306.

30. Longacre (*Joseph,* p. 196) describes Joseph's reply in v. 17 as "unctuous and well soaped-over with civility."

31. See M. Fishbane, *Biblical Interpretation in Ancient Israel* (Oxford: Clarendon, 1985), pp. 242-44.

3. JUDAH'S PLEA FOR BENJAMIN (44:18-34)

18 *Then Judah approached him, saying: "Please, my lord, let your servant speak a word in my lord's ears, and be not angry with your servant, for you are Pharaoh's equal.*[1]

19 *My lord asked his servants: 'Have you a father or brother?'*

20 *And we said to my lord: 'We have an elderly father, and a child of his advanced age is young.*[2] *His brother is dead. Since he is his mother's only surviving son, his father dotes on him.'*

21 *Then you said to your servants: 'Bring him down to me, that I may set my eyes on him.'*

22 *We explained to my lord: 'The lad cannot leave his father; if he were to leave him, his father would die.'*[3]

23 *But you stated to your servants: 'If your youngest brother does not come down with you, you shall not see my face again.'*

24 *When we returned to your servant, my father,*[4] *we reported my lord's words to him.*

25 *When our father said: 'Return and purchase a little food for us,'*

26 *we said: 'We cannot go down. Only if our youngest brother is with us, can we go down, for we cannot see the man's face unless our youngest brother is with us.'*

27 *Then your servant, my father,*[5] *said to us: 'You*[6] *know that my wife bore me two sons.*

1. Lit., "your likeness is Pharaoh's likeness," with the subject of a nominal clause being a prepositional phrase (Blau, *Grammar of Biblical Hebrew,* p. 83, § 54 *[ḵāmôḵâ]*). For other instances of k^e . . . k^e passages (here *kî ḵāmôḵâ k*^{e}*par'ōh*) that involve the function of classifying groups or persons, see Gen. 18:25; Lev. 24:16, 22; Deut. 1:17; Josh. 8:33; 1 Chr. 25:8; 26:13; 2 Chr. 31:15; and S. J. DeVries, "The three comparisons in 1 Kings xxii 46 and its parallel and 2 Kings iii 7b," *VT* 39 1989) 285-86. Judah's purpose is to classify Joseph as comparable to Pharaoh in terms of rank. B. A. Levine (*Numbers 1–20,* AB [New York: Doubleday, 1993], p. 393) suggests that "such phrasing probably reflects the spoken, conversational language of biblical times."

2. Waltke and O'Connor (*Biblical Hebrew Syntax,* p. 492) identify *qāṭān* as an adjectival present perfective, in which the use of the verb, more than the adjective, directs attention to the subject's involvement.

3. Conditional sentences may be expressed by consecutive perfect verb forms in the protasis and apodosis. See GKC, § 159g; Williams, *Hebrew Syntax,* p. 85, § 512.

4. SP, Pesh., and 2 Hebrew mss. read "our father." Cf. vv. 25, 27, 30.

5. LXX and Vulg. read "our father." See also vv. 24, 25, 30.

6. On the addition of the pronoun *'attem* before the pl. verb *y*^{e}*ḏa'tem* to give emphasis not only to the verb but to the whole expression, see Davidson, *Hebrew Syntax,* p. 152, § 107, Rem. 1.

28 *One disappeared from my presence and I assumed that he must surely*[7] *have beeen ravaged by beasts; I have not seen him since.*

29 *Now, if you take this one too from me, and tragedy befalls him, you will bring down my white head in grief to the underworld.'*

30 *And so,*[8] *if I were to come to your servant, my father, and the lad, with whom his life is bound up, were not with me,*

31 *when he sees the lad is missing, he would die,*[9] *and your servants would bring the white head of your servant, my father, in sorrow to the underworld.*

32 *Besides, your servant has pledged himself for the boy to my father,*[10] *saying: 'If I do not bring him back to you,*[11] *I shall stand condemned before my father forever.'*

33 *And so, please let*[12] *your servant stay here instead of the lad as a slave to my lord, and let the lad return with his brothers.*

34 *For how can I return to my father if the lad is not with me? I could not look on the ill fate*[13] *that would overtake*[14] *my father."*

7. N. H. Snaith ("The Meaning of the Hebrew *'aḵ,*" *VT* 14 [1964] 224-25) points to Gen. 44:28; Judg. 3:24; 20:39; 1 Sam. 16:6, where *'aḵ* introduces supposed truth which in fact is incorrect. See also Williams, *Hebrew Syntax,* p. 65, § 389, for the asseverative meaning of *'aḵ.*

8. For this meaning of *w^{e}ʿattâ* in v. 30, and again in v. 33, see H. A. Brongers, "Bemerkungen zum Gebrauch des adverbialen *w^{e}ʿattāh* im alten Testament," *VT* 15 (1965) 296 (v. 30), 294 (v. 33).

9. For the perfect consecutive *(wāmēṯ)* as the apodosis announcing future events ("he would die") see GKC, § 112oo. The same feature is present in *w^{e}hôrîḏû,* "would bring."

10. See J. A. L. Lee, "Equivocal and Stereotyped Renderings in the LXX," *RB* 87 (1980) 111, on Gk. *ekdéchomai* for Heb. *ʿāraḇ.* The Greek reads, "for your servant has received (in charge) [*ekdédektai*] from his father [*pará toú patrós*]." Lee suggests that the misleading construction in the LXX came about through word-for-word adherence to the Hebrew (*pará* for Heb. *mēʿim*) instead of a reading more natural to the Greek.

11. LXX adds, "and present him before you," in line with the presence of this phrase in the earlier parallel, 43:9.

12. On the use of the jussive in humble request (twice in this verse), see GKC, § 109b.

13. For *pen* meaning "I could not, cannot," see GKC, § 152w; and Redford, *Study of the Biblical Story of Joseph,* p. 40. For *rā'â ḇārāʿ/b^{e}rāʿâ,* lit., "look at the evil of," cf. Num. 11:15.

14. See A. R. Ceresko, "The Function of *Anṭanaclasis* (*mṣ'* 'to find'//*mṣ'* 'to reach, overtake, grasp') in Hebrew Poetry, Especially in the book of Qoheleth," *CBQ* 44 (1982) 556. *Antanaclasis* is the repetition of the same word with a different meaning. A set of roots in Ugaritic, related to Heb. *mṣ',* i.e., *mṣa/mẓa/mǵy,* have the meaning "to reach, arrive, overtake," and with this set of roots one should connect *yimṣāʿ* in Gen. 44:34.

The lengthiest human speech recorded in Genesis is that of Judah before Joseph. It is made up of two sections considerably unequal in length. The first is a review of the recent past (vv. 18-32). The second (vv. 33-34) focuses on the present.

18-32 In the first section Judah recapitulates selected portions of previous conversations with Joseph and with his father. Only four of the fifteen verses in the first section contain no direct quote of previous discourse (vv. 18, 24, 30, 31). Judah quotes Joseph addressing the brothers three times (vv. 19, 21, 23). This is an illustration of what may be called an *XYY* quotation, where *X* is the speaker, and *Y* is both the original speaker, now quoted, and the listener.[15] Three times Judah quotes the brothers, twice speaking to Joseph (vv. 20, 22) and once to their father (v. 26). Twice he quotes Jacob speaking to his sons (vv. 25, 27-29). These quotations are an illustration of an *XYZ* quotation, where *X* is the speaker, *Y* the quoted, original speaker, and *Z* the listener. Once he quotes himself speaking to his father (v. 32). This is an illustration of a *XXY* quotation, in which *X* is the speaker quoting his own words, and *Y* is the present listener. Thus vv. 18-32 comprise the renarration of nine previous speeches.

Sprinkled freely throughout these verses is the word *servant(s)*. It occurs ten times (including both sing. [vv. 18 (twice), 24, 27, 30, 32] and pl. [vv. 19, 21, 23, 31]), and twice again in the second section (v. 33). Where "servant" is applied to Jacob (vv. 24, 27, 30) by Judah, Jacob is first identified by his relationship to Joseph ("your servant"), and then by his relationship to Judah ("my father"). Judah is careful to follow protocol in so identifying himself, his brothers, and even his father, when addressing a superior. Also, he is careful to address Joseph in a way becoming the latter's high standing in Egyptian society. Six times (vv. 18 [twice], 19, 20, 22, 24), and once again in v. 33, Judah addresses him as "my lord." One other repeated word in Judah's speech is *father.* Judah uses it thirteen times in vv. 18-32 (19, 20 [twice], 22 [twice], 24, 25, 27, 30 [twice], 31, 32 [twice]), and two times in v. 34. Its repeated use is perhaps Judah's way of persuading Joseph to be concerned about Jacob's needs and fears at this moment.

Of course, Judah thoughtfully recalls only the portions of previous conversations that will be helpful in gaining Benjamin's release. He is careful in the first subsection (vv. 19-23) to reemphasize the great love that Jacob has for Benjamin, especially since the "death" of Jacob's firstborn son by Benjamin's mother (information that Joseph knows is wrong but that Judah believes is correct). In fact, Judah makes his mistake even more obvious when he states, quoting his brothers, that Joseph is "dead." Earlier they had used the more ambiguous "he is no more" [*'ênennû*] in 42:13, 32, as had Jacob himself, 42:36).

15. For these different forms of quotation see Savran, *Telling and Retelling,* pp. 24-25, 38, and esp. pp. 58-63 for his insightful discussion of quotations in Gen. 44:19-34.

Also, note that Judah says nothing about the reason why Joseph earlier insisted that they return to Canaan and then return to Egypt with their youngest brother. We know it was a test to determine whether they were spies (42:9, 14-16, 20). By leaving out this piece of information, Judah makes it appear that Joseph was selfish in his insistence that they bring Benjamin back with them to Egypt. In the second subsection (vv. 24-29) Judah again places special emphasis on their father's inability to survive without Benjamin, but carefully deleting Jacob's initial refusal to release Benjamin (42:38). Benjamin's failure to return to Canaan will bring about their father's death. Judah suggests again in the third subsection (vv. 30-31) what a fatal blow Benjamin's detention in Eygpt would be to their father. Only at the end of this first section (v. 32) does he mention his own involvement in Benjamin's well-being.

33-34 The second, and much briefer, part of Judah's speech is his proposal that Benjamin be allowed to go back to Canaan and that Judah be detained in Egypt in his place. Judah will become Benjamin's surrogate. Judah's proposal to his father regarding Benjamin, stated first to Jacob (43:9) and subsequently to Joseph (44:32), is actually somewhat different from what he counterproposes here. He first promised "to bring back" Benjamin. That is, he would personally conduct Benjamin back to his home. But what Judah is suggesting in v. 33 will not allow him "to bring back" Benjamin to his father. In effect, Judah will become what Simeon once was, but on a permanent basis. Understandably, Judah had not shared the possibility in as many words with his father that "the man" in Egypt might exact a life for a life.

A spiritual metamorphosis for the better has certainly taken place in Judah. His speech to Joseph in ch. 44 represents a profound advancement over his speech about Joseph in 37:26ff. He who once callously engineered the selling of Joseph to strangers out of envy and anger is now willing to become Joseph's slave so that the rest of his brothers, and especially Benjamin, may be freed and allowed to return to Canaan to rejoin their father.

Among modern commentators only G. W. Coats focuses on factors other than a genuine change in Judah's attitude and deportment.[16] He suggests that Judah's offer does not arise from any character change within, but from the exigencies of circumstances over which he has no control. He made an oath to his father. His options are twofold: Take his chances staying in Egypt (note that Judah uses a softer word, *stay* [*yēšeḇ*, lit., "dwell"], rather than a stronger word, like "be bound" or "enslaved"), or live under the guilt of a broken surety oath. But is not Judah's taking of the oath in the first place dictated by the knowledge that vicarious suffering is a real possibility in the near future? Whence springs this willingness to become Benjamin's substitute, if not from a dynamic, spiritual change within Judah?

16. Coats, *From Canaan to Egypt,* p. 43.

I. JOSEPH REVEALS HIMSELF TO HIS BROTHERS (45:1-28)

1. THE MOMENT OF DISCLOSURE (45:1-8)

1 *Joseph, unable to give vent to his emotions*[1] *in the presence*[2] *of all his attendants,*[3] *cried out: "Get everybody away from me." So no one was with him when Joseph made himself known*[4] *to his brothers.*

2 *But he wept so loudly*[5] *that the Egyptians*[6] *heard, and Pharaoh's house heard.*[7]

3 *Joseph said to his brothers: "I am Joseph! Is my father still alive?" But his brothers were unable to reply, so stunned*[8] *were they by him.*

4 *Then Joseph instructed his brothers: "Come closer to me." When they*

1. On this translation of *l*^{e}*hiṯʾappēq* see the commentary below.

2. For the vocable *l*^{e}*ḵōl* meaning "in the presence of all" see R. Gordis, "Studies in the Esther Narrative," *JBL* 95 (1976) 46, who connects this construction with *l*^{e}*ḵōl* in Esth. 1:18, "And the noblewomen of Persia and Media will say this very day that they had heard what the queen had said in the presence of all [*l*^{e}*ḵōl*] the king's lords."

3. Lit., "all those standing beside him" (*l*^{e}*ḵōl hanniṣṣāḇîm ʿālâw*). The verb *nāṣaḇ* in the Niphal, followed by the preposition *ʿal,* appears elsewhere in Genesis in 18:2; 24:13, 43; 28:13. Gen. 45:1 is the only instance in Genesis in which one finds *ʿal* used in an idiom where servants or courtiers stand "by/beside" a superior, but see elsewhere Exod. 18:13, 14; Judg. 3:19; 1 Sam. 22:6, 7, 17; and for heavenly servants who stand around Yahweh, cf. 1 K. 22:19; Job 1:6; 2:1; Zech. 4:14; 6:5. See H. N. Wallace, *The Eden Narrative,* HSM 32 (Atlanta: Scholars, 1985), p. 96 n. 69, and p. 81 for an example from the Ugaritic texts (*UT,* 137.21 [*CTA,* 2.1.21]): *bʿl qm ʿl il,* "Baal stood by El."

4. The only other instance of the Hithpael of *yādaʿ* in the OT is in Num. 12:6, part of a poem spoken by Yahweh on the occasion of Miriam's and Aaron's criticism of Moses.

5. Lit., "he gave his voice in weeping." The idiom appears in the Ugaritic texts. Thus J. Gray (*The KRT Text in the Literature of Ras Shamra,* 2nd ed. [Leiden: Brill, 1964], pp. 22 and 66) renders *UT,* 125.12-13: *ybky wyšnn ytn gh bky,* "Weeping and gnashing his teeth, he utters his voice in weeping." Cf. also *UT,* 51:V:70 (*CTA,* 4.V.70): *wytn qlh bʿrpt,* "and he [Baal] uttered his voice in the clouds." Cf. also 2 K. 1:13, 14. Unlike expressions such as "raise/lift one's voice in weeping," which refer to the onset of weeping, "give one's voice in weeping" normally expresses loudness. See W. Weinberg, *Essays on Hebrew,* ed. Paul Citrin, South Florida Studies in the History of Judaism 6 (Atlanta: Scholars, 1993), p. 72.

6. MT "Egypt"; LXX "all the Egyptians," i.e., those who, in the previous verse, were waiting on Joseph.

7. LXX and Pesh. read "was informed" (*wayyiššāmaʿ*) (Niphal) for MT *wayyišmaʿ* (Qal), but the MT makes good sense.

8. For the Niphal of *bāhal* ("be stunned, dismayed, terrified") cf. Exod. 15:15; Judg. 20:41; 1 Sam. 28:21; 2 Sam. 4:1; Job 4:5; 21:6, and frequently in the Psalter (6:3 [Eng. 2]; 6:4 [Eng. 3]; 6:11 [Eng. 10]; 30:8 [Eng. 7]; 48:6 [Eng. 5]; 83:18 [Eng. 17]; 90:7; 104:29). The expression *bāhal* (Niphal) plus *mipp*^{e}*nê* appears only in Gen. 45:3 and Job 23:15.

had done so, he said: "I am Joseph, your brother, whom you sold[9] *into Egypt.*

5 *Now then, do not be distressed*[10] *or reproach yourselves*[11] *that you sold me here, because for life preservation*[12] *God sent me ahead of you.*

6 *For it is now*[13] *two years that the famine has been in the land, and there are five more years to go in which*[14] *there will be neither plowing nor harvesting.*[15]

7 *Therefore God sent me ahead of you to ensure for you a remnant*[16] *on earth and to keep alive*[17] *for you many*[18] *survivors.*[19]

9. Lit., "I am Joseph . . . who you sold me." On the use of the retrospective pronoun "me" see GKC, § 138d; Waltke and O'Connor, *Biblical Hebrew Syntax,* p. 334.

10. The verb *ʿāṣaḇ* has appeared in Genesis in the Hithpael with a divine subject (6:6) and with a human subject (34:7). Here it is used in the Niphal *(tēʿāṣᵉḇû).* Gen. 34:7 is close in structure to 45:5, apart from stem use, in that in both instances *ʿāṣaḇ* is followed by *yiḥar (wayyiḥar, wᵉʾal-yiḥar)* and then a *kî* clause.

11. Lit., "and let it not burn/flare up in your eyes." For the idiom *ḥārâ bᵉʿênê* see Gen. 31:35.

12. Lit., "for place of life" *(lᵉmiḥyâ).* The noun occurs in Judg. 6:4 and 17:10 with the meaning "sustenance"; in Lev. 13:10, 24 in reference to a "patch" of raw, exposed flesh; and in Ezra 9:8, 9 with the meaning "reviving."

13. For the use of the demonstrative *zeh* to add force to temporal expressions, see Davidson, *Hebrew Syntax,* p. 5, § 6, Rem. 2.

14. After words of time *ʾᵃšer* is the equivalent of "when, in which"; see Waltke and O'Connor, *Biblical Hebrew Syntax,* p. 334.

15. *ḥārîš* and *qāṣîr* are to be understood as a merism, as in Exod. 34:21. See M. J. Dahood, "Vocative *lamedh* in Exodus 2,14 and Merismus in 34,21," *Bib* 62 (1981) 414. Merism (or merismus) is a linguistic phenomenon that expresses a unity either by marking the extremities with the formula "from *X* (and) unto *Y*," or by listing two members of a class to represent the whole class with the formula "*X* and *Y*," or "neither *X* nor *Y*." See A. M. Honeyman, "*Merismus* in Biblical Hebrew," *JBL* 71 (1952) 15. For the combination *ḥrš/qṣr* in and outside Biblical Hebrew, see Y. Avishur, *Stylistic Studies of Word-Pairs in Biblical and Ancient Semitic Literatures,* AOAT 210 (Kevelaer: Butzon & Bercker; Neukirchen-Vluyn: Neukirchener, 1984), pp. 449-50; and J. Khanjian, *RSP,* 2:396.

16. *šᵉʾērîṯ,* "remnant (left over)" with the meaning of descendants who have survived a catastrophe, occurs in the Pentateuch only here. See Redford, *Study of the Biblical Story of Joseph,* p. 53. Cf. 2 Sam. 14:7 for the same meaning.

17. *lᵉhaḥᵃyôṯ* appeared in 6:20 to describe the survival of two of each of the animal and bird species from drowning in the flood.

18. Lit., "great" *(gᵉḏōlâ).* Speiser (*Genesis,* p. 338) adds, "with reference to something supernatural."

19. The last phrase in MT, *lip̱lêṭâ gᵉḏōlâ,* "many survivors" (so RSV; see NEB "a great band of survivors"; cf. AV, NIV, "a great deliverance"; NAB, "an extraordinary deliverance") is rendered by LXX *kaí ekthrépsai hymṓn katáleipsin megálēn,* "even to nourish a great remnant of you," thus reading *pᵉlêṭâ* instead of *lip̱lêṭâ* as the object of the

8 *So it was not*[20] *you who sent me down here, but*[21] *God. He has established me as a father to Pharaoh, master*[22] *over all his household, and ruler over the entire land of Egypt."*

1 In a previous meeting with his brothers Joseph was able to "control" himself and regain his composure (43:31). Now, however, he is on the verge of losing that control altogether and dissolving into tears. Accordingly, he orders everybody except his brothers to leave the room immediately. Joseph's words are identical to those uttered by David's son Amnon, when, in his bedroom feigning sickness, he ordered everybody out except his half-sister Tamar (2 Sam. 13:9). Thus "the same words that were a preface to a great moment of fraternal reconciliation [in Genesis] are now [in 2 Samuel] a prologue to a sexual violation of the fraternal bond."[23]

Get everybody away from me. Joseph's order, found in the middle of the verse, might explain the best translation of *l^ehiṯ'appēq* in the first part of the verse. As I have mentioned, the verb appears in the same stem in 43:31, where it clearly means "control oneself, restrain one's feelings." If, however, one translates it similarly in 45:1 (i.e., "Joseph was no longer able to control himself in the presence of all his attendants"), it sounds as if his attendants are preventing his self-control, when in fact they are preventing his emotional self-revelation to his brothers. Accordingly he orders them to leave before making that self-disclosure. Thus I have translated, following Gordis,[24] "Joseph could not give vent to his emotions," i.e., he wants to express his emotions rather than control them.

2 For a third time the Genesis narrative records Joseph weeping. The previous occasions are 42:24 and 43:30. The first two are hidden weepings.

---

infinitive. LXX uses *katáleimma* for *š^e'ēriṯ* and *katáleipsis* for *p^elēṭâ,* without any preceding preposition, as in MT (see GKC, § 117n).

20. The usual place of the negative is prior to the verb, but it may be placed before the emphatic word *('attem)* in the negative clause. See Davidson, *Hebrew Syntax,* p. 171, § 127a. G. E. Whitney ("Alternative Interpretations of *LŌ'* in Exodus 6:3 and Jeremiah 7:22," *WTJ* 48 [1986] 154) extends the meaning of the negative to "so now it was not only you who sent me here, but God."

21. After a negative, "but" is expressed by *kî 'im* (32:29), or simply *kî,* as here.

22. On the basis of Ugar. *adanu,* "father," there is mounting evidence to see at times in Heb. *'āḏôn* the meaning "father." Cf. M. J. Dahood, "Two Textual Notes on Jeremia," *CBQ* 23 (1961) 463; J. Blau and J. C. Greenfield, "Ugaritic Glosses," *BASOR* 200 (1970) 16 and n. 23. Note, however, that *'āḇ* and *'āḏôn* are used in parallel cola in Mal. 1:6, as in Gen. 44:18, but *'āḏôn* can only be "master" there. Cf. D. Hillers, "Additional Note," *BASOR* 200 (1970) 18. Also, M. Dahood, *RSP,* 3:12, 13.

23. R. Alter, *The World of Biblical Literature* (San Francisco: Basic Books, 1992), p. 114.

24. R. Gordis, *The Word and the Book* (New York: Ktav, 1976), pp. 188-89.

He left so he could weep without being observed. Here he orders everybody else to leave so that his uncontrollable sobbing will not become a public spectacle. Everybody near can hear, but they cannot observe. Both his Egyptian servants and Pharaoh's house hear the weeping. That the occupants of Pharaoh's house could also hear Joseph's weeping indicates that Joseph's house (44:14) and the king's house were close to each other. Is something wrong? Has there been an accident?

Verses 2 and 16 have verbal similarities. Thus v. 2 has *wayyittēn ʾeṯ-qōlô,* literally "and he gave his voice in weeping," which is followed by "the Egyptians heard" *(wayyišmᵉʿû)* and "Pharaoh's house heard" *(wayyišmaʿ bêṯ parʿō). qōl, šāmaʿ,* and *bêṯ parʿō* are used again in v. 16: literally, "the voice was heard [in/by] Pharaoh's house" *(haqqōl nišmaʿ bêṯ parʿō).* These three verbal similarities may be categorized as a case of synchroneity. Thus as vv. 3-15 are a dovetailed follow-up to v. 2, so are, simultaneously, vv. 17-20 a follow-up to v. 16.[25]

3 Now comes the moment of disclosure, two words in Hebrew, one pronoun and one proper name: *ʾᵃnî yôsēp̱, I am Joseph!* Then without allowing his brothers to respond he follows that with another nominal clause: *Is my father still alive?* Heretofore Joseph could refer to Jacob only as "your father" (43:27). Now he styles him *my father.* Joseph had asked this question earlier of his brothers (43:27) and received a positive answer (43:28). Some have therefore suggested that Joseph's question in 45:3 is uncalled for, or perhaps from a tradition different from that of ch. 43. This explanation seems unnecessary. Joseph wants to know for sure that what he was told earlier by his brothers, while he was still incognito to them, is indeed true. How is he to know that his brothers have not been deceiving him all along in their earlier talk about their father? "Please tell me again," he says, "if my father is in good health." The brothers are immobilized by shock. As a result they never do answer Joseph's question, which he does not repeat.

4 Joseph requests his brothers to *Come closer (nāg̱aš).* This verb was used earlier of the brothers' approaching Joseph in 43:19; 44:18. In all three texts the emphasis is on the brothers' deference to Joseph. He does not approach them; they approach him. For a second time he says to his brothers, *I am Joseph.* Those writers who distinguish two traditions about Joseph's self-revelation to his brothers attribute v. 3 to E and v. 4 to J.[26] There may be legitimate evidence in ch. 45 for discerning multiple sources (e.g., in vv. 9-15 Joseph invites Jacob and his family to immigrate to Goshen [E?], while in vv.

25. S. Talmon, "The Presentation of Synchroneity and Simultaneity in Biblical Narrative," *Scripta Hierosolymitana* 27 (1978) 20-21.

26. For example, Jenks, *The Elohist and North Israelite Traditions,* pp. 30, 72 n. 58, who cites Noth's *History of Pentateuchal Traditions,* tr. B. W. Anderson (Englewood Cliffs, NJ: Prentice-Hall, 1972), pp. 30, 36.

16-20 Pharaoh issues that invitation [J?]), but vv. 3-4 should not be included in that evidence. R. Alter rightly states: "The obtuseness of conventional source criticism is nowhere better illustrated than in its attributing to a duplication of sources this brilliantly effective repetition so obviously justified by the dramatic and psychological situation."[27]

In Joseph's first self-disclosure he said simply: "I am Joseph." Here he repeats that, but adds the condemning clause, *your brother, whom you sold into Egypt.* Nobody but Joseph and his brothers would be aware of this telltale bit of family history. Is Joseph still speaking through an interpreter (none is mentioned), or does he slip into his native tongue? With nobody else around, and in such an emotional, fragile moment, this conversation would no doubt be in Hebrew.

5 Now that Joseph has unnerved his brothers, he must calm them. To that end, he tells them, *do not be distressed* (*ʿāṣaḇ,* the verb used to describe God's inner feelings at the human evil in Noah's time, 6:6; nouns built off this root ["pain"] also occur in 3:16, 17; 5:29), or *reproach yourselves,* that is, engage in penance or self-flagellation.[28]

He explains to them that God had, in fact, sent him ahead of them *for life preservation.* The Hebrew word for this last phrase in *miḥyâ,* literally, "place of life." It appears in Judg. 6:4 and 17:10 with the meaning "means of livelihood" or "sustenance." Closest to our verse is 2 Chr. 14:12. It is possible, but not necessary, to repoint *miḥyâ* to *m*ᵉ*ḥayyeh,* a Piel participle meaning "a preserver of life" (see 1 Sam. 2:6; Neh. 9:6).

The concepts expressed in v. 5 are not those of the narrator, but of Joseph. This is Joseph's reasoned statement on the purpose of his experiences thus far. We are not told precisely at what point it dawned upon Joseph that he was a lifesaver sent by God at the most propitious moment, rather than a victim of barbaric men and brutal circumstances. Nothing thus far in the narrative has prepared us for this eloquent and magnificent theologizing on his pilgrimage. We must assume that Joseph perceived bit by bit the hand of God in this nightmare. It is doubtful, as I said before, that he embraced this conviction as a seventeen-year-old on his way to Egypt.

Joseph does not yet elaborate on whose *life* he is to save. His brothers'? His father's? His homeland's? The Egyptians'? He will be more specific in v. 7.

6 The famine is closer to its beginning than to its ending. Only *two years* of famine have passed. There are yet *five more years* to come. During these five years there will be *neither plowing nor harvesting.* Despite Speiser's impressive note to the contrary,[29] we believe Joseph is painting a picture of a

27. Alter, *Art of Biblical Narrative,* p. 175.

28. On the sequence *ʿāṣaḇ . . . ḥārâ* see Gen. 34:7, where these two verbs describe the feelings of Dinah's brothers after they learn of her rape.

29. Speiser, *Genesis,* p. 338.

famine so severe that all kinds of agricultural activity will cease. Perhaps during the first two years of the famine farmers have continued to till their ground, but after that it will become a futile investment of their time and energy.

7 Joseph repeats in v. 7a what he had said in v. 5b, *God sent me ahead of you.* Then he proceeds to elaborate on his "for life preservation" of v. 5 with *to ensure for you a remnant* [*š^{e}'ērîṯ*] *on earth and to keep alive for you many survivors* [*p^{e}lēṭâ*]. It becomes clear here that the lives Joseph will save are the lives of his own flesh and blood. The two Hebrew words here translated *remnant* and *survivors* occur elsewhere in the OT in combination (see 2 K. 19:31 par. Isa. 37:32; 1 Chr. 4:43; Ezra 9:14).[30] Others in Canaan may perish because of the famine, but the family of Jacob will not be among them. Unlike the earlier patriarchal stories in which the greatest threat to the promises of God was the bearers of those promises, here it is a famine that looms as the enemy. May a natural catastrophe do to the promises of God what a lying Abraham and a conniving Jacob could not do — thwart them? The answer is decidedly negative. In using terms like *remnant* and *survivors,* Joseph is employing words that elsewhere in the OT are freighted with theological significance. It may well be that in the deliverance of his brothers and his father Joseph perceives that far more is at stake than the mere physical survival of twelve human beings. What really survives is the plan of redemption announced first to his great grandfather. At least the reader is cognizant of that fact.

Westermann questions what possible significance the use of *š^{e}'ērîṯ,* "remnant," could have here.[31] "A remnant of what?" he asks. He opines that v. 7b is a later expansion, arising in the late prophetic period when the anticipation of salvation and deliverance ran high. Now, to be sure, the argument advanced by some of the older commentators, such as Driver and Skinner,[32] that *š^{e}'ērîṯ* should here be translated "descendants" because in 45:7 all members of his family have been kept alive, is unconvincing, and is thus not a powerful objection to the point raised by Westermann and others. One may argue,

30. The two words occur (a) in construct state: 1 Chr. 4:43, "and they destroyed the remnant of the Amalekites that had escaped" (*š^{e}'ērîṯ happ^{e}lēṭâ,* lit. "remnant of the escaped"); (b) in syndetic parataxis: Ezra 9:14, "so that there should be no remnant nor any to escape" *(l^{e}'ên š^{e}'ērîṯ ûp^{e}lēṭâ);* (c) in parallelism; Isa. 10:20, "the remnant of Israel and the survivors of the house of Jacob" *(š^{e}'ar yísrā'ēl ûp^{e}lêṭaṯ bêṯ ya'^{a}qōḇ);* also 37:32 for the same order and 15:9 in reverse order; (d) as name and its adjective: Exod. 10:5, "and they [the locusts] shall eat what is left to you" *(happ^{e}lēṭâ hanniš'ereṯ).* Jer. 50:26-30 has two parallel stanzas (vv. 26-28, 29-30) that urge the enemy to inflict punishment on the Babylonians. Part of stanza one, v. 26, reads "let nothing be left to her" *('al-t^{e}hî-lāh š^{e}'ērîṯ).* Part of stanza two, v. 29, reads "let no one escape" (*'al-y^{e}hî-lāh* [see textual note in *BHS*] *p^{e}lēṭâ*). Cf. Avishur, *Stylistic Studies in Word-Pairs,* pp. 84-85, 164, 317.

31. Westermann, *Genesis,* 3:144.

32. S. R. Driver, *Genesis,* p. 362; Skinner, *Genesis,* p. 487.

however, that "remnant" is a legitimate and accurate translation of *šᵉʾērîṯ* even in Gen. 45:7 in that the family of Jacob, "in narrowly escaping destruction is like a remnant which is the bearer of hopes for the future existence."[33]

8 For a third time Joseph employs the verb *sent,* here emphasizing that the subject is *not you . . . but God.* It is interesting that Joseph leaves to last the positions of eminence he has had bestowed on him. He begins not with how important he is, the success he has achieved, or the honors that have come his way. This is no selfish display for Joseph. Instead, he begins by divulging to his brothers why, in his analysis, he was in Egypt in the first place. Joseph talks more about God than about Joseph.

Of the three titles Joseph uses about himself in this verse, the most intriguing is *father to Pharaoh.* This could be the equivalent of the Egyptian title "God's Father," in which "God" is the Pharaoh, the living king. The title may or may not be used to indicate family relationship. When used by nonrelated individuals especially, it designated one who stood in the relation of "father" to the king by virtue of, say, his outstanding wisdom and ability. That is, Joseph was a father figure to Pharaoh.[34] Is it not ironic that Joseph, so concerned about the welfare of his father, is himself a "father"?

Redford dismisses any connection between Egyptian "God's Father" and "a father to Pharaoh" in v. 8, principally because the Egyptian phrase is (a) a priestly title, (b) a term for the king's father-in-law, or (c) the progenitor of a dynasty, none of which particularly fits 45:8.[35] A few places in the OT use "father" for someone who exercises paternal influence over another. It is applied to a priest (Judg. 17:10; 18:19), to a prophet (2 K. 6:21; Isa. 22:21), and to the commander of an army (2 K. 5:13).[36]

33. G. Hasel, *The Remnant: The History and Theology of the Remnant Idea from Genesis to Isaiah,* 2nd ed. (Berrien Springs, MI: Andrews University, 1975), p. 154 n. 69; see further pp. 153-59; also H. P. Müller, *Ursprünge und Strukturen alttestestamentlicher Eschatologie,* BZAW 109 (Berlin: Töpelmann, 1969) p. 46.

34. See W. Ward, "Egyptian Titles in Genesis 39–50," *BSac* 114 (1957) 51-53; idem, "The Egyptian Offices of Joseph," *JSS* 5 (1960) 149. The closest parallel to the use of "father" in Gen. 45:8 (i.e., one with a political role) is Isa. 22:21: "he [viz., Eliakim] will be a father to those who live in Jerusalem and to the house of Judah."

35. Redford, *Study of the Biblical Story of Joseph,* p. 91. Redford expresses strong opposition to A. Osman's *Stranger in the Valley of Kings* (San Francisco: Harper & Row, 1987), which identifies Yuya, a vizier of Thutmose IV (late 15th century B.C.), with Joseph, and on whose sarcophagus appeared the title "the holy father of the Lord of the Two Lands." See Redford's scathing review in *BAR* 15 (March/April, 1989) 18.

36. For an example from the Phoenician texts cf. the autobiographical account by the vizier Azitawada: *wʾp bʾbt pʿln kl mlk bṣdqy,* "and indeed every king treated me as a father [if *bʾbt* is a pl. of majesty, or else, 'reckoned me among the fathers'] because of my righteousness." See J. C. L. Gibson, *Textbook of Syrian Semitic Inscriptions,* 3 vols. (Oxford: Clarendon, 1971-82), 3:48-49, 58 (A i.12 = *KAI,* 26.I.12); E. Lipiński, "North Semitic

Joseph's words to his brothers on this occasion, especially vv. 5, 7, and 8a, recall a number of statements in Proverbs to the effect that there is a divinely established order that no machinations of humankind can thwart (16:4, 7, and esp. 19:21, "Many are the plans in a man's heart, but it is the Lords's purpose that prevails" [NIV]). Rom. 8:28 makes essentially the same point in the NT.[37] But the idea is by no means confined to Proverbs. For example, one need only read through Isa. 40–55 and note its emphasis on God as the Lord of history, especially when these nations come into contact with Israel or Judah. What Joseph's words emphasize here and in Gen. 50:20 is "the ironies and accidents that shape the course of history and bring unintended consequences out of human purposes."[38]

2. JOSEPH'S MESSAGE FOR JACOB (45:9-15)

9 *"Hurry, go up to my father and tell*[1] *him: 'Your son Joseph says, God has established me as master over all of Egypt; come down to me immediately.*[2]

Texts," in *Near Eastern Religious Texts Relating to the Old Testament,* ed. W. Beyerlin, tr. J. Bowden, OTL (Philadelphia: Westminster, 1978), p. 241 and n. r.

37. See G. von Rad, "The Joseph Narrative and Ancient Wisdom," in *The Problem of the Hexateuch and Other Essays,* tr. E. W. Trueman Dicken (New York: McGraw-Hill, 1965), pp. 292-300, and esp. 296-300; and Humphreys, *Joseph and His Family,* who states on p. 187, "An ambiguity is here attained between the purposeful and meaningful quality in human motive and actions on the one hand, and the absolute sovereignty and control of the deity over the course of affairs on the other. Both are to be affirmed, and the tensions between them is unresolved." A parallel to the emphasis in Gen. 45 on the overruling providence of God is found in the teaching of the Egyptian sage Amenemope (11th century B.C.?): "Do not spend the night fearful of the morrow. At daybreak what is the morrow like? Man knows not what the morrow is like. God is (always) in his success, whereas man is in his failure; one thing are the words which men say, another is that which the god does" (translation of J. A. Wilson in *ANET,* p. 423). Wilson notes (p. 423 n. 30) that the last two lines of the above quote are the Egyptian equivalent of Thomas à Kempis's famous dictum: *Homo proposuit sed Deus disponit* ("Man proposes, but God disposes").

38. D. Patrick, *The Rendering of God in the Old Testament,* OBT (Philadelphia: Fortress, 1981), pp. 83-84; also J. Rogerson, "Can a Doctrine of Providence Be Based on the Old Testament?" in *Ascribe to the Lord,* Fest. P. C. Craigie, ed. L. Eslinger and G. Taylor, JSOTSup 67 (Sheffield: Sheffield Academic, 1988), pp. 529-43. See also B. Albrektson, *History and the Gods: An Essay on the Idea of Historical Events as Divine Manifestations in the Ancient Near East and in Israel* (Lund: Gleerup, 1967), p. 81, who concedes only that a verse like Gen. 45:8 shows the Yahwist's shorter perspective, i.e., his belief in purposeful divine actions but not a belief in a divine plan that embraces all history.

1. For *waw* plus perfect *(wa'ᵃmartem)* used as a jussive or as surrogate for the imperative, see Blau, *Grammar of Biblical Hebrew,* p. 86, § 60.1. Cf. also n. 13 below.

2. Lit., "do not stand (around)," *'al-taʿᵃmōḏ,* i.e., "don't stay there." For a com-

10 *You are to dwell in the territory of Goshen*[3] *adjacent to me — you, your sons, your grandsons, your flocks and herds, everything you have.*

11 *There I will take care*[4] *of you — for there are still five years of famine to come — lest you suffer want,*[5] *you,*[6] *your household, and everything you have.'*

12 *You see for yourselves, and Benjamin my brother can see for himself, that it is I who am speaking to you.*[7]

13 *Tell my father about my exalted status*[8] *in Egypt, and everything you have seen here; but hurry and bring my father down here."*

14 *Thereupon he flung himself*[9] *on the neck*[10] *of Benjamin his brother and wept, and Benjamin wept on his neck.*

15 *Then Joseph kissed all his brothers, weeping over each of them. Only then did his brothers talk with him.*

---

mand issued as a positive injunction ("come down to me"), and then repeated in apposition as a negative prohibition, see Andersen, *Sentence in Biblical Hebrew,* p. 44.

3. For MT *gōšen* LXX reads *Gesem Arabías,* as in Neh. 6:1. See the commentary below.

4. *wᵉḵilkaltî* is the Pilpel of *kûl* and means "sustain, maintain," hence (a) "nourish, feed" (Gen. 45:11; 47:12; 50:21); and (b) "sustain a cause, manage affairs" (Ps. 112:5; Prov. 18:14). On the use of the verb in Zech. 11:16, see R. Gordis, *The Word and the Book* (New York: Ktav, 1976), pp. 174-75.

5. MT *tiwwārēš* is a Niphal from *yāraš,* lit., "lest you be dispossessed," i.e., "impoverished." It is possible (see *BHS*) to repoint the verb as *tûrēš* (from *rûš*), "lest you be in want." In either case the meaning is the same, i.e., "be reduced to poverty." Targ. Onqelos *tštyṣy,* "lest you perish," read the Niphal as a Hiphil (and cf. Exod. 15:9, where the Hiphil of this root means "destroy"). There can be more dire consequences brought on by famine than impoverishment. See also Redford, *Study of the Biblical Story of Joseph,* p. 63.

6. When the pronominal subject contained in a finite verb is extended by a parallel second subject, the pronominal subject is generally repeated in its separate form prior to the second subject. For this same phenomenon cf. the previous verse (v. 10) and 38:12; also Blau, *Grammar of Biblical Hebrew,* p. 91, § 78.

7. Lit., "Behold, your eyes are seeing, and the eyes of my brother Benjamin, that it is my mouth which is speaking to you." On the relative use of the article with the participle *(hamᵉḏabbēr)* see Waltke and O'Connor, *Biblical Hebrew Syntax,* pp. 248, 263. Targ. Onqelos renders the latter part of this verse "that I speak to you in your language" *(blyšnkwn 'n' mmlyl ʿymkwn),* suggesting that Joseph substantiated his identity by talking to his brothers in Hebrew.

8. *kᵉḇôḏî,* lit., "my glory." Westermann renders "the dignity that is mine," and Speiser "my high station." For *kāḇôḏ* with this nuance, see F. Nötscher, "Heisst *kābōd* auch 'Seele'?" *VT* 2 (1952) 359-60; C. Westermann, *"kbd," THAT,* 1:798, 799-800.

9. In some instances *nāpal* has a reflexive, voluntary nuance (Gen. 14:10; 17:3; 33:4; 46:29), for which see C. Cohen, "Genesis 14:1-11 — An Early Israelite Chronographic Source," in *The Biblical Canon in Comparative Research,* Scripture in Context 4, ed. K. L. Younger, W. W. Hallo, and B. F. Batto (Lewiston, NY: Mellen, 1991), p. 76 n. m.

10. "Neck" is in the pl. both times in this verse *(ṣawwᵉ'rê, ṣawwā'rāyw)* because the Hebrew word includes both the neck and the shoulder blades (Speiser, *Genesis,* p. 339).

9-11 Joseph's message to his father is to be delivered to Jacob by Joseph's brothers. The message consists of the following components: (1) the commissioning of a messenger, (v. 9a: *Hurry, go up to my father and tell him*); (2) a message formula (v. 9b: *Your son Joseph says*); (3) the actual message, consisting of two parts: a report in the perfect (v. 9c), and a summons in the imperative (vv. 9d-10); (4) motivation (v. 11).[11]

Joseph is careful to begin his message to his father by placing proper and initial emphasis on *God.* It is God who is responsible for both Joseph's preservation and elevation. Joseph mentioned no less than three titles, now applied to himself, when talking to his brothers (v. 8). He is less specific about his position when relaying a message to Jacob. He is now simply *master over all of Egypt.* It is imperative that the message be brief and simple. At a later and more appropriate time Joseph will tell his father the details. Joseph does not even tell his brothers to inform Jacob that he is alive. The brothers will share that themselves without prompting.

Joseph tells Jacob that he, his family, and his animals are to settle in *the territory of Goshen.* This place name has not yet been found in an Egyptian text. Since there was a town in Canaan called Goshen (Josh. 15:51), and another "land of Goshen" south of Judah (Josh. 10:41; 11:16), it is likely that *Goshen* is a Semitic name and not Egyptian. *Goshen* is a district on the eastern edge of the Delta, which is known in ancient records as Wadi Tumilat. That it was a district favorable to herdsmen of the Sinai is made clear in a letter sent by one of Merneptah's officials in that area back to the Pharaoh. According to the letter, the Egyptians had "finished letting the Bedouin tribes of Edom (the Shasu) pass the Fortress of Mer-ne-Ptah . . . which is in Tjeku (Ṯeku), to the pools of Per-Atum (Pithom) . . . which are in Tjeku (Ṯeku), to keep them alive and to keep their cattle alive."[12]

Joseph still refers to Jacob as *my father* (as he did in v. 3), rather than "our father." In his message to Jacob he refers to the eleven as *your sons* rather than "my brothers." Thus he conveys intimacy toward his father and distance from his brothers.

12-13 Joseph now addresses his brothers directly, first with a word of reassurance (v. 12), then with information they are to pass on to Jacob. That information includes Joseph's high-ranking position in Egypt and his desire that they bring Jacob to Egypt as swiftly as possible. These data are much like what he already told his brothers in v. 9. There is one formal

11. See C. Westermann, *Basic Forms of Prophetic Speech,* tr. H. C. White (Philadelphia: Westminster, 1967), pp. 106-7. What I have called "motivation" is not part of Westermann's schemata. For this structure in the NT's great commission see B. J. Malina, "Structure and Form of Matt xxviii.16-20," *NTS* 17 (1970) 87-103.

12. Translation of de Vaux, *Early History of Israel,* p. 302; cf. *ANET,* p. 259a.

difference, however, between v. 9 and v. 13. The imperative form dominates Joseph's speech in v. 9 ("hurry" *[mahărû]*; "go up" *[waʿălû];* "come down" *[rĕḏâ]*). In v. 13 the *waw* plus perfect verb form dominates Joseph's speech ("tell" *[wĕhiggaḏtem];* "hurry *[ûmihartem];* "bring my father down" *[wĕhôraḏtem]*), although I have translated them as imperatives, for their intent is to give a command. Possibly the shift from imperative to *waw* plus perfect (in lieu of further imperatives) is Joseph's way of avoiding brusqueness.[13]

Perhaps the brothers think they are hallucinating. Special emphasis is given to Benjamin and his ability to observe for himself that this man is indeed Joseph. Joseph leaves open the possibility of extra commentary by his brothers with his all-inclusive *and everything you have seen here.* Again, Jacob is twice styled as *my father.*

Joseph's use of the verb *wĕhôraḏtem* in "and bring my father down here" recalls Jacob's earlier use of the Hiphil of *yāraḏ* in his expression of concern about going down to the netherworld/Sheol (*wĕhôraḏtem,* 42:38) should anything happen to Benjamin. Judah later quotes this concern of Jacob to Joseph, using the same verb in the same form (44:29). Now Joseph wants his father to know that he is going down to life, not to death; to Egypt, not to the netherworld.

In vv. 9-11 the brothers are to tell Jacob of the compassion he and his family may expect to receive from Joseph. He will provide a home for them and food for them. Throughout this communication Joseph downplays his own history, and even there quickly gives the credit to God. In v. 13 Joseph is a bit more self-oriented. It is not Goshen that Jacob is invited to come and see, but rather Joseph's *exalted status* or high station.

14-15 So far in this newly discovered relationship there has been monologue and tears. Joseph has done both. There has been talking but no touching. But at this point there is touching (vv. 14-15a) and dialogue (v. 15b), and more tears from Joseph. Starting with Benjamin, Joseph moves to each of the brothers, kissing each of them. Did they weep too, or is Joseph the only tear shedder? Only such gestures by Joseph restore to the brothers the capacity for speech. But what they talked about is not recorded. They have a lot of catching up to do to fill in the gaps of more than twenty years of separation. The announcement by the narrator that his brothers talked with and to Joseph *(kēn dibbĕrû ʾeḥāyw ʾittô)* is a signal that the breach between the brothers, which has long existed since 37:4 ("they could not speak to him peaceably," *wĕlōʾ yāḵĕlû dabbĕrô lĕšālōm*), is now in the process of

13. See the discussion of vv. 9-13 by Longacre, *Joseph,* pp. 127-31, who also explains the shift from imperative to *waw* plus perfect as a way of showing that the unit moves from a hortatory discourse to a procedural discourse. See also idem, "Discourse Perspective on the Hebrew Verb: Affirmation and Restatement," in *Linguistics and Biblical Hebrew,* ed. W. R. Bodine (Winona Lake, IN: Eisenbrauns, 1992), pp. 187-88.

closing. The resurfacing of dialogue between Joseph and his brothers spells the end of alienation.[14]

3. PHARAOH CONFIRMS JOSEPH'S INVITATION (45:16-20)

16 *The report[1] reached Pharaoh's palace:[2] "Joseph's brothers have arrived." Pharaoh and his courtiers were pleased.*

17 *And Pharaoh said to Joseph: "Tell your brothers, 'This do: load[3] your animals[4] and go immediately[5] to the land of Canaan.*

18 *Bring your father and your households[6] and come back to me. I will assign to you the very best[7] in Egypt, where you shall live off the fat[8] of the land.'*

14. "This third-person statement [viz. v. 15c] brings closure to the motif of communicative estrangement" (H. C. White, *Narration and Discourse in the Book of Genesis* [Cambridge: Cambridge University, 1991], p. 271).

1. BDB, p. 877a, identifies this nuance of *qôl,* "voice", here and in Eccl. 10:20. The same nuance is present in Ugar. *ql.* See M. J. Dahood, "Hebrew-Ugaritic Lexicography IX," *Bib* 52 (1971) 345.

2. In answer to the question "where?" the accusative of place is common in prose, esp. with the words *bayiṯ,* "house," and *petaḥ,* "door." See Davidson, *Hebrew Syntax,* p. 98, § 69a.

3. *ṭāʿan,* "to load," is a hapax legomenon. See M. Delcor, "Quelques cas de survivances du vocabulaire nomade en hébreu biblique," *VT* 25 (1975) 310; V. Sasson, "The word *trkb* in the Arad ostracon," *VT* 30 (1980) 46-47. H. R. Cohen (*Biblical Hapax Legomena,* p. 127 n. 50) connects it with Akk. *ṣenu,* usually used with boats. For its occurrence in Ugaritic, see *UT,* 67:I:26 (*CTA,* 5.I.26).

4. For *beʿîr* see Exod. 22:4; Num. 20:4, 8, 11; Ps. 78:48. In 44:3, 13 these animals were identified as *ḥ*ᵃ*mōr.*

5. Lit., "go, come" *(l*ᵉ*ḵû ḇōʾû).* Where there is the juxtaposition of two imperative verbs often the first imperative "becomes semantically empty, functioning merely as a hortatory particle" (Andersen, *Sentence in Biblical Hebrew,* p. 56), thus here, "come — go!" Cf. Speiser, *Genesis,* p. 339: " 'go . . . arrive,' lose no time getting there." Targ. Onqelos read the second imperative (*ḇōʾû,* Qal imperative) as a Hiphil to get the translation "and go, take them *('wbylu)* to the land of Canaan."

6. Lit., "your houses" *(bottêḵem).*

7. The abstract noun with genitive conveys superlative meaning. See Davidson, *Hebrew Syntax,* p. 49, § 34, Rem. 5; Waltke and O'Connor, *Biblical Hebrew Syntax,* p. 271; M. Mannati, "*Tûb-Y.* en Ps. XXVII 13: *La bonté de Y.,* ou *les biens de Y.?*" *VT* 19 (1969) 488-89.

8. For "eating/living off the fat" *('āḵal 'eṯ-ḥēleḇ)* see Ps. 81:7; Ezek. 34:3; 39:19; and J. Heller, "Die Symbolik des Fettes im AT," *VT* 20 (1970) 108. In Gen. 45:18 *ḥēleḇ* should be understood metaphorically, i.e., "its best part." See J. Milgrom, *Leviticus 1–16,* AB (New York: Doubleday, 1991), pp. 207, 210. Note that Targ. Onqelos does read, "you shall eat the best of the land" *(ṭwb' d'r').*

19 *And further you are instructed (to say),*[9] *'This do: take wagons*[10] *from Egypt for your little ones and wives, and to transport your father on your way back down here.*
20 *Forget about your possessions,*[11] *for the best in the land of Egypt shall be yours.' "*

The previous seven verses (9-15) detailed Joseph's invitation to his father to come down and join him in Egypt, particularly in the region of Goshen, where Jacob will be taken care of by Joseph. This invitation is followed by Pharaoh's own speech (really two speeches, vv. 17-18, 19-20) to Jacob to come down and settle in Egypt. He does not mention Goshen, as did Joseph. Because of the duplicate account of invitations extended to Jacob, and because 46:31 has Joseph informing Pharaoh about the arrival of his brothers and father in Egypt (i.e., 46:31 is unaware of Pharaoh's invitation), many commentators see vv. 9-15 and 16-20 in conflict with each other. Their solution to this enigma is to propose two accounts of the invitation to Jacob: vv. 9-15 (J), vv. 16-20 (E), or vv. 9-15 (E), vv. 16-20 (J).[12]

But why is recourse to sources even necessary here? It is logical to read Pharaoh's invitation as a royal confirmation of Joseph's previously issued

9. MT *wᵉʾattâ ṣuwwêṯâ* is a 2nd person perfect Pual, "you have been commanded (or ordered)." This may be retained by inserting an understood "(to say)." Following LXX and Vulg., both *BHK* and *BHS* suggest *wᵉʾattâ ṣawwēh ʾōṯām,* thus reading the verb as a Piel imperative: "and you, instruct them." While Speiser (*Genesis,* p. 339) leans toward the LXX, Redford (*Study of the Biblical Story of Joseph,* p. 63 n. 1), following Gunkel and König, favors the MT. The Pual of *ṣāwâ* is attested elsewhere in the OT (Exod. 34:34; Lev. 8:35; 10:13; Num. 3:16; 36:2; Ezek. 12:7; 24:8; 37:7).

10. W. F. Albright (*Vocalization of the Egyptian Syllabic Orthography* [New Haven: American Oriental Society, 1934], p. 38) connects Egyp. *ʿa-ga-ra-ta* with Canaanite *ʿagal(ᵃ)t(a)* and Heb. *ʿᵃgālâ.* For pictures of wagons drawn by draught animals, see *ANEP,* nos. 167, 367, 813.

11. Lit., "let not your eye look with pity (or compassion) on your vessels." The phrase "you must show no pity" *(lōʾ ṯāḥōs ʿênᵉḵā ʿal)* is frequent in Deuteronomy (7:16, regarding the total extermination of the Canaanites; 13:9, the execution of one's relative or friend; 19:13, the killing of a person returned from a city of refuge; 19:21, the execution of a false witness; 25:12, cutting off the hand of a woman accused of immodesty). The phrase is used where there is a possibility that the punisher would be lenient or be unwilling to inforce the punishment. Also in Ezekiel (5:11; 7:4, 9; 8:18; 9:5, 10) it is an expression of God's resolve to punish backslidden Israel (or, in one case, not punish her, 20:17). See also Isa. 13:18. Cf. M. Weinfeld, *Deuteronomy and the Deuteronomic School,* (repr. Winona Lake, IN: Eisenbrauns, 1992), p. 2; M. Greenberg, *Ezekiel 1–20,* AB (Garden City, NY: Doubleday, 1983), p. 115.

12. For the former see Skinner, *Genesis,* pp. 487-89; Speiser, *Genesis,* pp. 340-41. For the latter see Noth, *History of Pentateuchal Traditions,* pp. 30, 36, 266; Jenks, *The Elohist and North Israelite Traditions,* p. 30.

invitation.[13] Joseph takes the initiative in the extension of courtesy, and Pharaoh ratifies it. It is unlikely that Joseph, even if he is Pharaoh's majordomo, has sufficient authorization to invite Asiatic immigrants to the Delta area of Egypt.

Joseph's superior is then delighted to provide official royal authorization for the relocation of Joseph's kin. Why not? Is this not a small favor to repay to a man who saved one's empire from catastrophe?

The report (v. 16) that came to Pharaoh's attention refers not only to Joseph's invitation to Jacob (vv. 9ff.), but to all that transpired in Joseph's self-disclosure to his brothers (vv. 1ff.). Joseph's courtiers did not see what was going on (v. 1), but they heard what was going on (v. 2). Again, in a speech to Pharaoh, Joseph is referred to by his Hebrew name. Pharaoh is not told, "Zaphenath-paneah's brothers have arrived." This use is comparable to 41:55, where Pharaoh himself refers to Joseph as Joseph. Again, the narrator has Egyptians use the Hebrew name Joseph.

If anything, Pharaoh's invitation is more generous than Joseph's. Joseph focused on the male members of his family: "you, your sons, your grandsons." Pharaoh explicitly mentions everybody, including *little ones* and *wives.* Joseph designated the invitation as an invitation to settle in Goshen. Pharaoh appears to open the door even wider with phrases like *the very best in Egypt, the fat of the land, the best in the land of Egypt.* These may be general descriptions of Goshen, but it is likely that they range beyond that one region. Finally, Pharaoh offers *wagons* so that the aged Jacob, the young children, and the women will not have to make the trip on foot.

Both of Pharaoh's speeches are introduced with the demonstrative, followed by the imperative: *This do.* We have seen this construction twice thus far in the Joseph story (42:18; 43:11). Close to it is the demonstrative followed by a finite form of the verb (37:32).

4. THE BROTHERS RETURN TO JACOB (45:21-28)

21 *The sons of Israel did so. In accordance with Pharaoh's order*[1] *Joseph gave them wagons and supplied them with provisions for the trip.*[2]

13. So Coats, *Genesis,* p. 293; Westermann, *Genesis,* 3:141-42, 146-47. Coats also states: "the plurality in the chapter lends itself to artistic structure in a single source but not to convincing evidence for distinguishing two parallel sources" (*From Canaan to Egypt,* p. 67).

1. Lit., "according to the mouth of" (*'al pî).* See BDB, p. 805b.

2. Y. Muffs ("Abraham the Noble Warrior: Patriarchal Politics and Laws of War in Ancient Israel," *JJS* 33 [1982] 89) connects the phrase *ṣᵉḏâ laddāreḵ,* "provisions for the trip" (here, earlier in 42:25, and again in Josh. 9:11) with the expression *akal ḫarrāni-šunu* ("the rations for the road") in an Akkadian text from Hatti. There the phrase refers to the daily rations allotted to an ally's troops.

22 *To all of them he gave one by one*[3] *changes of clothes, but to Benjamin he gave three hundred pieces of silver*[4] *and five changes of clothing.*[5]

23 *He sent to his father the following:*[6] *ten donkeys loaded with some of the best produce of Egypt, ten she-asses loaded with corn, bread, and provisions*[7] *for his father*[8] *for the trip.*

24 *As he sent his brothers on their way, he said to them: "Let there be no arguments*[9] *on the trip."*

25 *So they left Egypt, and headed for the land of Canaan*[10] *and Jacob their father.*

26 *When they told him, "Joseph is still living, and is*[11] *ruler over the entire*

3. The force of *lā'îš* is uncertain. Most translations of this verse obscure the fact that the verse has three indirect objects (not two), and all are introduced by the preposition *l*ᵉ: *l*ᵉ*ḵullām, lā'îš, ûl*ᵉ*ḇinyāmin.* Perhaps one should read the first two together as "to each and all of them."

4. On the use of *chrysoús* in the LXX to translate *kesep̱* (instead of the more ordinary silver coin *drachmḗ*), possibly to enhance the value of the gift to Benjamin, see J. A. L. Lee, *Lexical Study of the Septuagint Version of the Pentateuch* (Chico, CA: Scholars, 1983), pp. 64-65.

5. Both times in this verse Targ. Onqelos reads "long robes as clothes" *('wsṭlwy dlbwš'). 'wsṭlwy* seems to be a transliteration from the Greek and Latin *stola,* a long outer garment descending to the ankles.

6. On the form *k*ᵉ*zō'ṯ,* see GKC, § 102g.

7. *māzôn* occurs again only in 2 Chr. 11:23. The verb from which it is built, *zûn,* is a hapax legomenon (Jer. 5:8). An Ebla text now provides the personal name *zu-NI-a,* "My sustenance is Ya." See R. Althann, *A Philological Analysis of Jeremiah 4–6 in the Light of Northwest Semitic,* BibOr 38 (Rome: Biblical Institute, 1983), p. 138. Of the three nouns ("corn, bread, provisions") LXX has only the second *(ártous).* Even if this reading of the Ebla text is dubious, the antiquity of the word is still substantiated by Akk. *zanānu,* "provide food or sustenance, provide a city or temple with means of support"; accordingly it is inappropriate to style *māzōn* a late Aramaism. See D. J. Wiseman, "Rahab of Jericho," *TynBul* 14 (1964) 11.

8. The sequence *ûl*ᵉ*'āḇîw* ("to his father") . . . *nōś*ᵉ*'îm* ("loaded"):: *nōś*ᵉ*'ōṯ* ("loaded") . . . *l*ᵉ*'āḇîw* ("for his father") is one of many A:B::B:A word patterns (a stylistic device) in the OT (A. R. Ceresko, "The A:B::B:A Word Pattern in Hebrew and Northwest Semitic with Special Reference to the Book of Job," *UF* 7 [1975] 78).

9. The basic meaning of *rāgaz* is "be agitated, disquieted." An extended meaning is "quarrel." SP reads a Hithpael, *tiṯragg*ᵉ*zû,* for MT Qal, *tirg*ᵉ*zû,* ("do not quarrel among yourselves, one with another"). Speiser (*Genesis,* p. 339) says: "Very likely, the general sense is, 'let there be no recriminations.' "

10. *'ereṣ k*ᵉ*na'an* is an accusative of place in answer to "whither?" See Davidson, *Hebrew Syntax,* p. 98, § 69b; Waltke and O'Connor, *Biblical Hebrew Syntax,* p. 170.

11. Noting that *kî* introduces the second clause of the brothers' words to their father *(w*ᵉ*ḵî hû' mōšēl),* but not the first clause ("Joseph is still living"), leads Andersen (*Sentence in Biblical Hebrew,* p. 116) to suggest that the *kî* is assertative: "Joseph is still alive, and he *surely* is ruler." See also Blau, *Grammar of Biblical Hebrew,* p. 106, § 103.3.

land of Egypt," he was numb,[12] *for he did not believe them.*

27 *But when they had shared with him everything that Joseph had said to them, and when he saw the wagons that Joseph had sent to transport him, the spirit of their father revived.*[13]

28 *"It is enough,"*[14] *said Israel. My son Joseph is still alive! I must go down and see him*[15] *before I die."*

Joseph's brothers, designated as *sons of Israel,* carry out Pharaoh's bidding with Joseph's assistance (v. 21). In addition to the promised items Joseph supplies each of his brothers with a change of clothes. Benjamin comes out considerably better than his brothers. He receives *five changes of clothing* and *three hundred pieces of silver.* Once again the motifs of clothing[16] and silver, each prominent at different points in the Joseph narrative, surface. He who once was stripped of his clothes by his brothers now clothes those same brothers. Unlike the previous occasion when Joseph furtively slipped money into the sacks of the brothers, he now openly gives three hundred silver shekels to Benjamin. Joseph does not state why he gives the money to Benjamin, nor does he say anything about what the shekels should be used for.[17] The one previous place where clothing and silver appeared side by side was ch. 37. Joseph is already demonstrating his forgiveness of that dastardly event both by his words (45:5ff.) and by his deeds (vv. 21ff.).

The description of Joseph's going-away gifts to his brothers (v. 22a)

12. The verb *pûg* is rare in the OT. Besides Gen. 45:26 it is found in Ps. 38:9 (Eng. 8); 77:3 (Eng. 2); Hab. 1:4 Cf. M. D. Johnson, "The paralysis of torah in Habakkuk i 4," *VT* 35 (1985) 259-60. In Ps. 38:9 (8) the verb (in Niphal) parallels *nid̲kêt̲î,* which means "broken, crushed" (RSV: "utterly spent and crushed"; NEB: "all battered and benumbed"). In Ps. 77:3 (Eng. 2) the verb refers to an exhausting paralysis. Thus the basic meaning of the verb "seems to be that of being frozen or numbed, a condition of inability to function" (Johnson). See also Redford, *Study of the Biblical Story of Joseph,* pp. 63-64.

13. Targ. Onqelos reads this last phrase, "the holy spirit [*rwḥ qwdš*] rested on their father Jacob," suggesting that through divinely stimulated reflection and intuitiveness, the truth about Joseph finally dawned on Jacob.

14. *rab̲* as an exclamation, "enough!" appears in Exod. 9:28; Num. 16:3, 7; Deut. 1:6; 2:3; etc. See Blau, *Grammar of Biblical Hebrew,* p. 82, § 53.1.

15. A. F. Rainey ("The Prefix Conjugation Patterns of Early Northwest Semitic," in *Lingering over Words,* Fest. W. L. Moran, ed. T. Abusch, J. Huehnergard, and P. Steinkeller [Atlanta: Scholars, 1990], p. 419) cites *wᵉʾerʾennû* as an instance of the attraction of the longer pronominal suffixes of 3rd sing., masc. and fem., to the Hebrew cohortative (first person).

16. For other references to clothing as a part of the Joseph story, see 37:3, 31-33; 38:14, 19; 39:12-18; 41:14.

17. "Joseph trusts that the other brothers will perceive this predilection" (Westermann, *Genesis,* 3:147).

and to Benjamin (v. 22b) is followed by the listing of his gifts for his father: *ten donkeys* and *ten*[18] *she-asses,* all loaded with desperately needed *provisions* (v. 23). Are these twenty animals in addition to the brothers own donkeys? Most likely so. Knowing full well his brothers' capacity for duplicity and disagreement, he urges them not to quarrel or debate among themselves (v. 24), as he had previously observed them doing (42:22).

Only one item is recorded in vv. 25-28 about the brothers' return to Jacob: *Joseph is still living!* Once he hears that, Jacob has little concern about the new clothes, Benjamin's purse, or even the grain carried by the animals. In ch. 37 Jacob did believe his sons when they were lying to him. In ch. 45 Jacob disbelieves his sons when they are being truthful with him. Bad news he accepts; good news he rejects. Jacob's response on hearing that Joseph is alive is parallel to the response of the disciples when they were told that Jesus was alive — shock, unbelief, which eventually turns to uncontrollable joy.

The sons' lengthy conversation with Jacob about Joseph (v. 27a) and the sighting of the wagons (v. 27b)[19] provide prima facie evidence for Jacob that Joseph was indeed alive. No longer did he need to pinch himself to see if he was dreaming (v. 27c). The sons might have been making up the story about Joseph, but the *wagons* supply irrefutable confirmation of the authenticity of their story, more so than the clothing or the three hundred shekels.

Now convinced that Joseph is alive, Jacob resolves to go down to Egypt immediately. He suggests the possibility that his time is growing shorter (v. 28c). If he waits too long, advancing age or death will prohibit such a voyage. This is too touching a moment for Jacob to say: "your brother Joseph is still alive." *My son Joseph* is how he speaks of the boy whom he has not seen for so long.

It is fitting that Jacob be styled as *Israel* in the last verse (usually interpreted as a sure evidence of J). Israel is Jacob's new name, a name that speaks of a new destiny and a new future. Here is Israel with a new hope and a new expectation. Joseph is alive. Israel will meet him shortly. Here is Israel in v. 28 making the decision as the head of the family to go to Egypt to see Joseph.[20]

18. Had he given them eleven donkeys and she-asses, there would have been a set of animals for each brother. Does Benjamin remain behind with Joseph (Lowenthal, *Joseph Narrative in Genesis,* p. 108)?

19. On the interesting ways in which some of the rabbinic literature interacted with how the wagons provided irrefutable evidence of Joseph's existence to Jacob (could not the sons have secured some wagons as part of a ruse?), see J. L. Kugel's discussion of the texts, *In Potiphar's House,* pp. 102-5.

20. Longacre, *Joseph,* p. 151.

J. JACOB AND HIS FAMILY SETTLE IN EGYPT (46:1-34)

1. JACOB LEAVES CANAAN FOR EGYPT (46:1-7)

1 *So Israel set out, along with all his relatives and belongings, and reached Beer-sheba, where he offered sacrifices to the God of his father Isaac.*

2 *God spoke to Israel in a night vision.*[1] *He said: "Jacob, Jacob!" to which he replied: "I'm here!"*

3 *And he said: "I am the God, the God of your father.*[2] *Do not be fearful about going down*[3] *to Egypt, for into a great nation I will form you there.*

4 *I myself will go down with you to Egypt, and furthermore I myself will surely bring you back up.*[4] *Joseph's hand shall close your eyes."*[5]

5 *So Jacob left Beer-sheba, and the sons of Israel carried Jacob their father, along with their little ones*[6] *and wives, in the wagons that Pharaoh*[7] *had sent to carry him.*

6 *They took their cattle and their possessions acquired in the land of Canaan and set out for Egypt — Jacob and all his offspring with him.*

1. Lit., "visions" *(mar'ōṯ)*. Words pl. in form but sing. in meaning are not uncommon in Biblical Hebrew. See GKC, § 124e, and M. Greenberg, *Ezekiel 1–20,* AB (Garden City, NY: Doubleday, 1983), p. 41. LXX reads a sing., *horámati* (presupposing Heb. *mar'aṯ*).

2. *hā'ēl 'ĕlōhê 'āḇîḵā* is a case of apposition involving repetition. In such instances the appositive repeats the lead word. See Waltke and O'Connor, *Biblical Hebrew Syntax,* p. 234. On the significance of the article in *hā'ēl,* see O. Loretz, "Die Epitheta *'l 'lhj jśr'l* (GN 33, 20) und *'l 'lhj 'bjk* (GN 46, 3)," *UF* 7 (1975) 583, who argues for its retention, versus F. M. Cross, *Canaanite Myth and Hebrew Epic* (Cambridge: Harvard University, 1973), pp. 12 n. 38, 46 n. 13, who argues for its deletion.

3. The form of the infinitive is strange *(mērᵉḏâ),* and not the expected *mēreḏeṯ* (see, e.g., Job 33:34). See GKC, § 69m, who observes that "the change of the *ē* into vocal *šᵉwa* is to be explained . . . from its position between the principal and secondary tone."

4. Note the Qal infinitive absolute *('ālōh)* connected with the same root in the Hiphil *('a'alḵā),* on which see GKC, § 113w; Waltke and O'Connor, *Biblical Hebrew Syntax,* p. 582. On the emphasizing *gam* before an infinitive absolute, see Andersen, *Sentence in Biblical Hebrew,* p. 166.

5. Lit., "and Joseph shall put (or lay) his hand upon your eyes."

6. On LXX *aposkeuḗ* ("baggage"; "a soldier's baggage, family and other persons attached to him"; "a soldier's family (wife, children, and other household members") to render *ṭap* ("family"?), see J. A. L. Lee, *Lexical Study of the Septuagint Version of the Pentateuch,* pp. 105-6.

7. LXX reads "Joseph."

7 *His sons and his grandsons, his daughters and granddaughters, and all his offspring he brought with him to Egypt.*[8]

1 Presumably Israel/Jacob still resides in Hebron (37:14; 35:27), and it is from there that he *set out* or "journeyed" (*wayyissa';* cf. 12:9; 13:11; 20:1; 35:21]) to Beer-sheba. From there he "goes down" (*yāraḏ,* v. 4) to Egypt. His reason for making the journey is obvious. He wants to see Joseph, whom he supposed was long dead. Thinking he himself has but a little while longer to live, he resolves to go to Egypt. Joseph has invited him to come, and he accepts gladly.

The previous chapter mentioned that his sons informed him of Joseph's invitation (45:27), but said nothing about Pharaoh's invitation. It is difficult to know whether the omission of this detail is due to the brothers or to the narrator. Did they ignore the generous words of Pharaoh when talking with their father, or did the narrator delete this section of their communication with Jacob? In any case, Pharaoh's invitation is subordinated to Joseph's invitation. What excites Jacob is the word of hospitality from his son who "was dead and is alive" (cf. Luke 15:24).

Upon reaching Beer-sheba Jacob presents sacrifices to his Lord, designated as *the God of his father Isaac.* A father on his way to see his son pauses to worship the God of his own father. It was at this same site that God appeared to Isaac and reminded him that he was the "God of his father Abraham" (26:23-25). Apart from Gen. 31:54 (also in connection with Jacob and the God of his father [v. 53b]), this is the only instance of the verb *zāḇaḥ* ("offer [a sacrifice]") in Genesis. Isaac built the altar (*mizbēaḥ,* 26:25) at Beer-sheba, and a generation later his son offered sacrifices *(zᵉḇāḥîm)* at that place. It is significant that Jacob's sacrifice precedes God's speech. The act of worship is thus cast as a spontaneous expression of gratitude by Jacob, rather than a response by Jacob to any promise from God.

2 God speaks to Jacob during the *night,* the time of darkness, as he did to Abraham (15:5ff.), and even to foreigners like Abimelech (20:3) and Laban (31:24). Jacob himself knows from previous experience the meaning of a nocturnal meeting with deity (28:10ff.; 32:22ff. [Eng. 21ff.]). The repetition of Jacob's name recalls the same phenomenon with his grandfather at Moriah (22:11; cf. also Exod. 3:4; 1 Sam. 3:10; Acts 9:4).

It is somewhat surprising to find the patriarch designated as both *Israel* and *Jacob* in the description of this brief theophany, which source critics

8. Vv. 6b-7 are an apposition sentence: *wayyāḇō'û miṣrāymâ ya'ᵃqōḇ . . .: bānāyw . . . hēḇî' 'ittô miṣrāymâ,* a stylistic feature (cf. 8:18-19) and therefore not tediously redundant or even necessarily reflective of different sources. See Andersen, *Sentence in Biblical Hebrew,* p. 40.

identify as most certainly Elohistic. In this particular verse, and in the preceding one, the narrator uses "Israel," while in the actual theophany God calls him "Jacob," which, I suggested earlier, is used when the fretful, apprehensive, suffering patriarch is in view. The rule of thumb is that J uses "Israel," while E (and P) uses "Jacob." Here is an instance where that neat separation breaks down.[9] Note later in v. 5 that "the sons of *Israel* carried *Jacob* their father."

It has been some time since the narrator informed us that God appeared and spoke to Jacob. The most recent occurrence recorded in Genesis is found in 35:9ff. Many years earlier God came to Jacob at Bethel and gave him a reminder and reconfirmation of his destiny. Now years later the divine voice speaks again, and Jacob has no apparent problems deciphering it.

The whole life of Abraham, in terms of receiving divine promises, is ringed by speeches of God which focus exclusively on the promises of God to Abraham and his progeny. God's first talk to Abraham (12:1-3) and final talk to Abraham (22:15-18) are God's promises. Similarly, God's first talk to Jacob (28:13-16) and his last talk to Jacob (46:2-4) are promises.

3-4 These two verses contain one of the four "do not be fearful" oracles in Genesis (see 15:1; 21:17; and 26:24). This particular oracle is composed of four parts: (1) self-identification of the deity: *I am the God,* [a general name for deity] *the God of your father* [a specific name for deity]; (2) assurance: *Do not be fearful;* (3) object of fear: *about going down to Egypt;* (4) promise: *for into a great nation I will form you. . . . Joseph's hand shall close your eyes.*[10] Of these four parts, the last is easily the longest and most prominent.

If Jacob is fearful about going down to Egypt, he did not disclose that in either 45:28 or 46:1. The prospect of seeing his son overrides concern over any mishap they may encounter on the way to Egypt or in Egypt. Jacob does not need to be coaxed to leave Canaan. He is prepared to pull up his roots and leave for the empire to the south. God's word to Jacob about not being fearful about going down to Egypt is a considerable change from his earlier explicit charge to Jacob's father's Isaac not to go down to Egypt (26:2). What God denied Isaac he permits for Jacob. For Isaac Egypt was off-limits. For Jacob Egypt is the land in which God will bless Jacob and his progeny, and form them into a nation. Thus the sojourn of Jacob and his family to Egypt

9. The presence of "Israel" in v. 2a, normally taken to be from E, presents a problem. Speiser (*Genesis,* p. 346) refers to its use in v. 2a as "an accidental carry-over from the preceding verse," which is an unconvincing explanation. Redford (*Study of the Biblical Story of Joseph,* p. 20) attributes vv. 1-2a to J, and 2b-4 to E.

10. See E. W. Conrad, "The 'Fear Not' oracles in Second Isaiah," *VT* 34 (1984) 143-45, for this outline of 46:3, 4.

is not in fundamental opposition to God's purposes. Rather, the sojourn is part of the development of God's plan for this chosen family, first articulated to Abraham in 12:1ff.[11]

Jacob first offered sacrifices to "the god of his father" (v. 1), and now he is addressed by deity whose self-identification is *I am the God* [*hā'ēl*], *the God of your father.* The general name of God *('ēl)* has appeared elsewhere in the Jacob story (see 31:13; 35:1, 3). Perhaps the addition of the article *(hā-)* destroys the titular use of the word, and alters its sense from "El" to "the God (of). . . ."[12] The narrator (v. 1) used the full title, "the God of his father Isaac." God identifies himself simply as "the God of your father," leaving out the name of Isaac. "This is the only national promise in the patriarchal narratives which is not attributed to Yahweh or El Shaddai, but to the God, the God of your Father."[13]

The surprise of v. 3 is the last clause: *for into a great nation I will form you there.* This clause indicated to Jacob that his journey to Egypt will not be a quick excursion. He will move from the ranks of the visitor into those of the immigrant. Egypt will become his home away from home. While this is by no means the first time that God announces his intention to make a great nation from the patriarchs and their progeny, and even Ishmael (see 12:2; 17:20; 18:19; and esp. 21:13, 18, which also use the verb *śîm* ["make"] and the noun *gôy* ["nation"] in conjunction with Ishmael), it is the first time he announces that this formation will take place well outside the borders of the promised land in Egypt. Egypt will become the womb for this great nation. Of all God's promises throughout Genesis to make a great nation of somebody's descendants, the one to Jacob in 46:3 and the one to Ishmael in 17:20 and 21:13, 18 are most similar in that neither includes the promise of a national territory.[14] For the bedouin-like Ishmael the absence is self-explanatory. In the case of Jacob, this theophany emphasizes only the establishment of a great nation but in an unusual geographical milieu. That Jacob is the root from which a great nation is to be formed in the relatively secluded Egyptian region of Goshen, rather than in Canaan, implies that this nation will be insulated from outside influences that may impinge on their group identity.[15]

It is not enough that Jacob is accompanied by his family and possessions to Egypt. God himself will be his personal escort (v. 4a). Jacob does

11. See J. H. Sailhammer, *The Pentateuch as Narrative* (Grand Rapids: Zondervan, 1992), p. 224.

12. See N. Wyatt, "The Problem of the 'God of the Fathers,'" *ZAW* 90 (1978) 103.

13. Z. Weisman, "National Consciousness in the Patriarchal Promises," *JSOT* 31 (1985) 65.

14. See ibid., p. 66.

15. See Lowenthal, *Joseph Narrative in Genesis,* p. 113.

not intuit that information; he knows it by revelation. This is the reason Jacob need not be intimidated. Egypt is not inaccessible to the God of Israel. Regarding the clause in v. 4b, *I myself will bring you back,* the reader, but not Jacob himself, knows that this clause does not mean that Jacob will physically leave Egypt alive and well. We know he would later leave Egypt in a coffin (ch. 50). *you* can only refer to Jacob's remains and Jacob's descendants. In fact, there are three referents of "you/your" in v. 4: "I will accompany you [Jacob and his family], I will bring you [the nation] back, then Joseph's hand shall close your [Jacob's] eyes." Here is an intriguing illustration of the oscillation between the individual and the collective, a well-known feature of OT thought. There is no problem here at all of passing from the individual to the community and back to the individual without any awareness of the transitions.

From the emphasis on the national ("I will bring you back") the verse turns to the tender *(Joseph's hand shall close your eyes).* The brother who once knew what it was like to have his brothers place their hands on him in fraternal rage will place his hand upon his father in filial devotion. The announcement of his forthcoming death, placed in an amiable context, is much like that of his grandfather's (see 15:13-16). Abraham's "going to your fathers in peace; buried in a good old age" parallels this word in 46:4c about Jacob's demise and Joseph. Jacob knows all about eyes. He had a father with fading eyesight (27:1), and a wife with tender eyes (29:17). V. 4c is also part of the divine promise to Jacob. V. 4a, b emphasizes God's presence with Jacob from the present occasion until the end of his life. V. 4c emphasizes Joseph's presence with his father in the waning days of his father's life, whenever that comes.

5 Jacob is not deterred from traveling further by the recent disclosure that his life will end in Egypt. He has no thoughts of turning back. He is not terrorized by the possibility that he will die beyond the borders of his homeland. He, along with his daughters-in-law and grandchildren, is helped back onto the wagons to continue their trek to Egypt.

6-7 This is a drastic relocation. Jacob is transplanting his entire belongings to Egypt, and leaving his birth land, as had his grandfather Abraham. Either by ignorance or by intention he disregards Pharaoh's suggestion that they leave their goods (*k^{e}lêḵem,* 45:20) behind when he packs their possessions *(r^{e}ḵûšām)* as well. Especially interesting in the listing by groups of the traveling party is the reference to *daughters.* We know of only one — Dinah. That there were daughters other than Dinah is confirmed by 34:9, 16, 21. Note also that the granddaughters of v. 7 are his sons' daughters, not his daughters' daughters. Absent from v. 7 is any reference to Jacob's wives and concubines. Rachel is dead, but what about Leah, Zilpah, and Bilhah?

The repetition of *all his offspring* in vv. 6 and 7 emphasizes that none of Jacob's offspring is excluded from the divine blessing. Jacob's family has certainly had as much, if not more, fraternal friction as that of Abraham and of Isaac. Yet Jacob has no Ishmael, as Abraham had, and no Esau, as Isaac had. Jacob's decidedly dysfunctional family is on the verge of coming together again in genuine community.

2. JACOB'S EXTENDED FAMILY (46:8-27)

8 *These are the names of the descendants of Israel who came to Egypt, Jacob and his descendants. Jacob's firstborn was Reuben.*

9 *Reuben's sons: Hanoch, Pallu, Hezron, and Carmi.*[1]

10 *Simeon's sons: Jemuel, Jamin, Ohad,*[2] *Jachin, Zohar,*[3] *and Shaul,*[4] *the son of a Canaanite woman.*

11 *Levi's sons: Gershon, Kohath,*[5] *and Merari.*[6]

12 *Judah's sons: Er, Onan, Shelah, Perez, and Zerah. Now Er and Onan had died in the land of Canaan. Perez's sons were Hezron and Hamul.*

1. Here, and in Exod. 6:14; Num. 26:6; and 2 Chr. 5:3, Carmi is a Reubenite. Josh. 7:1 identifies Achan as "the son of Carmi, son of Zabdi, son of Zerah, of the tribe of Judah." Either there is a Judahite Carmi and a Reubenite Carmi, or else there has been some mixture in tribal backgrounds. Cf. Jo Ann Hackett, "Religious Traditions in Israelite Transjordan," in *Ancient Israelite Religion,* Fest. F. M. Cross, ed. P. D. Miller, Jr., P. D. Hanson, and S. D. McBride (Philadelphia: Fortress, 1987), p. 136 n. 16.

2. Num. 26:12-14 and 1 Chr. 4:24 do not have the name Ohad among Simeon's sons as do Gen. 46:10 and Exod. 6:15, possibly because the clan bearing the name of Ohad later disappeared.

3. This son's name is Zohar *(ṣōḥar)* here, but Zerah *(zeraḥ)* in Num. 26:13 and 1 Chr. 4:24. Since one of Judah's sons is also Zerah (v. 12), and also the fifth son listed, it is possible, given Simeon's later absorption into Judah, that descendants of Zohar were linked with both tribes.

4. O. Margalith ("More Samson legends," *VT* 36 [1986] 399 n. 6) notes that Saul is transcribed *Samouēl* in some LXX mss., an evidence he cites of the easy change between "Samuel" and "Saul" in the account of the birth of the child (Samuel? Saul?) to Hannah (1 Sam. 1:17ff.); on this problematic narrative see, e.g., P. K. McCarter, Jr., *I Samuel,* AB (Garden City, NY: Doubleday, 1980), pp. 61-66.

5. On the connection of the Hebrew personal name *qᵉhāṯ* and the Ugaritic personal name *'aqht* ("ruler"?), son of Danel, cf. J. Gray, *The Legacy of Canaan,* 2nd ed. (Leiden: Brill, 1965), p. 111 n. 1.

6. On the apparent contradiction between Gen. 46:11, which states that Levi's sons moved to Egypt during the great famine, and the LXX of the difficult Hebrew phrase in Num. 26:59 ("Jochebed, Levi's daughter, who bore these to Levi in Egypt" for the Hebrew "Jochebed, Levi's daughter, whom she [?] bore her to Levi in Egypt"), see S. Levin, "An Unattested 'Scribal Correction' in Numbers 26,59?" *Bib* 71 (1990) 25-33.

13 *Isaachar's sons: Tola, Puvah,*[7] *Jashub,*[8] *and Shimron.*[9]

14 *Zebulon's sons: Sered, Elon,*[10] *and Jahleel.*[11]

15 *These are the sons of Leah that she bore to Jacob in Paddan-aram, along with Dinah his daughter. In all, his sons and daughters numbered thirty-three.*[12]

16 *Gad's sons: Ziphion,*[13] *Haggi, Shuni, Ezbon,*[14] *Eri, Arodi,*[15] *and Areli.*[16]

17 *Asher's sons: Imnah,*[17] *Ishvah, Ishvi, Beriah, and Serah*[18] *their sister. Beriah's sons were Heber*[19] *and Malchiel.*

7. *pûʾâ* in 1 Chr. 7:1; *puwwâ* here, *puwâ* in Num. 26:23. Judg. 10:1-2 speaks of the judge Tola, son of Puah, and places him in the hill country of Ephraim.

8. Following SP and LXX *(yāšûḇ)* rather than MT *yôḇ,* "Iob," and *yāšûḇ* in Num. 26:24 and 1 Chr. 7:1.

9. In Josh. 11:1 Shimron is a Canaanite enclave and its king in league with Jabin of Hazor, while in Josh. 19:15 it is part of the territory assigned to Zebulon. Cf. R. Boling and G. E. Wright, *Joshua,* AB (Garden City, NY: Doubleday, 1982), p. 305.

10. In Judg. 12:11-12 Elon is a Zebulonite judge. His name means "oak" or "terebinth."

11. If one emends *yaḥl^{e}ʾēl* to *y^{e}ḥîlāʾēl,* the meaning "May he live long, O El" becomes possible. See M. J. Dahood, "Vocative *lamedh* in Exodus 2,14 and Merismus in 34,21," *Bib* 62 (1981) 413 n. 5. Westermann (*Genesis,* 3:153) reads *yḥl lʾl,* "let him wait for God."

12. In Hebrew the more frequent sequence of combined numbers is the lower preceding the higher. Thus in 5:20 "62" is "two and sixty". In 12:4 "75" is "five and seventy." In 7:11 "17" is "seven, ten." It is occasionally the opposite sequence, esp. when *šānâ* ("year") is used; thus "88" is "eighty and eight" (16:16), and "99" is "ninety and nine" (17:1); here Leah's descendants are "thirty and three." Cf. the total given for the number of city-states taken by Israel under Joshua (Josh. 12:9-24). V. 24 ends "thirty-one kings in all" (lit., "total kings: thirty and one." B. Levine (*Numbers 1–20,* AB [New York: Doubleday, 1993], pp. 262-63) suggests that the listing of totals such as one finds in Josh. 12:24 or Gen. 46:15 may indicate that original ideographic numerals were subsequently replaced by words.

13. SP and LXX read *ṣ^{e}pôn* for MT *ṣipyôn.* See Num. 26:15, which agrees with the reading of SP and LXX in Gen. 46:16.

14. In Num. 26:16 the equivalent name is "Ozni" *(ʾoznî).* Here MT has *ʾeṣbōn;* SP and Pesh. read *ʾeṣbaʿôn.* LXX *Thasoban (= teṣbôn)* may be accounted for by the confusion of the letters *aleph* and *taw,* which were quite similar in the Hebrew script.

15. In Num. 26:17 "Arodi" is "Arod."

16. "Areli" *(ʾarʾēlî)* may be understood as "My God is a Light (or Fire)." See E. Lipiński, "Notes on the Mesha Inscription," *Or* 40 (1971) 334.

17. Possibly a hypochorism (i.e., a shortened form) for *yimnâ-ʾēlēl* or *yimnâ-yāh,* "May El (or Yah[weh]) destine." See M. J. Dahood, "Stichometry and Destiny in Psalm 23,4," *Bib* 60 (1979) 418 n. 9.

18. Serah is also mentioned in Num. 26:46 and 1 Chr. 7:30; apart from Jacob's wives and concubines, she is, along with Dinah, the only female in this genealogy. On her presence in Num. 26:46 see Milgrom, *Numbers,* JPS Torah Commentary (Philadelphia: Jewish Publication Society, 1990), p. 226.

19. For possible connections between Heber of Gen. 46:17 and Eber of Num. 24:24 see W. Wifall, Jr., "Asshur and Eber, or Asher and Heber?" *ZAW* 82 (1970) 110-14.

18 *These are the sons of Zilpah, whom Laban gave to Leah his daughter, and these she bore to Jacob — sixteen persons in all.*

19 *The sons of Rachel, Jacob's wife: Joseph and Benjamin.*

20 *Joseph became the father of two sons, Manasseh and Ephraim, whom Asenath daughter of Potiphera, priest of On, bore to him in the land of Egypt.*

21 *Benjamin's sons: Bela, Becher, Ashbel, Gera, Naaman,*[20] *Ehi, Rosh, Muppim, Huppim,*[21] *and Ard.*[22]

22 *These are the sons of Rachel who were born*[23] *to Jacob — fourteen persons in all.*

23 *Dan's son:*[24] *Hushim.*[25]

24 *Naphtali's sons: Jahzeel, Guni, Jezer, and Shillem.*[26]

25 *These are the sons of Bilhah, whom Laban gave to Rachel his daughter, and these she bore to Jacob — seven persons in all.*[27]

20. Naaman means "darling"; the Ugaritic cognate *nʿmn* is an epithet for Aqhat (e.g., *UT,* 2 Aqht VI:45) and Keret (e.g., *UT,* 128:II:20; Krt 40, 61). See H. L. Ginsberg, "The North-Canaanite Myth of Anat and Aqhat," *BASOR* 97 (1945) 4 n. 8. In Num. 26:40 Naaman and Ard are sons of Bala.

21. "Hupham" in Num. 26:39. For other instances of rhyming names ("Muppim, Huppim") cf. Mahlon and Chilion in Ruth 1:2; Uz and Buz in Gen. 22:21; and Hendan, Eshban, Ithran, and Cheran in Gen. 36:26.

22. The list of the Benjamite clans in Num. 26:38-41 omits the following names found in Gen. 46:21: Becher, Gera, Ehi, Rosh, Muppim. In addition, Num. 26 identifies Ard and Naaman as grandsons of Benjamin. It is possible that Ehi, Rosh, and Muppim are not genuine names; they may be an inaccurate reading of the names Ahiram and Shephupham, which do appear in Num. 26:38-39 but not in Gen. 46:21 (G. B. Gray, *Critical and Exegetical Commentary on the Book of Numbers,* ICC [Edinburgh: T. & T. Clark, 1903], p. 393).

23. SP and Pesh.: "which she bore." By changing MT's Pual 3rd masc. perfect into a Qal 3rd fem. perfect, SP and Pesh. make the formula in 46:22 exactly parallel to the one in 46:15.

24. The word is pl. ("sons") even though only one son is listed, most likely because of the frequent use of pl. *bᵉnê* throughout this genealogy.

25. Num. 26:42 reverses the first two consonants of the name, reading *šḥm,* "Shuham," for *ḥšm,* "Hushim."

26. 1 Chr. 7:13 has "Shallum" for "Shillem" and "Zahziel" for "Jahzeel." But the spellings of these names in Num. 26:48, 49 agrees with Gen. 46:24 over against the spellings in 1 Chr. 7:13.

27. This formula is the same as that used in 46:18, a summarizing statement about Leah's daughters, just as the formula used in v. 22 (Rachel's children; see n. 23 above) parallels the formula used in v. 15 (Leah's children).

28. Lit., "those coming out of his thigh" *(yōṣᵉʾê yᵉrēḵô),* with *yārēḵ* being a euphemism for the genitals. Cf. Exod. 1:5; Judg. 8:30; and M. Malul, "More on *paḥad yiṣḥāq* (Genesis XXXI 42, 53) and the oath by the thigh," *VT* 35 (1985) 194 n. 9. N. J. Tromp (*Primitive Conceptions of Death and the Nether World in the Old Testament,* BibOr

26 *Jacob's people who migrated to Egypt, that is, his own issue,*[28] *but excluding the wives of Jacob's sons, numbered sixty-six in all.*

27 *The sons of Joseph, born*[29] *to him in Egypt, were two.*[30] *Thus all the people in Jacob's family who came to Egypt totalled seventy*[31] *in all.*

Jacob does not go down to Egypt alone. Vv. 8-27 supply the specifics hinted at in v. 7 (sons, grandsons, daughters, granddaughters). Again, as in v. 2, we find *Israel* and *Jacob* in the same verse (v. 8).

This genealogy has six parts. First is the introduction (v. 8ab), then respectively the sons of Jacob by Leah (vv. 8c-15), the sons of Jacob by Zilpah (vv. 16-18), the sons of Jacob by Rachel (vv. 19-22), the sons of Jacob by Bilhah (vv. 23-25). The genealogy ends with a summarizing statement (vv. 26-27), which gives a qualified total in v. 26 and a grand total in v. 27.

Through Leah Jacob obtains thirty-three descendants (six sons, twenty-five grandsons, two great-grandsons). But from this list one must exclude Er and Onan (v. 12) who died in Canaan (38:7, 10), and thus the total number of Jacob's male children who went with him to Egypt is thirty-one. That number is raised to thirty-two with the inclusion of Dinah (v. 15). Unless there is another, unnamed daughter (cf. v. 15c, "in all, his sons and *daughters* numbered thirty-three"), then the total of thirty-three can be obtained only with the inclusion of Jacob himself. Yet v. 15 identifies the above names as "the sons [or 'descendants'] of Leah that she bore to Jacob."

Through Zilpah he obtains sixteen descendants (two sons, eleven grandsons, one granddaughter, two great-grandsons). Through Rachel he obtains fourteen descendants (two sons, twelve grandsons). Through Bilhah he obtains seven descendants (two sons, five grandsons). As a whole, the list contains twelve sons, fifty-three grandsons, one granddaughter, and four great-grandsons. The wives produce twice as many descendants (46/47) as the concubines (23).[32] Of Jacob's children Dan is the least fruitful (one son),

---

21 [Rome: Pontifical Biblical Institute, 1969], p. 181 and n. 26) prefers "inward parts" for *yārēḵ* in Gen. 46:26.

29. Note pl. subject ("sons of Joseph") with sing. verb *(yullaḏ),* as in 35:26. Sperber (*Historical Grammar of Biblical Hebrew,* pp. 89-93) cites frequent instances from Biblical Hebrew in which the verb and the substantive that belongs to it do not agree with one another in number. Sperber rejects the constant tendency of *BHK* (and, I may add, of *BHS*) to "correct" such passages.

30. LXX "nine." LXX does not list all nine, but it does list Manasseh and his son Galaad, Ephraim and his sons Sutalaam and Taam, and Sutalaam's son Edom.

31. LXX "seventy-five"; cf. Exod. 1:5 (LXX); Acts 7:14. See the commentary below.

32. Leah has 32 descendants (33 including Dinah) and Rachel 14, for a total of 46 (47 including Dinah). Zilpah has 16 descendants and Bilhah 7, for a total of 23. Thus Leah has twice the descendants of her handmaid Zilpah, and Rachel has twice the descendants of her handmaid Bilhah.

Benjamin is the most fruitful (ten sons). Only with Judah and Asher does the genealogy extend into the fourth generation.

Each of the four sections delineating Jacob's offspring (vv. 8c-25) ends with a summarizing formula (vv. 15, 18, 22, 25), stating by categories how many descendants Jacob realized through the respective maternal lines. There is one interesting addition in these formulaic statements. In the concubine groups, we are reminded that Laban gave Zilpah to Leah and Bilhah to Rachel. We are not told that Laban gave Rachel and Leah to Jacob, which he did. It has been sometime in the Genesis narrative since Laban was present (see ch. 31). Why does the narrator remind us at this point of Laban? It is most unlikely he is writing to a people who will be in the dark about Zilpah and Bilhah without further clarification. The resurrection of Laban's name momentarily throws us into the past. It takes us back from a Jacob with seventy kin to a Jacob with no kin. It recalls the similar crisis Jacob faced there. In ch. 31 Jacob was preparing to leave Paddan-aram for Canaan under less than happy circumstancs. Here Jacob is preparing to leave Canaan for Egypt under equally unsettling circumstances. In ch. 31 he had to deal with Laban. In ch. 46 he has to deal with a famine. In ch. 31 he fled with his family. In ch. 46 he moves with his family.

Several items distinguish the section given over to Jacob's family through Rachel (vv. 19-22). First, it is the only unit which has an introductory formula (*The sons of Rachel,* v. 19), as well as the summarizing formula (v. 22). Second, Rachel is the mother of Jacob's most fruitful son — Benjamin. Third, for every other son of Jacob the genealogy reads: "Reuben's sons: . . . ," "Simeon's sons: . . ." etc. For Joseph alone his family is introduced with, "Joseph became the father of. . . ." Fourth, Joseph is the only son of Jacob whose wife is named in this genealogy: *Asenath.* Just as the reference to Laban in vv. 18, 25 is to distant history, the reference to Asenath in v. 20 is to recent history. Fifth, of the fifty-three grandsons mentioned in the genealogy, only Joseph's sons and those of Judah have been mentioned elsewhere in Genesis. The majority of these grandsons are but names, included in genealogies but absent from narratives. Nevertheless, God has a role for each — for the famous and for the otherwise unknown.

The first number given to Jacob's descendants is *sixty-six* (v. 26). This group is identified as those *who migrated to Egypt* with Jacob. Excluded from that caravan are Er and Onan, for they are already dead (v. 12; see 38:7, 10), as well as Joseph, Manasseh, and Ephraim, who are already in Egypt. Thus, eliminating those five names from the seventy listed brings the number to sixty-five, but sixty-six is obtained by the addition of Dinah.[33]

33. Thus 32 (Leah) plus 16 (Zilpah) plus 11 (Rachel, and excluding Joseph, Ephraim, and Manasseh) plus 7 (Bilhah) equals 66; or, less likely, 31 (Leah, excluding Jacob and Dinah) plus 16 (Zilpah) plus 12 (Rachel, excluding Ephraim and Manasseh) plus 7 (Bilhah) equals 66.

The second number computed for Jacob's offspring is *seventy* (v. 27).[34] The increase from sixty-six in v. 26 to seventy in v. 27 is arrived at by the inclusion of Jacob himself, Joseph, and Joseph's two children. The LXX's seventy-five[35] comes about by the deletion of Jacob and Joseph and the addition of nine sons of Joseph instead of two.[36]

It is clear that seven (and multiples thereof) is prominent in this genealogy, whose total number of entries is 70.[37] Rachel has fourteen descen-

34.

Gen. 46 (MT)	
Leah's children:	
Reuben and 4 sons	5
Simeon and 6 sons	7
Levi and 3 sons	4
Judah, 3 sons, 2 grandsons	6
Issachar and 4 sons	5
Zebulon and 3 sons	4
Dinah	1
[Jacob]	1
Subtotal:	33
Zilpah's children:	
Gad and 7 sons	8
Asher, 4 sons, 1 daughter, 2 grandsons	8
Subtotal:	16
Rachel's children:	
Joseh and 2 sons	3
Benjamin and 10 sons	11
Subtotal:	14
Bilhah's children:	
Dan and 1 son	2
Naphtali and 4 sons	5
Subtotal:	7
Total:	70

Jub. 44:12-33	
Leah's children:	
Reuben and 4 sons	5
Simeon and 6 sons	7
Levi and 3 sons	4
Judah, 1 son, 2 grandsons	4
Issachar and 4 sons	5
Zebulon and 3 sons	4
[Jacob]	1
Subtotal:	30
Zilpah's children:	
Gad and 7 sons	8
Asher, 4 sons, 1 daughter	6
Subtotal:	14
Rachel's children:	
Joseph and 2 sons	3
Benjamin and 10 sons	11
Subtotal:	14
Bilhah's children:	
Dan and 5 sons	3
Naphtali and 5 sons	6
Subtotal:	12
Total:	70

35. In agreement with the number "70" are Exod. 1:5 (MT) and Deut. 10:22 (MT). "75" is read by the LXX in Gen. 46:27; Exod. 1:5; Deut. 10:22 and in the Hebrew fragment from the Dead Sea Scrolls 4QEx[a]. See F. F. Bruce, *Book of the Acts,* NICNT, rev. ed. (Grand Rapids: Eerdmans, 1988), p. 137 n. 34; idem, *Acts of the Apostles,* 3rd ed. (Grand Rapids: Eerdmans, 1990), p. 196; J. T. Milik, *Ten Years of Discovery in the Wilderness of Judaea,* tr. J. Strugnell, SBT 1/26 (Naperville, IL: Allenson, 1959), p. 24. S. Kamim ("The Hebraica Veritas in Jerome's Thought," in *Sha'arei Talmon,* Fest. S. Talmon, ed. M. Fishbane and E. Tov [Winona Lake: IN: Eisenbrauns, 1992], p. 251 n. 25) notes Jerome's apology for the "error" in Acts 7:14 in his *Hebraicae Quaestiones in Libro Geneseos.*

36. See n. 20 above.

37. On "70" as a number of a group cf. Gen. 10; Exod. 24:1, 9; Num. 11:16, 24, 25; Judg. 1:7; 8:30; 9:2; 1 Sam. 6:9; 2 K. 10:6; Luke 10:1, 17.

dants, and Bilhah has seven. Together they have twenty-one. Together Leah and Bilhah have forty-nine descendants. The seventh son of Jacob listed in this genealogy is Gad. Gen. 29–30 (see 30:11) is the only other Jacobite genealogy in which Gad is placed in the seventh position. Interestingly, the numerical value of the seventh-placed Gad is seven (*g* = 3; *d* = 4).[38]

The genealogy of Jacob in Gen. 46:8ff. and those in Num. 26:5ff. and 1 Chr. 2–8 obviously have some major differences, as we have indicated briefly in some of the notes above. Confining ourselves to Gen. 46 and Num. 26, we note the following types of differences. The first is differences in spelling. The following examples will suffice: Jemuel (Gen. 46:10) and Nemuel (Num. 26:12); Puwwah (Gen. 46:13) and Puah (Num. 26:13); Iob (Gen. 46:13) and Jashub (Num. 26:24); Ziphion (Gen. 46:16) and Zephon (Num. 26:15); Ezbon (Gen. 46:16 and Ozni (Num. 26:15).

The second type of difference is names found in one genealogy but missing in the other. Thus Gen. 46:10 lists Ohad as the third of Simeon's six children. Num. 26:12-14 gives only five children for Simeon, and there is no Ohad. Gen. 46:17 lists four sons of Asher, of whom the second is Ishvah. Num. 26:44 lists three sons of Asher and omits Ishvah. There are also names in the Numbers' genealogy (Ahiram, Shephupham, sons of Benjamin [vv. 38, 39]) that appear nowhere in Gen. 46.

The third difference is in overall numbers. Gen. 46:21 lists ten sons for Benjamin. Apart from the surprise that a still relatively young Benjamin has fathered ten children in so few years, we note that Num. 26:38-39 attribute only five sons to Benjamin. Two individuals listed in Gen. 46:21 as sons of Benjamin and brothers to Bela (Ard, Naaman) are listed in Num. 26:40 as sons of Bela and grandsons of Jacob. All of this suggests that there is a bit of artificiality in Gen. 46:8-27, and that the genealogy need not be pressed for historical exactness.

If source critics are correct in attributing this genealogy to P (as is done with all the genealogies in the Pentateuch), one that P either concocted or borrowed, then one must ask how it fits into its present context. Now to be sure, Jacob is about to embark on a journey to Egypt. And what more appropriate place to insert a list of his family than here? There is more, however. Vv. 1-7 emphasized that Jacob will have one kind of company when he heads down to Egypt — God himself. Vv. 8-27 focus on another kind of company Jacob will have when he heads down to Egypt — his nuclear family. Thus one might say that the number accompanying Jacob on this journey is seventy-one, for he has God to guide him and his family to support him.[39]

38. See J. M. Sasson, "A Genealogical 'Convention' in Biblical Chronography?" *ZAW* 90 (1978) 181.

39. On the brief recapitulation of Gen. 46:8-27 to open the book of Exodus (1:1-7), see M. Greenberg, *Understanding Exodus* (New York: Behrman House, 1969), pp. 18-20;

3. JACOB AND JOSEPH MEET (46:28-34)

28 *Judah he sent ahead of him to Joseph to show*[1] *the way before him to Goshen.*[2] *When they*[3] *arrived at Goshen,*

29 *Joseph harnessed his chariot,*[4] *and off he went*[5] *to Goshen to meet*

B. S. Childs, *Book of Exodus,* OTL (Philadelphia: Westminster, 1974), pp. 1-3; S. Talmon, "The Presentation of Synchroneity and Simultaneity in Biblical Narrative," *Scripta Hierosolymitana* 27 (1978) 14-15.

1. *lᵉhôrōṯ* presents problems. The Hiphil infinitive, if from *yārâ* II, must be rendered, "to point out" (BDB, p. 435a). SP and Pesh. read a Niphal infinitive of *rā'â, lᵉhērā'ōṯ,* "to appear." (See 2 Sam. 17:17; 1 K. 18:2; Ezek. 21:29 for this form.) LXX *synantḗsai autṓ* suggests *lᵉhiqqārôṯ,* "to present himself" (see *BHS*). Comments by skilled Hebraists such as Skinner (*Genesis,* p. 495): "The Hebrew here gives no tolerable sense"; and Speiser (*Genesis,* p. 345): "Little can be done with Hebrew *lhwrt*" indicate the perplexity of the verb form. Skinner, Speiser, and Westermann all prefer the reading of the LXX, even though that reading does not fit smoothly with the syntax of the rest of the sentence. The most frequent meaning of this root in the Hiphil is "to teach." An extension of this meaning produces the idea of "pointing out, directing." Cf. *HALAT,* 2:417; and J. Weingreen, *From Bible to Mishna* (New York: Holmes and Meier, 1976), pp. 108-9. I suggest that the strongest support for the reading of the LXX in this verse ("to present himself") is the use of *wayyērā'* ("when he saw him") in the following verse.

2. LXX reads not "Goshen" but the enigmatic "to the city of Heroes [*Hērṓōn polin,* Heropolis?], into the land of Ramesses" (Heropolis = Pithom).

3. SP, Vulg., and Pesh. read a sing., "when he arrived," which reflects their reading of *lᵉhôrōṯ* as "to appear before him [Joseph]."

4. For the verb *'āsar* used for preparing/harnessing a "chariot," see Exod. 14:6 and 2 K. 9:21 (these two references use *reḵeḇ* for "chariot," not *merkāḇâ* as here). An exact parallel to the verb and noun in Gen. 46:29 is found n the second Phoenician inscription from Arslan Tash (upper Syria, 7th century B.C.): *bʿl 'sr mrkbty.* "Baal has harnessed my chariot." See Y. Avishur, "Studies of Stylistic Fetures Common to the Phoenician Inscriptions and the Bible," *UF* 8 (1976) 18; J. C. L. Gibson, *Textbook of Syrian Semitic Inscriptions,* 3 vols. (Oxford: Clarendon, 1971-82), 3:89-90. See also the lines in the Ugaritic text (*UT,* 123.21-23; *CTA,* 22.A.22-23) *ilnym asr mr*[*kbt . . .*] *tʿln mr* [*kbt hm*]: "The gods hitched up/tied up their chariots . . . they get up to their chariot" (Avishur, ibid.; and M. Dijkstra and J. C. de Moor, "Problematic Passages in the Legend of Aqhâtu," *UF* 7 [1975] 214-15).

5. The same verb *(ʿālâ)* is used in v. 29 for Joseph's "going up" to meet Israel and in v. 31 for Joseph's "going up" to inform Pharaoh of his family's arrival. See S. Shibayama, "Notes on *Yārad* and *ʿĀlāh:* Hints on Translating," *JBR* 34 (1966) 360-62. In Egyptian "to go up (the Nile)" means to go south, and "to go down (the Nile)" means to go north, because the Nile runs from south to north. It is clear why *ʿālâ* is used in v. 29, for Goshen was higher than the Nile Valley (Skinner, *Genesis,* p. 495). But that explanation does not fit *ʿālâ* in v. 31, which describes Joseph's going to a lower place than Goshen, suggesting one should render *ʿālâ* there as "go south," thus reflecting Egyptian linguistic idiom.

Israel his father. When he saw him he flung himself on his neck and wept on his neck steadily.[6]

30 *Then Israel said to Joseph: "Now I can die,*[7] *now that I have seen your face and know you are alive."*

31 *Joseph then said to his brothers and to his father's household:*[8] *"I will go and inform Pharaoh and tell him, 'My brothers and my father's household, who were once in the land of Canaan, have come to me.*

32 *The men are shepherds, livestock-men are they. Their flocks and herds and everything they own they have brought.'*

33 *So when Pharaoh sends for you and inquires about your occupation,*

34 *You shall answer: 'Livestock-men have your servants been from our youth until this very moment, both we and our ancestors.' Thus you will be allowed to remain in the land of Goshen, because an abomination to Egyptians is every shepherd."*[9]

28 *Judah* precedes the party heading to Egypt both positionally and syntactically. Special prominence is given to Judah in this verse by his placement at the very beginning of the sentence, even though he is the direct object. It is ironic that Judah is selected to play the lead role, to be the mediator in the forthcoming reuniting of long-separated father and son, for he earlier had played the lead role in separating father from son (37:26ff.).[10] After this mention, Judah plays no further role in the meeting between Jacob and Joseph. Judah is sent by his father as a courier to Joseph, to be a liaison between the two. Jacob knows from previous experience what it means in an intense moment to send a party ahead *(šālaḥ lᵉp̱ānāyw)* to meet a family member one has not seen in a good while. Recall the events surrounding the preparation for his meeting with Esau (32:4 [Eng. 3]). There it was Esau. Here it is Joseph. Some twenty years have separated brother from brother and father from son. In both instances Jacob sends a party ahead of him to meet the relative.

6. For *ʿōḏ* with stress on the idea of continuance, see BDB, p. 729a (AV "a good while"); cf. Ruth 1:14; Ps. 84:5 (Eng. 4).

7. GKC, § 108b, describes *'āmûṯâ* as a cohortative used "as a more or less emphatic statement of a fixed determination . . . *now let me die (I am willing to die).*" Concerned with Jacob's apparent death wish, which was considered inappropriate, Targ. Onqelos reads his words as a subjunctive clause: "If I were to die now I would be comforted" *('ylw 'n' m'yt bzymn' hd' mnḥm 'n').*

8. LXX omits "and to his father's household." The MT may reflect dittography here (the phrase appears in the latter half of the verse), and thus LXX would show the more original reading.

9. Targ. Onqelos softens Egyptian contempt for the shepherd ancestors of Israel by reading "for the Egyptians keep all shepherds at a distance" *('ry mrḥqyn mṣr'y kl r'y ʿn').*

10. See Sarna, *Genesis,* p. 317; Humphreys, *Joseph and His Family,* p. 85.

29 No record is given of any speech of Judah to Joseph. No details are provided about Judah's arrival in Egypt. From this point onward he is unmentioned in the narrative. Joseph makes immediate preparations to leave and head for Goshen.

There are no words exchanged between father and son, now united after many years of separation. There is much weeping and touching. Conversation can wait. Joseph has already had more than one weeping spell (42:24; 43:30; 45:14, 15). Others still await him (50:1, 17). When Jacob was informed by his other sons that Joseph was "dead," he wept over Joseph (37:35). Now it is Joseph's turn to weep, not because Jacob is dead, but because he is alive. Tears of sorrow (ch. 37) are replaced by tears of joy (ch. 46).

Joseph is clearly most eager to be reunited with his father. He goes to see his father rather than waiting for his father to come all the way to his residence. Joseph harnesses his own chariot rather than delegating that work to his subordinates, much as his great-grandfather Abraham earlier had saddled his donkey himself before making a trip involving a family member, something the two servants with him would normally do (22:3).

As some scholars have observed, the phrase *When he saw him (wayyērāʾ ʾēlâw)* may also be translated "when he appeared to him." At least six other times in Genesis this expression describes a divine appearance to a patriarch (to Abraham: 12:7; 17:1; 18:1; to Isaac: 26:2, 24; to Jacob: 35:9); this is the only place in Genesis that it describes the meeting of two people. Its use here does not, however, convey the same nuance one finds in the other citations (i.e., a solemn occasion in which a superior discloses himself to an inferior). If Joseph is the subject of the following verbs ("he flung"; "he wept"), then seeing is the prelude to the emotional reunion of father and son. Seeing plays the same role here as in Jesus' parable of the two sons: "but while he was still a long way off, his father *saw* him" (Luke 15:20).

30 In many ways Jacob's words, upon seeing Joseph, parallel those of Simeon in the temple: "Lord, now let your servant depart[11] in peace . . . for my eyes have seen your salvation" (Luke 2:29-30). Jacob can now happily accept death, knowing that he will no more go to his grave with unanswered questions about his beloved Joseph's circumstances.

Jacob had a previous experience of seeing a face, the result of which he was never again the same. The face that time was God's. He named that place Peniel. He had seen God's face, yet he continued to live. Having seen Joseph's face, he needs to live no longer.

Jacob may feel he is now prepared to die, but he will have seventeen more years of life before that moment comes (47:28). Earlier he had seventeen

11. *apolýein* (lit., "set free, release") is used in the LXX for the death (i.e., release from life) of Abram (Gen. 15:2) and Aaron (Num. 20:29).

years with Joseph (37:2). After a long hiatus he has another seventeen years with Joseph.

31-32 Joseph is cautious enough to make sure that every necessary diplomatic step is taken. He wants nothing to happen that would prevent his family's remaining in Goshen. It is incumbent that Pharaoh be informed about the family's arrival and presence in Goshen. In addition to the announcement of their arrival, Joseph will tell Pharaoh about his family's vocation (they are *shepherds*), and the animals they have brought with them. This is Joseph's way of hinting to Pharaoh that Goshen is the ideal territory in which to allow his family to settle. By adding the data about the animals, Joseph is underlining to Pharaoh that his family perceives this as a permanent move, and that what his family was in Canaan, they wish to be in Egypt. They want to change residences, but not occupations.

33-34 Joseph's final piece of advice to his family is patterned along the lines of frequent counsel given by Moses to his people. For example, in connection with Passover observance he states: "And when your children say to you, 'What do you mean by this service?' you shall say, 'It is the sacrifice of the Lord's passover' " (Exod. 12:26-27). One person (Joseph, Moses) tells a group (his family, the Israelites) that in the future they will be asked a question. That question is then stated either indirectly (Joseph) or directly (Moses). Then the individual who cites the question provides an answer, "you shall say. . . ."

In the answer they are primed to recite, Joseph's family is to reinforce that cattle breeding has been in their family for generations: *both we and our ancestors.*[12] It will not hurt their case to designate themselves as *your servants* before Pharaoh.

The thrust of Joseph's last statement is not clear: *an abomination to Egyptians is every shepherd.* Might not such an acknowledgment by Jacob and his children that they are shepherds or cattle-breeders result in their exclusion from Egypt, if in fact such people are an abomination in Egypt? There is slim, if any, indication in Egyptian literature that Egyptians held shepherds in contempt, unless one sees here a popular understanding (Manetho, Josephus) of the term *hyksos* (invaders from Asia in the 17th century B.C. who ruled over Egypt for approximately a century, with their capital at Avaris in the Delta), later held in contempt by Egyptians as "shepherd kings." If Joseph is associated with a group of people, a family, that engages in a despised occupation, what does that do to his own reputation and his ability to expedite his responsibilities?[13] Perhaps it is best to under-

12. The claim is not fabricated. Abraham (13:7, 8), Isaac (26:14), and Jacob (32:16ff.) all had herdsmen.

13. See Humphreys, *Joseph and His Family,* pp. 182-83.

stand Joseph's remark as applying only to non-Egyptian shepherds, that is, reflecting Egyptian xenophobia. Perhaps this statement by Joseph reflects the tension that existed in Egypt as well between the urbanites and those living in the open country. It also reflects the earlier tension between Abel, who was a shepherd (*rōʿēh ṣōʾn,* 4:2, the same expression as at the end of v. 34), and Cain, who was a farmer. Cain and the Egyptians are workers of the land. Abel and Joseph's family are shepherds of the flocks. What in Gen. 4 was a fraternal division is in Gen. 46 an international division.[14]

In Exod. 8:22 (Eng. 26) Moses stated that offering sacrifices in Egypt would be an abomination in the eyes of the Egyptians. Both Exod. 8:22 (Eng. 26) and Gen. 46:34 use the word *tôʿēḇâ* (see also its use in 43:32) to point out what Egyptians considered abhorrent, i.e., pastoral pursuits. Precisely why the Egyptians would so view the sacrifices from the flocks of the Hebrews is not stated. In any case, Joseph is encouraging his family to be absolutely honest with Pharaoh regarding their occupation. They are not to try and be something they are not. Dishonesty is an issue that long plagued Jacob and his family. It is Judah who shows his family the way to Goshen. But it falls to his brother Joseph to make it possible for his family to settle in Goshen.

K. JACOB AND PHARAOH BECOME LANDOWNERS (47:1-26)

1. PHARAOH MEETS FIVE OF JOSEPH'S BROTHERS (47:1-6)

1 *Joseph then went and told Pharaoh: "My father and my brothers, along with their flocks and herds and everything they have, have come from the land of Canaan. They are now in the land of Goshen."*

2 *He had selected five*[1] *of his brothers from their entire group*[2] *and had*

14. See R. B. Coote and D. R. Ord, *The Bible's First History* (Philadelphia: Fortress, 1989), p. 197.

1. Some commentators (e.g., Speiser, *Genesis,* p. 348) and translations (e.g., NJPS) consistently translate "five" in the Joeph story as "several" or "few," taking "five" as a round number.

2. Lit., "from the edge (or end)," *miqṣēh,* which is "a condensed term for what is included within extremities, = the whole" (BDB, p. 892a). Cf. also this use of *miqṣēh* in 1 K. 12:31 ("from among all the whole range of the people"); 13:33; 2 K. 17:32; Ezek. 33:2 ("and the people of the land take a man from among them [RSV]/from their midst" [W. Zimmerli, *Ezekiel,* tr. R. E. Clements and J. D. Martin, Hermeneia, 2 vols. (Philadelphia: Fortress, 1979-83), 2:179]). All these passages use a pl. form of *qᵉṣēh*

presented them to[3] *Pharaoh.*

3 *When Pharaoh asked his brothers,*[4] *"What is your occupation?" they replied to Pharaoh, "we your servants are shepherds,*[5] *as were our forefathers."*[6]

4 *They continued:*[7] *"To sojourn in the land we have come, for there is no feed for your servants' sheep, so intense is the famine in the land of Canaan. Please permit your servants to dwell in the land of Goshen."*

5 *Then Pharaoh said to Joseph: "So your father and brothers have come to you.*[8]

6 *The land of Egypt lies open to you. In the choice parts of the land settle your father and brothers. Let them settle in the land of Goshen.*[9]

(*miqṣôṯ,* 1 K. 12:31; *miqṣêhem,* Ezek. 33:2). A good parallel to the sing. of *qᵉṣēh* in Gen. 47:2 is Num. 22:41, where *wayyar' miššam qᵉṣēh hā'ām* does not mean "he saw from there the mass of people" (J. Gray, *1 & 2 Kings,* OTL, 2nd ed. [London: SCM; Philadelphia: Westminster, 1970], p. 317) but "from there he could see a portion of the people" (J. Milgrom, *Numbers,* JPS Torah Commentary [Philadelphia: Jewish Publication Society, 1990], pp. 193-94). Balak permits Balaam to see only a portion of the Israelites, lest their size intimidate Balaam and even nullify his curse against them. Cf. also S. Talmon, "Divergences in calendar-reckoning in Ephraim and Judah," *VT* 8 (1958) 50-51.

3. On the use of *lip̄nê* in the context of gaining an audience with one's superiors, see M. D. Fowler, "The Meaning of *lip̄nê* in the Old Testament," *ZAW* 99 (1987) 386.

4. LXX, SP, and Pesh. have "the brothers of Joseph." The difference between the MT and the versions may be explained by the fact that in the Hebrew text proper names of persons and places, esp. those which occur often, were frequently abbreviated. Thus *'ᵃḥê y'* was read as *'eḥāyw* (MT) or *'ᵃḥê yôsēp̄* (LXX, SP, Pesh.). See G. R. Driver, "Abbreviations in the Massoretic Text," *Textus* 1 (1960) 121.

5. MT has a sing. *(rō'ēh ṣō'n).* For words sing. in form but with a collective meaning, see Davidson, *Hebrew Syntax,* p. 19, § 17; Waltke and O'Connor, *Biblical Hebrew Syntax,* p. 115.

6. Pesh. adds, "from our youth," in line with the presence of the phrase in 46:34.

7. Lit., "they said to Pharaoh" or "they further said to Pharaoh."

8. The order of the LXX differs considerably from that of the MT for vv. 5-6. The LXX has (1) v. 5a, "then Pharaoh said to Joseph"; (2) v. 6b, "let them settle . . . overseers of my own flocks"; (3) an insert, "When Jacob and his sons came to Joseph in Egypt, and Pharaoh said to Joseph"; (4) v. 5b, "your father and your brothers have come to you"; (5) v. 6a, "The land of Egypt lies before you . . . settle your father and brothers." See the commentary below.

9. Pharaoh's words to Joseph in vv. 5b and 6abc consist of four independent sentences. Andersen (*Sentence in Biblical Hebrew,* p. 37) notes: "The ubiquitous Hebrew 'and' is less common in vernacular speech than in narrative and other more literary discourse. This may account for the rather jerky effect of the high level of asyndeton in Pharaoh's speech."

If you know[10] *of capable men*[11] *among them, appoint them as overseers of my own livestock."*

1 Judah represented his father before Joseph. Joseph now represents his family before Pharaoh. He informs Pharaoh that his family has arrived in Egypt and are now in Goshen. This is the first speech of Joseph to Pharaoh since that recorded in 41:25ff. He revises slightly the original draft of the speech. To his family Joseph had said: "I will go and tell Pharaoh, my brothers and my father's household . . . have come to me" (46:31). In this speech he changes "my brothers and my father's household" to *my father and my brothers,* thus highlighting the appearance of his father. (He makes no direct mention of daughters, grandsons, or granddaughters.) He also replaces "have come to me" with *They are now in the territory of Goshen,* thus laying the foundation for the brothers' request to be allowed to settle in Goshen (v. 4). They have come to Egypt, not to Joseph. Pharaoh, however, later says to Joseph that "your father and brothers have come to you" (v. 5b).

2 On his own Joseph picks *five* (or "several," or a "few")[12] of his brothers to present them to Pharaoh. Which five? Why only five? What are the criteria for selection? Those whom he believes would make the best impression on Pharaoh? Following A. B. Ehrlich, Speiser is inclined to think that Joseph took the more outstanding brothers because "the context is made emphatic through inversion" (i.e., lit., "from the edge/extremity of his brothers he took five").[13] Rabbinic tradition takes the opposite position. For example, Gen. Rabbah 95:4 has the interpretation that he took five of the more inferior, less formidable brothers, fearing that Pharaoh would make soldiers out of the stronger brothers had Joseph taken them. According to that tradition, Joseph took with him Reuben, Simeon, Levi, Benjamin, and Issachar.

10. *wᵉyeš* here has the sense of *kî yeš,* "that there are." For the conjunctive use of *waw* in *wᵉyeš* see M. Greenberg, *Ezekiel 1–20,* AB (Garden City, NY: Doubleday, 1983), p. 238, who observes a similar use of the *waw* in Ezek. 13:11: "Say to those who daub on untempered plaster *that* it will fall [*wᵉyippōl*]." Cf. also *niḥašštî wayᵉḇārᵃḵēnî,* "I have grown rich, for (Yahweh) has blessed me," in Gen. 30:27.

11. See M. Weinfeld, "The Royal Guard According to the Temple Scroll," *RB* 87 (1980) 395 n. 6, who connects the phrase *'anšê ḥayil* with the same phrase in Exod. 18:21. Both times the meaning is "capable men." Exod. 18:21 lists three characteristics of an individual who belongs to the *ḥayil* category: he fears God; he is trustworthy; he is above bribery. Gen. 47:6 demonstrates that the honesty and trustworthiness of the *ḥayil* are recognized outside Israel. See C. Gottlieb, "The Words of the Exceeding Wise: Proverbs 30:31," in *The Biblical Canon in Comparative Perspective,* Scripture in Context 4, ed. K. L. Younger, Jr., W. W. Hallo, and B. F. Batto (Lewiston, NY: Edwin Mellen, 1991), pp. 282ff., and her discussion of *'ēšeṯ ḥayil* ("capable woman"?) in Prov. 31:10 and Ruth 3:11.

12. See n. 1 above.

13. Speiser, *Genesis,* p. 350.

It makes most sense to translate the verbs in this sentence as pluperfects (hence *had selected . . . had presented*). Joseph does not travel from Goshen to Pharaoh's palace, announce the arrival of his family in Egypt, return to Goshen, select five of his brothers, then make a second trip to Pharaoh.

3 Joseph was correct in his supposition (46:33) that Pharaoh would begin his conversation with a leading question: *What is your occupation?* The question is addressed, of course, only to a delegation of the brothers. Joseph delays in presenting his father to Pharaoh, possibly to avoid the embarrassment of having his esteemed father stand before Pharaoh to beg a favor, as did the brothers in v. 4. The brothers' answer also varies from Joseph's instructions. He had urged them to identify themselves as "cattle-breeders" (*'anšê miqneh,* 46:34). They identify themselves, instead, as *shepherds (rōʿēh ṣō'n).* In fact, they use the specific term which Joseph had identified as a vocational abomination among the Egyptians (46:34). If they are playing with potential fire, no damage was caused by their revised version. In later conversation Pharaoh casts no negative aspersions on Jacob and his family in spite of their vocation.

4 In addition to such revisions, the brothers' response to Pharaoh also includes amplifications. They share with Pharaoh why they have come to Egypt (*to sojourn,* or seek temporary residency, in Egypt and respite from *the famine in the land of Canaan*), and what their request is *(Please permit your servants to dwell in the territory of Goshen).* They are throwing themselves on Pharaoh's good graces and mercy. Three times they refer to themselves before Pharaoh as *your servants* (vv. 3, 4 [twice]). They never mention that they have come to Egypt because Joseph invited them (45:9ff.), or because Pharaoh too invited them (45:17ff.). It is need, more than privilege or courtesy, that brings them to Egypt.

5-6 In the translation above I have noted the textual problem in vv. 5-6. If one allows priority to the LXX for these two verses, as do many commentators,[14] then the following situation emerges. What unfolds in 47:1-6 is two accounts of Joseph before Pharaoh. In the J account (vv. 1-4, 5a, 6b), Joseph announces his family's arrival in Goshen and introduces several of them to Pharaoh. Pharaoh first speaks to them, then to Joseph, assuring Joseph of his permission for his kin to reside in Goshen, even offering incentives for his brothers. This is followed by P's account, which begins with a section missing in MT and vv. 5b, 6a, and continues to v. 12. In this version Pharaoh shares with Joseph the arrival of his family in Egypt and promises them the pick of the land.

The main reason for preferring LXX over MT is that v. 6b is a logical sequel to v. 4. At the end of v. 4 the brothers say, *permit your servants to dwell in the territory of Goshen.* To which vv. 5a and 6b respond, *Then Pharaoh said to Joseph, "Let them settle in the land of Goshen."* V. 4 is the request; vv. 5a and 6b are the answer.

14. For example, Speiser, *Genesis,* pp. 350-51; Skinner, *Genesis,* pp. 497-98.

Those who would favor the LXX at this point overlook the problem this division creates. For source critics, P's account is especially a conundrum. It declares that Pharaoh first heard about the arrival of Jacob and his family in Egypt. He, in turn, relayed this information to Joseph (vv. 5b, 6a). This account clashes severely with the data presented earlier. There it was stated that Judah sought out Joseph, found him, and took him to his family in Goshen (46:28ff.) Pharaoh plays no role. But the problem extends beyond the clash in J and P of how Joseph found out about his family's appearance in Egypt. P's account appears incredible if it is a distinct source. It affirms that Joseph found out secondhand about his kin's arrival. That never happened before in any of the brothers' visits to Egypt to procure corn.[15]

Joseph began this dialogue by speaking to Pharaoh (v. 1), Pharaoh then speaks to Joseph's brothers (v. 3a). The brothers speak to Pharaoh (vv. 3b-4). Lastly, Pharaoh speaks to Joseph (vv. 5-6). In the first and last of these speeches talker and listener are reversed (Joseph-Pharaoh; Pharaoh-Joseph). Why should Pharaoh address Joseph, and not his family? He did so because he delegates to Joseph the authority to accept Jacob's family into Egypt, and to supervise their settlement in Goshen.

It is conceivable that the brothers will rise in rank in Egypt as their brother Joseph did. Their feet have hardly touched Egyptian soil, and already they are tantalized with the possibility of being placed in charge of the royal cattle. Pharaoh is interested not in *'anšê miqneh* ("cattle-breeders," 46:32) but in *'anšê-ḥayil* (*capable men,* 47:6). This terminology indicates that the best Egyptian cattle were pastured in the area of Goshen. An Egyptian Pharaoh requesting the services of Hebrew herdsmen to tend his animals may be compared with a Hebrew Solomon requesting the services of Phoenician craftsmen to help him build a temple. Perhaps shepherding is a vocation that the upper-class Egyptian felt beneath his dignity. In this way shepherding was an "abomination" to them (46:34).

Pharaoh is magnanimous. His offer (vv. 5-6) goes beyond the request of Joseph's brothers in v. 4. They had asked only for permission to sojourn in the land, and to dwell in Goshen. Pharaoh's words *The land of Egypt lies open to you. In the choice parts*[16] *of the land settle your father* are, in the words of the NT, "immeasurably more than all we ask or imagine" (Eph. 3:20, NIV). His words also evidence his benignity toward Joseph.

15. On the unity of thought in the MT of vv. 5-6 see Westermann, *Genesis,* 3:168-69; Redford, *Study of the Biblical Story of Joseph,* pp. 159-60; Sarna, *Genesis,* p. 319.

16. *mêṭāḇ* appears only in the construct in Biblical Hebrew *(mêṭaḇ)* with superlative meaning (Exod. 22:4, "the best of his field and the best of his vine yard"; and 1 Sam. 15:9, 15, "the best of the sheep").

2. PHARAOH MEETS JACOB (47:7-12)

7 *Then Joseph brought in Jacob his father and presented him to Pharaoh. Jacob blessed Pharaoh.*

8 *Pharaoh asked Jacob: "How many years*[1] *have you lived?"*

9 *Jacob replied to Pharaoh: "My years as a sojourner amount to one hundred and thirty. Few and difficult have been the years*[2] *of my life.*[3] *They come nowhere near comparing with the years of my fathers' sojournings."*[4]

10 *Then Jacob blessed Pharaoh and went out from Pharaoh's presence.*

11 *And Joseph settled his father and brothers and gave them property in Egypt, in the choice parts of the land, the region of Rameses, as Pharaoh had ordered.*[5]

12 *Joseph sustained his father and brothers, and his father's entire household, with food, each according to the number of children.*[6]

1. For other questions about age introduced by *kammâ y^e^mê* see 2 Sam. 19:35 (Eng. 34); Ps. 119:84.

2. Both uses of the phrase "the years of" in this sentence, as well as "my years as," read lit., "the days of the years of. . . ." S. J. DeVries (*Yesterday, Today and Tomorrow* [Grand Rapids: Eerdmans, 1975], pp. 45, 46) cites the pl. of *yôm* in "few and difficult have been the years of my life" (lit., "few and difficult have been the days of the years of my life") as a use of *yôm* in the pl. in reference to a gnomic present, with the qualifiers of *yôm* in the predicate position.

3. The sentence "Few and difficult . . ." is in apposition to the preceding one ("My years as a sojourner . . .") and makes explicit some detail lacking in the first sentence. The apposition sentence adds the unanticipated comment that Jacob's life was both brief and difficult. See Andersen, *Sentence in Biblical Hebrew,* p. 47.

4. The phrase "the years of my father's sojournings" reads lit., "the days of the years of the lives of my fathers' sojournings," and shows that as many as three constructs may follow one another, each depending on the one after it as its genitive. See GKC, § 128a.

5. On the force of the LXX rendering of *ṣiwwâ* by *prostáttō,* see A. Pelletier, "L'autorité divine d'après le Pentateuque grec," *VT* 32 (1982) 240. Pelletier notes that the Greek translators of the Pentateuch were sensitive to the variety of nuances inherent in the Hebrew verb for "command," and thus they exploited the resources of the Greek language to explicate each of these nuances. *prostáttō* emphasizes the dignity of the one issuing the command (for references, see ibid., p. 242 n. 10).

6. Lit., "by the mouth of the little ones" *(l^e^pî haṭṭāp̱).* G. R. Driver ("Two Problems in the Old Testament Examined in the Light of Assyriology," *Syria* 33 [1956] 70-73) connects *haṭṭāp̱* with Aram. *ṭippā',* "little drop," and Assyrian *ṭuppu,* "bit, piece." This provides him with the translation "in full measure," or "within a drop." This suggestion is reflected in NEB "with all the food they needed," REB "with the food they needed"; see also Redford, *Study of the Biblical Story of Joseph,* pp. 51-52; *HALAT,* 2:362. In the "Addenda and Corrigenda" to BDB, p. 1123b, the authors note that the Heb. *ṭāp̱* may

7 When Joseph presented his brothers to Pharaoh (v. 2), the narrator used the verb *yāṣag* (Hiphil; see 43:9). When Joseph presents his father to Pharaoh, the narrator uses the verb *ʿāmaḏ* (Hiphil; see 43:15 for the Qal). No great inference may be extracted from this divergence, except to note that *ʿāmaḏ* (Hiphil) *lip̄nê* is a common expression in priestly contexts where somebody or something (a leper, Lev. 14:11; a goat, 16:7; an animal, 27:11) is brought before somebody else (the king, Yahweh, the priest).

Pharaoh's conversations with the sons (vv. 3-6) and with the father (vv. 8-10) differ in some respects. For one thing Pharaoh's conversation with Jacob is preceded and followed by *Jacob blessed Pharaoh,* something the sons did not do. The trend among some translators of the Hebrew text of Genesis has been to render *bāraḵ* in vv. 7, 10 not with the traditional "bless" but with "paid respects to" (Speiser, NAB, NJB) or "greeted" (NJPS) in v. 7, and "took leave" (Speiser, NJB) or "bade farewell" (NAB, NJPS) in v. 10.[7] Now it is true that sometimes in the OT *bāraḵ* means "greet." For example, Prov. 27:14 says, "He who blesses [i.e., greets] his neighbor with a loud voice, rising early in the morning, will be counted as cursing" (RSV).[8] Cf. also Ruth 2:4, where the reapers' words to Boaz, "May Yahweh bless you [*bāraḵ,* Piel]," should be understood as a greeting formula between employer and employees. Again, one finds the Piel of *bāraḵ* to express a greeting in 2 K. 4:29 ("do not *salute* him; and if anyone *salutes* you . . ." [RSV]), and in 2 K. 10:15 ("and he *greeted* him" [RSV]). Both Gen. 47:7 and 2 K. 4:29 have in common the use of *bāraḵ* (Piel) for two parties in which the speaker and the addressee are total strangers.

I prefer the translation "bless" in 46:7, 10, or at least "greet with a blessing."[9] This is something the sons would hesitate to do (and hence its

include, or imply, women as well as children in some passages, Gen. 47:12 being one of them. The LXX translates *ṭāp̄* by *aposkeuḗ,* which occurs 16 times in the Pentateuch, usually as a rendering of *ṭāp̄,* and it too has a broader meaning, including wife, children, and other household members. See J. A. L. Lee, *Lexical Study of the Septuagint Version of the Pentateuch,* pp. 101-7, esp. p. 104. For "each according to the number of children," see Coote and Ord, *Bible's First History,* p. 197; *HALAT,* 2:362 *(nach der Kinderzahl);* Westermann, *Genesis,* 3:165. Speiser's "down to the youngest" and NJPS's "down to the little ones" is another attempt to make sense of the obscure Hebrew.

7. The following versions retain "bless" in both verses: AV, NKJV, RSV, NRSV, NEB, REB, JB, NIV (with a footnote that the verb may be translated "greeted" in v. 7 and "said farewell to" in v. 10).

8. See H. C. Brichto, *The Problem of "Curse" in the Hebrew Bible,* JBLMS 13 (Philadelphia: Society of Biblical Literature, 1968), p. 190, for the rendering of the Piel of *bāraḵ* in Prov. 27:14 as "greet, salute." See also C. W. Mitchell, *The Meaning of BRK "To Bless" in the Old Testament,* SBLDS 95 (Atlanta: Scholars, 1987), pp. 106-8.

9. See B. A. McKenzie, "Jacob's Blessing on Pharaoh: An Interpretation of Gen. 46:31–47:26," *WTJ* 45 (1983) 390-95, for this interpretation of *bāraḵ* in Gen. 47:7, 10.

absence in v. 2), but it falls within the jurisdiction of the paterfamilias. Here is one of the relatively rare places in the OT where we find the pattern *A* (the inferior) blessing *B* (the superior).[10] Jacob is inferior to Pharaoh as regards position, but may be superior to Pharaoh in the matter of age, and at least is well beyond the Egyptian ideal of the 110-year life. Perhaps Jacob prayed that the pharaoh may be blessed with a long life. The OT has several instances of a subject entering the presence of royalty and exclaiming "O king, live forever!" (2 Sam. 16:16; 1 K. 1:31; Dan. 2:4; 5:10; 6:7 [Eng. 6]). Such a blessing might also explain why in the next verse Pharaoh inquires about how long Jacob has lived.

Pharaoh has enriched Jacob's family. He has promoted son Joseph to a prominent position in Egypt. On several occasions he has sent much-needed grain back to Canaan with Jacob's other sons. He has invited Jacob and his family to Egypt with freedom to settle anywhere. Jacob is profoundly grateful for the assistance Pharaoh has provided. The appropriate response is to bless Pharaoh. "He has enriched us. May God enrich him." Vv. 13-26, which detail Joseph's agrarian reforms, serve as a stunning illustration of the consequence of Jacob's blessing on Pharaoh.

Blessing has surfaced repeatedly in Genesis, and most often the dispenser of blessing is God. Here is one of the few places where both the subject and object of "bless" are human beings. Jacob blesses Pharaoh. Jacob knows what it means to be the object of blessing. Chs. 27 and 28 provide most of the instances in Genesis of one person (Isaac) blessing another person (Jacob). Jacob, once the recipient of blessing, now becomes the source of blessing.

8 Pharaoh's question to Jacob's sons had to do with their occupation (v. 3). Pharaoh's question to Jacob has to do with Jacob's age. Pharaoh had no need to ask about Jacob's occupation, since occupation probably passes from father to son. What Jacob does, Jacob's children do. There is no particular reason why Pharaoh should lead with this question, other than to see in it "an act of sharing."[11] But Jacob did bring seventy of his progeny with him, some of whom are three generations removed from Jacob. Jacob did come to Egypt riding on a wagon, courtesy of Pharaoh, and onto which his sons "boosted" him (46:5). Maybe to Pharaoh Jacob just looked very old.

9 Jacob's response is something of a surprise. He has lived 130 years (and will have 17 more to go for a total of 147 years [47:28]).[12] Thus his life

10. See J. Scharbert, *"brk," TDOT,* 2:291-92. Apart from Gen. 47:7, 10, the only other cases of subjects blessing the king are Exod. 12:32 (Moses and Pharaoh); 1 K. 8:66 (the people and Solomon); Ps. 72:15 (the psalmist and the king).

11. Westermann, *Genesis,* 3:170.

12. I noted in the genealogy of 46:8-27 the prominence of seven. Note that Jacob's 147 years may be factored as 3×7^2. See further the commentary on 47:28.

span will be somewhat less than the 180 of his father Isaac (35:28) and the 175 of his grandfather Abraham (25:7), but is the difference great enough to call his years "few"? Note that in his response Jacob shifts Pharaoh's "How many years have you lived?" (lit., "like what are the days of the years of your life") to "My year as a sojourner" (lit., "the days of the years of my sojourning"). That is, he exchanges "sojourning" for "life" in his answer, thus giving to the former "the elegian connotation that for him [viz., Jacob] life on earth is but a sojourn."[13]

Jacob's concern is not that he will apparently fail to live longer than either his father or grandfather. What does concern him is that his life thus far has been *difficult.* Just as the sons answered Pharaoh's question, then supplied unsolicited information, so Jacob answers Pharaoh's question, then supplies an autobiographical summary of his life. When we first encountered Jacob, he was struggling inside his mother's womb with his twin brother. As we come to the end of Jacob's life, he is struggling for his life in a famine-devastated Canaan. In between these first and last moments of struggle have been many trying experiences for Jacob. His life has had more sorrow than joy.

This is not the kind of information a stranger would share with Pharaoh. What, we would like to know, was his response to this tiny but personal revelation from Jacob? What about Joseph, who certainly overheard it?

10 Pharaoh makes no response to Jacob, or at least none is recorded. Jacob pronounces a second blessing on Pharaoh, and then leaves. Thus Jacob apparently ends the conversation, rather than Pharaoh. He exits, and presumably his five (or six) sons follow him. Jacob, however, has not experienced so much sorrow as to make him bitter and cynical. He has a double blessing for Pharaoh. Mixed in with his bad memories is a sense of gratitude to God for this pagan king who has become the means of the physical salvation of his family.

11-12 Following Pharaoh's orders, Joseph settles his family in Goshen, identified here as *the region of Rameses.* This phrase appears to be an editorial comment,[14] for this terminology was not used until the thirteenth-century pharaohs of the 19th Dynasty. The region of Rameses (cf. Exod. 1:11; 12:37; Num. 33:3, 5) may be identified with Qantir or Tanis in the northeastern delta of the Nile. It became the residence city of the kings of the 19th Dynasty and was built by and named after Ramses II (1304-1227 B.C.). The only way to defend the presence of this place name as early as the setting of the Joseph story, that is, as something other than an editorial insertion or an anachronism, is to suggest that the city bore this name prior to the Ramesside Dynasty, a name that simply meant "Re has created it."[15]

13. Lowenthal, *Joseph Narrative in Genesis,* p. 124.
14. See K. A. Kitchen, "Joseph," *ISBE,* 2:1129.
15. See R. W. Pierce, "Rameses," *ISBE,* 4:39.

Joseph exceeds the brothers' original request. They would be content to sojourn *(gûr)* in Goshen. Instead, Joseph gives them *property ('ᵃḥuzzâ)*. All of this confirms God's promise to Jacob that he would make of Jacob a great nation in Egypt (46:3). This Hebrew word has already appeared in Genesis: when God so spoke to Abraham (17:8), when Abraham requested property in which to bury Sarah (23:4, 9, 20), and in reference to Edomite territory (36:43). It will be used again in 48:4 (Jacob quoting God Almighty to Joseph); in 49:30, in a reference back to ch. 23; in 50:13, also a reference back to ch. 23. Unlike *naḥᵃlâ,* which refers to inalienable property transmitted by inheritance, *'ᵃḥuzzâ* refers to inalienable property received from a sovereign, or at least from one who has the power to release or retain land.[16] That is why this noun is often used with the verb "give" (Gen. 47:11; Lev. 14:34; Num. 27:4; 32:5; Deut. 32:49; etc.).

How different is Jacob's descent to Egypt from his grandfather's (ch. 12)! Both seek out the safety of Egypt because of famine. To save himself Abraham engages in deceit. To save his family Jacob engages in blessing. The Pharaoh at Abraham's visit was only too happy to see Abraham return to his own country. The Pharaoh at Jacob's visit insists that Jacob stay and settle on some choice land. Abraham retreats from Egypt. For Jacob Egypt is his new home. Abraham leaves Egypt alive (and happy to be so!). Jacob will leave Egypt dead.

3. JOSEPH'S AGRARIAN PROGRAM (47:13-26)

13 *There was no food anywhere*[1] *because the famine was so intense, so that the land of Egypt and the land of Canaan languished*[2] *because of the famine.*

14 *So Joseph collected*[3] *all the money that was to be found*[4] *in the land*

16. See J. Milgrom, *Leviticus 1–16,* AB (New York: Doubleday, 1991), pp. 866-67; idem, *Numbers,* JPS Torah Commentary (Philadelphia: Jewish Publication Society, 1990), p. 231.

1. For the use of a circumstantial clause to introduce a new episode, see Andersen, *Sentence in Biblical Hebrew,* pp. 79ff.

2. The root behind *tēlah* may be *lhh,* though this root is not attested elsewhere (BDB, p. 529b). SP *wtl'* suggests that *lhh* is a by-form of *l'h,* "be weary." KB, p. 382, connects it with *yālâ,* "be in consternation." *HALAT,* 2:394, follows this interpretation, but on p. 495 allows for the root *lhh/l'h* and the translation "languish, faint."

3. *lāqaṭ* (Piel here) is used several times in Ruth 2 for Ruth's "gleaning" after the reapers. Its frequent use in Ruth 2 demonstrates that the basic idea contained in the verb is "gather" or "collect." Gen. 47:14 provides the only instance where the verb is used in connection with the collection of money.

4. For the gerundive meaning of the Niphal participle *(hannimṣā'),* see Waltke and O'Connor, *Biblical Hebrew Syntax,* p. 620.

of Egypt and in the land of Canaan as payment for the rations, and
Joseph deposited[5] *the money in Pharaoh's palace.*
15 *When all the money in the land of Egypt and in the land of Canaan*
was gone,[6] *all the Egyptians came to Joseph and said: "Give us food.*
Why[7] *should we die right before you?*[8] *The money has run out."*[9]
16 *Joseph responded: "Bring your livestock, and I will give you food*[10]
in exchange for[11] *your livestock, if your money has run out."*
17 *So they brought their livestock to Joseph, and Joseph gave them food*
in exchange for horses, flocks, herds, and donkeys. He helped them
survive[12] *with food in exchange for their livestock for that year.*
18 *When that year was over,*[13] *they came to him the next year and said*

5. Lit., "brought" or "had brought" *(wayyāḇēʾ).*

6. *tāmam,* besides indicating what is finished or completed, also means "perish" (i.e., "be at an end"). Cf. Num. 14:33, 35; 17:28; 32:13; Deut. 2:14, 15, 16; etc.

7. At times *lammâ,* "why," is used to introduce a hypothetical deprecation: "Why should such a thing happen, when it might well be avoided?" Cf. J. Barr, "Why? in Biblical Hebrew," *JTS* 36 (1985) 19.

8. Presumably the people could have used the expression *lᵉpāneyḵā* for "before you," but instead they use *negdeḵā. BDB,* p. 617, notes that *neged* is "rather stronger and distincter than *lipnê*" — "why should we die *in thy sight*?"

9. Here the Egyptians use the phrase *ʾāp̄ēs kāsep̄* (lit., "money is at an end") for "money running out," as does Joseph in v. 16. But in v. 18 the Egyptians shift the phrase from *ʾāp̄ēs kāsep̄* to *tam hakkesep̄. ʾāp̄ēs* may be read as either a perfect or a participle. See Ts. Betser, "*ʾāp̄ēs kāsep̄* and Its Consequences," *Beth Mikra* 28 (1982/83) 177-79 (Hebrew), who argues that *ʾāp̄ēs* in the mouth of the Egyptians is a perfect ("the money has run out"), whereas Joseph uses *ʾāp̄ēs* in the next verse as a participle ("if your money is running out"). The Egyptians accordingly shift to the perfect *tam* in v. 18 in order to make clear to Joseph that their claim about their lack of money in v. 15 is not fraudulent. The use of the verb *tāmam* as the first word of the sentence followed by its subject *hakkesep̄* forms an *inclusio* with the last two words of the verse *ʾāp̄ēs kāsep̄;* see Y. Avishur, *Stylistic Studies of Word-Pairs,* pp. 239, 642.

10. LXX, SP, and Targ. Jonathan insert "food." One may retain MT by translating *ʾettᵉnâ* as "I will make/give distributions," without a direct object, a translation Speiser suggests, but for which he provides no evidence.

11. One of several illustrations of the *bᵉ* ("in") of equivalence or of price in these verses. See C. H. Gordon, " 'In' of Predication or Equivalence," *JBL* 100 (1981) 612-13. For *nāṯan bᵉ* meaning "give in exchange for, in place of" see Ezek. 27:13, 16; Joel 4:3 (Eng. 3:3, "have given a boy for a harlot"). The direct object *leḥem,* "food," is present with *nāṯan* in v. 17.

12. The normal meaning of *nāhal* is "to lead (to watering holes)" as in the familiar Ps. 23:2. The sheep will not survive if the shepherd is not able to guide them to water sources. The last part of v. 17 is lit., "he guided them with food in exchange for all their livestock through/in that year." The verb "connotes special solicitude" (Lowenthal, *Joseph Narrative,* p. 126).

13. The same verb is used later in the verse for "the money has run out." The year is over *(tittōm),* and the money is exhausted *(tam).*

to him: "We cannot conceal from my lord that since the money has run out and our herds belong to my lord,[14] *nothing remains for my lord but*[15] *our bodies*[16] *and our farmlands.*

19 *Why*[17] *should we die before your eyes, we and our land?*[18] *Buy us and our farmlands in exchange for bread, and we along with our farmlands will become Pharaoh's serfs. Only give us seed*[19] *so that we may live and not die, and that the farmland not become a desert."*[20]

20 *Joseph bought up all the Egyptians' farmland for Pharaoh because*[21] *each Egyptian had sold his field, so severe*[22] *was the famine for them. Thus the land became Pharaoh's.*

14. The Hebrew of "the money has run out" *(tam hakkesep̱)* and "our herds belong to our lord" *(ûmiqnēh habbᵉhēmâ 'el-'ᵃḏōnî)* demonstrate that the predicate of a verbless clause may form a chiasmus with a verb. See Andersen, *Sentence in Biblical Hebrew,* p. 127. Two kinds of wealth are no more.

15. "Except" or "but" can be expressed after *lō'* ("not") and a verb by *kî 'îm* (Num. 26:65; 1 Sam. 30:17; 2 Chr. 21:17). Perhaps *biltî 'îm* is used here because *kî 'îm* already appeared in the first half of the sentence (translated here as "that since"). Cf. also Judg. 7:14 and Amos 3:3 (the only place where *biltî 'im* is followed by a verb).

16. *gᵉwîyâ* often means the "corpse" of a person (1 Sam. 31:10, 12; Ps. 110:6) or of an animal (Judg. 14:8, 9). Or it may refer to the humanlike body of an angelic being (Ezek. 1:11, 23). Is it used here because the famine-struck Egyptians are near death? H.-J. Fabry, in his discussion of this word in *TDOT,* 2:433-38, observes that the term "characterizes man in his existential weakness, oppression, or trouble. . . . The OT sees man in the aspect of *geviyyah* when in time of real distress, e.g., during the years of the Egyptian famine he must . . . lose the status of a free, fully enfranchised citizen" (p. 435).

17. On the force of *lāmmâ,* see n. 7 above.

18. The expression "Why should we die . . . we and our land" is strange. This expression is called a zeugma, i.e., the use of a verb ("die") to govern two words, with only one of which ("we") it makes sense. LXX avoids "the land dying" by reading "that we die not, and the land be made desolate [*kaí hē gḗ erēmōthḗ*]."

19. LXX inserts "so that we may sow" *(hína speírōmen).*

20. On the ingressive force of *tēšām* ("become a desert") see H.-P. Müller, "Aramaisierende Bildungen bei Verba Mediae geminatae — ein Irrtum der Hebraistik?" *VT* 36 (1986) 424-25. Targ. Onqelos renders *šāmam,* which normally implies total destruction, including the loss of all human life, by *l' tbwr* ("and the land shall not lie fallow") to show that *šāmam* refers only to the desolation of the soil.

21. For the sequence *kî . . . kî* (lit., "because . . . because") see A. Schoors, "The Particle *kî,*" *OTS* 21 (1981) 266: "The sequence *kî . . . kî* expresses two causes at a different level, i.e., a proximate and a more remote one, but it can present two coordinate causes as well."

22. For a comparison of *ḥāzaq 'al* in Gen. 47:20 and in Mal. 3:13 see N. H. Waldman, "Some Notes on Malachi 3:6; 3:13; and Psalm 42:11," *JBL* 93 (1974) 545-46. Waldman would render *ḥāzaq 'al* in both the verses as "be too much for, be too strong for" (Gen. 47:20, "since the famine was too much for them; Mal. 3:13, "your words have been too much for me").

21 *The people he reduced to servitude,*[23] *from one end*[24] *of Egypt to the other.*

22 *Only*[25] *the priests' farmland did he not buy, for it was the priests' allotment*[26] *from Pharaoh, and they would live off*[27] *the allotment which Pharaoh gave them. That explains why*[28] *they did not sell their farmland.*

23 *Joseph said to the people: "Now that I have bought you and your*

23. MT has "he moved them to the cities." I follow LXX *(katedoulṓsato)* and SP, which read a *d* instead of an *r* twice: *heʿe̱biḏ . . . laʿa̱bāḏîm* for MT *heʿe̱bîr . . . leʿārîm.* For another instance where LXX read a *d* for a Heb. *r* cf. Gen. 22:13, where MT has *'ayil 'aḥar* ("another ram"), for which LXX has *kriós heís* ("one ram," presupposing Heb. *'ayil 'eḥāḏ*). Jer. 15:14 is another place where LXX read *ʿāḇar* as *ʿāḇaḏ* (MT "I will transfer"; LXX *katadoulṓsō,* "I will enslave you"). See E. Tov, *The Text-Critical Use of the Septuagint in Biblical Research* (Jerusalem: Simor, 1981), pp. 145, 196. For SP's reading *(w't hʿm hʿbyd 'tw lʿbdym),* which agrees with LXX, see E. Tov, *Textual Criticism of the Hebrew Bible* (Minneapolis: Fortress: Aassen/Mastricht: Van Gorcum, 1992), p. 92. The MT is followed by some versions (e.g., NJPS, "he removed the population town by town") and by some commentators (e.g., Coote and Ord, *Bible's First History,* pp. 198, 200: "he removed them to the cities"; for Coote and Ord, being made slaves and being forced to move into the city are essentially the same thing). I follow the LXX only because it follows more logically on the people's promise, "we . . . will become Pharaoh's serfs," than does "he moved them to the cities."

24. *miqṣēh* was used back in v. 2 in reference to the total number of Joseph's brothers. GKC, § 139e n. 3, says that Hebrew may express "the one — the other" by repeating the substantive *(miqṣēh . . . weʿaḏ qāṣēhû).*

25. For *raq* in vv. 22 and 26 see B. Jongeling, "La particule *raq,*" *OTS* 18 (1973) 99, who observes that the particle applies only to the phrase "the priest's farmland" (i.e., "it was only the priest's farmland that he did not buy" rather than "but he did not buy the priests' farmland"). Similarly, Andersen (*Sentence in Biblical Hebrew,* p. 170) says of *raq* in this verse, "a clause which makes a blanket statement can be subsequently limited by excluding some of what it has comprehensively embraced."

26. For *ḥōq* with the unusual meaning of "religious due, right, privilege" (here translated "allotment") and "legal right" (translated "law" in v. 26), see P. Victor, "A note on *ḥoq* in the Old Testament," *VT* 16 (1966) 359. The noun comes from the verb *ḥāqaq,* "to inscribe, engrave," and refers to that which is ordained by written statute. See B. Levine, *Leviticus,* JPS Torah Commentary (Philadelphia: Jewish Publication Society, 1991), p. 37; J. Milgrom, *Leviticus 1–16,* AB (New York: Doubleday, 1991), p. 395. For this meaning of *ḥōq,* see, in addition to Gen. 47:22, Exod. 29:28; Lev. 6:11, 15; 7:34; 10:15; 24:9; Num. 18:8, 11, 19. Modern translators render the word in Genesis as "allotment" (Speiser, *Genesis,* p. 350); "a fixed income" (Westermann, *Genesis,* 3:166, 175); "a fixed allowance" (Humphreys, *Joseph and His Family,* p. 146; Lowenthal, *Joseph Narrative,* p. 128); "a statutory grant" (Coote and Ord, *Bible's First History,* p. 198); "fixed revenue" (P. Walters, *The Text of the Septuagint* [Cambridge: Cambridge University, 1973], p. 209).

27. Lit., "ate." For a *weqāṭaltî* form after a nominal clause and with an imperative sense, see GKC, § 112l; Waltke and O'Connor, *Biblical Hebrew Syntax,* p. 535.

28. Lit., "Therefore, they did not sell their farmland."

farmland[29] *for Pharaoh, here*[30] *is seed for you to sow the farmland.*

24 *But of the crops,*[31] *you must give one-fifth of it to Pharaoh. Four-fifths*[32] *are*[33] *to be yours as seed for the field, to provide food for you and those of your households, and to feed the little ones."*[34]

25 *"You have rescued our lives,"*[35] *they said. "Having found acceptance in my lord's eyes, we will be slaves to Pharaoh."*

26 *So Joseph established it as law — still in force today — concerning the farmland of Egypt, that to Pharaoh belongs a fifth.*[36] *Only the priests' farmland alone*[37] *did not become Pharaoh's.*

Some time after settling his family in Goshen (vv. 11, 12), Joseph turns his attention to national concerns (vv. 13-26). Even though there *was no food in Egypt* (v. 13), except in storage, Joseph's family is nicely settled in "the choice

29. Lit., "Behold, I have bought you today [*hayyôm*], and your farmland," which makes difficult syntax, and implies possibly that originally Joseph purchased only the people. DeVries (*Yesterday, Today and Tomorrow,* p. 159 n. 69) notes that "*hayyôm* does not date the declaration so much as epitomize its intent and effect."

30. The interjection *hē'* occurs only here and in Ezek. 16:43, and its sense is not clear. The Mishnaic equivalent means "behold" (M. H. Segal, *Grammar of Mishnaic Hebrew* [Oxford: Clarendon, 1927], p. 148).

31. *battᵉḇû'ōt* is lit., "in the product (or yield or revenue)." The phrase is elliptical for "yield of crops." The preposition *b* is partitive, "of, from among," (BDB, p. 100a; *HALAT,* 4:1457, 1458).

32. Lit., "four of the hands (or portions)" (*'arba' hayyaḏoṯ*). Cf. in 43:34 *ḥameš yāḏôṯ*. See J. Gray, *Legacy of Canaan,* VTSup 5, 2nd ed. (Leiden: Brill, 1965), p. 105 n. 3, for Ugaritic examples of *yd* meaning "portions"; idem, *The KRT Text in the Literature of Ras Shamra,* 2nd ed. (Leiden: Brill, 1964), p. 51.

33. Note the sing. verb (*yihyeh*) with the pl. subject. When the subject precedes, it is treated almost as a *casus pendens,* "the four-fifths, it shall be." See Davidson, *Hebrew Syntax,* p. 160, § 116.

34. This last phrase, two words in the Hebrew text, is absent from LXX, but I find no compelling reason to delete it. It would reassure the adults to know that even their children would be provided for. The latter are often the heaviest casualties in a famine.

35. For the Hiphil of *ḥāyâ* elsewhere in the Joseph narrative cf. 45:7 and 50:20. In all three instances the Hiphil of *ḥāyâ* has the meaning "rescue, preserve alive, let live." It is Joseph's sagacity that preserves the lives of both his brothers and the Egyptians.

36. LXX reads "to give a fifth to Pharaoh," presupposing *lᵉhammēš lᵉpar'ōh* rather than MT *lᵉparōh laḥōmeš*.

37. With regard to the combination *raq . . . lᵉḇaddām,* Andersen (*Sentence in Biblical Hebrew,* p. 171) notes: "The use of *lĕbaddām* as a restrictive 'adverb' modifying *priests* excuses *raq* from a similar role, and virtually drives it into the camp of the antithetical conjuctions — *but.*"

parts" of Egypt (v. 6). They seem to have a reasonably rosy future, while that of the Egyptian masses is bleak.[38]

Joseph takes responsibility for some essential agrarian reforms. If Egypt is to continue to survive its unpredictable climate, then more than grain handouts is needed. The basic system of land tenure will need to be revised. This is Joseph's long-range proposal for what will likely be a recurring event.

To that end Joseph takes from the people their money (v. 14), their livestock (vv. 15-17), and eventually their farmlands and the people's own freedom (vv. 18-21). In exchange for these, Joseph gives the people much-needed grain. The first measure (and possibly the second), the giving of money (and cattle), extends even to the land of Canaan (vv. 13-15). The result of this reform is that former landowners now become tenants of Pharaoh, farming the land for him and paying him one-fifth of the produce as tax (vv. 20-26). Temple lands were excepted from this feudalistic system (vv. 22, 26d).

Each time the citizenry give Joseph something of theirs, he gives something back of value. In exchange for their money, Joseph gives them *rations* (*šeḇer,* v. 14).[39] In exchange for their cattle he gives them *food* (*leḥem,* v. 17).[40] In exchange for their land and persons, Joseph gives them *seed* (*zeraʿ,* v. 23). The first two will meet their immediate needs. The third will meet their future needs.

Joseph is not a callous, unethical taskmaster. True, the people forfeit ownership of their land to Pharaoh, but Joseph allows them, when this measure can be put into practice, to keep 80 percent of the harvest for themselves. Only 20 percent remains Pharaoh's. (Cf. the 10 percent that is Yahweh's in OT religion.)[41] The people are evidently grateful for this arrangement, for they say to Joseph, *You have rescued our lives* (v. 25). Joseph is a nondiscriminating savior. His concern for Egyptians is no less than his concern for his own family. And apparently Joseph's reforms were acceptable to later Egyptians as well, or at least to later Pharaohs. Joseph's

38. The contrasts between vv. 1-12 and 13-26 are stark. As Humphreys (*Joseph and His Family,* p. 54) notes, in these two units "land and privilege gained balance land and freedom lost."

39. *šeḇer* has appeared in the Joseph story in 42:1, 2, 19, 26; 43:2; 44:2, all in reference to what Joseph gave to his own family. The noun is formed from the verb *šāḇar,* "to break (in pieces)," hence *šeḇer* is that which is broken, i.e., threshed — "grain."

40. *leḥem,* "(prepared food/bread") occurs only in this chapter in the Joseph narrative (vv. 13, 15, 17, 19).

41. Lowenthal (*Joseph Narrative,* p. 193) asks, "And what kind of 'serfdom' is it that grants four-fifths of the produce to the 'serf'?"

decree was still a law in Egypt in the writer's day (*still in force today,* v. 26).[42] Joseph's reforms outlived Joseph.

The text is clear about Joseph mandating this tax. It is not as clear in stating whether he supervised its collection. This responsibility would belong either to the overseer of granaries or to the chief of the treasury, who would make daily reports of his activities to the vizier. The vizier himself was not responsible for collections of tax payments on field produce.[43]

It is difficult to settle on a particular period in Egyptian history when the land-reform system, outlined in Gen. 47:13-26, prevailed in Egypt. At what particular juncture, if any, did vast amounts of privately held property pass to the crown? Is there any period in Egyptian history in which a one-fifth tax on land produce was imposed on the citizenry? What about exemption for priests from taxes on crops? Several Egyptologists have favored a period following the expulsion of the Hyksos, and beginning with the 18th Dynasty (ca. 1550 B.C.). Perhaps at this period the crown began to confiscate the estates of the noble families.[44] At the other extreme, Redford attempts to provide evidence that ties in the procedures of Gen. 47:13-26 with the Saite period (26th Dynasty, 7th-6th century B.C.).[45] He appeals especially to texts from this period that state unequivocally that temples of Egypt were not taxed. De Vaux makes the interesting observation that the measures introduced in Egypt by Joseph were condemned by Samuel, when their introduction in Israel became a possibility. He warned the people that if they persisted in their request for a king, they would receive a king who would take over their farmland, tithe their crops, and take sons and daughters for his slaves (1 Sam. 8:13-16).[46] One would assume that the story approving of this practice (Joseph) would precede a second story condemning this practice (Samuel), rather than vice versa.

42. Cf. B. S. Childs, "A Study of the Formula, 'Until This Day,'" *JBL* 82 (1963) 283-84, for the particular force of etiologies that follow the *waw*-consecutive imperfect of a transitive verb with direct or indirect object. Childs notes that in such instances "the formula appears almost as a gloss, and serves as a witness to the extension in time of the phenomenon rather than indicating its causality."

43. See the lengthy footnote in W. A. Ward, "The Egyptian Office of Joseph," *JSS* 5 (1960) 147 n. 3, in which he follows Steindorff and Seele in the belief that it was the overseer of granaries, rather than the chief of the treasury, who was responsible for collections of tax payments on field produce. In any case, Joseph is not performing the duties of the vizier, for this function was not in the hands of the vizier.

44. See G. Steindorff and K. Sethe, *When Egypt Ruled the East,* 2nd ed. (Chicago: University of Chicago, 1957), p. 88; J. H. Breasted, *History of Egypt* (New York: Scribner's Sons, 1942), pp. 237-38; K. A. Kitchen, "Joseph," *ISBE,* 2:1129b, all of whom connect Gen. 47:13ff. with Egyptian policy in the 18th Dynasty.

45. Redford, *Study of the Biblical Story of Joseph,* pp. 236-39.

46. De Vaux, *Early History of Israel,* pp. 306-7.

Even those commentators who disagree about the period of Egyptian history that illuminates Gen. 47:13-26 do agree on one point. That point is their contention that vv. 13-26 are patently intrusive in the Joseph story, and that they contribute nothing to the development of the Joseph narrative. They claim that the editor(s) of Genesis so admired the Egyptian system of the one-fifth tax that he recounted it, and artificially ascribed it to Israel's ancestor Joseph, probably because such a political organization did not yet exist in Israel,[47] or because he wanted to confer another honor on his hero Joseph. Even commentators like Westermann and Coats, who are committed to the unity of the Joseph narrative, label this particular unit as secondary.[48]

The unit underscores that the Egyptians are saved and Pharaoh prospers because of the measures taken by Joseph. Emphasis is on the latter result. In the immediately preceding paragraph (vv. 7-12) we encountered twice the fact that Jacob blessed Pharaoh (vv. 7, 10). No further commentary was provided on that double blessing. Might it be possible to read vv. 13-26 as the fruit of that blessing?[49] Pharaoh spared Joseph. He promoted Joseph to a position of authority in his empire. He sent a personal invitation to Joseph's family to settle in Goshen. He permitted the sending of grain to them in Canaan in their time of need. Upon their arrival in Egypt, he extended to them a royal welcome. Jacob's response to all these displays of compassion is to bless Pharaoh. The result of that blessing is the transference to Pharaoh of resources not previously at his disposal. The giver now becomes the receiver. The one who gave land (47:1-12) is in return given land (47:13-26). It is significant, however, that vv. 1-12 come before vv. 13-26. Had that order been reversed, and had the text told first of Pharaoh's getting land, and then giving land, then the door would have been opened to the possibility that Pharaoh gave only because he received. His motive could then have been interpreted as returning one favor for another, rather than as sheer gratitude and compassion. In some ways, then, the pharaoh of the Joseph story comes across as a caring, magnanimous, and charitable individual. But even more important, ch. 47 attributes much of the pharaoh's holdings not to his magnanimity but to the blessing of Jacob (vv. 1-12) and to Joseph's wise management in times of potential chaos (vv. 13-26).

47. See F. W. Golka, "The aetiologies in the Old Testament: Part 1," *VT* 26 (1976) 416.

48. Westermann, *Genesis,* 3:173-77; Coats, *Genesis,* pp. 298-300.

49. See B. A. McKenzie, "Jacob's Blessing on Pharaoh," *WTJ* 45 (1983) 395-98.

L. JACOB BLESSES A SON AND GRANDSONS (47:27–48:22)

1. JACOB'S LAST REQUEST OF JOSEPH (47:27-31)

27 *So Israel settled*[1] *in the land of Egypt, in the land of Goshen; they acquired property in it, were fruitful, and became very numerous.*

28 *Jacob lived seventeen years in the land of Egypt, so that Jacob's life came to*[2] *one hundred and forty-seven years.*

29 *When the time drew near for Israel*[3] *to die, he called for his son Joseph and said to him: "If you really want to please me,*[4] *put your hand under my thigh as a promise of your constant loyalty*[5] *to me: do not allow me to be buried in Egypt!*

30 *When I lie down with my ancestors, have me taken out of Egypt and entomb me in their burial place." "I*[6] *will do as you have said," he answered.*

1. Unlike the following three verbs in this verse (*wayyē'āḥᵃzû,* "they acquired"; *wayyip̱ᵉrû,* "they were fruitful"; *wayyirbû,* "they became very numerous"), *wayyēšeḇ,* "settled," is in the sing. This shift in the number of the verb, with the same subject for all four, indicates a merging of Israel the individual and Israel the people. Accordingly, it is necessary that v. 27 begin by identifying the patriarch as "Israel" rather than "Jacob."

2. Lit., "the days of Jacob, the years of his life, were [*wayᵉhî*] . . . ," i.e., pl. subject and sing. verb. SP reads a pl. verb *(wayyihyû).* In the very next verse "days of Israel" is coupled with a pl. verb *(wayyiqrᵉḇû).* Was *wayᵉhî* used at the midpoint of v. 28 because *wayᵉḥî* ("he lived") was used at its beginning?

3. Lowenthal (*Joseph Narrative,* p. 132) states, "At great or crucial moments of his life, Jacob's patriarchhood is reinstated by the name 'Israel.'" See also Longacre, *Joseph,* p. 151: "the time draws near for 'Israel' (clan-head) to die."

4. Lit., "if I have found favor in your eyes." The expression is normally used by a person of lower status to a superior. For other instances of a superior using this formula in addressing one of lower authority see David with Jonathan (1 Sam. 20:3, 29) and David with Nabal (1 Sam. 25:8). E. F. Campbell suggests that in such places the formula "may be used as a criterion for determining who holds the dominant position in a relationship where there might be reason for doubt" (*Ruth,* AB [Garden City, NY: Doubleday, 1975], p. 92). There seems to be no doubt here. This is a father making a request of a son, not a sojourner making a request of a powerful politician or high-placed government official.

5. *ḥeseḏ we'ᵉ̆meṯ* is a hendiadys; cf. F. I. Andersen, "Yahweh, the Kind and Sensitive God," in *God Who Is Rich in Mercy,* Fest. D. B. Knox, ed. P. T. O'Brien and D. G. Peterson (Grand Rapids: Baker, 1987), p. 57.

6. The use of the independent pronoun in the phrase *'ānōḵî 'eʿᵉ̆śeh,* otherwise redundant, for the subject is already expressed by the verb, gives extra force to Joseph's words, occurring as they do in response to a preceding request. See Davidson, *Hebrew Syntax,* p. 151, § 107, Rem. 1.

31 *"Swear to me," he said. So he swore to him. Then Israel bowed*[7] *at the head of his*[8] *bed.*[9]

27 This verse swings the reader back to v. 11. There, Joseph settled *(wayyôšēḇ)* his father and brothers in Egypt. Here, Israel *settled (wayyēšeḇ)* in Egypt. There, they were given property *('ᵃḥuzzâ),* a fact repeated in v. 27 *(wayyē'āḥᵃzû).* The region of Rameses of v. 11 is *the territory of Goshen* of v. 27. Thus the story of Pharaoh's acquiring property in Egypt (vv. 13-26) is bracketed by references to Joseph's family receiving property in Egypt (vv. 11-12, 27). Both recipients receive their land from Joseph in one way or other. The shift in verbs from *gûr,* v. 4 ("sojourn") to *yāšaḇ* here ("settle") indicates that the first experience of land possession takes place in Egypt rather than in Canaan. On the one hand, such an unexpected development is the necessary outcome of God's earlier promise to make Jacob and his descendants into a great nation even in Egypt (46:3). On the other hand, such possessions may lead to the temptation of self-sufficiency. That is, Israel's ancestors are no longer sojourners whose only security is trust in God's promises, but are now dwellers whose security is in their landholdings and in their connections with a powerful head-of-state via Joseph.[10]

The added remark in v. 27 is that in Goshen Jacob's family *were fruitful and became very numerous.* The combination of *pārâ* and *rāḇâ* has been common in Genesis (1:28 is the first). In Genesis these verbs normally describe a goal. Here they describe a fait accompli. Even in Egypt God's blessings are on his own.[11] Jacob blessed Pharaoh (vv. 7, 10), one result of which is spelled

7. Possibly something different from "bowed" is necessary here for *wayyištaḥû.* Does Jacob "bow" at the head of his bed, or does he fall down exhausted on his bed? D. M. Golomb argues for the latter in "The Targumic Renderings of the Verb *lᵉhištaḥᵃwôt:* A Targumic Translation Convention," in *Working with No Data: Semitic and Egyptian Studies Presented to Thomas O. Lambdin,* ed. D. M. Golomb (Winona Lake, IN: Eisenbrauns, 1987), p. 108 and n. 10, p. 113.

8. For the rendering of the Hebrew definite article (*hammiṭṭâ,* "the bed") into English as a pronominal adjective, see Davidson, *Hebrew Syntax,* p. 26, § 21d; Waltke and O'Connor, *Biblical Hebrew Syntax,* p. 243 n. 8.

9. For MT *hammiṭṭâ,* "the bed," LXX has *tḗs rhabdou autoú,* which suggests *maṭṭēhû,* "his staff." The LXX reading is reflected in Heb. 11:21. It is likely that the translators of the LXX read *mṭh* as "staff" simply because *maṭṭeh* is a more common Hebrew word than *miṭṭâ,* and it has already appeared in Genesis (ch. 38). See J. Barr, "Vocalization and the Analysis of Hebrew among the Ancient Translators," in *Hebräische Wortforschung,* Fest. W. Baumgartner, VTSup 16 (Leiden: Brill, 1967), p. 3; idem, "St. Jerome and the Sounds of Hebrew," *JSS* 12 (1967) 31-32.

10. See W. Brueggemann, *The Land,* OBT (Philadelphia: Fortress, 1977), pp. 9-10; B. C. Birch, *Let Justice Roll Down* (Louisville: Westminster/John Knox, 1991), p. 113.

11. See W. Brueggemann, in Brueggemann and H. W. Wolff, *Vitality of Old Testament Traditions,* 2nd ed. (Atlanta: John Knox, 1982), p. 106.

out in vv. 13-26. Now it is God who is blessing Jacob. Of course, v. 27b goes well beyond Jacob's own generation, and even that of his children. Although they are aliens in a strange land, and although they are surrounded by famine, the Israelites are blessed. Neither geography nor natural catastrophe can throttle God's commitment to his own.

28 In Jacob's thinking, he did not live unusually long — something he earlier admitted to Pharaoh (v. 9). But by Egyptian standards he outlived the law of averages. Egyptian literature has many references to 110 years as the ideal span of life for an Egyptian (see 50:22, 26 for Joseph).[12] Jacob's life exceeds that limit by thirty-seven years.[13]

I observed earlier that the writer of the Joseph story devoted hardly any attention to the journeys Jacob and the brothers made to Egypt and back to Canaan. In one verse they are in Canaan. In the next verse, or in the second half of the verse, they are in Egypt. The same ignoring of nonessential information is found here. Only minimal detail is given to any episode over this lengthy period. Genesis is as silent on Jacob's last seventeen years as it was on Joseph's first seventeen years (37:2). The reference to *seventeen years* advances the Joseph narrative into a more distant time frame. The famine is over by now. Joseph is even further consolidated in his position of authority, and the text is now ready to describe Jacob's last days.[14]

29 Jacob/Israel is now on the verge of death. He has one final request.

12. References to such an ideal life span in Egyptian texts are documented in Vergote, *Joseph en Égypte,* pp. 200-201; cf., e.g., the instructions of Ptah-hotep, the vizier of King Izezi of the 5th Dynasty in the mid-2400s B.C., to his son: "What I have done on earth is not inconsiderable. I attained one hundred and ten years of life which the king gave me, with favor foremost among the ancestors, through doing right for the king up to the point of veneration" (translation of J. Wilson in *ANET,* p. 414).

13. Sarna (*Genesis,* p. 324) notes that the life spans of the patriarchs may be factored in the following manner: Abraham, $175 = 5 \times 5 \times 7$; Isaac, $180 = 6 \times 6 \times 5$; Jacob, $147 = 7 \times 7 \times 3$. Each time the squared number increases by one, and the coefficient number decreases by two. Also, 17 is the total of these factored numbers for all three patriarchs ($5 + 5 + 7$; $6 + 6 + 5$; $7 + 7 + 3$). Sarna states, "Through their factorial patterns, the patriarchal chronologies constitute a rhetorical device expressing the profound biblical conviction that Israel's formative age was not a concatenation of haphazard incidents but a series of events ordered according to God's grand design." Working from a different direction, i.e., sexagesimal mathematics, D. W. Young ("On the Application of Numbers from Babylonian Mathematics to Biblical Life Spans and Epochs," *ZAW* 100 [1988] 335, 350, 351, 359) reckoned that Jacob's 147 years is the sum of the reciprocals of the numbers 1 to 6 ($60 + 30 + 20 + 15 + 12 + 10$). Such a number, as common to ancient Babylonian children in their early mathematical training as 144 (12×12) would be to children today, is but one way in which the author highlights Jacob, the progenitor of Israel's tribes.

14. See J. H. Sailhamer, *The Pentateuch as Narrative* (Grand Rapids: Zondervan, 1992), p. 228.

He does not want to *be buried in Egypt.*[15] Moses will forsake Egypt alive. Jacob will forsake Egypt dead. Who better to make sure that his father's remains do not stay in Egypt than Joseph? Joseph has the authority, and the remaining sons have done little to bolster Jacob's confidence in them.

To guarantee that Joseph will fulfill his request, Jacob asks Joseph to place his hand under Jacob's *thigh* (genitals?)[16] and promise to take Jacob's remains from Egypt. Before Joseph places his hands on Jacob's eyes (in death), Jacob wants Joseph to place his hand under his thigh (in life). Jacob appeals to Joseph's sense of *loyalty (ḥeseḏ).* Obviously Jacob cannot compel Joseph to do this, for Jacob will be dead at the time! All that the father can appeal to is his son's sense of loyalty to him. Joseph has already shown so much *ḥeseḏ* to Jacob and his family. In his father's death will Joseph cease to display that loyalty?

30 Jacob wants to be buried with his *ancestors.*[17] Because 50:5 states

15. The desire to end one's life in one's own land because of a strong love for and identification with that land is known from the Egyptian story of Sinuhe, an Egyptian official in the Middle Kingdom (mid to late 1900s B.C.), who fled from Egypt to Asia in voluntary exile. In spite of his prosperity abroad, he says, "Whichever god decreed this flight, have mercy, bring me home! Surely you will let me see the place in which my heart dwells! What is more important than that my corpse be buried in the land in which I was born! Come to my aid!" (M. Lichtheim, *Ancient Egyptian Literature,* 3 vols. [Berkeley: University of California, 1973-82], 1:228). See also C. H. Gordon, *Before the Bible* (London: Collins, 1962), pp. 102-8. The same theme may be present in an Aramaic inscription discovered near Zenjirli in Syria in 1888, and dating back to 730 B.C. In it Barrakkab pays tribute to his late father, Panammu II, who gained the throne with the help of Tiglath-pileser III of Assyria. The portion of line 18 that has survived describes events following Panammu's death: "and he [Tiglath-pileser III] set up an image for him by the way, and brought my father across from Damascus to Assyria. In my days. . . ." Then follows a long lacunae that may have read: "he sent my father back to his own land, and I wept for him and. . . ." See J. C. L. Gibson, *Textbook of Syrian Semitic Inscriptions,* 3 vols. (Oxford: Clarendon, 1971-82), 2:85; G. A. Cooke, *Text-Book of North-Semitic Inscriptions* (Oxford: Clarendon, 1903), p. 179.

16. See M. Malul, "More on *paḥad yiṣḥāq* (Genesis XXXI 42, 53)" *VT* 35 (1985) 196-200, on "an oath by the thigh." For "thigh" as a euphemism for the genitals, see Gen. 46:26; Exod. 1:5; Judg 8:30; and cf. M. Malul, "Touching the sexual organs as an oath ceremony in an Akkadian letter," *VT* 37 (1987) 491-92; R. D. Freedman, " 'Put Your Hand Under My Thigh' — The Patriarchal Oath," *BAR* 2:2 (1976) 3-4, 42; Z. W. Falk, "Gestures Expressing Affirmation," *JSS* 4 (1959) 269. On false swearing, which has the consequence of infertility, the withdrawal of procreative power, see J. Khanjian, *RSP,* 2:375-76.

17. One should distinguish between the phrase "be gathered to one's kin" (Gen. 25:8 [Abraham]; 25:17 [Ishmael]; 35:29 [Isaac]; 49:29, 33 [Jacob]; Num. 27:13; 31:2; Deut. 32:50 [Moses]; Num. 20:24; Deut. 32:50 [Aaron]) and "sleep with one's ancestors/fathers," which is used here in Gen. 47:30. The former follows death, precedes burial, and means to be reunited with one's ancestors in the afterlife. The second phrase, used more extensively in Kings and Chronicles than elsewhere, is often followed by "they buried him" (1 K. 15:8), or by "was buried" (1 K. 2:10), or by "and was buried with his

that Jacob had said to Joseph, "bury me in the tomb I hewed out for myself," some have emended *their burial place (qᵉḇurāṯām)* to "my burial place" *(qᵉḇurāṯî).*[18] This change forces an absolute consistency on the story that is not necessary. Besides, *in their burial place* may be a reference to an area very near to the grave of his ancestors, rather than to the identical grave. Jacob's choice of the pronominal suffix "their" on "burial place" is dictated by his opening words in the verse, "When I lie down with my ancestors." With such a beginning clause referring to the object "my ancestors," it is expected that Jacob will continue with ". . . and entomb me in *their* burial place (i.e., the ancestors'), rather than with ". . . and entomb me in *my* burial place."

But why even be concerned about the transportation of one's corpse to the homeland, except for sentimental purposes? Jacob knows that there is to be no permanent residence in Egypt for his people. Egypt is to Jacob and his family what the ark was to Noah — a temporary shelter from the disaster on the outside. Even if represented only by his decayed remains, he wants to be a part of that redemptive act of God.

31 Jacob insists that Joseph's word be cemented with an oath: *Swear*[19] *to me.* Jacob had used these same words many years earlier to Esau when he plotted to get Esau's birthright (*hiššāḇᵉʿâ lî,* 25:23). That first incident was laced with subterfuge. Here everything is transparent. In ch. 25 Jacob was conniving and opportunistic. Here he is desperate. There he was in the family tent. Here he is in his home on his deathbed.

Why is an oath necessary if Joseph has already promised to treat his father with *ḥeseḏ?* Again, there are parallels with 25:29-33. Esau's "I am about to die, of what use is a birthright?" needs to be made official with an oath. Esau swore to him. Joseph's promise to Jacob, *I will do as you have said,* needs also to be firmed up by an oath. The oath will reinforce in Joseph's memory his promise to Jacob: Joseph, in taking the oath, makes himself directly accountable to God and places himself under God's wrath if he reneges on his promise. Thus "the oath heightens the general dimension of moral

---

fathers" (1 K. 14:31). Thus "sleep with one's ancestors" does not itself refer to burial. Because "sleep with one's ancestors" is never used with *môṯ,* "die," one might suppose that the phrase in question refers to dying, and always to a natural death as opposed to a violent one. See B. Alfrink, "L'expression *šākab ʿim ʾᵃbôṯāyw,*" *OTS* 2 (1943) 106-18; N. J. Tromp, *Primitive Conceptions of Death and the Nether World in the Old Testament,* BibOr 21 (Rome: Pontifical Biblical Institute, 1969), pp. 169-70.

18. See *BHK, BHS;* cf. Skinner, *Genesis,* p. 503.

19. G. Giesen (*Die Wurzel* šbʿ "schwören": Eine semasiologische Studie zum Eid im Alten Testament, Bonner biblische Beiträge 56 [Königstein: Hanstein, 1981], pp. 84-86) cites *šāḇaʿ* in Gen. 25:33 and 47:31 as the two instances where the root is used in a profane context (an oath between persons) as a supplement and a support to a promise already made.

responsibility which is characteristic of biblical loyalty, for such swearing was done with radical seriousness."[20]

2. JOSEPH VISITS HIS AILING FATHER (48:1-7)

1 *Shortly thereafter Joseph was told:*[1] *"Your father is now*[2] *failing."*[3] *He took his two sons with him, Manasseh and Ephraim.*[4]

2 *Someone informed*[5] *Jacob: "Your son Joseph has come to you."*[6] *Israel then rallied his strength*[7] *and sat up in bed.*

20. See K. Sakenfeld, *The Meaning of Ḥesed in the Hebrew Bible,* HSM 17 (Missoula, MT: Scholars, 1978), pp. 36-38; idem, *Faithfulness in Action,* OBT (Philadelphia: Fortress, 1985), pp. 28-29.

1. LXX, Pesh., Vulg., and Targ. Jonathan presuppose *wayyē'āmēr* (Niphal); MT has *wayyō'mer* (Qal), "and he said." One need not follow the versions, or repoint the MT to a passive Qal; *wayyō'mer lᵉyôsēp̱* and *wayyaggēḏ lᵉyaʿᵃqōḇ* in v. 2 are illustrations of an authentic Hebrew impersonal construction. See GKC, § 144d and n. 2 (which, curiously, leaves *wayyō'mer* of v. 1 as is, but changes *wayyaggēḏ* of v. 2 to *wayyuggaḏ*); Davidson, *Hebrew Syntax,* p. 152, § 108; R. Gordis, *The Word and the Book* (New York: Ktav, 1976), pp. 296, 327 n. 3.

2. This clause illustrates the use of *hinnēh* to indicate vivid immediacy, often in clauses with participles. See Waltke and O'Connor, *Biblical Hebrew Syntax,* p. 675.

3. The LXX renders the Hebrew participle *ḥōleh* by the verb *enochléō,* its one occurrence in the Pentateuch *(ho patḗr sou enochleítai).* In Classical and Koine Greek the verb means "trouble, annoy, be a bother," but in the passive it develops into "be bothered" and "be unwell, ill," the meaning it has in 48:1. See Lee, *Lexical Study of the Septuagint,* p. 66.

4. LXX adds, "and went to Jacob."

5. LXX again has a passive (presupposing *wayyuggaḏ*), rather than MT's active *wayyaggēḏ;* see n. 1 above. MT uses the verb *wayyō'mer* to tell how Joseph found out about Jacob (v. 1), but the verb *wayyaggēḏ* to tell how Jacob found out about Joseph (v. 2). In effect, the LXX reads both verbs as *nāḡaḏ,* using *apēngélē* (an aorist passive of *apangéllō*) in both verses. If there is a difference between direct speech introduced by *'āmar* and *nāḡaḏ,* it is that "the verb *n-g-d* intentionally wishes to convey a specific block of information. It is a deliberate, not accidental or casual, transfer of a clearly defined body of information. The words 'say' and 'speak' allow for randomness in discourse. . . . On the other hand words that one 'tells' have a focus of specificity" (S. A. Meier, *Speaking of Speaking: Marking Direct Discourse in the Hebrew Bible,* VTSup 46 [Leiden: Brill, 1992], p. 185).

6. The phrase *hinnēh . . . bā' 'ēleyḵā* is much like the one in Exod. 18:6, *'ᵃnî . . . bā' 'ēleyḵā,* "I . . . am coming to you," except that Exod. 18:6 reads the pronoun *'ᵃnî* rather than the interjection *hinnēh.* Both the LXX and SP read *hinnēh* in Exod. 18:6, probably in conformity with Gen. 48:2. See U. Cassuto, *Commentary on the Book of Exodus,* tr. I. Abrahams (Jerusalem: Magnes, 1967), p. 215; B. Childs, *Book of Exodus,* OTL (Philadelphia: Westminster, 1974), p. 320.

7. The basic meaning of *ḥāzaq* in the Hithpael is "exert oneself" (Deut. 12:23) or "take pains to do something" (Num. 13:20). Cf. J. Milgrom, *Numbers,* JPS Torah Commentary (Philadelphia: Jewish Publication Society, 1990), p. 102.

3 *Jacob said to Joseph: "El Shaddai appeared to me at Luz, in the land of Canaan, and blessed me,*

4 *and said to me: 'Look, I will make you fertile and numerous,*[8] *and establish you as an assembly of peoples, and will give this land to your offspring as an everlasting holding.'*

5 *Now your two sons, who were born to you in the land of Egypt before I joined you in Eygpt, shall be mine.*[9] *Ephraim and Manasseh, as much as Reuben and Simeon, shall be mine.*

6 *But progeny you father after them belong*[10] *to you. By their brothers' name their heritage shall be recorded.*[11]

7 *When I was coming from Paddan,*[12] *to my sorrow*[13] *Rachel*[14] *died, during the journey to Canaan, only a short distance from Ephrath. I buried her there on the way to*[15] *Ephrath, that is,*[16] *Bethlehem."*

1 Jacob is elderly. Reference has been made to his imminent death (47:29) but not to sickness. All that 47:31 suggested was that Jacob was bedridden. We have translated *ḥōleh* as *failing*. By itself *ḥālâ* does not mean terminally ill (for that mcaning, something like *lāmûṯ,* "unto death" [e.g., 2 K. 20:1 par. Isa. 38:1], or *ʿaḏ lāmûṯ* [2 Chr. 32:24], is added). But the situation is serious enough to report it to Joseph. We do not know who brought this news to

8. When an additional clause is joined by "and" to a participial construction (*mapr*ᵉ*ḵā,* "I will make you fertile"), a finite verb is usually employed (*w*ᵉ*hirbîṯiḵā,* "and numerous"). See Davidson, *Hebrew Syntax,* p. 135, § 100e; Waltke and O'Connor, *Biblical Hebrew Syntax,* pp. 535-36. Here the finite verb expresses a logically consequent situation to that expressed in the participial construction.

9. *lî hēm* shows that independent personal pronouns *(hēm)* that resume the subject of a verbless claus function generally as copulas; i.e., they are equivalent to the corresponding form of the verb "to be." Cf. G. Khan, *Studies in Semitic Syntax* (Oxford: Oxford University, 1988), p. 72.

10. Hebrew grammar permits a fem. collective noun *(môlaḏt*ᵉ*ḵā)* with a masc. pl. verb *(yihyû).* See Waltke and O'Connor, *Biblical Hebrew Syntax,* p. 109.

11. Lit., "by the name of their brothers they shall be called in (the matter of) their inheritance." See the commentary below.

12. SP and LXX add "Aram," to harmonize with the other uses of the full name Paddan-aram in Genesis (25:20; 28:2, 5-7; 31:18, 33:18; 35:9, 26; 46:15).

13. This translation is an intcrprctation of *ʿālay* ("[as a sorrow] upon me"). It may be read "Rachel died upon/beside me." Grammarians normally understand *ʿālay* in v. 7 as the adversative use of the preposition *ʿal,* expressing disadvantage. See Williams, *Hebrew Syntax,* p. 51, § 288; Waltke and O'Connor, *Biblical Hebrew Syntax,* p. 217.

14. One need not add, as do SP and LXX, "your mother" after "Rachel."

15. MT has lit., "on the way of Ephrath."

16. The use of the pronoun *hiwʾ* before Bethlehem indicates that this place name is already familiar to the reader. Cf. 14:2, 3, 7, 8, 17; 23:2, 19.

Joseph. More than likely it was one of his brothers, or possibly the courier by whom Jacob earlier got in touch with Joseph (47:29). This verse shows that Joseph continued to live apart from his family. He did not move to Goshen to join his kin.

Upon hearing of his father's condition, Joseph went to Goshen, accompanied by his two sons. The two sons are listed in the order of their birth: *Manasseh and Ephraim.* A few verses later (v. 5) Jacob will mention them in reverse order (Ephraim, Manasseh), pointing to the special blessing for the second-born. Although the account of Joseph's sons' birth is described in 41:50-52 (before the start of the seven-year famine), and although Joseph is reunited with his father from whom he has long been separated in 46:29, and although Jacob's time in Egypt amounted to seventeen years (47:28), 48:1ff. is the first passage to delineate any intercourse between grandfather and grandsons via Joseph (cf. Jacob's inability to recognize his grandsons in v. 8, caused perhaps by physical handicap).

2 Only Joseph's arrival is announced to Jacob. Nothing is said yet about his two grandsons who have also come. *Someone informed Jacob* — again the text is silent about who announces Joseph's appearance in Goshen. Joseph's arrival is enough to rally bedridden Jacob. Jacob had to exert himself: he *rallied his strength (wayyiṯḥazzēq),* for it took a great effort for him even to sit up. Jacob has deteriorated from "dwelling" in Goshen (*yēšeḇ,* 47:27) to "dwelling" in bed (*yēšeḇ,* 48:2).[17]

3-4 Jacob may be losing his health, but he is not losing his memory. He can recall the incident of many years earlier when God appeared to him at Luz (35:9-15). He repeats the promises of God about fertility, multiplication, that his seed will be an assembly of nations, and finally the promise of land. The only essential element of that theophany he does not repeat is the name change from Jacob to Israel. In this way, Jacob minimizes his role and maximizes God's role in that event. He does not say to Joseph: "Son, let me tell you what God did for me at Luz." Rather, he implies: "Son, let me tell you about our God and the precious promises he made for you, and the family, and our family's families."

Most source critics grant that vv. 3-7 are from P, principally because of indubitable Priestly terms *(El Shaddai, fertile, numerous, an assembly of peoples).* Even if that is the case, why should the narrator have Jacob recall this particular theophany, and why place it here at all? One should note that many of the promises given at Luz are currently being realized while Jacob's family is in Egypt. In Egypt they are *fertile* (or "fruitful," *pārâ,* 47:27; 48:4).

17. The prepositions that follow the verb allow for a different English equivalent. In 47:27 *yāšaḇ bᵉ* means "to dwell, reside in," while in 48:2 *yāšaḇ ʿal* means "to sit on/up."

In Egypt they are *numerous* (or "multiplying," *rāḇâ,* 47:27; 48:4). In Egypt they are acquiring land as an everlasting *holding* (*'ḥz,* 47:27; 48:4). Of course, the difference between the *'ᵃḥuzzâ* in Canaan and that in Egypt is that the former is to be *ʿôlām, forever.* Jacob's repetition of this particular encounter with God may be a gentle reminder to Joseph that Egypt is a temporary abode. It is in Canaan, and only in Canaan, that the promises of God can be realized. What God has graciously done for his people in Egypt is but a foretaste of what he will do for them in Canaan.

5 Jacob started talking about the past (vv. 3-4). He now shifts to the future (vv. 5-6). He will return to the past in v. 7. Most certainly surprising Joseph, Jacob elevates Joseph's two children from grandsons to sons. To make it clear and unmistakable to Joseph what Jacob is doing, Jacob picks out his two oldest children for comparison — Reuben and Simeon. Ephraim and Manasseh may now claim Jacob as "father" as legitimately as any of his other sons. In one move Joseph's sons become coinheritors with their uncles! This is, of course, the event that explains why, in subsequent times, the descendants of Joseph held two tribal allotments, rather than Joseph himself.

Jacob's declaration that Joseph's sons are his may be compared with a law in the Code of Hammurapi (§ 170): "If the father during his lifetime has ever said 'My children!' [lit., 'my sons'] to the children whom the slave bore him, thus having counted them with the children of his first wife. . . ."[18] Like Jacob, the adoptive father uses the term "my sons."[19] Perhaps it is best to say that this case involves adoption only in its broadest sense. For Gen. 48:5 does not record the adoption of a stranger by a childless man, but rather the recognition by a grandfather of his grandsons as his own sons. Also, the acceptance of the child of a wife's maidservant (as in the case of § 170 in Hammurapi's Code) is not the adoption of a stranger's son but rather the legitimation of a natural son. Thus Westermann says of this incident, "it is meant as legitimation, because the sons remain with their parents, and it is a subsequent legitimation which refers only to their future as fathers of tribes."[20]

18. See *ANET,* p. 173.

19. For a parallel from Ugarit to an intrafamily adoption in which a grandfather (Abdiya) adopts a grandson (Ana-Teshub, son of Abdiya's daughter), see I. Mendelsohn, "A Ugaritic Parallel to the Adoption of Ephraim and Manasseh," *IEJ* 9 (1959) 180-83.

20. Westermann, *Genesis,* 3:185. On the larger issue of adoption, see G. R. Driver and J. C. Miles, *Assyrian Laws* (Oxford: Clarendon, 1935), p. 249; idem, *Babylonian Laws,* 2 vols. (Oxford: Clarendon, 1952-55), 1:383-405; H. Donner, "Adoption oder Legitimation? Erwägungen zur Adoption im alten Testament auf dem Hintergrund der altorientalischen Rechte," *Oriens Antiquus* 8 (1969) 87-117; J. H. Tigay, "Adoption," *EncJud,* 2:298-301; A. Philipps, "Some aspects of family law in pre-exilic Israel," *VT* 23 (1973)

No reason is given for Jacob's action, but a partial explanation will be provided in vv. 8ff. What is his motive? What is Joseph's response? Joseph knows what it means to be elevated. He has gone from a household slave to Pharaoh's majordomo. Now his sons will experience an elevation of their own. Jacob has other grandsons with him in Goshen, fifty-one to be exact. Is not this act by Jacob a final demonstration of his gratitude to Joseph? By making Joseph's sons Jacob's sons, Jacob is in effect elevating Joseph to the level of himself. That is, both men are now ancestral fathers of the tribes of Israel that will come from them.

6 Jacob adds the proviso that any subsequent children born to Joseph — Genesis records none — will be Joseph's children. For inheritance purposes such offspring will be counted as Ephraimites or Manassites. Emphasis is given to *progeny (môlaḏtᵉḵā)* by virtue of the word being placed first in the sentence: *But progeny you father after them belong to you.*

The closing clause of the verse, *by their brothers' name their heritage shall be recorded,* simply indicates that any other subsequent children of Joseph and their descendants will be subsumed under privileges and territory extended to the tribes of Ephraim and Manasseh. Thus the case is made that the situation of Ephraim and Manasseh is unique.

7 Again Jacob relives a past event, the death of his beloved wife Rachel as they traveled from *Paddan*(-aram) back to Canaan (35:16-20). A dying man talks about a dead woman. It is not clear why Jacob recalls Rachel's death and shares it with Joseph. Jacob does not repeat that Rachel died in giving birth to Benjamin, Joseph's brother. Are these two people (Joseph and Rachel) the individuals for whom Jacob has the highest affection? Jacob has just talked to Joseph about his sons. He follows that by talking to Joseph about his mother. Jacob has recently spoken of his own future burial (*qāḇar,* 47:29-30). He buried his spouse in Canaan. Will not Joseph bury his father there too?

It may be that we should see some connection between Jacob's appropriation of Joseph's children as his own and his recall of his wife's death. Had Rachel lived longer, she would have given birth to other children. In taking Joseph's two children, Jacob increases (posthumously) Rachel's offspring to four. If that is the case, then Rachel's prayer at the birth of Joseph ("May Yahweh add another son for me," 30:24b) has been answered with Benjamin, and again with Ephraim and Manasseh.

358-61; S. Paul, "Adoption Formulae: A Study of Cuneiform and Biblical Legal Clauses," *MAARAV* 2 (1979/80) 173-85; H. J. Boecker, *Law and the Administration of Justice in the Old Testament and Ancient East,* tr. J. Moiser (Minneapolis: Augsburg, 1980), pp. 118ff.; A. Viberg, *Symbols of Law,* ConBOT 34 (Stockholm: Almqvist & Wiksell, 1992), pp. 166-75; F. Knobloch, "Adoption," *ABD,* 1:76-79.

3. EPHRAIM AND MANASSEH BEFORE JACOB (48:8-16)

8 *When Israel saw Joseph's sons he asked,*[1] *"Who are these?"*[2]

9 *"My sons are they," Joseph replied to his father, "whom God has given me here." He said: "Bring them*[3] *to me so that I may bless them."*

10 *Now Israel's eyes became heavy*[4] *with age*[5] *and he could not see.*[6] *So he brought his sons close to him, and he kissed them and embraced them.*

11 *Israel said to Joseph: "To see*[7] *your face again is something for which I cannot take credit,*[8] *and now*[9] *God has permitted me to see your offspring as well!"*

1. Lit., "he said" *(wayyō'mer).* Genesis has more than fifty instances where questions appear that are not introduced by *šā'al,* "ask," and only eight with *šā'al.* See the references in S. A. Meier, *Speaking of Speaking: Marking Direct Discourse in the Hebrew Bible,* VTSup 46 (Leiden: Brill, 1992), p. 161 n. 2.

2. LXX and SP read, "Who are these to you?" i.e., who are these in relation to you, what relationship do they have to you?

3. The normal 3rd person masc. pl. pronominal suffix on an imperative should be *-ēm.* In *qāḥem-nā'* ("bring them"), *ēm* has lost the tone because of *maqqeph,* and so is reduced to *-em.* See GKC, § 58g.

4. For *kāḇēḏ* used with parts of the body cf. Job 23:2 (hand); Isa. 6:10; 59:1; Zech. 7:11 (ear); Exod. 9:7 (heart); Ezek. 3:5-6 (tongue); Exod. 4:10 (mouth). The same is true for Akk. *kabātu/kubtu,* "to be heavy," said of the feet *(šēpā kabtā),* of the ears *(uznā kabtā),* of the eye *(īnā kabtā),* of the mouth *(kabātu ša pî).* Cf. H. Tawil, "Some Literary Elements . . . of East and West Semitic Royal Inscriptions," *Or* 43 (1974) 61-62. On the ingressive use of the stative, see Waltke and O'Connor, *Biblical Hebrew Syntax,* p. 492.

5. *mizzōqen* provides an instance of the use of the preposition *min* with causative sense ("with, from, because of"). See Davidson, *Hebrew Syntax,* p. 142, § 101c.

6. One way of underscoring a point is to repeat the same material ("Now Israel's eyes became heavy") by means of the negation of an antonymn ("he could not see"). For other examples in Genesis see 11:30; 37:24; 42:31; and Andersen, *Sentence in Biblical Hebrew,* pp. 43-44.

7. *r^{e}'ōh* provides an illustration of an alternative form of the infinitive construct of a verb ending in *h;* the usual form is *r^{e}'ôṯ.* Cf. GKC, §§ 75n, 115b.

8. The Piel of *pālal* occurs only 3 other times in the OT (1 Sam. 2:25; Ezek. 16:52; Ps. 106:30), and in each of these texts most versions read "intercede, mediate," or the like. E. A. Speiser ("The Stem *PLL* in Hebrew," *JBL* 82 [1963] 301-6 [esp. p. 304]) arrives at "I never expected" by understanding *pillāltî* as a factitive Piel formed from *p^{e}lîlîm,* "assessment, estimate," and *p^{e}lîlâ,* "judgment." Another approach is taken by C. Toll, "Ausdrücke für 'Kraft' im Alten Testament mit besonderer Rücksicht auf die Wurzel BRK," *ZAW* 94 (1982) 120. He translates, "I had no strength to see you, but God has allowed me to see your offspring" ("Ich hatte keine Kraft, dich zu sehen, aber Gott hat mich auf deine Nachkommen sehen lassen"). It is not at all clear, however, that "intercede/mediate" is the best English equivalent of the Piel of *pālal.* Speiser appears to

12 *Joseph removed them from his knees*[10] *and bowed*[11] *with his face to the ground.*

13 *And Joseph took the two of them, Ephraim with his right hand, to Israel's left, and Manasseh with his left hand, to Israel's right, and brought them*[12] *to him.*

14 *Israel extended his right hand*[13] *and placed it on Ephraim's head — although*[14] *he was the younger*[15] *— and his left hand on Manasseh's head by crossing*[16] *his hands — although*[17] *Manasseh*[18] *was the firstborn.*

---

overlook the fact that the verb in question is used primarily in legal or quasi-legal contexts with the idea of being accountable, or responsible, or liable. Thus if the basic idea underlying the verb is that of sole responsibility, then the Piel would designate the moving of that responsibility onto either the verb's object or the verb's subject, thus here something like "I did not take upon myself the seeing of your face" or "I cannot claim credit for this." See R. Westbrook, "Lex Talionis and Exodus 21,22-25," *RB* 93 (1986) 59-61; idem, "Adultery in Ancient Near Eastern Law," *RB* 97 (1990) 569 n. 101; A. Berlin, "On the Meaning of *pll* in the Bible," *RB* 96 (1989) 344-51.

9. On the use of *wᵉhinnēh* to report a clause which reports a surprise development, see Andersen, *Sentence in Biblical Hebrew,* pp. 95, 161.

10. Understanding the text to suggest that Joseph's sons were standing between Jacob's legs when he blessed them, Targ. Onqelos chose deliberately not to translate "from his knees" ("and Joseph brought them out from before him"), since spreading one's legs bordered on indecent exposure.

11. LXX, SP, and Pesh. read a pl., which suggests that it is the grandsons who genuflect, but I see no problem with retaining the MT, and restricting the bowing to Joseph.

12. On the basis of LXX, Pesh., and Vulg., I follow *BHS* and insert *'ōṯām,* "them," after the verb, as in v. 10.

13. The OT frequently uses *yᵉmîn* for "right hand" (Exod. 15:6; Deut. 33:2; Ps. 17:7; 20:7 [Eng. 6]; 44:4 [Eng. 3]); here *yᵉmîn* is synonymous with *yaḏ yᵉmînô* in v. 17.

14. In a noun clause connected by a *waw* copulative to a verbal clause, the *waw* may indicate a simultaneous contradictory fact. See GKC, § 141e.

15. For and *ṣā'îr* and *bᵉḵôr* cf. 43:33. For *bᵉḵîrâ* and *ṣᵉ'îrâ* cf. 19:30-38 and 29:26.

16. On the basis of an Arabic cognate meaning "bind the legs of beast" and "plait locks of hair," BDB, p. 968b, derives this from *śāḵal* II, "lay crosswise," rather than *śāḵal* I, "be prudent," and cf. *HALAT,* 4:1239. Targ. Onqelos is an early translation that does read the verb as *śāḵal* I: "he placed his hand wisely" *('ḥkymynyn lydwhy).* For the use of a perfect in a circumstantial clause *(śikkēl),* see Davidson, *Hebrew Syntax,* p. 63, §41, Rem. 3.

17. On the use of the particle *kî* to subordinate a concessive, circumstantial clause, see Andersen, *Sentence in Biblical Hebrew,* p. 90.

18. In the majority of nominal clauses with a proper noun, the proper noun follows the other word(s) in the clause. In the minority, where the proper noun precedes, as here, the proper noun has contrastive force. Here it is of special importance that Manasseh was the firstborn, not Ephraim, who received the right hand of blessing. See J. Hoftijzer's review of Andersen's *Hebrew Verbless Clause in the Pentateuch* in *VT* 23 (1973) 494.

15 *Then he blessed them*[19] *and said:*
"May the God before whom walked my fathers Abraham and Isaac,
the God who has shepherded me throughout my entire life,[20]
16 *The angel*[21] *who delivers me from every distress, may he bless the lads,*
that my name may live on[22] *in them, as well as the names of my fathers Abraham and Isaac,*
and that they may multiply[23] *exceedingly in the land."*

8 Two problems arise from this brief verse. The first is the apparent contradiction between *When Israel saw* [*wayyar'*] *Joseph's sons* and the statement in v. 10 that Jacob's eyesight was fading so badly that he was not able to see *(lō' yûḵal lir'ôṯ).* Could he see, or could he not? The second problem is reconciling Jacob's question to Joseph about Joseph's sons *(Who are these?)* with the fact that (a) 46:5 says that Jacob knew Joseph had two boys, that he knew they were born in Egypt, that he knew their names; and (b) 45:28 claims that Jacob had by this time lived in Egypt for seventeen years. Might a grandfather live in one place for almost two decades and not recognize his grandchildren?

To respond to the first issue, I suggest that vv. 8 and 10 claim retention of some vision for Jacob. He is not totally blind. He can pick out two bodies standing by his son. But he cannot recognize them until they are standing right in front of him (the second problem). Seventeen years earlier Jacob would have had no need to ask that question. Note that in v. 11 Jacob speaks of his euphoria in "seeing" one more time Joseph's face. So he is not completely blind.

It may also be that Jacob's question should be understood as part of

19. This is the reading of LXX, which makes more sense than MT ("he blessed Joseph"), since v. 16 refers clearly to "the lads."

20. Lit., "ever since I was [*mē'ôḏî,* for which cf. Num. 22:30] until this day." See BDB, p. 729b. LXX, Vulg. and Pesh. read *minnᵉ'ûray,* "from my youth," for *mē'ôḏî.* Cf. the similar *bᵉ'ôḏî,* while "I have being" in Ps. 104:33; 146:2, where it is synonymous with "life."

21. SP reads *hammeleḵ,* "the king," for MT *hammal'āḵ,* "the angel" or "the messenger." "Angel" of v. 16, parallel to "God" of v. 15, represents the form in which God appeared to Jacob.

22. Or "be called, recalled" *(yiqqārē').*

23. *dāgâ* is a hapax legomenon. It seems to be related to the noun *dāg,* "fish" (who multiply quickly?). Cf. F. E. Greenspahn, *Hapax Legomena in Biblical Hebrew,* SBLDS 74 (Chico, CA: Scholars, 1984), pp. 107-8. If this connection is correct, then one could render the verb "may they become fishlike multitudes." Cf. Targ. Onqelos: "May they increase like the fish of the sea."

the formal prelude to the forthcoming blessing. That prelude includes formal recognition by Joseph that the young men are his sons. One thinks of the question at a baptism, "What name is given to this child?" or the question at a wedding, "Who giveth this woman to this man?" — neither of which is prompted by the ignorance of the clergyperson.[24]

The only other possible solution is to suppose that these verses have been artificially placed in their current position (i.e., at Jacob's deathbed), but that their original position was at some point shortly after Jacob arrives in Egypt, say, around 46:30.

9 Joseph responds to his father's question with *My sons are they,* thereby giving prominence to the sons by placing the noun ahead of the pronoun in this nominal sentence.[25] They are not sons whom his wife, Asenath, has given to him, but sons whom *God* has given him. Joseph calls Ephraim and Manasseh *My* sons, not "our" sons. The question-and-answer dialogue between Jacob and Joseph is much like that earlier between Esau and Jacob: Esau — "Who are these with you?" Jacob — "The children whom God has graciously given your servant" (33:5).

10 In the later years of his life Jacob has the same problem as did Isaac his father — failing eyesight (27:1). Therefore, Joseph brings his sons right up to Jacob, within arm's reach, so that he may bless them. Jacob, first the subject of blessing (47:7, 10), then the object of blessing (48:3), is again the subject of blessing. Before Jacob blesses his grandchildren he shows his affections for them by kissing and embracing them. (These two verbs were used in 33:4 when Esau and Jacob were united with each other after a long separation.) Jacob may be losing his eyesight, but he is not losing his emotional attachment to his family. The difference between the two verbs in 33:4 and 48:10 is their sequence. In 33:4 the sequence is "embraced" *(wayeḥabbeqēhû),* then an intervening verb, then "kissed" *(wayyiššāqēhû).* The same sequence for these two verbs occurs in 29:13, when Laban greeted Jacob and embraced and kissed him. 48:10 reverses this sequence. The embrace is a sequel to the kissing, not a prelude, indicating Jacob's desire to hold his grandsons in his embrace for an extended period.[26]

24. Sarna (*Genesis,* p. 327) states, "we have here the second stage of the legal adoptive process, namely, the establishment of the true identity of the candidates for adoption by formal interrogation of the natural father."

25. In the majority of nominal clauses having a noun and a pronoun, the pronoun usually precedes the noun. In reversing this normal order with *bānay hēm,* Joseph emphasizes the special relationship he has with these two young men. They are not just "boys" (v. 16), but they are his sons. See Hoftijzer, *VT* 23 (1973) 488-90.

26. Both sequences occur in the Ugaritic texts: *y[ḥb]q wynšq,* "he embraced and kissed (her)" (*UT,* 1 Aqht [= *CTA,* 19].63-64, 70-71); *bm nšq whr bḥbq ḥmḥmt,* "from kissing and conception, from the embrace of pregnancy" (*UT,* 52 [= *CTA,* 23].51, 56); *bm*

11 The grandsons now stand before him, but Jacob addresses Joseph. He still finds it unbelievable that he has seen not only Joseph but Joseph's sons as well. Both father and son are quick to give credit and glory to God. Joseph's "my sons . . . whom God has given me here" is matched by Jacob's *God has permitted me to see.*[27] It is not a case of either man being lucky. God has been gracious to both of them. Jacob had earlier referred to Ephraim and Manasseh as Joseph's "two sons" (*šᵉnê-ḇāneyḵā,* v. 5), but now he calls them *your offspring (zarʿeḵā).* Jacob had used "offspring" earlier in the chapter when recalling to Joseph the theophany at Luz (*lᵉzarʿᵃḵā,* v. 4).

Jacob may lament that his days have been few and evil, and that he has not lived as long or as well as his father and grandfather (47:9). Yet Jacob is the only patriarch in these narratives who meets and has any dealings with his grandchildren. We do not read of any exchange between Abraham and Isaac's children, or between Isaac and Jacob's children. In having this privilege, Jacob is exceeded only by Joseph, who saw perhaps three generations beyond him (50:23).

12 If Joseph removes Ephraim and Manasseh from Jacob's knees, then that would indicate that they were still relatively small and young, little lads. In fact, they must be near twenty, for they were born to Joseph before Jacob came to Egypt seventeen years earlier. It is unlikely that a bedridden, elderly, blind, and sickly man could support two young men on his knees. The phrase must mean, then, that Ephraim and Manasseh stood by their grandfather's bed, near his knees.[28]

Jacob had earlier wondered, hesitantly, whether he would one day "bow" before Joseph (37:10). That never happened. Instead, here it is Joseph who bows before Jacob. The only place Jacob does any bowing is on his bed (47:31). Joseph may be the second most powerful man in Egypt, but he never loses his respect for his father, and he never ceases to be gracious toward him.

13 Now that the preliminaries are over, Joseph brings his two sons back to the edge of Jacob's bed. (The verb *wayyaggēš, brought,* is used twice here, vv. 10 and 13.) He takes Ephraim, the second-born, with his right hand and positions him before Jacob's left hand. He takes Manasseh, the firstborn, with his left hand and positions him before Jacob's right hand. In this way, Joseph thinks, the important right hand of blessing will be placed on Manasseh, and the less important left hand of blessing will be placed on Ephraim. (On

---

nšq aṯth bḥhqh ḥmḥmt, "in the kissing of his wife [she'll conceive], in his embracing became pregnant" (*UT,* 2 Aqht [= *CTA,* 17].I.40-41). These Ugaritic passages are cited by Avishur, *Stylistic Studies of Word-Pairs,* p. 356.

27. On the use of a "permissive" Hiphil *(herʾâ),* see C. L. Seow, *Grammar for Biblical Hebrew* (Nashville: Abingdon, 1987), p. 121.

28. See Westermann, *Genesis,* 3:187.

the inauspicious quality of the left side cf. Ezek. 4:4; Eccl. 10:2.) Joseph thus "firmly stage-manages the blessing scene for his doting father."[29]

Of course, Joseph does what he does for two reasons. One, he is trying to give his father (with impaired vision) some assistance. He lines the sons up in their correct positions, something that Jacob could not see well enough to do by himself. Two, Joseph is a traditionalist. He has no reason to believe that anything out of the normal is about to occur. The subtlety of Jacob naming Ephraim ahead of Manasseh back in v. 5 slipped by Joseph unnoticed, even though Jacob named his own children chronologically — Reuben, then Simeon.

14 To the surprise of everybody, Jacob crosses his hands and places his right hand on the younger boy and his left hand on the older boy. From this action of Jacob comes the eventual precedence of Ephraim over Manasseh. Jacob may be losing his sight, but he is not losing his insight. For some undisclosed reason Jacob ignores the law of primogeniture. Manasseh thus joins a long list of firstborn in Genesis who for one reason or other are passed by — Cain, Ishmael, Esau, Reuben, and Zerah. The text is strangely silent about the stimulus for Jacob's surprise move. How does he know to cross his hands and bless with the right hand the younger boy? Is he guided by "a supernatural impulse"?[30] Does he do a right thing inadvertently?[31] In any case, "the blind patriarch shows an insight into the future denied to his clear-sighted (and occasionally clairvoyant) but for once earthbound son."[32]

In the case of Ishmael and Isaac, God told Abraham directly that Isaac was to be his "firstborn" (21:12). In the case of Esau and Reuben, they forfeited their firstborn position because of their behavior. Here, however, Manasseh has done nothing to lose his position, and Jacob has received no revelation of Ephraim's elevation. Perhaps we have here another instance from the Ancient Near East of a (grand)father's right to disregard the law of primogeniture, and choose his own "firstborn."[33] (If such was practiced in Canaan, it was later prohibited by law — see Deut. 21:15-17.)

The act of hand imposition in this incident is conveyed by the verb *šîṯ* (vv. 14, 17) and by the verb *śîm* (v. 18), both of which mean "put, place." In contrast, throughout priestly literature, wherever there is a laying on of one hand (Lev. 1:4) or of both hands (16:21), the verb that is consistently used is *sāmaḵ*. It is possible that *šîṯ/śîm* and *sāmaḵ* are synonyms. But it is also

29. Sternberg, *Poetics of Biblical Narrative,* p. 352.

30. So Skinner, *Genesis,* p. 505; cf. Speiser, *Genesis,* p. 360.

31. Cf. Brueggemann, *Genesis,* p. 363.

32. Sternberg, *Poetics of Biblical Narrative,* p. 353.

33. See I. Mendelsohn, "On the Preferential Status of the Eldest Son," *BASOR* 156 (1959) 38-40.

possible that *šîṯ/śîm* may refer to laying one's hands on the head of another lightly, while *sāmaḵ* implies the use of more pressure.[34] If this distinction can be maintained, then we have a Jacob who earlier "embraced" Ephraim and Manasseh (i.e., a strong, sustained, physical touch), but who now lightly places his hands on their head in an act of blessing. Through placing his hands on Joseph's children, Jacob simply engages in an act by which he designates who the recipients of blessing are, and an act by which the actual blessing is bestowed.[35]

15-16 Jacob now pronounces a blessing on his two grandsons. The first half of the blessing (vv. 15-16a) is actually a testimony covering three generations. First Jacob bears witness to the religious devotion of his father and grandfather. They walked before God. How appropriate it is for one grandfather, now a father who is blessing his (grand)children, to recall his own father and grandfather. So, Jacob begins by highlighting the God of his fathers and the obedience they lived out before that God.

Jacob does not continue his testimony with "and the God before whom I walked." Rather, when he comes to this autobiographical section he shifts the emphasis from himself and anything he has done to God and what he has done for Jacob. If Abraham and Isaac walked before God, God has walked before Jacob. When describing his fathers' behavior before God, Jacob uses a verb form that conveys completed action *(hiṯhallᵉḵû),* which is what one expects. But when Jacob describes God's behavior toward Jacob, he uses participles, which express continuous action, either in present time or in past time, and here are an equivalent to a relative clause. God *has shepherded (rōʿeh)* him, and delivered *(gōʾēl)*[36] him. From Rebekah's womb to his deathbed in Egypt, Jacob testifies that God has been there with him, leading him, liberating him.

In one breath Jacob refers to *God* (v. 15b) and in the next breath to *The angel* (v. 16a). In the Genesis narratives an angel, or heavenly messenger, appears at moments fraught with danger and turmoil — Hagar alone in a desert

34. The distinction is made by J. Milgrom, *Leviticus 1–16,* AB (New York: Doubleday, 1991), pp. 150-51, on the basis of a few passages in the OT where *śāmaḵ (yaḏ)* means "to lean on/against" (Judg. 16:29; Amos 5:19), i.e., exert pressure, and on postbiblical Jewish traditions. For a contrary view, see D. P. Wright, "Hands, Laying on of," *ABD,* 3:47-48.

35. See C. W. Mitchell, *The Meaning of BRK "To Bless" in the Old Testament,* SBLDS 95 (Atlanta: Scholars, 1987), p. 84.

36. This is the only occurrence of the root *g'l* in Genesis. As one would expect, it is used frequently in the Psalter in laments and songs of thanksgiving, but much more frequently in collective psalms than in individual ones. Gen. 48:16 is a rare instance of this verb used by an individual about himself. See N. P. Lemche, *Early Israel,* VTSup 37 (Leiden: Brill, 1985), pp. 344-48.

(16:7-11); Hagar with a near-dead son in the desert (21:17); Abraham holding a knife over Isaac (22:11-18); a servant making a long journey to another country (24:7, 40); Jacob preparing to leave his father-in-law (31:11); Jacob alone by a river, running from Laban and frightened by the prospects of meeting Esau (32:25-31 [Eng. 24-30]). No wonder then that Jacob would here speak of the angel who delivers him *from every distress (mikkol-rāʿ).*[37]

After an elaborate subject for the blessing (vv. 15-16a), Jacob follows with a brief verb and object: *may he bless the lads.* Ephraim and Manasseh, previously designated as "sons" and "seed," are now *lads (n^eʿārîm).* Joseph was once referred to as a *naʿar* (37:2; 41:12); and Jacob's most precious, irreplaceable *naʿar* was Benjamin (43:8; 44:22, 30-34). Thus to Jacob's two lads (Joseph, Benjamin) are added two more lads (Ephraim, Manasseh). It is not necessary for Jacob to use their names.[38]

Jacob's blessing has three parts to it: (1) the invocation of God (vv. 15-16a); (2) the prayer for blessing (v. 16b); and (3) the results of the blessing and the prayer (v. 16c, d).

One result relates directly to the sons themselves. To be blessed means to *multiply,* to be fertile. What God had promised to Jacob (*hirbîṯiḵā,* 48:4) Jacob wants to see realized in these two lads *(yiḏgû lārōḇ).*

Jacob's other hoped-for result is that his name, and the names of his father and grandfather, will *live on* (lit., "be named, called, recalled") in Ephraim and Manasseh. In other words, his prayer is that from this time on Ephraim and Manasseh will be known as sons of Jacob. The Hebrew phrase *w^eyiqqārēʾ ḇāhem š^emî* is equivalent to that found in a law dealing with the adoption of a freeborn child in the Code of Hammurapi: "If a seignior adopted a boy in his own name. . . ."[39] In such instances the idiom *qārāʾ šēm,* or a variant, carries the force of "continue/perpetuate the family line."[40]

37. Some commentators have drawn a parallel between Jacob's threefold invocation of deity ("God . . . God . . . angel") with the prayer of Aaron: "May Yahweh bless . . . May Yahweh make . . . May Yahweh lift up" (Num. 6:24-26). See Westermann, *Genesis,* 3:189. The correspondence shows "the link between patriarchal tradition and the liturgy of Israel."

38. See J. MacDonald, "The Status and Role of the *Naʿar* in Israelite Society," *JNES* 35 (1976) 148, who states from his study of the noun in the narratives of the OT that the *naʿar* "was of high birth. Indeed no examples can be found of one of lowly birth" (p. 149); the term is "descriptive of a high-born male young" (p. 150).

39. *ANET,* p. 174, § 185 (Akk. *šumma awîlum ṣiḫram ina mēšu ana mârûtim ilqi*). Cf. Ezra 2:61 (par. Neh. 7:63), which speaks of a person of the rejected priestly families who "had taken a wife from the daughters of Barzillai the Gileadite, and was called by their name"; that is, he was adopted into the family of Barzillai and assumed that name. Gen. 48:16 uses *qārāʾ* (Niphal) plus *b^e;* Ezra 2:61 uses *qārāʾ* (Niphal) plus *ʿal.*

40. H. C. Brichto, "Kin, Cult, Land and Afterlife — A Biblical Complex," *HUCA* 44 (1973) 21ff.

4. JACOB REJECTS JOSEPH'S CORRECTIVE (48:17-22)

17 *When Joseph saw that his father was about to lay*[1] *his right hand on Ephraim's head, it seemed wrong to him;*[2] *so he took hold of his father's hand to remove it from Ephraim's head to Manasseh's.*

18 *Joseph said to his father: "That is not right, father; the other one is the firstborn;*[3] *lay your right hand on his head."*

19 *But his father refused and said: "I know it, son, I know.*[4] *He too shall become a people, and he too shall become great.*[5] *Nevertheless,*[6] *his younger brother shall become greater than he, and his descendants shall become a company of peoples."*[7]

20 *He blessed them on that day,*[8] *saying,*
"By you[9] *all Israel shall offer blessing,*[10] *saying,*
'May God make you like Ephraim and Manasseh,' "

1. *yāšîṯ* is a future, not a past ("had laid"), and indicates that at least vv. 17-19a are a parenthesis, informing the reader of what Joseph did prior to Jacob's conferring the blessing, and thus Jacob is not correcting his father after the fact (cf. Westermann, *Genesis,* 3:188-89).

2. Lit., "it was evil [or 'bad,' Heb. *rāʿa'*] in his eyes." For an earlier occurrence of *wayyēraʿ bᵉʿênê* with the same nuance see 21:11, 12 (Sarah's insistence that Abraham get rid of Hagar and Ishmael, and Abraham's emotional response to her request).

3. On this nominal clause (*zeh habbᵉḵōr,* pronoun followed by definite noun), see Hoftijzer, *VT* 23 (1973) 491, who argues that *zeh* is the only pronominal core constituent that could be used here, for it implies clearly that Manasseh ("the other one") is the firstborn.

4. On verbal repetition in apposition cf. also *nēlēḵ . . . nēlēḵ,* "we will go . . . we will go" in Exod. 10:9; and Andersen, *Sentence in Biblical Hebrew,* pp. 37-38.

5. On conjoined predictive clauses that refer to concomitant future events by means of a prefixed verb *(yihyeh, yigdāl),* see Andersen, *Sentence in Biblical Hebrew,* pp. 99-100.

6. Adversative clauses may be introduced by the adverb *'ûlām.* Cf. Gen. 28:19; and Williams, *Hebrew Syntax,* p. 93, § 553.

7. Lit., "the fullness of the nations," or "a plethora of nations." Given that the Hebrew text opens the possibility of the intermixture of non-Israelite peoples with the tribe of Ephraim, Targ. Onqelos renders the last part of this verse, "and his descendants shall rule over nations" *(wbnwhy šlytyn bʿmmy').*

8. S. J. DeVries (*Yesterday, Today and Tomorrow* [Grand Rapids: Eerdmans, 1975], pp. 99, 116) cites "on that day" as an instance of this phrase as a transition formula between episodes, and as introducing a supplement to the blessing contained in v. 19.

9. For MT *bᵉḵā* (sing.) LXX reads *En hymín* (pl., presupposing Heb. *bāḵem*). The sing. in MT is a distributive, "by each of you."

10. I follow MT Piel *(yᵉḇārēḵ).* LXX, SP, and Vulg. read it as a Niphal *(yibbārēḵ),* which occurs nowhere else in the OT. A Hiphil *(yaḇrēḵ)* or a Pual *(yᵉbōraḵ)* is also possible. H. C. Brichto (*The Problem of "Curse" in the Hebrew Bible,* JBLMS 13 [Philadelphia: Society of Biblical Literature, 1968], p. 196) cites Jer. 29:22 as a parallel to Gen. 48:20: "And from them a *qᵉlālāh* will be taken up by all the exiles of Judah, who are in Babylon," to wit: "May Yahweh make you like Zedekiah and Ahab, whom the king of Babylon roasted in fire!"

as he placed Ephraim ahead of Manasseh.

21 *Then Israel said to Joseph: "I am about to die. But God will be with you*[11] *and restore you to your fathers' land.*

22 *As for me, I give you*[12] *one mountain slope*[13] *more than*[14] *your brothers which I captured from the Amorites with my sword and bow."*[15]

17 Joseph assumes that his father, because of poor eyesight, has mixed up Ephraim and Manasseh. That is why Jacob had to cross his hands, and use his right hand to touch "Manasseh" (in reality, Ephraim).

For one of the few times in his life, Joseph is wrong in his assumption that here protocol should be followed. Joseph can "see" in the sense of observe his father's actions *(wayyar')*, but such seeing is limited to external, surface observations. There is surely some connection between the use of the noun *rāʿ* ("distress") in v. 16 and the verb *rāʿaʿ (it seemed wrong)* in v. 17. Jacob testified in v. 16 that the angel had delivered him from every crisis (lit.,

11. The two uses of "you" in this verse are pl. *(ʿimmāḵem, 'eṯkem),* as is "your" in "your fathers" *('ᵃḇōṯêḵem),* but "you" in the following verse is sing. *(lᵉḵā),* indicating that Jacob speaks through Joseph to his entire family in v. 21.

12. On the use of the perfect to express future actions *(nāṯattî),* see GKC, § 106m ("when the speaker intends by an express assurance to represent them as finished, or as equivalent to accomplished facts").

13. *šᵉḵem 'aḥaḏ* presents several difficulties. First, is *šᵉḵem* "Shechem" or "shoulder, mountain slope, ridge of land"? Second, why is the numeral *'aḥaḏ* ("one") in the construct state after the noun, instead of the expected *'eḥāḏ?* GKC, § 130g, believes that the numeral is not construct in form, but is a rhythmical shortening of the usual (tone-lengthened) form. (SP reads the numeral as fem., *'aḥaṯ,* ostensibly for the Samaritans a reference to Gerizim!) Third, should *'aḥaḏ* modify *šᵉḵem* (as in my translation), or what follows, as in Speiser's "I give you, as the one above your brothers, Shechem" (*Genesis,* pp. 356, 358)? Hebrew syntax allows either translation. Speiser's suggestion that "shoulder" is impossible because the numeral would have to be fem. is wide of the mark. In the one instance where the gender of *šᵉḵem* is demonstrated it is clearly masc. — "to serve him with one shoulder [i.e., one purpose; *šᵉḵem 'eḥaḏ*]" (Zeph. 3:9). LXX avoids the numeral completely with its *Sikima exaíreton,* "Shechem, a select portion" (*exaíretos,* "picked out, selected, chosen," from *exaírō,* "exalt, lift up"; see W. Bauer, *Greek-English Lexicon of the New Testament and Other Early Christian Literature,* tr. W. F. Arndt and F. W. Gingrich, ed. Gingrich and F. W. Danker, 2nd ed. [Chicago: University of Chicago, 1979], pp. 271-72). Possibly LXX's translation reflects the location of Shechem between two mountains.

14. For *ʿal* meaning "more than" see BDB, p. 755a, § 2. R. Gordis (*Book of Job: A Commentary* [New York: Jewish Theological Seminary of America, 1978], p. 260) perceives this meaning for *ʿal* in Job 23:2, but M. Pope (*Job,* AB, 3rd ed. [Garden City, NY: Doubleday, 1973], pp. 170-71) does not.

15. For the pair *bᵉḥarbî ûḇᵉqaštî* ("sword and bow") see Avishur, *Stylistic Studies of Word-Pairs,* p. 258.

"evil"). Now Joseph laments that what his father is about to do "is evil." Joseph fails to understand that what Jacob is doing is no exception to this testimony. Even in blessing his second-born grandson with his right hand, Jacob is guided by God and delivered from doing any kind of *rāʿ*.

18 Joseph is more concerned about moving Jacob's right hand to Manasseh's head than in moving Jacob's left hand to Ephraim. Joseph does not use names when talking to his father about his two sons; Manasseh is simply *the other one* (*zeh,* lit., "this one").

Nothing in the blessing of vv. 15-16 gives Joseph any concern. It is what his father has done, not what he has said, that upsets Joseph. Although some scholars interpret vv. 15-16 as secondary,[16] and think that vv. 17-18 originally followed v. 14, it is also possible to interpret vv. 17-19 as a parenthesis (as already noted). Yet another possibility is that by delaying Joseph's response until after the blessing, the text suggests that Joseph is so upset by what he sees his father do that he never hears what his father says. Joseph knows well enough that a blessing, once pronounced, cannot be retracted. Isaac could not withdraw his blessing on Jacob, even though he was tricked into pronouncing it. More importantly, there is nothing in the blessing to which Joseph might object. In fact, the blessing that follows the right-hand imposition on Ephraim does not single him out for special favors. It is a blessing on *both* Ephraim and Manasseh as equals: "may he bless the *lads,* that my name may live on in *them* . . . and that *they* may multiply exceedingly."

19 Jacob's *I know it, son, I know,* is similar to Pilate's "What I have written, I have written." Jacob's *yāḏaʿtî* ("I know") near the end of his life may be compared with his *lōʾ yāḏaʿtî* (28:16, "I did not know") near the beginning of his adult life. He begins his life with a confession of ignorance, and comes to the end of his life with a "calm self-assurance."[17]

Only now does Jacob realize the nature of the special and favored role that will be assigned to Ephraim. Ephraim shall be greater than Manasseh, and his descendants will be exceedingly numerous, as his name suggests. In other words, the difference between Ephraim and Manasseh is a comparative one.[18]

16. Westermann, *Genesis,* 3:191.

17. See, e.g., ibid., 3:188-89.

18. The subordination of Manasseh to Ephraim is evident in data from the early chapters of Numbers. For example, Ephraim precedes Manasseh in the genealogy (Num. 1:10), in the census results (1:32-33 and 34-35, respectively: Ephraim with 40,500 descendants, Manasseh with 32,200), and in the list of tribal chieftains (7:48-53, 54-59). Also in the tribal divisions around the tabernacle, Ephraim is in the middle position on the west side between Manasseh and Benjamin (2:18-24). The firstborn would usually take on the privileged middle position (thus Reuben, firstborn of Leah, on the south between Gad and Simeon; and Dan, firstborn of Bilhah, on the north between Asher and Naphtali). By contrast, later in

20 For a second time (or, resuming his benediction) Jacob blesses his (grand)sons. The first (vv. 15-16) was a blessing about them. Hence it is spoken in the third person — bless *the lads,* live in *them,* let *them* multiply. This one is spoken to the boys, and hence is in the second person — "By *you.* . . . May God make *you.*" His use of the of the second singular pronominal suffix *(bᵉḵā)* is distributive, almost as if he wishes to bless each of the grandsons as individuals, rather than in tandem. What follows is a blessing formula. I understand *By you* to mean "by you (as example)." Whenever anyone living in Israel (i.e., the nation) wishes to bless someone and make them fruitful, one is to use the formula: *May God make you like Ephraim and Manasseh.* Again, this blessing formula does not aim to exalt Ephraim over Manasseh. It declares the blessedness of these two tribes together.[19]

21 Jacob again announces that he is about to die.[20] He seems to speak here to all his family, if that is the significance of the plural suffixes. God will be with them, says Jacob; and this is an echo of a key phrase at the beginning of the Joseph story — "Yahweh was with Joseph." A father speaking to his family believes that God will restore his family to their *fathers' land.* To have referred to this land as "the land of Canaan" would arouse much less emotion than the designation *your fathers' land.*

22 To conclude, Jacob gives to Joseph a piece of property *(šᵉḵem)* above and beyond what he is giving to his other sons. Part of the enigma of this verse is the qualifying phrase *which I captured from the Amorites with my sword and bow.* It was equally a conundrum for the targumists. Thus Targ. Jonathan reads, "which I took from the hands of the Amorites when you entered it [i.e., Shechem], and I stood by and helped you with my sword and with my bow." Targ. Neofiti I is most interesting: "and I took it from the hands of my brother Esau *neither* with my sword *nor* with my bow, but rather with my merits and my good deeds."[21] The targumists were well aware of

---

Numbers, the census of the second generation places Manasseh (26:29-34) ahead of Ephraim (26:35-37), and attributes 20,200 more descendants to Manasseh (52,700) than to Ephraim (32,500). This inversion also results in the placement of Manasseh in the crucial seventh position in the tribal order in 26:1-65, a position occupied by Ephraim in 1:32. Thus in its earlier history at least, Manasseh appears to have surpassed Ephraim in size.

19. See DeVries, *Yesterday, Today and Tomorrow* p. 99 n. 187, for this insight on v. 20.

20. Joseph also uses the phrase *'ānōḵî mēṯ* in 50:24. I see no significance in Jacob's use of *'ānōḵî* for "I" in v. 21, but *'ᵃnî* for "I" in v. 22. Redford (*Study of the Biblical Story of Joseph,* pp. 173-74) does not include these two in his survey of uses of the 1st person sing. pronoun in Gen. 37–50.

21. See M. Klein, "Converse Translation: A Targumic Technique," *Bib* 57 (1976) 525-27. M. Aberbach and B. Grossfeld (*Targum Onkelos to Genesis* [New York: Ktav, 1982], pp. 278-79) note that some versions of Targ. Onqelos read the last phrase as "by

the fact that Jacob had looked with disgust on his sons' raid on Shechem (34:30; 49:5-7). How then could this passage be read as attributing bellicosity to Jacob in seizing *šᵉḵem?* We do know of military adventures by Abraham (ch. 14), but none by Jacob.

Historians have tried to recover the incident to which this verse refers. For example, de Vaux points to Abimelech's conquest of Shechem as the only conquest of Shechem by Israelites mentioned in the OT (Judg. 9). He sees the verse as a legitimation for Abimelech's action.[22] Gottwald sees in 48:22 a reference to an original Josephite seizure of land around Shechem. By contrast, Gen. 34 describes an earlier *ʿapiru* or proto-Israelite contact with Shechem.[23] It is very unlikely that Gen. 48:22 is to be connected with 33:19 (cf. Josh. 24:32) which tells us about some property in Shechem Jacob *bought* from the locals for one hundred pieces of money.[24] It is impossible to be certain about the event to which the last half of this verse refers. It has not been recorded in Genesis. In the light of the fact that the OT has no other record of a conquest of Shechem, and that Joshua supervised a covenant renewal service there (Josh. 24) but never had to conquer it, Gen. 48:22 may be a crystallized reference to a pre-Mosaic conquest of Shechem.[25]

---

my prayer and my supplication" by connecting *bᵉqaštî,* "my bow," with the verb *bāqaš* (to seek, request [in prayer from God]). The authors also note that "during the Talmudic age purely military exploits, which had signally failed to overcome Roman domination of Palestine, were discredited, and even the glorious victories of the Hasmoneans are virtually ignored in the Talmud" (p. 279).

22. De Vaux, *Early History of Israel,* pp. 637-38.

23. Gottwald, *Tribes of Yahweh,* pp. 541-42, 551-52.

24. Noth (*History of Pentateuchal Traditions,* pp. 83-85) believes that 48:22 and 33:19 do refer to the same piece of land. While in the present context the story in 48:22 takes place in Egypt, according to Noth this context is wholly artificial. In the "original" story Jacob died in Canaan surrounded by his descendants, and the setting is probably Shechem.

25. See G. E. Wright, *Shechem: The Biography of a Biblical City* (New York: McGraw-Hill, 1965), pp. 131-32; Sarna, *Genesis,* p. 330; R. G. Boling and G. E. Wright, *Joshua,* AB (Garden City, NY: Doubleday, 1982), p. 252. There are other explanations. For example, Lowenthal (*Joseph Narrative,* p. 143) cites the medieval Jewish commentator Abrabanel and his view that Jacob is here speaking sarcastically, esp. in reference to his sons. Jacob's own "sword and bow," by contrast, were ways of peace. It has also been suggested that the claim in 48:22 is purely fictional, concocted in circles that reacted against the idea of purchasing property from Canaanites (Gen. 33:19ff.). Josh. 24:12 ("it was not by our sword or bow") would be a theological reaction against the militaristic and self-congratulatory statement of Gen. 48:22 and a harmonization with Gen. 33:19ff. Cf. E. Nielsen, *Shechem: A Traditio-Historical Investigation* (Copenhagen: Gad, 1959), pp. 283-86. Nielsen also suggests, but not too strongly, that *lāqaḥ mîyaḏ* means "to receive from one's hand, to buy," elsewhere (2 K. 5:20; Prov. 31:16), and if one understands the preposition *bᵉ* to mean "in exchange for, in return for," a possible reading would be "which I have received from the hand of the Amorite by placing in return my military capacity at his control."

In a chapter given over to a narration of the preferential status of Ephraim over his brothers, the concluding note is one about Joseph's preferential status over his brothers. Joseph is to his eleven brothers as Ephraim is to Manasseh. Although the family is miles away from Canaan, Jacob deeds a bit of it to Joseph. Jacob started a lot of problems by an extra gift to Joseph — the multicolored coat, which created friction. For a second time Jacob gives to Joseph an extra gift: *one mountain slope.*[26] We know how the brothers reacted to the coat. We do not know how they reacted to the gift of real estate.

M. THE TESTAMENT OF JACOB (49:1-33)

1. REUBEN (49:1-4)

1 *Jacob summoned his sons and said: "Gather yourselves so that I may inform you what is ahead for you*[1] *in the coming days:*

2 *Assemble together and pay attention, O sons of Jacob,*
pay attention to Israel your father.

3 *You, Reuben, my firstborn,*
my strength and the beginning of my manly vigor,
excelling in authority[2] *and excelling in power!*

26. It is possible to connect Jacob's gift to Joseph with § 165 in Hammurapi's Code, which speaks of a gift that a father makes to *ablišu,* "his heir," as a sign of his special favor. While the translation in *ANET,* p. 173, identifies the heir as the firstborn, G. R. Driver (*The Babylonian Laws,* 2 vols. [Oxford: Clarendon, 1952-55], 1:345-46) thinks otherwise. He identifies *ablišu* as the favorite son, who may or may not be the firstborn. The law states that the gift is of landed property alone (as in Gen. 48:22). It cannot be movable property; it must be "a field, orchard, or house."

1. The words *'ēṯ 'ăšer-yiqrā'* show a clause introduced by the relative in which the relative clause functions as a principal part (i.e., object) of the main verbal clause ("I may inform you"). See Waltke and O'Connor, *Biblical Hebrew Syntax,* p. 331.

2. *yeṯer śĕ'ēṯ* may stand as is, with *śĕ'ēṯ* being compared with *miśśĕ'ēṯô* in Ps. 62:5 (Eng. 4) ("from his eminence [or excellence]"), and with *śĕ'ēṯô* in Job 13:11 ("his majesty"), which is parallel with *paḥdô,* "his dread." See, however, the comments of M. Pope, *Job,* 3rd ed., AB (Garden City, NY: Doubleday, 1973), pp. 98-99. Or it may be that here is an instance of shared consonants, and *yeṯer śĕ'ēṯ* should be read as *yeṯer rĕ'š'ûṯ,* "excelling in authority." See M. J. Dahood, "Northwest Semitic Notes on Genesis," *Bib* 55 (1974) 81; S. Gevirtz, "The Reprimand of Reuben," *JNES* 30 (1971) 90. Dahood's and Gevirtz's reading is lent credibility by the parallelism of *rš't* and *'z* in Phoenician. The Phoenician text is quoted by Gevirtz and by Y. Avishur, "Word Pairs Common to Phoenician and Biblical Hebrew," *UF* 7 (1975) 23. Dahood, however, opts for "an excess of murder, and an excess of violence," in *Psalms,* AB, 2nd ed. (Garden City, NY: Doubleday,

4 *You are as uncontrollable*[3]*, as water, you shall no longer excel,*[4]
for you climbed[5] *into your father's bed;*[6]
indeed,[7] *you defiled the couch of his concubine."*[8]

1973), 2:100, which appear to me to be strained meanings for *r^{e}'š'ûṯ* and *ʿāz.* See also Avishur, *Stylistic Studies of Word-Pairs,* pp. 25, 457, 460. On the phenomenon of shared consonants in OT Hebrew see W. G. E. Watson, "Shared Consonants in Northwest Semitic," *Bib* 50 (1969) 525-533; *Idem.,* "More on Shared Consonants," *Bib* 52 (1971) 44-50.

3. Cf. Judg. 9:4, *'^{a}nāšîm rêqîm ûp̱ōḥ^{a}zîm,* lit., "empty and reckless men," a reference to Abimelech's hired mercenaries, and Zeph. 9:4, the only occurrence of the verb *pāḥaz,* and both are participles. While MT points the word as a noun *(paḥaz;* see BDB, p. 808), it is possible that we have here an abbreviation in which the pronominal affix in the verb *(-ṯ)* has been omitted, and thus MT *pḥz* is actually *pḥzt.* Thus I read it as a verb, a reading reflected in LXX *exýbrisas,* "you have broken out with violence," and in SP. Cf. G. R. Driver, "Once Again Abbreviations," *Textus* 4 (1964) 94.

4. The Hiphil (*tôṯar,* from *yāṯar*) need not be emended to a Niphal *(tiwwāṯēr)* as in Pesh and LXX. The form is an elative Hiphil. That is, the Hiphil, the causative conjugation, which by definition is transitive, may also be intransitive, as here.

5. Cf. the line in the Ugaritic Epic of Aqhat: *lʿršh yʿl [wyšk]b,* "he mounted his couch and lay down" (*UT,* 2 Aqht [= *CTA,* 17] I:39-40, describing Danel's intercourse with his wife). A reference to licentious behavior involving "going up to a bed" may be found in the notoriously difficult Isa. 57:8, "you have uncovered your bed, you have gone up to it, you have made it wide" (RSV), on which see S. M. Paul, "Polysensuous Polyvalency in Poetic Parallelism," in *Shaʿarei Talmon,* Fest. S. Talmon, ed. M. Fishbane and E. Tov (Winona Lake, IN: Eisenbrauns, 1992), pp. 155-56. For most in the ancient world, and in many places today, a bed consists of a mat or sheet placed on the floor, plus some other type of covering. In wealthier homes the bed would be raised above the floor. Thus Reuben had to climb into his father's bed.

6. Lit., "beds of your father," *mišk^{e}ḇê 'āḇîḵā.* GKC, § 124b, calls this a pl. of local extension to denote localities in general, although he also allows for the possibility that the reference is to a double bed.

7. *'āz* does not introduce a second action following the first, as is often the case; rather, it stands before a clause that repeats and emphasizes the foregoing. See P. Ruben, "The Song of Deborah," *JQR* 10 (1898) 544; D. R. Hillers, "A Note on Judges 5,8a," *CBQ* 27 (1965) 125. See BDB, p. 23: "in poetry *'z* is sometimes used to throw emphasis on a particular feature of the description."

8. The Hebrew is difficult. It reads lit.: "You profaned my couch; he climbed"; or, "you profaned; my couch he climbed." The translation adopted here reflects an emendation of MT *y^{e}ṣûʿî ʿālâ* to *y^{e}ṣûaʿ yaʿ^{a}lâ,* lit., "the couch of his doe." Cf. Prov. 5:19, where "doe" is used figuratively of a wife. See M. J. Dahood, "Hebrew-Ugaritic Lexicography III," *Bib* 46 (1965) 319; idem, "Northwest Semitic Notes on Genesis," *Bib* 55 (1974) 81; idem, *Bib* 45 (1964) 282. Perhaps "couch" should be read as a pl., *y^{e}ṣûʿê* (which is the form in the related passage, 1 Chr. 5:1), thus balancing *mišk^{e}ḇê.* For an alternate vocalization see M. Tsevat, "Alalakhiana," *HUCA* 29 (1958) 127. S. Gevirtz (*JNES* 30 [1971] 97-98) emends least. He reads *ʿālâ* not as a verb but as a noun in the absolute state which is related to an Arabic verb meaning "to suckle." This interpretation produces: "When you ascended your father's bed, then you fouled the suckler's couch." Dahood's

1 For one last time Jacob summons around his deathbed his sons, who are all still living. He has blessed Pharaoh (47:7, 10); he has blessed Joseph (48:15); and he has blessed Ephraim and Manasseh (48:20). What remains is a blessing (*bāraḵ,* 49:28) for all his sons. There is no dialogue in vv. 1-27, only unbroken monologue; nor is there any solicitation of paternal blessing by any of Jacob's sons to match Jacob's earlier deception in order to gain his father's blessing (ch. 27). The verb *qārā'* is used twice in v. 1, once by the narrator ("Jacob summoned [*wayyiqrā'*] his sons"), and once by Jacob himself ("what is ahead for you," *yiqrā' 'eṯḵem*).[9]

What he is about to share with them is in the form of an inspired prophecy about the destiny of each son as extended into the tribe emanating from that son. Each saying has to do with *the coming days (be'aḥarîṯ hayyāmîm).* This expression occurs thirteen times in the OT, eight of which are in the prophetic books (nine if one includes Daniel).[10] Of these texts, the most similar to Gen. 49:1 is Deut. 31:29 (and the surrounding verses). Both begin with a command to assemble (*hē'āsepû* [Gen. 49:1], *hiqqāḇesû* [Gen. 49:2]; *haqhîlû* [Deut. 31:28]). Both contain the expression "in the coming days." In both someone is told to listen to what is about to be said (*šim'û* [Gen. 49:1, 2]; *tišma'* [Deut. 32:1]). Thus Jacob addressing his sons is comparable to Moses addressing the assembly of Israel.

It is fitting that Jacob's last words are prophecies, for his life began with a prophecy (25:23). What is missing in Gen. 49 is anything like "The word of Yahweh came unto Jacob, saying, 'Go, speak to your sons.'" There is no discernible impetus for these disclosures of the distant future by Jacob, no divine afflatus resting on him. Jacob speaks almost intuitively, as he did at the blessing of Ephraim and Manasseh. Jacob, now the discloser and interpreter of future events, is exercising a gift from God that his son Joseph had exercised on occasion (usually in interpreting the dreams of others).

2 Jacob speaks in the third person. (He switches to first person in the next verse when he addresses an individual son.) He refers to himself as *Jacob*

---

redivision of the consonantal text, in my judgment, is the sanest one, for which see also W. G. E. Watson, "Shared Consonants," *Bib* 50 (1969) 532; M. O'Connor, *Hebrew Verse Structure* (Winona Lake, IN: Eisenbrauns, 1980), p. 170.

9. BDB, pp. 894-96, distinguishes between *qārā'* I, "call, summon, proclaim, read," and *qārā'* II, "encounter, befall," and suggests that the latter is parallel to *qārâ,* "encounter, meet, befall."

10. See Gen. 49:1; Num. 24:14; Deut. 4:30; 31:29; Isa. 2:2; Jer. 23:20; 30:24; 48:47; 49:39; Ezek. 38:16; Hos. 3:5; Mic. 4:1; Dan. 10:14. In Gen. 49:1 at least, the expression is not a *terminus technicus* for the eschaton, but an indefinite, long period. See J. P. M. van der Ploeg, "Eschatology in the Old Testament," *OTS* 17 (1972) 90; E. Lipiński, "*b'ḥryt hymym* dans les textes préexiliques," *VT* 20 (1970) 445-48, esp. pp. 446-47; G. W. Buchanan, "Eschatology and the 'End of Days,'" *JNES* 20 (1961) 188-93.

and as *Israel your father,* thus using both of his names. The Joseph story opens and concludes with the plural imperative *Pay attention* (*šimʿû,* lit., "hear," 37:6; 49:2). Joseph has something to say and reveal to his brothers. Jacob has something to say and reveal to his sons. He appears like the wise father of Proverbs who counsels his child(ren) to hear *(šᵉmaʿ bᵉnî)* his instructions (Prov. 1:8; 4:1, 10; 5:7; 7:24; 8:32).

3-4 The saying directed to Reuben has two parts. The first is a word about privilege. Reuben is Jacob's *firstborn,*[11] once a source of inestimable joy to his father. The second is a word about accountability. Because Reuben slept with Jacob's concubine (35:22), he forfeits all the privileges that go with primogeniture. This forfeiture is fulfilled historically in later times when the Reubenites living in Transjordan are integrated into the tribe of Gad.[12]

From this first oracle the teaching is clear that the behavior of one individual affects the destiny of his descendants. God does visit the iniquities of the fathers upon the children to the third and fourth generation of those who live licentiously, as did Reuben (Exod. 20:5). This promise works in a positive direction as well. Recall God's words to Abraham, "And by your descendants shall all the nations of the earth be blessed, because you have obeyed my voice" (22:18); or God's words to Isaac, "I will multiply your descendants . . . because Abraham obeyed my voice" (26:4-5). Or, we may go as far back as the story of Sodom and Gomorrah (Gen. 18–19), which teaches that a nucleus of righteous people guarantees the survival of a city for one's children and grandchildren.

I am aware that most commentators (e.g., Skinner, Westermann) view Gen. 49 as originally a series of tribal sayings that have been collected and artificially connected with each tribe's eponymous ancestor. This interpretation creates a number of problems for these commentators. For example, if we assume that v. 4 refers obliquely to some tribal offense of the Reubenites, then we are at a loss to identify it. Von Rad states, "If what is said in v. 4

11. Is there any significance in the designation "firstborn" *(bᵉḵōr)* in a chapter devoted to blessing *(bāraḵ)?* Note the reversal of consonants: *bkr/brk.* Does this reversal point possibly to a reversal of Reuben's status? The phrase *rēʾšîṯ ʾônî,* "the beginning of my manly vigor," is synonymous with *bᵉḵôr.* While the basic meaning of *ʾôn* is "vigor, wealth," in a few texts it connotes specifically sexual potency (Deut. 21:17, *rēʾšîṯ ʾōnô;* Ps. 78:51, *rēʾšîṯ ʾônîm*). For other parallel uses of *kōaḥ* ("strength") and *ʾôn* ("manly vigor") cf. Isa. 40:26, RSV: "by the greatest of his might [*mērōḇ ʾônîm*], and because he is strong in power [*wᵉʾammîṣ kōaḥ*]"; Isa. 40:29, RSV: "he gives power [*kōaḥ*] to the faint, and to him who has no might [*ûlᵉʾên ʾônîm*] he increases strength"; Job 40:16, RSV: "behold his strength [*kōḥô*] in his loins, and his power [*wᵉʾōnô*] in the muscles of his belly." For *ʾôn,* "strength," in the sense of "firstborn," see M. Weinfeld, *Deuteronomy and the Deuteronomic School* (repr. Winona Lake, IN: Eisenbrauns, 1992), p. 112 n. 3.

12. See de Vaux, *Early History of Israel,* pp. 576-81.

about the ancestor contains some recollection of a severe crime committed by the tribe of Reuben, it is completely incomprehensible to us, for the mention in ch. 35.22 is only a fragment."[13] Does not this approach create more problems than it solves?

If v. 4 refers to the crime of an individual, then we are faced with the oddity of Jacob confronting Reuben about sexual promiscuity and morally reprimanding him long after the dastardly deed took place. All that was said in 35:22b was, "and Israel found out." Did the recall of some of his own conduct force him to relent as disciplinarian of Reuben? Anything conciliatory said by Reuben to Jacob (42:37) has not softened Jacob's harsh rebuke of Reuben. The pattern of sexual violation followed by a word of judgment on the offender has a parallel in the incident in 9:20-27. The act of violation is described in vv. 22-23, and the curse on the offender is detailed in vv. 24-25. The only difference between the two episodes is that in 9:20-27 the curse comes immediately after the violation. In the second incident involving Jacob and Reuben, the violation (35:22) is separated from the judgment by many chapters (49:4).[14]

2. SIMEON AND LEVI (49:5-7)

5 *"Simeon and Levi:*[1]
Brothers they destroyed.[2]
They treated violently[3] *their covenanters.*[4]

13. Von Rad, *Genesis,* p. 423.

14. See S. Gevirtz, "A Father's Curse," *Mosaic* 2 (1968) 56-61.

1. I take "Simeon and Levi" not as part of the oracle but as its heading. This leaves five bicola in the logion that follows.

2. Following SP and LXX, which read *killû* rather than MT *kᵉlê* (lit., "vessels of"). May MT *kly* preserve archaic *killayû?*

3. The final vowel on *ḥāmᵉsû* would not be shown in the old orthography; hence MT *ḥms*. See F. I. Andersen, *Or* 35 (1966), 107.

4. *mᵉḵērōṯêhem* is baffling. The ancient versions were as puzzled by it as are modern scholars. Among contemporary writers note the following interpretations: (1) Speiser (*Genesis,* p. 365) connects it with the root *mkr,* "sell, trade," and translates "wares." (2) Dahood isolates the root *krt* in the noun, and translates "circumcision knives" ("*MKRTYHM* in Genesis 49:5," *CBQ* 23 [1961] 54-56; idem, "Hebrew-Ugaritic Lexicography IV," *Bib* 47 [1966] 418; idem, "Comparative Philology Yesterday and Today," *Bib* 50 (1969) 74; idem, "Northwest Semitic Notes on Genesis," *Bib* 55 [1974] 81; see also H. R. Moeller, "Four Old Testament Problem Terms," *BT* 13 [1962] 219-20). (3) Close to the previous suggestion is the translation "knives," which is based primarily on the similarity between the MT form and the Greek word *máchaira.* See C. H. Gordon, "Homer and Bible," *HUCA* 26 (1955) 60; O. Margalith, "*mᵉkērōtēhem* (Genesis xlix 5)" *VT* 34 (1984) 101-2. (4) J. Barr (*Comparative Philology and the Text of the Old Testament* [London: Oxford University, 1968], pp. 57, 270)

6 *Into their council let my soul not enter,*[5]
with their company let not my being[6] *be united.*[7]

---

connects the noun with Ethiopic *mkr,* "to advise," and translates "their counsels." (5) M. Cohen ("*mᵉkērōtēhem* [Genèse xlix 5]," *VT* 31 [1981] 472-82) connects the noun with the root *krh,* "accumulate," and translates *leurs biens* ("their goods"). (6) D. Young ("A Ghost Word in the Testament of Jacob [Genesis 49:5]?" *JBL* 100 [1981] 335-42) relates the Hebrew word to cuneiform *kirru,* a container for liquids used in sacred rituals, and thus a parallel to *kᵉlê:* "their *kirru*-vessels implements of injustice." (7) F. I. Andersen ("Moabite Syntax," *Or* 35 [1966] 106-7) understands the noun in question as a Piel participle of *kāraṯ* (as in "cut a covenant"), functioning as a noun parallel to "brothers." The context of Gen. 49:5-7 makes explanations (3), (4), and (7) the most plausible, esp. number (7), supplying as it does a parallel word for *'aḥîm.*

5. Cf. *wtʿrb sd,* "and you will enter the council," in the Ugaritic Aqhat Epic. See M. Dijkstra and J. C. de Moor, "Problematical Passages in the Legend of Aqhâtu," *UF* 7 (1975) 214.

6. Lit., "my glory" *(kᵉḇōḏî).* LXX *hḗpata* suggests *kᵉḇēḏî,* "my liver." *kᵉḇēḏî* is possible because of the fem. verb with which it is connected *(tēḥaḏ).* The fem. gender of this word is clear from Ugar. *kbd,* whose pl. is *kbdt,* and Akk. *kabattu. kāḇôḏ* may be used in the OT for the person of a man (see M. Greenberg, *Ezekiel 1–20,* AB [Garden City, NY: Doubleday, 1983], p. 51), but that is unlikely here since *kāḇôḏ* is masc. and the verb is fem. *(tēḥaḏ)* — unless *tēḥaḏ* is the result of attraction exerted by the first verb *tāḇō',* also fem. For other parallel uses of *nep̱eš* ("soul") and *kāḇôḏ* ("being"), cf. Ps. 7:6 (Eng. 5), "let the enemy pursue my soul [*nap̱šî*] . . . and lay my being [*ûḵᵉḇôḏî*] in the dust," where *nep̱eš/kāḇôḏ* are parallel terms in the first and third cola. Cf. also Lam. 2:11-12, "my liver is poured out on the ground [*nišpaḵ lā'āreṣ kᵉḇēḏî*] . . . as their life is poured out [*bᵉhištappēḵ nap̱šām*]." It is also possible that one could read "my soul" and "my being" as vocatives: "Enter not their council, O my soul; be not united with their company, O my being." For sentences with verb, prepositional phrase, and vocative in last position, see M. O'Connor, "The poetic inscription from Khirbet el-Qôm," *VT* 37 (1987) 226-27.

7. What is the root behind *tēḥaḏ?* If it is taken as the 3rd fem. sing. imperfect Qal of *yāḥaḏ,* then the meaning is "be united." This meaning forms a perfect parallel with the first verb in the bicolon: *bō' bᵉ,* "enter." In fact, "be united, joined with" is an excellent translation for the idiom *bō' bᵉ* as can be observed in Deut. 23:2, 3, 4, 9 (Eng. 3, 4, 5, 10); Job 3:6. See H. L. Ginsberg, "Lexicographical Notes," in *Hebräische Wortforschung,* Fest. W. Baumgartner, ed. B. Hartmann, et al., VTSup 16 (Leiden: Brill, 1967), pp. 71-72; M. Pope, *Job,* 3rd ed., AB (Garden City, NY: Doubleday, 1973), p. 30. Dahood has suggested that the Hebrew language possessed a root *ḥdw/y,* meaning "to see," which he branded a "Canaanism." He reads the verb as a Niphal jussive — "let not my liver be seen in their assembly." See "A New Translation of Gen. 49,6a," *Bib* 36 (1955) 229; idem, "The Value of Ugaritic for textual criticism," *Bib* 40 (1959) 168-69; idem, review of *The Torah* in *Bib* 45 (1964) 282. A third suggestion is to link *tēḥaḏ* with the verb *ḥāḏâ,* "to rejoice," and Akk. *ḫadû,* "to be happy, rejoice" (which often occurs with *kabattu,* "liver," and *libbu,* "heart" — "I [lit., my liver] shall not be happy in their company." See W. G. E. Watson, "Hebrew 'to be happy' — an idiom identified," *VT* 31 (1981) 92-95; G. Rendsburg, "Double Polysemy in Genesis 49:6 and Job 3:6," *CBQ* 44 (1982) 48-50. Rendsburg is one of the few scholars who does not emend *kᵉḇōḏî* to *kᵉḇēḏî* in this verse. He does so by reading *tēḥaḏ* as a 3rd masc. sing. with

For in their anger they murdered a man,
at will[8] *they hamstrung*[9] *an ox.*
7 *Cursed be their fury so*[10] *fierce,*
and their rage[11] *so cruel.*
I will scatter them in[12] *Jacob,*
I will disperse them in Israel."

---

preformative *t-*. On the LXX rendering of the verb in question, see J. Barr, "*Erízō* and *Ereídō* in the Septuagint: A Note Principally on Gen. XLIX.6," *JSS* 19 (1974) 198-215. Barr argues for *erísai* ("vie, strive, contend") as the correct Greek reading without committing himself to an understanding of the Hebrew word.

8. Another problematical word: *ûḇirṣōnām.* Dahood ("Northwest Semitic Notes on Genesis," *Bib* 55 [1974] 81) repoints MT to *b^{e}rūṣnām,* the infinitive construct of *rûṣ* followed by the pl. suffix *-nm.* This reading provides a good parallel for *b^{e}'appām,* "in their anger." If it is connected with *rāṣôn* (BDB, p. 953b), then somehow "goodwill" has to evolve into "self-will." J. Kugel (*Idea of Biblical Poetry* [New Haven: Yale University, 1981], p. 32 n. 3) translates "and in a good humor, hough an ox." They can laugh over a killing. The words *'ap* and *rāṣôn* occur together again only in Ps. 30:6 (Eng. 5), NRSV: "in his anger [*b^{e}'appô*] is distress, in his favor [*birṣônô*] there is life." After a study of the noun *rāṣôn,* N. Walker notes ("The Renderings of *Rāṣôn,*" *JBL* 81 [1962] 184), "the root meaning of *RĀṢÔN* is two-sided, namely, *will* and *pleasure,* whether of oneself or another. Doing one's own will and pleasure invovles one's own *desire,* but doing the will and pleasure of another results in *acceptance, approval, delight* of another, and his returning *favor* and *blessings.*"

9. See W. Krebs, "'. . . sie haben Stiere gelähmt' (Gen. 49:6)," *ZAW* 78 (1966) 359-61, who observes that *'āqar* (Piel) denotes a method of laming large animals, and that a similar expression with the same meaning occurs in Greek and in Arabic, where it referred often to some formal action in connection with animal sacrifice.

10. I take *kî* as an emphatic in both this line and the next, following O'Connor, *Hebrew Verse Structure,* p. 171. It is also possible to read *kî* as causal, introducing a motive clause after a curse (as in Gen. 3:14, 17-19). Cf. J. Muilenburg, "The Linguistic and Rhetorical Usages of the Particle *kî* in the Old Testament," *HUCA* 32 (1961) 152; A. Schoors, "The Particle *kī,*" *OTS* 21 (1981) 276.

11. For other instances of *'ap* and *'eḇrâ* in parallel cf. Ps. 7:7 (Eng. 6), RSV: "Arise, O Lord, in thy anger [*b^{e}'appeḵā*], lift thyself up against the fury [*b^{e}'aḇrôṯ*] of my enemies"; Ps. 85:4 (Eng. 3), RSV: "Thou didst withdraw all thy wrath [*'eḇrāṯeḵā*]; thou didst turn from thy hot anger [*'appeḵā*]." Also Ps. 90:11; Amos 1:11; Hab. 3:8. See Avishur, *Stylistic Studies of Word-Pairs,* p. 157. C. H. Gordon (*UT,* pp. 135-37, § 13.116) cites Gen. 49:7 as an instance of a "ballast variant" in Hebrew poetry. By this he means, "If a major word in the first stichos is not paralleled in the second, then one or more of the words in the second stichos [*viz., 'eḇrâ*] tend to be longer than their counterparts in the first stichos [*viz., 'ap*]."

12. D. N. Freedman reads the two uses of the preposition *b^{e}* as "from" — "from Jacob . . . from Israel" ("Early Israelite History in the Light of Early Israelite Poetry," in *Unity and Diversity: Essays in the History, Literature, and Religion of the Ancient Near East,* ed. H. Goedicke and J. J. M. Roberts [Baltimore: Johns Hopkins University, 1975], p. 17). This reading is not necessary, however, in the light of the fact that the verb *ḥālaq* followed by the preposition *b^{e}* is either locative ("among") or partitive ("of"; cf. GKC, § 119m). See J. W. Olley, "How Is Isa. 53,12a to Be Understood?" *Bib* 68 (1987) 345-46.

In his words addressed to Simeon and Levi, Jacob recalls a previous incident in which they were involved, as he did with Reuben. The antecedent for Jacob's rebuke against sons two and three is obviously the incident recorded in Gen. 34, Simeon's and Levi's massacre of the male population of Shechem in retaliation for the humiliation of their sister Dinah. Here is another illustration, as in the Reuben oracle, of the principle that the behavior of one generation affects the circumstances of later generations.

Jacob's oracle to Simeon and Levi is composed of (a) an address or a heading (v. 5a); (b) an accusation (v. 5b-c); (c) a statement of dissociation from the criminals (v. 6a-b); (d) justification for this dissociation (v. 6d-e); (e) the pronouncement of a curse (v. 7a-b); (f) the particulars of this curse (v. 7c-d). Vv. 5-7b refer to past history. V. 7c-d is future history.

There is little problem in connecting most of the language of vv. 5-6 with Gen. 34. The only phrase that lacks a clear reference is *at will they hamstrung an ox.* Heb. *ʿiqqᵉrû (hamstrung)* refers to an act of crippling, but not execution. R. Péter describes the process as follows: "It involves the practice of provoking paralysis by cutting the tendons of the leg in order to prevent the animal being used as a beast of burden."[13] Gen. 34 did not mention Simeon and Levi incapacitating the Shechemites' animals. Note, however, the close relationship in sound between *ʿiqqᵉrû* (from *ʿāqar*) in 49:6, and Jacob's words to Simeon and Levi in 34:30, *ʿᵃḵartem* [from *ʿāḵar*] *ʾōṯî* ("you have brought trouble upon me"). In Gen. 34 he indicts them with *ʿāḵar,* and in Gen. 49 he indicts them with *ʿāqar.*[14]

Note that in v. 5 two plural nouns as direct objects of verbs balance each other: *ʾaḥîm, Brothers,* and *mᵉḵērōṯêhem, their covenanters.* In v. 6 two singular nouns as direct objects of verbs balance each other: *ʾîš* (lit., "man") and *šôr* (lit., "ox"). If *ʾîš* is to be connected with a verb meaning "to be strong" — and this is by no means certain[15] — then *ʾîš* (i.e., "strong man") is a perfect parallel with *šôr,* the symbol of strength in the world of domesticated animals.[16] Unless we understand "man" and "ox" as collectives, then in v. 5 Jacob remonstrates with Simeon and Levi for their violence against a group, whereas in v. 7 he remonstrates with them for their violence against an individual. (Hamor? Shechem? Jacob himself?)

It should be observed that Jacob addresses Reuben directly in the second person: "You, Reuben, my firstborn, . . . you shall no longer excel, For you climbed . . . you defiled." But with Simeon and Levi Jacob speaks indirectly in

13. R. Péter, "*pr* and *swr:* Note de lexicographie hébraïque," *VT* 25 (1975) 494.

14. The verb *ʿāqar* is not far removed from the verb used to describe Jacob's own usurpation of Esau's position — *ʿāqaḇ* (25:26; 27:36).

15. T. E. McComiskey (*TWOT,* 1:38) and N. P. Bratsiotis (*TDOT,* 1:222) cite this as a possibility.

the third person: *they destroyed . . . They treated violently . . . their council . . . their company . . . their anger . . . they murdered . . . they hamstrung . . . their fury . . . their rage; I will scatter them . . . I will disperse them.*

Two items call for special attention in v. 7. One is Jacob's use of *Cursed ('ārûr).* This word has been used in Genesis by God (3:14; 4:11) and by people (9:25). Noah's "Cursed be" and Jacob's "Cursed be" are in many ways similar. Something is done by a son (or sons) to a father that puts the father in a precarious situation. The father pronounces a curse on the perpetrator(s) that really touches the perpetrator's descendants more than the perpetrator himself (Canaan, the tribes of Simeon and Levi).

The second item of interest is Jacob speaking in v. 7c-d as if he were God: *I will scatter them . . . I will disperse them.* The first of these verbs is a Piel *(ḥālaq),* and the second is a Hiphil *(pûṣ).* The normal meaning of *ḥālaq* is "divide, assign, apportion." The only other place where it means "scatter" is Lam. 4:16. Its meaning here is sure, however, by virtue of its parallel, *pûṣ.* This second verb is frequently used in the OT to describe the dispersal of Israel among the nations (Deut. 4:27; 28:64; Jer. 9:15; Ezek. 11:16; 12:15; 20:23; 22:15; 36:19 [all *pûṣ* in the Hiphil followed by *bᵉ*]).[17] Joseph may deny being in God's place, but Jacob will not. His threatened action came about. Eventually Simeon is integrated into the tribe of Judah, and hence *scatter* here means "dissolve." Levi is dispersed in the sense that the Levites are never given a territory of their own, but are divided up among the remaining tribes.

This is the only oracle in Gen. 49 in which two sons/tribes are addressed simultaneously, suggesting some kind of a connection between the Levitical priesthood and the tribe of Simeon. On the basis of the incident recorded in Gen. 34 and alluded to in 49:5-7, some commentators have sought to establish a distinction between a secular tribe of Levi and the more traditional picture of a sacral tribe of Levi. This distinction is both unnecessary and unlikely. A number of texts generally assigned to the Priestly source describe the Levites' activities around the sanctuary with militaristic, belligerent overtones. They serve as guards around the sanctuary and are under orders to execute any encroacher on temple sancta (e.g., Num. 1:51b, "and if any one comes near [i.e., encroaches] he shall be put to death [i.e., by these Levitical guards]"). We may add the Levitical participation in the extirpation of those involved in the golden calf incident (Exod. 32:25-29).[18]

16. Cf. the four-faced divine beings seen by Ezekiel (ch. 1). Each has the face of a man, of a lion, of an ox, and of an eagle. The ox *(šôr)* is the most powerful of domestic animals.

17. The verb was used in Gen. 11:4 (Qal), 9 (Hiphil), for the dispersal of the tower builders.

18. See E. Nielsen, "The Levites in Ancient Israel," *ASTI* 3 (1964) 16-27, esp. 20-22; J. Milgrom, *Studies in Levitical Terminology* (Berkeley: University of California, 1970), 1:48.

Further confirmation of a secular/sacral tribe of Levi may occur in a reading of Moses' blessing on Levi in Deut. 33:8-11. The first two lines of v. 11 may be translated: "Bless, O Lord, his substance, and accept the work of his hands." It is possible that one should understand "bless" as a euphemism here, i.e., *bāraḵ* means "curse" rather than "bless," as in Job 1:5, 11; 2:5, 9. Thus *bāraḵ* in Moses' word to the tribe of Levi would be equal to Jacob's use of *'ārûr* ("cursed") with Levi. One then could render Deut. 33:11ab as "Curse, O Yahweh, his strength; but the work of his hands accept." Thus, "while the priestly tribe of Levi is set apart to do the work of YHWH on behalf of the entire tribal assembly in ancient Israel, she is also reminded of the folly of her 'secular' ways in the more distant part."[19]

3. JUDAH (49:8-12)

8 *"Judah:*[1] *you are the one whom your brothers praise,*
your hand[2] *is on the neck of your enemies,*
your father's sons bow before you.[3]
9 *A lion's cub is Judah;*
you have grown,[4] *my son, on prey.*

19. D. L. Christensen, "Dtn 33, 11 — A Curse in the 'Blessing of Moses,' " *ZAW* 101 (1989) 278-82. The quote is from p. 282.

1. For "Judah" as the title of the oracle rather than a vocative see Andersen, *Hebrew Verbless Clause in the Pentateuch,* p. 42.

2. Normally it is the foot, not the hand, that is on the neck of the prostrate foe. This has led Andersen to suggest that *yāḏᵉḵā,* "your hand," may in fact be defective spelling of the preceding *plene* reading *yôḏûḵā,* "they praise." This reading produces "you . . . your brothers praise; they praised you when you broke your enemies' neck." See his article, "Orthography in Repetitive Parallelism," *JBL* 89 (1970) 344. For variations of the trope "your hand is on the neck of your enemies" cf. Exod. 23:27b; Ps. 18:41a (Eng. 40a). In the War Scroll from Qumran (1QM) this phrase reappears, but it is augmented by a verb and a parallel line: "put your hand [*ydkh*] on the neck of your enemies, and your foot [*wrglkh*] upon the backs of the slain" (12:10). The presence of the idiom "put the hand on the neck of" in the Qumran texts should make Andersen's changes unnecessary. The threefold use of the sequence *y-d* in the first part of this verse *(yᵉhûḏâ, yôḏûḵā, yāḏᵉḵā)* provides one of the instances of paronomasia in this poem (on which see W. F. Albright, *Yahweh and the Gods of Canaan* [Garden City, NY: Doubleday, 1968], p. 20).

3. On the rendering of "bow before you" in many of the Targs. as "they will continually approach and/to enquire about your welfare," see D. M. Golomb, "The Targumic Renderings of the Verb *lᵉhištaḥᵃwôt:* A Targumic Translation Convention," in *Working with No Data,* Fest. T. O. Lambdin, ed. D. M. Golomb (Winona Lake, IN: Eisenbrauns, 1987), pp. 110, 111, 116. In the Targs. Onqelos and Pseudo-Jonathan it is the only place where this phrase or idiom is used.

4. Lit., "you have gone up" *(ʿālîṯā).* For *ʿālâ* in the sense "to grow (up)" cf. M. Greenberg, *Ezekiel 1–20,* AB (Garden City, NY: Doubleday, 1983), p. 350, who draws

He crouches down, lies down[5]*like a lion,*
like the king of beasts[6] *— who dares rouse*[7] *him*[8] *up?*
10 *The scepter*[9] *shall not pass from Judah,*
nor the mace from between his feet,[10]
until[11] *he possesses that which belongs to him,*[12]

---

attention to Ezek. 19:3, which he renders "she raised up [*watta'al*] one of her cubs." If the meaning "go up" is retained, then the reference is to a lion returning to its mountain lair with its captured prey.

5. This verb *(rāḇaṣ)* was used back in 4:7 — the sin which is "crouched" ready to pounce on Cain. Here it means reclined for sleep, not for a leaping at or on prey. The sense conveyed by *rāḇaṣ* is defined by the preceding verb *kāra'* (which is used again with "lion" in Num. 24:9, where the verb is followed by *šāḵaḇ,* "rest").

6. On the parallelism of *'aryēh,* "lion," and *lāḇî',* "king of beasts," cf. Num. 23:24 *(lāḇî', 'ᵃrî);* Num. 24:9 *('ᵃrî, lāḇî');* cf. also Isa. 5:29; Nah. 2:12, 13 (Eng. 11, 12); and Avishur, *Stylistic Studies of Word-Pairs,* p. 142.

7. *kᵉ'aryēh* is obviously parallel to *kᵉlāḇî';* the verb at the end of the sentence *(yᵉqîmennû)* is explained by the previous verbs *kāra'* and *rāḇaṣ,* i.e., *qûm* means to rouse another from sleep or rest. Cf. P. D. Miller, Jr., "Synonymous-Sequential Parallelism in the Psalms," *Bib* 61 (1980) 259-60. For other references in which *kāra'* appears near *qûm* cf. 1 K. 8:54, Solomon "arose" from "kneeling"; also Job 4:4, Job's words have "upheld" the faint and braced "tottering" knees.

8. If *lāḇî'* is fem. ("lioness"), the masc. suffix on *yᵉqîmennû* is to be explained as a disregard for gender agreement because of an intervening relative particle. See G. R. Driver, "Ezekiel: Linguistic and Textual Problems," *Bib* 35 (1954) 151 n. 3.

9. Because LXX renders *šēḇeṭ* and *mᵉḥōqēq* by *árchōn* ("ruler") and *hēgoúmenos* ("leader"), and because of the parallelism of *mᵉḥōqqēnû* and *šōpṭēnû* in Isa. 33:22, some writers have suggested amending *šēḇeṭ* to *šōpēṭ,* "ruler, judge." Note that the reading of 2 Sam. 7:7 *(šiḇṭê yiśrā'ēl)* is replaced by *šipṭê yiśrā'ēl* in the parallel passage, 1 Chr. 17:6. It is likely, however, that the latter reading is the *lectio facilior,* i.e., the easier reading. See P. K. McCarter, Jr., *II Samuel,* AB (Garden City, NY: Doubleday, 1984), p. 192. He argues, against the majority, that the Chronicler altered the text. MT *šēḇeṭ* may be retained by reading the word as *šōḇēṭ,* "ruler," and explaining the form as a dialectal variant of *šōpēṭ* (see M. J. Dahood, *Proverbs and Northwest Semitic Philology* [Rome: Pontifical Biblical Institute, 1963], p. 43 n. 1; idem, *Bib* 44 [1963] 229). Or, one may posit a substantive *šōḇēṭ,* a denominative Qal participle from *šēḇeṭ,* "staff," i.e., "staff bearer." See P. V. Reid, "*šbṭy* in 2 Samuel 7:7," *CBQ* 37 (1975) 17-20, who retains "scepter" in Gen. 49:10; and P. K. McCarter, Jr., *II Samuel,* AB (Garden City, NY: Doubleday, 1984), p. 192. A third option is to distinguish between two Hebrew homographs, *šēḇeṭ,* "staff," and *šēḇeṭ,* "ruler, judge." The first reflects early Semitic *šbṭ* and the second *ṯbṭ,* a phonetic variant of *ṯpṭ*. See S. Gevirtz, "On Hebrew *šēḇeṭ* = 'Judge,' " in *The Bible World,* Fest. C. H. Gordon, ed. G. Rendsburg, et al. (New York: Ktav, 1980), pp. 61-66.

10. I see no reason to understand "feet" as a euphemism for the sexual organ, as argued by E. M. Good, "The 'Blessing' on Judah, Gen. 49:8-12," *JBL* 82 (1963) 429; and by C. M. Carmichael, "A Ceremonial Crux: Removing a Man's Sandal as a Female Gesture of Contempt," *JBL* 96 (1977) 329; idem, "Some Sayings in Genesis 49," *JBL* 88 (1969) 439-40.

11. For the combination *'aḏ kî* earlier in Genesis, cf. 26:13.

12. This line has provoked more difference of opinion among Hebraists than

and the obedience[13] *of nations comes to him.*
11 *He who hitches*[14] *to the vine*[15] *his*[16] *ass,*
and to the bramble[17] *the progeny of his she-ass;*[18]

---

perhaps any other in the entire book of Genesis. Accordingly I discuss it at length in the commentary below.

13. *yiqhâ* (or *yᵉqāhâ*) occurs again (perhaps!) only in Prov. 30:17. The rendering of LXX, Vulg., and Pesh. suggests *tiqwat̲,* "the hope (or expectation) of nations." If *yiqqᵉhat̲* is a denominative *qitlat* formation from putative *yāqâ,* which in turn is explained by Ugar. *wqy,* ought not the form to be *yiqyat̲?* W. Moran (*Bib* 39 [1958] 413 n. 6) suggests that *yqht* may conceal a verbal stem, *yuqhat̲û* or *yiqqahit̲û,* "be subjected" (as in the Ugaritic personal name Aqhat). The meaning of Heb. *yiqhâ/yᵉqāhâ* is put beyond doubt by Arab. *wqh/wqy,* "to obey" (H. Kruse, "David's covenant," *VT* 35 [1985] 154 n. 39).

14. S. Mandelkern (*Veteris Testamenti Concordantiae* [Graz: Akademische Druck- u. Verlagsanstalt, 1955], p. 133) and BDB, p. 63, interpret *'ōsᵉrî* as an active participle construct. It may also be the infinitive used as a finite verb (read as *'āsōrî*); see M. O'Connor, *Hebrew Verse Structure* (Winona Lake, IN: Eisenbrauns, 1980), p. 173. The verbal form may be compared with lines 25-26 of the Moabite inscription: *w'nk krty hmkrtt lqrḥh b'sry yśr'l,* "and I cut the dissected parts in behalf of Qarhoh binding Israel." This is the translation of E. Lipiński, "Notes on the Mesha' Inscription," *Or* 40 (1971) 337-38. Lipiński connects Moabite *b'sry* with *'sry* in Gen. 49:11, and identifies both as infinitives with an *-i* ending, akin to the Akkadian adverbial ending *-i.* See also W. L. Moran, "The Hebrew Language in Its Northwest Semitic Background," in *The Bible and the Ancient Near East,* Fest. W. F. Albright, ed. G. E. Wright (Garden City, NY: Doubleday, 1961), pp. 60, 62, who appeals to several absolute infinitives with an *-i* ending in the Amarna Letters. The older interpretation that the form in question is a participle, coming as it does in an independent clause (all of Moran's examples come from subordinate clauses), is also a valid possibility. See D. A. Robertson, *Linguistic Evidence in Dating Early Hebrew Poetry,* SBLDS 3 (Missoula, MT: Society of Biblical Literature, 1972), pp. 69-76. For other instances of participle (with *-y* ending) plus prepositional phrase and noun (as object of the participle), see Isa. 22:16; Ps. 101:5; 113:7.

15. *gep̱en* is a common Hebrew word meaning "vine," but may its use here have any connection with Ugar. *gpn,* used for a type of saddle? Cf. J. C. Greenfield, "Ugaritic *mdl* and Its Cognates," *Bib* 45 (1964) 527 n. 2. Although *gpn,* when used in the Ugaritic texts, refers to the saddling of an ass for riding on a journey, Gen. 49:11 speaks of the binding of an ass to a vine or tree so that it would not move from its spot. See U. Cassuto, *Biblical and Oriental Studies,* tr. I. Abrahams, 2 vols. (Jerusalem: Magnes, 1973-75), 2:184 n. 7.

16. Note in v. 11 the chiastic arrangement of the two forms of the masc. sing. pronominal suffix, the rarer form *-ōh* balanced by the more common *-ô: 'îrōh . . . 'ᵃt̲ōnô . . . lᵉḇušô . . . sût̲ōh.* See A. R. Ceresko, "The A:B::B:A Word Pattern in Hebrew and Northwest Semitic," *UF* 7 (1975) 78.

17. *śōrēqâ,* "bramble, choice vine," is a hapax legomenon, although it is close to *śārōq,* "vine tendrils" (Isa. 16:8) and *śōrēq,* "choice vine" (Isa. 5:2; Jer. 2:21). The word is also cognate with Mishnaic Heb. and Aram. *srg* (from *śrg*), "to plait, saddle, strap" (see Greenfield, ibid.).

18. Speiser (*Genesis,* p. 366) reads "choice, purebred ass" for (lit.) "the young of (his) she-ass" and ties it with the phrase from Mari, *mār atānim,* meaning also "choice, purebred ass." A comment should be made about the presence of the *-î* in the expression *bᵉnî 'ᵃt̲ōnô* (as opposed to the normal construct from *ben 'ᵃt̲ōnôt̲* found in Zech. 9:9). The *-î* on the end of *bᵉnî* is as unexpected, perhaps, as the *-î* on the end of the participle with

he washes with[19] *wine his robe,*
and with grapes' blood his mantle.[20]
12 *Darker of eyes than*[21] *wine,*
whiter of teeth[22] *than milk."*[23]

---

which the verse begins, *'ōsᵉrî.* Scattered throughout the OT are twenty-seven places where -*î* is affixed to a participle, of which *'ōsᵉrî* is one, and six places where it is affixed to a noun, of which *bᵉnî 'ᵃṯōnô* is one. D. Robertson ("The Morphemes -y (-ī) and -w (-ō) in Biblical Hebrew," *VT* 19 [1969] 211-23) argues convincingly that, on the one hand, -*î* is a morpheme associated with nouns or participles in apposition (and here "he who hitches" is in apposition to "Judah" in v. 10); on the other hand, it is a morpheme associated with bound structures (i.e., construct phrases), e.g., *bᵉnî 'ᵃṯōnô*). That this morpheme appears on the *nomen regens* of a construct chain in two poetical passages generally considered early (Gen. 49:11 and Deut. 33:16, *šōḵᵉnî sᵉneh,* "the dweller of the bush") indicates that the morpheme in question is ancient. See S. C. Layton, *Archaic Features of Canaanite Personal Names in the Hebrew Bible,* HSM 47 (Atlanta: Scholars, 1990), pp. 107-21.

19. Here I retain the usual rendering of *bᵉ* as "with" or "in." Is Judah dyeing his clothes the color of wine (i.e., a rich, if not royal, red)? Is this a demonstration of affluence? More likely it is a sign of the plenty that comes from blessing. Westermann (*Genesis,* 3:231) says correctly, "The meaning is: 'There is so much wine there that one could. . . .' " Dahood has argued for understanding *bᵉ* as having here separative value — "*of* wine he washes his garments, his robe *of* the blood of grapes" ("Northwest Semitic Notes on Genesis," *Bib* 55 [1974] 81; idem, *Psalms,* AB, 2nd ed. [Garden City, NY: Doubleday, 1973], 2:63).

20. *sûṯōh,* "his mantle," is a hapax legomenon, and may be connected with Eblaite *su-du, sūt-u,* "robe." See M. J. Dahood, "Eblaite and Biblical Hebrew," *CBQ* 44 (1982) 10. In *Psalms,* 2:183, Dahood discovers *sûṯ* in the enigmatic *pissaṯ* of Ps. 72:16, and links Heb. *sûṯ* with Phoenician *swt.* Phoenician *swt* is found in the late 9th-century B.C. Kilamuwa inscription, line 8: "He gave a maid for the price of a sheep, and a man for the price of a garment [*bswt*]" (J. C. L. Gibson, *Textbook of Syrian Semitic Inscriptions,* 3 vols. [Oxford: Clarendon, 1971-82], 3:34-35); also, H. R. Cohen, *Biblical Hapax Legomena in the Light of Akkadian and Ugaritic,* SBLDS 37 (Missoula, MT: Scholars, 1978), p. 64 n. 95.

21. The cola might read: "dark of eyes from wine, white of teeth from milk." Cognate to Heb. *haḵlîlî* is Akk. *ekêlu,* "to be dark." See C. H. Gordon, "The Wine-Dark Sea," *JNES* 37 (1978) 51-52. This interpretation differs from mine in two respects. First, it interprets v. 12 not as a description of the beauty of the individual referred to in the previous verses but as continuing the emphasis on abundance in the previous verse, i.e., much wine and milk is available, enough to darken the eyes and whiten the teeth of the one drinking them. Second, this interpretation reads the *min* on *mîyāyin* and *mēḥālāḇ* not as a comparative ("than wine . . . than milk") but as "from" in the sense of "because of." See A. Brenner, *Colour Terms in the Old Testament,* JSOTSup 21 (Sheffield: JSOT, 1982), pp. 86-88.

22. Translations (e.g., RSV, NIV) that read "his eyes are darker than wine, his teeth are whiter than milk" add the pronominal adjective, apparently on the basis of the context and LXX.

23. "Wine" and "milk" occur together three times in the OT, once in parallelism (Gen. 49:11), and twice in syndetic parataxis (with *'im* in Cant. 5:1, "I drink my wine with my milk"; with *waw* in Isa. 55:1, "Come, buy wine and milk").

This is the second longest oracle in vv. 1-27, and is matched in length only by the oracle to Joseph (vv. 22-26). Jacob addresses Judah directly in the second person in vv. 8-9b. In vv. 9c-12 Jacob shifts to the third person and speaks not to Judah, but about Judah. The change from third person to second person (see, e.g., Exod. 15:1-5 [third person] and 15:6-17 [second person]; Ps. 23:1-4a [third person] and 23:4-5 [second person]; Jonah 2:2a [third person] and 2:2b-9 [second person]) is more common than the change from second person to third person. The Judah oracle combines both forms of address found in the previous two oracles. The oracle to Reuben was delivered completely in the second person (vv. 3-4). The oracle to Simeon and Levi was delivered completely in the third person (vv. 5-7).

It is quite obvious that Jacob's words to his first three sons are to be connected with previous reprehensible behavior by the son(s) addressed. Reuben's tryst with Bilhah and Simeon's and Levi's slaughter of the Shechemites form the background for Jacob's message. Nevertheless, a reading of vv. 8-12 appears to reveal little that can be clearly connected with previous episodes in Judah's life. Two earlier events in which Judah played a less than commendable role are his part in the selling of Joseph and the deceiving of Jacob (37:26-28, 31-32), and his involvement with his daughter-in-law (ch. 38). Any clear-cut references to these earlier debacles are not to be found in 49:8-12. Those who would argue for a relationship between 37:26-28, 31-32; 38 and 49:8-12 are forced to do so by the isolation of similarities that may be accidental rather than deliberate.[24] For instance, the connection between the staff that Judah gave to the harlot in ch. 38 and the mace between the feet of Judah, or his offspring, is certainly strained. Is it legitimate to read *šîlōh* (Shiloh) in 49:10 as "Shelah," the third son of Judah (ch. 38)? Is there really a connection between "his ass" *(ʿîrōh)* and Judah's son Er, or between "progeny of his she-ass" *(bᵉnî ʾᵃṯōnô)* and Judah's son Onan? The same may be asked about the site Enaim (Heb. *ʿênayim*) at which Tamar positioned herself (38:14), and the reference to the one in 49:12 whose "eyes" (Heb. *ʿênayim*) are darker than wine. Why is 49:8-12 so roundabout in its recall of chs. 37–38, when 49:3-7 were so unmistakably direct? If Judah's previous actions are now being decried by Jacob, why is there no simple "you sold your brother" or "you went into your daughter-in-law"?

8 In the first verse of the oracle Judah is given a more honorable position than his brothers by his brothers. They praise Judah (note the play

24. For representatives of this position see E. M. Good, "The 'Blessing' on Judah, Gen. 49:8-12," *JBL* 82 (1963) 427-32; C. M. Carmichael, "Forbidden Mixtures," *VT* 32 (1982) 394-415; idem, "Some Sayings in Genesis 49," *JBL* 88 (1969) 438-44; idem, *Law and Narrative in the Bible* (Ithaca: Cornell University, 1985), pp. 185-93; G. A. Rendsburg, "David and his circle in Genesis xxxviii," *VT* 36 (1986) 446 n. 21.

on sound here — *y^e^hûḏâ yôḏûḵā*) and bow before him. What Jacob raised derogatorily as a possibility with Joseph (37:10) he now affirms with Judah. The reason for the exaltation of Judah is because of Judah's impressive accomplishments — *your hand is on the neck of your enemies.* The verse may be interpreted as describing a present circumstance *(you are the one whom your brothers praise)* or a future circumstance ("your brothers will praise you"). The same goes for the last phrase of the verse ("your father's sons bow/will bow"). If it is a present situation, then most likely we have a statement from the time of the Judges. If it projects a future situation, then the reference would be to the time of David when Judah assumed hegemony over the other tribes. Earlier, when the brothers were debating the best way to rid themselves of Joseph, Judah protested "let not our hand be upon him" (37:7). Both 37:7 and 49:8 use the expression *yāḏ b^e^*. Judah refused to put his hand on Joseph, but is praised by his father for putting his hand on his real enemies.

9 Here Jacob shifts from a description of what Judah had done to what Judah is like. Judah is described as lionesque. In fact, three words for *lion* are used: *gûr 'aryēh, 'aryēh,* and *lāḇî'*. Scripture uses a lion to represent both a group (Num. 23:24; 24:9) and an individual (Rev. 5:5). The analogy is also applied elsewhere to the tribe of Gad (Deut. 33:20) and to Dan (Deut. 33:22).[25] What is pictured here is a lion that has grown into adulthood. *grown . . . on prey* is the equivalent of "your hand is on the neck of your enemies" in v. 8. The lion, having recently eaten, has retired to its sleeping quarters to digest its meal. Even while it is reposing, nothing else tries to invade its territory, so powerful is the lion.

10 The crux in vv. 8-12 is v. 10, particularly the third line of the verse. The first two lines suggest that Judah will continue to enjoy eminence,[26]

25. The styling of both Dan in Deut. 33:22 and of Judah in Gen. 49:9 as *gûr 'aryēh* led S. Gevirtz to suggest that 48:8-12 is really a poetic statement of a political reality, i.e., the conquest and settlement by Judah of territory that was once Danite ("Adumbrations of Dan in Jacob's Blessing on Judah," *ZAW* 93 [1981] 21-37). Gevirtz is unwilling to accept the possibility of two tribes being designated as a "lion's cub" even in a society that took delight in the conferring of animal names on people.

26. *šēḇeṭ* and *m^e^ḥōqēq* are interchangeable, parallel words, and do not represent two distinct emblems, at least in the sense that one can attribute a distinct shape or function to each. Both words indicate some kind of staff or rod used by one in authority. For pictures of kings holding such emblems before them see *ANEP,* no. 379 (Egyptian); nos. 442, 447 (Mesopotamian); no. 461 (North Syrian). Particularly apropos to Gen. 49:10 is the bas-relief of Darius, king of Persia, on his throne with his mace between his feet (*ANEP,* no. 463). It is possible that Ezekiel's dirge over the princes of Israel (19:1-14) has Gen. 49:8-12 in mind. In addition to the word *šēḇeṭ* (vv. 11, 14), Ezek. 19 shares the following words with Gen. 49:8-12: *l^e^ḇîyā',* "lion(ness)" (Ezek. 19:2, evidently a variant of *lāḇâ',* Gen. 49:9); *rāḇaṣ,* "crouch"; *gûr,* "cub"; *'ālâ,* "raise"; *'aryēh,* "lion"; *gep̱en,* "vine"; and *ṭārap̱ ṭerep̱,*

the tribe will never lose its place of primus inter pares, *until he possesses that which belongs to him.*

Without emending the Hebrew text in any way, one may read this line as "until Shiloh comes." But this reading is strange for several reasons. First, it combines a feminine subject ("Shiloh") with a masculine verb ("comes"). More importantly, what would such an expression mean? As a person, whom would Shiloh represent? Elsewhere in the OT Shiloh is only a place. Why represent an individual by a city, and why represent someone in a message to Judah by a city that falls within the territory of Ephraim?

It is also possible to read the Hebrew phrase as "until he [i.e., Judah] comes to Shiloh." Taking Shiloh as a representative term for northern Israel, the verse would point to the extension of the Davidic kingdom in Judah to include the northern tribes. In other words, the phrase foretells a great future for David and his kingdom.[27] A modification of this interpretation suggests that the verse originally foretold the expansion of Judean tribes over Israel as well. When Solomon's empire broke up and this expansion became less and less of a possibility, however, some annotator inserted the sarcastic remark, "until a man of Shiloh comes" (*ʿaḏ kî-yāḇōʾ ʾîš šîlōh,* i.e., inserting *ʾîš,* which had dropped out through haplography).[28] The problem with the first interpretation is that the people of Israel never did become monotribal although they were for a while a united kingdom. The problem with the modification is that it is arbitrary, since it has no textual support. Even if it be granted that the placement of these blessings in the mouth of the patriarch Jacob is entirely fictive, what would be accomplished by this blatant anachro-

---

"catch prey." Unlike the lionesque Judah in Gen. 49, the lions of Ezek. 19 are rapacious and cruel. Noting the metamorphosis that the figure of the raging lion underwent in prophetic Scripture, M. Greenberg remarks: "Jacob's endowment of Judah with royalty evidently hovered in Ezekiel's consciousness as he composed this dirge over Judah's rulers" (*Ezekiel 1–20,* p. 358).

27. See J. Lindblom, "The political background of the Shiloh oracle," in *Congress Volume: Copenhagen, 1953,* VTSup 1 (Leiden: Brill, 1953), pp. 78-87, who suggests that the oracle dates to the time when David was king in Hebron. See also J. Becker, *Messianic Expectations in the Old Testament,* tr. D. E. Green (Philadelphia: Fortress, 1980), pp. 35-36; J. A. Emerton, "Some Difficult Words in Genesis 49," in *Words and Meanings,* Fest. D. Winton Thomas, ed. P. R. Ackroyd and B. Lindars (Cambridge: Cambridge University, 1968), pp. 83-88.

28. See M. Treves, "Shiloh (Genesis 49:10)," *JBL* 85 (1966) 353-56. Close to Treves's interpretation is that of L. Sabottka, "Noch einmal Gen. 49,10," *Bib* 51 (1970) 225-29: "His throne will indeed come to Shiloh" ("Sein Thron wird wahrlich kommen nach Silo"). Sabottka's solution is questionable at two points: his reading of *ʿaḏ* as "throne" (on the basis of Ugaritic), and his reading of *kî* as an emphatic *(wahrlich)* instead of a conjunction. See B. Margulis, "Emendation and Exegesis: A Reply to L. Sabottka (*Bib* 51 [1970] 225-229)," *Bib* 52 (1971) 226-28.

nism, by having the patriarch speak of Shiloh, a city that, unlike others nearby such as Bethel and Shechem, had no apparent significance before the conquest?

The early versions were as baffled by the phrase as are modern commentators. For example, the LXX could easily have read "until Shiloh comes." Instead, it read "until there come the things stored up for him" *(héōs án élthē tá apokeímena autṓ).* This reading presupposes Heb. *šellōh* for MT *šîlōh,* that is, "that which belongs to him" (the relative particle *še* plus the preposition *l^e* plus the pronominal suffix, and the "him" would be a coming scion of Judah). How did the LXX come up with this reading? Did the Alexandrian translators, familiar with the targumic and rabbinic traditions on Gen. 49:10, create a redaction of the Hebrew text so as to produce a messianic sense?[29] Or is this an instance where a biblical word was explained according to its meaning in Aramaic or postbiblical Hebrew? That is, at the time of the tranlators, *šel* was used in places where Biblical Hebrew employed *'^{a}šer l^e*.[30]

There is no doubt about how the Qumran community understood Gen. 49:10. In 4Q Patriarchal Blessings (4QPBless) the interpretation of Gen. 49:10 reads as follows:

> "A ruler shall not depart from the tribe of Judah while Israel has dominion. There will not be cut off a king [lit., 'enthroned one,' *ywšb*] in it belonging to (the line of) David. For the staff [*hmḥqq*] is the covenant of the kingship; the thousands of Israel are the feet, until the coming of [*'d bw'*] the Messiah of Righteousness, the branch of David, for to him and to his seed has been given the covenant of the kingship over his people for everlasting generations."[31]

29. See L. Monsengwo-Pasinya, "Deux textes messianiques de la Septante: Gn 49,10 et Ez 21,32," *Bib* 61 (1980) 357-76.

30. See E. Tov, *The Text-Critical Use of the Septuagint in Biblical Research* (Jerusalem: Simor, 1981), pp. 125-26. H. Cazelles ("Shiloh, The Customary Laws and the Return of the Ancient Kings," in *Proclamation and Presence: Old Testament Essays in Honour of Gwynne Henton Davies,* ed. J. I. Durham and J. R. Porter [London: SCM, 1970], pp. 248-49) defends the reading of the MT as *šellōh* (and thus the LXX's rendering too) by appealing to the orthography of Qumran, which indicates the doubling of a consonant by preceding it with a *mater lectionis:* hence *š-y-l-h = š-l-l-h.*

31. Translations of 4QPBless are found in Millar Burrows, *More Light on the Dead Sea Scrolls* (New York: Viking, 1958), p. 401; J. M. Allegro, "Further Messianic References in Qumran Literature," *JBL* 75 (1956) 174-76; G. Vermes, *Scripture and Tradition in Judaism* (Leiden: Brill, 1961), p. 53 and notes. Cf. D. R. Schwartz, "The Messianic Departure from Judah (4Q Patriarchal Blessings)," *TZ* 37 (1981) 257-66, who interprets the text as prophesying the exile of the legitimate Davidic monarchic line. The Davidic messiah will depart this exile and establish his kingship.

Both LXX and 4QPBless would agree then that the phrase be understood as "until he comes to whom it [the scepter, the kingship] belongs." The Hebrew would have to be read as "until that which is his comes." If that is what Gen. 49:10 is saying, then we are faced with a Hebrew grammatical anomaly for which the Hebrew Bible offers no parallel.

Other scholars have attempted to isolate in *šîlōh* some word meaning "prince" or "ruler." This sense is accomplished by appeal to the Akkadian word *šēlu,* "ruler, counselor,"[32] or by emending to *mōšᵉlōh,* "his (or its) ruler" (cf. *mōšᵉlô* in Isa. 52:5 [Ketib], and in Jer. 30:21). This second suggestion assumes that the text is corrupt (a *mem* has dropped out). So, the colon reads, "until its ruler comes."[33]

Yet another viable option is faithful to the consonantal pattern of 49:10: *š(y)lh.* The cluster may be divided into *šy* and *lh.* Reading *šy* as *šay* and *lh* as *lōh,* the result is "tribute to him." If *yāḇōʾ* is revocalized as a Hophal *(yûḇāʾ),* then the phrase would read, "until tribute is brought to him." Thus the phrase forecasts the tribute and the subjection of the world to Judah, or to one of Judah's own.[34] *šay* indicating a gift offered as homage is present in Isa. 18:7; Ps. 68:30 (Eng. 29); 76:12 (Eng. 11).

There are, then, four major approaches to Gen. 49:10c: (1) attempt to make sense of MT by retaining "Shiloh"; (2) follow the reading of the ancient versions ("that which is his"); (3) emend *šîlōh* to *šay lōh* ("tribute to him"); (4) discover in "Shiloh" some Semitic word meaning "ruler" or "prince." Of course, many other interpretations have been suggested, including those who see Judah's son Shelah in Shiloh, and those who resort to yet other redivisioning of the consonants.[35]

32. Although not original with him, this suggestion gained popularity when G. R. Driver advanced it in "Some Hebrew Roots and their Meanings," *JTS* 23 (1922) 70. For some unexplained reason Driver vocalized the Hebrew text as *šayyālōh,* and did not follow the vocalization of the Akkadian cognate that he discerned. W. L. Moran ("Gen 49,10 and Its Use in Ez 21,32," *Bib* 39 [1958] 406ff.) has dismissed this connection, for in his judgment Akk. *šēlu/šilu* never has the meaning "prince, ruler, king." Rather, in the vast majority of instances it means "hole," (cf. W. von Soden, *Akkadisches Handwörterbuch,* 3 vols. [Wiesbaden: Harrassowitz, 1965-81], 3:1237).

33. Many scholars have advanced similar approaches, e.g., most recently, Westermann, *Genesis,* 3:219, 231.

34. See Moran, *Bib* 39 (1958) 405-25. In agreeing with Moran one need not agree with all his reasons for rejecting the reading "Shiloh." For example, Moran's suggestion (p. 411) that "Shiloh" cannot be meant in 49:10 because nowhere else in the OT is it spelled *šylh* is weak, for Shiloh is spelled several different ways in the MT *(šilô, šîlô, šilōh)* and therefore another variant spelling is hardly suspect.

35. For the former see n. 24 above; for the latter see B. Margulis, "Gen. XLIX 10/Deut. XXXIII 2-3," *VT* 19 (1969) 202-10: *ʿāḏēḵā yāḇōʾ bʾlšay li/wt liqᵉhal ʿammîm,* "unto thee [Judah] shall come the son-of-Jesse, to become a community of

11-12 The oracle continues by saying that the one spoken of in v. 10 *hitches to the vine his ass, and to the bramble the progeny of his she-ass.* The meaning of the vine image (v. 11a-b) and of the wine image (v. 11c-d) is uncertain. It is clear that the vine-wine metaphor is quite prominent with the reference to the vine in v. 11a, washing with wine and grapes' blood in v. 11b-c, and eyes darker than wine in v. 12a. Good and Carmichael take v. 11 as containing metaphorical allusions to Judah's dalliance with Tamar. Thus Judah's tethering his ass to the vine alludes to Judah's encounter with the roadside harlot, and washing the cloak with grapes' blood alludes to Judah's "washing" Joseph's coat with blood.[36]

If one understands vv. 11 and 12 as further descriptions of the messianic scion mentioned in v. 10, then these two verses would describe the individual's wealth (v. 11) and his beauty (v. 12). Tethering an ass to a vine (which the ass would readily consume) would be like lighting a cigarette with a dollar bill. Laundering one's clothing with wine might also point to opulence.

It is clear that *wine* is not exactly the same as *grapes' blood.* The first refers to the finished product. The second refers to the crushing of the grapes. May we have here a pastoral image, but within which there is the intimation of violence? May there be both a laundering of wine and a laundering of blood?[37] To his own this one will bring joy and fullness; to those who reject him he brings terror.

The NT does not appropriate any part of this messianic oracle. The most likely allusion to this text occurs in reference to Jesus' triumphal entry into Jerusalem (Matt. 21:1-9; Mark 11:1-10; Luke 19:28-38; John 12:12-18). The major OT citation in these passages is Zech. 9:9. One description of the animal on which Jesus sits or rides in Zech. 9:9 is "a colt, the foal of she-asses" (*ʿayir ben-ʾaṯōnôṯ*). *ben-ʾaṯōnôṯ* recalls *ben ʾaṯōnô* of Gen. 49:11. Only Mark (11:2) mentions Jesus' command to "untie" the colt. Does this point back in any way to Gen. 49:11, *he hitches* [lit., binds] *to the vine his ass*?[38]

---

nations." To reach this reading Margulis must (1) combine *ʿaḏ kî* into *ʿāḏēḵā;* (2) restore *bʾi* because of haplography *(ybʾ bʾ);* (3) take *b* as equal to *ben,* "son of'" and (4) understand Jesse's name to begin with an *aleph* (a spelling present in 1 Chr. 2:1). Vulg.'s reading *qui mittendus est* ("the one to be sent") is championed by H. Kruse, "David's covenant," *VT* 35 (1985) 154-55, who reads *šylh* as *šylḥ* (which he connects with *šilḥô,* "his root, his offspring," in Cant. 4:13), and thus translates "until the coming of his offspring." But one cannot so easily dispatch an *h* from the text by arbitrarily replacing it with a *ḥ*.

36. See n. 24 above.

37. See R. Alter, *Art of Biblical Poetry* (New York: Basic Books, 1985), p. 16.

38. See J. Blenkinsopp, "The Oracle of Judah and the Messianic Entry," *JBL* 80 (1961) 56; J. D. M. Derrett, "Law in the New Testament: The Palm Sunday Colt," *NovT* 13 (1971) 241-58, esp. 256-57.

4. ZEBULON (49:13)

13 *"Zebulon: Near[1] the seashore[2] he will settle,*
himself near the shore of ships;[3]
his flank[4] shall be by[5] Sidon."

For the first time Gen. 49 does not reflect the order of birth of Jacob's children as recorded in chs. 29–30. If it had been in sequence, then the next son to be addressed would be either Dan, the first son by Bilhah, or Issachar, the fifth son by Leah. Zebulon is the tenth son overall, and the sixth and last son by Leah. Thus the birth order in Gen. 49, unlike the birth order given in Gen. 29–30, starts with Jacob's blessings on all six sons by Leah, i.e., from Reuben to Zebulon. It is curious that in ch. 49 the blessing on Zebulon precedes the blessing on Issachar, even though Issachar is Leah's fifth child and Zebulon is her sixth. The only other place where Zebulon precedes Issachar is in the Blessing of Moses (Deut. 33:18). One possible reason for the placement of Zebulon in this fifth position by the final editors of Genesis is to suggest a parallel with Dan, who is the fifth son of Jacob in Gen. 29–30. What both tribes appear to have in common is connections with the sea.[6]

1. For *lᵉ* meaning "near, at" see references cited by R. Gordis, *Book of Job* (New York: Jewish Theological Seminary of America, 1978), p. 83.

2. Heb. *hôp̱ yammîm* may be compared with Ugar. *tmḫṣ lim ḫp y*[*m*] *tṣmt adm ṣat š*[*p*]*š*, "She smote the people of the west [people of the seashore], she silenced the men of the east" (*UT,* ʿnt [= *CTA,* 3] II:7-8). See M. J. Dahood, "Eblaite, Ugaritic, and Hebrew Lexical Notes," *UF* 11 (1979) 146. Gibson (*Canaanite Myths and Legends,* 2nd ed. [Edinburgh: T. & T. Clark, 1977], p. 47) is uncertain about the reading *ḫp y[m]* and hence leaves it blank in his translation: "she smote the people of . . . . . . silenced the men of the sun-rise."

3. It is not necessary to delete or emend the second *lᵉhôp̱,* as is done by many writers (Speiser suggests it as a possibility) and even by *BHK* and *BHS.* The repetition in sequence of *lᵉhôp̱ yammîm* and *lᵉhôp̱ ʾonîyôṯ* corresponds to the sequence in 2 Aqht (= *CTA,* 17] VI:43-44, *bntb pšʿ . . . bntb gan,* "on the path of rebellion . . . on the path of presumption." In both texts the *nomen rectum* is repeated, but the *nomen regens* varied. See M. J. Dahood, "Ugaritic-Hebrew Parallel Pairs," in *RSP,* 1:118; S. E. Loewenstamm, *Bib* 56 (1975) 110.

4. The *k* in *wᵉyarḵāṯô* is an exception to the rule that the seven consonants, *b-g-d-k-p-t,* take a *dagesh lene* when they follow a closed syllable. See H. Bauer and P. Leander, *Historische Grammatik der Hebräischen Sprache des Alten Testaments* (Hildesheim: Olms, 1962), § 75f.

5. For the replacement of *ʿaḏ* by *ʿal* (recognized already by the Masoretes in Gen. 49:13; Josh. 2:7; 13:16; Judg. 7:22; etc.), see J. C. Greenfield, "The Prepositions *ʿAD/ʿAL* in Aramaic and Hebrew," *BSOAS* 40 (1977) 371-72; and B. J. Roberts, *The Old Testament Text and Versions* (Cardiff: University of Wales, 1951), p. 36. R. Gordis (*The Word and the Book* [New York: Ktav, 1976], p. 62 n. 15) challenges and corrects Roberts's understanding of the Masoretic marginal note. Gordis renders the meaning as follows: "There are those who believe *(sbyryn)* it better to read *ʿd* but you, the scribe, do not make the same mistake; follow the Masoretic text and write *ʿl!*"

6. See J. M. Sasson, "A Genealogical 'Convention' in Biblical Chronography?" *ZAW* 90 (1978) 183-84.

The territory of Zebulon (Josh. 19:10-16) did not actually touch the coast of the Mediterranean, nor did it border on Sidon. But if *Sidon* is taken as a collective term for Phoenicia, then the statement is quite apt. The verse may suggest the penetration of the Zebulonites into the Plain of Acco, most likely under the patronage of Canaanite cities in the region (Judg. 1:30).[7] More probably, the *seashore* here is the seashore of Chinnereth/Galilee. The reference to Sidon does not rule this out because "the W flank of the S Galilee highland, settled by the Zebulunites, actually borders on Phoenician territory in the Plain of Acco."[8]

I am inclined to read v. 13 not as a curse or judgment leveled at Zebulon because of his vain flirtation with maritime trafficking, but as a word of praise and promise addressed to the tribe. Zebulon will become a conqueror who will extend his territory to the west and to the north. This interpretation is substantiated with post-Joshua references like Judg. 1:30 and Judg. 4–5, especially 5:18, in which Zebulon is praised as one of the two most valiant participants in the fight which Deborah led against the Canaanites.

Zebulon is one of three Hebrew tribes (along with Dan and Asher) who are described as navigational. As C. H. Gordon has noted, "In *modus vivendi* such ancient Israelites were more akin to Phoenicians and Philistines than to the inland Hebrews."[9] Claims often made that the ancient Hebrews loathed the high seas and were exclusively landlubbers are exaggerated.

Although Jesus by birth was of the tribe of Judah, through his residence in Nazareth he was of the tribe of Zebulon by domicile. The Gospels record Jesus' interest in ships and fishing, and the body of water on which he fished is the same body of water with which the Zebulonites are associated here in the Blessing of Jacob.

5. ISSACHAR (49:14-15)

14 *"Issachar: A sturdy[1] ass[2]*
who crouches[3] between the pack saddles.[4]

7. See Y. Aharoni, *The Land of the Bible: A Historical Geography,* tr. A. F. Rainey, 2nd ed. (Philadelphia: Westminster, 1979), p. 18.

8. K. Ellinger, "Zebulun," *IDB,* 4:941.

9. C. H. Gordon, *Before Columbus* (New York: Crown, 1971), p. 112.

1. *gārem* is difficult. It means "bone," but it is used much less frequently than *ʿeṣem* (e.g., 2:23; 50:25). The word is used of the creature Behemoth in Job 40:18; see also Prov. 17:22; 25:15. It is from the meaning "bone" that most commentators (e.g., Westermann) derive the metaphorical meaning "strong" (though BDB, p. 175, gives the meaning "strength/strong" only in Gen. 49:14). It is possible, however, that *gerem* functions like

another word for "bone," *ʿeṣem,* i.e., it has the double meaning of "bone" and "strength." W. Brueggemann ("Of the Same Flesh and Bone [Gn 2,23a]," *CBQ* 32 [1970] 532-34) renders *ʿeṣem* as "bone-power." Cf. Vulg. *usinus fortis,* "a strong ass." SP reads *gērîm* for MT *gārem,* hence "an ass of strangers." This reading may be behind W. F. Albright's suggestion, "an alien donkey driver" (*BA* 36 [1973] 50) (and reading *-m* on *grm* as an enclitic?). See also Albright, *Yahweh and the Gods of Canaan* (Garden City, NY: Doubleday, 1968), p. 266: "Issachaar is a (resident) alien donkey-driver/ Who camps between the (camp-fire) hearths." To get that interpretation, Albright reads MT *ḥ^{a}mōr gārem rōḇeṣ* as *ḥammōr gēr marbîṣ. ḥammōr* is taken as "donkey-driver," a *nomen professionis,* and the *-m* on MT *gārem* is read as a participial prefix with the following word, *marbîṣ.* Andersen (*Hebrew Verbless Clause in the Pentateuch,* pp. 44 and 123 n. 6) follows Albright's reading and redivision as he renders "Issachar: Ass-driver became resident; Tinker settled down." See also S. Gevirtz, "Asher in the Blessing of Jacob ," *VT* 37 (1987) 156 n. 5; and R. G. Boling and G. E. Wright, *Joshua,* AB (Garden City, NY: Doubleday, 1982), p. 449. S. I. Feigin ("*ḤAMəR GĀRÎM,* 'Castrated Ass,' " *JNES* 5 [1946] 230-33) reads the word as a *qaṭîl* formation of the verb *gāram* (i.e., a passive participle) — "castrated ass." Feigin appeals to Syriac and Arabic, where even "castrate" is unlikely. Another suggestion is to read *gārem* as "stubborn," thus, "Issachar is a stubborn ass," a meaning applied to *gārem* in Gen. 49:14 and Job 40:18 by D. Wolfers, "The Lord's second speech in the book of Job," *VT* 40 (1990) 482-83, although Wolfers provides no real documentation for "stubborn." The more usual rendering "strong" could also be obtained by a slight emendation of the text, i.e., *gārem* to *gīdîm,* "a sinewy ass," as proposed by F. M. Cross and D. N. Freedman, *Studies in Ancient Yahwistic Poetry,* SBLDS 21 (Missoula, MT: Scholars, 1975), p. 86 n. 50. For the connection of Hebrew *gerem* with *garmāʾ,* the standard Aramaic word for "bone," see G. A. Rendsburg, "Israelian Hebrew Features in Genesis 49," *MAARAV* 8 (1992) 163-64.

2. I see no reason to read MT *ḥ^{a}mōr* as *ḥammôr,* "donkey-driver" (as does Albright, *BA* 36 [1973] 50). Of the ancient versions, only the LXX read something other than *ḥ^{a}mōr: tó kalón epethýmēsen,* "he desired that which is good," which involves reading a *d* (i.e., *ḥmd*) for an *r* (MT *ḥmr*). On this kind of reading see E. Tov, *The Text-Critical Use of the Septuagint in Biblical Research* (Jerusalem: Simor, 1981), pp. 107, 140, 157.

3. The same verb was used in v. 9 of Judah. It describes the position of a lion (v. 9) or an ass (v. 14), and both times is used for an animal in a resting posture.

4. *mišp^{e}ṯāyim* appears again only in Judg. 5:16. BDB, p. 1046, gives "fire-places, ash-heaps" as possible translations. It may be be connected with Ugar. *mṯpdm* (also with the dual ending) meaning "hearth (stationary or movable)" in *UT,* ʿnt III:79 (= *CTA,* 3.IV.79), as first pointed out by W. F. Albright, "A Catalogue of Early Hebrew Lyric Poems," *HUCA* 23/1 (1950/51) 22. In an earlier note ("The Earliest Forms of Hebrew Verse," *JPOS* 2 [1922] 78 n. 2) Albright connected the word with the cognate *ʾašpōṯ,* "ash heap, refuse heap" (1 Sam. 2:8; Job 2:8, pl. in Lam. 4:5 [*ʾašpattôṯ*]), and translated "piles of rubbish, manure." The problem with this argument for the meaning of the Hebrew word as "hearths," or the like, on the basis of Ugar. *mṯpdm* is that the Ugaritic word means rather something that is placed over something else, such as paint on wood or bags over an animal's back. See J. Aistleitner, *Wörterbuch der Ugaritischen Sprache* (Berlin: Akademie, 1963), p. 341, no. 2918; *HALAT,* 2:616 (*Sattelkörbe,* "saddlebags"). Both "hearths" and "saddlebags" have been argued for the other instance of this noun in Judg. 5:16 — "why then do you squat beneath hearths?" (R. G. Boling, *Judges,* AB [Garden City, NY: Doubleday, 1975], p. 112); "why do you remain sitting under the pack-saddles?" (J. A. Soggin, *Judges,* tr. J. Bowden, OTL [Philadelphia: Westminster, 1981], p. 90), who defines the Hebrew word as "baskets or other items which hang down from the two sides of the

15 *He sees the very best settling place,*[5]
and the land most pleasant.
He bends his shoulder as a burden carrier,[6]
and becomes a laboring worker."[7]

---

saddles of asses and mules." For an earlier study reaching the same conclusion see J. E. Hogg, "The Meaning of *hmšptym* in Gen. 49:14 and Judg. 5:16," *AJSL* 43 (1926/27) 299-300. On LXX's unusual rendering of *mišp^{e}ṯayim* in Judg. 5:16 by "between lips," see Tov, *Text-Critical Use of the Septuagint,* pp. 242-43. The LXX obviously read *śph* for *šph.* A. D. Crown, without too much evidence, reads "squatting on its haunches" ("Judges v 15b-16," *VT* 17 [1967] 241-42).

5. *m^{e}nuḥâ* (fem.) should require the fem. form of the adjective, which, in fact, is masc. *(ṭôḇ,* not *ṭôḇâ).* J. Kugel ("The Adverbial Use of *Kî ṭôḇ,*" *JBL* 99 [1980] 435) explains the lack of gender correspondence as due to the fact that *kî ṭôḇ* is used adverbially — "and he was very pleased with (the) place." This would not apply to the second *kî* in v. 15, for there the genders correspond *('āreṣ, nā'ēmâ).* Dahood ("Hebrew-Ugaritic Lexicography V," *Bib* 48 [1967] 427-28) goes a different route by explaining *m^{e}nuḥâ* as the masc. substantive *mānôaḥ* with the accusative ending *-āh.* The ancient versions (SP, LXX, Vulg.) support a fem. reading. Thus the word might be an abbreviation, the simplest type of which is the omission of terminations, such as the fem. ending *-â.* See G. R. Driver, "Abbreviations in the Massoretic Text," *Textus* 1 (1960) 114-15. For the word pair *n'm/ṭwb* in the OT and Ugaritic see Avishur, *Stylistic Studies of Word-Pairs,* pp. 387-88. Here the adjective/noun *ṭôḇ* parallels the verb *nā'ēmâ,* unless one emends MT to *n^e'îmâ* (Avishur, p. 387 n. 1).

6. This reading is arrived at by slightly emending MT *lisbōl* (preposition plus infinitive construct) to *l^{e}sēḇel* (preposition plus noun). This change provides synonymous parallelism with *mas-'ōḇēḏ,* "a slaving laborer" (on this parallelism of a simple term in the first line with a double compound in the second line, see S. A. Geller, *Parallelism in Early Biblical Poetry,* HSM 20 [Missoula, MT: Scholars, 1979], p. 268). See M. Held, "The Root *ZBL/SBL* in Akkadian, Ugaritic and Biblical Hebrew," *JAOS* 88 (1968) 95-96. Note the sequence of *sēḇel . . . šeḵem* in Ps. 81:7 (Eng. 6) — "I relieved your shoulder of the burden" (RSV). If a noun is not necessary after the preposition *l^e* to balance the noun after the preposition *l^e* in the next phrase, and no change is made in the vocalization, then the first part of the sentence reads, "He bends his back to carry a load." See D. K. Stuart, *Studies in Early Hebrew Meter,* HSM 13 (Missoula, MT: Scholars, 1976), p. 149 n. 33.

7. On *mas-'ōḇēḏ* see A. F. Rainey, "Compulsory Labour Gangs in Ancient Israel," *IEJ* 20 (1970) 191-202. Rainey points to a cuneiform inscription from Megiddo (14th century B.C.) that talks of corvée laborers in the plain of Jezreel, particularly in the town of Shunem. He notes (p. 194): "Since this tribe [viz., Issachar] actually settled in the region around Shunem and east of Yapu (Japhia), the coincidence that corvée work was imposed on it is hard to disassociate from the practice reflected in Biridiya's letter." See also de Vaux, *Early History of Israel,* pp. 663-64, for some implications of this Amarna letter for Gen. 49:14-15. For this Amarna text see *ANET,* p. 485. The most recent translation is that of W. L. Moran, *The Amarna Letters* (Baltimore: Johns Hopkins University, 1992), p. 363: "Say [to the ki]ng, my lord and my [Su]n: Message of Biridiya, the loyal servant of the king. I fall at the feet of the king, my lord and my Sun, 7 times and 7 times. May the king, my lord, take cognizance of his servant and his city. In fact, only I am cultivating: *aḫ-ri-šu* in Šunama, and only I am furnishing corvée workers *[amīlūti massa].* But consider

One may interpret Jacob's words to Issachar in two possible ways. The prevailing view is that Jacob paints Issachar as a group of people who put creaturely comforts (v. 15a-b) ahead of any other value, and as a result it cost them their independence (v. 15c-d). They became serfs to the local Canaanites, i.e., the feudal barons ruling in the Jezreel valley.

This sin is as old as Adam and Eve. The woman saw that the tree was good for food *(rāʾâ kî ṭôḇ),* and the Issacharites saw a resting place that was good *(rāʾâ kî ṭôḇ).* This theme surfaces again in the Sodom and Gomorrah stories, where pandering to lust became epidemic. It also appears in Jacob's brother Esau. He put the needs of his stomach ahead of the voice of his conscience and paid for it dearly. The hersdmen of Lot (ch. 13) can identify with the choice of Issachar and his progeny.

The basic reason for this majority view is the last phrase of v. 15, *wayᵉhî lᵉmas-ʿoḇēḏ* ("he submitted to forced labor" [Westermann]; "and he became a willing serf" [Speiser]). Now it cannot be denied that this expression carries such connotations elsewhere. For example, cf. Exod. 1:11, "they put gang-formen [*śārê missîm*] in charge of them to oppress them with forced labor [*bᵉsiḇlōṯām*]."[8] Both Gen. 49:15 and Exod. 1:11 feature the words *ms* and *sbl.* See also Josh. 16:10, "the Canaanites . . . became subjects for forced labor"[9] *(wayᵉhî lᵉmas-ʿōḇēḏ),* the same expression we have in Gen. 49:15; cf. too 1 K. 9:21, RSV: "their descendants who were left after them in the land . . . these Solomon made a forced levy of slaves" (*lᵉmas-ʿōḇēḏ;* repeated in 2 Chr. 8:8 but without *ʿōḇēḏ*). Finally, note the slightly different phrase in Deut. 20:11, which states how the residents of a city that offer to surrender are to be treated: "all the people who are found in it shall do forced labor [*lāmas*] for you and shall serve you [*waʿᵃḇāḏûḵā*]" (RSV). Thus it appears that *mas* or *mas-ʿōḇēḏ* is something onerous imposed on one person by another. But the OT appears to have no instances of an individual or a group freely choosing such circumstances. In all the examples cited the group who is classified as *mas-ʿōḇēḏ* is so because of circumstances over which they have no control. The majority interpretation of Jacob's words to Issachar would suggest that Gen. 49:15 is an exception to this usage.

This majority interpretation has sufficient problems to warrant an alternative interpretation of v. 15. For one thing, nowhere does the OT comment on

---

the mayors that are near me. They do not act as I do. They do not cultivate in Šunama, and they do not furnish corvée workers *[amīlūti massa].* Only I: *ia₈-ḫu-du-un-ni* (by myself) furnish corvée workers *[amīlūti massa].* From Yapu they come, from *[my] resources* here, (and) from Nuribta. And may the king, my lord, take cognizance of his city."

8. Translation of B. S. Childs, *Book of Exodus,* OTL (Philadelphia: Westminster, 1974), p. 4.

9. Translation of Boling, *Joshua,* p. 10.

the subjugation of the Issacharites to local power figures. The only possible evidence is extrabiblical (i.e., Amarna text no. 365), but even here this conclusion is only implied and possible. Moreover, when Judg. 1 lists the tribes that did not successfully drive out the local Canaanites (Manasseh, v. 27; Ephraim, v. 29; Zebulon, v. 30; Asher, v. 31; Naphtali, v. 33), some of which were contiguous with Issachar, it does not mention the tribal area of Issachar. Also, the Song of Deborah celebrates Issachar's valued contribution in battle (Judg. 5:15). Finally, in Gen. 49, when Jacob clearly says a word of judgment on one of his sons, the reason for the father's displeasure is explicit (Reuben, v. 4; Simeon and Levi, vv. 5-6). No such qualifying explanation is given with Issachar.

I have chosen to translate *a laboring worker,* a reading already reflected in LXX's "and he became a farmer" *(kaí egenḗthē anḗr geōrgós).* Thus here l^{e}mas-ʿōḇēḏ has an archaic, nontechnical meaning that in later biblical usage took on the overtones of enforced servitude and the like. In Gen. 49:15 Jacob predicts for Issachar and his descendants, strong as they are, a *modus vivendi* in which they do not shy away from assuming tasks of some physical magnitude.[10]

6. DAN (49:16-18)

16 *"Dan shall judge*[1] *his people*
as any other[2] *of the tribes of Israel.*[3]
17 *May Dan be a serpent by*[4] *the wayside,*

10. See J. D. Heck, "Issachar: Slave or Freeman?" (Gen. 49:14-15)," *JETS* 29 (1986) 385-96.

1. J. A. Emerton alone suggests *yāḏôn* (from *dānan*) for MT *yāḏîn:* "Dan, his people will be *strong,* as one of the tribes of Israel" ("Some Difficult Words in Genesis 49," in *Words and Meanings,* Fest. D. Winton Thomas, ed. P. R. Ackroyd and B. Lindars [Cambridge: Cambridge University, 1968], pp. 90-91). But the MT reading provides another instance of paronomasia in this poem: "Dan shall judge" *(dān yāḏîn),* such as we saw above in v. 8, *y^{e}hûḏâ . . . yôḏûḵā,* and therefore is quite acceptable.

2. Lit., "as one [*'aḥaḏ*] of the tribes of Israel." The use of *'aḥaḏ šiḇṭê yiśrā'ēl* (Gen. 49:16) and *yaḥaḏ šiḇṭê yiśrā'ēl* (Deut. 33:5) suggests that *'aḥaḏ* may mean "community." Cf. M. J. Dahood, "Eblaite, Ugaritic, and Hebrew Lexical Notes," *UF* 11 (1979) 143-44.

3. Here is another instance, as in the preceding verse (15bc, d), of a compound term *(šiḇṭê yíśrā'ēl)* in the second line replaces a simple term in the preceding line *(ʿammô)* (S. A. Geller, *Parallelism in Early Hebrew Poetry,* HSM 20 [Missoula, MT: Scholars, 1979], p. 269).

4. The MT attests the prepositions *ʿal, 'el,* with suffixed *-y* 56 times, all in poetry. Here the form is *ʿ^{a}lê* (twice). The majority of these forms are in Job (21 times), and 6 of them are in older poetry (Gen. 49:17 [twice]; 49:22 [twice]; Deut. 32:2 [twice]). The frequency of this form of the preposition in Syro-Arabian contexts such as Job has led G. Rendsburg to

a viper[5] *by the road,*[6]
who bites[7] *at the horse's hooves*[8]
so that its rider falls off[9] *backward."*
18 *"For your saving action I wait, Yahweh."*

16-17 Dan is the fifth son of Jacob (and the first by Bilhah) in the narrative account of chs. 29–30. In this particular list, and again only in 1 Chr. 2:1-2, he occupies the significant seventh position. It is only in connection with the oracle to Dan that one finds the sentiments expressed in v. 18, a statement of trust directed toward Yahweh, and the only time Yahweh is addressed in the poem. Also, apart from Judah and Joseph, Dan is the only tribal leader in ch. 49 to receive two separate blessings.[10]

The reconstruction of the history of the tribe of Dan is a formidable task, and it is essentially beyond the scope of a Genesis commentary. Both Gordon and Yadin appeal to 49:16a-b as suggesting that Dan (originally a segment of the sea peoples?) was admitted to equality with the other tribes at

---

conclude that they were used by the author of Job "to color his Hebrew in an Arabian manner" ("Sabaic Notes to Hebrew Grammar," *Abr-Nahrain* 27 [1989] 109-10).

5. *šᵉpîp̄ōn* occurs only here in the OT. H. R. Cohen (*Biblical Hapax Legomena in the Light of Akkadian and Ugaritic,* SBLDS 37 [Missoula, MT: Scholars, 1978], p. 109 n. 3) connects it with Akk. *šibbu/šippu.* LXX renders freely v. 17b as "lying in ambush by the road" *(enkasthḗmenos epí tríbou).* Not sure of the meaning of *šᵉpîp̄ōn,* the LXX translation derived it from the root *špp* (cf. also *tērḗsei* for *yᵉšûpᵉḵā* in Gen. 3:15). Targ. Onqelos reads "like a venomous snake" *(kḥywy ḥwrmn)* for Heb. *naḥaš* ("serpent"), probably to make it parallel with its rendering of *šᵉpîp̄ōn* as *pytn'* ("viper"), and thus accentuate the poisonous potential of Dan the serpent — his bite can be fatal.

6. *dereḵ* and *'ōraḥ* ("wayside" and "road") occur frequently in parallelism (Ps. 25:4; Prov. 2:20; 3:6; 4:18-19; 9:15; 15:19; Isa. 2:3 [par. Mic. 4:2]; 30:11), in construct (Isa. 3:12), and in reverse order (Ps. 139:3; Prov. 2:8, 13; 12:28). See Avishur, *Stylistic Studies of Word-Pairs,* pp. 168-69.

7. While many creatures bite, the OT almost always confines this activity to snakes. Thus the verb *nāšaḵ* occurs 10 out of 12 times in relation to a snake. U. Cassuto (*Biblical and Oriental Studies,* tr. I. Abrahams, 2 vols. [Jerusalem: Magnes, 1972-75], 2:39) draws attention to a similar comparison in the Ugaritic text dealing with the struggle between Baal and Mot (I AB vi.19 = *UT,* 49:VI:19; *CTA,* 6.VI.19) — "they bite like serpents" *(ynṯkn kbṯnm).*

8. Lit., "the heels of."

9. MT *wayyippōl,* a Qal, may just as easily be read as *wayyappēl,* a Hiphil: "(so that) he makes its rider fall off backward." See F. M. Cross and D. N. Freedman, *Studies in Ancient Yahwistic Poetry,* SBLDS 21 (Missoula, MT: Scholars, 1975), p. 87. This causative reading is reflected in Targ. Onqelos's rendering "he throws (over) [*wymgr*] their riders backward."

10. See J. M. Sasson, "A Genealogical 'Convention' in Biblical Chronography?" *ZAW* 90 (1978) 183.

a time later than the formation of the original confederation.[11] In contrast, de Vaux appeals to 49:16a-b to suggest that at some point Dan, originally part of the tribe of Benjamin,[12] became an autonomous tribe after its move to and conquest of Laish (Judg. 18).[13] This interpretation explains Dan judging his people *as any other of the tribes of Israel.*

In v. 16a *judge* means "plead the cause, defend," not condemn. Hence, v. 16 needs to be read as a statement of praise directed at Dan. Only one writer seems to read v. 16 as applying not to Dan at all, but to God — "He governs his people according to one judgment, he rules his people Israel according to one judgment."[14] This interpretation involves not a few shifts in the MT, and it produces a complicated reading out of a simple one.

Verse 17 compares Dan to a *serpent* or *viper* who lunges at and bites the hooves of a passing horse, causing the horse to bolt and throw its rider. We have already run across serpent symbolism in Genesis.[15] The first *nāḥāš* we encountered was in 3:1, 2, 4, 13, 14. The word *hooves* (lit., "heels," *ʿiqqᵉḇê*) is familiar from the Jacob story. In his own way Jacob grabbed the heel of his uterine brother, just as this viper snaps at the heel of the horse. The imagery in 49:17 seems to suggest that Dan, although small, will be quite capable of holding his own. His strength will be greater than his size. As small as he is, he will be able to strike panic into an animal as large as a horse.[16]

18 In the midst of his blessing on his sons Jacob says: *For your saving action I wait, Yahweh.* This statement sounds odd at this point in the poem. It

11. C. H. Gordon, "The Mediterranean Factor in the Old Testament," in *Congress Volume: Bonn, 1962,* VTSup 9 (Leiden: Brill, 1962), pp. 21-22; Y. Yadin, "And Dan, Why did he Remain in Ships?" *Australian Journal of Biblical Archaelogy* 2 (1968) 9-23; see also F. Spina, "The Dan Story Historically Reconsidered," *JSOT* 4 (1977) 60-71.

12. Is there any connection between *šᵉp̄îp̄ōn* ("viper") in v. 17b and Shephupham, a son of Benjamin according to Num. 26:39, and Muppim, a son of Benjamin listed in Gen. 46:21, but written as Shuppim in 1 Chr. 7:12?

13. See de Vaux, *Early History of Israel,* pp. 775-83.

14. Translation of M. O'Connor, *Hebrew Verse Structure* (Winona Lake, IN: Eisenbrauns, 1980), pp. 174-75. On the use of this verb where "judge" means "save, defend" (as in Prov. 31:19; Jer. 5:28; 22:15-16), see M. Weinfeld, " 'Justice and Righteousness' — *mšpṭ wṣdqh* — The Expression and its Meaning," in *Justice and Righteousness: Biblical Themes and Their Influence,* Fest. B. Uffenheimer, ed. H. G. Reventlow and Y. Hoffman, JSOTSup 137 (Sheffield: JSOT, 1992), p. 242.

15. See K. R. Joines, *Serpent Symbolism in the Old Testament* (Haddonfield, NJ; Haddonfield House, 1974), pp. 6-7.

16. The reference to Dan as a snake or viper is especially interesting when compared with Deut. 33:22: "Dan is a lion's whelp who shies away from a viper [*bšn*]." This is the reading of Cross and Freedman, *Studies in Ancient Yahwistic Poetry,* pp. 102, 119 n. 74. Thus in Gen. 49 Dan is a viper but in Deut. 33 his tribe is one who avoids vipers, as would a lion cub.

reminds one of Jeremiah's lament in Jer. 20:7-18. In between a charge against God plus a wish for vengeance on his enemies (vv. 7-12) and a curse on the day of his birth (vv. 14-18), we find this: "Sing to Yahweh; praise Yahweh; for he has delivered the life of the needy from the hand of evildoers" (v. 13)!

Freedman understands v. 18 as a liturgical element that breaks the sequence of blessings in the body of the poem.[17] Westermann makes the unlikely suggestion that the verse was inserted by a (post-) exilic writer who, shocked by the tribal sayings, contrasts them with the genuine faith of the Israel of his generation.[18] O'Connor retains the verse as part of the oracle, and thus the words to Dan (v. 17) are bracketed by two references to deity (vv. 16, 18).[19] Few consider the statement to be genuinely Jacob's. But if it is, it is a ringing testimony by the elderly patriarch to his renewed faith in God that he shall one day be delivered by his God and experience eternal salvation. Interestingly, this is the only place in Genesis where any form of the root *yšʿ* is used. Although the illustrations of salvation and deliverance are scattered throughout Genesis, only here is the Hebrew word that most clearly means "salvation" used.[20]

In the light of the fact that Jacob compares Dan to a snake who bites horses, some have attempted to connect Jacob's blessing on Dan with two Ugaritic texts that also speak about snakebites. In one of them (*KTU,* 1.100), a divine mare, called the "Mother-of-horses," calls out to Shapshu, the sun-goddess, for help because her offspring are dying from snakebites. Shapshu, in turn, relays her message to the gods, each of whom does something to remedy the problem. Only the actions of the god Ḥoron (god of the nether-world) resolve the problem, and so the divine mare and Ḥoron are married. In the second text (*KTU,* 1.107) a deity or human hero named *Śrǵzz,* like the mare, turns to Shapshu for assistance when those around him are afflicted with snakebites. This text is unfortunately not nearly as well preserved as

17. D. N. Freedman, "The Poetic Structure of Deuteronomy 33," in *The Bible World,* Fest. Cyrus H. Gordon, ed. G. Rendsburg, et al. (New York: Ktav, 1980), p. 34.

18. Westermann, *Genesis,* 3:235.

19. O'Connor, *Hebrew Verse Structure,* p. 428.

20. The verb *yāšaʿ* occurs infrequently in the Pentateuch; with God as the subject, twice in the Hiphil (Exod. 14:30; Deut. 20:4) and twice in the Niphal (Num. 10:9; Deut. 33:29). (In Exod. 2:17 Moses is the subject.) By contrast, the same verb appears in the Psalter over fifty times. The noun that Jacob uses here for God's "saving action" *(yᵉšûaʿ)* occurs only two more times in the Pentateuch (Exod. 15:2 and Deut. 32:15), and all three of these passages are poetic. Thus salvation terminology (and this applies to other words besides *yāšaʿ*) is rare in the prose narrative of the Pentateuch. It is also apparent that the real locus of salvation language in the OT is the poetic tradition. See further the remarks of J. Barr, "An Aspect of Salvation in the Old Testament," in *Man and His Salvation: Studies in Memory of S. G. F. Brandon,* ed. E. J. Sharpe and J. R. Hinnels (Manchester: Manchester University, 1973), pp. 39-52.

1.100, hence some conjecture is necessary to restore the text. But Shapshu apparently took some measures to heal the victims bitten by the snakes and to render the snakes impotent.

The parallel between these two Ugaritic texts and Gen. 49:16-18 is more than simply the references to snakes and horses bitten by snakes. That a passage in Genesis referring to horses being bitten by snakes (v. 17) is followed by Jacob's recitation in which he signals his intention to wait for Yahweh's saving actions (v. 18) may also parallel these two texts, both of which include appeals to the gods and were probably meant to be recited. Indeed, 1.107.43 indicates explicitly that this text was recited: [ ]*sp ḫph ḫ*[ ], "[ ]Repeat, for the entire recita[tion]." In the light of these similarities, v. 18 may allude to the sort of recitations one finds in 1.107, minus the magical praxis to which the Canaanite texts allude.[21]

7. GAD (49:19)

19 *"Gad: Raiders shall raid him,*[1]
but he shall inflict defeat (at) their heels."[2]

Settled east of the Jordan, Gad had to fight constantly against Ammonite and desert marauders, as is evident from the Jephthah story in Judges (11:1–12:7).[3]

21. These two texts have been studied frequently by Ugaritologists, but the study that discerns a possible parallel between the texts and Gen. 49:16-18 is that of B. A. Levine and J.-M. de Tarragon, " 'Shapshu Cries Out in Heaven': Dealing with Snake-Bites at Ugarit (*KTU* 1.100, 1.107)," *RB* 95 (1988) 481-518, esp. 509. The extensive n. 2 on pp. 482-83 supplies bibliography of earlier studies.

1. Note the play on *gd* in this line: *gāḏ gᵉḏûḏ yᵉgûḏennû . . . yāguḏ*. J. Sasson ("Wordplay in the OT," *IDBS*, p. 969) calls attention to metaphonic puns produced by the occurrence of verbal forms in which the second use of the verb is quite different from the first use of the verb. He cites Isa. 1:19-20 and Gen. 49:19. In Gen. 49:19a *gāḏaḏ* means "raid"; in v. 19b *gāḏaḏ* means "inflict defeat."

2. MT ends v. 19 with *ʿāqēḇ*, "heel," and begins v. 20 with *mēʾāšēr*, "From Asher." *BHS*, most commentators, and most translations follow LXX, Pesh., and Vulg., which transpose *m* from the beginning of *mēʾāšēr* to the end of *ʿāqēḇ*; hence, *ʿᵃqāḇām*, "their heels." This redivision of the consonants also brings v. 20 into line with all the other blessings in the chapter, which start with a personal name without any kind of prefix. I see no reason to discern the meaning "to take vengeance" for *ʿqb* in v. 19b, as suggested by G. R. Driver, "Notes and Studies," *JTS* 38 (1937) 406: "But he (in turn) as (his own) Avenger chargeth upon them."

3. Even into the days of Saul the Ammonites harassed the residents of Gad (1 Sam. 11:1ff.). This episode is dramatically expanded in 4QSamᵃ. See F. M. Cross, "The Ammonite Oppression of the Tribes of Gad and Reuben: Missing Verses from 1 Samuel 11 Found in 4QSamuelᵃ," in *History, Historiography and Interpretation*, ed. H. Tadmor and M. Weinfeld (Jerusalem: Magnes, 1983), pp. 148-58.

In the Song of Deborah (Judg. 5:17) those of Gilead (Gad) are rebuked for remaining on their side of the Jordan (conceivably because they were preoccupied with their own problems at the time) and not coming to the assistance of tribes on the west side of the Jordan. In addition to pressure from the Ammonites, the Gadites also had to deal with the Moabites to the south. In the famous Moabite Stone from the mid-9th century B.C., Mesha, king of Moab, claims: "Now the men of Gad had always dwelt in the land of Ataroth, and the king of Israel had built Ataroth for them; but I fought against the town and took it and slew all the people of the town as satiation for Chemosh and Moab."[4] This oracle predicts Gad's ability to bounce back, to retaliate against those who would seek his territory. In later texts *g^{e}d̲ûd̲* ("raider[s]") refers to a divisional unit within an army (1 Chr. 7:4; 2 Chr. 25:13), but here the reference is to a raiding party, a strike force. The term may be applied to nomadic peoples (1 Sam. 30:8, 15, 23), but it may equally apply to sedentary peoples (1 K. 11:24; 2 K. 5:2, from Aram-Damascus; 13:20-21, from Moab; 24:2, from Nebuchadnezzar's multinational force; 2 Sam. 4:2, from Israel itself).[5] Thus the raiding parties may have been sent against Gad in Transjordan from any place, urban or nomadic.

Gad is not big enough to engage in frontal warfare. He must attack from the rear (v. 19b). Mobility rather than number is Gad's major asset. Vulnerable as the tribe was, especially from the east with the emergence of the kingdom of Ammon, Jacob's words to Gad are prophetic.

8. ASHER (49:20)

20 *"Asher: Rich*[1] *is his food,*
he himself shall provide royal delicacies."[2]

4. Translation of W. F. Albright, *ANET,* p. 320.

5. See Gottwald, *Tribes of Yahweh,* pp. 540-41.

1. "Rich" *(š^{e}mēnâ)* is fem. while "food" *(leḥem)* is masc. (SP changes to a masc., *šmn*). *leḥem* seems to be masc. everywhere else in the OT, except possibly for 1 Sam. 10:4 (*š^{e}t̲ê leḥem,* where one would expect *š^{e}nê leḥem,* unless some word has dropped out). May *š^{e}mēnâ* be connected with Ugar. *šmt* (from *šmnt*), "fatness"? In that case, the disagreement in gender would disappear — "Asher: his food/nourishment is fatness." Cf. C. Rabin, "Etymological Miscellanea," in *Studies in the Bible,* ed. Rabin, Scripta Hierosolymitana 8 (Jerusalem: Magnes, 1961), p. 392: "they of Asher eat [*lāḥĕmû*] fatness." Targ. Onqelos renders the expression as "Asher: his land shall be good" *(ṭb' 'rʿyh)* by understanding *laḥmô* as a reference to the land that produces the food, rather than to the food itself. The rendering of *lḥm* by "land" (*'rʿyh,* which is fem.) led Dahood to conclude that *lḥm* in Gen. 49:20 denotes "grainfield," and this would explain why *š^{e}mēnâ* is fem. (*Bib* 43 [1962] 546).

2. For *ma^{ʿa}d̲annîm,* "dainties, delicacies," cf. Lam. 4:5. What appears to be the fem. pl. form of this word *(ma^{ʿa}d̲annôt̲)* is found in 1 Sam. 15:32 and Job 38:31, on which see M. Pope, *Job,* AB, 3rd ed. (Garden City, NY: Doubleday, 1973), p. 300. A related

Asher is the blessed/happy tribe, evidenced by its agricultural bounty, to which v. 20 alludes. Asher occupies a fertile piece of land (the western slopes of the Galilean highland) and is therefore prosperous. Asher's involvement in maritime enterprises (Judg. 5:17) also expanded that prosperity. The first line of the verse praises Asher for the exquisite quality of his culinary products. 1 K. 4:7 speaks of those who were responsible for providing food for Solomon and his household for one month each, and one may ask whether Gen. 49:20 reflects that custom. That is, the tribe of Asher out of its abudance fulfills its responsibility of sharing and providing the royal family with food necessities.

Yet, since Judg. 1:32 speaks of Asher as dwelling among the Canaanites, the reference here may be a pejorative one, that is, Asher provides food for Canaanite or Phoenician courts. If that is the correct interpretation of v. 20b, then it is a stunning reversal of the meaning of the name *Asher* — "happy, blessed." Now, however, the blessed tribe is using that God-given bounty to sustain Canaanite-Phoenician city kings. The Song of Deborah (Judg. 5:17) chides Asher for neutrality and passivity in a time when it could have lent assistance to its beleaguered fellow tribe, the Ephraimites. "Asher was probably deterred by consideration for its customers, after the dream of possessing their cities had long since vanished in thin air."[3] One must not assume, however, that Gen. 49:20b speaks of the relationship between Asher and its neighbors in the days of the judges. One may understand the verse simply as Jacob's prophecy that Asher and the Asherites will be blessed by God with abundance and prosperity, and will produce food luxuriant and rich enough for royalty.

S. Gevirtz suggests a different interpretation by revocalizing *šᵉmēnâ* to *šemminnâ* (3rd masc. sing. of *mnh* or *mny,* Piel, "apportion, ration, dole out"), with the prefixed relative particle *šᵉ*-. This produces the translation, "Asher, who rations his bread, he gives delicacies to (the) king."[4] For Gevirtz, v. 20 is a sarcastic reference to the times of Solomon in which the tribe of Asher, which has already seen its territory reduced and as a result is impoverished to the point that food rationing is necessary, is still obligated to provide the royal house with

---

word, *ʿēḏnâ,* appears in Gen. 18:12 with the meaning "(sexual) delight"; cf. also the garden of Eden (*ʿēḏen).* Lam. 4:4, 5 are of particular interest because they contain the two nouns at the end of v. 20a and v. 20b: "young children ask for bread [*leḥem*]; no one gives it to them. Those who once fed on delicacies [*lᵉmaʿăḏannîm*] are destitute in the streets" (D. R. Hillers, *Lamentations,* rev. ed., AB [New York: Doubleday, 1992], p. 135). The two words occur in parallel in Ugaritic (*UT,* Krt [= *CTA,* 14.II] 83-84) — "Let *bread* be baked for a fifth, *food* for a sixth month" *(yip lḥm dḫmš mǵd ṯdṯ yrḫm).* See J. Coppens, "La bénédiction de Jacob: Son cadre historique à la lumière des parallèles ougaritiques," in *Volume du Congrès: Strasbourg, 1956,* VTSup 4 (Leiden: Brill, 1957), p. 99; Avishur, *Stylistic Studies of Word-Pairs,* pp. 379-80.

3. K. Ellinger, "Asher," *IDB,* 1:249.

4. S. Gevirtz, "Asher in the Blessing of Jacob," *VT* 37 (1987) 154-63.

food way beyond their means to supply. But to reach that interpretation, Gevirtz must not only revocalize the text but also appeal to the Piel of *mānâ* in a meaning that appears only in late texts (Dan. 1:10, appointing food; cf. 1:11, appointing supervisors). In addition he must discern the relative particle *šᵉ*- on a verb in the Piel (a rare phenomenon — Judg. 5:7, *šaqqamtî*).

9. NAPHTALI (49:21)

21 *"Naphtali: A productive[1] hind[2]*
which[3] brings[4] forth beautiful[5] fawns."[6]

1. Revocalizing MT *šᵉluḥâ* (a Qal fem. passive participle, lit., "let loose") as *šōlᵉḥâ*. "Productive" is a closer parallel to "which brings forth" than "let loose" would be. See M. J. Dahood, "Northwest Semitic Notes on Genesis," *Bib* 55 (1974) 81-82, who observes that the pairing *šlḥ/ntn* suggests synonyms. In numerous places these two verbs appear (in Hebrew, Ugaritic, and Phoenician) with essentially the same meaning. The Ugaritic text cited most frequently is *UT,* 2 Aqht (= *CTA,* 17] VI:26-28: "Ask for life, O Aqhat the youth, ask for life and I'll give it to thee [*watnk*], for deathlessness, and I'll bestow it on thee [*wašlḥk*]" (translation of Avishur, *Stylistic Studies of Word-Pairs,* pp. 542-43). Avishur also refers to the Phoenician letter from Saqqara (*KAI,* 50.3-4): *'pqn hksp 'š šlḥt ly wtntw ly,* "I brought out the silver which *you (or she) sent* [*šlḥt*] *and gave it* [*wtntw*] to me." On this particular word pair, see also U. Cassuto, *Biblical and Oriental Studies,* tr. I. Abrahams, 2 vols. (Jerusalem: Magnes, 1972-75), 2:64; and S. Gevirtz, "Naphtali in 'The Blessing of Jacob,'" *JBL* 103 (1984) 517-18.

2. *'ayyālâ* is one of the debated words of the verse. I see no reason to emend it to *'ēlâ* ("terebinth") as in NEB, even if LXX read *stélechos,* "tree trunk, branch." *'ayyālâ* is usually identified as a member of the deer family, specifically the adult male of the red deer. Gevirtz (*JBL* 103 [1984] 514) challenges this identification and suggests instead "mountain sheep/ewe" because twice *'ayyālâ* occurs with "mountain goat" (Job 39:1; Prov. 5:19), and because of the close association between *'ayyālâ* and *'ayil,* "ram." Note, also, that the Arabic equivalent of Heb. *'ayyālâ,* i.e., *'iyyalun,* is much like the Arabic word for "mountain goat" *(wa'lun).* See F. Firmage, *ABD,* 6:1153. Although seldom domesticated, the *aialu* ("stag") appears in a 15th-century B.C. Alalakh tablet in a series listing rations for domestic animals. See W. G. Lambert, "The Domesticated Camel in the Second Millennium — Evidence from Alalakh and Ugarit," *BASOR* 160 (1960) 42.

3. For the article on a participle functioning as a relative pronoun see Dahood, *Psalms,* 3:205.

4. The participle is masc. *(hannōṯēn),* and yet it modifies a fem. noun *('ayyālâ)* and follows a fem. passive participle (MT). Gevirtz (*JBL* 103 [1984] 520) provides instances of sequentially ordered gender discrepancies that make the emendation of *hannōṯēn* to a fem. unnecessary.

5. *šāp̄er* is to be connected either with Ugar. *špr,* and rendered as "beautiful, lovely" (see M. J. Dahood, "Hebrew-Ugaritic Lexicography XI," *Bib* 54 [1973] 363), or with Akk. *supūru,* "fold, pen," i.e., "sheep of the fold" (S. Gevirtz, *JBL* 103 [1984] 516; Andersen, *Hebrew Verbless Clause in the Pentateuch,* pp. 44, 123 n. 5). The problem of connecting Akk. *supūru* with Heb. *šāp̄er* is the rarity of Akk. *s* = Heb. *š,* and the abundance

A major problem of this verse is its translation. Note the wide range of differences among the following:

(1) The one reflected above (supported by Speiser, Dahood, O'Connor, Westermann, and Sarna).[7]
(2) "Naphtali is a spreading terebinth,
putting forth lovely boughs" (NEB; cf. Cross and Freedman, Stuart).[8]
(3) "Naphtali is a racing stag
Which bellows with trumpet notes" (Albright).[9]
(4) "Naphtali is a hind let loose,
Giving forth sweet songs [of freedom]" (Barnes).[10]
(5) "Naphtali: A hind is released,
Sheep of the fold are sold" (Andersen).[11]
(6) "Naphtali a mountain-ewe was born
who gives (birth to) lambs of the fold" (Gevirtz).[12]

---

of *špr* as "good, beautiful" in Northwest Semitic (Ugaritic, Aramaic). See G. A. Rendsburg, "Israelian Hebrew Features in Genesis 49," *MAARAV* 8 (1992) 165-66.

6. *'imrê* is also difficult. Some, e.g., NEB, read *'ᵃmîrê* (from *'āmîr,* Isa. 17:6), "branches." Others read *'imrê,* "words" (e.g., NJPS). My translation points to *'imrê* as the construct pl. of the noun *'immār,* not otherwise extant in Biblical Hebrew but cognate with Akk. *immeru,* Aram. *'immar,* and Ugar. *imr,* "sheep, lamb." Gevirtz (*JBL* 103 [1984] 515) supplies numerous examples of nouns that have a doubling of the second root consonant in the absolute pl., but which write that consonant only once when it appears in a pl. construct — thus *'ayyālôt,* absolute pl. (Ps. 29:9) and *'aylôt,* construct pl. (Cant. 2:7); *ballāhôṯ,* absolute pl. (Ezek. 26:21) and *balhôṯ,* construct pl. (Job 24:17). Gevirtz does not supply any instances of this phenomenon with masc. nouns. Cf. *HALAT,* 1:65. F. I. Andersen and D. N. Freedman (*Hosea,* AB [Garden City, NY: Doubleday, 1980], p. 632) do not comment on Dahood's suggestion ("Hebrew-Ugaritic Lexicography I," *Bib* 44 [1963] 296) that the noun is also present in Hos. 13:2: "for them these are the sacrificial lambs [*'immārê-m zabḥî* for MT *'ōmᵉrîm zōbeḥê*], with men kissing calves," but they reject the similar proposal of W. Kuhnigk, *Nordwestsemitische Studien zum Hoseabuch,* BibOr 27 (Rome: Pontifical Biblical Institute, 1974), p. 219. Cf. also Rendsburg, *MAARAV* 8 (1992) 164-65, for agreement with Gevirtz.

7. Speiser, *Genesis,* pp. 363, 367; M. J. Dahood, "Northwest Semitic Notes on Genesis," *Bib* 55 (1974) 81-82; M. O'Connor, *Hebrew Verse Structure* (Winona Lake, IN: Eisenbrauns, 1980), p. 176; Westermann, *Genesis,* 3:218, 236; Sarna, *Genesis,* p. 342.

8. F. M. Cross and D. N. Freedman, *Studies in Ancient Yahwistic Poetry,* SBLDS 21 [Missoula, MT: Scholars, 1975], p. 89; D. K. Stuart, *Studies in Early Hebrew Meter,* HSM 13 (Missoula, MT: Scholars, 1976), pp. 145, 150 n. 40.

9. W. F. Albright, "From the Patriarchs to Moses: II. Moses out of Egypt," *BA* 36 (1973) 52.

10. W. E. Barnes, "A Taunt-Song in Gen. XLIX 20, 21," *JTS* 33 (1932) 355.

11. Andersen, *Hebrew Verbless Clause in the Pentateuch,* p. 44.

12. Gevirtz, *JBL* 103 (1984) 520.

Where comment is made, all of the above, except for Gevirtz, interpret v. 21 as positive: Naphtali will be productive, and will have numerous and beautiful progeny. Gevirtz reads the verse as the author's way of stating his disappointment with the tribe. Born to be free (v. 21a), Naphtali has instead become domesticated (v. 21b).

Naphtali, a tribe about which little is known, is praised in Judg. 4:6, 10; 5:18b for its yeoman cooperation with Deborah in her tribe's fight with Canaanites. He was willing to abandon the safety of his own highlands in this hilly, wooded Galilean country in support of a vulnerable brother. To the best of our knowledge, this is one of the few areas of Canaan that show no signs of Canaanite occupation. This reference puts the tribe of Naphtali in a good light, and would suggest that Jacob's word to Naphtali hints at the tribe's abilities in fighting.

Other references give a different perspective on Naphtali. Thus the Naphtalites were unsuccessful in driving out the people of Beth-shemesh and Ben-anath (Judg. 1:33), although they do subject the indigenous people to forced labor. Earlier, the second census in Numbers (26:48-50) lists a decrease of 8,000 from the first census (1:42-43), 45,400 versus 53,400. Naphtali is one of five tribes (Reuben, 2,700; Simeon, 37,100; Gad, 5,150; Ephraim, 8,000) to show a decline.

As a result of the above data, it is difficult to be certain whether Jacob's blessing on Naphtali is positive or negative. Thus Ellinger maintains that "Naphtali as the last of the Galilean tribes gets a somewhat gloomy comment; it is compared to an unleashed hind and this probably suggests the danger of its impulsive strength."[13] In contrast, the evidence might lead one to the conclusion that "it is uncertain whether Jacob's reference to Naphtali as an 'unleashed hind' in his blessing to the tribes is pejorative or a reference to the tribe's residence in fighting."[14]

The positioning of the Danite division on the north side of the tent of meeting might contribute something to this discussion (Num. 1:25-31). The Danites, who have developed a reputation for military exploits (Gen. 49:16-17) are placed between its subordinate tribes, Asher and Naphtali, who are recalled more for their pacific nature (49:20, 21).[15] It would appear that early in its existence the tribe of Naphtali lived a peaceful, nomadic life-style (49:21), but subsequently became more settled and produced new villages (Deut. 33:23, Moses' blessing on the tribe of Naphtali).[16]

13. K. Ellinger, "Naphtali," *IDB,* 3:509.

14. S. P. Jeansonne, "Naphtali," *ABD,* 4:1021.

15. J. Milgrom, *Numbers,* JPS Torah Commentary (Philadelphia: Jewish Publication Society, 1990), p. 341.

16. R. G. Boling and G. E. Wright, *Joshua,* AB (Garden City, NY: Doubleday, 1982), pp. 460-61.

10. JOSEPH (49:22-26)

22 *"The foal*[1] *of a wild she-ass*[2] *is Joseph,*
the foal of a wild she-ass at a spring,
(the foal of)[3] *wild asses*[4] *by a rocky rim.*[5]

1. *bēn* is a legitimate vocalization of the construct, "son of." It need not be changed to *ben* as suggested by *BHS,* which would delete the first phrase *bēn pōrāṯ* altogether, and read the second *bēn pōrāṯ* in the verse as *ben pārâ.* On the repetition of single words or phrases within a strophe, see J. Muilenburg, "A Study in Hebrew Rhetoric: Repetition and Style," in *Hearing and Speaking the Word: Selections from the Works of James Muilenburg,* ed. T. F. Best (Chico, CA: Scholars, 1984), p. 204. Muilenburg calls Gen. 49:22-26 "a model of Hebrew repetitive style." Other biconsonantal nouns in Biblical Hebrew illustrate the same variation, e.g., *šēm* or *šem* for "name of."

2. The first significant problem here is the interpretation of *bēn pōrāṯ.* The translation above connects it with Ugar. *prt,* "cow, heifer." See V. Salo, "Joseph, Sohn der Färse," *TZ* 12 (1968) 94-95; M. J. Dahood, "Hebrew-Ugaritic Lexicography VIII," *Bib* 51 (1970) 401. Support for this view is found in Hos. 8:9, which compares Ephraim to a "wild ass" *(pere'),* and in Hos. 13:15, which describes Ephraim as "wild" *(yaprî'),* on which see F. I. Andersen and D. N. Freedman, *Hosea,* AB (Garden City, NY: Doubleday, 1983), p. 640. See also D. W. Young, "With Snakes and Dates: A Sacred Marriage Drama at Ugarit," *UF* 9 (1977) 304 n. 107. The connection of Jacob's designation for Joseph with Ephraim may indicate that Ephraim is to be considered the stronger and more important of the two Joseph tribes (Ephraim and Manasseh) in later biblical history. On the presence of the fem. sing. nominal ending *-āṯ* or *aṯ,* esp. in early (archaic) poetry and reflecting a time in the Hebrew language prior to the shift of *-āṯ/aṯ* to *-â,* see G. A. Rendsburg, "Morphological Evidence for Regional Dialects in Ancient Hebrew," in *Linguistics and Biblical Hebrew,* ed. W. R. Bodine (Winona Lake, IN: Eisenbrauns, 1992), pp. 77-78; idem, *MAARAV* 8 (1992) 167-68. Others identify *pōrāṯ* as the active participle of *pārâ,* "be fruitful" (instead of the more standard *pōreh*), hence "son of a fruit bearer," i.e., "a fruitful bough" (BDB, p. 826; GKC, § 80g). This is the reading of Westermann ("Joseph is a young and verdant tree") and RSV ("Joseph is a fruitful bough"). This reading has the support of some of the ancient versions, e.g., LXX (*Huiós ēyxēménos,* "Joseph is a son increased") and Targ. Onqelos (*bry dysgy ywsp bry dytbrk kgwpn,* "Joseph is my son who shall be numerous, my son who shall be blessed like a vine"). The main problem with this interpretation is that it must attribute the unusual meaning "branches" or "daughter-vines" to *bānôṯ* in v. 22c to continue the analogy of a fruitful bough or tree. Close to this interpretation is J. Allegro's reading: "A Euphratean poplar is Joseph" ("A Mesopotamian Background to the Joseph Blessing of Gen. xlix," *ZAW* 64 [1952] 249-51), and the reading of A. Caquot, "A son (is) a fertile (plant), O Joseph" ("*Ben porat* [Genèse 49,22]," *Semitics* 30 [1980] 43-56). W. F. Albright (*BA* 36 [1973] 27) renders simply, "Son of Euphrates is Joseph." (In Biblical Hebrew "Euphrates" is *pᵉrāṯ.*) The reading I follow is strengthened by the appearance of the personal names *prt, prtn, bn prtn* in Ugaritic texts, as noted by F. Gröndahl, *Die Personennamen der Texte aus Ugarit* (Rome: Pontifical Biblical Institute, 1967), pp. 27-28 (where the general category of names under discussion is *Tiernamen als Personennamen,* "animal names as personal names"); see also pp. 175, 289. Support for this reading is also found in the interpretation of *bānôṯ ṣāʿăḏâ* in v. 22c, to which I shall

23 *They harry*[6] *and contend*[7] *with him,*
archers[8] *try to do him in.*

---

turn shortly. Lastly, an animal designation for Joseph continues the extensive use of animal metaphors throughout the chapter. The structure *bēn pōrāṯ yôsēp̱* is an exact parallel to Jacob's earlier *gûr ʾaryēh yᵉhûḏû* (v. 9).

3. For ellipsis as a feature of staircase parallelism, see W. G. E. Watson, *Classical Hebrew Poetry: A Guide to Its Techniques,* JSOTSup 26 (Sheffield: JSOT, 1984), p. 155; S. Gevirtz, "Of Patriarchs and Puns: Joseph at the Fountain, Jacob at the Ford," *HUCA* 46 (1975) 40-41. The observation of this feature in 49:22 removes the problem of gender disagreement between *bēn* (masc. sing., twice) and *bānôṯ* (fem. pl.), in that 22c should be read as *bēn bānôṯ ṣāʿᵃḏâ,* "the foal of wild asses."

4. *bānôṯ ṣāʿᵃḏâ* is not transparent in meaning. Those who render "his branches run over the wall" (e.g., RSV) first have to read *bānôṯ* ("daughters") as "branches," then make sense of a fem. pl. noun (= a collective sing.?) as subject of a verb that is 3rd fem. sing. *(ṣāʿᵃḏâ).* Barr (*Comparative Philology and the Text of the Old Testament* [Oxford: Clarendon, 1968], pp. 30-31) sees no problem here, however, if one interprets *ṣāʿᵃḏâ* as an isolated survival of the fem. termination in *-â* for the third pl., with parallels to this form in the Aramaic portions of the OT. Various attempts to interpret *bānôṯ* in other ways all seem unnecessary; cf., e.g., (1) Old Assyrian *binu,* "poplar" (J. Allegro, *ZAW* 64 [1952] 251; (2) Ugar. *bnt,* "form" (J. Sanmartín, "Zum Begriff 'Struktur' [*BNT*] im Ugaritischen," *UF* 10 [1978] 446); (3) to read it as the old third fem. pl. of the perfect (Gordis, *Book of Job* [New York: Jewish Theological Seminary of America, 1978], p. 177); (4) to see it as an instance of a pl. subject with the fem. sing. of the verbal predicate (GKC, § 145k). Following the suggestion of Ehrlich, Speiser (*Genesis,* p. 368) connected *bānôṯ ṣāʿᵃḏâ* with Arab. *banât ṣaʿdat,* "wild asses." The Hebrew of Gen. 49:22 would be an example of a Hebraized Arabic loanword. See also S. Gevirtz, "Of Patriarchs and Puns," *HUCA* 46 (1975) 37-38. The advantage of this last interpretation is that it most consistently advances the meaning and animal analogy of v. 22ab, if I have interpreted *bēn pōrāṯ* correctly.

5. *šûr* means "wall" in 2 Sam. 22:30 (par. Ps. 18:30 [Eng. 29]); cf. *šûrâ* (wall of vines or olives) in Job 24:11; Jer. 5:10. In 2 Sam. 22:30 *šûr* clearly designates a "(manmade) rock wall." In Gen. 49:22 *šûr* would probably indicate a natural rock wall such as one would find in ravines or canyons, i.e., the desert environment of the wild ass. One might also read *šôr,* "ox," or even the place name Shur (cf. Gen. 16:7), esp. in the light of the comparison of Ishmael to a "wild ass of a man (*pereʾ ʾāḏām*), and Hagar's location in the wilderness by a spring (*ʿayin)* on the road to Shur *(šûr).* The linkage between Joseph in Gen. 49 and Ishmael in Gen. 16 is suggestively advanced by Gevirtz, *HUCA* 46 (1975) 42ff. I am inclined to go with "rocky rim" only because it provides a balance with "spring." That is, the wild ass is most vulnerable to the hunter (v. 23) either when it comes to a spring for water or when it is silhouetted on the rocky rim of a canyon (Young, *UF* 9 [1977] 304 n. 107).

6. For *mārar* here the meaning is "(try to) prevail upon one militarily" rather than "embitter." See L. Kutler, "A 'Strong' Case For Hebrew *MAR,*" *UF* 16 (1984) 112. "The archers shewed bitterness toward him" (BDB, p. 600) is less likely. Dahood (*Psalms,* AB, 2nd ed. [Garden City, NY: Doubleday, 1973], 2:104) reads "they shot poisoned arrows at him." I am not certain that one can support Dahood's reading, but the sense he gives the passage is on target. Indeed, Gen. 49:23 is the one indisputable place in the OT where *mārar* is used with weapons. See also D. Pardee, "The Semitic root *mrr* and the Etymology of Ugaritic *mr(r)//brk,*" *UF* 10 (1978) 261 n. 72.

24 *But his bow*[9] *was broken*[10] *forever,*[11]
his powerful hands[12] *trembled,*[13]

---

7. This translation reflects LXX *eloidóroun* (i.e., *way^{e}rîbuhû*) rather than MT *wārōbbû;* cf. *BHS* and Cross and Freedman, *Studies in Ancient Yahwistic Poetry,* p. 90 n. 75. There is some evidence for a rare verb in Biblical Hebrew, *rāḇaḇ, rāḇâ,* "to shoot (arrows, shafts)." See Gen. 21:20; 2 Sam. 22:15 (par. Ps. 18:15 [Eng. 14]); and P. K. McCarter, Jr., *II Samuel,* AB (Garden City, NY: Doubleday, 1984), p. 457; Dahood, *Psalms,* 1:19. W. F. Albright (*BA* 36 [1973] 26) sees in *wārōbbû* some remains of the tribe of Rabbayu or Rabbu (lit., "archers") known from the Mari letters, and situated on both sides of the upper Euphrates in northern Syria and northwestern Mesopotamia. This term would parallel *ba'^{a}lê ḥiṣṣîm* of v. 23b.

8. Lit., "lords (or masters) of arrows." "Archers" is metaphorical for "slanderers," as can be seen too in Ps. 89:51-52 (Eng. 50-51), and in the LXX here: "against whom the calumniators brought false accusations, though the masters of bows took aim at him." Gevirtz points out (*VT* 37 [1987] 160) that the double pl. *ba'^{a}lê ḥiṣṣîm* is not necessarily an evidence of late Biblical Hebrew, although the construction is frequent in Chronicles (R. Polzin, *Late Biblical Hebrew: Toward an Historical Typology of Biblical Hebrew Prose,* HSM 12 [Missoula, MT: Scholars, 1976], p. 42). The construction occurs in Judg. 5, Phoenician, Ugaritic, and the Amarna tablets from Byblos. For other OT uses of the double pl. syntagma, see Rendsburg, *MAARAV* 8 (1992) 168-69.

9. If one translates v. 24a as "but his bow stayed taut" (e.g., Westermann, NJPS), then the reference is to Joseph. My translation takes the reference to be to Joseph's enemies, principally because the previous verse pictured the enemies as the one shooting at Joseph, the foal of a wild she-ass. The sing. pronominal suffix in "his bow" would be understood as a sing. form used collectively or distributively (Speiser, *Genesis,* pp. 368-69).

10. Following LXX *synetríbē* (i.e., *wattiššāḇēr,* a Niphal), rather than MT *wattēšeḇ* (a Qal). This reading involves restoring an *-r* to MT *wttšb.* See D. K. Stuart, *Studies in Early Hebrew Meter,* HSM 13 (Missoula, MT: Scholars, 1976), pp. 142, 145. By contrast, Dahood ("Third Masculine Singular with Performative *t-* in Northwest Semitic," *Or* 48 [1979] 99) does not appeal to LXX to get *šāḇar,* but rather revocalizes *wattēšeḇ* to *watt^{e}šōḇēḇ,* which he identifies as an instance of the 3rd masc. sing. with preformative *t-.* He appeals to the Polel form *y^{e}šôḇēḇ D(from šûḇ)* in Ps. 23:3 ("he restores my soul") to get "The Perennial restored his bow." Dahood's rendering of the verb as an instance of a 3rd masc. sing. *taqṭul* is, however, open to serious question. See, e.g., A. Schoors, "A Third Masculine Singular *taqtul* in Biblical Hebrew?" in *Text and Context: Old Testament and Semitic Studies for F. C. Fensham,* ed. W. Claasen, JSOTSup 48 (Sheffield: JSOT, 1988), pp. 195-200, esp. p. 195. I am aware that good sense can be made from the MT as it stands, i.e., "and his bow abode [*yāšaḇ*] as a firm one" (BDB, p. 443). My reason for not following MT is stated in n. 9 above.

11. *'êṯān* means "perennial, ever flowing" (adj.); "steady flow, permanence" (noun). Dahood has argued for a divine epithet in *'êṯān.* In MT *tšb b'tn,* according to Dahood, the *b* was inadvertently written twice: "The Perennial restored his bow." See Dahood, *Or* 48 (1979) 99; idem, "The Minor Prophets and Ebla," in *The Word of the Lord Shall Go Forth,* Fest. D. N. Freedman, ed. C. Meyers and M. O'Connor (Winona Lake, IN: Eisenbrauns, 1983), p. 64 n. 25. He varies this translation with "But his bow was shattered by the Mighty One" ("Is *'Eben Yiśrā'ēl* a Divine Title [Gen 49,24]," *Bib* 40 [1959] 1002-7) by reading MT as *wattiššaḇ* or *wattuššaḇ* and connecting it with an otherwise unattested verb in Biblical Hebrew, *šbb,* "to smash, shiver." Dahood cites several passages in Ugaritic where *yṯb* parallels *yṯbr*

by the hands of Jacob's Mighty One,[14]
by the name of[15] *the Shepherd,*[16] *Israel's Rock.*[17]
25 *From the God of your father who supports you,*
from[18] *Shaddai who blesses you,*

(1 Aqht 107-8, 122-23; but cf. both *CTA,* 19.III.108, 123; and *KTU,* 1.19.III.2, 17, which restore *ytbr* in both lines). But much more OT evidence suggests that one should understand *'êṯān* as referring to something that is permanent: wadis with a perennial stream (Ps. 74:15; Amos 5:24), abodes that are permanently secure (Num. 24:21), or nations that have an apparently unlimited future (Jer. 5:15).

12. Lit., "the arms of his hands." The reference is to the strength of the archers' arms that enables them to draw the bow with the hand. *yāḏ* and *zᵉrôaʿ* mean not only "hand" and "arm" but metaphorically "power" and "strength." See BDB, pp. 283, 390; and J. K. Hoffmeier, "The Arm of God Versus the Arm of Pharaoh in the Exodus Narratives," *Bib* 67 (1986) 378-87.

13. *pāzaz* is used only here in the Qal, and but once more in the Piel (2 Sam. 6:16). BDB, p. 808, suggests "be supple, agile." See Y. Avishur, "*KRKR* in Biblical Hebrew and in Ugaritic," *VT* 26 (1976) 259 n. 6.

14. *'ᵃḇîr yaʿᵃqōḇ* cannot be rendered "the Bull of Jacob" (cf. Ps. 132:2, 5; Isa. 49:26; 60:16; and "Bull of Israel" in Isa. 1:24), for this translation is possible only if *'ᵃḇîr* is vocalized as *'abbîr.* The lack of gemination in the middle consonant may be a deliberate repudiation of any idea that "Bull" was the name of a proto-Israelite deity transferred to Yahweh. Even if one grants *'abbîr,* note that "Bull" is here a symbol of protecting power, and not, as in Canaanite usage, of procreative power, i.e., fertility. See J. Gray, *Legacy of Canaan,* rev. ed., VTSup 5 (Leiden: Brill, 1965), p. 158, and his comments about El *(tr 'el);* and S. Olofsson, *God Is My Rock: A Study of Translation Technique and Theological Exegesis in the Septuagint,* ConBOT 31 (Stockholm: Almqvist & Wiksell, 1990), pp. 87-92; N. M. Sarna, "The Divine Title *'abhîr yaʿăqôbh,*" in *Essays on the Occasion of the Seventieth Anniversary of the Dropsie University,* ed. A. I. Katsh and L. Nemoy (Philadelphia: Dropsie University, 1979), pp. 389-96.

15. With Pesh. I read *miššēm* for MT *miššam,* "from there." See S. Talmon, "*Yād wāšēm:* An Idiomatic Phrase in Biblical Literature and Its Variations," *HS* 25 (1984) 8-17, esp. pp. 13-14 for his comment on v. 24. On *yd . . . šm* in Ugaritic literature, see M. J. Dahood, *RSP,* 1:196 (though Gen. 49:24 is not cited). Avishur (*Stylistic Studies of Word-Pairs,* p. 675) cites this reading under the category "Textual Emendations Based on Word Pairs."

16. The words *'byr* ("Mighty One") and *rʿh* ("Shepherd") are preserved in the OT in two pairing modes only: here in parallelism, and in 1 Sam. 21:8 in construct (*'abbîr hārōʿîm,* "the mighty of shepherds"). See Avishur, *Stylistic Studies of Word-Pairs,* p. 166. The LXX reads *ho katischýsas Israēl,* "thence is he that strengthened Israel," which would seem to indicate that *rō'eh* was not in the *Vorlage* of the LXX.

17. The usual expression for God as "Israel's Rock" is *ṣûr yiśrā'ēl* (33 times). This is the only instance of *'eḇen yiśrā'ēl.* Accordingly, many have attempted to eliminate the phrase as a divine title; most recently, Dahood, *Bib* 40 (1959) 1002-7. A less drastic attempt than that of Dahood to eliminate *'eḇen yiśrā'el* is advanced by A. S. van der Woude, "*ṣûr,*" *THAT,* 2:542; he understands *'eḇen* to be *ben,* "son," with prosthetic *aleph:* "through the work of the strength of Jacob, through the help of the Shepherd of the sons of Israel"; so also D. N. Freedman, "Divine Names and Titles in Early Hebrew Poetry" in *Magnalia Dei: The Mighty Acts of God,* Fest. G. E. Wright, ed. F. M. Cross, W. E. Lemke, P. D.

with the bounty of heaven above,
the bounty of the deep that crouches below,
the bounty of breast and womb,
26 *may the bounty of your father surpass*
the bounty of my progenitors/mountains[19] *of old,*

Miller, Jr. (Garden City, NY: Doubleday, 1976), p. 65. For Freedman, *’bn* is a by-form of *bn,* and is to be read as a pl., *’ibnē,* with the final *yod* possibly represented by the initial *yod* of *yiśrā’ēl* serving double duty. The reason for the infrequency of *’eḇen* as a divine name may have been the prophetic polemic against idolatry that made use of sacred stones (see A. S. Kapelrud, *TDOT,* 1:50-51). Also, as a divine metaphor for refuge and shelter, *’eḇen,* "stone," seems less appropriate than *ṣûr,* "rock": one seeks protection in rocks rather than in stones. See Olofsson, *God Is My Rock,* pp. 94-95.

18. On the basis of some Hebrew mss., SP, LXX, and Pesh., the emendation of *w*^{e}*’ēṯ* to *w*^{e}*’ēl* is often made (see *BHS*). MT may be retained, however, if one understands *’eṯ* as meaning at times "from" (cf. Akk. *šâmu ’itti,* "to buy from"). See M. J. Dahood, "Northwest Semitic Notes on Genesis," *Bib* 55 (1974) 77. Also, N. Wyatt, "The Problem of the 'God of the Fathers,'" *ZAW* 90 (1978) 101, who attributes instrumental force to both particles — "by El, by Shaddai." Phoenician provides one instance of this meaning for *’t: tsrḥ[w] hrbt b‘lt gbl ’yt h’dm h’ wzr‘w ’t pn kl ’ln gbl,* "may the Lady, the Mistress of Byblos, [remove (?)] that man and his seed *from* before all the gods of Byblos" (inscription of Yehaumilk, *KAI,* 10.15-16). See S. Gevirtz, "On Canaanite Rhetoric: The Evidence of the Amarna Letters from Tyre," *Or* 42 (1973) 171. This meaning is also present in Classical Hebrew as shown by Arad Ostracon 24:rev. 18-19: *hnh šlḥty lh‘yd hym h’nšm ’t ’lyš‘,* "Look, I have sent men today from Elyasha to testify" (M. J. Dahood, *Or* 46 [1977] 331). This meaning for *’eṯ* in Biblical Hebrew is established by Gen. 4:1, "I have acquired a man from [*’eṯ*] Yahweh" (see my *Genesis, Chapters 1–17,* NICOT [Grand Rapids: Eerdmans, 1990], p. 221); and Gen. 6:13, "I am going to annihilate them from the earth" (ibid., p. 279 n. 2). The same meaning for *’eṯ* may be found in Jer. 51:59 in which Jeremiah sends word to Babylon (of its forthcoming destruction) via Seraiah, the brother of Baruch, who went to Babylon "with/from" Zedekiah, king of Judah. The LXX translates *’eṯ* here as *parà,* "from," indicating that Zedekiah was not a part of the delegation. This reading is followed by W. L. Holladay, *Jeremiah,* Hermeneia, 2 vols. (Philadelphia/Minneapolis: Fortress, 1986-89), 2:432, who needlessly emends MT *’eṯ* to *mē’eṯ.* Cf. R. Althann, "Does *’et (’aet-)* sometimes signify 'from' in the Hebrew Bible?" *ZAW* 103 (1991) 121-24.

19. *hôray ‘aḏ-* calls for comment. If *hôray* is connected with the verb *hārâ,* "conceive, become pregnant," then something like "my progenitors of old" is possible. Following LXX *oréōn monímōn,* "steadfast mountains," most modern scholars emend MT to *har*^{a}*rê ‘aḏ,* "everlasting mountains" (cf. Hab. 3:6; *BHS;* BDB, p. 223). "Mountains" may be obtained from MT as is by pointing *hwry* as *hā(w)rê,* with the use of *ḥôlem* to represent *ā* (as with *hā*[*w*]*lōḵ* in Josh. 6:13, and *gōlā*[*w*]*n* in Josh. 20:8). Following the detection by C. H. Gordon in biblical poetry of "Janus" parallelism (one word with two different meanings in a verse, one meaning connecting with what precedes, the other with what follows), G. Rendsburg has brought a fresh interpretation to this phrase. Pointed as *hôray,* "progenitors," the word parallels "father," and is thus used retrospectively. Pointed as *hā(w)rê,* "mountains," the word parallels "hills," and is thus used prospectively. See G. Rendsburg, "Janus Parallelism in Gen. 49:26" *JBL* 99 (1980) 291-93; Watson, *Classical*

the delight[20] *of the eternal hills.*
May they rest upon Joseph's head,
on the skull of the Nazir[21] *of his brothers."*[22]

22 I have chosen to translate the opening phrase in v. 22 as an animal metaphor rather than as a vegetation metaphor. Apart from the linguistic data noted above, my decision is encouraged by two other factors. One is the plethora of animal metaphors found elsewhere in the poem (Judah/lion, v. 9; Issachar/bony ass, v. 14; Dan/serpent, v. 17; Naphtali/hind, v. 21/; Benjamin/wolf, v. 27). The botanical metaphor would be unique. Second, the animal metaphor forms a better bond with the following verse. Archers do not shoot at fruitful branches, but they do take aim at wild animals grazing on hills ("a rocky rim") and around drinking spots ("spring"). This, then, is

---

Hebrew Poetry, p. 159. For "everlasting pools" see G. R. Driver, *JTS* 20 (1969) 567. S. M. Paul ("Polysensuous Polyvalency in Poetic Parallelism," in *Shaʿarei Talmon,* Fest. S. Talmon, ed. M. Fishbane and E. Tov [Winona Lake, IN: Eisenbrauns, 1992], pp. 150-51) notes that both of these interpretations were already perceived by Targ. Yerushalmi when it rendered, "May the blessings of your father's be added to the blessings wherewith your *fathers,* Abraham and Isaac, who are like *mountains,* blessed you." For yet another interpretation, see N. Jay, "Sacrifice, descent and the Patriarchs," *VT* 38 (1988) 69, for whom the masc. form *hôray* ("my progenitors"), otherwise found only in the fem. sing. ("mother," *hôrāṯām,* Hos. 2:7; *hôrāṯî,* Cant. 3:4), is an illustration of the Hebrew use of the masc. whenever the referent includes both males and females. Jacob prays, according to Jay, that the blessings of Jacob the father may surpass the blessings of his mother's family, i.e., Laban and his line of descent.

20. I understand *taʾᵃwâ* as a fem. noun meaning "desire, delight" (as in Gen. 3:6) from the verb *ʾāwâ,* "incline, desire." It is also possible to translate the noun as "boundary" or "abode," thus "the abode of the eternal hills." This was already suggested by BDB, p. 1063, but then rejected. For this reading see also J. Reider, "Etymological Studies in Biblical Hebrew," *VT* 2 (1952) 113-14; M. J. Dahood, *Proverbs and Northwest Semitic Philology* (Rome: Pontifical Biblical Institute, 1963), p. 42.

21. Or, "on the skull of the one consecrated among [or 'set apart from'; *nᵉzîr*] his brothers." The verb *nāzar* means "dedicate, consecrate." The noun *nēzer* means "diadem," worn by a king on his head as a sign of his consecration (2 Sam. 1:10; 2 K. 11:12; Ps. 89:40 [Eng. 39]; 132:18), or by the priests (Lev. 8:9). It also means "Naziriteship, consecration, dedication" (Num. 6:4, 5, 7, 8, 12-13). Then there is the noun *nāzîr,* "Nazirite," one who is set apart, consecrated. One could be set apart either by one's high rank (Gen. 49:26; Deut. 33:16) or by specific vows of abstinence (Num. 6:2; Judg. 13:5; Amos 2:11). See J. Milgrom, *Leviticus 1–16,* AB (New York: Doubleday, 1991), p. 512.

22. These last three verses (vv. 24-26) are rich in parallel pairs also found in poetry from Ugarit. On "bow/hand" (v. 24) see M. J. Dahood, *RSP,* 3:74. On "heaven/deep" (v. 25) see Dahood, *RSP,* 1:358-59; and Avishur, *Stylistic Studies of Word-Pairs,* p. 407. On "breast/womb" (v. 25) see Dahood, *RSP,* 3:156-57. On "head/skull" (v. 26) see Dahood, *RSP,* 1:335.

Jacob's designation of Joseph. Joseph, once *bēn rāḥēl* (son of Rachel, son of a ewe), is now *bēn pōrāṯ, son or foal of a wild she-ass.*

23 The enemies who attack Joseph may be understood as enemies of Joseph the individual or of Joseph the tribe. If the first, then the reference is to the brothers' harsh treatment of Joseph. They certainly tried to make life bitter for Joseph. Note the use of *śāṭam* here *(try to do him in)* and in 50:15. What the brothers sought to do to Joseph (49:23) they feared he would do to them or feel about them (50:15). This verb *(śāṭam)* occurs but six times in the OT, and three of them involve Jacob in some way (27:41; 49:23; 50:15).[23]

If Joseph the tribe is meant, then the reference is harder to determine. One possibility would be the intratribal war involving Ephraim and Benjamin (Judg. 19–21), less likely Ephraim and the men of Gilead (Judg. 12). Also possible is the Ephraimite occupation of Amalekite hill country in the time of the Judges (Judg. 12:15).

24 The first two cola of this verse may refer (as we noted above) either to Joseph or to Joseph's enemies mentioned in the previous verse. Some (e.g., Westermann) would argue for Joseph because v. 24 speaks of "his bow, his hands," rather than "their bow, their hands." In either case, the thrust of the whole verse remains the same. God turned back the assaults of the wicked against Joseph; or God gave to Joseph the strength to fend off his attackers.

In the OT and in ancient Near Eastern literature the *bow* may symbolize (1) the military power of an enemy; to break one's bow is to reduce one to military impotence (Jer. 49:35; 51:56; Hos. 1:5); (2) universal peace and the cessation of war (Hos. 2:20; Ps. 46:10 [Eng. 9]); (3) vigor (1 Sam. 2:4; 2 K. 9:24 ["he drew his bow with full strength," lit., "he filled his hand with the bow"]; Job 29:19-20); (4) sexual vigor. The last meaning is clearer in nonbiblical texts. An incantation for potency includes this line: "may the quiver [a feminine symbol] not become empty; may the bow [a masculine symbol] not become slack."[24] In an Akkadian text describing a treaty between Ashurnirari V of Assyria and Mati'ilu of Arpad, one of the threatened penalties for treaty violation by Mati'ilu states, "If Mati'ilu sins against this treaty with Ashurnirari, king of Assyria, . . . may Ishtar, the goddess of men, the lady of women, take away their bow, cause their [steri]lity. . . ."[25] Interestingly, Gen. Rabbah 98:20 understands "his bow" in 49:24 as the *membrum virile,*[26] with the comment, "For R. Samuel

23. The other three uses of *śāṭam* are Job 16:9, RSV: "[God] hated me"; Job 30:21, RSV: "with the might of thy hand dost thou persecute me"; Ps. 55:4 (Eng. 3), RSV: "and in anger they cherish enmity against me." The verb appears to refer to both feelings of animosity and active hate.

24. See R. D. Biggs, *ŠÀ.ZI.GA, Ancient Mesopotamian Potency Incantations* (Locust Valley, NY: Augustin, 1967) p. 37.

25. *ANET,* p. 533.

26. See N. M. Waldman, "The Breaking of the Bow," *JQR* 69 (1978) 82-88;

said, 'His "bow" grew taut but then became flaccid. That is in line with this verse: "And his bow returned in strength" (Gen. 49:29).' "[27] A more faithful and simpler reading of the verse understands it as the thwarted and unsuccessful attempts of Joseph's attackers to eliminate him; thus "break the bow" in v. 24 fits best the first sense given above, that of destroying military power.

This particular oracle has more names for deity than any other in the poem. In one sense the saying is more about Joseph's God than about Joseph. He is *Jacob's Mighty One (*’^{a}*ḇîr), the Shepherd (rōʿeh),* and *Rock (’eḇen)* of Israel. The first speaks of his strength, the second of his tenderness and care, the third of his firmness and stability. Jacob has had many experiences with stones, dating back to his first meeting with God at Bethel, and Heb. *’eḇen* has already been highlighted (28:11, 18, 22). There, the *’eḇen* was a pillow and a pillar. Here, the *’eḇen* is a personal God.

25 Names for deity continue with *the God of your father* and *Shaddai.* If my translation is correct, v. 24b-c described what Joseph's Lord did to Joseph's enemies. V. 25 begins to describe what Joseph's Lord will do for Joseph. He will be both Joseph's protector (v. 24) and his benefactor (vv. 25-26). The blessings ahead for Joseph include agricultural blessings (v. 25c-d) and family blessings (v. 25e).

Perhaps we should see some play on words in *Shaddai* (*šadday,* v. 25b) and *breasts* (*šāḏayim,* v. 25e). Also, the word *womb (reḥem)* would recall his own family history for Jacob. Once God opened Leah's womb (29:31), and subsequently Rachel's womb (30:22). These are gifts from above. Jacob received them. They are ahead, even in greater measure, for Joseph. One might have expected the order in v. 25e to be "the bounty of womb and breasts," that is, first the place in which the fetus is cradled, second the source of the newborn's nourishment. Elsewhere in the OT where these two nouns occur near each other "womb" precedes "breasts" (Job 3:11, 12; Hos. 9:14), except for Ps. 22:10b-11a (Eng. 9b-10a). The same order of the two words in Gen. 49 and Ps. 22 is found in an Ugaritic text (*UT,* 52 [*CTA*, 23]:13): *wšd šd ilm šd aṯrt wrḥm<y>,* "O breast, breast of the gods, breast of Asherah and the one of womb!" (Dahood, *RSP,* 3:156). *šāḏayim* may appear first in Gen. 49:25 to provide a similar sound to *šāmayim,* "heavens," occurring earlier in the verse; *rāḥam* also sounds similar in its ending to *t*^{e}*hôm,* "the deep."

26 In conclusion Jacob prays that the blessing of the patriarchs may be upon Joseph. Actually, they are to be *upon Joseph's head, on the skull of*

M. Pope, "Rainbow," *IDBS,* p. 725, who suggests the phallic symbolism in this verse by assuming, incorrectly in my judgment (see n. 9 above), that the reference is to Joseph rather than to his assailants.

27. Translation of J. Neusner, *Genesis Rabbah,* 3 vols. (Atlanta: Scholars, 1985), 3:369.

the Nazir. This connection of *head* and *Nazir* is interesting when one remembers that the uncut hair (on the head) of the Nazirite is his distinction (Num. 6), and, along with abstaining from wine, is a prohibition binding on both temporary Nazirites (Num. 6) and permanent Nazirites (Samson, Samuel).

The oracle begins by describing Joseph as the hunted, as engaging in war with the enemy. The oracle concludes with a reference to Joseph as a *nāzîr.* At least in the cases of Samson and Samuel, the Nazirite is connected with warfare (but about which Num. 6:1-21 says nothing). It is difficult to be certain whether Nazirites were a category of especially dedicated warriors. That Joseph (or the Joseph tribes) is styled as *the Nazir* is more than likely a metaphorical use of the term. Joseph stands "separated from his brothers."[28] It is Joseph's high rank, conferred on him by his father, rather than the following of any prescribed prohibitions, that sets him apart from his brothers. He who was once separated from his brothers through spite is now separated from his brothers by blessing.

11. BENJAMIN (49:27)

27 *"Benjamin:*[1] *A ravenous*[2] *wolf,*
devouring prey from[3] *morning,*
and until evening dividing spoil."[4]

Benjamin, Jacob's last-born, receives Jacob's last word of blessing. The animal metaphor chosen for Benjamin is not wide of the mark as an apt description of Benjamin's descendants. He is pictured as a wolf who during the day consumes

28. See J. Milgrom, "Nazirite," *EncJud,* 12:907-8; Gottwald, *Tribes of Yahweh,* p. 773 n. 458, for this an understanding of *n^e^zîr* in Gen. 49:26.

1. On the reading of Benjamin as a title ("Benjamin:") instead of "Benjamin is," see Andersen, *Hebrew Verbless Clause in the Pentateuch,* pp. 44, 55 (no. 31).

2. J. Obermann ("Survival of an Old Canaanite Participle and Its Impact on Biblical Exegesis," *JBL* 70 [1951] 204 n. 9) points to this verse as an instance of an asyndetic imperfect *(yiṭrāp̱)* used in an attributive sense when forming a relative clause; thus "a wolf (who) tears," i.e., "a ravenous wolf."

3. The two actions of v. 27b-c are concurrent. That is, during the night the wolf hunts for prey, which he then devours and divides during the day ("from morning and until evening") in his lair. See M. J. Dahood, *Bib* 45 (1964) 282-83; idem, "The Phoenician Background of Qoheleth," *Bib* 47 (1966) 281; idem, "Hebrew-Ugaritic Lexicography VIII," *Bib* 51 (1970) 392; idem, "Northwest Semitic Notes on Genesis," *Bib* 55 (1974) 82; idem, *Ugaritic-Hebrew Philology,* BibOr 17 (Rome: Pontifical Biblical Institute, 1965), p. 27. For another rendition cf. D. W. Young, "With Snakes and Dates," *UF* 9 (1977) 311.

4. On the tricolon with strong parallelism in the last two lines (A/B/B′) ("devouring prey" [B]/"dividing spoil" [B′]), see W. G. E. Watson, *Classical Hebrew Poetry,* JSOTSup 26 (Sheffield: JSOT, 1984), pp. 181, 183.

and divides with his lair the prey he has caught the night before. We saw in Gen. 46 that Benjamin has the most "little ones" to feed of Jacob's children. The saying points primarily to a future day when the tribe of Benjamin shall become a predataor, engage in military raids, and realize booty from its victories.

This characterization seems to be documented in the Benjamite judge Ehud (Judg. 3:15-30), and specifically his successful battle against the Transjordanian Moabites. Note also the description of the tribe of Benjamin in Judg. 20 and the tribe's strength in that premonarchical civil war against other tribes. They were able, for a while at least, to hold their own, though vastly outnumbered (Judg. 20:14-21). Later Benjamites had the reputation of being "mighty warriors, bowmen" (1 Chr. 8:40; 12:2). It is not difficult to understand, therefore, why Israel's first king should be drawn from the tribe of Benjamin, given its reputation for militancy (1 Sam. 9:1). Benjamin's safety is not in his prowess, however. The saying about Benjamin in Deut. 33:12c tells us where Benjamin's safety lies — it is in dwelling "between God's shoulders," i.e., on God's back. The picture may be that of a father carrying a son on his back, and hence a beautiful metaphor for God's protective, fatherly care of Benjamin.[5]

12. JACOB'S LAST INSTRUCTION (49:28-33)

28 *All these are the twelve tribes of Israel, and this is what their father said to them as he blessed them, blessing each with his own blessing.*[1]

29 *Then he gave them instructions, saying to them. "I will shortly be gathered*[2] *to my kin.*[3] *Inter me with*[4] *my fathers in the cave on Ephron the Hittite's plot of land,*

5. See J. D. Heck, "The Missing Sanctuary of Deut 33:12," *JBL* 102 (1984) 523-29. Cf. also R. G. Boling and G. E. Wright, *Joshua,* AB (Garden City, NY: Doubleday, 1982), pp. 432-34.

1. Lit., "each which according to his blessing he blessed them." LXX, Pesh., and 3 Hebrew mss. omit *'ᵃšer*.

2. On the use of the participle in a temporal/conditional clause in connection with a future event ("will shortly be gathered, inter me"), see Waltke and O'Connor, *Biblical Hebrew Syntax,* p. 628.

3. *'ammî* (MT) or *'ammay?* In v. 33 it is pl. (*'ammāyw*). The only reason for emending from a sing. pronominal suffix to a pl. is that the other 9 times this expression occurs in the OT (Gen. 25:8, 17; 35:29; 49:33; Num. 20:24; 27:13; 31:2; Deut. 32:50 [twice]) use the pl. pronominal suffix. It is not necessary, however, to level all biblical expressions to an exact phraseology and thus rob the writer of any opportunity to vary one's style. See R. M. Good, *The Sheep of His Pasture,* HSM 29 (Chico, CA: Scholars, 1983), p. 90.

4. For the use of *'el* in two asyndetic phrases (here "with . . . in") separated only by an *athnach* see S. E. McEvenue, *The Narrative Style of the Priestly Writer,* AnBib 50 (Rome: Pontifical Biblical Institute, 1971), p. 24.

30 *in the cave on the plot of land at Machpelah, east of Mamre, in the land of Canaan, the plot of land that Abraham purchased from Ephron the Hittite as a burial place —*

31 *That is where they interred Abraham and his wife Sarah, as well as Isaac and his wife Rebekah; and there I buried Leah —*

32 *the plot of land and the cave on it were purchased*[5] *from Heth's children."*

33 *When Jacob had finished giving instructions*[6] *to his sons, he drew his feet up onto the bed, took his last breath, and was gathered to his kin.*

28 This verse summarizes vv. 1-27, and clearly designates what Jacob has said to his sons as blessing. Three times some form of *brk* is used: *way*^{e}*ḇārēḵ, k*^{e}*ḇirḵāṯô, bērēḵ.* The narrator's statement also identifies, in colophon style, the sons of Jacob as the *tribes of Israel.* The distinguishing traits of the ancestor of the tribe extend into the life-style of the tribe that emanates from him. This is the third in a triad of Jacob's blessings. First was on Pharaoh (ch. 47), second on Joseph's children (ch. 48), and last on Jacob's sons.[7]

29-32 Unfortunately, most commentators (e.g., Westermann) isolate their discussion of 49:1-28a from 49:28b-33. Whether or not the two units go back to separate traditions, which is by no means certain, they share a common feature with each other (via contrast), and that is their time orientation. Vv. 1-28 focus primarily on Jacob's knowledge of the future, on the destiny of the tribes named for his sons. Vv. 29-32 focus on Jacob's recall of the past. He recalls the names of patriarchs and a matriarch, and even of a Hittite foreigner of two generations ago. He recalls the name of places *(the cave at Machpelah),* geography *(east of Mamre),* and business transactions expedited by his grandfather. Jacob is as sharp on his control of family history (vv. 29-32) as he is on

5. Perhaps one should read *miqnaṯ* for MT *miqnēh. miqnēh* is the construct of *miqneh,* "cattle." *miqnaṯ* is the construct of *miqnâ,* "purchase." See BDB, p. 889. Other possibilities would be *māqneh* (Hiphil participle) or *m*^{e}*qanneh* (Piel participle) but these are unlikely. *HALAT,* 2:594, leaves MT as is, but cites Gen. 49:32 as the only place in the OT where *miqneh* designates "landed property" *(Grundbesitz).* Elsewhere it refers to livestock property *(Viehbesitz).*

6. Of the many places where *ṣāwâ* occurs in the Pentateuch, most frequently in the Piel, this is the only time the LXX renders it by *epitáttō,* probably in order "to express the irrevocable character of the last wishes of a dying patriarch" (A. Pelletier, "L'autorité divine d'après le Pentateuque grec," *VT* 32 [1982] 240).

7. On the phenomenon of testamental blessings as a category of person blessing person, see C. W. Mitchell, *The Meaning of BRK "To Bless" in the Old Testament,* SBLDS 95 (Atlanta: Scholars, 1991), p. 112. See also R. E. Clements, *In Spirit and in Truth. Insights from Biblical Prayers* (Atlanta: John Knox, 1985), pp. 27-37, who notes the often thin line in the OT between prayer and prophecy.

his control of family prophecy (vv. 1-28). He is clear both about the distant future of his family and its descendants (vv. 1-28), and his own immediate future (vv. 28-33). In particular, Jacob's mention of *the land of Canaan* (v. 30) is significant; by now in the Joseph story this expression has become "the trump-card of the narrator, who uses this card to impress on his readers that Israel really has to settle in the land of Canaan and in no other country."[8]

33 Jacob joins those who "breathed their last, and then were gathered to their kindred." These formulae have been used already with Abraham (25:8), Ishmael (25:17), and with Isaac (35:29). Present with these three, but absent in the note about Jacob's passing in 49:33, is the verb "died." The emphasis is not on dying but on rejoining.[9] He gathered his feet beside him (Qal of *'āsap*),[10] then *was gathered to his kin* (Niphal of *'āsap̱*), after which Joseph *(yôsēp̱)* falls of the neck of his departed father (50:1).

8. N. P. Lemche, *The Canaanites and Their Land,* JSOTSup 110 (Sheffield: Sheffield Academic, 1991), p. 112.

9. See B. Alfrink, "L'expression *ne'ᵉsap 'el-'ammāyw,*" *OTS* 5 (1948) 118-31; N. J. Tromp, *Primitive Conceptions of Death and the Nether World in the Old Testament,* BibOr 21 (Rome: Pontifical Biblical Institute, 1969), pp. 168-69; T. J. Lewis, *Cults of the Dead in Ancient Israel and Ugarit,* HSM 39 (Atlanta: Scholars, 1989), pp. 164-65. The Bible appears to use different terms for three stages of the death process: one dies (here "took his last breath"), one is gathered to one's kin, and lastly one is buried. Thus "to be gathered to one's kin" takes place after dying but before burial, and carries with it the idea of "being reunited with one's ancestors." See J. Milgrom, *Numbers,* JPS Torah Commentary (Philadelphia: Jewish Publication Society, 1990), pp. 169-70. But if one understands "to be gathered to one's kin" as the antonymn of "to be cut off from one's kin" (Gen. 17:14; Exod. 12:15, 19; Lev. 7:25; etc.), the former expression could indicate death without guilt, just as the latter expression would indicate death with guilt. See Good, *Sheep of His Pasture,* pp. 90-92. The verb *'āsap̱* in the sense of "be gathered (to one's ancestors)" may also be attested at least once in Ugaritic. In the Keret text (*CTA,* 14), col. 1, much of which describes Keret's loss in quick succession of seven wives, lines 18-19 read: "the fifth Reseph carried off" *(mḫmšt yitsp ršp).* This is the translation of J. C. L. Gibson, *Canaanite Myths and Legends,* 2nd ed. (Edinburgh: T. & T. Clark, 1977), p. 82. Other translations of these three words are "One-fifth pestilence gathered unto itself" (Ginsberg, *ANET,* p. 143); "a fifth Rashap shall gather to himself" (W. F. Albright, "New Canaanite Historical and Mythological Data," *BASOR* 63 [1936] 27-28, 28 n. 17).

10. While the idiom *'āsap 'el* is common, it usually refers to the gathering of persons (Gen. 42:17; Josh. 2:18; 2 K. 23:1; 2 Chr. 34:28; Zech. 14:2), and once to the storing of food (Gen. 6:21). Here Jacob resumes a sleeping posture, almost fetal-like, on his deathbed.

N. THE DEATH OF JACOB AND JOSEPH (50:1-26)

1. JOSEPH MOURNS JACOB'S DEATH (50:1-6)

1 *Joseph flung himself*[1] *on his father's face and wept over him as he kissed him.*

2 *Then Joseph ordered*[2] *his servants who were physicians to embalm*[3] *his father, and the physicians embalmed Israel.*

3 *They finished their work in forty days, the time required for embalming;*[4] *the Egyptians mourned him for seventy days.*

4 *When the mourning period had passed, Joseph spoke to Pharaoh's representatives: "Please, if you would do me the kindness,*[5] *convey*[6] *to Pharaoh this request:*

5 *My father placed me under oath,*[7] *saying, 'I shall shortly die. In the*

1. Elsewhere in Genesis the expression for emotional outpouring, when both parties are living and presumably standing or sitting, is "and he fell on his neck" (33:4, Esau meeting Jacob; 45:14, Joseph meeting Benjamin; 47:29, Joseph meeting Jacob). Here is the one place where somebody (lit.) "falls on" *(nāpal ʿal)* somebody else's face. The translations range from Westermann's "he bent over his father's face" to Coote and Ord's (*Bible's First History* [Philadelphia: Fortress, 1989], p. 203) "he fell all over his father's face," to NEB's "Then Joseph throwing himself upon his father."

2. Both MT *(ṣāwâ)* and LXX *(prostáttō)* use the same verbs to render "ordered" in 47:11 (in Pharaoh's mouth) and in 50:2 (in Joseph's mouth). LXX, however, uses *epitáttō* to render *ṣāwâ* in 49:33 (in Jacob's mouth). Of *prostáttō* A. Pelletier notes: "This verb always preserves a certain emphasis due to the dignity of the one who commands: God, his priest, Moses, Pharaoh, Joseph" ("L'autorité divine d'après le Pentateuque grec," *VT* 32 [1982] 240).

3. The verb *ḥānaṭ* meaning "embalm" is used only in Gen. 50:2, 26. A verb with the same radicals appears in Cant. 2:13, "the fig ripens [*ḥnṭ*] her fruits" or "the fig tree spices its figs." The attraction of "spices" is that it allows for the connection between "embalm" and aromatic spices that were used in the embalming process. The translation "spices" is, however, suspect because figs are not distinguished by a spicy smell. A more appealing suggestion (at least for Cant. 2:13) is to connect *ḥānaṭ* with the Arabic factitive stem *ḥannaṭa,* applied to the ripening of fruits. Is the Hebrew word for "wheat," *ḥiṭṭâ* (from *ḥinṭâ*) related to this verb? If so, then the Hebrew word for "wheat" may be connected with this root by virtue of its coloration in ripening. See M. Pope, *Song of Songs,* AB (Garden City, NY: Doubleday, 1977), p. 397. Cf. also R. E. Murphy, *Song of Songs,* Hermeneia (Minneapolis: Fortress, 1990), pp. 76, 139. No Egyptian background is discernible for Heb. *ḥānaṭ* (see *HALAT,* 1:320a). The regular Egyptian word for "embalm" is *wt*.

4. An abstract pl. *(haḥᵃnuṭîm)*, lit., "the enbalmings."

5. Lit., "if I have found favor in your eyes." As in other places in Genesis (18:3; 33:10) and elsewhere (e.g., Judg. 6:17), the formal protasis *'im-nā' māṣā'ṯî ḥēn* at times assumes the sense of being a formula of entreaty.

6. LXX adds *perí emoú,* "for me, on my behalf."

7. On the contribution of the root *šbʿ* to the dynamics of vv. 2-5 see G. Giessen,

grave I hewed[8] *for myself in the land of Canaan, there you shall inter me.' Allow me now to go up and inter my father;*[9] *then I shall come back."*

6 *Pharaoh replied:*[10] *"Go and inter your father*[11] *as he placed you under oath."*

1 Joseph is the only one whose mourning over the death of his father is reported. What of his brothers? They are certainly experiencing grief equal to Joseph's. That Joseph alone *flung himself on his father's face* may be intended as a fulfillment of an earlier word to Jacob by God that it would be Joseph who would close the eyes of his father (46:4). It would appear that "such honor is reserved beforehand to the survivor acknowledged to have been closest to the departed."[12] All weepings of Joseph thus far have been weepings of joy — he is reunited with his brothers, with Benjamin, then with his father. This weeping is one of sorrow. Earlier, when his father was still alive, Joseph "fell on his father's neck" (46:29). In Jacob's death Joseph literally "falls on his father's face.

2 Joseph gives orders to have his father embalmed, and those to whom this assignment is given are called *physicians* (*hārōp̄eʾîm,* lit., "the healers"). The LXX rendered the Hebrew word with *hoi entaphiastaí,* "those who bury." However, embalmers are not those who bury a body, but those who prepare a body for burial. There is no evidence that physicians officiated at the embalming, although they may have gained valuable knowledge of physiology and anatomy for their practice of medicine from the embalming practices of the Egyptians. This procedure was mostly a religious observance, and therefore a priestly function. But in view of the frequent use of magical incantations and spells as a part of the praxis of ancient medicine, it is likely that Egyptian physicians served

Die Wurzel šbʿ "schworen," Bonner biblische Beiträge 56 (Bonn: Hanstein, 1981), pp. 105-6. After the verb *hišbîʿanî* SP adds "before his death."

8. Pesh. reads "which I purchased" *(qānîṯî).* LXX reads "which I dug" *(ṓryxa).* The latter translation connects *kārîṯî* with *kārâ* I, "to dig"; the former with *kārâ* II, "to buy," found in Deut. 2:6; Hos. 3:2 (on which see the extensive note in F. I. Andersen and D. N. Freedman, *Hosea,* AB [Garden City, NY: Doubleday, 1983], pp. 298-99); Neh. 5:8; Isa. 57:8 (perhaps); and finally Job 6:27; 40:30, with the meaning "barter." On the use of *kārâ* I, meaning to dig a well, see Gen. 26:25. The verb is again used in 2 Chr. 16:14 in connection with one's grave: "They buried him [Asa] in his grave chamber which he *had cut out* for himself in the city of David" (translation of J. M. Myers, *I & II Chronicles,* AB [Garden City, NY: Doubleday, 1965], p. 92).

9. SP adds "as he placed me under oath," as in the first part of the verse.

10. LXX adds "to Joseph," i.e., indirectly, for Joseph sent a delegation to Pharaoh.

11. On the use of the imperative to grant permission after a cohortative to express a wish or a request ("allow me to go up and inter"), and hence my translation of *wayyōʾmer* by "replied," see Waltke and O'Connor, *Biblical Hebrew Syntax,* p. 572.

12. E. I. Lowenthal, *The Joseph Narrative in Genesis* (New York: Ktav, 1973), p. 147.

in some kind of a priestly capacity. Embalming was, above all, a religious ritual, and one in which such medical/priestly personnel would be involved.

One of the first acts in the embalming process was cutting a long slit down the side of the abdomen so that certain viscera could be removed. According to the first-century B.C. Roman historian Diodorus (*Histories* 1.91), the person who made this cut was called "the so-called one who slits" *(legómenos paraschiótēs).* This was this person's only responsibility in the embalming process. Is this where Gen. 50:2 gets its designation "physicians" — associating those who make an incision into the body with the art of medicine? That is unlikely; in such a case the writer, if referring to those who make the incision, could easily have used a derivative of any word meaning "cut."

The Egyptian verb for "embalm" is, as noted above, *wt.* In the medical literature of Egypt this verb has another meaning. It may be used to describe wrapping the mummy in bandages. The Egyptian medical profession adopted this word as a way of saying "bind up with a bandage" or "wrap with a poultice." The noun designates a "binder [of wounds]." Applied to Gen. 50:2, it is possible to see that in the sense they were "bandagers," the morticians who embalmed Jacob could be called *physicians.*[13]

3 It took the embalmers *forty days* (a frequently used biblical number)[14] to complete their work. Interestingly, *the Egyptians mourned him for seventy days.* More than likely this is not seventy more days after the completion of the embalming. Rather, the period of mourning extends beyond the embalming process by thirty days. Diodorus (*Histories* 1.72) informs us that the period of mourning in Egypt for a king was seventy-two days. Might there be any connection between the seventy days of mourning for Jacob and Jacob's seventy descendants (46:27)? Seventy years is a popular time period in the OT, but not seventy days.[15]

Are we to believe that the entire nation of Egypt went into mourning for two-and-a-half months for a transplanted Hebrew living in Goshen? This must be something mandated by Pharaoh as an expression of his respect for the father of the son who saved his empire from starvation.

13. I have gleaned most of my information on v. 2 from W. A. Ward, "Egyptian Titles in Genesis 39–50," *Bib Sac* 114 (1957) 55-59. See also Redford, *Study of the Biblical Story of Joseph,* pp. 240-41; Vergote, *Joseph en Égypte,* pp. 197-200; C. R. Youngblood, "The Embalming Process in Ancient Egypt," *Biblical Illustrator* 14/2 (1988) 80-83.

14. See Gen. 7:17; 8:6; Num. 13:25; 1 Sam. 17:16. For "forty days and nights" see Gen. 7:4, 12; Exod. 24:18, 34:28; Deut. 9:9, 11, 18, 25; 10:10; 1 K. 19:8. "Forty" occurred earlier in the Jacob story — the forty cows Jacob sent ahead to Esau (Gen. 32:16 [Eng. 13]), one of only three places in the OT (see also Deut. 25:3; 2 K. 8:9) where the number "40" is applied to something other than a unit of time.

15. Mourning would ordinarily last 7 days among the Hebrews and their forefathers (Gen. 50:10; 1 Sam. 31:13), but could be extended to 30 days when mourning the death of individuals of renown such as Moses (Deut. 34:8) and Aaron (Num. 20:29).

4 Joseph, who otherwise seems to have direct access to Pharaoh, now goes through intermediaries. Perhaps he is hesitant to approach Pharaoh directly because of his recent contact with the corpse of his father. Here one might compare Esth. 4:2. Mordecai has torn his clothes and put on sackcloth and ashes upon hearing of Haman's plan to destroy all the Jews. V. 2 states that Mordecai, in such a condition, could come only as far as the King's Gate, for no one in sackcloth was allowed to enter the King's Gate, i.e., the palace door.

Joseph's *if you would do me the kindness* (lit., "if I have found favor in your eyes") is the same expression his father used with him on his deathbed, and with which he prefaced a request (47:29). In preparation for my comments on Joseph's effective use of quotation in v. 5, note that he has shifted Jacob's *'im-nā' māṣā'ṯî ḥēn* (47:29), part of Jacob's entreaty to Joseph, to his own entreaty to Pharaoh, rather than including it in the quotation.

5 Joseph repeats the oath that he made to Jacob (*šāḇa'* is used in 47:31 and 50:5). He leaves out at least two things from that original conversation with his father. He repeats nothing like "my father had me place my hand under his thigh" — hardly an intelligible phrase to Pharaoh. Nor does Joseph repeat these words of his father: "do not bury me in Egypt . . . carry me out of Egypt." Joseph does not want to make it appear in any way that his father has a disliking for Egypt, or is in any way ungrateful. Egypt has been a great place to live. It just is not the best place to be interred. It was crucial for Jacob that he be allowed to lie with his fathers (47:30).[16] Joseph also shifts Jacob's "bury me in my fathers' burying place" to *In the grave I hewed for myself in the land of Canaan, there you shall inter me*. By deleting the part of Jacob's request that has ancestral, religious aspects and replacing it with a reference to Jacob's own prepared gravesite in another country, Joseph may have been trying to make his request to Pharaoh more appealing, given the emphasis an Egyptian would place on his own burial place, stocking it with the necessary requirements for the good life in the hereafter.[17]

6 Pharaoh is agreeable and is impressed by Joseph's filial devotion. Joseph has given his word that he will return. Pharaoh believes him, and he also believes that once a promise is made, it must be fulfilled. Thus Joseph is party to two promises — a promise to his father to bury him in Canaan, and a promise to his superior not to use this family matter as a means of permanently leaving Egypt. In his answer to Joseph's request, Pharaoh repeats Joseph's words with *Go and inter your father as he placed you under oath,* and he stops there. He does not end

16. This expression "to lie with the fathers" occurs 40 times in the OT, and in all but two (the death of Jacob, 47:30; the death of Moses, Deut. 1:16) it is used in connection with the death of kings. See also G. A. Lee, "Gather," *ISBE,* 2:414, and bibliography cited there.

17. See G. W. Savran, *Telling and Retelling* (Bloomington: Indiana University, 1988), p. 43.

with "and then come back to me," as Joseph said he would. This is another indication of Pharaoh's implicit trust in Joseph's truthfulness.

2. JOSEPH BURIES HIS FATHER IN CANAAN (50:7-14)

7 *So Joseph went up to inter his father, and with him went up all of Pharaoh's subordinates,*[1] *senior members of his household, as well as every dignitary*[2] *in the land of Egypt,*

8 *and all Joseph's household,*[3] *his brothers, and his father's household.*[4] *Only their little ones,*[5] *sheep, and cattle did they leave behind in the land of Goshen.*

9 *Chariots and horsemen went up with him too; it was a very large retinue.*[6]

10 *When they reached Goren-ha-atad,*[7] *which is in the region*[8] *of the*

1. Lit., "Pharaoh's servants," which Speiser renders "officials" and Westermann "courtiers."

2. "Senior members" and "dignitary" translate, respectively, *ziqnê bēṯô,* lit., "elders of his household," and *ziqnê 'ereṣ-miṣrāyim,* lit., "elders of the land of Egypt." See Speiser, *Genesis,* p. 376. I am inclined to believe that the phrase "Pharaoh's subordinates" is a general one, explicated by the two subsequent phrases, "senior members of his household" and "every dignitary in the land of Egypt." If, in contrast, they represent three groups of personnel, then the listing of "servants" before "elders" would suggest the (unlikely) superiority of the former to the latter. See T. M. Willis, "Yahweh's Elders (Isa 24,23): Senior Officials of the Divine Court," *ZAW* 103 (1991) 378 and n. 11.

3. LXX's rendering of *wᵉḵōl bêṯ* by *kaí pása hē panoikía* provides an instance of the use of a double translation *(pasa, pan-),* in which the Hebrew phrase is rendered by one compound term in the Greek *(panoikía),* but one of the components of the compound term is repeated *(pasa).* See Z. Talshir, "Double Translations in the Septuagint," in *VI Congress of the International Organization for Septuagint and Cognate Studies,* ed. C. E. Cox (Atlanta: Scholars, 1987), pp. 33-34, who argues that such doublets are best explained on account of the desire to render the Hebrew text as literally as possible.

4. Pesh. adds "went up with him," apparently repeating the *wayya'ᵃlû 'ittô* of the preceding verse. The first part of the verse distinguishes among Joseph's household (which must be understood as a nuclear family), his brothers, and Jacob's household. It is not clear, however, whether the verse implies that the families of Joseph's brothers were also units that had separated from their father's house. See N. P. Lemche, *Early Israel,* VTSup 37 (Leiden: Brill, 1985), p. 254.

5. While signifying primarily small children, *ṭap* might include women as well. See D. Daube, *The Exodus Pattern in the Bible* (London: Faber and Faber, 1963), pp. 47-48.

6. Lit., "camp," which Speiser renders "train" and Westermann "company." This is the only place where the noun refers to a funeral company (BDB, p. 334). For *maḥᵃneh* as a large body of people rather than an encampment, see Gen. 33:8; Num. 2:9; 1 Sam. 13:17; Ps. 27:3.

7. Or, "when they reached the threshing floor [*gōren*] of Atad"; or, "when they

Jordan, they raised a loud and solemn lament; and he observed for his father a seven-day period of mourning.

11 *When the inhabitants of the land, the Canaanites, saw the mourning at Goren-ha-atad, they said: "How grievously the Egyptians are mourning!"*[9] *So the place was called*[10] *Abel-mizraim.*[11] *It is in the region of the Jordan.*

12 *His sons expedited all his wishes.*[12]

13 *His sons carried him to the land of Canaan and interred him in the cave on the plot of land at Machpelah, the piece of property that Abraham had purchased as a burial site from Ephron the Hittite. It is in the vicinity of*[13] *Mamre.*

14 *Then Joseph returned to Egypt — he, his brothers, and everyone who accompanied him to inter his father — after he had interred his father.*[14]

---

reached the threshing floor of the bramble [*hā'āṭāḏ*]." *'āṭāḏ* occurs only in Judg. 9:14, 15 and Ps. 58:10 (Eng. 9).

8. See B. Gemser, "*Be'ēber hajjardēn:* in Jordan's Borderland," *VT* 2 (1952) 349-55.

9. On the force of this nominal clause see J. Hoftijzer, "The nominal clause reconsidered," *VT* 23 (1973) 498. It reads lit., "a mourning, heavy, [is] this for the Egyptians." Hoftijzer remarks, "the core sequence leaves no doubt that the only fitting description of this mourning is that it is a grievous mourning." For *kāḇēḏ* meaning "oppressive, grievous," see BDB, p. 458.

10. The verb is a 3rd sing. perfect (*qārā',* "he named") used impersonally. It is the only perfect verb form in the immediate context. All the other verbs around it are imperfects with *waw.* According to B. O. Long (*The Problem of Etiological Narrative in the Old Testament,* BZAW 108 [Berlin: de Gruyter, 1968], pp. 13-14), the *qāṭal* form of the verb brings to an end the narrative movement in the clause explaining the origin of the name.

11. Lit., "mourning of Egypt." Another Hebrew word, *'āḇēl,* means "meadow" or "brook" (Num. 33:49; Judg. 11:33; 2 Sam. 20:15; 2 Chr. 16:4). It is the first part of the name of a number of towns in Canaan: Abel-beth-maachah ("meadow near Beth-maachah," 2 Sam. 20:15); Abel-keramim ("meadow of vineyards," Judg. 11:33); Abel-mayim ("meadow of waters," 2 Chr. 16:4); Abel-meholah ("meadow of dance," Judg. 7:22; 1 K. 4:12; 19:16); Abel-shitim ("meadow of acacia," Num. 33:49). Accordingly Abel-mizraim is lit., "meadow (or brook) of Egypt." See W. F. Albright, "Two Little Understood Amarna Letters from the Middle Jordan Valley," *BASOR* 89 (1943) 15 n. 44, for explication of "Yabilima" as a town meaning "Streams," and its relationship with *'āḇēl.* We are, however, dealing with two different words here, *'ēḇel,* "mourning" (vv. 10a, 11a-b), and *'āḇēl,* "meadow," in Abel-mizraim, v. 11c. Note, however, that *'āḇēl* is a good Hebrew word meaning "mourning" (see Gen. 37:35; Esth. 6:12; Lam. 1:4; Job 29:25 [?]; Ps. 35:14; Isa. 57:18; 61:2, 3). A similar pun on a place name using the root *'bl* occurs in Ugaritic (*UT,* 3 Aqht obv. 8 [= *CTA,* 18.IV.8]: *qrt ablm ablm* [*qrt zbl yrḫ*], "the city of mourners, Abiluma, [the City of Prince Moon]."

12. LXX adds, "and interred him there," which anticipates v. 13.

13. See J. F. Drinkard, Jr., "*'AL PĔNÊ* as 'East of,' " *JBL* 98 (1979) 286 n. 18.

14. This last phrase is missing in LXX. Westermann (*Genesis,* 3:197) argues that

7-9 Three different groups participate in Jacob's funeral procession: (1) high-ranking members of Pharaoh's bureaucracy, v. 7; (2) male survivors of Jacob's family, v. 8 (what of Leah and his concubines — are they still living?);[15] (3) a military escort, v. 9. The largeness of the procession is reinforced by the threefold use of *kōl* in vv. 7 and 8. The third group is particularly interesting. The chariots *(reḵeḇ)* and horsemen *(pārāšîm),* who accompany the deceased Israel to his place of burial as a sign of respect and honor, may be compared with later chariots and horsemen who pursue Israel (the nation) as they leave for Canaan, with the intent of overtaking them (Exod. 14:9, 17, 18, 23, 26, 28).

That the military escort is described as *hammaḥ*ᵃ*neh kāḇēḏ m*ᵉ*'ōḏ, a very large retinue* (lit., "camp"), has earlier echoes in the Jacob narrative. While he was still alive, Jacob found himself in the midst of other military camps (cf. 32:3, 8, 9, 11 [Eng. 2, 7, 8, 10]), one a divine camp, the other a camp of his own making. There is also a contrast between this Egyptian retinue that accompanies Jacob, and a later *maḥ*ᵃ*nēh miṣrayim* that wishes to capture Jacob's descendants (Exod. 14:20).

10 The procession makes its way from Egypt to Canaan. A number of well-known sites might have been mentioned as falling within the itinerary, but no famous cities are mentioned. The only place at which the funeral march halted was Goren-ha-atad. Here they remained for seven days while Joseph mourned his father's passing. Seven days was the normal period for mourning (see 1 Sam. 31:13 par. 1 Chr. 10:12; 2 Sam. 11:27; Job 2:13; Jdt. 16:24; Sir. 10:12).[16] The thirty days of mourning for Moses (Deut. 34:8) and for Aaron (Num. 20:29) are exceptional. Other texts refer to fasting as part of the mourning ceremony. For example, 2 Sam. 1:12 records a one-day fast by David after the death of Saul and Jonathan, and 1 Sam. 31:13 speaks of a seven-day fast performed by the residents of Jabesh-gilead after the burial of the bones of Saul and his three sons. Perhaps mourning included a number of acts, of which fasting would only be one, and hence the reason for not mentioning it explicitly in v. 10.[17] I fail to see any significance in the fact that the entourage's expression of grief is conveyed by the noun *mispēḏ (lament),* while Joseph's own expression of grief is conveyed by

---

these words are not a gloss and may have intentionally been written at the end for emphasis.

15. See n. 5 above.

16. The seven days of mourning may be compared with the seven days of birth preceding circumcision (17:12), the seven days of marriage (29:27), and the seven days of consecration of the priests (Lev. 8:33), all of which seem to refer to what today would be called rites of passage. See J. Milgrom, *Leviticus 1–16,* AB (New York: Doubleday, 1991), p. 538.

17. See H. A. Brongers, "Fasting in Israel in Biblical and Post-Biblical Times," *OTS* 20 (1977) 4.

'ēḇel (mourning).[18] The camp's number is "great, very large" (*kāḇēḏ,* v. 9), as is their lamenting (*kāḇēḏ,* v. 10). The Canaanites also perceive the grieving to be "great, grievous" (*kāḇēḏ,* v. 11).

The site *Goren-ha-atad* is unidentifiable. This is the only place in the OT where it is mentioned. It is described as being *bᵉʿēḇer hayyardēn,* for which most translations have "beyond the Jordan," that is, Transjordan or East Jordan. If we retain that translation, then that means that the funeral march did not take the normal route from Egypt to Canaan, but — for some unknown reason — took a detour and traveled around the Dead Sea and up the east side of the Jordan, much as a later march of Jacob's descendants did under Moses' leadership. After the seven-day grieving period, the party continued on to Hebron, by either crossing the Jordan or by swinging around the lower tip of the Dead Sea.

Some exegetes suggest that vv. 10-11 are a cryptic reference to a burial of Jacob east of the Jordan. This material from J (vv. 1-11, 14) is then seen to clash with P (vv. 12-13), which reports Jacob's burial at Hebron in the patriarchal, family tomb. For example, Noth makes much of Gen. 50:10 for further support for his contention of a special East Jordan Jacob tradition.[19]

This position has two problems. First, v. 11 identifies the residents of Goren-ha-atad as *Canaanites.* This would be the only instance in the OT where peoples living east of the Jordan are so identified. Second, because v. 10 reports only a mourning for Jacob at Goren-ha-atad, but not a burial of Jacob there, exegetes holding this position have to assume that a later editor, faced with two patently contradicting traditions, defused the contradiction by excising the report of Jacob's burial from v. 10. The critics, however, would be the first to say that later editors did not normally feel free to alter their traditions in such a way, nor did they feel any hesitancy in allowing duplications to stand. As noted above (see fn. 8), Gemser has made a strong case for reading *bᵉʿēḇer hayyardēn* as *in the region of the Jordan,* and the phrase is comparable to *ʿal-pᵉnê (in the vicinity of)* in v. 13. This interpretation allows for a location of Goren-ha-atad on either side of the Jordan. Thus it is incorrect to say that a sixth-century A.D. mosaic map at Medeba indicating an Alon Atad ("terebinth of Atad") near Beth Agla, between Jericho and the Dead Sea, cannot be the Atad of Gen. 50:10, 11, for "it is on the wrong side of the Jordan."[20]

11 The funeral party's mourning must have included actions as well

18. For *'ēḇel* to express a son's mourning for his father, see Gen. 27:41. For the two words in parallelism cf. Mic. 1:8cd, RSV: "I will make lamentation [*mispēḏ*] like the jackals, and mourning [*wᵉ'ēḇel*] like the ostriches."

19. See M. Noth, *History of Pentateuchal Traditions,* tr. B. W. Anderson (Englewood Cliffs, NJ: Prentice-Hall, 1972), pp. 88-89.

20. As argued by G. H. Oller, "Atad," *ABD,* 1:508. See also S. Cohen, "Atad," *IDB,* 1:305, who suggests that the viewpoint is from Transjordan, and thus "beyond" means "west of."

as words, for it is something the local residents *saw* rather than "heard." In addition to weeping or crying, clothes might be torn and sackcloth donned (Gen. 37:34; 2 Sam. 1:11). There might be fasting (2 Sam. 1:12). Some people might be walking around bareheaded and barefoot (Ezek. 24:17). Some may be lacerating themselves (Jer. 16:6) or shaving their hair (Ezek. 7:18).

Upon seeing this ritual, the residents state: *How grievously the Egyptians are mourning!* Moved by this scene, they rename the vicinity *Abel-mizraim,* thus providing another instance of etiological narrative in Genesis.[21] There is no indication that the Goren-ha-atadites have any knowledge of who is being mourned. It is not the identity of the deceased but rather the identity of the mourners that catches the attention of the local citizenry. Thus the new name is not Abel-ya'aqob (mourning of Jacob), but *Abel-mizraim.* The word *'āḇēl* had been used earlier when describing Jacob's emotions over the apparent loss of son Joseph (37:35).

12 Jacob's sons are unexpectedly reintroduced to the narrative. Just about everything thus far in the chapter has been carried out by Joseph. Yet 49:29 reminds us that Jacob had given last-minute orders to all of his sons about his burial.

13-14 The sons carry out their father's last wish. They bury him in the cave of Machpelah where Jacob's father, and grandfather, and one of his wives (Leah) are buried. Thus Jacob leaves one part of his family and joins another part of his family. Perhaps the recall of Abraham's purchase[22] of this real estate from Ephron the Hittite (see Gen. 23) is prompted by the use of the word *'ᵃḥuzzâ* ("burial site"). For the last seventeen years Jacob has lived on an *'ᵃḥuzzâ* in Egypt, courtesy of Pharaoh (47:11). Now Jacob is giving up not only one part of his family for another part of his family, but one *'ᵃḥuzzâ* for another *'ᵃḥuzzâ.* "Life in the land first becomes possible through a grave; through a grave the group put down roots in the land. The grave is the maternal origin and the final refuge."[23]

Joseph honors the promise he earlier made to Pharaoh (v. 5). He has honored a promise made to his father. He now follows that with honoring a promise made to his superior. In every instance Joseph is a man of his word. But can Pharaoh be certain of that? Representatives of Pharaoh (v. 7) plus chariots and horsemen (v. 9) provide not only a larger cast of mourners and protection for this funeral cortege, but also function as deterrents should Joseph decide to stay in Canaan. Note that in vv. 7, 8 the mention of members of Jacob's household (v. 8) follows the mention of the Egyptian participants.

21. See Long, *Problem of Etiological Narrative,* pp. 13-14.

22. Throughout Gen. 23 the verb *nāṯan* is used for buying (23:4) and selling (23:11) property, and means "give for money." Other references (29:10; 49:30; and here in 50:13) use the verb *qānâ,* "to buy, purchase," making clear that Abraham acquired his grave site by purchase.

23. H. Gese, *Essays on Biblical Theology,* tr. K. Crim (Minneapolis: Augsburg, 1981), p. 37.

Conversely, in v. 14 mention of members of Jacob's household precedes mention of the Egyptian participants. Yet, although there are many returnees, the emphasis of v. 14 is on Joseph's return, highlighted by the use of a singular verb *(wayyāšāḇ)* rather than a plural one.

3. THE WILL OF GOD TRIUMPHS IN ADVERSITY (50:15-21)

15 *When Joseph's brothers saw*[1] *that their father was deceased, they said: "Joseph surely*[2] *will loathe*[3] *us, and requite*[4] *us for all the harm we did*[5] *to him!"*

16 *They dispatched a message*[6] *to Joseph, saying: "Your father left these instructions before he died:*

1. MT *wayyir'û* is an ambiguous form. If from *r'h,* it means "they saw"; but if from *yr',* it means "they were afraid" (1 Sam. 4:7; 7:7; etc.). But thus far in Genesis, the 3rd pl. form of *yr'* ("and they were afraid") has been written *wayyîrᵉ'û* (20:8; 43:18) or *wayyîrā'û* (pausal, 42:35). There is no good reason for emending the MT. Here "see" must have the sense of "knowing"; it cannot mean "to observe with the eye," for the brothers have already been present at their father's interment.

2. I take *lû* as asseverative in meaning. See F. Nötscher, "Zum emphatischen Lamed," *VT* 3 (1953) 374 ("Surely Joseph will show hostility toward us"); G. R. Driver, "Notes on Two Passages in the Odes of Solomon," *JQR* 25 (1974) 435. Others would take *lû* as optative or conditional, here introducing a conditional protasis ("if Joseph were to turn on us"), but with the apodosis absent. See GKC, § 159y; R. Gordis, *Koheleth — The Man and His World,* 3rd ed. (New York: Schocken, 1968), p. 259; J. Huehnergard, "Asseverative *la* and Hypothetical *lu/law* in Semitic," *JAOS* 103 (1983) 571. The difference between the two comes down to how sure the brothers are of forthcoming revenge by Joseph. Is it for certain ("surely"), or is it hypothetical ("what if")? The brothers' measures, narrated in the following verses, incline me to think that they are trying to fend off an inevitable retribution.

3. The root *śṭm* has been used twice so far in Genesis, once with Jacob as object (27:41), once with Joseph as object (49:23). The more popular verb for "hate" *(śānē')* is used in 24:60; 26:27; 29:31, 33; 37:4, 5, 8. See my earlier comments on this verb in 49:23, which might explain the preference for *śāṭam* over *śānē'* here.

4. Lit., "he shall surely return" *(hāšēḇ yāšîḇ). šûḇ* may carry implications of requital. See P. K. McCarter, Jr., *I Samuel,* AB (Garden City, NY: Doubleday, 1980), pp. 132-33. See other passages cited by W. L. Holladay, *The Root Šûbh in the Old Testament* (Leiden: Brill, 1958), p. 95. Note the back-to-back use of *šûḇ* in v. 14 (Qal) and v. 15 (Hiphil). Joseph will return to Egypt (v. 14), and may return vengeance (v. 15) on his brothers. One of the closer parallels to *šûḇ* in this verse is 1 Sam. 25:21, in which David laments that Nabal has returned him evil for good *(wayyāšeḇ lî rā'â taḥaṯ ṭôḇâ).* Both verses use the Hiphil of *šûḇ,* followed by the preposition *lᵉ* plus pronominal suffix, and the noun *rā'â.* In David's case, the verb *šûḇ* deals with returning evil for good. In the brothers' case, the verb deals with returning evil for evil, or as we would say today, "tit for tat."

5. The verb for "doing" evil in vv. 15 and 17 is *gāmal.* For other instances of "render [*gāmal*] good/evil" cf. 1 Sam. 24:18; Isa. 63:7; Prov. 3:30; 31:12. The verb is sometimes used to express retribution of a judicial kind (2 Sam. 19:37; 22:21; Joel 4:4

17 *Speak thus to Joseph, 'Forgive, I implore you, the crime of your brothers and their sin,*[7] *for*[8] *they treated you so harmfully.' So now,*[9] *forgive*[10] *the crime of the servants of your father's God." Joseph broke into tears upon hearing their words to him.*

18 *At that the brothers also*[11] *went in and fell before him, saying, "See,*[12] *let us be your slaves."*

19 *Then Joseph remarked to them: "Do not be afraid. God's surrogate am I?*[13]

[Eng. 3:4]; Ps. 13:6 [Eng. 5]). See K. Seybold, "Zwei Bemerkungen zu *gmwl/gml,*" *VT* 22 (1972) 112-17; A. Lauha, "'Dominus beneficit.' Die Wortwurzel *gml* und die Psalmenfrömmigkeit," *ASTI* 11 (1977-78) 57-62.

6. Lit., "they instructed, commanded" *(way^{e}ṣawwû).* LXX reads "they approached" *(paregénonto),* which would reflect Heb. *wayyigg^{e}šû.* The Hebrew may be retained as is, for *ṣawwâ* also means "to send a message," as in Exod. 6:13; Jer. 27:4; Esth. 3:12. Where the verb has this meaning, it is normally followed by an object, then the prepositional phrase introduced by *'el,* as illustrated by Exod. 6:13 *(way^{e}ṣawwēm 'el).* Esth. 3:12 shows that the verb may carry the same meaning, even if the accusative (of the person) is omitted, as in Gen. 50:16.

7. The pair *pš'* ("crime") and *ḥṭ'* ("sin") occur in syndetic parataxis (here, Exod. 34:7; Job 13:23; Isa. 1:28); in syndetic combination (Jer. 33:8 [where the order is *ḥṭ'* . . . *pš'*]; Dan. 9:24); in parallelism (Ps. 32:1; Isa. 43:27 *[ḥṭ' . . . pš'];* Mic. 1:5). Jacob used both words earlier when he inquired angrily of Laban about the nature of his crime/offense *(piš'î)* and sin *(ḥaṭṭā'ṯî)* in Gen. 31:36. On this pair of roots see Avishur, *Stylistic Studies of Word-Pairs,* p. 285.

8. Some would translate *kî* as concessive, "forgive . . . even though they did evil to you." See T. C. Vriezen, "Einige Notizen zur Übersetzung des Bindeswort *kî,*" *Von Ugarit nach Qumran,* Fest. O. Eissfeldt, ed. J. Hempel and L. Rost, BZAW 77 (Berlin: Töpelmann, 1958), p. 267. But the more usual causal sense is quite plausible. See A. Schoors, "The Particle *kî,*" *OTS* 21 (1981) 271-72; A. Aejmelaeus, "Function and Interpretation of *kî* in Biblical Hebrew," *JBL* 105 (1986) 205, 207. Cf. Dan. 9:9 for a parallel to Gen. 50:17. Aejmelaeus well remarks (p. 207), "sin is not a concession to forgiveness, but rather the reason for the need of forgiveness."

9. M. Weinfeld (*Deuteronomy and the Deuteronomic School* [repr. Winona Lake, IN: Eisenbrauns, 1992], pp. 175-76) notes that the expression *w^{ec}attâ,* attributed to Jacob in v. 17 and later used by Joseph himself (v. 21), occurs frequently in Deuteronomic orations to indicate a turning point (e.g., Deut. 4:1), as it is in the speeches of the teaching, wise father in Proverbs as he addresses his child (Prov. 5:7; 7:24).

10. Although the verb *nāśā'* occurs frequently in the OT with "sin" meaning to "forgive" (see references under BDB, p. 671, § 3.c), only three times does it involve one person asking forgiveness from another person: here, Pharaoh from Moses (Exod. 10:17), Saul from Samuel (1 Sam. 15:25). The one whose forgiveness is sought is assumed to be one who has been favored by God. See J. Milgrom, *Leviticus 1–16,* AB (New York: Doubleday, 1991], p. 623.

11. The inclusion of *gam* shows that two different groups came to see Joseph: first the messengers, then the brothers. See Andersen, *Sentence in Biblical Hebrew,* p. 162.

12. For *hinnennû* instead of the expected *hin^{e}nû* (Josh. 9:25; 2 Sam. 5:1; Jer. 3:22, Ezra 9:15) see GKC, § 58k, for the uncontracted forms of pronominal suffix with *nun.*

13. Lit., "instead of/in place of God am I?"

20 *You have done*[14] *something malicious against me; God*[15] *has done something beneficial in order that he might do what has now happened*[16] *— the survival of many people.*

21 *So now, do not be afraid. I will provide*[17] *for you and your little ones." Thus he consoled*[18] *them by speaking affectionately.*[19]

15 The text says that the brothers *saw* that Jacob was dead. This cannot mean that they learned for the first time that their father was not alive, unless we accept a flagrant disagreement between vv. 1-11, 14 (J) — the brothers went with Joseph to Canaan to bury their father — and vv. 15-21 (E).[20] *saw*

14. Here *ḥāšaḇ* means more than "plan, devise." It includes the actual implementation of those plans, and thus means something like "do, realize." See J. Hoftijzer, "David and the Tekoite woman," *VT* 20 (1970) 434.

15. Most modern versions (e.g., RSV) insert a bland "and [i.e., but] God intended something beneficial." The asyndetic form is more powerful in drawing the contrast. On the thrust of the antithetical clause in apposition with asyndeton, see Andersen, *Sentence in Biblical Hebrew,* pp. 57, 153.

16. Lit., "in order that he might do as this day." S. J. DeVries (*Yesterday, Today and Tomorrow* [Grand Rapids: Eerdmans, 1975], p. 52 n. 77) says, "*kayyôm hazzeh* compares a past saving act with present good in Gen. 50:20, Deut. 2:30, 4:20, 38, 8:18, 10:15, 1 Kings 3:6, 8:24 = II Chron. 6:15, Jer. 11:5, 32:20." Similarly, Weinfeld, *Deuteronomy and the Deuteronomic School,* p. 175: "The speakers employ this term when recalling past events with specific reference to their own present time."

17. N. Avigad ("The Contribution of Hebrew Seals to an Understanding of Israelite Religion and Society," in *Ancient Israelite Religion,* Fest. F. M. Cross, ed. P D. Miller, Jr., P. D. Hanson, and S. Dean McBride [Philadelphia: Fortress, 1987], p. 196) observes that one of the names appearing on a Hebrew seal (8th to 6th century B.C.?) is *klklyhw,* "Yahweh has sustained/provided for," which he connects with the use of *kûl* in the Pilpel in Gen. 45:11 and 50:21, and with the proper name Chalcol in 1 Sam. 5:11.

18. For *yᵉnaḥēm* see H. Van Dyke Parunak, "A Semantic Survey of *NḤM,*" *Bib* 56 (1975) 512-32.

19. Lit., "and spoke to (or upon) their heart." G. Fischer notes that the expression is used in difficult situations, or where there is the smell of danger, or where there is guilt ("Die Redewendung *dbr 'al-lb* im AT — Ein Beitrag zum Verstandnis von Jes 40,2," *Bib* 65 [1984] 244-50). In Gen. 34:3; Judg. 19:3; and Hos. 2:16 (Eng. 14) it refers to persuading or enticing a woman. In 2 Sam. 19:8 (Eng. 7); 2 Chr. 30:22; 32:6 it refers to a king encouraging his people. Closest to Gen. 50:21 is Isa. 40:2 and Ruth 2:13, where in both places the phrase parallels *nāḥam* as here. Cf. E. F. Campbell, Jr., *Ruth,* AB (Garden City, NY: Doubleday, 1975), pp. 100-101; R. L. Hubbard, Jr., *Book of Ruth,* NICOT (Grand Rapids: Eerdmans, 1988), p. 169. Note, e.g., Hubbard's translation of Ruth 2:13 (p. 153): "Ruth replied, 'May I continue to please you, sir, since you have allayed my fears [*niḥamtānî*] and since you have spoken kindly [*dibbartā 'al-lēḇ*] to your maidservant.' " The phrase is evocative of caring, supportive words spoken in behalf of another. See also P. Joüon, "Locutions hébraiques avec la préposition *'al* devant *lēḇ, lēḇāḇ,*" *Bib* 5 (1924) 49-53.

20. For the connection of Gen. 50:15ff. with E, see A. W. Jenks, *The Elohist and*

means something like, "when the full reality of their father's passing dawned on them."

Their suspicion is that Joseph *will loathe* them. The Joseph narrative started with the brothers hating him (*śānē'*, 37:4, 5, 8). At the end of the narrative the tables are turned, and they think Joseph will hate them *(śāṭam).* Their hatred for Joseph is real, but Joseph's hatred of them is only imaginary.

If, in fact, Joseph did loathe his brothers, such loathing would not have been triggered by Jacob's death. It would have a longer history than that, extending as far back as the incident of ch. 37. Maybe we should read the brothers' feelings not as two coordinate statements, but as a cause-and-effect statement: "Joseph will demonstrate his contempt for us by returning on us all the evil we heaped on him." Joseph has given them no premonition or reason to think that his spirit is retaliatory, that he has been laying low and waiting for the most propitious moment for vengeance. This, incidentally, is the first time the brothers acknowledge their guilt for what they did to Joseph — *all the harm* [*hārā'â*] we did to him. Joseph himself had discouraged remorse in his brothers by his reconciling words of 45:5 ("do not worry, or reproach yourselves").

16 Rather than face Joseph directly, the brothers send *a message* to him. Writing letters and sending messages, rather than facing one's foe directly, is one way to avoid direct confrontation with one's adversary. David did this (2 Sam. 11:14, 15), and so did Jezebel (1 K. 21:9) and Jehu (2 K. 10:1, 6). The closest parallel to Joseph's brothers sending a message to Joseph, rather than going themselves, is to be found with Jacob sending messengers with a message to Esau (Gen. 32:4ff. [Eng. 3ff.]). In both cases the one sending the message (Joseph's brothers, Jacob) is extremely apprehensive about how the offended brother (Joseph, Esau) will react when at last the two groups meet.

The brothers adroitly refer to Jacob as *Your father* (i.e., Joseph's). Their choice of *'āḇîḵā* rather than *'āḇînû* ("our father") is deliberate. They want to

---

North Israelite Traditions, SBLMS 22 (Missoula, MT: Scholars, 1977), pp. 31-32, who makes much of the recurrent use of *Elohim* throughout this unit.

21. Heb. *peša'* ("crime") is a word whose use originated in the political sphere, where it referred to the rebellion of a vassal against an overlord (1 K. 12:19; 2 K. 1:1; 3:5, 7; 8:20, 22). By extension it is applied in the religious realm, where it denotes Israel's rebellion against God (1 K. 8:50; Isa. 1:2; 43:27; Jer. 2:8; 33:8; Ezek. 2:3; Hos. 7:13; 8:1). It therefore denotes brazen sin, sin that offends either a human being or God. For that reason, in the Israelite cult *peša'* sin is removed only on Yom Kippur (Lev. 16:16, 21). Apart from Lev. 16, the OT has six references to the forgiveness of *peša'* sin: Gen. 50:17 (twice); 1 Sam. 25:28; 1 K. 8:50; Ps. 25:7; 51:3 (Eng. 1). On this term see the studies of Š. Porúbčan, *Sin in the Old Testament: A Soteriological Study* (Rome: Herder, 1963), pp. 24-26; R. Knierim, *Die Hauptbegriffe für Sünde im Alten Testament* (Gütersloh: Gerd Mohn, 1967), pp. 114-84, esp. pp. 114-15 for the author's analysis of this word in Gen. 50:17; idem, *"peša',"* *THAT,* 2:488-95; S. Lyonnet and Léopold Sabourin, *Sin, Redemption, and Sacrifice: A Biblical and Patristic Study,* AnBib 48 (Rome: Pontifical Biblical Institute, 1970), p. 13.

make their case as strong as possible by suggesting to Joseph: "Joseph, it was your very own father who. . . ." They continue with the second person singular pronominal suffix in the next verse — "your father's God."

17 The thrust of the message that they send to Joseph is that Jacob, before he died, left parting instructions that Joseph was to forgive the crime[21] and sin that his brothers had committed against Joseph. We cannot know whether this is a total fabrication by the brothers, or whether Jacob did indeed make some last statement about Joseph's need to pardon his brothers. The evidence favors the first possibility, since such an instruction from Jacob is nowhere earlier recorded. Nor has there been even a hint of Jacob's discovery of the brothers' mistreatment of Joseph. Also, the brothers have done little over the last number of years to lend credibility to their speech. If they misstate the truth at the beginning to Jacob (ch. 37), what is to prevent them from misstating the truth about Jacob at the end? And why would Jacob share this with them, and not directly with Joseph?

If they are telling the truth,[22] that means Jacob is cast in the role of intercessor. Scripture has many instances of A asking B to forgive the sins of A. There are not as many illustrations where A asks B to forgive the sins of C. A good parallel to Gen. 50:17 would be Exod. 32:32, the golden calf incident at Mt. Sinai's base. Moses even uses the expression *wᵉʿattâ,* "and now," as does Gen. 50:17b.[23]

Certainty is impossible in this matter; the ambiguity may be deliberate. The best one can say is that the brothers' quotation of their father's earlier words is unverifiable. As such, this quotation is parallel to three other places in the OT that give an unverifiable quotation. First, in 2 Sam. 15:8 Absalom quotes an earlier quotation of his own to David to the effect that if Yahweh takes him back to Jerusalem, he will worship Yahweh at Hebron. Did Absalom ever say that, or is it simply a ruse to get to Hebron to start the coup against his father? Second, in 2 Sam. 16:3, Ziba, steward of Saul's grandson Mephibosheth, quotes Mephibosheth's words to David that in effect suggest that Mephibosheth has gone over to Absalom's side in order to regain Saul's kingdom. Mephibosheth later denies this (2 Sam. 19:27), but who can tell? Third, in 1 K. 1:17 Bathsheba quotes David to the effect that he had promised his kingdom to Solomon. Despite David's own later witness to this promise (1 K. 1:30), the reader is left in doubt as to whether David really said this, given his advancing senility referred to earlier in the chapter. Did David say this, or is he being manipulated? In the case of Gen. 50:17 one must classify the quotation as unverifiable, although it does not seem believable.[24]

22. Among modern commentators this interpretation is rare. For an advocate of this position, see Lowenthal, *Joseph Narrative in Genesis,* pp. 151-55.

23. Cf. Pharaoh's words to Moses in Exod. 10:17, *wᵉʿattâ śāʾ nāʾ ḥaṭṭāʾṯî,* lit., "and now, forgive, please, my sin."

24. On the phenomenon of unverifiable quotations, see Savran, *Telling and Retelling* pp. 82, 106-8.

One may give the brothers credit for using a strong word to describe how they treated Joseph. Privately they used the word "harm" *(rāʿâ),* and so did Jacob according to the brothers. They also have Jacob use the phrase *the crime of your brothers and their sin.* When making a personal request of Joseph, the brothers use only *crime (pešaʿ).* This is the word for sinful action in its most transparent manifestation. It is revolt and rebellion.[25]

They do make one slight modification in their version of Jacob's instruction. They had him say, *Forgive . . . your brothers.* When they move from repetition to request, they say, *So now, forgive . . . the servants of your father's God.* Their appeal is not to bloodlines but to spiritual roots and relationships. Joseph would certainly not recriminate against some fellow believers, those who worship the God of Jacob.

Joseph's response to this communication is to break into tears. Why? We do not know. Is he distressed, after all he has done for his brothers, that they still perceive him as a potential killer, and as one who thrives on retribution? Has the recall of the lately departed father brought up Joseph's grief again? Is he just sad, or is he relieved that they finally confess? I am inclined to believe that one must understand this verse by seeing it as a sequel to the event narrated in 45:1ff., rather than as a variant, in which Joseph revealed his identify to his brothers, tried to calm their fears, and testified to God's involvement in the events and experiences of previous years. "It is as though the whole ordeal has been in vain: if they have learned anything about him beyond externals — and the fear may well have haunted them all those years — the effect has evaporated."[26] Hence, Joseph's tears.

18 In v. 1 it was Joseph who did the falling (on Jacob). Here it is the brothers who do the falling (before Joseph) — they *fell before him.* They had done the same thing earlier (see 44:14), although on most occasions before Joseph they "prostrated" themselves (42:6; 43:26, 28). What is needed here is falling, not bowing.

They also shift their self-designation from "the servants of your father's God" to simply *your slaves.* The former expression suggests that these men share an equal status with Joseph. They are all children of the same God. The latter expression suggests subordination, something they had advocated earlier (44:9).

The brothers, seeking forgiveness from Joseph, start with a communication (vv. 15-17), and then follow with a personal appearance (v. 18). The two are so close to each other that Joseph has no time to respond to their message before they themselves are in his presence.

19 In his response Joseph nowhere says: "I forgive you," as they had requested. He has already forgiven them. The past is water over the dam

25. See n. 21 above.
26. Sternberg, *Poetics of Biblical Narrative,* p. 178.

as far as Joseph is concerned. What he does do is attempt to allay their fears with his *Do not be afraid* (lit., "fear not"). He does not upbraid them for asking for reconciliation. There is no "ask not," but rather "fear not." This expression occurs in Genesis usually in God's mouth (15:1; 21:17; 26:24; 46:3). Once it is used by Rachel's midwife to Rachel (35:17). It is the second time the brothers have heard *'al-tîrā'û*. Much earlier Joseph's steward had to put them at ease with the same words (43:23).

Joseph follows his words of reassurance with a rhetorical question: *God's surrogate am I?* This is the second time this question appears in Genesis. When provoked by his wife to father children for Rachel or else, Jacob responded: *hᵃṯaḥaṯ 'ĕlōhîm 'ānōḵî* (30:2), exactly as we have in 50:19 (except Joseph uses the pronoun *'ănî*). There are two differences between Joseph's question and Jacob's, both of which are addressed to family members. One is the interesting difference in the way LXX renders the Hebrew in 30:2 and 50:19. The Greek translation of 30:2 parallels the Hebrew *(Mḗ antí theoú egṓ eimi).* The Greek translation of 50:19, however, is considerably different. It reads "for I am God's" *(toú gár theoú eimi egṓ).* In other words, LXX has Joseph saying to his brothers: "You need have no fear of retribution, for I have God's view of things, and am therefore above retaliation."

The second difference is that Jacob qualifies his question: "Am I in God's place, who has restrained you from having children?" "Am I God," asks Jacob, "who has power to close and open your womb?" But Joseph leaves his question dangling. It could have been extended to say: "Am I in God's place to impose retribution? Vengeance is Yahweh's. He will repay, if necessary" (cf. Deut. 32:35; Rom. 11:19).

While the phrase *taḥaṯ 'ĕlōhîm* is not explicit in the text, it is implicit in the serpent's question to Eve. In essence, he tantalizes her with, "Would you like to be in God's place?" "Would you like to be your own God?" There is a considerable contrast between Adam and Eve and Joseph. Genesis begins by telling us about a primeval couple who tried to become like God, and ends by telling us about a man who denied he was in God's place.[27] Adam and Eve attempted to wipe out the dividing line between humanity and deity. Joseph refuses to try to cross that line. Joseph will only be God's instrument, never his substitute.[28]

20 Only once before has Joseph explained to his brothers his experiences in a decidely theological, reflective way. In 45:7-8 he testified that it was God who sent him to Egypt ahead of them to preserve a remnant among Jacob's descendants.

Joseph states that his brothers *have done something malicious against*

27. See B. T. Dahlberg, "On recognizing the unity of Genesis," *TD* 24 (1976) 363.
28. Lowenthal, *Joseph Narrative in Genesis,* p. 156.

me (ḥ^{a}šab̲tem ʿālay rāʿâ).[29] The brothers' evil intentions and imaginations against Joseph parallel similar evil inner thoughts and plannings among Noah's contemporaries *(w^{e}k̲ol-yēṣer maḥš^{e}b̲ôt̲ libbô raq raʿ,* 6:5).

In contrast to the brothers' evil machinations is the *something beneficial* God has done for Joseph *('^{ĕ}lōhîm ḥ^{a}šāb̲â l^{e}ṭōb̲â).* It may well be that we need to follow Brueggemann's suggestion and look to the Psalter for the full explication of this verse, rather than to wisdom literature as von Rad has done.[30] It is especially in Psalms of lament that one reads frequently of God who defeats and frustrates the plans *(maḥš^{e}b̲ôt̲)* of the wicked. Indeed, *ḥāšab̲* in the Qal occurs more often in Psalms (11 times) than in any other book except Jeremiah (12 times).

As attractive as it is, Brueggemann's proposal overlooks one point. The text reads literally, "You planned [or 'reckoned,' or 'did'] against me evil; God planned [or 'did'] it for good." That is, the second occurrence of *ḥāšab̲* (now with God as the subject) has a pronominal suffix (3rd fem. sing.) attached to it. The antecedent for "it" can only be *rāʿâ* or an implied *maḥ^{a}šāb̲â.* It appears then, that Joseph states that God took the evil his brothers planned against him and turned it into good.

What is this good? The last part of v. 20 answers that question: *the survival of many people.* We cannot be certain who is meant by *many people (ʿam-rāb̲).*[31] To be sure, it includes Jacob's family. The suffering and humiliation inflicted on Joseph by Jacob's family becomes the means of the salvation of Jacob's family. One speculates whether *many people* might also include the citizenry of Egypt.[32] They too survived because of Joseph, or, better,

29. For other instances of *ḥāšab̲ ʿal . . . rāʿâ* cf. Jer. 48:2; Mic. 2:3 (with God as subject!); Hos. 7:15 (Piel, but using the preposition *'el*). Close to *ḥāšab̲ rāʿâ* is *ḥāšab̲ 'āwen* (Ezek. 11:2; Mic. 2:1; Ps. 36:5 [Eng. 4]).

30. See W. Brueggemann, "Genesis L 15-21: A theological exploration," *Congress Volume: Salamanca, 1983,* ed. J. A. Emerton, VTSup 36 (Leiden: Brill, 1985), pp. 40-53, esp. pp. 47-49; repr. in *Old Testament Theology: Essays on Structure, Theme, and Text,* ed. P. D. Miller, Jr. (Minneapolis: Fortress, 1992), pp. 203-18; von Rad, *Genesis,* pp. 435-39, esp. pp. 438-39. N. Niehoff ("Do Biblical Characters Talk to Themselves? Narrative Modes of Representing Inner Speech in Early Biblical Fiction," *JBL* 111 [1992] 579) draws attention to the threefold use of the verb *ḥāšab̲* in Genesis when attributed to humans: Laban considering his daughters Rachel and Leah as outsiders (31:15); Judah mistakenly taking Tamar for a harlot (38:15); Joseph's brothers plotting harm against Joseph (50:20). Niehoff notes that in these three instances the verb does not "describe a conscientious deliberation of an individual but rather refers to one's illusionary perception of reality. . . . In all of these cases the narrator subsequently shows how the figures' own conceptions are wrong and contradict God's plan for the world."

31. Cf. *'ād̲ām rāb̲* in Job 36:28 for a kindred expression.

32. See H. W. Wolff, "Kerygma of the Yahwist" (tr. W. A. Benware), in W. Brueggemann and Wolff, *The Vitality of Old Testament Traditions,* 2nd ed. (Atlanta: John Knox, 1982), p. 59.

because of what Joseph's God did with and through Joseph. Because of God's providential turning of sour events into divinely used events in the life of one man, the chosen survive, and the unchosen survive. God sends his blessings on the just and the unjust (Matt. 5:45).

Of von Rad's famous dictum about v. 20 — "Such a bold mixture of divine activity and guilty human deeds was never attempted again by the teachers" — we find the last part most interesting.[33] Now, by "teachers" von Rad refers to the teachers of the wisdom schools. However, the theme of a beneficent divine plan at work through calamity and confusion is by no means confined to Gen. 50:20. One thinks of Daniel, Esther, Ruth, and many others who illustrate the same theme.

Perhaps the best parallel to Gen. 50:20 is the case of Judas Iscariot in the NT. He is both evil and important (much as there are others who are good and important). In lifting up his heel against his friend, Judas is marked as the archetypal traitor. He is additionally a figure of sinister importance in the working out of the divine will. Judas is to Jesus what Joseph's brothers were to Joseph.

21 The brothers had prefaced their request with *wᵉʿattâ* (lit., "and now," v. 17b). Joseph prefaces his words of reassurance with his own *wᵉʿattâ (So now).* Both times one might paraphrase the Hebrew into English as "this being the case." Used by Joseph, it follows a rhetorical question of justification ("God's surrogate am I?"), and leads into a request formed imperatively ("Do not be afraid").

Joseph promises to continue to *provide* (the Pilpel of *kûl*) for his family and their children. Joseph had used "provide, take care of" (the Pilpel of *kûl*) in 45:11. The famine is probably over, but Joseph continues to be his family's "keeper" long after the famine. His concern for his family does not stop with the lifting of the famine. Finally, the narrator adds his own comment about Joseph's ministry to his family (v. 21b).

4. THE DEATH OF JOSEPH (50:22-26)

22 *Joseph stayed on in Egypt, he*[1] *and his father's household. Joseph lived one hundred and ten years.*

23 *Joseph lived to see Ephraim's sons down to the third generation.*[2]

33. G. von Rad, *Wisdom in Israel,* tr. J. D. Martin (Nashville: Abingdon, 1972), p. 200.

1. LXX adds "and his brothers," and thus distinguishes the brothers from Jacob's household.

2. For *šillēšîm* ("those of the third generation") cf. Exod. 20:5; 34:7; Num. 14:18; Deut. 5:9. *bᵉnê* before *šillēšîm* presents some problems. *šillēšîm* designates the great-grandchildren of Joseph. The "sons of" *(bᵉnê)* the third generation would be the great-g[...] grandchildren. SP, LXX, and Pesh. read "sons" *(bānîm),* thus limiting the phras[...]

Also the sons of Machir, son of Manasseh, were born on Joseph's knees.[3]

24 *Joseph said to his brothers: "I am about to die. God will surely come to your assistance,*[4] *and bring you up from this land to the land that he promised on oath to*[5] *Abraham, to Isaac, to Jacob."*

25 *Then Joseph put the sons of Israel under oath,*[6] *saying: "When God comes to your assistance, be sure to take up my remains*[7] *from here."*

26 *Joseph died at the age of one hundred and ten. They embalmed him, and he was placed*[8] *in the coffin in Egypt.*

---

generations. One may retain MT by understanding *bᵉnê* not to mean "sons of" but rather "those belonging to," as argued by GKC, § 128v.

3. For the meaning of the phrase "to be born on the knees of," see my comments on 30:3. Note also that the latter half of this verse illustrates a clause in specifying apposition to the first clause. Thus v. 23b specifies the great-grandchildren alluded to in v. 23a. On this phenomenon, see Andersen, *Sentence in Biblical Hebrew,* pp. 47-48.

4. The problem of the best English translation for Heb. *pāqaḏ* is borne out by Speiser: "There is probably no other Hebrew verb that has caused translators as much trouble as *pqd*" ("Census and Ritual Expiation in Mari and Israel," *BASOR* 149 [1958] 21), and B. Grossfeld: "Hebrew PQD is perhaps the most versatile root in the entire Biblical text" ("The Translation of Biblical Hebrew *pqd* in the Targum, Peshitta, Vulgate and Septuagint," *ZAW* 96 [1984] 93). Both Speiser and Grossfeld agree that the basic meaning of this root is "to take note of, to notice, to consider, to attend to with care." See also H. S. Gehman, "*'Episképomai, epískepsis, epískopos* and *episkopḗ* in the Septuagint in Relation to *pqd* and other Hebrew Roots — a Case of Semantic Development Similar to that of Hebrew," *VT* 22 (1972) 197-207, esp. 200-201. In an earlier study on this root (*TWOT,* 2:1802) I remarked, "The basic meaning is to exercise oversight over a subordinate, either in the form of inspecting or of taking action to cause a considerable change in circumstances of the subordinate, either for the better or for the worse."

5. For the formula *šāḇaʿ* (Niphal) plus the preposition *lᵉ* and a person, plus the accusative of a thing (usually land), meaning "promise on/by oath to," see Exod. 33:1; Num. 11:12; 14:16, 23; 32:11; Judg. 2:1; and frequently throughout Deuteronomy (e.g., 6:18). Cf. BDB, p. 989, § 2 under Niphal.

6. *wayyašbaʿ* is the Hiphil of *šāḇaʿ* (the Niphal stem of this verb appeared in v. 24), and in this stem means "to put under oath, to cause one to take an oath."

7. Lit., "bones," which is used, by synecdoche, for "body, corpse." For this meaning of *ʿeṣem,* in the pl., cf. Exod. 13:19; Josh. 24:32; 2 Sam. 21:12, 13; Amos 6:10; and BDB, p. 782, § 1f.

8. MT *wayyîśem* (lit., "and he put") is problematic. The verb form may be explained as a Qal passive from a metaplastic root *yśm,* cognate to *św/ym.* See M. Dahood, "Qoheleth and Northwest Semitic Philology," *Bib* 43 (1962) 354 n. 6. This interpretation vocalizes the verb as *wayyûyśām.* Or it may be read as a Hophal *(wayyûśam)* as in SP (so *BHS*). Cf. Gen. 24:33. While each case must be decided on its own merits, one should normally prefer a revocalization of the MT that retains the verb in question rather than a revocalization that results in the creation of a putative verb. Note that in 24:33 for the Ketib, an anomalous *wyyśm,* the Masoretes supply a Qere *(wayyûśām).* But here in Gen. 50:26 for the Ketib *wyyśm,* the Masoretes supply no corresponding Qere. This is one argument used by Gordis (*The Word*

22 Joseph lives for 110 years. The first seventeen of those were lived in Canaan. The last ninety-three are lived in Egypt. We do know at what age any of his brothers died, and whether they outlived Joseph or died before he did. Their obituary notices are screened out of the biblical story.

It has often been pointed out that many Egyptian texts cite 110 years as the ideal life span.[9] Since the Joseph story is set in Egypt, it is appropriate that he should live the Egyptian equivalent of "three score and ten." This is a life span that Joseph shares with Joshua (Josh. 24:29; Judg. 2:8), and thus the total is not exclusively Egyptian.

If one examines the life span of the three patriarchs in Gen. 12–50, the years of the patriarchs are formed as square numbers that constitute a succession.[10] Thus the following pattern emerges:

Abraham: $175 = 7 \times 5^2$
Isaac: $180 = 5 \times 6^2$
Jacob: $147 = 3 \times 7^2$

Gevirtz has carried this observation one step further by noting that Joseph's 110 years are the sum of these consecutive square numbers ($110 = 5^2 + 6^2 + 7^2$). He also notes that the first man in Genesis, Adam, has a life span of 930 years ($= 30^2 + 30$), and the last man in Genesis, Joseph, has a life span of 110 years ($= 10^2 + 10$).[11]

This numerical pattern may be extended as follows:

Abraham: $175 = 7 \times 5^2$
Isaac: $180 = 5 \times 6^2$
Jacob: $147 = 3 \times 7^2$
Joseph: $110 = 1 \times 5^2 + 6^2 + 7^2$

That is, Joseph is the successor in the pattern 7-5-3-1, and the sum of his predecessors ($5^2 + 6^2 + 7^2$).[12] In this way, Joseph is linked intimately with his

---

and the Book [New York: Ktav, 1976], p. 33) to challenge a widely held view that the Qere readings represent corrections of the Ketib. If they were, why then was the Ketib not supplied with a corrected Qere in 50:26? On these two uses of the Hophal of *śwyym* in Gen. 24:33 and 50:26, see BDB, p. 964, under Hophal. GKC, § 73f, understands the verbal form in 50:26 as a Qal passive, although he hedges with "may perhaps be seen in."

9. See, e.g., Vergote, *Joseph en Égypte,* pp. 200-201; J. A. Wilson, *ANET,* p. 414.

10. See J. Meysing, "The Biblical Chronologies of the Patriarchs," *Christian News from Israel* 14 (1963) 26.

11. S. Gevirtz, "The Life Spans of Joseph and Enoch and the Parallelism *šibʿātayim — šibʿîm wĕšibʿāh,*" *JBL* 96 (1977) 570-71.

12. See J. G. Williams, "Number Symbolism and Joseph as Symbol of Completion," *JBL* 98 (1979) 86-87; C. J. Labuschagne, "The Life Spans of the Patriarchs," *OTS* 25 (1989) 121-27, esp. 126-27.

family line. He is certainly no marginal figure, and he comes close to being considered a fourth patriarch. That Joseph's life span of 110 years reflects the ideal length of life by Egyptian standards is not an attempt by the author to give the Joseph story an Egyptian flavor. Rather, it appears that the narrator is suggesting that Joseph symbolically brings to a conclusion the patriarchal narratives.

It is hardly likely that the above data may be explained as simple coincidence. To the contrary, the writers apparently used symbolic numbers as a composition technique. Thus the roots of the Jewish Kabbalah (the esoteric teachings of Judaism and Jewish mysticism that flourished in the Middle Ages), and in particular gematria (one form of which involves explaining a word or group of words according to the numerical value of the letters) are found in the biblical text.[13] A proper and restrained use of number symbolism functions as a deterrent against an overly literal treatment of symbolic numbers in the Bible.[14]

23 This verse precedes chronologically v. 22. It informs us that Joseph lived long enough to see his great-grandchildren through Ephraim. According to Job 42:16, Job lived to see four generations. To see one's (grand)children is the crowning joy of a full life (Ps. 128:6; Prov. 17:6; Isa. 53:10).

This theme echoes in ancient Near Eastern literature as well. In the second Nerab inscription one reads "and with my eyes I see the children of the fourth generation."[15] In the memorial inscription of Nabonidus's mother we read: "My descendants to four generations alive I have seen."[16]

Some of his great-grandsons *(the sons of Machir, son of Manasseh)* he adopted. This is the meaning of *were born on Joseph's knees.* Bilhah's children were born on Rachel's knees, and thus became her children (30:3). Jacob took the two sons of Joseph, Ephraim and Manasseh, and adopted them as sons when he "took them between his knees" (48:12). Naomi took the newly born

13. See G. Scholem, "Kabbalah," *EncJud,* 10:489-553; idem, "Gematria," *EncJud,* 7:369-74.

14. C. J. Labuschagne, "The literary and theological function of divine speech in the Pentateuch," in *Congress Volume: Salamanca, 1983,* ed. J. A. Emerton, VTSup 36 (Leiden: Brill, 1985), pp. 154-73, esp. p. 171. It is possible that Matthew's division of Jesus' genealogy into three sections of fourteen (Matt. 1:1-17) may have been inspired by gematria, for in the Hebrew orthography the numerical value of David's name was fourteen (4 + 6 + 4), and thus the structuring of the genealogy of Jesus in an artificial way that highlights Jesus as the Son of David. See R. E. Brown, *The Birth of the Messiah* (Garden City, NY: Doubleday, 1977), pp. 74-81.

15. See *KAI,* 226.5.

16. References in J. C. Greenfield, "The Etymology of *'amtaḥat,*" *ZAW* 77 (1965) 91 n. 11; H. Tawil, "Some Literary Elements in the Opening Sections of the Hadad, Zākir, and the Nerab II Inscriptions in the Light of East and West Semitic Royal Inscriptions," *Or* 43 (1974) 63-64; A. L. Oppenheim, *ANET,* p. 561; M. Weinfeld, *Deuteronomy 1–11,* AB (New York: Doubleday, 1991), pp. 296-97.

son of Ruth on her lap, and those present said: "A son has been born for Naomi" (Ruth 4:16-17).[17]

It is telling that Joseph should adopt the children of Machir as his own. Whatever the historical context of this may be,[18] there is immediate connection between Joseph and Machir in the Joseph narrative. *Machir* means "one who is sold." *mākar* is the verb used to describe what happened to Joseph (37:28; 45:5). In a sense Joseph was Machir (i.e., "sold").

24 Joseph may live to see his great-grandchildren, but he will not live forever. He speaks to his brothers (all of them?). Although he is the second youngest of thirteen children, some of his siblings may outlive him. For all his obedience and faithfulness to God, he does not enjoy longevity beyond that of his brothers.

Joseph's last words to his family are a testimony: *God will surely come to your assistance* [lit., "visit," *pāqaḏ*],[19] *and bring you up from this land to the land that he promised on oath to Abraham, to Isaac, to Jacob* (i.e., his great-grandfather, grandfather, and father).[20] There is not a hint that God will give the land to Joseph's family because of any merits they have. The land is theirs because of divine grace and promise only. Gen. 50:24 is much like Deut. 6:10, "And when the Lord your God brings you into the land which he swore to your fathers, to Abraham, to Isaac, and to Jacob. . . ." This kind of verse is more striking in Deuteronomy than it is in Genesis. Deuteronomy, we recall, brims with the teaching that land acquisition is a reward, a blessing for obedience. But is this always the case? Deut. 6:10 suggests there are other explanations — unmitigated grace and promise, for example.

25 God placed himself under oath to the patriarchs (v. 24). Joseph now asks his brothers to place themselves under oath to him. His request is much like that of his father (49:29-32). He too wants to be buried in his native land. Jacob made his request with *ṣāwâ* ("instructed, ordered"). Joseph uses a stronger verb (*šāḇaʿ*, "to put under oath, swear"), perhaps because of lingering suspicions he has about his brothers' integrity.

26 Joseph is *embalmed,* as was Jacob, and *placed in the coffin.* The word for *coffin* is *'ārôn,* the word used for the "ark" (i.e., chest) of the

17. Cf. the example from Mari: *ina birit paḫalliya urabbûšuma ana* [is]*kussê bît abišu utērrusû,* "I have brought him up on my knees [lit., 'between my thighs or testicles'] and have returned him to the throne of his family," quoted by Greenfield, *ZAW* 77 (1965) 91 n. 12.

18. See de Vaux, *Early History of Israel,* pp. 312-13, 585-87, 649-50, 784-86.

19. On *pqd* as an act of the favor of Yahweh according to an earlier promise (cf. 21:1), see G. André, *Determining the Destiny: PQD in the Old Testament,* ConBOT 16 (Lund: Gleerup; Uppsala: Almqvist & Wiksell, 1980), pp. 207-8.

20. Note in this brief pericope (vv. 22-26) Joseph stands in the middle of a seven-generation span: Abraham, Isaac, Jacob, Joseph, Manasseh, Machir, sons of Machir. Joseph is the grandson of a grandfather, and the grandfather of a grandson.

covenant. Perhaps it is best to understand *'ārôn* as a sarcophagus here (the only time *'ārôn* has this nuance in the OT); the use of the definite article on coffin *(the coffin)* may be a way of specifying that the coffin in which Joseph was placed was similar to a sarcophagus used in Egypt for a high-ranking Egyptian. The Egyptian language had a number of words for coffin, and one might have expected one of them to be used here, given the presence of other Egyptian words throughout the Joseph narrative. Does this terminology lend credence to the possibility that the Joseph story, although situated geographically in Egypt, was composed in ancient Hebrew?

Later Jewish tradition did not miss the parallel between Joseph being placed in an *'ārôn,* and the two tables of the Decalogue also being placed in an *'ārôn* (Deut. 10:5): "All this time in the desert Israel carried two shrines with them, the one the coffin containing the bones of the dead man Joseph, the other the Ark containing the covenant of the Living God. The wayfarers who saw the two receptacles wondered, and they would ask, 'How doth the ark of the dead come next to the ark of the Ever-living?' The answer was, 'The dead man enshrined in the one fulfilled the commandments enshrined in the other.' "[21] The tradition goes on to document Joseph's faithful observance of the Decalogue even though he precedes its announcement at Sinai. For example, Joseph's rejection of Potiphar's wife's advances is linked with the commandment about adultery and coveting.

THE NEW TESTAMENT APPROPRIATION

a. The Joseph Narrative and Acts 7:9-16

Two sections of Stephen's lengthy speech in Acts 7 are given over to a discussion of Genesis material: vv. 2-8, Abraham; vv. 9-16, Joseph. Stephen focuses on the first and last generation in Gen. 12–50, omitting completely Isaac, and mentioning Jacob only as a footnote to his son Joseph.

Interestingly, Stephen refers to the brothers of Joseph as "patriarchs." Because they were jealous of Joseph (*zēlóō,* and see Gen. 39:11), they sold him into Egypt. Stephen says nothing about the involvement of the Midianites and Ishmaelites, even though 37:28 speaks of the brothers (or the Midianites) selling Joseph to Ishmaelites, and 37:36 speaks of Midianites selling Joseph into Egypt (the exact phrase used in Acts 7:9b). Ignoring the material in Gen. 37, Stephen uses instead Joseph's statement of Gen. 45:4. It is clear from the outset that Stephen is drawing a line of vivid contrast between Joseph and his patriarchal brothers.

21. L. Ginzberg, *Legends of the Jews,* 7 vols. (Philadelphia: Jewish Publication Society, 1969), 2:183.

Because God was with Joseph (Acts 7:9c), God delivered Joseph out of all his afflictions *(thlípseōn).* What Reuben could not do for Joseph, God did for Joseph. Stephen goes on to use words that, although accurate, do not appear in Genesis. Note, for example, Stephen's assertion that God gave wisdom *(sophían)* to Joseph before Pharaoh, and that Pharaoh appointed Joseph "ruler" *(hēgoúmenon)* over Egypt (v. 10).[1]

In v. 11 Stephen makes the point that "our fathers" (i.e., Joseph's patriarchal brothers) could find no food or sustenance *(chortásmata)* when the famine came. He says nothing about the Egyptians' inability to find food. Furthermore, Stephen refers to this famine as a time of "great tribulation" *(thlípsis megálē)* for the brothers, the word the writer used two verses earlier for Joseph's own sufferings. God delivered Joseph from his tribulations (*thlípseis,* v. 10). How will he deliver the brothers from their tribulation (*thlípsis,* v. 11)?

Stephen recalls subsequent visits of family members (v. 13), including Jacob (vv. 14-15), to Egypt. But Stephen does not comment on how God (through Joseph) delivered the patriarchs from death; nor is there any reference to the congenial arrangements for settlement in Goshen. He even mentions the death of Joseph's brothers (v. 15b), something Gen. 50 does not do.

The remark in v. 16 that the bodies of Jacob and his sons ("our fathers") were brought back to Shechem and placed in the tomb that Abraham had bought from the sons of Hamor at Shechem is of particular interest for two reasons. First, the reference to Jacob and Joseph's brothers being buried in Shechem does not seem to agree with Gen. 49:29-33 and 50:13, which claim that Jacob was buried in the cave of Machpelah at Hebron, although one might assume that the subject of the verbs of v. 16a refers only to the sons of Jacob, not including Jacob himself. Second, nowhere does the OT refer to Abraham purchasing property at Shechem, but Gen. 33:19 does tell of Jacob purchasing a plot of land at Shechem from the sons of Hamor. Has Stephen confused Shechem with Hebron, and Abraham with Jacob? It is difficult, but not impossible, to harmonize these traditions.[2] Could it be that Acts 7:16 reflects the possibility of a Samaritan tradition, especially with the reference to Shechem, which Luke has used in Acts 7:16?[3] The weakness with that argument is that elsewhere the Samaritan Pentateuch clearly records the burial of Abraham, Isaac, and Jacob at Hebron. Thus it is unlikely that the replacement of Hebron by Shechem in Acts 7:16

1. The problem here is the absence in LXX of Gen. 41:40, 43 to any equivalent to *hēgoúmenon.* See E. Richard, "The Old Testament in Acts: Wilcox's Semitisms in Retrospect," *CBQ* 42 (1980) 333-34.

2. As does W. H. Mare, "Acts 7: Jewish or Samaritan in Character?" *WTJ* 34 (1971) 19-20, using strained arguments.

3. C. H. H. Scobie, "The Use of Source Material in the Speeches of Acts III and VII," *NTS* 25 (1979) 407-8.

betrays Samaritan influence. We are left then only with the explanation that Stephen has telescoped two purchases of land, one by Abraham in Shechem, one by Jacob in Shechem.[4]

Throughout the pericope (vv. 9-10) Joseph is in bold contrast with his brothers. Near the end of his speech Stephen accuses his audience with "as your fathers did, so do you" (v. 51). Since "fathers" (in a negative light) are so prominent in Acts 7:9-16 (cf. vv. 11, 12, 14, 15), and elsewhere in the speech, it may be that Stephen means to connect the brothers of Joseph with his murderous audience. They wanted to kill Joseph, and Stephen's audience wishes to kill Stephen. In a broader sense, Joseph is also a forerunner of Stephen — God is with both, and upon both, and upon both shines the glory of God.[5]

b. The Joseph Narrative and Heb. 11:21-22

The writer of Hebrews devotes but one verse each to Jacob (v. 21) and to Joseph (v. 22) in his list of heroes of faith in the OT, and both are deathbed scenes. V. 21 goes back to Gen. 47:31 (LXX), and v. 22 goes back to Gen. 50:24-25.

On his deathbed Jacob, by faith, blessed the two sons of Joseph (whom the writer does not name). Joseph on his deathbed made mention of the Exodus of the Israelites, and gave directions concerning his burial.

What Jacob's faith and Joseph's faith have in common is their future orientation, the deep conviction that God has a future for his people beyond the circumstances of the present. Jacob's hands and Joseph's bones[6] will play some part in that future.[7]

c. The Joseph Narrative and Matt. 1–2

While Matt. 1–2 does not refer explicitly to the OT Joseph, Matthew appears to make the case that the NT Joseph is reliving the experiences of the OT

4. F. F. Bruce, *Book of the Acts,* NICNT, rev. ed. (Grand Rapids: Eerdmans, 1988), p. 137 n. 35; L. Johnson, *Acts of the Apostles,* Sacra Pagina (Collegeville, MN: Liturgical, 1992), p. 119.

5. See E. Richard, "The Polemical Character of the Joseph Episode in Acts 7," *JBL* 98 (1979) 255-67; J. J. Kilgallen, "The Function of Stephen's Speech (Acts 7,2-53)," *Bib* 70 (1989) 181.

6. M. Wilcox, "The Bones of Joseph: Hebrews 11:22," in *Scripture: Meaning and Method: Essays Presented to A. T. Hanson,* ed. B. P. Thompson (Hull: Hull University, 1987), pp. 114-30.

7. G. W. Buchanan, *To the Hebrews,* AB (Garden City, NY: Doubleday, 1972), pp. 196-97; H. W. Attridge, *Hebrews,* Hermeneia (Philadelphia: Fortress, 1989), pp. 336-37; F. F. Bruce, *Epistle to the Hebrews,* rev. ed., NICNT (Grand Rapids: Eerdmans, 1990), pp. 305-7.

Joseph. Both Josephs receive revelation in dreams, and both go down to Egypt. Both are involved with a king (Pharaoh, Herod). Both are followed by children who are destined to be saviors and rescuers of the oppressed. Thus the parallel is: OT Joseph-drcams-wicked Pharaoh-infant Moses :: NT Joseph-dreams-wicked Herod-infant Jesus.[8]

d. The Joseph Narrative and Matt 21:33-46/Mark 12:1-12/Luke 20:9-19

While it is unlikely a conscious appropriation of material from the Joseph story, one cannot help but notice the parallel between the words of the wicked tenant farmers in the parable when they saw the son of the vineyard sent by his father to collect the landlord's share and the words used by Joseph's brothers after he has been sent to them by his father. In both instances the larger group say among themselves, "Come! Let us kill him," *deute apokteínōmen autón* (Gen. 37:20; Matt. 21:38; Luke 20:14).

8. R. E. Brown, *The Birth of the Messiah* (Garden City, NY: Doubleday, 1977), pp. 111-12; idem, *A Coming Christ in Advent* (Collegeville, MN: Liturgical, 1988), pp. 34-35.

INDEX OF SUBJECTS

INDEX OF AUTHORS

181, 202, 206, 223, 229, 290, 309, 310, 337, 361, 373, 398, 403, 413, 442, 443, 478, 480, 482, 499, 530, 542, 547, 605, 609, 629, 644, 645, 654, 661, 666, 672, 683, 699
Driver, S. R., 47, 114, 215, 233, 252, 286, 296, 297, 304, 311, 328, 403, 457, 576

Eback, J., 127
Ehrlich, A. B., 4, 251, 278
Eichrodt, W., 9, 18, 111, 525
Eisenbeis, W., 350
Eissfeldt, O., 126, 273, 309, 375, 378
Ellinger, K., 128, 664, 674, 677
Ellington, J., 160
Emerton, J. A., 6, 15, 115, 219, 271, 321, 401, 430, 433, 434, 442, 659, 668
Eph'al, I., 171
Eskhult, M., 537, 538
Eslinger, L., 331
Evans, C. D., 182
Evans, G., 134, 367

Fabry, H.-J., 493, 615
Falk, Z. W., 92, 507, 624
Falkenstein, A., 487
Fawcett, S. W., 153
Feigin, S. I., 665
Feliks, J., 284
Fensham, F. C., 75, 80, 81, 97, 132, 369, 504
Fewell, D. N., 35, 48, 364, 372
Fichtner, J., 267
Finkelstein, J. J., 282, 307
Firmage, F., 675
Fisch, H., 52
Fishbane, M., 26, 190, 214, 225, 227, 234, 379, 381, 566
Fischer, G., 352, 355, 701
Fisher, E. J., 447
Fisher, L. R., 248
Fitzmyer, J. A., 69, 88, 273, 314, 360, 416, 484
Fohrer, G., 281
Fokkelman, J. P., 103, 119, 218, 225, 234, 239, 242, 244, 246, 248, 249, 256, 261, 272, 284, 289, 299, 303, 313, 315, 382
Fontinoy, C., 318
Forbes, A. D., 58, 124, 178, 272
Fowler, M. D., 605
Fox, M. V., 413, 556
Frank, R. M., 502
Franken, H. J., 348
Frankena, R., 299
Free, J. L., 414
Freedman, D. N., 178, 225, 297, 334, 349, 361, 401, 441, 444, 543, 650, 665, 669, 670, 671, 676, 678, 680, 681, 682, 691
Freedman, R. D., 139, 624
Frick, F. S., 134, 351, 367, 383, 500
Friedrich, J., 271
Fuchs, E., 295, 296
Fuhs, H. F., 112, 113
Furman, N., 444, 469

Gadd, C. J., 294
Gai, A., 279, 280, 502
Gamberoni, J., 276
Gammie, J., 282
Garber, P. L., 452
Garcia-Treto, F. O., 311
Gaster, T. H., 181, 477
Gaston, L., 96, 188
Gehman, H. S., 708
Geller, S. A., 330, 332, 338, 339, 343, 494, 518, 666, 668
Gemser, B., 202, 695
Gerleman, G., 65, 350
Gese, H., 698
Getty, M. A., 188
Gevirtz, S., 156, 214, 219, 222, 228, 285, 311, 319, 331, 338, 524, 644, 645, 648, 654, 658, 665, 674, 676, 679, 680, 682, 709
Gibson, J. C. L., 36, 163, 308, 338, 408, 428, 577, 600, 624, 656, 663, 689
Giesen, G., 625, 690
Gilmer, H. W., 312
Ginsberg, H. L., 4, 5, 203, 219, 227, 324, 334, 408, 447, 595, 649
Ginzberg, L., 712
Glenn, M. G., 237
Globe, A., 271
Gluck, J. J., 453
Goetze, A., 130, 338
Gold, V. R., 439
Goldin, J., 432, 453
Golka, F. W., 620
Golomb, D. M., 622, 653
Good, E. M., 44, 71, 135, 334, 347, 440, 654, 657

INDEX OF SCRIPTURE REFERENCES

OLD TESTAMENT

INDEX OF HEBREW WORDS